Frommer's

New England

14th Edition

by Leslie Brokaw, Paul Karr, Herbert Bailey
Livesey, Marie Morris, Laura M. Reckford

WILEY
Wiley Publishing, Inc.

Published by:

Wiley Publishing, Inc.
111 River St.
Hoboken, NJ 07030-5774

ISBN 978-0-470-27437-8

Editor: Matthew Brown
Production Editor: Katie Robinson
Cartographer: Andy Dolan
Photo Editor: Richard Fox
Production by Wiley Indianapolis Composition Services

Front cover photo: Vermont, Groton State Forest: woman paddling a red canoe along Boulder Beach, autumn foliage.
Back cover photo: Cape Cod: man surrounded with various lobster buoys attached to home.

For information on our other products and services or to obtain technical support, please contact our Customer Care Department within the U.S. at 800/762-2974, outside the U.S. at 317/572-3993 or fax 317/572-4002.

Wiley also publishes its books in a variety of electronic formats. Some content that appears in print may not be available in electronic formats.

Manufactured in the United States of America

5 4 3 2 1

Contents

13   New Hampshire   542

by Paul Karr

14   Maine   589

by Paul Karr

Appendix: Fast Facts, Toll-Free Numbers & Websites   668

Index   678

List of Maps

About the Authors

Leslie Brokaw (chapters 9-11) lives in Boston and teaches at Emerson College. She writes a film column for the *Boston Globe* and covers travel, business, and entertainment for a wide variety of other publications and websites. Brokaw, the author of *Frommer's Montreal & Quebec City*, spent her early career at *Inc.* magazine as a writer and Web editor.

Paul Karr (chapters 2–3 and 12–14) is also the author of *Frommer's Nova Scotia, New Brunswick & Prince Edward Island; Frommer's Maine Coast; Frommer's Vermont, New Hampshire & Maine;* and a contributor to *Frommer's Canada*.

Herbert Bailey Livesey (chapters 9–11) has written about food and travel for over 30 years. Among the many magazines that have published his articles are *Travel + Leisure, Food & Wine, Playboy, New York,* and *Yankee.* He has authored and contributed to several books and travel guides, including *Frommer's Canada* and *Frommer's Europe.*

Marie Morris (chapters 5–6) lives in Boston and is a graduate of Harvard, where she studied history. She has worked for the *New York Times, Boston* magazine, and the *Boston Herald,* and is also the author of *Frommer's Boston.*

Laura M. Reckford (chapters 7–8) is a writer and editor who lives on Cape Cod. Formerly the managing editor of *Cape Cod Life Magazine,* she has also been on the editorial staffs of *Good Housekeeping* and *Entertainment Weekly.*

An Invitation to the Reader

In researching this book, we discovered many wonderful places—hotels, restaurants, shops, and more. We're sure you'll find others. Please tell us about them, so we can share the information with your fellow travelers in upcoming editions. If you were disappointed with a recommendation, we'd love to know that, too. Please write to:

Frommer's New England, 14th Edition
Wiley Publishing, Inc. • 111 River St. • Hoboken, NJ 07030-5774

An Additional Note

Please be advised that travel information is subject to change at any time—and this is especially true of prices. We therefore suggest that you write or call ahead for confirmation when making your travel plans. The authors, editors, and publisher cannot be held responsible for the experiences of readers while traveling. Your safety is important to us, however, so we encourage you to stay alert and be aware of your surroundings. Keep a close eye on cameras, purses, and wallets, all favorite targets of thieves and pickpockets.

Frommer's Star Ratings, Icons & Abbreviations

Every hotel, restaurant, and attraction listing in this guide has been ranked for quality, value, service, amenities, and special features using a **star-rating system.** In country, state, and regional guides, we also rate towns and regions to help you narrow down your choices and budget your time accordingly. Hotels and restaurants are rated on a scale of zero (recommended) to three stars (exceptional). Attractions, shopping, nightlife, towns, and regions are rated according to the following scale: zero stars (recommended), one star (highly recommended), two stars (very highly recommended), and three stars (must-see).

In addition to the star-rating system, we also use **seven feature icons** that point you to the great deals, in-the-know advice, and unique experiences that separate travelers from tourists. Throughout the book, look for:

Finds	Special finds—those places only insiders know about
Fun Fact	Fun facts—details that make travelers more informed and their trips more fun
Kids	Best bets for kids and advice for the whole family
Moments	Special moments—those experiences that memories are made of
Overrated	Places or experiences not worth your time or money
Tips	Insider tips—great ways to save time and money
Value	Great values—where to get the best deals

The following **abbreviations** are used for credit cards:

AE	American Express	DISC	Discover	V	Visa
DC	Diners Club	MC	MasterCard		

Frommers.com

Now that you have this guidebook to help you plan a great trip, visit our website at **www.frommers.com** for additional travel information on more than 4,000 destinations. We update features regularly to give you instant access to the most current trip-planning information available. At Frommers.com, you'll find scoops on the best airfares, lodging rates, and car rental bargains. You can even book your travel online through our reliable travel booking partners. Other popular features include:

- Online updates of our most popular guidebooks
- Vacation sweepstakes and contest giveaways
- Newsletters highlighting the hottest travel trends
- Podcasts, interactive maps, and up-to-the-minute events listings
- Opinionated blog entries by Arthur Frommer himself
- Online travel message boards with featured travel discussions

What's New in New England

BOSTON & CAMBRIDGE The highway construction that dominated downtown Boston for nearly 2 decades officially ended in late 2007. In its place are the mile-long ribbon of parks known as the **Rose Kennedy Greenway,** newly configured surface roads—and more construction. Walk around or through it to reach the increasingly accessible, enjoyable waterfront.

The transit authority, or **MBTA** (© **800/392-6100** or 617/222-3200; www.mbta.com), introduced **automated fare collection** on subways and buses in 2007. **Ferries** and the **commuter rail** should be part of the system by 2009.

By the time you read this, the *haute* boutique **Regent Boston,** Battery Wharf, off Commercial Street on the edge of the North End (© **800/545-4000;** www. regenthotels.com), and the over-the-top **Mandarin Oriental, Boston,** on Boylston Street next to the Prudential Center (© **866/526-6567;** www.mandarin oriental.com), should be entertaining guests in ultraluxurious style.

Boston Restaurant Week is now 4 weeks, but it's not Restaurant Month: It's 2 weeks in August and 2 in March. I prefer the seasonal raw materials available to chefs in the summer, but the offer ($20.08 or $20.09 for lunch, $10 or so more for dinner) is a great deal at any time. The Greater Boston Convention & Visitors Bureau lists participating establishments on its website (www.bostonusa.com).

La Voile, 261 Newbury St. (© **617/ 587-4200;** www.lavoileboston.net), may look familiar to travelers who have spent a lot of time in Cannes. The owners of the French/Mediterranean brasserie created it by shipping an existing restaurant across the Atlantic.

The **Boston Tea Party Ship & Museum** (© **617/269-7150;** www. bostonteapartyship.com), which closed after a fire in 2001, plans to expand and reopen in 2009. I've written some version of that sentence at least six times, so call ahead before visiting.

The original **Filene's Basement,** at Downtown Crossing, closed for construction in 2007 with plans to reopen sometime in 2009. Bargain shoppers can hit the Back Bay location, at 497 Boylston St. (© **800/843-8474;** www.filenes basement.com), but it doesn't offer the automatic-markdown policy that makes the century-old original catnip for thrifty fashionistas.

Boston Ballet (© **617/695-6955;** www.bostonballet.org) will spend the 2008–09 season on its longtime home stage, the Citi Wang Theatre, before moving all of its productions (not just *The Nutcracker,* which is already there) to the **Opera House.**

The **Isabella Stewart Gardner Museum,** 280 The Fenway (© **617/ 566-1401;** www.gardnermuseum.org), has followed the lead of the Museum of Fine Arts and started scheduling one evening a month of after-work drinking and music in the galleries.

Boston's nightlife backbone, **Lansdowne Street,** was in transition at press time. Avalon and Axis, stalwarts of the lively strip across from Fenway Park, closed in late 2007, roiling the straight and gay club scenes. In an everything-old-is-new-again twist (the original link in the chain was in Cambridge), the **House of Blues** is expected to replace the popular nightclubs in early 2009. Visit www.hob.com or ask at your hotel before heading out for live music, Southern food, or the famed Sunday gospel brunch.

SIDE TRIPS FROM BOSTON The **Hancock–Clarke House,** 36 Hancock St. (© **978/862-1703;** www.lexington history.org), one of Lexington's best-known historic attractions, closed for restoration in 2008 and is expected to reopen in 2009.

The Cape Ann Historical Museum, not so long ago the Cape Ann Historical Association, is now the **Cape Ann Museum,** 27 Pleasant St., Gloucester (© **978/283-0455;** www.capeannmuseum.org).

CAPE COD One of the most delightful new additions to the Cape Cod dining scene in years is **Osteria La Civetta,** at 133 Main St. in Falmouth (© **508/540-1616),** run by a family from Bologna, Italy. This is European-style dining and service. The food here is exquisite, especially specialties like the lasagna alla bolognese, with homemade pasta.

Restaurant Heather, 20 Joy St. in South Cape Plaza, Mashpee (© **508/539-0025),** is another wonderful new restaurant in the Upper Cape. Chef/owner Heather Allen specializes in wowing diners with creative preparations made with local ingredients. A favorite is the spinach ravioli with lobster, scallops, and boursin cheese.

The newest hot spot in Hyannis is **Embargo,** 453 Main St. (© **508/771-9700),** which specializes in martinis and tapas. This is a popular spot for happy hour from 4:30 to 6pm nightly.

MARTHA'S VINEYARD & NANTUCKET The big news in Edgartown is the $77-million renovation that will take place over the next several years at the historic **Harbor View Hotel,** 131 N. Water St. (© **800/225-6002).** One of the projects is to convert 21 smaller hotel rooms into 13 luxury suites, some with private gardens and outdoor showers. Parts of the hotel will remain open in season during the renovation.

One of the Vineyard's top fine-dining establishments, **L'étoile** (© **508/627-5187),** has moved out of its longtime home at the Charlotte Inn and down the street to 22 North Water St. (just off Main St.). Chef Michael Brisson is still in charge and earning rave reviews. The restaurant at Charlotte Inn is now **Catch at the Terrace** (© **608/627-7200),** which is also receiving high marks from reviewers.

Designer Vanessa Noel has expanded her Nantucket empire once again. Having started with a shoe store, she now has two hotels and a restaurant. **Vanessa Noel Hotel,** 5 Chestnut St. (© **508/228-5300),** seeks to be a boutique hotel by offering amenities like Bulgari toiletries and flatscreen TVs. The new hotel next door, **Hotel Green** (same number), has an ecological theme, with organic cottons and such. Her new restaurant is called **Café V** (© **508/228-8133),** a champagne and caviar bar, in the Vanessa Noel Hotel, that serves breakfast and a light dinner nightly.

CENTRAL & WESTERN MASSACHUSETTS In Worcester, the **Higgins Armory Museum,** 100 Barber Ave. (© **508/853-6015),** has added an outpost of the London Brass Rubbings Centre next to the gift shop, where visitors can make rubbings from plates featuring knights, dragons, and crests.

Old Sturbridge Village, 1 Old Sturbridge Village Rd. (© **800/733-1830),** opened a hands-on craft center for visitors in 2007 and plans to begin offering rides on a newly commissioned horse-drawn stagecoach in 2008. The **Oliver Wright Tavern,** closed for a few years, reopened in 2007. An aggressive 2006–07 fundraising campaign raised $1.83 million and has brought new financial stability to the popular village, which re-creates a rural settlement of the 1830s.

Also in Sturbridge, the newish **Cedar Street Restaurant,** 12 Cedar St. (© 508/347-5800), has become the brightest dining spot in the area. Entrees such as duck with juniper-honey drizzle and toasted pistachio dust, and buttermilk fried chicken with red-eye gravy and braised Swiss chard are as good as you'll find anywhere.

The **Springfield Marriott,** 2 Boland Way (© 800/228-9290), got a snazzy renovation to its lobby and guest rooms, giving the hotel a markedly sparkling and modern overhaul.

The education center of **Historic Northampton,** 46 Bridge St. (© 413/584-6011), no longer has its three 18th- and early-19th-century homes open to the public. It does, however, maintain a small museum, and its website (www.historic-northampton.org) has been beefed up to include detailed virtual exhibits and tours.

Also in Northampton, the popular **Green Street Café,** 64 Green St. (© 413/586-5650), was closed for much of 2007 over a rental dispute but has reopened with a new lease and a small attached wine bar.

The Hampshire Hospitality chain, which runs a number of the hotels in the Pioneer Valley, opened its newest, the **Courtyard By Marriott,** 423 Russell St. (Rte. 9; © 800/321-2211 or 413/256-5454), on the Hadley/Amherst border in May 2007. Rooms have a sleek decor more common to pricier proper-ties, and the property is convenient to the UMass campus.

The village of Turners Falls, in the upper Pioneer Valley near the Vermont and New Hampshire border, has seen its profile rise in recent years, with an influx of artists and an active partnership among cultural and commercial groups. Worth a visit is the **Hallmark Museum of Con-temporary Photography,** 85 Ave. A (also at 52 and 56 Ave. A; © 413/863-0009), which opened one gallery in January 2006 and then another across the street in January 2008. Bicyclists will enjoy the **Franklin County Bikeway's Canalside Trail,** a 4-mile path that opened in early 2008.

New dining highlights in the Berk-shires include Great Barrington's **Allium,** 42 Railroad St. (© 413/528-2118), an offshoot of a growing northern Berkshire chainlet that aims to focus on local and seasonal ingredients, and, across the street, **Pearl's,** 47 Railroad St. (© 413/528-7767), a follow-up to the owners' stylish Zinc in Lenox (which leapt to the upper echelon of Berkshires dining nearly as soon as *it* opened). In Williamstown, a new **Jae's Inn,** 777 Cold Spring Rd. (© 413/458-8032), opened on Route 7. It's a sister operation to its accomplished sibling, Jae's, in North Adams.

In Williamstown, the **Sterling and Francine Clark Art Institute,** 225 South St. (© 413/458-2303), is getting an additional wing. The first phase of the wing is scheduled to open in summer 2008.

CONNECTICUT Up in Washington, in the Litchfield Hills, the **Mayflower Inn & Spa,** 118 Woodbury Rd. (© 860/868-9466), has given its well-heeled pil-grims another reason to make its 58 acres of woods and extravagant bedrooms of tapestry rugs and mahogany wainscoting a destination—an on-site spa. Open since 2006, the spa features scrubs, wraps, and "rituals" in a facility decorated in white marble, bleached wood, and Arts and

Crafts–style windows overlooking tranquil lawns.

The biggest buzz in southern Connecticut's dining scene is New Haven's **Bespoke,** 266 College St. (① **203/562-4644**), open since fall 2006. It's on par with the best of Manhattan dining, but without the comparable cost. The chef/owner was previously behind the late-lamented Roomba, and he brings to his new menu a wider-ranging variety, with memorable entrees such as roasted sea bass in a carrot-curry broth and the "Two-Way" duck.

Old Lyme's **Florence Griswold Museum,** 96 Lyme St. (① **860/434-5542**), reopened in 2006 after 14 months of extensive restoration and refurnishing. Its first floor is now accurately furnished as it was in 1910, when artists who came to be known as the "American Impressionists" boarded here. They expressed their gratitude by leaving samples of their work—sometimes directly on the walls. Renovations also brought in green geothermal cooling and heating systems.

The tribal nations of southeastern Connecticut can't build fast enough on their **Foxwoods Resort** (① **800/369-9003**) and **Mohegan Sun** ① **888/226-7711**) casinos. A new hotel, the **MGM Grand at Foxwoods,** was set to open May 2008 as part of $700-million development project. One wrinkle on the horizon: There are rumblings in Massachusetts for not one, not two, but *three* similar ventures on that side of the border. Massachusetts Governor Deval Patrick is so determined to get gaming up and running in 2008 that he included $124 million in projected casino licensing fees in his budget—well before plans had even passed muster in the legislature. What effect more gaming options in the region might have on the Connecticut operations is, of course, a billion-dollar question.

RHODE ISLAND The state's "Renaissance City" continues to reinvent itself.

The latest sign is a snazzy new luxury hotel, the **Renaissance Providence,** 5 Ave. of the Arts (labeled on most maps as Brownell St.; ① **800/468-3571**). It's the result of an over-$100-million renovation of a dilapidated neoclassical temple partially built by the Masons in the late 1920s, which stood empty for 78 years after that project ran out of cash. The end result is spectacular. Its restaurant-bar, **Temple,** 120 Francis St. (Ave. of the Arts; ① **401/919/5050**), was an instant hit with young professionals and older sophisticates, as well as with hotel guests.

Also in Providence, a 3-month renovation at the **Courtyard by Marriott,** 32 Exchange Terrace (① **800/321-2211**), was completed in early 2008.

In Newport, the newest high-end lodging is the **Hilltop Inn,** 2 Kay St. (① **800/846-0393**), a property which was recently purchased and renovated by the owners of well-appointed Francis Malbone House. Turn-of-the-last-century ceramic tiles and elaborate woodwork abound.

Newport's must-dine list has one new addition: **Fluke Wine Bar,** 41 Bowen's Wharf (① **401/849-7778**). Open since summer 2007, its third level offers a bar, views of the harbor, and a convivial crowd to enjoy them. The chef has a New Orleans background, resulting in spicy versions of quahog chowder, potato croquettes, and the like.

VERMONT In Manchester, the **Equinox Resort,** Route 7A (① **800/362-4747**), has been sold to a hotel consortium in Connecticut; updates are reportedly on the way. Check the resort website and my online updates on Frommers.com for any news.

Among the Equinox's early new moves was the acquisition of the **1811 House,** formerly one of Vermont's best B&B's. It remains mostly what it was, so far; how it will finally be integrated into the resort concept remains to be seen.

Just a stone's throw away from the growing Equinox empire, the **Reluctant Panther,** 17–39 West Rd. (© **800/ 822-2331**), has reopened after a devastating fire and is better and more convivial than ever. The reconstruction of the main inn house excellently replaces the 1850s-era original (though it's no longer purple, as was its predecessor); rooms have become bigger and better, and the inn restaurant—always a plus—has stepped forward into the top ranks of southern Vermont dining.

In northern Vermont, Burlington's overwhelmingly popular **Five Spice Café** was forced to close after a fire. It's a shame, because this was Vermont's best place for an Asian-fusion meal and one of the only places in northern New England where you could eat dim sum meals. It's rumored around town that the Five Spice will reopen in a new location, but nothing has happened yet. Stay tuned.

Also in Burlington, the popular **Frog Hollow Gallery** has relocated to a more central location; in fact, it's as central as can be—right on the Church Street Marketplace.

NEW HAMPSHIRE Here's a switch: Granite Staters approving government and regulation and control of something. As of September 2007, there's **a statewide smoking ban**—not only in restaurants and bars, but at any public event.

On Mount Washington, the **Mount Washington Cog Railway** (© **800/ 922-8825** or 603/278-5404) has added a winter excursion through the lovely snow-covered vistas. Shorter than the normal excursion, it takes an hour and costs about $31 per adult, less for kids and seniors.

A new fancy restaurant, **Victory 96 State Street,** 96 State St. (© **603/766- 0960**), has opened in downtown Portsmouth just a stone's throw from the historic Stawbery Banke district. Its bar area is especially appealing.

MAINE   The Portland Public Market has moved. Portland's once-proud public market closed its doors in early 2007 and the property was sold. But a new market has sprung up right in the center of the city: the **Public Market House,** at 28 Monument Square.

No more $1 popcorn. Sadly, the plucky little **Bayview Street Cinema,** in downtown Camden, has been shuttered, depriving the state of one of its finest independent movie houses.

1

The Best of New England

One of the greatest challenges of traveling in New England is choosing from an abundance of superb restaurants, accommodations, and attractions. Where to start? Here's an entirely biased list of our favorite destinations and experiences. Over years of traveling through the region, we've discovered that these are places worth more than just a quick stop—they're all worth a major detour.

1 The Best of Small-Town New England

- **Marblehead** (MA): The "Yachting Capital of America" has major picture-postcard potential, especially in summer, when the harbor fills with boats of all sizes. From downtown, a short distance inland, make your way toward the water down the narrow, flower-dotted streets. The first glimpse of blue sea and sky is breathtaking. See "Marblehead" in chapter 6.

- **Provincetown** (Cape Cod, MA): At the far tip of the Cape's curl, in intensely beautiful surroundings, is Provincetown. Provincetown's history goes back nearly 400 years, and in the last century, it's been a veritable headquarters of bohemia—a gathering place for famous writers and artists. It's also, of course, one of the world's top gay and lesbian resort areas. But Provincetown is a place for everyone who enjoys savory food, fun shopping, and fascinating people-watching. See "The Lower Cape" in chapter 7.

- **Nantucket** (MA): With grand 19th-century homes and cobblestone streets, it looks as though the whalers just left. Traveling to the island of Nantucket is like taking a trip to a parallel universe; you get historic charm but with 21st-century amenities. The island also has shops full of luxury goods, loads of historical sites open to the public, and miles of public beaches and bike paths. See "Nantucket" in chapter 8.

- **Oak Bluffs** (Martha's Vineyard, MA): Stroll down Circuit Avenue in Oak Bluffs with a Mad Martha's ice cream cone and then ride the Flying Horses Carousel. This island harbor town is full of fun for kids and parents. Don't miss the colorful "gingerbread" cottages behind Circuit Avenue. Oak Bluffs also has great beaches, bike paths, and the Vineyard's best nightlife. See "Martha's Vineyard" in chapter 8.

- **Stockbridge** (MA): Norman Rockwell made a famous painting of the main street of this, his adopted hometown. Facing south, it uses the southern Berkshires as backdrop for the sprawl of the Red Lion Inn and the other late-19th-century buildings that make up the commercial district. Then as now, they service a beguiling mix of unassuming saltboxes and Gilded Age mansions that have sheltered farmers, artists, and aristocrats since the days of the French and Indian Wars. See "The Berkshires" in chapter 9.

New England

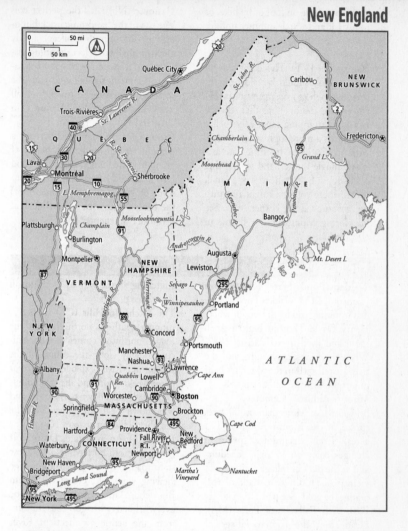

- **Washington** (CT): A classic, with a Congregational church facing a village green surrounded by clapboard Colonial houses—all of them with black shutters. See "The Litchfield Hills" in chapter 10.
- **Essex** (CT): A walk past white-clapboard houses to the active waterfront on this narrow, unspoiled stretch of the Connecticut River rings all the right bells. There is not an artificial

note, a cookie-cutter franchise, nor a costumed docent to muddy its near-perfect image. Rides on a 1920s steam locomotive or Mississippi-style riverboat are options. See "The Connecticut River Valley" in chapter 10.
- **Woodstock** (VT): Woodstock has a stunning village green, a whole range of 19th-century homes, woodland walks leading just out of town, and a settled, old-money air. This is a good

place to explore on foot or by bike, or to just sit and watch summer unfold. See "Woodstock & Environs" in chapter 12.

- **Montpelier** (VT): This is the way all state capitals should be: slow paced, small enough so you can walk everywhere, and full of shops that still sell nails and strapping tape. Montpelier also shows a more sophisticated edge, with its Culinary Institute, an art-house movie theater, and several fine bookshops. But at heart it's a small town, where you just might run into the governor at the corner store. See "Exploring Montpelier & Barre" in chapter 12.

- **Hanover** (NH): It's the perfect college town: the handsome brick buildings of Dartmouth College, a tidy green, a small but select shopping district, and a scattering of good restaurants. Come in the fall, and you'll be tempted to join in the touch football game on the green. See "Hanover" in chapter 13.

- **Castine** (ME): Soaring elm trees, a peaceful harborside setting, plenty of grand historic homes, and a few good inns make this a great spot to soak up some of Maine's coastal ambience off the beaten path. See "The Blue Hill Peninsula" in chapter 14.

2 The Best Places to See Fall Foliage

- **Walden Pond State Reservation** (Concord, MA): Walden Pond is hidden from the road by the woods where Henry David Thoreau built a small cabin and lived from 1845 to 1847. When the leaves are turning and the trees are reflected in the water, it's hard to imagine why he left. See p.158

- **Mount Auburn Cemetery** (Cambridge, MA): More than 5,000 trees spread across Mount Auburn's 175 acres. Each deciduous specimen changes color on its own schedule, and at the peak of foliage season, each seems to be a different shade of red, orange, or gold. See p. 131.

- **Bash-Bish Falls State Park** (MA): Head from the comely village of South Egremont up into the forested hills of the southwest corner of Massachusetts. The roads, which change from macadam to gravel to dirt and back, wind between crimson clouds of sugar maples and white birches feather-stroked against banks of black evergreens. The payoff is a three-state view from a promontory above a 50-foot cascade notched into a bluff, with carpets of russet and gold

stretching all the way to the Hudson River. See p. 335.

- **The Litchfield Hills** (CT): Route 7, running south to north through the rugged northwest corner of Connecticut, roughly along the course of the Housatonic River, explodes with color in the weeks before and after Columbus Day. Leaves drift down to the water and whirl down the foaming river. See "The Litchfield Hills" in chapter 10.

- **I-91** (VT): An interstate? Don't scoff (the traffic can be terrible on narrow state roads). If you like your foliage viewing wholesale, cruise I-91 from Brattleboro to Newport. You'll be overwhelmed with gorgeous terrain, from the gentle Connecticut River Valley to the sloping hills of the Northeast Kingdom. See chapter 12.

- **Vermont Route 100** (VT): Route 100 winds the length of Vermont from Readsboro to Newport, plying the Mad River Valley for a stretch. It's the major north-south route through the center of the Green Mountains, and it's surprisingly undeveloped along most of its length. You won't have it to yourself along the southern stretches on autumn weekends, but as you head farther north, you'll leave the crowds behind. See chapter 12.

- **Crawford Notch** (NH): Route 302 passes through this scenic valley, where you can see the brilliant red maples and yellow birches high on the hillsides. In fall, Mount Washington, in the background, is likely to be dusted with an early snow. See "The White Mountains" in chapter 13.

- **Camden** (ME): The dazzling fall colors that cover the rolling hills are reflected in Penobscot Bay on the east side, and in the lakes on the west. Ascend the peaks for views out to the color-splashed islands in the bay. Autumn usually comes a week or so later on the coast, so you can stretch out your viewing pleasure. See "Penobscot Bay" in chapter 14.

3 The Best Ways to View Coastal Scenery

- **Strolling Around Rockport** (MA): The town surrounds the small harbor and spreads out along the rugged, rocky coastline of Cape Ann. From the end of Bearskin Neck, the view is spectacular—fishing and pleasure boats in one direction, roaring surf in the other. The surf's the thing at Halibut Point State Park, at the tip of the peninsula. See "Cape Ann" in chapter 6.

- **Getting Back to Nature on Plum Island** (MA): The Parker River National Wildlife Refuge, in Newburyport, offers two varieties of coastal scenery: picturesque salt marshes packed with birds and other animals, and gorgeous ocean beaches where the power of the Atlantic is evident. See "Newburyport, Ipswich & Plum Island" in chapter 6.

- **Biking or Driving the Outer Cape** (MA): From Eastham through Wellfleet and Truro, all the way to Provincetown, Cape Cod's outermost towns offer dazzling ocean vistas and a number of exceptional bike paths, including the Province Lands, just outside Provincetown, that are bordered by spectacular swooping dunes. See "The Outer Cape" in chapter 7.

- **Heading "Up-Island" on Martha's Vineyard** (MA): Many visitors never venture beyond the port towns of Vineyard Haven, Oak Bluffs, and Edgartown. Though each has its charms, the scenery actually gets more spectacular "up-island," in towns like Chilmark, where you'll pass moorlike meadows and family farms surrounded by stone walls. Follow State Road and the scenic Moshup Trail to the westernmost tip of the island, where you'll experience the dazzling colored cliffs of Aquinnah and the quaint fishing port of Menemsha. See "Martha's Vineyard" in chapter 8.

- **Cruising Newport's Ocean Drive** (RI): After a tour of the fabulously overwrought "cottages" of the hyperrich that are strung along Bellevue Avenue, emerging onto the shoreline road that dodges the spray of the Atlantic is a cleansing reminder of the power of nature over fragile monuments to the conceits of men. To extend the experience, take a 3.5-mile hike along the Cliff Walk that skirts the edge of the bluff commanded by the largest mansions. See "Newport" in chapter 11.

- **Sitting in a Rocking Chair** (ME): The views are never better than when you're caught unawares—such as suddenly looking up from an engrossing book on the front porch of an oceanside inn. Throughout the Maine chapter, look for mention of inns right on the water, such as Beach House Inn (p. 604), Samoset Resort

(p. 633), East Wind Inn (p. 633), and the Claremont (p. 659).

- **Hiking Monhegan Island** (ME): The village of Monhegan is clustered around the harbor, but the rest of this 700-acre island is all picturesque wildlands, with miles of trails crossing open meadows and winding along rocky bluffs. See "Midcoast Maine" in chapter 14.

- **Driving the Park Loop Road at Acadia National Park** (ME): This is the region's premier ocean drive. You'll start high along a ridge with views of Frenchman Bay and the Porcupine Islands, then dip down along the rocky shores to watch the surf crash against the dark rocks. Plan to do this 20-mile loop at least twice to get the most out of it. See p. 647.

4 The Best Places to Rediscover America's Past

- **Paul Revere House** (Boston, MA): We often study the history of the American Revolution through stories of governments and institutions. At this little home in the North End, you'll learn about a real person. The self-guided tour is particularly thought-provoking, allowing you to linger on the artifacts that hold your interest. Revere had 16 children with two wives, supported them with his thriving silversmith's trade—and put the whole operation in jeopardy with his role in the events that led to the Revolution. See p. 124.

- **Old State House** (Boston, MA): Built in 1713, the once-towering Old State House is dwarfed by modern skyscrapers. It stands as a reminder of British rule (the exterior features a lion and a unicorn) and its overthrow—the Declaration of Independence was read from the balcony, which overlooks a traffic island where a circle of bricks represents the site of the Boston Massacre. See p. 122.

- **Faneuil Hall** (Boston, MA): Although Faneuil Hall is best known nowadays as a shopping destination, if you head upstairs, you'll be transported back in time. In the second-floor auditorium, park rangers talk about the building's role in the Revolution. Tune out the sound of sneakers squeaking across the floor, and you can almost hear Samuel Adams (his statue is out front) exhorting the Sons of Liberty. See p. 116.

- **"Old Ironsides"** (Boston, MA): Formally named USS *Constitution,* the frigate was launched in 1797 and gained fame battling Barbary pirates and seeing action in the War of 1812. Last used in battle in 1815, it was periodically threatened with destruction until a complete renovation in the late 1920s started its career as a floating monument. The staff includes sailors on active duty who wear 1812 dress uniforms. See p. 124.

- **North Bridge** (Concord, MA): British troops headed to Concord after putting down the uprising in Lexington, and the bridge (a replica) stands as a testament to the Minutemen who fought here. The Concord River and its peaceful green banks give no hint of the bloodshed that took place. On the path in from Monument Street, placards and audio stations provide a fascinating narrative. See "Concord" in chapter 6.

- **Plymouth Rock** (Plymouth, MA): Okay, it's a fraction of its original size and looks like something you might find in your garden. Nevertheless, Plymouth Rock makes a perfect starting point for exploration. Close by is

Mayflower II, a replica of the alarmingly small original vessel. The juxtaposition reminds you of what a dangerous undertaking the Pilgrims' voyage was. See "Plymouth" in chapter 6.

- **Sandwich** (MA): The oldest town on Cape Cod, Sandwich was founded in 1637. Glassmaking brought notoriety and prosperity to this picturesque town in the 19th century. Visit the Sandwich Glass Museum for the whole story, or tour one of the town's glassblowing studios. Don't leave without visiting the 76-acre Heritage Museums and Gardens, which has a working carousel, a sparkling antique-car collection, and a wonderful collection of Americana. See "The Upper Cape" in chapter 7.

- **Nantucket** (MA): It looks as though the whalers just left, leaving behind their grand houses, cobbled streets, and a gamut of enticing shops offering luxury goods from around the world. The Nantucket Historical Association owns more than a dozen properties open for tours, and the Whaling Museum is one of the most fascinating sites in the region. Tourism may be rampant, but not its tackier side effects, thanks to stringent preservation measures. See "Nantucket" in chapter 8.

- **Old Sturbridge Village** (MA): Authentic buildings re-create a rural settlement of the 1830s. In the winter, the participatory "Dinner in a Country Village" promotion lets guests stay after hours and prepare a meal of the era on a massive hearth by candlelight, then enjoy the fruits of their labor—roast chicken, "beef olives," gourd soup, trifle, and fresh-roasted coffee. See "Sturbridge & Old Sturbridge Village" in chapter 9.

- **Deerfield** (MA): Arguably the best-preserved Colonial village in New England, the historic section of this town has over 80 houses dating back to the 17th and 18th centuries. None of the clutter of modernity has intruded here. Thirteen museum houses on the main avenue can be visited through tours conducted by the organization known as Historic Deerfield. See "The Pioneer Valley" in chapter 9.

- **Newport** (RI): A key port of the clipper trade long before the British surrendered their colony, Newport retains abundant recollections of its maritime past. In addition to its great harbor, clogged with tugs, ferries, yachts, and majestic sloops, the City by the Sea has kept three distinctive enclaves preserved: the waterside homes of Colonial seamen, the hillside Federal houses of port-bound merchants, and the ostentatious mansions of America's post–Civil War industrial and financial grandees. See "Newport" in chapter 11.

- **Plymouth Notch** (VT): President Calvin Coolidge was born in this high upland valley, and the state has done a superb job preserving his hometown village. You'll get a good sense of the president's roots, but also gain a greater understanding of how a New England village works. See p. 497.

- **Shelburne Museum** (Shelburne, VT): Think of this sprawling museum as New England's attic. Located on the shores of Lake Champlain, the Shelburne features not only the usual exhibits of quilts and early glass, but also whole buildings preserved like specimens in formaldehyde. Look for the lighthouse, the railroad station, and the stagecoach inn. This is one of northern New England's "don't miss" destinations. See p. 530.

- **Portsmouth** (NH): Portsmouth is a salty coastal city that just happens to boast some of the most impressive historic homes in New England. Start at Strawbery Banke, a historic compound of 42 buildings dating from 1695 to 1820. Then visit the many other grand homes in nearby neighborhoods, like the house John Paul Jones occupied while building his warship during the Revolution. See "Portsmouth" in chapter 13.

- **Victoria Mansion** (Portland, ME): The Donald had nothing on the Victorians when it came to excess. You'll see Victorian decorative arts at their zenith in this Italianate mansion built during the Civil War years by a prosperous hotelier. It's open to the public for tours in summer and also puts on outstanding Christmas-season programs in December. See p. 611.

5 The Best Activities for Families

- **Exploring the Museum of Fine Arts** (Boston, MA): Parents hear "magnificent Egyptian collections." Kids think: "Mummies!" Even the most hyper youngster manages to take it down a notch in these quiet, refined surroundings, and the collections at the MFA simultaneously tickle visitors' brains. See p. 119.

- **Experimenting in the Museum of Science** (Boston, MA): Built around demonstrations and interactive displays that never feel like homework, this museum is wildly popular with kids—and adults. Explore the exhibits, then take in a show at the planetarium or the Mugar Omni Theater. Before you know it, everyone will have learned something, painlessly. See p. 120.

- **Catching a Free Friday Flick at the Hatch Shell** (Boston, MA): Better known for the Boston Pops Fourth of July concert, the Esplanade is also famous for family films (like *Shrek* or *Pocahontas*) shown on Friday nights in summer. The lawn in front of the Hatch Shell turns into a giant, carless drive-in as hundreds of people picnic and wait for dark. See p. 140.

- **Visiting the Heritage Museums and Gardens** (Cape Cod, MA): This site with museum buildings spread over 76 acres will delight both children and adults. Kids will especially love the gleaming antique cars, the collections of soldiers and Native American clothing, and the 1912 carousel that offers unlimited rides. Outdoor concerts free with admission take place most Sunday afternoons in season. See p. 199.

- **Whale-Watching off Provincetown** (Cape Cod, MA): Boats leave MacMillan Wharf for the 8-mile journey to Stellwagen Bank National Marine Sanctuary, a rich feeding ground for several types of whales. Nothing can prepare you for the thrill of spotting these magnificent creatures feeding, breaching, and even flipper-slapping. See p. 254.

- **Deep-Sea Fishing:** Charter fishing boats these days usually have high-tech fish-finding gear—imagine how your kids will react to reeling in one big bluefish after another. The top spots to mount such an expedition are Barnstable Harbor or Rock Harbor in Orleans, on Cape Cod; Point Judith, at the southern tip of Rhode Island; and the Maine coast. See chapters 7, 11, and 14, respectively.

- **Riding the Flying Horses Carousel in Oak Bluffs** (Martha's Vineyard, MA): Some say this is the oldest carousel in the country, but your kids might not notice the genuine horsehair, sculptural details, or glass eyes. They'll be too busy trying to grab the brass ring to win a free ride. After your ride, stroll around the town of Oak

Bluffs. Children will be enchanted with the "gingerbread" houses, a carry-over from the 19th-century revivalist movement. See p. 278.

• **Biking Nantucket** (MA): Short, flat trails crisscross the island, and every one leads to a beach. The shortest rides lead to Children's Beach, with its own playground, and Jetties Beach, with a skate park and water-sports equipment for rent; older kids will be able to make the few miles to Surfside and Madaket. See "Nantucket" in chapter 8.

• **Visiting Mystic Seaport and Mystic Aquarium** (CT): The double-down winner in the family-fun sweepstakes has to be this combination: a visit to the waterfront settlement of the Seaport, which captures the look and feel of a 19th-century seafaring village, and a trip to the Aquarium, with performing sea lions and a display of glowing, fluorescent coral. These are the kinds of G-rated attractions that have no age barriers. See p. 407.

• **Visiting the Ben & Jerry Ice Cream Factory** (Waterbury, VT): Kids and ice cream are a great combination, and the half-hour tours that leave every 10 minutes in summer won't tax anybody's patience. Browse the small ice cream museum, enjoy the playground and cow-viewing area,

and make sure to save room for the free samples. See p. 514.

• **Exploring the Shelburne Museum** (Shelburne, VT): This museum contains one of the nation's most singular collections of American decorative, folk, and fine art. Kid favorites include the Circus Building, with a 35,000-piece three-ring miniature circus; an operating vintage carousel; a collection of dolls and dollhouses; and automata, large (sometimes 3 feet tall), often comical wind-up toys. See p. 530.

• **Riding the Mount Washington Cog Railway** (Crawford Notch, NH): It's fun! It's terrifying! It's a great glimpse into history. Kids love this ratchety climb to the top of New England's highest peak aboard trains that were specially designed to scale the mountain in 1869. As a technological marvel, the railroad attracted tourists by the thousands a century ago. They still come to marvel at the sheer audacity of it all. See p. 584.

• **Exploring Monhegan Island** (ME): Kids from 8 to 12 especially enjoy overnight excursions to Monhegan Island. The mail boat from Port Clyde is rustic and intriguing, and the hotels are an adventure. Leave at least an afternoon to sit atop the high, rocky bluffs scouting the glimmering ocean for whales. See "Midcoast Maine" in chapter 14.

6 The Best Country Inns

• **Hawthorne Inn** (Concord, MA; © 978/369-5610): Everything here—the 1870 building, the garden setting a stone's throw from the historic attractions, the antiques, the eclectic decorations, the accommodating innkeepers—is top of the line. See p. 160.

• **Coonamessett Inn** (Falmouth, MA; © 508/548-2300): Picture windows overlooking a pond and 7 verdant

acres make this former (from 1796) homestead a very special place to stay. Separate sitting rooms and knotty pine walls add to its comfort and charm. Plus, Sunday brunch is a real treat. See p. 206.

• **Captain's House Inn** (Chatham, Cape Cod, MA; © 800/315-0728): An elegant country inn dripping with good taste, this is among the best small inns in the region. Most rooms have fireplaces, elegant paneling, and antiques; they're sumptuous yet cozy. Your British hostess serves a stupendous high tea. This could be the ultimate spot to enjoy Chatham's Christmas Stroll festivities. See p. 235.

- **Charlotte Inn** (Edgartown, Martha's Vineyard, MA; ✆ **508/627-4751**): Edgartown tends to be the most formal enclave on Martha's Vineyard, and this compound of exquisite buildings is by far the fanciest address in town. The rooms are distinctively decorated: One boasts a baby grand, another its own thematic dressing room. The restaurant, **Catch at the Terrace,** is also top-notch. See p. 280.

- **The Porches** (North Adams, MA; ✆ **413/664-0400**): It may be stretching the definition of the "country inn" category, but this is too much fun to ignore. It was put together with six 19th-century workmen's houses lined up opposite the Massachusetts Museum of Contemporary Art, a new veranda running across their length. The wit of the designers is evident in the use of paint-by-the-numbers pictures and sublimely kitschy accessories, but laptop rentals, DVD players, and Internet access ensure no 21st-century deprivation. See p. 358.

- **Mayflower Inn & Spa** (Washington, CT; ✆ **860/868-9466**): Not a tough call at all for this part of the region: Immaculate in taste and execution, the Mayflower is as close to perfection as any such enterprise is likely to be (although points off for whiffs of excess pretension). A genuine Joshua Reynolds hangs in the hall. See p. 375.

- **Griswold Inn** (Essex, CT; ✆ **860/767-1776**): "The Griz" has been accommodating sailors and travelers as long as any inn in the country, give or take a decade. In all that time, it has been a part of life and commerce in the lower Connecticut River Valley, always ready with a mug of suds, a haunch of beef, and a roaring fire. The walls are layered with nautical paintings and memorabilia, and they've even gotten up the nerve to add a wine bar to the mix. See p. 400.

- **The Equinox Resort** (Manchester Village, VT; ✆ **800/362-4747**): This is southern Vermont's grand resort, with nearly 200 rooms in a white-clapboard compound that seems to go on forever. The rooms are pleasant enough, but the real draws are the grounds and the resort's varied activities—it's set on 2,300 acres with pools, tennis courts, an 18-hole golf course, and even its own mountainside. Tried everything on vacation? How about falconry classes or backcountry driving at the Range Rover school? See p. 474.

- **Windham Hill Inn** (West Townshend, VT; ✆ **800/944-4080**): Welcome amenities such as air-conditioning in the rooms and a conference room in the barn have been added, while preserving the charm of this 1823 farmstead. It's at the end of a remote dirt road in a high upland valley, and guests are welcome to explore 160 private acres on a network of walking trails. See p. 489.

- **Twin Farms** (Barnard, VT; ✆ **800/894-6327**): Just north of Woodstock may be the most elegant inn in New England. Its rates are a tad breathtaking, but guests are certainly pampered here. Novelist Sinclair Lewis once lived on this 300-acre farm, and today it's an aesthetic retreat that offers serenity and exceptional food. See p. 493

- **The Pitcher Inn** (Warren, VT; ✆ **802/496-6350**): Even though this place was built in 1997, it's possessed of the graciousness of a longtime, well-worn inn. It combines traditional New England form and scale with modern and luxe touches, plus a good dollop of whimsy. See p. 510.

- **Basin Harbor Club** (Vergennes, VT; ℰ **800/622-4000**): Established in 1886, this waterside gem is a classic family resort, with golf, tennis, boating on Lake Champlain, jackets-required dining, stunning views, and evening lectures on the arts. Bring books and board games, and relearn what summer's all about. See p. 532.

- **White Barn Inn** (Kennebunkport, ME; ℰ **207/967-2321**): Many of the White Barn's staff hail from Europe, and guests are treated with a Continental graciousness that's hard to match. Rooms, suites, and cottages here are all a delight, and the meals (served in the barn) are among the best in Maine. See p. 605.

- **Claremont** (Southwest Harbor, ME; ℰ **800/244-5036**): The 1884 Claremont is a Maine classic. This waterside lodge has everything a Victorian resort should, including sparely decorated rooms, creaky floorboards in the halls, great views of water and mountains, and a perfect croquet pitch. See p. 659.

7 The Best Moderately Priced Accommodations

- **Newbury Guest House** (Boston, MA; ℰ **800/437-7668**): This lovely property would be a good deal even if it weren't ideally located on Newbury Street, Boston's version of Rodeo Drive. Rates even include breakfast. See p. 101.

- **Pilgrim Sands Motel** (Plymouth, MA; ℰ **800/729-7263**): The ocean views and two pools (indoor and outdoor) make this a great deal, whether you're immersing yourself in Pilgrim lore or passing through on the way from Boston to Cape Cod. See p. 193.

- **White Horse Inn** (Provincetown, Cape Cod, MA; ℰ **508/487-1790**): The very embodiment of Provincetown funkiness, this inn has hosted such celebrities as filmmaker John Waters and poet laureate Robert Pinsky. Rooms are short on amenities but long on artiness. The apartments, cobbled together by innkeeper Frank Schaefer, are highly original and a lot of fun. See p. 258.

- **Nauset House Inn** (East Orleans, Cape Cod, MA; ℰ **800/771-5508**): This romantic 1810 farmhouse is like a sepia-toned vision of old Cape Cod. Recline in a wicker divan surrounded by fragrant flowers while the wind whistles outside. Better yet, stroll to Nauset Beach and take a quiet walk as the sun sets. Your genial hosts also prepare one of the finest breakfasts in town. See p. 241.

- **Hopkins Inn** (New Preston, CT; ℰ **860/868-7295**): This yellow farmhouse bestows the top view of Lake Waramaug, and is at its best on soft summer days when robust Alpine dishes can be taken out on the terrace. The somewhat spartan rooms don't tempt winding-down guests with either phones or TVs. The Hopkins Vineyard is adjacent. See p. 377.

- **Bee and Thistle Inn** (Old Lyme, CT; ℰ **800/622-4946**): Known for decades for its cuisine, this 1756 house also has a detached cottage and 11 pretty guest rooms, two of which have fireplaces. Easily one of the area's most romantic weekend getaways, it sits on 5 acres beside the small Lieutenant River. See p. 399.

- **Inn at the Mad River Barn** (Waitsfield, VT; ℰ **800/631-0466**): It takes a few minutes to adapt to the spartan rooms and no-frills accommodations here. But you'll soon discover that the real action takes place in the living room and dining room, where skiers relax and chat after a day on the slopes, and share heaping helpings at mealtime. See p. 510.

8 The Best Restaurants

- **Legal Sea Foods** (Boston, MA, and other locations; © 617/266-6800): Newcomers ask where to go for fresh seafood, then react suspiciously when I recommend a world-famous restaurant instead of a local secret. No, it's no secret—but it's a wildly successful chain for a reason. See p. 105.

- **Mamma Maria** (Boston, MA; © 617/523-0077): The best restaurant in the restaurant-choked North End is a far cry from the spaghetti-and-meatballs workhorses that crowd this Italian-American neighborhood. The Northern Italian cuisine at this elegant town house is something to write home about. See p. 108.

- **902 Main** (South Yarmouth, Cape Cod, MA; © 508/398-9902): With fabulous service, an elegant atmosphere, and to-die-for food, this is the place to go for fine dining in the Mid-Cape. Entrees like filet mignon with portobello mushrooms, rack of lamb with truffle mashed potatoes, and haddock with organic beets range will set you swooning. See p. 221.

- **Atria** (Edgartown, Martha's Vineyard, MA; © 508/627-5840): This fine-dining restaurant set in an 18th-century sea captain's home gets rave reviews for its gourmet cuisine and its high-quality service. This is one of those places where you can just relax and have a fantastic and memorable meal, because the staff knows exactly what they are doing. See p. 285.

- **Centre Street Bistro** (Nantucket, MA; © 508/228-8470): Two of the best chefs on the island, Ruth and Tim Pitts, combine their talents at this cozy little hole-in-the-wall restaurant. The best part is that this place features wonderful, creative cuisine at fairly reasonable prices, compared to other island fine-dining restaurants. See p. 309.

- **Zinc** (Lenox, MA; © 413/637-8800): Setting the Berkshires culinary standard ever since its opening, this stylish, contemporary bistro impresses on every repeat visit. It looks great, for starters, with its zinc bar, buffed woods, and flowers everywhere. Most everything that arrives on a plate is supremely satisfying, joining familiarity with the French repertoire with cunning twists in execution. There are 24 wines by the glass and an irresistible five-cheese tasting. See p. 350.

- **Bespoke** (New Haven, CT; © 203/562-4644): The preeminent new-ish restaurant in Connecticut, Bespoke has been open since 2006. Food arrives in one dazzling display after another: seafood chowder in a coconut milk broth; roasted sea bass in a carrot-curry broth; and "Two-Way" duck, an Asian-style leg confit and breast with rhubarb-celery salad. The chef is from the late-lamented Roomba, a revelatory exercise in the then-fresh Nuevo Latino arena. See p. 386.

- **Union League Café** (New Haven, CT; © 203/562-4299): This august setting of arched windows and high ceilings is more than 150 years old and was long the sanctuary of an exclusive club. It still looks good, but the tone has been lightened into an approximation of a Lyonnaise brasserie. See p. 388.

- **Scales & Shells** (Newport, RI; © 401/846-3474): Ye who turn aside all ostentation, get yourselves hence. There's nary a frill nor affectation anywhere near this place, and because the wide-open kitchen is right at the entrance, there are no secrets, either. What we have here are marine critters mere hours from the depths, prepared and presented free of any but the slightest artifice. This might well be the purest seafood joint on the southern New England coast. See p. 450.

- **Chantecleer** (Manchester Center, VT; ✆ **802/362-1616**): Swiss chef Michel Baumann has been turning out dazzling dinners here since 1981, and the kitchen hasn't gotten stale in the least. The dining room in an old barn is magical, the staff helpful and friendly. It's a great spot for those who demand top-notch Continental fare but don't like the fuss of a fancy restaurant. See p. 478.
- **T. J. Buckley's** (Brattleboro, VT; ✆ **802/257-4922**): This tiny diner on a dark side street serves up outsize tastes prepared by a talented chef. Forget about stewed-too-long diner fare; get in your mind big tastes blossoming from the freshest of ingredients prepared just right. See p. 487.
- **Hemingway's** (Killington, VT; ✆ **802/422-3886**): Killington seems an unlikely place for a serious culinary adventure, yet Hemingway's will meet the loftiest expectations. The menu changes frequently to ensure only the freshest of ingredients. If it's available, be sure to order a bowl of the wild mushroom and truffle soup. See p. 487.
- **Arrows** (Ogunquit, ME; ✆ **207/ 361-1100**): The emphasis at this elegant spot is on local products—often many ingredients from nearby organic vegetable gardens. Prices are not for the fainthearted, but the experience is top-rate, from the cordial service to the silver and linens. Expect New American fare informed by an Asian sensibility. See p. 602.
- **White Barn Inn** (Kennebunkport, ME; ✆ **207/967-2321**): The setting in an ancient, rustic barn is magical. The tables are set with floor-length tablecloths, and the chairs feature imported Italian upholstery. The food? To die for. Start with lobster spring rolls, then enjoy entrees such as roasted duck with juniper sauce or Maine lobster over fettuccine with a cognac coral butter sauce. See p. 604.
- **Fore Street** (Portland, ME; ✆ **207/ 775-2717**): Fore Street is one of northern New England's most celebrated restaurants. The chef's secret? Simplicity, and lots of it. Some of the most memorable meals are prepared over an apple-wood grill. See p. 614.
- **Hugo's** (Portland, ME; ✆ **207/ 774-8538**): Chef Rob Evans has performed a CPR job on this once-proud bistro that's been nothing short of amazing; it now stands among Maine's finest restaurants. The tasting menus are especially wonderful, and there's an affiliated Belgian-fries shop just down the street for guilty-pleasure dining as well. See p. 614.

9 The Best Local Dining Experiences

- **Durgin-Park** (Boston, MA; ✆ **617/ 227-2038**): A meal at this landmark restaurant might start with a waitress dropping a handful of cutlery in front of you and saying, "Here, give these out." The surly service usually seems to be an act, but it's so much a part of the experience that some people are disappointed when the waitresses are nice (as they often are). In any case, it's worked since 1827. See p. 110.
- **Woodman's of Essex** (Essex, MA; ✆ **800/649-1773**): This busy North Shore institution is not for the faint of heart—or the hard of artery, unless you like eating corn and steamers while everyone around you is gobbling fried clams and onion rings. The food at this glorified clam shack is fresh and delicious, and a look at the organized pandemonium behind the counter is worth the (reasonable) price. See p. 174.

- **Black Eyed Susan's** (Nantucket, MA; ℂ 508/325-0308): This is extremely exciting food in a funky bistro atmosphere. The place is small, popular with locals, and packed. Sitting at the diner counter and watching the chef in action is a show in itself. No credit cards, no reservations, and no liquor license are all an inconvenience, but if you can get past all that, you're in for a top-notch dining experience. See p. 309.
- **Louis' Lunch—The Very First (Well, Probably) Burgers** (New Haven, CT; ℂ 203/562-5507): Not a lot of serious history has happened in New Haven, but boosters claim it was here that hamburgers were invented in 1900. This little lunch-eonette lives on, moved from its original site in order to save it. The patties are freshly ground daily, thrust into vertical grills, and served on white toast. Garnishes are tomato, onion, and cheese. No ketchup and no fries, so don't even ask. See p. 387.
- **Pizza** (New Haven, CT): The city's claim to America's first pizza is a whole lot shakier than its claim to the first burgers, but New Haven has few equals as purveyor of the ultrathin, charred variety of what they still call "apizza" in these parts, pronounced "ah-peetz." Old-timer **Frank Pepe's,** 157 Wooster St. (ℂ 203/865-5762), is usually ceded top rank among the local parlors, but it is joined by such contenders as **Sally's,** 237 Wooster St. (ℂ 203/624-5271), and **Modern Apizza,** 874 State St. (ℂ 203/776-5306). See p. 386.
- **Abbott's Lobster in the Rough** (Noank, CT; ℂ 860/536-7719): Places like this frill-free lobster shack abound along more northerly reaches of the New England coast, but here's a little bit o' Maine a Sunday drive from Manhattan. Shore dinners rule, so roll up sleeves, tie on napkins, and dive into platters of boiled shrimp and steamed mussels, and dunk hot lobster chunks in pots of drawn butter. See p. 410.
- **Johnnycakes and Stuffies** (RI): Most worthy regional food faves eventually become known to the wider world (witness Buffalo wings). But the Ocean State still has some taste treats that are mysteries beyond its borders. "Johnnycakes" are flap-jacks made with cornmeal, which come small and plump or wide and lacy, depending upon family tradition. "Stuffies" are the baby-fist-size quahog (*KWAH*-og or *KOE*-hog) clams barely known elsewhere in New England. The flesh is chopped up, combined with minced bell peppers and bread crumbs, and packed back into both halves of the shell. See chapter 11.
- **Blue Benn Diner** (Bennington, VT; ℂ 802/442-5140): This 1945 Silk City diner has a barrel ceiling, acres of stainless steel, and a vast menu. Don't overlook specials scrawled on paper and taped all over the walls. And leave room for a slice of delicious pie, such as blackberry, pumpkin, or chocolate cream. See p. 470.
- **Bove's** (Burlington, VT; ℂ 802/864-6651): A Burlington landmark since 1941, Bove's is a classic red-sauce-on-spaghetti joint that's a throwback to a lost era. The red sauce is rich and tangy, and the garlic sauce packs enough garlic to knock you clear out of your booth. See p. 534.
- **Al's French Frys** (South Burlington, VT; ℂ 802/862-9203): This is where Ben and Jerry go to eat french fries—as does every other potato addict in the state. See p. 534.
- **Lou's** (Hanover, NH; ℂ 603/643-3321): Huge crowds flock to Lou's, just down the block from the Dartmouth campus, for breakfast on

weekends. Fortunately, breakfast is served all day here, and the sandwiches on fresh-baked bread are huge and delicious. See p. 562.

- **Becky's** (Portland, ME; © **207/773-7070**): Five different kinds of home fries on the menu? It's breakfast nirvana at this local institution on the working waterfront. It's a favored hangout of fishermen, high-school kids, businessmen, and just about everyone else. See p. 616.
- **Silly's** (Portland, ME; © **207/772-0360**): Hectic and fun, this tiny, informal, kitschy restaurant serves up delicious finger food, like pita wraps, hamburgers, and pizza. The milkshakes alone are worth the detour. See p. 617.

10 The Best of the Performing Arts

- **Symphony Hall** (Boston, MA; © **617/266-1492**): Home to the Boston Symphony Orchestra, the Boston Pops, and other local and visiting groups and performers, this is a perfect (acoustically and otherwise) destination for classical music. See p. 140.
- **Hatch Shell** (Boston, MA; © **617/626-1250**): This amphitheater on the Charles River Esplanade plays host to free music, dance performances, and films almost all summer. Around the Fourth of July, the Boston Pops provide the entertainment. Bring a blanket to sit on. See p. 140.
- *The Nutcracker* (Boston, MA; © **800/447-7400** for tickets): New England's premier family-oriented holiday event is Boston Ballet's extravaganza. When the Christmas tree grows through the floor, even fidgety preadolescents forget that they think they're too cool to be here. See p. 140.
- **The Comedy Connection at Faneuil Hall** (Boston, MA; © **617/ 248-9700**): Even in the Athens of America, it's not all high culture. The biggest national names and the funniest local comics take the stage at this hot spot. See p. 143.
- **The Berkshire Theatre Festival** (Stockbridge, MA; © **413/298-5576**): An 1887 "casino" and converted barn mount both new and classic plays from June to late August in one of the prettiest towns in the Berkshires. Name artists on the order of Joanne Woodward and Kevin Kline are often listed as actors and directors in the annual playbill. See p. 340.
- **The Jacob's Pillow Dance Festival** (Becket, MA; © **413/243-0745**): Celebrated dancer/choreographer Martha Graham made this her summertime performance space for decades. Guest troupes are among the world's best, often including Mark Morris Dance Group, Les Grands Ballets Canadiens, and Twyla Tharp. The growing campus includes a store, pub, dining room, and tent restaurant. See p. 343.
- **Tanglewood Music Festival** (Lenox, MA; © **617/266-1492**): By far the most dominating presence on New England's summer cultural front, the music festival that takes place on this magnificent Berkshires estate is the summer playground for the Boston Symphony Orchestra. Room is also made for such guest soloists as Itzhak Perlman and Yo-Yo Ma, as well as popular artists including James Taylor, Bonnie Raitt, and Wynton Marsalis. See p. 346.
- **Williamstown Theatre Festival** (Williamstown, MA; © **413/597-3400**): Classic, new, and avant-garde plays are all presented during the June-through-August season at this

venerable festival. There are two stages, one for works by established playwrights, the smaller second venue for less mainstream or experimental plays. See p. 357.

- **Summer in Newport** (RI): From Memorial Day to Labor Day, only a scheduling misfortune will deny visitors the experience of an outdoor musical event. In calendar order, the highlights (well short of all-inclusive) are the Newport Music Festival, in July; the Dunkin' Donuts Newport Folk Festival and JVC Jazz Festival, in August; and the Waterfront Irish Festival, in September. See p. 433.

11 The Best Destinations for Antiques Hounds

- **Charles Street** (Boston, MA): Beacon Hill is one of the city's oldest neighborhoods, and at the foot of the hill is a thoroughfare that's equally steeped in history. Hundreds of years' worth of furniture, collectibles, and accessories jam the shops along its 5 blocks. River Street, which runs parallel to Charles (follow Chestnut St. 1 block), is worth a look, too. See p. 138.

- **Main Street, Essex** (MA): The treasures on display in this North Shore town run the gamut, from "one step above yard sale" to "one step below nationally televised auction." Follow Route 133 west of Route 128 through downtown and north almost all the way to the Ipswich border. See "Cape Ann" in chapter 6.

- **Route 6A: The Old King's Highway** (Cape Cod, MA): Antiques buffs, as well as architecture and country-road connoisseurs, will have a field day along scenic Route 6A. Designated a Regional Historic District, this former stagecoach route winds through a half-dozen charming villages and is lined with scores of antiques shops. The largest concentration is in Brewster, but you'll find good pickings all along this meandering road, from Sandwich to Orleans. See chapter 7.

- **Brimfield Antique and Collectible Shows** (Brimfield, MA): The otherwise sleepy town west of Sturbridge erupts with three monster shows every summer, in mid-May, mid-July, and early September. Upward of 6,000 dealers set up tented and table-top shops in fields around town. Call ℂ **800/628-8379** for details, and book room reservations far in advance. See p. 315.

- **Sheffield** (MA): This southernmost town in the Berkshires is home to at least two dozen dealers in collectibles, Americana, military memorabilia, English furniture of the Georgian period, silverware, and weather vanes . . . even antique birdhouses. Most of them are strung along Route 7, with a worthwhile detour west along Route 23 in South Egremont. See p. 334.

- **Woodbury** (CT): More than 30 high-end dealers along Main Street offer a diversity of precious treasures, near-antiques, and simply funky old stuff. American and European furniture and other pieces are most evident, but there are forays into crafts and assorted whimsies as well. Pick up the directory of the Woodbury Antiques Dealers Association, available in most shops. See p. 373.

- **Newfane and Townshend** (VT): A handful of delightful antiques shops are hidden in and around these picture-perfect towns. But the real draw is the Sunday flea market, held just off Route 30 north of Newfane, where you never know what might turn up. See p. 488.

- **Portsmouth** (NH): Picturesque downtown Portsmouth is home to a half-dozen or so antiques stores and some fine used-book shops. For more meaty browsing, head about 25 miles northwest on Route 4 to Northwood, where a dozen good-size shops flank the highway. See "Portsmouth" in chapter 13.

- **Route 1, Kittery to Scarborough** (ME): Antiques scavengers delight in this 37-mile stretch of less-than-scenic Route 1. Antiques minimalls and high-class junk shops alike are scattered all along the route, though there's no central antiques zone. See "The Southern Maine Coast" in chapter 14.

2

New England in Depth

by Paul Karr

Reduced to the simplest terms, New England consists of two regions: Boston and Not-Boston.

Boston, of course, is in the same league as other major metropolitan areas and boasts first-class hotels, restaurants, and historic and modern architecture. Of all U.S. cities, Boston has perhaps the richest history, ranging from the days of America's settlement in the 17th century through the War of Independence in 1776 and on into the nation's cultural renaissance in the mid- and late 19th century. The Boston area is also a national seat of education, with dozens of prestigious colleges and universities. The presence of so many august institutions lends the city a youthful air in contrast to its staid heritage.

The extensive territory of Not-Boston arcs widely, from the Connecticut and Rhode Island shoreline through the rolling Berkshire Mountains of western Massachusetts, on through the Green and White mountains, and into the vast state of Maine. This region, while widely spread, traces it roots back to a Puritan ethic, and its longtime residents still tend to display shared traits and values such as a stubborn independence, a respect for thrift and straight-shooting, and an almost genetic mistrust of outsiders.

Some writers maintain that New England's character is still informed by a Calvinist doctrine, which decrees that nothing will change one's fate and that hard work is a virtue. The New Englander's perverse celebration of the often-brutish climate is often trotted out as evidence of the region's enduring Calvinism.

But that's not to say travelers should expect rock-hard mattresses and nutritional but tasteless meals. Luxurious country inns and restaurants serving food rivaling what you'll find in Manhattan have become part of the landscape in the past 2 decades. Be sure to visit these places. But also set aside enough time to spend an afternoon rocking and reading on a broad inn porch, or to wander out of town on an abandoned county road with no particular destination in mind.

"There's nothing to do here," an inn manager in Vermont once explained. "Our product is indolence." That's an increasingly rare commodity these days. Take the time to savor it.

1 New England Today

It's a common question, so don't be embarrassed about asking it. You might be on Martha's Vineyard, or traveling through a pastoral Vermont valley, or exploring an island off the Maine coast.

You'll see houses and people. And you'll wonder: "What do these people do to earn a living?"

As recently as a few decades ago, the answer was probably living off the land.

They might have fished, harvested timber, or managed a gravel pit. Of course, many still do operate such businesses, but this work is no longer the economic mainstay it once was. Today, scratch a rural New Englander and you're just as likely to find an editor for a magazine that's published in Boston or New York, a farmer who grows specialized produce for gourmet restaurants, or a banking consultant who handles business by fax and e-mail. And you'll find lots of folks whose livelihood is dependent on tourism.

This change in the economy is but one of the tectonic shifts facing the region. The most visible and wracking change involves development and growth. For a region long familiar with economic poverty, a spell of recent prosperity and escalating property values has threatened to bring to New England that curious homogenization already marking much of the rest of the nation. Once a region of distinctive villages, green commons, and courthouse squares, New England's landscape in certain places is beginning to resemble suburbs everywhere else—a pastiche of strip malls dotted with fast-food chains, big-box discount and home-improvement stores, and the like.

This change pains longtime residents. New England towns have long maintained their identities in the face of considerable pressure. The region has always taken pride in its low-key, practical approach to life. In smaller communities, town meetings are still the preferred form of government. Residents gather in a public space to speak out about—sometimes rather forcefully—and vote on the issues of the day, such as funding for their schools, road improvements, fire trucks, or even symbolic gestures such as declaring their towns nuclear-free. "Use it up, wear it out, make it do, or do without" is a well-worn phrase that aptly sums up the attitude of many longtime New Englanders—and it's the polar opposite of the designer-outlet ethos filtering in.

It's still unclear how town meetings and that sense of knowing where your town starts and the next one begins will survive the slow but inexorable encroachment of Wal-Marts and Banana Republics. Of course, suburban Connecticut communities in the orbit of New York City and Boston have long since capitulated to sprawl, as have pockets elsewhere in the region—including mall-heavy areas outside Hartford, Connecticut; Portland, Maine; and Burlington, Vermont, not to mention Maine's Route 1 or the outlets along interstate highways in Massachusetts and Connecticut.

But the rest of New England is still figuring out how best to balance the principles of growth and conservation—how to allow the economy to edge into the modern age without sacrificing those qualities that make New England such a distinctive place.

Development is a hot but not necessarily inflammatory issue—this isn't like the property-rights movement in the West (at least, not yet). Few seem to think that development should be allowed at all costs. And few seem to think that the land should be preserved at all costs.

Pinching off all development means the offspring of longtime New England families will have no jobs, and New England will be fated to spend its days as a sort of quaint theme park. But if development continues unabated, many of the characteristics that make New England unique—and attract tourist dollars—will vanish. Will the Berkshires or the Maine coast be able to sustain tourism industries if they're blanketed with strip malls and fast-food joints, making them look like every other place in the nation? Not likely. The question is how to respect the conservation ethic while leaving room for growth. And that question won't be resolved in the near future.

Except for a several-year slump in the early 1990s, New England has been

Local Wisdom
Live free or die.

—New Hampshire state motto

enjoying a generally rosy period of economic growth since the mid-1980s; even when the economy has dipped back downward, as it has done of late, property values continue to rise as city folks increasingly seek a piece of what makes rural New England special. Commentators point out that this change, while welcome after decades of slow growth, will bring new conflicts. The rise of the information culture will make it increasingly likely that telecommuters and info-entrepreneurs will settle in New England's most remote and pristine villages, running their businesses via modem or satellite. How will these affluent newcomers adapt to clear-cutting in the countryside or increasing numbers of tour buses cruising their village greens?

Change doesn't come rapidly to New England. But there's a lot to sort out, and friction will certainly continue to build, one strip mall at a time.

2 Looking Back at New England

Viewed from a distance, New England's history mirrors that of its namesake, England. The region rose from nowhere to gain tremendous historical prominence, captured a good deal of overseas trade, and became an industrial powerhouse and center for creative thought. And then the party ended relatively abruptly, as commerce and culture sought more fertile grounds to the west and south.

To this day, New England remains linked to its past. Walking through Boston, layers of history are evident at every turn, from the church steeples of Colonial times (dwarfed by glass-sided skyscrapers) to verdant parklands that bespeak the refined sensibility of the late Victorian era.

History is even more inescapable in off-the-beaten-track New England. Travelers in Down East Maine, northern New Hampshire, Connecticut's Litchfield Hills, the Berkshires, and much of Vermont will find clues to what Henry Wadsworth Longfellow called "the irrevocable past" every way they turn, from stone walls running through woods to Federal-style homes.

Here's a brief overview of some historical episodes and trends that shaped New England:

INDIGENOUS CULTURE

Native Americans have inhabited New England since about 7000 B.C. While New York's Iroquois Indians had a presence in Vermont, New England was inhabited chiefly by Algonquins who lived a nomadic life. Connecticut was home to some 16 Algonquin tribes, who dubbed the region Quinnetukut.

After the arrival of the Europeans, French Catholic missionaries succeeded in converting many Native Americans, and most tribes sided with the French in the French and Indian Wars in the 18th century. Afterward, the Indians fared poorly at the hands of the British and were quickly pushed to the margins. Today they are found in greatest concentration at several reservations in Maine. The Pequots have established a thriving gaming industry in Connecticut. Other than that, the few clues left behind by Indian cultures have been more or less obliterated by later settlers.

THE COLONISTS

Viking explorers from Newfoundland may or may not have sailed southward into New England—stories abound—but what's certain is that the European colonists arrived in the very early 17th century and eventually displaced entirely the native American culture that existed in the region.

It began in 1604, when some 80 French colonists spent a winter on a small island on what today is the Maine–New Brunswick border. They did not care for the harsh weather of their new home and left in spring to resettle in present-day Nova Scotia. In 1607, 3 months after the celebrated Jamestown, Virginia, colony was founded, another group of 100 settlers (this time from England) established a community at Popham Beach, in present-day Phippsburg, Maine. The Maine winter demoralized these would-be colonists as well, and they returned to England the following year.

The colonization of the region began in earnest with the arrival of the Pilgrims at Plymouth Rock in 1620. The Pilgrims—a religious group that had split from the Church of England—established the first permanent colony, although it came at a hefty price: Half the group perished during the first winter. But the colony began to thrive over the years, in part thanks to helpful Native Americans.

The success of the Pilgrims lured other settlers from England, who established a constellation of small towns outside of Boston that became the Massachusetts Bay Colony. Roger Williams was expelled from the colony for his religious beliefs; he founded the city of Providence, Rhode Island. Other restless colonists expanded their horizons in search of lands for settlement. Throughout the 17th century, colonists from Massachusetts pushed northward into what are now New Hampshire and Maine, and southward into Connecticut. The first areas to be settled were lands near protected harbors along the coast and on navigable waterways.

The more remote settlements came under attack in the 17th and early 18th centuries in a series of raids by Indians conducted both independently and in concert with the French. These proved temporary setbacks; colonization continued throughout New England into the 18th century.

THE AMERICAN REVOLUTION

Starting around 1765, Great Britain launched a series of ham-handed economic policies to reign in the increasingly feisty colonies. These included a direct tax—the Stamp Act—to pay for a standing army. The crackdown provoked strong resistance. Under the banner of "No taxation without representation," disgruntled colonists engaged in a series of riots, resulting in the Boston Massacre of 1770, when five protesting colonists were fired upon and killed by British soldiers.

In 1773, the most infamous protest took place in Boston. The British had imposed the Tea Act (the right to collect duties on tea imports), which prompted a group of colonists dressed as Indians to board three British ships and dump 342 chests of tea into the harbor. This incident was dubbed the Boston Tea Party.

Hostilities reached a peak in 1775, when the British sought to quell unrest in Massachusetts. A contingent of British soldiers was sent to Lexington to seize military supplies and arrest two high-profile rebels—John Hancock and Samuel Adams. The militia formed by the colonists exchanged gunfire with the British, thereby igniting the Revolution ("the shot heard 'round the world").

Notable battles in New England included the Battle of Bunker Hill outside Boston, which the British won but at tremendous cost; and the Battle of

Bennington in Vermont, in which the colonists prevailed. Hostilities formally ended in February 1783, and in September, Britain recognized the United States as a sovereign nation.

FARMING & TRADE

As the new republic matured, economic growth in New England followed two tracks. Residents of inland communities survived by farming and trading in furs. Vermont, in particular, has always been an agrarian state, and remains a prominent dairy producer to this day.

On the coast, boatyards sprang up from Connecticut to Maine, and ship captains made tidy fortunes trading lumber for sugar and rum in the Caribbean. Trade was dealt a severe blow following the Embargo Act of 1807, but commerce eventually recovered, and New England ships could be encountered everywhere around the globe.

The growth of the railroad in the mid–19th century was another boon. The train opened up much of the interior and led to towns springing up overnight, such as White River Junction, Vermont. The rail lines allowed local resources—such as the fine marbles and granites from Vermont—to be easily shipped to markets to the south.

AN INDUSTRIAL REVOLUTION

New England's Industrial Revolution found seed around the time of the embargo of 1807. Barred from importing English fabrics, Americans built their own textile mills. Other common household products were also manufactured domestically, especially shoes. Towns like Lowell, Massachusetts; Lewiston, Maine; and Manchester, New Hampshire, became centers of textile and shoe production. In Connecticut, the manufacture of arms and clocks emerged as major industries. Today industry no longer plays the prominent role it once did— manufacturing first moved to the South, then overseas.

TOURISM BOOM, ECONOMIC BUST

In the mid- and late 19th century, New Englanders discovered a new cash crop: the tourist. All along the Eastern Seaboard, it became fashionable for the gentry, and eventually the working class, to set out for excursions to the mountains and the shore. Regions such as the Berkshires, the White and Green mountains, and Block Island were lifted by the tide of summer visitors. The tourism wave crested in the 1890s in Newport, Rhode Island, and Bar Harbor, Maine, both of which were flooded by the affluent. Several grand resort hotels from tourism's golden era still host summer travelers in the region.

But this economic rebirth would not last long. While railways allowed New England to thrive in the mid–19th century, the trains also eventually played a pivotal role in undermining the region's prosperity. The driving of the Golden Spike in 1869 in Utah, linking America's Atlantic and Pacific coasts by rail, was heard loud and clear in New England, and it had a discordant ring. Transcontinental rail meant farmers and manufacturers could ship goods from the fertile Great Plains and California to faraway markets, making it harder for New England's hardscrabble farmers to survive. Likewise, the coastal shipping trade was dealt a fatal blow by this new transportation network. And the tourists set their sights on the Rockies and other stirring sites in the West.

Beginning in the late 19th century, New England lapsed into an extended economic slumber. Families commonly walked away from their farmhouses (there was no market for resale) and set off for regions with more promising opportunities. The abandoned, decaying farmhouse became almost an icon for New England, and vast tracts of open farmland were reclaimed by forest. With

Local Wisdom

Ask not what your country can do for you; ask what you can do for your country.

—John F. Kennedy

the rise of the automobile, the grand resorts further succumbed, and many closed their doors as inexpensive motels siphoned off their business.

TOURISM & TECH: A SECOND WIND

During the last 2 decades of the 20th century, much of New England rode an unexpected wave of prosperity. A massive real-estate boom shook the region in the 1980s, driving land prices sky-high as prosperous buyers from New York and Boston acquired vacation homes or retired to the most alluring areas. In the 1990s, the sudden rise of high-tech companies in the Boston area, riding the Internet wave, sent ripples from Boston out into the hinterlands of Maine and New Hampshire. New York City's rebound as a world-class

tourism destination brought fresh jobs, money, and homeowners pouring into Connecticut, Rhode Island, and Vermont. Tourism also rebounded as the newly harried urbanites of the Eastern Seaboard opted for shorter, more frequent vacations closer to home during economic dips.

Though the recent boom has been welcome news to many long-term residents, those in the most remote regions of New England never benefited at all from this boom. Especially hard-hit were places like northeastern Vermont and far Down East Maine, where many residents still depend on local resources—timber, fisheries, and farmland—to eke out a living, though land prices have begun rising even here as city dwellers seek ever-quieter places to recreate or retire.

3 New England's Architecture & Art

ARCHITECTURE

You can often trace the evolution of a town by its architecture, as styles evolve from basic structures to elaborate Victorian mansions. The primer below should aid with basic identification.

- **Colonial** (1600–1700): The New England house of the 17th century was a simple, boxy affair, often covered in shingles or rough clapboards. Don't look for ornamentation; these homes were designed for basic shelter from the elements, and are often marked by prominent stone chimneys. You can see examples at Plimoth Plantation and in Salem, near Boston.
- **Georgian** (1700–1800): Ornamentation comes into play in the Georgian

style, which draws heavily on classical symmetry. Georgian buildings were in vogue in England at the time and were embraced by affluent colonists. Look for Palladian windows, formal pilasters, and elaborate projecting pediments. Deerfield (in the Pioneer Valley of Massachusetts) is a good destination for seeing early Georgian homes, and Providence, Rhode Island, and Portsmouth, New Hampshire, have abundant examples of later Georgian styles.
- **Federal** (1780–1820): Federal homes (sometimes called Adams homes) may best represent the New England ideal. Spacious yet austere, they are often rectangular or square, with low-pitched roofs and little ornamentation

on the front, although carved swags or other embellishments are frequently seen near the roofline. Look for fan windows and chimneys bracketing the building. Excellent Federal-style homes are found throughout the region in towns such as Kennebunkport, Maine.

- **Greek Revival** (1820–60): The most easy-to-identify Greek Revival homes feature a projecting portico with massive columns, like a part of the Parthenon grafted onto an existing home. The less dramatic homes may simply be oriented such that the gable faces the street, accenting the triangular pediment. Greek Revival didn't catch on in New England the way it did in the South, but some fine examples exist, notably in Newfane, Vermont.
- **Carpenter Gothic** and **Gothic Revival** (1840–80): The second half of the 19th century brought a wave of Gothic Revival homes, which borrowed their aesthetic from the English country home. Aficionados of this style and its later progeny featuring gingerbread trim owe themselves a trip to Oak Bluffs at Martha's Vineyard in Massachusetts, where cottages are festooned with scrollwork and exuberant architectural flourishes.
- **Victorian** (1860–1900): This is a catchall term for the jumble of mid- to late-19th-century styles that emphasized complexity and opulence. Perhaps the best-known Victorian style—almost a caricature—is the tall and narrow Addams Family–style house, with mansard roof and prickly roof cresting. You'll find these scattered throughout the region. The Victorian style also includes squarish **Italianate** homes with wide eaves and unusual flourishes, such as the outstanding Victoria Mansion in Portland, Maine.

Stretching the definition of Victorian a bit is the **Richardsonian Romanesque** style, which was popular for railroad stations and public buildings. The classic Richardsonian building, designed by H. H. Richardson himself in 1872, is Trinity Church, in Boston.

- **Shingle** (1880–1900): This uniquely New England style quickly became preferred for vacation homes on Cape Cod and the Maine coast. They're marked by a profusion of gables, roofs, and porches, and are typically covered with shingles from roofline to foundation.
- **Modern** (1900–present): Outside of Boston, New England has produced little in the way of notable modern architecture. In the 1930s, Boston became a center for the stark **International Style** with the appointment of Bauhaus veteran Walter Gropius to the faculty at Harvard. Some intriguing experiments in this style are found on the MIT and Harvard campuses, including Gropius's Campus Center and Eero Saarinen's Kresge Auditorium.

ART

New England is also justly famous for the art it has produced, particularly the seascapes painted on Cape Cod, along the coast of Maine, as well as those by **Hudson River School** artists such as Thomas Cole and his student Frederic Church. Some of the other artists who have memorably painted New England landscapes and seascapes include **Winslow Homer** (1836–1910), **John Marin** (1870–1953), **Fairfield Porter** (1907–1975), **Neil Welliver** (1929–2005), and **Andrew Wyeth** (b. 1917), the latter of the iconic *Christina's World,* painted in a coastal Maine field.

To showcase these works, and the works of other local and traveling artists, there are a surprising number of excellent art museums and galleries throughout New England, even in such unlikely places as Williamstown, Massachusetts; St. Johnsbury, Vermont; and Portland and Rockland, Maine. Consult individual chapters for more details on local art offerings.

4 New England in Popular Culture: Books, Film, TV, Music

BOOKS

New Englanders have generated whole libraries, from the earliest days of hellfire-and-brimstone Puritan sermons to Stephen King's horror novels set in fictional Maine villages.

Among the more enduring writings from New England's earliest days are the poems of Massachusetts Bay Colony resident **Anne Bradstreet** (ca. 1612–72) and the sermons and essays of **Increase Mather** (1639–1723) and his son, **Cotton Mather** (1663–1728).

After the American Revolution, Hartford dictionary writer **Noah Webster** (1758–1843) issued a call to American writers: "America must be as independent in literature as she is in politics, as famous for arts as for arms." He struck an early blow for pragmatism by taking the "u" out of British words like "labour" and "honour."

The tales of **Nathaniel Hawthorne** (1804–64) captivated a public eager for a native literature. His most famous story, *The Scarlet Letter,* is a narrative about morality set in 17th-century Boston, but he wrote numerous other books that wrestled with themes of sin and guilt, often set in the emerging republic.

Henry Wadsworth Longfellow (1807–82), the Portland poet who settled in Cambridge, caught the attention of the public with evocative narrative poems focusing on distinctly American subjects. His popular works included "The Courtship of Miles Standish," "Paul Revere's Ride," and "Hiawatha." Poetry in the mid–19th century was the equivalent of Hollywood movies today—Longfellow could be considered his

generation's Steven Spielberg (apologies to literary scholars).

The zenith of New England literature occurred in the mid- and late 19th century with the Transcendentalist movement. These writers and thinkers included **Ralph Waldo Emerson** (1803–82), **Bronson Alcott** (1799–1888), and **Henry David Thoreau** (1817–62). They fashioned a way of viewing nature and society that was uniquely American. They rejected the rigid doctrines of the Puritans, and found sustenance in self-examination, the glories of nature, and a celebration of individualism. Perhaps the best-known work to emerge from this period was Thoreau's *Walden.*

Among other regional writers who left a lasting mark on American literature was **Emily Dickinson** (1830–86), a native of Amherst, Massachusetts, whose precise and enigmatic poems placed her in the front rank of American poets. **James Russell Lowell** (1819–91), of Cambridge, was an influential poet, critic, and editor. Later poets were imagist **Amy Lowell** (1874–1925), from Brookline, Massachusetts, and **Edna St. Vincent Millay** (1892–1950), from Camden, Maine.

The bestselling *Uncle Tom's Cabin,* the book Abraham Lincoln half-jokingly accused of starting the Civil War, was written by **Harriet Beecher Stowe** (1811–86) in Brunswick, Maine. She lived much of her life as a neighbor of **Mark Twain** (himself an adopted New Englander) in Hartford, Connecticut. Another bestseller was the children's book *Little Women,* by **Louisa May Alcott** (1832–88), whose father, Bronson, was part of the Transcendentalist movement.

New England's later role in the literary tradition may best be symbolized by the poet **Robert Frost** (1874–1963). Though born in California, he lived most of his life in Massachusetts, New Hampshire, and Vermont. In the New England landscape and community, he found a lasting grace and rich metaphors. (Among his most famous lines: "Two roads diverged in a wood, and I—I took the one less traveled by, / And that has made all the difference.")

New England continues to attract writers drawn to the noted educational institutions and the privacy of rural life. Prominent contemporary writers and poets who live in the region at least part of the year include **Nicholson Baker, Bill Bryson, Christopher Buckley, Donald Hall, John Irving, P. J. O'Rourke,** and **John Updike.** Maine is also the home of **Stephen King,** who is considered not so much a novelist as the state's leading industry.

FILM & TV

New England is frequently captured through the lens of Hollywood, thanks in equal parts to its natural beauty; its Calvinist, slightly spooky history; and the unusual number of star actors, actresses, and directors who were raised here and continue to push forward projects incorporating local storylines or landscapes.

Lillian Gish's 1920 silent film *Way Down East* was perhaps the first movie to bring cinematic attention to the region, and films now regularly depict Boston's grimy underbelly (*The Departed* and *Mystic River*); local Red Sox mania (*Fever Pitch*); and working-class struggle and identity crises (*Good Will Hunting*). Plus

there are a host of horror films written by Maine's Stephen King—from *Carrie, Cujo,* and *The Dead Zone,* as well as a welter of TV miniseries—which make it sometimes seem as if the only inhabitants of small New England towns are supernatural forces. However, King also penned the story upon which the lovely film *The Shawshank Redemption*—also purportedly set in Maine—was based.

Several television series have also been based in New England, most notably this wildly popular trifecta: *Cheers* (1982–93), set in a chummy Boston bar (which is still there beside Boston Common); *Newhart* (1982–90), in which actor Bob Newhart comically attempted to run a Vermont bed-and-breakfast inn; and *Murder, She Wrote* (1984–96), which saw crime novelist Angela Lansbury stumbling across and solving real-life crimes with seeming ease from her perch in fictional Cabot Cove, Maine. *Wings* (1990–97), a TV program set at a small airstrip on Massachusetts's Nantucket Island, propelled several actors to further fame.

More recently, *Boston Public* (2000–04) and *Boston Legal* (still running) have explored facets of public schools and legal practice, respectively, in the city.

MUSIC

New England musicians have contributed mightily to the American music scene. An exhaustive list of stars is impossible here, but a few of the notable local lights include:

- Folk-pop singer **James Taylor,** born in Boston, long ensconced on Martha's Vineyard, and now residing in his beloved Berkshires

---

Impressions

The woods are lovely, dark and deep. / But I have promises to keep, / And miles to go before I sleep, / And miles to go before I sleep.

—Robert Frost, "Stopping by Woods on a Snowy Evening"

Moments

Now the first of December was covered with snow;
and so was the turnpike from Stockbridge to Boston;
Lord, the Berkshires seemed dream-like, on account of that frosting . . .

—James Taylor, "Sweet Baby James"

- The longstanding rock band **Aerosmith,** with roots in Boston and New Hampshire
- Crooner **Rudy Vallee,** born in Vermont and raised in Westbrook, Maine
- The wildly popular '70s rock group **Boston,** fronted by residents of that city
- Pop stars **Michael Bolton** and **John Mayer,** both born in Connecticut
- Jam-band **Phish,** formed in Burlington, Vermont, by college friends
- Texas-based country-folk musician **Slaid Cleaves,** raised in western Maine
- Nashville singer-songwriter **Patty Griffin,** also born and raised in Maine

5 Eating and Drinking in New England

All along the coast you'll be tempted by seafood in its various forms. You can get fried clams by the bucket at divey shacks along remote coves and busy highways. The more upscale restaurants offer fresh fish, grilled or gently sautéed.

Live lobster can literally be bought off the boat at lobster pounds, especially along the Maine coast. The setting is usually rustic—maybe a couple of picnic tables and a shed where huge vats of water are kept at a low boil.

Inland, take time to sample the local products. This includes delectable maple syrup, sold throughout the northern reaches. Cheese is a Vermont specialty, especially cheddar. Look also for Vermont's famed apple cider and Maine's wild blueberries.

In summer, small farmers across New England set up stands at the end of their driveways offering fresh produce straight from the garden. You can usually find berries, fruits, and sometimes home-baked breads. These stands are rarely tended; just leave your money in the coffee can.

Restaurateurs haven't overlooked New England's bounty. Many chefs serve up delicious meals consisting of local ingredients—some places even tend their own gardens. Some of the fine dishes we've enjoyed while researching this guide include curried pumpkin soup, venison medallions with shiitake mushrooms, and wild boar with juniper berries.

But you don't have to have a hefty budget to enjoy the local foods. A number of regional classics fall under the "road food" category. Here's an abbreviated field guide:

- **Beans:** Boston is forever linked with baked beans (hence the nickname "Beantown"), which are popular throughout the region. A Saturday-night supper traditionally consists of baked beans and brown bread.
- **Clam chowder:** The obligatory Boston dish of choice, clam chowder consists simply of chopped clams, milk, and some butter, flour and/or salt pork to thicken the mixture up into soup form. Interestingly, Rhode Islanders eat a *reddish* version incorporating tomatoes or tomato soup in lieu of the milk.
- **Johnnycakes:** A Colonial recipe largely lost to time, the Johnnycake still survives in Rhode Island's wayside diners. They're heavy pancakes made from cornmeal and molasses

rather than the usual wheat flour and sugar.

- **Lobster rolls:** Lobster rolls consist of lobster meat plucked from the shell, mixed with just enough mayonnaise to hold it all together, then served on a hot-dog roll.
- **Maple syrup:** Nothing says New England like sweet local maple syrup. You can get the stuff in all six of the New England states, but the best is supplied in New Hampshire and Vermont. Come in late spring for open-house days at the local sap houses, where sugar makers boil up the sweet stuff and ladle it onto pancakes, ice cream, or snow.
- **Moxie:** Early in this century, Moxie outsold Coca-Cola. Part of its allure was the fanciful story behind its 1885 creation: A traveler named Moxie was said to have observed South American Indians consuming the sap of a native plant, which gave them extraordinary strength. The drink was "re-created" by Maine native and Massachusetts resident Dr. Augustin Thompson. It's still popular in New England, although some folks liken the taste to a combination of medicine and topsoil.
- **Necco wafers:** Still made in Cambridge by the New England Confectionery Company, these powdery wafers haven't changed a bit since 1847. The candies are available widely throughout New England.

Finally, no survey of comestibles would be complete without mention of something to wash it all down: beer. New England has more **microbreweries** than any other region outside the Pacific Northwest.

Popular brewpubs that rank high on the list include the Great Providence Brewing Co., the Commonwealth Brewing Co. (Boston's first brewpub), the Portsmouth Brewery, Federal Jack's Brewpub (Kennebunkport), Vermont Pub & Brewery (Burlington), the Windham Brewery at the Latchis Hotel (Brattleboro), and a clutch of minibreweries in Portland, Maine—at least a half-dozen, at last count, all making mighty good beer.

3

Planning Your Trip to New England

For such a small area, New England is a surprisingly diverse region; you can do anything from deep-sea fish to leaf-peep on mountaintops, and dine on anything from flapjacks with real maple syrup (at 6am, preferably wearing flannels) to world-class restaurant fare. Yet all five states can be reached in roughly an hour or less by either plane or car from New York City.

As such, it's a wonderful destination for both the family and the peripatetic traveler. In most of the region, crime is almost nonexistent. In fact, your primary worries involve choosing the right time of year to visit; determining the most efficient way to get from point A to point B (New England is still a bit mass-transit challenged); and choosing from among the many natural treasures, roadside diners, and historical tours and walks available here. In this chapter, many of the critical aspects of planning your trip are covered. You can also turn to the "Fast Facts, Toll-Free Numbers & Websites" appendix on p. 668.

1 Visitor Information

All of the New England states maintain excellent tourism information offices and kiosks throughout their key areas.

If you're a highly organized traveler, call or e-mail in advance and ask for information to be mailed to you before departure; we have provided plenty of local tourism and chamber of commerce addresses and phone numbers in the chapters that follow. (You can also swing by the office when you reach town—and hope that it's open.)

State tourism offices are happy to send out loads of maps and free visitor information packets to travelers who call, write, or e-mail to them. Here's the contact information for each state's tourism authority:

- **Connecticut Commission on Culture & Tourism,** One Financial Plaza, 755 Main St., Hartford, CT 06103 (© **888/288-4748;** www.ctvisit.com).
- **Maine Office of Tourism,** #59 State House Station, Augusta, ME 04333

(© **888/624-6345** or 207/287-5711; www.visitmaine.com).
- **Massachusetts Office of Travel and Tourism,** 10 Park Plaza, Suite 4510, Boston, MA 02116 (© **800/227-6277** or 617/973-8500; www.massvacation.com).
- **Rhode Island Tourism Division,** 315 Iron Horse Way, Suite 101, Providence, RI 02908 (© **800/556-2484;** www.visitrhodeisland.com).
- **New Hampshire Division of Travel and Tourism Development,** 172 Pembroke Rd. (P.O. Box 1856), Concord, NH 03302 (© **800/386-4664** or 603/271-2665; www.visitnh.gov).
- **Vermont Department of Tourism and Marketing,** National Life Building, 6th floor, Drawer 20, Montpelier, VT 05620 (© **800/837-6668** or 802/828-3237; www.travel-vermont.com).

2 Entry Requirements

PASSPORTS

New regulations issued by the Department of Homeland Security now require virtually every air traveler entering the U.S. to show a passport. As of January 23, 2007, all persons, including U.S. citizens, traveling by air between the United States and Canada, Mexico, Central and South America, the Caribbean, and Bermuda are required to present a valid passport. As of January 31, 2008, U.S. and Canadian citizens entering the U. S. at land and sea ports of entry from within the western hemisphere will need to present government-issued proof of citizenship, such as a birth certificate, along with a government-issued photo ID, such as a driver's license. A passport is not required for U.S. or Canadian citizens entering by land or sea, but it is highly encouraged to carry one.

For information on how to obtain a passport, go to **"Passports"** in the **"Fast Facts, Toll-Free Numbers & Websites"** appendix (p. 672).

VISAS

The U.S. State Department has a **Visa Waiver Program (VWP)** allowing citizens of the following countries to enter the United States without a visa for stays of up to 90 days: Andorra, Australia, Austria, Belgium, Brunei, Denmark, Finland, France, Germany, Iceland, Ireland, Italy, Japan, Liechtenstein, Luxembourg, Monaco, the Netherlands, New Zealand, Norway, Portugal, San Marino, Singapore, Slovenia, Spain, Sweden, Switzerland, and the United Kingdom. (*Note:* This list was accurate at press time; for the most up-to-date list of countries in the VWP, consult www.travel.state.gov/visa.) Canadian citizens may enter the United States without visas; they will need to show passports (if traveling by air) and

proof of residence, however. *Note:* Any passport issued on or after October 26, 2006, by a VWP country must be an **e-Passport** for VWP travelers to be eligible to enter the U.S. without a visa. Citizens of these nations also need to present a round-trip air or cruise ticket upon arrival. E-Passports contain computer chips capable of storing biometric information, such as the required digital photograph of the holder. (You can identify an e-Passport by the symbol on the bottom center cover of your passport.) If your passport doesn't have this feature, you can still travel without a visa if it is a valid passport issued before October 26, 2005, and includes a machine-readable zone, or between October 26, 2005, and October 25, 2006, and includes a digital photograph. For more information, go to **www.travel.state.gov/visa**.

Citizens of all other countries must have (1) a valid passport that expires at least 6 months later than the scheduled end of their visit to the U.S., and (2) a tourist visa. To obtain a visa, applicants must schedule an appointment with a U.S. consulate or embassy, fill out the application forms (available from www.travel.state.gov/visa), and pay a $131 fee. Wait times can be lengthy, so it's best to initiate the process as soon as possible.

As of January 2004, many international visitors traveling on visas to the United States will be photographed and fingerprinted on arrival at Customs in airports and on cruise ships in a program created by the Department of Homeland Security called **US-VISIT.** Exempt from the extra scrutiny are visitors entering by land or those (mostly in Europe; see above) that don't require a visa for short-term visits. For more information, go to the Homeland Security website at **www.dhs.gov/dhspublic**.

Skipping the Airport Security Lines as a Registered Traveler

In 2003, the **Transportation Security Administration (TSA;** www.tsa.gov) approved a pilot program to help ease the time spent in line for airport security screenings. In exchange for information and a fee, persons can be prescreened as registered travelers, granting them a front-of-the-line position when they fly. The program is run through private firms—the largest and most well known is Steven Brill's **Clear** (www.flyclear.com), and it works like this: Travelers complete an online application providing specific points of personal information, including name, addresses for the previous five years, birth date, social security number, driver's license number, and a valid credit card (you're not charged the **$99 fee** until your application is approved). Print out the completed form and take it, along with proper ID, with you to an "enrollment station" (this can be found in over 20 participating airports and in a growing number of American Express offices around the country, for example). It's at this point where it gets seemingly sci-fi. At the enrollment station, a Clear representative will record your biometrics necessary for clearance; in this case, your fingerprints and your irises will be digitally recorded.

Once your application has been screened against no-fly lists, outstanding warrants, and other security measures, you'll be issued a clear plastic card that holds a chip containing your information. Each time you fly through participating airports (and the numbers are steadily growing), go to the Clear Pass station located next to the standard TSA screening line. Here you'll insert your card into a slot and place your finger on a scanner to read your print—when the information matches up, you're cleared to cut to the front of the security line. You'll still have to follow all the procedures of the day, like removing your shoes and walking through the x-ray machine, but Clear promises to cut 30 minutes off your wait time at the airport.

Each time I've used my Clear Pass, my travel companions are still waiting to go through security while I'm already sitting down, reading the paper and sipping my overpriced smoothie. Granted, registered traveler programs are not for the infrequent traveler, but for those of us who fly on a regular basis, it's a perk I'm willing to pay for.

—David A. Lytle

For specifics on how to get a visa, go to "Visas" in the "Fast Facts, Toll-Free Numbers & Websites" appendix (p. 675).

MEDICAL REQUIREMENTS

Unless you're arriving from an area known to be suffering from an epidemic (particularly cholera or yellow fever), inoculations or vaccinations are not required for entry into the United States.

CUSTOMS
WHAT YOU CAN BRING INTO THE U.S.

Every visitor more than 21 years of age may bring in, free of duty, the following: (1) 1 liter of wine or hard liquor; (2) 200 cigarettes, 100 cigars (but not from Cuba), or 3 pounds of smoking tobacco; and (3) $100 worth of gifts. These exemptions are offered to travelers who spend at least 72 hours in the United States and who have not claimed them within the preceding 6 months. It is forbidden to bring into the country almost any meat products (including canned, fresh, and dried meat products such as bullion, soup mixes, and so on). Generally, condiments, including vinegars, oils, and spices; coffee; tea; and some cheeses and baked goods are permitted. Avoid rice products, as rice can often harbor insects. Bringing fruits and vegetables is not advised, though not prohibited. Customs will allow produce depending on where you got it and where you're going after you arrive in the U.S. Foreign tourists may carry in or out up to $10,000 in U.S. or foreign currency with no formalities; larger sums must be declared to U.S. Customs on entering or leaving, which includes filing form CM 4790. For details regarding U.S. Customs and Border Protection, consult your nearest U.S. embassy or consulate, or **U.S. Customs** (www.customs.ustreas.gov).

WHAT YOU CAN TAKE HOME FROM NEW ENGLAND

U.S. Citizens: For specifics on what you can bring back and the corresponding fees, download the invaluable free pamphlet *Know Before You Go* online at www.cbp.gov. (Click on "Travel," and then click on "Know Before You Go! Online Brochure.") Or contact the U.S. Customs & Border Protection (CBP), 1300 Pennsylvania Ave., NW, Washington, DC 20229 (✆ **877/287-8667**), and request the pamphlet.

Canadian Citizens: For a clear summary of Canadian rules, write for the booklet *I Declare,* issued by the Canada Border Services Agency (✆ **800/461-9999** in Canada, or 204/983-3500; www.cbsa-asfc.gc.ca).

U.K. Citizens: For information, contact **HM Customs & Excise** at ✆ **0845/010-9000** (from outside the U.K., 020/8929-0152), or consult their website at **www.hmce.gov.uk**.

Australian Citizens: A helpful brochure available from Australian consulates or Customs offices is *Know Before You Go*. For more information, call the **Australian Customs Service** at ✆ **1300/363-263**, or log on to **www.customs.gov.au**.

New Zealand Citizens: Most questions are answered in a free pamphlet available at New Zealand consulates and Customs offices: *New Zealand Customs Guide for Travellers, Notice no. 4*. For more information, contact **New Zealand Customs,** The Customhouse, 17–21 Whitmore St., Box 2218, Wellington (✆ **04/473-6099** or 0800/428-786; **www.customs.govt.nz**).

3 When to Go

The well-worn joke about the climate in New England is that it has just two seasons—winter and August. Though this bromide might have originated as a ploy to keep outsiders from moving up here (and it worked, partly), there's also a kernel of truth to it. But don't worry. The ever-shifting seasons here are precisely what make New England so distinctive, and three of the four are genuinely enjoyable. The fourth (which is not the one you might have guessed) is, well, tolerable.

SUMMER   The peak summer season in New England runs from Fourth of July weekend until Labor Day weekend. That's a pretty slim sandwich, only about 8½ weeks. But, my gosh, does the population of each of these states ever swell between the starting line and summer's checkered flag! Vast crowds surge into New England on each of these two holiday weekends, and a constant stream also moves northward daily in between them.

It's no wonder. Summers here are exquisite, particularly since the daylight lasts so long—until 9 or 9:30 pm in late June and early July. Forests are verdant and lush; the sky is a deep blue, the cumulus clouds puffy and almost painfully bright white. In the mountains, warm days are the rule, followed by cool nights. On the coast, ocean breezes keep temperatures down even when it's triple-digit steaming in the big cities. (Of course, these sea breezes sometimes also produce thick, soupy fogs that linger for days.) In general, expect moderation: In Portland, Maine, the thermometer tops 90°F (32°C) for only 4 or 5 days each year, at most.

Local weather in this region is largely determined by the winds. Summer's southwesterly winds bring haze, heat, and humidity (to everywhere except the seashore); northwesterly winds bring cool bright weather and knife-sharp views. These systems tend to alternate during the summer, the heat and humidity building slowly and stealthily for a few days—then swiftly getting kicked out on their ears by stiff, cool winds pressing down from Canada. Then the pattern repeats. Rain is rarely far away in summer—some days it's in the form of an afternoon thunderstorm, sometimes a steady drizzle that brings a 3- or 4-day soaking. On average, about 1 day in 3 here will bring some rain. But, hey, that's what keeps the Green Mountains green.

For most of this region (we'll get to Vermont in a moment), midsummer is prime time. Expect to pay premium prices at hotels and restaurants. (The exception is around the empty ski resorts, where you can often find bargains.) Also be aware that early summer brings out scads of biting black flies and mosquitoes, a state of affairs that has spoiled many north-country camping trips. Come prepared for these guys. They've been up here a lot longer than we have, and they seem to like it just fine.

What to do? Play some golf. Go hiking in the woods. Swim in the ocean. Catch a minor-league baseball game. Or indulge in one of our favorite activities: rocking in a chair on a screened porch, reading a book, playing guitar, or just listening intently to the sounds of loons or crickets and watching the night sky for stars you never knew existed.

AUTUMN   Don't be surprised to smell the tang of fall approaching even as early as mid-August, when you'll also begin to notice a few leaves turning blaze-orange on the maples at the edges of wetlands or highways. Fall comes early to New England, puts its feet up on the couch, and stays for some time. The foliage season begins in earnest in the northern part of the region by the third week in September; in the southern portions, it reaches its peak by mid-October. But it's beautiful everywhere.

Fall in New England is one of the great natural spectacles in the world. When its rolling hills tart up in brilliant reds and stunning oranges, grown men pull to the sides of roads and fall to their knees weeping (and snapping, and taking video; the scenery is garish in a way that seems deviously designed to tease and embarrass shy, understated New England. The best part? This spectacle is nearly as regular as clockwork, with only a few years truly "bad" for foliage (due to oddly warm or wet weather). Though you can never predict exactly *when* it will strike, you can more or less guess *where* and set your clock to be here for it.

Keep in mind, however, that this is the most popular time of year to travel—bus tours flock like migrating geese to New England in early October. As a result, hotels are invariably booked solid at that time. (Local radio stations have been known to put out calls for residents to open up their doors to stranded travelers who otherwise might have to sleep in their cars.) Reservations are essential. Don't be surprised if you're assessed a foliage surcharge of $10 or $50 or more per room at your inn or hotel; deal with it. You can't buy scenery like this.

Some states maintain seasonal **foliage hotlines and/or websites** to let you know when the leaves are at their peak: Call **Maine** (© **888/624-6345;** www.mainefoliage.com), **New Hampshire** (© **800/258-3608**), or **Vermont** (© **800/VERMONT;** www.travel-vermont.com/seasons/report.asp). The **U.S. Forest Service** also maintains a foliage hotline at (© **800/354-4595**), updating conditions within the White Mountain National Forest in **New Hampshire.**

WINTER New England winters are like wine—some years are good, some are lousy. During a good season, mounds of light, fluffy snow blanket the deep woods and fill the ski slopes. A "good" winter offers a profound peace and tranquillity as the fresh snow muffles all noise and brings such a thunderous silence to the entire region that the hiss and pop of a wood fire at a country inn can seem noisome. During these good winters, exploring the forest on snowshoes or cross-country skis is an experience bordering on the magical.

During the *other* winters, though—the yucky ones—the weather fairies instead bring a nasty mélange of rain, freezing rain, and sleet (um, frozen rain). The woods become filled with crusty snow, the cold is damp and bone-numbing, and it's bleak, bleak, bleak as gunpowder-gray clouds lower and linger for weeks.

There are some cures for this malaise. The higher in elevation you go into the mountains of northern New England, or the farther north you head (to places like Jay, Vermont), the better your odds of finding snow.

On the other hand, meteorologically speaking, the coast in winter is a crapshoot, at best, more likely to yield rain (or sticky, heavy "snowball" snow) than powdery snow. Yes, winter vacations on the ocean can be spectacular—think Winslow Homerian waves crashing savagely onto an empty beach—but after a day or two of trying to navigate your car around big gray slushy snow banks, you, too, will soon be heading for Stowe.

Naturally, ski areas get crowded during the winter months. Some of them get *very* crowded. Expect maximum pricing, so-so food, and a herd mentality; this is the price you must pay for enjoying great skiing in the region. The resorts get especially packed during school vacations, which is just when many resorts choose to employ the rather mercenary tactic of jacking up rates at hotels *and* on the slopes.

By the way, if you visit a small town in this region during winter, there is another pleasure to enjoy during deepest winter: public ice skating and ice hockey. You'll find locals skating on town greens, lakes, ponds, rivers, and probably on top of swimming pools, for all we know—anywhere that will hold a little water. How do you find these spots? Easy. Look for a clump of cars beside an iconic little warming hut with a wood-burning or oil-burning stove inside, sending up smoke puffs like a signal to the masses.

You call this rustic? I call it heaven.

SPRING After the long, long winters, spring in New England is a tease. She promises a lot and comes dressed in impressive finery (see: delicate purple lilacs, which blossom for just a week). But in many years, spring lasts only a week, sometimes less than that (we're not kidding), "occurring" around mid-May but sometimes as late as June. There's a reason New Englanders hardly ever use the word *spring* in conversation with peers. They just call this time of year "mud season."

Boston's Average Temperatures & Rainfall

	Jan	Feb	Mar	Apr	May	June	July	Aug	Sept	Oct	Nov	Dec
Temp. (°F)	30	31	38	49	59	68	74	72	65	55	45	34
Temp. (°C)	–1	–1	3	9	15	20	23	22	18	13	7	1
Rainfall (in.)	3.8	3.5	4.0	3.7	3.4	3.0	2.8	3.6	3.3	3.3	4.4	4.2

Burlington, Vermont, Average Temperatures & Rainfall

	Jan	Feb	Mar	Apr	May	June	July	Aug	Sept	Oct	Nov	Dec
Temp. (°F)	25	27	38	53	66	76	80	78	69	57	44	30
Temp. (°C)	–4	–3	3	12	19	24	27	26	21	14	7	–1
Rainfall (in.)	2.2	1.7	2.3	2.9	3.3	3.4	4.0	4.0	3.8	3.1	3.1	2.2

It happens quickly. One morning the ground is muddier than muddy, the trees are barren, and gritty snow is still collected in shady hollows. The next day, it's in the 80s and humid, maple trees are blooming with little red cloverlike buds, kids are swimming in the lakes where the docks have just been put in, and somewhere in New Hampshire a blue cover is being ripped off an aboveground pool.

Travelers need to be awfully crafty to experience spring in New England—and once they get here, they often have trouble finding a room. That's because a good number of innkeepers and restaurateurs close up for a few weeks for repairs or to venture someplace warm. The upside? Rates are never cheaper than they are in spring. It's simply jaw-dropping how little you can pay in March for the same room that would cost 3 to 10 times *more* in the middle of summer or October.

NEW ENGLAND CALENDAR OF EVENTS

February

U.S. National Toboggan Championships, Camden, ME. This is a raucous and lively athletic event where being overweight is actually an advantage. Held at the toboggan chute of the Camden Snow Bowl. Call ℂ **207/ 236-3438.** Early February.

Dartmouth Winter Carnival, Hanover, NH. Huge, elaborate ice sculptures grace the village green during this festive celebration of winter, which includes numerous sporting events. Call ℂ **603/646-1110.** Mid-February.

Stowe Derby, Stowe, VT. The oldest downhill/cross-country ski race in the nation pits racers who scramble from the wintry summit of Mount Mansfield into the village on the Stowe Recreation path. Call ℂ **802/253-7704.** Late February.

March

New England Spring Flower Show, Dorchester, MA. This annual harbinger of spring presented by the Massachusetts Horticultural Society (ℂ **617/536- 9280;** www.masshort.org) draws huge crowds starved for a glimpse of green. Second or third week in March.

College Sports Extravaganza, Boston. In 2009, Boston plays host to the semifinals and finals of the **Men's Hockey East Tournament,** to an **NCAA Men's Basketball East Regional**—both at the TD Banknorth Garden (ℂ **617/624-1000;** www. tdbanknorthgarden.com)—and to the **NCAA Women's Frozen Four** (hockey), at Boston University's Agganis Arena (ℂ **617/358-7000;** www.bu.edu/ agganis). Expect giddy crowds, sold-out hotels, and packed sports bars. Hockey East (www.hockeyeast.com), late March; Frozen Four (www.ncaa.com), March 20–22; East Regional, March 26–28 (www.ncaa.com).

Maine Boatbuilders Show, Portland, ME. More than 200 exhibitors and 9,000 boat aficionados gather, as winter fades, to make plans for the coming summer. A great place to meet boat builders and get ideas for your dream craft. Call ✆ **207/774-1067.** Mid- to late March.

April

Patriots Day, Boston area (Paul Revere House, Old North Church, Lexington Green, Concord's North Bridge), MA. The events of April 18 and 19, 1775, which signified the start of the Revolutionary War, are commemorated and reenacted. Participants dressed as Paul Revere and William Dawes ride to Lexington and Concord to warn the Minutemen. Battle reenactments take place at Lexington and Concord. Call the Lexington Chamber of Commerce (✆ **781/862-1450;** www.lexington chamber.org) or the Concord Chamber of Commerce (✆ **978/369-3120;** www.concordchamberofcommerce.org). Third Monday in April; a state holiday in Massachusetts and Maine.

Daffodil Festival, Nantucket, MA. Spring's arrival is trumpeted with masses of yellow blooms adorning everything in sight, including a cavalcade of antique cars. Call ✆ **508/228-1700.** Late April.

May

Brimfield Antique and Collectible Show, Brimfield, MA. Up to 6,000 dealers fill several fields near this central Massachusetts town, with similar fairs in July and September. Call ✆ **800/628-8379** or go to www.brimfield show.com. Mid-May, also mid-July and early Sept.

Cape Maritime Week, Cape Cod, MA. A multitude of cultural organizations mount special events—such as lighthouse tours—highlighting the region's nautical history. Call ✆ **508/362-3828.** Mid-May.

Lilac Festival, Shelburne, VT. See the famed lilacs (more than 400 bushes) at the renowned Shelburne Museum when they're at their most beautiful. Call ✆ **802/985-3346.** Mid-May to late May.

Figawi Sailboat Race, Hyannis (on Cape Cod) to Nantucket, MA. The largest and wildest sailboat race on the East Coast. Intensive partying in Hyannis and on Nantucket surrounds this popular event. Call ✆ **508/362-5230.** Late May.

June

Old Port Festival, Portland, ME. A block party in the heart of Portland's historic district with live music, food vendors, and activities for kids. Call ✆ **207/772-6828.** Early June.

Yale-Harvard Regatta, on the Thames River in New London, CT. One of the oldest collegiate rivalries in the country. Check the schedule for the heavyweight men's crew at **http://yale bulldogs.cstv.com**. Early June.

Taste of Hartford, Hartford, CT. One of New England's largest outdoor festivals, where many area restaurants serve up their specialties. You'll also get a "taste" of local music, dance, magic, and comedy. Call ✆ **860/728-3089.** Early June.

Market Square Weekend, Portsmouth, NH. This lively street fair attracts 300 vendors and revelers from throughout southern New Hampshire and Maine into downtown Portsmouth to dance, listen to music, sample food, and enjoy summer's arrival. Call ✆ **603/436-3988.** Early June.

Motorcycle Week, Loudon and Weirs Beach, NH. Tens of thousands of bikers descend on the Lake Winnipesaukee region early each summer to compare their machines and cruise the strip at Weirs Beach. The Gunstock Hill Climb and the Loudon Classic race are the centerpieces of the week's activities. Call ✆ 603/366-2000. Early June.

Nantucket Film Festival, Nantucket, MA. This annual event focuses on storytelling through film and includes showings of short and feature-length films, documentaries, staged readings, panel discussions, and screenplay competitions. You may see a celebrity or two. Call ✆ 508/228-1700. Mid-June.

Provincetown Film Festival, Provincetown, MA. Focusing on alternative film, this fete has brought out celebrities like John Waters and Lily Tomlin. Call ✆ 508/487-FILM. Mid-June.

Boston Pride March, Back Bay to Beacon Hill, Boston. The largest gay pride parade in New England is the highlight of a weeklong celebration of diversity. The parade, on the second Sunday of the month, starts at Copley Square and ends on Boston Common. Call ✆ 617/262-9405 or go to www.bostonpride.org. Early June.

Jacob's Pillow Dance Festival, Becket, MA. The oldest dance festival in America features everything from ballet to modern dance and jazz. For a season brochure, call ✆ 413/243-0745 or go to www.jacobspillow.org. Late June through August.

Williamstown Theater Festival, Williamstown, MA. This nationally distinguished festival presents everything from the classics to comedies and contemporary works. Scattered among the drama are readings and cabarets. Call ✆ 413/597-3400 or go to www.wtfestival.org. Late June through August.

July

Tanglewood Music Festival, near Lenox, MA. The Boston Symphony Orchestra makes its summer home at this fine estate, bringing symphonies, chamber groups, and soloists to the Berkshire Hills. Call the orchestra's home base in Boston at ✆ 617/266-1492 or go to www.tanglewood.org. July through August.

Boston Harborfest, downtown Boston, along Boston Harbor, and the Boston Harbor Islands, MA. The city puts on its Sunday best for the Fourth of July, which has become a gigantic weeklong celebration of Boston's maritime history. Events include concerts, tours, cruises, fireworks, the Boston Chowderfest, and the annual turnaround of USS *Constitution.* Contact Boston Harborfest (✆ 617/227-1528; www.bostonharborfest.com). First week in July.

Boston Pops Concert and Fireworks Display, Hatch Memorial Shell on the Esplanade, Boston. The big day culminates in the famous Boston Pops' Fourth of July concert. People wait from dawn 'til dark for the music to start. Visit **www.july4th.org**. July 4th.

Wickford Art Festival, Wickford, RI. More than 200 artists gather in this quaint village for one of the East Coast's oldest art festivals. Call ✆ 401/294-6840 or go to www.wickfordart.org. Mid-July.

Sail Boston 2009, Boston Harbor and waterfront. The Tall Ships—magnificent sailing vessels from around the world—parade into the heart of the harbor, berth at piers that are open to the public, and leave town in another stately procession. Festivals, fireworks, and tours of the ships await the millions of visitors who flood eastern Massachusetts for this uniquely enjoyable event. Make reservations as early as possible. For more info, visit www.sailboston.com. July 8–13.

Friendship Sloop Days, Rockland, ME. This 3-day event is a series of boat races that culminates in a parade of sloops. Call ✆ **207/596-0376.** Mid-July.

Vermont Quilt Festival, Northfield, VT. Displays are only part of the allure of New England's largest (and oldest) quilt festival. You can also attend classes and have your heirlooms appraised. See descriptions at www.vqf.org, or call ✆ **802/485-7092** for more information. Mid-July.

Revolutionary War Days, Exeter, NH. Learn all you need to know about the War of Independence during this historic community festival, which features a Revolutionary War encampment and dozens of reenactors. Call ✆ **603/772-2411.** Mid- July.

Barnstable County Fair, East Falmouth (on Cape Cod), MA. An old-time county fair complete with rides, food, and livestock contests. Call ✆ **508/563-3200.** Late July.

Marlboro Music Festival, Marlboro, VT. This is a popular 6-week series of classical concerts featuring talented student musicians and seasoned artists performing in the peaceful hills outside of Brattleboro. Call ✆ **802/254-2394** (or 215/569-4690 in winter) for information. Weekends from July to mid-August.

Maine Lobster Festival, Rockland, ME. Fill up on the local harvest and a boiled lobster or two at this event marking the importance and delectability of Maine's favorite crustacean. Call ✆ **207/596-0376.** Late July to early August.

Greater Hartford Festival of Jazz, downtown Hartford, CT. Join locals for free performances at the pavilion in Bushnell Park. Visit www.hartford jazz.com. Late July.

August

Southern Vermont Art & Craft Fair, Manchester, VT. More than 200 artisans show off their fine work at this popular festival, which also features creative food and good music. Held on the grounds of Hildene, a grand historic home. Call ✆ **802/362-2100.** Early August.

Newport Folk Festival. Newport, RI. Thousands of music lovers congregate at Fort Adams State Park for a heavy dose of performances on an August weekend. It's one of the nation's premier festivals. Go to www.newport folk.com. Early August.

Annual Star Party, St. Johnsbury, VT. The historic Fairbanks Museum and Planetarium hosts special events and shows, including night-viewing sessions during the Perseid Meteor Shower. Call ✆ **802/748-2372.** Mid-August.

Wild Blueberry Festival, Machias, ME. A festival marking the harvest of the region's wild blueberries. Call ✆ **207/794-3543** or 207/255-6665. Mid-August.

JVC Jazz Festival, Newport, RI. This 3-day jazz festival brings together some of the best in the music industry to play for a sizzling weekend at Fort Adams State Park. Go to www. festivalnetwork.com. Mid-August.

Martha's Vineyard Agricultural Fair, West Tisbury, MA. An old-fashioned country fair featuring horse pulls, livestock shows, musicians, and woodsman contests, along with plenty of carnival action. Call ✆ **508/693-4343.** Third weekend in August.

Pops Goes the Summer, Barnstable County Fairgrounds, Falmouth, MA. Cape Cod Symphony Orchestra concert followed by a huge fireworks display. Call ✆ **508/548-8500.** Late August.

September

Windjammer Weekend, Camden, ME. Come visit Maine's impressive fleet of old-time sailing ships, which host open houses throughout the weekend at this scenic harbor. Call ℂ **207/236-4404.** Labor Day weekend.

Vermont State Fair, Rutland, VT. All of Vermont seems to show up for this grand event, with a midway, live music, and plenty of agricultural exhibits. Call ℂ **802/775-5200.** Early September.

Norwalk Seaport Oyster Festival, Norwalk, CT. This waterfront festival celebrates Long Island Sound's seafaring past. Highlights include oyster-shucking and slurping contests, harbor cruises, concerts, and fireworks. Call ℂ **203/838-9444** or go to www.seaport.org. Weekend after Labor Day.

Eastern States Exhibition, West Springfield, MA. "The Big E" is New England's largest agricultural fair, with a 4-H horse show, ox pulling, carnival food, a midway, and entertainment from the likes of Joan Jett. Call ℂ **413/737-2443** or go to www.thebige.com. Mid- to late September.

Provincetown Arts Festival, Provincetown, MA. One of the country's oldest art colonies celebrates its past and present with local artists opening their studios. Call ℂ **508/487-3424.** Late September.

Common Ground Country Fair, Unity, ME. A sprawling, old-time state fair with a twist: The emphasis is on organic foods, recycling, crafts, and wholesome living. Call ℂ **207/568-4142.** Late September.

October

Fryeburg Fair, Fryeburg, ME. Cotton candy, tractor pulls, live music, and huge vegetables and barnyard animals at Maine's largest agricultural fair. Call ℂ **207/985-3268.** One week in early October.

Mystic Seaport Chowderfest, Mystic, CT. A festival of soup ("chowda" in these parts) served from bubbling cauldrons set on wood fires. Call ℂ **860/572-5315,** or visit www.mysticseaport.org. Mid-October.

Head of the Charles Regatta, Boston and Cambridge, MA. High school, college, and postcollegiate rowing teams and individuals—some 4,000 in all—race in front of hordes of fans along the Charles River's banks and bridges. Call ℂ **617/868-6200** or visit www.hocr.org. Late October.

Salem Haunted Happenings, Salem, MA. Parades, parties, fortune-telling, cruises, and tours lead up to a ceremony on Halloween. Contact **Destination Salem** (ℂ **877/SALEM-MA**), or check the website (www.hauntedhappenings.org) for specifics. All month.

November

Northampton Independent Film Festival, Northampton, MA. The cultural center of the state's Pioneer Valley hosts a creative film fest and brings in guests from the region. Visit **www.niff.org** for details. Early November.

Thanksgiving Celebration, Plymouth, MA. The town observes the holiday that put it on the map with a "stroll through the ages," showcasing 17th- and 19th-century Thanksgiving preparations in historic homes. Nearby Plimoth Plantation, where the colony's first years are re-created, wisely offers a Victorian Thanksgiving feast (reservations required). Call Destination Plymouth (ℂ **800/872-1620;** www.visit-plymouth.com) or Plimoth Plantation (ℂ **800/262-9356** or 508/746-1622; www.plimoth.org). Week including Thanksgiving Day.

Victorian Holiday, Portland, ME. From late November until Christmas,

Portland decorates its Old Port in a Victorian Christmas theme. Enjoy the window displays, take a free hayride, and listen to costumed carolers. Call ✆ **207/772-6828** or 207/780-5555. Late November to Christmas.

December

Black Nativity, Converse Hall, Tremont Temple Baptist Church, 88 Tremont St., Boston, MA. (✆ **617/723-3486;** www.blacknativity.org). Poet Langston Hughes wrote the "gospel opera," and a cast of more than 100 brings it to life. Most weekends in December.

Christmas Prelude, Kennebunkport, ME. This scenic coastal village greets Santa's arrival in a lobster boat and marks the coming of Christmas with street shows, pancake breakfasts, and tours of the town's splendid inns. Call ✆ **207/967-0857.** Early December.

Christmas Stroll, Nantucket, MA. The island briefly stirs from its winter slumber for one last shopping/feasting spree, attended by costumed carolers and Santa in a horse-drawn carriage. The weekend event is the pinnacle of Nantucket Noel, a month of festivities starting in late November. Call ✆ **508/228-1700.** Early December.

Candlelight Stroll, Portsmouth, NH. Historic Strawbery Banke gets in a Christmas way with old-time decorations and more than 1,000 candles lighting the 10-acre grounds. Call ✆ **603/433-1100.** First two weekends in December.

Boston Tea Party Reenactment, Old South Meeting House and Congress Street Bridge, Boston. A lively, all-ages audience-participation happening re-creates the events of December 16, 1773. Call ✆ **617/482-6439** or visit www.oldsouthmeetinghouse.org. Mid-December.

Christmas Season Festivities, Newport, RI. The whole city collaborates to use only clear bulbs to illuminate the harbor and wharves, the restored colonials, and the Victorian splendor of Bellevue Avenue. It's all designed to simulate candlelight and the atmosphere of olden days. There also are wreath sales, a blessing of the fleet, caroling evenings, holiday concerts, gingerbread-house viewings, and more. Visit **www.christmasinnewport.org.** Every day in December.

Woodstock Wassail Celebration, Woodstock, VT. Enjoy classic English grog, along with parades and dances, at this annual event. Call ✆ **802/457-3555.** Mid-December.

Christmas Eve and Christmas Day, festivities throughout New England. Nantucket, MA, features carolers in Victorian garb, art exhibits, and tours of historic homes. December 24 and 25.

First Night, Boston. The original arts-oriented, no-alcohol, citywide New Year's Eve celebration includes a parade, ice sculptures, art exhibitions, theatrical performances, and indoor and outdoor entertainment. Fireworks light up the sky above Boston Common at 7pm and over Boston Harbor at midnight. For details, contact **First Night** (✆ **617/542-1399;** www.firstnight.org) or check the newspapers when you arrive. December 31.

New Year's Eve, regionwide. Portland, ME; Providence, RI; Hartford, CT; Portsmouth, NH; Burlington, VT; and many other cities and towns, celebrate the coming of the New Year. Check with local chambers of commerce for details. December 31.

4 Getting There & Getting Around

GETTING TO NEW ENGLAND
BY PLANE

Nearly all the major airlines fly into Boston's **Logan International Airport** (BOS), your likely hub of arrival or connection if you're coming by air. There's a complete listing of airlines servicing New England in the appendix (p. 675). For more information about Logan, contact the airport at © **800/235-6426** or check the airport's website at www.massport.com/logan.

Commercial carriers serve other important locales in the region as well, such as Bradley International Airport (BDL), in Hartford, Connecticut; and in places like Burlington, Vermont (BTV); Manchester, New Hampshire (MHT); Portland (PWM) and Bangor, Maine (BGR); and Providence, Rhode Island (PVD). Airlines most commonly fly to these airports from New York or Boston, although direct connections from other cities, such as Chicago, Cincinnati, and Philadelphia, are available. Even smaller towns and cities are served by feeder airlines and charter companies, including those flying into air strips in Rutland, Vermont (RUT); Rockland, Maine (RKD); and Trenton, Maine (BHB), near Bar Harbor. (Remember that many of the scheduled flights to these smaller New England cities from Boston are aboard smaller prop planes; check ahead with the airline or your travel agent if this is an issue for you.)

While flights into these smaller airports are convenient, they can be pricey. Some savvy visitors to New England find cheaper fares and a wider choice of flight times by flying into Boston's Logan Airport, then renting a car or connecting by bus to their final destination. (Boston is about 2 hr. by car from Portland, less than 3 hr. from the White Mountains.)

Tips Discount Flights to New England

No, it's not a mirage. Discount airfares aren't easy to find when flying into small regional airports around New England, but they do exist. The airport in Manchester, New Hampshire (MHT), for instance, has grown in prominence thanks to Southwest Airlines, which brought competitive, low-cost airfares to New England along with improved service. A few other airlines have followed suit lately. My advice? When you're pricing tickets and itineraries into Boston, compare airline prices in other parts of the region:

- Check with **Southwest** (© **800/435-9792;** www.southwest.com), which flies into Manchester (as well as into Providence, Rhode Island) from all over the country.
- Check with discount airline **JetBlue** (© **800/538-2583;** www.jetblue.com), which now offers direct service into both Burlington, Vermont, and Portland, Maine, from New York City's Kennedy Airport (JFK)—sometimes at very attractive fares. Remember, you can fly into JFK from practically anywhere in the world.
- Check **Continental** (© **800/523-3273;** www.continental.com), which flies into Manchester, Burlington, and Portland from Newark's Liberty International Airport (EWR).

Tips Flying into New England: The Skinny

Here's the breakdown of which airlines fly into the region's amalgam of airstrips, airfields, and larger airports:

- **Continental** flies into Bangor and Portland, Maine; and Manchester, New Hampshire, from Newark Liberty International Airport outside New York City.
- **JetBlue** flies into Portland, Maine, and Burlington, Vermont, from New York City's John F. Kennedy International Airport.
- **Northwest** flies into Burlington, Vermont; Portland, Maine; and Manchester, New Hampshire.
- **Southwest** flies nonstop into Manchester, New Hampshire, from numerous faraway destinations, including even from California and Hawaii.
- **United** flies into Burlington, Vermont; Portland, Maine; and Manchester, New Hampshire.
- **US Airways** and its commuter subsidiaries (Colgan Air and U.S. Airways Express) fly into Burlington, Vermont; West Lebanon/Hanover and Manchester, New Hampshire; Portland, Augusta, Rockland, Bangor, Bar Harbor, and even Presque Isle, Maine, from Boston, Philadelphia, and New York's LaGuardia.

On the other hand, Boston's airport can become very congested, delayed flights are endemic, and traffic can be nightmarish (Route 1A north is one good escape route). So travelers might find that the increased expense of using smaller airports to be more than offset by the less stressful experience of speedier check-ins, departures, and arrivals.

And new routes and connections into smaller airports are popping up all the time. Check the "Getting There" information at the beginning of each chapter in this book for the latest details. Also see "Flying into New England: The Skinny" above.

Overseas visitors may want to take advantage of the APEX (Advance Purchase Excursion) reductions offered by all major U.S. and European carriers. In addition, some large airlines offer transatlantic or transpacific passengers special discount tickets under the name **Visit USA,** which allows mostly one-way travel from one U.S. destination to another at very low prices. Unavailable in the U.S., these discount tickets must be purchased abroad in conjunction with your international fare. This system is the easiest, fastest, cheapest way to see the country.

BY CAR

Coming from the New York City area by car (your most likely entry point, unless you're coming from Canada), several interstate highway corridors serve New England. **I-91** heads more or less due north from Hartford, Connecticut, through Massachusetts and along the Vermont–New Hampshire border. **I-95** parallels the Atlantic coast through Boston, after which it strikes northeast across New Hampshire and along the southern Maine coast before heading north toward the Canadian border. The Massachusetts Turnpike **(I-90)** makes a wandering east-west jaunt from Boston to the lovely Berkshire hills (for a price— it's a toll road).

From Boston, you head south on I-95 to reach Rhode Island, north on I-95 for Maine, northwest up **I-93** for New Hampshire and the White Mountains, or southwest on **I-84** directly into the heart of Connecticut. Most of these highways flow smoothly through rural countryside, except on summer weekends or at rush hour around the big metro areas. In Concord, New Hampshire, **I-89** splits off from I-93 and heads into Vermont. Stay on I-89 if you want to reach Montpelier and Burlington; exit northward onto **I-91** at White River Junction if you want to visit St. Johnsbury and the Northeast Kingdom.

If scenery is your priority, the most picturesque way to enter New England is from the west. Drive through New York's scenic Adirondack Mountains to Port Kent, New York, on Lake Champlain, then catch the car ferry across the lake to Burlington.

Note that travel times may be longer than you think, since there are few fast roads in New England and lots of local ones. From Boston to Portland takes about 2 hours, and to Bar Harbor about 5 hours.

For listings of the major car rental agencies in New England, please see the "Fast Facts, Toll-Free Numbers & Websites" appendix (p. 668).

BY TRAIN

From Boston and New York City, commuter train lines radiate out to the suburbs (which can include southern New Hampshire and coastal Connecticut, respectively), but elsewhere train service in northern New England is basically limited to three **Amtrak** (© **800/872-7245;** www.amtrak.com) lines: two running to Vermont and one to Maine.

Amtrak's **Vermonter** service departs from Washington, D.C., once each day, with stops in Baltimore, Philadelphia, and New York City before following the Connecticut River northward. The train calls at Brattleboro, Bellows Falls, Claremont (in New Hampshire), White River Junction, Randolph, Montpelier, Waterbury, and Essex Junction (near Burlington), finally arriving in St. Albans some 10 hours after leaving Manhattan.

The **Ethan Allen Express** departs New York's Penn Station once to twice daily and travels somewhat more quickly, moving north along the Hudson River before veering northeast into Vermont, stopping at Fair Haven (near Castleton) and terminating at Rutland after about 5½ hours.

Amtrak relaunched rail service to Maine in late 2001, restoring a line that had been idle since the 1960s. The **Downeaster** service operates four to five times daily between North Station in

---

Avoiding "Economy Class Syndrome"

Deep vein thrombosis, or as it's know in the world of flying, "economy-class syndrome," is a blood clot that develops in a deep vein. It's a potentially deadly condition that can be caused by sitting in cramped conditions—such as an airplane cabin—for too long. During a flight (especially a long-haul flight), get up, walk around, and stretch your legs every 60 to 90 minutes to keep your blood flowing. Other preventative measures include frequent flexing of the legs while sitting, drinking lots of water, and avoiding alcohol and sleeping pills. If you have a history of deep vein thrombosis, heart disease, or another condition that puts you at high risk, some experts recommend wearing compression stockings or taking anticoagulants when you fly; always ask your physician about the best course for you. Symptoms of deep vein thrombosis include leg pain or swelling, or even shortness of breath.

Boston and Portland, Maine; if you're coming from elsewhere on the East Coast, you will need to change train stations in Boston—a slightly frustrating exercise requiring either a taxi ride through congested streets or a ride and transfer on Boston's aging subway system. The Downeaster makes stops in Haverhill, Massachusetts; Exeter, Durham, and Dover, New Hampshire; and Wells, Saco, and Old Orchard Beach, Maine. Travel time is a little under 2½ hours between Boston and Portland. Bikes are allowed to be loaded or off-loaded at Boston, Wells, and Portland.

International visitors might want to buy a **USA Rail Pass,** good for 5, 15, or 30 days of unlimited travel on **Amtrak** (© **800/USA-RAIL;** www.amtrak.com). The pass is available online or through many overseas travel agents. See the Amtrak website for the cost of travel within the western, eastern, or northwestern United States. Reservations are generally required and should be made as early as possible. Regional rail passes are also available.

GETTING AROUND
BY CAR

If you're visiting from abroad and plan to rent a car in the United States, you probably won't need the services of an additional automobile organization. If you're planning to buy or borrow a car, automobile-association membership is recommended. **AAA, the American Automobile Association** (© **800/ 222-4357;** http://travel.aaa.com), is the country's largest auto club and supplies its members with maps, insurance, and, most important, emergency road service. *Note:* Foreign driver's licenses are usually recognized in the U.S., but you should get an international one if your home license is not in English.

The major airports in New England (see "Getting To New England," earlier in this chapter) all host national car-rental chains. For the agencies' contact information, see the "Fast Facts, Toll-Free Numbers & Websites" appendix, p. 668. The websites Orbitz.com, Hotwire.com, Travelocity.com, and Priceline.com all offer competitive online car-rental rates.

A famous New England joke ends with the punch line, "You can't get there from here," but you may conclude it's no joke as you try to navigate through the region. Travel can be convoluted and often confusing, and it's handy to have someone adept at map reading in the car if you veer off the main routes for country-road exploring. North-south travel is fairly straightforward, thanks to the four major interstates in the region. Traveling east to west (or vice versa) across the region is a more vexing proposition and will likely involve stitching together a route of several state or county roads. Don't fight it; just relax and understand that this is part of the New England experience, like rain in the Northwest or rattlesnakes in the Southwest.

On the other hand, New England is of a size that touring by car can be done quite comfortably, at least if you're not determined to see all six states in a week (see chapter 4 for our suggested itineraries). Note that Maine is much larger than the other states; when making travel plans, beware of two-sided maps that alter the scale from one side to the other.

Traffic is generally light compared to that of most urban and suburban areas along the East Coast, but there's a big exception: Traffic anywhere in or around Boston can be sluggish anytime, and Friday afternoons and evenings in the summer are positively infuriating; the tentacles of Beantown traffic now extend all the way to I-495, which you may need to use to get from the New York area to, say, coastal Maine. Come prepared for unexpected delays if you'll be anywhere near Boston.

New England Driving Distances

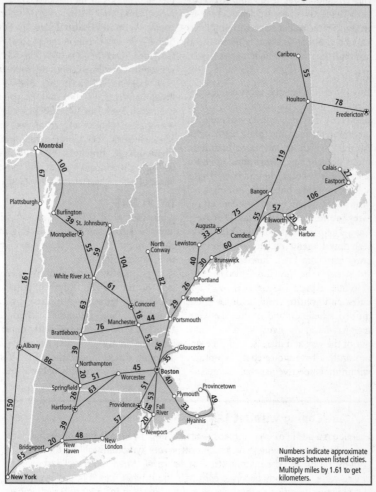

Numbers indicate approximate mileages between listed cities.
Multiply miles by 1.61 to get kilometers.

Other choke points, such as Route 1 along the Maine coast (during summer weekends) or attractive New England back-road routes (during the height of foliage season), can back up for miles at certain times of the year. To avoid the worst of the tourist traffic, try to avoid being on the road during big summer holidays; if your schedule allows it, travel on weekdays rather than weekends and hit the road early or late in the day to avoid the midday crunch.

If you're a connoisseur of back roads and off-the-beaten-track exploring, **DeLorme atlases** are invaluable. These are now produced for all 50 states, but the first one was Maine, and the company's headquarters is here. The atlases offer an extraordinary level of detail, right down to logging roads and public boat launches on small ponds. DeLorme's headquarters and map store (© **800/561-5105** or 800/642-0970; www.delorme.com) are in Yarmouth, Maine, but their products are also available widely at bookstores and convenience stores throughout the region.

BY BUS

Bus travel is often the most economical form of public transit for short hops between U.S. cities, but it's certainly not an option for everyone (particularly when Amtrak, which is far more luxurious, offers similar rates). **Greyhound** (© **800/231-2222;** www.greyhound.com) is the sole nationwide bus line. International visitors can obtain information about the **Greyhound North American Discovery Pass.** The pass can be obtained from foreign travel agents or through www.discoverypass.com for unlimited travel and stopovers in the U.S. and Canada.

While express bus service to major cities and tourist areas is quite good, quirky schedules and routes between regional destinations may send you miles out of the way and increase trip time significantly. I have indicated all bus routes within the respective regional chapters.

For quick information on travel schedules and fares, call the major players. In New Hampshire, Maine, and Vermont, contact **Vermont Transit Lines** (© **800/552-8737;** www.vermonttransit.com) or **Concord Coach** (© **800/639-3317;** www.concordtrailways.com). In southern New England, **Bonanza** (© **888/751-8800** or 401/331-7500) and its parent company, **Peter Pan** (© **800/343-9999;** www.peterpanbus.com), serve western Massachusetts and Connecticut, while **Plymouth & Brockton** (© **508/746-0378;** www.p-b.com) serves the South Shore of Massachusetts and Cape Cod.

BY PLANE

I have described the major airport, airlines, and routes serving New England above, in the "By Plane" section of "Getting To New England."

Overseas visitors can also take advantage of the APEX (Advance Purchase Excursion) reductions offered by all major U.S. and European carriers. In addition, some large airlines offer transatlantic or transpacific passengers special discount tickets under the name **Visit USA,** which allows mostly one-way travel

---

Tips Coping with Jet Lag

Jetlag is a pitfall of traveling across time zones. If you're flying north–south and you feel sluggish when you touch down, your symptoms will be the result of dehydration and the general stress of air travel. When you travel east–west or vice-versa, your body becomes confused about what time it is, and everything from your digestive system to your brain is knocked for a loop. Traveling east is more difficult on your internal clock than traveling west because most peoples' bodies are more inclined to stay up late than to fall asleep early.

Here are some tips for combating jet lag:

- **Reset your watch** to your destination time before you board the plane.
- **Drink lots of water** before, during, and after your flight. Avoid alcohol.
- **Exercise and sleep well** for a few days before your trip.
- If you have trouble sleeping on planes, **fly eastward on morning flights.**
- **Daylight** is the key to resetting your body clock. At the website for **Outside In** (www.bodyclock.com), you can get a customized plan of when to seek and avoid light.

Tips Hey, Google, Did You Get My Text Message?

It's bound to happen: The day you leave this guidebook back at the hotel for an unencumbered stroll through Harvard Square, you'll forget the address of the lunch spot you had earmarked. If you're traveling with a mobile device, send a text message to ℘ **46645 (GOOGL)** for a lightning-fast response. For instance, type "carnegie deli new york" and within 10 seconds you'll receive a text message with the address and phone number. This nifty trick works in a range of search categories: Look up weather ("weather philadelphia"), language translations ("translate goodbye in spanish"), currency conversions ("10 usd in pounds"), movie times ("harry potter 60605"), and more. If your search results are off, be more specific ("the abbey gay bar west hollywood"). For more tips and search options, see www.google.com/intl/en_us/mobile/sms/. Regular text message charges apply.

from one U.S. destination to another at very low prices. Unavailable in the U.S., these discount tickets must be purchased abroad in conjunction with your international fare. This system is the easiest, fastest, cheapest way to see the country.

BY TRAIN

As noted above, **Amtrak** provides limited rail travel to and from the region. But it's not really a valid option for getting around. (Coastal Connecticut is the exception—both Metro North commuter lines and Amtrak trains stop here.) See the "Getting To New England" section,

earlier in this chapter, for details about the main train lines that service New England.

International visitors can buy a **USA Rail Pass,** good for 15 or 30 days of unlimited travel on **Amtrak** (℘ **800/ USA-RAIL;** www.amtrak.com). The pass is available online or through many overseas travel agents. See Amtrak's website for the cost of travel within the western, eastern, or northwestern United States. Reservations are generally required and should be made as early as possible. Regional rail passes are also available.

5 Money & Costs

Here's a scene I've seen repeated dozens of times around New England. It's late Saturday afternoon, maybe early in July. A young (or not-so-young) couple has driven up from the city by car or motorcycle, "just for the day," in sparkling clear weather. But something magical has happened. They've fallen in love with each other all over again and with the quaint lovely New England-ness of (insert town name here). They've decided to stay for the night in a feather bed, eat a nice meal, and maybe watch the sun set over the (ocean/mountains/lake) and head home

tomorrow morning, fully assured that all is right with the world.

Except that here they stand, before a tourist information center staff member, looking despondent (or even desperate) as the staffer holds a phone in one hand, waiting for an answer.

"Isn't there *anything* cheaper?" pleads one of the lovebirds. "No, and that's a good price," responds the person behind the desk as kindly as possible. "You won't find anything better. Now, do you want me to book it, or not?"

Yes, travelers are in for a little sticker shock in New England, at least during peak travel seasons. In midsummer, there's simply no such thing as a cheap motel room in places like Winnipesaukee, Portland, Portsmouth, southwestern Vermont, Camden, or Bar Harbor. Even no-frills mom-and-pop motels can and do sometimes happily charge $100 a night or more for a bed that could fairly be described as a notch above car-camping. Blander-than-bland chain hotels demand even more.

To be fair, innkeepers in some of these tourist areas must reap nearly all their annual profits in what amounts to just a 2- or 3-month season.

Anyhow, take heart. Except during peak foliage season and holidays, the cost of rooms, meals, and day-to-day expenses is generally a lot less here than you'd pay in a major non–New England city. You can find excellent entrees at upscale, creative restaurants for around $20, comparing favorably with similar dishes at big-city restaurants that would top $30.

Still, lodging here is more expensive than in almost any other rural part of the United States, and planning can prove tricky for budget travelers.

So you'll need money to enjoy yourself here. It's always advisable to bring money in a variety of forms on a vacation: a mix of cash, credit cards, and traveler's checks. You should also exchange enough petty cash to cover airport incidentals, tipping, and transportation to your hotel before you leave home, or withdraw money upon arrival at an airport ATM.

Foreign travelers will want to note that the most common **bills** in the U.S. are the $1 (known as a dollar or a "buck"), $5, $10, and $20 denominations. There are also $2 bills (seldom encountered), $50 bills, and $100 bills—these last two not usually welcome as payment for small purchases.

Coins come in seven denominations: 1¢ (1 cent, or a penny); 5¢ (5 cents, or a nickel); 10¢ (10 cents, or a dime); 25¢ (25 cents, or a quarter); 50¢ (50 cents, or a half-dollar); the gold-colored Sacagawea coin, worth $1; the gold-colored presidential coins, also worth $1; and the rare silver dollar.

The easiest and best way to get cash away from home is from an ATM (automated teller machine), also sometimes known as a "cash machine." ATMs are easy to locate in cities, towns, and regions that cater to tourists. To find one, check the back of your card to determine what networks it "belongs" to. The **Cirrus** (© 800/424-7787; www.mastercard.com) and **PLUS** (© 800/843-7587; www.visa.com) networks span the country; you can find them even in remote regions of New Hampshire.

Credit cards are the most widely used form of payment in the United States: **Visa** (Barclaycard in Britain), **MasterCard** (EuroCard in Europe, Access in Britain, Chargex in Canada), **American Express, Diners Club,** and **Discover.** They also provide a convenient record of all your expenses, and they generally offer relatively good exchange rates.

6 Health

STAYING HEALTHY

New Englanders, by and large, consider themselves a healthy bunch, which they ascribe to clean living, brisk northern air, vigorous exercise (leaf raking, snow shoveling, and so on), and few excesses other than the stresses and strains of being a

Red Sox fan (now greatly alleviated, thank goodness). Other than picking up a stray cold or flu, you shouldn't face any serious health risks when traveling in the region.

Exceptions? Well, yes—you may find yourself at higher risk when exploring the outdoors, particularly in the backcountry. A few things to watch for when venturing off the beaten path:

- **Poison ivy:** This shiny, three-leafed plant is common throughout the region. If you touch it, you could develop a nasty, itchy rash that might seriously erode further enjoyment of your vacation. Some people experience a dangerously bad reaction, while others are barely affected if at all. If you're unfamiliar with what poison ivy looks like, ask at a ranger station or visitor information booth. Many have posters or books to help you with identification.

- **Giardia:** That crystal-clear stream coursing down a backcountry peak might look pure, but it could be contaminated with animal feces. Disgusting, yes, and also dangerous. When ingested by humans, *Giardia* cysts can cause serious diarrhea and loss of weight. The symptoms might not surface until well after you've left the backcountry and returned home. Carry your own water for day trips, or bring a small filter (available at any camping or sporting goods store) to treat backcountry water. Failing that, at least boil your water or treat it with iodine pills before using it—even for cooking, drinking, or washing. If you feel diarrhea coming on, see a doctor immediately.

- **Lyme disease:** Lyme disease has been a growing problem in New England since 1975, when it was identified in the town of Lyme, Connecticut; thousands of cases are reported nationwide annually, and they're no trifling matter: Left untreated, Lyme disease can damage the heart. The disease is transmitted by tiny deer ticks, which are difficult to see—but check your socks and body daily anyway (ideally with a partner). If you spot a bull's-eye-shaped rash, 3 to 8 inches in diameter (the rash may feel warm but usually doesn't itch), see a doctor right away. Lyme disease is more easily treated in early phases than later. Other symptoms may include muscle and joint pain, fever, or fatigue.

- **Rabies:** Since 1989, rabies has increasingly been spreading northward into New England. The disease is spread by animal saliva and is especially prevalent in skunks, raccoons, bats, and foxes. It is *always* fatal if left untreated in humans. Infected animals tend to display erratic and aggressive behavior; the best advice is to keep a safe distance between yourself and any wild animal you might encounter. If you're bitten, wash the wound as soon as you can and immediately seek medical attention. Treatment is no longer as painful as it used to be, but still involves a series of shots.

Those planning longer excursions into the backcountry of New England might find a compact first-aid kit with basic salves and medicines very handy to have along. Towns and villages throughout the region are reliably stocked with pharmacies, chain grocery stores, and Wal-Mart-type big-box stores where you can stock up on common medicines (such as calamine lotion and aspirin) to cope with minor ailments along the way.

WHAT TO DO IF YOU GET SICK AWAY FROM HOME

We list **emergency numbers** under "Fast Facts: New England," p. 668.

If you suffer from a chronic illness, consult your doctor before your departure. Pack **prescription medications** in your carry-on luggage, and carry them in their original containers, with pharmacy labels—otherwise, they won't make it through airport security. Visitors from outside the U.S. should carry generic names of prescription drugs. For U.S. travelers, most reliable healthcare plans provide coverage if you get sick away from home. Foreign visitors may have to pay all medical costs upfront and be reimbursed later.

If you get sick, consider asking your hotel concierge to recommend a local doctor—even his or her own. You can also try the emergency room at a local hospital. Many hospitals also have walk-in clinics for emergency cases that are not life-threatening; you may not get immediate attention, but you won't pay the high price of an emergency room visit. There are large, good hospitals in all cities in this region, as well as in many small towns. Check with your hotel or the local tourism office if you're concerned about proximity to hospitals.

7 Safety

New England—with the notable exception of parts of Boston and Hartford—boasts some of the lowest crime rates in the country. The odds of anything bad happening during your visit here are very slight. But all travelers are advised to take the usual precautions against theft, robbery, and assault.

Travelers should avoid any unnecessary public displays of wealth. Don't bring out fat wads of cash from your pocket, and save your best jewelry for private occasions. If you are approached by someone who demands money, jewelry, or anything else from you, do what most Americans do: Hand it over. Don't argue. Don't negotiate. Just comply. Afterward, immediately contact the police by dialing © **911** from almost any phone.

The crime you're statistically most likely to encounter is theft of items from your car. Don't leave anything of value in plain view, and lock valuables in your trunk.

Late at night, you should look for a well-lighted area if you need gas or you need to step out of your car for any reason.

Take the usual precautions against leaving cash or valuables in your hotel room when you're not present. Many hotels have safe-deposit boxes. Smaller inns and hotels often do not, although it can't hurt to ask to leave small items in the house safe.

8 Specialized Travel Resources

TRAVELERS WITH DISABILITIES Most disabilities shouldn't stop anyone from traveling to New England. Thanks to provisions in the Americans with Disabilities Act, most public places are required to comply with disability-friendly regulations. Almost all public establishments (including hotels, restaurants, museums, and so on, but not including certain National Historic Landmarks) and at least some modes of public transportation provide accessible entrances and other facilities for those with disabilities.

The **America the Beautiful— National Park and Federal Recreational Lands Pass—Access Pass** (formerly the **Golden Access Passport**) gives visually impaired or permanently disabled persons (regardless of age) free lifetime entrance to federal recreation sites administered by the National Park Service, including the Fish and Wildlife Service, the Forest Service, the Bureau of Land Management, and the Bureau of Reclamation. This may include national parks, monuments, historic sites, recreation areas, and national wildlife refuges.

The America the Beautiful Access Pass can be obtained only in person at any NPS facility that charges an entrance fee.

You need to show proof of a medically determined disability. Besides free entry, the pass offers a 50% discount on some federal-use fees charged for such facilities as camping, swimming, parking, boat launching, and tours. For more information, go to www.nps.gov/fees_passes.htm or call the United States Geological Survey (USGS), which issues the passes, at (© **888/275-8747.**

For more on organizations that offer resources to disabled travelers, go to www.frommers.com/planning.

GAY & LESBIAN TRAVELERS

Parts of New England are surprisingly friendly to gay and lesbian culture, while other parts are still deeply antipathetic toward the culture. As elsewhere in the country, the larger cities tend to be more accommodating to gay travelers than smaller towns.

Boston, of course, has the region's largest gay population, many concentrated in the **South End** neighborhood; in fact, many locals credit gays and lesbians with transforming Southie from a downtrodden, working-class 'hood into its current incarnation as home to many of the city's quirkiest antiques shops, restaurants, and B&Bs.

Provincetown, Massachusetts (at the very end of Cape Cod), is without a doubt the most gay-friendly town in New England. Rainbow flags fly proudly throughout the town, and it's safe to say this is a must-visit place for any first-time gay or lesbian traveler to the region.

Northampton, Massachusetts—home to Smith College—boasts a substantial and thriving lesbian community.

Overall, **Vermont** has traditionally been the most welcoming of the New England states to gay travelers; it is a specific destination for visitors who want to utilize or support the state's law acknowledging civil unions. For information on Vermont civil unions, visit the state-run website www.sec.state.vt.us/otherprg/civilunions/civilunions.html.

Ogunquit, on the southern Maine coast, is a hugely popular destination among gay travelers and features a lively beach and bar scene in the summer. In the winter, it's less active and more mellow. A well-designed website, **www.gayogunquit.com,** is one good place to find information on gay-owned inns, restaurants, and nightclubs in town.

Finally, **Portland, Maine,** has a substantial gay population and hosts a gay-pride festival each summer. In early 1998, Maine narrowly repealed a statewide gay-rights law that had been passed earlier by the state legislature. In Portland, however, the vote was nearly four to one against the repeal and in support of equal rights. Portland also has a municipal ordinance that prohibits discrimination in jobs and housing based on sexual orientation.

For more gay and lesbian travel resources, visit www.frommers.com/planning.

SENIOR TRAVEL

New England is well suited to older travelers, with a wide array of activities for seniors and discounts commonly available. Members of **AARP** (formerly known as the American Association of Retired Persons), 601 E St. NW, Washington, DC 20049 (© **888/687-2277;** www.aarp.org), get discounts on hotels, airfares, and car rentals. AARP offers members a wide range of benefits, including *AARP: The Magazine* and a monthly newsletter. Anyone over 50 can join.

The U.S. National Park Service offers an **America the Beautiful—National Park and Federal Recreational Lands Pass—Senior Pass** (formerly the **Golden Age Passport**), which gives seniors 62 years or older lifetime entrance to all properties administered by the National Park Service—national parks, monuments, historic sites, recreation areas, and

Frommers.com: The Complete Travel Resource

Planning a trip or just returned? Head to **Frommers.com,** voted Best Travel Site by *PC Magazine.* We think you'll find our site indispensable before, during and after your travels—with expert advice and tips; independent reviews of hotels, restaurants, attractions, and preferred shopping and nightlife venues; vacation giveaways; and an online booking tool. We publish the complete contents of over 135 travel guides in our **Destinations** section, covering over 4,000 places worldwide. Each weekday, we publish original articles that report on **Deals and News** via our free **Frommers.com Newsletters.** What's more, **Arthur Frommer** himself blogs five days a week, with cutting opinions about the state of travel in the modern world. We're betting you'll find our **Events** listings an invaluable resource; it's an up-to-the-minute roster of what's happening in cities everywhere—including concerts, festivals, lectures, and more. We've also added weekly **podcasts, interactive maps,** and hundreds of new images across the site. Finally, don't forget to visit our **Message Boards,** where you can join in conversations with thousands of fellow Frommer's travelers and post your trip report once you return.

national wildlife refuges—for a one-time processing fee of $10. The pass must be purchased in person at any NPS facility that charges an entrance fee. Besides free entry, the America the Beautiful Senior Pass offers a 50% discount on some federal-use fees charged for such facilities as camping, swimming, parking, boat launching, and tours. For more information, go to www.nps.gov/fees_passes.htm or call the United States Geological Survey (USGS), which issues the passes, at ⓒ **888/275-8747.**

For more information and resources on travel for seniors, see www.frommers.com/planning.

FAMILY TRAVEL

Families will have little trouble finding fun, low-key things to do with kids in New England. The natural world seems to hold tremendous wonder for the younger set—an afternoon exploring mossy banks and rocky streambeds can be a huge adventure. Older kids may like the challenge of climbing a mountain peak or learning to paddle a canoe in a straight line, and the beach is always good for hours of afternoon diversion.

Be sure to ask about **family discounts** when visiting attractions. Many places offer a flat family rate, which is less than paying for each ticket individually. Some parks and beaches charge by the car rather than the head.

Also, when planning your trip, be aware that certain small inns cater only to couples and prefer that families not stay there, or at least prefer that children be over a certain **minimum age.** This guidebook notes the recommended age for children where restrictions apply, but it's always best to ask first, to be safe. At any rate, if you mention that you're traveling with kids when making reservations, often you'll get accommodations nearer the game room or the pool, making everyone's life a bit easier.

Recommended destinations for families include Lake Winnipesaukee and Lake Sunapee in New Hampshire (great

---

---

for splashing around and kid-friendly attractions), York Beach and Acadia National Park in Maine (ditto), and Waterbury, Vermont, for its famous ice cream factory. North Conway, New Hampshire, makes a good White Mountains base for families with young kids; the town has lots of motels with pools, as well as mini train rides, streams, easy hikes, and the distraction known as Story Land.

To locate accommodations, restaurants, and attractions that are particularly kid-friendly, refer to the "Kids" icon throughout this guide.

Frommer's National Parks with Kids includes useful material on traveling with kids to Acadia National Park in Maine and Cape Cod National Seashore in Massachusetts.

For a list of more family-friendly travel resources, visit www.frommers.com/planning.

STUDENT TRAVEL

Check out the **International Student Travel Confederation (ISTC)** (www.istc.org) website for comprehensive travel services information and details on how to get an **International Student Identity Card (ISIC),** which qualifies students for substantial savings on rail passes, plane tickets, entrance fees, and more. It also provides students with basic health and life insurance and a 24-hour helpline. The card is valid for a maximum of 18 months. You can apply for the card online or in person at **STA Travel** (© **800/781-4040** in North America; © 132 782 in Australia; © 0871 2 300 040 in the U.K.; www.statravel.com), the biggest student travel agency in the world; check out the website to locate STA Travel offices worldwide. If you're no longer a student but are still under 26, you can get an **International Youth Travel Card (IYTC)** from the same people, which entitles you to some discounts. **Travel CUTS** (© **800/592-2887;** www.travelcuts.com) offers similar services for both Canadians and U.S. residents. Irish students may prefer to turn to **USIT** (© **01/602-1904;** www.usit.ie), an Ireland-based specialist in student, youth, and independent travel.

9 Sustainable Tourism

Sustainable tourism is conscientious travel. It means being careful with the environments you explore and respecting the communities you visit. Two overlapping components of sustainable travel are **ecotourism** and **ethical tourism.** The **International Ecotourism Society** (TIES) defines ecotourism as responsible travel to

⌒Kids It's Easy Being Green

Here are a few simple ways you can help conserve fuel and energy when you travel:

- Each time you take a flight or drive a car, greenhouse gases release into the atmosphere. You can help neutralize this danger to the planet through "carbon offsetting"—paying someone to invest your money in programs that reduce your greenhouse gas emissions by the same amount you've added. Before buying carbon offset credits, just make sure that you're using a reputable company, one with a proven program that invests in renewable energy. Reliable carbon offset companies include **Carbonfund** (www.carbonfund.org), **TerraPass** (www.terrapass.org), and **Carbon Neutral** (www.carbonneutral.org).

- Whenever possible, choose nonstop flights; they generally require less fuel than indirect flights that stop and take off again. Try to fly during the day—some scientists estimate that nighttime flights are twice as harmful to the environment. And pack light—each 15 pounds of luggage on a 5,000-mile flight adds up to 50 pounds of carbon dioxide emitted.

- Where you stay during your travels can have a major environmental impact. To determine the green credentials of a property, ask about trash disposal and recycling, water conservation, and energy use; also question if sustainable materials were used in the construction of the property. The website **www.greenhotels.com** recommends green-rated member hotels around the world that fulfill the company's stringent environmental requirements. Also consult **www.environmentallyfriendlyhotels.com** for more green accommodation ratings.

- At hotels, request that your sheets and towels not be changed daily. (Many hotels already have programs like this in place.) Turn off the lights and air-conditioner (or heater) when you leave your room.

- Use public transport where possible—trains, buses, and even taxis are more energy-efficient forms of transport than driving. Even better is to walk or cycle; you'll produce zero emissions and stay fit and healthy on your travels.

- If renting a car is necessary, ask the rental agent for a hybrid, or rent the most fuel-efficient car available. You'll use less gas and save money at the tank.

- Eat at locally owned and operated restaurants that use produce grown in the area. This contributes to the local economy and cuts down on greenhouse gas emissions by supporting restaurants where the food is not flown or trucked in across long distances. Visit **Sustain Lane** (www.sustainlane.org) to find sustainable eating and drinking choices around the U.S.; also check out **www.eatwellguide.org** for tips on eating sustainably in the U.S. and Canada.

natural areas that conserves the environment and improves the well-being of local people. TIES suggests that ecotourists follow these principles:

- Minimize environmental impact.
- Build environmental and cultural awareness and respect.
- Provide positive experiences for both visitors and hosts.
- Provide direct financial benefits for conservation and for local people.
- Raise sensitivity to host countries' political, environmental, and social climates.
- Support international human rights and labor agreements.

You can find some eco-friendly travel tips and statistics, as well as touring companies and associations—listed by destination under "Travel Choice"—at the **TIES** website, www.ecotourism.org. Also check out **Ecotravel.com,** which lets you search for sustainable touring companies in several categories (water based, land based, spiritually oriented, and so on).

While much of the focus of eco-tourism is about reducing impacts on the natural environment, ethical tourism concentrates on ways to preserve and enhance local economies and communities, regardless of location. You can embrace ethical tourism by staying at a locally owned hotel or shopping at a store that employs local workers and sells locally produced goods. **Responsible Travel** (www.responsible-travel.com) is a great source of sustainable travel ideas; the site is run by a spokesperson for ethical tourism in the travel industry. **Sustainable Travel International** (www.sustainabletravelinternational.org) promotes ethical tourism practices and manages an extensive directory of sustainable properties and tour operators around the world.

In the U.K., **Tourism Concern** (www.tourismconcern.org.uk) works to reduce social and environmental problems connected to tourism. The **Association of Independent Tour Operators (AITO)** (www.aito.co.uk) is a group of specialist operators leading the field in making holidays sustainable.

Volunteer travel has become increasingly popular among those who want to venture beyond the standard group-tour experience to learn languages, interact with locals, and make a positive difference while on vacation. Volunteer travel usually doesn't require special skills—just a willingness to work hard—and programs vary in length from a few days to a number of weeks. Some programs provide free housing and food, but many require volunteers to pay for travel expenses, which can add up quickly.

Before you commit to a volunteer program, it's important to make sure any money you're giving is truly going back to the local community, and that the work you'll be doing will be a good fit for you. **Volunteer International** (www.volunteerinternational.org) has a helpful list of questions to ask to determine the intentions and the nature of a volunteer program.

ANIMAL-RIGHTS ISSUES
Whale-watching is increasingly popular in New England, particularly in Maine and Massachusetts. For those who may be concerned about the sensitivity of the animals to these visits, there are a number of animal-rights organizations that provide good information. The organization **Tread Lightly** (www.treadlightly.org) is one. For more specific information about the current status of various species of whales, visit the **Whale and Dolphin Conservation Society** (www.wdcs.org).

10 Packages for the Independent Traveler

One good source of package deals is the airlines themselves. Most major airlines offer air/land packages, including **American Airlines Vacations** (© 800/321-2121; www.aavacations.com), **Delta Vacations** (© 800/221-6666; www.delta vacations.com), **Continental Airlines Vacations** (© 800/301-3800; www.co vacations.com), and **United Vacations** (© 888/854-3899; www.unitedvacations. com). Several big **online travel** **agencies**—Expedia, Travelocity, Orbitz, Site59, and Lastminute.com—also do a brisk business in packages.

Travel packages are also listed in the travel section of your local Sunday newspaper. Or check ads in the national travel magazines such as *Arthur Frommer's Budget Travel Magazine, Travel + Leisure, National Geographic Traveler,* and *Condé Nast Traveler.*

11 Special-Interest Trips

One rewarding way to spend a vacation is to learn a new outdoor skill or add to your knowledge while on holiday. You can find plenty of options in New England, ranging from formal weeklong classes to 1-day workshops.

There are lots of options; here are a few of the best:

- **Learn to fly-fish on New England's fabled rivers.** Among the region's most respected schools are those offered by **Orvis** (© **888/235-9763**) in Manchester, Vermont; and by **L.L.Bean** (© **800/343-4552**) in Freeport, Maine. (L.L.Bean also offers a number of shorter workshops on various outdoor skills through its **Outdoor Discovery Program;** call © **888/552-3261**.)
- **Learn about birds and coastal ecosystems in Maine.** Budding and experienced naturalists can expand their understanding of marine wildlife while residing on 333-acre Hog Island in Maine's wild and scenic Muscongus Bay through the **Maine Audubon Society,** 20 Gilsland Farm Rd., Falmouth, ME 04105 (© **207/781-2330;** www. maineaudubon.org). You're brought by boat, then stay on the island for 3 to 7 nights. Famed birder Roger Tory Peterson once taught birding classes here, and I can personally vouch for Maine Audubon's other outdoors and educational programs, too. Call or visit their lovely headquarters near Portland.

- **Sharpen your outdoor skills.** The **Appalachian Mountain Club,** 5 Joy St., Boston, MA 02108 (© **800/ 372-1758** or 617/523-0636; www. outdoors.org), offers a full roster of outdoor adventure classes, many taught at the club's Pinkham Notch Camp at the base of New Hampshire's Mount Washington. You could learn outdoor photography, wild mushroom identification, or backcountry orienteering. In winter, ice-climbing and telemark-skiing lessons are taught in the White Mountains. Course fees often include accommodations, and most are reasonably priced. Call or write for a catalog.

New England also especially lends itself to outdoorsy adventures that combine fresh air and exercise with Mother Nature as your instructor in a vast, beautiful classroom. For special-interest trips of an even more active type, see "The Active Traveler," below.

12 The Active Traveler

New England is a superb destination for those who don't consider a vacation to be a vacation unless it takes place far, far away from buildings and cars. Hiking, canoeing, and skiing are among the most popular outdoor activities here, but you can also try rock climbing, sea kayaking, mountain biking, road biking, sailing, winter mountaineering, and snowmobiling. The farther north you go in this region, the more remote and wild the terrain becomes. For pointers on where to head, see the "Enjoying the Great Outdoors" sections in the subsequent chapters; also, more detailed information on local services and outfitters is included in each regional section, when appropriate.

GENERAL ADVICE

The ideal way to enjoy the outdoors here is to head for public lands where the natural landscape has been best preserved. The wildest areas in New England include the Green Mountain National Forest in Vermont, the White Mountain National Forest in New Hampshire, and Baxter State Park and Acadia National Park in Maine. Use this book to help pick the best area for what you want to experience. You can often find adventure-travel outfitters and suppliers in towns around the fringes of these parks.

Once you've zeroed in the area you will visit, a bit of advice: Stay put. I've run across too many gung-ho travelers who try to bite off too much—some biking in Vermont, a little hiking in the White Mountains or Berkshire Hills, and then maybe some kayaking and lobsters in Maine. All in a week! That's a good formula for developing a close personal relationship with the highway, not relaxation. I advise you to pick one area, settle in for a few days or a week, and explore locally by foot, canoe, or kayak. This will give you time to enjoy an extra hour lounging at a remote backcountry lake or camping

in the backcountry. You'll also learn a lot more about the area. In my experience, few travelers regret planning to do too little on their vacations to New England, but plenty of visitors regret having tried to do too much.

Travelers used to hire guides just to ensure that they would later be able to find their ways back *out* of the woods. With development encroaching on so many once-pristine areas of New England, it's now sometimes useful to have guides help you find your way *into* the woods and away from civilization's long reach. Clear-cuts, second-home developments, and trails teeming with weekend hikers are obstacles to be avoided—and a good dose of local knowledge is the cure; it's the best way I know to find the most alluring (and least congested) spots.

Basically, you've got three options: Hire a guide, sign up for a guided trip, or dig up the essential information yourself.

HIRING A GUIDE

Guides of all kinds can be hired throughout the region, from grizzled fishing hands who know local rivers like their own living rooms to young canoe guides attracted to the jobs because of their enthusiasm for the environment.

Alexandra and Garrett Conover of Maine's **North Woods Ways,** 2293 Elliotsville Rd., Willimantic, ME 04443 (© **207/997-3723**), are among the most experienced in the region. The couple offers canoe trips on northern Maine rivers (including a "Thoreau's Maine Woods" trip) and are well versed in North Woods lore.

Maine also has a centuries-old tradition of guides leading "sports" into the backwoods for hunting and fishing, although many now have branched out to include recreational canoeing and more specialized interests, such as bird-watching. Professional guides are certified by

Your Car: *Do* Leave Home Without It

If you're *really* green-friendly, options even exist for a vacation in New England *without a car* (yes, you read that right). Here are four suggestions:

- From New York City or Boston, take an **Amtrak** (www.amtrak.com) train to Vermont and explore small towns like Brattleboro for their brick architecture, good restaurants, and quirky shops. Cross the river to hike Wantastiquet Mountain. Another day, rent a canoe and explore the Connecticut River, or get a bike and head off into the hilly countryside. There's a canoe touring center just north of town, and a bike rental outfit or two on the main street.

- From Boston, take a Concord Coach bus directly to the **Appalachian Mountain Club's Pinkham Notch Visitor Center** (© 603/466-2721), high in the White Mountains. Spend a night or two, then backpack for 2 days across demanding, rugged mountains, staying at AMC's backcountry huts (all meals provided). At the end of your sojourn, catch the AMC shuttle back to North Conway or Pinkham Notch, and then hail the return bus back to Boston.

- Bus, fly, or train it to Portland, Maine, where you can sign up for a guided sea-kayak excursion. The **Maine Island Kayak Co.** (© 207/766-2373) on Peaks Island is reached by a quick and pleasant 20-minute ferry ride (the terminal is at the corner of Commercial and Franklin streets, and offers trips throughout the state all summer long. You can even camp within city limits on remote Jewell Island at the edge of Casco Bay, or head out for a few days along more remote parts of the coast. Portland's museums, restaurants, and bars don't require wheels to each, either.

- Bus or fly to **Bar Harbor,** Maine, and then settle into one of the numerous inns or B&Bs downtown. (There's a free shuttle bus from the airport to downtown, and other free buses running around the island from spring through late fall; the bus connects downtown Bar Harbor with more than a half-dozen routes into and around the park, making travel hassle-free.) Rent a mountain bike and explore the elaborate network of carriage roads at Acadia National Park, then cruise along picturesque Park Loop Road. Another day, sign up for a sea-kayak tour or whale-watching excursion. By night, enjoy lobster or other fine meals at Bar Harbor's fine restaurants. Mountain bikes may be easily rented along Cottage Street in Bar Harbor.

the state; you can learn more about hiring Maine guides by contacting the **Maine Professional Guides Association,** P.O. Box 336, Augusta, ME 04332. The association's website (www.maineguides.org) features links to many of its members.

In Vermont, contact the **Vermont Outdoor Guide Association,** P.O. Box 10, N. Ferrisburg, VT 05473 (© **800/425-8747** or 802/425-6211; www.voga.org), whose members can help arrange adventure-travel tours, instruction, and lodging.

The VOGA website is a good place to get ideas for an outdoor vacation, with links to outfitters and outdoor-oriented inns.

Elsewhere, contact chambers of commerce for suggestions about guides.

GUIDED TOURS

The phenomenon of guided tours in New England has exploded in recent years, in both number and variety. These range from 2-night guided inn-to-inn hiking trips to weeklong canoe and kayak expeditions, camping each night along the way. A few reputable outfitters to start with include the following:

- **Allagash Canoe Trips,** P.O. Box 932, Greenville, ME 04441 (© **207/237-3077;** www.allagashcanoetrips.com), leads 5- to 7-day canoe trips down Maine's noted and wild Allagash River and other local rivers. You provide a sleeping bag and clothing; everything else is taken care of.
- **BattenKill Canoe Ltd.,** 6328 Historic Rte. 7A, Arlington, VT 05250 (© **800/421-5268** or 802/362-2800; www.battenkill.com), runs guided canoeing and walking excursions in Vermont (as well as abroad). Nights are spent at quiet inns.
- **Bike the Whites,** P.O. Box 1785, North Conway, NH 03865 (© **800/421-1785;** www.bikethewhites.com), offers self-guided biking tours between three inns in the White Mountains, with each day requiring about 20 miles of biking. Luggage is shuttled from inn to inn.
- **Country Walkers,** P.O. Box 180, Waterbury, VT 05676 (© **800/464-9255** or 802/244-1387; www.countrywalkers.com), has a glorious color catalog (more like a wish book) outlining supported walking trips around the world. Among the offerings: walking tours in coastal Maine and north-central Vermont. Trips

generally run 4 to 5 nights and include all meals and lodging at appealing inns.

- **Maine Island Kayak Co.,** 70 Luther St., Peaks Island, ME 04108 (© **207/766-2373;** www.maineislandkayak.com), has a fleet of seaworthy kayaks for camping trips up and down the Maine coast, as well as to places like Canada and Belize. The firm has a number of 2- and 3-night expeditions each summer and has plenty of experience training novices.
- **New England Hiking Holidays,** P.O. Box 1648, North Conway, NH 03860 (© **800/869-0949** or 603/356-9696; www.nehikingholidays.com), has an extensive inventory of trips, including weekend trips in the White Mountains, as well as more extended excursions to the Maine coast, Vermont, and overseas. Trips typically involve moderate day hiking coupled with nights at comfortable lodges.
- **Vermont Bicycle Touring,** P.O. 614 Monkton Rd., Bristol, VT 05443 (© **800/245-3868;** www.vbt.com), is one of the more established and well-organized touring operations, with an extensive bike tour schedule in North America, Europe, and New Zealand. VBT offers several trips apiece in both Vermont and Maine, including a 6-day Acadia trip with some overnights at the grand Claremont Hotel.

FOR MORE INFORMATION

Guidebooks to the region's backcountry are plentiful and diverse. **L.L.Bean's** headquarters in Freeport, Maine (plus a half-dozen outlet stores scattered in northern New England), as well the **Green Mountain Club's** head office in Waterbury, Vermont (see below), each stock excellent selections of local guidebooks, as do bookshops throughout the region. An exhaustive collection of New England outdoor guidebooks for sale may be found online at **www.mountainwanderer.com**, a company based right in the White Mountains of New Hampshire. The **Appalachian Mountain Club,** 5 Joy St., Boston, MA 02108 (© **800/262-4455** or 617/523-0636; www.outdoors.org), publishes a number of definitive guides to hiking and boating in the region.

Map Adventures, P.O. Box 15214, Portland, ME 04112 (© **207/879-4777**), is a small firm that publishes a growing line of good recreational maps covering popular New England areas, including the Stowe and Mad River Valley areas, the Camden Hills of Maine, Acadia National Park, and the White Mountains. See what they offer online at **www.mapadventures.com**.

Local outing clubs are also a good source of information, and most offer trips to nonmembers. The largest of the bunch is the Appalachian Mountain Club (see address above), whose chapters run group trips almost every weekend throughout the region, with northern New Hampshire especially well represented. Another active group is the **Green Mountain Club,** 4711 Waterbury–Stowe Rd., Waterbury Center, VT 05677 (© **802/244-7037;** www.greenmountainclub.org).

13 Tips on Accommodations

"The more we travel," said an unhappy couple one morning at a New Hampshire inn, "the more we realize why we go back to our old favorites time and again." The reason for their chagrin? They had been forced to switch rooms at 2am when rain had begun dripping right onto them through the ceiling. I hasten to add that this story is not an isolated incident. Small, quaint inns here often come with their own drips, creaks, and quirks.

Of course, New England is famous for its plethora of country inns and bed-and-breakfasts (B&Bs), which offer a wonderful alternative to the sort of cookie-cutter, chain-hotel rooms that line U.S. highways from coast to coast. But (as the unhappy couple learned) there are reasons why some people *prefer* the cookie-cutter hotels. In a chain hotel, you can be reasonably sure that water won't drip through your ceiling in the middle of the night. Likewise, the beds will be firm, the sink will be relatively new, and you'll have a TV, a telephone, and counter space next to the bathroom sink.

Every **inn** and **B&B** listed in this guide yields a decent, and often a high-quality, experience. Just keep in mind that each place is different, and you need to match the personality of the place with your *own* personality. Some inns are more polished and fussier than others; this is a rural area, so a lot of them (even some calling themselves "resorts") lack basic amenities to which business travelers have grown accustomed in chain hotels. (In-room phones and air-conditioning lead the list.)

For tips on surfing for hotel deals online, visit www.frommers.com/planning.

SERVICE CHARGES

Rather than increase room rates in the face of rising competition, hotels, inns, and B&Bs are increasingly tacking on nickel-and-dime fees to their guests' bills. Most innkeepers will tell you about these fees when you reserve or check in; a few will surprise you at checkout.

The most common surcharge is an involuntary "service charge" of 10% to

Fun Fact   Inn vs. B&B: Everybody Wins

The difference between an inn and a B&B may be confusing for some travelers, since the gap between the two narrows by the day. A couple of decades ago, inns were full-service affairs, whereas B&Bs consisted of private homes with an extra bedroom or two and a homeowner looking for a little extra income. These old-style B&Bs still exist around the region. I've occupied a few evenings sitting in a well-used living room with the owner, watching TV as if visiting with a forgotten aunt.

Today B&Bs are more commonly professionally run affairs, where guests have private bathrooms, a separate common area, and attentive service. The owners have apartments tucked away in the back, prepare sumptuous breakfasts in the morning (some B&Bs offer "candlelight breakfasts"), and offer a high level of service. All the B&Bs in this guide are of the more professionally run variety (although several or more still have shared bathrooms). Other guidebooks are available for those searching for home-stay lodging.

The sole difference between inns and B&Bs—at least, as defined by this guide—is that inns serve dinner (and sometimes lunch). B&Bs provide breakfast only. Readers shouldn't infer that B&Bs are necessarily more informal or in any way inferior to a full-service inn. Indeed, all the places listed under "The Best Bed & Breakfasts," in chapter 1, have the air of gracious inns that just happened to have overlooked serving dinner. That's true for many of the other B&Bs listed in this guide; with a little luck, you'll stumble into Ralph Waldo Emerson's idea of simple contentment: "Hospitality consists in a little fire, a little food, and an immense quiet."

15%. Coupled with state lodging taxes (even "sales-tax-free" New Hampshire hits tourists with an 8% levy), that bumps the cost of a bed up by nearly 25%. (The rates listed in this guide don't include service charges or sales tax.)

Other charges may include a pet fee ($10 or more per day extra), a foliage-season surcharge ($10–$50 per room), and a "resort fee" (of 15%–20% tax at certain resorts). Some hotels even tack on a $1 per day fee for the presence of an in-room safe, whether it is used or not.

4

Suggested New England Itineraries

Getting to know New England requires equal amounts of patience and persistence. Your most memorable experience might come at a roadside lobster pound marked only with a scrawled paper sign, at the end of a mountainside hiking trail that overlooks a peaceful lake, or while exploring a cobblestone alley that's not on any map.

Racing around with a checklist and a beat-the-clock attitude is a recipe for disaster. The happiest visitors to New England are those who stay awhile in one spot, getting to know a manageable area through well-crafted day trips. Read on for strategies that can help you organize your time.

1 The Regions in Brief

BOSTON Oliver Wendell Holmes dubbed Boston the "hub of the solar system," and the label stuck. Today "The Hub" is the region's largest and most vibrant city. This alluring metropolis of historic and modern buildings, world-class museums, and top-notch restaurants is an important stop for travelers on any trip to New England.

CAPE COD & THE ISLANDS The ocean is writ large on Cape Cod, a low peninsula with miles of sandy beaches and grassy dunes that whisper in the wind. The carnival-like atmosphere of Provincetown is a draw, as are the genteel charms of Martha's Vineyard and Nantucket, two islands just offshore.

THE PIONEER VALLEY Extending through Massachusetts along the Connecticut River, the area takes its name from the early settlers who arrived here in the 17th century. Among the many picturesque towns is unspoiled Historic Deerfield.

THE BERKSHIRES Massachusetts's rolling hills at the state's western edge are home to historic old estates, graceful villages, and an abundance of festivals and cultural events, including the Tanglewood Music Festival and Jacob's Pillow Dance Festival.

THE LITCHFIELD HILLS The historic northwest corner of Connecticut has sleepy villages, hidden hiking trails, and a surfeit of New England charm—all just a couple of hours from New York City.

THE CONNECTICUT COAST The eastern coast is home to the historic towns of Mystic and New London, where you can get a glimpse of the shipbuilding trade at the Mystic Seaport museum and the Navy submarine base in nearby Groton.

NEWPORT, RHODE ISLAND, AREA The lifestyles of the truly rich and famous are on parade in Newport, once home to the likes of the Astors and Vanderbilts. A tour of the oceanfront mansions never fails to astonish.

GREEN MOUNTAINS Extending the length of Vermont from Massachusetts to Canada, this mostly gentle chain of forested hills and low mountains allows for great hiking, scenic back-road drives, fantastic inns, and superb bicycling. The apples and the maple syrup here taste pretty good, too; be sure and stock up.

LAKE CHAMPLAIN Pastoral and scenic, the region of Vermont that forms half the lakeshore of Lake Champlain has idyllic drives and a sense of gracious openness—along with a lot of dairy cows and great views of New York's Adirondacks.

NORTHEAST KINGDOM This is Vermont at its most remote and lost-in-time best. The state's northeastern counties are rugged, hilly, and unpolished, but there are some improbable grace notes such as the little city of St. Johnsbury: It has not one but *two* excellent museums. You can also find great cheddar cheese right at the source.

COASTAL NEW HAMPSHIRE Yes, New Hampshire *does* have a coastline—though only 18 miles of it—and packed into this tiny area you'll find plenty of sand, surf, honky-tonk beach boardwalks, and sailboat views. As a bonus, there's also the historic and entertaining little city of Portsmouth: a smaller (possibly even better) version of Boston, a great place to shop and drink a beer or a cup of coffee.

THE UPPER VALLEY The Connecticut River Valley dividing Vermont and New Hampshire is a world unto itself, full of villages, rolling hills, covered bridges, river views, and small-town bakeries. It's got smarts, too: Dartmouth College is here.

LAKES REGION Lake Winnipesaukee is the crown jewel of New Hampshire's Lakes Region, but other lakes and ponds scattered in the area also add in charm what they lack in size. *On Golden Pond* was filmed on one of them, though this region's fame and beauty long predate Hollywood's recent discovery of them.

WHITE MOUNTAINS Since the mid-1800s, New Hampshire's towering White Mountains have drawn travelers magnetically with their rugged, windswept peaks, forests dotted with glacial boulders, and clear, rushing streams. You can find New England's best backcountry hiking and camping here . . . but also its wildest weather. Keep a radio and a cellphone handy.

WESTERN MAINE This oft-overlooked region—centered on Bethel, but taking in a wide swath of territory north and south of that village—is as different from nearby North Conway as could be. It's home to brawny hills, wide fast rivers, unbelievably scenic lakes, great foliage, and endless opportunities for quiet hiking and skiing. You might even see a moose.

COASTAL MAINE Maine's rocky coast is the stuff of legend, art, and poetry. The southern coast has the best beaches; to the north, the Down East region offers spectacular rocky headlands and huge Acadia National Park. Great views, lighthouses, lobster shacks, and local color abound.

MAINE'S NORTH WOODS The mostly uninhabited North Woods of Maine are still almost entirely owned by timber companies, yet there are some spectacular places tucked within them. Two of Maine's hidden jewels are worth a visit: big, wild Baxter State Park, home to the state's largest peak (impressive Mount Katahdin); and giant Moosehead Lake, an isolated province of both fishing camps and luxury inns. Numerous smaller lakes and ponds, accessible only by seaplane, shine like coins in the woods, and the Allagash River is a once-in-a-lifetime paddling adventure.

2 Boston & Vicinity in 1 Week

Basing yourself in Boston or Cambridge is a good way to get to know eastern Massachusetts while not limiting yourself to one destination. On this itinerary, you'll get a taste of Boston and Cambridge, then set out on day trips to the history-rich suburbs. You'll go in roughly chronological order: Start in Plymouth with the Pilgrims; move on to Lexington and Concord to learn about the rebellious colonists; and finally, visit the North Shore, which flourished after the Revolution. If you're renting a car, note that you don't need it for the full week—pick it up on (and don't start paying for it until) Day 4.

Days ❶ & ❷: Boston ✸✸✸

Begin exploring downtown Boston by walking at least part of the 2.5-mile **Freedom Trail** (p. 121). The whole shebang can be an all-day affair, but I suggest concentrating on the first two-thirds of the trail, from **Boston Common** through **Faneuil Hall.** Break for lunch at **Faneuil Hall Marketplace** (p. 84), then head into the North End for a stroll on the main drag, **Hanover Street,** and a visit to the **Paul Revere House** (p. 124), one of my favorite Boston attractions. From there it's an easy walk to Long Wharf or Rowes Wharf, where you can take a **sightseeing cruise** (p. 126) or, if you want to save both time and money, a **ferry ride** (p. 88) to the Charlestown Navy Yard and back. Have dinner at the **Legal Sea Foods** (p. 105) on Long Wharf, or return to the North End for Italian food.

On Day 2, prearrange tickets for a **Boston Duck Tour** (p. 126), ideally one that leaves from the Prudential Center in the early afternoon. Be at the **Museum of Fine Arts** (p. 119) when it opens; consider taking a tour to give you an overview before you explore on your own. Head to the Back Bay for lunch and your Duck Tour, then make a beeline for the retail delights of **Newbury Street.** Newbury dead-ends at the **Public Garden** (p. 125), where you can unwind and perhaps go for a spin on a **Swan Boat** (p. 125). For dinner, check out Boston's take on French cuisine at **Brasserie Jo** or **La Voile.**

Day ❸: Cambridge ✸✸

Start in **Harvard Square** (p. 129) with a student-led or self-guided tour of the main Harvard campus. Up next are the treasures of the university's **art museums,** currently assembled under one roof at the Sackler Museum as the other two undergo extensive renovations (p. 129); you may prefer the **natural history museums,** especially if children are along. Then head to lovely Brattle Street and the **Longfellow National Historic Site** (p. 130). From there, walk along Mass. Ave. toward Porter Square, a route with some excellent shopping opportunities. In fact, this whole day represents a fantastic chance to mix shopping and snacking with sightseeing. Have dinner at **Mr. Bartley's Burger Cottage** (p. 115), then hit a bookstore or two.

Day ❹: Plymouth ✸✸

Spend a day with the Pilgrims. Start with a 17th-century reality check at **Plimoth Plantation** (p. 190), which opens at 9am. The hands-on activities are almost as much fun as mingling with the "settlers," who stay in character as they chat with visitors. In downtown Plymouth, have lunch at the **Lobster Hut** (p. 194), where the deck overlooks the harbor, then explore a bit, starting at **Plymouth Rock** (p. 189). Take in some historic attractions—the *Mayflower II* (p. 190) is next to the Rock, and the **Pilgrim Hall Museum** (p. 190) is nearby—before returning to Boston or Cambridge for dinner.

Suggested New England Itineraries

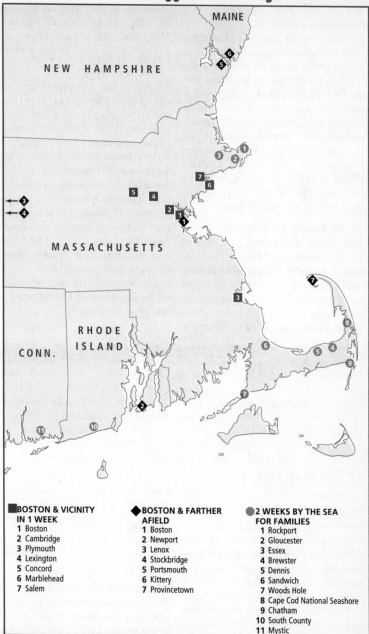

MAINE

NEW HAMPSHIRE

MASSACHUSETTS

RHODE ISLAND

CONN.

■ **BOSTON & VICINITY IN 1 WEEK**
1 Boston
2 Cambridge
3 Plymouth
4 Lexington
5 Concord
6 Marblehead
7 Salem

◆ **BOSTON & FARTHER AFIELD**
1 Boston
2 Newport
3 Lenox
4 Stockbridge
5 Portsmouth
6 Kittery
7 Provincetown

● **2 WEEKS BY THE SEA FOR FAMILIES**
1 Rockport
2 Gloucester
3 Essex
4 Brewster
5 Dennis
6 Sandwich
7 Woods Hole
8 Cape Cod National Seashore
9 Chatham
10 South County
11 Mystic

Day ❺: Lexington ☆ & Concord ☆☆☆

Spend most of the morning in **Lexington** (p. 149), acquainting yourself with the earliest events of the Revolutionary War and visiting the historic **Buckman Tavern** (p. 152). Have an early lunch in Concord and explore the beautiful town, picking and choosing the destinations and events that particularly interest you. I suggest starting with the **Concord Museum** (p. 156), touring **Orchard House** (p. 156), and stopping at **Walden Pond** (p. 158) on the way back into town, perhaps for a picnic dinner.

Day ❻: Boston & Cambridge

After 2 days on the road, stick close to "home." Head to Dorchester and the **John F. Kennedy Library and Museum** (p. 119), which is accessible by public transit and offers free parking (you're paying for that rental car, so you might as well get some use out of it). Spend the afternoon at the **Museum of Science** (p. 120), allowing enough time for an IMAX film, if that appeals to you.

Day ❼: Marblehead ☆☆☆ & Salem ☆☆

Begin your day on the picturesque streets of Old Town **Marblehead** (p. 161), a top destination for both sightseeing and shopping. If your hotel room rate doesn't include breakfast, arrive hungry and make a dent in a stack of pancakes at the **Driftwood Restaurant** (p. 164). The **Jeremiah Lee Mansion** (p. 162) is a must if you enjoy house tours. Spend the afternoon in **Salem** (p. 165), where the can't-miss destination is the **Peabody Essex Museum** (p. 167); if time allows, also visit the **Salem Witch Museum** (p. 169). This itinerary leaves you in a handy location for returning to Boston or for heading out to explore the wonders of northern New England.

3 Boston & Farther Afield

The 10-towns-in-6-days bus tours that clog the highways and byways of the Northeast every fall miss the point: The goal of a savvy traveler to New England is an experience that's deeper than it is wide. But even I'll admit to a fondness for day trips that take me just a bit out of my comfort zone. Each of these excursions is about as long as you'd want a day trip to be—and can easily work as an overnight journey. Tackle this itinerary before or after a visit to Boston and Cambridge, or as a tune-up for another of the trips in this chapter. On the first 3 days, an extra driver will come in handy; on the 4th day, there's no driving at all.

Day ❶: Newport ☆☆☆

If you don't hit traffic, you can cover the 75 or so miles between Boston and Newport in a little over an hour. The city's top attractions are the "cottages"—Newportspeak for "mansions"—that line Bellevue Avenue along the magnificent shore. Don't attempt to tour more than two **cottages** (p. 436) in a day, partly because they all start to run together, and partly because you'll want to leave time for exploring the picturesque downtown area. Between the glorious scenery and the serendipitous shopping, Newport is a perfect place to while away an afternoon. Linger into the evening for a drink or dinner near the water.

Day ❷: The Berkshires ☆☆

Try to schedule this trip to coincide with a morning rehearsal or afternoon concert by the **Boston Symphony Orchestra** at **Tanglewood** (p. 141), in Lenox. It's a long ride (at least 2 hr.) from Boston, so you'll want to get an early start, especially if you're attending a rehearsal. Spread out a blanket, picnic on the lawn, and enjoy the scene, one of the hallmarks of summer in New England. After rehearsal or before and after a concert, select one western Massachusetts town to explore, but just one—crowds and traffic dictate that you not try to get too ambitious. Our choice is **Stockbridge** (p. 340), because we're suckers for the **Norman Rockwell Museum** (p. 341).

Day ❸: Portsmouth ★★ & Kittery ★

A little over an hour from Boston is a gem of historic architecture, maritime sights and sounds, funky shops and cafes, and beautiful scenery. Portsmouth is worth a trip just for **Strawbery Banke** (p. 544), where the historic buildings are the displays. Build in some time to explore the cobblestone downtown area, then cross the Piscataqua River for some serious shopping at the **Kittery** outlets and a bite to eat at **Bob's Clam Hut** (p. 596).

Day ❹: Provincetown ★★★

Ferries (conventional and high-speed) connect Boston to **Provincetown** (p. 250) every day in the summer and on weekends in the spring and fall. The trip by car is absolutely punishing, especially on a busy weekend, but an ocean voyage is always a good idea. On a day trip, you'll have time for world-class people-watching, strolling along **Commercial Street,** perusing the novelty shops and art galleries, lunching on seafood, and—if you're quick—a trip to one of the famous beaches. However, you'll have to forgo the hopping gay nightlife scene unless you've planned a longer excursion.

4 A Week by the Sea for Families

A family can easily spend a pleasant week or so exploring the beaches, boats, cobblestones, shops, museums, and attractions of coastal Maine and New Hampshire.

Days ❶ & ❷: Portland ★★★

Portland is a joy for families. The **Children's Museum of Maine** (p. 608) is almost exactly in the center of town, making it a good jumping-off point for a city tour. The excellent **Portland Museum of Art** (p. 610), right next door, provides teens and college-age family members with something different to do.

In the historic **Old Port** (p. 608), Exchange Street is the key shopping address. Kids will enjoy the ice cream shops, boats, and quirky gift stores. The city tourist office is on Commercial Street.

The **Maine Narrow Gauge Railroad Co. & Museum** (p. 610) combines a short train ride to the foot of the cliffs framing Portland's east end with a museum.

Another great experience is a cruise on the **Casco Bay Ferry** (p. 611) lines. You can take anything from a 20-minute run to a half-day "mail boat" cruise. Two good destinations are **Peaks Island**—a favorite among parents pushing strollers, with easy-to-cruise streets and Portland views—and **Long Island,** which has an excellent beach.

For baseball fans, an outing to Hadlock Field to watch the **Portland Sea Dogs** (p. 612) can't be beat; it's one of our favorite minor-league parks.

Finally, young and old alike enjoy the sunrises, sunsets, picnics, sailboat views, and swing sets of the park along the **Eastern Promenade** (p. 608).

Day ❸: Cape Elizabeth ★★

Plan to spend at least one afternoon hitting the string of beaches and lighthouses off Route 77 in the quiet town of **Cape Elizabeth** and surroundings, just 15 minutes from Portland.

Kids will especially enjoy the **Portland Head Light** (p. 610) and romping around in the sand and surf on **Crescent, Scarborough,** and **Willard beaches.**

Day ❹: Old Orchard Beach ⭐

Drive 20 minutes south of Portland and you come to **Old Orchard Beach.** This place may strike you as corny at first, but it rarely fails to entertain. On the pier out over the water, you can find cotton candy, french fries, and arcade games. There's also a long beach to stroll along.

Day ❺: Ogunquit ⭐⭐

About 40 minutes south of Old Orchard is **Ogunquit** (p. 597), which offers enough distractions for a few days. In addition to a main street full of shops, restaurants, and cafes, it has a main beach that's a vast stretch of powdery sand at low tide and has some of Maine's warmest ocean water (which isn't saying much!). **Perkins Cove** (p. 598) has sea views, ice cream and candy shops, an excellent small bookstore, and lots of souvenirs for sale.

Day ❻: York ⭐⭐⭐ and Kittery ⭐

Only a 10-minute drive south, these twin towns offer a lot for families. **York** (p. 590) has a dynamite lighthouse (with homemade ice cream nearby), an amusement arcade, several excellent beaches, and the **Goldenrod** (p. 596), a candy store where kids can watch taffy being pulled. You can buy boxes to take home—half the fun is deciding which candies to buy. **Kittery** (p. 590) is more for adults, but its extensive set of outlet stores also appeals to teen shopaholics.

Day ❼: Portsmouth ⭐⭐

Portsmouth (p. 543) is a good base for exploring local parks and beaches. Be sure to visit New Castle Island for its historic streets; the outstanding collection of oceanside state parks lining Route 1A in Rye; and **Strawbery Banke** (p. 544) by the downtown Portsmouth waterfront, with its historic buildings and restorations. Nearby is the lively **Children's Museum of Portsmouth,** with hands-on exhibits of arts and science. In town, there are plenty of shops and restaurants.

5 Two Weeks by the Sea for Families

Spend your first week in New Hampshire and Maine, as described above, then head south. The water off Massachusetts and Rhode Island is warmer than the northern New England surf (though it's all relative), but the attractions and distractions are just as enjoyable.

Days ❽ & ❾: Cape Ann ⭐⭐

Use your first day to explore this lovely peninsula. Visit downtown **Rockport** (p. 180) for souvenirs and fudge. Push on to **Halibut Point State Park** (p. 182), at the tip of Cape Ann, which boasts spectacular views and plenty of room to run around. Walk the waterfront boulevard that extends north from Stage Fort Park in **Gloucester** (p. 176). Before or after blowing off some steam by running around **Stage Fort Park,** head west on

Route 133 for fried clams at the legendary **Woodman's of Essex** (p. 174).

On Day 2, head to the beach early, before the parking lots fill up. The rocky coast yields to welcoming strips of sand at several inviting spots. A good destination for families is Gloucester's **Wingaersheek Beach** (p. 174), where kids will happily while away the day. Plan on an early dinner, because you have a long drive ahead of you tomorrow.

More Suggested New England Itineraries

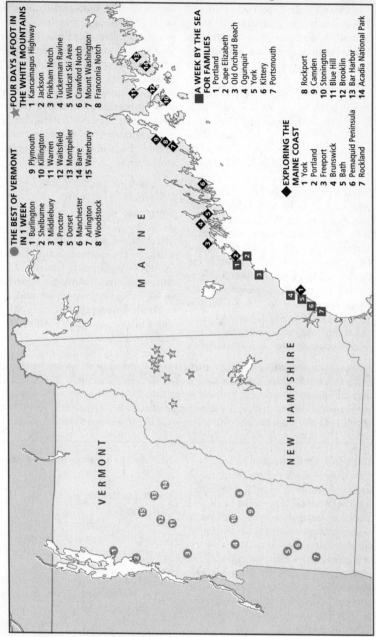

● THE BEST OF VERMONT
IN 1 WEEK
1 Burlington
2 Shelburne
3 Middlebury
4 Proctor
5 Dorset
6 Manchester
7 Arlington
8 Woodstock
9 Plymouth
10 Killington
11 Warren
12 Waitsfield
13 Montpelier
14 Barre
15 Waterbury

★ FOUR DAYS AFOOT IN
THE WHITE MOUNTAINS
1 Kancamagus Highway
2 Jackson
3 Pinkham Notch
4 Tuckerman Ravine
5 Wildcat Ski Area
6 Crawford Notch
7 Mount Washington
8 Franconia Notch

■ A WEEK BY THE SEA
FOR FAMILIES
1 Portland
2 Cape Elizabeth
3 Old Orchard Beach
4 Ogunquit
5 York
6 Kittery
7 Portsmouth
8 Rockport
9 Camden
10 Stonington
11 Blue Hill
12 Brooklin
13 Bar Harbor
14 Acadia National Park

◆ EXPLORING THE
MAINE COAST
1 York
2 Portland
3 Freeport
4 Brunswick
5 Bath
6 Pemaquid Peninsula
7 Rockland

Days ⑩, ⑪ & ⑫: Cape Cod 🌟🌟🌟

Base yourselves in **Brewster** (p. 227) or **Dennis** (p. 222); they're convenient but not in the heart of the tourist frenzy. On your first day, stick close to your home base and the child-friendly beaches that front Cape Cod Bay. On Day 4, venture to Falmouth by way of Sandwich. Be at the **Heritage Museums and Gardens** in Sandwich (p. 199) at 9am, and don't expect to get away without a carousel ride. Push on to the **Woods Hole Aquarium** (p. 205). Mix and match your routes in each direction, combining the speed and boredom of Route 6 with the pokey pace and abundant distractions of routes 6A and 28 to accommodate the level of interest in the back seat. Day 5 may just be another local beach day, but a fun option is **Cape Cod National Seashore** (p. 262) in the Outer Cape, followed by a stroll around lovely downtown **Chatham** (p. 232).

Let the family energy level dictate how you fill out your days. This area abounds with options for outdoor fun; depending on your kids' ages and interests, you might try biking, kayaking, or fishing. Just be sure to allow for some quality beach time and that timeless Cape combo, miniature golf and soft-serve ice cream. If it's summer, sports fans will want to take in a **Cape Cod Baseball League** game (p. 229). Starting times are in the afternoon as well as the evening, a boon for parents who are working around naps.

Days ⑬ & ⑭: South County & Mystic

Work your way west from Cape Cod along the Rhode Island coast, taking advantage of a good excuse to experience relatively undiscovered **South County** (p. 451). You'll reach Connecticut in time to explore the **Mystic Aquarium** (p. 407). That leaves a full day for a visit to **Mystic Seaport** (p. 408); fuel up first with a hearty breakfast at **Kitchen Little** (p. 411).

6 The Best of Vermont in 1 Week

You can enjoy a good taste of Vermont in less than a week. This trip involves about 2 or 3 hours of driving daily, if you don't linger (though I wholeheartedly recommend it). You can also scout out places to which you'd like to return and explore in depth.

Days ❶ & ❷: Burlington 🌟🌟

Check in to the hotel and head out to explore **Burlington** (p. 526). Depending on the weather, rent bikes or in-line skates, or just put on some comfortable walking shoes—this is a great destination for pedestrians.

Budget plenty of time for exploring the pedestrian-only **Church Street Marketplace** (p. 529)—keep an eye out for the popcorn guy hawking sugared kettle corn in summer—as well as the University of Vermont campus.

Each night, have dinner at one of Burlington's many excellent midpriced restaurants. In the evening, you can check out the **Vermont Mozart Festival** (p. 528).

Day ❸: Shelburne 🌟🌟 & Middlebury 🌟

Head south to **Shelburne** in the morning, and spend most of the day exploring the remarkable **Shelburne Museum** (p. 530).

Afterward, drive south to the classic town of **Middlebury** (p. 503) and spend the night at a country inn. The historic **Otter Creek** (p. 504) district, set on a steep hillside by the rocky creek, is well worth exploring and has some great crafts for sale. If you're an art lover, explore the campus and art museum of little **Middle-bury College** (p. 504). For dinner, we like **American Flatbread** (p. 511), though it's open only 2 nights a week.

Day ❹: In & Around Dorset 🐦🐦 & Manchester 🐦🐦

From Middlebury, drive south on Route 7, detouring to Proctor to visit the **Vermont Marble Museum** (p. 502). You'll be amazed at the famous sculptures and edifices carved, built, enhanced, or faced with the local stone.

Later, continue west on Route 4 almost to the New York border, then go south on Highway 30 through **Dorset** and **Manchester,** both classic Vermont small towns with scenic vistas. If you're a history fan, you'll love **Hildene** (p. 472), the former estate of Robert Todd Lincoln, son of the assassinated president.

Spend the night in Manchester, Dorset, or Arlington—being sure to leave time late in the day for **outlet shopping** (p. 479) in Manchester and a stop at the flagship **Orvis** outdoors shop.

Day ❺: Woodstock 🐦🐦🐦

Today head east on Highway 30 into the Green Mountains, then follow Highway 35 north to the town of **Woodstock** (p. 489). (Break out those maps if you crave back roads.)

Be sure to sit a spell on Woodstock's lovely town green, taking some photographs of the covered bridge. You can walk from the center of town to the underrated **Billings Farm and Museum** (p. 490). Drop in to a local pub or coffee shop for a pint or a cup, and try to stay overnight here or nearby.

Day ❻: The Mad River Valley

After exploring Woodstock in the morning, head west on Route 4 with a detour to **Plymouth** 🐦🐦 to visit the **President Calvin Coolidge State Historic Site** (p. 497), which is also the site of yet another **cheese factory.**

Continue through **Killington** and up scenic Route 100 to the **Mad River Valley** (p. 508). If it's winter and you're a skier, you may be in heaven; the ski hill here is Vermont's most laid-back.

Overnight in **Warren** 🐦🐦 or **Waitsfield** 🐦🐦—dropping in to the cute **Warren General Store** (p. 509) for souvenirs—and, if time permits, rent a bike.

Day ❼: Back to Burlington 🐦🐦

Spend your final day of this tour working your way back to Burlington.

On the way, spend an hour or two in the lovely little capital city of **Montpelier** 🐦🐦. If you're interested, check out the immense working quarries in **Barre.**

You may be pressed for time, but your kids won't let you miss the **Ben & Jerry's factory tour** (p. 514) in **Waterbury** 🐦🐦. There's plenty of shopping around here, too, so give in.

End your trip with dinner in **Burlington** (p. 534) at one of the restaurants you missed on your first visit—even if it's just **Al's** (p. 534).

---

7 Four Days Afoot in the White Mountains

New Hampshire's White Mountains reveal extraordinary natural grandeur from the roadside, and they provide the opportunity to explore mountain crags and crystalline streams.

Day ❶: The "Kanc" 🐦🐦🐦

Start at the town of Lincoln, at exit 32 of I-93, and drive to North Conway via the scenic **Kancamagus Highway** (p. 567), stopping for some short hikes or a picnic. Indulge in a few shopping forays in town, and savor the views of the Mount Washington Valley. Head to the village of **Jackson** (p. 577) for the night.

Relax before dinner at **Jackson Falls**, or take a bike ride up **Carter Notch Road** or other back roads in the hills above the village.

Day ❷: Pinkham Notch ⓖⓖ

Stay another night in Jackson, and spend the day exploring by foot around **Pinkham Notch** (p. 579). Stop at **Glen Ellis Falls** (p. 579) en route to the base of Mount Washington. Park at Pinkham Notch and hike to dramatic **Tuckerman Ravine** (p. 579) for a picnic lunch.

Return to your car and continue north to **Wildcat Ski Area** (p. 580). Take the chairlift to the summit for spectacular views of Mount Washington, the Presidential Range, and the Carter Range. Return to Jackson for the night.

Day ❸: Mount Washington ⓖⓖⓖ

Retrace your path down Route 16 and back to Route 302, turn right, and drive through **Crawford Notch** (p. 583). If weather and time allow, hike to one of the scenic waterfalls.

Go to the **Mount Washington Cog Railway** (p. 584) on the far side of the Notch. Take the train ride to the summit of **Mount Washington** (dress warmly). On your return, stop by the grand **Mount Washington Hotel** (p. 585) for a celebratory snack.

Day ❹: Franconia Notch ⓖⓖ

Continue west on Route 302 to Route 3. Turn left (south) onto I-93, then drive through scenic **Franconia Notch** (p.586). Visit some of the scenic attractions (such as the **Flume Gorge** [p. 586] or the **tram ride to Cannon Mountain** [p. 587]) as time permits.

8 Exploring the Maine Coast

The inlets and peninsulas of the Maine coast make it impossible to plot a straight course. This trip takes you a little more than halfway up (really across) the coast, allowing time for serendipitous detours and delays. Tack on some extra time at the end to really explore Acadia.

Day ❶: York ⓖⓖ

Drive into Maine from the south on I-95, and head immediately for **York Village** (p. 590) (the first exit). Spend some time snooping around the historic homes of the **Old York Historical Society** (p. 592), and stretch your legs on a walk through town or the woods.

Drive north through **York Beach**, stock up on saltwater taffy at the **Goldenrod** (p. 596), and spend the night near the beach.

Days ❷ & ❸: Portland ⓖⓖⓖ

Using the right route, getting to Portland can be as fun as being there. You can hit the antiques shops along parts of Route 1 as you drive north. If you're in a hurry or

traveling in summer, avoid the crowds on Route 1 by taking I-95.

In **Portland** (p. 607) by afternoon, collect tourism information and devise a schedule. Plan to stay in the city or on a nearby beach, shopping for jewelry, souvenirs, or even kites; taste-testing chowder and microbrewed beer; and just soaking up the salty air and atmosphere. Don't forget a walk along the **Eastern Promenade** (p. 608) or a **day cruise** (p. 611) on a local ferry.

Day ❹: Freeport ⓖⓖⓖ, Brunswick ⓖ & Bath ⓖⓖ

Head north early to beat the shopping crowds at the outlet haven of Freeport.

You can't leave too early for **L.L.Bean** (p. 620)—it never closes!

From Freeport, continue north to **Wiscasset,** the so-called "Prettiest Village in Maine," or to the **Boothbay** region (p. 623). Spend a relaxing night in a picturesque B&B.

Days ❺ & ❻: Camden ☙☙☙ & Penobscot Bay

Heading north from the Bath-Brunswick area, detour down to **Pemaquid Point** (p. 627) for a late picnic as you watch the surf roll in. Then head back to Route 1 and set your sights on the heart of Penobscot Bay.

Rockland ☙, which you'll reach first, is the workaday part of the equation. The best places here are the arty cafes and the excellent museum and restaurants. Nearby **Rockport** ☙☙ is a tiny harbor town with excellent views and a small main street.

Finally, head a few miles north to wander around downtown **Camden,** poking into shops and galleries. Hike up one of the impressive hills at **Camden Hills State Park** (p. 635), hop a **ferry** to an island (North Haven and Isleboro are both great for biking), or sign up for a daylong sail on a **windjammer.** We also like getting ice cream and hot dogs down by the harbor.

Day ❼: Blue Hill ☙☙☙ & Deer Isle

From Camden, drive up and around the head of Penobscot Bay and then down the bay's eastern shore. The roads here are great for aimless drives, but head for **Stonington** ☙☙, far down at the end of the peninsula.

Next, head to scenic **Blue Hill** (p. 642) for dinner and lodging. I love the views from here, and the combination of a Maine fishing town and new-blood bookshops and restaurants is quite appealing. Also take a spin around the peninsula to smaller towns such as **Blue Hill Falls** and **Brooklin,** where you'll see boatyards, old-fashioned general stores (post offices included), and ingenuity holding it all together. *This* is the real Maine.

Days ❽, ❾, ❿ & ⓫: Bar Harbor ☙☙ & Acadia National Park ☙☙☙

Bar Harbor is a great base for exploring **Mount Desert Island,** which is well worth 4 (or more) days on a Maine itinerary. You may want to stay at least 2 nights in Bar Harbor, especially if you have family members along. It provides access to comforts and services such as a movie theater, souvenir shops, bike and kayak rentals, free shuttle buses all over the island, and numerous restaurants. Yes, it's a lot more developed (perhaps too much so) than the rest of the island, but think of it as a supply depot.

Hike, bike, boat, or do whatever you must to explore the island and **Acadia National Park** (p. 644), one of America's finest. What it lacks in size, it makes up for through intimate contact with nature. Explore the island at your own pace: Take a beginner's **kayak trip** down the eastern shore, a **hike** out to **Bar Island,** or a **mountain-bike trip** along one of the many **carriage roads** built by the Rockefeller family. Only bicycles and horses are allowed on these roads, making them a tranquil respite from the island's highways, which—almost unbelievably—do get crowded in summer.

The scenic **Park Loop Road** is a great introduction to what's in store for you later (crashing waves, big mountains, drop-dead-gorgeous views). Make sure to get a park pass that lasts more than a day.

While exploring the rest of the island, be sure to hit some of the nonpark towns, too. **Northeast Harbor** ☙☙ and **Southwest Harbor** ☙☙ are fishing towns that tourism has partly transformed into tiny centers of art, music, and shopping. However, they still have small stores where fishermen shop for slickers and Wonder Bread.

What about those things you wanted to do but didn't have time for? Do them on your last day in Acadia. Watch a sunrise from the top of **Cadillac Mountain** (p. 649). Cap off your visit with a cold-water dip at **Sand Beach** (p. 648) and tea and popovers at **Jordan Pond House** (p. 650). Take a quick last hike up **The Bubbles** (p. 651). Or just enjoy one last lobster atop a wooden pier.

5

Boston & Cambridge

by Marie Morris

Boston greeted the 21st century by putting on a new face. The 2-decade, $15-billion highway-construction project known as the "Big Dig" wrapped up, leaving new parks, open spaces, surface roads, and buildings in place of the mile-long elevated expressway that had separated the waterfront from downtown for half a century. A subterranean highway now carries traffic through Boston, a modern metropolis that's also steeped in history. Rich in Colonial lore and 21st-century technology, it's a living landmark that changes every day.

Cambridge and Boston are so close that many people believe they're the same—a notion both cities' residents and politicians are happy to dispel. Cantabrigians are often considered more liberal and better educated than Bostonians, which is another idea that's sure to get you involved in a heated discussion. Harvard dominates Cambridge's history and geography, but there's more to the city than just the university.

Take a few days (or weeks) to get to know the Boston area, or use it as a gateway to the rest of New England. Here's hoping your experience is memorable and delightful.

1 Orientation

ARRIVING

BY PLANE Most major domestic carriers serve Boston's Logan International Airport, which the locals usually call just "Logan." Many major international carriers also fly into Boston. **Southwest** (© 800/435-9792) and several other major carriers serve New Hampshire's **Manchester–Boston International Airport** (© 603/624-6556; www.flymanchester.com; airport code MHT) and **T. F. Green Airport,** in the Providence suburb of Warwick, Rhode Island (© 888/268-7222; www.pvdairport.com; airport code PVD). The Manchester airport operates free shuttle van service to and from Boston (the Sullivan Square Orange Line T stop) and suburban Woburn, Massachusetts; check the website for details. **Vermont Transit** (© 800/552-8737; www.vermonttransit.com) buses connect the Manchester airport to Boston's South Station, and some continue to Logan Airport. The fare is $20 one-way, $39 round-trip. Allow 60 to 90 minutes. To and from T. F. Green, **Peter Pan Bonanza** (© 888/751-8800; www.peterpanbus.com) runs buses; the fare is $20 one-way, $37 round-trip. You can also take a cab or local bus to downtown Providence and transfer to either the MBTA commuter rail or Amtrak. Allow at least 2 hours.

Logan International Airport (© 800/23-LOGAN; www.massport.com/logan; airport code BOS) is in East Boston at the end of the Sumner, Callahan, and Ted

Williams tunnels, 3 miles across the harbor from downtown. Each of the four terminals has ATMs, Internet kiosks, pay phones with dataports, fax machines, and information booths (near baggage claim). Wireless Internet access is available all over the airport for $8 a day through **Logan Wifi** (© 617/561-9434; www.loganwifi.com). Terminals C and E have bank branches that handle currency exchange; A and C have children's play spaces.

You can get into town by bus, subway (the "T"), cab, van, or boat. If you're taking the Silver Line bus or the subway, look for MBTA fare kiosks tucked into corners near the exits closest to the public transit pick-up area in each terminal.

The Silver Line **bus** stops at each airport terminal and runs directly to South Station, where you can connect to the Red Line subway and the commuter rail to the southern suburbs. It takes about 20 minutes, not including waiting time. The **subway** takes just 10 minutes to reach downtown, not including the shuttle-bus ride to the subway. Free **shuttle buses** run from each terminal to the Airport station on the Blue Line of the T daily from 5:30am to 1am. The Blue Line stops at State Street and Government Center, downtown points where you can exit or transfer (free) to the other lines. The fare for the bus or subway is $1.70 (with a pass or CharlieCard) or $2 (with a CharlieTicket or cash).

A **cab** from the airport to downtown or the Back Bay costs about $20 to $35 and can be as high as $45 in bad traffic. The ride into town takes 10 to 45 minutes, depending on traffic and the time of day. If you must travel during rush hour or on Sunday afternoon, allow extra time, or plan to take the subway or water shuttle (and pack accordingly).

The Logan Airport website (www.massport.com/logan) lists numerous companies that operate **shuttle-van service** to local hotels. One-way prices start at $14 per person and are subject to fuel surcharges as gas prices fluctuate.

The trip to the downtown waterfront (near cabstands and several hotels) in a weather-protected **boat** takes 7 minutes and costs $10 one-way. Service runs from early morning through early evening daily, year-round; hours are shorter on weekends and in the winter. The free no. 66 shuttle bus connects all terminals to the Logan ferry dock; call ahead from the dock for water taxi pickup. Three on-call water taxi operators serve the downtown waterfront and other points around Boston Harbor: **City Water Taxi** (© 617/422-0392; www.citywatertaxi.com), **Rowes Wharf Water Transport** (© 617/406-8584; www.roweswharfwatertransport.com), and **Boston Harbor Water Taxi** (© 617/593-9168; www.bostonharborwatertaxi.com). The MBTA (© 800/392-6100 or 617/222-3200; www.mbta.com) contracts out scheduled ferry service to **Harbor Express,** which runs to Long Wharf, behind the Marriott Long Wharf hotel.

Some hotels have **limousines** or **shuttle vans;** ask when you make your reservations. To arrange private service, call ahead for a reservation, especially at busy times. Your hotel can recommend a company, or try **Boston Coach** (© 800/672-7676; www.bostoncoach.com) or **Carey Limousine Boston** (© 800/336-4646 or 617/623-8700; www.carey.com).

BY CAR   Boston is 218 miles from New York City; driving time is about 4½ hours. From Washington, D.C., it takes about 8 hours to cover the 468 miles; the 992-mile drive from Chicago takes around 21 hours.

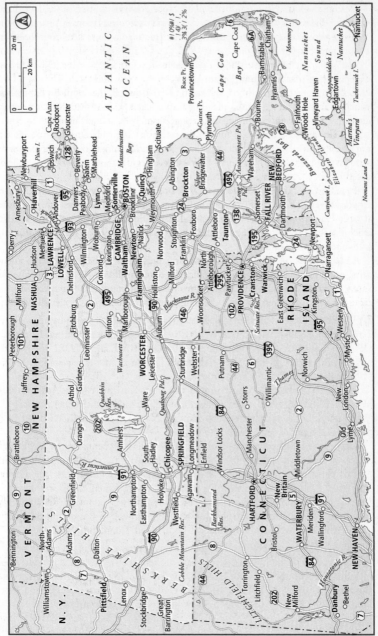

Driving to Boston is not difficult, but between the cost of parking and the hassle of traffic, the savings on airfare may not be worth the aggravation. If you're thinking of using the car to get around town, think again—you won't need one to explore Boston and Cambridge.

The major highways are **I-90,** the Massachusetts Turnpike ("Mass. Pike"), an east-west toll road that runs from Logan Airport to the New York State Thruway; **I-93/ U.S. 1,** which extends north to Canada; and **I-93/Route 3,** the Southeast Expressway, which connects with the south, including Cape Cod. **I-95** (MA Rte. 128) is a beltway about 11 miles from downtown that connects to I-93 and to highways to Rhode Island, Connecticut, and New York to the south and New Hampshire and Maine to the north. *Note:* The Mass. Pike's FastLane program is compatible with some out-of-state systems, including New York's **EZPass;** your regular transponder works in designated lanes.

To reach Cambridge, take **Storrow Drive** or **Memorial Drive** (on either side of the Charles River). The Mass. Pike's Allston/Cambridge exit connects with Storrow Drive. It has a Harvard Square exit; cross the Anderson Bridge to John F. Kennedy Street to reach the square. Memorial Drive intersects with Kennedy Street; turn away from the bridge to reach the square.

AAA (✆ **800/AAA-HELP;** www.aaa.com) provides members with maps, itineraries, and other information, and arranges free towing if you break down. The privately operated Mass. Pike arranges its own towing; if you break down, wait in your car until a patrol arrives. To reach the state police from a cellphone, call ✆ ***911.**

BY TRAIN   Boston has three rail centers: **South Station,** on Atlantic Avenue; **Back Bay Station,** on Dartmouth Street across from the Copley Place mall; and **North Station,** on Causeway Street. **Amtrak** (✆ **800/USA-RAIL** or 617/482-3660; www. amtrak.com) serves all three. Each train station is also a rapid-transit station. See the "Boston Transit & Parking" map on p. 87.

Amtrak serves Boston from the south and from Portland, Maine. **Acela Express** high-speed service, when it's on time, reaches New York in just under 4 hours and Washington, D.C., in about 6 hours. Standard Northeast Corridor service takes 4 to 5 hours and 8 hours, respectively.

South Station is a stop on the Red Line, which runs to Cambridge by way of Park Street, the hub of the **subway** (✆ **800/392-6100** or 617/222-3200; www.mbta.com). At Park Street you can connect to the Green, Blue, and Orange lines. The Orange Line links Back Bay Station with Downtown Crossing (where there's a walkway to Park St. station) and other points. The **commuter rail** serves Ipswich, Rockport, and Fitchburg from North Station, and points south and west of Boston, including Plymouth, Massachusetts, and Providence, Rhode Island, from South Station.

BY BUS   The **South Station Transportation Center,** on Atlantic Avenue next to the train station, is the city's bus-service hub. It's served by regional and national lines, including **Greyhound** (✆ **800/231-2222** or 617/526-1801; www.greyhound.com), **Bonanza** (✆ **800/556-3815** or 617/720-4110; www.bonanzabus.com), and **Peter Pan** (✆ **800/237-8747** or 800/343-9999; www.peterpanbus.com).

VISITOR INFORMATION

BEFORE YOU LEAVE HOME   The **Greater Boston Convention & Visitors Bureau** (✆ **888/SEE-BOSTON** or 617/536-4100; 0171/431-3434 in the U.K.; www.bostonusa.com) offers a comprehensive information kit ($10) with a planner, guidebook, map, and coupons, and a separate *Kids Love Boston* guide ($5). Free smaller planners for specific seasons or events are often available.

The **Cambridge Office for Tourism** (© **800/862-5678** or 617/441-2884; www. cambridge-usa.org) distributes information about Cambridge.

The **Massachusetts Office of Travel and Tourism** (© **800/227-6277** or 617/973-8500; www.massvacation.com) distributes the *Getaway Guide*, a free magazine with information on attractions and lodgings statewide, a map, and a seasonal calendar.

An excellent resource for travelers with disabilities is **VSA Arts Massachusetts** (© **617/350-7713;** TTY 617/350-6836; www.vsamass.org). Its **Access Expressed** network maintains a website (www.accessexpressed.net) with a searchable directory of cultural venues.

IN PERSON   The **Boston National Historical Park Visitor Center,** 15 State St. (© **617/242-5642;** www.nps.gov/bost), across the street from the Old State House and the State Street T, is a good place to start exploring. Park rangers staff the center and lead free tours of the "heart" of the Freedom Trail in the spring, summer, and fall. The center is wheelchair accessible and has restrooms; it's open daily from 9am to 5pm. The ranger-staffed center at the **Charlestown Navy Yard** (© **617/242-5601**) keeps the same hours.

The Freedom Trail begins at the **Boston Common Information Center,** 148 Tremont St., on the Common. The center is open Monday through Saturday from 8:30am to 5pm, Sunday from 9am to 5pm. The **Prudential Information Center,** on the main level of the Prudential Center, is open Monday through Friday from 8:30am to 6pm, Saturday and Sunday from 10am to 6pm. The **Greater Boston Convention & Visitors Bureau** (© **888/SEE-BOSTON** or 617/536-4100) operates both centers.

The outdoor information booth at **Faneuil Hall Marketplace,** between Quincy Market and the South Market Building, is staffed in the spring, summer, and fall from 10am to 6pm Monday through Saturday, noon to 6pm Sunday.

In Cambridge, there's an **information kiosk** (© **800/862-5678** or 617/497-1630) in the heart of Harvard Square, near the T entrance at the intersection of Mass. Ave., John F. Kennedy Street, and Brattle Street. It's open Monday through Saturday from 9am to 5pm, Sunday from 1 to 5pm.

CITY LAYOUT

Parts of Boston reflect the city's original layout, a seemingly haphazard plan that can disorient even longtime residents. Old Boston abounds with alleys, dead ends, one-way streets, streets that change names, and streets named after extinct geographical features. On the plus side, every "wrong" turn **downtown,** in the **North End,** or on **Beacon Hill** is a chance to see something you might otherwise have missed.

FINDING AN ADDRESS   There's no rhyme or reason to the street pattern, compass directions are virtually useless, and there aren't enough street signs. The best way to find an address is to call ahead and ask for directions, including landmarks, or leave time for wandering around. If the directions involve a T stop, be sure to ask which exit to use—most stations have more than one.

STREET MAPS   Free maps of downtown Boston and the transit system are available at visitor centers around the city. *Where* and other tourism-oriented magazines, available free at most hotels, include maps of central Boston and the T. *Streetwise Boston* ($6.95) and *Artwise Boston* ($7.95) are sturdy, laminated maps available at most bookstores.

BOSTON NEIGHBORHOODS IN BRIEF

See the map on p. 92 to locate these areas. When Bostonians say **"downtown,"** they usually mean the first six neighborhoods below. With a couple of exceptions (noted here), Boston is generally safe, but you should take the same precautions as in any large city, especially at night.

The Waterfront This narrow area along **Atlantic Avenue** and **Commercial Street,** once filled with wharves and warehouses, now boasts luxury condos, marinas, restaurants, offices, and hotels. Most of the **Rose Kennedy Greenway** is here, as are the New England Aquarium and docks for harbor cruises and whale watches.

The North End One of the city's oldest neighborhoods has been an immigrant stronghold for much of its history. It's now less than half Italian-American, but you'll still hear Italian spoken and find many Italian restaurants, *caffès,* and shops. **Hanover Street** is the main street of the North End, which adjoins Faneuil Hall Marketplace and the Waterfront. Clubs and restaurants cluster on and near **Causeway Street** in the **North Station** area (btw. N. Washington St. and Beacon Hill), where you shouldn't wander the side streets alone late at night.

Faneuil Hall Marketplace & Haymarket Employees aside, Boston residents tend to be scarce at Faneuil Hall Marketplace (also called Quincy Market). An irresistible draw for out-of-towners and suburbanites, the cluster of restored market buildings adjacent to the North End is the city's most popular attraction. **Haymarket,** along Blackstone Street, is home to an open-air produce market on Friday and Saturday.

Government Center Here, modern design strays into Boston's traditional red-brick facade. Across **Cambridge Street** from Beacon Hill, Government Center is home to state and federal office towers, Boston City Hall, and a central T stop.

Financial District In the city's banking, insurance, and legal center, skyscrapers surround the landmark Custom House Tower. This area is frantic during the day, bust after work on weekdays, and nearly empty at night. **State Street** separates it from Faneuil Hall Marketplace.

Downtown Crossing The Freedom Trail runs through this shopping and business district adjacent to Boston Common, which hops during the day and slows at night. The intersection that gives Downtown Crossing its name is where Winter Street becomes Summer Street at **Washington Street,** the most "main" street downtown.

Beacon Hill Narrow, tree-lined streets and architectural showpieces make up this largely residential area near the State House. **Charles Street** is the main drag of "the Hill." Two of the city's loveliest and most exclusive spots are here: Mount Vernon Street and Louisburg (pronounced "Lewisburg") Square. Massachusetts General Hospital is off **Cambridge Street.** On the south side, **Beacon Street** borders Boston Common, as does **Park Street,** which is just 1 block long but looms large in the geography of the T.

Charlestown One of the oldest areas of Boston is where you'll see the Bunker Hill Monument and USS *Constitution* ("Old Ironsides"). Yuppification has brought some diversity to the mostly white residential neighborhood, but pockets remain that have earned their reputation for insularity. To get here, follow **North Washington Street** from the North End.

Seaport District/South Boston Waterfront Across **Fort Point Channel** from downtown, it's where you'll find the Boston Convention & Exhibition Center, World Trade Center, Institute of Contemporary Art, federal courthouse, Museum Wharf, and one end of the Ted Williams Tunnel.

Chinatown The fourth-largest Chinese community in the country abounds with Asian restaurants, groceries, and other businesses. As the "Combat Zone," or red-light district, has nearly disappeared, Chinatown has expanded to fill the area between Downtown Crossing and the Mass. Pike extension. Its main street is **Beach Street.** Also in this neighborhood, the tiny **Theater District** extends about 1½ blocks in each direction from the intersection of Tremont and Stuart streets; be careful here at night.

South End Cross **Huntington Avenue** or Stuart Street to reach this landmark district packed with Victorian row houses and little parks. Known for its ethnic, economic, and cultural diversity, as well as for its galleries and boutiques, the South End has a large gay community and some of the city's best restaurants. Main thoroughfares include **Tremont** and **Washington streets** and **Harrison Avenue,** which originate downtown, and **Columbus Avenue.** *Note:* The South End is not South Boston, the residential neighborhood across I-93.

Back Bay Fashionable since its creation out of landfill in the mid–19th century, the Back Bay overflows with gorgeous architecture and chic shops. It extends from **Arlington Street,** in the plush area near the **Public Garden,** to the student-dominated sections near Massachusetts Avenue, or **Mass. Ave.** Unlike downtown, it's laid out in a grid. The main streets include the prime shopping areas of **Boylston** and **Newbury streets** and largely residential Commonwealth Avenue, or **Comm. Ave.,** and **Beacon Street.** The cross streets go in alphabetical order.

Huntington Avenue Landmarks dot the "Avenue of the Arts" (or, with a Boston accent, "Otts"). Not a formal neighborhood, Huntington Avenue is where you'll find Symphony Hall (at the corner of **Mass. Ave.**), Northeastern University, and the Museum of Fine Arts. Parts of Huntington can be a little risky; if you're leaving the museum at night, grab a cab or the Green Line, and try to travel in a group.

Kenmore Square The landmark white-and-red Citgo sign above the intersection of **Comm. Ave., Beacon Street,** and **Brookline Avenue** tells you you're approaching Kenmore Square. Boston University students throng its shops, bars, restaurants, and clubs. The college-town atmosphere goes out the window when the Red Sox are in town and baseball fans flock to Fenway Park, 3 blocks away.

Cambridge The backbone of Boston's neighbor across the Charles River is **Mass. Ave.,** which originates in Roxbury and extends as far as Lexington. The Red Line subway parallels Mass. Ave. in the areas you're likeliest to visit, around the **Kendall/MIT, Central, Harvard,** and **Porter** T stops.

2 Getting Around

It's impossible to say this often enough: When you reach your hotel, *leave your car in the garage and walk or use public transportation.* If you must drive in town, ask at the front desk for the quickest route (which may not be obvious from a map or mapping website).

Tips **All's Fare on the T**

MBTA (© **800/392-6100** or 617/222-3200; www.mbta.com) passengers pay their fares with stored-value CharlieTickets or CharlieCards. Buses and trolleys also accept cash. Fares are lower if you pay with a CharlieCard than if you use a CharlieTicket or cash. The **CharlieCard** (a plastic "smart card" with an embedded chip) registers when you hold it in front of the rectangular fare reader; the **CharlieTicket** (heavy paper with a magnetic strip) goes into and pops out of a slot on the turnstile or farebox. Self-service kiosks at the entrance to each subway station and in each terminal allow you to add value to CharlieTickets and CharlieCards, using cash or a credit or debit card. They dispense CharlieTickets but not CharlieCards. To get a CharlieCard, ask a T employee, order one in advance, or visit a retail location (check the website for a list of convenience stores, newsstands, and other outlets). Consider ordering CharlieCards or CharlieTickets online before you leave home; at press time, shipping is free, and you won't have to buy one immediately upon arriving.

BY PUBLIC TRANSPORTATION

The Massachusetts Bay Transportation Authority, or **MBTA** (© **800/392-6100** or 617/222-3200; www.mbta.com), is known as the "T," and its logo is the letter in a circle. It runs subways, trolleys, buses, and ferries in Boston and many suburbs, as well as the commuter rail. Its website includes maps, schedules, and other information.

Newer stations on the Red, Blue, and Orange lines are wheelchair accessible; the Green Line is being converted. All T buses have lifts or kneelers; call © **800/LIFT-BUS** for information. To learn more, call the **Office for Transportation Access** (© **800/543-8287** or 617/222-5976, or TTY 617/222-5854).

BY SUBWAY & TROLLEY   Red, Blue, and Orange line trains and Green Line trolleys make up the **subway** system, which runs partly aboveground. The commuter rail to the suburbs is purple on system maps and is sometimes called the Purple Line. The Silver Line is a fancy name for a bus line; the Waterfront branch runs from South Station to the airport via the South Boston waterfront, including the convention center and the World Trade Center. The fare on the subway and Waterfront Silver Line is $1.70 with a CharlieCard, $2 with a CharlieTicket or cash. Transfers to local buses are free. Service begins around 5:15am and ends around 12:30am. On New Year's Eve, closing time is 2am and service is free after 8pm. A sign on the token booth in every station gives the time of the last train in either direction.

The oldest system in the country, the T dates to 1897. The Green Line is the most unpredictable—leave early if you're taking it to a vital appointment, and bring cab fare in case you have to jump off. Note that downtown stops are so close together that walking is often faster. The system is generally safe, but always watch out for pickpockets, especially during the holiday season.

BY BUS   T buses and "trackless trolleys" (buses with electric antennae) provide service around town and to and around the suburbs. The fare for local buses and the Washington Street Silver Line is $1.25 with a CharlieCard (transferring to the subway costs 45¢), $1.50 with a CharlieTicket or cash. Express-bus fares are higher. Important local routes include **no. 1** (Mass. Ave. from Dudley Sq. in Roxbury through the Back Bay

Boston Transit & Parking

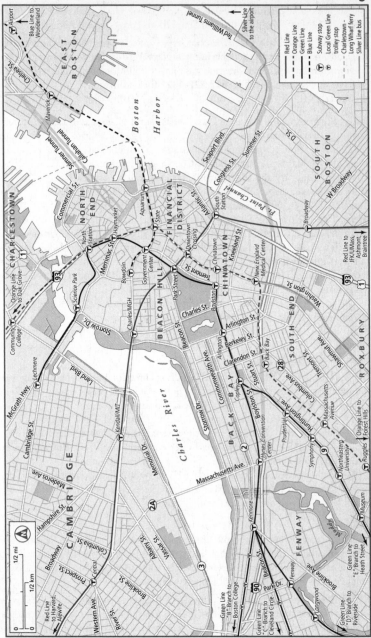

and Cambridge to Harvard Sq.), **nos. 92** and **93** (btw. Haymarket and Charlestown), and **no. 77** (Mass. Ave. from Harvard Sq. north to Porter Sq. and Arlington).

BY FERRY   The MBTA Inner Harbor ferry connects **Long Wharf** (near the New England Aquarium) with the **Charlestown Navy Yard**—it's a good way to get back downtown from "Old Ironsides" and the Bunker Hill Monument. The fare is $1.70. Visit www.mbta.com or call ℂ **617/227-4321** for information.

BY TAXI

Taxis are expensive and not always easy to flag—find a cabstand or call a dispatcher. Stands are usually near hotels. There are also busy ones at Faneuil Hall Marketplace (on North St. and in front of 60 State St.), South Station, Back Bay Station, and on Mass. Ave. in Harvard Square near the Coop and in front of Au Bon Pain.

To call ahead, try the **Independent Taxi Operators Association** (ℂ 617/426-8700; www.itoataxi.com), **Boston Cab** (ℂ 617/536-5100 or 617/262-2227), **Town Taxi** (ℂ 617/536-5000; www.towntaxiboston.com), **City Cab** (ℂ 617/536-5100), or **Metro Cab** (ℂ 617/242-8000; www.boston-cab.com). In Cambridge, call **Ambassador Brattle** (ℂ 617/492-1100) or **Yellow Cab** (ℂ 617/547-3000). Boston Cab can dispatch a wheelchair-accessible vehicle; advance notice is recommended. If you want to report a problem or have lost something in a Boston cab, contact the police department's **Hackney Hot Line** (ℂ **617/536-8294;** www.cityofboston.gov/police; click "Taxi Issues" for the complaint form).

The fare structure: the first ¼-mile (when the flag drops), $2.25; each additional ⅛ of a mile, 30¢. Wait time is extra, and the passenger pays tolls as well as a total of $7.50 in fees on trips leaving Logan Airport. Charging a flat rate in the city is not allowed; the police department maintains a list (available at www.massport.com/logan) of flat rates for trips to the suburbs.

BY WATER TAXI OR WATER SHUTTLE   Three companies operate daily year-round; one-way fares from and to various points around the harbor start at $10. Reservations are recommended but not required; you can call from the dock for pick-up. Check ahead to see which operator serves the stops you need. The companies are **City Water Taxi** (ℂ 617/422-0392; www.citywatertaxi.com), **Rowes Wharf Water Taxi** (ℂ **617/406-8584;** www.roweswharfwatertransport.com), and **Boston Harbor Water Taxi** (ℂ **617/593-9168;** www.bostonharborwatertaxi.com).

Weekday-only **Seaport Express** (ℂ **617/939-4802;** www.seaporttma.org) connects Rowes Wharf, the Seaport World Trade Center, and Central Wharf. The one-way fare is $2; check the schedule on the website.

BY CAR

If you plan to visit only Boston and Cambridge, you do not need a car. Construction, expensive parking, daredevil drivers, and confusing geography make Boston, in particular, a motorist's nightmare. If you arrive by car, park at the hotel and walk or use public transit. For day trips, you'll probably want a car.

RENTALS   The major car-rental firms have offices at Logan Airport and in Boston; some have other area branches. Boston levies a $10 surcharge on car rentals that goes toward the construction of a new convention center. If you're traveling at a busy time, especially during foliage season, reserve well in advance. Most agencies offer shuttle service from the airport to their offices.

PARKING It's difficult to find your way around Boston and practically impossible to park in some areas. Most spaces on the street are metered (and patrolled until exactly 6pm Mon–Sat), have strict time limits, or both. Parking downtown usually costs $1 an hour; bring plenty of quarters. Time limits range from 15 minutes to 2 hours. The penalty is a $45 ticket, but should you blunder into a tow-away zone, retrieving the car will take at least $100 and a lot of running around. The city tow lot is at 200 Frontage Rd., South Boston (© **617/635-3900;** T: Red Line to Andrew, then grab a cab).

It's best to leave the car in a garage or lot and walk. A full day at most lots costs no more than $25, but some downtown facilities charge as much as $45. Some restaurants offer discounts at nearby garages; ask when you make reservations.

The city-run **Boston Common Garage,** off Charles Street (© **617/954-2096**), accepts vehicles under 6 feet, 3 inches tall. Enter the garage in the state **Transportation Building,** 10 Park Plaza (© **617/973-7054**), from Charles Street South. The **Prudential Center Garage** (© **617/267-1002**) has entrances on Boylston Street, Huntington Avenue, and Exeter Street, and at the Sheraton Boston Hotel. Parking is discounted if you buy something at the Shops at Prudential Center and have your ticket validated. The **Copley Place Garage,** off Huntington Avenue (© **617/375-4488**), offers a similar deal. Many businesses in Faneuil Hall Marketplace validate parking at the **75 State St. Garage** (© **617/742-7275**).

Good-size garages downtown are at **Government Center,** off Congress Street (© **617/227-0385**); **Sudbury Street** off Congress Street (© **617/973-6954**); the **New England Aquarium** (© **617/367-3847**); and **Zero Post Office Square,** in the Financial District (© **617/423-1500**). In the Back Bay, there's a large garage near the Hynes Convention Center, on **Dalton Street** (© **617/247-8006**).

DRIVING RULES When traffic permits, you may turn right at a red light after stopping, unless a sign says otherwise. Seat belts are mandatory for adults and children, children under 12 may not ride in the front seat, and infants and children under 5 must be in car seats. Pedestrians in the crosswalk and vehicles already in a rotary (traffic circle or roundabout) have the right of way.

FAST FACTS: Boston & Cambridge

American Express Offices are at 1 State St. (© **617/723-8400**), opposite the Old State House; 170 Federal St., Financial District (© **617/439-4400**); 432 Stuart St., Back Bay (© **617/236-1331**); and 39 John F. Kennedy St., Harvard Square, Cambridge (© **617/868-2600**).

Area Codes Boston proper, **617** and **857**; immediate suburbs, **781** and **339**; northern and western suburbs, **978** and **351**; southern suburbs, **508** and **774**. *Note:* To complete a local call, you must dial all 10 digits.

Car Rentals See "Getting Around," above.

Drinking Laws The legal drinking age is 21. In many bars, particularly near college campuses, and at sporting events, you will probably be asked for ID.

Embassies & Consulates See "Embassies & Consulates," in the appendix.

Emergencies Call ℭ **911** for fire, ambulance, or police. For the state police, call ℭ **617/523-1212** or, from a cellphone, ℭ ***911**. The Boston police direct emergency number is ℭ **617/343-4911**.

Hospitals **Massachusetts General Hospital**, 55 Fruit St. (ℭ **617/726-2000**), and **Tufts Medical Center**, 750 Washington St. (ℭ **617/636-5000**), are closest to downtown. In Cambridge is **Mount Auburn Hospital**, 330 Mt. Auburn St. (ℭ **617/492-3500**).

Hot Lines AIDS Hotline (ℭ **800/235-2331**), Poison Control (ℭ **800/682-9211**), Rape Crisis (ℭ **877/627-7700** or 617/492-7273), Samaritans Suicide Prevention (ℭ **617/247-0220**), Samariteens (ℭ **800/252-8336** or 617/247-8050).

Information See "Visitor Information," earlier in this chapter. For directory assistance, dial ℭ **411**.

Internet Access Visit **www.jiwire.com** to find public Wi-Fi hotspots. For wired access, The ubiquitous **FedEx Kinko's** charges 10¢ to 20¢ a minute at locations including 2 Center Plaza, Government Center (ℭ **617/973-9000**); 187 Dartmouth St., Back Bay (ℭ **617/262-6188**); and 1 Mifflin Place, off Mount Auburn Street near Eliot Street, Harvard Square (ℭ **617/497-0125**). **Tech Superpowers,** 252 Newbury St., third floor (ℭ **617/267-9716**; www.newburyopen.net), offers access by the hour ($5/hour; $3/15 min. minimum) with or without a computer.

Newspapers & Magazines The daily papers are the *Boston Globe* and *Boston Herald*. The "Sidekick" section of the daily *Globe* and the "Edge" section of the Friday *Herald* contain cultural listings. The arts-oriented *Boston Phoenix*, published on Thursday, has entertainment and restaurant listings.

Where, a free monthly magazine, contains information on shopping, nightlife, attractions, museums, and galleries. Newspaper boxes around both Boston and Cambridge dispense the free weekly *Phoenix* and *Weekly Dig*, and the biweekly *Improper Bostonian* and *Stuff@Night*. *Boston* magazine is a lifestyle-oriented monthly.

Pharmacies Downtown Boston has no 24-hour pharmacy. The **CVS** locations at 587 Boylston St., off Copley Square in the Back Bay (ℭ **617/437-8414**), and at the Porter Square Shopping Center, off Mass. Ave. in Cambridge (ℭ **617/876-5519**), are open 24/7, as are their pharmacies. The pharmacy at the **CVS** at 155–157 Charles St. (ℭ **617/523-1028**), next to the Charles/MGH Red Line T stop, is open until midnight. Some emergency rooms can fill your prescription at the hospital's pharmacy.

Police Call ℭ **911** for emergencies. For the state police, call ℭ **617/523-1212** or, from a cellphone, ℭ ***911**.

Restrooms The visitor center at 15 State St. has public restrooms, as do most tourist attractions, hotels, department stores, shopping centers, coffee bars, and public buildings. Free-standing, self-cleaning pay toilets (25¢) are scattered around downtown, but check carefully before using them; despite regular patrols, IV-drug users have been known to take advantage of the generous time limits.

Safety On the whole, Boston and Cambridge are safe cities for walking. As in any urban area, stay out of parks (including Boston Common, the Public Garden, and the Esplanade) at night unless you're in a crowd. Areas to avoid at night include Boylston Street between Tremont and Washington, and Tremont Street from Stuart to Boylston. Try not to walk alone late at night in the Theater District and around North Station. Public transportation is busy and safe, but service stops between 12:30 and 1am.

Smoking Massachusetts prohibits smoking in all workplaces, including clubs, bars, and restaurants. Take it outside—you'll have plenty of company.

Taxes The 5% sales tax does not apply to food, prescription drugs, newspapers, or clothing that costs less than $175; the tax on meals and takeout food is 5%. The lodging tax in Boston and Cambridge is 12.45%.

Taxis See "Getting Around," earlier in this chapter.

Transit Info Call ℂ 617/222-3200 for the T (subways, local buses, commuter rail), and ℂ 800/23-LOGAN for MassPort (airport transportation).

3 Where to Stay

With enough flexibility, you probably won't have too much difficulty finding a suitable place to stay in or near the city. Year-round, it's always a good idea to **make a reservation,** and the earlier you book, the better your chances of landing a (relative) bargain. Definitely book ahead if you plan to travel **between April and November,** when conventions, college graduations, and vacations increase demand. During **foliage season,** the busiest and priciest time of year—even more expensive than the summer—plan early or risk staying far from Boston, or staying home.

Although the Boston area has gained hundreds of rooms in the past decade, the average rate in 2007 topped $200. Rates at most downtown hotels are lower on weekends than on weeknights, when business and convention travelers fill rooms; leisure hotels offer discounts during the week. If you don't mind cold and the possibility of snow, aim for January through March, when you'll find great deals, especially on weekends.

Before you rule out a hotel because of its location, consult a map. Especially downtown, neighborhoods are so small that the borders are somewhat arbitrary. The division to consider is **downtown vs. the Back Bay vs. Cambridge** and not, say, Downtown Crossing vs. the adjacent Financial District. For example, if your interests lie primarily in Cambridge, the Back Bay is not the most convenient place to stay.

The state **hotel tax** is 5.7%. Boston and Cambridge (like Worcester and Springfield) add a 2.75% convention-center tax to the 4% city tax, bringing the total tax to 12.45%.

The Convention & Visitors Bureau **Hotel Hot Line** (ℂ **800/777-6001**) can help make reservations even at the busiest times. It's staffed Monday through Friday until 8pm, Saturday and Sunday until 4pm. If you're driving from the west, stop at a Mass. Pike rest area in Natick, Charlton, or Lee and try the **reservation service** at the visitor center.

BED-AND-BREAKFASTS Most lodgings require a minimum stay of at least 2 nights. The following organizations can help you find a B&B:

- **Bed & Breakfast Agency of Boston** (ℂ **800/248-9262,** 0800/89-5128 from the U.K., or 617/720-3540; fax 617/523-5761; www.boston-bnbagency.com)

Boston Accommodations

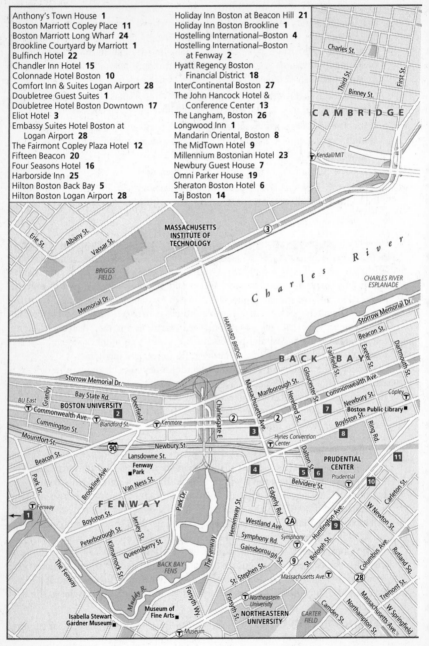

Anthony's Town House **1**
Boston Marriott Copley Place **11**
Boston Marriott Long Wharf **24**
Brookline Courtyard by Marriott **1**
Bulfinch Hotel **22**
Chandler Inn Hotel **15**
Colonnade Hotel Boston **10**
Comfort Inn & Suites Logan Airport **28**
Doubletree Guest Suites **1**
Doubletree Hotel Boston Downtown **17**
Eliot Hotel **3**
Embassy Suites Hotel Boston at Logan Airport **28**
The Fairmont Copley Plaza Hotel **12**
Fifteen Beacon **20**
Four Seasons Hotel **16**
Harborside Inn **25**
Hilton Boston Back Bay **5**
Hilton Boston Logan Airport **28**
Holiday Inn Boston at Beacon Hill **21**
Holiday Inn Boston Brookline **1**
Hostelling International–Boston **4**
Hostelling International–Boston at Fenway **2**
Hyatt Regency Boston Financial District **18**
InterContinental Boston **27**
The John Hancock Hotel & Conference Center **13**
The Langham, Boston **26**
Longwood Inn **1**
Mandarin Oriental, Boston **8**
The MidTown Hotel **9**
Millennium Bostonian Hotel **23**
Newbury Guest House **7**
Omni Parker House **19**
Sheraton Boston Hotel **6**
Taj Boston **14**

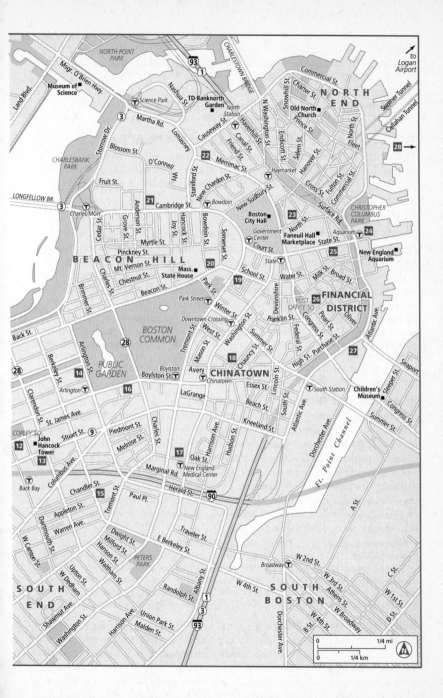

- **Host Homes of Boston** (© **800/600-1308** or 617/244-1308; fax 617/244-5156; www.hosthomesofboston.com)
- **Bed & Breakfast Reservations North Shore/Greater Boston/Cape Cod** (© **800/832-2632**, 617/964-1606, or 978/281-9505; fax 978/281-9426; www.bbreserve.com)
- **Bed and Breakfast Associates Bay Colony** (© **888/486-6018,** 08/234-7113 from the U.K., or 781/449-5302; fax 781/455-6745; www.bnbboston.com)

THE WATERFRONT & FANEUIL HALL MARKETPLACE

These areas are convenient to the Financial District and other downtown destinations, but not as handy if you plan to spend a lot of time in the Back Bay or Cambridge. *Tip:* Ask for a room on a high floor—the Big Dig is more or less complete, but construction continues throughout the downtown area.

VERY EXPENSIVE

Boston Marriott Long Wharf ✪   The landmark Marriott's chief appeal is its location, a stone's throw from the New England Aquarium. It attracts business travelers with its proximity to the Financial District and woos families with its pool and easy access to downtown and waterfront attractions. Rooms are large and quite sunny (the stand-alone building has no neighbors to block the light), and units close to the harbor afford good views of the wharves and the waterfront.

296 State St. (at Atlantic Ave.), Boston, MA 02109. © **800/228-9290** or 617/227-0800. Fax 617/227-2867. www.marriottlongwharf.com. 400 units. Apr–Nov $249–$450 double; Dec–Mar $159–$279 double; $450–$490 suite year-round. Packages available. AE, DC, DISC, MC, V. Parking $34. T: Blue Line to Aquarium. **Amenities:** Restaurant (seafood); cafe and lounge; bar and grill; indoor pool; exercise room; Jacuzzi; game room; concierge; tour desk; 24-hr. business center; limited room service; laundry service; same-day dry cleaning. *In room:* A/C, TV, high-speed Internet access ($10/day), coffeemaker, hair dryer, iron, safe.

InterContinental Boston ✪   The luxury brand's first New England hotel opened in 2006. The 22-story glass-sheathed building (the hotel occupies the bottom 12 floors) faces the Rose Kennedy Greenway, near the Financial District, the convention center, and Boston Harbor. Guest rooms on the east (back) side have lovely water views. All are decorated in polished contemporary style, with plush earth-tone fabrics and dramatic artwork. Rooms are large, with oversize work desks, and the huge bathrooms hold separate tubs and showers. The spa, health club, dining options, and upper-story condos amplify the residential feel. With top-notch service and amenities, this brand consistently earns repeat business from its predominantly corporate clientele. At these prices, I'd expect nothing less.

510 Atlantic Ave., Boston, MA 02210. © **800/424-6835** or 617/747-1000. Fax 617/747-5120. www.intercontinental boston.com. 424 units. $350–$600 double; $800–$6,000 suite. Children under 18 stay free in parents room. Extra person $35. Packages available. AE, DC, DISC, MC, V. Valet parking $39. T: Red Line to South Station. Pets under 25 lb. accepted; $100/stay. **Amenities:** Restaurant (24-hr. Provençal brasserie); 2 bars (sushi/tequila, rum/champagne); indoor pool; 24-hr. health club; spa; concierge; business center; 24-hr. room service; babysitting; laundry service; same-day dry cleaning. *In room:* A/C, TV w/pay movies, Wi-Fi ($15/day), minibar, hair dryer, iron, safe, robes.

Millennium Bostonian Hotel ✪✪   Three brick 19th-century buildings make up this relatively small hotel, which offers excellent service and features that make it competitive with larger rivals. Its boutique atmosphere appeals to both business travelers and vacationers. A $25-million renovation in 2008 left the guest rooms all cool neutrals and clean lines, with pillow-top beds, and separate tubs and showers in the new bathrooms. Rooms vary in size; in half of them, French doors open onto small private balconies. My favorites overlook Faneuil Hall Marketplace, which is lively but not noisy, thanks to good soundproofing.

At Faneuil Hall Marketplace, 26 North St., Boston, MA 02109. ℭ 866/866-8086 or 617/523-3600. Fax 617/523-2454. www.millenniumhotels.com. 201 units. $229–$459 double; from $495 suite. Extra person $20. Children under 18 stay free in parent's room. Packages available. AE, DC, DISC, MC, V. Valet parking $40. T: Green or Blue Line to Government Center, or Green or Orange Line to Haymarket. **Amenities:** Restaurant; lounge; small fitness room; access to nearby health club ($10); in-room exercise equipment delivery on request; concierge; tour desk; car-rental desk; business center; salon; 24-hr. room service; massage; babysitting; laundry service; same-day dry cleaning. *In room:* A/C, TV w/pay movies, high-speed Internet access ($10/day), minibar, hair dryer, iron, safe, umbrella, robes.

MODERATE

Harborside Inn ✸✸   The Harborside Inn offers an unbeatable combination of location and value. The renovated 1858 warehouse is near Faneuil Hall Marketplace, the harbor, and the Financial District. The nicely appointed guest rooms, renovated in 2007, have hardwood floors and enough room for a table and chairs. City-view units are more expensive than rooms that face the skylit atrium, but the former can be noisier. Rooms on the upper floors of the eight-story building have lower ceilings but better views.

185 State St. (btw. Atlantic Ave. and the Custom House Tower), Boston, MA 02109. ℭ 888/723-7565 or 617/723-7500. Fax 617/670-6015. www.harborsideinnboston.com. 54 units. $109–$299 double. Extra person $15. Packages and long-term rates available. Rates may be higher during special events. AE, DC, DISC, MC, V. Off-site parking $26; reservation required. T: Blue Line to Aquarium or Orange Line to State. **Amenities:** Lounge; access to nearby health club ($15); concierge; limited room service; laundry service; dry cleaning. *In room:* A/C, TV, Wi-Fi ($10/day), hair dryer, iron.

AT THE AIRPORT
EXPENSIVE

The **Embassy Suites Hotel Boston at Logan Airport,** 207 Porter St., Boston, MA 02128 (ℭ **800/EMBASSY** or 617/567-5000; www.embassysuites.com), is a 273-unit hotel with an indoor pool, exercise room, and business center. Each suite in the 10-story hotel has a living room with a pullout couch. Room rates, which start at $169, include breakfast, high-speed Internet access, and shuttle service to the airport and the Airport T stop.

Hilton Boston Logan Airport ✸✸   This hotel, smack in the middle of the airport, draws most of its guests from meetings, conventions, and canceled flights. It's convenient and well equipped for business travelers, and an excellent fallback for vacationers who don't mind commuting to downtown. Guest rooms are large; the best units, on higher floors of the 10-story building, afford sensational views. Soundproofing throughout the hotel, opened in 1999 and renovated in 2007, is excellent. Walkways lead directly to Terminals A and E.

85 Terminal Rd., Logan International Airport, Boston, MA 02128. ℭ 800/HILTONS or 617/568-6700. Fax 617/568-6800. www.hiltonfamilyboston.com/hilton-boston-logan-airport.php. 599 units. $99–$399 double; from $500 suite. Children under 18 stay free in parent's room. Packages available. AE, DC, DISC, MC, V. Valet parking $35; self-parking $30. T: Blue Line to Airport, then take shuttle bus. Pets accepted; deposit required. **Amenities:** Restaurant (American); Irish pub; coffee counter; indoor lap pool; health club; concierge; 24-hr. shuttle to airport destinations (including car-rental offices and ferry dock); business center; 24-hr. room service; massage; laundry service; same-day dry cleaning. *In room:* A/C, TV w/pay movies, Wi-Fi ($10/day), minibar, coffeemaker, hair dryer, iron.

MODERATE
Comfort Inn & Suites Logan Airport   The airport lies about 3½ miles south of the well-equipped Comfort Inn. Room rates at the eight-story hotel, which opened in

2000, offer a good range of features for business and leisure travelers. The somewhat inconvenient location translates to reasonable rates, and the North Shore is easily accessible if you plan to take a day trip.

85 American Legion Hwy. (Rte. 60), Revere, MA 02151. ☎ **877/485-3600** or 781/485-3600. Fax 781/485-3601. www.comfortinnboston.com. 208 units. $109–$239 double; $139–$279 suite. Rates include continental breakfast. Children under 18 stay free in parent's room. Senior and AAA discounts available. AE, DC, DISC, MC, V. Free parking. T: Blue Line to Airport; take airport shuttle bus to terminal, then hotel shuttle. Pets accepted ($20/night). **Amenities:** Restaurant (Mexican/American); lounge; indoor pool; exercise room; shuttle to airport; business center; limited room service; coin-op laundry; laundry service; same-day dry cleaning. *In room:* A/C, TV w/pay movies, high-speed Internet access, coffeemaker, hair dryer, iron.

FINANCIAL DISTRICT
VERY EXPENSIVE

The Langham, Boston 🏵🏵 This is one of the best business hotels in the city, with a busy weekend clientele of vacationers attracted by excellent rates for luxurious accommodations and amenities, including a pool. Elegantly decorated and large enough to hold a generous work area, the luxurious guest rooms have 153 configurations. The most desirable units in the nine-story building overlook the lovely park in Post Office Square (buildings surround the other three sides).

250 Franklin St. (at Post Office Sq.), Boston, MA 02110. ☎ **800/791-7781** or 617/451-1900. Fax 617/423-2844. http://boston.langhamhotels.com. 325 units. $185–$495 double; $545–$2,950 suite. Extra person $30. Packages available. AE, DC, DISC, MC, V. Valet parking $39 Sun–Thurs, $25 Fri–Sat. T: Blue or Orange Line to State, or Red Line to Downtown Crossing or South Station. Pets accepted; $50 fee. **Amenities:** Restaurant (Mediterranean); cafe w/Sun jazz brunch and Sat "Chocolate Bar Buffet" (Sept–June); bar w/live piano most nights; 40-ft. indoor pool; well-equipped health club; Jacuzzi; sauna; concierge; business center; 24-hr. room service; in-room massage; laundry service; same-day dry cleaning. *In room:* A/C, TV w/pay movies, high-speed Internet access ($10/day), minibar, coffeemaker, hair dryer, iron, safe, umbrella, robes.

DOWNTOWN CROSSING/BEACON HILL/NORTH STATION
VERY EXPENSIVE

Fifteen Beacon 🏵🏵 Nonstop pampering, high-tech appointments, and outrageously luxurious rooms make this boutique hotel *the* name to drop with the expense-be-hanged set. The 10-story hotel has attracted demanding travelers, especially businesspeople, since it opened in 2000. Management bends over backward to keep them returning, with attentive service and lavish perks. The guest rooms, individually decorated in austere but plush style that's more SoHo than Beacon Hill, contain queen-size canopy beds with Frette linens, surround-sound stereo systems, gas fireplaces, and 4-inch TVs in the bathroom. "Studio" units have a sitting area.

15 Beacon St., Boston, MA 02108. ☎ **877/XV-BEACON** or 617/670-1500. Fax 617/670-2525. www.xvbeacon.com. 60 units (some with shower only). From $395 double; from $1,200 suite. AE, DISC, MC, V. Valet parking $38. T: Red or Green Line to Park St., or Blue Line to Government Center. Pets under 20 lb. accepted; refundable deposit required. **Amenities:** Restaurant (steakhouse); bar; fitness room; access to nearby health club ($15); concierge; courtesy car; 24-hr. room service; in-room massage; babysitting; laundry service; same-day dry cleaning. *In room:* A/C, TV w/pay movies, fax/copier/printer, high-speed Internet access, minibar, hair dryer, iron, safe, umbrella, robes.

EXPENSIVE

The **Holiday Inn Boston at Beacon Hill,** 5 Blossom St., at Cambridge Street (☎ **800/HOLIDAY** or 617/742-7630), offers all the features you'd expect of the international chain, including a heated outdoor pool.

Hyatt Regency Boston Financial District 🏵 *Value* This centrally located 22-story hotel, a busy convention and business destination during the week, offers excellent weekend packages that make it a magnet for vacationers. The second-floor lobby leads to four atriums that create the effect of several small hotels in one. Guest rooms are lovely, with enough space for a sitting area and, in most units, a king-size pillow-top bed (one-quarter of the units have two doubles). *Tip:* Ask for a unit on a high floor and you won't be too close to construction on nearby Washington Street.

1 Ave. de Lafayette (off Washington St.), Boston, MA 02111. (© **800/223-1234** or 617/912-1234. Fax 617/451-0054. www.hyattregencyboston.com. 500 units. $189–$469 double; $350–$1,500 suite. Extra person $25. Children under 18 stay free in parent's room. Packages available. AE, DC, DISC, MC, V. Valet parking $41; self-parking $30. T: Red or Orange Line to Downtown Crossing, or Green Line to Boylston. **Amenities:** Restaurant (American/Continental); bar; 52-ft. indoor pool; health club; sauna; concierge; tour desk; business center; 24-hr. room service; massage; babysitting; laundry service; same-day dry cleaning. *In room:* A/C, TV w/pay movies, Wi-Fi ($10/day), coffeemaker, hair dryer, iron, robes.

Omni Parker House ⋆ The Parker House offers a great combination of over 150 years of history (since 1855!) and extensive renovations. Regular interior and exterior renovations keep the property in excellent shape. Guest rooms, a patchwork of more than 50 configurations, aren't huge, but they are thoughtfully laid out and nicely appointed. Business travelers can book a room with an expanded work area; sightseers can economize by requesting a smaller, less expensive unit.

60 School St., Boston, MA 02108. (© **800/THE-OMNI** or 617/227-8600. Fax 617/742-5729. www.omniparkerhouse. com. 551 units (some with shower only). $189–$289 double; $249–$399 suite. Children under 18 stay free in parent's room. Packages and AARP discount available. AE, DC, DISC, MC, V. Valet parking $38. T: Green or Blue Line to Government Center, or Red Line to Park St. Pets accepted; deposit required. **Amenities:** 2 restaurants (New England); bar; exercise room; concierge; airport shuttle; business center; 24-hr. room service; laundry service; same-day dry cleaning. *In room:* A/C, TV w/pay movies and Nintendo, Wi-Fi ($10/day), coffeemaker, hair dryer, iron, robes, safe.

MODERATE

Bulfinch Hotel ⋆ One block from North Station, the Bulfinch abounds with details that enhance its "budget boutique" feel. Rooms are on the small side, but custom furnishings create the illusion of more space. Plush fabrics (including suede headboards), flatscreen TVs, and marble bathrooms set off the contemporary, uncluttered design. The hotel, which opened in 2004, offers business features such as work desks and cordless phones. The best units are junior suites—oversize doubles—known as "nose rooms" because they're in the pointed end of the triangular building.

107 Merrimac St., Boston, MA 02114. (© **877/267-1776** or 617/624-0202. Fax 617/624-0211. www.bulfinchhotel. com. 80 units (most with shower only). $169–$399 double; $199–$489 junior suite. Children under 18 stay free in parent's room. Packages and AAA, AARP, and military discounts available. AE, DC, DISC, MC, V. Parking $25 in nearby garage. T: Green or Orange Line to North Station. Pets accepted; $50 fee. **Amenities:** Restaurant and lounge (tapas); exercise room; concierge; room service; same-day dry cleaning. *In room:* A/C, TV, high-speed Internet access, coffeemaker, hair dryer, iron.

CHINATOWN/THEATER DISTRICT
MODERATE

Doubletree Hotel Boston Downtown ⋆ *(Value)* Within walking distance of both downtown and the Back Bay, the Doubletree is a better deal than most competitors in either neighborhood. The six-story building is a former high school with high ceilings and compact, well-designed rooms. Ask for a unit that faces away from busy Washington Street, and your view will be of a cityscape rather than of the hospital across the street. Don't confuse this hotel with its all-suite corporate sibling near Cambridge (p. 101). This Doubletree, which opened in 2000, adjoins the Wang YMCA of Chinatown, and room rates include access to its extensive facilities.

821 Washington St., Boston, MA 02111. ℭ **800/222-TREE** or 617/956-7900. Fax 617/956-7901. http://doubletree. hilton.com. 267 units (some with shower only). $129–$299 double; $189–$359 suite. Extra person $10. Children under 17 stay free in parent's room. Packages and AAA, AARP, and military discounts available. AE, DC, DISC, MC, V. Valet parking $36. T: Orange Line to New England Medical Center. **Amenities:** Restaurant and lounge (American/ Asian); cafe; access to adjoining YMCA w/Olympic-size pool; concierge; business center; limited room service; same-day dry cleaning. *In room:* A/C, TV w/pay movies, Wi-Fi ($10/day), minibar, coffeemaker, hair dryer, iron, safe.

BACK BAY/SOUTH END
VERY EXPENSIVE

The 148-unit **Mandarin Oriental, Boston** (ℭ **866/526-6567** or 617/531-0888; www.mandarinoriental.com), on Boylston Street at Fairfield Street, next to the Prudential Center, was under construction at press time and slated to open in late 2008. Part of a 14-story hotel-condo development, it has a 16,000-square-foot spa, two restaurants (including the relocated L'Espalier), a lounge, and the ultraluxurious brand's over-the-top appointments and service.

Eliot Hotel 🌟🌟🌟   This exquisite hotel combines the flavor of Yankee Boston with European-style service and amenities. On tree-lined Comm. Ave., it feels more like a classy apartment building than like a hotel, with a romantic atmosphere that belies the top-notch business features. Almost every unit is a spacious suite (16 rooms are standard doubles) furnished with antiques. French doors separate the living rooms and bedrooms, and bathrooms are outfitted in Italian marble. The 1925 building is near Boston University and MIT (across the river), and the atmosphere contrasts pleasantly with the bustle of Newbury Street, a block away.

370 Comm. Ave. (at Mass. Ave.), Boston, MA 02215. ℭ **800/44-ELIOT** or 617/267-1607. Fax 617/536-9114. www. eliothotel.com. 95 units (8 with shower only). $235–$395 double; $355–$545 1-bedroom suite for 2; $580–$890 2-bedroom suite. Extra person $30. Children under 18 stay free in parent's room. Packages available. AE, DC, MC, V. Valet parking $36. T: Green Line B, C, or D to Hynes Convention Center. Pets accepted. **Amenities:** Restaurant (eclectic); sashimi bar; access to nearby health club; concierge; business center; 24-hr. room service; in-room massage; babysitting; laundry service; dry cleaning. *In room:* A/C, TV w/pay movies, Wi-Fi ($10/day), minibar, hair dryer, iron, umbrella, robes.

The Fairmont Copley Plaza Hotel 🌟🌟   The "grande dame of Boston" is a true grand hotel with a well-earned reputation for excellent service. Built in 1912, the six-story Renaissance Revival building faces Copley Square. The spacious guest rooms have a residential feel, thanks largely to a $34-million overhaul completed in 2004. The custom-made traditional furnishings reflect the elegance of the opulent public spaces. Rooms that face the lovely square afford better views than those that overlook busy Dartmouth Street.

138 St. James Ave., Boston, MA 02116. ℭ **800/441-1414** or 617/267-5300. Fax 617/247-6681. www.fairmont. com/copleyplaza. 383 units. From $259 double; from $699 suite. Extra person $30. Packages available. AE, DC, MC, V. Valet parking $32. T: Green Line to Copley, or Orange Line to Back Bay. Pets accepted; $25/day. **Amenities:** Restaurant (steakhouse); lounge; exercise room; access to nearby health club ($15); concierge; tour desk; courtesy car; business center; 24-hr. room service; laundry service; same-day dry cleaning. *In room:* A/C, TV w/pay movies, high-speed Internet access ($14/day), minibar, hair dryer, iron, safe, umbrella, robes.

Four Seasons Hotel 🌟🌟🌟   Many hotels offer top-notch guest rooms, public areas, fitness facilities, service, and restaurants in a beautiful location. But no other hotel in Boston—indeed, in New England—combines every element of a luxury hotel as seamlessly as the Four Seasons. If I were traveling with someone else's credit cards, I'd head straight here. The 16-story brick-and-glass building (the hotel occupies eight floors) blends traditional and contemporary style. The best units overlook the Public

Garden; city views from the back of the hotel aren't as desirable. The staff is famously accommodating to businesspeople, families, and celebrities. Small pets even enjoy a special menu and amenities.

200 Boylston St., Boston, MA 02116. ℂ 800/819-5053 or 617/338-4400. Fax 617/423-0154. www.fourseasons. com/boston. 272 units. $475–$600 double; from $750 1-bedroom suite; from $1,225 2-bedroom suite. Packages available. AE, DC, DISC, MC, V. Valet parking $41. T: Green Line to Arlington. Pets under 15 lb. accepted. **Amenities:** Restaurant (New England), The Bristol (see "Bars & Lounges," later in this chapter); 44-ft. pool; health club and spa; concierge; tour desk; limo to downtown; business center; 24-hr. room service; in-room massage; babysitting; laundry service; same-day dry cleaning. *In room:* A/C, TV w/pay movies, high-speed Internet access ($10/day), minibar, hair dryer, iron, safe, robes.

Taj Boston 𝒢   Taj Boston, which succeeded the original Ritz-Carlton, is quickly making a name for itself. The traditional hotel overlooking the Public Garden became part of the India-based luxury chain in 2007. Completely restored for its 75th anniversary in 2002, the lovely property is undergoing upgrades and updates. The elegantly appointed guest rooms have dark-wood furnishings and feather duvets. You'll pay more for a room with a view. The best units are the suites, which have wood-burning fireplaces. The Taj is competitive with other top-tier hotels, but state-of-the-art fitness facilities help some newer properties mount a serious challenge.

15 Arlington St., Boston, MA 02116. ℂ 877/482-5267 or 617/536-5700. Fax 617/536-1335. www.tajhotels.com. 273 units. From $325 double; from $425 Club Level or suite. Children under 13 stay free in parent's room. Extra person $20. Packages available. AE, DC, DISC, MC, V. Valet parking $42. T: Green Line to Arlington. Pets accepted. **Amenities:** Restaurant; bar; lounge; exercise room; concierge; courtesy car; airport shuttle; business center; 24-hr. room service; in-room massage; babysitting; laundry service; same-day dry cleaning; club-level rooms. *In room:* A/C, TV w/pay movies, high-speed Internet access ($11/day), minibar, hair dryer, iron, safe.

EXPENSIVE

The largest convention hotel in New England is the 1,147-unit **Boston Marriott Copley Place,** 110 Huntington Ave., Boston, MA 02116 (ℂ **800/228-9290** or 617/236-5800; www.copleymarriott.com). Part of the Copley Place shopping complex, it offers complete business features and a good-size pool.

Colonnade Hotel Boston 𝒢𝒢 *Kids*   The centrally located, independently owned Colonnade is a luxurious spot of European-style calm in the Back Bay's retail frenzy. The attentive, gracious staff caters to an international clientele of businesspeople, sightseers, shoppers, and families. An $18-million renovation completed in 2008 made the 11-story concrete-and-glass hotel even more desirable—the large guest rooms, decorated in muted earth tones, have pillow-top beds, marble-clad bathrooms, and sleek residential-style furnishings. Floor-to-ceiling windows face the bustling Prudential Center or the South End's urban patchwork. The seasonal "rooftop resort" and swimming pool are a welcome change of pace in warm weather.

120 Huntington Ave., Boston, MA 02116. ℂ 800/962-3030 or 617/424-7000. Fax 617/424-1717. www.colonnade hotel.com. 285 units. $175–$459 double; $575–$1,750 suite. Children under 12 stay free in parent's room. Packages and winter discounts available. AE, DC, DISC, MC, V. Parking $36. T: Green Line E to Prudential. Pets accepted. **Amenities:** Restaurant (Brasserie Jo, p. 113); bar; heated outdoor rooftop pool; fitness center; concierge; 24-hr. business center; 24-hr. room service; in-room massage; babysitting; laundry service; same-day dry cleaning. *In room:* A/C, TV/DVD w/pay movies, Wi-Fi, minibar, hair dryer, iron, safe.

Hilton Boston Back Bay 𝒢𝒢   Across the street from the Prudential Center complex, the Hilton is primarily a business hotel, but families also find it comfortable. The carefully maintained rooms in the 26-story tower are large, soundproof, and furnished in modern style. The weekend packages, especially in winter, can be a great deal. The closest competitor is the Sheraton (see below), across the street. It's three times the Hilton's size (which generally means less personalized service), has a better pool, and books more vacation and function business.

40 Dalton St., Boston, MA 02115. © **800/874-0663**, 800/HILTONS, or 617/236-1100. Fax 617/867-6104. www. bostonbackbay.hilton.com. 385 units (66 with shower only). $149–$399 double; from $450 suite. Extra person $20; rollaway $20. Children under 18 stay free in parent's room. Packages and AAA discount available. AE, DC, DISC, MC, V. Valet parking $39; self-parking $35. T: Green Line B, C, or D to Hynes Convention Center. Pets accepted. **Amenities:** Restaurant (American/Continental); bar; indoor pool; fitness center; concierge; courtesy car; 24-hr. business center; 24-hr. room service; laundry service; same-day dry cleaning. *In room:* A/C, TV w/pay movies, high-speed Internet access ($10/stay), minibar, coffeemaker, hair dryer, iron.

Sheraton Boston Hotel ☆

Its central location, range of accommodations, convention and function facilities, direct access to the Hynes Convention Center and the Prudential Center complex, and huge pool make this 29-story hotel one of the most popular in the city. Because it's so big, it often has rooms available when smaller properties are full. If you're on a budget, though, you may be able to get a better deal elsewhere; shop around. The fairly large guest rooms are decorated in sleek contemporary style and contain Starwood's signature pillow-top beds. Units on higher floors afford gorgeous views.

39 Dalton St., Boston, MA 02199. © **800/325-3535** or 617/236-2000. Fax 617/236-1702. www.sheraton.com/ boston. 1,215 units. $209–$409 double; from $309 suite. Children under 17 stay free in parent's room. Packages available. 25% discount for students, faculty, and retired persons with ID, depending on availability. AE, DC, DISC, MC, V. Valet parking $39. T: Green Line E to Prudential, or B, C, or D to Hynes Convention Center. Dogs under 40 lb. accepted with prior approval. **Amenities:** Restaurant (New England); lounge; heated indoor/outdoor pool; health club; Jacuzzi; sauna; concierge; airport shuttle; business center; limited room service; laundry service; same-day dry cleaning. *In room:* A/C, TV w/pay movies, high-speed Internet access ($10/day), coffeemaker, hair dryer, iron.

MODERATE

Chandler Inn Hotel ☆ *Value*

The comfortable Chandler Inn is a bargain for its location, just 2 blocks from the Back Bay. Standard units are tastefully decorated in contemporary style and contain a queen-size or double bed or two twins, without enough room to squeeze in a cot. Bathrooms are tiny. The top three floors of the eight-story building hold deluxe guest rooms with plasma TVs and marble bathrooms. This is a gay-friendly hotel—Fritz, the bar next to the lobby, is a neighborhood hangout—that books up early for foliage season and events such as the Marathon and Boston Pride March.

26 Chandler St. (at Berkeley St.), Boston, MA 02116. © **800/842-3450** or 617/482-3450. Fax 617/542-3428. www. chandlerinn.com. 56 units. $109–$225 double; $179–$279 deluxe double. Children under 12 stay free in parent's room. AE, DC, DISC, MC, V. Parking $18 at nearby garage. T: Orange Line to Back Bay. Pets under 25 lb. accepted; $50 fee. **Amenities:** Lounge; access to nearby health club ($10). *In room:* A/C, TV, Wi-Fi, hair dryer.

The John Hancock Hotel & Conference Center *Finds*

This eight-story hotel near Back Bay Station is a limited-service lodging that's popular with groups that use the abundant meeting space. The compact, comfortable guest rooms were spruced up and had their furniture replaced in 2007. They're not fancy, but they're well maintained and big enough not to feel claustrophobic; bathrooms, however, are tiny. The 1925 building has been a hotel since 1986. The eponymous insurance firm books the whole place in the weeks before the Boston Marathon.

40 Trinity Place (off Stuart St.), Boston, MA 02116. © **617/933-7700**. Fax 617/933-7709. www.jhcenter.com. 64 units. $189 double. Rates include continental breakfast. Children under 18 stay free in parent's room. Extra person $15. Off-season discounts available. AE, DC, DISC, MC, V. Parking $20 in nearby garage. Closed to the public 1st 3 weeks of Apr. T: Orange Line to Back Bay or Green Line to Copley. *In room:* A/C, TV, Wi-Fi, hair dryer, iron.

The MidTown Hotel ⚡ *Kids* *Value*   Popular with families, budget-conscious businesspeople, and tour groups, this centrally located hotel is a good deal, and its parking fee is the lowest around. On a busy street opposite the Prudential Center, the
two-story establishment has been completely renovated since 2006. Guest rooms are
large, bright, and attractively outfitted, although bathrooms are on the small side.
Some units have connecting doors that allow families to spread out. The best rooms
are on the side of the building that faces away from Huntington Avenue.

220 Huntington Ave., Boston, MA 02115. ✆ 800/343-1177 or 617/262-1000. Fax 617/262-8739. www.midtown
hotel.com. 159 units. $119–$259 double; $139–$279 suite. Extra person $15. Children under 18 stay free in parent's
room. Packages and AAA, AARP, and government discounts may be available. AE, DC, DISC, MC, V. Parking $12. T:
Green Line E to Prudential, or Orange Line to Mass. Ave. Pets accepted. **Amenities:** Heated outdoor pool; access to
nearby health club ($5–$10); concierge; airport shuttle; laundry service; same-day dry cleaning. *In room:* A/C, TV
w/pay movies, Wi-Fi ($10/day), coffeemaker, hair dryer, iron.

Newbury Guest House ⚡⚡ *Value*   After just a little shopping in the Back Bay, you'll
appreciate what a find this cozy place is: a bargain on Newbury Street. The comfortably furnished, nicely appointed guest rooms take up three 1880s brick town houses.
Largest and most expensive are the bay-window units, which overlook the lively street.
This place operates near capacity all year, prompting my only caveat: Reserve early.

261 Newbury St. (btw. Fairfield and Gloucester sts.), Boston, MA 02116. ✆ 800/437-7668 or 617/437-7666. Fax
617/670-6100. www.newburyguesthouse.com. 32 units (some with shower only). $135–$195 double. Extra person
$20. Rates include continental breakfast and may be higher during special events. Minimum 2 nights on weekends.
Packages available. AE, DC, DISC, MC, V. Parking $20 (reservation required). T: Green Line B, C, or D to Hynes Conven-
tion Center. **Amenities:** Access to nearby health club ($25). *In room:* A/C, TV, Wi-Fi, hair dryer, iron.

INEXPENSIVE

Hostelling International–Boston   This hostel near the Berklee College of Music
caters to students, youth groups, and other travelers in search of comfortable, no-frills
lodging. Accommodations are dorm-style, with six beds per room; a couple of private
units sleep one or two. The air-conditioned hostel has two kitchens, 29 bathrooms,
and a large common room. It provides linens, or you can bring your own; sleeping
bags are not permitted. The enthusiastic staff organizes free and inexpensive cultural,
educational, and recreational programs.

Open in summer only, **Hostelling International–Boston at Fenway,** 575 Commonwealth Ave. (✆ **617/267-8599;** www.hifenway.org; T: Green Line B, C, or D to
Kenmore), holds 485 beds in a well-equipped building that's a Boston University
dorm during the school year. Rates are $35 per bed for HI-AYH members, $38 for
nonmembers. Private rooms for one to three guests cost $89 to $99.

12 Hemenway St., Boston, MA 02115. ✆ 800/909-4776 or 617/536-9455. Fax 617/424-6558. www.bostonhostel.
org. 205 beds. Members of Hostelling International–American Youth Hostels $28–$45 per bed; nonmembers $31–$48
per bed. Members $70–$100 per private unit; nonmembers $73–$106 per private unit. Children 3–12 half-price; children under 3 free. Rates include continental breakfast. MC, V. T: Green Line B, C, or D to Hynes Convention Center.
Amenities: Access to nearby health club ($6); coin laundry; Wi-Fi. *In room:* A/C, lockers, no phone.

OUTSKIRTS & BROOKLINE

Staying in this area means commuting to downtown Boston. Because of the unwieldy
public transit connections, it's not a great choice if your destination is Cambridge.

EXPENSIVE

Doubletree Guest Suites ⚡⚡ *Value*   This hotel is one of the best deals in town—
every unit is a two-room suite. It's near Cambridge and the bike path along the

Charles River—not in a real neighborhood, but there's shuttle service to local destinations. The large suites, which were renovated in 2007, surround a 15-story atrium. Most bedrooms have a king-size bed and writing desk. Each living room contains a sofa bed and dining table. The Hyatt Regency Cambridge, the hotel's nearest rival, is more convenient but generally more expensive.

400 Soldiers Field Rd., Boston, MA 02134. ✆ 800/222-TREE or 617/783-0090. Fax 617/783-0897. www.double tree.com. 308 units. $129–$309 double. Extra person $20. Children under 18 stay free in parent's room. Packages and AARP and AAA discounts available. AE, DC, DISC, MC, V. Valet parking $27; self-parking $20. Pets accepted with prior approval. **Amenities:** Restaurant (American); lounge; Scullers Jazz Club (see later in this chapter); indoor pool; exercise room; free access to nearby health club; Jacuzzi; sauna; concierge; shuttle service; 24-hr. business center; limited room service; coin laundry; laundry service; same-day dry cleaning. *In room:* A/C, TV w/pay movies, Wi-Fi ($10/day), fridge, coffeemaker, hair dryer, iron.

MODERATE

Options in this price range and area are chain hotels, including the **Brookline Courtyard by Marriott,** 40 Webster St., Brookline (✆ **866/296-2296,** 800/321-2211, or 617/734-1393), and the **Holiday Inn Boston Brookline,** 1200 Beacon St., Brookline (✆ **800/HOLIDAY** or 617/277-1200).

INEXPENSIVE

Anthony's Town House
Many patrons at this four-story brownstone guesthouse, a family business since 1944, are Europeans accustomed to homey accommodations with shared bathrooms, and budget-minded Americans won't be disappointed. Each floor has three high-ceilinged rooms furnished in Queen Anne or Victorian style, plus a bathroom with enclosed shower; the staff will supply a VCR, DVD player, hair dryer, or iron on request. The large front rooms have bay windows, and two family units hold as many as five comfortably. The guesthouse is about 15 minutes from downtown by T, and 2 blocks from a busy commercial strip.

1085 Beacon St., Brookline, MA 02446. ✆ 617/566-3972. Fax 617/232-1085. www.anthonystownhouse.com. 10 units, none with private bathroom. $78–$108 double; from $125 family room. Extra person $10. Weekly rates and winter discounts available. No credit cards. Limited free parking. T: Green Line C to Hawes St. *In room:* A/C, TV, Wi-Fi, no phone.

Longwood Inn
In a residential area near the Boston-Brookline border, this three-story guesthouse offers comfortable accommodations at modest rates. Rooms were redecorated in 2007 and kept the homey style that suits the Victorian architecture. Guests have the use of a full kitchen, dining room, and TV lounge. The apartment has its own bathroom and kitchen. Tennis courts, a running track, and a playground at the school next door are open to the public. Public transit is within easy reach, and the Longwood Medical Area and Coolidge Corner are a short walk away.

123 Longwood Ave., Brookline, MA 02446. ✆ 617/566-8615. Fax 617/738-1070. www.longwood-inn.com. 22 units, 19 with private bathroom (some with shower only). Apr–Nov $114–$134 double; Dec–Mar $79–$99 double; 1-bedroom apt (sleeps 4-plus) $99–$139. Weekly rates available. AE, DISC, MC, V. Free parking. T: Green Line D to Longwood or C to Coolidge Corner. **Amenities:** Coin laundry. *In room:* A/C, TV, Wi-Fi.

CAMBRIDGE
VERY EXPENSIVE

The Charles Hotel ✦✦✦
This nine-story brick hotel, a block from Harvard Square, has been *the* place for business and leisure travelers in Cambridge since it opened in 1985. Much of its fame derives from its excellent restaurants, jazz bar, day spa, and service. In the posh guest rooms, which were renovated in 2006, the style is

Cambridge Accommodations & Dining

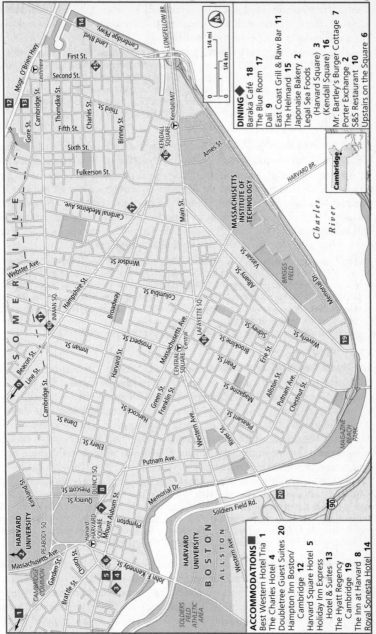

DINING ◆
Baraka Café **18**
The Blue Room **17**
Dali **9**
East Coast Grill & Raw Bar **11**
The Helmand **15**
Japonaise Bakery **2**
Legal Sea Foods
  (Harvard Square) **3**
  (Kendall Square) **16**
Mr. Bartley's Burger Cottage **7**
Porter Exchange **2**
S&S Restaurant **10**
Upstairs on the Square **6**

ACCOMMODATIONS ■
Best Western Hotel Tria **1**
The Charles Hotel **4**
Doubletree Guest Suites **20**
Hampton Inn Boston/
  Cambridge **12**
Harvard Square Hotel **5**
Holiday Inn Express
  Hotel & Suites **13**
The Hyatt Regency
  Cambridge **19**
The Inn at Harvard **8**
Royal Sonesta Hotel **14**

contemporary country, with custom adaptations of Shaker furniture. The austere design contrasts with the indulgent amenities, which include down quilts and Bose Wave radios; bathrooms hold phones and TVs.

1 Bennett St., Cambridge, MA 02138. © 800/882-1818 or 617/864-1200. Fax 617/864-5715. www.charleshotel. com. 293 units. $259–$599 double; $309–$4,000 suite. Extra person $20. Packages available. AE, DC, MC, V. Valet or self-parking $34. T: Red Line to Harvard. Pets under 25 lb. accepted; $50 fee. **Amenities:** 2 restaurants (Italian, New England); 2 bars; Regattabar jazz club (p. 144); access to adjacent health club w/pool, Jacuzzi, and exercise room; adjacent spa and salon; concierge; car-rental desk; business center; 24-hr. room service; in-room massage; babysitting; laundry service; same-day dry cleaning. *In room:* A/C, TV/DVD, high-speed Internet access ($11/day), minibar, hair dryer, iron, safe.

Royal Sonesta Hotel ★★ *Kids*   This luxurious hotel is close to only a few things but convenient to everything. Features for both businesspeople and families, such as the business center and indoor/outdoor pool with retractable roof, are excellent. The CambridgeSide Galleria mall and the Museum of Science are nearby, and Kendall Square is 10 minutes away on foot. Most of the spacious rooms have lovely views of the river or the city. (Higher prices are for better views.) Everything is custom designed in modern yet comfortable style. The closest competition is Hotel Marlowe, across the street, which offers less extensive fitness options and fewer river views.

40 Edwin H. Land Blvd., Cambridge, MA 02142. © 800/SONESTA or 617/806-4200. Fax 617/806-4232. www.sonesta. com/boston. 400 units (some with shower only). $239–$279 standard double; $259–$299 superior double; $279–$319 deluxe double; $339–$1,000 suite. Extra person $25. Children under 18 stay free in parent's room. Packages available. AE, DC, DISC, MC, V. Valet or self-parking $27. T: Green Line to Lechmere; 10-min. walk. Pets accepted with prior approval. **Amenities:** Restaurant (new American/Mediterranean); cafe; indoor/outdoor pool; 24-hr. health club and spa; bike rental (seasonal); concierge; courtesy van; 24-hr. business center; 24-hr. room service; massage; laundry service; dry cleaning. *In room:* A/C, TV w/pay movies, Wi-Fi, minibar, coffeemaker, hair dryer, iron, safe, umbrella.

EXPENSIVE

The Hyatt Regency Cambridge ★ *Kids*   The location of this dramatic pyramidal brick building is a plus and a minus. Across the street from the Charles River, it's convenient to Harvard and Kendall squares and Boston University. Shuttle service, access to the bike path along the river, and plentiful amenities help make up for the distance to the T. The best of the spacious guest rooms afford breathtaking views of Boston and the river. A business destination during the week, the Hyatt Regency courts families on weekends. The closest competitor is the Doubletree, which is even farther from public transit but consists of all suites.

575 Memorial Dr., Cambridge, MA 02139. © 800/233-1234 or 617/462-1234. Fax 617/491-6906. www.cambridge. hyatt.com. 469 units (some with shower only). $179–$359 double; $300–$750 suite. Extra person $25. Children under 18 stay free in parent's room. Packages available. AE, DC, DISC, MC, V. Valet parking $39; self-parking $35. **Amenities:** Restaurant and lounge (eclectic); 75-ft. indoor lap pool; health club; Jacuzzi; sauna; bike rental; concierge; shuttle to Cambridge destinations; business center; limited room service; in-room massage; laundry service; same-day dry cleaning. *In room:* A/C, TV w/pay movies, fax, Wi-Fi ($10/day), coffeemaker, hair dryer, iron.

The Inn at Harvard ★★   The Inn at Harvard is adjacent to Harvard Yard, and its Georgian-style architecture would fit nicely on campus. The elegant hotel is popular with business travelers and university visitors. The guest rooms were extensively renovated in 2006; they have pillow-top beds, and each has a work area with an Aeron chair. The four-story skylit atrium holds the "living room," a well-appointed lounge that's suitable for a meeting if you don't want to conduct business in your room.

1201 Mass. Ave. (at Quincy St.), Cambridge, MA 02138. © 800/458-5886 or 617/491-2222. Fax 617/520-3711. www.theinnatharvard.com. 111 units (some with shower only). $179–$419 double; $1,500 presidential suite. AAA and AARP discounts available. AE, DC, DISC, MC, V. Valet parking $45. T: Red Line to Harvard. **Amenities:** Restaurant

(New England); Harvard Faculty Club dining privileges; fitness center; limited room service; laundry service; same-day dry cleaning. *In room:* A/C, TV, Wi-Fi ($10/day), hair dryer, iron, umbrella, robes.

MODERATE

Two chain hotels in East Cambridge offer comfortable, predictable accommodations and free parking within easy walking distance of the Green Line Lechmere station. At the **Hampton Inn Boston/Cambridge,** 191 Msgr. O'Brien Hwy. (© **800/ HAMPTON** or 617/494-5300; www.bostoncambridge.hamptoninn.com), rates include expanded continental breakfast. Rooms at the **Holiday Inn Express Hotel & Suites,** 250 Msgr. O'Brien Hwy. (© **888/887-7690** or 617/577-7600; www.hi express.com/boscambridgema), hold a fridge and microwave; rates include continental breakfast.

Best Western Hotel Tria ✦   This four-story establishment blends chain convenience and boutique features. Set back from the busy street in a commercial neighborhood, it offers accommodations at least one floor up from the parking lot. Guest rooms are spacious and well maintained, decorated in comfy, contemporary style. A shopping center with a Whole Foods Market is nearby. Boston lies about a 15-minute drive or a 30-minute T ride away; Lexington and Concord are less than a half-hour away by car.

220 Alewife Brook Pkwy., Cambridge, MA 02138. © **866/333-8742** or 617/491-8000. Fax 617/491-4932. www. hoteltria.com. 69 units. Mid-Mar to Oct $149–$299 double; Nov to mid-Mar $119–$179 double. Extra person $10. Rates include continental breakfast and may be higher during special events. Children under 17 stay free in parent's room. AE, DC, MC, V. Parking $12. T: Red Line to Alewife, then a 10-min. walk. Pets accepted; reservation required; $25 fee; $100 deposit. **Amenities:** Indoor pool; exercise room; Jacuzzi; tour desk; shuttle service; same-day dry cleaning. *In room:* A/C, TV, Wi-Fi, coffeemaker, hair dryer, iron, robes.

Harvard Square Hotel   At busy times, including pretty much every night in the fall, rates for the modest accommodations here seem high—but you really can't beat the location. Smack in the middle of "the Square," the six-story brick hotel is a favorite with visiting parents and budget-conscious business travelers. The unpretentious guest rooms were renovated in 2006 and 2007; they're relatively small but comfortable and neatly decorated in contemporary style. Each has a flatscreen TV (important when every inch counts), and some overlook Harvard Square.

110 Mount Auburn St., Cambridge, MA 02138. © 800/458-5886 or 617/864-5200. Fax 617/492-4896. www.harvard squarehotel.com. 73 units, some with shower only. $99–$249 double. Extra person $10. Children under 17 stay free in parent's room. Corporate rates, AAA and AARP discounts available. AE, DC, DISC, MC, V. Parking $35. T: Red Line to Harvard. **Amenities:** Harvard Faculty Club dining privileges; free access to nearby health club; car-rental desk; laundry service; dry cleaning. *In room:* A/C, TV, Wi-Fi ($10/day), fridge, coffeemaker, hair dryer, iron, umbrella.

4 Where to Dine

Travelers from around the world relish the variety of skillfully prepared seafood available in the Boston area. Lunch is an excellent, economical way to check out a fancy restaurant without breaking the bank. At restaurants that accept reservations, it's always a good idea to make them, particularly for dinner.

WATERFRONT
EXPENSIVE

Legal Sea Foods ✦✦✦ SEAFOOD   This well-known chain may not be the secret insider tip you were expecting, but trust me. The family-owned business enjoys an international reputation because it serves only the freshest, best-quality fish and shellfish,

Boston Dining

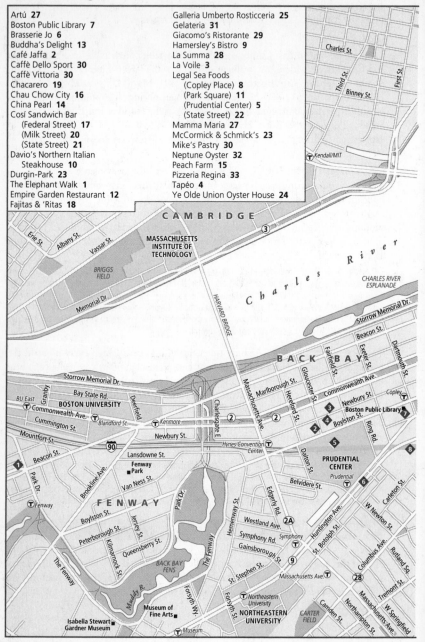

Artú **27**
Boston Public Library **7**
Brasserie Jo **6**
Buddha's Delight **13**
Café Jaffa **2**
Caffè Dello Sport **30**
Caffè Vittoria **30**
Chacarero **19**
Chau Chow City **16**
China Pearl **14**
Cosí Sandwich Bar
  (Federal Street) **17**
  (Milk Street) **20**
  (State Street) **21**
Davio's Northern Italian
  Steakhouse **10**
Durgin-Park **23**
The Elephant Walk **1**
Empire Garden Restaurant **12**
Fajitas & 'Ritas **18**

Galleria Umberto Rosticceria **25**
Gelateria **31**
Giacomo's Ristorante **29**
Hamersley's Bistro **9**
La Summa **28**
La Voile **3**
Legal Sea Foods
  (Copley Place) **8**
  (Park Square) **11**
  (Prudential Center) **5**
  (State Street) **22**
Mamma Maria **27**
McCormick & Schmick's **23**
Mike's Pastry **30**
Neptune Oyster **32**
Peach Farm **15**
Pizzeria Regina **33**
Tapéo **4**
Ye Olde Union Oyster House **24**

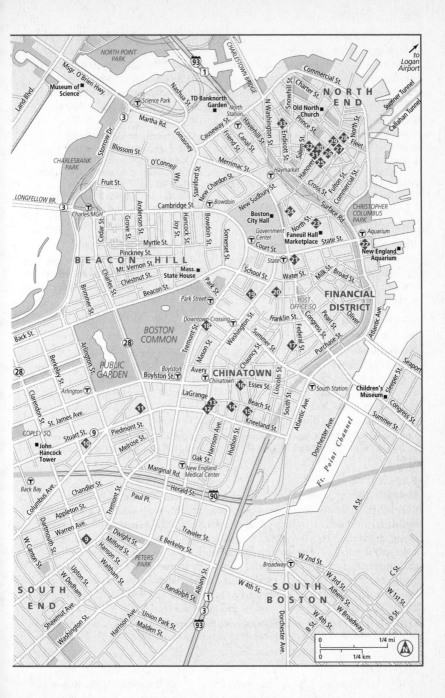

to
Logan
Airport

NORTH POINT PARK

Msgr. O'Connell Hwy.

Museum of Science

Land Blvd.

Nashua St.

Science Park

TD Banknorth Garden

North Station

Martha Rd.

Lomasney

Causeway St.

Friend St.

Canal St.

Haverhill St.

N. Washington St.

Charter St.

Commercial St.

Snowhill St.

Salem St.

Prince St.

Old North Church

Endicott St.

NORTH END

Sumner Tunnel

Callahan Tunnel

CHARLESBANK PARK

Storrow Dr.

Blossom St.

O'Connell Wy.

Merrimac St.

Haymarket

Hanover St.

Cross St.

Fulton St.

Commercial St.

North St.

Fleet

Salem St.

CHRISTOPHER COLUMBUS PARK

Aquarium

Fruit St.

New Chardon St.

New Sudbury St.

Surface Rd.

LONGFELLOW BR.

Charles/MGH

Cambridge St.

Bowdoin

Boston City Hall

Government Center

Faneuil Hall Marketplace

North St.

State St.

Aquarium

New England Aquarium

Cedar St.

Grove St.

Anderson St.

Joy St.

Hancock St.

Bowdoin St.

Somerset St.

Court St.

State

Water St.

Milk St.

Broad St.

Myrtle St.

Pinckney St.

Mt. Vernon St.

BEACON HILL

Mass. State House

Park St.

School St.

FINANCIAL DISTRICT

Atlantic Ave.

Charles St.

Chestnut St.

Beacon St.

Park Street

POST OFFICE SQ.

Oliver

Brimmer St.

Park St.

Downtown Crossing

Franklin St.

Congress St.

Pearl St.

Purchase St.

BOSTON COMMON

Tremont St.

Mason St.

Washington St.

Summer St.

Federal St.

Seaport

Back St.

Arlington St.

Berkeley St.

PUBLIC GARDEN

Boylston St.

Avery

Chinatown

CHINATOWN

Essex St.

Lincoln St.

South St.

Atlantic Ave.

South Station

Children's Museum

Sleeper St.

congress St.

Boylston

Arlington

LaGrange

Beach St.

Kneeland St.

Dorchester Ave.

Ft. Point Channel

Summer St.

COPLEY SQ.

Clarendon St.

St. James Ave.

Stuart St.

Piedmont St.

Melrose St.

Harrison Ave.

Hudson St.

John Hancock Tower

Back Bay

Columbus Ave.

Dartmouth St.

Chandler St.

Paul Pl.

Oak St.

Marginal Rd.

New England Medical Center

Herald St.

A St.

Appleton St.

Warren Ave.

Tremont St.

Traveler St.

E Berkeley St.

Broadway

W 2nd St.

W 3rd St.

C St.

W Canton St.

Dwight St.

Milford St.

Hanson St.

Waltham St.

PETERS PARK

SOUTH BOSTON

Athens St.

W 1st St.

SOUTH END

W Dedham St.

Upton St.

Shawmut Ave.

Washington St.

Harrison Ave.

Union Park St.

Malden St.

Randolph St.

Albany St.

W 4th St.

W Broadway

B. St.

Dorchester Ave.

D. St.

0   1/4 mi

0   1/4 km

which it processes at its own state-of-the-art plant. The menu includes regular selections plus whatever looked good at the market that morning, prepared in every imaginable way, and it's all splendid. The clam chowder is great, the fish chowder lighter but equally good. Entrees run the gamut from grilled fish served plain or with Cajun spices (try the arctic char) to seafood fra diavolo on fresh linguine to mammoth lobsters. And a friend who makes his living as a wine writer tells me the wine list here is the best at any restaurant chain in the country.

255 State St. ⓒ 617/227-3115. www.legalseafoods.com. Reservations recommended. Main courses $11–$19 at lunch, $14–$35 at dinner; lobster market price. AE, DC, DISC, MC, V. Mon–Thurs 11am–10pm; Fri–Sat 11am–11pm; Sun noon–10pm. T: Blue Line to Aquarium. Also at 800 Boylston St., in the Prudential Center. ⓒ 617/266-6800. T: Green Line B, C, or D to Hynes Convention Center, or E to Prudential. 36 Park Place (btw. Columbus Ave. and Stuart St.), Park Sq. ⓒ 617/426-4444. T: Green Line to Arlington. Copley Place, 2nd level. ⓒ 617/266-7775. T: Orange Line to Back Bay or Green Line to Copley. 20 University Rd., behind The Charles Hotel, Cambridge. ⓒ 617/491-9400. T: Red Line to Harvard. 5 Cambridge Center, Cambridge. ⓒ 617/864-3400. T: Red Line to Kendall/MIT.

THE NORTH END

Many North End restaurants don't serve dessert, but you can satisfy your sweet tooth at a *caffè*. Favorites include **Caffè Vittoria,** 296 Hanover St. (ⓒ 617/227-7606), and **Caffè dello Sport,** 308 Hanover St. (ⓒ 617/523-5063). For gelato, head to **Gelateria,** 272 Hanover St. (ⓒ 617/720-4243), which serves 50 flavors of the Italian version of ice cream.

VERY EXPENSIVE

Mamma Maria 𝕶𝕶𝕶 NORTHERN ITALIAN   In a town house overlooking North Square and the Paul Revere House, the best restaurant in the North End offers innovative seasonal cuisine in a sophisticated yet comfortable setting. The menu changes seasonally, and portions are more than generous. Fork-tender *osso buco* is almost enough for two, but you'll want it all for yourself. You can't go wrong with main-course pastas, either, and the fresh seafood specials are uniformly marvelous. The pasta, bread, and desserts are homemade, and the wine list is excellent.

3 North Sq. ⓒ 617/523-0077. www.mammamaria.com. Reservations recommended. Main courses $26–$40; AE, DC, DISC, MC, V. Sun–Thurs 5–9:30pm; Fri–Sat 5–10:30pm. Valet parking available. T: Green or Orange Line to Haymarket.

EXPENSIVE

Neptune Oyster 𝕶 SEAFOOD   Tiny and cramped, Neptune feels like one of those off-the-radar places out-of-towners fantasize about—or it would, if it weren't so crowded. Superfresh, inventively prepared seafood keeps this restaurant busy and loud almost all the time; even in winter, I suggest planning for lunch or an early dinner on a weekday if you don't enjoy waiting. Check out the daily specials, then start with oysters, comparing specimens from both coasts. Main courses include some menu standards, at least two of which aren't seafood, and dishes that make good use of whatever's fresh that day. Neptune is just off the Freedom Trail and easy to find: Look for the lemons and oysters in the front window and the crowd inside.

63 Salem St. ⓒ 617/742-3474. www.neptuneoyster.com. Reservations not accepted. Main courses $13–$34; lobster market price. AE, MC, V. Sun–Wed 11:30am–10pm; Thurs–Sat 11:30am–midnight. T: Green or Orange Line to Haymarket.

MODERATE

Artú ITALIAN   Artú is a neighborhood favorite as well as a good stop for Freedom Trail walkers. It's known for superb roasted meats and bounteous home-style pasta dishes. Roast lamb, penne alla puttanesca, and chicken stuffed with ham and cheese are all terrific. Panini are big in size and flavor—prosciutto, mozzarella, and tomato is sublime, and chicken parmigiana is tender and filling. Artú isn't great for quiet conversation, especially during dinner in the noisy main room, but do you really want to talk with your mouth full?

6 Prince St. ℂ 617/742-4336. www.artuboston.com. Reservations recommended at dinner. Main courses $8–$14 at lunch, $14–$23 at dinner; sandwiches $6–$8. AE, MC, V. Daily 11am–11pm; bar menu until 1am. T: Green or Orange Line to Haymarket.

Giacomo's Ristorante ★★ ITALIAN/SEAFOOD   The line snakes down the street, especially on weekends. No reservations, cash only, a tiny dining room with an open kitchen—what's the secret? Terrific food, plenty of it, and the "we're all in this together" atmosphere. To start, try fried calamari or mozzarella with excellent marinara sauce. Take the chef's advice or put together your own main dish from the list of daily ingredients on a board on the wall. The best suggestion is salmon and sun-dried tomatoes in tomato cream sauce over fettuccine. Nonseafood offerings such as butternut squash ravioli are equally memorable. Service is friendly but incredibly swift. (Those hungry people want your seat.) After a 40-minute dinner, dessert at a *caffè* is practically a necessity.

355 Hanover St. ℂ 617/523-9026. Reservations not accepted. Main courses $14–$18; specials market price. No credit cards. Mon–Thurs 5–10pm; Fri–Sat 5–10:30pm; Sun 4–10pm. T: Green or Orange Line to Haymarket.

La Summa ★ SOUTHERN ITALIAN   Away from the restaurant rows of Hanover and Salem streets, La Summa maintains a cozy neighborhood atmosphere. It's worth seeking out for wonderful homemade pasta and desserts; more elaborate entrees are scrumptious, too. Try any seafood special, lobster ravioli, *pappardelle e melanzane* (eggplant strips tossed with ethereal fresh pasta), or the house special—veal, chicken, sausage, shrimp, artichokes, pepperoncini, olives, and mushrooms in white-wine sauce. Desserts, especially tiramisu, are terrific.

30 Fleet St. ℂ 617/523-9503. Reservations recommended on weekends. Main courses $11–$24. AE, DC, DISC, MC, V. Sun–Fri 4:30–10:30pm; Sat 4:30–11pm. T: Green or Orange Line to Haymarket.

INEXPENSIVE

An excellent eat-and-run spot just off the Freedom Trail is the cafeteria-style **Galleria Umberto Rosticceria,** 289 Hanover St. (ℂ **617/227-5709**). Join the line for tasty pizza, *arancini* (a rice ball filled with ground beef, peas, and cheese), potato croquettes, or calzones. Lunch is served Monday through Saturday; cash only.

Pizzeria Regina ★★ PIZZA   In business since 1926, Regina's looks like a movie set, but it's the real thing. The line stretches up the street at busy times; even during off hours, business is seldom slow. Busy waitresses weave through the boisterous dining room, delivering peerless pizza hot from the brick oven. The list of toppings includes nouveau ingredients such as sun-dried tomatoes, but that's not authentic. House-made sausage, maybe some pepperoni, and a couple of beers—now, *that's* authentic.

11½ Thacher St. ℂ 617/227-0765. www.pizzeriaregina.com. Reservations not accepted. Pizza $10–$17. AE, MC, V. Mon–Thurs 11am–11:30pm; Fri–Sat 11am–midnight; Sun noon–11pm. T: Green or Orange Line to Haymarket.

FANEUIL HALL MARKETPLACE & FINANCIAL DISTRICT

The **food court in Quincy Market,** at the center of Faneuil Hall Marketplace, is a great place to pick up picnic fare. Eat here, or cross Atlantic Avenue and dine in Christopher Columbus Waterfront Park.

Tips **It's Nothing Personal**

State law requires the scary disclaimer that appears on menus to alert you to the potential danger of eating raw or undercooked meat (such as rare burgers), seafood (raw oysters, for instance), poultry, or eggs.

EXPENSIVE

The national chain **McCormick & Schmick's Seafood Restaurant** has a branch at Faneuil Hall Marketplace in the North Market Building (© **617/720-5522**).

Ye Olde Union Oyster House ✸ NEW ENGLAND/SEAFOOD   America's oldest restaurant in continuous service, the Union Oyster House opened in 1826. Its tasty New England fare is popular with tourists on the adjacent Freedom Trail as well as savvy locals. They're not here for anything fancy; the best bets are simple, classic preparations. Try oyster stew or a cold seafood sampler of oysters, clams, and shrimp. Follow with a broiled or grilled dish such as scrod or salmon, or perhaps fried seafood or grilled pork loin. A "shore dinner" (chowder, steamers, lobster, corn, and dessert) is an excellent introduction to local favorites. **Tip:** A plaque marks John F. Kennedy's favorite booth (no. 18), where he often read the Sunday papers.

41 Union St. (btw. North and Hanover sts.). © 617/227-2750. www.unionoysterhouse.com. Reservations recommended. Main courses $8–$22 lunch, $17–$29 dinner; lobster market price. Children's menu $5–$12. AE, DC, DISC, MC, V. Sun–Thurs 11am–9:30pm (lunch until 5pm); Fri–Sat 11am–10pm (lunch until 6pm). Union Bar daily 11am–midnight (lunch until 3pm, late supper until 11pm). Validated and valet parking available. T: Green or Orange Line to Haymarket.

MODERATE

Durgin-Park ✸✸ _Kids_ NEW ENGLAND   For huge portions of delicious food, a rowdy atmosphere where CEOs share tables with students, and famously cranky waitresses, Bostonians have flocked to Durgin-Park since 1827. The line stretches down the stairs to the first floor of Faneuil Hall Marketplace's North Market building, and many diners are actually disappointed when the waitresses are nice (as they often are). Come here for prime rib the size of a hubcap, piles of fried seafood, fish dinners broiled to order, and bounteous portions of roast turkey. Steaks and chops are broiled on an open fire over wood charcoal. This is the place to try Boston baked beans. For dessert, strawberry shortcake is justly celebrated.

340 Faneuil Hall Marketplace. © 617/227-2038. Reservations accepted for parties of 15 or more. Main courses $7–$25; daily specials $19–$40. Children's menu $8–$9. AE, DC, DISC, MC, V. Mon–Sat 11:30am–10pm; Sun 11:30am–9pm (lunch daily until 2:30pm). Validated parking available. T: Green or Blue Line to Government Center, or Orange Line to Haymarket.

INEXPENSIVE

Cosí Sandwich Bar ✸ ITALIAN/ECLECTIC   Flavorful fillings on delectable bread make Cosí a downtown lunch favorite. This location of the national chain, just off the Freedom Trail, makes a delicious refueling stop. Tasty Italian flatbread is filled with your choice of meat, fish, vegetables, cheese, and spreads. The more fillings you choose, the more you pay; the total can climb, so don't go wild if you're on a budget. The Federal Street location has seasonal patio seating.

53 State St. (at Congress St.). © 617/723-4447. www.getcosi.com. Sandwiches $6–$10; soups and salads $4–$7. AE, DC, MC, V. Mon–Thurs 7am–6pm; Fri 7am–5pm. T: Orange or Blue Line to State. Also at 14 Milk St. © 617/426-7565. T: Red or Orange Line to Downtown Crossing. 133 Federal St. © 617/292-2674. T: Red Line to South Station.

CHINATOWN/THEATER DISTRICT

The best way to sample Chinese food is by trying **dim sum,** the traditional midday meal featuring a variety of appetizer-style dishes. It's especially popular on weekends, when the variety of offerings is greatest. My favorite destinations are **China Pearl,** 9 Tyler St., 2nd floor (© **617/426-4338**), **Chau Chow City,** 83 Essex St. (© **617/338-8158**), and **Empire Garden Restaurant,** also known as Emperor's Garden, 690–698 Washington St., 2nd floor (© **617/482-8898**).

MODERATE

Peach Farm ⚝ SEAFOOD/CANTONESE/SZECHUAN Chinatown's go-to place for fresh seafood is a subterranean hideaway with no decor to speak of and service so fast that just saying "calamari" seems to make spicy dry-fried salted squid appear on your table. Gobble it up while it's hot, then explore: delicious, messy clams with black-bean sauce; braised chicken hot pot; emerald-green stir-fried pea-pod stems. Spicy salt shrimp—you can eat them whole, shells, heads, and all—is addictive; my favorite is that same spicy salt preparation applied to meltingly tender scallops. Fresh fish steamed with ginger and scallions, a Cantonese classic, comes to your table thrashing in a plastic bucket and reappears moments later, perfectly cooked.

4 Tyler St. © 617/482-3332. Reservations recommended for large groups at dinner. Main courses $5–$34 (most items less than $15); fresh seafood market price. MC, V. Daily 11am–3am. T: Orange Line to Chinatown.

INEXPENSIVE

Buddha's Delight ⚝ VEGETARIAN/VIETNAMESE Fresh, healthful, cheap, and filling—what's not to like? Brave the run-down stairwell, ask for a table near the window, and try "chicken," "pork," and even "lobster"—in quotes because the chefs substitute fried and barbecued tofu and gluten for meat, poultry, and fish. The more-than-reasonable facsimiles are good stand-ins for your usual protein. To start, try fried "pork" dumplings or a delectable salad. Move on to "shrimp" with rice noodles, any of the house specialties, or excellent chow fun.

3 Beach St., 2nd floor. © 617/451-2395. Main courses $6–$13; lunch specials $6.50. MC, V. Sun–Thurs 11am–9:30pm; Fri–Sat 11am–10:30pm. T: Orange Line to Chinatown.

Fajitas & 'Ritas ⚝ TEX-MEX This colorful, entertaining restaurant serves nachos, quesadillas, burritos, and fajitas, exactly the way you want them. Mark your food and drink selections on a checklist, and your busy server quickly returns with big portions of tasty food. Everything is superfresh, because this place is so popular that nothing sits around for very long. As the name indicates, 'ritas (margaritas) are a house specialty. Primarily a casual business destination at lunch, it's livelier at dinner (probably

---

Tips The Lunch Line

Lunchtime favorite **Chacarero,** 26 Province St., between School and Bromfield streets (© **617/367-1167;** www.chacarero.com; T: Blue or Orange Line to State), serves other things, but the line is so long because of the scrumptious Chilean sandwiches, served on house-made bread. Order chicken, beef, or vegetarian "with everything"—tomatoes, cheese, avocado, hot sauce, and (unexpected but delicious) green beans—and dig in. For less than $8, you feel like a savvy Bostonian.

thanks to the margaritas) and a perfect stop before or after a movie at the nearby AMC Loews Boston Common theater.

25 West St. (btw. Washington and Tremont sts.). © 617/426-1222. www.fajitasandritas.com. Reservations accepted only for parties of 8 or more. Main dishes $5–$9 at lunch, $6–$13 at dinner. AE, DC, DISC, MC, V. Mon–Tues 11:30am–9pm; Wed–Thurs 11:30am–10pm; Fri–Sat 11:30am–11pm; Sun noon–8pm. T: Red or Green Line to Park St., or Orange Line to Downtown Crossing.

SOUTH END
VERY EXPENSIVE
Hamersley's Bistro 🍴🍴 ECLECTIC   This is the place that put the South End on Boston's culinary map, a pioneering restaurant that's both classic and contemporary. It's one of the area's top special-occasion restaurants, yet the huge volume of repeat business makes it feel like a neighborhood hangout. The seasonal menu offers entrees noted for their emphasis on local ingredients and classic techniques. The signature roast chicken with garlic is a bit tame, but the inventive seafood dishes and flavorful meat preparations have no such problem. The wine list and desserts are excellent, and there's seasonal outdoor seating.

553 Tremont St. © 617/423-2700. www.hamersleysbistro.com. Reservations recommended. Main courses $26–$42; tasting menu varies. AE, DISC, MC, V. Mon–Fri 6–10pm; Sat 5:30–10pm; Sun 11am–2pm (brunch) and 5:30–9:30pm. Closed Jan 1–12. Valet parking available. T: Orange Line to Back Bay.

BACK BAY
VERY EXPENSIVE
Davio's Northern Italian Steakhouse 🍴🍴 STEAKS/CREATIVE NORTHERN ITALIAN   Robust cuisine in a business-chic setting makes this excellent restaurant a hit with diners in search of top-notch Northern Italian cuisine, picture-perfect steakhouse offerings, and inventive-comfort-food sides. Davio's is a great compromise for Italophiles (the lobster risotto is the best in town) dining with hard-core carnivores. The exceptional wine list includes some rare Italian vintages, and the excellent breads and desserts are made in-house. Despite the open kitchen, the bar in the middle of the room, and the lively lounge area, the noise level allows for conversation, even at busy times. *Tip:* When the Yankees are in town to play the Red Sox, you can often see at least a few of them here.

75 Arlington St. © 617/357-4810. www.davios.com. Reservations recommended. Main courses $9–$43 at lunch (most less than $25), $21–$52 at dinner; 5-course tasting menu $95. AE, DC, DISC, MC, V. Mon–Fri 11:30am–3pm; Sun–Tues 5–10pm (lounge menu until 11pm); Wed–Sat 5–11pm (lounge menu until midnight). Validated and valet parking available. T: Green Line to Arlington.

EXPENSIVE
The Spanish tapas restaurant **Dalí** (p. 114) has a Back Bay outpost called **Tapéo,** at 266 Newbury St. (© 617/267-4799).

La Voile 🍴 FRENCH/MEDITERRANEAN   Talk about authentically French: The owners created La Voile by shutting down La Voile au Vent in Cannes and shipping it to Boston, complete with chef. Start with a house-made terrine or bone marrow, then try classic *blanquette de veau* (veal in cream sauce), *choucroute Alsacienne* (the bistro standby of sausages over sauerkraut), or roasted chicken, which gets a goose-fat bath before going in the oven. Bouillabaisse comes in a gravylike sauce, not broth. Service could be a little more polished, but this cozy place below street level has understandably been a hit since it opened in late 2007. Check ahead to see whether lunch is available.

261 Newbury St. ℂ **617/587-4200.** www.lavoileboston.net. Reservations recommended. Main courses $15–$43 (most less than $26). AE, MC, V. Tues–Sun 5:30–10:30pm. Valet parking available. T: Green Line to Copley.

MODERATE

Brasserie Jo ★★ REGIONAL FRENCH   The Boston branch of this Chicago favorite serves food that's classic—house-made pâtés, fresh baguettes, superb shellfish, salade Niçoise, Alsatian onion tart, coq au vin—but never boring. The casual, all-day brasserie and bar fits well in this neighborhood, where shoppers can always use a break but might not want a full meal. It's also a good bet before or after a Boston Symphony or Pops performance, and it's popular for business lunches. The noise level can be high when the spacious room is full—have your tête-à-tête at a table near the bar.

In the Colonnade Hotel, 120 Huntington Ave. ℂ **617/425-3240.** www.brasseriejoboston.com. Reservations recommended at dinner. Main courses $6–$15 at lunch, $15–$27 at dinner; *plats du jour* $18–$32. AE, DC, DISC, MC, V. Mon–Fri 6:30am–11pm; Sat 7am–11pm; Sun 7am–10pm; late-night menu daily until 1am. Valet and garage parking available. T: Green Line E to Prudential.

INEXPENSIVE

The Boston Public Library, 700 Boylston St. (ℂ **617/536-5400;** www.bpl.org), is home to a restaurant, **Novel,** that serves lunch and afternoon tea on weekdays only and to the less expensive **Sebastian's Map Room Café,** which serves meals and snacks Monday through Saturday from 9am to 5pm.

Café Jaffa MIDDLE EASTERN   A long, narrow brick room with a glass front, Café Jaffa looks more like a snazzy pizza place than the excellent Middle Eastern restaurant it is. Reasonable prices, high quality, and large portions draw crowds for traditional dishes such as falafel, baba ghanoush, and hummus, as well as burgers and steak tips. For dessert, try the baklava if it's fresh (give it a pass if not).

48 Gloucester St. ℂ **617/536-0230.** Main courses $5–$18. AE, DC, DISC, MC, V. Mon–Thurs 11am–10:30pm; Fri–Sat 11am–11pm; Sun 1–10pm. T: Green Line B, C, or D to Hynes Convention Center.

KENMORE SQUARE
MODERATE

The Elephant Walk ★★ FRENCH/CAMBODIAN   France meets Cambodia on the menu at this madly popular spot 4 blocks from Kenmore Square. Many Cambodian dishes have part-French names, such as *poulet à la citronelle* (chicken sautéed with lemongrass) and *curry de crevettes* (shrimp curry with picture-perfect vegetables). Or try *loc lac,* fork-tender beef cubes in addictively spicy sauce. On the French side, you'll find classics like filet mignon with pommes frites. Vegetarians and diners who can't have gluten are well taken care of, and the pleasant staff will help out if you need guidance.

900 Beacon St. ℂ **617/247-1500.** www.elephantwalk.com. Reservations recommended for dinner Sun–Thurs; not accepted Fri–Sat. Main courses $7–$28; tasting menus $30 and $40. AE, DC, DISC, MC, V. Mon–Fri 11:30am–2:30pm; Sun brunch 11am–3pm; Sun–Thurs 5–10pm; Fri–Sat 5–11pm. Valet parking available at dinner. T: Green Line C to St. Mary's St.

CAMBRIDGE

The Red Line runs from downtown Boston to Harvard Square. Many of the restaurants listed here can be reached on foot from there. To go in search of inexpensive ethnic food, head for Central and Inman squares.

Note: See the "Cambridge Accommodations & Dining" map, on p. 103, for the locations of the restaurants reviewed below.

VERY EXPENSIVE

Upstairs on the Square 𝕲𝕲 ECLECTIC   Overlooking a park off Harvard Square, Upstairs on the Square is the perfect combination of comfort food and fine dining. It consists of two lovely spaces; I prefer the more casual Monday Club Bar, a dining room where firelight flickers on jewel-toned walls. The food—unusual salads and sandwiches, satisfying soups, fried chicken, inventive pastas, steak with ever-changing versions of potatoey goodness—is homey and satisfying, and the bar is a tweedy Cambridge scene. The top-floor Soirée Room, a jewel box of pinks and golds under a low, mirrored ceiling, is the place for that big anniversary dinner. In both rooms, you'll find outstanding wine selections and desserts.

91 Winthrop St. ℂ 617/864-1933. www.upstairsonthesquare.com. Reservations recommended. Main courses $10–$28 downstairs, $25–$42 upstairs; prix fixe lunch (downstairs only) $20; tasting menus (upstairs only) $50–$86. AE, DC, DISC, MC, V. Downstairs Mon–Fri 11:30am–2:30pm; Sat–Sun brunch 10am–3pm; afternoon tea Fri–Sat 3–5pm; daily 5pm–2am (dinner until 11pm). Upstairs Mon–Thurs 5:30–10pm; Fri–Sat 5:30–11pm. Validated and valet parking available. T: Red Line to Harvard.

EXPENSIVE

Legal Sea Foods has branches in Harvard Square and in Kendall Square; see "Water-front," above.

The Blue Room 𝕲𝕲𝕲 ECLECTIC   The Blue Room sits below plaza level in an office-retail complex, a slice of foodie paradise in high-tech heaven. The cuisine deftly combines top-notch ingredients and aggressive flavors, and the crowded dining room isn't as noisy as it looks. Main courses tend to be grilled over a wood fire, roasted, or braised, with at least one well-conceived vegetarian choice. Chicken, roasted with Moroccan spices and served with garlic mashed potatoes, is fantastic. Seafood is always a good choice, and pork chops are juicy and succulent. In warm weather, there's patio seating.

1 Kendall Sq. ℂ 617/494-9034. www.theblueroom.net. Reservations recommended. Main courses $21–$26. AE, DC, DISC, MC, V. Sun–Thurs 5:30–10pm; Fri–Sat 5:30–11pm; Sun brunch 11am–2:30pm. Closed 1st week of July. Validated parking available. T: Red Line to Kendall/MIT, then a 10-min. walk.

Dalí 𝕲𝕲𝕲 SPANISH   This festive restaurant casts an irresistible spell—people wait an hour or more for a table and hardly complain. The authentic Spanish fare includes excellent paella, but most people come in a group and explore the three dozen or more tapas offerings, all perfect for sharing. They include delectable garlic potatoes, salmon balls with not-too-salty caper sauce, pork tenderloin with blue goat cheese, and delicious sausages, plus monthly specials. The staff sometimes seems rushed but never fails to supply bread for sopping up juices and sangria for washing it all down. I like to finish with "ubiquitous flan" or *tarta de chocolates*.

The owners of Dalí also run **Tapéo**, 266 Newbury St. (ℂ **617/267-4799**), between Fairfield and Dartmouth streets in Boston's Back Bay.

415 Washington St., Somerville. ℂ **617/661-3254**. www.DaliRestaurant.com. Reservations accepted only Sun–Thurs until 6:30pm, Fri until 6pm, Sat for parties of 6 or more until 6pm. Tapas $4.50–$16 (most $10 or less); main courses $20–$25; late-night menu $4.50–$9. AE, DC, MC, V. Daily 5:30–11pm; bar serves food until 12:30am. T: Red Line to Harvard; follow Kirkland St. to intersection of Washington and Beacon sts. (20-min. walk or $5 cab ride).

East Coast Grill & Raw Bar 𝕲𝕲 SEAFOOD/BARBECUE   Huge portions, a dizzying menu, and funky decor have made the East Coast Grill incredibly popular since 1985. The kitchen handles fresh seafood (an encyclopedic variety), barbecue, and grilled fish and meats with equal authority and imagination. The influence of founder Chris Schlesinger, a national expert on grilling and spicy food, is apparent in the exuberant menu descriptions ("super fresh catch o' the moment," "wings of mass destruction"). More than at perhaps any other restaurant in town, it's imperative to check the specials board here—thank me later.

1271 Cambridge St., Inman Sq. © 617/491-6568. www.eastcoastgrill.net. Reservations accepted only for parties of 5 or more Sun–Thurs. Main courses $15–$30; fresh seafood market price. AE, MC, V. Sun–Thurs 5:30–10pm; Fri–Sat 5:30–10:30pm; Sun brunch 11am–2:30pm. Validated parking available. T: Red Line to Central, 10-min. walk on Prospect St., or Red Line to Harvard, then no. 69 (Harvard-Lechmere) bus to Inman Sq.

MODERATE

Baraka Café ★ ALGERIAN/TUNISIAN/MEDITERRANEAN A tiny, aromatic destination for adventurous diners, Baraka Café specializes in flavorful, highly spiced (though not necessarily hot) cuisine. Locals talk about it as though it's a secret, but one look at the line that forms on weekend evenings will tell you it's not. The drawbacks—no alcohol, cash only, tiny dining room, deliberate service—are insignificant when the food is this good. It's easy to fill up on house-made breads and appetizers, but save room for the likes of fork-tender lamb chops and eggplant stuffed with a tasty concoction of olives, spinach, scallions, and two cheeses. Daily specials show off the kitchen's considerable abilities better than the limited regular menu.

80½ Pearl St., Central Sq. © 617/868-3951. www.barakacafe.com. Reservations not accepted. Main courses $5–$9 at lunch, $9–$16 at dinner. No credit cards. Tues–Sat 11:30am–3pm; Tues–Sun 5:30–10pm. T: Red Line to Central.

The Helmand ★★ AFGHAN The unusual cuisine, elegant setting, and reasonable prices make this spacious spot near the CambridgeSide Galleria mall the worst-kept secret in Cambridge. The delectable flavors and textures evoke Middle Eastern, Indian, and Pakistani cuisine. Many dishes are vegetarian, and meat is often one element of a dish rather than the centerpiece. Every meal comes with delectable bread made fresh in a wood-fired brick oven near the entrance. Main courses include grilled meats, poultry, and fish plus several versions of what Americans would call stew. For dessert, don't miss the Afghan version of baklava.

143 First St. © 617/492-4646. www.helmandrestaurantcambridge.com. Reservations recommended. Main courses $12–$20. AE, MC, V. Sun–Thurs 5–10pm; Fri–Sat 5–11pm. T: Green Line to Lechmere.

INEXPENSIVE

The food court on the lower level of the **Porter Exchange** mall, 1815 Mass. Ave., Porter Square, is home to half a dozen or so Japanese businesses that attract expats from all over the Boston area. All open in the late morning and close by 9pm. The superauthentic dining options are mostly fast-food counters with small seating areas; regardless of where you eat, finish up with French- and Japanese-style pastries at **Japonaise Bakery** (© 617/547-5531).

Mr. Bartley's Burger Cottage ★★ AMERICAN Great burgers and the best onion rings in the world make Bartley's a perennial favorite with a cross-section of Cambridge. Founded in 1960, this family business is a high-ceilinged, crowded room plastered with memorabilia. Anything you can think of to put on ground beef is available, from American cheese to grilled pineapple. Good dishes that don't involve meat include veggie burgers and creamy, garlicky hummus.

1246 Mass. Ave. © 617/354-6559. www.mrbartleysburgers.com. Burgers $9–$13; main courses, salads, and sandwiches $5–$9. No credit cards. Mon–Sat 11am–9pm. Closed Dec 25–Jan 1. T: Red Line to Harvard.

S&S Restaurant ★★ DELI *Es* is Yiddish for "eat," and this Cambridge classic is as straightforward as its name ("eat and eat"). Founded in 1919 by the current owners' great-grandmother, the wildly popular brunch spot draws huge crowds at busy times on weekends. It looks contemporary, but the brunch offerings are traditional: fantastic omelets, pancakes, waffles, fruit salad, cinnamon rolls. You'll also find traditional deli items (corned beef, pastrami, potato pancakes, blintzes), and breakfast anytime. Arrive early for brunch, or plan to spend a chunk of your Saturday or Sunday people-watching and getting hungry.

1334 Cambridge St., Inman Sq. ⓒ 617/354-0777. www.sandsrestaurant.com. Main courses $4–$18. AE, MC, V. Mon–Wed 7am–11pm; Thurs–Fri 7am–11pm; Sat 8am–11pm; Sun 8am–10pm (brunch Sat–Sun until 4pm). T: Red Line to Central; 10-min. walk on Prospect St. Or Red Line to Harvard, then no. 69 (Harvard–Lechmere) bus to Inman Sq.

5 Seeing the Sights in Boston

At press time, the **Boston Tea Party Ship & Museum** (ⓒ 617/269-7150; www.bostonteapartyship.com), which closed after a fire in 2001, was scheduled to reopen in mid-2009. Chronically delayed plans called for the construction of two more ships, doubling the size of the museum, and adding a tearoom. Check at your hotel or call ahead before setting out.

DISCOUNT PASSES   If you concentrate on the included attractions, a **CityPass** (ⓒ 888/330-5008; www.citypass.com) offers great savings. It's a booklet of tickets to the Harvard Museum of Natural History, Kennedy Library, Museum of Fine Arts, Museum of Science, New England Aquarium, and Prudential Center Skywalk Observatory. The price (at press time, $44 for adults, $24 for children 3–11) represents a 50% savings for adults who visit all six attractions, and having a ticket means you can go straight to the entrance without waiting in line. The passes, good for 1 year from the date of purchase, are on sale at participating attractions, from the website, through the **Greater Boston Convention & Visitors Bureau** (ⓒ 800/SEE-BOSTON; www.bostonusa.com), and from some hotel concierges and travel agents.

CityPass's main competition is the **Go Boston Card** (ⓒ 800/887-9103; www.gobostoncard.com). It includes admission to more than 60 Boston-area and New England attractions and a 2-day trolley pass. If you strategize wisely, this card can be a great value. It costs $55 for 1 day, $85 for 2 days, $115 for 3 days, $155 for 5 days, and $195 for 7 days, with discounts for children and winter travelers. A spin-off, the Explorer Pass, lets you select three of the nine included attractions and is good for 30 days. It costs $65 for adults and $39 for children—a potentially good deal, but do the math. Cards and passes are available through the website, at the Visitor Information Centers on Boston Common and at the Prudential Center, from the BosTix booths in Faneuil Hall Marketplace (closed Mon) and Copley Square, at many concierge desks, and as part of numerous hotel packages.

THE TOP ATTRACTIONS

Faneuil Hall Marketplace ★★ *Kids*   Since Boston's most popular attraction opened in 1976, cities all over the country have imitated the "festival market" concept. The complex of shops, food counters, restaurants, bars, and public spaces is such a magnet for tourists and suburbanites that you could be forgiven for thinking that the only Bostonians in the crowd are employees.

Boston Attractions

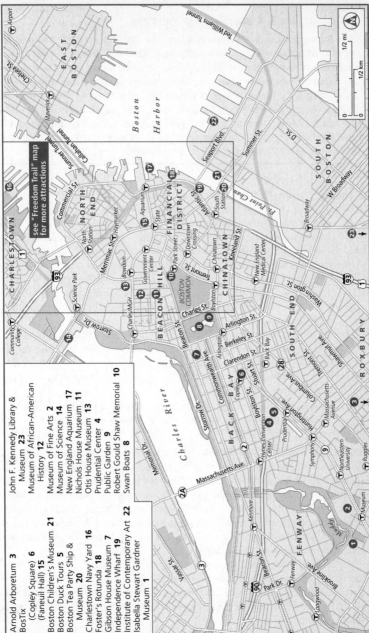

Arnold Arboretum 3
BosTix
(Copley Square) 6
(Faneuil Hall) 15
Boston Children's Museum 21
Boston Duck Tours 5
Boston Tea Party Ship &
Museum 20
Charlestown Navy Yard 16
Foster's Rotunda 18
Gibson House Museum 7
Independence Wharf 19
Institute of Contemporary Art 22
Isabella Stewart Gardner
Museum 1

John F. Kennedy Library &
Museum 23
Museum of African-American
History 12
Museum of Fine Arts 2
Museum of Science 14
New England Aquarium 17
Nichols House Museum 11
Otis House Museum 13
Prudential Center 4
Public Garden 9
Robert Gould Shaw Memorial 10
Swan Boats 8

see "Freedom Trail" map
for more attractions

Kids   Up, Up & Away: A Great View

The **Prudential Center Skywalk** ✸✸, on the 50th floor of 800 Boylston St. (© **617/859-0648**; www.topofthehub.net), offers a 360-degree view of Boston and beyond. When it's clear, you can see as far as the mountains of New Hampshire and the beaches of Cape Cod. Away from the windows, interactive audiovisual displays chronicle the city's history. It's open 10am to 10pm daily (call before visiting; the space sometimes closes for private events). Admission is $11 for adults, $9 for seniors, and $7.50 for children under 12, and includes a narrated audio tour. Adults must show an ID to enter the Prudential Tower. T: Green Line E to Prudential, or B, C, or D to Hynes Convention Center.

The five-building complex incorporates brick-and-stone plazas that teem with crowds shopping, eating, performing, watching performers, and people-watching. In warm weather, it's busy from just after dawn until well past dark. **Quincy Market** (you'll hear the whole complex called by that name) is the central Greek Revival–style building; its central corridor is an enormous food court. On either side, glass canopies cover restaurants, bars, and pushcarts that hold everything from crafts created by New England artisans to hokey souvenirs. Here you'll also see a bar that exactly replicates the set of the TV show *Cheers.* In the plaza between the **South Canopy** and the South Market building is an **information kiosk,** and throughout the complex you'll find a mix of chain stores and unique shops. One constant since the year after the original market opened (1826) is **Durgin-Park,** a traditional New England restaurant with traditionally crabby waitresses (p. 110). **Faneuil Hall** ✸ itself—nicknamed the "Cradle of Liberty"—sometimes gets overlooked, but it's well worth a visit. National Park Service rangers give free 20-minute talks every half-hour from 9am to 5pm in the second-floor auditorium.

Btw. North, Congress, and State sts. and I-93. © **617/523-1300.** www.faneuilhallmarketplace.com. Marketplace Mon–Sat 10am–9pm; Sun noon–6pm. Food court opens earlier; some restaurants and bars close later. T: Green or Blue Line to Government Center, Orange Line to Haymarket, or Blue Line to Aquarium or State.

Isabella Stewart Gardner Museum ✸✸   Isabella Stewart Gardner (1840–1924) was an incorrigible individualist long before such behavior was acceptable for a woman in polite Boston society, and her legacy is a treasure for art lovers. "Mrs. Jack" designed her exquisite home in the style of a 15th-century Venetian palace and filled it with European, American, and Asian painting and sculpture. You'll see works by Titian, Botticelli, Raphael, Rembrandt, Matisse, and Mrs. Gardner's friends James McNeill Whistler and John Singer Sargent. Titian's magnificent *Europa* is one of the most important Renaissance paintings in the United States.

The building holds a hodgepodge of furniture and architectural details imported from European churches and palaces. The *pièce de résistance* is the magnificent skylit courtyard, filled year-round with fresh flowers from the museum greenhouse. A special exhibition gallery features two or three changing shows a year, often by contemporary artists in residence.

280 The Fenway. © **617/566-1401.** www.gardnermuseum.org. Admission $12 adults, $10 seniors, $5 college students; free for children under 18 and adults named Isabella with ID. Tues–Sun, some Mon holidays 11am–5pm. T: Green Line E to Museum.

John F. Kennedy Library and Museum ★★ *Kids*   The Kennedy era springs to life at this dramatic complex overlooking Dorchester Bay. It captures the 35th president's accomplishments in video and audio recordings as well as fascinating displays of memorabilia and photos. Far from being a static experience, it changes regularly, with temporary shows and reinterpreted displays that highlight and complement the permanent exhibits. A visit begins with a 17-minute film about Kennedy's early life. The exhibits start with the 1960 campaign and end with a tribute to Kennedy's legacy. There's a film about the Cuban Missile Crisis, along with displays on Attorney General Robert F. Kennedy, the civil-rights movement, the Peace Corps, the space program, First Lady Jacqueline Bouvier Kennedy, and the Kennedy family.

Columbia Point. ✆ **866/JFK-1960** or 617/514-1600. www.jfklibrary.org. Admission $12 adults, $10 seniors and students with ID, $9 youths 13–17; free for children under 13. Surcharges may apply for special exhibitions. Daily 9am–5pm (last film at 3:55pm). T: Red Line to JFK/UMass, then free shuttle bus (every 20 min.). By car, take Southeast Expwy. (I-93/Rte. 3) south to exit 15 (Morrissey Blvd./JFK Library), turn left onto Columbia Rd., and follow signs to free parking lot.

Museum of African American History ★★ *Kids*   The final stop on the **Black Heritage Trail** (p. 121) offers a comprehensive look at the history and contributions of blacks in Boston and Massachusetts. Changing and permanent exhibits incorporate art, artifacts, documents, historic photographs, and other objects—including many family heirlooms. The museum occupies the **Abiel Smith School** (1834), the first American public grammar school for African-American children, and the **African Meeting House,** 8 Smith Court. The oldest standing black church in the United States, the meetinghouse opened in 1806. Once known as the "Black Faneuil Hall," it also schedules lectures, concerts, and church meetings.

46 Joy St. ✆ **617/725-0022.** www.afroammuseum.org. Free admission; suggested donation $5. Mon–Sat 10am–4pm. T: Red or Green Line to Park St. or Red Line to Charles/MGH.

Museum of Fine Arts ★★★ *Kids*   One of the world's great museums, the MFA works constantly to become even more accessible and interesting. Every installation reflects a curatorial attitude that makes even those who go in with a feeling of obligation leave with a sense of discovery and wonder. That includes children, who can launch a scavenger hunt, admire the mummies, or participate in family-friendly programs scheduled year-round.

The MFA is especially noted for its **Impressionist paintings** ★★★ (including dozens of Monets), Asian and Old Kingdom Egyptian collections, classical art, Buddhist temple, and medieval sculpture and tapestries. The American and European paintings and sculpture are a remarkable assemblage of timeless works that may seem as familiar as the face in the mirror or as unexpected as a comet. There are also magnificent holdings of prints, photography, furnishings, and decorative arts, including the finest collection of Paul Revere silver in the world. The museum has two restaurants, a cafe, and a cafeteria. Pick up a floor plan at the information desk, or take a free **guided tour** (weekdays except Mon holidays at 10:30am–3pm; Wed at 6:15pm; Sat–Sun 11am–3pm).

Note that the MFA's admission fees are among the highest in the country. A Boston CityPass (see the introduction to this section) is a great deal if you plan to visit enough of the other included attractions.

An enormous expansion project began in 2005. While construction proceeds, the museum is rearranging some collections and closing some exhibition spaces. Check ahead before visiting if you have your heart set on seeing a particular work of art. And check out the dramatic revamped entrance from the Fenway, which reopened in 2008, 2 years ahead of schedule.

465 Huntington Ave. © 617/267-9300. www.mfa.org. Admission $17 adults, $15 seniors and students when entire museum is open ($2 discount when only West Wing is open); $6.50 children 7–17 on school days until 3pm, otherwise free. Admission good for 2 visits within 10 days. Voluntary contribution ($17 suggested) Wed 4–9:45pm. Surcharges may apply for special exhibitions. Free admission for museum shop, library, restaurants, and auditoriums. Entire museum Sat–Tues 10am–4:45pm; Wed 10am–9:45pm; Thurs–Fri 10am–5pm. West Wing only Thurs–Fri 5–9:45pm. T: Green Line E to Museum or Orange Line to Ruggles.

Museum of Science ✦✦✦ (Kids)   For the ultimate pain-free educational experience, head to the Museum of Science. The demonstrations, experiments, and interactive displays introduce facts and concepts so effortlessly that everyone learns something. Take a couple of hours or a whole day to explore the permanent and temporary exhibits, most of them hands-on and all of them great fun. Among the hundreds of exhibits, you might find out how much you'd weigh on the moon, battle urban traffic (in a computer model), or climb into a space module. Activity centers focus on individual and interdisciplinary fields of interest—natural history (with live animals), computers, and the human body. Temporary exhibits change regularly, and just about any time you hear about a national or international touring show, this is one of its stops.

The separate-admission theaters are worth planning for, even if you're skipping the exhibits. Buy all your tickets at once, because shows sometimes sell out. The **Mugar Omni Theater** ✦✦✦, which shows IMAX movies on a five-story screen, is an intense experience. The **Charles Hayden Planetarium** ✦✦ takes you into space with daily star shows, as well as shows on special topics that change several times a year. On weekends, rock-music laser shows take over.

Science Park, off O'Brien Hwy. on bridge btw. Boston and Cambridge. © 617/723-2500. www.mos.org. Admission to exhibit halls $17 adults, $15 seniors, $14 children 3–11. Mugar Omni Theater, Hayden Planetarium, or laser shows $9 adults, $8 seniors, $7 children 3–11. Discounted combination tickets available. July 5 to Labor Day Sat–Thurs 9am–7pm, Fri 9am–9pm; day after Labor Day to July 4 Sat–Thurs 9am–5pm, Fri 9am–9pm. Extended hours during school vacations. T: Green Line to Science Park.

New England Aquarium ✦ (Kids)   This entertaining complex is home to more than 15,000 fish and aquatic mammals. At busy times, it seems to contain at least that many people—try to make this your first stop of the day, especially on weekends. You'll want to spend at least half a day, and afternoon crowds can make getting around painfully slow. Also consider buying a Boston CityPass (p. 116); it allows you to skip the ticket line. The **Simons IMAX Theatre** ✦✦✦, which has its own hours and admission fees, is worth planning ahead for, too. It shows 3-D films that concentrate on the natural world. Discounts are available when you combine a visit to the aquarium with an IMAX film or a whale watch (see "Organized Tours," below).

The focal point of the main building is the four-story, 200,000-gallon **Giant Ocean Tank.** It holds a replica of a Caribbean coral reef, a vast assortment of sea creatures and, twice a day, scuba divers who feed the sharks. Other exhibits focus on freshwater and tropical specimens, the Amazon, jellyfish, and the ecology of Boston Harbor. The hands-on **Edge of the Sea** exhibit contains a tide pool with sea stars, sea urchins, and horseshoe crabs, and the **Medical Center** is a working veterinary hospital.

Central Wharf (off Atlantic Ave. at State St.). © 617/973-5200. www.newenglandaquarium.org. Admission $19 adults, $11 children 3–11. Free admission for outdoor exhibits, cafe, and gift shop. July to Labor Day Mon–Thurs 9am–6pm, Fri–Sun and holidays 9am–7pm; day after Labor Day to June Mon–Fri 9am–5pm, Sat–Sun and holidays 9am–6pm. Simons IMAX Theatre: © 866/815-4629 or 617/973-5206. Tickets $10 adults, $8 children 3–11. Thurs–Sat 10am–8pm; Sun–Mon 10am–6pm. T: Blue Line to Aquarium.

> **Tips A Note on Online Ticketing**
>
> Many museums and other attractions sell tickets online, subject to a service charge, through their websites or an agency. This can be handy, but it can also cost you some flexibility and perhaps some money. If there's any chance that your plans will change, make sure you **understand the refund policy** before you enter your credit card info—you may not be able to return or exchange pre-paid tickets.

THE FREEDOM TRAIL ✦✦✦

A line of red paint or red brick down the center of the sidewalk, the 2½-mile Freedom Trail links 16 historic sights. Markers identify the stops, and plaques point the way from one to the next. The trail begins at **Boston Common,** where the Information Center, 148 Tremont St., distributes pamphlets that describe a self-guided tour.

A 2-hour narrative commissioned by the Freedom Trail Foundation (© 617/357-8300; www.thefreedomtrail.org) includes interviews, sound effects, and music, and allows visitors to tour the trail at their own pace. It costs $15 (credit cards only); buy it as an MP3 download, or rent a handheld digital audio player, for use with or without headphones, that can be picked up at the Boston Common Visitor Center and dropped off there or at several other sites. The foundation's costumed **Freedom Trail Players** lead 90-minute tours ($12 adults, $10 seniors and students, $6 children under 13) on two different, overlapping routes around downtown and the North End. Make reservations online, allowing time to explore the interactive website.

You can also explore the 1.6-mile **Black Heritage Trail** ✦✦ from here. Two-hour guided tours start at the **Robert Gould Shaw Memorial,** on Beacon Street across from the State House. They're available Monday through Saturday from Memorial Day to Labor Day and by request at other times; contact the visitor center (© 617/742-5415; www.nps.gov/boaf) for starting times or to make a reservation. Or go on your own, using a brochure (available at the Museum of African American History and the Boston Common and State Street visitor centers) that includes a map and descriptions of the buildings. The trail includes stations on the Underground Railroad and homes of famous citizens. The only stops that are open to the public are the **African Meeting House** and the **Abiel Smith School,** which make up the **Museum of African American History** (p. 119).

As you follow the Freedom Trail, you'll come to the **Boston National Historical Park Visitor Center,** 15 State St. (© 617/242-5642; www.nps.gov/bost). From here, rangers lead free tours of the heart of the trail from April to September. The first-come-first-served tours are limited to 30 people and not offered in bad weather. The wheelchair-accessible center has restrooms and a bookstore. It's open daily from 9am to 5pm.

The hard-core history fiend who peers at every artifact and reads every plaque along the trail will wind up at Bunker Hill some 4 hours later, weary but rewarded. The family with restless children will probably appreciate the enforced efficiency of the 90-minute ranger-led tour.

Space doesn't permit detailing every stop on the trail, but here's a concise listing:

- **Boston Common.** In 1634, when their settlement was just 4 years old, the town fathers paid the Rev. William Blackstone £30 for this property. In 1640, it was set aside as common land. Be sure to stop at Beacon and Park streets, where a **memorial** ✯✯✯ designed by Augustus Saint-Gaudens celebrates Col. Robert Gould Shaw and the Union Army's 54th Massachusetts Colored Regiment, who fought in the Civil War. You may remember the story of the first American army unit made up of free black soldiers from the movie *Glory.*

- **Massachusetts State House** (✆ 617/727-3676; www.mass.gov/statehouse). Charles Bulfinch designed the "new" State House, and Gov. Samuel Adams laid the cornerstone of the state capitol in 1795. Take a self-guided tour or call ahead to schedule a conducted tour (weekdays 10am–3:30pm).

- **Park Street Church,** 1 Park St. (✆ 617/523-3383; www.parkstreet.org). The plaque at the corner of Tremont Street describes this Congregational church's storied past. From mid-June through August, it's open for tours Tuesday through Saturday from 9am to 3:30pm. Year-round Sunday services are at 8:30am, 11am, 4pm, and 6pm.

- **Old Granary Burying Ground.** This cemetery, established in 1660, contains the graves of Samuel Adams, Paul Revere, John Hancock, and the wife of Isaac Vergoose, believed to be the "Mother Goose" of nursery-rhyme fame. It's open daily from 9am to 5pm (until 3pm in winter).

- **King's Chapel,** 58 Tremont St. (✆ 227-2155; www.kings-chapel.org). Completed in 1754, this church was built by erecting the granite edifice around the existing wooden chapel. The **burying ground** (1630), facing Tremont Street, is the oldest in Boston. It's open daily from 8am to 5:30pm (until 3pm in winter).

- **Site of the First Public School.** A colorful mosaic in the sidewalk on (of course) School Street honors the school, founded in 1634. Inside the fence that surrounds adjacent Old City Hall is the 1856 statue of **Benjamin Franklin,** the first portrait statue erected in Boston.

- **Old Corner Bookstore Building,** 3 School St. Built in 1718, it's on a plot of land that was once home to the religious reformer Anne Hutchinson.

- **Old South Meeting House,** 310 Washington St. (✆ 617/482-6439; www.old southmeetinghouse.org). Originally built in 1670 and replaced by the current structure in 1729, it was the starting point of the Boston Tea Party. It's open daily, April to October from 9:30am to 5pm, November to March from 10am to 4pm. Admission is $5 for adults, $4 for seniors, and $1 for children 6 to 18.

- **Old State House Museum** ✯, 206 Washington St. (✆ 617/720-1713; www. bostonhistory.org). Built in 1713, this building was the seat of Colonial government in Massachusetts before the Revolution, and the state capitol until 1798. The fascinating exhibits spotlight city history. The museum is open daily from 9am to 6pm in July and August, until 4pm in January, and until 5pm the rest of the year. Admission is $5 for adults, $4 for seniors and students, and $1 for children 6 to 18.

- **Boston Massacre Site.** On a traffic island in State Street, across from the T station under the Old State House, a ring of cobblestones marks the place where the skirmish took place on March 5, 1770.

- **Faneuil Hall** ✯ (✆ 617/242-5675; www.nps.gov/bost). Built in 1742, and enlarged using a Charles Bulfinch design in 1805, it was a gift to the city from the merchant Peter Faneuil. National Park Service rangers give free 20-minute talks every half-hour from 9am to 5pm in the second-floor auditorium.

The Freedom Trail

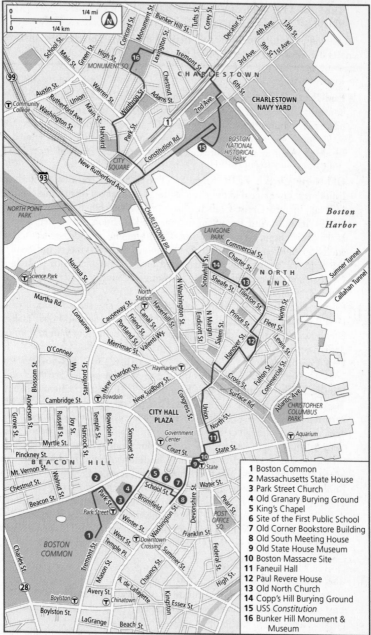

1 Boston Common
2 Massachusetts State House
3 Park Street Church
4 Old Granary Burying Ground
5 King's Chapel
6 Site of the First Public School
7 Old Corner Bookstore Building
8 Old South Meeting House
9 Old State House Museum
10 Boston Massacre Site
11 Faneuil Hall
12 Paul Revere House
13 Old North Church
14 Copp's Hill Burying Ground
15 USS *Constitution*
16 Bunker Hill Monument & Museum

Tips **Out to Sea**

A fun way to return to downtown from Charlestown is on the **ferry** that connects the Navy Yard to Long Wharf (near the Aquarium). It costs $1.70.

- **Paul Revere House** ★★★, 19 North Sq. (© **617/523-2338;** www.paulrevere house.org). The oldest house in downtown Boston (built around 1680) presents history on a human scale. It's open April 15 through October daily from 9:30am to 5:15pm, November through April 14 from 9:30am to 4:15pm (closed Mon Jan–Mar). Admission is $3 for adults, $2.50 for seniors and students, and $1 for children 5 to 17.
- **Old North Church** ★, 193 Salem St. (© **617/523-6676;** www.oldnorth.com). Paul Revere saw a signal in this church's steeple and set out on his "midnight ride." Officially named Christ Church, this is the oldest church building in Boston (1723). It's open daily from 9am to 5pm; a $3 donation is requested. Free tours of the church begin every 15 minutes. The 50-minute behind-the-scenes tour ($8 adults, $5 children under 17; buy tickets online) includes visits to the steeple and the crypt; it's available on weekdays and on weekend afternoons from June to October, and the rest of the year by appointment. Sunday services (Episcopal) are at 9 and 11am.
- **Copp's Hill Burying Ground,** off Hull Street. The second-oldest cemetery (1659) in the city, it contains the graves of Cotton Mather and Prince Hall, who established the first black Masonic lodge. It's open daily from 9am to 5pm (until 3pm in winter).
- **USS** *Constitution* ★★, Charlestown Navy Yard (© **617/242-5670;** www.old ironsides.com). Active-duty sailors in 1812 dress uniforms give free tours of "Old Ironsides." They begin every half-hour between 10am and 3:30pm in summer Tuesday through Sunday, and in winter Thursday through Sunday. The **USS** *Constitution* **Museum** ★ (© **617/426-1812;** www.ussconstitutionmuseum.org) is open daily May through October 15 from 9am to 6pm, October 16 through April from 10am to 5pm. Admission is free; donations are encouraged. National Park Service rangers staff the adjacent **Charlestown Navy Yard Visitor Center** (© **617/242-5601**) and give free 1-hour guided tours of the base.
- **Bunker Hill Monument** (© **617/242-5641;** www.nps.gov/bost), Charlestown. The 221-foot granite obelisk honors the memory of the men who died in the Battle of Bunker Hill on June 17, 1775. A punishing flight of 294 stairs leads to the top. National Park Service rangers staff the monument, which is open daily from 9am to 5pm (climbing stops at 4:30pm). Admission to the monument and to the museum across the street is free.

HOUSE MUSEUMS

The most fascinating historic home in Boston is the **Paul Revere House** (p. 124). To see three other interesting residences, you must take a guided tour. Check ahead for open days and hours.

On Beacon Hill, you'll find two houses as notable for their Charles Bulfinch architecture as for their occupants. Tours of the 1796 **Otis House Museum** ★★, 141 Cambridge St. (© **617/227-3956;** www.spnea.org), home of a young lawyer who was later mayor of Boston, discuss post-Revolutionary social, business, and family life. Tours cost $8. The 1804 **Nichols House Museum** *, 55 Mount Vernon St. (© 617/ 227-6993; www.nicholshousemuseum.org), holds beautiful antique furnishings collected by several generations of the Nichols family. Tours cost $7.

Nearby, in the Back Bay, the **Gibson House Museum**, 137 Beacon St. (© 617/ 267-6338; www.thegibsonhouse.org), is a lavishly decorated 1859 brownstone that embodies the word *Victorian*. Tours cost $7.

PARKS & GARDENS

The best-known park in Boston is the spectacular **Public Garden** ***, bordered by Arlington, Boylston, Charles, and Beacon streets. Something lovely is in bloom at the country's first botanical garden at least half of the year. For 5 months, the lagoon is home to the celebrated **Swan Boats** (© 617/522-1966; www.swanboats.com). The pedal-powered vessels—the attendants pedal, not the passengers—come out of hibernation on the Saturday before Patriots Day (the 3rd Mon of Apr). They operate in summer daily from 10am to 5pm; in spring daily from 10am to 4pm; and from Labor Day to mid-September Monday through Friday from noon to 4pm and Saturday and Sunday from 10am to 4pm. The 15-minute ride costs $2.75 for adults, $2 for seniors, and $1.25 for children 2 to 15.

Even more spectacular is the **Arnold Arboretum** **, 125 Arborway, Jamaica Plain (© 617/524-1718; www.arboretum.harvard.edu). One of the oldest parks in the United States, founded in 1872, it is open daily from sunrise to sunset. Admission is free. The 265-acre Frederick Law Olmsted design contains more than 15,000 ornamental trees, shrubs, and vines from all over the world. Lilac Sunday, in May, is the only time picnicking is allowed. To get here, take the Orange Line to Forest Hills and follow signs to the entrance.

ORGANIZED TOURS

WALKING TOURS **   From May to October, the nonprofit **Boston by Foot** ** (© 617/367-2345, or 617/367-3766 for recorded info; www.bostonbyfoot.com) conducts excellent historical and architectural tours that focus on neighborhoods or themes. The rigorously trained volunteer guides encourage questions. Buy tickets ($12 adults, $8 children 6–12; Boston Underfoot $14 per person) from the guide; reservations are not required. The 90-minute tours take place rain or shine.

Historic New England (© 617/227-3956; www.historic.org) offers a fascinating tour that describes life in the mansions and garrets of Beacon Hill in 1800. "Magnificent and Modest" ($12, including museum tour) starts at the Otis House Museum,

---

(Finds Eyes in the Skies

For a smashing view of the airport, the harbor, and the South Boston waterfront, stroll along the water or Atlantic Avenue to Northern Avenue. On either side of this intersection are buildings with free observation areas. Be ready to show an ID. The first, on the 14th floor of Independence Wharf, 470 Atlantic Ave., is open daily from 11am to 5pm. Foster's Rotunda, on the ninth floor of 30 Rowes Wharf, in the Boston Harbor Hotel complex, is open Monday to Friday from 11am to 4pm.

Kids Boston by Duck

The most unusual and enjoyable way to see Boston is with **Boston Duck Tours** ✹✹✹ (© 800/226-7442 or 617/267-DUCK; www.bostonducktours.com). The tours, offered from late March to November, are pricey but great fun. Sightseers board a "duck," a reconditioned World War II amphibious landing craft, behind the Prudential Center on Huntington Avenue or at the Museum of Science. The 80-minute narrated tour begins with a quick but comprehensive jaunt around the city. Then the duck lumbers down a ramp, splashes into the Charles River, and takes a spin around the basin. Tickets cost $29 for adults, $25 for seniors and students, $19 for children 3 to 11, and $3 for children under 3. Tours run every 30 to 60 minutes from 9am to a half-hour before sunset. You can buy tickets online or in person (at the Prudential Center, the Museum of Science, and Faneuil Hall). Try to buy same-day tickets early in the day, or ask about the limited number of tickets available starting 30 days in advance. Reservations are not accepted (except for groups of more than 19). No tours December through mid-March.

141 Cambridge St., at 11am on Saturday from May to October. Reservations are recommended.

TROLLEY TOURS   Because Boston is so pedestrian friendly, a trolley tour isn't the best choice for the able-bodied and unencumbered making a long visit. But if you're short on time, unable to walk long distances, or traveling with children, a trolley tour can be worth the money. The narrated tour can give you an overview before you focus on specific attractions, or you can use your all-day pass to hit as many places as possible in 8 hours or so.

The various companies cover the major attractions and offer informative narratives in their 90- to 120-minute tours. Most offer free reboarding if you want to visit the sites. Tickets cost $29 to $40 for adults, $16 or less for children (subject to fuel surcharges). Boarding spots are at hotels, historic sites, and tourist information centers. Each company paints its cars a different color. They include orange-and-green **Old Town Trolley Tours** (© 617/269-7150; www.trolleytours.com); **Beantown Trolleys** (© 800/343-1328 or 617/720-6342; www.grayline.com), which say "Gray Line" but are red; and silver **CityView Trolleys** (© 617/363-7899; www.cityviewtrolleys.com). The **Super Trolley Tours** (© 617/742-1440; www.bostonsupertrolleytours.com) vehicle is white; its narration is available translated into Japanese, Spanish, French, German, and Italian.

SIGHTSEEING CRUISES ✹✹   The season runs from April to October, with spring and fall offerings often restricted to weekends. Check websites for discount coupons before you leave home. If you're prone to seasickness, check the size of the vessel (larger equals more comfortable) before buying tickets.

Boston Harbor Cruises, 1 Long Wharf (© 877/733-9425 or 617/227-4321; www.bostonharborcruises.com), is the largest company. Ninety-minute historic sightseeing cruises depart daily at 11am, 1, 3, and 6 or 7pm (the sunset cruise), with extra excursions at busy times. Tickets are $19 for adults, $17 for seniors, and $15 for children 4 to 12; sunset-cruise tickets are $1 more. The 45-minute USS *Constitution* cruise schedule gives you time to visit Old Ironsides. Tours leave Long Wharf hourly from 10:30am to 4:30pm, and on the hour from the Navy Yard from 11am to 5pm. Tickets are $14 for adults, $12 for seniors, and $10 for children.

Massachusetts Bay Lines (© 617/542-8000; www.massbaylines.com) offers 55-minute harbor tours. Cruises leave Rowes Wharf on the hour from 11am to 6pm (until 5pm after Labor Day); the price is $16 for adults, $12 for children and seniors. The 90-minute sunset (7pm, 6pm after Labor Day) and moonlight (8:45pm, weekends only) cruises each cost $19 for adults, $16 for children and seniors.

The **Charles Riverboat Company** (© 617/621-3001; www.charlesriverboat.com; T: Green Line to Lechmere) offers 60-minute narrated cruises around the lower Charles River basin five times daily, a daily tour of the Charles River lock system and Boston Harbor at 10am, and a daily sunset cruise (call for times). Boats leave from the CambridgeSide Galleria mall, and tickets cost $13 for adults, $10 for seniors, $6 for children.

WHALE-WATCHING ★★   For information on Cape Ann excursions, see "A Whale of an Adventure," in chapter 6.

The **New England Aquarium** (p. 120) runs whale-watching trips (© 617/973-5200 for information, 617/973-5206 for tickets) daily from May to mid-October and on weekends in April and late October. They travel several miles out to Stellwagen Bank, the feeding ground for whales as they migrate from Newfoundland to Provincetown. Allow 3½ to 5 hours. Tickets are $36 for adults, $33 for seniors and college students, $30 for children 3 to 11. Children must be at least 3 years old and 30 inches tall. Reservations are strongly recommended; you can also buy tickets online.

With its onboard exhibits and vast experience, the Aquarium offers the best whale-watches in Boston. If they're booked, try **Boston Harbor Cruises** (© 877/SEE-WHALE or 617/227-4321; www.bostonharborcruises.com), which operates high-speed catamarans, or **Massachusetts Bay Lines** (© 617/542-8000; www.massbaylines.com).

ESPECIALLY FOR KIDS

Destinations with something for every family member include **Faneuil Hall Marketplace** (© 617/523-1300) and the **Museum of Fine Arts** (© 617/267-9300), which offers special weekend and after-school programs. Hands-on exhibits and large-format films are the headliners at the **New England Aquarium** (© 617/973-5200) and the **Museum of Science** (© 617/723-2500). A **Red Sox game** (see "Spectator Sports," later in this chapter) is another sure-fire kid pleaser.

The allure of seeing people the size of ants draws young visitors to the **Prudential Center Skywalk** (© 617/236-3318). They can see actual ants—though they might prefer dinosaurs—at the Museum of Comparative Zoology, part of the **Harvard Museum of Natural History** (© 617/495-3045; see "Exploring Cambridge," below).

Older children who have studied American history will enjoy a visit to the **John F. Kennedy Library and Museum** (© 617/929-4523). Middle-schoolers who enjoyed Esther Forbes's *Johnny Tremain* might get a kick out of the **Paul Revere House** (© 617/523-2338). Young visitors who have read Robert McCloskey's children's classic *Make Way for Ducklings* will relish a visit to the **Public Garden,** as will fans of E. B. White's *The Trumpet of the Swan,* who certainly will want to ride on the **Swan Boats.** Considerably less tame and much longer are **whale watches** (see "Organized

Welcome to the North End

The Paul Revere House and the Old North Church are the best-known buildings in the **North End** ✿✿✿, Boston's "Little Italy" (although it's *never* called that). Home to natives of Italy and their assimilated children, numerous Italian restaurants and private social clubs, and many historic sights, this is one of the oldest neighborhoods in the city. It was home in the 17th century to the **Mather family** of Puritan ministers, who certainly would be shocked to see the merry goings-on at the festivals and street fairs that take over different areas of the North End on weekends in July and August.

The Italians (and their yuppie neighbors who have made inroads since the 1980s) are only the latest immigrant group to dominate the North End. In the 19th century, this was an Eastern European Jewish enclave and later an Irish stronghold. In 1890, President Kennedy's mother, Rose Fitzgerald, was born on Garden Court Street and baptized at St. Stephen's Church.

Modern visitors might be more interested in a Hanover Street *caffè*, the perfect place to have coffee or a soft drink and feast on sweets. **Mike's Pastry** ✿✿✿, 300 Hanover St. (© 617/742-3050; www.mikespastry.com), is a bakery that does a frantic takeout business and has tables where you can sit down and order one of the confections on display in the cases. The signature item is cannoli (tubes of crisp-fried pastry filled with sweetened ricotta cheese); the cookies, cakes, and other pastries are excellent, too. You can also sit and relax at **Caffè dello Sport** or **Caffè Vittoria,** on either side of Mike's.

Before you leave the North End, stroll down toward the water and see whether there's a **bocce** game going on at the courts on Commercial Street near Hull Street. The European pastime is both a game of skill and an excuse to hang around and shoot the breeze—in Italian and English—with the locals (mostly men of a certain age). It's so popular that the neighborhood has courts both outdoors, in the Langone Playground at Puopolo Park, and indoors, at the back of the Steriti Rink, 561 Commercial St.

Tours," above, and "A Whale of an Adventure," in chapter 6); **sightseeing cruises** fall somewhere in the middle.

The **Boston Tea Party Ship & Museum** (© 617/338-1773; www.bostonteaparty ship.com) closed after a fire in late 2001. It's currently renovating, expanding, and planning to reopen in 2009. It makes an entertaining stop on the way to or from the Children's Museum.

The walking-tour company **Boston by Foot** ✿✿ (© 617/367-2345, or 617/367-3766 for recorded info; www.bostonbyfoot.com) has a special program, **Boston by Little Feet,** geared to children 6 to 12. The 1-hour walk gives a child's-eye view of the architecture along the Freedom Trail and of Boston's role in the American Revolution. Children must be accompanied by an adult. Tours ($8 per person) run May through October and meet at the statue of Samuel Adams on the Congress Street side of Faneuil Hall Friday and Saturday at 10am, Sunday at 2pm, rain or shine.

Boston Children's Museum 🏃🏃 *Kids*   A delightful destination for kids under 11, the Children's Museum is great fun for adults, too. Children can stick with the family or wander on their own. The centerpiece of the warehouse, which was renovated and expanded in 2007, is a two-story-high maze that incorporates motor skills and problem-solving. The hands-on exhibits include, among many others, **Johnny's Workbench,** a souped-up version of puttering in the garage; physical experiments (such as creating giant soap bubbles); and **Boats Afloat,** which has an 800-gallon play tank and a replica of the bridge of a working boat. A special room, **Playspace,** is packed with toys and activities for children under 4 and their caregivers. Check ahead for information on traveling exhibitions and other special programs.

300 Congress St. (Museum Wharf). ℭ 617/426-8855. www.bostonchildrensmuseum.org. Admission $10 adults, $8 seniors and children 2–15, $2 children age 1, free for children under 1; Fri 5–9pm $1 for all. Sat–Thurs 10am–5pm; Fri 10am–9pm. T: Red Line to South Station. Walk north on Atlantic Ave. 1 block (past Federal Reserve Bank), turn right onto Congress St., walk 2 blocks. Or Silver Line to Courthouse; walk toward downtown and turn left at the Fort Point Channel. Call for information on discounted parking.

6 Exploring Cambridge

Harvard Square 🏃🏃 is a people-watching paradise of students, instructors, commuters, shoppers, and sightseers. Restaurants and stores pack the three streets that radiate from the center of the square and the streets that intersect them. On weekend afternoons and evenings year-round, you'll hear music and see street performers. To get away from the urban bustle, stroll down to the paved paths along the Charles River.

From Boston, take the Red Line toward Alewife. In Cambridge, the subway stops at Kendall/MIT, and Central, Harvard, and Porter squares. If you're staying in or visiting the Back Bay, a more interesting route is the no. 1 bus (Harvard–Dudley), which runs along Mass. Ave.

By car from Boston, follow Mass. Ave., or take Storrow Drive along the south bank of the river to the Harvard Square exit. Memorial Drive runs along the north side of the river near MIT, Central Square, and Harvard. Traffic in and around Harvard Square is almost as bad as in downtown Boston. After you reach Cambridge, park and walk.

HARVARD UNIVERSITY

Harvard is the oldest college in the country, and if you suggest aloud that it's not the best, you may encounter the attitude that inspired the saying "You can always tell a Harvard man, but you can't tell him much." The university encompasses the college and 10 graduate and professional schools in more than 400 buildings around Boston and Cambridge. Free student-led tours of the main campus leave from the **Information Center,** in Holyoke Center, 1350 Mass. Ave. (ℭ **617/495-1573**), during the school year twice a day weekdays and once on Saturday (except during vacations), and during the summer four times a day Monday through Saturday. Check ahead for exact times; reservations aren't necessary. You're also free to wander on your own. The center has maps, illustrated booklets, and self-guided walking-tour directions. Before visiting, check out the university's website, www.harvard.edu.

Harvard Art Museum   In June 2008, Harvard's Fogg and Busch-Reisinger museums closed for renovations scheduled to last 5 years. In the interim, the Sackler Museum is showing highlights from all three institutions' collections. Before you add this stop to your itinerary, check the website for specifics of what's on exhibit—I, for one, can't wait to see what kind of lemonade the inventive curators will make from this lemon-scented situation, but you may feel differently.

The collections of the Fogg, Busch-Reisinger, and Sackler museums encompass a quarter-million works, from ancient sculptures to contemporary photos. The **Arthur M. Sackler Museum** houses Harvard's world-famous collections of Asian, ancient, Islamic, and Later Indian art. Here you'll find internationally renowned Chinese jades, superb Roman sculpture, Greek vases, Korean ceramics, Japanese woodblock prints, and Persian miniature paintings and calligraphy. The **Fogg Museum**'s holdings include everything from 17th-century Dutch and Flemish landscapes to Impressionist masterpieces to contemporary sculpture. The **Busch-Reisinger Museum**'s specialty is the art of northern and central Europe, specifically Germany; the early-20th-century holdings are particularly notable. Exhibit spaces also serve as teaching and research facilities; keep an ear out for instructors leading classes.

485 Broadway. ✆ 617/495-9400. www.artmuseums.harvard.edu. Admission $9 adults, $7 seniors, $6 students, free for children under 18; free to all before noon Sat. Mon–Sat 10am–5pm; Sun 1–5pm. Closed major holidays. T: Red Line to Harvard, cross Harvard Yard diagonally from the T station and exit onto Quincy St., turn left, and walk to the next corner. Or turn your back on the Coop and follow Mass. Ave. to Quincy St., then turn left and walk 1 long block.

Harvard Museum of Natural History and Peabody Museum of Archaeology & Ethnology ✦ (Kids)

These fascinating museums house the university's collections of items and artifacts related to the natural world. The world-famous academic resource offers interdisciplinary programs and exhibitions that tie in elements of all the associated fields. On weekends, staffed "Investigation Stations" help visitors learn through hands-on activities. You'll certainly find something interesting here, be it a dinosaur skeleton, the largest turtle shell in the world, a Native American artifact, or the world-famous Glass Flowers.

The **Glass Flowers** ✦✦✦ are 3,000 models of more than 840 plant species devised between 1887 and 1936 by the German father-and-son team of Leopold and Rudolph Blaschka. You may have heard about them, and you may be skeptical, but it's true: They look real. Children love the **zoological collections** ✦✦, where dinosaurs share space with preserved and stuffed insects and animals that range in size from butterflies to giraffes. The **Peabody Museum** ✦ boasts the **Hall of the North American Indian,** which displays 500 artifacts representing 10 cultures. Photographs, textiles, pottery, and art and crafts of all ages and descriptions fill the galleries.

Museum of Natural History: 26 Oxford St. ✆ 617/495-3045. www.hmnh.harvard.edu. Peabody Museum: 11 Divinity Ave. ✆ 617/496-1027. www.peabody.harvard.edu. Admission to both $9 adults, $7 seniors and students, $6 children 3–18; free to MA residents Sun until noon year-round and Wed 3–5pm. Daily 9am–5pm. T: Red Line to Harvard. Cross Harvard Yard, keeping John Harvard statue on right, and bear right before Science Center. First left is Oxford St. Check website for parking info.

A HISTORIC HOUSE

Longfellow National Historic Site ✦

The books and furniture inside the yellow mansion have remained intact since the poet Henry Wadsworth Longfellow died here in 1882. During the siege of Boston in 1775–76, the house served as the headquarters of Gen. George Washington, with whom Longfellow was fascinated. On the absorbing tour—the only way to see the house—you'll learn about the history of the building and its famous occupants.

105 Brattle St. ✆ 617/876-4491. www.nps.gov/long. Guided tours $3 adults, free for children under 17. Call ahead to confirm hours and tour times. June–Oct Wed–Sun 10am–4:30pm. Tours 10:30 and 11:30am and 1, 2, 3, and 4pm. Closed Nov–May. T: Red Line to Harvard, then follow Brattle St. about 7 blocks; house is on the right.

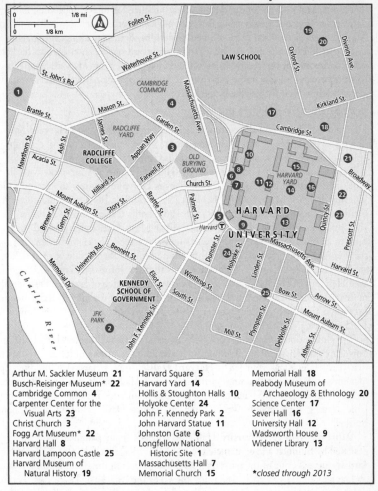

Arthur M. Sackler Museum **21**
Busch-Reisinger Museum* **22**
Cambridge Common **4**
Carpenter Center for the
    Visual Arts **23**
Christ Church **3**
Fogg Art Museum* **22**
Harvard Hall **8**
Harvard Lampoon Castle **25**
Harvard Museum of
    Natural History **19**

Harvard Square **5**
Harvard Yard **14**
Hollis & Stoughton Halls **10**
Holyoke Center **24**
John F. Kennedy Park **2**
John Harvard Statue **11**
Johnston Gate **6**
Longfellow National
    Historic Site **1**
Massachusetts Hall **7**
Memorial Church **15**

Memorial Hall **18**
Peabody Museum of
    Archaeology & Ethnology **20**
Science Center **17**
Sever Hall **16**
University Hall **12**
Wadsworth House **9**
Widener Library **13**

*closed through 2013

A CELEBRATED CEMETERY

Dedicated in 1831, **Mount Auburn Cemetery** ⋆, 580 Mt. Auburn St. (© 617/547-7105; www.mountauburn.org), was the first of America's rural, or garden, cemeteries. Since the day it opened, Mount Auburn has been a popular place to retreat and reflect. The graves of Henry Wadsworth Longfellow, Oliver Wendell Holmes, Mary Baker Eddy, Winslow Homer, and many other prominent New Englanders are here. In season, you'll see gorgeous flowering trees and shrubs. Stop at the **visitor center** in Story Chapel (daily 9am–4pm Apr–Oct except during burials; closed Sun Nov–Mar) for an overview and a look at the changing exhibits, or ask at the office or front gate for brochures and a map. You can rent a CD or tape of a 60-minute driving or 75-minute walking tour ($7; a $15 deposit is required) and listen in your car or on a portable player. The **Friends of Mount Auburn Cemetery** conduct workshops and lectures and coordinate walking tours; call the main number for topics, schedules, and fees. The cemetery is open daily from 8am to 5pm October through April, 8am to 7pm May through September; there is no admission fee. Pets, picnicking, and jogging are not allowed. Bus route nos. 71 and 73 start at Harvard station and stop near the gates; they run frequently on weekdays, less often on weekends. From Harvard Square by car (5 min.) or on foot (30 min.), take Mount Auburn Street or Brattle Street west; just after they intersect, the gate is on the left.

A STROLL AROUND CAMBRIDGE

To explore Harvard and the surrounding area, begin your walk in **Harvard Square.** Town and gown meet at this lively intersection, where you'll get a taste of the improbable mix of people drawn to the crossroads of Cambridge.

Start at the Harvard T station, with the **Harvard Coop** at your back. Walk half a block, crossing Dunster Street. To your right is **Holyoke Center,** an administration building designed by the Spanish architect Josep Luis Sert, the dean of the university's Graduate School of Design from 1953 to 1969, and a disciple of Le Corbusier.

Across the street is **Wadsworth House,** 1341 Mass. Ave., a yellow wood structure built in 1726 as a residence for Harvard's fourth president. Its claim to fame is a classic: George Washington slept here. Turn left and follow the outside of the brick wall along Mass. Ave. to another T entrance. Pass through **Johnston Gate,** which guards the oldest part of **Harvard Yard.** "The Yard" was just a patch of grass with grazing animals when Harvard College was established in 1636 to train young men for the ministry. The Continental Army, under Washington's command, spent the winter of 1775–76 here.

With Johnston Gate at your back, to your right is **Massachusetts Hall** (1720), the university's oldest surviving building. It houses the president's office and rooms for first-year students. To your left is **Harvard Hall** (1765), a classroom building. The matching side-by-side buildings behind Harvard Hall are **Hollis** and **Stoughton halls.** Hollis dates to 1763 and has been home to many students who went on to great fame, among them Ralph Waldo Emerson, Henry David Thoreau, and Charles Bulfinch.

Across the Yard is **University Hall,** the college's main administration building, designed by Bulfinch and constructed in 1812–13. It's the backdrop of the **John Harvard statue** ★★, one of the most photographed objects in the Boston area. Designed by Daniel Chester French in 1884, it's known as the "Statue of Three Lies" because the inscription reads "John Harvard—Founder—1638." In fact, the college was established in 1636; Harvard (one of many people involved) wasn't the founder, but donated money and his library; and this isn't John Harvard, anyway. No portraits of him survive, so the model was, according to various accounts, either his nephew or a student. Walk over to the statue and join the throng of tourists posing for pictures with the benevolent-looking gentleman.

Walk around University Hall into the adjoining quadrangle; you're leaving the "Old Yard" for the "New Yard," where commencement and other university-wide ceremonies take place. On your right is **Widener Library,** the centerpiece of the world's largest university library system. It was built in 1913 as a memorial to Harry Elkins Widener, a 1907 Harvard graduate who died when the *Titanic* sank in 1912. Legend has it that he was unable to swim 50 yards to a lifeboat, and his mother donated $2 million for the library on the condition that every undergraduate pass a 50-yard swimming test.

Facing the library is **Memorial Church,** built in 1931 and topped with a tower and weather vane 197 feet tall. You're welcome to look around this Georgian Revival–style edifice unless services are going on. The entrance is on the left. The south wall, toward the Yard, lists the names of Harvard graduates who died in World Wars I and II, Korea, and Vietnam. One is Joseph P. Kennedy, Jr. ('38), the president's older brother.

Continue across the Yard onto Quincy Street. To your right is the curvilinear **Carpenter Center for the Visual Arts,** 24 Quincy St. Designed by the Swiss-French architect **Le Corbusier** and completed in 1963, it's the only Le Corbusier building in North America.

Facing the Carpenter Center, turn left and follow Quincy Street, crossing Broadway (the architect Norman Foster once called this area an "architectural zoo"), and walk another block. To your left is **Memorial Hall,** a massive Victorian structure built from 1870–74. The hall of memorials (enter from Kirkland or Cambridge sts.) is a transept where you can read the names of the Harvard men who died fighting for the Union during the Civil War—but not those who died for the Confederacy. Next door is the **Science Center,** Zero Oxford St., a 10-story monolith that supposedly resembles a Polaroid camera. (Edwin H. Land, founder of Cambridge-based Polaroid Corporation, was one of its main benefactors.) Sert also designed this structure, which was built in 1970–72.

Keep "Mem Hall" and the Science Center to your right and follow the walkway for the equivalent of a block and a half as it curves around toward Mass. Ave. The **Harvard Law School** campus is on your right. Carefully cross Mass. Ave. to **Cambridge Common.** Memorials and plaques dot this well-used plot of greenery and bare earth. Turn left and head back toward Harvard Square; after a block or so, you'll walk near or over **horseshoes** embedded in the concrete. This is the path William Dawes, Paul Revere's fellow alarm-sounder, took from Boston to Lexington on April 18, 1775.

Turn right onto Garden Street and find **Christ Church,** Zero Garden St. The oldest church in Cambridge, it was designed by Peter Harrison of Newport, Rhode Island (also the architect of King's Chapel in Boston), and opened in 1761. Note the square wooden tower. Inside the vestibule, you can still see bullet holes made by British muskets.

With the church at your back, turn right and return to Mass. Ave. Turn right again, then walk 2 blocks into the middle of the square and 1 more block on John F. Kennedy Street. Turn left onto Mount Auburn Street. Stay on the left side of the street as you cross Dunster, Holyoke, and Linden streets.

The corner of Mount Auburn and Linden streets is a good vantage point for viewing the **Harvard Lampoon Castle,** designed by Wheelwright & Haven in 1909. Listed on the National Register of Historic Places, this is the home of Harvard's undergraduate humor magazine, the *Lampoon.* The main tower looks like a face, with windows as the eyes, nose, and mouth, topped by what looks like a miner's hat.

Cross Mount Auburn Street and walk south (away from Holyoke Center) on Holyoke Street or Dunster Street to get a sense of some of the rest of the campus. Turn right on Winthrop Street or South Street, continue to John F. Kennedy Street, and turn left. Cross the street at some point, and follow it toward the Charles River, almost to Memorial Drive, passing the Kennedy School of Government. On your right is **John F. Kennedy Park.** Walk away from the street to the fountain, engraved with excerpts from the president's speeches. This is an excellent place to take a break and plan the rest of your day.

7 Spectator Sports & Getting Outside

SPECTATOR SPORTS

Boston enjoys a well-deserved reputation as a great sports town. The Red Sox, Celtics, and New England Patriots (who play in suburban Foxboro) have been more successful and popular than the Bruins recently, but local fans are nothing if not loyal—just ask all those Celtics fans who waited 22 years between NBA championships. Fans are also passionate about college sports, particularly hockey, in which the Division I schools are fierce rivals.

BASEBALL No other experience in sports matches watching the **Red Sox** play at **Fenway Park** ★★★, which they do from April to early October, and later if they make the playoffs. The quirkiness of the oldest park in the major leagues (1912) only adds to the mystique, and the euphoria that accompanied the team's 2004 and 2007 World Series titles has hardly abated. Tickets are wildly expensive, but one of the most imaginative management teams in baseball strives to make visiting Fenway worth big bucks. Yawkey Way turns into a sort of carnival midway for ticket holders before games, with concession stands, live music, and other diversions.

The **ticket office** (© 877/REDSOX-9; www.redsox.com) is at 4 Yawkey Way, off Brookline Avenue. Tickets go on sale in December; order early. They're the most expensive in the majors—a few upper bleacher seats go for $12, but most are in the $25-to-$90 range. Forced to choose between tickets for a low-numbered grandstand section (say, 10 or below) and bleacher seats, go for the bleachers and the better view. A limited number of same-day standing-room tickets ($20–$30) are available before each game, and fans sometimes return presold tickets, especially if a rainout causes rescheduling. It can't hurt to check, particularly if the team isn't playing well; visit the website and navigate to "Red Sox Replay," or check at the ticket office.

Tours (© 617/236-6666) start on the hour Monday through Saturday from 9am to 4pm, Sunday from noon to 3pm (or 3 hr. before game time, whichever is earlier), in the summer; winter hours end 1 hour earlier, with no tours on Sunday. There are no tours on holidays or before day games. The cost is $12 for adults, $11 for seniors, and $10 for children under 15.

BASKETBALL The Boston Celtics' unlikely run to the 2008 NBA title captivated even the most jaded fans. The season runs from early October to April or May. Especially when a top contender is visiting, you may have trouble getting tickets. Prices are as low as $10 for some games and top out at $275. For information, call **TD Banknorth Garden** (© 617/624-1000; www.nba.com/celtics); for tickets, contact **Ticketmaster** (© 617/931-2000; www.ticketmaster.com). To reach the Garden, take the Green or Orange Line to North Station. *Note:* Spectators may not bring any bags, including backpacks and briefcases, into the arena.

FOOTBALL The **New England Patriots** (© 800/543-1776; www.patriots.com) were playing to sellout crowds even before they won three Super Bowls in 4 years (2002, 2004, and 2005) and famously fizzled out in 2008. The Pats play from August to December or January at Gillette Stadium on Route 1 in Foxboro, about 45 minutes south of the city. Tickets ($49–$169) sell out well in advance. Call or check the website for information on individual ticket sales and public-transit options.

HOCKEY Tickets to see the **Boston Bruins** are expensive ($19–$155) but worth it for serious fans. For information, call **TD Banknorth Garden** (© 617/624-1000;

www.bostonbruins.com); for tickets, call **Ticketmaster** (© **617/931-2000;** www.
ticketmaster.com). To reach the Garden, take the Green or Orange Line to North Station. *Note:* Spectators may not bring any bags, including backpacks and briefcases,
into the arena.

Economical fans will be pleasantly surprised by the quality of local **college
hockey** ✮. Even for sold-out games, standing-room tickets are usually available
shortly before game time. Local teams include **Boston College,** Conte Forum, Chestnut Hill (© **617/552-GOBC;** www.bceagles.collegesports.com); **Boston University,**
Agganis Arena, 928 Commonwealth Ave. (© **617/353-3838;** www.bu.edu/athletics);
Harvard University, Bright Hockey Center, North Harvard Street, Allston (© **877/
GO-HARVARD** or 617/495-2211; www.gocrimson.com); and **Northeastern University,** Matthews Arena, St. Botolph Street (© **617/373-4700;** www.gonu.com).

THE MARATHON   Every year on Patriots Day (the 3rd Mon in Apr), the **Boston
Marathon** ✮✮✮ rules the roads from Hopkinton to Copley Square in Boston. An
especially nice place to watch is tree-shaded Comm. Ave. between Kenmore Square and
Mass. Ave., but you'll be in a crowd wherever you stand, particularly near the finish line
in front of the Boston Public Library. For information about qualifying, contact the
Boston Athletic Association (© **617/236-1652;** www.bostonmarathon.org).

ROWING   In late October, the **Head of the Charles Regatta** ✮ (© **617/868-
6200;** www.hocr.org) attracts some 4,000 oarsmen and oarswomen. The largest crew
event in the country draws hundreds of thousands of spectators who socialize and
occasionally even watch the action.

GETTING OUTSIDE

The **Department of Conservation & Recreation** (www.state.ma.us/dcr) oversees
activities on the state's public lands (you'll also see the name of the obsolete Metropolitan District Commission on many signs). The website describes properties and activities, and has a planning area to help you make the most of your time.

BEACHES   The beaches in Boston proper, with their icy water and periodic safety-
related closings, are not worth the trouble. If you want to swim, book a hotel with a
pool. If you want sand between your toes, hit the beach on the North Shore or at
Walden Pond in Concord. See chapter 6 for information on suburban beaches.

BIKING   Even expert cyclists who feel comfortable with Boston's layout will be better off in Cambridge, which has bike lanes, or on the area's many bike paths. The 18-
mile **Dr. Paul Dudley White Charles River Bike Path** follows the river from the
Museum of Science to Watertown and back. You can enter and exit at many points
along the way. Bikers share the path with lots of pedestrians, joggers, and in-line
skaters. On warm-weather Sundays from 11am to 7pm, **Memorial Drive** from Central Square to west Cambridge is closed to cars.

State law requires that children under 12 wear helmets. Bicycles are forbidden on
buses and the Green Line, and on other lines during rush hours.

Most rental shops charge around $10 per hour or $25 per day. They include **Back
Bay Bicycles,** 366 Comm. Ave., near Mass. Ave. (© **617/247-2336;** www.backbay
bicycles.com); **Boston Bicycle,** 842 Beacon St., about 3 blocks from Kenmore Square
(© **617/236-0752**); and **Cambridge Bicycle,** 259 Mass. Ave. (© **617/876-6555;**
www.cambridgebicycle.com). For more information, contact **MassBike** (© **617/
542-2453;** www.massbike.org).

Finds   **A Vacation in the Islands**

Majestic ocean views, hiking trails, historic sights, rocky beaches, nature walks, campsites, and picnic areas abound in New England. The **Boston Harbor Islands** ☆☆ (✆ 617/223-8666; www.bostonislands.com) have them all. The unspoiled beauty of the national park area is a welcome break from the urban landscape, but even many longtime Bostonians haven't visited. Bring a sweater or jacket, and note that fresh water is available only on Georges Island. (Management strongly suggests that you bring your own.)

Thirty-four islands dot the Outer Harbor, and at least a half-dozen are open to the public. Ferries run to the **Georges Island,** home of Fort Warren (1834), which held Confederate prisoners during the Civil War. You can investigate on your own or take a ranger-led tour. The island has a visitor center, refreshment area, fishing pier, picnic area, and wonderful view of Boston's skyline. Allow at least half a day, longer if you plan to take the water taxi ($5) to **Lovell, Peddocks, Bumpkin,** or **Grape Island;** all have picnic areas and campsites.

Harbor Express (✆ 617/222-6999; www.harborexpress.com) serves Georges Island from Long Wharf; the trip takes 45 minutes, and round-trip tickets are $14 for adults, $10 for seniors, and $8 for children 3 to 11. Cruises depart daily on the hour from 9am to 5pm in the summer, less frequently in the spring and fall. In the off season, check ahead for winter wildlife excursions (scheduled occasionally). There's no admission charge to visit the islands.

The Boston Harbor Islands National Recreation Area (www.nps.gov/boha) is the focus of a public-private project designed to make the islands more interesting and accessible. For more information, visit the website, consult the staff at the **kiosk on Long Wharf,** or contact the **Friends of the Boston Harbor Islands** (✆ 617/740-4290; www.fbhi.org).

GOLF   The **Massachusetts Golf Association** (✆ 800/356-2201 or 774/430-9100; www.mgalinks.org) represents more than 400 courses around the golf-mad state. Given a choice, play on a weekday, when you'll find lower prices and smaller crowds than on weekends.

One of the best public courses in the area, **Newton Commonwealth Golf Course,** 212 Kenrick St., Newton (✆ **617/630-1971;** www.sterlinggolf.com), is a challenging 18-hole Donald Ross design. It's 5,305 yards from the blue tees, par is 70, and greens fees are $30 weekdays, $37 weekends. Within the city limits is the legendary 6,009-yard **William J. Devine Golf Course,** in Franklin Park, Dorchester (✆ **617/ 265-4084**). As a Harvard student, Bobby Jones sharpened his game on the 18-hole, par-70 course. Greens fees are $39 weekdays, $48 weekends. Less challenging but with more of a neighborhood feel is 9-hole, par-35 **Fresh Pond Golf Course,** 691 Huron Ave., Cambridge (✆ **617/349-6282;** www.freshpondgolf.com). The 3,161-yard layout adjoins the Fresh Pond Reservoir (there's water on four holes) and charges $22, or $32 to go around twice, on weekdays; $26 and $38 on weekends.

GYMS   The concierge at your hotel can recommend a health club and perhaps arrange a discounted visit. Hotels with good health clubs (see "Where to Stay," earlier in this chapter) include the Four Seasons Hotel, the Hilton Boston Logan Airport, the InterContinental Boston, and the Royal Sonesta Hotel. The best combination of facilities and value is at the **Wang YMCA of Chinatown,** 8 Oak St. W., off Washington Street (© 617/426-2237; www.ymcaboston.org). A day pass costs $10.

ICE SKATING   The rink at the Boston Common **Frog Pond** (© 617/635-2120; www.cityofboston.gov/parks) is an extremely popular cold-weather destination. It's an open surface with an ice-making system and a clubhouse. Admission is $4 for adults, free for children under 14; skate rental costs $8 for adults, $5 for kids. Try to go on a weekday; huge crowds descend on weekends.

IN-LINE SKATING   Unless you're confident of your ability and your knowledge of Boston traffic, stay off the streets. A favorite car-free spot is the **Esplanade,** between the Back Bay and the Charles River. It continues onto the bike path that runs to Watertown and back, but once you leave the Esplanade, the pavement in many spots is in disrepair. Your best bet is to wait for a spring, summer, or fall Sunday, when **Memorial Drive** in Cambridge closes to cars. It's a perfect surface. The **InLine Club of Boston** offers event and safety information on its website (www.sk8net.com).

   Expect to pay about $15 for rentals. Try the **Beacon Hill Skate Shop,** 135 Charles St. S. (© 617/482-7400), or one of the vendors who set up shop on Memorial Drive on warm-weather Sundays.

JOGGING   The **Dr. Paul Dudley White Charles River Bike Path** (see "Biking," above) is the area's busiest jogging trail. It's so popular because it's car-free (except at intersections), scenic, and generally safe. The bridges along the river allow for circuits of various lengths, but be careful around abutments, where you can't see far ahead. Don't jog at night, and try not to go alone. Visit the DCR website (www.state.ma.us/dcr) to view a map that gives distances. If the river's not convenient, check with the concierge or desk staff at your hotel for a map with suggested routes.

SAILING   The best deal in town is **Community Boating, Inc.,** 21 David Mugar Way, on the Esplanade (© 617/523-1038; www.community-boating.org). It's open April through November, and the fleet includes 13- to 23-foot sailboats as well as windsurfers and kayaks. Visitors pay $100 for 2 days of unlimited use in the Charles River basin.

TENNIS   Public courts are available throughout the city at no charge. Well-maintained courts near downtown that seldom get busy until after work are along the Southwest Corridor Park in the South End (there's a nice one near **W. Newton St.**) The courts on **Boston Common** and in **Charlesbank Park,** overlooking the river next to the bridge to the Museum of Science, are more crowded during the day.

8 Shopping

Boston-area shopping represents a tempting blend of classic and contemporary. Boston and Cambridge boast tiny boutiques and sprawling malls, esoteric bookshops and national chain stores, classy galleries and snazzy secondhand-clothing outlets.

   Note: Massachusetts has no sales tax on clothing priced below $175 or on food. All other items are taxed at 5% (as are restaurant meals and takeout food). The state no longer prohibits stores from opening before noon on Sunday, but many still wait until noon or don't open at all—call ahead before setting out.

BACK BAY   This is New England's premier shopping district. Dozens of upscale galleries, shops, and boutiques make **Newbury Street** ★★★ a world-famous destination. Nearby, an enclosed walkway across Huntington Avenue links **Copley Place** (© 617/375-4400) and the **Shops at Prudential Center** (© 800/SHOP-PRU). This is where you'll find the tony department stores **Barneys New York** (© 617/385-3300), **Lord & Taylor** (© 617/262-6000), **Neiman Marcus** (© 617/536-3660), and **Saks Fifth Avenue** (© 617/262-8500). At press time, the Back Bay is home to the only open Boston location of **Filene's Basement,** 497 Boylston St (© 800/843-8474; www.filenesbasement.com).

If you're passionate about art, set aside a couple of hours for strolling along Newbury Street. Besides being a prime location for upscale boutiques, it boasts an infinite variety of styles and media in the dozens of art galleries at street level and on the higher floors. (Remember to look up.) Most galleries are open Tuesday through Sunday from 10 or 11am to 5:30 or 6pm. For specifics, pick up a copy of the free monthly *Gallery Guide* at businesses along Newbury Street.

DOWNTOWN   Faneuil Hall Marketplace (© 617/523-1300) is the busiest attraction in Boston not only for its smorgasbord of food outlets, but also for its shops, boutiques, and pushcarts. Although it has more upscale chain outlets than only-in-Boston shops, it's a fun experience.

If the hubbub here is too much for you, stroll over to **Charles Street,** at the foot of Beacon Hill. A short but commercially dense (and picturesque) street, it's home to perhaps the best assortment of gift and antiques shops in the city. Be sure to check out the contemporary home accessories at **Koo De Kir,** 65 Chestnut St., just off Charles (© **617/723-8111;** www.koodekir.com); the well-edited selection at **Upstairs Downstairs Antiques,** 93 Charles St. (© **617/367-1950**); and the engagingly funky gifts at **Black Ink,** 101 Charles St. (© **617/723-3883**).

One of Boston's oldest shopping areas is **Downtown Crossing.** Now a traffic-free pedestrian mall along Washington, Winter, and Summer streets near Boston Common, it's home to **Macy's;** tons of smaller clothing, shoe, and music stores; food and merchandise pushcarts; and a branch of **Borders.** At press time, the original **Filene's Basement** ★★★, 426 Washington St. (© **617/542-2011**), is closed while the building above undergoes complete reconstruction. The famed automatic markdown policy (25% off the already-discounted price after 2 weeks on sale, up to 75% after 8 weeks) applies only here. Check ahead to see whether this location has reopened, or hit the Back Bay location (see above).

(Tips Present at the Creation: Craft Shows

New England is a hotbed of fine crafts, and the Boston area affords many opportunities to explore the latest trends in every imaginable medium and style. Prominent artisans often have exclusive relationships with galleries; an excellent way to get an overview is to attend a show and sale. The best-known exhibitions are prestigious weekend events that benefit nonprofit organizations. **Crafts at the Castle** (© **617/523-6400,** ext. 5987; www.fsgb.org/catc.htm) takes place in late November or early December at the Hynes Convention Center. **CraftBoston** (© **617/266-1810;** www.craftboston.org) is in April or May at the Seaport World Trade Center.

Finds **By the Book**

Bookworms flock to Cambridge; Harvard Square in particular caters to general and specific audiences. Check out the basement of the **Harvard Book Store,** 1256 Mass. Ave. (© **800/542-READ,** or 617/661-1515; www.harvard. com), for great deals on remainders and used books. **Curious George Books & Toys,** 1 John F. Kennedy St. (© **617/498-0062;** www.curiousg.com), specializes in children's merchandise. Jammed shelves line the tiny **Grolier Poetry Book Shop,** 6 Plympton St. (© **617/547-4648**). Barnes & Noble runs the book operation at the **Harvard Coop,** 1400 Mass. Ave. (© **617/499-2000;** www. thecoop.com), which stocks textbooks, academic works, and a large general selection. One T stop away is the excellent independent shop **Porter Square Books,** in the Porter Square Shopping Center, 25 White St. (© **617/491-2220**).

In Boston, you'll find a huge selection of used and rare titles at the **Brattle Book Shop,** 9 West St. (© **800/447-9595** or 617/542-0210; www.brattle bookshop.com), near Downtown Crossing. Downtown Crossing has a **Borders,** 24 School St. (© **617/557-7188;** www.borders.com), and the Back Bay has both a **Barnes & Noble** (© **617/247-6959**), in the Shops at Prudential Center, and a **Borders,** 511 Boylston St. (© **617/236-1444**). There's also a **Borders** (© **617/679-0887**) at the CambridgeSide Galleria mall.

CAMBRIDGE   The bookstores, boutiques, and T-shirt shops of **Harvard Square** lie about 15 minutes from downtown Boston by subway. Despite the neighborhood association's efforts, chain stores have swept across the Square. You'll find a mix of national and regional outlets, and more than a few persistent independent retailers. They include the delightful children's store **Calliope,** 33 Brattle St. (© **617/876-4149**); **Colonial Drug,** 49 Brattle St. (© **617/864-2222**), which stocks hard-to-find perfume and other high-end cosmetics; and **Oona's,** 1210 Mass. Ave. (© **617/491-2654**), a trove of lovely "experienced" clothing and accessories.

For a less generic experience, walk along **Mass. Ave.** in either direction to the next T stop. The stroll takes about an hour. Heading north toward Porter Square, be sure to stop at **Joie de Vivre,** 1792 Mass. Ave. (© **617/864-8188**), a top-notch gift shop, and eco-aware **Greenward,** 1776 Mass. Ave. (© **617/395-1338**). Going southeast to Central, pop into **WardMaps.com,** 12 Bow St. (© **617/497-0737;** www.wardmaps. com), just outside the Square, and **Pearl Art & Craft Supplies,** 579 Mass. Ave. (© **617/547-6600**), an excellent link in the national discount chain.

And if you just can't manage without a trip to a mall, head to East Cambridge. Take the Green Line to Lechmere, or the Red Line to Kendall/MIT and the free shuttle bus to the **CambridgeSide Galleria,** 100 CambridgeSide Place (© **617/621-8666**).

9 Boston & Cambridge After Dark

For up-to-date entertainment listings, consult the "Sidekick" section of the daily *Boston Globe,* the "Edge" section of the Friday *Boston Herald,* or the daily arts sections of both papers. Four free publications, available at newspaper boxes around town, publish nightlife listings: the *Boston Phoenix,* the *Improper Bostonian, Stuff@Night* (a *Phoenix* offshoot), and the *Weekly Dig.* The *Phoenix* website (www.bostonphoenix. com) archives the paper's season preview issues; especially before a summer or fall visit, it's a worthwhile planning tool.

GETTING TICKETS   Some companies and venues sell tickets over the phone or online; many will refer you to a ticket agency. The major agencies that serve Boston are **Ticketmaster** (© 617/931-2000; www.ticketmaster.com) and **Telecharge** (© 800/432-7250; www.telecharge.com). Many smaller venues use independent companies that don't charge as much. To avoid fees—and possible losses if your plans change and you can't get your money back—visit the box office in person. If you wait until the day before or day of a performance, you'll sometimes have access to tickets that were held back and have just gone on sale.

DISCOUNT TICKETS   Visit a **BosTix** (© 617/482-2849; www.bostix.org) booth, at Faneuil Hall Marketplace (on the south side of Faneuil Hall) or in Copley Square (at the corner of Boylston and Dartmouth sts.), where same-day tickets to musical and theatrical performances are half-price, subject to availability. Credit cards are not accepted, and there are no refunds or exchanges. Check the board or the website for the day's offerings. The booths, which are also Ticketmaster outlets, are open Tuesday through Saturday from 10am to 6pm (half-price tickets go on sale at 11am), Sunday from 11am to 4pm. The Copley Square location is also open Monday from 10am to 6pm. *Tip:* Sign up for email updates (you can always unsubscribe later), and you may have a crack at discounted advance tickets.

THE PERFORMING ARTS

The city's premier classical performance venue is **Symphony Hall,** 301 Mass. Ave. (© 617/266-1492; www.bso.org), which turned 100 in 2000. It plays host to other notable groups and artists when the Boston Symphony Orchestra and the Boston Pops are away. The **Hatch Shell** on the Esplanade (© 617/727-5215; www.mass. gov/dcr) is an amphitheater best known as the home of the Pops' Fourth of July concerts. On summer nights, free music and dance performances and films take over the stage to the delight of crowds on the lawn.

Other venues that attract big-name visitors include the **Berklee Performance Center,** 136 Mass. Ave. (© 617/747-8890; www.berkleebpc.com); the **Boston Center for the Arts,** 539 Tremont St. (© 617/426-2787; www.bcaonline.org); the **Cutler Majestic Theatre,** 219 Tremont St. (© 617/824-8000; www.maj.org); New England Conservatory's **Jordan Hall,** 30 Gainsborough St. (© 617/585-1260; www.newengland conservatory.edu/jordanhall); and **Sanders Theatre,** 45 Quincy St., Cambridge (© 617/496-2222; www.fas.harvard.edu/~memhall).

THE MAJOR COMPANIES

In addition to the companies listed below, the **Boston Lyric Opera** (© 617/542-6772; www.blo.org) performs classical and contemporary works. The season runs from November to May. Performances are at the **Shubert Theatre,** 265 Tremont St.

Boston Ballet ★★   Boston Ballet's reputation seems to jump a notch every time someone says, "So it's not just *The Nutcracker.*" One of the top dance companies in the country, Boston Ballet performs an eclectic mix of classic story ballets and contemporary works during the rest of the season (Oct–May). The holiday classic runs from Thanksgiving to New Year's at the **Opera House,** 539 Washington St. Beginning

---

(Finds) Dessert Alert

Finale is one of the best debuts Boston's Theater District has seen in many years. It's a "desserterie" that serves a mouth-watering variety of glorious desserts in elegant, romantic surroundings with lots of velvet and soft lighting. Yes, it's a tad expensive. No, this is not a balanced meal. But the sweet tooths (sweet teeth?) who flock here don't care. The original is at 1 Columbus Ave., in the pointy end of the Park Plaza Building (© **617/423-3184;** www.finaledesserts. com), with branches at 30 Dunster St., Harvard Square (© **617/441-9797**), and 1306 Beacon St., Coolidge Corner, Brookline (© **617/232-3233**). Finale also serves real food, such as salads and pizzas, but the desserts are the real draw.

---

in the fall of 2009, the Opera House will be the company's full-time home. *Tip:* The pitch of the seats at the current venue, the **Citi Wang Theatre,** makes the top two balconies less than ideal for watching ballet; paying more for a better seat is a good investment. Performing at the Citi Wang Theatre, 270 Tremont St., and the Opera House, 539 Washington St. © 800/447-7400 (Telecharge) or 617/695-6955. www.bostonballet.org. Tickets $45–$110. Senior, student, and child rush tickets (2 hr. before curtain) $20, except for *Nutcracker.* T: Green Line to Boylston.

Boston Pops 🎭🎭   From May to early July, tables and chairs replace Symphony Hall's floor seats, and drinks and light refreshments are served. The Pops play a range of music from light classical to show tunes to popular music, often with celebrity guest stars. Performances are Tuesday through Sunday evenings. Special holiday performances in December ($32–$118) usually sell out well in advance, but it can't hurt to check. The regular season ends with two **free outdoor concerts** at the Hatch Shell on the Esplanade along the Charles River: the July 3 rehearsal and the traditional Fourth of July concert. Symphony Hall, 301 Mass. Ave. (at Huntington Ave.). © 617/266-1492 or 617/CONCERT (program information). SymphonyCharge © 888/266-1200 (outside 617) or 617/266-1200. www.bso.org. Tickets $40–$87 for tables; $19–$52 for balcony seats. T: Green Line E to Symphony, or Orange Line to Mass. Ave.

Boston Symphony Orchestra 🎭🎭🎭   The Boston Symphony, one of the world's greatest, was founded in 1881. James Levine is the music director. You might want to schedule your trip to coincide with a particular performance, or with a visit by a celebrated guest artist or conductor. The season runs from October to April, with performances most Tuesday, Thursday, and Saturday evenings; Friday afternoons; and some Friday evenings. Explanatory talks (included in the ticket price) begin 75 minutes before the curtain. If you can't get tickets in advance, check at the box office for returns from subscribers 2 hours before showtime. A limited number of rush tickets are available on the day of the performance for Tuesday and Thursday evening and Friday afternoon programs. Some Wednesday evening and Thursday morning rehearsals are open to the public. Symphony Hall, 301 Mass. Ave. (at Huntington Ave.). © 617/266-1492 or 617/CONCERT (program information). SymphonyCharge © 888/266-1200 (outside 617) or 617/266-1200. www.bso.org. Tickets $29–$114. Rush tickets $9 (on sale 10am Fri, 5pm Tues and Thurs). Rehearsal tickets $19. T: Green Line E to Symphony, or Orange Line to Mass. Ave.

THEATER & PERFORMANCE ART

Boston is one of the last cities for pre-Broadway tryouts, allowing an early look at a classic (or classic flop) in the making. It's also a popular destination for touring companies

Finds **Boston Common Culture**

An excellent summer diversion is a free, top-quality performance on historic Boston Common. Bring a picnic, spread out a blanket, and enjoy the sunset. The **Commonwealth Shakespeare Company** (© **617/482-9393;** www.commshakes. org) performs Tuesday through Sunday nights in July and early August. The **Boston Landmarks Orchestra** (© **617/520-2200;** www.landmarksorchestra.org) schedules "accessible classical" concerts in local parks, including the Common, on evenings from July to September.

of established hits. You'll find most of the shows headed to or coming from Broadway in the **Theater District,** at the **Colonial Theatre,** 106 Boylston St. (© 617/426-9366); the **Opera House,** 539 Washington St. (© 617/880-2400); the **Shubert Theatre,** 265 Tremont St. (© 617/482-9393); the **Citi Wang Theatre,** 270 Tremont St. (© 617/482-9393; www.wangcenter.org); and the **Wilbur Theater,** 246 Tremont St. (© 617/423-4008). The promoter often is **Broadway Across America** (© 866/523-7469; www.broadwayacrossamerica.com).

The excellent local theater scene boasts the **Huntington Theatre Company,** which performs at the Boston University Theatre, 264 Huntington Ave. (© **617/266-0800;** www.huntington.org), and the **American Repertory Theatre,** which makes its home at Harvard University's Loeb Drama Center, 64 Brattle St., Cambridge (© **617/ 547-8300;** www.amrep.org).

The off-Broadway performance-art sensation **Blue Man Group** is a trio of cobalt-colored entertainers who use music, percussion, food, and audience participants—props include social commentary, Twinkies, marshmallows, breakfast cereal, toilet paper, and lots of blue paint. Older children and teenagers enjoy the mayhem as much as adults. Shows are at the **Charles Playhouse,** 74 Warrenton St. (© **617/426-6912;** www.blueman.com), in the Theater District. Tickets are $58 and $48 at the box office and through Ticketmaster (© **617/931-ARTS;** www.ticketmaster.com).

THE CLUB & MUSIC SCENE

The Boston-area club scene changes constantly, and somewhere out there is a good time for everyone—or at least every early bird. Bars close at 1am, clubs at 2am. The subway shuts down between 12:30 and 1am. Check the "Sidekick" section of the *Globe,* the *Phoenix,* the "Edge" section of the Friday *Herald, Stuff@Night,* or the *Improper Bostonian* while you're planning.

The drinking age is 21; a valid driver's license or passport is required as proof of age. The law is strictly enforced, especially near college campuses—in other words, practically everywhere. Even if you're not drinking, many clubs require patrons to be 21 (or, in some cases, 18 or 19). Wherever you go, be prepared to show ID if you appear to be younger than 35 or so.

Big-name rock and pop artists play **TD Banknorth Garden,** 100 Legends Way (Causeway St.; © **617/624-1000;** www.tdbanknorthgarden.com), when it's not in use by the Bruins (hockey), the Celtics (basketball), the circus (in Oct), and touring ice shows. Concerts are in the round or on the arena stage.

COMEDY

The Comedy Connection ★★ The oldest original comedy club in town (established in 1978) draws top-notch talent from near and far. There's one show Sunday through Thursday, two shows Friday and Saturday. The cover seldom tops $20 during the week but jumps for a big name appearing on a weekend. *Note:* In 2008, the Comedy Connection left its longtime home at Faneuil Hall Marketplace (and dropped the "at Faneuil Hall" part of its name). At press time, more specifics about the new location were up in the air; call ahead or check the website for information. In the Wilbur Theatre, 246 Tremont St. ✆ **617/248-9700.** www.comedyconnectionboston.com. Cover $15–$45, 2-item minimum. T: Green Line to Boylston or Orange Line to New England Medical Center.

The Comedy Studio ★★ *Finds* Nobody here is a sitcom star—yet. With a stellar reputation for searching out undiscovered talent, the no-frills Comedy Studio draws connoisseurs, students, and network scouts. Sketches and improv spice up the standup. Shows are Tuesday (magicians) through Sunday at 8pm. At the Hong Kong restaurant, 1238 Mass. Ave., Cambridge. ✆ **617/661-6507.** www.thecomedystudio.com. Cover $8–$10. T: Red Line to Harvard.

DANCE CLUBS

The *Improper Bostonian* and the *Phoenix* club listings are good resources for info about this ever-changing scene, but a savvy concierge is even better. *Tip:* Note that most club websites let you put your name on the VIP list. Can't hurt, might help.

The Estate A can't-miss destination for visiting "celebrities," such as Paris Hilton, the Estate is a cavernous space with a balcony overlooking the large dance floor. It attracts a lively 20-something crowd with well-known local DJs and an excellent sound system. The lower level is the **Suite**—all house music, all the time. In both clubs, the dress code is "casual chic and fashionable," which appears to mean shirts with collars on men and something tight and black on women. The key to jumping the inevitable line is to reserve a table and look sharp. Open Thursday through Sunday (note that Thurs and Sun are gay nights); check ahead for specifics. 1 Boylston Place. ✆ **617/351-7000.** www.theestateboston.com. Cover $10–25. T: Green Line to Boylston.

The Roxy ★★ This former hotel ballroom boasts excellent DJs and all sorts of live music, a huge dance floor, a stage, and a balcony that's perfect for checking out the action below. Concerts (recently, Elliott Yamin and Spoon) and occasional boxing cards take good advantage of the sight lines. Offerings change regularly, so call or surf for the latest schedule. Open at 10pm Friday and Saturday, and other days depending

---

Finds **Make Some Noise in a Museum**

Two museums schedule events that attract 20- and 30-somethings with live music, cocktails, food, and mingling; a visit is an equally good couple or group activity. On the first Friday of each month—every Friday in the summer—the **Museum of Fine Arts,** 465 Huntington Ave. (✆ **617/267-9300;** www.mfa.org), schedules "mfafirstfridays" from 5:30 to 9:30pm. General admission to the museum ($15 after 5pm) includes admission. The **Isabella Stewart Gardner Museum's** "After Hours" series ($12), from 5 to 9pm on the third Thursday of each month, includes self-guided tours and gallery talks.

on bookings. In the Courtyard Boston Tremont hotel, 279 Tremont St. ℂ **617/338-7699.** www.roxy plex.com. Cover $10–$20. T: Green Line to Boylston or Orange Line to New England Medical Center.

FOLK & ECLECTIC

Club Passim 🌟🌟🌟   Joan Baez, Suzanne Vega, and Tom Rush all started out in this legendary basement coffeehouse. There's live music nightly, and coffee and food (but no alcohol) until 10:30pm. Open Sunday through Thursday from 11am to 11pm, Friday and Saturday until midnight. 47 Palmer St., Cambridge. ℂ **617/492-7679.** www.passim center.org. Cover $5–$27; most shows $15 or less. T: Red Line to Harvard.

Johnny D's Uptown Restaurant & Music Club 🌟🌟🌟 *Finds*   This family-owned establishment draws a congenial, low-key crowd for performers on international tours as well as local acts. The music ranges from zydeco to rock, blues to ska. It's only two stops past Harvard Square on the Red Line (about a 15-min. ride at night). Open daily from 11:30am to 1am. Brunch starts at 9am on weekends; dinner runs from 4:30 to 9:30pm Tuesday through Saturday (a reservation guarantees you a seat for the show), with lighter fare until 11pm. 17 Holland St., Davis Sq., Somerville. ℂ **617/776-2004** or 617/776-9667 (concert line). www.johnnyds.com. Cover $3–$20, usually $8–$12. T: Red Line to Davis.

JAZZ & BLUES

On summer Thursdays at 6pm, the **Boston Harbor Hotel** (ℂ **617/439-7000**) stages performances on the "Blues Barge," which floats in the water behind the hotel. The theater at the Cambridge Multicultural Arts Center, 41 Second St., Cambridge (ℂ **617/577-1400;** www.cmacusa.org; T: Green Line to Lechmere), becomes the **Real Deal Jazz Club & Cafe** at least a couple of times a month year-round.

Regattabar 🌟🌟   The Regattabar's lineup of local and international artists is often considered the best in the area, but be sure to check the lineup at Scullers (see below). Madeleine Peyroux and McCoy Tyner have appeared recently. The third-floor room holds about 200 and can get a little noisy. Buy tickets in advance or try your luck at the door an hour before showtime. In The Charles Hotel, 1 Bennett St., Cambridge. ℂ **617/661-5000,** or 617/395-7757 for tickets. www.regattabarjazz.com. Tickets $12–$35. T: Red Line to Harvard.

Scullers Jazz Club 🌟🌟🌟   Overlooking the Charles River, Scullers books top singers and instrumentalists—recent notables include Abbey Lincoln, Herb Alpert, and Bobby Caldwell. Patrons tend to be more hard-core and quieter than the crowds at the Regattabar, but it depends on who's performing. The box office is open Monday through Saturday from 11am to 6pm. Ask about dinner and overnight packages. In the Doubletree Guest Suites hotel, 400 Soldiers Field Rd. ℂ 617/562-4111. www.scullersjazz.com. Tickets $15–$50. Validated parking available.

Wally's Cafe 🌟🌟   This Boston institution, near a busy corner in the South End, opened in 1947. Its New Orleans–style all-about-the-music atmosphere draws a notably diverse crowd—black, white, straight, gay, affluent, indigent—for nightly live music by local ensembles, students and instructors from the Berklee College of Music,

---

(*Tips* **Got a Light? Not So Fast!**

Massachusetts state law forbids smoking in all workplaces, including bars, nightclubs, and restaurants.

Tips **Rock of Ages**

Bring your driver's license or passport when you go club-hopping, no matter how old you think you look—you must be 21 to drink alcohol, and the law is strictly enforced. Most bouncers won't risk a fine or license suspension, especially at 18-plus shows.

---

and the occasional international star. 427 Mass. Ave. ℭ **617/424-1408.** www.wallyscafe.com. 1-drink minimum. T: Orange Line to Mass. Ave.

ROCK & ALTERNATIVE

The Middle East 𝒢𝒢𝒢   One of the best rock clubs in New England books an impressive variety of progressive and alternative acts in two rooms (upstairs and downstairs) every night. Showcasing top local talent as well as bands with international reputations, it's a popular hangout that gets crowded, hot, and *loud.* In the same complex are the **Corner,** a former bakery that features acoustic artists, and **ZuZu** (ℭ **617/ 492-9181**), a Middle Eastern restaurant with its own music schedule. 472–480 Mass. Ave., Central Sq., Cambridge. ℭ **617/864-EAST,** or 617/931-2000 (Ticketmaster). www.mideastclub. com. Cover $7–$15 (ZuZu cover $3 Fri–Sat only). T: Red Line to Central.

Paradise Rock Club 𝒢   The medium-size Paradise, by the Boston University campus, draws enthusiastic, student-intensive crowds for top local rock and alternative performers. You might also see well-known up-and-comers who aren't ready to headline a big show. 967 Comm. Ave. ℭ **617/562-8800,** or 877/MUSIC-77 for tickets. www.thedise.com. T: Green Line B to Pleasant St.

Toad 𝒢𝒢 (Value   Essentially a bar with a stage, this narrow space attracts a savvy three-generation clientele with big local names and no cover. Toad enjoys good acoustics but not much elbow room—a plus when restless musicians wander into the crowd. 1912 Mass. Ave., Cambridge. ℭ **617/497-4950** (info line). www.toadcambridge.com. T: Red Line to Porter.

T. T. the Bear's Place 𝒢   A mainstay of the Central Square live-music scene since it opened in 1985, "T. T.'s" has an uncanny knack for booking hot new talent. Bookings range from cutting-edge alternative and roots music to up-and-coming indie rockers. New bands predominate early in the week, with more established artists on weekends. 10 Brookline St., Cambridge. ℭ **617/492-0082,** or 617/492-BEAR (concert line). www. ttthebears.com. Cover $3–$17. T: Red Line to Central.

BARS & LOUNGES

The Beehive   A funky two-level space beneath the Boston Center for the Arts (p. 140), this restaurant and lounge schedules live music, usually jazz, every night. Early in the week, the crowd tends toward laid-back and local; weekends are more of a see-and-be-seen scene for suburbanites. 541 Tremont St. ℭ **617/423-0069.** www.beehive boston.com. T: Orange Line to Back Bay.

The Black Rose   Purists might sneer at The Black Rose's touristy location, but performers don't. Sing along with the authentic entertainment at this jampacked pub and restaurant at the edge of Faneuil Hall Marketplace. 160 State St. ℭ **617/742-2286.** www.irishconnection.com. Cover $3–$5. T: Orange or Blue Line to State.

Fun Fact **House of Blues: Encore!**

Part of Boston's best-known nightlife destination may be a construction site during your visit. Two longtime Lansdowne Street nightclubs, most recently called Avalon and Axis, are gone, and a new **House of Blues** is in the works in the space that once held 11–36 Lansdowne St. The chain got its start in Harvard Square in 1992 and closed that location in 2003, vowing to reopen in the area; the search for a new location only took about 4 years. Visit **www.hob.com** to see whether the new location is open.

The Bristol 🎭🎭🎭 An elegant room with cushy seating and a fireplace, The Bristol is an oasis anytime, and it features a fabulous dessert buffet on weekend nights. There's live jazz every evening, and food until 11:30pm (12:30am Fri–Sat). In the Four Seasons Hotel, 200 Boylston St. ✆ 617/351-2037. T: Green Line to Arlington.

Casablanca 🎭🎭 Students and professors crowd this legendary Harvard Square watering hole, especially on weekends. It offers an excellent jukebox, excellent food, and excellent eavesdropping. 40 Brattle St., Cambridge. ✆ 617/876-0999. T: Red Line to Harvard.

Cask 'n Flagon 🎭 A long fly ball away from Fenway Park, "the Cask," which opened in 1969, is one of the best-known sports bars in this sports-mad city. It's much bigger than it looks from Brookline Avenue, but lines on game days are still comically long. The crowds watching major events on numerous TVs in the memorabilia-drenched bar are large and enthusiastic year-round. 62 Brookline Ave. ✆ 617/536-4840. www.casknflagon.com. T: Green Line B, C, or D to Kenmore.

Cheers (Beacon Hill) Try to hide your shock when, upon entering "the *Cheers* bar," you realize it looks nothing like the bar on the TV show. (A spin-off in Faneuil Hall Marketplace fills that niche—see the next listing.) This one-time neighborhood bar is far better known as a destination for legions of out-of-towners, who find good pub grub and plenty of souvenirs. 84 Beacon St. ✆ 617/227-9605. www.cheersboston.com. T: Green Line to Arlington.

Cheers (Faneuil Hall Marketplace) Blatantly but good-naturedly courting fans of the sitcom, this bar centers on an area that exactly replicates the set of the TV show. You know you want to. Quincy Market Building, South Canopy. ✆ 617/227-0150. www.cheers boston.com. T: Green or Blue Line to Government Center, or Orange Line to Haymarket.

DeLux Cafe 🎭 Ultracool but never obnoxious about it, the DeLux is one of the classiest dives around. The funky decor (check out the Elvis shrine), selection of microbrews, and veggie-friendly ethnic menu attract a cross-section of the South End, from off-duty chefs to yuppies. 100 Chandler St. ✆ 617/338-5258. T: Orange Line to Back Bay.

Eastern Standard A cavernous brasserie with a mile-long marble bar, Eastern Standard is an all-things-to-all-people destination. It serves three meals daily, offers outdoor seating, and has a hopping bar scene every night during the week and almost all day on weekends. The specialty cocktails are numerous and diverse, and the bartenders know their way around the wine list. On Red Sox game nights, be ready to spend a lot of time on your feet. In the Hotel Commonwealth, 528 Commonwealth Ave. ✆ 617/532-9100. www.easternstandardboston.com. T: Green Line B, C, or D to Kenmore.

Flat Top Johnny's ★★   A spacious, loud room with a bar and 12 red-topped pool tables, Flat Top Johnny's has a casual neighborhood feel despite being in a rather sterile office-retail complex. Open weekdays noon to 1am, weekends 3pm to 1am. 1 Kendall Sq., Cambridge. ℂ 617/494-9565. www.flattopjohnnys.com. T: Red Line to Kendall/MIT.

The Fours   One of Boston's best and best-known sports bars, The Fours is about one football field away from TD Banknorth Garden. Festooned with sports memorabilia and TVs, it's a madhouse before Celtics and Bruins games—and a promising place to pick up an extra ticket. 166 Canal St. ℂ 617/720-4455. T: Green or Orange Line to North Station.

Game On! Sports Cafe   Yes, it's actually *in* Fenway Park, and, no, you can't just sneak into the stands. The overgrown sports bar and restaurant boasts the latest techno toys, including high-def TVs and a booming sound system, on two deafeningly loud levels of a onetime bowling alley. On game days, the line stretches out the door. 82 Lansdowne St. ℂ 617/351-7001. www.gameonboston.com. T: Green Line D to Fenway, or B, C, or D to Kenmore.

Grendel's Den ★   A vestige of prefranchise Harvard Square, this cozy subterranean space is *the* place to celebrate turning 21. Recent grads and grad students dominate, but Grendel's has been so popular for so long that it also gets its share of Gen Y's parents. 89 Winthrop St., Cambridge. ℂ 617/491-1050. www.grendelsden.com. T: Red Line to Harvard.

Hard Rock Cafe *Kids*   This link in the chain is a fun one—just ask the other tourists. The gigantic space across the street from Faneuil Hall Marketplace abounds with memorabilia of Nirvana, Madonna, local favorites Aerosmith and the Cars, and others. 24 Clinton St. ℂ 617/424-ROCK. www.hardrock.com. T: Orange Line to Haymarket, or Green or Blue Line to Government Center.

John Harvard's Brew House ★★   This subterranean Harvard Square hangout pumps out terrific English-style brews in a clublike setting and prides itself on its food. 33 Dunster St., Cambridge. ℂ 617/868-3585. www.johnharvards.com. T: Red Line to Harvard.

Mr. Dooley's Boston Tavern ★★   Sometimes an expertly poured Guinness is all you need. If one of the nicest bartenders in the city pours it, so much the better. This Financial District spot offers many imported beers on tap, live music, and a menu of pub favorites. 77 Broad St. ℂ 617/338-5656. www.somerspubs.com. Cover $3–$5 Fri–Sat. T: Orange Line to State or Blue Line to Aquarium.

The Plough & Stars ★   Although it's comically small, The Plough is a huge presence on the local pub and live-music scenes. A neighborhood hangout during the day, it's a hipster magnet at night. Saturday is bluegrass night. 912 Mass. Ave., Cambridge. ℂ 617/576-0032. www.ploughandstars.com. T: Red Line to Central or Harvard.

Silvertone Bar & Grill ★   One of the few real hangouts in the Downtown Crossing area, this tiny subterranean bar attracts an incredibly loud after-work crowd. The dining room is noted for reasonably priced comfort food (try the sublime macaroni and cheese). Closed Sunday. 69 Bromfield St. ℂ 617/338-7887. www.silvertonedowntown.com. T: Red or Green Line to Park Street.

Top of the Hub ★★★   The 52nd-story view of greater Boston from this appealing lounge is especially lovely at sunset. There's music and dancing nightly. Dress is casual but neat. Prudential Center, 800 Boylston St. ℂ 617/536-1775. T: Green Line E to Prudential.

6

Side Trips from Boston: Lexington & Concord, the North Shore & Plymouth

by Marie Morris

Besides being, in the words of Oliver Wendell Holmes, "the hub of the solar system," Boston is the hub of a network of wonderful day trips and longer excursions. The destinations in this chapter are lively communities where you'll find sights and attractions of great beauty and historical significance. Exploring can take as little as half a day or as long as a week or more.

WEST OF BOSTON If time is short, combine a visit to Cambridge (see chapter 5) with a trip to Lexington and Concord for a hefty dose of American history. The route that Paul Revere took out of Boston on April 18, 1775, is tough to follow—he started by crossing the harbor in a rowboat, for one thing—but his fellow rider William Dawes cut through Harvard Square. Both proceeded to warn the colonists that British troops were on the march.

NORTH OF BOSTON Great prosperity came to eastern Massachusetts after the Revolution, as the new nation took advantage of the lifting of British trade barriers. Today the spoils of the China trade adorn mansions and public edifices in seaside locales such as Marblehead, Salem, and Cape Ann. Fishing is still an important industry, but these days the area caters more to commuters and tourists than to those who make their living from the sea. A worthwhile detour from the north or west is Lowell, a once-decrepit mill town where tourism is now the largest industry.

SOUTH OF BOSTON The communities between Boston and Cape Cod are mostly commuter suburbs. The prime sightseeing destination is Plymouth, one of the oldest permanent European settlements in North America. It's a pleasant place where you can walk in the footsteps of the Pilgrims—and of the countless out-of-towners who flock here in summer and at Thanksgiving. Farther south, the old whaling port of New Bedford makes an interesting detour.

Tips **Follow the Leader**

If you lack the time or inclination to make your own arrangements, consider an escorted tour. One reliable company is Gray Line's **Brush Hill Tours,** 435 High St., Randolph (© **800/343-1328** or 781/986-6100; www.brushhilltours.com), which offers a wide variety of half- and full-day excursions.

1 Lexington (★)

9 miles NW of downtown Boston; 6 miles NW of Cambridge; 6 miles E of Concord

A country village turned prosperous suburb, Lexington takes great pride in its history. It's a pleasant town with some engaging destinations, but it lacks the atmosphere and abundant attractions of nearby Concord. Being sure to leave time for a tour of the Buckman Tavern, you can schedule as little as a couple of hours to explore downtown Lexington, possibly en route to Concord. A visit can also fill a half or full day. The town contains part of Minute Man National Historical Park, which is definitely worth a visit.

The shooting phase of the Revolutionary War started here, with a skirmish on the town green. It began when British troops clashed with local militia members, who were known as "Minutemen" for their ability to assemble on short notice. British soldiers marched from Boston to Lexington late on April 18, 1775. Tipped off, Paul Revere and William Dawes rode ahead to sound the warning. They did their job so well that the alarm came long before the advancing forces. The Lexington Minutemen, under the command of Capt. John Parker, got the word shortly after midnight, but the redcoats were still several hours away. The colonists repaired to their homes and the Buckman Tavern. Five hours later, some 700 British troops under Major Pitcairn arrived.

A tense standoff ensued. Three times Pitcairn ordered them to disperse, but the patriots—fewer than 100, and some accounts say 77—refused. Parker called: "Stand your ground. Don't fire unless fired upon, but if they mean to have a war, let it begin here!" Finally the captain, perhaps realizing as the sky grew light how badly outnumbered his men were, gave the order to fall back.

As the Minutemen began to scatter, a shot rang out. One British company charged into the fray, and the colonists attempted to regroup as Pitcairn tried unsuccessfully to call off his troops. Nobody knows who started the shooting, but when it was over, 8 militia members, including a drummer boy, lay dead, and 10 were wounded.

ESSENTIALS

GETTING THERE   From downtown Boston, take Storrow Drive or Memorial Drive to Route 2. Follow Route 2 from Cambridge through Belmont, exit at Route 4/225, and follow signs to downtown Lexington. Or take Route 128 (I-95) to exit 31A and follow signs. If it's not rush hour, allow about 35 minutes. **Massachusetts Avenue** (the same "Mass. Ave." you saw in Boston and Cambridge) runs through the center of town. There's metered parking on the street and in several municipal lots, and free parking at the National Heritage Museum and the National Historical Park.

The **MBTA** (✆ **800/392-6100** or 617/222-3200; www.mbta.com) runs bus route nos. 62 (Bedford) and 76 (Hanscom) to Lexington from Alewife station, the last stop on the Red Line. The one-way fare is $1.25 with a CharlieCard or $1.50 with a CharlieTicket, and the trip takes about 25 minutes. Buses leave every hour during the day and every half-hour during rush periods Monday through Saturday, with no service on Sunday. The seasonal Liberty Ride tour connects Lexington and Concord.

VISITOR INFORMATION   The Chamber of Commerce **visitor center,** 1875 Mass. Ave. (✆ **781/862-2480;** www.lexingtonchamber.org), distributes maps and information. The **Greater Merrimack Valley Convention & Visitors Bureau** (✆ **800/443-3332** or 978/459-6150; www.merrimackvalley.org) includes Lexington.

> **(Tips** Poetry in Motion
>
> Before you visit Lexington and Concord, you might want to read or (reread) **"Paul Revere's Ride,"** Henry Wadsworth Longfellow's classic but historically questionable poem that dramatically chronicles the events of April 18 and 19, 1775.

GETTING AROUND   Downtown Lexington is easily negotiable on foot, and most of the attractions are within walking distance. If you prefer not to walk to the Munroe Tavern and the National Heritage Museum (see below), bus nos. 62 and 76 pass by on Mass. Ave.

The **Liberty Ride** (② 781/862-0500, ext. 702; www.libertyride.us) is a 90-minute narrated trolley tour that connects the attractions in Lexington and Concord. It operates from 10:30am to 3pm Saturday and Sunday of Patriots Day weekend and daily from Memorial Day weekend through late October; check ahead to confirm the schedule. The fare (good for a full day) is $20 for adults, $10 for children 5 to 17, free for children under 5. There's free parking at the National Heritage Museum and the national park visitor center, and your ticket entitles you to discounts at local businesses.

SPECIAL EVENTS   **Patriots Day,** a state holiday observed on the third Monday in April, commemorates the start of the Revolution. Celebrations include a reenactment of the battle and other festivities. Visit **www.battleroad.org** for information.

EXPLORING THE HISTORIC SITES

Minute Man National Historical Park is in Lexington, Concord, and Lincoln. At the Lexington end of the park is the **Minute Man Visitor Center** ⊛, off Route 2A, about ½ mile west of I-95 exit 30B (② **781/674-1920;** www.nps.gov/mima). This area of the park includes the first 4 miles of the Battle Road, the route the defeated British troops took as they left Concord. Begin your visit here by watching "The Road to Revolution," a multimedia program that explains Paul Revere's ride and the events of April 19, 1775. (Winter visitors can start in Concord.) Also here are informational displays and a 40-foot mural illustrating the battle. On summer weekends, rangers lead tours of the park; call ahead for times. The **Battle Road Trail,** a 5½-mile interpretive path, carries pedestrian, wheelchair, and bicycle traffic. Panels and granite markers along the trail display information about the military, social, and natural history of the area. In season (Oct–Apr), this center is open daily from 9am to 5pm, but schedules vary. Call ahead (use the phone number for the North Bridge Visitor Center, ② **978/369-6993,** if there's no answer here) for open days and hours. For more information, see "Concord," below.

Start your visit to downtown Lexington at the **visitor center,** on the town common or Battle Green. It's open daily from 9am to 5pm (10am–4pm Dec–Mar). A diorama and accompanying narrative illustrate the Battle of Lexington. The **Minuteman statue** (1900) on the green is of Capt. John Parker, who commanded the militia. The **Old Revolutionary Monument** (1799) marks the grave of seven of the eight colonists who died in the conflict, which the **Line of Battle Boulder** commemorates. The **Memorial to the Lexington Minutemen** bears the names of the men who fell in the battle. Across Mass. Ave., near Clarke Street, is the **Old Belfry,** a reproduction of the free-standing bell that sounded the alarm the day of the battle. **Ye Olde Burying**

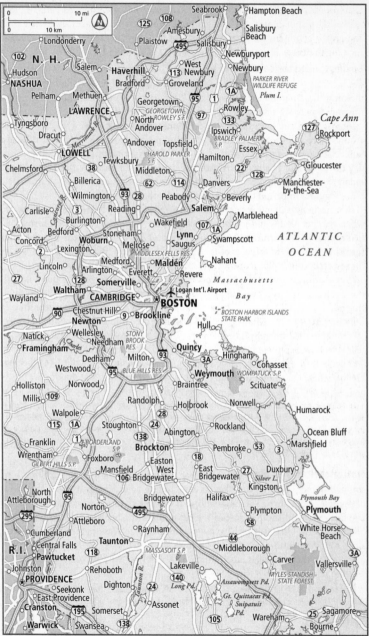

Ground, at the west end of the green, dates to 1690 and contains Parker's grave. A stop at the visitor center and a walk around the monuments takes about half an hour and gives a good sense of what went on here and why the participants are still held in such high esteem.

Lexington Historical Society 𝕶𝕶 *Kids* The historical society's signature properties were among the country's first **historic houses** when restoration of the three buildings began around the turn of the 20th century. A guided tour (30–45 min.) is the only way to see the houses.

Across from the Battle Green is the **Buckman Tavern** 𝕶𝕶, 1 Bedford St., built around 1710. If time is short and you have to pick just one house to visit, make it this one. The interior of the tavern has been restored to approximate its appearance on the day of the battle. The colonists gathered here to await word of British troop movements, and they brought their wounded here after the conflict. The tour of the tavern, by guides in period dress, is educational and entertaining.

Within easy walking distance, the **Hancock-Clarke House,** 36 Hancock St., is where Samuel Adams and John Hancock were staying when Paul Revere arrived. They fled to nearby Woburn. The 1698 house with a 1738 addition contains some original furnishings as well as artifacts of the Battle of Lexington. *Note:* This house will close for restoration in 2008, reopening for the 2009 season.

The British took over the **Munroe Tavern** 𝕶, 1332 Mass. Ave. (about 1 mile from the Green), to use as their headquarters and, after the battle, as their field hospital. In this building (1690), you'll learn more about the royal troops and see furniture carefully preserved by the Munroe family, including the table and chair President George Washington used when he dined here in 1789. The historically accurate gardens in the rear (free admission) are beautifully planted and maintained.

The historical society makes its headquarters downtown in the 1846 Lexington Depot, where changing exhibits on local history are open to the public.

Depot Square (off Mass. Ave. near the Battle Green). (℄ **781/862-1703** or 781/862-5598 for information about group tours, offered by appointment only. www.lexingtonhistory.org. **Buckman Tavern:** Daily Apr–Oct. Tours every 30 min. 10am–4pm. Closed Nov–Mar. **Hancock-Clarke House:** Sat–Sun Apr to mid-June; daily mid-June to Oct. Tours every 30 min. 11am–2pm. Closed Nov–Mar. **Munroe Tavern:** Sat–Sun Apr to mid-June; daily mid-June to Oct. Tours every 30 min. 11am–3pm. Closed Nov–Mar. Admission $6 adults for 1 house, $8 for 2, $10 for all 3; $4 children 6–16 for 1 house, $5 for 2, $7 for all 3.

National Heritage Museum 𝕶𝕶 *Kids* This fascinating museum explores history through popular culture. It makes an entertaining complement to the Colonial focus of the rest of the town. The installations in the six exhibition spaces change regularly; you can start with another dose of the Revolution, the permanent exhibit *Sowing the Seeds of Liberty.* Other topics have ranged from George Washington to mail-order catalogs to 19th-century inventions. Lectures, concerts, and family programs are also offered, and the cafe serves lunch (Tues–Sat). The Scottish Rite of Freemasonry sponsors the museum.

33 Marrett Rd., Rte. 2A (at Mass. Ave.). (℄ **781/861-6559.** www.nationalheritagemuseum.org. Free admission. Mon–Sat 10am–5pm; Sun noon–5pm. Bus: 62 or 76 from downtown Lexington to Rte. 2A.

SHOPPING

A stroll along **Mass. Ave.** near the center of town won't disappoint. Check out **Waldenbooks,** 1713 Mass. Ave. (℄ **781/862-7870**); **Upper Story Books,** 1730 Mass. Ave. (℄ **781/862-0999**); and the **Crafty Yankee,** 1838 Mass. Ave. (℄ **800/286-3037** or

Lexington

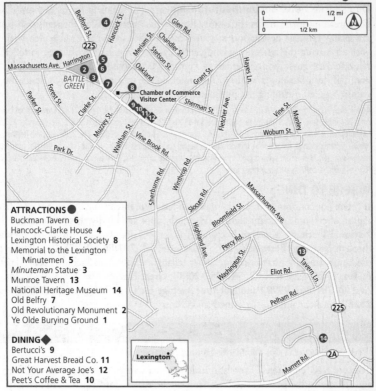

ATTRACTIONS ●
Buckman Tavern **6**
Hancock-Clarke House **4**
Lexington Historical Society **8**
Memorial to the Lexington
    Minutemen **5**
Minuteman Statue **3**
Munroe Tavern **13**
National Heritage Museum **14**
Old Belfry **7**
Old Revolutionary Monument **2**
Ye Olde Burying Ground **1**

DINING ◆
Bertucci's **9**
Great Harvest Bread Co. **11**
Not Your Average Joe's **12**
Peet's Coffee & Tea **10**

781/863-1219). One of the best-known yarn shops in eastern Massachusetts is **Wild & Woolly Studio,** 7A Meriam St., off Mass. Ave. (© **781/861-7717**).

WHERE TO STAY

Starwood introduced two brands to the Boston-area market in 2008 with the opening of **Aloft Lexington** (© **877/GO-ALOFT** or 781/861-1391; www.aloftlexington. com) and **Element Lexington** (© **877/ELEMENT** or 781/761-1750; www.element lexington.com). Aloft rooms have 9-foot ceilings that make the good-size units feel even larger; the hotel has a pool and a 24-hour restaurant. Rates start at $219 on week-days, with weekend and off-season discounts. The extended-stay Element brand targets business travelers; units have full kitchens and Westin's signature Heavenly Beds. High-season weekday rates start at $259. The newly built hotels are on the same property (which formerly held a Sheraton) at 727 Marrett Rd. It's just off I-95/Route 128 exit 30B, far enough from the interstate that traffic noise isn't a serious problem.

WHERE TO STAY NEARBY

Bedford is 15 minutes from downtown Lexington on Route 4/225, across I-95. The **Boston/Bedford Travelodge,** 285 Great Rd., Bedford (© **781/275-6120;** www. travelodge.com), is an affordable motel with an outdoor pool. A double room runs about $79 in high season.

Doubletree Hotel Boston/Bedford Glen ⚐ The sights in Lexington and Concord are convenient to this three-story hotel, which neatly makes the transition from a weekday business destination to a weekend family resort. There's also plenty to do without leaving the attractively landscaped 24-acre property. Doubletree completely renovated the guest rooms after taking over in 2007, adding marble baths, cushy beds, and high-tech business amenities. The hotel shuttle transports guests to destinations within 5 miles, including the Burlington Mall.

44 Middlesex Tpk., Bedford, MA 01730. ℂ 800/HOTELS-1 or 781/275-5500. Fax 781/275-8956. www.doubletree. com. 284 units. Sun–Thurs $129–$249 double; Fri–Sat $109–$229 double. Extra person $15. Children under 19 stay free in parent's room. Packages and senior and AAA discounts available. AE, DC, DISC, MC, V. **Amenities:** Restaurant (New England); lounge; indoor pool; indoor/outdoor tennis courts; fitness center; Jacuzzi; sauna; shuttle; concierge; business center; 24-hr. room service; laundry service; dry cleaning. *In room:* A/C, TV w/pay movies, high-speed and Wi-Fi access, fridge, coffeemaker, hair dryer, iron.

WHERE TO DINE

If you're not continuing to Concord, which has more interesting dining options, Lexington offers some pleasant choices. The fresh soups and sandwiches at the cafe at the **National Heritage Museum** (see above) make it a popular spot for lunch Tuesday through Saturday. **Bertucci's,** 1777 Mass. Ave. (ℂ **781/860-9000**), is a branch of the family-friendly pizzeria chain. Other reliable chain outlets include **Peet's Coffee & Tea,** 1749 Mass. Ave. (ℂ **781/357-2090**); **Great Harvest Bread Co.,** 1736 Mass. Ave. (ℂ **781/861-9990**); and **Not Your Average Joe's,** 1727 Mass. Ave. (ℂ **978/674-2828**), for pizza and creative American cuisine.

2 Concord

18 miles NW of Boston; 15 miles NW of Cambridge; 6 miles W of Lexington.

Concord (say "conquered") revels in its legacy as a center of groundbreaking thought and its role in the country's political and intellectual history. A visit can easily fill a day; if your interests are specialized or time is short, a half-day excursion is reasonable. For an excellent overview of town history, start your visit at the **Concord Museum.**

After just a little time in this lovely town, you may find yourself adopting the local attitude toward two of its most famous residents: Ralph Waldo Emerson, a well-respected uncle figure, and Henry David Thoreau, everyone's favorite eccentric cousin. Long before they wandered the countryside, the first official battle of the Revolutionary War took place at the North Bridge, now part of Minute Man National Historical Park. By the middle of the 19th century, Concord was the center of the Transcendentalist movement. Homes of Emerson, Thoreau, Nathaniel Hawthorne, and Louisa May Alcott are open to visitors, as is the authors' final resting place, Sleepy Hollow Cemetery.

ESSENTIALS

GETTING THERE From Lexington (10 min. by car), take Route 2A west from Mass. Ave. (Rte. 4/225) at the National Heritage Museum; follow the BATTLE ROAD signs. From Boston and Cambridge (30–40 min.), take Route 2 into Lincoln and stay in the right lane. Where the main road makes a sharp left, go straight onto Cambridge Turnpike, and follow signs to HISTORIC CONCORD. To go directly to Walden Pond, use the left lane, take what's now Route 2/2A another mile or so, and turn left onto Route 126. There's parking throughout town and at the attractions.

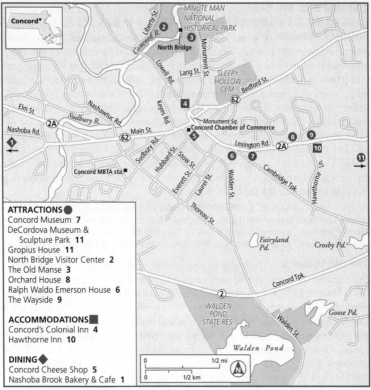

The **commuter rail** (© **800/392-6100** or 617/222-3200; www.mbta.com) takes about 45 minutes from North Station in Boston, with a stop at Porter Square in Cambridge. The round-trip fare is $13. The station is about ¾ of a mile over flat terrain from the town center. There is no bus service from Boston to Concord. For information about **Liberty Ride** tours, which cover Concord and Lexington, see "Getting Around," p. 150.

VISITOR INFORMATION   The **Chamber of Commerce,** 15 Walden St., Suite 7 (© **978/369-3120;** www.concordchamberofcommerce.org), maintains a visitor center at 58 Main St., next to Middlesex Savings Bank, 1 block south of Monument Square. It's open daily 10am to 4:30pm from April through October; public restrooms in the same building are open year-round. Guided walking tours are available. Weekday and group tours are available by appointment. The town website (**www.concord ma.gov**) includes visitor information. You can also contact the **Greater Merrimack Valley Convention & Visitors Bureau** (© **800/443-3332** or 978/459-6150; www. merrimackvalley.org).

GETTING AROUND   Major attractions are within walking distance of downtown. If you're trying to stop everywhere in a day or are visiting Walden Pond or Great Meadows, you'll need a car.

SEEING THE SIGHTS
LITERARY LANDMARKS & HISTORIC ATTRACTIONS

Concord Museum 𝕲𝕲 *Kids*   Just when you're (understandably) suspecting that everything interesting in this area started on April 18, 1775, and ended the next day, this superb museum sets you straight. It's a great place to start your visit to the town. The **History Galleries** 𝕲𝕲 explore the question "Why Concord?" Artifacts, murals, films, maps, documents, and other presentations illustrate the town's role as a Native American settlement, Revolutionary War battleground, 19th-century intellectual center, and focal point of the 20th-century historic preservation movement. One of the lanterns that signaled Paul Revere from the Old North Church is on display. You'll also see the contents of Ralph Waldo Emerson's study and a large collection of Henry David Thoreau's belongings. Pick up a **family activity pack** 𝕲 as you enter and use the games and reproduction artifacts (including a quill pen and powder horn) to give the kids a hands-on feel for life in the past.

Cambridge Tpk. at Lexington Rd. ⓒ **978/369-9609** (recorded info) or 978/369-9763. www.concordmuseum.org. Admission $10 adults, $8 seniors and students, $5 children 6–18. June–Aug daily 9am–5pm; Apr–May and Sept–Dec Mon–Sat 9am–5pm, Sun noon–5pm; Jan–Mar Mon–Sat 11am–4pm, Sun 1–4pm. Follow Lexington Rd. out of Concord Center and bear right at museum onto Cambridge Tpk.; entrance is on left. Parking allowed on road.

The Old Manse 𝕲   The engaging history of this home touches on the military and the literary, but it's mostly the story of a family. The Rev. William Emerson built the Old Manse in 1770 and watched the Battle of Concord from his yard. For almost 170 years, the house was home to his widow, her second husband, their descendants, and two famous friends. Nathaniel Hawthorne and his bride, Sophia Peabody, moved in after their marriage in 1842 and stayed for 3 years. As a wedding present, Henry David Thoreau sowed the vegetable garden (re-created today) for them. William's grandson Ralph Waldo Emerson wrote the essay "Nature" here. Today you'll see mementos and memorabilia of the Emerson and Ripley families and of the Hawthornes, who scratched notes on two windows with Sophia's diamond ring.

269 Monument St. (at North Bridge). ⓒ **978/369-3909**. www.oldmanse.org. Guided tour $8 adults, $7 seniors and students, $5 children 6–12, $25 families. Patriots Day weekend to Columbus Day Mon–Sat 10am–5pm, Sun and holidays noon–5pm (last tour at 4:30pm). Closed mid-Oct to mid-Apr. From Concord Center, follow Monument St. to North Bridge parking lot (on right); Old Manse is on left.

Orchard House 𝕲𝕲𝕲 *Kids*   *Little Women* (1868), Louisa May Alcott's best-known and most popular work, was written and set at Orchard House. Seeing the family home brings the Alcotts to life for legions of female visitors and their pleasantly surprised male companions. Fans won't want to miss the excellent tour, copiously illustrated with heirlooms. Serious buffs can check in advance for information on special events and holiday programs, some of which require reservations.

Louisa's father, the writer and educator Amos Bronson Alcott, created Orchard House by joining and restoring two homes. Bronson and his wife, the social activist Abigail May Alcott, and their family lived here from 1858 to 1877, socializing in the same circles as Emerson, Thoreau, and Hawthorne. Models for the characters in *Little Women* included Anna ("Meg"), an amateur actress, and May ("Amy"), a talented artist. Elizabeth ("Beth"), a gifted musician, died before the family moved to this house.

399 Lexington Rd. ⓒ **978/369-4118**. www.louisamayalcott.org. Guided tour $9 adults, $7 seniors and students, $5 children 6–17, $25 families. Apr–Oct Mon–Sat 10am–4:30pm, Sun 1–4:30pm; Nov–Mar Mon–Fri 11am–3pm, Sat 10am–4:30pm, Sun 1–4:30pm. Closed Jan 1–15. Follow Lexington Rd. out of Concord Center and bear left at Concord Museum; house is on left. Overflow parking across the street.

Ralph Waldo Emerson House   This house offers a taste of the days when a philosopher could attain the status we now associate with rock stars. Emerson, also an essayist and poet, lived here from 1835 until his death, in 1882. He moved here after marrying his second wife, Lydia Jackson, whom he called "Lydian"; she called him "Mr. Emerson," as the staff still does. The tour gives a good look at his personal side and at the fashionably ornate interior decoration of the time. You'll see original furnishings and some of Emerson's personal effects.

28 Cambridge Tpk. © 978/369-2236. Guided tours $7 adults, $5 seniors and students. Call to arrange group tours (10 people or more). Patriots Day weekend to late Oct Thurs–Sat 10am–4:30pm, Sun 1–4:30pm. Closed late Oct to mid-Apr. Follow Cambridge Tpk. out of Concord Center; just before Concord Museum, house is on right.

Sleepy Hollow Cemetery 🏛   Follow the signs for AUTHOR'S RIDGE and climb the hill to the graves of some of the town's literary lights, including the Alcotts, Emerson, Hawthorne, and Thoreau. Emerson's bears no religious symbols, just an uncarved quartz boulder. Thoreau is buried nearby; at his funeral, in 1862, his old friend Emerson concluded his eulogy with these words: " . . . wherever there is knowledge, wherever there is virtue, wherever there is beauty, he will find a home."

Entrance on Rte. 62 W. © 978/318-3233. www.concordma.gov. Daily 7am to dusk, weather permitting. No buses allowed.

The Wayside ★   The Wayside was Nathaniel Hawthorne's home from 1852 until his death, in 1864. The Alcotts also lived here (the girls called it "the yellow house"), as did Harriett Lothrop, who wrote the *Five Little Peppers* books under the pen name Margaret Sidney and owned most of the current furnishings. The Wayside is part of Minute Man National Historical Park, and the fascinating 45-minute ranger-led tour illuminates the occupants' lives and the house's crazy-quilt architecture. The exhibit in the barn (free admission) consists of audio presentations and figures of the authors. Call ahead to double-check hours, which are subject to change.

455 Lexington Rd. © 978/318-7863. www.nps.gov/mima. Guided tour $5 adults, free for children under 17. May–Oct; open days and hours vary. Closed Nov–Apr. Follow Lexington Rd. out of Concord Center past Concord Museum and Orchard House. Parking across the street.

MINUTE MAN NATIONAL HISTORICAL PARK 🏛🏛

This 970-acre park preserves the scene of the first Revolutionary War battle, on April 19, 1775. After the skirmish at Lexington, the British continued to Concord in search of stockpiled arms (which the colonists had already moved). Warned of the advance, the Minutemen crossed the North Bridge, evading the "regulars" standing guard, and awaited reinforcements. The British searched nearby homes and burned any guns they found, and the colonials, seeing the smoke, mistakenly thought the soldiers were burning the town. The gunfire that ensued, the opening salvo of the Revolution, is remembered as "the shot heard round the world."

The park is open daily year-round. A visit can take as little as half an hour—for a jaunt to the North Bridge (a reproduction)—or as long as half a day (or more), if you stop at both visitor centers and perhaps participate in a ranger-led program. Park management suggests beginning your visit at the Minute Man Visitor Center (see "Lexington," above), which is closed in the winter. Alternatively, start at the **North Bridge Visitor Center** 🏛, 174 Liberty St., off Monument Street (© **978/369-6993;** www.nps.gov/mima), which overlooks the Concord River and the bridge. A diorama and video illustrate the battle; exhibits include uniforms, weapons, and tools of Colonial and British soldiers. Park rangers lead programs and answer questions. Outside, picnicking is allowed, and the scenery (especially the fall foliage) is lovely. The center is open daily from 9am to 5pm (11am–3pm in winter).

To go straight to the bridge, follow Monument Street until you see the parking lot on the right. Walk a short distance to the bridge, stopping along the unpaved path to read and hear the narratives. On one side of the bridge is a plaque commemorating the British soldiers who died in the Revolutionary War. On the other side is Daniel Chester French's **Minute Man** statue, engraved with a stanza of the poem Emerson wrote for the dedication ceremony in 1876.

NEARBY SIGHTS
DeCordova Museum and Sculpture Park ☆☆
Indoors and out, this museum shows the work of American contemporary and modern artists, with an emphasis on living New England residents. The main building, on a leafy hilltop, overlooks a pond and the sculpture park. Exhibits center on imaginative themes as well as the work of individual artists. Picnicking is allowed in the sculpture park; bring your lunch or buy it at the cafe (open Tues noon–3pm, Wed–Sun 11am–4pm). Free tours of the main galleries start at 1pm Thursday and 2pm Sunday year-round; sculpture-park tours run May through October on Saturday and Sunday at 1pm.

51 Sandy Pond Rd., Lincoln. ✆ 781/259-8355. www.decordova.org. Museum: $12 adults; $8 seniors, students, and children 6–12. Tues–Sun and Mon holidays 11am–5pm. Sculpture park: Free admission when museum is closed. Daily daylight hours. From Rte. 2 east, take Rte. 126 south to Baker Bridge Rd. (1st left after Walden Pond). When it ends, go right onto Sandy Pond Rd.; museum is on left. From I-95, take exit 28B, follow Trapelo Rd. 2½ miles to Sandy Pond Rd., then follow signs.

Gropius House ☆
Architect Walter Gropius (1883–1969), founder of the Bauhaus school of design, built this hilltop home for his family in 1938 after accepting a job at the Harvard Graduate School of Design. He used traditional materials such as clapboard, brick, and fieldstone, with components then seldom seen in domestic architecture, including glass blocks and chrome (on the banisters). Marcel Breuer designed many of the furnishings, which were made for the family at the Bauhaus. Decorated as it was in the last decade of Gropius's life, the house affords a revealing look at his life, career, and philosophy.

68 Baker Bridge Rd., Lincoln. ✆ 781/259-8098. www.historicnewengland.org. Admission $10 adults, $9 seniors, $5 students and children. Tours on the hour June–Oct 15 Wed–Sun 11am–4pm; Oct 16–May Sat–Sun 11am–4pm. From Rte. 2 east, take Rte. 126 south to left on Baker Bridge Rd. (1st left after Walden Pond); house is on right. From I-95, take exit 28B, follow Trapelo Rd. to Sandy Pond Rd., go left onto Baker Bridge Rd.; house is on left.

WILDERNESS RETREATS
The titles of Henry David Thoreau's first two published works can serve as starting points: *A Week on the Concord and Merrimack Rivers* (1849) and *Walden* (1854).

To see the area from water level, there's no need to take a week; 2 hours or so should suffice. Rent a **canoe or kayak** ☆ at the **South Bridge Boat House,** 496–502 Main St. (✆ 978/369-9438; www.canoeconcord.com), just over half a mile west of the center of town, and paddle to the North Bridge and back. Rates are about $15 per hour on weekends, less on weekdays.

At **Walden Pond State Reservation** ☆☆, 915 Walden St., Rte. 126 (✆ 978/369-3254; www.mass.gov/dcr), a pile of stones marks the site of the cabin where Thoreau lived from 1845 to 1847. Today the picturesque reservation is an extremely popular destination for walking (a path circles the pond), swimming, and fishing. Although crowded, it's well preserved and insulated from development, making it less difficult than you might expect to imagine Thoreau's experience. Call for the schedule of interpretive programs. No dogs or bikes are allowed. Parking costs $5. In good weather, the lot fills early every day—call before setting out, because the rangers turn away visitors if the park has reached capacity (1,000). From Concord Center, take Walden Street (Rte. 126) south, cross Route 2, and follow signs to the parking lot.

Another Thoreau haunt, an especially popular destination for birders, is **Great Meadows National Wildlife Refuge** ★, 73 Weir Hill Rd., Sudbury (© **978/443-4661;** www.fws.gov/northeast/greatmeadows). The Concord portion of the 3,400-acre refuge includes 2.5 miles of walking trails around man-made ponds that attract abundant wildlife. More than 200 species of native and migratory birds have been recorded. The refuge is open daily from sunrise to sunset; admission is free. Dogs are not allowed. Follow Route 62 (Bedford St.) east out of Concord Center for 1⅓ miles, then turn left onto Monsen Road.

SHOPPING

Downtown Concord, off **Monument Square,** is a terrific shopping destination. Here you'll find the **Toy Shop of Concord,** 4 Walden St. (© **978/369-2553**); the **Grasshopper Shop,** 36 Main St. (© **978/369-8295**), which carries women's clothing and accessories; jewelry at **Mascio-Ricci,** 48 Monument Sq. (© **978/371-1191**); and the **Concord Bookshop,** 65 Main St. (© **978/369-2405**). The compact shopping district in **West Concord,** along Route 62, boasts the old-fashioned **West Concord 5 & 10,** 106 Commonwealth Ave. (© **978/369-9011**), which carries everything from light bulbs to lace.

WHERE TO STAY

The **Best Western at Historic Concord,** 740 Elm St. (© **800/780-7234** or 978/369-6100; www.bestwestern.com), is just off Route 2, about 2 miles from the center of town. The motel has a fitness room and a seasonal outdoor pool. Doubles go for $119 to $149, which includes continental breakfast and wireless Internet access.

Concord's Colonial Inn ★   The main building of the Colonial Inn has overlooked Monument Square since 1716. Like many historic inns, it's not luxurious, but it is comfortable and centrally located. Additions since it became a hotel in 1889 have left the inn large enough to offer modern conveniences (including wireless Internet access) and small enough to feel friendly. It's popular with businesspeople as well as vacationers, especially during foliage season. The 15 original guest rooms—one of which (no. 24) supposedly is haunted—are in great demand. Reserve early if you want to stay in the main inn, which is decorated in Colonial style. Rooms in the 1970 Prescott House have country-style decor, and four free-standing buildings hold one-, two-, and three-bedroom suites suitable for long-term stays.

Two lounges serve light meals; outdoor tables afford a front-row seat for the action on Monument Square. The restaurant serves salads, sandwiches, and pasta at lunch, and traditional American fare at dinner. Afternoon tea is served Friday through Sunday; reservations required (© **978/369-2373**).

48 Monument Sq., Concord, MA 01742. © 800/370-9200 or 978/369-9200. Fax 978/371-1533. www.concords colonialinn.com. 56 units (some with shower only). Apr to early Sept $179–$229 main inn, $149–$199 Prescott House; mid-Sept to Oct $199–$249 main inn, $169–$219 Prescott House; Nov–Mar from $159 main inn, from $129 Prescott House. Long-term discounts available. AE, DC, DISC, MC, V. **Amenities:** Restaurant (American); 2 lounges; bar w/live jazz and blues nightly; access to nearby health club ($10); concierge; tour desk; business center; same-day dry cleaning. *In room:* A/C, TV/DVD, Wi-Fi, coffeemaker, hair dryer, iron.

Tips North of Boston: Planning Pointers

For convenience and flexibility, drive to destinations north of Boston if you can. Renting a car may be cheaper than the commuter rail if your group is large enough; even if it isn't, flexibility is priceless. The trip from Boston to Cape Ann on I-93 and Route 128 by car takes about an hour. A more leisurely excursion on Routes 1A, 129, and 114 takes you through Marblehead to Salem. You can also follow Route 1 to I-95 and Route 128, but don't attempt it during rush hour. To take Route 1A, leave downtown through the Callahan or Ted Williams Tunnel. If you miss the entrance and wind up on I-93, follow signs to Route 1 and pick up Route 1A in Revere. The **North of Boston Convention & Visitors Bureau** (© 800/742-5306 or 978/977-7760; www.northofboston.org) publishes a visitor guide that covers many destinations in this chapter. The website of the **Essex National Heritage Area** (© 978/740-0444; www.essexheritage.org) is another good resource.

Hawthorne Inn ★★   This is the quintessential country inn. Built around 1870, it sits on a tree-shaded property across the street from Nathaniel Hawthorne's home, the Wayside. Antiques and handmade quilts enhance the rooms, which aren't huge but are meticulously maintained and gorgeously decorated. My favorite is the Walden Room, which has black wallpaper, but they're all delightful. Original art is on display throughout, and there's a small pond in the peaceful garden. Personable innkeepers Gregory Burch and Marilyn Mudry, who have been in business for more than 3 decades, acquaint interested guests with the philosophical, spiritual, military, and literary aspects of Concord's history.

462 Lexington Rd., Concord, MA 01742. © **978/369-5610.** Fax 978/287-4949. www.concordmass.com. 7 units (some with shower only). $165–$315 double. Rates include continental breakfast. Extra person $30. Off-season discounts available. AE, DISC, MC, V. From Concord Center, take Lexington Rd. ¼ mile east; inn is on right. *In room:* A/C, Wi-Fi, hair dryer, iron, robes.

WHERE TO DINE

See also the **Colonial Inn,** above. For basic to lavish picnic provisions, stop in downtown Concord at the **Concord Cheese Shop,** 29 Walden St. (© **978/369-5778;** www.concordcheeseshop.com).

Nashoba Brook Bakery & Café ★ AMERICAN   The enticing variety of artisan breads, baked goods, pastries, and made-from-scratch soups, salads, and sandwiches makes this airy cafe a popular destination throughout the day. The industrial-looking building off West Concord's main street backs up to little Nashoba Brook, which is visible through the glass back wall. Order and pick up at the counter, then grab a seat along the window or near the children's play area. Or order takeout—this is great picnic food.

152 Commonwealth Ave., West Concord. © **978/318-1999.** www.slowrise.com. Sandwiches $7; other menu items $2–$8. MC, V. Mon–Fri 7am–5:30pm; Sat 7am–5pm; Sun 8am–5pm. From Concord Center, follow Main St. (Rte. 62) west, across Rte. 2; bear right at traffic light in front of train station and go 3 blocks. For overflow parking, turn right onto Commonwealth Ave. and right onto Winthrop St.

3 Marblehead ★★★

15 miles NE of Boston; 4 miles SE of Salem

Like an attractive person with a great personality, Marblehead has it all. Scenery, history, architecture, and shopping combine to make it one of the area's most popular day trips for both locals and visitors. The narrow streets of historic "Old Town" lead down to the magnificent harbor that helps make Marblehead the self-proclaimed "Yachting Capital of America." Plaques on many homes give the dates of construction as well as the names of the builders and original occupants—a history lesson without any studying.

Many of the houses have stood since before the Revolutionary War, when Marblehead was a center of merchant shipping. Two historic homes are open to visitors. Allow at least a full morning to visit Marblehead, but be flexible, because you may want to hang around.

ESSENTIALS

GETTING THERE   From Boston, take Route 1A north until you see signs in Lynn for Swampscott and Marblehead. Take Lynn Shore Drive to Route 129, and follow it into Marblehead. Or take I-93 or Route 1 to Route 128, then Route 114 through Salem into Marblehead. Except at rush hour, allow 35 to 40 minutes. Parking is tough, especially in Old Town—grab the first spot you see.

MBTA (© **800/392-6100** or 617/222-3200; www.mbta.com) bus no. 441/442 runs from Haymarket (Orange or Green Line) in Boston to downtown Marblehead. During weekday rush periods, bus no. 448/449 connects Marblehead to Downtown Crossing. The trip takes about an hour; the one-way fare is $2.80 with a CharlieCard, $3.50 with a CharlieTicket.

VISITOR INFORMATION   The **Marblehead Chamber of Commerce,** 62 Pleasant St. (© **781/631-2868;** www.visitmarblehead.com), is open weekdays from 9am to 5pm. The **information booth** (© **781/639-8469**) on Pleasant Street near Spring Street is open mid-May through October, weekdays from noon to 5pm, weekends from 10am to 6pm. Before you visit, download a description of a walking tour from the chamber website.

GETTING AROUND   Wear good walking shoes—the car or bus can get you to Marblehead, but it can't negotiate many of the narrow streets of Old Town. The downtown area is fairly compact and moderately hilly.

SPECIAL EVENTS   Sailing regattas take place all summer. The National Offshore One Design (NOOD) Regatta, or **Race Week,** falls in mid- to late July and attracts yachting enthusiasts from all over the country. During the **Christmas Walk,** on the first weekend in December, Santa Claus arrives by lobster boat.

EXPLORING THE TOWN

A stroll through the winding streets of **Old Town** ★★★ invariably leads to shopping, snacking, or gazing at something picturesque, be it the harbor or a beautiful home. Be sure to spend some time in **Crocker Park** ★★, on the water off Front Street. Especially in warm weather, when boats jam the harbor, the view is breathtaking. The park has benches and allows picnicking. The view from **Fort Sewall,** at the other end of Front Street, is just as mesmerizing. The ruins of the fort, built in the 17th century and rebuilt late in the 18th, are another excellent picnic spot.

Just inland, the **Lafayette House** is a private home at the corner of Hooper and Union streets. Legend has it that one corner of the first floor was chopped off in 1824 to allow Lafayette's carriage to negotiate the turn. In Market Square, on Washington Street near State Street, is the **Old Town House,** a public meeting and gathering place since 1727.

By car or bicycle, the swanky residential community of **Marblehead Neck** 𝒢 is worth a look. Follow Ocean Avenue across the causeway. Here you can visit the **Audubon Bird Sanctuary** (𝒸 **800/AUDUBON** or 781/259-9500; www.mass audubon.org); look for the tiny sign at the corner of Risley Avenue. Admission is free. Or continue to **Castle Rock** for another eyeful of scenery. At the end of "the Neck," at Harbor and Ocean avenues, is **Chandler Hovey Park,** which has a (closed) lighthouse and a panoramic view. Many inns and B&Bs provide bikes for guests' use; to rent, visit **Marblehead Cycle,** 25 Bessom St., 1 block off Pleasant Street (𝒸 **781/631-1570;** www.marbleheadcycle.com). Bikes go for $14 for a half-day, $20 for a full day.

Abbot Hall   A 5-minute stop here (look for the clock tower) is just the ticket if you want to be able to say you did some sightseeing. The town offices and Historical Commission share Abbot Hall with Archibald M. Willard's famous painting *The Spirit of '76* 𝒢, on display in the Selectmen's Meeting Room. The thrill of recognizing the ubiquitous drummer, drummer boy, and fife player is the main reason to stop here. Cases in the halls contain artifacts from the Historical Society's collections.

Washington Sq. 𝒸 **781/631-0528.** www.marblehead.org. Free admission. Year-round Mon–Tues and Thurs 8am–5pm, Wed 7:30am–7:30pm, Fri 8am–1pm; May–Oct also open Fri 1–5pm, Sat 9am–6pm, Sun 11am–6pm. From the historic district, follow Washington St. up the hill.

Jeremiah Lee Mansion 𝒢𝒢   Built in 1768 for a wealthy merchant, the Lee mansion is an extraordinary example of pre-Revolutionary Georgian architecture. Rococo woodcarving and other details complement historically accurate room arrangements; the most exciting feature for aficionados is the original hand-painted wallpaper. Ongoing restoration and interpretation by the Marblehead Museum & Historical Society place the 18th- and 19th-century furnishings and artifacts in context. The friendly guides welcome questions and are well versed in the history of the home. The lawn and gardens are open to the public.

Across the street is a visitor center that houses two galleries; one shows changing exhibits and the other paintings by the noted folk artist J. O. J. Frost, a Marblehead native. Call ahead for the schedule of **summer walking tours.**

161 Washington St. 𝒸 **781/631-1768.** www.marbleheadmuseum.org. Guided tours $5 adults, $4.50 seniors and students. June–Oct Tues–Sat 10am–4pm. Closed Nov–May. Visitor center: 170 Washington St. Free admission. June–Oct Tues–Sat 10am–4pm; Nov–May Tues–Fri 10am–4pm. From Abbot Hall, follow Washington St. down the hill; mansion is on left.

King Hooper Mansion/Marblehead Arts Association & Gallery   Shipping tycoon Robert Hooper got his nickname because he treated his sailors so well, but it's easy to think he was called "King" because he lived like royalty. Around the corner from the home of Jeremiah Lee (whose sister-in-law was the second of Hooper's four wives), the 1728 mansion gained a Georgian addition sometime after 1745. The **Marblehead Arts Association** stages exhibits, schedules special events, and runs a gift shop that sells members' work. The mansion has a lovely garden; enter through the gate at the right of the house.

Marblehead

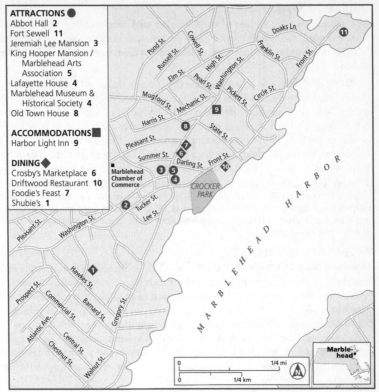

ATTRACTIONS ●
Abbot Hall **2**
Fort Sewell **11**
Jeremiah Lee Mansion **3**
King Hooper Mansion /
  Marblehead Arts
  Association **5**
Lafayette House **4**
Marblehead Museum &
  Historical Society **4**
Old Town House **8**

ACCOMMODATIONS ■
Harbor Light Inn **9**

DINING ◆
Crosby's Marketplace **6**
Driftwood Restaurant **10**
Foodie's Feast **7**
Shubie's **1**

8 Hooper St. ✆ **781/631-2608**. www.marbleheadarts.org. Free admission. May–Oct Tues–Sat 11am–5pm, Sun noon–5pm; Nov–Apr Tues–Sat noon–4pm, Sun 1–5pm. Where Washington St. curves at the foot of hill near Lee Mansion, look for the colorful sign.

SHOPPING ★★

One of Marblehead's claims to fame is its excellent retail scene. Shops, boutiques, and galleries abound in **Old Town** and on **Atlantic Avenue** and the east end of **Pleasant Street.**

The most unusual shop in town is **Antiquewear,** 82 Front St. (✆ **781/639-0070**), near the town pier. It sells 19th-century buttons ingeniously fashioned into women's and men's jewelry of all descriptions. Other good stops include **Arnould Gallery & Framery,** 111 Washington St. (✆ **781/631-6366**); **Artists & Authors,** 108 Washington St. (✆ **781/639-0400;** www.artists-authors.com), which carries rare books and fine art; **Cargo Unlimited,** 82 Washington St. (✆ **781/631-1112;** www.cargounlimited.com), for home furnishings and accessories; **Erlich Gallery,** 96 Washington St. (✆ **781/631-1202;** www.erlichgallery.com); and the **Marblehead Toy Shop,** 44–48 Atlantic Ave. (✆ **781/631-9900**).

WHERE TO STAY

The accommodations listings of the **Chamber of Commerce** (📞 781/631-2868; www.visitmarblehead.com) include many of the town's innumerable inns and B&Bs. Contact the chamber or consult one of the agencies listed in chapter 5 under "Where to Stay."

Harbor Light Inn 👯 Two Federal-era mansions make up this gracious inn, a stone's throw from the Old Town House. From the wood floors to the 1729 beams (in a third-floor room) to the swimming pool, it's both historic and relaxing. Rooms are comfortably furnished in period style, with some lovely antiques; most have canopy or four-poster beds. Eleven have working fireplaces, and five have double Jacuzzis. The best rooms, on the top floor at the back of the building (away from the street), have gorgeous harbor views. The undeniably romantic inn also attracts business travelers.

58 Washington St., Marblehead, MA 01945. 📞 781/631-2186. Fax 781/631-2216. www.harborlightinn.com. 21 units (7 with shower only). $145–$335 double; $195–$375 suite. Rates include breakfast. Corporate rate available midweek. 2- to 3-night minimum weekends and holidays. AE, MC, V. Free parking. **Amenities:** Bar; heated outdoor pool; access to nearby health club ($5); Jacuzzi; concierge; airport shuttle; in-room massage. *In room:* A/C, TV/VCR, Wi-Fi, hair dryer, iron, umbrella, robes.

A SEASIDE INN NEARBY

Diamond District Bed & Breakfast 👯 This comfortable Georgian-style mansion, built in 1911 as a private home, attracts both business and leisure travelers. The Atlantic is a block away; the 3-mile public beach (a good place to burn off the inn's generous breakfast) is popular for jogging, skating, and biking, as well as swimming. It's visible from many of the good-size rooms, tastefully decorated with elaborate Victorian touches. The best are third-floor units with ocean views and Jacuzzis. Two rooms have cozy electric fireplaces. The large living room and porch overlook houses on Lynn Shore Drive and, just past them, the ocean. The whirlpool spa, on the back lawn, also has a water view.

142 Ocean St., Lynn, MA 01902. 📞 800/666-3076 or 781/595-2200. Fax 781/599-5122. www.diamonddistrict inn.com. 11 units (some with shower only). $155–$285 double. Rates include breakfast. Extra person $20. Winter discounts available. 2-night minimum on busy weekends. AE, DC, DISC, MC, V. Take Rte. 1A north to signs for Swamp-scott/Marblehead; after rotary, take Lynn Shore Dr. north, past 2 lights and Christian Science Church. Turn left onto Wolcott Rd., then right onto Ocean St.; inn is on the right. **Amenities:** Outdoor whirlpool. *In room:* A/C, TV, dataport.

WHERE TO DINE

You're better off heading to Salem if you want a sit-down meal, but I prefer sitting down outdoors—for a picnic. Stock up at **Foodie's Feast,** 114 Washington St. (📞 781/639-1104; www.foodiesfeast.com); **Crosby's Marketplace,** 115 Washington St. (📞 781/631-1741; www.crosbysmarkets.com); or **Shubie's,** 16 Atlantic Ave. (📞 781/631-0149; www.shubies.com).

See "Salem," below, for information about the **Rockmore Restaurant.**

Driftwood Restaurant 🐟 DINER/SEAFOOD At the foot of State Street next to Clark Landing (the town pier) is an honest-to-goodness local hangout. Join the crowd at a table or the counter for generous portions of breakfast (served all day) or lunch. Try pancakes or hash, chowder or a seafood "roll" (a hot-dog bun filled with, say, fried clams or lobster salad). The house specialty, served on weekends and holidays, is fried dough, a sort of New England beignet. At busy times, you may have to wait outside for a table.

63 Front St. 📞 781/631-1145. Main courses $3–$12; breakfast items under $7. No credit cards. Daily 5:30am–2pm.

4 Salem ★★

16 miles NE of Boston; 4 miles NW of Marblehead

Settled in 1626 (4 years before Boston) and later known around the world as a center of merchant shipping, Salem is internationally famous today for a 7-month episode in 1692. The witchcraft trials led to 20 deaths, centuries of notoriety, countless lessons on the evils of prejudice, and innumerable bad puns ("Stop by for a spell" is a favorite slogan). Today the city abounds with witch-associated attractions. Most are historically accurate, but you'll also see a fair number of goofy souvenirs and opportunistic tourist traps. An excellent antidote is the **Peabody Essex Museum.** Salem is a family-friendly destination that's worth at least a half-day visit, perhaps after a stop in Marblehead; it can easily fill a day.

Visitors concentrating on wall-to-wall witches will miss another important part of the city's history. Salem's merchant vessels circled the globe in the 17th and 18th centuries, returning laden with treasures. The city peaked between the Revolutionary War and the War of 1812, with the opening of the China trade—many overseas merchants even believed that Salem was an independent country. One reminder of that era, a replica of the 1797 East Indiaman tall ship *Friendship,* is anchored near the Salem Maritime National Historic Site.

ESSENTIALS

GETTING THERE   From Marblehead, take Route 114 west into downtown Salem. From Boston, take I-93 or Route 1 to Route 128, then Route 114 east. Or take Route 1A north from Boston, being careful in Lynn, where the road turns left and immediately right. There's metered street parking and a reasonably priced garage opposite the visitor center.

From Boston, the **MBTA** (© 800/392-6100 or 617/222-3200; www.mbta.com) runs commuter trains from North Station and bus no. 450 from Haymarket (Orange or Green Line). The train is more comfortable but runs less frequently. It takes 30 to 35 minutes; the round-trip fare is $11. The station is about 5 blocks from the downtown area. The one-way fare for the 35- to 55-minute bus trip is $2.80 with a CharlieCard, $3.50 with a CharlieTicket.

The **Salem Ferry** (© 978/741-0220; www.salemferry.com) operates daily from Memorial Day weekend through October. The 50-minute catamaran trip connects Central Wharf, next to Boston's New England Aquarium (T: Blue Line to Aquarium) to the Blaney Street Wharf, off Derby Street, a 15-minute walk or quick hop on the Salem Trolley (see below) from downtown. The peak adult fare (before 4 pm from late June to early Sept) is $13 one-way, $23 round-trip, with discounts for seniors, children, families, and evening passengers. The one-way off-season fare is $10 for all.

VISITOR INFORMATION   A good place to start is the **National Park Service Regional Visitor Center,** 2 New Liberty St. (© 978/740-1650; www.nps.gov/sama), open daily from 9am to 5pm. Exhibits highlight early settlement, maritime history, and the leather and textiles industries. The center distributes brochures and pamphlets, including one that describes a walking tour of the historic district, and shows a free film on Essex County that provides a good overview.

The city tourism office, **Destination Salem** (© 877/SALEM-MA or 978/744-3663; www.salem.org), produces a free visitor guide that includes a good map. The **Salem Chamber of Commerce,** 265 Essex St. (© 978/744-0004; www.salemchamber.org), maintains a rack of brochures and pamphlets. It's open weekdays 9am to 5pm. The municipal website (www.salem.com) and an excellent community web-site (www.salemweb.com) offer information for out-of-towners.

GETTING AROUND   In the congested downtown area, walking is the way to go. If it's hot or you plan lots of sightseeing, you might prefer to ride. **Salem Trolley** (**© 508/744-5469;** www.salemtrolley.com) offers a 1-hour narrated tour and unlim-ited reboarding at any of its 12 stops. The tour starts at the Essex Street side of the vis-itor center. It operates from 10am to 5pm (last tour at 4pm) daily April through October; check ahead for November hours. Tickets ($12 adults, $10 seniors, $5 chil-dren 6–14) are good all day.

SPECIAL EVENTS   The city's month-long Halloween celebration, **Haunted Hap-penings** (www.hauntedhappenings.org), includes parades, parties, tours, and a ceremony on the big day. In August, the 2-day **Salem Maritime Festival** fills the area around the Salem Maritime National Historic Site (see listing below) with live music, food, and demonstrations of nautical crafts. The festival kicks off **Heritage Days,** a weeklong event that celebrates Salem's multicultural history with musical and theatri-cal performances, a parade, and fireworks. Contact Destination Salem (see "Visitor Information," above) or Escapes North (www.escapesnorth.com) for details.

EXPLORING SALEM

The **historic district** extends well inland from the waterfront; ask at the visitor cen-ter for the walking-tour pamphlet. Many 18th-century houses, some with original fur-nishings, still stand. Ship captains lived near the water at the east end of downtown, in relatively small houses crowded close together. The captains' employers, the ship-ping-company owners, built their homes away from the water (and the accompany-ing aromas). Many lived on the grand thoroughfare of **Chestnut Street**, now a National Historic Landmark.

Salem Historical Tours (**© 978/744-5469;** www.salemhistoricaltours.com) offers the Haunted Footsteps Ghost Tour nightly from April through October. The 90-minute exploration of the spooky and paranormal costs $14 for adults, $10 for sen-iors and students, $8 for children 6 to 14.

By car or trolley, the **Salem Willows** (**© 978/745-0251;** www.salemwillows.com) amusements are 5 minutes away; many signs point the way. The strip of rides and snack bars has a honky-tonk air, and the waterfront park is a good place to bring a pic-nic and wander along the shore. Admission is free; metered parking is available. To enjoy the great view without the arcades and rides, have lunch one peninsula over at **Winter Island Park.**

The House of the Seven Gables (Kids)   Nathaniel Hawthorne's cousin lived here, and stories and legends of the house and its inhabitants inspired his 1851 book. If you haven't read the eerie novel, don't let that keep you away—begin with the audiovisual program, which tells the story. The house, built by Capt. John Turner in 1668, holds six rooms of period furniture, including pieces referred to in the book, and a secret staircase. Tours include a visit to Hawthorne's birthplace and descriptions of what life was like for the house's 18th-century inhabitants. The costumed guides are helpful and eager to answer questions. Also on the grounds, overlooking Salem Harbor, are period gardens, the Retire Beckett House (1655), the Hooper-Hathaway House (1682), and a counting house (1830).

54 Turner St. **© 978/744-0991.** www.7gables.org. Guided tour of house and grounds $12 adults, $11 seniors, $7.25 children 5–12. Surcharges may apply for special exhibitions. July–Oct daily 10am–7pm (until 11pm Oct weekends);

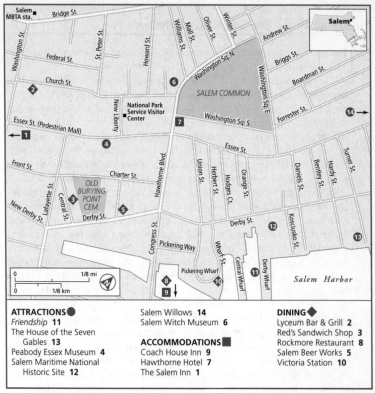

ATTRACTIONS ●

Friendship **11**
The House of the Seven
  Gables **13**
Peabody Essex Museum **4**
Salem Maritime National
  Historic Site **12**

Salem Willows **14**
Salem Witch Museum **6**

ACCOMMODATIONS ■

Coach House Inn **9**
Hawthorne Hotel **7**
The Salem Inn **1**

DINING ◆

Lyceum Bar & Grill **2**
Red's Sandwich Shop **3**
Rockmore Restaurant **8**
Salem Beer Works **5**
Victoria Station **10**

Nov–June daily 10am–5pm. Closed 1st 3 weeks of Jan. From downtown, follow Derby St. east 3 blocks past Derby Wharf.

Peabody Essex Museum ★★ *Kids*   A local favorite since 1799, the Peabody Essex has transformed itself into a national presence. All by itself, this captivating museum is reason enough to visit Salem.

Impressive collections of art from New England and around the world are the Peabody Essex's calling card, but they're just part of the story. The museum owns two dozen houses, including a well-preserved 18th-century Qing dynasty house, **Yin Yu Tang** ★, which was shipped here from China and reassembled. The only example of Chinese domestic architecture outside that country, the house captures 2 centuries of rural life. It sits outside a huge wing designed by Moshe Safdie that opened in 2003.

The 1.4 million items in the permanent collections blend contemporary acquisitions with "the natural and artificial curiosities" Salem's sea captains and merchants brought back from around the world to the Peabody Museum (1799) and local and domestic objects collected by the Essex Institute (1821), the county historical society. The displays help you understand the significance of each object, and interpretive materials (including interactive and hands-on activities) let children get involved. Noteworthy collections include American, African, Indian, Asian, and East Asian art and objects; photography; and the practical arts and crafts of East Asian, Pacific

Trying Times: The Salem Witch Hysteria

The Salem witch trials took place in 1692, a product of old-world superstition, religious control of government, and plain old boredom.

The crisis began quietly in Salem Village (now the town of Danvers). The Rev. Samuel Parris's household included his 9-year-old daughter, Elizabeth; her cousin Abigail; and a West Indian slave named Tituba who told stories to amuse the girls during the long, harsh winter. Entertained by tales of witchcraft, sorcery, and fortunetelling, the girls and their friends began to act out the stories, claiming to be under a spell, rolling on the ground and wailing. The settlers, aware that thousands of people in Europe had been executed as witches in the previous centuries, took the behavior seriously.

At first, only Tituba and two other women were accused of casting spells. The infighting typical of the Puritan theocracy surfaced soon enough, and an accusation of witchcraft became a handy way to settle a score. Anyone "different" was a potential target, from the elderly to the deaf to the poor. A special court convened in Salem proper, and although the girls recanted, the trials began. Defendants had no counsel, and pleading not guilty or objecting to the proceedings was considered equivalent to confessing. From March 1 to September 22, the court convicted 27 of the more than 150 people accused.

In the end, 19 people went to the gallows, and one man who refused to plead, Giles Corey, was pressed to death by stones piled on a board on his chest. Finally, cooler heads prevailed. Leading cleric Cotton Mather and his father, Harvard president Increase Mather, led the call for tolerance. With the jails overflowing, the court called off the trials and freed the remaining prisoners, including Tituba.

The episode's lessons about open-mindedness and tolerance have echoed through the years. Salem was the backdrop for Arthur Miller's 1953 play *The Crucible*, a story about the witch trials as well as an allegory about the McCarthy Senate hearings—another kind of witch hunt in a time when those lessons needed to be taught again.

Island, and Native American peoples. Portraits of area residents include Charles Osgood's omnipresent rendering of Nathaniel Hawthorne.

East India Sq. ⓒ 800/745-4054 or 978/745-9500. www.pem.org. Admission $15 adults, $13 seniors, $11 students, free for children under 17. Yin Yu Tang admission $4 with museum admission. Surcharges may apply for special exhibitions. Daily 10am–5pm. Take Hawthorne Blvd. to Essex St., following signs for visitor center. Enter on Essex St. or New Liberty St.

Salem Maritime National Historic Site ⚑ *(Kids)*   An entertaining introduction to Salem's seagoing history, this complex includes an exciting attraction: a real live ship. The *Friendship* ⚑⚑ is a full-size replica of a 1797 East Indiaman merchant vessel, a three-masted 171-footer that disappeared during the War of 1812. The guided ranger tour includes a tour of the ship.

Central Wharf holds a warehouse (ca. 1800) that houses the orientation center. Tours, which vary seasonally, expand on Salem's maritime history. Yours might include the Derby House (1762), a wedding gift to shipping magnate Elias Hasket Derby from his father. Legend (myth, really) has it that Nathaniel Hawthorne was working at the 1819 Custom House when he found an embroidered scarlet "A." If you prefer to explore on your own, you can see a free film and wander around Derby Wharf, the West India Goods Store, the Bonded Warehouse, the Scale House, and Central Wharf.

174 Derby St. ⓒ **978/740-1660.** www.nps.gov/sama. Free admission. Guided tour $5 adults, $3 seniors and children 6–16. Daily 9am–5pm. Take Derby St. east; just past Pickering Wharf, Derby Wharf is on the right.

Salem Witch Museum ⭐⭐ *Kids*   This is one of the most memorable attractions in eastern Massachusetts—it's both interesting and scary. The main draw of the museum (a former church) is a three-dimensional audiovisual presentation with life-size figures. The show takes place in a huge room lined with displays that are lighted in sequence. The 30-minute narration tells the tale of the witchcraft trials and the accompanying hysteria. The well-researched presentation recounts the story accurately, if somewhat overdramatically. One of the victims was crushed to death by rocks piled on a board on his chest—smaller kids may need a reminder that he's not real.

19½ Washington Sq., on Rte. 1A. ⓒ **978/744-1692.** www.salemwitchmuseum.com. Admission $8 adults, $7 seniors, $5.50 children 6–14. Daily July–Aug 10am–7pm; Sept–June 10am–5pm; check ahead for Oct hours. Follow Hawthorne Blvd. to the northwest corner of Salem Common.

SHOPPING

Pickering Wharf, at the corner of Derby and Congress streets (ⓒ **978/740-6990;** www.pickeringwharf.com), is a waterfront complex of shops, boutiques, restaurants, and condos. It's popular for strolling, snacking, and shopping, and the central location makes it a local landmark.

Several shops specialize in witchcraft accessories. Bear in mind that Salem is home to many practicing witches who take their beliefs very seriously. The **Broom Closet,** 3–5 Central St. (ⓒ **978/741-3669;** www.broomcloset.com), and **Crow Haven Corner,** 125 Essex St. (ⓒ **978/745-8763;** www.crowhavencorner.net), stock everything from crystals to clothing.

Shops throughout New England sell the chocolate confections of **Harbor Sweets** ⭐⭐, Palmer Cove, 85 Leavitt St., off Lafayette Street (ⓒ **978/745-7648;** www.harborsweets.com). The retail store overlooks the floor of the factory. The deliriously good sweets are expensive, but candy bars and small assortments are available. Closed Sunday.

WHERE TO STAY

The busiest and most expensive time of year is **Halloween week;** reserve well in advance if you plan to travel anytime in October.

In nearby **Danvers,** on or near Route 1 north of I-95, many of the major motel chains have locations that lie 30 minutes or less from downtown Salem.

Coach House Inn   Built in 1879 for a ship's captain, this welcoming inn is 2 blocks from the harbor and 9 blocks from downtown. The three-story mansion, set back from the street by a well-kept lawn, is tastefully furnished in just-frilly-enough style. The good-size guest rooms have high ceilings and four-poster beds, and most have (nonworking) fireplaces. Breakfast arrives at your door in a basket. The inn is 15 to 20 minutes on foot or 5 minutes by car from the center of town, up the street from Salem State College.

284 Lafayette St. (Routes 1A and 114), Salem, MA 01970. © **800/688-8689** or 978/744-4092. Fax 978/745-8031. www.coachhousesalem.com. 11 units, 9 with private bathroom (2 with shower only). $115–$185 double; $170–$240 2-room suite. Rates include continental breakfast. 2- to 3-night minimum weekends and holidays. AE, DISC, MC, V. Free parking. *In room:* A/C, TV, Wi-Fi, fridge, coffeemaker.

Hawthorne Hotel ✦   This historic hotel, built in 1925, is both convenient and comfortable. It attracts vacationers and business travelers, and is popular for functions. The six-story building is centrally located and well maintained, with a traditional atmosphere. The attractively furnished guest rooms vary in size from snug to spacious, and some bathrooms are small. The best units, on the Salem Common (north) side of the building, have better views than rooms that face the street. Ask to be as high up as possible, because the neighborhood is busy.

18 Washington Sq. W. (at Salem Common), Salem, MA 01970. © **800/729-7829** or 978/744-4080. Fax 978/ 745-9842. www.hawthornehotel.com. 89 units (30 with shower only). $107–$209 double; $209–$315 suite. Extra person $12. Children under 16 stay free in parent's room. Packages and off-season and senior discounts available. 2-night minimum May–Oct weekends. AE, DC, DISC, MC, V. Limited self-parking. Pets accepted; $10/day; $100 deposit. **Amenities:** Restaurant (American); tavern; exercise room; access to nearby heath club; concierge; airport shuttle; business center; limited room service; laundry service; same-day dry cleaning. *In room:* A/C, TV, Wi-Fi, hair dryer, iron, umbrella.

Salem Inn ✦✦   The Salem Inn occupies the comfortable niche between too-big hotel and too-small B&B. Rooms in its three buildings are large and tastefully decorated; some have fireplaces, canopy beds, and whirlpool baths. The best units are the honeymoon and family suites in the 1874 Peabody House. The variety allows the innkeepers to match accommodations with guests, whether they're honeymooners, sightseers, or families. The peaceful rose garden at the rear of the main building is open to all guests.

7 Summer St. (Rte. 114), Salem, MA 01970. © **800/446-2995** or 978/741-0680. Fax 978/744-8924. www.Salem InnMA.com. 41 units (some with shower only). Nov–Sept $119–$179 double; $169–$229 suite; Oct $180–$225 double, $225–$295 suite. Rates include continental breakfast. 2- to 3-night minimum during holidays and special events. Packages available. AE, DC, DISC, MC, V. Free parking. Pets accepted by prior arrangement ($15–$25/night). *In room:* A/C, TV, Wi-Fi, coffeemaker, hair dryer, iron.

WHERE TO DINE

Pickering Wharf has a food court as well as a restaurant, **Victoria Station** (© **978/ 744-7644;** www.victoriastationinc.com), where the deck has a great view of the marina and the menu emphasizes seafood and traditional American dishes. **Red's Sandwich Shop,** 15 Central St. (© **978/745-3527;** www.redssandwichshop.com), is a local favorite that serves diner-style breakfast and lunch daily. The restaurant and cafe at the **Peabody Essex Museum** (p. 167) serve lunch.

Lyceum Bar & Grill ✦✦ CONTEMPORARY AMERICAN   The elegance of the Lyceum's dining rooms matches the quality of the food, which attracts local businesspeople and out-of-towners. Grilling is the signature cooking technique, but the kitchen is adept with the full range of preparations and delectable (local, when possible) ingredients. At lunch, inventive salads and sandwiches make a fortifying but not incapacitating break from sightseeing. At dinner, flavorful meat and fish dishes are equally delicious. Save room for a traditional yet sophisticated dessert—the brownie sundae is out of this world.

Milling Around: A Trip to Lowell

A 19th-century textile center that later fell into disrepair, Lowell is a 21st-century success story. A city built around restored mills and industrial canals will never be a glamorous vacation spot, but thousands of visitors a year find Lowell a fascinating and rewarding destination. The sights concentrate on the history of the Industrial Revolution and the textile industry. They include boardinghouses where the "mill girls" lived; the workers, some as young as 10, averaged 14-hour days weaving cloth on power looms.

Start at the **Lowell National Historical Park Visitor Center,** 246 Market St. (② **978/970-5000;** www.nps.gov/lowe), open daily from 9am to 5pm. Rangers lead free programs and tours, and canal cruises and free trolley tours operate in summer. Ask for a map of the area, and use it to find your way around downtown. Two interesting museums are within walking distance: the **American Textile History Museum,** 491 Dutton St. (② **978/441-0400;** www.athm.org), and the **New England Quilt Museum** ⊛, 18 Shattuck St. (② **978/452-4207;** www.nequiltmuseum.org). For more information, consult the **Greater Merrimack Valley Convention & Visitors Bureau,** 9 Central St., Suite 201, Lowell (② **800/443-3332** or 978/459-6150; www.merrimack valley.org).

To drive to Lowell, take Route 3 or I-495 to the Lowell Connector and follow signs north to exit 5B and the historic district. The **commuter rail** (② **800/392-6100** or 617/222-3200; www.mbta.com) from Boston's North Station takes about 45 minutes and costs $14 round-trip.

43 Church St. (at Washington St.). ② **978/745-7665.** www.lyceumsalem.com. Reservations recommended. Main courses $8–$14 lunch, $17–$29 dinner. AE, DISC, MC, V. Mon–Fri 11:30am–3pm; Sun brunch 11am–3pm; daily 5:30–10pm. Validated parking available.

Rockmore Restaurant ⊛ SEAFOOD/AMERICAN   If you're going to eat at a restaurant with a gimmick, it might as well be a good gimmick. This is: It's on a float in the middle of Salem Harbor. The Rockmore serves burgers, sandwiches, and fresh seafood in an extremely casual atmosphere, usually to local boaters. The food is fine, but nobody's here for the food. (Did I mention it's on a *float?*) If you're not traveling by boat, ferry service is available from the Congress Street Bridge, next to Pickering Wharf, or from Village Street in Marblehead.

Salem Harbor. ② **978/740-1001.** www.therockmore.com. Main courses $8–$18. AE, DISC, MC, V. Memorial Day weekend to Labor Day weekend daily 11am–10pm, weather permitting.

Salem Beer Works PUB GRUB   Beer is the headliner at this popular downtown restaurant, but the food is also worth mentioning. Piled-high burgers, salads, sandwiches, and buckets of fried delicacies such as onion rings, jalapeño poppers, and pickles complement the house-made brews.

278 Derby St. ② **978/745-BEER.** www.beerworks.net. Main courses $6–$17. AE, DISC, MC, V. Sun–Thurs 11:30am–midnight; Fri–Sat 11:30am–1am.

5 Cape Ann

Gloucester, Rockport, Essex, and Manchester-by-the-Sea make up Cape Ann, a rocky peninsula so enchantingly beautiful that when you hear the slogan "Massachusetts's *Other* Cape," you may forget what the first one was. Cape Ann and Cape Cod do share some attributes—scenery, shopping, seafood, and traffic. The smaller cape's proximity to Boston and manageable scale make it a wonderful day trip and a good choice for a longer stay.

With the decline of the fishing industry that brought great prosperity to the area in the 19th century, Cape Ann has played up its long-standing reputation as a haven for artists. Along with galleries and crafts shops, you'll find historical attractions, beaches—and oh, that scenery!

Although all four towns have large year-round populations, this is hardly a four-season destination. Many establishments close in fall or early winter through April or May; some open on weekends in December.

The **Cape Ann Transportation Authority** (© 978/283-7916; www.canntran. com) runs buses from town to town on Cape Ann and operates special summer routes.

The **Cape Ann Chamber of Commerce,** 33 Commercial St., Gloucester (© 800/ 321-0133 or 978/283-1601; www.capeannvacations.com), and the **North of Boston Convention & Visitors Bureau** (© 800/742-5306 or 978/977-7760; www.northof boston.org) provide abundant visitor information.

MANCHESTER-BY-THE-SEA

The scenic route to Gloucester from points south is Route 127, which runs through Manchester-by-the-Sea, a lovely village incorporated in 1645. Now a prosperous suburb of Boston, Manchester is probably best known for **Singing Beach** (see "Life's a Beach . . . with Very Cold Water!" below). The **commuter rail** (© 800/392-6100 or 617/222-3200; www.mbta.com) from Boston costs $14 and stops in the center of the compact downtown area, where there are many shops and restaurants. Nearby **Masconomo Park** overlooks the harbor.

The home of the Manchester Historical Society is the **Trask House,** 10 Union St. (© 978/526-7230; www.manchesterhistorical.com), a 19th-century sea captain's home. Tours show off the period furnishings, including pieces produced in Manchester, and the society's costume collections. It's specialized but intriguing to devotees of house tours. The society also operates the **Seaside No. 1 Fire House Museum,** which holds two antique engines and memorabilia of the town fire and police departments. Both buildings are open weekends in July and August from noon to 3pm, and by appointment.

MAGNOLIA

Pay close attention as you head north from Manchester or south from Gloucester on Route 127—Magnolia is easy to miss, but the village (technically, part of Gloucester) is worth a detour. Notable for its lack of waterfront commercial property, the village center is unremarkable. The homes surrounding it, many of them former summer residences now occupied year-round, are magnificent.

Just up the coast are two noteworthy geological formations; grab your camera. **Rafe's Chasm** is a huge cleft in the shoreline rock, opposite the reef of **Norman's Woe,** which figures in Henry Wadsworth Longfellow's scary poem "The Wreck of the

Gloucester

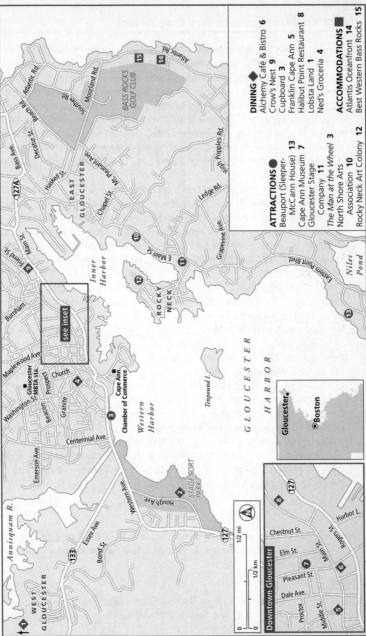

DINING ◆
Alchemy Café & Bistro **6**
Crow's Nest **9**
Cupboard **3**
Franklin Cape Ann **5**
Halibut Point Restaurant **8**
Lobsta Land **1**
Ned's Groceria **4**

ACCOMMODATIONS ■
Atlantis Oceanfront **14**
Best Western Bass Rocks **15**

ATTRACTIONS ●
Beauport (Sleeper-
  McCann House) **13**
Cape Ann Museum **7**
Gloucester Stage
  Company **11**
The Man at the Wheel **3**
North Shore Arts
  Association **10**
Rocky Neck Art Colony **12**

Downtown Gloucester

Life's a Beach . . . with Very Cold Water!

Paradoxically, Cape Ann is almost as well known for its sandy beaches as for its rocky coastline. Things to know: First, the water is *cold*. Second, parking can be scarce, especially on weekends, and pricey—as much as $22. If you can't set out before breakfast, wait until midafternoon and hope that the early birds have had enough. During the summer, lifeguards are on duty from 9am to 5pm at larger public beaches. Surfing is generally permitted outside of those hours. The beaches listed here all have bathhouses and snack bars. Swimming or not, watch out for greenhead flies in July and August. They don't sting—they take little bites of flesh. Bring or buy insect repellent.

The best-known North Shore beach is **Singing Beach** *(★★*, off Masconomo Street in Manchester-by-the-Sea. Because it's accessible by public transportation, it attracts the most diverse crowd—carless singles, local families, and other beach bunnies of all ages. From the train station, they walk about ½ a mile on Beach Street to find sparkling sand and lively surf. Take the commuter rail (*©* **800/392-6100** or 617/222-3200; www.mbta.com) from Boston's North Station.

Nearly as famous and popular is **Crane Beach** *(★*, off Argilla Road in Ipswich, part of a 1,400-acre barrier beach reservation. Fragile dunes and a white-sand beach lead down to Ipswich Bay. The surf is calmer than that at less sheltered Singing Beach, but still quite chilly. Pick up Argilla Road south of Ipswich Center near the intersection of Routes 1A and 133 or take the Ipswich Essex Explorer bus (see "Ipswich," p. 186). Also on Ipswich Bay is Gloucester's **Wingaersheek Beach** *(★*, on Atlantic Street off Route 133. From exit 13 off Route 128, the beach is about 15 minutes away (mind the speed limits). Wingaersheek has beautiful white sand, a glorious view, and more dunes. Because these beaches are harder to get to, they attract more of a local crowd, as well as lots of day-tripping families.

Most other good beaches in Gloucester have almost no nonresident parking. Two exceptions are **Half Moon Beach** and **Cressy's Beach,** at Stage Fort Park, off Route 127 near Route 133 and downtown. The sandy beaches and the park snack bar are popular local hangouts.

Hesperus." About ¾ of a mile out of the center, look for a small parking area on the right. After a ¼-mile walk through the woods, you'll find a gorgeous panorama of stone and surf.

ESSEX *(★*

West of Gloucester (past Rte. 128) on Route 133 lies a beautiful little town known for Essex clams, salt marshes, a long tradition of shipbuilding, a plethora of antiques shops, and one celebrated restaurant.

Legend has it that **Woodman's of Essex** *(★★★*, 121 Main St. (*©* **800/649-1773** or 978/768-6057; www.woodmans.com), was the birthplace of the fried clam in 1916. Today the thriving family business is a great spot to join legions of locals and visitors from around the world for lobster "in the rough," chowder, steamers, corn on the cob, onion rings, and (you guessed it) superb fried clams. Expect the line to be long, even in winter, but it moves quickly and offers a view of the regimented commotion in the food-preparation area. Eat in a booth, upstairs on the deck, or out back at a picnic table. You'll want to be well fed before you explore the numerous antiques shops along Main Street. Long a cash-only business, Woodman's now accepts credit cards (AE, MC, V).

The water views in town are of the Essex River, a saltwater estuary. The offerings of **Essex River Cruises** ✹, Essex Marina, 35 Dodge St. (© **800/748-3706** or 978/768-6981; www.essexcruises.com) include narrated 90-minute tours that put you in prime birding territory. They run daily May through October. The pontoon boat, which allows for excellent sightseeing, is screened and has restrooms. Tickets cost $23 adults, $20 seniors, $10 children 4 to 12; reservations are suggested.

GLOUCESTER ✹✹

The ocean has been Gloucester's lifeblood since long before the first European settlement in 1623. The most urban of Cape Ann's communities, Gloucester (which rhymes with "roster") is a working city, not a cutesy tourist town. Miles of gorgeous coastline surround the densely populated downtown area. Gloucester is home to one of the last commercial fishing fleets in New England, an internationally celebrated artists' colony, a large Portuguese-American community, and just enough historic attractions. Allow at least half a day, perhaps combined with a visit to the tourist magnet of Rockport; a full day would be better, especially if you plan a cruise or whale watch.

ESSENTIALS

GETTING THERE   From Boston, the quickest route is I-93 (or Rte. 1, if it's not rush hour) to Route 128, which ends at Gloucester. From Salem, a slower but prettier approach is Route 1A across the bridge at Beverly to Route 127. It runs through Manchester to Gloucester. The Manchester exits from Route 128 allow access to Route 127. There's street parking and a free lot on the causeway to Rocky Neck. Gloucester is 33 miles northeast of Boston, 16 miles northeast of Salem, and 7 miles south of Rockport.

The **commuter rail** (© **800/392-6100** or 617/222-3200; www.mbta.com) runs from Boston's North Station. The trip takes about 1 hour; the round-trip fare is $15. The station is across town from downtown, about 10 blocks, so allow time for getting to the waterfront. The **Cape Ann Transportation Authority** (© **978/283-7916;** www.canntran.com) runs buses from town to town, as well as special summer routes.

⌒Moments *The Perfect Storm*

Long after the release of the blockbuster movie, Sebastian Junger's best-selling book *The Perfect Storm* remains a popular reason to visit Gloucester. The thrilling but tragic nonfiction account of the "no-name storm" of 1991 centers on the ocean and a neighborhood tavern. The **Crow's Nest,** 334 Main St. (© **978/281-2965**), a bit east of downtown, is a no-frills place with a horseshoe-shaped bar and a crowd of regulars who seem amused that their hangout is a tourist attraction. The Crow's Nest plays a major role in Junger's story, but its ceilings aren't high enough for it to be a movie set—so the crew built an exact replica nearby.

VISITOR INFORMATION   The **Gloucester Tourism Office** (© 800/649-6839 or 978/281-8865; www.gloucesterma.com) operates the excellent **Visitors Welcoming Center** at Stage Fort Park, off Route 127 at Route 133. It's open in summer daily from 9am to 5pm. The **Cape Ann Chamber of Commerce,** 33 Commercial St. (© **800/321-0133** or 978/283-1601; www.capeannvacations.com), is open year-round (summer weekdays 8am–6pm, Sat 10am–6pm, Sun 10am–4pm; winter weekdays 8am–5pm). It also operates a seasonal information booth on Rogers Street at Harbor Loop.

GETTING AROUND   Downtown is fairly compact and walkable, but there's more to Gloucester than that. If you can manage it, travel by car. You'll be able to make the best use of your time, especially if you plan several stops. The **Cape Ann Transportation Authority** (see above) serves Gloucester.

SPECIAL EVENTS   Gloucester holds festivals and street fairs on weekends all summer. The best known is **St. Peter's Fiesta,** a colorful 4-day event at the end of June. The Italian-American fishing colony's festival includes parades, carnival rides, music, food, sporting events, and the blessing of the fleet. The **Schooner Festival,** a floating party with plenty of land-based revelry, takes place over Labor Day weekend.

EXPLORING THE TOWN

Start at the water, as visitors have done for centuries. The French explorer Samuel de Champlain called the harbor "Le Beauport" in 1604—some 600 years after the Vikings first visited—and its configuration and proximity to good fishing gave it the reputation it enjoys to this day. Fishing is still Gloucester's leading industry (as your nose will tell you), with tourism a close second. The city is exceptionally welcoming—residents seem genuinely happy to see out-of-towners and to offer directions and insider info. The **Gloucester Maritime Trail** brochure, available at visitor centers, describes four excellent self-guided tours.

On Stacy Boulevard (west of downtown) is a reminder of the sea's danger. Leonard Craske's bronze statue of the **Gloucester Fisherman,** known as "The Man at the Wheel," bears the inscription "They That Go Down to the Sea in Ships 1623–1923." To the west is a memorial to the women and children who waited at home. As you take in the glorious view, consider this: More than 10,000 fishermen lost their lives during the city's first 300 years.

Stage Fort Park, off Route 127 near the intersection with Route 133, offers an excellent view of the harbor and has a busy seasonal snack bar, the **Cupboard** (© **978/281-1908**). The park is a good spot for picnicking, swimming, or playing on the cannons in the Revolutionary War fort.

To reach **East Gloucester,** follow signs as you leave downtown or go directly from Route 128, exit 9. On East Main Street, you'll see signs for the world-famous **Rocky Neck Art Colony** 🐦🐦, the oldest continuously operating art colony in the country. Park in the lot on the tiny causeway and head west along Rocky Neck Avenue, which abounds with studios, galleries, restaurants, and people. The attraction is the presence of working artists, not just shops that happen to sell art. In summer, most galleries are open daily from 10am to 10pm. The prestigious **North Shore Arts Association,** 197R E. Main St. (© **978/283-1857;** www.northshoreartsassoc.org), founded in 1922, is open from late May to Columbus Day Monday through Saturday from 10am to 5pm, Sunday from noon to 5pm. Admission is free.

Kids A Whale of an Adventure

The waters off the Massachusetts coast are prime **whale-watching** ⟨★★⟩ territory, and Gloucester is a center of cruises. Stellwagen Bank, which runs from Gloucester to Provincetown about 27 miles east of Boston, is a rich feeding ground for the magnificent mammals, which dine on sand eels and other fish that gather on the ridge. The whales often perform by jumping out of the water, and dolphins occasionally join the show. Naturalists on board narrate the trip for the companies listed here, pointing out the whales and describing birds and fish that cross your path.

This is not a particularly time- or cost-effective activity, especially if restless children are along, but it's so popular for a reason: The payoff is, literally and figuratively, huge. This is an experience that kids (and adults) will remember for a long time.

The season runs from April or May to October. Bundle up—it's much cooler at sea than on land—and wear a hat and rubber-soled shoes. Pack sunglasses, sunscreen, and a camera. If you're prone to motion sickness, take precautions, because you'll be at sea for 4 to 6 hours.

This is an extremely competitive business—they'd deny it, but the companies are virtually indistinguishable. Most guarantee sightings, offer morning and afternoon cruises and deep-sea fishing excursions, honor other firms' coupons, and offer Internet, AARP, and AAA discounts. Check ahead for sailing times, prices (at least $40 for adults, slightly less for seniors and children), and reservations, which are strongly recommended. In downtown Gloucester, **Cape Ann Whale Watch** (© 800/877-5110 or 978/283-5110; www.caww.com) is the best-known operation. Also downtown are **Capt. Bill & Sons Whale Watch** (© 800/33-WHALE or 978/283-6995; www.captbilland sons.com) and **Seven Seas Whale Watch** (© 888/238-1776 or 978/283-1776; www.7seas-whalewatch.com). At the Cape Ann Marina, off Route 133, is **Yankee Whale Watch** (© 800/WHALING or 978/283-0313; www.yankee fleet.com).

Also in East Gloucester, the **Gloucester Stage Company** ★, 267 E. Main St. (© **978/281-4099;** www.gloucesterstage.com), is one of the best repertory troupes in New England. It schedules six plays a season (late May to early Sept).

Beauport (Sleeper-McCann House) ⟨★★⟩   Aficionados of house tours will want to build their schedules around a visit to this magnificent property on the stylish Back Shore, the product of a uniquely creative mind. Interior designer and antiquarian Henry Davis Sleeper accumulated vast collections of American and European decorative arts and antiques in his summer home. From 1907 to 1934, he decorated the 40-plus rooms to illustrate literary and historical themes. The entertaining tour concentrates more on the house in general than on the countless objects. You'll see architectural details from other buildings, magnificent arrangements of colored glassware, the "Red Indian Room" (with a majestic view of the harbor), and even the kitchen and servants' quarters.

75 Eastern Point Blvd. ℂ **978/283-0800.** www.historicnewengland.org. Guided tour $10 adults, $9 seniors, $5 students and children 6–12. Tours on the hour. June to mid-Oct Tues–Sat 10am–4pm. Closed mid-Oct to May and Sun–Mon year-round. Take E. Main St. south to Eastern Point Blvd. (a private road), continue ½ a mile to house, park on left.

Cape Ann Museum ⟐

This meticulously curated museum makes an excellent introduction to Cape Ann's history and artists. It devotes an entire gallery to the extraordinary work of **Fitz Henry Lane** ⟐⟐⟐ (formerly known as Fitz Hugh Lane), the Luminist painter whose light-flooded canvases show off the best of his native Gloucester. The nation's single largest collection of his paintings and drawings is here. Other galleries feature works on paper by 20th-century artists such as Maurice Prendergast and Milton Avery, work by other contemporary artists, and granite-quarrying tools and equipment. There's also an outdoor sculpture court. The maritime and fisheries galleries display entire vessels, exhibits on the fishing industry, ship models, and historic photographs and models of the Gloucester waterfront. The Capt. Elias Davis House (1804), decorated and furnished in Federal style, is part of the museum.

27 Pleasant St. ℂ **978/283-0455.** www.capeannmuseum.org. Admission $8 adults, $6 seniors and students, free for children under 12. Mar–Jan Tues–Sat 10am–5pm, Sun 1–4pm. Closed Feb. Follow Main St. west through downtown and turn right onto Pleasant St.; the museum is 1 block up on right. Metered parking on street or in lot across street.

SCHOONER ADVENTURES

The schooner *Thomas E. Lannon* ⟐ (ℂ **978/281-6634;** www.schooner.org) is a lovely reproduction of a Gloucester fishing vessel. The 65-foot-tall ship sails from Seven Seas Wharf downtown; 2-hour excursions ($38 for adults, $33 for seniors, $25 for children under 17) leave about four times a day from mid-June to mid-September, less often on weekends from mid-May to mid-June and mid-September to mid-October. Reservations are recommended. The company offers music and dining cruises, including sunset lobster bakes.

The two-masted schooner *Adventure* ⟐ (ℂ **978/281-8079;** www.schooneradventure.org), a 122-foot fishing vessel built in Essex in 1926, was completing an extensive restoration project at press time and scheduled to be sailing in 2009. The "living museum," a National Historic Landmark, is open to the public and on view at Rowe's Wharf downtown; check ahead for information.

SHOPPING

Rocky Neck (see "Exploring the Town," above) offers great browsing. If you admired the wardrobe design in *The Perfect Storm,* check out the shirts and caps at **Cape Pond Ice,** 104 Commercial St., near the Chamber of Commerce (ℂ **978/283-0174;** www.capepondice.com). Downtown, Main Street between Pleasant and Washington streets is a good destination. Agreeable stops include **Mystery Train,** 21 Main St. (ℂ **978/281-8911;** www.mysterytrainrecords.com), which carries used music and films; **Ménage Gallery,** 134 Main St. (ℂ **978/283-6030**), which shows work by artists and artisans; and the **Dogtown Book Shop,** 132 Main St. (ℂ **978/281-5599**), noted for its used and antiquarian selection.

WHERE TO STAY

Gloucester abounds with B&Bs; for guidance, check with the Cape Ann Chamber of Commerce (ℂ **978/283-1601**). The 40-unit **Vista Motel,** 22 Thatcher Rd. (Rte. 127A), Gloucester (ℂ **866/VISTA-MA** or 978/281-3410; www.vistamotel.com), is a comfortable establishment on a hilltop near the Rockport border. Summer rates range from $135 for standard rooms to $180 for efficiencies and include wireless Internet access and continental breakfast.

Atlantis Oceanfront Motor Inn   Across the street from the water, the Atlantis enjoys stunning views from every window. The well-maintained, good-size guest rooms are decorated in comfortable, contemporary style. Every unit has a terrace or balcony. The view from second-floor accommodations is a little better. The Atlantis doesn't have the resort feel of its pricier neighbor, the Bass Rocks Ocean Inn (see below), but the views are the same.

125 Atlantic Rd., Gloucester, MA 01930. ℂ 800/732-6313 or 978/283-0014. Fax 978/281-8994. www.atlantis motorinn.com. 40 units (7 with shower only). Late June to Labor Day $165–$195 double; spring and fall $140–$170 double. Children under 13 stay free in parent's room. Extra person $10; rollaway or crib $15. Off-season midweek discounts available. Minimum stay may be required. Closed Nov to mid-Apr. AE, MC, V. Follow Rte. 128 to the end (exit 9, East Gloucester), turn left onto Bass Ave. (Rte. 127A), and follow it ½ mile. Turn right and follow Atlantic Rd. **Amenities:** Coffee shop (breakfast only); heated outdoor pool. *In room:* A/C, TV, Wi-Fi, fridge, coffeemaker, hair dryer, iron.

Best Western Bass Rocks Ocean Inn   The Bass Rocks Ocean Inn offers gorgeous views and modern accommodations in a traditional setting. The spacious guest rooms take up a sprawling, comfortable two-story motel across the road from the rocky shore. An 1899 Colonial Revival mansion known as the "wedding-cake house" holds a handful of one-bedroom suites and the public areas. The inn has an old-fashioned resort feel that distinguishes it from the neighboring Atlantis (see above). Each motel room has a balcony or patio; second-floor rooms have slightly better views. In the afternoon, the staff serves coffee, tea, lemonade, and cookies.

107 Atlantic Rd., Gloucester, MA 01930. ℂ 800/WESTERN or 978/283-7600. Fax 978/281-6489. www.bassrocks oceaninn.com. 48 units. Summer $239–$350 double; $450 suite. Spring and fall $159–$229 double, $300–$350 suite. Children under 13 stay free in parent's room. Extra person $10; rollaway or crib $12. Rates include continental breakfast. 3-night minimum summer weekends, some spring and fall weekends. Closed Nov to late Apr. AE, DC, DISC, MC, V. Follow Rte. 128 to the end (exit 9, East Gloucester), turn left onto Bass Ave. (Rte. 127A), and follow it ½ mile; turn right and follow Atlantic Rd. **Amenities:** Heated outdoor pool; game room. *In room:* A/C, TV/VCR, Wi-Fi, fridge, coffeemaker, hair dryer, iron.

WHERE TO DINE

See "Essex," earlier, for information on the celebrated **Woodman's of Essex,** which is about 20 minutes from downtown Gloucester. The Stage Fort Park snack bar, the **Cupboard,** 41 Hough Ave. (ℂ **978/281-1908**), serves excellent fried seafood and blue-plate specials in the summer. **Lobsta Land,** 10 Causeway St., near exit 12 off Route 128 (ℂ **978/281-0415**), is a summer-only destination for familiar and unusual seafood dishes and amazing french fries.

Alchemy Café and Bistro ☆ CREATIVE AMERICAN   Friends who live in Gloucester tipped me off to this funky-yet-elegant place. The unusually varied, vegetarian-friendly menu makes this a good destination for lunch (try a fish taco or pulled-pork sandwich), cocktails and appetizers, or a special dinner. The service could be more polished, but it's hard to quibble when even the pickiest eater in your party can find just the right dish.

3 Duncan St., off Main St. ℂ **978/281-3997.** www.alchemybistro.com. Reservations recommended at dinner. Main courses $8–$19 at lunch, $13–$28 at dinner; pizza from $10. Children's menu $6. AE, MC, V. Sun–Thurs 11:30am–9:30pm; Fri–Sat 11:30am–10pm (lunch served until 4pm). From intersection of Rogers and Main sts. (just north of downtown), follow Main St. south ½ mile; Duncan St. is on left.

The Franklin Cape Ann ★★ BISTRO   A sophisticated offshoot of a neighborhood favorite in Boston's South End, the Franklin is a welcome addition to the fried-seafood-focused local dining scene. It does serve seafood, but in inventive preparations such as panko-crusted scallops accompanied by delectable lemon sauce, and honey-and-lavender-glazed salmon. Meat dishes are equally creative. The two-story restaurant also offers fabulous martinis and live jazz at least 1 night a week, making it a popular late-evening destination.

118 Main St. ℂ 978/283-7888. www.franklincafe.com. Reservations recommended. Main courses $16–$23. AE, MC, V. Daily 5:30pm–1:30am; bar daily 5pm–2am.

Halibut Point Restaurant SEAFOOD/AMERICAN   Halibut Point is a friendly tavern that serves generous portions of good food. The "Halibut Point Special"—a cup of chowder, a burger, and a beer—hits the high points. The clam chowder is terrific, and some people come to Gloucester just for the spicy Italian fish chowder. There's also a raw bar. Main courses are simple (mostly sandwiches) at lunch, more elaborate at dinner. Be sure to check the specials board—you didn't come all this way to a fishing port not to have fresh fish, did you?

289 Main St. ℂ 978/281-1900. www.halibutpoint.com. Main courses $5–$13 lunch, $9–$18 dinner. AE, DISC, MC, V. Daily 11:30am–11pm.

ROCKPORT

This lovely little town at the tip of Cape Ann was settled in 1690. Over the years, it has been a fishing port, a center of granite excavation, and a thriving summer community whose specialty seems to be selling fudge and refrigerator magnets to out-of-towners. But there's more to Rockport than just gift shops. It's home to a lovely state park, and it's popular with photographers, sculptors, jewelry designers, and painters. Winslow Homer, Fitz Henry Lane, and Childe Hassam are among the famous artists who have captured the local color. At times, especially on summer weekends, you'll be hard pressed to find much local color in this tourist-weary destination. But for every year-round resident who seems genuinely startled when people with cameras around their necks descend each June, there are dozens who are proud to show off their town.

Rockport makes an entertaining half-day trip, perhaps combined with a visit to Gloucester. Out of season, from January to mid-April, Rockport is pretty but somewhat desolate, though some businesses stay open and keep reduced hours.

ESSENTIALS

GETTING THERE   Rockport is north of Gloucester along Route 127 or 127A. At the end of Route 128, turn left at the signs for Rockport to take 127, which is shorter but more commercial. To take 127A, continue on 128 to the sign for East Gloucester and turn left. Parking is tough, especially on summer Saturday afternoons, but metered spots are available throughout downtown. Make one loop around downtown and then head to the free parking lot on Upper Main Street (Rte. 127). The shuttle bus to downtown costs $1. Rockport is 40 miles northeast of Boston, 7 miles north of Gloucester.

The **commuter rail** (ℂ 800/392-6100 or 617/222-3200; www.mbta.com) runs from Boston's North Station. The trip takes 60 to 70 minutes; the round-trip fare is $16. The station is about 6 blocks from the downtown waterfront. **Cape Ann Transportation Authority** (ℂ 978/283-7916; www.canntran.com) buses serve Rockport.

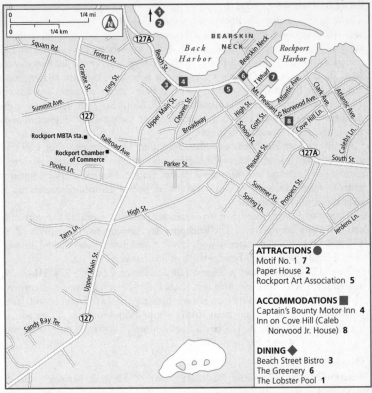

ATTRACTIONS ●
Motif No. 1 **7**
Paper House **2**
Rockport Art Association **5**

ACCOMMODATIONS ■
Captain's Bounty Motor Inn **4**
Inn on Cove Hill (Caleb
  Norwood Jr. House) **8**

DINING ◆
Beach Street Bistro **3**
The Greenery **6**
The Lobster Pool **1**

VISITOR INFORMATION   The **Rockport Chamber of Commerce,** 3 Whistlestop Mall (© **888/726-3922** or 978/546-6575; www.rockportusa.com), is open daily from 9am to 5pm. The chamber operates an information booth on Upper Main Street (Rte. 127) daily from July 1 through Labor Day and on weekends from mid-May to June and early September through mid-October. It's about a mile from the town line and a mile from downtown—look for the WELCOME TO ROCKPORT sign. The Rockport Chamber is a division of the Cape Ann Chamber of Commerce (see "Gloucester," earlier in this chapter), which is also a good source of information.

GETTING AROUND   For traffic and congestion, Boston has nothing on Rockport on a summer weekend afternoon. If you can schedule only one weekday trip, make it this one. When you arrive, park and walk, especially downtown. The Cape Ann Transportation Authority (see above) runs within the town.

SPECIAL EVENTS   The **Rockport Chamber Music Festival** (© **978/546-7391;** www.rcmf.org) takes place in June at the Rockport Art Association, 12 Main St. Events include performances, family concerts, lectures, and discussions. The annual **Christmas pageant,** on Main Street in early December, is a kid-friendly event with carol singing and live animals.

EXPLORING THE TOWN

The most famous sight in Rockport has something of an "Emperor's New Clothes" aura—it's a wooden fish warehouse on the town wharf, or T-Wharf, in the harbor. The barn-red shack known as **Motif No. 1** is the most frequently painted and photographed object in a town filled with lovely buildings and surrounded by rocky coastline. The color certainly catches the eye in the neutrals of the surrounding seascape, but you may find yourself wondering what the big deal is. Originally constructed in 1884 and destroyed during the blizzard of 1978, Motif No. 1 was rebuilt using donations from residents and visitors. It stands again on the same pier, duplicated in every detail, reinforced to withstand storms.

Nearby is **Bearskin Neck,** named after an unfortunate ursine visitor who washed ashore in 1800. It holds perhaps the highest concentration of gift shops anywhere. The narrow peninsula has one main street (South Rd.) and several alleys crammed with galleries, snack bars, antiques shops, and ancient houses. The peninsula ends in a plaza with a magnificent water view.

Throughout town, more than two dozen **art galleries** ⟨⋆⟩ display the work of local and nationally known artists. The **Rockport Art Association,** 12 Main St. (© **978/546-6604;** www.rockportartassn.org), sponsors exhibitions and special shows. It's open daily in the summer, Tuesday through Sunday in the winter.

The 1922 **Paper House,** 52 Pigeon Hill St., Pigeon Cove (© **978/546-2629**), is an unusual experience. Everything in it (including the furniture) was built entirely out of 100,000 newspapers. Every item is made from papers of a different period. It's open April through October, daily from 10am to 5pm. Admission is $1.50 for adults, $1 for children. Follow Route 127 north from downtown about 1½ miles until you see signs at Curtis Street pointing to the left.

SHOPPING

Bearskin Neck is the obvious place to start. Dozens of little shops stock clothes, gifts, toys, jewelry, souvenirs, inexpensive novelties, and expensive handmade crafts and paintings. Another enjoyable stroll is along **Main** and **Mount Pleasant streets.** Good stops include the nonprofit **Toad Hall Bookstore,** 47 Main St. (© **978/546-7323;** www.toadhallbooks.org); **Tidal Edge Gallery,** 3 School St., off Main Street (© **978/ 546-3196**); and **Willoughby's,** 20 Main St. (© **978/546-9820**), a women's clothing and accessories shop.

Two favorite stops are retro delights. Downtown, you can watch taffy being made at **Tuck's Candy Factory,** 7 Dock Sq. (© **800/569-2767** or 978/546-6352; www. tuckscandy.com), a local landmark since the 1920s. Near the train station, **Crackerjacks,** 27 Whistlestop Mall, off Railroad Avenue (© **978/546-1616**), is an old-fashioned variety store with a great crafts department.

A TRIP TO THE EDGE OF THE SEA

The very tip of Cape Ann is accessible to the public and well worth the 2½-mile trip north on Route 127 to **Halibut Point State Park** ⟨⋆⋆⟩ (© **978/546-2997;** www. mass.gov/dcr). The surf-battered point got its name not from the fish, but because sailing ships heading for Rockport and Gloucester must "haul about" when they reach the jutting promontory. This is a great place to wander around and admire the scenery. On a clear day, you can see Maine.

About 10 minutes from the parking area, you'll come to a huge water-filled quarry next to a visitor center, where staffers dispense information, brochures, and bird lists.

Swimming in the quarry is absolutely forbidden. There are walking trails, tidal pools, a World War II observation tower, and a rocky beach where you can climb around on giant boulders. To take a self-guided tour, pick up a brochure at the visitor center or the Chamber of Commerce. Check ahead for information about guided tours and other special programs. The park is open daily from Memorial Day to Labor Day, 8am to 8pm; otherwise daily dawn to dusk. Parking costs $2 from Memorial Day to Columbus Day.

WHERE TO STAY

When Rockport is busy, it's very busy, and when it's not, it's practically empty. The town's dozens of **B&Bs** fill in good weather and empty or even close in the winter. If you haven't made summer reservations well in advance, cross your fingers and call the Chamber of Commerce to ask about cancellations. Most innkeepers will arrange for guests to be picked up at the train station; if you're not driving, be sure to ask about this service when you reserve.

In Town

Captain's Bounty Motor Inn   This modern, well-maintained motor inn is on the water. In fact, it's almost *in* the water, and nearly as close to the center of town as to the harbor. Each rather plain unit in the three-story building overlooks the water and has its own balcony. Rooms are spacious and soundproof, with good cross-ventilation but no air-conditioning. The best units are on the adults-only top floor. Although it's hardly plush and the pricing structure is a bit peculiar (note the charge for children), you can't beat the location.

1 Beach St., Rockport, MA 01966. ✆ **978/546-9557.** Fax 978/546-9993. www.captainsbountymotorinn.com. 24 units. Late May to late Sept $160 double, $170 efficiency, $200 efficiency suite; spring and fall $115–$135 double, $125–$140 efficiency, $145–$155 efficiency suite. Extra adult $10; $5 for each child. 2- to 3-night minimum weekends and holidays. MC, V. Closed Nov–Mar. Pets accepted; $10/night. *In room:* TV/DVD, Wi-Fi, fridge.

Inn on Cove Hill (Caleb Norwood Jr. House) ✦   This attractive Federal-style inn was built in 1771 using the proceeds of pirates' gold found nearby. Although it's just 2 blocks from the town wharf, the inn is set back from the road and has a hideaway feel. Guest rooms are decorated in period style; most have Colonial furnishings and handmade quilts, and some have canopy beds. Innkeeper Betsy Eck overhauls one room each winter. Water views from the back of the house are worth the climb to the third floor. The generous breakfast is served in the dining room or, in good weather, in the pleasant garden. A harbor-view apartment across the street is available for long-term (1 week or more) stays.

37 Mount Pleasant St., Rockport, MA 01966. ✆ **888/546-2701** or 978/546-2701. Fax 978/546-1095. www.innon covehill.com. 7 units (some with shower only). $120–$175 double. Extra person $25. Rates include continental breakfast. 2-night minimum mid-May to mid-Oct and most weekends. MC, V. *In room:* A/C, TV, no phone.

On the Outskirts

Emerson Inn by the Sea ✦✦   Somewhere in an old guest register, you might find Ralph Waldo Emerson's name—the philosopher stayed at the original (1840) inn. He wouldn't recognize it today: The oceanfront building expanded in 1912, and innkeepers Bruce and Michele Coates have transformed it into a miniresort. Still, the inn retains a relaxing old-fashioned feel, with modern conveniences like an outdoor pool. Traditional furnishings such as four-poster beds grace the rooms, which are nicely appointed but not terribly large. If you can manage the stairs, the view from the top floor is worth the exertion. The best units have private balconies, fireplaces, or hot tubs; the regular oceanview rooms offer the same scenery. Two three-bedroom cottages nearby each rent for $1,800 to $4,500 a week. The Grand Café restaurant (© **978/546-9500**) enjoys a good reputation for contemporary American cuisine. It serves dinner daily in the summer and on weekends in the off season; reservations are required.

1 Cathedral Ave., Rockport, MA 01966. © **800/964-5550** or 978/546-6321. Fax 978/546-7043. www.emerson innbythesea.com. 35 units (some with shower only). May–Oct $299–$379 "best" double; $229–$229 oceanview double; $159–$179 double without view. Off-season discounts available. Extra person $25; crib or cot $25. Rates include full breakfast May–Oct, continental breakfast Nov–Apr. Weekly rates available. 2- or 3-night minimum weekends May–Oct. AE, DC, DISC, MC, V. Follow Rte. 127 north from the center of town for 2 miles; turn right at sign on Phillips Ave. **Amenities:** Dining room; outdoor pool; sauna; business center. *In room:* A/C, TV, Wi-Fi, hair dryer.

WHERE TO DINE

A good way to experience the town is to arrive before the tourist hordes descend and enjoy a hearty breakfast. Two tasty destinations are **Beach Street Bistro,** 18 Beach St., across from Front Beach (© **978/546-0055**), and **Flav's Red Skiff,** 15 Mount Pleasant St. (© **978/546-7647**). For a nice dinner, head to the Grand Café, the public dining room at the **Emerson Inn by the Sea** (see above), or to Gloucester.

The birthplace of the fried clam, **Woodman's of Essex** (see "Essex," earlier in this chapter), is about half an hour from Rockport.

The Greenery SEAFOOD/AMERICAN   In a great location near Bearskin Neck, the Greenery is pricey, but part of what you're paying for is the view. The cafe at the front serves light fare to stay or go; the dining rooms, at the back, overlook the harbor views. The food ranges from tasty quiche at lunch to lobster at dinner to steamers and fresh-caught fish anytime. As in any town with a fishing fleet, check out the daily specials. When the restaurant is busy, the cheerful service tends to drag. This is a good place to launch a picnic on the beach.

15 Dock Sq. © 978/546-9593. www.greenery-restaurant.com. Reservations recommended for dinner. Main courses $10–$25; breakfast items $2–$14. AE, DC, DISC, MC, V. Spring–fall daily 8am–9:30pm; call for winter hours.

6 Newburyport, Ipswich & Plum Island

The area between Cape Ann and the New Hampshire border is magnificent, with outdoor sights and sounds that can only be described as natural wonders, and enough impressive architecture to keep any city slicker happy.

In a part of the world where the word *charming* is used almost as often as *hello,* Newburyport is a singular example of a picturesque waterfront city. Downtown Newburyport is on the Merrimack River. On the town's Atlantic coast, Plum Island contains one of the country's top nature preserves. On the other side of Ipswich Bay, Ipswich is a lovely town that's home to Crane Beach, on another wildlife reservation.

NEWBURYPORT 🎔🎔

To get here directly from Boston, take I-93 (or Rte. 1 if it's not rush hour) to I-95— *not* Route 128, as for most other destinations in this chapter—and follow it to exit 57, a solid 45-minute ride. Signs point to downtown, where you can park and explore. The **commuter rail** (© **800/392-6100** or 617/222-3200; www.mbta.com) from North Station takes about 75 minutes and costs $16 round-trip.

Newburyport has a substantial year-round population that lends it a less touristy atmosphere than its appearance might suggest. Start your visit at the **Greater**

Newburyport Chamber of Commerce and Industry, 38R Merrimac St. (© **978/ 462-6680;** www.newburyportchamber.org), in the red-brick downtown shopping district. It also runs a seasonal information booth on Merrimac Street near Green Street. The website includes copious information and an event calendar, as well as a downloadable map of a walking tour.

Market Square, at the foot of State Street near the waterfront, is the center of a neighborhood packed with boutiques, gift shops, plain and fancy restaurants, and antiques stores. You can also wander to the water, take a stroll on the boardwalk, and enjoy the action on the river. Architecture buffs will want to climb the hill to High Street, where the **Charles Bulfinch**–designed building (1805) that houses the Superior Court is only one of several Federal-era treasures.

If you haven't gone out to sea yet, now is a good time, and here's a good place: **Newburyport Whale Watch** ★★, Hilton's Dock, 54 Merrimac St. (© **800/848-1111** or 978/499-0832; www.newburyportwhalewatch.com), offers 4½-hour cruises on a 100-foot boat with onboard marine biologists as guides. Ticket prices are competitive with rates at the Gloucester outfits (see "A Whale of an Adventure," on p. 177), and reservations are recommended.

Or head to the ocean using an inland route: From downtown, take Water Street south until it becomes Plum Island Turnpike and follow it to the Parker River National Wildlife Refuge.

PARKER RIVER NATIONAL WILDLIFE REFUGE ★★

The 4,662-acre refuge on **Plum Island** is a complex of barrier beaches, dunes, and salt marshes, one of the few remaining in the Northeast. The refuge is flat-out breathtaking, whether you're exploring the marshes or the seashore. More than 800 species of plants and animals (including more than 300 bird species) visit or make their home on the narrow finger of land between Broad Sound and the Atlantic Ocean. Get your bearings at the **visitor center,** 6 Plum Island Turnpike (© **978/465-5753;** http:// parkerriver.fws.gov), which houses interactive displays and other exhibits. It's open daily 11am to 4pm.

The refuge offers some of the best **birding** ★★★ anywhere, as well as observation of mammals and plants. Wooden boardwalks with observation towers and platforms wind through marshes and along the shore—most lack handrails, so this isn't an activity for rambunctious children. Birders come from around the world hoping to see native and migratory species such as owls, hawks, martins, geese, warblers, ducks, snowy egrets, swallows, monarch butterflies, Canada geese, foxes, beavers, and harbor seals.

The ocean beach closes April 1 to allow piping plovers, listed by the federal government as a threatened species, to nest. The areas not being used for nesting reopen July 1; the rest open in August, when the birds are through. The currents are strong and can be dangerous, and there are no lifeguards—swimming is allowed but not encouraged. Surf fishing is popular, though; striped bass and bluefish are found in the area. A permit is required for night fishing and vehicle access to the beach.

The refuge is open from dawn to dusk year-round. The daily entrance fee is $5 for motorists, $2 for bikers and pedestrians. The seven parking lots fill quickly on weekends when the weather is good, so plan to arrive early. South of lot 4 (Hellcat Swamp), the access road is flat and well maintained but not paved.

IPSWICH ✹

Across Ipswich Bay from Plum Island is the town of Ipswich. It's accessible from Route 1A (which you can pick up in Newburyport or at Rte. 128 in Hamilton) and from Route 133 (which intersects with Rte. 128 in Gloucester and I-95 in Georgetown). The **MBTA** (© **800/392-6100** or 617/222-3200; www.mbta.com) commuter rail serves Ipswich; the round-trip fare is $14, and the trip from Boston takes about an hour. The **Cape Ann Transportation Authority** (© **978/283-7916;** www.ipswichessex explorer.com) runs the summer-only Ipswich Essex Explorer bus, which connects the station to the attractions, including Crane Beach. The fare is $1.50; an all-day pass costs $4.

The **Ipswich Visitor Information Center,** in the Hall Haskell House, 36 S. Main St., Rte. 133 (© 978/356-8540), is open weekends in May and daily from Memorial Day weekend through October. The **Ipswich Chamber of Commerce** (© **978/ 356-9055;** www.ipswichma.com) operates the center and offers abundant information on its website.

Settled in 1630, Ipswich is dotted with **17th-century houses** ✹—reputedly the largest concentration in the United States. Many are private homes; ask at the visitor center for a map of a tour that passes three dozen of them, or rent the audio version ($8). House-tour aficionados can go inside the **John Whipple House,** 1 South Village Green (© **978/356-2811;** www.ipswichmuseum.net), and the **Heard House Museum,** 54 S. Main St (© **978/356-2811**). Tours ($5, or $7 for both houses) are offered Wednesday through Saturday from Memorial Day weekend through Columbus Day weekend; call for schedules.

Ipswich is also known for two more contemporary structures. The **Clam Box,** 246 High St., Rte. 1A/133 (© **978/356-9707;** www.ipswichma.com/clambox), is a restaurant shaped like—what else?—a red-and-white-striped takeout clam box. It's a great place to try Ipswich clams, and not easy to sneak past if you have children in the car. Heading south from Newburyport, it's on the right. Closed December through February.

South of Ipswich Center, near the intersection of routes 1A and 133, look carefully for the Argilla Road sign (on the east side of the street). If you're traveling west on Route 133 from Gloucester and Essex, watch for a sign on the right pointing to Northgate Road, which intersects with Argilla Road. Follow it east to the end, where you'll find the 1,400-acre Crane Estate.

The property is home to **Crane Beach** (see "Life's a Beach . . . with Very Cold Water!" on p. 174), the **Crane Wildlife Refuge** ✹✹, a network of hiking trails, and **Castle Hill,** 290 Argilla Rd. (© **978/356-4351;** www.thetrustees.org). One of the Boston area's most popular wedding locations, the exquisite Stuart-style seaside mansion known as the Great House was built by Richard Teller Crane, Jr., who made his fortune in plumbing and bathroom fixtures early in the 20th century. You have several options for seeing the property. One-hour house tours ($10 for adults, $5 for children under 18) run Wednesday through Saturday from 10am to 1pm from June to mid-October. Ninety-minute landscape tours of Castle Hill ($5) start at 10am Thursday and Saturday from June to mid-October. Year-round, you can explore the estate ($8 per car on summer weekends, otherwise $5 per car) without entering the house.

Children who can't get excited about a tour might be pacified by a stop just before Castle Hill. **Russell Orchards Store and Winery** ✹, 143 Argilla Rd. (© **978/356-5366;** www.russellorchards.com), is open daily May through November. It has a picnic

Finds   **More Whale Tales: A Trip to New Bedford**

The masses that flock to eastern Massachusetts aren't yet swarming the cobblestone streets of New Bedford, which makes it a good destination for families on the verge of crowd-phobia. The **New Bedford Whaling National Historical Park,** which encompasses the downtown historic district, commemorates the city's past as the world's leading whaling port.

The downtown area near the waterfront has been restored, and the attractions are reasonably close together. Start your visit at the **National Park Service Visitor Center,** 33 William St. (© 508/996-4095; www.nps.gov/ nebe), open daily from 9am to 5pm. The exhibits include a film about whaling and the city's history. Take a guided walking tour (daily in summer, some off-season weekends) or pick up a brochure that describes self-guided excursions around the historic district.

The centerpiece of the Historical Park is the **New Bedford Whaling Museum** *★*, 18 Johnny Cake Hill (© 508/997-0046; www.whalingmuseum. org). It's the world's premier whaling museum, which sounds terribly specialized but is actually quite absorbing. On display in the lobby is the skeleton of a 65-foot juvenile blue whale. Admission to the lobby is free, but the rest of the museum is worth a visit. Children love the half-scale model of the whaling bark *Lagoda,* the world's largest ship model. The museum is open daily from 9am to 5pm, until 9pm one Thursday a month. Admission is $10 for adults, $9 for seniors and students, and $6 for children 6 to 14.

The **Seamen's Bethel,** 15 Johnny Cake Hill (© 508/992-3295), a nondenominational chapel described in Herman Melville's classic novel *Moby-Dick,* is across the street. Up the hill from the water, the **Rotch-Jones-Duff House & Garden Museum,** 396 County St. (© 508/997-1401; www.rjdmuseum.org), is an 1834 Greek Revival mansion with magnificent formal gardens. Admission is $5 for adults, $4 for seniors and students, $2 for children under 13.

To get there, take the Southeast Expressway south to I-93 (Rte. 128), then Route 24 south. Follow signs to Route 140 south to I-195. From Plymouth, take Route 44 west to Route 24 south. **Dattco** (© 800/229-4879; www. dattco.com) buses take 75 minutes from Boston's South Station ($23 roundtrip). For more information, contact the **New Bedford Office of Tourism** (© 800/508-5353 or 508/979-1745; www.destinationnewbedford.org) or the **Bristol County Convention & Visitors Bureau** (© 800/288-6263 or 508/997-1250; www.bristol-county.org).

area, farm animals, and an excellent country store. Depending on the season, you might go on a hayride or taste fruit wines. Be sure to try some cider and doughnuts.

7 Plymouth *★★*

Everyone educated in the United States knows at least a little about Plymouth—about how the Pilgrims, fleeing religious persecution, left Europe on the *Mayflower* and landed at Plymouth Rock in 1620. Many also know that the Pilgrims endured disease and privation, and that just 51 people from the original group of 102 celebrated the first Thanksgiving in 1621 with Squanto, a Pawtuxet Indian associated with the Wampanoags, and his cohorts.

What you won't know until you visit is how small everything was. The *Mayflower* (a replica) seems perilously tiny, and when you contemplate how dangerous life was at the time, it's hard not to marvel at the settlers' accomplishments. The *Mayflower* passengers weren't even aiming for Plymouth. They originally set out for what they called "Northern Virginia," near the mouth of the Hudson River. On November 11, 1620, rough weather and high seas forced them to make for Cape Cod Bay and anchor at Provincetown. The captain then announced that they had found a safe harbor and refused to continue to their original destination. On December 16, Provincetown having proven an unsatisfactory location, the weary travelers landed at Plymouth.

Plymouth is in many ways a model destination, where the 17th century coexists with the 21st, and most historic attractions are both educational and fun. Tourists jam the downtown area in summer, but the year-round population is so large that Plymouth feels more like the working community it is than like a warm-weather day-trip destination. It's a manageable excursion from Boston, particularly enjoyable if you're traveling with children. It also makes a good stop between Boston and Cape Cod.

ESSENTIALS

GETTING THERE By car, follow the Southeast Expressway (I-93) from Boston to Route 3. From Cape Cod, take Route 3 north. Take exit 6A to Route 44 east, and follow signs to the historic attractions. The 40-mile trip from Boston takes 45 to 60 minutes if it's not rush hour. Take exit 5 to the **Regional Information Complex** for maps, brochures, and information. Take exit 4 to go directly to **Plimoth Plantation.**

The **commuter rail** (© 617/222-3200; www.mbta.com) serves Cordage Park, on Route 3A north of downtown, from South Station. The round-trip fare is $16. Plymouth and Brockton **buses** (© 508/746-4795 or 508/746-0378; www.p-b.com) take about an hour from South Station. They run more often than the train, but they cost more ($13 one-way, $23 round-trip) and drop off and pick up passengers at the park-and-ride lot at Route 3, exit 5. The **Plymouth Area Link** bus (© 508/746-0378; www.gatra.org/pal.html) connects the train station and bus stop with downtown. The fare is $1, free for children under 7.

VISITOR INFORMATION If you haven't visited the Regional Information Complex (see "Getting There," above), pick up a map at the **visitor center** (© 508/747-7525), open seasonally at 130 Water St., across from the town pier. To plan ahead, contact Plymouth Visitor Information, known as **Destination Plymouth** (© 800/USA-1620 or 508/747-7533; www.visit-plymouth.com). The **Plymouth County Convention & Visitors Bureau** (© 800/231-1620 or 508/747-0100; www.seeplymouth.com) publishes a vacation guide.

GETTING AROUND The downtown attractions are accessible on foot. A shallow hill slopes from the center of town to the waterfront. **Plymouth Rock Trolley** (© 508/747-4161; www.plymouthrocktrolley.com) offers a 40-minute narrated tour and unlimited reboarding daily from Memorial Day to October and weekends until Thanksgiving. It serves marked stops downtown (every 20 min.) and Plimoth Plantation (once an hour in summer). Tickets are $15 for adults, $12 for children 3 to 12.

Plymouth

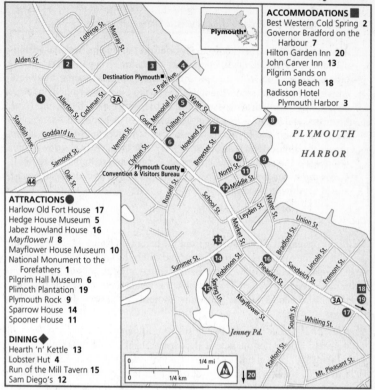

ACCOMMODATIONS ■
Best Western Cold Spring **2**
Governor Bradford on the
  Harbour **7**
Hilton Garden Inn **20**
John Carver Inn **13**
Pilgrim Sands on
  Long Beach **18**
Radisson Hotel
  Plymouth Harbor **3**

PLYMOUTH

HARBOR

Destination Plymouth ■

Plymouth County
Convention & Visitors Bureau ■

ATTRACTIONS ●
Harlow Old Fort House **17**
Hedge House Museum **5**
Jabez Howland House **16**
Mayflower II **8**
Mayflower House Museum **10**
National Monument to the
  Forefathers **1**
Pilgrim Hall Museum **6**
Plimoth Plantation **19**
Plymouth Rock **9**
Sparrow House **14**
Spooner House **11**

DINING ◆
Hearth 'n' Kettle **13**
Lobster Hut **4**
Run of the Mill Tavern **15**
Sam Diego's **12**

EXPLORING THE HISTORIC SITES

No matter how many times you suffered through elementary-school pageants wearing a big black hat and paper buckles on your shoes, you can still learn something about Plymouth and the Pilgrims. The logical place to begin (good luck talking children out of it) is where the Pilgrims first set foot—at **Plymouth Rock** ★★. The rock, accepted as the landing place of the *Mayflower* passengers, was originally 15 feet long and 3 feet wide. It was moved on the eve of the Revolution and several times thereafter. In 1867, it assumed its present position at tide level. The Colonial Dames of America commissioned the portico around the rock, designed by McKim, Mead & White and erected in 1920. The rock isn't much to look at, but the accompanying descriptions are interesting, and the atmosphere curiously inspiring.

To get away from the waterfront crowds, cross though Brewster Park (from the Rock, walk away from the *Mayflower II* and turn away from the water) and make your way to **Town Brook Park,** at Jenney Pond, across Summer Street from the John Carver Inn. It's a good place to unwind—ducks and geese live in the pond, and there's room to run around.

A short distance from the waterfront is the **National Monument to the Forefathers** (© **508/866-2580**), a granite behemoth inscribed with the names of the

> ## Tips A Presidential History Twofer
>
> A worthwhile detour en route to Plymouth is the **Adams National Historical Park** in Quincy, about 10 miles south of Boston. The park preserves the birthplaces of Presidents John Adams and John Quincy Adams, the house where four generations of the family lived, and eight other buildings associated with the political dynasty. A trolley connects the buildings, which are open for guided tours daily from 9am to 5pm in season (mid-Apr to mid-Nov). Admission is $5 for adults, free for children under 16. The grounds and the visitor center, 1250 Hancock St. (© **617/770-1175;** www.nps.gov/adam), are open in the winter Tuesday through Friday 10am to 4pm. The center is across the street from the Quincy Center stop on the Red Line; call or surf ahead for driving directions.

Mayflower passengers. Heading away from the harbor on Route 44, look carefully on the right for the turn onto Allerton Street, and climb the hill. The 81-foot-high monument is elaborately decorated with figures representing moral and political virtues and scenes of Pilgrim history. The monument is incongruous in its little park in a residential neighborhood, but it's also quite impressive. The view from the hilltop is excellent.

Mayflower II ☆ *Kids*   Berthed a few steps from Plymouth Rock, *Mayflower II* is a full-scale reproduction of the type of ship that brought the Pilgrims from England to America in 1620. Even at full scale, the 106½-foot vessel, constructed in England from 1955 to 1957, seems remarkably small. Although little technical information about the original *Mayflower* survives, the designer of *Mayflower II* incorporated the few references in Governor Bradford's account of the voyage with other research to re-create the ship as authentically as possible. Costumed guides provide interesting first-person narratives about the vessel and voyage. Displays describe and illustrate the journey and the Pilgrims' experience, including 17th-century navigation techniques.

State Pier. © **508/746-1622.** www.plimoth.org. Admission $10 adults, $9 seniors, $7 children 6–12. Plimoth Plantation (good for 2 consecutive days) and *Mayflower II* admission $28 adults, $25 seniors and students, $18 children 6–12, $110 families (2 adults and up to 4 children 6–17; not available online). Apr–Nov daily 9am–5pm.

Pilgrim Hall Museum ☆   This is a great place to get a sense of the day-to-day lives of Plymouth's first European residents. Many original possessions of the early Pilgrims and their descendants are on display, including Myles Standish's sword, Governor Bradford's Bible, and an uncomfortable chair (you can sit in a replica) that belonged to William Brewster. Regularly changing exhibits explore aspects of the settlers' lives, and hands-on activities such as treasure hunts get kids interested. Check ahead for information about exhibits that make use of the new wing completed in 2008.

75 Court St. © **508/746-1620.** www.pilgrimhall.org. Admission $7 adults, $6 seniors and AAA members, $4 children 5–17, $20 families. Feb–Dec daily 9:30am–4:30pm. Closed Jan. From Plymouth Rock, walk north on Water St. and up the hill on Chilton St.

Plimoth Plantation ☆☆ *Kids*   Allow at least half a day to explore this re-creation of the 1627 village, which children and adults find equally interesting. Enter by the hilltop fort that protects the "villagers" and walk down the hill to the farm area, visiting homes and gardens constructed with careful attention to historical detail. The "Pilgrims" are actors who, in speech, dress, and manner, assume the personalities of members of the original community. You can watch them framing a house, splitting wood, shearing sheep, preserving foodstuffs, or cooking stew over an open hearth, all as it was done in the 1600s. Wear comfortable shoes—you'll be walking a lot.

The plantation is as accurate as research can make it. The planners combined accounts of the original colony with archaeological research, old records, and the history written by the Pilgrims' leader, William Bradford (who often used the spelling "Plimoth"). There are daily militia drills with matchlock muskets that are fired to demonstrate the community's defense system. In fact, little defense was needed, because the Native Americans were friendly. Local tribes included the Wampanoags, who are represented near the village at a replica of a homesite (included in plantation admission). Museum staffers show off native foodstuffs, agricultural practices, and crafts.

At the main entrance are two modern buildings that house exhibits, a gift shop, a bookstore, a cafeteria, and an auditorium that shows a film produced by the History Channel. There's also a picnic area. Call or surf ahead for information on special events, lectures, tours, workshops, theme dinners, and family programs.

137 Warren Ave. (Rte. 3). (℃ **508/746-1622**. www.plimoth.org. Admission (good for 2 consecutive days) $24 adults, $22 seniors, $14 children 6–12. Plimoth Plantation and *Mayflower II* admission $28 adults, $25 seniors and students, $18 children 6–12, $110 families (2 adults and up to 4 children 6–17; not available online). Apr–Nov daily 9am–5pm. From Rte. 3, take exit 4, Plimoth Plantation Hwy.

THE HISTORIC HOUSES

You can't stay in Plymouth's historic houses, but they're worth a visit to see the changing styles of architecture and furnishings since the 1600s. Costumed guides explain the homemaking and crafts of earlier generations. When they're not undergoing renovation, most of the houses are open Memorial Day through Columbus Day, during Thanksgiving celebrations, and around Christmas; call for schedules.

Tip: Unless you have a sky-high tolerance for house tours, pick just one or two from eras that you find particularly interesting. This advice applies especially if you're sightseeing with children.

Six homes are usually open to visitors. The 1640 **Sparrow House,** 42 Summer St. (℃ **508/747-1240;** www.sparrowhouse.com; admission $2 adults, $1 children), and the 1667 **Jabez Howland House,** 33 Sandwich St. (℃ **508/746-9590;** www.pilgrim johnhowlandsociety.org; $4 adults, $2 children), are most engaging for those curious about the original settlers. Other houses that are open to the public include the 1749 **Spooner House,** 27 North St. (℃ **508/746-0012;** $4.50 adults, $2 children), and the 1754 **Mayflower Society House,** 4 Winslow St. (℃ **508/746-2590;** www. themayflowersociety.com; $4). The **Harlow Old Fort House,** 119 Sandwich St., and the 1809 **Hedge House Museum,** 126 Water St., were closed for renovation at press time. Contact the **Plymouth Antiquarian Society** (℃ **508/746-0012;** www.plymouth antiquariansociety.org), which owns both buildings (and the Spooner House), for updates.

ORGANIZED TOURS & CRUISES

To walk in the Pilgrims' footsteps, take a **Colonial Lantern Tour** ⋆ (℃ **508/ 747-4161,** or 774/454-8126 for reservations; www.lanterntours.com). Participants carry pierced-tin lanterns on a 90-minute walking tour of the original settlement under the direction of a knowledgeable guide. It might seem a bit hokey at first, but it's fascinating. Tours—of Pilgrim history or "Ghostly Haunts & Legends"—run nightly April through Thanksgiving. Tickets are $15 for adults, $12 for seniors and children 6 to 16; check the meeting place when you call for reservations. The company offers special tours for Halloween and Thanksgiving.

Narrated cruises run from April through November. **Capt. John Boats,** 10 Town Wharf (© **800/242-2469** or 508/747-2400; www.captjohn.com), offers several options. The *Pilgrim Belle* paddle-wheeler is the vessel for 75-minute narrated tours of the harbor ($14 adults, $12 seniors, $10 children), which leave from State Pier. **Whale watches** ($37 adults, $31 seniors, $25 children) run from April through October. Dining and entertainment cruises and ferry service to Provincetown (p. 177) are available.

A BELOVED ATTRACTION NEARBY

Edaville USA ꕤ, 7 Eda Ave., South Carver (© **877/EDAVILLE** or 508/866-8190; www.edaville.com), is a longtime favorite with young New Englanders. The main attraction is an entertaining 20-minute train ride on a 2-mile loop of narrow-gauge railroad tracks that takes you past cranberry bogs. Also on the premises are a carousel, kiddie rides, and cafe. It's a retro experience—no high-tech multimedia stuff, just good clean fun.

The railroad, which dates to 1947, reopened in 1999 after being shuttered for 7 years, and management has tinkered with the schedule ever since. It's currently open only for special events (such as visits by Thomas the Tank Engine), which take place on many summer weekends, as well as for the Cranberry Festival on Columbus Day weekend and the Holiday Festival of Lights on weekends in November and daily in December. Check ahead for schedules and admission fees. The railroad is extremely crowded when the weather is good; try to arrive when it opens. From Plymouth, follow Route 44 west to Route 58 south, continue about 7 miles to Rochester Road, and turn right.

SHOPPING

Water Street, on the harbor, boasts an inexhaustible supply of souvenir shops. A less kitschy destination, just up the hill, is Route 3A, known as Court, Main, and Warren Street as it runs through town. **Lily's Apothecary,** 6 Main St. Extension, in the old post office (© **508/747-7546;** www.lilysapothecary.com), carries a big-city-style selection of skin- and hair-care products. **Main Street Antiques,** 46 Main St. (© **508/ 747-8887**), is home to dozens of dealers. **Pilgrim's Progress,** 13 Court St. (© **508/ 746-6033;** www.pilgrimsprogressclothing.com), carries women's and men's clothing. **British Imports,** 1 Court St. (© **508/747-2972;** www.britishsupplies.com), attracts homesick Marmite fans from miles around.

WHERE TO STAY

Just about every establishment in town participates in a **Destination Plymouth** (© **800/USA-1620;** www.visit-plymouth.com) program that piles on the deals and discounts. Especially in the off season, this can represent great savings. On busy summer weekends, it's not unusual for every room in town to be taken; make reservations well in advance.

The 175-unit **Radisson Hotel Plymouth Harbor,** 180 Water St. (© **800/333-3333** or 508/747-4900; www.radisson.com), is the only chain hotel downtown. On a hill across the street from the waterfront, it offers the usual amenities, including a pool in the atrium lobby. Doubles in high season start at $139. The **Hilton Garden**

Inn, 4 Home Depot Dr. (© **877/782-9444** or 508/830-0200; www.hiltongarden inn.com), is at Route 3 exit 5, about 10 minutes from downtown. The hotel has an exercise room, an indoor pool, and extensive business features; doubles go for $139 and up in high season.

Best Western Cold Spring ⊛ Convenient to downtown and the historic sites, this fastidiously maintained motel and the adjacent cottages surround nicely landscaped lawns. Rooms are pleasantly decorated and big enough for a family to spread out; if you want some privacy, book a two-bedroom cottage. The tolerable distance from the water makes the Cold Spring a good deal: The two-story complex is 1 long block inland, set back from the street in a quiet part of town.

188 Court St. (Rte. 3A), Plymouth, MA 02360. © **800/678-8667** or 508/746-2222. Fax 508/746-2744. www.bwcold spring.com. 58 units (10 with shower only), 2 2-bedroom cottages. Apr–Nov $99–$159 double; $139–$199 suite; $109–$159 cottage. Extra person $10. Rollaway $10. Crib $5. Children under 12 stay free in parent's room. Rates include continental breakfast. Packages and AAA and off-season discounts available. AE, DC, DISC, MC, V. Closed Dec–Mar. Pets accepted ($10 fee). **Amenities:** Outdoor pool. *In room:* A/C, TV, Wi-Fi, coffeemaker, hair dryer, iron.

Governor Bradford on the Harbour The Governor Bradford occupies a great location across the street from the waterfront and only a block from Plymouth Rock and the *Mayflower II*. Each attractively decorated room contains modern furnishings. You'll pay more for units on the top floor of the three-story building, which offer excellent water views.

98 Water St., Plymouth, MA 02360. © **800/332-1620** or 508/746-6200. Fax 508/747-3032. www.governorbradford. com. 94 units (some with shower only). From $125 double. Rates include continental breakfast. Extra person $10. Children under 16 stay free in parent's room. Off-season and AARP discounts available. AE, DISC, MC, V. **Amenities:** Small outdoor pool; coin laundry. *In room:* A/C, TV, dataport, fridge.

John Carver Inn *Kids* A three-story Colonial-style building with a landmark portico, this hotel offers comfortable, modern accommodations and plenty of amenities, including a spa. The indoor "theme pool," a big hit with families, has a large water slide and a Pilgrim ship model. Business features, including meeting space, make this the Radisson's main competition for corporate travelers. The good-size guest rooms are decorated in Colonial style. The best units are the lavish suites with private Jacuzzis; "four-poster" rooms contain king-size beds. The inn is within walking distance of the main attractions on the edge of the downtown business district.

25 Summer St., Plymouth, MA 02360. © **800/274-1620** or 508/746-7100. Fax 508/746-8299. www.johncarverinn. com. 85 units. Early Apr to mid-June and mid-Oct to Nov $119–$219 double, $259–$299 suite; mid-June to mid-Oct $159–$249 double, $299–$329 suite; Dec to early Apr $109–$199 double, $239–$279 suite. Extra person $20; rollaway $20; crib free. Children under 19 stay free in parent's room. Packages and senior and AAA discounts available. AE, DC, DISC, MC, V. **Amenities:** Restaurant (American/seafood); indoor and outdoor pools; fitness center; game room; Jacuzzi; concierge; business center; limited room service; laundry service; dry cleaning. *In room:* A/C, TV w/pay movies, Wi-Fi, hair dryer, iron.

Pilgrim Sands on Long Beach ⊛⊛ *Kids* This attractive motel sits on its own beach 3 miles south of town, within walking distance of Plimoth Plantation. If you want to avoid the bustle of downtown and still be near the water, it's an excellent choice. The good-size rooms are tastefully furnished and well maintained, and most have wireless Internet access. If you can swing it, book a beachfront room—the view is worth the money, especially when the surf is rough.

150 Warren Ave. (Rte. 3A), Plymouth, MA 02360. © **800/729-7263** or 508/747-0900. Fax 508/746-8066. www. pilgrimsands.com. 64 units. Summer $155–$195 double; spring and early fall $114–$169 double; Apr and late fall $94–$134 double; Dec–Mar $84–$99 double. $159–$309 suite year-round. Extra person $6–$8 (suite $10–$15). Up

to 2 children under 7 stay free in parent's room. Rates include continental breakfast. 2-night minimum holiday weekends. Rates may be higher on holiday weekends. AE, DC, DISC, MC, V. **Amenities:** Coffee shop; indoor and outdoor pools; access to nearby health club ($10); Jacuzzi; business center; private beach. *In room:* A/C, TV, high-speed Internet access (most with Wi-Fi), fridge, hair dryer.

WHERE TO DINE

Plimoth Plantation (p. 190) has a cafeteria and a picnic area, and occasionally schedules theme dinners. The family-friendly **Hearth 'n' Kettle** chain has a branch at the John Carver Inn (see above), and there's a lively Southwestern restaurant, **Sam Diego's** (© **508/747-0048**), at 51 Main St.

Lobster Hut ✦ SEAFOOD   A busy self-service restaurant with a great view, the Lobster Hut is popular with both locals and sightseers. Order and pick up at the counter, then head to an indoor table or out onto the large deck that overlooks the bay. To start, try clam chowder or lobster bisque. The seafood "rolls" (hot-dog buns with your choice of filling) are excellent. The many fried seafood options include clams, scallops, shrimp, and haddock. There are also boiled and steamed items, burgers, chicken tenders—and lobster, of course. Beer and wine are served, but only with meals.

25 Town Wharf. © **508/746-2270.** Reservations not accepted. Lunch specials (Mon–Fri until 4pm) $8–$11; main courses $6–$19; sandwiches $3–$11 (most under $8); clams and lobster priced daily. MC, V. Summer daily 11am–9pm; winter daily 11am–7pm. Closed Jan.

Run of the Mill Tavern ✦ AMERICAN   This friendly restaurant sits 3 blocks inland, across from Town Brook Park. You won't mind not having a water view—the food is tasty and reasonably priced, making the comfortable tavern a popular hangout. The unconventional clam chowder, made with red potatoes, is fantastic. Other appetizers include nachos, potato skins, and mushrooms. Entrees are well-prepared versions of familiar meat, chicken, and fish dishes, plus burgers, fresh seafood (fried, broiled, or baked), and sandwiches (at lunch). On some Saturday nights, there's live Irish music.

6 Spring Lane, off Summer St. © **508/830-1262.** Reservations accepted only for parties of 6 or more. Main courses $8–$19; children's menu $4–$6. AE, DC, DISC, MC, V. Sun–Thurs 11:30am–9:30pm; Fri–Sat 11:30am–10pm (lunch menu until 4pm). Bar closes at 1am.

7

Cape Cod

by Laura M. Reckford

Only 75 miles long, Cape Cod is a curving peninsula that encompasses miles of beaches, hundreds of freshwater ponds, more than a dozen richly historic New England villages, scores of classic clam shacks and ice cream shops—and it's just about everyone's idea of the perfect summer vacation spot.

More than 13 million visitors flock to the Cape to enjoy summertime's nonstop carnival. In full swing, the Cape is, if anything, perhaps a bit too popular for some tastes. Connoisseurs are discovering the subtler appeal of the off season, when prices plummet along with the population. For some select travelers, the prospect of sunbathing en masse on sizzling sand can't hold a candle to a long, solitary stroll on a windswept beach with only the gulls as company. Come Labor Day, the crowds clear out—even the stragglers are gone by Columbus Day—and the whole place hibernates until Memorial Day weekend, the official start of "the season."

I've listed mostly summer rates for the accommodations in this chapter, because that's when the vast majority of travelers plan their trips, but if you decide to explore the Cape off season, you'll get the added benefit of lower prices everywhere you go.

The **Cape Cod Chamber of Commerce,** Routes 6 and 132, Hyannis (**② 888/332-2732** or 508/862-0700; fax 508/362-2156; www.capecodchamber. org), is a clearinghouse of information. You can also stop in at the Route 25 Visitor Center (**② 508/759-3814;** fax 508/759-2146), open daily year-round.

1 The Upper Cape

Because the Upper Cape towns are so close to Boston by car (just over an hour), they've become bedroom as well as summer communities. They are perhaps a bit more staid than those towns farther east, but they are also spared some of the fly-by-night qualities that come with a transient populace. Shops and restaurants tend to stay open year-round.

SANDWICH ★★

Sandwich is both the oldest town on the Cape and the most quaint. Towering oak trees, 19th-century churches, and historic houses line its winding Main Street. A 1640 gristmill still grinds corn beside bucolic Shawme Pond. Farther east, Sandy Neck, one of the Cape's most beautiful beaches, extends out into Cape Cod Bay.

Sandwich's claim to fame is its prominence as the home to the nation's first glass factories in the early to mid–19th century. The town still supports a number of highly skilled glassmakers.

Cape Cod

PEMBROKE
Pembroke
Marshfield
MARSHFIELD
Brant Rock
Green Harbor
3A
DUXBURY
Millbrook
Bryantville
53
Duxbury
3
South
Duxbury
Silver L.
Guret Pt.
27
North
Plympton
Kingston
Plymouth Harbor
KINGSTON
North Plymouth
PLYMPTON
Plympton
Plymouth
White Horse
Beach
Billington Sea
Manomet
North
Carver
44
Great South Pd.
58
Carver
PLYMOUTH
3A
Vallerville
CARVER
Long Pd.
MIDDLEBOROUGH
MYLES STANDISH
STATE FOREST
Ellisville
Sampson Pd.
Halfway Pd.
South
Carver
White
Island
Shores
Cedarville
White
Island Pd.
Great Herring Pd.
495
3
SCUSSET BEACH S.P.
West
Wareham
25
Sagamore
Town Neck Beach
ROCHESTER
WAREHAM
Wareham
Sandwich
East
Sandwich
Sandy Neck Beach
Weweantic
Buzzards
Bay
Cape Cod Canal
Sandy Neck
Onset
MARION
Rochester
6
Bourne
MASSACHUSETTS
MIL. RES.
West
Barnstable
6A
Monument
Beach
SANDWICH
149
Marion
Lawrence Pd.
BARNSTAB
195
Pocasset
BOURNE
Forestdale
Wakeby Pd.
Mystic L.
MATTAPOISETT
Wings Neck
28
130
Wequaquet L.
Mattapoisett
Scraggy Neck
Cataumet
OTIS A.N.G.B.
Marstons
Mills
Centerville
North Falmouth
Mashpee
Santuit
North Bay
Craigville
Beach
28A
Ashumet Pd.
Old Silver Beach
Coonamessett Pd.
151
Cotuit
Osterville
MASHPEE
West Falmouth
FALMOUTH
Waquoit
28
Teaticket
East
Falmouth
South
Mashpee
Sippewissett
Grews Pond
Great Pd.
Popponesset
New Seabury
West I.
Falmouth
Surf Drive Beach
Falmouth
Heights
Beach
Menauhant
Beach
Waquoit
Bay
SOUTH CAPE BEACH S.P.
BUZZARDS
BAY
Woods Hole
Nobska Pt.

CAPE
BA

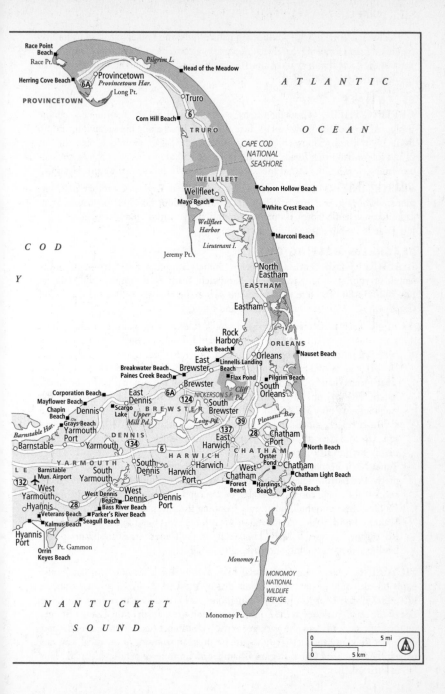

Race Point Beach
Race Pt.
Herring Cove Beach
6A
PROVINCETOWN
Provincetown
Provincetown Har.
Long Pt.
Pilgrim L.
Head of the Meadow
Truro
6
Corn Hill Beach
TRURO

A T L A N T I C

O C E A N

CAPE COD
NATIONAL
SEASHORE

WELLFLEET
Wellfleet
Cahoon Hollow Beach
Mayo Beach
White Crest Beach
*Wellfleet
Harbor*
Marconi Beach
Lieutenant I.
Jeremy Pt.

North
Eastham
EASTHAM
Eastham

C O D

Y

Rock
Harbor
Skaket Beach
East
Brewster
Breakwater Beach
Paines Creek Beach
Linnells Landing
Beach
Orleans
ORLEANS
Nauset Beach
Flax Pond
Pilgrim Beach
Corporation Beach
Brewster
Mayflower Beach
East
Dennis
6A
*Cliff
Pd.*
NICKERSON S.P.
South
Orleans
Chapin
Beach
Dennis
124
B R E W S T E R
South
Brewster
Long Pd.
Scargo
Lake
*Upper
Mill Pd.*
Grays Beach
137
Pleasant Bay
Chatham
Port
Barnstable Har.
Yarmouth
Port
D E N N I S
East
Harwich
39
28
North Beach
Barnstable
Yarmouth
134
6
Oyster
Pond
C H A T H A M
Y A R M O U T H
H A R W I C H
West
Chatham
Chatham
L E
Barnstable
Mun. Airport
South
Yarmouth
South
Dennis
Harwich
Harwich
Port
West
Chatham
Chatham Light Beach
132
West
Yarmouth
West Dennis
Beach
West
Dennis
Dennis
Port
Forest
Beach
Hardings
Beach
South Beach
Hyannis
28
Bass River Beach
Veterans Beach
Parker's River Beach
Kalmus Beach
Seagull Beach
Hyannis
Port
Orrin
Keyes Beach
Pt. Gammon

Monomoy I.

MONOMOY
NATIONAL
WILDLIFE
REFUGE

Monomoy Pt.

N A N T U C K E T

S O U N D

0   5 mi
0   5 km

The town is popular with families and nature buffs who find excellent spots for hiking, biking, and canoeing. Sandwich also makes a convenient base for exploring other parts of the Cape that may offer more lively activities, like the nightlife of Hyannis or the ocean beaches of Wellfleet.

ESSENTIALS

GETTING THERE   Cross the Cape Cod Canal on either the Bourne or Sagamore Bridge. At the Bourne Bridge rotary, take Sandwich Road along the canal; it turns into Route 6A as it nears Sandwich Center. If you cross the Sagamore Bridge, take exit 1 or 2, and follow Sandwich Road/Route 6A or Route 130, respectively, to Sandwich Center. Sandwich is 3 miles east of the Sagamore Bridge, 16 miles northwest of Hyannis.

VISITOR INFORMATION   The **Cape Cod Canal Region Chamber of Commerce,** 70 Main St., Buzzards Bay (© **508/759-6000;** fax 508/759-6965; www. capecodcanalchamber.org), is open year-round, daily 9am to 5pm. An excellent walking guide is available at most inns in town.

BEACHES & GETTING OUTSIDE

BEACHES   For the beaches listed below, nonresident parking stickers—$40 for the length of your stay—are available at **Sandwich Town Hall Annex,** 145 Main St. (© **508/833-8012**). Note that there's no swimming allowed within the Cape Cod Canal—the currents are much too swift and dangerous.

- **Sandy Neck Beach** ★★★, off Sandy Neck Road in East Sandwich: This 6-mile stretch of silken barrier beach with low, rounded dunes is one of the Cape's most beautiful beaches; in summer, its parking lot tends to fill up early. It's also popular with endangered piping plovers—and their nemesis, off-road vehicles (ORVs). That means that ORV trails are closed for some of the summer while the chicks hatch. ORV permits ($140 per season for nonresidents) can be purchased at the gatehouse (© **508/362-8300**). ORV drivers must be equipped with supplies like a spare tire, jack, shovel, and tire-pressure gauge. Parking costs $10 per day in season. Up to 3 days of camping in self-contained vehicles is permitted at $10 per night plus an ORV permit.

- **Town Neck Beach,** off Town Neck Road in Sandwich: A bit rocky but ruggedly pretty, this narrow beach offers a busy view of passing ships, plus restrooms and a snack bar. Parking costs $10 per day, or you can hike from town (about 1½ miles) via the community-built boardwalk spanning the salt marsh.

- **Wakeby Pond,** Ryder Conservation Area, John Ewer Road (off South Sandwich Rd. on the Mashpee border): The beach, on the Cape's largest freshwater pond, has lifeguards, restrooms, and parking ($10 per day).

BICYCLING   The **Cape Cod Canal bike path** ★★★ is actually two flat 7-mile paths on each side of the canal, maintained by the U.S. Army Corps of Engineers (© **508/759-5991** for recreation hot line). For easy access for the path on the Cape side of the canal, park free at the Bourne Recreation Area, north of the Bourne Bridge, on the Cape side. You can also park free at the Sandcatcher Recreation Area at the end of Freezer Road in Sandwich. For the path on the mainland side of the canal, you can park at the **Cape Cod Canal Region Chamber of Commerce** parking lot at 70 Main St., in Buzzards Bay.

BOATING   To explore by canoe, rent one in Falmouth (see below) and paddle around Old Sandwich Harbor, out to Sandy Neck, or through the salt-marsh maze of Scorton Creek, which leads out to Talbot Point.

FISHING   Sandwich has eight fishable ponds; for licenses, inquire at **Town Hall** in the center of town (© **508/888-0340**). No permit is required to fish from the banks of the Cape Cod Canal. Call the **Army Corps of Engineers** (© **508/759-5991**) for canal tide and fishing information.

NATURE & WILDLIFE AREAS   The **Shawme-Crowell State Forest,** off Route 130 in Sandwich (© **508/888-0351**), offers 298 campsites and 742 acres to roam. Entrance is free; parking costs $2. The **Sandwich Boardwalk** links the town and Town Neck Beach by way of salt marshes that attract many birds, including great blue herons.

The 57-acre **Green Briar Nature Center & Jam Kitchen** ⚘, 6 Discovery Hill Rd., off Rte. 6A (© **508/888-6870**), has a mile-long path crossing marsh and stands of white pine.

MUSEUMS

Heritage Museums and Gardens ⭐⭐⭐ *Finds* *Kids*   This is one of those rare museums that appeals equally to adults and children. The 76 beautifully landscaped acres are crisscrossed with walking paths and riotous with color in late spring, when the museum's famous collection of towering rhododendrons are in bloom. Scattered buildings house a wide variety of collections, from Native American artifacts to Cape Cod Baseball League memorabilia. The high point for most kids will be a ride on the 1912 carousel. There's also a replica Shaker round barn packed with gleaming antique automobiles. Outdoor summer concerts are usually held Sundays around 2pm.

Grove and Pine sts. (about ½ mile southwest of the town center). © 508/888-3300. Admission $12 adults, $10 seniors, $6 children 6–16, free for 5 and under. AE, DISC, MC, V. Apr–Oct daily 10am–5pm; Thurs 9am–8pm.

Sandwich Glass Museum ⭐⭐ *Finds*   Even if you don't consider yourself a glass fan, make an exception for this fascinating museum, which captures the history of the town above and beyond its legendary industry. A brief video introduces Deming Jarves's brilliant 19th-century endeavor to bring glassware—a hitherto rare commodity available only to the rich—within reach of the middle classes. All went well until Midwestern factories undercut Jarves by using coal to fire their furnaces. Unable to keep up with their level of mass production, Jarves switched back to hand-blown techniques just as his workforce was ready to revolt. An excellent little gift shop stocks Sandwich glass replicas and original glassworks. In summer, volunteers demonstrate glassblowing techniques.

129 Main St. (in the center of town). © 508/888-0251. www.sandwichglassmuseum.org. Admission $4.75 adults, $1 children 6–14, free for children under 6. Apr–Dec daily 9:30am–5pm; Feb–Mar Wed–Sun 9:30am–4pm. Closed Jan, Thanksgiving, and Christmas.

WHERE TO STAY

Many motels line Route 6A in Sandwich, but the one with the best location is **Sandy Neck Motel,** at 669 Rte. 6A, East Sandwich (© **800/564-3992** or 508/362-3992; www.sandyneck.com), which sits at the entrance to the road leading to Sandy Neck, the best beach in these parts. Rates are $89 to $99 for a double, $135 to $235 for one-and two-room efficiencies. The motel is closed November to mid-April.

The Belfry Inne and Bistro 𝄞𝄞   This inn comprises three buildings in the center of Sandwich Village. The turreted 1879 rectory, called The Drew House, is a Victorian "painted lady," done up in shades of pink. The rooms are romantic, with queen-size retrofitted antique beds, a claw-foot tub (or Jacuzzi), and a scattering of fireplaces and private balconies. Next door is the Abbey, a former church that owner Chris Wilson has converted into six unique deluxe guest rooms, and one fine restaurant called the **Belfry Bistro** (see below), as well as a more casual restaurant called the **Painted Lady Cafe.** The Abbey rooms are painted vivid colors and tucked cleverly into sections of the old church. All the Abbey rooms have Jacuzzis. Mr. Wilson also owns the Village House, next door, which has eight rooms decorated in a French country style.

8 Jarves St. (in the center of town), Sandwich, MA 02563. ⓒ **800/844-4542** or 508/888-8550. Fax 508/888-3922. www.belfryinn.com. 22 units. Summer $119–$235 double; 2-room efficiencies $250. Rates include full breakfast. AE, MC, V. **Amenities:** Two restaurants (New American bistro and casual cafe). *In room:* TV, Wi-Fi, Jacuzzis (in some).

The Dan'l Webster Inn and Spa 𝄞𝄞   This large, popular inn is a dependable bet for a comfortable stay or a hearty meal. The main building sits on the site of a Colonial tavern favored by Daniel Webster, the famous orator and Boston lawyer. Guest rooms are ample and nicely furnished with reproductions. Deluxe suites, some in nearby historic houses, offer perks like balconies, gas fireplaces, oversize whirlpool tubs, and heated tile bathroom floors. The inn's common spaces are convivial, if bustling; the restaurant is a tour-bus lunch spot that turns out surprisingly sophisticated fare.

149 Main St. (in the center of town), Sandwich, MA 02563. ⓒ **800/444-3566** or 508/888-3622. Fax 508/888-5156. www.danlwebsterinn.com. 54 units. Summer $199–$229 double; $219–$399 suite. Off-season rates include full breakfast. AE, DC, DISC, MC, V. **Amenities:** Restaurant (New American); tavern/bar; small outdoor heated pool; access to health club (2 miles away); spa w/massage and facials; room service 7:30am–10pm in season (11am–9pm off season). *In room:* A/C, TV, dataport, hair dryer, iron.

Isaiah Jones Homestead 𝄞   Of the many B&Bs in Sandwich Center, this one is a particularly good value, though the fancier rooms tend to be more expensive (and more elegant) than those at other small B&Bs in town. The innkeepers have carefully appointed this courtly 1849 Victorian with fine antiques and reproductions. Many rooms have additional romantic touches like fireplaces and oversized whirlpool baths. Two minisuites in the Carriage House have sitting alcoves. The room named for industrial magnate Deming Jarves boasts an inviting floral-curtained half-canopy bed and a whirlpool tub. A gourmet three-course breakfast is served daily.

165 Main St. (in the center of town), Sandwich, MA 02563. ⓒ **800/526-1625** or 508/888-9115. Fax 508/888-9648. www.isaiahjones.com. 7 units. Summer $150–$275 double. Rates include full breakfast. AE, DC, DISC, MC, V. No children under 12. *In room:* A/C, hair dryer, no phone.

Spring Hill Motor Lodge 𝄞   This motel boasts all sorts of amenities, like night-lit tennis court and a large pool. The interiors are cheerfully contemporary, the grounds beautifully landscaped. In addition to the motel rooms, there are four cottages that are light, airy, and comfortable.

351 Rte. 6A (about 2½ miles east of the town center), East Sandwich, MA 02537. ⓒ **800/647-2514** or 508/888-1456. Fax 508/833-1556. www.sunsol.com/springhill. 24 units (20 tub/shower), 4 cottages (shower only). Summer $125–$165 double; $225–$275 efficiency; $185–$265 for 1-bedroom cottage; $235–$350 for 2-bedroom cottage. AE, DC, DISC, MC, V. **Amenities:** Heated outdoor pool; night-lit tennis court. *In room:* A/C, TV, fridge, coffeemaker.

Wingscorton Farm Inn 𝄞𝄞 (Kids) (Finds)   This Colonial farmhouse on 7 acres will delight youngsters and animal lovers of all ages. It's been a working farm since 1758 and still houses a brood of sheep, goats, dogs, cats, chickens, a pet turkey, and a potbellied pig. The paneled guest rooms have canopy beds, working fireplaces, and braided rugs. Modernists might prefer the carriage house, with its skylight-suffused loft bedroom, kitchen (with woodstove), and private deck. A private bay beach is a short walk down a country lane.

11 Wing Blvd. (off Rte. 6A, about 5 miles east of the town center), East Sandwich, MA 02537. © 508/888-0534. Fax 508/888-0545. 4 units, carriage house. Summer $225 suite; $250 carriage house. Full breakfast. AE, MC, V. Pets welcome. *In room:* A/C, TV, fridge, no phone.

WHERE TO DINE

Aqua Grille ✿ SEAFOOD   Overlooking the town's picturesque marina and not-so-picturesque power plant, this place wants to be the premier spot for fish in Sandwich. The towering lobster salad, with *haricot verts,* tomato, avocado, chives, and crème fraîche, is the perfect antidote to a steamy summer night. Those with larger appetites may want to try the baby-back pork spare ribs with peach barbecue sauce, which comes with—what else?—potato salad and Boston baked beans. Ask for a table that doesn't face the power plant.

14 Gallo Rd. (next to Sandwich Marina). © 508/888-8889. www.aquagrille.com. Reservations recommended. Main courses $8–$20. AE, DC, MC, V. Apr–Oct Mon–Fri 11:30am–2:30pm and 4:30–9pm, Sat–Sun noon–9pm; call for off-season hours.

The Bee-Hive Tavern ✿ INTERNATIONAL   A cut above the rather characterless restaurants clustered along this stretch of road, the Bee-Hive employs atmospheric old-time touches: Green-shaded banker's lamps illuminate the dark wood booths, and vintage prints convey a clubby feel. The food is straightforward but tasty and well priced, too. Steaks, chops, and fresh fish are among the pricier choices, while burgers, sandwiches, and salads cater to lighter appetites (and wallets). At lunch, try the lobster roll, one of the Cape's best.

406 Rte. 6A (about ½ mile east of the town center), East Sandwich. © 508/833-1184. Main courses $7–$16. MC, V. Mon–Sat 11:30am–9pm; Sun 8am–3pm and 5–9pm.

The Belfry Bistro ✿✿ *Finds* NEW AMERICAN   Sandwich's most upscale dining option is in a renovated abbey, formerly a Catholic church. The Gothic space is quite spectacular, with flying buttresses supporting the ceiling's high arches. Once seated, guests can concentrate on the snowy, dense linens; intimate lighting; and pleasing menu. Portions are generous and elegantly presented. The menu changes seasonally, but among the appetizers you might find a Thai crab and baby shrimp cake or mini barbecue pork empanadas, which are braised and wrapped in pastry. The entrees run from an unusual black grouper roasted in a banana leaf to the traditional grilled filet of beef over whipped potatoes with green beans. Because this restaurant hosts many weddings and other events, it is sometimes closed to the public, so be sure to call ahead. While The Belfry Bistro serves dinner only, the more casual **Painted Lady Café** next door serves lighter, less expensive fare ($8–$25), like brie-cheese burgers and chicken potpie, from 11:30am to 9pm.

8 Jarves St. (in the center of town). © 508/888-8550. Reservations recommended. Main courses $20–$32. AE, MC, V. Feb–Dec Tues–Sat 5–10pm; call for off-season hours. Closed Jan.

The Dan'l Webster Inn ✿✿ *Kids* AMERICAN   You have a choice of four main dining rooms—from a casual, Colonial-motif tavern to a skylight-topped conservatory fronting a splendid garden. The atmospheric Tavern at the Inn, with its own pub-style menu, is the most popular. A restaurant on this scale could probably get away with ho-hum food, but the output is on par with that of the Cape's best boutique restaurants. Try a classic dish like the *fruits de mer* in white wine.

149 Main St. (in the center of town). ℂ **508/888-3622.** Reservations recommended. Main courses $18–$29; Tavern menu $7–$14. AE, DC, DISC, MC, V. Daily 8am–9pm; call for off-season hours.

Marshland Restaurant on 6A (*Value* DINER   Locals have been digging this diner for 2 decades. This is home-cooked grub, slung fast and cheap. You'll gobble up the hearty breakfast and be back in time for dinner.

109 Rte. 6A. ℂ **508/888-9824.** Most items under $10. No credit cards. Daily 6am–8:30pm. Open year-round.

FALMOUTH & WOODS HOLE ✶✶✶

Falmouth is a classic New England town, complete with church steeples encircling the town green and a walkable and bustling Main Street. With over 32,000 year-round residents, it's the second-largest town on the Cape, after Barnstable.

Woods Hole ✶✶✶, one of eight villages in Falmouth, has been a world-renowned oceanic research center since 1871, when the U.S. Commission of Fish and Fisheries set up a primitive seasonal collection station. Today the various scientific institutes crowded around—the National Marine Fisheries Service, the Marine Biological Laboratory, and the Woods Hole Oceanographic Institute—employ thousands of scientists. They offer a unique opportunity to get in-depth—and often hands-on—exposure to marine biology. Woods Hole is also one of the hipper communities on the Cape, with a number of restaurants, bars, and shops making crowded Water Street (don't even think of parking here in summer) a very pleasant place to stroll.

Falmouth Heights ✶✶✶, a cluster of shingled Victorian summer houses on a bluff east of Falmouth's harbor, is as popular as it is picturesque; its narrow ribbon of beach is a magnet for all, especially families.

ESSENTIALS

GETTING THERE   After crossing the Bourne Bridge, take Route 28 south. It's 18 miles south of the Bourne Bridge, 20 miles southwest of Hyannis.

Falmouth's bus station near the center of town is serviced by **Bonanza Bus Lines** (59 Depot Ave.; ℂ **508/548-7588;** www.bonanzabus.com). There are daily buses from Boston, Logan Airport, Providence, and New York.

GETTING AROUND   To get around Falmouth and Woods Hole (where parking in summer is impossible due to ferry traffic to Martha's Vineyard), use the **Whoosh Trolley,** which makes a circuit every 20 minutes down Falmouth's Main Street to Woods Hole. You can flag it down anywhere along the route.

The **Sea Line Shuttle** (ℂ **800/352-7155**) connects Woods Hole and Falmouth with Hyannis year-round (except holidays). The fare ranges from $1 to $3.50, depending on distance.

VISITOR INFORMATION   Contact the **Falmouth Chamber of Commerce,** Academy Lane, Falmouth, MA 02541 (ℂ **800/526-8532** or 508/548-8500; fax 508/548-8521; www.falmouth-capecod.com).

SPECIAL EVENTS

The **Falmouth Road Race** (www.falmouthroadrace.com), on the second Sunday in August, is a 7.3-mile run from the Captain Kidd Bar in Woods Hole to The British Beer Company in Falmouth Heights. It all started nearly 30 years ago when two

ACCOMMODATIONS ■
Beach Breeze Inn **8**
Coonamessett Inn **1**
Inn on the Sound **11**
Red Horse Inn **7**
Seaside Inn **12**
The Tides **10**

DINING ◆
Betsy's Diner **6**
The British Beer Company **12**
The Clam Shack **9**
La Cucina Sul Mare **3**
Osteria la Civetta **2**
Roo Bar **4**
Peking Place **5**

buddies decided to race from one bar to the other. Now the race attracts 10,000 participants from all over the world. Those who want to run need to apply to a lottery in April.

BEACHES & GETTING OUTSIDE

BEACHES While Old Silver Beach, Surf Drive Beach, and Menauhant Beach will sell a day pass, most other Falmouth public beaches require a parking sticker. Day passes to Old Silver are $20 and passes to Surf Drive and Menauhant are $10. Renters can obtain temporary beach parking stickers for $60 per week or $90 per month at **Falmouth Town Hall,** 59 Town Hall Sq. (✆ **508/548-7611**), or at the **Surf Drive Beach Bathhouse** in season (✆ **508/548-8623**). The town beaches for which a parking fee is charged all have lifeguards, restrooms, and concession stands. Falmouth's public shores include:

- **Falmouth Heights Beach** ★★★, off Grand Avenue in Falmouth Heights: Once a rowdy spot, this is now primarily a family beach. Parking is sticker-only. This neighborhood supported the Cape's first summer colony. The grand Victorian mansions still overlook the beach.

- **Grews Pond** 👫👫, in Goodwill Park off Palmer Avenue in Falmouth: This fresh-water pond in a large town forest stays fairly uncrowded, even in the middle of summer. While everyone else is trying to find parking at Falmouth's popular saltwater beaches, here you can park for free and wander shady paths around the pond. There's a playground, picnic tables, barbecue grills, lifeguard, and restrooms.
- **Menauhant Beach** 👫, off Central Avenue in East Falmouth: A bit off the beaten track, Menauhant is a little less mobbed than Falmouth Heights Beach and better protected from the winds. Parking costs $10.
- **Old Silver Beach** 👫👫👫, off Route 28A in North Falmouth: Western-facing (great for sunsets) and relatively calm, this warm Buzzards Bay beach is a popular, often crowded, choice. It's the chosen spot for the college crowd. Families with young children cluster on the opposite side of the street where a shallow pool formed by a sandbar is perfect for toddlers. Parking costs $20.
- **Surf Drive Beach** 👫👫👫, off Shore Street in Falmouth: About a half-mile from downtown, this is an easy-to-get-to choice. The tidal beach between the jetties is a shallow, calm area called "the kiddie pool." Parking is limited and costs $10.

BICYCLING   The **Shining Sea Bicycle Path** 👫👫👫 (© **508/548-8500**) is a 5-mile beauty skirting Vineyard Sound from Falmouth to Woods Hole with plenty of swim-mable beach along the way. (Unfortunately, most of the beach along this stretch is rocky.) You can park at the trail head on Locust Street in Falmouth or at any spot in town (parking in Woods Hole is scarce). The closest bike shop is **Corner Cycle** at Palmer Avenue and North Main Street (© **508/540-4195**) near the Village Green. A project to extend the bikeway along old rail lines all the way to North Falmouth will begin in 2008, and construction is expected to take a year.

BOATING   **Patriot Party Boats,** 227 Clinton Ave. (at Scranton Ave. on the har-bor), Falmouth (© **800/734-0088** or 508/548-2626; www.patriotpartyboats.com, www.theliberte.com), offers scenic cruises around Vineyard Sound aboard the three-masted schooner *Liberté* 👫👫. Two-hour sails cost $20 to $25 for adults and $15 to $20 for children 12 and under. Also offered in July and August are 2-hour sunset cruises on the *Patriot Too.*

    Cape Cod Kayak (© **508/563-9377**; www.capecodkayak.com) rents kayaks and offers lessons and eco-tours. A fun kayak excursion begins at the boat ramp next to Edward's Boat Yard in Waquoit. It takes about 15 minutes south down the Child's River to reach Waquoit Bay and **Washburn Island** 👫👫👫, a protected reserve with wooded trails. It takes another half-hour of paddling to reach the pristine beaches on either the east or north sides of Washburn.

FISHING   Falmouth has six fishable ponds. A free guide is available from the Fal-mouth Chamber of Commerce. Freshwater fishing and shellfishing licenses can be obtained at **Falmouth Town Hall,** 59 Town Hall Sq. (© **508/548-7611**, ext. 219). Freshwater fishing licenses can also be obtained at **Eastman's Sport & Tackle,** 150 Main St. (© **508/548-6900**).

    Surf Drive Beach is a great spot for surf-casting, once the crowds have dispersed. Other good locations are the jetties off Nobska Point in Woods Hole and Bristol Beach on Menauhant Road in East Falmouth.

    To go after bigger prey, head out with a group on one of the **Patriot Party Boats** (© **800/734-0088** or 508/548-2626; www.patriotpartyboats.com), which leave twice daily in season. The clunky *Patriot Too*, with an enclosed deck, is ideal for family-style "bottom fishing" (4-hr. sails $35 adults, $25 children under 12; equipment provided).

NATURE & WILDLIFE AREAS   **Ashumet Holly and Wildlife Sanctuary** 𝕣𝕣, operated by the Massachusetts Audubon Society at 186 Ashumet Rd., off Route 151 (ℭ 508/362-1426), is an intriguing 49-acre collection of more than 1,000 holly trees, along with over 130 species of birds and a kettle pond that's covered with a carpet of Oriental lotus blossoms in summer. The trail fee is $3 for adults and $2 for seniors and children under 16.

Near the center of Falmouth (follow Depot Rd. to the end) is the 650-acre **Beebe Woods** 𝕣𝕣, a treasure for hikers and dog walkers. From here, you can wend your way to the 90-acre **Peterson Farm** 𝕣𝕣 (entrance off Woods Hole Rd.; take a right at the Quisset farm stand), with paths through woods and fields, as well as a flock of sheep and a llama grazing in a meadow. Bluebird boxes (special birdhouses for bluebirds) line the path on the way to a quiet pond.

The 2,250-acre **Waquoit Bay National Estuarine Research Reserve (WBNERR),** at 149 Waquoit Hwy. in East Falmouth (ℭ 508/457-0495; www.waquoitbay reserve.org), maintains a 1-mile nature trail. Also inquire about the boat ride to **Washburn Island** 𝕣𝕣𝕣, offered Saturdays in season by reservation. After the 20-minute boat trip to the island, naturalist-led guided walks are offered.

WATERSPORTS   Falmouth is something of a sailboarding mecca, prized for its unflagging southwesterly winds. While Old Silver Beach in North Falmouth is the most popular spot for windsurfing, the sport is allowed there only prior to 9am and after 5pm. The Trunk River area on the west end of Falmouth's Surf Drive Beach and a portion of Chapoquoit Beach are the only public beaches where windsurfers are allowed during the day.

SEA SCIENCE

Woods Hole Oceanographic Institution Exhibit Center and Gift Shop   This

world-class research organization—locally referred to by its acronym, WHOI (pronounced "Hooey")—is dedicated to the study of marine science. Kids might enjoy looking through microscopes at organisms or listening to sounds of marine animals on a computer. *Titanic* fans might be interested in the brief video, displays, and life-size model of the submersible that discovered the wreck. Walking tours of WHOI are offered twice a day on weekdays in July and August (reservations required; call ℭ 508/289-2252).

15 School St. (off Water St.), Woods Hole. ℭ 508/289-2663. $2 donation requested. Late May to early Sept Mon–Sat 10am–4:30pm, Sun noon–4:30pm; call for off-season hours. Closed Jan–Mar.

Woods Hole Science Aquarium 𝕣 *Kids*   A little beat-up after more than a century

of service, this aquarium—the first such institution in the country—may not be state-of-the-art, but it's a treasure nonetheless. The displays, focusing on local waters, might make you think twice before taking a dip. Children show no hesitation, though, in getting up to their elbows in the "touch tanks." A key exhibit illuminates the effect of plastic trash on the marine environment. A brand-new, state-of-the-art seal tank is being constructed in 2008. There are usually two seals in rehabilitation here, and they are fed at 11am and 4pm.

Albatross St. (off the western end of Water St.), Woods Hole. ℭ 508/495-2001. Donations accepted. Mid-June to early Sept Tues–Sat 11am–4pm; mid-Sept to mid-June Mon–Fri 10am–4pm. You need a picture ID to enter.

WHERE TO STAY
Moderate

Beach Breeze Inn   This inn has a great location, just steps from Surf Drive Beach and a short and pleasant stroll to Main Street, with its many shops and restaurants. Guests here beat the summer traffic blues, because with beach and town within walking distance, you never need to use your car! Rooms are sunny and spacious, with motel-style privacy; many of them have separate entrances. The inn was built in 1858 and spent many years as a run-down boardinghouse. In recent years, it has been thoroughly freshened up and is now a terrific lodging option, particularly for families.

321 Shore St. (about ¼ mile south of Main St.), Falmouth, MA 02540. © **800/828-3255** or 508/548-1765. www.beachbreezeinn.com. 20 units. Summer $169–$279 double; $1,250–$1,600 weekly efficiencies. MC, V. **Amenities:** Unheated pool. *In room:* TV, fridge. Open year-round.

Coonamessett Inn   A gracious inn built around the core of a 1796 homestead, the Coonamessett Inn is Falmouth's most traditional lodging choice. Set on 7 lush acres overlooking a pond, the inn is known for its comfortable rooms, which are decorated in what might be called "Cape Cod modern"—knotty pine walls jazzed up with colorful curtains, for example. The units with the best light are nos. 1 through 6 of the Village Rooms; they have large picture windows overlooking a pond. Most rooms have a separate sitting room attached with an overstuffed couch. On-site is a restaurant featuring a tavern as well as a more formal dining room. The buffet brunch here on Sundays draws people from all over town.

Jones Rd. and Gifford St. (about ½ mile north of Main St.), Falmouth, MA 02540. © **508/548-2300**. Fax 508/540-9831. www.capecodrestaurants.org. 27 units, 1 cottage. Summer $150–$200 double; $175–$230 2-bedroom suite; $200–$260 cottage. Rates include continental breakfast. AE, MC, V. **Amenities:** 2 restaurants (1 fancy, 1 tavern w/entertainment). *In room:* A/C, TV, coffeemaker, hair dryer.

Inn on the Sound   *(Finds)*   The ambience here is as breezy as the setting, high on a bluff beside Falmouth's premier sunning beach, with a sweeping view of Vineyard Sound from the large front deck. There's none of the usual frilly/cutesy stuff in these well-appointed guest rooms, most of which have ocean views, several with their own private decks. The focal point of the inn's living room is a handsome boulder hearth (nice for those chilly winter nights). Most guests enjoy having their breakfast, which features lots of home-baked goodies, on the front deck.

313 Grand Ave., Falmouth Heights, MA 02540. © **800/564-9668** or 508/457-9666. Fax 508/457-9631. www.innon thesound.com. 9 units (6 tub/shower, 2 shower only). Summer $195–$325 double. Rates include full breakfast. AE, DISC, MC, V. No children under 16. *In room:* TV, hair dryer, robes, no phone.

Sands of Time Motor Inn & Harbor House   This property, across the street from the ferry terminal for Martha's Vineyard, consists of a two-story motel in front of a shingled 1879 Victorian mansion. The motel rooms feature crisp, above-average decor, plus private balconies overlooking the harbor. The rooms in the Harbor House are more lavish—some with four-poster beds and working fireplaces.

549 Woods Hole Rd., Woods Hole, MA 02543. © **800/841-0114** or 508/548-6300. Fax 508/457-0160. www. sandsoftime.com. 36 units, 2 with shared bathroom. Summer $179–$200 double. Rates include continental breakfast. AE, DC, DISC, MC, V. Closed Nov–Mar. **Amenities:** Small heated pool; 2 tennis courts. *In room:* A/C, TV.

Inexpensive

For a basic motel with a great location, try the **Tides Motel** (© **508/548-3126**), at the west end of Grand Avenue in Falmouth Heights. The 1950s-style no-frills (no air-conditioning, no phone) motel is a good value. It sits on the beach at the head of Falmouth Harbor facing Vineyard Sound. Rates in season are $160 to $170 for a double, $215 for a suite. The Tides is closed late October to mid-May.

The **Red Horse Inn,** 28 Falmouth Heights Rd., ⊛ (© **508/548-0053;** www.redhorseinn.com) is a family-friendly option just a short walk from Falmouth Harbor in Falmouth Heights. The 22 rooms are priced from $150 to $250, and kids will love the large outdoor pool.

The **Seaside Inn,** at 263 Grand Ave., Falmouth Heights (© **800/827-1976** or 508/540-4120; www.seasideinnfalmouth.com), is a reasonably priced motel in a superb location, across the street from Falmouth Heights Beach and next to the British Beer Company, a family-style restaurant and pub. The 23 rooms with air-conditioning, TVs, and phones with free calls are priced at $139 to $229 for a double, $184 to $294 for a deluxe room.

WHERE TO DINE
Expensive
Fishmonger's Cafe ⊛ NATURAL   This sunny cafe jutting out into the harbor attracts local young people, scientists, and tourists for an array of imaginatively prepared dishes, with vegetarian choices a specialty. Lunch could be a tempeh burger or a regular beef version. The eclectic, changing dinner menu includes some Thai entrees. Regulars sit at the counter to enjoy a bowl of the fisherman's stew, while newcomers usually go for the tables by the window, where you can watch boats come and go from Eel Pond.

56 Water St. (at the Eel Pond drawbridge), Woods Hole. © 508/540-5376. Reservations not accepted. Main courses $15–$25. AE, MC, V. Mid-June to Oct Mon–Fri 11:30am–3pm, 5:30–9pm, Sat and Sun 9am–3pm, 5:30–10pm; call for off-season hours. Closed mid-Dec to mid-Feb.

La Cucina Sul Mare ⊛⊛ ITALIAN   Locals and tourists alike line up outside this popular Main Street restaurant, craving its hearty Italian fare. The interior features cheerful murals and a tin ceiling, and large picture windows overlook Main Street. Chef/owner Mark Ciflone's signature dishes include classic Italian specialties like lasagna, braised lamb shanks, *osso buco,* lobster *fra diablo* over linguine, *zuppa de pesce,* rigatoni a la vodka, chicken Parmesan, and veal piccata, among others. The desserts here are homemade and truly delicious.

237 Main St., Falmouth. © 508/548-5600. Reservations not accepted, but you can call a half-hour before arrival to put your name on the list. Main courses $15–$25. AE, MC, V. Tues–Sun 11:30am–3pm and 5–10pm. Open year-round.

Osteria La Civetta ⊛⊛⊛ *Finds* NORTHERN ITALIAN   One of the most delightful new additions to the Cape Cod dining scene in years is this authentic and intimate restaurant run by the Toselli family of Bologna, Italy. Osteria is the Italian word for a tavernlike establishment, and a *civetta* is an owl, a symbol of good luck in Bologna. This is European-style dining and service, and, for some patrons, that may take some getting used to. Courses are ordered a la carte. Meat is not served on the same plate as pasta; even vegetables are ordered separately. Because diners are expected to have multiple courses, servings are smaller than at the average American restaurant. But diners can share courses for a meal that is not more expensive than at other fine-dining establishments in the area. The food here is exquisite. Homemade pasta makes the lasagna alla bolognese a great choice. Another favorite is the handmade *tagliatelle al funghi e tartufo nero,* which has mushrooms, porcini, and black truffle oil. Desserts are also made on-site—my favorite is the chocolate salami; don't ask, just order and eat.

133 Main St. (across from the post office) Falmouth. ℭ **508/540-1616**. Reservations recommended. Main courses $15–$25. MC, V. Wed–Sun 11:30am–2pm, 6–10pm.

Phusion Grille ℱ NEW AMERICAN/ASIAN   Because of its innovative menu and terrific location on Eel Pond in Woods Hole, Phusion Grille has the potential to be one of Falmouth's best restaurants. But there tends to be a different chef every summer, and the food can be a bit inconsistent; sometimes it is wonderful, sometimes underwhelming. The interior is all blond wood and Asian screens, but nothing blocks the water views out the wraparound floor-to-ceiling windows. The menu changes nightly depending on the catch of the day, but keep an eye out for the bouillabaisse and the sautéed sea scallops tossed with artichokes and a lobster sherry cream sauce. There's also a sushi bar.

71 Water St., Woods Hole. ℭ **508/457-3100**. Reservations not accepted. Main courses $21–$27. AE, MC, V. Tues–Sun 11am–2pm and 5–10pm; call for off-season hours. Closed mid-Oct to Apr.

RooBar ℱ NEW AMERICAN   A change in chefs has bumped RooBar off its perch as the top restaurant in town, though it still is the place to come for excellent service and hip atmosphere. It has an intriguing menu with lots of creative dishes; you can have a three-course gourmet meal with items like Thai wontons and snapper pie, which is braised snapper in a puff pastry. Or you can have a simple, inexpensive meal: just a cheeseburger or wood-oven grilled pizza with unusual toppings like scallops and prosciutto. The arty decor of this stylish bistro features hand-blown glass lamps over the bar and metal sconce sculptures on the walls. They don't take reservations, but if you call a half-hour ahead, you can put your name on the waiting list.

285 Main St. (at Cahoon Court). ℭ **508/548-8600**. Reservations not accepted. Main courses $11–$26. AE, MC, V. Daily 5–10pm; call for off-season hours. Open year-round.

Moderate
Chapoquoit Grill ℱℱ NEW AMERICAN   One of the few worthwhile dining spots in sleepy West Falmouth, this little roadside bistro has Californian aspirations: wood-grilled slabs of fish accompanied by trendy salsas, and crispy personal pizzas delivered straight from the brick oven. People drive here from miles around for the consistently good, flavorful food. A no-reservations policy means long waits nightly in season and weekends year-round.

410 Rte. 28A, West Falmouth. ℭ **508/540-7794**. Reservations not accepted. Main courses $10–$18. MC, V. Daily 5–10pm.

Iriecorna Jamaican Restaurant ℱ JAMAICAN   This tiny but ambitious Jamaican-owned restaurant is unique on Cape Cod. Owner Leroy Lewin welcomes you and is solicitous in his attempts to please. The food is delicious and well priced. There's jerk chicken and dumplings, whole flounder in a brown stew, and even curried goat. For vegetarians, there's Rasta Pasta with stir-fried veggies and tofu. Rum drinks are a specialty.

420 E. Falmouth Hwy (Rt. 28 at the corner of Meetinghouse Rd., in the Town and Country Shoppes Plaza), East Falmouth. ℭ **508/457-7774**. Reservations accepted. Main courses $11–$18. MC, V. Daily 11am–11pm.

Landfall ℱ AMERICAN   A waterfront location, terrific decor, and good service make this seafood restaurant a fun choice when you are in Woods Hole, though note that Landfall also has steep prices. Besides the usual fish and pasta dishes, there's "light" fare—the best choice—which includes burgers and fish and chips. This is a

Dining in Nearby Mashpee

Restaurant Heather ★★★ (📞 508/539-0025), recently opened by Heather Allen (former chef of the excellent Regatta of Cotuit), is a contender for the best dining establishment on the Cape. The first surprise is the space, all curving walls and cozy sitting areas. The second surprise is the excellent service, something unusual to find on the Cape. The third and perhaps best surprise is the food: Every dish is a triumph of creativity, combining favorites with unusual preparations and unexpected spices. The menu varies with the seasons. On the appetizer list in the fall, for example, you might find a creamy and curried pumpkin bisque or a cracked spinach ravioli that gets its melt-in-your mouth flavor from lobster, scallops, and boursin cheese. For main courses, there could be a crispy duckling with a ginger glaze, or a roasted salmon with potato gnocchi. Desserts like the cinnamon and apple cake are all house-made. For those on a budget, Heather does a fabulous $21 three-course prix fixe menu every night but Saturday from 5 to 6pm. Restaurant Heather is at 20 Joy St. (off Rt. 28, in South Cape Village plaza across from Mashpee Commons), Mashpee, and is open Tuesday through Sunday 5am to 9:30pm. Reservations are recommended. Main courses run between $18 and $34.

good place to bring the kids; a children's menu comes with games and crayons. Or come for a drink at the half-dory bar to enjoy this massive wooden building constructed of salvage, both marine and terrestrial. A large bank of windows looks out onto the harbor, and the Martha's Vineyard ferry, when docking, appears to be making a beeline straight for your table.

Luscombe Ave. (½ block south of Water St.), Woods Hole. 📞 508/548-1758. Reservations recommended. Main courses $7–$26. AE, MC, V. Mid-May to Sept daily 11:30am–9pm; call for off-season hours. Closed late Nov to mid-Apr.

Peking Palace ★★ CHINESE/JAPANESE/THAI This popular Chinese restaurant also serves Japanese and Thai food. There are also three regional Chinese cuisines (Cantonese, Mandarin, and Szechuan), as well as Polynesian. The decor is modern and sophisticated. Sip a fanciful drink to give yourself time to take in the menu, and be sure to solicit your server's opinion: That's how I encountered some heavenly spicy chilled squid.

452 Main St. (a few blocks east of the center of town), Falmouth. 📞 508/540-8204. Reservations for parties of six or more only. Main courses $5–$15. AE, MC, V. Daily 11:30am–midnight. Open year-round.

Inexpensive

Betsy's Diner ★ *(Finds* *(Kids* AMERICAN This is hearty food like your mother used to make, if your mother was a variation of June Cleaver. The menu features turkey dinner, breakfast all day, and homemade pies. Some say the fried clams here are the best in town. Each red vinyl booth is equipped with its own jukebox with retro hits.

457 Main St. (in the center of town). 📞 508/540-0060. No reservations accepted. All items under $11. AE, MC, V. Mon–Sat 6am–9pm, Sun 6am–2pm; call for off-season hours.

The British Beer Company ★ PUB FARE/PIZZA The view is great at this faux British pub across the street from Falmouth Heights beach. The best choices are the fish and chips, burgers, and pizzas. The lobster bisque is also good and has won local awards. Of course, there is beer—23 drafts available, including Guinness and John Courage, as well as bottled selections.

263 Grand Ave. (across from the beach), Falmouth Heights. © 508/540-9600. Reservations not accepted. All items under $15. AE, DC, DISC, MC, V. Daily noon–10pm.

The Clam Shack ☆ *Kids* SEAFOOD   This classic clam shack at the head of Falmouth harbor offers steaming plates of fried seafood that you carry to a picnic table inside, outside, or up on the roof deck. It's basic fare, but the fish is fresh and you can't beat the view.

227 Clinton Ave. (off Scranton Ave., about 1 mile south of Main St.). © 508/540-7758. Reservations not accepted. Main courses $5–$15. No credit cards. Daily 11:30am–7:45pm. Closed early Sept to late May.

FALMOUTH AFTER DARK

The Boathouse (© 508/548-7800), at 88 Scranton Ave. on Falmouth Inner Harbor, features live bands in season, from classic rock to jazz, and dancing is popular here. God knows whom you'll meet in the rough-and-tumble old **Cap'n Kidd** ☆, 77 Water St., in Woods Hole (© 508/548-9206): maybe a lobsterwoman, maybe a Nobel Prize winner. You'll find good grub, too. Everyone heads to **Liam Maguire's Irish Pub** ☆, on 273 Main St. in Falmouth (© 508/548-0285), for a taste of the Emerald Isle. There's live music on weekends year-round, often by Liam himself. **Grumpy's**, at 29 Locust St. (© 508/540-3930), is a good old bar/shack with live music (rock, blues, and jazz) Thursday to Saturday nights. Cover is $2 to $10.

2 The Mid-Cape

Visitors who want to be centrally located on Cape Cod choose the Mid-Cape, which is just over an hour from Boston (without traffic), an easy (less than an hour) drive to the Outer Cape, and a 1-hour ferry ride from Nantucket. This is the Cape's most populous area and also the prime location for its cheapest motels, which line Route 28 from Hyannis to Dennis.

Hyannis is the Cape's unofficial capital. It's a sprawling concrete jungle of strip malls and chain stores where the Kennedy mystique of the 1960s had the unfortunate side effect of spurring heedless development over the ensuing decades—a period during which the Cape's year-round population doubled to more than 200,000. The summer population is about three times that, and you'd swear every single person had daily errands to run in Hyannis. And yet this overrun town still has plenty of pockets of charm, especially the waterfront area and Main Street.

The real beauty of the Mid-Cape lies in its smaller places: old-money hideaways like **Osterville** ☆ to the west, and charming villages like **West Barnstable** ☆☆ and **Yarmouth Port** ☆☆, which can be found along the **Old King's Highway (Rte. 6A)** ☆☆☆ on the northern bay side of the Cape. A drive along this winding two-lane road reveals the early architectural history of the region, from humble Colonial saltboxes to ostentatious captains' mansions. Scores of intriguing antiques shops subtly compete to draw a closer look, and each village seems a throwback to a kinder, gentler era.

HYANNIS & ENVIRONS ☆

Hectic Hyannis is the commercial center and transportation hub of the Cape, with the large Cape Cod Mall and busy Barnstable Municipal Airport. It also has a diverse

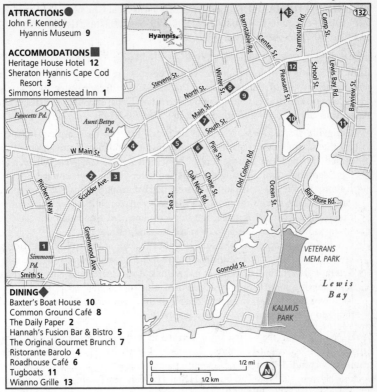

ATTRACTIONS●
John F. Kennedy
Hyannis Museum **9**

ACCOMMODATIONS■
Heritage House Hotel **12**
Sheraton Hyannis Cape Cod
Resort **3**
Simmons Homestead Inn **1**

DINING◆
Baxter's Boat House **10**
Common Ground Café **8**
The Daily Paper **2**
Hannah's Fusion Bar & Bistro **5**
The Original Gourmet Brunch **7**
Ristorante Barolo **4**
Roadhouse Café **6**
Tugboats **11**
Wianno Grille **13**

selection of restaurants, bars, and nightclubs. But if you were to confine your visit to this one town, you'd get a warped view of the Cape. Along Routes 132 and 28, you could be visiting Anywhere, USA: The roads are lined with the standard chain stores and mired with maddening traffic.

While Hyannis's impersonal hotels and motels have more beds at better prices than anywhere else on the Cape, there's little reason to choose them unless you happen to have missed the last ferry out to Nantucket. I recommend staying in Hyannisport or heading due north to Barnstable Village, where you'll find myriad charming B&Bs along the scenic Old King's Highway. Once you're settled, you can visit Hyannis to sample some of the Cape's best restaurants and nightlife. See "Barnstable Village & Environs," below.

ESSENTIALS
GETTING THERE After crossing the Sagamore bridge, head east on Route 6 or 6A. Route 6A passes through Barnstable Village; Route 132 (exit 6 off Rte. 6) leads to Hyannis. You can also fly into Hyannis, and there is good bus service from Boston and New York.

VISITOR INFORMATION   Contact the **Hyannis Area Chamber of Commerce,** 1481 Rte. 132, Hyannis, MA 02601 (© **800/449-6647,** 877/492-6647, or 508/362-5230; fax 508/362-9499; www.hyannis.com).

BEACHES & GETTING OUTSIDE

BEACHES   Most of the Nantucket Sound beaches are fairly protected and offer little in the way of surf. Parking costs $12 to $15 a day, usually payable at the lot; for a weeklong parking sticker ($40), visit the Recreation Department at 141 Basset Lane, at the **Kennedy Memorial Skating Rink** (© **508/790-6345**).

- **Craigville Beach** ✹✹✹, off Craigville Beach Road in Centerville: This broad expanse of sand has lifeguards and restrooms. A destination for the bronzed and buffed, it's known as "Muscle Beach." It's a short walk to Craigville Village, a former Methodist camp meeting site with Carpenter Gothic–style cottages.
- **Kalmus Beach** ✹✹, off Gosnold Street in Hyannisport: This 800-foot spit of sand stretching toward the mouth of the harbor makes an ideal launching site for windsurfers. The surf is tame, the slope shallow, and the conditions ideal for young kids. There are lifeguards, a snack bar, and restrooms.
- **Orrin Keyes Beach** ✹✹ (also known as Sea Beach), at the end of Sea Street in Hyannis: This little beach at the end of a residential road is popular with families.
- **Veterans Beach,** off Ocean Street in Hyannis: A small stretch of harborside sand adjoining the John F. Kennedy Memorial, this spot is not tops for swimming. Parking is usually easy, though, and it's walkable from town. The snack bar, restrooms, and playground will see to a family's needs.

FISHING   Among the charter boats berthed in Barnstable Harbor is the 36-foot *Drifter* (© **508/398-2061**), offering half- and full-day trips. **Hy-Line Cruises** offers seasonal sonar-aided "bottom" or blues fishing on boats leaving from its Ocean Street dock in Hyannis (© **508/790-0696**). **Helen H Deep-Sea Fishing,** at 137 Pleasant St., Hyannis (© **508/790-0660**), offers year-round expeditions aboard a 100-foot boat with a heated cabin and full galley.

GOLF   The **Hyannis Golf Club,** Route 132 (© **508/362-2606**), offers a 46-station driving range and an 18-hole championship course. Smaller but scenic is the 9-hole **Cotuit High Ground Country Club,** 31 Crockers Neck Rd., Cotuit (© **508/428-9863**).

WATERSPORTS   **Eastern Mountain Sports,** 1513 Iyannough Rd./Rte. 132 (© **508/362-8690;** www.ems.com), offers rental kayaks—as well as tents and sleeping bags—and sponsors free clinics and walks, like a full-moon hike. Kayaks rent for about $50 a day.

SIGHTSEEING TOURS BY STEAMER

Hy-Line Harbor Cruises   For a fun and informative introduction to the harbor and its residents, take a leisurely 1-hour tour aboard one of Hy-Line's 1911 steamer replicas. The Sunday "Ice Cream Float" includes a design-your-own Ben & Jerry's sundae.

Ocean St. Dock, Hyannis. © **508/790-0696.** www.hy-linecruises.com. Tickets $12–$21 adults, $19 seniors, $15 children 12 and under. Parking is $3 per car. Late June to Sept departures daily; call for schedule. Closed Nov to mid-Apr.

THE KENNEDY LEGACY

Don't even bother trying to track down the Kennedy Compound in Hyannisport; it's effectively screened from view. You'll see more at the following museum. Or, if you absolutely must satisfy your curiosity, take a harbor cruise (see "Sightseeing Tours by Steamer," above).

John F. Kennedy Hyannis Museum *Overrated* This multimedia display captures the Kennedys during the glory days from 1934 to 1963.

397 Main St., Hyannis. © **508/790-3077.** Admission $5 adults, $2.50 for children 10–16 and seniors. Mid-Apr to Oct Mon–Sat 9am–4:30pm; Sun and holidays noon–4:30pm; last admission at 3:30pm; call for off-season hours.

SHOPPING

Although Hyannis is undoubtedly the commercial center of the Cape, the stores here are fairly standard. Head to the wealthy enclaves west of Hyannis, such as Osterville, and along the Old King's Highway (Rte. 6A) to the north, to locate the real gems.

Tao Water Art Gallery, 1989 Rte. 6A, West Barnstable (© **508/375-0428**), is a former garage converted into a very Zen-like space. It features paintings by Chinese artists as well as museum reproductions of Chinese antiques and jade.

It's worth a special trip to see the salvaged antique lumber that is turned into cupboards, tables, and chairs at **West Barnstable Tables,** 2454 Meetinghouse Way (off Rte. 149 near the intersection of Rte. 6A), West Barnstable (© **508/362-2676**).

WHERE TO STAY

There are a variety of large, generic but convenient hotels and motels in Hyannis.

Heritage House Hotel, 259 Main St. (in the center of town), Hyannis (© **800/ 352-7189** or 508/775-7000; www.heritagehousehotel.com), is ideally located on Main Street, walking distance from restaurants, shops, and the ferries to Nantucket and Martha's Vineyard. There are an indoor and an outdoor pool, hot tub and saunas, and a restaurant/lounge on-site. The 143 rooms are priced at $199 for double occupancy.

If you prefer more amenities, there's the **Sheraton Hyannis Cape Cod Resort,** at the West End Circle just off Main Street (© **800/598-4559** or 508/775-7775; www.sheraton.com). Summer rates are $199 to $309 double. Out the back door is an 18-hole, par-3 executive golf course. There are also four tennis courts, an indoor and an outdoor pool, four restaurants, and a fitness center.

A great choice for families is the **Cape Codder Resort and Spa,** 1225 Iyannough Rd./Rte. 132 (at the intersection of Bearse's Way), Hyannis (© **888/297-2200** or 508/771-3000; www.capecodderresort.com). It features two restaurants (VJ's Grille Room and Hearth 'n Kettle for families), plus a wine bar and a spa (massage and other body treatments). Kids love the indoor wave pool with two water slides. Summer rates in the 261 rooms are $199 to $239 for a double, $389 for a suite.

Simmons Homestead Inn *Finds* The first thing passersby notice is all the classic red sports cars: 50 at last count. A former ad exec and race-car driver, innkeeper Bill Putman likes to collect. He's made his sports-car collection into a small museum open to the public called **Toad Hall,** after *The Wind in the Willows.* (Admission is $8 adults, $4 children; free for guests) Each room in this rambling 1820s house has an animal theme represented by stuffed toys, sculptures, even needlepoint and wallpaper. Guests who prefer privacy may book the spiffily updated "servants' quarters," a spacious wing with its own deck. This is the kind of place where you'll find everyone milling around the hearth sipping complimentary wine while they compare notes and nail down dinner plans. To help his guests plan their days, Putman has typed up extensive notes on day trips, bike routes, and his own quirky restaurant reviews.

288 Scudder Ave. (about ¼ mile west of the West End rotary), Hyannisport, MA 02647. ℭ 800/637-1649 or 508/778-4999. Fax 508/790-1342. www.simmonshomesteadinn.com. 14 units. Summer $180–$250 double; $320 2-bedroom suite. Rates include full breakfast. AE, DISC, MC, V. Open year-round. Dogs welcome. **Amenities:** 6-person hot tub; loaner bikes; billiards parlor. *In room:* Hair dryer, iron, no phone.

WHERE TO DINE
Expensive
Hannah's Fusion Bar and Bistro 🐾🐾 INTERNATIONAL/ASIAN   After serving as chef at the RooBar and starting the restaurant Phusion (see above), both in Falmouth, Chef Binh Phu has created a following for his innovative cuisine. Those people will likely flock to his new restaurant, a labor of love for this Vietnamese native. Binh's genius comes from his creativity in blending ingredients. For example, main courses might include Mongolian coffee-encrusted pork tenderloin or pan-seared ginger and lemon grass–marinated Atlantic salmon. There's also a special sushi menu. His all-chocolate dessert menu features delicacies like Key lime pie with a chocolate trellis.

615 Main St., Hyannis (the west end of town). ℭ 508/778-5565. Reservations recommended. Main courses $18–$30. AE, DC, DISC, MC, V. Apr–Oct Wed–Sun 11:30am–2:30pm, 5–10pm; call for off-season hours. Open year-round.

Naked Oyster Bistro and Raw Bar 🐾🐾 NEW AMERICAN   Overlook the fact that this fun bistro is located in an office complex and enjoy the experience. The specialty here is fresh local seafood, and oyster fans will be fascinated by the selection of "dressed oysters," from the traditional Rockefeller to a more exotic baked *oishi* with wasabi and soy. On the menu, Executive Chef David Kelley features spicy options like sautéed Thai shrimp and blackened Cajun swordfish, as well as hearty dishes like grilled filet mignon with garlic mashed potatoes. Portions are large and service is professional and cheerful. On weeknights there is a young-professionals scene lining up at the long mahogany bar, and some say the bartenders serve the best martinis in town.

20 Independence Dr., Hyannis (off Rt. 132 at Park Place). ℭ 508/778-6500. Reservations recommended. Main courses $14–$24. AE, MC, V. Apr–Oct Tues–Sat 11:30am–9:30pm, Sun 2–8pm. Open year-round.

The Regatta of Cotuit 🐾🐾🐾 NEW AMERICAN   With new chef/owner Weldon Fizell, this remains one of the best restaurants on Cape Cod. In addition to fine-dining cuisine in the Federal-era rooms of this 1790 house, there is a less expensive "tap room" menu and, appropriately, a newly renovated, more casual bar room. The food and service are always top-notch here. Specials might include roasted buffalo tenderloin with blackberry Madeira sauce served with braised fresh greens and a Stilton sage bread pudding.

4631 Rte. 28 (near the intersection of Rte. 130), Cotuit. ℭ 508/428-5715. Reservations recommended. Main courses $24–$34; tap room menu $10–$27. AE, MC, V. Apr–Dec daily 5–10pm; Jan–Mar Wed–Sun 5–10pm.

Ristorante Barolo 🐾🐾 NORTHERN ITALIAN   This is the best Italian restaurant in town. Part of a smart-looking brick office complex, this place does everything right, from offering extra-virgin olive oil for dunking the crusty bread to getting those pastas perfectly al dente. Entrees include a number of tempting veal choices, as well as such favorites as *Linguine al Frutti di Mare*, with littlenecks, mussels, shrimp, and calamari. The desserts are brought in daily from Boston's famed North End.

1 Financial Place (297 North St., just off the West End rotary), Hyannis. ℭ 508/778-2878. Reservations recommended. Main courses $10–$27. AE, DC, MC, V. June–Sept Sun–Thurs 4:30–10pm, Fri–Sat 4:30–11pm; call for off-season hours.

Roadhouse Café ★★ AMERICAN/NORTHERN ITALIAN   This is neither a roadhouse nor a cafe, but it is a solid entry in the Hyannis dining scene. The menu is split between American standards and real Italian cooking. Among the appetizers are beef carpaccio with fresh-shaved Parmesan, and vine-ripened tomatoes and buffalo mozzarella drizzled with balsamic vinaigrette. The vinaigrette also makes a tasty marinade for native swordfish headed for the grill. A less expensive, lighter-fare menu, including what some have called "the best burger in the world," is served in the snazzy bistro in back, which also features live jazz Monday nights (see "Hyannis & Environs After Dark," below).

488 South St. (off Main St., near the West End rotary), Hyannis. ✆ **508/775-2386.** Reservations recommended. Main courses $15–$26. AE, DC, DISC, MC, V. Daily 4pm–10:30pm.

Moderate

Tugboats ★ *Kids* AMERICAN   Yet another harborside perch for munching and ogling, this one's especially appealing. Forget fancy dining and chow down on blackened-swordfish bites (topping a Caesar salad, perhaps) or lobster fritters. Among the desserts is a Key lime pie purportedly lifted straight from Papa's of Key West.

21 Arlington St. (at the Hyannis Marina, off Willow St.), Hyannis. ✆ **508/775-6433.** Reservations not accepted. Main courses $11–$18. AE, DC, DISC, MC, V. Late May to Oct daily 11:30am–10:30pm; Apr to late May Tues–Sun 11:30am–10:30pm. Closed Nov–Mar.

Wianno Grille ★ *Kids* PUB/SEAFOOD   When you're in the mood for an informal meal in sleek surroundings, this new restaurant near the Barnstable Airport may be just the ticket. Calling itself an "upscale pub," the Wianno Grille offers straightforward fare like fish and chips, burgers, sandwiches, and salads, as well as heartier dishes such as barbeque ribs, sirloin, and lamb chops. The main floor has an almost roomlength bar and cozy booths. Downstairs has larger tables more suitable for families. Sunday brunch is popular here.

380 Barnstable Rd. (at the Staples Plaza, just off the airport rotary), Hyannis. ✆ **508/778-5587.** Reservations accepted. Main courses $8–$25. AE, MC, V. Daily 11:30am–10pm.

Inexpensive

Baxter's Boat House ★ *Value* *Kids* SEAFOOD   A shingled shack on a jetty jutting out into the harbor, Baxter's caters to the boating crowd with fried clams and fish virtually any way you like it, served on paper plates at picnic tables.

177 Pleasant St. (near the Steamship Authority ferry), Hyannis. ✆ **508/775-7040.** Main courses $8–$14. AE, MC, V. Late May to early Sept Mon–Sat 11:30am–10pm, Sun 11:30am–9pm; mid-Apr to late May and mid-Sept to mid-Oct Thurs–Sun 11:30am–9pm. Closed mid-Oct to Apr.

Common Ground Cafe ★ *Value* AMERICAN   There are really good sandwiches here at this New Age-y cafe run by a commune. The barn-board walls and wide-board floors surround alcoves with private booths containing amorphous tree-stump tables. But enough about atmosphere; this place makes the best iced tea on Cape Cod (the house blend—a mixture of mint teas and lemon). Besides yummy sandwiches, there are delicious salads, and the burrito with turkey is a winner.

420 Main St., Hyannis. ✆ **508/778-8390.** Most items under $10. AE, DC, DISC, MC, V. Mon–Thurs 10am–9pm; Fri 10am–3pm.

The Daily Paper ★ *Value* DINER   The newest diner in town has all the expected accoutrements, like red banquets and a long diner counter with plenty of swivel stools, but there is also excellent grub here, including what one diner called "the best toast

I've ever had." Breakfast is served to 11:30am Monday through Saturday and all day on Sunday. There is also a kids' menu.

644 West Main St., Hyannis. © 508/790-8800. Most items under $10. MC, V. Mon–Sat 6am–2pm; Sun 7am–1pm.

The Original Gourmet Brunch ★ *Finds* AMERICAN   Though the name feels very 1970s, this classic breakfast joint hearkens back to the 1950s, when small, quirky family-owned restaurants were all that Cape Cod had to offer. When you travel the narrow red brick path off Main Street into this humble low-ceilinged establishment, you may first notice the oddly slanted floors. Next you'll see the walls covered with autographed photos of celebrities that have rubbed elbows with owner Joe Cotellessa, the man who probably seated you. The menu offers over 100 combinations of omelets, from peanut butter and jelly to bacon and asparagus. There are also Belgian waffles, quiche, and award-winning chili.

517 Main St., Hyannis. © 508/771-2558. Reservations not accepted. All items under $11. MC, V. Daily 7am–2pm.

HYANNIS & ENVIRONS AFTER DARK

From July to early September, try to catch a show at the **Cape Cod Melody Tent** ★★, West End rotary, Hyannis (© **508/775-9100**). Built as a summer theater in 1950, this billowy big top proved even better suited to variety shows. A nonprofit venture since 1990, the Melody Tent has hosted the major performers of the past 50 years, from jazz greats to comedians, crooners to rockers. There's children's theater Wednesday at 11am.

For a hip hangout for grown-ups (Hyannis nightlife tends to attract mostly 20-somethings), check out **Island Merchant** (302 Main St., Hyannis; © **508/771-1337;** www.theislandmerchant.com), where there is nightly entertainment, whether DJ or live—blues, rock, funk or soul. There are great "island-influenced" sandwiches, like smoked pulled pork, and desserts, like Key lime pie. Island Merchant is open Wednesday to Monday 4pm to 1am. There's no cover.

Embargo (453 Main St., Hyannis; © **508/771-9700;** capecodbar.com), the new hot spot in Hyannis, specializes in martinis and tapas. This is a popular place for happy hour, 4:30 to 6pm nightly. On Tuesday, it's half-price tapas all night. Dinner at Embargo is served 4:30 to 11pm daily. There's live music Tuesday and Thursday and a DJ on Friday and Saturday nights. Embargo is open year-round, and there's no cover.

The congenial **Baxter's Boat House,** 177 Pleasant St. (see "Where to Dine," above), Hyannis (© **508/775-7040**), with low-key blues piano, draws an attractive crowd. A good place for after-dinner entertainment is **Roadhouse Café** ★, 488 South St. (see "Where to Dine," above), Hyannis (© **508/775-2386**), a dark-paneled bar that stocks 48 boutique beers. Insiders show up Monday nights to hear local jazz great Dave McKenna. **RooBar,** 586 Main St., Hyannis (© **508/778-6515**), feels very Manhattan, with ultracool servers; a long, sleek bar area; and lots of attitude. The bistro food is good, too.

The cramped dance floor makes for instant camaraderie at **Harry's** ★★, 350 Stevens St. (at the corner of Main St.), Hyannis (© **508/778-4188**), which features live blues and rockabilly nightly in season, and about 5 nights a week of music the year. The cover is $3 to $4 Thursday through Saturday.

BARNSTABLE VILLAGE & ENVIRONS ★★

Just a couple of miles from Hyannis, the bucolic village of Barnstable houses the county courthouse and government offices for the region. In this peaceful setting are some of the most charming B&Bs around. The bay area along historic Route 6A, the Old King's Highway, unfolds in a blur of greenery and well-kept Colonial houses.

BEACHES & GETTING OUTSIDE

BEACHES   Barnstable's primary bay beach is **Sandy Neck,** accessed through East Sandwich (see "The Upper Cape," earlier in this chapter).

BOATING   You can rent a canoe from **Eastern Mountain Sports** (see "Watersports," under "Hyannis & Environs," earlier in this chapter) and paddle around Scorton Creek, Sandy Neck, and Barnstable Harbor.

FISHING   Barnstable has 11 ponds for freshwater fishing; for permits, visit **Town Hall,** 367 Main St., Hyannis (© **508/790-6240**), or **Sports Port,** 149 W. Main St., Hyannis (© **508/775-3096**). Shellfishing permits are available from the **Department of Natural Resources,** 1189 Phinney's Lane, Centerville (© **508/790-6272**). Surfcasting without a license is permitted on Sandy Neck. Among the charter boats berthed in Barnstable Harbor is the ***Drifter*** (© **508/398-2061**), a 36-foot boat offering half- and full-day trips.

WHERE TO STAY

Ashley Manor Inn 🛏   A lovely country inn along the Old King's Highway, this 1699 mansion still retains many of its original features, including a hearth with beehive oven and wide-board floors, many of them brightened with Nantucket-style splatter paint. The rooms, all but one with working fireplace, are spacious and inviting. A deluxe unit has a separate entrance, whirlpool bath, and canopy bed. The 2-acre property includes a Har-Tru tennis court. Breakfast on the brick patio is worth waking up for.

3660 Rte. 6A (just east of Hyannis Rd.), Barnstable, MA 02630. © **888/535-2246** or 508/362-8044. Fax 508/362-9927. www.ashleymanor.net. 6 units. Summer $165 double; $200–$215 suite. Rates include full breakfast. AE, DISC, MC, V. **Amenities:** Har-Tru tennis court; loaner bikes. *In room:* A/C, dataport, coffeemaker, hair dryer.

Beechwood Inn 🛏🛏 *(Finds)*   Look for a butterscotch-colored 1853 Queen Anne Victorian all but enshrouded in weeping beech trees. Admirers of late-19th-century decor are in for a treat: The interior is dark with a red-velvet parlor and a tin-ceilinged dining room. Two of the upstairs bedrooms embody distinctive period styles from the 1860s and 1880s. Each affords a distant view of the bay. Rooms range from quite spacious (Lilac) to romantically snug (Garret).

2839 Rte. 6A (about 1½ miles east of Rte. 132), Barnstable, MA 02630. © **800/609-6618** or 508/362-6618. Fax 508/362-0298. www.beechwoodinn.com. 6 units (4 with tub/shower, 2 with shower only). Summer $180–$210 double. Rates include full breakfast. AE, DISC, MC, V. *In room:* A/C, minifridge, hair dryer, no phone.

Lamb and Lion Inn 🛏   This is an unusual property: part B&B, part motel. From the roadside, it's one of those charming old Cape Cod cottages (ca. 1740) along the Old King's Highway. Inside it's a motel-like space with units encircling a pool and hot tub. The rooms are all individually decorated, and six rooms have kitchenettes. All rooms in the main inn building are air-conditioned. The multilevel barn suite, with three loft-type bedrooms, is a funky historic space (built in 1740), filled with rustic nooks and crannies.

2504 Main St. (Rte. 6A), Barnstable, MA 02630. © **800/909-6923** or 508/362-6823. Fax 508/362-0227. www.lambandlion.com. 10 units (6 with tub/shower, 4 with shower only). Summer $165–$275 double. Rates include continental breakfast. MC, V. Well-behaved pets allowed (40-lb. limit). **Amenities:** Pool; hot tub. *In room:* A/C, TV.

WHERE TO DINE

Barnstable Restaurant and Tavern ✿✿ NEW AMERICAN/PUB   Talk about atmosphere: This 200-year-old former stagecoach stop has it in spades. But it is also a place for the kind of high-quality dining you might not expect at a ye olde pub. Chef Rob Calderone has put together a menu of sophisticated options such as roast lamb with mustard sauce, roast duck with orange liqueur sauce, and sole piccata. A raw bar spotlights local oysters and clams. Families looking for a reasonably priced meal will be pleased by the prices for burgers, sandwiches and fried seafood. On sunny days, sitting outside on the terrace across the street from the old granite courthouse is a great option, particularly for Sunday brunch.

3176 Main St./Rte 6A (in the center of town), Barnstable Village. ✆ 508/362-2355. Reservations accepted. Main courses $9–$25. AE, DC, MC, V. Daily 11:30am–9pm. Open year-round.

Dolphin Restaurant ✿✿ NEW AMERICAN   Never mind the corny decor in what looks like just another run-of-the-mill eatery. The finesse is to be found in the menu, where amid the more typical fried fish you'll find such delicacies as Chilean sea bass with roasted corn salsa and lime vinaigrette, and roast duck served with the glaze of the evening, perhaps mango.

3250 Rte. 6A (in the center of town), Barnstable. ✆ 508/362-6610. Main courses $17–$23. AE, MC, V. May–Oct Mon–Sat 11:30am–3pm and 5–9:30pm, Sun 5–9:30pm.

Mattakeese Wharf ✿ SEAFOOD   This place, with great views and average food, is always packed; don't even bother on summer weekends. The outdoor seating fills up first, and no wonder, with Sandy Neck sunsets to marvel over. The bouillabaisse is always good, and you can't go wrong if you stick to the varied combinations of pasta, seafood, and sauce—from Alfredo to *fra diablo*. There's live piano music most nights in season.

271 Mill Way (about ½ mile north of Rte. 6A), Barnstable. ✆ 508/362-4511. Reservations recommended. Main courses $14–$28. AE, DC, DISC, MC, V. June to mid-Oct daily 11:30am–10pm; call for off-season hours. Closed mid-Oct to mid-Apr.

YARMOUTH ✿✿

Yarmouth represents the Cape at its best—and its worst. **Yarmouth Port** ✿✿, on Cape Cod Bay, is an enchanting village, whereas the sound-side villages of West and South Yarmouth are a lesson in unbridled development run amuck. This section of Route 28 is a nightmarish gauntlet of mostly tacky accommodations and attractions.

ESSENTIALS

GETTING THERE   After crossing the Sagamore bridge, head east on Route 6 or 6A. The section of Route 6A north of Route 6's exit 7 passes through the village of Yarmouth Port. The villages of West Yarmouth, Bass River, and South Yarmouth are located along Route 28, east of Hyannis; to reach them from Route 6, take exit 7 (Yarmouth Rd.) or exit 8 (Station St.) south.

VISITOR INFORMATION   Contact the **Yarmouth Area Chamber of Commerce,** 657 Rte. 28, West Yarmouth, MA 02673 (✆ **800/732-1008** or 508/778-1008; fax 508/778-5114; www.yarmouthcapecod.com).

BEACHES & GETTING OUTSIDE

BEACHES   Yarmouth boasts 11 saltwater and two pond beaches open to the public. The body-per-square-yard ratio can be pretty intense along the sound, but so's the social scene, and no one seems to mind. The beachside parking lots charge $12 to $15 a day and sell weeklong stickers ($45).

- **Bass River Beach** ⟨, off South Shore Drive in Bass River (South Yarmouth): At the mouth of the largest tidal river on the eastern seaboard, this sound beach offers restroom facilities and a snack bar, plus a wheelchair-accessible fishing pier. The beaches along the south shore (Nantucket Sound) tend to be clean and sandy with comfortable water temps, but they can also be crowded. You need a beach sticker to park here.

- **Grays Beach,** off Center Street in Yarmouth Port: This isn't much of a beach, but tame waters make this tiny spit of dark sand good for young children. It adjoins the Callery–Darling Conservation Area with a 2.5-mile trail. The Bass Hole boardwalk offers one of the most scenic walks in the Mid-Cape. Parking is free, and there's a picnic area.

- **Parker's River Beach,** off South Shore Drive in Bass River: The usual amenities are available, like restrooms and a snack bar, plus a gazebo for the sun-shy.

- **Seagull Beach** ⟨, off South Sea Avenue in West Yarmouth: Rolling dunes, a boardwalk, and all the necessary facilities, like restrooms and a snack bar, attract a young crowd. Bring bug spray, though: Greenhead flies get the munchies in July.

FISHING   Of the five fishing ponds in the Yarmouth area, Long Pond near South Yarmouth is known for its largemouth bass and pickerel; for details and a license (shellfishing is another option), visit **Town Hall,** at 1146 Rte. 28 in South Yarmouth (⟨ **508/398-2231**), or **Riverview Bait and Tackle,** at 1273 Rte. 28 in South Yarmouth (⟨ **508/394-1036**). Full-season licenses for out-of-state residents cost $39. You can cast for striped bass and bluefish off the pier at Bass River Beach (see "Beaches," above).

NATURE & WILDLIFE AREAS   For a pleasant stroll, follow the 2 miles of trails maintained by the **Historical Society of Old Yarmouth.** Park behind the post office. The in-season trail fee (50¢ adults, 25¢ children) includes a keyed trail guide. Your path will cross the 1873 Kelley Chapel, said to have been built by a Quaker grandfather to comfort his daughter after the death of her child.

MUSEUMS

The Edward Gorey House ⟨⟨ *Finds*   The Cape's newest attraction is a museum devoted to the life and works of whimsically mischievous illustrator Edward Gorey, whose best-known work may be the animated opening to the television series *Mystery!* on PBS. He was also the author of many illustrated books, including *The Doubtful Guest* and *The Gashlycrumb Tinies.* Gorey died in the spring of 2000 and his home on the Yarmouth Port Common off Route 6A (the Old Kings Hwy.) has been converted into an intimate museum displaying original artworks, photographs, and first editions from his career as an author, playwright, illustrator, and costume and set designer. Gorey's passion for animals is also a focus of the collection.

8 Strawberry Lane (off Rte. 6A, on the Common), Yarmouth Port. ⟨ 508/362-3909. www.edwardgoreyhouse.org. Admission $5 adults, $3 students and seniors, $2 children 6–12, free for under 6. Mar–Jan Wed–Sat 11am–4pm, Sun noon–4pm. Closed Feb.

Winslow Crocker House ⟨⟨   The only property on the Cape currently preserved by the prestigious Society for the Preservation of New England Antiquities, this house, built around 1780, deserves every honor. Not only is it a lovely example of the shingled Georgian style, it's packed with outstanding antiques collected in the 1930s by

Mary Thacher, a descendant of the town's first land grantee. Anthony Thacher and his family had a rougher crossing than most: Their ship foundered off Cape Ann in 1635, and though their four children drowned, Thacher and his wife were able to make it to shore, clinging to the family cradle. You'll come across a 1690 replica in the parlor.

250 Rte. 6A (about ½ mile east of the town center), Yarmouth Port. © 617/227-3957, ext. 256. www.spnea.org. Admission $4 adults, $4 seniors, $2.50 children 6–12, free to Yarmouthport residents and SPNEA members. June–Oct 1st Sat each month, tours hourly 11am–5pm (last tour at 4pm). Closed Nov–May.

SHOPPING

Driving Route 6A, the Old King's Highway, in Yarmouth Port, you'll pass a number of antiques stores and shops for the home. Check out **Town Crier Antiques,** 153 Rte. 6A (in the center of town), Yarmouth Port (© 508/362-3138), for fun stuff including well-priced quilts, glassware, and attendant paraphernalia. The most colorful bookshop on the Cape is **Parnassus Books,** 220 Rte. 6A, Yarmouth Port (© 508/362-6420), housed in an 1858 Swedenborgian church. New stock, including the Cape-related reissues published by Parnassus Imprints, is offered alongside the older treasures. The outdoor racks, maintained on an honor system, are open 24 hours a day.

WHERE TO STAY

There are so many hotels and motels lining Route 28 and along the shore in West and South Yarmouth that it can be hard to make sense of the choices. For those staying on Route 28, the town runs frequent beach shuttles in season. Families looking for a reasonably priced beach vacation may want to consider one of the following options, all near or on the beach.

The attractive 101-unit white clapboard **Tidewater Motor Lodge,** 135 Main St. (Rte. 28), West Yarmouth (© 800/338-6322 or 508/775-6322; www.tidewaterml. com), has indoor and outdoor pools. Double rates go for $130 in summer. The 114-unit **All Seasons Motor Inn,** 1199 Main St. (Rte. 28), South Yarmouth (© 800/527-0359 or 508/394-7600; www.allseasons.com), has a game room and indoor and outdoor pools. Summer rates are $145 to $165 for a double room. The 63-unit **Ocean Mist** ⟨★⟩, 97 S. Shore Dr., South Yarmouth (© 800/248-6478 or 508/398-2633; www.capecodtravel.com/oceanmist), is right on the beach. There's also an indoor pool, in case it rains. Doubles range from $189 to $209 double, and suites are $259.

Captain Farris House ⟨★★⟩   Sumptuous is the only way to describe this 1845 inn, improbably set a block off bustling Route 28. Fine antiques and striking contemporary touches elevate the interiors beyond the average B&B decor. Some suites are apartment-size, with fireplaces and whirlpool tubs. Welcoming touches include chocolates, fresh flowers, and plush robes. Next door, the Elisha Jenkins House contains an additional suite with its own deck.

308 Old Main St. (just west of the Bass River Bridge), Bass River, MA 02664-4530. © 800/350-9477 or 508/760-2818. Fax 508/398-1262. www.captainfarris.com. 10 units (9 with tub/shower, 1 with shower only). Summer $150–$190 double; $195–$275 suite. Rates include full breakfast. AE, DISC, MC, V. *In room:* A/C, TV/VCR, dataport, hair dryer, iron.

Red Jacket ⟨★★⟩ (Kids   Of the huge resort motels lining Nantucket Sound in South Yarmouth, Red Jacket has the best location. It's at the end of the road and borders Parker's River on the west, so sunsets are particularly fine. Families who want all the fixings will find them, though the atmosphere can be a bit impersonal. All rooms have a balcony or private porch.

1 S. Shore Dr. (P.O. Box 88), South Yarmouth, MA 02664. © 800/672-0500 or 508/398-6941. Fax 508/398-1214. www.redjacketinns.com/redjacket. 150 units, 14 cottages. Summer $275–$350 double; $650–$900 cottages. Cottages weekly: $3,000–$5,500. MC, V. Closed Nov to mid-Apr. **Amenities:** Restaurant; bar/lounge; ice cream shop; indoor and outdoor heated pools; putting green; tennis court; exercise room; whirlpool; sauna; full concierge service. *In room:* A/C, TV/VCR, hair dryer, fridge.

WHERE TO DINE

At **Hallett's,** 139 Rte. 6A, Yarmouth Port (© **508/362-3362**), an 1889 drugstore, you can get a float from the original marble soda fountain.

Expensive

abbicci ★★ MEDITERRANEAN   This newly renovated sophisticated spot serves cuisine that's a cut above most of the New England-y fare you'll find around these parts. While the exterior is a modest 18th-century Cape, the contemporary interior features a stylish bar area and cozy smaller rooms lined with banquets. The menu offers seafood dishes, as well as veal, lamb, and, of course, pasta, all in a delicate Northern Italian style. A taste of the gnocchi Gorgonzola; or the *saltimbocca,* veal with prosciutto and a sage, and you'll be transported straight to Tuscany. There is also a tapas menu, priced from $5 to $12. Save room for house-made desserts, like the Napoleon with spiced red-wine poached pears. This small restaurant can get overrun on summer weekends, so expect a wait even with a reservation. A three-course prix fixe menu in the fall and winter costs $25.

43 Main St./Rte. 6A (near the Cummaquid border), Yarmouth Port. © **508/362-3501.** Reservations recommended. Main courses $23–$39. AE, MC, V. Daily 4–9:30pm (dinner), Mon and Fri–Sat noon–3pm (lunch), Sun 11am–3pm (brunch). Open year-round.

Inaho ★★ (Finds) JAPANESE   What better application of the Cape's oceanic bounty than fresh-off-the-boat sushi? From the front, Inaho is a typical Cape Cod cottage, but park in the back so you can enter through the Japanese garden. The decor is minimalist with traditional shoji screens and crisp navy-and-white banners softened by tranquil music and service. On chilly days, opt for the tempura or a steaming bowl of shabu-shabu.

157 Main St./Rte. 6A (in the village center), Yarmouth Port. © **508/362-5522.** Reservations recommended. Main courses $13–$23; sushi pieces and rolls $3–$7. MC, V. Tues–Sun 5–10pm; call for off-season hours.

902 Main ★★★ NEW AMERICAN   This wonderful restaurant continues to excel. With fabulous service, an elegant atmosphere, and to-die-for food, this is the place to go for fine dining in the Mid-Cape. Entrees like filet mignon with portobello mushrooms, rack of lamb with truffle mashed potatoes, and haddock with organic beets will make you swoon.

902 Main St./Rte. 28, South Yarmouth. © **508/398-9902.** Reservations required. Main courses $18–$33. AE, MC, V. Daily 5–10pm.

Old Yarmouth Inn NEW ENGLAND   If a traditional Cape Cod atmosphere is what you are looking for, you can't do much better than this old stagecoach inn serving Yankee basics like prime rib and baked scrod. The food is fresh and hearty and the preparations are tasty. It can be crowded on weekends in season. There's also a lighter-fare menu. One of the most requested dishes is the deluxe lobster roll, with big chunks of fresh lobster. The Sunday brunch, a combination buffet and a la carte meal, is popular.

223 Rte. 6A (in the center of Yarmouth Port). © **508/362-9962.** Reservations recommended. Main courses $14–$25. AE, DC, DISC, MC, V. June–Oct Tues–Sat 11:30am–2:30pm, Sun 10am–1:30pm, daily 4:30–9pm; call for off-season hours.

DENNIS ★★

In Dennis, as in Yarmouth, virtually all the good stuff—pretty drives, inviting shops, and restaurants with real personality—is in the north, along Route 6A. Route 28, on the other hand, is chockablock with generic motels and strip malls.

ESSENTIALS

GETTING THERE   After crossing the Sagamore Bridge, head east on Route 6 or 6A. Route 6A passes through the villages of Dennis and East Dennis (which can also be reached via northbound Rte. 134 from exit 9 off Rte. 6). Route 134 South leads to South Dennis; if you follow Route 134 all the way to Route 28, the village of West Dennis will be a couple of miles to your west, and Dennisport a couple of miles east. Or fly into Hyannis.

VISITOR INFORMATION   Contact the **Dennis Chamber of Commerce,** 242 Swan River Rd., West Dennis, MA 02670 (© **800/243-9920** or 508/398-3568; www.dennischamber.com).

BEACHES & RECREATIONAL PURSUITS

BEACHES   Dennis harbors more than a dozen saltwater and two freshwater beaches open to nonresidents. The bay beaches are charming and a big hit with families. The beaches on the Sound tend to attract wall-to-wall families, but the parking lots are usually not too crowded because many beachgoers stay within walking distance. The lots charge $15 per day; for a 1-week permit ($50), visit **Town Hall** on Main Street in South Dennis (© **508/394-8300**).

- **Chapin Beach** ★★, off Route 6A in Dennis: A nice, long bay beach with occasional boulders and surrounded by dunes. No lifeguard, but there are restrooms.
- **Corporation Beach** ★★, off Route 6A in Dennis: This bay beach boasts a wheel-chair-accessible boardwalk, lifeguards, snack bar, restrooms, and a children's play area.
- **Mayflower Beach** ★★, off Route 6A in Dennis: This 1,200-foot bay beach has the necessary amenities, plus an accessible boardwalk. The tide pools attract lots of children.
- **Scargo Lake,** a large kettle-hole pond (formed by a melting fragment of a glacier) has two pleasant beaches: Scargo Beach, accessible right off Route 6A; and Princess Beach, off Scargo Hill Road, where there are restrooms and a picnic area.
- **West Dennis Beach** ★★, off Route 28 in West Dennis: This long (½-mile) but narrow beach along the sound has lifeguards, a playground, a snack bar, rest-rooms, and a special kite-flying area. The eastern end is reserved for residents; in any case, the western end tends to be less packed.

BICYCLING   The 25-mile **Cape Cod Rail Trail** ★★★ (© **508/896-3491**) starts here, on Route 134, a half-mile south of Route 6, exit 9. Once a Penn Central track, this paved bikeway extends all the way to Wellfleet (with a few on-road lapses), pass-ing through woods, marshes, and dunes. At the trail head is **Bob's Bike Shop,** 430 Rte. 134, South Dennis (© **508/760-4723**), which rents bikes and in-line skates and does repairs. Rates are $10 for a couple of hours and up to $22 for the full day. Another bike path runs along Old Bass Road, 3.5 miles north to Route 6A.

FISHING   Fishing is allowed in Fresh Pond and Scargo Lake; for a license (shellfish-ing is also permitted), visit **Town Hall,** on Main Street in South Dennis (© **508/394-8300**), or **Riverview Bait and Tackle,** at 1273 Rte. 28 in South Yarmouth

(© **508/394-1036**). Plenty of people drop a line off the Bass River Bridge along Route 28 in West Dennis. Several charter boats operate out of the Northside Marina in East Dennis's Sesuit Harbor, including the ***Albatross*** (© **508/385-3244**).

NATURE & WILDLIFE AREAS   Behind the town hall parking lot on Main Street in South Dennis, a half-mile walk along the **Indian Lands Conservation Trail** leads to the Bass River, where blue herons and kingfishers often take shelter. Dirt roads off South Street in East Dennis, beyond the Quivet Cemetery, lead to Crow's Pasture, a patchwork of marshes and dunes bordering the bay; this circular trail is about a 2.5-mile round-trip.

WATERSPORTS   On small, placid Swan River, **Cape Cod Waterways,** 16 Rte. 28, Dennisport (© **508/398-0080**), rents canoes, kayaks, and paddle boats for exploring 200-acre Swan Pond (less than a mile north) or Nantucket Sound (2 miles south). A full-day canoe or kayak rental costs $50.

MUSEUMS
Cape Cod Museum of Art ✦✦   Part of the prettily landscaped Cape Playhouse complex, this museum has done a great job of acquiring hundreds of works by representative area artists dating back to the turn of the 20th century.

60 Hope Lane (off Rte. 6A in the center of town). © **508/385-4477**. www.cmfa.org. Admission $8 adults, free for children under 18, admission by donation Weds 10am–1pm and Thurs 5–8:30pm. MC, V. Mon–Sat 10am–5pm; Sun noon–5pm.

SHOPPING
Dennisport has a growing cluster of flea market–style antiques shops, but you may want to save your time and money for the better shops along Route 6A, where you'll also find fine contemporary crafts.

More than 136 dealers stock the co-op **Antiques Center of Cape Cod,** 243 Rte. 6A, about 1 mile south of Dennis Village center, Dennis (© **508/385-6400**); it's the largest such enterprise on the Cape.

Dennis along Route 6A has become a magnet for interesting small galleries. Among the finest is **Scargo Stoneware Pottery and Art Gallery,** 30 Dr. Lord's Rd. S. (off Rte. 6A, about 1 mile east of the town center), Dennis (© **508/385-3894**).

WHERE TO STAY
Corsair & Cross Rip Resort Motels ✦ (Kids)   Of the many family-oriented motels lining this part of Nantucket Sound, these two neighbors are among the nicest, with fresh contemporary decor, two beach-view pools, and their own chunk of sand. As a rainy-day backup, there's an indoor pool, a game room, and a toddler playroom equipped with toys.

41 Chase Ave. (off Depot St., 1 mile southeast of Rte. 28), Dennisport, MA 02639. © **800/201-1072** or 508/398-2279. Fax 508/760-6681. www.corsaircrossrip.com. 47 units (all with tub/shower). Summer $225–$275 double. Special packages and family weekly rates available. AE, MC, V. Closed mid-Oct to Apr. **Amenities:** 2 outdoor pools; indoor pool; outdoor Jacuzzi; game room; toddler playroom and kids' playground; coin-op washers and dryers. *In room:* A/C, TV w/HBO, fax, dataport, fridge, coffeemaker, hair dryer, iron.

Isaiah Hall B&B Inn ✦✦   This inn's location on a quiet side street in a residential neighborhood bodes well for a good night's sleep, but it's also just a short walk to restaurants, entertainment options, and Corporation Beach. Breakfasts are served at the long plank table that dominates the 1857 country kitchen. Room styles range from 1940s knotty pine to spacious and spiffy.

152 Whig St. (1 block northwest of the Cape Playhouse), Dennis, MA 02638. ℂ 800/736-0160 or 508/385-9928. Fax 508/385-5879. www.isaiahhallinn.com. 10 units (5 with tub/shower, 5 with shower only). Summer $135–$155 double; $285 suite. Rates include full breakfast. AE, DISC, MC, V. Closed mid-Oct to late Apr. No children under age 7. *In room:* A/C, TV/VCR, dataport, hair dryer.

Lighthouse Inn ✸✸ *(Kids)*   Set on placid West Dennis Beach on Nantucket Sound, this resort has been welcoming families for over 60 years. In 1938, Everett Stone acquired a decommissioned 1855 lighthouse and built an inn and a 9-acre cottage colony around it. With amusements such as miniature golf and shuffleboard right on the premises, as well as a heated outdoor pool and tennis courts, there's plenty to do. The rooms aren't what you'd call fancy, but some have great views. Lunch is served on the deck overlooking Nantucket Sound, a delightful setting in which to enjoy a club sandwich. The Sand Bar, a classic bar with cabaret-style entertainment, serves as on-site nightspot.

1 Lighthouse Inn Rd. (off Lower County Rd., ½ mile south of Rte. 28), West Dennis, MA 02670. ℂ 508/398-2244. Fax 508/398-5658. www.lighthouseinn.com. 44 units, 24 cottages (all with tub/shower). Summer $244–$270 double; $447–$583 2-bedroom cottage; $480–$690 3-bedroom cottage. MC, V. Rates include full breakfast and all gratuities. Closed mid-Oct to mid-May. **Amenities:** 2 restaurants (large dining room, pool snack bar); bar w/entertainment; outdoor heated pool w/sunning deck, chairs, umbrellas, and pool house/changing rooms; outdoor tennis court; InnKids, a free supervised play program (ages 3–11), offered July and Aug; game room; shuffleboard; volleyball; and minigolf. *In room:* A/C, TV, fridge, hair dryer, iron, safe.

WHERE TO DINE

For a time-travel treat, visit **Sundae School** ✸, 381 Lower County Rd., at Sea Street, about ½ mile south of Route 28, Dennisport (ℂ **508/394-9122**). The spacious barn has been retrofitted with a turn-of-the-20th-century marble soda fountain and other artifacts from the golden age of ice cream.

Expensive

Blue Moon Bistro ✸✸ MEDITERRANEAN   Beautiful presentations of innovative cuisine are the hallmarks at this Dennis Village venue, one of the newer eateries in the Cape's fine-dining roster. The restaurant's deep blue ceiling and dark wood floors contribute to the warm and inviting atmosphere; crisp, white tablecloths hint at the elegant dining to come. Chef/owner Peter Hyde, who was trained in Europe, gives a twist to traditional recipes. Instead of a crab cake, his is a crab and cod cake with spicy red peppers. His Mediterranean fish soup includes chorizo for added pizzazz. There are always a couple of vegetarian options on the menu in addition to fish and meat, including the luscious grilled beef tenderloin wrapped in house-smoked bacon. Don't miss the house-made desserts.

605 Main St./Rte 6A (in the center of town), Dennis Village. ℂ **508/385-7100.** Reservations recommended. Main courses $16–$30. AE, MC, V. June to late Aug Wed–Sat 11:30am–3pm and 4:30–11pm, Tues and Sun 5–9:30pm; Apr–May and late Aug to Nov Wed–Sun 4–11pm. Closed Dec–Mar.

(Kids) Especially for Kids

If the kids get sick of all the miscellaneous go-cart and minigolf concessions on Route 28, they can take in a show. On Friday mornings in season, at 9:30 and 11:30am, the **Cape Playhouse** ✸✸ (ℂ **508/385-3911**), 820 Rte. 6A, Dennis, hosts visiting companies that mount theater geared toward children 4 and up. At only $7 to $8, tickets go fast.

Gracie's Table 🎯 SPANISH TAPAS   Just steps from the Cape Playhouse and Cape Cinema, Gracie's Table offers something different on Cape Cod: Spanish-style dining. Preparations by chef/owner Ann Austin are inspired by cuisine from the Basque region, as well as southwest France. While there are plenty of full meals to choose from, the specialty here is tapas, small unusual dishes. The best way to enjoy tapas is for each diner to choose several smaller dishes and share the different tastes with dining companions. Tapas choices include hot lobster roll, sushi style; potato and chorizo tortilla; and tuna carpaccio with horseradish sorbet. The dining room is sleek and sophisticated, and is staffed by professional servers, pleased to recommend their favorite tapas.

800 Main St./Rte 6A (at Theatre Marketplace in front of the Cape Playhouse complex), Dennis Village. 📞 508/385-5600. Reservations recommended. Tapas $5–$15; main courses $15–$30. AE, MC, V. Daily 5–9pm; call for off-season hours.

The Ocean House New American Bistro and Bar 🎯🎯 *Finds* NEW AMERICAN This restaurant set on the beach overlooking Nantucket Sound has long had a stellar reputation, and now it's better than ever. There's a buzz around this creative cuisine, making this oceanfront restaurant a must-visit location. One appealing thing about The Ocean House is that you can come for a multicourse fine-dining meal or just nibble on some appetizers. Favorites are the lemon grass–battered gray sole and the grilled beef tenderloin with Maytag blue cheese. With the dining room's large arches framing the beach beyond, this is a wonderful place to spend the evening. For bargain-hunters, a special three-course fall dinner is $25 per person.

3 Chase Ave. (at Depot St., on the beach), Dennisport. 📞 508/394-0700. Reservations strongly recommended. Main courses $18–$34. MC, V. June–Sept Tues–Sun 5–10pm; call for off-season hours. Closed Jan to mid-Mar.

The Red Pheasant Inn 🎯🎯 CONTEMPORARY AMERICAN   An enduring Cape favorite since 1977, this handsome space—an 18th-century barn-turned-chandlery—has managed not only to keep pace with trends, but also to remain a frontrunner. Popular dishes include roast rack of lamb, sole meunière, and in the fall, game specials like venison. Two massive brick fireplaces tend to be the focal point in the off season. In fine weather, you'll want to sit out in the garden room.

905 Main St. (about ½ mile east of the town center). 📞 508/385-2133. Reservations required. Main courses $18–$30. DISC, MC, V. Apr–Dec daily 5–9pm; Jan–Mar Wed–Sun 5–9pm.

Moderate

Center Stage Café & Backstage Pub 🎯 NEW AMERICAN   In the same complex as the Cape Playhouse and Cape Cinema, this place could get away with so-so food and service. Instead, the Center Stage has become a destination in itself, in addition to being *the* place to go after a show. The beauty of this place is you can get anything from a burger or sandwich to a full multicourse meal. Hours are extended for convenient bites before or after a show. From a fresh lobster roll to a barbecue chicken pizza to a Delmonico steak, it's all here. The cozy and convivial bar is a great place to grab a drink before or after a show.

36 Hope Lane (on the grounds of the Cape Playhouse). 📞 508/385-7737. www.centerstagedennis.com. Reservations suggested. Main courses $8–$22. AE, MC, V. June to late Aug Mon–Sat 11:30am–2pm, 4:30–10pm; Apr–May and late Aug to Nov Wed–Sun 4–10pm. Closed Dec–Mar.

Gina's by the Sea 🎯🎯 ITALIAN   A landmark amid Dennis's "Little Italy" beach community since 1938, this intimate restaurant specializes in traditional Italian comfort food. Save room for Mrs. Riley's Chocolate Rum Cake, made daily by the owner's mother. This popular place fills up fast, so if you want to eat before 8:30pm, arrive before 5:30pm.

134 Taunton Ave. (about 1½ miles northwest of Rte. 6A; turn north across from the Public Market and follow the signs). ℂ **508/385-3213.** Reservations not accepted. Main courses $10–$23. AE, MC, V. June to late Aug daily 5–10pm; Apr–May and late Aug to Nov Thurs–Sun 5–10pm. Closed Dec–Mar.

Scargo Cafe ℛ INTERNATIONAL   Formerly a sea captain's house, this lively bistro has a menu split into "traditional" and "adventurous" categories. Traditionalists will find surf and turf, and the popular grilled lamb loins served with mint jelly (talk about traditional!); adventurous dishes include "wildcat chicken" (a sauté of sausage, mushrooms, and raisins, flambéed with apricot brandy). Serving food until 11pm, Scargo is one of only a couple of options in the neighborhood to go to after a show at the Cape Playhouse across the street.

799 Main St./Rte. 6A (opposite the Cape Playhouse). ℂ **508/385-8200.** Reservations accepted for parties of 6 or more. Main courses $14–$22. AE, DISC, MC, V. Mid-June to mid-Sept daily 11am–3pm and 4:30–11pm; mid-Sept to mid-June daily 11am–10pm.

INEXPENSIVE

Sesuit Harbor Cafe ℛ AMERICAN   Right on the beach in a busy boatyard, this clam shack promises one of those authentic Cape Cod experiences that are becoming harder and harder to find. It's worth seeking out the family-owned establishment for its picture-postcard views and tasty food. Specialties include clam chowder, lobster rolls, and fried clams. You'll find good breakfasts here, too. Order from the counter and find a seat at one of the picnic tables outside.

257 Sesuit Neck Rd. (Rte. 6A to Bridge St., take a right on Sesuit Neck and follow to the harbor), East Dennis. ℂ **508/385-6134.** Reservations not accepted. Main courses $7–$17. MC, V. Daily 7am–8:30pm. Closed mid-Oct to late Apr.

DENNIS AFTER DARK

The oldest continuously active straw-hat theater in the country, and still one of the best, the **Cape Cod Playhouse** ℛℛ, 820 Rte. 6A (ℂ **877/385-3911** or 508/385-3911; www.capeplayhouse.com), was the 1927 brainstorm of Raymond Moore, who'd spent a few summers as a playwright in Provincetown and quickly tired of the strictures of "little theater." Salvaging an 1838 meetinghouse, he plunked it amid a meadow and got his New York buddy, designer Cleon Throckmorton, to turn it into a proper theater. It was an immediate success, and a parade of stars has trod the boards in the decades since, from Humphrey Bogart to Julie Harris. Not all of today's headliners are quite as impressive, but the theater can be counted on for a varied season of polished work. Performances are staged from mid-June to early September. Tickets range from $25 to $45.

The **Cape Cinema** ℛℛ, 36 Hope Lane, off Route 6A in the center of town (ℂ **508/385-22503** or 508/385-5644; www.capecinema.com), is an Art Deco surprise, with a Prometheus-themed ceiling mural. George Mansour, curator of the Harvard Film Archive, sees to the art-house programming. The setting and seating—black leather armchairs—may spoil you forever.

3 The Lower Cape

The Lower Cape has fewer year-rounders than the Mid- and Upper Cape towns, so the communities on this part of Cape Cod are more summer-oriented. There are also several upscale and expensive resorts and restaurants in this area.

Along the easternmost portion of historic Route 6A, **Brewster** still enjoys much the same cachet that it had as a high roller in the maritime trade. But for the cars, it looks much as it might have in the late 19th century, with its general store still serving as a social center. Perhaps because excellence breeds competition, Brewster has spawned several fine restaurants and has become something of a magnet for gourmands.

Realtors tout **Chatham,** the Cape's most chichi town, as "the Nantucket of the Cape." Its Main Street offers appealing shops and eateries, complemented by a scenic lighthouse and plentiful beaches nearby.

As the gateway to the Outer Cape, where all roads merge, **Orleans** is a bustling town in the summer. The village of East Orleans is a destination itself, offering a couple of fun restaurants and—best of all—a good chunk of magnificent, unspoiled Cape Cod National Seashore.

BREWSTER 🟢🟢

With miles of placid Cape Cod Bay beaches and acres of state park, Brewster is an attractive place for families. Route 6A, the Old King's Highway, becomes Brewster's Main Street and houses a bevy of B&Bs, pricey restaurants, and the Cape's finest antiques shops. The town has managed to absorb a huge development within its borders, the 380-acre condo complex known as Ocean Edge. Brewster also welcomes the tens of thousands of campers and day-trippers headed for Nickerson State Park.

ESSENTIALS

GETTING THERE   After crossing the Sagamore Bridge, head east on Route 6 or 6A. Route 6A on the north side of the Cape passes through the villages of West Brewster, Brewster, and East Brewster. You can also reach Brewster by taking Route 6 to exit 10 north, along Route 124.

VISITOR INFORMATION   Contact the **Brewster Chamber of Commerce Visitor Center,** behind Brewster Town Hall, 2198 Main St./Rte. 6A, Brewster (© **508/896-3500;** fax 508/896-1086; www.brewstercapecod.org).

BEACHES & GETTING OUTSIDE

BEACHES   Brewster's eight bay beaches have minimal facilities. When the tide is out, the beach extends as much as 2 miles, leaving behind tide pools to splash in and explore. On a clear day, you can see the whole curve of the Cape, from Sandwich to Provincetown. Purchase a beach parking sticker ($15 per day, $50 per week) at the **Visitor Center** behind Town Hall, at 2198 Main St. (Rte. 6A; © **508/896-4511**).

- **Breakwater Beach** , off Breakwater Road, Brewster: Only a brief walk from the center of town, this calm, shallow beach (the only one with restrooms) is ideal for young children.
- **Flax Pond** 🟢🟢 in Nickerson State Park (see "Nature & Wildlife Areas," below): This freshwater pond has a bathhouse and offers watersports rentals. The park contains two more ponds with beaches—Cliff and Little Cliff. Access and parking are free.
- **Linnell Landing Beach** 🟢, on Linnell Road in East Brewster: This is a ½-mile, wheelchair-accessible bay beach.
- **Paines Creek Beach** 🟢, off Paines Creek Road, West Brewster: With 1½ miles to stretch out on, this bay beach has something to offer sun lovers and nature lovers alike. Your kids will love it if you arrive when the tide's coming in—the current will give an air mattress a nice little ride.

Moments **Biking the Cape Cod Rail Trail**

The 25-mile **Cape Cod Rail Trail** ★★★ is one of New England's longest and most popular bike paths. Once a bed of the Penn Central Railroad, the trail is relatively flat and straight. On weekends in summer, you'll have to contend with dogs, in-line skaters, families, and bikers who whip by you on their way to becoming the next Lance Armstrong. Still, if you want to venture away from the coast and see some of the Cape's countryside without having to deal with motorized traffic, this is one of the best ways to do it.

The trail starts in South Wellfleet on Lecount Hollow Road or in South Dennis on Route 134, depending on which way you want to ride. Beginning in South Wellfleet, the path cruises by purple wildflowers, flowering dogwood, and small maples, where red-winged blackbirds and goldfinches nest. In Orleans, you'll have to ride on West Road until the City Council decides to complete the trail. Fortunately, the roads provide a good view of the boats lining Rock Harbor. Clearly marked signs lead back to the Rail Trail. You'll soon enter Nickerson State Park bike trails, or continue straight through Brewster to a series of swimming holes—Seymour, Long, and Hinckleys ponds. A favorite picnic spot is the Pleasant Lake General Store in Harwich. Shortly afterward, you'll cross over Route 6 on Route 124 before veering right through farmland, soon ending in South Dennis.

—*by Stephen Jermanok*

BICYCLING   The **Cape Cod Rail Trail** ★★★ intersects with the 8-mile **Nickerson State Park** trail system at the park entrance, where there's plenty of free parking; you could follow the Rail Trail back to Dennis (about 12 miles) or onward toward Wellfleet (13 miles). In season, **Idle Times** (© 508/255-8281) provides rentals within the park. Another good place to jump in is on Underpass Road about a half-mile south of Route 6A. Here you'll find **Brewster Bicycle Rental,** 442 Underpass Rd. (© **508/896-8149**), and **Brewster Express,** which makes sandwiches to go. Just up the hill is the well-equipped **Rail Trail Bike & Blade,** 302 Underpass Rd. (© **508/896-8200**). All three shops offer free parking. Bicycle rentals start at around $14 for 4 hours and go up to about $22 for 24 hours.

BOATING   You can rent a canoe from **Goose Hummock** ★ in Orleans (© 508/255-2620) and paddle around Paines Creek and Quivett Creek, as well as Upper and Lower Mill ponds.

FISHING   Brewster offers more ponds for fishing than any other town: 14 in all. Among the most popular are Cliff and Higgins ponds (within Nickerson State Park). For a license, visit the town clerk at **Town Hall,** 2198 Rte. 6A (© **508/896-3701**).

GOLF   The 18-hole championship **Ocean Edge Golf Course,** at 832 Villages Dr. (© **508/896-5911**), is Brewster's most challenging, followed closely by **Captain's Golf Course,** at 1000 Freemans Way (© **508/896-5100**).

NATURE & WILDLIFE AREAS   Admission is free to the two trails maintained by the Cape Cod Museum of Natural History (see below). The **South Trail,** covering a

---

Take Me Out to the Ballgame

The **Cape Cod Baseball League** (www.capecodbaseball.org), an elite amateur league, will delight sports fans of all ages. The Cape has 10 teams, some with intense rivalries. Games are in July and August. Admission is a small donation. Games are afternoons and evenings. A highlight, besides the superb play, is watching dozens of kids trying to catch the elusive foul ball.

.75-mile round-trip south of Route 6A, crosses a natural cranberry bog beside Paines Creek to reach a hardwood forest of beeches and tupelos; toward the end of the loop, you'll come upon a "glacial erratic," a huge boulder dropped by a receding glacier. Before heading out on the .25-mile **North Trail,** stop in at the museum for a free guide describing the local flora. Also accessible from the museum parking lot is the **John Wing Trail,** a 1.5-mile network traversing 140 acres of preservation land, including upland, salt marsh, and beach. (*Note:* This can be a soggy trip. Be sure to heed the posted warnings about high tides, especially in spring, or you might very well find yourself stranded.)

As it crosses Route 6A, Paines Creek Road becomes Run Hill Road. Follow it to the end to reach **Punkhorn Park Lands,** an undeveloped 800-acre tract popular with mountain bikers; it features several kettle ponds, a "quaking bog," and 45 miles of dirt paths.

The short jaunt around the **Stony Brook Grist Mill** is especially scenic. In spring, you can watch the alewives (freshwater herring) vaulting upstream to spawn, and in the summer, the millpond is surrounded and scented by honeysuckle.

The 1,955-acre **Nickerson State Park,** at Route 6 and Crosby Lane (✆ **508/896-3491**), encompasses 418 campsites (reservations pour in a year in advance, but some are held open for new arrivals willing to wait a day or two), eight kettle ponds, and 8 miles of bicycle paths.

WATERSPORTS Sailboats, kayaks, canoes, and more are available seasonally at **Jack's Boat Rentals** (✆ **508/896-8556**), on Flax Pond in Nickerson State Park.

A BREWSTER MUSEUM

Cape Cod Museum of Natural History ⭐⭐⭐ *Kids* Long before *ecology* became a buzzword, noted naturalist writer John Hay helped found a museum dedicated to Cape Cod's unique landscape. The children's exhibits include a "live hive"—like an ant farm, only with busy bees and marine-room tanks. The bulk of the museum is outdoors, where 85 acres invite exploration (see "Nature & Wildlife Areas," above). There's an on-site archaeology lab on Wing Island, thought to have sheltered one of Brewster's first settlers—the Quaker John Wing, driven from Sandwich in the mid–17th century by religious persecution—and before him, native tribes dating back 10 millennia. The museum sponsors lectures, concerts, marsh cruises, bike tours, seal cruises, and "eco-treks"—including a sleepover on uninhabited Monomoy Island off Chatham.

869 Rte. 6A (about 2 miles west of the town center). ✆ **800/479-3867** (eastern MA only), or 508/896-3867. www.ccmnh.org. Admission $8 adults, $7 seniors, $3.50 children 3–12. June–Sept daily 10am–4pm; Oct–Mar Wed–Sun 11am–3pm; Apr–May Wed–Sun 10am–4pm.

SHOPPING

No one should miss **The Brewster Store,** 1935 Main St./Rte. 6A, in the center of town (ⓒ **508/896-3744**), built as a church in 1852. You'll find everything from penny candy to comics to the bestselling Brewster Store coffee. Neighbors meet on the wide front porch to catch up on village gossip.

WHERE TO STAY

Michael's Cottages and Bed and Breakfast ⓖ Ⓥalue   These cottages on an immaculately groomed compound are small yet centrally located. Across the street is Brewster's Drummer Boy Park, which has a playground, historic windmill, and antique house. Brewster's summer band concerts are held there as well. The closest beach is Paines Creek, about 1 mile away. In July and August, rentals are available by the week only.

618 Main St./Rte. 6A, Brewster, MA 02631. ⓒ **800/399-2967** or 508/896-4025. Fax 508/896-3158. www.michaels inbrewster.com. 7 units (2 with tub/shower, 5 with shower only). Summer $150–$175 double. Weekly rates $775–$850 double; $1,375 2-bedroom. B&B rooms include continental breakfast. AE, DISC, MC, V. *In room:* A/C, TV, fridge, coffeemaker, hair dryer.

Ocean Edge Resort & Club ⓖ   Looking like an enormous seaside estate, Ocean Edge offers numerous amenities, from beach, pools, tennis, and golf. Replete with New England–style charm—lovely quilts, sliding glass doors that lead to patios or balconies—hotel rooms off the mansion are extremely large and comfortable. Spread across the 400-acre property, one- to three-bedroom villas offer the freedom of a private residence (full kitchens, washer/dryers, and fireplaces in some) and the convenience of not having to drive (shuttle buses run all over the property). However, you might want to go out for groceries or to a local restaurant once in a while; the food served here is fine but not impressive.

2907 Main St./Rte. 6A, Brewster, MA 02631. ⓒ **800/896-9000.** Fax 508/896-9123. www.oceanedge.com. 335 units. Summer $335–$375 hotel room (double), $395–$550 1-bedroom villa, $800–$1,800/night or $2,400–$7,500/week 2- to 3-bedroom villa. Minimum-stay restrictions may apply during peak periods. AE, DISC, MC, V. **Amenities:** 4 restaurants; 6 pools (2 indoor, 4 outdoor) and 2 toddler pools; 18-hole championship golf course; 11 tennis courts; fitness center; babysitting; laundry and dry-cleaning services; conference/banqueting facilities; housekeeping service. *In room:* A/C, TV, Wi-Fi, full kitchen or kitchenette (in villas), coffeemaker, hair dryer, iron, safe (in hotel rooms).

Old Sea Pines Inn ⓖⓖ Ⓚids Ⓥalue   This reasonably priced, large historic inn is a great spot for families. The inn's former days as the Sea Pines School of Charm and Personality for Young Women can still be seen in the handful of rather minuscule boarding school–scale rooms on the second floor. These bargain rooms with shared bathrooms are the only ones in the house without air-conditioning, but at $105 per night in season, who cares? The annex rooms are downright playful, with colorful accouterments, such as pink TVs. Sunday evenings from mid-June through mid-September, Old Sea Pines is the site of a dinner/theater performance by the Cape Cod Repertory Theatre.

2553 Main St. (about 1 mile east of the town center), Brewster, MA 02631. ⓒ **508/896-6114.** Fax 508/632-0084. www.oldseapinesinn.com. 24 units, 5 with shared bathroom. Summer $105–$160 double; $155–$185 suite. Rates include full breakfast and afternoon tea. AE, DC, DISC, MC, V. Closed Jan–Mar. *In room:* TV, hair dryer, iron.

WHERE TO DINE

The Bramble Inn Restaurant ⓖⓖⓖ NEW AMERICAN   Often named among the best restaurants on Cape Cod, The Bramble Inn is also one of the most expensive—but worth it for a special night out. The restaurant also has an a la carte bistro menu that is available Sunday to Thursday in the Hunt Room bar and in the court-yard garden. Fortunately, no matter which menu you order from, you'll be able to enjoy Ruth Manchester's extraordinary cuisine. Her assorted seafood curry (with lobster, cod, scallops, and shrimp in a light curry sauce with grilled banana, toasted almonds, coconut, and chutney) and her rack of lamb (with deep-fried beet-and-fontina polenta, pan-seared zucchini, and mustard port cream) have been written up in the *New York Times*.

2019 Main St. (about ½ mile east of Rte. 124). (© **508/896-7644**. Reservations required for fine dining, not for bistro. Fixed-price dinner $44–$64. AE, DISC, MC, V. June to early Sept daily 5:30–9pm; call for off-season hours. Closed Jan–Mar.

Chillingsworth &&& FRENCH   This longtime contender for the title of fanciest restaurant on the Cape has two dining options: formal dinner, with jackets recommended for men, and the more casual bistro. The dining room contains antique appointments dating back several centuries and a six-course Francophiliac table d'hôte menu that will challenge the most shameless gourmands. Specialties include steamed lobster over spinach and fennel with sea beans and lobster-basil butter sauce. Finish with warm chocolate cake with pistachio ice cream and chocolate drizzle. Or try the moderately priced bistro, which serves Sunday brunch and lunch and dinner daily in season in the adjoining greenhouse or on the shady lawn. There are also three deluxe guest rooms on the premises.

2449 Main St. (about 1 mile east of the town center). (© **800/430-3640** or 508/896-3640. www.chillingsworth.com. Reservations required for fine-dining; recommended for bistro. Jacket advised for men in fine-dining section. Fixed-price meals $60–$70; bistro $17–$28. AE, DC, MC, V. Mid-June to August Thurs–Sun 11:30am–2:30pm and Mon–Sun 6–9:30pm (bistro opens for dinner at 5:30pm). On Mon seating only for fine dining (7–7:30pm); call for off-season hours. Closed Dec–mid-May.

Moderate

The Brewster Fish House && NEW AMERICAN   Spare and handsome as a Shaker refectory, this small restaurant bills itself as "nonconforming" and delivers on the promise. Its approach to seafood borders on genius: Consider, for instance, squid delectably tenderized in a marinade of soy and ginger; or silky-tender, walnut-crusted ocean catfish accompanied by kale sautéed in Marsala. Beef and vegetarian options are always available as well. Better get there early (before 7pm) if you want to get in.

2208 Main St. (about ½ mile east of the town center). (© **508/896-7867**. Reservations not accepted. Main courses $17–$29. MC, V. May–Aug Mon–Sat 11am–3pm and 5–9:30pm, Sun noon–3pm and 5–9:30pm; call for off-season hours. Closed mid-Dec to Apr.

Inexpensive

Brewster Inn & Chowder House & ECLECTIC   To get the gist of the expression "chow down," just observe the early-evening crowd happily doing so at this century-old restaurant. The draw is hearty staples at prices geared to ordinary people rather than splurging tourists. This place also makes the best martinis in town, and there's a good old bar, **The Woodshed,** out back.

1993 Rte. 6A (in the center of town). (© **508/896-7771**. Main courses $12–$18. AE, DISC, MC, V. Late May to mid-Oct daily 11:30am–2:30pm, Sun–Thurs 5–9:30pm, Fri–Sat 5–10pm; call for off-season hours. Open year-round.

Cobie's & AMERICAN   Accessible to cars whizzing along Route 6A and within collapsing distance for cyclists exploring the Rail Trail, this picture-perfect clam shack has been dishing out exemplary fried clams, lobster rolls, foot-long hot dogs, black-and-white frappés, and all the other beloved summer staples since 1948.

3260 Rte. 6A (about 2 miles east of Brewster center). ℂ **508/896-7021.** Most items under $15. No credit cards. Late May to early Sept daily 11am–9pm. Closed early Sept to late May.

CHATHAM ✸✸✸

Chatham (pronounced "Chatt-um") is small-town America the way Norman Rockwell imagined it. Roses climb white picket fences in front of shingled Cape cottages, all within a stone's throw of the ocean. The Cape's fanciest town is also its prettiest. As a result, inn rooms are pricier here and rentals are snapped up more quickly. But those looking for a picture-perfect New England town will love Chatham's winding Main Street, which is filled with pleasing shops and leads to a beautiful beach with a lighthouse.

Sticking out like a sore elbow, Chatham was one of the first spots to attract early explorers. Samuel de Champlain stopped by in 1606 but got into a tussle with the prior occupants and then left in a hurry. The first colonist to stick around was William Nickerson of Yarmouth, who befriended a local *sachem* (tribal leader) and built a house beside his wigwam in 1656. To this day, listings for Nickersons occupy a half-page in the Cape Cod phone book.

Chatham is one of the few areas on the Cape to support a commercial fishing fleet—against increasing odds. Over-fishing has resulted in closely monitored limits to give the stock time to bounce back. Boats must now go out as far as 100 miles to catch their fill. Despite the difficulties, it's a way of life few locals would willingly relinquish.

ESSENTIALS

GETTING THERE   After crossing the Sagamore Bridge, head east on Route 6 and take exit 11 south (Rte. 137) to Route 28. From this intersection, South Chatham is about a half-mile west, and West Chatham is about 1½ miles east. Chatham itself is about 2 miles farther east on Route 28. The town lies 32 miles east of Sandwich, 24 miles south of Provincetown.

VISITOR INFORMATION   Visit the **Chatham Chamber of Commerce,** 533 Main St., Chatham, MA 02633 (ℂ **800/715-5567** or 508/945-5199; www.chatham info.com); or the new **Chatham Chamber booth** at the intersection of routes 137 and 28 (no phone).

BEACHES & GETTING OUTSIDE

BEACHES   Chatham has an unusual array of beach styles, from the peaceful shores of the Nantucket Sound to the treacherous, shifting shoals along the Atlantic. For beach stickers ($15 per day, $60 per week), call the **Permit Department** on George Ryder Road in West Chatham (ℂ **508/945-5180**).

- **Chatham Light Beach** ✸✸: Located directly below the lighthouse parking lot (where stopovers are limited to 30 min.), this narrow stretch of sand is easy to get to: Just walk down the stairs. Currents here can be tricky and swift, though, so swimming is discouraged.
- **Cockle Cove Beach, Ridgevale Beach,** and **Hardings Beach** ✸✸: Lined up along the sound, each at the end of its namesake road south of Route 28, these family-pleasing beaches offer gentle surf and full facilities. Ridgevale Beach also has kayak and sailboat rentals.
- **Forest Beach** ✸: No longer an officially recognized town beach (there's no lifeguard), this Sound landing near the Harwich border is still popular, especially among surfboarders.

Chatham

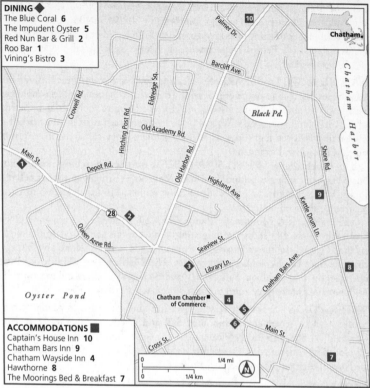

DINING ◆
The Blue Coral **6**
The Impudent Oyster **5**
Red Nun Bar & Grill **2**
Roo Bar **1**
Vining's Bistro **3**

ACCOMMODATIONS ■
Captain's House Inn **10**
Chatham Bars Inn **9**
Chatham Wayside Inn **4**
Hawthorne **8**
The Moorings Bed & Breakfast **7**

- **Oyster Pond Beach,** off Route 28: Only a block from Chatham's Main Street, this sheltered saltwater pond (with restrooms) swarms with children.
- **South Beach** 𝒌𝒌: A former island jutting out slightly to the south of the Chatham Light, this glorified sandbar can be dangerous, so heed posted warnings and content yourself with strolling.
- **North Beach** 𝒌𝒌: Extending all the way south from Orleans, this 5-mile barrier beach is accessible from Chatham only by boat; you can take the **Beachcomber** (© **508/945-5265**), a water taxi, which leaves from the fish pier. The round-trip costs $12 for adults, $8 for children 12 and under.

BICYCLING Though Chatham has no recreational paths, per se, a demarcated biking/skating lane makes a scenic 8-mile circuit of town, heading south onto "The Neck," east to the Chatham Light, up Shore Road all the way to North Chatham, and back to the center of town. A brochure prepared by the **Chatham Chamber of Commerce** (© **800/715-5567** or 508/945-5199) shows the route. Rentals are available at **Bikes & Blades,** 195 Crowell Rd., Chatham (© **508/945-7600**).

FISHING Chatham has five ponds and lakes that permit fishing; Goose Pond off Fisherman's Landing is among the top spots. For saltwater fishing without a boat, try the fishing bridge on Bridge Street at the southern end of Mill Pond. First, though, get a license at **Town Hall,** 549 Main St., in Chatham (© **508/945-5101**). If you hear the deep sea calling, sign on with the *Headhunter* (© 508/430-2312; www. capecodfishingcharters.com) or the *Banshee* (© 508/945-0403), both berthed in Stage Harbor. Sportfishing rates average around $725 for 8 hours. Shellfishing licenses are available at the **Permit Department,** on George Ryder Road in West Chatham (© 508/945-5180).

NATURE & WILDLIFE AREAS   Heading southeast from the Hardings Beach parking lot, the 2-mile-round-trip **Seaside Trail** offers beautiful parallel panoramas of Nantucket Sound and Oyster Pond River. Access to 40-acre Morris Island, southwest of the Chatham Light, is easy: Walk or drive across and start right in on a marked .75-mile trail. Heed the high tides, as advised, though—they can come in surprisingly quickly, leaving you stranded.

The **Beachcomber** ★★ (© 508/945-5265) runs **seal-watching cruises** out of Stage Harbor. Parking is behind the former Main Street School, on the left before the rotary. The cruises cost $22 for adults, $20 for seniors, $16 for children 3 to 15, and are free for children under 3.

The uninhabited **Monomoy Islands** ★★, 2,750 acres of brush-covered sand favored by some 285 species of migrating birds, are the perfect pit stop along the Atlantic Flyway. Harbor and gray seals are catching on, too: Hundreds now carpet the coastline from late November through May. The **Wellfleet Bay Wildlife Sanctuary,** operated by the Audubon Society (© 508/349-2615), offers guided trips. The Audubon's trips take place April through November; the cost is $30 to $60.

WATERSPORTS   Seaworthy vessels, from surf- and sailboards to paddle craft and Sunfish, can be rented from **Monomoy Sail and Cycle,** at 275 Rte. 28 in North Chatham (© 508/945-0811). Pleasant Bay, the Cape's largest bay, is the best place to play for those with sufficient experience; if the winds don't seem to be going your way, try Forest Beach on the South Chatham shore.

SHOPPING

Chatham's tree-shaded Main Street offers a terrific opportunity to shop and stroll. Headed for such prestigious outlets as Neiman Marcus, the hand-blown glassworks of James Holmes originate at **Chatham Glass Company,** 758 Main St., just west of the Chatham rotary (© 508/945-5547), where you can literally look over their shoulders as the pieces take shape. At **Chatham Pottery,** 2058 Rte. 28, east of the intersection with Route 137 (© 508/430-2191), striking graphics characterize the collaborative work of Gill Wilson (potter) and Margaret Wilson-Grey (glazer).

WHERE TO STAY

Chatham's accommodations tend to be more expensive than those of neighboring towns, but you can also find several good inexpensive motel options.

Practically across the street from the Chatham Bars Inn, the very basic **Hawthorne,** 196 Shore Rd. (© 508/945-0372; www.thehawthorne.com), boasts one of the best locations in town: right on the water, with striking views of Chatham Harbor, Pleasant Bay, and the Atlantic Ocean. An additional perk here is the free phone calls (both local and long distance) and Internet access. Rates for the 26 rooms are $165 to $195 double.

Chatham Seafarer, 2079 Rte. 28 (about ½ mile east of Rte. 137), West Chatham (© 800/786-2772 or 508/432-1739; www.chathamseafarer.com), is a well-run motel on Route 28. It's only about a half-mile from Ridgevale Beach and also has a pool. Rates are $145 to $165 double.

Another inexpensive option is **The Chatham Motel,** 1487 Main St./Rte. 28, Chatham (℃ **800/770-5545** or 508/945-2630; www.chathammotel.com), 1½ miles from Hardings Beach. It has an outdoor pool, and summer rates in the 32 rooms are $140 double, $225 suites.

Very Expensive

Chatham Bars Inn ✮✮ (Kids)   Set majestically above the beach in Chatham with commanding views out to a barrier beach and the Atlantic Ocean beyond is the grand Chatham Bars Inn. The colonnaded 1914 brick building is surrounded by 26 shingled cottages on 20 acres. This resort also has a heated outdoor pool, tennis courts, and three restaurants. Take in the sweeping ocean views from the breezy veranda, where you can order a drink and recline in an Adirondack chair. Many guest rooms have balconies with views of the beach or the landscaped grounds. Cottage rooms are cheery with painted furniture and Waverly fabrics.

Shore Rd. (off Seaview St., about ½ mile northwest of the town center), Chatham, MA 02633. ℃ **800/527-4884** or 508/945-0096. Fax 508/945-5491. www.chathambarsinn.com. 205 units. Summer $425–$630 double; $720–$980 1-bedroom suite; $790–$1,600 2-bedroom suite. AE, DC, MC, V. **Amenities:** 3 restaurants (the formal Main Dining Room, the fireplaced Tavern, and the seasonal Beach House Grill located right on the beach); outdoor heated pool; putting green (Seaside Links, a 9-hole course open to the public, adjoins the resort; guests play for a fee, $18); 3 all-weather tennis courts ($15 an hour); boat to the outer beach for a fee; Wellness Center offering spa and massage services and fitness equipment; complimentary children's program for ages 3½ and up, available morning through night in summer; room service (7am–10pm in season, 7am–9pm off season); babysitting; concierge. *In room:* A/C, TV/VCR/DVD, Wi-Fi, fridge, hair dryer, iron, safe.

Wequassett Inn Resort and Golf Club ✮✮✮ (Kids)   Fans of golf, sailing, and tennis will enjoy this 22-acre resort occupying its own little peninsula sticking out on Pleasant Bay. Though advertised as Chatham, the resort is actually just over the town line in Harwich. Adjacent is the private Cape Cod National Golf Club, where inn guests enjoy exclusive privileges. The resort's restaurant, **28 Atlantic,** was recently revamped and is now one of the Cape's top dining spots (see below). Tucked amid the woods along the shore, 15 buildings, built in the 1940s, harbor roomy quarters done up in a country style. They cost a bit more than the 56 more modern "villa" rooms because of their beachfront locations. All units have either a balcony or a patio. Beach-loving guests can choose the calm private bay beach just steps from the rooms or Chatham's North Beach, a 15-minute ride via the inn's Power Skiff ($12).

2173 Rte. 28 (about 5 miles northwest of Chatham center, on Pleasant Bay), Chatham, MA 02633. ℃ **800/225-7125** or 508/432-5400. Fax 508/432-5032. www.wequassett.com. 104 units. Summer $475–$825 double; $600–$1,365 suites. AE, DC, DISC, MC, V. Closed Dec–Mar. **Amenities:** 2 restaurants (28 Atlantic for fine dining and Outer Bar and Grille for casual fare, both open to the public); golf course next door ($105 a round plus $20 for a cart); pear-shaped heated outdoor pool; 4 all-weather Plexipave tennis courts ($15 an hour per person) plus a pro shop; fitness room (w/new machines and weights); rental bikes ($20–$40 per day) and watersports equipment (sailboards, Sunfish, Day-sailers, and Hobie Cats) for about $40 an hour; free horseshoes, basketball, and volleyball equipment; yoga and Pilates classes for $15; Children's Fun Club, $25 for half-day, $45 for full day; concierge; room service (daily 7am–10pm); massage; secretarial and babysitting services available. *In room:* A/C, TV, minibar, coffeemaker, hair dryer, iron.

Expensive

Captain's House Inn ✮✮✮ (Finds)   This 1839 Greek Revival house—along with a cottage and a carriage house—set on 2 meticulously maintained acres is a shining example of 19th-century style. The hospitality and amenities here make this one of the top B&Bs on Cape Cod. Guest rooms are richly furnished, with atmospheric touches like canopied four-posters, beamed ceilings, and brick hearths. The inn provides a wonderful array of extras, like robes, bottled water, newspapers, early-morning coffee, and room service. Many rooms have minifridges and Jacuzzis. The window-walled breakfast room is also the site of a traditional tea. Light lunches can be enjoyed poolside for an extra charge.

369–377 Old Harbor Rd. (about ½ mile north of the rotary), Chatham, MA 02633. ℂ 800/315-0728 or 508/945-0127. Fax 508/945-0866. www.captainshouseinn.com. 16 units (14 with tub/shower, 2 with shower only). Summer $250–$450 double. Rates include full breakfast and afternoon tea. AE, DISC, MC, V. **Amenities:** Outdoor heated pool; exercise room. *In room:* A/C, TV/VCR, dataport, coffeemaker, hair dryer, iron.

Chatham Wayside Inn ★★   Centrally located on Chatham's Main Street, this 1860 stagecoach stop, has undergone a thoroughly modern renovation. Don't expect any musty antique trappings: It's all lush carpeting, Waverly fabrics, and polished reproductions. The prize rooms have patios or balconies overlooking the town bandstand. The restaurant serves three meals a day and is open to the public.

512 Main St. (in the center of town), Chatham, MA 02633. ℂ 800/391-5734 or 508/945-5550. Fax 508/945-3407. www.waysideinn.com. 56 units. Summer $210–$425 double, $345–$425 suite; off-season packages available. DISC, MC, V. **Amenities:** Restaurant/bar; outdoor heated pool. *In room:* A/C, TV/VCR, hair dryer, iron.

Pleasant Bay Village ★★   Across the street from Pleasant Bay, a few minutes' walk from a bay beach, this is one fancy motel. Over the past 25 years, the owner has transformed the property into a Zen-like paradise, where waterfalls cascade through colorful rock gardens into a stone-edged pool surrounded by whimsical Oriental gardens. Guest rooms, done up in pastels, are unusually pleasant. Many bathrooms feature marble countertops and stone floors. The suites have fully equipped kitchens, including microwave ovens, as well as two televisions, one with a DVD player. In summer, the restaurant serves three meals a day. You can order lunch from the grill without having to leave your place at the heated pool.

1191 Orleans Rd./Rte. 28 (about 3 miles north of Chatham center), Chatham Port, MA 02633. ℂ 800/547-1011 or 508/945-1133. Fax 508/945-9701. www.pleasantbayvillage.com. 58 units. Summer $205–$256 double; $395–$525 1- or 2-bedroom suite (for 4 occupants). AE, MC, V. Closed Nov–Apr. **Amenities:** Restaurant (breakfast; July–Aug: lunch by the pool and dinner); heated pool and 8-person hot tub; game room (w/pinball). *In room:* A/C, TV, dataport, fridge, hair dryer, iron.

WHERE TO DINE
Very Expensive
28 Atlantic ★★★ NEW AMERICAN   This restaurant, on the grounds of the Wequassett Inn resort (see above), is one of the top places to eat on Cape Cod. The elegant, spacious dining room overlooks Pleasant Bay through immense floor-to-ceiling glass panels. Service is professional and stylish. And the food stands out as superb, from the *amuse bouche* (a little taste teaser) offered at the start of the meal, to the exceptional desserts served at the end. Menu items use local provender as much as possible, but there are also delicacies from around the world. You might start with the Cape lobster and roasted corn bisque with sherried Devonshire cream; move on to the composed salad of mâche, melon, prosciutto, grapes, goat-cheese mousse, and tawny port syrup; and then get to your main course, perhaps skillet-seared local bluefish with saffron smoked mussel risotto, wilted Swiss chard, and lobster oil. You're in for a treat here; it's all exquisite. For more casual dining, the Wequassett has a poolside cafe, the **Outer Bar** ★★, open to the public from 11:30am to 10pm; it's a stylish place to grab a drink or a light meal while listening to live jazz and basking in views of Pleasant Bay.

2173 Rte. 28 (at the Wequassett Inn, about 5 miles northwest of Chatham center, on Pleasant Bay). ℂ 508/430-3000. www.wequassett.com. Reservations recommended. Main courses $21–$44. AE, DC, DISC, MC, V. May–Nov daily 7am–10pm; call for off-season hours. Closed Dec–Mar.

Expensive

The Blue Coral ★ NEW AMERICAN   This restaurant features "seaside cuisine" on an outdoor courtyard just off Main Street. Specialties include a 3-pound lobster dinner with all the fixin's, and sushi-grade blue-fin tuna, pan seared with balsamic demiglaze. One of the most popular dishes is the lobster ravioli, served with a brandy cream sauce. There's live jazz and blues on Thursday through Sunday nights, in season.

483 Main St., Chatham. ℂ 508/348-0485. Reservations accepted. Main courses $18–$40. AE, DISC, MC, V. Daily 11:30am–2:30pm and 5–10pm. Closed late Sept to late June.

RooBar ★ NEW AMERICAN   Like its sister restaurants in Hyannis and Falmouth, this RooBar in Chatham is the place to see and be seen. This former Friendly's Restaurant is a sleek and stylish venue that features a garden patio area as well as a welcoming bar. The menu offers a wide range of options, from seafood specialties like seafood jambalaya to fine meat dishes like herb-grilled Delmonico. You may also opt for a brick-oven pizza topped with spicy prawns or barbecued chicken.

907 Main St., Chatham. ℂ 508/945-9988. Reservations accepted. Main courses $17–$28. AE, MC, V. Daily 5–10pm. Open year-round.

Moderate

Buca's Tuscan Roadhouse ★★ *Finds* NORTHERN ITALIAN   This popular Harwich restaurant is very close to the Chatham border and well worth the drive for anyone staying in the lower Cape. It's got a great atmosphere, somehow romantic and festive at the same time; wonderful food; and superior service. The only problem is getting a reservation, even in January. But once you do, you can relax and enjoy homemade pastas, fresh-off-the-boat fish, and tender cuts of meat—it doesn't get much better than this. From basics like eggplant parmigiana to cacciucco, a mélange of seafood in a garlic-y broth, the food is delicious. Wines by the glass are also exceptional.

4 Depot Rd. (on the corner of Rte. 28, close to the Chatham border), Harwich. ℂ 508/432-6900. Reservations recommended. Main courses $18–$25. AE, MC, V. June–Aug daily 5–10pm; call for off-season hours.

The Impudent Oyster ★ INTERNATIONAL   All but hidden off the main drag, this perennially popular eatery cooks up fabulous fish in exotic guises, ranging from Mexican to Szechuan, but mostly Continental. The flavorful specialties of the house are the *sole piccata* (native sole with lemon, fresh herb, and caper butter sauce), the steak *au poivre,* and the *pesca fra diablo* (local littlenecks, lobster, and other seafood served in a spicy sauce over fettuccine). A tavern menu is served at the bar from 3 to 5pm, featuring soup, salads, raw bar, chicken fingers, and burgers. This place is very busy in the summer, and if you don't make a reservation, you may be out of luck.

15 Chatham Bars Ave. (off Main St., in the center of town). ℂ 508/945-3545. Reservations recommended. Main courses $14–$20. AE, MC, V. Mon–Thurs 11:30am–3pm and 5–9:30pm; Fri–Sat 11:30am–3pm and 5–10pm; Sun noon–3pm and 5–9:30pm.

Vining's Bistro ★★ *Finds* FUSION   If you're looking for cutting-edge cuisine, venture upstairs at Chatham's minimall and into this ineffably cool cafe. The menu offers compelling juxtapositions such as the warm lobster tacos with salsa fresca and crème fraîche, or the spit-roasted chicken suffused with achiote-lime marinade and sided with a salad of oranges and jicama.

595 Main St. (in the center of town). ✆ 508/945-5033. Reservations not accepted. Main courses $16–$24. AE, DC, MC, V. June to mid-Oct daily 5:30–9:45pm; call for off-season hours. Closed Jan–Mar.

Inexpensive

Red Nun Bar & Grill *Value* DINER   There used to be lots of casual little hole-in-the-wall places like this on the Cape; now there are precious few. With just five tables and some bar seats, this is a good place to go early, late, or off season. They serve comfort food, like Mama's meatloaf, cheeseburgers, and a fish sandwich made from this morning's catch that was probably brought in by one of the guys bellied up to the bar. There's a good selection of beers on tap, too.

746 Main St. (near Monomoy Theatre and Veterans Field). ✆ 508/348-0469. Under $11. No credit cards. May–Sept Mon–Thurs 4pm–1am, Fri–Sun noon–1am; call for off-season hours. Closed Jan 15–Apr 1.

CHATHAM AFTER DARK

Chatham's free **band concerts** ✸✸ are arguably the best on the Cape and attract crowds in the thousands. This is small-town America at its most nostalgic, as the band plays standards of yesteryear that never go out of style. Held in Kate Gould Park (off Chatham Bars Ave.) from July to early September, the concerts kick off at 8pm every Friday. Come early to claim your square of lawn, which is already checkerboarded with blankets by late afternoon. Call ✆ **508/945-5199** for information.

A great leveler, the **Chatham Squire** ✸, 487 Main St. (✆ **508/945-0942**), attracts CEOs, seafarers, and collegians alike. There's great pub grub here, too! The piano bar **Upstairs at Christian's,** 443 Main St. (✆ **508/945-3362**), has the air of a vintage frat house, with scuffed leather couches and movie posters. Live music is offered nightly in season and weekends year-round.

ORLEANS ✸✸

Orleans is where the "Narrow Land" (the early Algonquin name for the Cape) starts to get very narrow indeed: From here on up—or "down," in paradoxical local parlance—the Cape is never more than a few miles wide from coast to coast. This is also where the oceanside beaches open up into a glorious expanse some 40 miles long, framed by dramatic dunes and serious surf.

The Cape's three main roads (routes 6, 6A, and 28) converge here, too, so on summer weekends, it acts as a rather frustrating funnel. Nevertheless, Main Street boasts some appealing restaurants and shops. The village of East Orleans, near the entrance to Nauset Beach, may be the best place to base yourself. The 10-mile beach, which is the southernmost stretch of the Cape Cod National Seashore preserve, is a magnet for families and young folks.

ESSENTIALS

GETTING THERE   After crossing the Sagamore Bridge, head east on Route 6 or 6A (the long but scenic route); both converge with Route 28 in Orleans. The town is 35 miles east of Sandwich, 25 miles south of Provincetown.

VISITOR INFORMATION   Contact the **Orleans Chamber of Commerce,** 44 Main St. (P.O. Box 153), Orleans, MA 02653 (✆ **800/865-1386** or 508/255-1386; www.capecod-orleans.com). There's an **information booth** at the corner of Route 6A and Eldredge Parkway (✆ **508/240-2484**).

BEACHES & GETTING OUTSIDE

BEACHES   From here all the way to Provincetown on the Cape's eastern side, you're dealing with the wild Atlantic Ocean. Current ocean conditions are clearly posted at

Fun Fact **Rock Harbor**

Yes, those are trees in the middle of the harbor at Rock Harbor, and, no, they are not live trees. For decades, dead trees have been erected in the harbor in order to mark the channel. At sunset, the row of narrow trees silhouetted against the horizon makes a pretty picture.

the entrance to Nauset Beach. Purchase 1-week parking permits ($50 for renters) from **Town Hall** on School Road (© **508/240-3775**). Day passes for Nauset Beach and Skaket Beach are $15 per car. Day-trippers who arrive early enough—better make that before 10am on weekends in July and August—can pay at the gate (© **508/240-3780**).

- **Crystal Lake** ⊛, off Monument Road about ¾ mile south of Main Street: Parking—if you can find a space—is free, but there are no facilities here.
- **Nauset Beach** ⊛⊛⊛, in East Orleans (© **508/240-3780**): Stretching southward all the way past Chatham, this barrier beach, which is part of the Cape Cod National Seashore but is managed by the town, has long been one of the Cape's gonzo beach scenes—good surf, big crowds, lots of young people. Full facilities, including a terrific snack bar, can be found within the 1,000-car parking lot. The in-season parking fee is $15 per car, which is also good for same-day parking at Skaket Beach (see below). Substantial waves make for good surfing and boogie-boarding in the special section to the far left reserved for that purpose. In July and August, there are concerts from 7 to 9pm in the gazebo.
- **Pilgrim Lake** ⊛, off Monument Road about 1 mile south of Main Street: This small freshwater beach is covered by a lifeguard in season. You must have a beach parking sticker.
- **Skaket Beach** ⊛, off Skaket Beach Road to the west of town: This peaceful bay beach is a better choice for families. When the tide recedes, little kids will enjoy splashing about in the tide pools left behind. Parking costs $15, and you'd better turn up early.

BICYCLING   Orleans presents the one slight gap in the 26-mile **Cape Cod Rail Trail** ⊛⊛⊛ (© **508/896-3491**): Just east of the Brewster border, the trail merges with town roads for about 1½ miles. The best way to avoid vehicular aggravation and fumes is to zigzag west to scenic Rock Harbor. Bike rentals are available at **Orleans Cycle** at 26 Main St. (© **508/255-9115**).

BOATING   **Arey's Pond Sailing School,** off Route 28 in South Orleans (© **508/255-7900**), offers sailing lessons on Little Pleasant Bay. Individual lessons are $65 per hour; weekly group lessons are around $189. The **Goose Hummock Outdoor Center,** at 15 Rte. 6A, south of the rotary (© **508/255-2620;** www.goose.com), rents out canoes, kayaks, and more, and the northern half of Pleasant Bay is the perfect place to use them.

FISHING   Fishing is allowed in Baker Pond, Pilgrim Lake, and Crystal Lake. For licenses, visit **Town Hall,** at Post Office Square in the center of town (© **508/240-3700,** ext. 305), or **Goose Hummock** (see above). Surf-casting—no license needed—is permitted on Nauset Beach South, off Beach Road. **Rock Harbor** ⊛⊛, a former packet landing on the bay (about 1¼ miles northwest of the town center), shelters

New England's largest sportfishing fleet: some 18 boats at last count. One call (℃ **800/287-1771** in MA, or 508/255-9757) will get you information on them all—or go look them over in person. Rock Harbor charter prices range from $550 for 4 hours to $750 for 8 hours. Individual prices are also available ($140 per person for 4 hr.; $150 per person for 8 hr.).

WATERSPORTS   The **Pump House Surf Co.,** at 9 Rte. 6A (℃ **508/240-2226**), rents and sells wet suits, body boards, and surfboards. Stop by for up-to-date reports on where to find the best waves. **Nauset Sports,** at Jeremiah Square, Route 6A at the rotary (℃ **508/255-4742**), also rents surfboards, boogie boards, skim boards, kayaks, and wet suits.

SHOPPING

Though shops are somewhat scattered, Orleans is full of great finds for browsers. You'll find some 400 vintage light fixtures at **Continuum Antiques,** 7 S. Orleans Rd., Route 28, south of the junction with Route 6A (℃ **508/255-8513**). Stop by **Kemp Pottery,** 9 Rte. 6A, just south of the rotary (℃ **508/255-5853**), and check out the turned and slab-built creations from soup tureens to fanciful sculptures.

WHERE TO STAY
Moderate
The Cove 🌟   Ask for a water-view room at this motel complex, on busy Route 28, that also fronts placid Town Cove. The interiors are adequate, if not dazzling, and a small heated pool and a restful gazebo overlook the waterfront. Some rooms have kitchenettes and balconies with cove views.

13 S. Orleans Rd. (Rte. 28, north of Main St.), Orleans, MA 02653. ℃ **800/343-2233** or 508/255-1203. Fax 508/255-7736. www.thecoveorleans.com. 47 units. Summer $149–$234 double; $185–$209 suite or efficiency. Open year-round. AE, DC, DISC, MC, V. **Amenities:** Small heated pool. *In room:* A/C, TV/DVD, fridge, coffeemaker, hair dryer, microwave.

A Little Inn on Pleasant Bay 🌟🌟 *(Finds)*   Sitting on a hill overlooking the bay, this is a lovely property. The four rooms in the peaceful main house, which dates to 1798, are decorated warm tiles, light woods, and subtle colors. An adjacent building, called the "Paddock," has three additional rooms. Breakfast served outside is an extravagant affair they call a "European buffet," with a spread of pastries, yogurt, muesli, cereals, fresh fruits, and assorted meats and cheeses.

654 S. Orleans Rd., South Orleans, MA 02662. ℃ **888/332-3351** or 508/255-0780. www.alittleinnon pleasantbay.com. 9 units. Summer $225–$300 double. Rates include continental breakfast and evening sherry. AE, MC, V. No children under 10. *In room:* A/C, TV (in Paddock rooms), hair dryer, no phone.

Nauset Knoll Motor Lodge 🌟🌟 *(Value)*   Overlooking Nauset Beach, one of Cape Cod's most popular beaches, this nothing-fancy motel with picture windows will suit beach lovers to a T. The simple, clean rooms are well maintained, and by staying here, you'll save on daily parking charges at Nauset Beach. The whole complex is owned by Uncle Sam and is under the supervision of the National Park Service.

237 Beach Rd. (at Nauset Beach, about 2 miles east of the town center), East Orleans, MA 02643. ℃ **508/255-2364.** www.capecodtravel.com. 12 units (all with tub/shower). Summer $150 double. MC, V. Closed late Oct to early Apr. *In room:* TV, no phone.

The Orleans Inn 🌟   You can't miss this mansard-roofed beauty, perched right on the edge of Town Cove. Try to get one of the rooms facing the water. Built in 1875, the inn has been lovingly restored and maintains its central place in the community.

The simple rooms, some with twin beds or sleeper sofas, are cheerful with modern amenities and extra touches like a box of chocolates on the bureau. Downstairs is a bar and restaurant with wonderful views of the cove.

Rte. 6A (P.O. Box 188; just south of the Orleans rotary), Orleans, MA 02653. © 508/255-2222. Fax 508/255-6722. www.orleansinn.com. 11 units. Summer $225–$250 double; $275–$300 suite. Rates include continental breakfast. AE, MC, V. **Amenities:** Restaurant/bar. *In room:* TV, fridge.

Inexpensive
Nauset House Inn *ft ft* *Value*   Just a half-mile from Nauset Beach, this reasonably priced country inn is a cozy setting for those seeking a quiet retreat. Several of the rooms in greenery-draped outbuildings feature such romantic extras as a sunken bath or private deck. The most romantic hideaway here, though, is a 1907 conservatory appended to the 1810 farmhouse inn. It's the perfect place to lounge when the rain pounds down, prompting the camellias to waft their heady perfume. Breakfast would seem relatively workaday, were it not for the setting—a pared-down, rustic refectory— and innkeeper Diane Johnson's memorable muffins and pastries.

143 Beach Rd. (P.O. Box 774; about 1 mile east of the town center), East Orleans, MA 02643. © 800/771-5508 or 508/255-2195. Fax 508/240-6276. www.nausethouseinn.com. 14 units, 6 with shared bathroom (4 with tub/shower, 4 with shower only). Summer $70 single; $80–$90 shared bathroom; $110–$175 double with private bathroom. Rates include full breakfast. DISC, MC, V. Closed Nov–Mar. No children under 12. *In room:* No phone.

WHERE TO DINE
Expensive
Abba *ft ft* INTERNATIONAL   Abba continues to earn raves for its fresh take on fine dining in the Lower Cape. Tables are closely packed inside, so I prefer the covered outdoor dining area behind the restaurant. Chef/co-owner Erez Pinhas of Israel creates what can only be described as fusion cuisine: a little Middle Eastern, a little European, a little New American, plus some Thai and New England thrown in. Where else can you start with a falafel, move on to a steaming plate of shrimp pad Thai, and then end with chilled melon soup? And everything is delicious.

West Rd. and Old Colony Way (2 blocks from Main St., toward Skaket Beach). © 508/255-8144. Reservations recommended. Main courses $18–$27. AE, MC, V. June–Aug Tues–Sun 5–10pm; call for off-season hours.

Moderate
Joe's Beach Road Bar & Grille at the Barley Neck Inn *ft* NEW AMERICAN This 1857 captain's house with adjoining tavern is a favorite with locals. While the front room has a more traditional ambience, the tavern space features a huge field-stone fireplace and World War II posters. With denim tablecloths and bandannas serving as napkins, the atmosphere is casual. The 28-foot mahogany bar is a popular meeting place. The menu varies from fancy dishes such as grilled Atlantic salmon filet with a red-pepper coulis and basil vinaigrette to Joe's pizza (with goat cheese, roasted peppers, and spinach) or highfalutin fish and chips—beer-battered, with saffron aioli.

At The Barley Neck Inn, 5 Beach Rd. (about ½ mile east of the town center), East Orleans. © 508/255-0212. www.barleyneck.com. Reservations accepted. Main courses $10–$25. AE, DC, MC, V. June to early Sept daily 5–10pm; call for off-season hours.

The Lobster Claw Restaurant *ft* *Kids* SEAFOOD   This sprawling family-owned business has been serving up quality seafood for almost 30 years. Get the baked stuffed lobster with all the fixings.

Rte. 6A (just south of the rotary), Orleans. © 508/255-1800. Main courses $10–$19. AE, DC, DISC, MC, V. Daily 11:30am–9pm. Closed Nov–Mar.

Mahoney's Atlantic Bar & Grill ☆ NEW AMERICAN   Seafood is the specialty at this casual restaurant. Dishes like tuna sashimi, grilled sea bass, and pan-seared lobster are why you came to Cape Cod. There are also poultry, meat, pasta, and vegetarian dishes. In season, some nights there's live jazz and blues.

28 Main St. (in the center of town). © 508/255-5505. www.mahoneysatlantic.com. Reservations recommended. Main courses $16–$25. AE, MC, V. May–Sept daily 5–10pm; Oct–Apr Tues–Sun 5–10pm.

Inexpensive

Cap't Cass Rock Harbor Seafood SEAFOOD   Most tourists figure that a silvered shack sporting this many salvaged lobster buoys has an inside track on the freshest of seafood. The supposition makes sense, but the stuff here is about par for the area and the preparations are basic. Nevertheless, it's fun to eat in a joint left untouched for decades as time—and dining fads—marched on.

117 Rock Harbor Rd. (on the harbor, about 1½ miles northwest of the town center). No phone. Most main courses under $12. No credit cards. Late June to mid-Oct Tues–Sun 11am–2pm and 5–9pm. Closed mid-Oct to late June.

ORLEANS AFTER DARK

Joe's Beach Road Bar & Grille ☆, at the Barley Neck Inn (© 508/255-0212; see "Where to Dine," above), is a big old barn of a bar that might as well be town hall: It's where you'll find all the locals exchanging juicy gossip and jokes. On Sunday evenings in season, there's live "Jazz at Joe's."

Thursday through Saturday, there's live music at the **Land Ho!** ☆☆ (© 508/255-5165), the best pub in town, and on Monday and Tuesday nights as well during high season. There's usually no cover charge.

4 The Outer Cape

It's only on the Outer Cape that the landscape and even the air feel really beachy. You can smell the seashore just over the horizon—in fact, everywhere you go, because you're never more than a mile or two away from sand and surf. You won't find any high-rise hotels along the shoreline or tacky amusement arcades—just miles of pristine beaches and dune grass rippling in the wind. That's because in the early 1960s, 27,000 acres here became the federally protected Cape Cod National Seashore.

WELLFLEET ☆☆☆

With the well-tended look of a classic New England village and surrounded by beaches, Wellfleet is the chosen destination for artists, writers, off-duty psychiatrists, and other contemplative types who hope to find more in the landscape than mere quaintness or rusticity. Distinguished literati such as Edna St. Vincent Millay and Edmund Wilson put this rural village on the map in the 1920s, in the wake of Provincetown's bohemian heyday.

To this day, Wellfleet remains remarkably unspoiled. Once you leave Route 6, commercialism is kept to a minimum, though the town boasts plenty of appealing shops, distinguished galleries, and a couple of very good New American restaurants. It's hard to imagine any other community on the Cape supporting so sophisticated an undertaking as the Wellfleet Harbor Actors' Theatre, or hosting such a wholesome event as public square dancing on the adjacent Town Pier. And where else could you find a thriving drive-in movie theater right next door to an outstanding nature preserve?

ESSENTIALS

GETTING THERE   After crossing the Sagamore Bridge, head east on Route 6 to Orleans, and after the rotary, continue north on Route 6 to Wellfleet. Wellfleet is 42 miles northeast of Sandwich, 14 miles south of Provincetown.

VISITOR INFORMATION   Contact the **Wellfleet Chamber of Commerce,** off Route 6, Wellfleet, MA 02663 (© **508/349-2510;** fax 508/349-3740; www. wellfleetchamber.com).

BEACHES & GETTING OUTSIDE

BEACHES   Wellfleet's fabulous ocean beaches tend to sort themselves demographically: Lecount Hollow is popular with families, Newcomb Hollow with high-schoolers, White Crest with the college crowd, and Cahoon Hollow with 30-somethings. Only the latter two permit parking by nonresidents ($15 per day). To enjoy the other two, as well as Burton Baker Beach on the harbor at Indian Neck and Duck Harbor on the bay, plus three freshwater ponds, you'll have to walk or bike in, or see if you qualify for a sticker ($60 per week for renters). Bring proof of residency to the seasonal Beach Sticker Booth on the Town Pier, or call the **Wellfleet Recreation Department** (© **508/349-9818**). Parking is free at all beaches and ponds after 4pm.

- **Marconi Beach** ☀☀, off Marconi Beach Road in South Wellfleet: A National Seashore property, this cliff-lined beach (with restrooms) charges an entry fee of $15 per day, or $45 for the season. *Note:* The bluffs are so high that the beach lies in shadow by late afternoon.

- **Mayo Beach,** Kendrick Avenue (near the Town Pier): Right by the harbor, facing south, this warm, shallow bay beach (with restrooms) is hardly secluded but will please young waders. Parking is free. You could grab a bite (and a paperback) at The Bookstore Restaurant across the street.

- **White Crest & Cahoon Hollow Beaches** ☀☀☀, off Ocean View Drive in Wellfleet: These two town-run ocean beaches—big with surfers—are open to all. Both have snack bars and restrooms. Parking costs $15 per day, $45 for the season.

BICYCLING   The end of the 25-mile **Cape Cod Rail Trail** ☀☀☀ (© **508/896-3491**), Wellfleet is also among its more desirable destinations: A country road off the bike path leads right to Lecount Hollow Beach. The deli at the adjoining **South Wellfleet General Store** (© **508/349-2335**) can see to your snacking needs.

BOATING   **Jack's Boat Rentals,** located on Gull Pond off Gull Pond Road, about a half-mile south of the Truro border (© **508/349-9808**), rents out canoes, kayaks, sailboards, and Sunfish, as well as sea cycles and surf bikes. Gull Pond connects to Higgins Pond by way of a placid, narrow channel lined with red maples and choked with water lilies. Needless to say, it's a great place to paddle. If you'd like a canoe for a few days, you'll need to go to the Jack's Boat Rentals location on Route 6 in Wellfleet (next to the Cumberland Farms). In addition to watercraft to go, Jack's is the place for information about **Eric Gustavson's guided kayak tours** (© **508/349-1429**) of kettle ponds and tidal rivers from Chatham to Truro.

The **Chequessett Yacht & Country Club,** on Chequessett Neck Road in Wellfleet (© **508/349-0198**), offers group sailing lessons. For experienced sailors, **Wellfleet Marine Corp.,** on the Town Pier (© **508/349-2233**), rents sailboats in season.

FISHING   For a license to fish at Long Pond, Great Pond, or Gull Pond, visit **Town Hall** at 300 Main St. (© **508/349-0301**). Surf-casting, which doesn't require a license, is permitted at the town beaches. Shellfishing licenses—Wellfleet's oysters are world-famous—can be obtained from the **Shellfish Department,** on the Town Pier off Kendrick Avenue (© **508/349-0300**).

In season, heading out from Wellfleet Harbor is the 60-foot party fishing boat *Navigator* (© **508/349-6003**). Charter boats include the *Erin-H* (© **508/349-9663;** www.virtualcapecod.com/erinh) and *Snooper* (© **508/349-6113**).

NATURE & WILDLIFE AREAS   Right in town, the short, picturesque boardwalk known as **Uncle Tim's Bridge,** off East Commercial Street, crosses Duck Creek to access a tiny island crisscrossed by paths.

The Cape Cod National Seashore maintains two spectacular self-guided trails. The 1.25-mile **Atlantic White Cedar Swamp Trail** 🌟🌟, off the parking area for the Marconi Wireless Station (see "Cape Cod National Seashore," later in this chapter), shelters a rare stand of the lightweight species prized by Native Americans as wood for canoes; the moss-choked swamp is a magical place, refreshingly cool even at the height of summer. A boardwalk will see you over the muck, but the return trip does entail a calf-testing half-mile trek through deep sand. Consider it a warm-up for magnificent **Great Island,** jutting 4 miles into the bay (off the western end of Chequessett Neck Rd.) to cup Wellfleet Harbor. Before attaching itself to the mainland in 1831, Great Island harbored a busy whaling post. Be sure to cover up, wear sturdy shoes, bring water, and venture to Jeremy Point—the very tip—only if you're sure the tide is going out.

You'll find 6 miles of very scenic trails lined with lupines and bayberries—Goose Pond, Silver Spring, and Bay View—within the **Wellfleet Bay Wildlife Sanctuary** 🌟🌟🌟, off Route 6 north of the Eastham border, in South Wellfleet (© **508/349-2615;** fax 508/349-2632; www.wellfleetbay.org). A spiffy, eco-friendly visitor center serves as both introduction and gateway to this 1,000-acre refuge, maintained by the Massachusetts Audubon Society. Passive solar heat and composting toilets are just a few of the waste-cutting elements incorporated into the seemingly simple building. You might see red-winged blackbirds and osprey as you follow the looping trails through pine forests, salt marsh, and moors. The sanctuary offers naturalist-guided tours and workshops for children. Inquire about canoeing, birding, and seal-watching excursions. Trail use is free for Massachusetts Audubon Society members; otherwise, the fee is $5 for adults and $3 for seniors and children 3 to 12. Trails are open July through August from 8am to 8pm, and September through June from 8am to dusk. The visitor center is open from Memorial Day to Columbus Day daily from 8:30am to 5pm; off season, it's closed Monday.

WATERSPORTS Surfing is restricted to White Crest Beach, and sailboarding to Burton Baker Beach at Indian Neck during certain tide conditions; ask for a copy of the regulations at the Beach Sticker Booth on the Town Pier.

SHOPPING

A stroll from Main Street down Bank Street and then along Commercial Street will take you past a dozen galleries worth a look. Crafts make a strong showing, too, as do contemporary women's clothing and eclectic home furnishings. But unlike Provincetown, which has something to offer virtually year-round, Wellfleet pretty much closes up come Columbus Day.

The **Cove Gallery,** 15 Commercial St., by Duck Creek (© **508/349-2530**)—with a waterside sculpture garden—carries the paintings and prints of many well-known artists, including Barry Moser and Leonard Baskin. John Grillo's work astounds every summer during his annual show in July. **Jules Besch Stationers,** 15 Bank St. (© **508/ 349-1231**), specializes in stationery products, including papers, gift cards, handmade journals, and unusual gift items.

WHERE TO STAY

Even'tide 🌟 *Kids* Set back from busy Route 6, this well-run motel is a good base for families. In case of rain, there's a 60-foot heated indoor pool—a rarity in this part of the Cape. There are seven cottages on the property with one-, two-, and three-bedroom units. In the pines are a barbecue and a picnic area. The Rail Trail goes right by, and a 1-mile footpath through the woods leads to Marconi Beach.

650 Rte. 6 (about 1 mile north of the Eastham border), South Wellfleet, MA 02663. © 800/368-0007 in MA only, or 508/349-3410. Fax 508/349-7804. www.eventidemotel.com. 40 units (39 with tub/shower, 1 with shower only). Summer $135–$170 double, $185–$210 efficiency. AE, DISC, MC, V. **Amenities:** Large heated indoor pool; playground; self-service laundromat. *In room:* A/C, TV, fridge, coffeemaker.

The Inn at Duck Creeke *Value* This historic complex is set on 5 woodsy acres overlooking a tidal creek and salt marsh. The 1880s captain's house features wide-board floors and charming but basic rooms, many with shared bathrooms; the carriage house contains a few light and airy cabin-style rooms; and the 1715 saltworks building has smaller rooms with antique decor. In the main building, each shared bathroom adjoins two rooms, which might not suit those in search of privacy. All rooms have fans, and those on the third floor have air-conditioning. The carriage house and saltworks building are quieter and can be downright romantic. But there's definitely a no-frills quality to this place—towels are thin, and so are walls. A big plus is that there are two good restaurants on-site: **Sweet Seasons** (see "Where to Dine," below) and the **Duck Creeke Tavern,** with live entertainment in season.

70 Main St. (P.O. Box 364), Wellfleet, MA 02667. © 508/349-9333. Fax 508/349-0234. www.innatduckcreeke.com. 27 units (14 tub/shower, 5 shower only, 8 with shared bathroom). Summer $85–$95 double with shared bathroom; $115–$130 double with private bathroom. Rates include continental breakfast. AE, MC, V. Closed Nov–Apr. **Amenities:** 2 restaurants (seafood restaurant and tavern). *In room:* No phone.

Surfside Cottages 🌟🌟 *Kids* This is where you want to be: smack dab on a spectacular beach with 50-foot dunes, within biking distance of Wellfleet Center and a short drive from Provincetown. All of the one-, two-, or three-bedrooms have kitchens, fireplaces, barbecues, outdoor showers, and screened porches. Some even have roof decks. From mid-May to mid-October, the cottages rent weekly. Bring your own sheets and towels; renting a set costs $10 per person.

Ocean View Dr. (at Lecount Hollow Rd.; P.O. Box 937), South Wellfleet, MA 02663. ©/fax **508/349-3959**. www. surfsidevacation.com. 18 cottages (with showers only). Summer $1,100–$1,875 weekly; off season $80–$130 per day. MC, V. Closed Nov to early Apr. Pets allowed off season. *In room:* Fridge, coffeemaker.

WHERE TO DINE

Hatch's Fish & Produce Market ⊛, 310 Main St., behind Town Hall (© **508/349-6734** for produce, 508/349-2810 for fish market), is the unofficial heart of Wellfleet. You'll find the best local bounty, from fresh-picked corn to fruit-juice Popsicles to steaming lobsters. Virtually no one passes through without picking up a little something, including the latest town gossip. It's closed from late September until May.

Mac's Seafood Market and Harbor Grill Restaurant ⊛ *Finds* *Kids* SEAFOOD On the town pier, this takeout shack with picnic tables features fresh local seafood unloaded from the boats just steps away. Besides grilled fish dinners, there's homemade chowders, sushi, and a raw bar. The same owners also have **Mac's Shack** (© 508/349-6333), a traditional clam shack open for dinner in season, located at 91 Commercial St. just east of town center and featuring fried seafood with all the fixings served on paper plates at picnic tables.

Wellfleet Town Pier. © **508/349-9611**. Main courses $10–$20. MC, V. Daily 7:30am–10pm. Closed mid-Oct to late May.

Moby Dick's Restaurant ⊛ *Kids* SEAFOOD   This is your typical clam shack. Order your meal at the register, sit at a picnic table, and a cheerful college student brings it to you. The fried fish, clams, scallops, and shrimp are all good; try the Moby's Seafood Special—a heaping platter of all of the above, plus coleslaw and fries. Then there's the clambake special with lobster, steamers, and corn on the cob. Bring the family and chow down.

Rte. 6, Wellfleet. © **508/349-9795**. www.mobydicksrestaurant.com. Reservations not accepted. Main courses $8–$20. MC, V. Mid-June to early Sept daily 11:30am–10pm; call for off-season hours. Closed mid-Oct to Apr.

Sweet Seasons Restaurant/Duck Creeke Tavern ⊛ NEW AMERICAN   Chef-owner Judith Pihl's Mediterranean-influenced fare is still appealing after more than 2 decades, as is this dining room's peaceful pond view. Some of the dishes can be a bit heavy by contemporary standards, but there's usually a healthy alternative: Wellfleet littlenecks and mussels in a golden, aromatic tomato-and-cumin broth, for instance, as opposed to Russian oysters with smoked salmon, vodka, and sour cream. Specialties of the house include creamy sage-and-asparagus ravioli, and Seasons shrimp with feta and ouzo.

At The Inn at Duck Creeke, 70 Main St. (about ⅛ mile west of Rte. 6). © **508/349-6535**. Reservations recommended. Main courses $19–$30. AE, MC, V. July–Sept Tues–Sun 5:30–10pm. Closed Oct–June.

The Wicked Oyster ⊛⊛ NEW AMERICAN   This old warehouse-style building on the way to Wellfleet Center has been converted into a cool and casual year-round restaurant. There are several sections: an enclosed front porch, an ample dining room, and a large bar area. With a busy to-go area for coffee and pastries, this place definitely has a bustling atmosphere. You'll see families with small children, 20-something couples, and older folks enjoying this comfortable and convenient restaurant. Breakfast is popular and features a multitude of omelets plus very strong coffee. At lunch, sandwiches and fried fish appear on the menu. Dinner choices range from burgers to more refined options, like pan-fried sole with lemon caper butter, spring risotto with mushrooms and asparagus, or, for large appetites, grilled angus tenderloin.

50 Main St. (just off Rte. 6, close to Wellfleet Center). ✆ 508/349-3455. Reservations recommended. Main courses $16–$26. MC, V. June–Aug daily 7am–2pm and 5:30–10pm; call for off-season hours. Open year-round.

Winslow's Tavern ✿✿ BISTRO This new upscale bistro offers summertime treats like grilled lobster and bistro classics like steak frites in a contemporary setting. Of course, they have Wellfleet oysters, the town's world famous bivalve. But they also have wonderful salads and light meals.

316 Main St. (in the center of town). ✆ 508/349-6450. Reservations for parties of 6 or more only. Main courses $13–$23. AE, MC, V. July–Aug daily noon–3pm and 5:30–10pm; call for off-season hours. Closed late Oct to mid-May.

WELLFLEET AFTER DARK

The Beachcomber ✿, 1220 Old Cahoon Hollow Rd., off Ocean View Drive (✆ 508/349-6055; www.beachcomber.com), arguably the best dance club on Cape Cod, is definitely the most scenic. It's right on Cahoon Hollow Beach—so close, in fact, that late beachgoers on summer weekends can count on a free concert of reggae, blues, ska, or rock. Cover varies. It's closed early September to late May.

The **Wellfleet Drive-In Theater,** 51 Rte. 6, just north of the Eastham border (✆ 800/696-3532 or 508/349-2520), built in 1957, is the only drive-in left on Cape Cod and one of a scant half-dozen surviving in the state. The rituals are as unbending and endearing as ever: the playtime preceding the cartoons, the countdown plugging the allures of the snack bar, and finally, two full first-run features. It's open daily from late May through mid-September; showtime is at dusk. Call for off-season hours.

The principals behind the **Wellfleet Harbor Actors' Theatre,** 1 Kendrick Ave., near the Town Pier (✆ 508/349-6835), aim to provoke—and usually succeed, even amid this very sophisticated, seen-it-all summer colony. Performances are given from late May through October, daily at 8pm.

TRURO ✿✿

With only 1,600 year-round residents (fewer than it boasted in 1840, when Pamet Harbor was a whaling and shipbuilding port), Truro amounts to little more than a smattering of stores and public buildings, and lots of low-profile houses hidden away in the woods and dunes. Edward Hopper lived in contented isolation in a South Truro cottage for nearly 4 decades. If you find yourself craving cultural stimulation or other kinds of excitement, head to Provincetown, which is only a 10-minute drive away.

ESSENTIALS

GETTING THERE After crossing the Sagamore Bridge, head east on Route 6 or 6A to Orleans and north on Route 6.

VISITOR INFORMATION Contact the **Truro Chamber of Commerce,** Route 6A (at Head of the Meadow Rd.), Truro, MA 02666 (✆ 508/487-1288). Truro is 46 miles east of Sandwich, 10 miles south of Provincetown.

BEACHES & GETTING OUTSIDE

BEACHES Parking at all of Truro's exquisite Atlantic beaches, except for one Cape Cod National Seashore access point (Corn Hill Beach), is reserved for residents and renters. To obtain a sticker ($30 for 1 week; $60 for 2 weeks), inquire at the beach-sticker office at 14 Truro Center Rd., behind the post office in Truro Center (✆ 508/487-3635).

- **Corn Hill Beach** ★★, off Corn Hill Road: Offering restrooms, this bay beach—near the hill where the Pilgrims found the seed corn that ensured their survival—is open to nonresidents for a parking fee of $10 per day.
- **Head of the Meadow** ★★★, off Head of the Meadow Road: Among the more remote National Seashore beaches, this spot (equipped with restrooms) is known for its excellent surf. A parking lot connected by a short boardwalk to the beach makes this beach more easily accessible than other National Seashore beaches. It is also connected by a short bike path to Pilgrim Heights (see "Bicycling," below). Parking costs $15 per day, or $45 per season.

BICYCLING Although it has yet to be linked up to the Cape Cod Rail Trail, Truro does have a stunning 2-mile bike path of its own: the **Head of the Meadow Trail** ★, off the road of the same name (look for a right turn about a half-mile north of where routes 6 and 6A intersect). Part of the old 1850 road toward Provincetown, it skirts the bluffs, passing Pilgrim and ending at High Head Road.

FISHING Great Pond, Horseleech Pond, and Pilgrim Lake—flanked by parabolic dunes carved by the wind—are all fishable; for a freshwater fishing license, visit **Town Hall** on Town Hall Road (✆ **508/487-2702**). You can also call the town hall for a shellfishing license. Surf-casting is permitted at Highland Light Beach, off Highland Road.

GOLF North Truro has the most scenic—and historic—9-hole course on the Cape. Created in 1892, the minimally groomed, Scottish-style **Highland Links,** at 10 Lighthouse Rd., off South Highland Road (✆ **508/487-9201**), shares a lofty bluff with the 1853 Highland Light.

NATURE TRAILS The Cape Cod National Seashore, which makes up 70% of Truro's land, offers three self-guided nature trails. The .5-mile **Pamet Trail** ★, off North Pamet Road, leads you past an old cranberry-bog building and bogs that have reverted to marshland. Park in the lot to the left of the Little America youth hostel and walk back to the fire road entrance about 500 feet down North Pamet Road. The **Pilgrim Spring Trail** ★ and **Small Swamp Trail** ★ (each a .75-mile loop) head out from the National Seashore parking lot just east of Pilgrim Lake. Both paths overlook Salt Meadow, a freshwater marsh favored by hawks and osprey.

A MUSEUM & AN ARTS CENTER

Highland House Museum and Highland Lighthouse Built as a hotel in 1907, the Highland House is a perfect repository of the odds and ends collected by the Truro Historical Society: ship's models, harpoons, primitive toys, a pirate's chest, and so on. In 1996, Highland Lighthouse was moved back from its perilous perch above a rapidly eroding dune. Now the lighthouse is within 800 feet of the museum and is also operated by the Truro Historical Society. Seasonal lighthouse tours run May through October. There is a 51-inch height requirement so, unfortunately, little ones can't climb up the tower.

27 Highland Light Rd. (off S. Highland Rd., 2 miles north of the town center on Rte. 6). ✆ **508/487-1121.** www.trurohistorical.org. Admission to both museum and lighthouse $6 adults, free for children under 12. Admission to museum or lighthouse $4; free for children under 12 at museum only. Museum June–Sept Mon–Sat 10am–4:30pm; Sun 1–4:30pm. Last ticket sold at 3:30pm. Lighthouse mid-June to mid-Oct daily 10am–5:30pm. Closed mid-Oct to mid-June.

Moments A Vineyard in the Dunes

This pastoral property just off Route 6 in Truro is one of the last working farms in the Outer Cape and the site of an honest-to-goodness vineyard. Horticulturists Kathy Gregrow and Judy Wimer, of **Truro Vineyard of Cape Cod** (11 Shore Rd./Rte. 6A, North Truro; ② **508/487-6200**), uncorked their first homegrown chardonnay and Cabernet Franc in the fall of 1996, the muscadet in 1997, the merlot in 1998. Inside the main house, the living room, with its exposed beams, is decorated with interesting oenological artifacts. Late May through October, free wine tastings are held daily from noon to 5pm. Guided tours of the property take place at 1 and 3pm.

WHERE TO STAY

Days Cottages *Value* Lined up along the bay beach in North Truro, these identical cottages—named after flowers—are all white clapboard with sea-foam green shutters. Although lacking frills, each has a living room, two small bedrooms, a kitchen, and a bathroom. The downside is that these accommodations are somewhat rough: The bedrooms are minuscule, and in some of the cottages, the fireplace has about 10 years' worth of graffiti written on the brick chimney. There is also the noise of passing cars on this busy stretch of road to contend with. The upside is miles of bay beach for walking and swimming, with views of Provincetown's quirky skyline in the distance. In season, beginning June 1, the cottages are rented only by the week, and they usually book up far in advance.

Rte. 6A (a couple of miles south of the Provincetown border), North Truro, MA 02652. ② **508/487-1062.** Fax 508/487-5595. www.dayscottages.com. 23 cottages (all with shower only). Summer $1,200 weekly. No credit cards. Closed mid-Oct to Apr. *In room:* Fridge.

Kalmar Village *Kids Value* Spiffier than many of the motels and cottages between Pilgrim Lake and Pilgrim Beach, this 1940s complex features little white cottages shuttered in black. There are picnic tables, grills, and daily maid service. Some cottages have air-conditioning. The clientele—mostly families—can splash the day away in the 60-foot freshwater pool or on the 400-foot private beach.

674 Shore Rd. (Rte. 6A, about ¼ mile south of the Provincetown border), North Truro, MA 02652. ② **508/487-0585.** Fax 508/487-5827. www.kalmarvillage.com. 16 units, 40 cottages. Summer $125–$300 double, $655–$1,065 efficiency; $1,385–$2,500 cottages weekly. DISC, MC, V. Closed mid-Oct to late May. **Amenities:** Outdoor pool; coin-op laundry. *In room:* TV, fridge.

WHERE TO DINE

Babe's Mediterranean Bistro MIDDLE EASTERN Babe's is the Outer Cape's newest place for ethnic cuisine. Chef/owner Peter Thrasher takes his inspiration from the Eastern Mediterranean and North Africa in preparing his cuisine. The menu, which uses vegetables from the chef's garden, changes often. Flavors taste wonderfully different, making this a perfect place for diners unafraid to explore. Dishes to try include *Muhammara,* a hummuslike spread served as an appetizer with special bread; chickpea and asparagus soup; Turkish lamb kabobs; *Izmiri Krofte,* a type of meatball dish with figs and peppers; and Moroccan chicken served in a clay pot with fresh herbs.

69 Shore Rd. (Rte. 6A), North Truro. ② **508/487-9955.** Reservations recommended. Main courses $14–$20. MC, V. June–Sept daily 5:30–10pm. Closed Oct–May.

Terra Luna ✦ FUSION   This serene restaurant, a '70s throwback, specializes in using organic and locally grown ingredients. It may be the only restaurant on the Cape serving pine-nut ricotta vegan lasagna (or vegan anything, for that matter). On the menu are well-priced Pacific Rim and/or neo-Italian fare, such as penne prosciutto sautéed with garlic, black pepper, and a splash of vodka. Main courses include local seafood dishes, like roasted local cod with homemade gnocchi and free-range chicken with savory bread pudding.

104 Shore Rd. (Rte. 6A), North Truro. ✆ **508/487-1019.** Reservations recommended. Main courses $17–$28. AE, MC, V. Late May to mid-Oct daily 5:30–10pm. Closed mid-Oct to late May.

SWEETS & TAKEOUT

Jams *Finds*   Seeing as this deli/bakery/grocery is basically the whole enchilada in terms of downtown Truro, and seasonal to boot, it's good that it's so delightful. It's full of tantalizing aromas: fresh, creative pizzas (from pesto to pupu); rotisseried fowl sizzling on the spit; or cookies straight from the oven. The pastry and deli selections deserve their own four-star restaurant but are all the more savory as part of a picnic.

14 Truro Center Rd. (off Rte. 6, in the center of town). ✆ **508/349-1616.** Call for hours. Closed early Sept to late May.

PROVINCETOWN ✦✦✦

You made it all the way to the end of the Cape, to one of the most interesting spots on the eastern seaboard. Explorer Bartholomew Gosnold must have felt much the same thrill in 1602, when he and his crew happened upon a "great stoare of codfysshes" here. The Pilgrims, of course, were overjoyed when they slogged into the harbor 18 years later. Never mind that they'd landed several hundred miles off course.

And Charles Hawthorne, the painter who "discovered" this near-derelict fishing town in the late 1890s and introduced it to the Greenwich Village intelligentsia, was besotted by this "jumble of color in the intense sunlight accentuated by the brilliant blue of the harbor."

He'd probably be aghast at the commercial circus his enthusiasm has wrought—though pleased, no doubt, to find the Provincetown Art Association & Museum, which he helped found in 1914, still going strong. The whole town, in fact, is dedicated to creative expression, both visual and verbal. The general atmosphere of open-mindedness plays a pivotal role, allowing a varied assortment of individuals to explore their creative urges.

That same open-mindedness may account for Provincetown's ascendancy as a gay and lesbian resort. In peak season, the streets are a celebration of the individual's freedom to be as "out" as imagination allows. But the street life also includes families, art lovers, and gourmands. In short, Provincetown has something for just about everyone.

ESSENTIALS

GETTING THERE   After crossing the Sagamore Bridge, head east on Route 6 or 6A to Orleans, then continue north on Route 6 to Provincetown. Provincetown is 56 miles northeast of Sandwich, 42 miles northeast of Hyannis.

If you plan to spend your entire vacation in Provincetown, you won't need a car—everything is within walking or biking distance. And because parking is a hassle, consider leaving your car at home and taking a boat from Boston or Plymouth. You'll get to skip the horrendous Sagamore Bridge traffic jams and arrive by sea like the Pilgrims did.

Provincetown

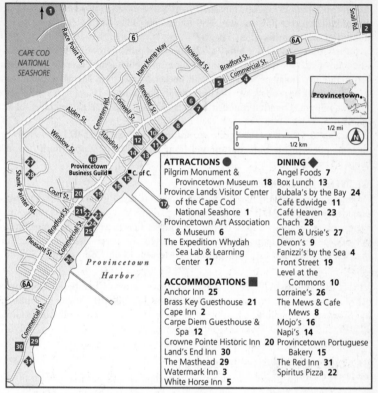

ATTRACTIONS ●
Pilgrim Monument &
   Provincetown Museum **18**
Province Lands Visitor Center
   of the Cape Cod
   National Seashore **1**
Provincetown Art Association
   & Museum **6**
The Expedition Whydah
   Sea Lab & Learning
   Center **17**

ACCOMMODATIONS ■
Anchor Inn **25**
Brass Key Guesthouse **21**
Cape Inn **2**
Carpe Diem Guesthouse &
   Spa **12**
Crowne Pointe Historic Inn **20**
Land's End Inn **30**
The Masthead **29**
Watermark Inn **3**
White Horse Inn **5**

DINING ◆
Angel Foods **7**
Box Lunch **13**
Bubala's by the Bay **24**
Café Edwidge **11**
Café Heaven **23**
Chach **28**
Clem & Ursie's **27**
Devon's **9**
Fanizzi's by the Sea **4**
Front Street **19**
Level at the
   Commons **10**
Lorraine's **26**
The Mews & Cafe
   Mews **8**
Mojo's **16**
Napi's **14**
Provincetown Portuguese
   Bakery **15**
The Red Inn **31**
Spiritus Pizza **22**

Bay State Cruises (℃ **617/748-1428;** www.boston-ptown.com) makes round-trips from Boston, daily from late June through September.

The high-speed *Provincetown Express* boat takes 90 minutes and makes three round-trips daily from mid-May to late September. It leaves Boston's World Trade Center at 8am, 1pm, and 5:30pm. On the return trip, it leaves Provincetown at 10am, 3pm, and 7:30pm. Tickets on the high-speed boat cost $44 one-way, $69 round-trip for adults. Seniors are $40 one-way and $65 round-trip. Children 4 to 11 are $28 one-way, $45 round-trip. Reservations are recommended.

The regular 3-hour boat, called *Provincetown II,* leaves Boston's Commonwealth Pier on Friday, Saturday, and Sunday at 9:30am and arrives in Provincetown at 12:30pm. At 3:30pm, the boat leaves Provincetown, arriving in Boston at 6:30pm. On the slow boat, round-trip fare is $33 for adults, free for children 4 to 11, and $24 for seniors.

Boston Harbor Cruises (℃ **617/227-4321;** www.bostonharborcruises.com) runs fast ferries from Long Wharf in Boston to Provincetown's Macmillan's Wharf. It's a 90-minute trip. In high season, there are three round-trips a day, leaving at 9am, 2pm, and 6:30pm from Boston, and leaving from Provincetown at 11am, 4pm, and 8:30pm. In the shoulder season, late May to mid-June and from early September to mid-October, there are one or two trips a day. Ferry tickets cost $45 one-way, $70 round-trip for adults. Tickets for seniors cost $40 one-way, $65 round-trip; and tickets for children cost $35 one-way, $60 round-trip. Bikes cost $5 each way. Reservations are a must on this popular boat.

Capt. John Boats (© 508/747-2400; www.provincetownferry.com) connects Plymouth and Provincetown daily mid-June through August; Tuesday, Wednesday, Saturday, and Sunday in September; and weekends only from late May to mid-June. The 90-minute boat ride leaves the state pier in Plymouth at 10am; it leaves Provincetown at 4:30pm. The adult round-trip fare is $37, seniors $30, children under 12 $25; bikes are $5 extra.

You can also fly into Provincetown. **Cape Air** (© 800/352-0714; www.flycape air.com) offers flights from Boston and from Nantucket in season. Both trips take about 25 minutes.

GETTING AROUND
Parking is at a premium. Illegally parked cars are ticketed (even on Sun), and repeat offenders will be towed. If your inn provides parking, you may want to keep your car there and get around on foot, bicycle, or shuttle. **Provincetown's Summer Shuttle** (© 508/487-3424) loops through town and to the beach daily from late June through October. You can also contact the **Mercedes Cab Company** (© 508/487-3333).

VISITOR INFORMATION   Contact the **Provincetown Chamber of Commerce,** 307 Commercial St., Provincetown, MA 02657 (© 508/487-3424; fax 508/487-8966; www.ptownchamber.com), or the gay-oriented **Provincetown Business Guild,** 115 Bradford St., P.O. Box 421, Provincetown, MA 02657 (© 800/637-8696 or 508/487-2313; fax 508/487-1252; www.ptown.org).

BEACHES & GETTING OUTSIDE
BEACHES   With nine-tenths of its territory (basically, all but the downtown area) protected by the Cape Cod National Seashore, Provincetown has miles of beaches. The 3-mile bay beach that lines the harbor, though certainly swimmable, is not all that inviting compared with the magnificent ocean beaches overseen by the National Seashore. The two official access areas (see below) tend to be crowded; however, you can always find a less densely populated stretch if you're willing to hike down the beach a bit.

- **Herring Cove** 🌟🌟🌟: This popular west-facing National Seashore beach is known for its spectacular sunsets. The long stretches of pristine sand front a calmer beach than Race Point (see below) because Herring Cove faces Cape Cod Bay. This is a haven for same-sex couples, who tend to gather to the far left side of the beach. Parking costs $15 per day, $45 per season.

- **Long Point:** Trek out over the breakwater at the far west end of Commercial Street and walk about 1½ miles over sand—or catch a water shuttle—$8 one-way, $12 round-trip, hourly in season—from Flyer's Boat Rental (see "Boating," below) to visit this very last spit of land, capped by an 1827 lighthouse. Locals call it "the end of the earth." Shuttles run hourly in July and August.

- **Race Point** 🌟🌟🌟: Facing the Atlantic Ocean, Race Point offers rougher surf than H ring Cove, and you might actually spot whales en route to Stellwagen Bank. Parking costs $15 per day, $45 per season.

BICYCLING   North of town, nestled amid the Cape Cod National Seashore preserve, is one of the more spectacular bike paths in New England, the 7-mile **Province**

Lands Trail ✿✿, a heady swirl of steep dunes anchored by wind-stunted scrub pines. With its free parking, the **Province Lands Visitor Center** ✿ ((✆ 508/487-1256) is a good place to start: You can survey the landscape from the observation tower to try to get your bearings before setting off amid the dizzying maze. Follow signs to a spur path leading to one of the beaches, Race Point or Herring Cove, lining the shore. Rentals are offered in season by **Gale Force Bikes,** at 144 Bradford St. (✆ 508/487-4849) in the West End. It's also an easy jaunt from town, where you'll find plenty of good bike shops—such as **Ptown Bikes,** at 42 Bradford St. (✆ 508/487-8735); reserve several days in advance.

BOATING   In addition to operating a Long Point shuttle from its own dock (see "Beaches," above), **Flyer's Boat Rental,** at 131 Commercial St. in the West End (✆ 508/487-0898), offers all sorts of craft, from kayaks and dinghies to sailboats of varying sizes; sailing lessons and fishing-gear rentals are also available.

FISHING   Surf-casting is permitted at Herring Cove Beach (off Rte. 6) and Race Point Beach (near the Race Point Coast Guard Station); many people drop a hand-line or light tackle right off the West End breakwater. For low-cost deep-sea fishing via party boat, board the *Cee Jay* (✆ 800/675-6724 or 508/487-4330; www.ceejay fishing.com).

NATURE TRAILS   Within the Province Lands (off Race Point Rd., ½ mile north of Rte. 6), the National Seashore maintains the 1-mile **Beech Forest Trail** ✿, a shaded path that circles a shallow freshwater pond blanketed with water lilies before heading into the woods. You can see the shifting dunes gradually encroaching on the forest.

A walk along the **West End breakwater** ✿✿ out to the end of **Long Point** is about 5 miles round-trip. Walking just to the end of the wide breakwater, located at the end of Commercial Street next to the Provincetown Inn, is quite popular. You'll see all ages maneuvering the layered boulders, about a 30-minute walk each way. If you want to continue to Long Point, the very tip of Cape Cod, it's about a 1½-hour walk across soft sand. At low tide, the distance can be shortened by cutting across the salt flats. **Wood End Lighthouse** is directly across the spit of sand near the breakwater. **Long Point Lighthouse** is at the end of the point. Hikers determined to reach the end of Long Point will want to bring a hat, water, and sunscreen. The inside of the arm has views of Provincetown and Provincetown Harbor and a couple of shipwrecks.

ORGANIZED TOURS & CRUISES

Art's Dune Tours ✿✿ is at the corner of Commercial and Standish streets (✆ 800/894-1951 or 508/487-1950; www.artsdunetours.com). In 1946, Art Costa started driving sightseers out to ogle the decrepit "dune shacks" where such transient luminaries as Eugene O'Neill, Jack Kerouac, and Jackson Pollock found their respective muses. The park service wanted to raze these eyesores, but luckily saner heads prevailed: They're now National Historic Landmarks. The tours typically take about 1 to 1½ hours. Tickets are $21 for adults, $16 for children 6 to 11. Additional tours offered include a sunset clambake dune tour ($83) and a barbecue tour ($73).

A recommended boat tour is aboard the *Bay Lady II* ✿ (✆ 508/487-9308; www. sailcapecod.com), which leaves from Macmillan Wharf. The sunset trip on this 73-foot reproduction gaff-rigged Grand Banks schooner is especially spectacular. Tickets cost $20 for adults, $12 to $20 for children under 12. There are four 2-hour sails daily from mid-May to mid-October.

Whale-Watching in P-town

Stellwagen Bank, 8 miles off Provincetown, is a rich feeding ground for whales. The **Portuguese Princess** ✪✪✪, MacMillan Wharf (© 800/442-3188 or 508/349-1900), offers naturalist-led whale-watching trips to Stellwagen and is partnered with the Center for Coastal Studies, a local group that studies the endangered right whale.

Tickets for the 3½-hour trips are $33 for adults, $30 for seniors, $25 for children 7 to 12, and free for children under 7. Call to reserve. Trips aren't offered from late October through March.

Tips for first-timers: Dress very warmly, in layers, and take along a waterproof windbreaker. If you're prone to seasickness, consider taking a motion-sickness pill at the start of the trip. (They are provided free as you board the vessel.)

MUSEUMS

The Expedition Whydah Sea Lab & Learning Center *(Overrated)*   Though the subject matter is fascinating, this site is a bit of a tourist trap. Cape Cod native Barry Clifford made headlines in 1984 when he tracked down the wreck of the 17th-century pirate ship *Whydah* (pronounced *Wid*-dah, like Yankee for "widow") 1,500 feet off the coast of Wellfleet, where it had lain undisturbed since 1717. Only 10% excavated to date, it has already yielded over 100,000 artifacts. In this museum/lab, visitors can supposedly observe the reclamation work being done, though it's unusual to actually see scientists or scholars at work.

MacMillan Wharf (just past the whale-watching fleet). © 508/487-8899. www.whydah.com. Admission $8 adults, $6 children 6–12. June–Sept daily 9:30am–9pm; Oct–Dec and mid-Apr to May weekends only 10am–5pm. Closed Jan to mid-Apr.

Pilgrim Monument & Provincetown Museum ✪✪   Anywhere you go in town, this granite tower looms, ever ready to restore your bearings. Climb up the 60 gradual ramps interspersed with 116 steps—a surprisingly easy lope—and you'll get a gargoyle's-eye view of the spiraling coast and, in the distance, Boston against a backdrop of New Hampshire's mountains. Definitely devote some time to the curious exhibits in the museum, chronicling P-town's checkered past as both fishing port and arts nexus. Among the memorabilia, you'll find polar bears brought back from MacMillan's expeditions and early programs for the Provincetown Players.

High Pole Hill Rd. (off Winslow St., north of Bradford St.). © 508/487-1310. www.pilgrim-monument.org. Admission $7 adults, $5 seniors and students, $3.50 children 4–12. July–Aug daily 9am–7pm; off season daily 9am–5pm. Last admission 45 min. before closing. Closed Dec–Mar.

Province Lands Visitor Center of the Cape Cod National Seashore ✪   Though much smaller than the Salt Pond Visitor Center, this satellite does a good job of explicating this special environment, where plant life must fight a fierce battle to maintain its hold amid shifting sands buffeted by salty winds. Be sure to circle the observation deck for great views. Inquire about special events, such as guided walks, family campfires, and canoe programs (reservations required).

Race Point Rd. (about 1½ miles northwest of the town center). © 508/487-1256. Free admission. Mid-Apr to late Nov daily 9am–5pm. Closed late Nov to mid-Apr.

Provincetown Art Association & Museum 😊😊😊 *Moments* This remarkable cache of 20th-century American art—now in an extraordinary modern building—began with five paintings donated by local artists, including Charles Hawthorne, the charismatic teacher who first "discovered" this picturesque outpost. Founded in 1914, only a year after New York's revolutionary Armory Show, the museum was the site of innumerable "space wars," as classicists and modernists vied for square footage. In today's less competitive atmosphere, it's not unusual to see a tame still life next to an unrestrained abstract. The museum sponsors a full schedule of concerts, lectures, readings, and classes.

460 Commercial St. (in the East End). © 508/487-1750. www.paam.org. Admission $5 adults. July–Aug daily noon–5pm and 8–10pm; call for off-season hours.

SHOPPING

ART GALLERIES Of the several dozen galleries in town, only a handful are reliably worthwhile. In season, most of the galleries and even some of the shops open around 11am, then close from around 5 to 7pm, reopening and greeting visitors up to as late as 10 or 11pm. Shows usually open on Friday evenings, prompting a "stroll" tradition spanning the many receptions.

Berta Walker is a force to be reckoned with, having nurtured many top artists through her association with the Fine Arts Work Center, before opening her own gallery in 1990, the **Berta Walker Gallery** 😊, 208 Bradford St. in the East End (© 508/487-6411). Closed from late October to late May.

DNA (Definitive New Art) Gallery 😊, 288 Bradford St. above the Provincetown Tennis Club in the East End (© 508/487-7700), has attracted such talents as photographer Joel Meyerowitz, Provincetown's favorite portraitist, known for such tomes as *Cape Light;* sculptor Conrad Malicoat, whose free-form brick chimneys and hearths can be seen around town; and local conceptualist/provocateur Jay Critchley. Readings by cutting-edge authors add to the buzz. Closed from mid-October to late May.

Julie Heller started collecting early P-town paintings as a child—and a tourist, at that. She chose so incredibly well, her roster at **Julie Heller Gallery** 😊, 2 Gosnold St. on the beach in the center of town (© 508/487-2169), reads like a who's who of local art. Hawthorne, Avery, Hofmann, Lazzell, Hensche—all the big names from Provincetown's past are here, as well as some contemporary artists. Closed weekdays January to April.

Schoolhouse Center for Art and Design, 494 Commercial St. in the East End (© 508/487-4800), is an impressive setup with two galleries, studios, arts programs, and an events series.

DISCOUNT SHOPPING **Marine Specialties,** 235 Commercial St., in the center of town (© 508/487-1730), is packed to the rafters with useful stuff, from discounted Doc Martens to cut-rate Swiss Army knives. Hung from the ceiling are some real antiques, including several carillons' worth of ship's bells.

FASHION **Giardelli/Antonelli Studio Showroom,** 417 Commercial St. in the East End (© 508/487-3016), is filled with Jerry Giardelli's unstructured clothing elements in vibrant colors and inviting textures. They demand to be mixed and matched with Diana Antonelli's statement jewelry.

Mad as a Hatter, 360 Commercial St. (© **508/487-4063**), has hats to suit every style and inclination. It's closed January to mid-February.

Moda Fina, 349 Commercial St. (© **508/487-6632**), specializes in women's clothing and accessories, including shoes and lingerie, and unique summer dresses.

WHERE TO STAY
Very Expensive

Anchor Inn Beach House 𝕽𝕽   This waterfront property centrally located on Commercial Street underwent a multimillion-dollar face-lift in 2001. Many rooms feature deluxe showers, whirlpool baths, and fireplaces. Sixteen guest rooms have waterfront balconies overlooking the harbor. Four have separate entrances through private porches. Some of the rooms, called "yacht cabins," are quite small but have fabulous views. Others are large suites with king-size beds, two-person whirlpool baths, and French doors leading to a private balcony. Breakfast is an elaborate affair that could include quiche or eggs Benedict.

175 Commercial St. (in the center of town), Provincetown, MA 02657. © **800/858-2657** or 508/487-0432. Fax 508/487-6280. www.anchorinnbeachhouse.com. 23 units. Summer $255–$275 double; $375 suite. Rates include continental breakfast. AE, MC, V. Closed Jan–Mar. *In room:* A/C, TV/VCR, CD player, dataport, fridge, hair dryer.

Brass Key Guesthouse 𝕽𝕽𝕽   Brass Key is the fanciest place to stay in Province-town. With Ritz-Carlton-style amenities and service in mind, the innkeepers have created a paean to luxury. They've thought of everything: down pillows, jetted showers, and free iced tea and lemonade delivered poolside. Rooms in the 1828 Federal-style Captain's House and the Gatehouse are decorated in a playful country style, while the Victorian-era building is classically elegant, with materials like mahogany, walnut, and marble. Most deluxe guest rooms have gas fireplaces and oversize whirlpool tubs. In high season, the clientele here is primarily gay men, though all are made to feel welcome.

67 Bradford St. (in the center of town), Provincetown, MA 02657. © **800/842-9858** or 508/487-9005. Fax 508/487-9020. www.brasskey.com. 41 units, 4 cottages. Summer $235–$485 double; $295–$445 cottage. Rates include continental breakfast and afternoon wine-and-cheese hour. AE, DISC, MC, V. Closed late Nov to early Apr. No children under 18. **Amenities:** Outdoor heated pool; 17-ft. hot tub. *In room:* A/C, TV/DVD, dataport, fridge, hair dryer, safe.

Crowne Pointe Historic Inn 𝕽𝕽   This property, Provincetown's newest luxury inn with a pool and a spa, is perched high on Bradford Street and features deluxe commons areas and attractive gardens. The staff is accommodating and professional. Rooms are spacious, and some of the deluxe rooms and suites have fireplaces, wet bars, and whirlpool spas. Buffet breakfast is served in the large living room, which has plenty of overstuffed couches for lounging while you plan your day.

82 Bradford St. (in the center of town), Provincetown, MA 02657. © **877/CROWNE1** or 508/487-6767. Fax 508/487-5554. www.crownepointe.com. 35 units. Summer $339–$469 double. Rates include continental breakfast and wine-and-cheese hour. AE, MC, V. **Amenities:** Heated outdoor pool; 10-person outdoor spa; sauna; steam room; soaking tub. *In room:* A/C, TV/DVD, dataport, hair dryer, iron.

Expensive

Land's End Inn 𝕽𝕽𝕽 *(Finds)*   Enjoying a prime perch atop Gull Hill in the far West End of Commercial Street, this whimsical 1907 bungalow is bursting with outlandish antiques. There are three deluxe rooms that make use of the inn's soaring towers. Some of the other rooms are small, but all are filled with kitschy Victorian and Art Deco *objets.* Though the inn caters to a predominantly gay clientele, all will feel welcome. The breakfast, an elaborate continental spread, features fresh fruits and homemade baked goods.

22 Commercial St. (in the West End), Provincetown, MA 02657. © 800/276-7088 or 508/487-0706. Fax 508/487-0755. www.landsendinn.com. 16 units. Summer $165–$195 double; $295–$495 tower rooms. Rates include continental breakfast and wine-and-cheese hour. AE, MC, V. Closed Nov–Apr. *In room:* A/C, no phone.

The Masthead 🌾🌾 *Kids*   This is one of the few places in town, other than the impersonal motels, that actively welcomes families, and the placid 450-foot private beach will delight young splashers. The cottages are fun, some with wicker furniture and antiques. In the water-view rooms perched above the surf, with their 7-foot picture windows overlooking the bay and Long Point, you may feel as though you're onboard a ship.

31–41 Commercial St. (in the West End), Provincetown, MA 02657. © 800/395-5095 or 508/487-0523. Fax 508/487-9251. www.themasthead.com. 21 units (3 with tub/shower, 16 with shower, 2 with shared bathroom), 4 cottages. Summer $86–$93 double with shared bathroom; $102–$249 double; $179–$235 efficiency; $265 2-bedroom apt. $1,750–$2,541 cottage weekly. AE, DC, DISC, MC, V. *In room:* A/C, TV, fridge, coffeemaker.

Watermark Inn 🌾🌾 *Kids*   If you'd like to experience P-town without being stuck in the thick of it (the carnival atmosphere can get tiring at times), this contemporary inn at the peaceful edge of town is the perfect choice. This beachfront hotel contains dazzling suites; the prize ones, on the top floor, have picture windows and sweeping deck views. Handmade quilts brighten up clean, monochromatic rooms.

603 Commercial St. (in the East End), Provincetown, MA 02657. © 508/487-0165. Fax 508/487-2383. www. watermark-inn.com. 10 units. Summer $195–300 suite. From mid-May to mid-Sept, suites rent by the week only ($1,240–$2,880 per week). AE, MC, V. *In room:* TV, fridge, coffeemaker.

Moderate
Cape Inn 🌾   This no-surprises motel on the waterfront at the far eastern edge of town is a good choice for first-timers not quite sure what they're getting into. Guests in waterfront rooms get a nice view of town. In season, free movies are shown in the restaurant/lounge on a 100-foot screen, and dinner is served in the restaurant. There's also a poolside bar and grill. Though this motel is a bit of a hike from the town's center, an in-season shuttle will whisk you down Commercial Street or to the beaches.

698 Commercial St. (at Rte. 6A, in the East End), Provincetown, MA 02657. © 800/422-4224 or 508/487-1711. Fax 508/487-3929. www.capeinn.com. 78 units. Summer $160–$179 double. Rates include continental breakfast. AE, DC, DISC, MC, V. Closed Nov–Apr. Dogs allowed. **Amenities:** Restaurant; outdoor pool. *In room:* A/C, TV, dataport, fridge, coffeemaker, hair dryer, iron.

Carpe Diem Guesthouse & Spa 🌾🌾   The theme of this stylish B&B on a side street in the center of town is "seize the day." There are two buildings, the newest featuring four suites and a spa (with massage, steam room, sauna, and hot tub). Guest rooms are exquisitely decorated with European antiques and brightly painted walls and wallpaper. All rooms have down comforters and pillows, as well as bathrobes, and all but one has a minifridge. There are deluxe garden suites with private entrances, Jacuzzis, and fireplaces. The full breakfast features homemade pastries served at the dining-room table.

12 Johnson St. (in the center of town), Provincetown, MA 02657. © 800/487-0132 or ©/fax 508/487-4242. www.carpediemguesthouse.com. 22 units. Summer $214–$400 double. Rates include full breakfast and wine-and-cheese hour. AE, DISC, MC, V. Open year-round. **Amenities:** Spa (steam room, sauna, hot tub). *In room:* A/C, TV/VCR, dataport.

Inexpensive

White Horse Inn 🏨 *(Value)*   Look for the house with the bright yellow door in the East End. The rates are terrific, especially given that this inn is the very embodiment of Provincetown's bohemian mystique. The rooms may be a bit austere, but each is enlivened by paintings collected over the decades. There's an aura of beatnik improv about the rooms, which were cobbled together out of salvage. Guests over the years have embodied a range of low and high art: Cult filmmaker John Waters stayed here often, as did poet laureate Robert Pinsky.

500 Commercial St. (in the East End), Provincetown, MA 02657. 📞 508/487-1790. 24 units, 10 with shared bathroom. Summer $60 single with shared bathroom; $70–$80 double; $125–$140 efficiency. No credit cards. *In room:* No phone.

WHERE TO DINE

Spiritus Pizza, 190 Commercial St. (📞 508/487-2808), is an extravagant pizza parlor open until 2am. The pizza's good, as are the fruit drinks and premium ice cream. For a peaceful morning repast, check out the little garden in back.

Peruse the scrumptious meat pies and pastries at **Provincetown Portuguese Bakery,** 299 Commercial St. (📞 508/487-1803). Both establishments are closed November to early April.

Very Expensive

The Red Inn 🏨 NEW AMERICAN   Located at the far west end of Commercial Street, this picture-perfect establishment has wraparound floor-to-ceiling windows and great beach views. The refined atmosphere makes this a favorite for special occasions, when your dinner might begin with a glass of champagne and end with a soufflé. This is fine dining on the calorie-rich side, with entrees like grilled thick pork chops with tomatillo salsa and pepper-crusted filet mignon with truffle mashed potatoes and Jack Daniel's sauce. Fresh fish and vegetarian main courses are always on the menu. There are also four beautiful guest rooms on site.

15 Commercial St. 📞 508/487-7334. Reservations required. www.theredinn.com. Main courses $21–$38. AE, DC, DISC, MC, V. Mid-June to early Sept daily 5:30–10pm, Sat–Sun 10am–2:30pm; call for off-season hours.

Expensive

Devon's 🏨🏨 NEW AMERICAN   You can tell who Devon is: He's the one seating people, acting as line cook, busing tables, taking reservations, and chatting with customers. The force behind Devon's is a multitalented restaurateur with a great attitude. The tiny restaurant itself, a former boat shack, has fewer than 10 tables inside, all next to the open kitchen. In good weather, the choice seats are on the patio out front. Service is professional and the food elegantly prepared and nicely presented. The menu changes often but features wonderful fish, steak, chicken, and vegetarian meals. One favorite is sole with a simple beurre blanc sauce. This is a romantic option, but you definitely need a reservation. It's also a good choice for breakfast for those staying in the far East End of town.

401½ Commercial St. (in the East End). 📞 508/487-4773. Reservations recommended. Main courses $18–$25. DISC, MC, V. June–Sept Thurs–Tues 8am–1pm and 6–10pm; call for off-season hours. Closed Nov–Apr.

Edwidge @ Night and Café Edwidge 🏨 NEW AMERICAN   Breakfast and dinner are run by two different teams at this second-floor restaurant, long a favorite with locals. For seating, you have a choice: inside where wooden booths, rafters, and close-set tables provide a casual feel; or outside on a narrow, breezy patio that offers

more private dining. Outstanding menu items for dinner include tuna tartare or lobster dumplings as appetizers, and for the main course, filet mignon with a blue cheese fritter or moqueta, a Brazilian seafood dish. If you want to have breakfast here, you must arrive early in order to get a table.

333 Commercial St. (in the center of town). © **508/487-4020.** Reservations recommended. Main courses $18–$29. MC, V. June–Sept daily 8–11am and 6–10pm; call for off-season hours. Closed Nov–Apr.

Front Street 𝕶𝕶 MEDITERRANEAN FUSION/ITALIAN For years, this restaurant has delivered high-quality food and service, and locals consider it a cherished locale. Located in a belowground space on Commercial Street, this cozy restaurant feels most comfortable in the chilly days of spring and summer. Chef Donna Aliperti is constantly improving her menu, inspired by trips to Italy and southern France. The fusion menu, available in season, has creative items like soft-shell crabs with corn-studded risotto and Chinese five-spice grilled duckling. There is also a traditional Italian menu with pastas available every night.

230 Commercial St. © **508/487-9715.** www.frontstreetrestaurant.com. Reservations recommended. Main courses $18–$25. DISC, MC, V. June–Sept daily 6–10pm; call for off-season hours.

Lorraine's 𝕶𝕶 MEXICAN/NEW AMERICAN Long heralded by year-rounders as a spot for creative food and a festive atmosphere, Lorraine's is on the far west end of Commercial Street. Even those who shy away from Mexican restaurants should try the truly unique food here. Maryland soft-shell crabs are lightly dusted in flour with Chimayo chile powder and pan-sautéed and served with a jalapeño aioli. For a main course, consider *viere verde*—sea scallops sautéed with tomatillos, flambéed in tequila, and cloaked in a green-chile sauce. For a treat, check out the extensive tequila menu; shots are served with a wonderful tomato juice–based chaser.

133 Commercial St. (in the West End). © **508/487-6074.** Reservations suggested. Main courses $17–$26. DISC, MC, V. June–Sept daily 6–10pm; call for off-season hours. Closed mid-Dec to Mar.

The Mews & Cafe Mews 𝕶𝕶 INTERNATIONAL/AMERICAN FUSION Bank on fine food and suave service at this beachfront restaurant, an enduring favorite since 1961. Upstairs is the cafe with its century-old mahogany bar and lighter menu. The dining room downstairs sits right on the beach. The best soup in the region is The Mews' scrumptious summertime special, chilled cucumber-miso bisque with curry shrimp timbale. Among the showier entrees is "captured scallops": prime Wellfleet specimens enclosed with a shrimp-and-crab mousse in a crisp wonton pouch and served atop a petite filet mignon with chipotle aioli. Desserts and coffees—take them upstairs in the cafe, to the accompaniment of soft-jazz piano—are delectable.

429 Commercial St. © **508/487-1500.** Reservations recommended. www.mews.com. Main courses $18–$29. AE, DC, DISC, MC, V. Mid-June to early Sept daily 6–10pm, Sun 11am–2:30pm; late Sept to mid-June daily 6–10pm only.

Moderate

Bubala's by the Bay 𝕶 ECLECTIC This trendy bistro promises "serious food at sensible prices." And that's what it delivers: from buttermilk waffles to creative focaccia sandwiches to fajitas, Cajun calamari, and pad Thai. This is a big operation for Provincetown, and the huge outdoor patio facing Commercial Street is particularly popular in the morning. In season, there's entertainment nightly from 10pm to 1am.

183 Commercial St. (in the West End). © **508/487-0773.** Main courses $10–$21. AE, DISC, MC, V. Apr–mid-Oct daily 8am–11pm. Closed late Oct to Apr.

Café Heaven ✿ AMERICAN   Prized for its leisurely country breakfasts (served until midafternoon, for reluctant risers), this modern storefront—adorned with big, bold paintings by acclaimed Wellfleet artist John Grillo—also turns out substantial sandwiches for lunch, such as avocado and goat cheese on a French baguette.

199 Commercial St. (in the center of town). ✆ 508/487-9639. Reservations not accepted. Most items $11–$15. No credit cards. July–Aug daily 8am–3pm; call for off-season hours. Closed Feb–May.

Fanizzi's By The Sea ✿ *Value* ITALIAN/SEAFOOD   This waterfront restaurant in the far East End of town is the perfect place to get away from all the hustle and bustle in the town center. The beauty of this casual restaurant is that you can have a burger and fries, order comfort food like Mom's meatloaf, or splurge on shrimp scampi, and it's all very reasonably priced. The view from the large wraparound plate glass windows is among the best in town. The $13 buffet brunch, served until 2pm on Sundays, is a good deal.

539 Commercial St. (in the far east end of town). ✆ **508/487-1964.** Reservations accepted. Main courses $9–$21. AE, MC, V. Mid-June to mid-Sept Mon–Sat 11:30am–10pm, Sun 10am–9pm; call for off-season hours.

Level at the Commons ✿✿ ECLECTIC/FRENCH BISTRO   It's a tossup: The sidewalk cafe provides an optimal opportunity for studying P-town's inimitable street life, while the plum-colored dining room is a refuge adorned with the owners' extraordinary collection of Toulouse-Lautrec prints. Either way, you'll get to partake of tasty and creative fare. At lunch, the lobster club sandwich on country bread is unbeatable. The Commons boasts the only wood-fired oven in town to date, which comes in handy in preparing the popular gourmet pizzas with unique toppings. At dinner, try the paella with roasted chicken, chorizo, clams, mussels, and shrimp. The Commons also serves as an all-day coffee shop, with cappuccinos and baked goods.

386 Commercial St. ✆ **508/487-7800.** www.commonsghb.com. Reservations recommended. Main courses $10–$26. AE, MC, V. Mid-June to mid-Sept daily 8am–4pm and 5:30–10:30pm; call for off-season hours. Closed Nov–Mar.

Napi's ✿✿ INTERNATIONAL   Restaurateur Napi Van Dereck can be credited with bringing P-town's restaurant scene up to speed—back in the early 1970s. His namesake restaurant still reflects that zeitgeist, with its rococo-hippie carpentry, select outtakes from his sideline in antiques, and some rather outstanding art. The cuisine is a lot less granola than it was, or maybe we've just caught up—hearty peasant fare never really goes out of style. And these peasants really get around, culling dumplings from China, falafel from Syria, and, from Greece, shrimp feta flambéed with ouzo and Metaxa. This restaurant has its own parking lot (around back), which is unusual in Provincetown.

7 Freeman St. (at Bradford St.). ✆ **800/571-6274** or 508/487-1145. Reservations recommended. Main courses $14–$26. DISC, MC, V. May to mid-Sept daily 5–10pm; mid-Sept to Apr daily 11:30am–4pm and 5–9pm.

Inexpensive

Chach ✿ *Finds* DINER   A diner run by a chef instead of a cook means the omelets are divine, the BLTs are heavenly, and there are all kinds of little surprises on the menu, like Mexican specials. It's a little off the beaten track, but it's worth seeking out Chach's for reasonably priced dining without the crowds you find on Commercial Street.

73 Shankpainter Rd. (off Bradford St., a few blocks south of town). ✆ 508/487-1530. Under $10. No credit cards. Apr–Feb Thurs–Tues 7am–3pm. Closed Mar.

A Cybercafe

To check your e-mail, surf online, or just hang out with techies, stop by **Cyber Cove**, an Internet lounge on the second floor of Whalers' Wharf on Commercial Street (© **508/487-7778**; www.cybercove-ptown.com).

Clem and Ursie's 🌟 *Kids* *Finds* SEAFOOD/BARBECUE   Grab a picnic table for a big family dinner of fried seafood and barbecue ribs. More elaborate choices include bouillabaisse and Japanese udon (fish, shellfish, and vegetables in a dashi broth over noodles). The children's menu offers a choice of $5 entrees with fries, drink, dessert, and a surprise. Takeout is popular here, as is the separate ice cream section.

85 Shankpainter Rd. (off Bradford St., a few blocks south of town). © **508/487-2333.** Main courses $6–$17. MC, V. Apr to mid-Oct daily 11am–10pm. Closed mid-Oct to Mar.

TAKEOUT & PICNIC FARE

Mojo's 🌟, 5 Ryder St. Ext. (© **508/487-3140**), is a seafood shack known for its lightly breaded fried fish and hand-cut fries. There are also veggie burgers, burritos, and chicken tenders. Eat at one of the six picnic tables on the patio or take it to the beach. Closed mid-Oct to early May.

The best gourmet shop is **Angel Foods,** 467 Commercial St., in the East End (© **508/487-6666**), which offers Italian specialties and other prepared foods.

The rollwiches—pita bread packed with a wide range of fillings—at **Box Lunch,** 353 Commercial St., in the center of town (© **508/487-6026**), are ideal for a strolling lunch.

PROVINCETOWN AFTER DARK

To order tickets for any of the shows at Provincetown's nightclubs and cabarets, call **Ptown Tix** (© **508/487-9793**; ptowntix.com).

An on-again, off-again contender for hottest club in town is **Club Euro,** 258 Commercial St., 2nd floor, beside Town Hall (© **508/487-8800**), the current home of "Two Fags and a Drag" and the ever-popular all-star musical comedy drag revue "Big Boned Barbies," starring Kandi Kane. It's closed October to May.

Perhaps the nation's premier gay bar, **The Atlantic House** 🌟, 6 Masonic Place, off Commercial Street (© **508/487-3821**), is open year-round. The "A-House" also welcomes straights, except in the leather-oriented Macho Bar upstairs. In the little bar downstairs, check out the Tennessee Williams memorabilia, including a portrait *au naturel.*

Come late afternoon, if you're wondering where all the beachgoers went, it's a safe bet that a number are attending the gay-lesbian tea dance held daily in season from 3:30 to 6:30pm on the pool deck at the **Boatslip Beach Club** 🌟, 161 Commercial St. (© **508/487-1669**). The action then shifts to the **Pied,** 193 Commercial St. (© **508/487-1527**; www.pied.com), for its After Tea T-Dance from 5 to 10pm, but returns to the Boatslip later in the evening for disco. Both are closed November through April.

Crown & Anchor 🌟, 247 Commercial St. (© **508/487-1430**; www.thecrown andanchor.net), houses a number of bars spanning leather, disco, comedy, drag shows, and cabaret. Facilities include a pool bar and game room. It's closed November through April.

One of P-town's top clubs, the **Post Office Café and Cabaret,** 303 Commercial St. (© **508/487-3892**), despite its cramped space, can be depended on for amusing drag and comedy shows. In recent years, the B-Girlz (Hard Kora, Barbie-Q, and Belle Bottom) have been the featured act. The cover is $20. It's closed November to April.

The chic women's bar, **Vixen,** at the Pilgrim House, 336 Commercial St. (© **508/ 487-6424**), features local and national jazz, blues, and comedy acts, including such favorites as Lea DeLaria and Melissa Ferrick a couple times a season. There are also pool tables. It's closed November to April.

Governor Bradford, 312 Commercial St. (© **508/487-2781**), is a good old bar, featuring pool tables, drag karaoke (summer nights at 9:30pm), and disco.

CAPE COD NATIONAL SEASHORE ★★★

No trip to Cape Cod would be complete without a visit to the **Cape Cod National Seashore** on the Outer Cape. Take an afternoon barefoot stroll along the "The Great Beach" and see why the Cape attracts so many artists and poets. On August 7, 1961, President John F. Kennedy signed a bill designating 27,000 acres in the 40 miles from Chatham to Provincetown as the Cape Cod National Seashore. However, as early as the 1930s, the National Park Service had been interested in Cape Cod's ocean beach; back then, the land would have cost taxpayers about $10 an acre! Unusual for a national park, the Seashore includes 500 private residences, the owners of which lease land from the park service. Convincing residents that a National Seashore would be a good thing for Cape Cod was an arduous task back then, and Provincetown still grapples with Seashore officials over town land issues.

ESSENTIALS
GETTING THERE   Take Route 6, the Mid-Cape Highway, to Eastham; it's about 50 miles from the Sagamore Bridge.

VISITOR INFORMATION   Pick up a map of the National Seashore at the **Salt Pond Visitor Center,** in Eastham (© **508/225-3421**). It's open daily: late May to early September from 9am to 5pm, early September to late May from 9am to 4:30pm. A $3-million rehab of the visitor center was completed in 2005. There is also the **Province Lands Visitor Center** (p. 254), a smaller site, in Provincetown. Both centers have ranger activities, gift shops, and restrooms. Seashore beaches are all clearly marked off Route 6. Additional beaches along this stretch are run by individual towns; you must have a sticker or pay a fee to park.

BEACHES & GETTING OUTSIDE
BEACHES   The Seashore's claim to fame is its spectacular beaches—in reality, one long beach—with dunes 50 to 150 feet high. This is the Atlantic Ocean, so the surf is rough (and cold), but a number of the beaches have lifeguards. A $45 pass will get you into all of them for the season, or you can pay a daily rate of $15. Most of the Seashore beaches have large parking lots, but you'll need to arrive early (before 10am) on busy summer weekends to claim a spot. If the beach you want to go to is full, try the one next door—most of the beaches are 5 to 10 miles apart. Don't forget your beach umbrella—the sun can get intense.

- **Coast Guard Beach** ★★★ and **Nauset Light Beach** ★★★, off Ocean View Drive, Eastham: Connected to outlying parking lots by a free shuttle, these pristine beaches have lifeguards and restrooms. With the old Coast Guard building on one and the striped lighthouse on the other, these two strands are among the most scenic in the Seashore.

- **Head of the Meadow Beach** 🐾🐾, off Head of the Meadow Road, Truro: Among the more remote National Seashore beaches, this spot (with restrooms) is known for its excellent surf. Because beachgoers don't have to traverse steep dunes to get here, Head of the Meadow is easier for seniors or those with disabilities to access.
- **Marconi Beach** 🐾🐾, off Marconi Beach Road in South Wellfleet: The bluffs are so high here that the beach lies in shadows by late afternoon. Restrooms are available.
- **Race Point Beach** 🐾🐾🐾 and **Herring Cove Beach** 🐾🐾🐾, off Route 6, Provincetown: Race Point has rough surf, and you might even spot a whale on its way to Stellwagen Bank, a breeding ground. Herring Cove, with much calmer waters, is a good place to watch sunsets and is popular with same-sex couples.

BICYCLING   Some say the best bike path on Cape Cod is the **Province Lands Trail** 🐾🐾🐾, 5 swooping and invigorating miles at Race Point Beach. There is also a 2-mile relatively flat path linking Head of the Meadow Beach to High Head Beach in Truro.

FISHING   Surf-casting is allowed from the ocean beaches. Race Point is a popular spot.

NATURE TRAILS   The Seashore has a number of walking trails—all free, all picturesque. In Eastham, **Fort Hill** 🐾🐾🐾, off Route 6, has one of the best scenic views on Cape Cod, as well as a popular boardwalk trail through a red maple swamp. Following the trail markers around Fort Hill, you'll pass "Indian Rock" (bearing the marks of untold generations who used it to sharpen their tools) and enjoy scenic vantage points overlooking the channel-carved marsh and out to sea. The Fort Hill Trail hooks up with the .5-mile Red Cedar Swamp Trail, offering boardwalk views of an ecology otherwise inaccessible.

The **Nauset Marsh Trail** 🐾 is accessed from the Salt Pond Visitor Center, on Route 6 in Eastham. **Great Island** 🐾🐾, on the bay side in Wellfleet, is one of the finest places to have a picnic; you could spend the day hiking the trails. On **Pamet Trail** 🐾, off North Pamet Road in Truro, hikers pass the decrepit old cranberry-bog building on the way to a trail through the dunes. Don't try the old boardwalk trail over the bogs here; it has flooded and is no longer in use. The **Atlantic White Cedar Swamp Trail** 🐾🐾 is located at the Marconi Wireless Station site (described below). **Small Swamp** 🐾 and **Pilgrim Spring** 🐾 trails are found at Pilgrim Heights Beach. **Beech Forest Trail** 🐾🐾 is located at Race Point in Provincetown.

SEASHORE SIGHTS   The **Old Harbor Lifesaving Station** 🐾, Race Point Beach off Race Point Road, Provincetown (🕾 **508/487-1256**), was 1 of 13 lifesaving stations mandated by Congress in the late 19th century. This shingled shelter with a lookout tower was part of a network responsible for saving some 100,000 lives. Before the U.S. Lifesaving Service was founded in 1872 (it became part of the Coast Guard in 1915), shipwreck victims lucky enough to be washed ashore were still doomed unless they could find a "charity shed"—a hut supplied with firewood—maintained by the Massachusetts Humane Society. The six valiant "Surfmen" manning each lifesaving station took a more active approach, patrolling the beach at all hours and rowing out into the surf to save all they could. Their old equipment is on view at this

> **Tips   Recommended Reading**
>
> Henry David Thoreau's *Cape Cod* is an entertaining account of the author's journeys on the Cape in the late 19th century. The writer/naturalist walked along the beach from Eastham to Provincetown, and you can follow in his footsteps. Henry Beston's *The Outermost House,* originally published in 1928 (Henry Holt, 2003), describes a year of living on the beach in Eastham in a simple one-room dune shack. The shack washed out to sea about 20 years ago, but "The Great Beach" remains. Michael Cunningham's *Land's End: A Walk in Provincetown* (Crown, 2002) is a brief, engrossing meditation, travelogue, and memoir about the little town at the tip of Cape Cod.

museum. Admission is free; there's a parking fee for Race Point Beach (see "Beaches," above). It's open daily from 3 to 5pm in July and August; call for off-season hours. It's closed November through April.

The **Marconi Wireless Station,** on Marconi Park Site Road (off Rte. 6), South Wellfleet (© 508/349-3785), tells the story of the first international telegraphic communication. It's from this spot that inventor Guglielmo Marconi sent the world's first wireless communiqué: "Cordial greetings from President Theadore [sic] Roosevelt to King Edward VII in Poldhu, Wales." It was also here, in 1912, that news of the *Titanic* first reached these shores. There's scarcely a trace left of this extraordinary feat of technology (the station was dismantled in 1920); still, the outdoor displays convey the leap of imagination that was required.

The **Captain Edward Penniman House** ✿, at Fort Hill off Route 6 in Eastham, is a grandly ornate 1868 Second Empire mansion. It's open for tours in season, but the exterior far outshines the interior. Call the visitor center (© 508/255-3421) for times. Check out the huge whale jawbone gate before crossing the street to the trails (see "Nature Trails," above).

Five lighthouses, all automated now, dot the Seashore. In 1996, both Nauset Light, in Eastham, and Highland Light, in Truro, were successfully moved from precarious positions on the edge of dunes in order to save the beloved lighthouses. **Nauset Light** ✿, with its cheerful red stripe, was originally moved to Eastham from Chatham in 1923. The lighthouse flashes an alternating red and white light that can be seen for 23 miles; public tours are offered.

Highland Light ✿✿, also known as **Cape Cod Light,** is the site of the first light in this area, dating back to 1798. The present structure was built in 1857. Follow signs from Route 6 in North Truro to the end of Highland Road. This lighthouse, set high on a cliff, was the first light seen by ships traveling from Europe. Now that the structure has been moved back from the eroding cliff, visitors are allowed to climb the staircase to the top with a guide. *Note:* There's a minimum 4-foot height requirement for climbing the lighthouse. Nearby is the 1907 **Highland House** ✿✿, home of the collections of the Truro Historical Society. Admission to both lighthouse and museum is $5 for adults, free for children under 12. Both are open June through September, daily from 10am to 5pm.

Wood End Light, on Long Point in Provincetown, is an unusual square lighthouse built as a "twin" to Long Point Light in 1873. Hearty souls can hike first across the breakwater at the west end of Commercial Street and then about ½ mile over soft sand to see this lighthouse.

Long Point Light, established in 1827, is isolated at the very tip of Cape Cod. It's about a 1½-hour walk from the breakwater, or a short boat ride from the center of Provincetown. Its fixed green light can be seen for 8 miles. This lighthouse was once the center of a thriving fishing community in the 1800s. Storms and erosion led the community to float their houses across the bay to Provincetown's West End, where a couple of the houses—some of the oldest in town—are still standing.

8

Martha's Vineyard & Nantucket

by Laura M. Reckford

Megastars and CEOs, vacationing families and penniless students all seek refuge on Martha's Vineyard and Nantucket, two picturesque islands off the coast of Cape Cod. Both islands have much to offer families with children and couples seeking a romantic getaway. Their fame as summer resorts doesn't begin to take into account their rich history, diverse communities, and artistic traditions. But the popularity of these islands means that if you must go in the middle of summer, expect crowds and even—yikes!—traffic jams.

While only about 25 nautical miles apart, each island has a distinct personality. Martha's Vineyard, large enough to support a year-round population spanning a broad socioeconomic spectrum, is not quite as rarefied as Nantucket. Vineyarders pride themselves on their liberal stances. True, a prime oceanside estate might fetch millions here, but the residents still dicker over the price of zucchini at the local farmers' market.

Nantucket, flash-frozen in the mid–19th century through zealous zoning, has long been considered a Republican haven. It's rich and traditional. Social scene aside, Nantucket has more pristine public shores than the Vineyard, as well as the best upscale shopping in the region. But there's something for everyone on both islands, and an island vacation is bound to be one that's cherished for many years.

1 Martha's Vineyard ⍟⍟⍟

With 100 square miles, Martha's Vineyard is New England's largest island, yet each of its six communities is blessed with endearing small-town charm. When the former First Family vacationed here, locals joked that the Clintons tested their reputed nonchalance toward famous faces. But don't visit the Vineyard for the celebrities. Instead, savor the decidedly laid-back pace of this unique place.

Most visitors don't take the time to explore the entire island, staying in the "down-island" towns of **Vineyard Haven** ⍟ (officially called Tisbury), **Edgartown** ⍟⍟⍟, and **Oak Bluffs** ⍟⍟⍟. The "up-island" towns—**West Tisbury** ⍟⍟, **Chilmark** ⍟ (including the fishing village of **Menemsha** ⍟⍟⍟), and **Aquinnah** ⍟ (formerly known as Gay Head)—tend to be less touristy.

By all means, admire the regal sea captains' homes in Edgartown. Stroll down Circuit Avenue in Oak Bluffs with a Mad Martha's ice cream cone, then ride the Flying Horses Carousel, said to be the oldest working carousel in the nation. Check out the cheerful "gingerbread" cottages behind Circuit Avenue, where the echoes of 19th-century revival meetings still ring out from the imposing tabernacle.

But don't forget to journey "up-island" to marvel at the red-clay cliffs of Aquinnah, a national historic landmark. Or bike the country roads of West Tisbury and

Chilmark. Buy a lobster roll in the fishing village of Menemsha. There's a surprising degree of diversity here, for those who take the time to discover it.

ESSENTIALS
GETTING THERE

BY FERRY Most visitors take a ferry from the mainland to the Vineyard. You'll most likely catch the ferry from the village of Woods Hole in the town of Falmouth on Cape Cod; boats also run from Falmouth Inner Harbor, Hyannis, New Bedford, Rhode Island, and Nantucket. It's easy to get a passenger ticket on almost any of the ferries, but space for cars is extremely limited, especially on summer weekends, when reservations must be made months in advance. Unless you absolutely must have your car with you, leave it on the mainland. Traffic and parking on the island can be brutal in summer, and it's easy to take shuttle buses (see below) from town to town or simply bike around.

From Woods Hole in Falmouth The state-run **Steamship Authority** (© **508/ 477-8600** or 508/693-9130 for reservations and information Apr 4–Sept 7 daily 7am–9pm, and reduced hours the rest of the year; www.steamshipauthority.com) operates daily, year-round, weather permitting.

Car Passage to Martha's Vineyard

Reservations are required to bring your car to Martha's Vineyard on Friday, Saturday, Sunday, and Monday from mid-June to mid-September, plus Memorial Day weekend. During these months, standby is in effect only on Tuesday, Wednesday, and Thursday. Technically, vehicle reservations can be made up to 1 hour in advance of ferry departure, but in summer ferries are almost always full. Be aware that your space may be forfeited if you have not checked into the ferry terminal 30 minutes prior to sailing time. Reservations may be changed to another date and time with at least 24 hours' notice; otherwise, you will have to pay for an additional ticket for your vehicle.

If you arrive without a reservation on a day that allows standby, come early and be prepared to wait in line for hours. Your passage is guaranteed if you're in line by 2pm on designated standby days. For up-to-date **Steamship Authority** information, check out their website (www.steamship authority.com).

The cost of a round-trip passenger ticket on the ferry to Martha's Vineyard is $14 for adults and $7.50 for children 5 to 12. Bringing a bike costs an extra $6 round-trip. You do not need a reservation on the ferry if you're traveling without a car, and there are no reservations needed for parking.

The Steamship Authority has the only ferries to Martha's Vineyard that accommodate cars. These large ferries make the 45-minute trip to Vineyard Haven throughout the year; some boats go to Oak Bluffs from late May to late October (call or check the website for seasonal schedules). The cost of a round-trip car passage from mid-May to mid-October is $130 to $150; in the off season, it drops to $80 to $100. The higher rates are for vehicles more than 17 feet long. Car rates do not include drivers or passengers. Although you can buy tickets over the phone, it's much faster to purchase them online at the boat line's website, **www.steamshipauthority.com**.

Many people prefer to leave their cars on the mainland, take the ferry (often with their bikes), and then travel around the island by shuttle bus or taxi, or rent a bicycle, car, or jeep on the island. You can park your car at the Woods Hole lots (always full in the summer) or at one of the many lots in Falmouth and Bourne that absorb the overflow of cars. Parking costs $10 per day. Free shuttle buses (some equipped for bikes) run regularly from the outlying lots to the Woods Hole ferry terminal. If you're leaving your car on the mainland, plan to arrive at the parking lots at least an hour before sailing time to allow for parking, taking the free shuttle bus to the ferry terminal, and buying your ferry ticket.

From Falmouth Inner Harbor, you can board the *Island Queen* (© **508/548-4800;** www.islandqueen.com) for a 35-minute cruise to Oak Bluffs (passengers only). The boat runs from late May to mid-October; round-trip fare is $12 for adults, $6 for children under 13, and an extra $6 for bikes. There are seven crossings a day in season (eight on Fri and Sun), and no reservations are needed. Parking runs $15 a day. Credit cards are not accepted.

The **Falmouth–Edgartown Ferry Service,** 278 Scranton Ave. (© **508/548-9400;** www.falmouthferry.com), operates a 1-hour passenger ferry, called the *Pied Piper,* from Falmouth Harbor to Edgartown. The boat runs from late May to mid-October; reservations are required. In season, there are five crossings a day (six on Fri). Round-trip fares are $30 for adults and $24 for children under 12. Bicycles are $8 round-trip. Parking is $18 per day.

From Hyannis Early June through late September, **Hy-Line,** Ocean Street Dock (© **508/778-2600;** www.hy-linecruises.com), operates a conventional ferry from the Ocean Street dock to Oak Bluffs on Martha's Vineyard. It runs three trips a day; travel time is about 1 hour and 45 minutes. A round-trip costs $32 for adults and $17 for children 5 to 12 ($10 extra for bikes). It's a good idea to reserve a parking spot in Hyannis; the all-day fee is $10.

Hy-Line also operates a **fast ferry** from Hyannis to Martha's Vineyard. It departs five to six times daily in season and takes 55 minutes. Round-trip tickets cost $71 for adults, $50 for children.

From Nantucket From early June to mid-September, **Hy-Line,** Ocean Street Dock (© **508/778-2600;** www.hy-linecruises.com), runs three passenger ferries to Oak Bluffs on Martha's Vineyard. There is no car-ferry service between the islands. The trip time is 1 hour and 10 minutes. The one-way fare is $29 for adults, $17 for children 5 to 12, and $5 extra for bikes.

From New Bedford The fast ferry M/V *Whaling City Express* travels to Martha's Vineyard in 1 hour. It makes six trips a day in season and is in service year-round, 7 days a week. A ticket costs $29 one-way and $58 round-trip for adults; $25 one-way and $50 round-trip for seniors; and $15 one-way, $30 round-trip for children under 12. Contact New England Fast Ferry for details (© **866/453-6800;** www.nefastferry. com).

From North Kingstown, Rhode Island From mid-June through October **Vine-yard Fast Ferry** (© **401/295-4040;** www.vineyardfastferry.com) runs the high-speed catamaran *Millennium* to Oak Bluffs two to three round-trips daily. The trip takes 90 minutes. The ferry leaves from Quonset Point, about 10 minutes from Route I-95, 15 minutes from T. F. Green Airport in Providence, and 20 minutes from the Amtrak station in Kingston. There is dockside parking. Rates are $69 round-trip for adults, $46 round-trip for children 4 to 12, free for children under 4, and $10 round-trip for bikes. Parking next to the ferry port is $8 per day.

BY PLANE You can fly into **Martha's Vineyard Airport,** also known as Dukes County Airport (© **508/693-7022**), in West Tisbury, about 5 miles outside Edgartown.

Airlines serving the Vineyard include **Cape Air/Nantucket Airlines** (© **800/352-0714** or 508/771-6944), which connects the island year-round with Boston (trip time 34 min.; hourly shuttle service in summer costs about $240 round-trip), Hyannis (trip time 20 min., $95), Nantucket (15 min., $86), and New Bedford (20 min., $90); and **US Airways** (© **800/428-4322**), which flies from Boston for about $215 round-trip and also has seasonal weekend service from La Guardia (trip time 1 hr. 15 min.), which costs approximately $400 round-trip.

Year-round charter service is offered by **Direct Flight** (© **508/693-6688**). **Westchester Air** (© **800/759-2929**) runs some charters out of White Plains, New York.

BY BUS   **Bonanza Bus Lines** (© **888/751-8800** or 508/548-7588; www.bonanza bus.com) connects the Woods Hole ferry port with Boston (from South Station), New York City, and Providence, Rhode Island. The trip from South Station in Boston takes about 1 hour and 35 minutes and costs about $19 one-way, $32 round-trip; from Boston's Logan Airport, the cost is $24 one-way, $42 round-trip; from New York, the bus trip to Woods Hole takes about 6 hours and costs approximately $52 one-way or $93 round-trip.

BY LIMO   **King's Coach** (© **800/235-5669** or 508/563-5669) will pick you up at Boston's Logan Airport and take you to meet your ferry in Woods Hole (or anywhere else in the Upper Cape area). The trip takes about 90 minutes, depending on traffic, and costs about $177 one-way plus a gratuity for a carload or a vanload of people. You'll need to book the service a couple of days in advance. **Falmouth Taxi** (© **508/ 548-3100**) also runs limo service from Boston and the airport to the Woods Hole ferry terminal.

GETTING AROUND

BY BICYCLE & MOPED   The best way to explore the Vineyard is on two wheels. There's a little of everything for cyclists, from paved paths to hilly country roads (see "Exploring the Vineyard on Two Wheels," later in this chapter, for details on where to ride).

Mopeds, which you need a driver's license to rent and a helmet to ride, are also a way to navigate Vineyard roads, but be aware they are considered quite dangerous on the island's busy, winding, and sandy roads—the number of accidents involving mopeds seems to rise every year. Also, islanders tend to feel quite negative about mopeds.

Bike-rental shops are clustered in all three down-island towns. Scooter- and moped-rental shops are only in Oak Bluffs and Vineyard Haven. Bike rentals cost about $20 a day (the higher prices are for suspension mountain bikes), scooters and mopeds $46 to $85. For bike rentals in Vineyard Haven, try **Martha's Bike Rentals,** Lagoon Pond Road (© 508/693-6593). For mopeds, try **Adventure/Thrifty Rentals,** Beach Road (© 508/693-1959). In Oak Bluffs, there's **Anderson's,** Circuit Avenue Extension (© 508/693-9346), which rents bikes only; and **Sun 'n' Fun,** Lake Avenue (© 508/ 693-5457). In Edgartown, you'll find bike rentals only at **R. W. Cutler Bike,** 1 Main St. (© 508/627-4052); **Edgartown Bicycles,** 190 Upper Main St. (© 508/627-9008); and **Wheel Happy,** 204 Upper Main St. and 8 S. Water St. (© 508/627-5928).

BY CAR   If you're here for a long visit or if you want to do some exploring up-island, you may want to bring a car or rent one on the island. Keep in mind that car-rental rates can soar during peak season, and gas is also much more expensive on the island. Representatives of national car-rental chains are located at the airport and in Vineyard Haven and Oak Bluffs. Local agencies also operate out of all three port towns, and many of them rent jeeps, mopeds, and bikes in addition to cars. The national chains include **Budget** (© **800/527-0700** or 508/693-1911), **Hertz** (© **800/654-3131**), and **Thrifty** (© **800/874-4389**).

For local agencies, in Vineyard Haven, you'll find **Adventure Rentals,** Beach Road (© **508/693-1959**); and in Edgartown, **AAA Island Rentals,** 141 Main St. (© **508/ 627-6800**). Operating out of the airport is **All Island Rent-a-Car** (© **508/693-6868**).

BY SHUTTLE BUS   In season, shuttle buses certainly run often enough to make them a practical means of getting around. They are also cheap, dependable, and easy.

The **Martha's Vineyard Regional Transit Authority** (© 508/693-9440; www.vineyardtransit.com) operates shuttle buses year-round on about a dozen routes around the island. The buses, which are white with purple logos, cost about $2 to $5, depending on distance. The formula is $1 per town. For example, Vineyard Haven to Oak Bluffs is $2, but Vineyard Haven to Edgartown (passing through Oak Bluffs) is $3. A 1-day pass is $6; a 3-day pass is $15. The Edgartown Downtown Shuttle and the South Beach buses circle throughout town or out to South Beach every 20 minutes in season. They also stop at the free parking lots just north of the town center—this is a great way to avoid circling the streets in search of a vacant spot on busy weekends. The main down-island stops are Vineyard Haven (near the ferry terminal), Oak Bluffs (near the Civil War statue in Ocean Park), and Edgartown (Church St., near the Old Whaling Church). From late June to early September, they run more frequently from 6am to midnight every 15 minutes or half-hour. Hours are reduced in spring and fall. Buses also go out to Aquinnah (via the airport, West Tisbury, and Chilmark), leaving every couple of hours from down-island towns and looping about every hour through up-island towns.

For bus tours of the island, call **Island Transport** (© 508/693-0058) or hop on one of the Island Transport buses that are stationed at the ferry terminals in Vineyard Haven and Oak Bluffs in the summer.

BY TAXI   Upon arrival, you'll find taxis at all ferry terminals and at the airport, and there are permanent taxi stands in Oak Bluffs (at the Flying Horses Carousel) and Edgartown (next to the Town Wharf). Most taxi outfits operate cars as well as vans for larger groups and travelers with bikes. Cab companies on the island include **Adam Cab** (© 800/281-4462 or 508/693-3332), **Accurate Cab** (© 888/557-9798 or 508/627-9798; the only 24-hr. service), **All Island Taxi** (© 800/693-TAXI or 508/693-2929), and **Marlene's Taxi** (© 508/693-0037). Rates from town to town in summer are generally flat fees based on where you're headed and the number of passengers on board. A trip from Vineyard Haven to Edgartown would probably cost around $17 for two people. Late-night revelers should keep in mind that rates double after midnight until 7am.

THE CHAPPAQUIDDICK FERRY   From June to mid-October, the **On-Time ferry** (© 508/627-9427) runs the 5-minute trip from Memorial Wharf on Dock Street in Edgartown to Chappaquiddick Island. It leaves every 5 minutes from 7am to midnight. Passengers, bikes, mopeds, dogs, and cars (three at a time) are all welcome. The one-way cost is $3 per person, $10 for one car/one driver, $6 for one bike/one person, and $5 for one moped or motorcycle/one person.

VISITOR INFORMATION

Contact the **Martha's Vineyard Chamber of Commerce** at Beach Road, Vineyard Haven (P.O. Box 1698 Vineyard Haven, MA 02568; © 508/693-0085; fax 508/693-7589), or visit their website at **www.mvy.com**. There are also information booths at the ferry terminal in Vineyard Haven, across from the Flying Horses Carousel in Oak Bluffs, and on Church Street in Edgartown. For information on current events, check the two local newspapers, the *Vineyard Gazette* (www.mv gazette.com) and the *Martha's Vineyard Times* (www.mvtimes.com), for information on current events.

In case of an **emergency,** call © **911** and/or head for the **Martha's Vineyard Hospital,** Linton Lane, Oak Bluffs (© **508/693-0410**), which has a 24-hour emergency room.

A STROLL AROUND EDGARTOWN ✿✿✿

A good way to acclimate yourself to the pace and flavor of the Vineyard is to walk the streets of Edgartown. This walk starts at the Dr. Daniel Fisher House and meanders along for about a mile; it takes about 2 to 3 hours.

If you're driving, park at the free lots at the edge of town (you'll see signs on the roads from Vineyard Haven and West Tisbury) and bike or take the shuttle bus (it costs only 50¢) to the Edgartown Visitor Center on Church Street.

The **Dr. Daniel Fisher House** ✿, 99 Main St. (© **508/627-8017**), is a prime example of Edgartown's trademark Greek Revival opulence. A key player in the 19th-century whaling trade, Dr. Fisher amassed a fortune sufficient to found the Martha's Vineyard National Bank. Built in 1840, his proud mansion boasts such classical elements as colonnaded porticos and a delicate roof walk.

Note: The only way to view the interior (now headquarters for the Martha's Vineyard Preservation Trust) is with a guided **Vineyard Historic Walking Tour** (© **508/ 627-8619**). This tour, which also takes in the neighboring Old Whaling Church, originates next door at the Vincent House Museum. Tours are offered June through September Monday through Saturday noon to 3pm. The cost is $7 to $10 for adults, free for children 12 and under.

The **Vincent House Museum** ✿, off Main Street between Planting Field Way and Church Street, is a transplanted 1672 full Cape and is considered the oldest surviving dwelling on the island. The **Old Whaling Church** ✿✿, 89 Main St., is a magnificent 1843 Greek Revival edifice designed by local architect Frederick Baylies, Jr., and was built as a whaling boat would have been, out of massive pine beams; it boasts 27-foot windows and a 92-foot tower. Maintained by the Preservation Trust and still supporting a Methodist parish, the building is now primarily used as a performance venue.

Continuing down Main Street and turning right onto School Street, you'll pass another Baylies monument, the 1839 **Baptist Church,** which, having lost its spire, was converted into a private home with a rather grand, column-fronted facade. Two blocks farther is the **Vineyard Museum** ✿✿, 59 School St. (© **508/627-4441**), a fascinating complex assembled by the Dukes County Historical Society. This cluster of buildings contains exhibits of Native American crafts, an entire 1765 house, an extraordinary array of maritime art, and the Gay Head Light Tower's decommissioned Fresnel lens.

Give yourself enough time to explore the museum's curiosities before heading south 1 block on Cooke Street. Cater-cornered across South Summer Street, you'll spot the first of Baylies's impressive endeavors, the 1828 **Federated Church.** One block left are the offices of the *Vineyard Gazette,* 34 S. Summer St. (© **508/627-4311**). Operating out of a 1760 house, this exemplary small-town newspaper has been going strong since 1846.

Walk down South Summer Street to Main Street and take a right toward the water, stopping at any inviting shops along the way. Veer left on Dock Street to reach the **Old Sculpin Gallery,** 58 Dock St. (© **508/627-4881**), open from late June to mid-September. The output of the Martha's Vineyard Art Association is displayed. The real draw is the stark old building itself, which started out as a granary and spent the better part of the 20th century as a boat-building shop.

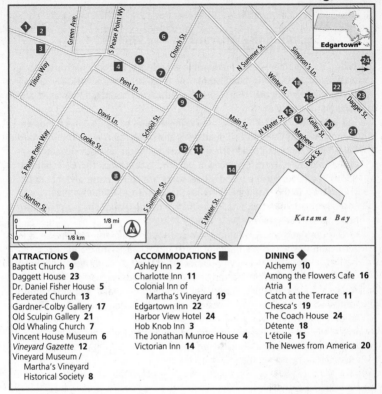

ATTRACTIONS ●
Baptist Church **9**
Daggett House **23**
Dr. Daniel Fisher House **5**
Federated Church **13**
Gardner-Colby Gallery **17**
Old Sculpin Gallery **21**
Old Whaling Church **7**
Vincent House Museum **6**
Vineyard Gazette **12**
Vineyard Museum /
    Martha's Vineyard
    Historical Society **8**

ACCOMMODATIONS ■
Ashley Inn **2**
Charlotte Inn **11**
Colonial Inn of
    Martha's Vineyard **19**
Edgartown Inn **22**
Harbor View Hotel **24**
Hob Knob Inn **3**
The Jonathan Munroe House **4**
Victorian Inn **14**

DINING ◆
Alchemy **10**
Among the Flowers Cafe **16**
Atria **1**
Catch at the Terrace **11**
Chesca's **19**
The Coach House **24**
Détente **18**
L'étoile **15**
The Newes from America **20**

Cross the street to survey the harbor from the second-floor deck at Town Wharf. You can watch the tiny On-Time ferry make its 5-minute crossing to **Chappaquiddick Island** 𝕬𝕬. Don't bother looking for the original **Dyke Bridge,** infamous scene of the Kennedy/Kopechne scandal; it has been dismantled and, at long last, replaced.

Stroll down North Water Street to admire the many formidable captain's homes, several of which have been converted into inns. Each has a tale to tell. The 1750 **Daggett House** (no. 59), which is now a private home, started out as a 1660 tavern, and the original beehive oven is flanked by a "secret" passageway. Nathaniel Hawthorne holed up at the **Edgartown Inn** (no. 56) for nearly a year in 1789, while writing *Twice Told Tales*—and, it is rumored, romancing a local maiden who inspired *The Scarlet Letter.* On your way back to Main Street, you'll pass the **Gardner–Colby Gallery** (no. 27), filled with beautiful island-inspired paintings.

After all that walking, stop for a drink at **The Newes from America,** 23 Kelley St., off North Water Street ✆ **508/627-4397**). This Colonial basement pub serves up specialty beers and the best French onion soup on the island (see "Where to Dine," later in this section).

BEACHES & OUTDOOR PURSUITS

BEACHES   Most down-island beaches in Vineyard Haven, Oak Bluffs, and Edgartown are open to the public and are just a walk or a short bike ride from town. In

Tips Exploring the Vineyard on Two Wheels

Biking on the Vineyard is a memorable experience, not only for the smooth, well-maintained paths, but also for the long stretches of virtually untrafficked up-island roads that reveal breathtaking country landscapes and sweeping ocean views.

A triangle of paved bike paths, roughly 8 miles to a side, links the down-island towns of Oak Bluffs, Edgartown, and Vineyard Haven. The Vineyard Sound portion along Beach Road, flanked by water on both sides, is especially enjoyable. From Edgartown, you can also follow the bike path to South Beach. For a more woodsy ride, there are paved paths and mountain-biking trails in the **Manuel F. Correllus State Forest** (© 508/693-2540), a vast spread of scrub oak and pine in the middle of the island. The bike paths are accessible off Edgartown–West Tisbury Road.

The up-island roads leading to West Tisbury, Chilmark, Menemsha, and Aquinnah are a cyclist's paradise, with unspoiled pastureland, old farm-houses, and brilliant sea views reminiscent of Ireland's countryside. But keep in mind that the terrain is often hilly, and the roads are narrow and a little rough around the edges. From West Tisbury to Chilmark Center, try **South Road**—about 5 miles—which passes stone walls rolling over moors, clumps of pine and wildflowers, verdant marshes and tidal pools, and, every once in a while, an Old Vineyard farmhouse. **Middle Road** is another lovely ride with a country feel and will also get you from West Tisbury to Chilmark. (It's usually less trafficked, too.)

season, shuttle buses make stops at **State Beach,** between Oak Buffs and Edgartown. Most of the Vineyard's magnificent up-island shoreline is privately owned or restricted to residents, and thus off-limits to visitors. Renters in up-island communities, however, can obtain a beach sticker (around $35–$50 for a season sticker) for those private beaches by applying with a lease at the relevant **town hall:** West Tisbury, © 508/696-0147; Chilmark, © 508/645-2100; or Aquinnah, © 508/645-2300. Also, many up-island inns offer the perk of temporary passes to the beautiful up-island beaches. In addition to the public beaches listed below, you might track down a few hidden coves by requesting a map of conservation properties from the **Martha's Vineyard Land Bank** (© 508/627-7141). Below is a list of visitor-friendly beaches.

- **Aquinnah Beach** 𝕲𝕲𝕲 (Moshup Beach), off Moshup Trail: Parking costs $20 a day in season at this peaceful half-mile beach just east (Atlantic side) of the colorful cliffs. Although it is against the law, nudists tend to gravitate toward this beach. Because of rapid erosion, climbing the cliffs or taking clay for a souvenir is forbidden. Restrooms are near the parking lot, which is a 10-minute walk from the beach.
- **East Beach** 𝕲𝕲, Wasque (pronounced *Way*-squee) Reservation, Chappaquiddick: Relatively few people bother biking or hiking (or four-wheel driving) this far, so you should be able to find all the privacy you crave. Take the On-Time Ferry to Chappaquiddick, then go straight 2½ miles and continue straight for another

My favorite up-island route is the 6-mile stretch from Chilmark Center out to Aquinnah via **State Road** and **Moshup Trail** 𝔾. The ocean views along this route are spectacular. Don't miss the **Quitsa Pond Lookout,** about 2 miles down State Road, which provides a panoramic vista of Nashaquitsa and Menemsha ponds, beyond which you can see Menemsha, Vineyard Sound, and the Elizabeth Islands. A bit farther, just over the Aquinnah town line, is the Aquinnah spring, a roadside iron pipe where you can refill your water bottle with the freshest and coldest water on the island. At the fork after the spring, turn left on Moshup Trail—in fact, a regular road—and follow the coast, which offers gorgeous views of the ocean and the sweeping sand dunes. You'll soon wind up in Aquinnah, where you can explore the red-clay cliffs and pristine beaches. On the return trip, you can take the handy bike ferry ($7 round-trip) from Aquinnah to Menemsha. It runs daily in summer and on weekends in May.

There are lots of bike-rental operations near the ferry landings in Vineyard Haven and Oak Bluffs, as well as a few rental shops in Edgartown. For information on rentals, see "Getting Around," earlier in this chapter.

A very good outfitter out of Boston called **Bike Riders** (𝄞 800/473-7040; www.bikeriderstours.com) runs 6-day island-hopping tours of Martha's Vineyard and Nantucket. Stays are at various inns on the islands. It's a perfect way to experience both islands.

½ mile on a dirt road. Biking on Chappaquiddick is one of the great Vineyard experiences, but the roads can be quite sandy and are best suited to a mountain bike. Along the dirt road, you'll pass **Mytoi,** a 14-acre Japanese garden open to the public, which is an oasis of flora and fauna. Because of its exposure on the east shore of the island, the surf here is rough. Pack a picnic; there are no stores on Chappy. There is a portable toilet in the parking lot. Most people park their car near the Dike Bridge and walk the couple of hundred yards out to the beach. Admission is $3 per person.

- **Joseph A. Sylvia State Beach** 𝔾𝔾𝔾, midway between Oak Bluffs and Edgartown: Stretching a mile and flanked by a paved bike path, this placid beach has views of Cape Cod and Nantucket Sound and is prized for its gentle and (relatively) warm waves, which make it perfect for swimming. The drawbridge is a local landmark, and visitors and islanders alike have been jumping off it for years. Be aware that State Beach is one of the Vineyard's most popular; in midsummer, it's packed. The shuttle bus stops here, and roadside parking is also available—but it fills up fast, so stake your claim early. Located on the eastern shore of the island, this is a Nantucket Sound beach, so waters are shallow and rarely rough. There are no restrooms, and only the Edgartown end of the beach, known as Bend-in-the-Road Beach, has lifeguards.

(Moments Menemsha Beach Sunset

This beach is the ideal place to watch a sunset. Get a lobster dinner to go at the famous **Home Port restaurant** right next to the beach in Menemsha (see "Where to Dine," later in this chapter), grab a blanket and a bottle of wine, and picnic here for a spectacular evening.

- **Lake Tashmoo Town Beach**, off Herring Creek Road, Vineyard Haven: The only spot on the island where lake meets ocean, this tiny strip of sand is good for swimming and surf-casting but is somewhat marred by limited parking and often brackish waters. Nonetheless, this is a popular spot, as beachgoers enjoy a choice between the Vineyard Sound beach with mild surf or the placid lake beach. Bikers will have no problem reaching this beach from Vineyard Haven; otherwise, you have to use a car to get here.

- **Menemsha Beach**, next to Dutchers Dock in Menemsha Harbor: The gentle surf of this small but well-trafficked strand, with lifeguards and restrooms, is popular with families. In season, it's virtually wall-to-wall umbrellas. Nearby food vendors in Menemsha—selling everything from ice cream and hot dogs to shrimp cocktail—are a plus here.

- **Oak Bluffs Town Beach,** Seaview Avenue: This sandy strip extends from both sides of the ferry wharf, which makes it a convenient place to linger while waiting for the next boat. This is an in-town beach, within walking distance for visitors staying in Oak Bluffs. The surf is consistently calm and the sand smooth, so it's also ideal for families with small children. Public restrooms are available at the ferry dock, but there are no lifeguards.

- **Owen Park Beach,** off Main Street in Vineyard Haven: A tiny strip of harborside beach adjoining a town green with swings and a bandstand will suffice for young children, who, by the way, get lifeguard supervision. There are no restrooms, but this is an in-town beach, which is probably a quick walk from your Vineyard Haven inn.

- **South Beach (Katama Beach)**, about 4 miles south of Edgartown on Katama Road: If you have time for only one trip to the beach and you can't get up-island, go with this popular 3-mile barrier strand that boasts heavy wave action (check with lifeguards for swimming conditions), sweeping dunes, and, most important, relatively ample parking space. It's also accessible by bike path or shuttle. Lifeguards patrol some sections of the beach, and there are sparsely scattered toilet facilities. The rough surf here is popular with surfers. ***Tip:*** As you face the water, families tend to head to the left, college kids to the right.

A word about Aquinnah: Almost every visitor to the Vineyard finds his way to the cliffs, and with all the tour buses lined up in the huge parking lot and the rows of tacky concession stands and gift shops, this can seem like a rather outrageous tourist trap. You're right; it's not the Grand Canyon. But the observation deck, with its view of the colorful cliffs, the adorable brick lighthouse, and the Elizabeth Islands beyond, will make you glad you made the effort. Instead of rushing away, stop for a cool drink and a clam roll at the snack bar with the deck overlooking the ocean.

FISHING   For shellfishing, get information and a permit from the appropriate town hall (for the telephone numbers, see "Beaches," above). Popular spots for surf-casting include **Wasque Point** on Chappaquiddick, South Beach, and the jetty at Menemsha Pond.

The party boat *Skipper* (© 508/693-1238) offers half-day trips out of Oak Bluffs harbor in season. The cost is $35 for adults, $25 for children 12 and under. Deep-sea excursions can be arranged aboard **Summer's Lease** (© 508/693-2880) out of Oak Bluffs. Up-island, there are **North Shore Charters** (© 508/645-2993; www.bassn blue.com) and **Flashy Lady Fishing Charters** (© 508/645-2462; www.flashylady charters.com) out of Menemsha, locus of the island's commercial fishing fleet.

Cooper Gilkes III, proprietor of **Coop's Bait & Tackle,** at 147 W. Tisbury Rd. in Edgartown (© 508/627-3909), which offers rentals as well as supplies, is another acknowledged authority. He's available as an instructor or charter guide.

GOLF   The 9-hole **Mink Meadows Golf Course,** off Franklin Street in Vineyard Haven (© 508/693-0600), is open to the general public, while the championship-level 18-hole **Farm Neck Golf Club,** off Farm Neck Road in Oak Bluffs (© 508/ 693-3057), is semiprivate.

NATURE TRAILS   About a fifth of the Vineyard's landmass has been set aside for conservation, and it's all accessible to bikers and hikers. The **West Chop Woods,** off Franklin Street in Vineyard Haven, comprise 85 acres with marked walking trails. Midway between Vineyard Haven and Edgartown, the **Felix Neck Wildlife Sanctuary** ⟨⟨ includes a 6-mile network of trails over varying terrain, from woodland to beach.

The 633-acre **Long Point Wildlife Refuge** ⟨⟨, off Waldron's Bottom Road in West Tisbury (gatehouse © 508/693-7392), offers heath and dunes, freshwater ponds, a popular family-oriented beach, and interpretive nature walks for children.

Up-island, along the sound, the **Menemsha Hills Reservation,** off North Road in Chilmark (© 508/693-7662), encompasses 210 acres of rocks and bluffs, with steep paths, lovely views, and even a public beach. **The Cedar Tree Neck Sanctuary,** off Indian Hill Road southwest of Vineyard Haven (© 508/693-5207), offers some 300 forested acres that end in a stony beach. Swimming and sunbathing are prohibited.

Some remarkable botanical surprises can be found at the 20-acre **Polly Hill Arboretum** ⟨⟨, 809 State Rd., West Tisbury (© 508/693-9426). The late legendary horticulturist Polly Hill developed this property over the past 40 years, and a trust now allows the public to wander the grounds Thursday to Tuesday from 7am until 7pm. This is a magical place, particularly mid-June to July, when the Dogwood Allée is in bloom. Wanderers will pass old stone walls on the way to The Tunnel of Love, an arbor of hornbeam. There are also witch hazels, camellias, magnolias, and rhododendrons. To get there from Vineyard Haven, go south on State Road, bearing left at the junction of North Road. The arboretum entrance is about a half-mile down, on the right. There is a requested donation of $5 for adults.

WATERSPORTS   **Wind's Up,** 199 Beach Rd., Vineyard Haven (© 508/693-4252), rents out canoes, kayaks, and various sailing craft, including windsurfers, and offers instruction on a placid pond; it also rents surfboards and boogie boards. Canoes and kayaks rent for $20 per hour.

MUSEUMS & HISTORIC LANDMARKS

Cottage Museum 🔍 This little museum, a cottage in the center of Oak Bluffs' famous "campground," displays 19th-century artifacts, like bulky black bathing costumes and a melodeon used for informal hymnal singalongs. The campground consists of a 34-acre circle with more than 300 multicolored, elaborately trimmed Carpenter Gothic cottages, which look very much the way they might have more than a hundred years ago. These adorable little houses were loosely modeled on the revivalists' canvas tents that inspired them. In the 1860s, when many of the cottages were built, campers typically attended three lengthy prayer services daily. Opportunities for worship remain at the 1878 Trinity Methodist Church within the park or, just outside, on Samoset Avenue, at the nonsectarian 1870 Union Chapel, a magnificent octagonal structure with superb acoustics.

At the very center of the Camp Meeting Grounds is the striking **Trinity Park Tabernacle** 🔍🔍. Built in 1879, the open-sided chapel is the largest wrought-iron structure in the country. Thousands can be accommodated on its long wooden benches, which are usually filled to capacity for the Sunday-morning services in summer, as well as for community sings (Wed in July–Aug) and occasional concerts.

1 Trinity Park (within the Camp Meeting Grounds), Oak Bluffs. ✆ **508/693-7784.** Admission $2 (donation). Mid-June to Sept Mon–Sat 10am–4pm. Closed Oct to mid-June.

Flying Horses Carousel 🔍🔍 *Kids* You don't have to be a kid to enjoy what is considered to be the oldest working carousel in the country. Built in 1876 at Coney Island, this National Historic Landmark predates the era of horses that "gallop." Lacking the necessary gears, these mounts merely glide smoothly in place to the joyful strains of a calliope. Take a moment to admire the intricate hand carving and real horsehair manes, and gaze into the horses' glass eyes for a surprise: tiny animal charms glinting within.

33 Circuit Ave. (at Lake Ave.), Oak Bluffs. ✆ **508/693-9481.** Tickets $1 per ride, or 8 rides for $10. Late May to early Sept daily 10am–10pm; call for off-season hours. Closed mid-Oct to mid-Apr.

The Martha's Vineyard Historical Society 🔍 All of Martha's Vineyard's colorful history is captured here, in a compound of historic buildings. To acclimate yourself chronologically, start with the pre-Colonial artifacts—from arrowheads to colorful Gay Head clay pottery—displayed in the 1845 **Captain Francis Pease House.** The **Gale Huntington Reference Library** houses rare documentation of the island's history, from genealogical records to whaling-ship logs. Some extraordinary memorabilia, including scrimshaw and portraiture, are on view in the adjoining **Francis Foster Maritime Gallery.**

To get a sense of daily life during the era when the waters of the East Coast were the equivalent of a modern highway, visit the **Thomas Cooke House,** a shipwright-built Colonial, built in 1765, where the Customs collector lived and worked. The Fresnel lens on display outside the museum was lifted from the Gay Head Lighthouse in 1952, after nearly a century of service. Though it no longer serves to warn ships of dangerous shoals (that light is automated now), it still lights up the night every evening in summer, just for show.

59 School St. (corner of Cooke St., 2 blocks southwest of Main St.), Edgartown. ✆ **508/627-4441.** www.marthas vineyardhistory.org. Admission in season $7 adults, $4 children 6–15. Mid-June to mid-Oct Tues–Sat 10am–5pm; mid-Oct to late Dec and mid-Mar to mid-June Wed–Fri 1–4pm, Sat 10am–4pm; early Jan to mid-Mar Wed–Fri by appointment, Sat 10am–4pm.

ORGANIZED TOURS & CRUISES

Hugh Taylor (James's brother) alternates with a couple of other captains in taking the helm of **Arabella** ⚓, docked in Menemsha Harbor at the end of North Road (© **508/645-3511**). This swift 50-foot catamaran makes daily trips to Cuttyhunk Island and offers sunset cruises around the Aquinnah cliffs. It's a great way to see lovely coves and vistas otherwise denied the ordinary tourist. Daily sails are $60 per person. From mid-June to mid-September, departures are daily at 10:30am and 6pm (or 2 hr. before sunset). Reservations are required.

The Trustees of Reservations, a statewide land conservation group, offers fascinating 2½-hour **Natural History Tours** ⚓⚓⚓ (© **508/627-3599;** www.thetrustees.org) by safari vehicle or kayak around Cape Poge on Chappaquiddick Island. The kayak tour on Poucha Pond and Cape Poge Bay is designed for all levels. The cost for the safari tour is $30 for adults, $15 for children 15 and under. The cost for the kayak tour is $35 for adults, $18 for children 15 and under. There's also a tour of the Cape Poge lighthouse that costs $20 for adults and $12 for children. Two-hour kayak tours around Long Point cost $20 for adults and $10 for children. Call © **508/693-7392** for details on the Long Point trips.

SHOPPING ⚓

ANTIQUES/COLLECTIBLES   For the most exquisite Asian furniture, lamps, porcelains, and jewelry, visit **All Things Oriental,** at 123 Beach Rd. in Vineyard Haven (© **508/693-8375**). The owner handpicks the treasures in China.

ARTS & CRAFTS   No visit to Edgartown would be complete without a peek at the wares of scrimshander Thomas J. DeMont, Jr., at **Edgartown Scrimshaw Gallery,** 43 Main St. (© **508/627-9439**). All the scrimshaw in the gallery is hand-carved using ancient mammoth ivory or antique fossil ivory.

The Field Gallery, State Road (in the center of town), West Tisbury (© **508/693-5595**), is where Marc Chagall meets Henry Moore and where Tom Maley's playful figures have enchanted locals and passersby for decades. You'll also find paintings by Albert Alcalay and drawings and cartoons by Jules Feiffer. The Sunday-evening openings are high points of the summer social season. Closed from mid-October to mid-May.

Don't miss the **Granary Gallery at the Red Barn,** Old County Road (off Edgartown–West Tisbury Rd., about ¼ mile north of the intersection), West Tisbury (© **800/472-6279** or 508/693-0455), which displays astounding prints by the late longtime summerer Alfred Eisenstaedt and dazzling color photos by local luminary Alison Shaw.

Another unique local artisans' venue is **Martha's Vineyard Glass Works,** State Road, North Tisbury (© **508/693-6026**). The three resident artists—Andrew Magdanz, Susan Shapiro, and Mark Weiner—have shown nationwide to considerable acclaim. Their output is decidedly avant-garde and may not suit all tastes, but it's an eye-opening array and all the more fascinating once you've witnessed a work in progress.

GIFTS/HOME DECOR   **Craftworks,** 149 Circuit Ave. (© **508/693-7463**), is filled to the rafters with whimsical, contemporary American crafts.

Carly Simon's **Midnight Farm,** 18 Water-Cromwell Lane, Vineyard Haven (© **508/693-1997**), offers a world of high-end, imaginative gift items from candles to children's clothes to furniture and glassware.

WHERE TO STAY

When deciding where to stay on Martha's Vineyard, you'll need to consider the type of vacation you prefer. The down-island towns of Vineyard Haven, Oak Bluffs, and Edgartown provide shops, restaurants, beaches, and harbors within walking distance, and frequent shuttles to get you all over the island. But all three can be overly crowded on busy summer weekends. Vineyard Haven is the gateway for most of the ferry traffic; Oak Bluffs is a raucous town with most of the Vineyard's bars and nightclubs; and many visitors make a beeline to Edgartown's manicured Main Street. Up-island inns provide more peace and quiet, but you'll probably need a car to get around. Also, you may not be within walking distance of the beach.

We've provided only summer rates below because the Vineyard is so seasonal. If you do visit in the off season, you may find substantial discounts at the establishments that remain open year-round.

EDGARTOWN
Very Expensive

Charlotte Inn 𝕮𝕮𝕮   Ask anyone to recommend the best inn on the island, and this is the name you're most likely to hear. It's one of only two Relais & Châteaux properties on the Cape and islands. Linked by formal gardens, each of the 18th- and 19th-century houses has a distinctive look and feel, though the predominant mode is English country. All but one of the rooms have TVs; some have VCRs. The bathrooms are luxurious, and some are bigger than most standard hotel rooms. **Catch at the Terrace** (𝕮 508/627-7200; www.catchrestaurant.com) is the on-site fine-dining restaurant.

27 S. Summer St. (in the center of town), Edgartown, MA 02539. 𝕮 508/627-4751. Fax 508/627-4652. 25 units (all with tub/shower). Summer $295–$695 double; $550–$895 suite. Rates include continental breakfast; full breakfast offered for extra charge ($15). AE, MC, V. Open year-round. No children under 14. **Amenities:** Fine-dining restaurant. *In room:* A/C, TV, hair dryer.

Harbor View Hotel 𝕮𝕮   This formerly grand 19th-century hotel is looking to regain its former glory by undergoing a multiyear renovation, estimated to cost $77 million. Among the changes, 21 smaller hotel rooms will be converted into 13 luxury suites, some with private gardens and outdoor showers. Parts of the hotel will remain open in season during the renovation. The shingle-style complex started out as two Gilded Age waterfront hotels, later joined by a 300-foot veranda that overlooks Edgartown Harbor and the lighthouse. Behind the hotel, there's a large pool surrounded by newer annexes, where some rooms and suites have kitchenettes. There is a new spa and fitness center scheduled to open in 2008. The hotel is just far enough from "downtown" Edgartown to avoid the traffic, but close enough for a pleasant walk past regal captain's houses. **The Coach House** (p. 286) serves three meals in an elegant setting.

131 N. Water St. (about ½ mile northwest of Main St.), Edgartown, MA 02539. 𝕮 800/225-6005 or 508/627-7000. Fax 508/627-8417. www.harbor-view.com. 124 units (all with tub/shower). Summer $350–$625 double; $775 one-bedroom suite; $825 two-bedroom suite; $1,250 three-bedroom suite. AE, DC, MC, V. Open year-round. **Amenities:** 2 restaurants (fine dining; more casual bar open daily for lunch and dinner—you can ask to be served by the pool); heated outdoor pool; 2 tennis courts; concierge; room service (seasonal only: breakfast, lunch, and dinner); babysitting; same-day laundry. *In room:* A/C, TV, Wi-Fi, fridge, hair dryer, iron, safe.

Hob Knob Inn 𝕮𝕮   Owner Maggie White's 19th-century Gothic Revival inn is an exquisite destination that vies for top honors as one of the Vineyard's best places to stay. Her style is peppy/preppy, with crisp floral fabrics and striped patterns creating a clean and comfortable look. The farm breakfast is a delight and is served at beautifully appointed individual tables in the sunny, brightly painted dining rooms. Bovine lovers will enjoy the agrarian theme, a decorative touch throughout the inn. The attentive staff will pack a splendid picnic basket or plan a charter fishing trip on Maggie's 27-foot Boston Whaler.

128 Main St. (on upper Main St., in the center of town), Edgartown, MA 02539. ℂ 800/696-2723 or 508/627-9510. Fax 508/627-4560. www.hobknob.com. 20 units, 4-bedroom cottage. Summer $300–$575 double. Rates include full breakfast and afternoon tea. AE, MC, V. Open year-round. **Amenities:** Exercise room; rental bikes ($20 per day); room service; massage (extra charge). *In room:* A/C, TV, hair dryer.

The Winnetu Inn & Resort 🌸🌸🌸   This large luxury hotel loaded with onsite activities sits on 11 acres overlooking South Beach in Katama. Guests can walk down a 250-yard path to get to the private beach, which is next to South Beach on the Atlantic Ocean. A 3-mile bike path links the inn to Edgartown, but the inn also runs a shuttle service that can pick up inn guests at the Edgartown ferry. Most rooms are two- and three-bedroom suites with kitchenettes, and there is one deluxe cottage with a four-person hot tub and a roof deck. Some guest rooms have ocean views and washer/dryers. Many have private decks or patios. The fine-dining restaurant, Lure, is a treat.

South Beach, Edgartown, MA 02539. ℂ 866/335-1133 or 508/310-1733. www.winnetu.com. 48 units. Summer $340 double; $470–$765 1-bedroom suite; $965–$1,475; $1,290–$1,475 2-bedroom suite. AE, MC, V. Closed Nov to mid-Apr. **Amenities:** Fine-dining restaurant; outdoor heated pool; putting green; tennis courts w/pro (6 Har-Tru, 4 all-weather); fitness room; childrens program (late June to early Sept complimentary 9am–noon; fee in evenings for ages 3 through preteens); free outdoor yoga classes; giant chess board; concierge; laundry facilities. *In room:* A/C, TV/DVD, fridge, coffeemaker, iron, microwave.

Expensive

Ashley Inn 🌸 *Value*   On Upper Main Street in Edgartown, this attractive B&B is just a short walk to the many shops and restaurants on Main Street and picturesque Edgartown Harbor. Innkeepers Fred and Janet Hurley have decorated the bedrooms in the 1860 captain's house with period antiques and quilts, and some rooms have canopy or four-poster beds. Thoughtful extras at this B&B include a little box of Chilmark Chocolates left on your pillow. A carriage house offers suites with a kitchen and whirlpool bath. In the morning, breakfast is served at individual tables in the dining room.

129 Main St., Edgartown, MA 02539. ℂ 508/627-9655. Fax 508/627-6629. www.ashleyinn.net. 10 units. Summer $205–$295 double. Rates include full breakfast. MC, V. Open year-round. *In room:* A/C, TV.

Colonial Inn of Martha's Vineyard 🌸🌸 *Kids*   This 1911 inn in the center of Edgartown has been transformed into a fine modern hotel, and recent extensive renovations have elevated it to what can accurately be described as "affordable luxury." Its lobby serves as a conduit to the Nevins Square shops beyond. The guest rooms are decorated in soothing, contemporary tones with pine furniture, crisp fabrics, hardwood floors, and beadboard wainscoting. Suites have VCRs (complimentary videos) and kitchenettes. Many rooms have gas fireplaces. Be sure to visit the roof deck, ideally around sunset or, if you're up for it, sunrise.

38 N. Water St., Edgartown, MA 02539. ℂ 800/627-4701 or 508/627-4711. Fax 508/627-5904. www.colonialinn mvy.com. 28 units. Summer $250–$425 double; $425–$895 suite or efficiency. Rates include continental breakfast and afternoon tea. AE, MC, V. Closed Dec–Mar, except for luxury suites in Residence Club, which are open year-round. Pets allowed in two designated suites for $30 per day. **Amenities:** Restaurant (Chesca's, see review below); fitness room and spa; shopping arcade. *In room:* A/C, TV, dataport, hair dryer, iron.

The Jonathan Munroe House 🏛🏛 *Finds*   With its graceful wraparound, colonnaded front porch, The Jonathan Munroe House stands out from the other inns and captains' homes on this stretch of upper Main Street. Inside, the formal parlor has been transformed into a comfortable gathering room with European flair. Guest rooms are immaculate, antique-filled, and dotted with clever details. Many rooms have fireplaces. At breakfast, don't miss the homemade waffles and pancakes, served on the sunny porch. Request the garden cottage if you are in a honeymooning mood.

100 Main St., Edgartown, MA 02539. ℂ 877/468-6763 or ℂ/fax 508/627-5536. www.jonathanmunroe.com. 6 units, 1 cottage. Summer $200–$265 double; $350 cottage. Rates include full breakfast and wine-and-cheese hour. AE, MC, V. Open year-round. No children under 12. *In room:* Wi-Fi, A/C, hair dryer.

Victorian Inn 🏛🏛   Do you long to stay at a quaint, reasonably priced inn that is bigger than a B&B but smaller than a Marriott? The Victorian Inn is a freshened-up version of those old-style hotels that used to exist in every New England town. There are enough rooms here so you don't feel as if you are trespassing in someone's home, yet there's a personal touch. With three floors of long, graceful corridors, the Victorian could serve as a stage set for a 1930s romance. Several rooms have canopy beds and balconies. The innkeepers are always quick to dispense helpful advice with good humor.

24 S. Water St. (in the center of town), Edgartown, MA 02539. ℂ 508/627-4784. www.thevic.com. 14 units. Summer $200–$385 double. Rates include full breakfast and afternoon tea. MC, V. Open year-round. Dogs welcome Nov–Mar. *In room:* A/C, TV, Wi-Fi, hair dryer, no phone.

Moderate

Edgartown Inn 🏛 *Value*   This lovely, centrally located 1798 Federal manse, a showplace even here on captain's row, offers perhaps the best value on the island. Nathaniel Hawthorne holed up here for nearly a year, and Daniel Webster also spent time here. The rooms are no-frills but pleasantly traditional; some have TVs and harbor views. Modernists may prefer the two cathedral-ceilinged quarters in the annex out back, which offer lovely light and a sense of seclusion. Service is excellent; be sure to say hello to Henry King, who has been on the staff for over 50 years.

56 N. Water St., Edgartown, MA 02539. ℂ 508/627-4794. Fax 508/627-9420. www.edgartowninn.com. 20 units, 4 with shared bathroom. Summer $125 shared bathroom; $170–$275 double. No credit cards. Closed Nov–Mar. No children under 8. *In room:* A/C, no phone.

OAK BLUFFS

Those looking for a basic motel with a central location can try **Surfside Motel,** across from the ferry dock on Oak Bluffs Avenue (ℂ **800/537-3007** or 508/693-2500). Summer rates are $150 to $175 for a double, $245 to $305 for suites. Well-behaved pets are allowed.

Expensive

The Oak House 🏛   An 1872 Queen Anne bayfront beauty has preserved all the luxury and leisure of the Victorian age. Innkeeper Betsi Convery-Luce trained at Johnson & Wales; her pastries are sublime. The common rooms are furnished in an opulent Victorian mode, as are the 10 guest rooms. Those toward the back are quieter, but those in front have Nantucket Sound views. This inn is very service oriented, and requests for feather beds, down pillows, or nonallergenic pillows are accommodated. Anyone intent on decompressing is sure to benefit from this immersion into another era—the one that invented the leisure class.

75 Seaview Ave. (on the sound), Oak Bluffs, MA 02557. ℂ 800/245-5979 or 508/693-4187. Fax 508/696-7385. www.vineyardinns.com. 10 units (1 tub/shower, 9 shower only). Summer $225–$275 double; $340–$350 suite. Rates include continental breakfast and afternoon tea. AE, DISC, MC, V. Closed late Oct to early May. *In room:* A/C, TV.

Moderate

The Dockside Inn ✿ (Kids)   Set close to the harbor, The Dockside is perfectly located for exploring the town of Oak Bluffs and is geared toward families. The welcoming exterior, with its colonnaded porch and balconies, duplicates the inns of yesteryear. Inside, the whimsical Victorian touches will transport you into the spirit of this rollicking town. Most of the cheerfully decorated rooms have either garden or harbor views; some have private decks. Location, charm, and flair make this a popular place, so book early.

9 Circuit Ave. Extension (Box 1206), Oak Bluffs, MA 02557. ℂ 800/245-5979 or 508/693-2966. Fax 508/696-7293. www.vineyardinns.com. 22 units. Summer $189–$225 suite; $295–$400 suite. Rates include continental breakfast. AE, DISC, MC, V. Closed late Oct to early Apr. *In room:* A/C, TV, hair dryer, iron.

The Oak Bluffs Inn ✿   This homey Victorian inn has a fun location at the top of Circuit Avenue, Oak Bluffs's main drag. The inn stands out with its colorful Victorian paint scheme and its prominent cupola, from which guests can enjoy a 360-degree view of Oak Bluffs. It's a 2-minute stroll from the inn to all the Oak Bluffs attractions, like the gingerbread cottages, the tabernacle, the Flying Horses Carousel, the waterfront park, and the ferries. Some of the rooms are a tad on the small side, but others are spacious and even have comfortable seating areas.

64 Circuit Ave. (at the corner of Pequot Ave.), Oak Bluffs, MA 02557. ℂ 800/955-6235 or 508/693-7171. Fax 508/693-8787. www.oakbluffsinn.com. 9 units. Summer $215–$300 double. Rates include continental breakfast. AE, MC, V. Closed Nov–Apr. *In room:* A/C, hair dryer, no phone.

Wesley Hotel ✿ (Value)   Formerly one of the grand hotels of Martha's Vineyard, this imposing 1879 property, right on the harbor, is now a solid entry in the good-value category, especially with its low off-season rates. It occupies a terrific location in Oak Bluffs, across the street from the harbor, in the center of the action. The only drawback here can be the noise from revelers on the boats in the harbor, or traffic on busy Lake Avenue. Most of the rooms are fairly compact and basic, though some are roomy with harbor views. The Wesley Arms, behind the main building, contains 33 air-conditioned rooms with private bathrooms, accessible by elevator. Eight suites and executive suites have kitchenettes. Reserve early to specify harbor views, which do not cost more than regular rooms. This is one of the few Vineyard hotels that does not require a minimum stay in season.

70 Lake Ave. (on the harbor), Oak Bluffs, MA 02557. ℂ 800/638-9027 or 508/693-6611. Fax 508/693-5389. www.wesleyhotel.com. 95 units (all with shower only). Summer $205–$245 double; $295 suite. AE, DISC, MC, V. Closed late Oct to Apr. *In room:* A/C, TV, no phone.

VINEYARD HAVEN (TISBURY)
Expensive

The Mansion House Inn ✿✿ (Finds)   After a fire burned down the 200-year-old Tisbury Inn several years ago, the owners decided to rebuild, making this one of the island's most full-service inns. The building, occupying a prominent corner location in Vineyard Haven, is a community hub, with a restaurant, health club, and shops. The three-story hotel is comfortable, with generous amenities. The rooms range in size from cozy to spacious, and prices vary accordingly. Many have kitchenettes, flatscreen TVs, and extra-large bathtubs. Some have harbor views. All the rooms are equipped with high-speed Internet service. One of the most unusual features of the inn is the 75-foot mineral-spring (no chlorine) swimming pool in the health club in the inn's basement. The restaurant, **Zephrus,** is open to the public for lunch and dinner, and also supplies room service for guests until late in the evening.

9 Main St., Vineyard Haven, MA 02568. © **888210-4504** or 508/693-2200. Fax 508/693-4095. www.mvmansion house.com. 40 units. $279–$329 double; $369–$516 suite. Rates include full buffet breakfast. AE, MC, V. **Amenities:** Restaurant (Zephrus, a fine-dining New American–style restaurant); health club and spa w/75-ft. pool. *In room:* A/C, Wi-Fi (fee), TV, fridge.

CHILMARK (INCLUDING MENEMSHA), WEST TISBURY & AQUINNAH
Very Expensive
Beach Plum Inn 🐠🐠 *Finds*   This country inn is set on 8 lush acres, with a lawn sloping gracefully down to Vineyard Sound. The room decor is predominantly cottage-y, though some rooms lean toward elegance. All but one room have decks or patios, some with views of Menemsha Harbor. Some units have canopied beds and are quite romantic. Linens are 275 thread-count and above; towels are Egyptian cotton. Five of the rooms have a whirlpool bath. The inn's restaurant is one of the best fine-dining spots on the island (see "Where to Dine," later).

Beach Plum Lane (off North Rd., ½ mile northeast of the harbor), Menemsha, MA 02552. © **877/645-7398** or 508/645-9454. Fax 508/645-2801. www.beachpluminn.com. 11 units. Summer $250–$400 double or cottage. Rates include full breakfast in season; continental breakfast off season. AE, DC, DISC, MC, V. Closed Nov–Apr. **Amenities:** Restaurant (fine dining); private beach passes; tennis court; croquet court; laundry service. Babysitting and in-room massage by arrangement. *In room:* A/C, TV, dataport, fridge, hair dryer, iron.

Expensive
Lambert's Cove Inn 🐠🐠   Set far off the main road and surrounded by apple trees and lilacs, this secluded estate suggests an age when time was measured in generations. In recent years, owners have upgraded the rooms and the decor, all done up in a sumptuous English country style. Some rooms have extras like Jacuzzi tubs, and all have sumptuous bedding. You'll find an all-weather tennis court on the grounds, a pool and hot tub, and the namesake beach 1 mile away. The inn's restaurant is known for skillfully prepared New American dinners.

Lambert's Cove Rd. (off State Rd., about 3 miles west of Vineyard Haven), West Tisbury, MA 02568. © **866/526-2466** or 508/693-2298. Fax 508/693-7890. www.lambertscoveinn.com. 15 units. Summer $220–$350 double. Rates include full breakfast. AE, MC, V. **Amenities:** Restaurant (New American cuisine dinner only; see review below); tennis court; heated pool, spa, private beach passes. *In room:* A/C, TV/DVD, CD, dataport., hair dryer, iron.

Menemsha Inn and Cottages 🐠🐠   Set in the pines near Menemsha Harbor, the Menemsha Inn is a place to revel in the outdoors (on 11 seaside acres) without distractions. The property is about a half-mile walk through a wooded path to the beach. There's no restaurant—just a restful breakfast room. Cottages have hair dryers, TVs, VCRs, DVDs, dataports, outdoor showers, barbecue grills, and kitchenettes. The most luxurious suites are located in the Carriage House, which has a spacious common room with a fieldstone fireplace. All rooms have private decks; most have water views. Guests have access to complimentary passes and shuttle bus service to the Lucy Vincent and Squibnocket private beaches.

Off North Rd. (about ½ mile northeast of the harbor), Menemsha, MA 02552. © **508/645-2521.** Fax 508/645-9500. www.menemshainn.com. 17 units, 12 cottages. Summer $265–$310 double; $575 suite; $2,200/week 2-bedroom cottage; $3,800–$4,200/week 3-bedroom cottage. Rates include continental breakfast for rooms and suites. AE, MC, V. Closed Nov–Apr. **Amenities:** Beach passes; tennis court; fitness room (step machine, treadmill, exercise bike, and free weights). *In room:* TV/VCR/DVD, dataport, fridge, hair dryer.

Moderate

The Captain R. Flanders House ★ *Finds*   Set amid 60 acres of rolling meadows crisscrossed by stone walls, this late-18th-century farmhouse has remained much the same for 2 centuries. The living room, with its broad-plank floors, is full of astonishing antiques. Two countrified cottages overlook the pond. The owners will provide you with a coveted pass to nearby Lucy Vincent Beach.

North Rd. (about ½ mile northeast of Menemsha), Chilmark, MA 02535. ☎ 508/645-3123. www.captainflanders. com. 5 units, 3 with shared bathroom; 2 cottages. Summer $80 single with shared bathroom; $175 double with shared bathroom; $195 double with private bathroom; $275 cottage. Rates include continental breakfast. AE, MC, V. Closed Nov to early May. **Amenities:** Private beach and shuttle bus passes. *In room:* No phone.

WHERE TO DINE

Outside Oak Bluffs and Edgartown, all of Martha's Vineyard is "dry," including Vineyard Haven, so bring your own bottle; some restaurants charge a small corkage fee.

EDGARTOWN
Very Expensive

Atria ★★★ NEW AMERICAN   This fine-dining restaurant set in an 18th-century sea captain's house gets rave reviews for its gourmet cuisine and high-caliber service. Pronounced with the emphasis on the second syllable (ah-TRE-ah), the name refers to the brightest of three stars forming the Southern Triangle constellation. You can sit in the elegant dining room, the rose-covered wraparound porch, or the brick cellar bar downstairs for more casual dining. The menu offers a variety of creative dishes with influences from around the country and around the world, with stops in the Mediterranean, the Middle East, and Asia. It features organic island-grown produce, off-the-boat seafood, local shellfish, and aged prime meats. Two popular starters are the miso soup with steamed crab dumplings and the Thai lemon-grass mussels. Unusual main courses include wok-fried Martha's Vineyard lobster or cracklin' pork shank with Southern collard greens. There is live entertainment in the bar, along the lines of acoustic guitar, on weekends.

137 Main St. (a short walk from the center of town). ☎ 508/627-5850. www.atriamv.com. Reservations recommended. Main courses $22–$33. AE, MC, V. June–Sept daily 5:30–10pm; call for off-season hours. Open year-round.

L'étoile ★★★ CONTEMPORARY FRENCH   The famous L'étoile has moved out of the Charlotte Inn and is now several blocks away, in the building that formerly housed the Tuscany Inn. Chef Michael Brisson is still in charge here, and he creates an ever-evolving menu devoted to local produce and seafood, along with delicacies flown in from the four corners of the earth. The menu changes often, but a typical meal here might begin with spice-crusted duck foie gras, then truffled beets with greens, and a main course of étuvée of native lobster with scallop and corn fritters. A small, less expensive bar menu ($15–$19) with items like spinach salad and roasted Cornish game hen is available in the bar nightly. A three-course chef's tasting menu is $98.

22 N. Water St. (off Main St.). ☎ 508/627-5187. Reservations recommended. Main courses $32–$57. MC, V. July to mid-Sept seatings daily 6–10pm; call for off-season hours. Closed late Nov to mid-Feb.

Lure ★★★ NEW AMERICAN   Though a bit out of the way—it's at the Winnetu Oceanside Resort, near Katama Beach—this restaurant does everything right. Executive Chef Ed Gannon, formerly of the Four Seasons Hotel in Boston, wows diners with his stylish preparations. Those fortunate enough to get a window seat or a spot on the deck can watch the sun set as they enjoy the fine cuisine and professional service. Menu selections make the most of local produce and seafood. You might begin

Moments   The Quintessential Lobster Dinner

When the basics—a lobster and a sunset—are what you crave, head to the **Home Port,** on North Road in Menemsha (📞 508/645-2679), a favorite of locals and visitors alike. At first glance, prices for the lobster dinners may seem a bit high, but note that they include an appetizer of your choice (go with the stuffed quahog), salad, amazing fresh-baked breads, a nonalcoholic beverage (remember, it's BYOB in these parts), and dessert. The decor is on the simple side, but who really cares? It's the riveting harbor views that have drawn fans to this family-friendly place for over 60 years. Locals not keen on summer crowds prefer to order their lobster dinners for pickup (less than half-price) at the restaurant door, then head down to Menemsha Beach for a private sunset supper. Reservations are required. Fixed-price platters range from $26 to $60. The Home Port is open mid-June to Labor Day daily at 5pm, with last reservations at 9pm. Call for off-season hours. It's closed mid-September to mid-May.

with Katama oysters, for example. As for main courses, there are unique choices like poached lobster with pea ravioli or wild king salmon with crabmeat-and-artichoke risotto. Homemade desserts like the caramelized apple charlotte are inspired.

At the Winnetu Oceanside Resort, Katama (South Beach). 📞 **508/627-3663.** Reservations recommended. Main courses $24–$37. MC, V. July–Aug daily 5:30–9:30pm; call for off-season hours. Closed Dec to mid-Apr.

Expensive

Alchemy 🐾🐾 FRENCH BISTRO   This spiffy restaurant is a slice of Paris on Main Street. Such esoteric choices as oyster brie soup and Burgundy Vintners salad share the bill with escargot-and-chanterelle fricassee. As befits a true bistro, there's a large selection of cocktails, liqueurs, and wines. In addition to lunch and dinner, a bar menu is served from 2:30 to 11pm. This choice isn't for everyone, but sophisticated diners will enjoy the Continental flair.

71 Main St. (in the center of town). 📞 **508/627-9999.** Reservations accepted. Main courses $22–$33. AE, MC, V. Apr–Nov daily noon–2:30pm and 5:30–10pm; call for off-season hours.

The Coach House 🐾🐾 NEW AMERICAN   This is a terrific place to have a drink or to dine, with its exquisite view of Edgartown Harbor and the lighthouse. The long and elegant bar is particularly smashing. The menu is simple but stylish. To start, there's soft-shell crab with arugula and teardrop tomatoes. As a main course, try the caramelized sea scallops with a salad of Asian pear and apple. Service is excellent; these are trained waiters, not your usual college surfer dudes. At the end of your meal, you may want to sit on the rockers on the Harbor View Hotel's wraparound porch and watch the lights twinkling in the harbor.

At the Harbor View Hotel (p. 280), 131 N. Water St. 📞 **508/627-7000.** Reservations recommended. Main courses $18–$35. AE, MC, V. Mon–Sat 7–11am and noon–2pm, Sun 8am–2pm, daily 6–10pm, call for off-season hours.

Détente 🐾🐾 NEW AMERICAN   Taking the French word for *relaxation* and *good relations,* this small Edgartown restaurant is working to be the choice for fine dining on the Vineyard. Fans of this intimate establishment cite the sophisticated wine bar and creative fine-dining cuisine. The menu is based on seasonal specials, featuring foods from local farms and markets. For starters, you can go light, with a spring watercress and spiced pecan salad, or heavy, with island lobster ravioli. The main courses are similarly varied, from pesto-marinated rack of lamb to orange curry–crusted monkfish. The wine list is extensive, with more choices available by the glass than anywhere else on the island.

Off Winter St. (in Nevins Sq. behind the Colonial Inn). © 508/627-8810. Reservations recommended. Main courses $28–$32. AE, MC, V. June–Aug Mon–Sat 5:30–10pm, Sun 11am–2pm and 5:30–10pm; call for off-season hours.

Moderate
Among the Flowers Cafe ★★ *Value* AMERICAN   Everything's fresh and appealing at this small outdoor cafe near the dock. The breakfasts are the best around, and the comfort-food dinners are among the most affordable options in this pricey town. There's almost always a wait, not just because it's so picturesque, but because the food is homey, hearty, and kind on the wallet.

Mayhew Lane. © 508/627-3233. Main courses $10–$18. AE, DC, DISC, MC, V. July–Aug daily 8am–9:30pm; May–June and Sept–Oct daily 8am–4pm. Closed Nov–Apr.

Chesca's ★★ *Finds* ITALIAN   This modern-decor restaurant at the Colonial Inn (p. 281) is a solid entry, with yummy food at reasonable prices. You're sure to find favorites like paella (with roasted lobster and other choice seafood), risotto (with roasted vegetables), and ravioli (with portobello mushrooms and asparagus). Smaller appetites can fill up on homemade soup and salad.

At the Colonial Inn, 38 N. Water St. © 508/627-1234. Reservations accepted for parties with 6 or more only. Main courses $18–$36. AE, MC, V. Late May to mid-October daily 5:30–10pm; Apr to late May Thurs–Sun; call for off-season hours. Closed mid-Oct to March.

Inexpensive
The Newes from America ★★ *Finds* PUB GRUB   The food is better than average at this subterranean tavern, built in 1742. Beers are a specialty here. Try a rack of five esoteric brews, or let your choice of food—from a wood-smoked oyster "Island Poor Boy" sandwich with linguiça (Portuguese-style sausage) relish to an 18-ounce porterhouse steak—dictate your draft. The menu comes handily annotated with recommendations. Don't miss the seasoned fries.

At The Kelley House, 23 Kelley St. © 508/627-4397. Main courses $9–$16. AE, MC, V. Daily 11:30am–11pm.

OAK BLUFFS
Expensive
Oyster Bar Grill ★★ NEW AMERICAN   Occupying a large space on Circuit Avenue, new owners have reinvented and reinvigorated this spot into a hip venue for the 30-something crowd. Specializing in seafood and—unusual for Martha's Vineyard—steak, the food preparations at the Oyster Bar are not fussy and are a bit less expensive than other similar island venues. The decor is also more casual. Live music on weekends in winter and year-round, and a hopping scene are centered on the huge oak bar. The Sunday brunch buffet attracts a large following.

67 Circuit Ave. © 508/693-6600. Reservations recommended. Main courses $16–$28. AE, MC, V. May–Nov Mon–Sat 4–11pm, Sun 11–3pm and 4–11pm; call for off-season hours.

Park Corner Bistro ★★★ *Finds* NEW AMERICAN   This superb restaurant in the center of Oak Bluffs is an intimate and cozy bistro that has a definite European aura. With just 10 tables, it's a romantic space for casual fine dining. Favorite appetizers are the beet salad and the Parmesan gnocchi, which is sautéed with chanterelle and black trumpet mushrooms. Move on to the Australian lamb loin with sweet corn flan and champagne corn emulsion. For dessert, don't miss the warm fruit cobbler with vanilla ice cream.

20 Kennebec Ave. (off Circuit Ave., across from the OB Post Office). © **508/696-9922**. Reservations recommended. Main courses $15–$28. AE, MC, V. July–Aug Mon–Sat 6–10pm, Sun noon–3pm and 6–10pm; call for off-season hours.

Sweet Life Cafe ✦✦✦ FRENCH/AMERICAN   Locals are crazy about this pearl of a restaurant, set in a restored Victorian house on upper Circuit Avenue. In season, the most popular seating is outside in the gaily lit garden. Fresh island produce is featured, with seafood specials an enticing draw. If the roasted lobster with potato-Parmesan risotto, roasted yellow beets, and smoked-salmon chive fondue is offered, order it.

63 Circuit Ave. © **508/696-0200**. Reservations recommended. Main courses $18–$35. AE, DISC, MC, V. Mid-May to Aug daily 5:30–10pm; Apr to mid-May and Sept–Nov Thurs–Mon 5:30–9:30pm. Closed Dec to mid-May.

Moderate

Lola's Southern Seafood ✦ SOUTHERN   This sultry New Orleans–style restaurant drips with atmosphere: crystal chandeliers; intricate wrought-iron, arched doorways; and starched linens in an ocher palette. Specialties include the chicken-and-seafood jambalaya and the baby back ribs. Meals are served family-style, with large helpings of side dishes. There's live entertainment nightly in season, while Sunday brunch also features live music. Off season, there's live music Friday and Saturday nights. A less-expensive pub menu ($10–$18) is served in the bar.

At the Island Inn, Beach Rd. © **508/693-5007**. www.lolassouthernseafood.com. Reservations accepted only for 5 or more. Main courses $19–$30. DC, MC, V. June–Aug daily 5–11pm; call for off-season hours. Closed Nov–Mar.

Inexpensive

Coop de Ville ✦ SEAFOOD   Of the several open-air harbor-front choices in Oak Bluffs, Coop de Ville has the best service and food. This outdoor fried-seafood shack serves up tasty beer-battered shrimp, grilled swordfish, lobster salad, and "world famous" chicken wings. It's a fun place to people-watch on sunny summer days as boaters cruise around the harbor.

Dockside Market Place, alongside Oak Bluffs Harbor. © **508/693-3420**. Most items $9–$20. MC, V. June–Aug daily 11am–10pm; call for off-season hours. Closed mid-Oct to Apr.

Sharky's Cantina ✦ MEXICAN   A swinging Mexican joint right on Circuit Avenue is the new hot spot in Oak Bluffs. Stretching from one end of the restaurant to the other, the large bar is packed five deep (with mostly young people) in the summer. It's within yelling distance of the dining area, where the margaritas wash down a standard array of quesadillas, tacos, enchiladas, and burritos. Although typical for a Mexican restaurant, the menu is an inexpensive rarity on the Vineyard. An unusual touch, the full menu is served until 12:30am.

31 Circuit Ave. © **508/693-7501**. Reservations accepted. Most items $6–$18. MC, V. Daily 11am–12:30am.

Slice of Life *Finds* DELI   This deli at the upper end of Circuit Avenue is the place to head for gourmet sandwiches, salads, and soups. There are just a handful of tables inside and more tables out on the screened porch in front. The eclectic menu includes burgers and pizza. All the food is very wholesome. There are also wine, beer, and specialty coffees.

50 Circuit Ave. ℂ 508/693-3838. Reservations not accepted. Most items under $10. MC, V. June–Aug daily 8am–8pm; call for off-season hours.

VINEYARD HAVEN (TISBURY)

Just around the corner from the Black Dog Tavern on Water Street, near the ferry terminal, is the **Black Dog Bakery** (ℂ **508/693-4786**). The doors open at 5am, and from midmorning on, it's elbowroom only as customers line up for freshly baked breads, muffins, and desserts that can't be beat. Don't forget some homemade doggie biscuits for your pooch.

Expensive

Black Dog Tavern ☆ NEW AMERICAN   How does a humble harbor shack come to be a national icon? Location helps. So do cool T-shirts. Soon after *Shenandoah* Capt. Robert Douglas decided, in 1971, that this hardworking port could use a good restaurant, influential vacationers stuck waiting for the ferry began to wander into this saltbox to tide themselves over with a bit of "blackout cake" or peanut-butter pie. The food is still home-cooking good, especially the seafood, and the blackout cake has lost none of its appeal. Though the lines grow ever longer, nothing much has changed at this beloved spot. Eggs Galveston for breakfast at the Black Dog Tavern is still one of the ultimate Vineyard experiences—go early, when it first opens, and sit on the porch, where the views are perfect.

Beach St. Extension (on the harbor), Vineyard Haven. ℂ **508/693-9223**. Reservations not accepted. Main courses $14–$27. AE, MC, V. June to early Sept daily 7–11am, noon–4pm, and 5–10pm; call for off-season hours.

Café Moxie ☆ NEW AMERICAN   A casual Vineyard-y atmosphere and top-notch food make this cafe a must-try. Starters like artichoke soup with fresh croutons and herbed potato gnocchi are deeply flavorful, as though all the ingredients were gathered from local gardens. Unusual combinations are a specialty, like the pan-seared scallops with pea risotto and warm apple-wood bacon sherry vinaigrette.

48 Main St. (in the center of town). ℂ **508/693-1484**. Reservations recommended. Main courses $22–$32. MC, V. Wed–Sat 11:30am–2:30pm; Tues–Sun 5:30–10pm. Closed Dec–Mar.

Le Grenier ☆☆ FRENCH   If Paris is the heart of France, Lyons is its belly—and that's where chef-owner Jean Dupon grew up on his *Maman*'s hearty cuisine. Dupon has the Continental moves down, as evidenced by such classics as steak au poivre; calves' brains Grenobloise with beurre noir and capers; and lobster Normande flambéed with Calvados, apples, and cream. Despite the fact that *Le Grenier* means (and, in fact, is housed in) "an attic," the restaurant is quite romantic, especially when aglow with hurricane lamps. Remember, you BYOB here.

96 Main St. (in the center of town). ℂ **508/693-4906**. Reservations suggested. Main courses $22–$32. AE, DC, DISC, MC, V. Daily 11am–2pm and 5:30–10pm. Open year-round.

Zephrus at the Mansion House Inn ☆☆ INTERNATIONAL   This hip restaurant is a great place to go for casual fine dining. Seating is at the sidewalk cafe on Main Street or inside by the hearth in view of the open kitchen. Main-course winners are pan-roasted pork tenderloin served with sweet 'tater tots, and shrimp and farfalle pasta. Though the menu is in constant flux, there is always a good vegetarian choice like the delicious vegetable risotto with truffle vinaigrette. Bring your favorite wine; the corkage fee is $5 per table.

9 Main St., Vineyard Haven ℂ **508/693-3416**. www.zephrus.com. Reservations recommended. Main courses $9–$20. AE, DC, DISC, MC, V. July–Aug daily 11:30am–3pm and 5:30–9pm; call for off-season hours.

Inexpensive

Art Cliff Diner ❀ ECLECTIC DINER   Expect the best diner food you've ever had at this quirky establishment. It's a short walk from the center of Vineyard Haven. Be aware that the hours are a little unreliable, and you should call to be sure it is open before making the trek. The food here is really scrumptious, whether you are having the just-caught fish of the day served with herbs from the chef's garden, or a simple burger, cooked just right. Desserts are homemade, of course.

39 Beach Rd. (a short walk from Main St.). ✆ 508/693-1224. Reservations not accepted. Main courses all under $15. No credit cards. July–Aug daily 7am–2pm; call for off-season hours. Closed Nov–Apr.

CHILMARK (INCLUDING MENEMSHA) & WEST TISBURY
Very Expensive

The Beach Plum Inn Restaurant ❀❀❀ INTERNATIONAL   This jewel of a restaurant is on a bluff overlooking the fishing village of Menemsha. Attention to quality has made this one of the island's top dining venues. Guests can dine inside in the spare but elegant dining room, or outside on the tiled patio. Chef James McDonough's most popular dishes include hazelnut-encrusted halibut with Marsala wine beurre blanc sauce. The most winning appetizer is the elaborate blackened lobster tips, served with mango cream sauce and house-cured gravlax with homemade wild rice and corn pancakes. For dessert, you'll flip for the chocolate quadruple-layer cake made with white and dark chocolate mousse and Chambord. In the spring and fall, there is usually an ethereal soufflé on the menu, either Grand Marnier or chocolate.

At the Beach Plum Inn, 50 Beach Plum Lane (off North Road), Menemsha. ✆ 508/645-9454. www.beachpluminn. com. Reservations required. Main courses $32–$42; 4-course fixed-price menu $68; off season only fixed-priced menu $50. AE, MC, V. Mid-June to early Sept daily seatings 5:30–6:45pm and 8–9:30pm; call for off-season hours. Closed Dec–Apr.

Lambert's Cove Inn Restaurant ❀❀ Finds NEW AMERICAN   One of the Vineyard's favorite chefs, Joe Silva, runs the kitchen at this romantic country inn. If you are staying in one of the down-island towns such as Edgartown or Oak Bluffs, driving through the wooded countryside to this secluded inn feels like an expedition to an earlier time. The interior of the restaurant is set up with crisp white tablecloths and antique furniture. In good weather, you can dine alfresco on a deck surrounded by flowering trees and shrubs. The menu features fresh seafood and island produce and meats. You might start with a crab and asparagus napoleon, or a simple but luscious cream-of-mushroom soup. Special dinner entrees include grilled marinated duck-breast casserole baked in a sherry lobster cream sauce. Desserts are homemade delicacies. Don't forget, the town of West Tisbury is "dry," so you must bring your own alcoholic beverages.

Lamberts Cove Rd. (off State Rd., about 3 miles west of Vineyard Haven), West Tisbury. ✆ 508/693-2298. Reservations recommended. Main courses $28–$38. AE, MC, V July–Aug daily 6–9pm; call for off-season hours.

Moderate

The Bite ❀❀ Finds SEAFOOD   It's usually places like The Bite that you crave when you think of New England. This is your quintessential "chowdah"-and-clam shack, flanked by picnic tables. The Bite makes superlative chowder, potato salad, fried fish, and so forth.

Basin Rd. (off North Rd., about ¼ mile northeast of the harbor), Menemsha. ✆ 508/645-9239. Main courses $18–$30. No credit cards. July–Aug daily 11am–8pm; call for off-season hours. Closed late Sept to Apr.

MARTHA'S VINEYARD AFTER DARK

All towns except Oak Bluffs and Edgartown are dry, and last call at bars and clubs is at midnight. Hit Oak Bluffs for the rowdiest bar scene and best nighttime street life. In Edgartown, you may have to hop around before you find the evening's most happening spot.

The Vineyard's top nightclub is at the airport, of all places. **Outerland** (formerly Hot Tin Roof) features comedy, rock, reggae, Latin, and blues from spring through fall. For schedule and more information, call ℂ **508/693-1137** or check out their website, www.outerlandmv.com.

Young and loud are the buzzwords at the **Lamppost** and the **Rare Duck,** 111 Circuit Ave., Oak Bluffs (ℂ **508/696-9352**), a pair of clubs in the center of town. The Lamppost features live bands and a dance floor; the Rare Duck, acoustic acts. This is where the young folk go, and the performers could be playing blues, reggae, R&B, or '80s. The cover is $1 to $5.

The Vineyard's first and only brewpub, **Offshore Ale Company,** 30 Kennebec Ave., Oak Bluffs (ℂ **508/693-2626**), is an attractively rustic place, with oak booths and peanut shells strewn on the floor. Local acoustic performers entertain 6 nights a week in season. The cover is $5.

The Ritz Cafe, 1 Circuit Ave., Oak Bluffs (ℂ **508/693-9851**), is a down-and-dirty hole-in-the-wall that features live music nightly in season and on weekends year-round. The cover is $2 to $3.

PERFORMING ARTS

The magnificent 1843 **Whaling Church,** 89 Main St., Edgartown (ℂ **508/627-4442**), functions primarily as a 500-seat performing-arts center offering lectures and symposia, films, plays, and concerts. Ticket prices vary; call for schedule.

The Vineyard Playhouse, 24 Church St., Vineyard Haven (ℂ **508/696-6300** or 508/693-6450; www.vineyardplayhouse.org), is an intimate black-box theater, where Equity professionals put on a rich season of favorites and challenging new work, followed, on summer weekends, by musical or comedic cabaret in the gallery/lounge. Children's theater selections are performed on Saturday at 10am. Townspeople often get involved in the outdoor Shakespeare production, a 3-week run starting in mid-July at the Tashmoo Overlook Amphitheatre, about 1 mile west of town.

2 Nantucket ⟨ℂ⟨ℂ⟨ℂ

Once the whaling capital of the world, this tiny island, 30 miles off the coast of Cape Cod, still counts its isolation as a defining characteristic. At only 3¹/₂×14 miles in size, Nantucket is smaller and more insular than Martha's Vineyard. But charm-wise, Nantucket stands alone—21st-century amenities wrapped in an elegant 19th-century package.

Sophisticated Nantucket Town features bountiful stores, quaint inns, cobblestone streets, interesting historic sites, and pristine beaches. The rest of the island is mainly residential, but for a couple of notable villages. **Siasconset** (nicknamed 'Sconset), on the east side of the island, is a tranquil community with picturesque, rose-covered cottages and a handful of businesses, including a pricey French restaurant. Sunset aficionados head to **Madaket,** on the west coast of the island, for the evening spectacular.

The lay of the land on Nantucket is rolling moors, cranberry bogs, and miles of exquisite public beaches. The vistas are honeymoon-romantic: an operating windmill, three lighthouses, and a skyline dotted with church steeples.

ESSENTIALS
GETTING THERE
BY FERRY   From Hyannis   Ferry service to Nantucket is fairly hassle-free, unless you're bringing a car in summer. But first-time visitors will find a car more a nuisance than a convenience, unless they're staying outside Nantucket Town.

From Hyannis (South St. Dock, take exit 7 off Rte. 6 and follow signs), the **Steamship Authority** (© 508/477-8600 in Hyannis, or 508/228-3274 in Nantucket; www.steamshipauthority.com) operates year-round ferry service for cars, passengers, and bicycles to Steamship Wharf on Nantucket using both high-speed and conventional ferries.

The Steamship Authority's **high-speed ferry** to Nantucket, *Iyanough* (© 508/495-3278), is for passengers only. It takes 1 hour and runs five times a day in season. Tickets cost $31 one-way ($61 round-trip) for adults, $23 one-way ($46 round-trip) for children 5 to 12. Parking costs $10 to $15 per day. Watch for the ferry parking signs on Route 6; if lots next to the dock are full, you may need to take exit 6 for a satellite lot, instead of exit 7 for the main lot. Satellite lots are on Lewis Bay Road, which is walking distance to the ferry terminal, and Yarmouth Road, from which you take a shuttle bus to the terminal. Passenger reservations are highly recommended on the high speed ferry.

Total trip time on the **conventional ferry** that carries cars is 2 hours and 15 minutes. There are six slow ferry trips a day in season. A round-trip fare for a car costs $370 to $420 from mid-May to mid-October, $250 to $290 the rest of the year. The higher rates are charged for vehicles more than 17 feet long. Car rates do not include drivers or passengers. Passenger tickets are $15 one-way ($30 round-trip) for adults, $7.75 one-way ($16 round-trip) for children 5 to 12; bikes cost $12 round-trip. Parking costs $10 to $12 per day; you do not need to make parking reservations.

No advance reservations are needed for passengers traveling without their cars on the conventional ferry. But if you bring your car in summer, you must reserve *months in advance*—only six boats make the trip daily, and they fill up fast. Arrive at least 1 hour before departure to avoid having your space given away. There is a $10 fee for canceling a reservation.

Hy-Line Cruises, Ocean Street Dock (© 888/778-1132 or 508/778-2600; for high-speed ferry reservations, call © 800/492-8082 or 508/778-0404; www.hy-line cruises.com), offers two types of passenger-only ferries from the Ocean Street Dock in Hyannis to Nantucket's Straight Wharf.

The Grey Lady, a year-round **high-speed** passenger ferry, makes the trip in 1 hour. The cost is $39 one-way ($71 round-trip) for adults, $29 one-way ($50 round-trip) for children 5 to 12, and $6 ($12 round-trip) for bicycles. The boat seats 260 and makes five to six round-trips daily in season; reserve in advance.

From early May through October, Hy-Line runs its standard 1-hour-and-50-minute **conventional ferry** service three times a day. Round-trip tickets are $39 for adults, $20 for children ages 5 to 12, and $10 extra for bikes. On busy holiday weekends, the slow ferry fills up, too, so order tickets in advance; buy or pick up your tickets at least half an hour before sailing time.

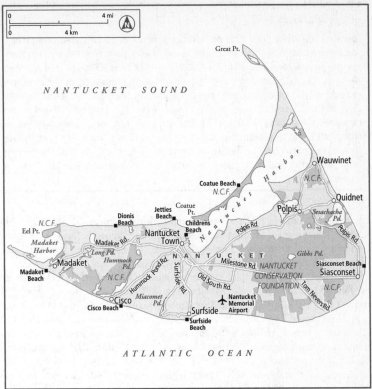

The standard ferry also has a **first-class section** with a private lounge, bathrooms, a bar, and a snack bar; a continental breakfast or afternoon cheese and crackers is also served onboard. No pets are allowed in the first-class section. Tickets in the first-class section are $52 for all ages.

Hy-Line's **"Around the Sound" cruise** is a 1-day round-trip excursion from Hyannis with stops on Nantucket and Martha's Vineyard. It runs from early June to late September. The price is $80 for adults, $50 for children 5 to 12, and $18 extra for bikes.

From Martha's Vineyard From Oak Bluffs on Martha's Vineyard, Hy-Line runs three passenger-only ferries to Nantucket from early June to mid-September (there is no car-ferry service btw. the islands). The trip time is 1 hour and 10 minutes. The one-way fare is $29 for adults, $17 for children 5 to 12, and $6 extra for bikes.

From Harwich Port You can avoid the summer crowds in Hyannis by boarding a passenger-only ferry with **Freedom Cruise Line,** 702 Rte. 28 in Harwich Port, across from Brax Landing (© **508/432-8999;** www.nantucketislandferry.com). From mid-May to mid-October, boats leave from Saquatucket Harbor in Harwich Port; the trip takes 1½ hours. Round-trip tickets are $51 for adults, $39 for children ages 2 to 11, $6 for children under 2, and $10 extra for bikes. Parking is free if you pick up your car the same day, but it's $15 for each night thereafter. Reservations are highly recommended.

(Tips) Parking

Because you won't need a car on Nantucket, consider parking your car in Hyannis before boarding the ferry to the island. If you are taking the **Hy-Line** ferry service from Ocean Street Dock (© **888/778-1132** or 508/778-2602) in July and August, it's a good idea to not only reserve tickets in advance, but also reserve a parking spot ahead of time. The all-day parking fee is $15 in season, and the lots are off Ocean Street, a short walk from the terminal. Travelers on **Steamship Authority** (© **508/477-8600**) vessels do not need a parking reservation. Parking at the Steamship Authority lots is $10 to $12 per day. Free shuttle buses take passengers to the Steamship terminal from off-site lots. The Hy-line and Steamship Authority ferry terminals are on opposite ends of Hyannis Harbor.

BY PLANE   You can fly into **Nantucket Memorial Airport** (© 508/325-5300), which is about 3 miles south of Nantucket Road on Old South Road. The flight to Nantucket takes 30 to 40 minutes from Boston, 15 minutes from Hyannis, and a little more than an hour from New York City airports.

Airlines providing service to Nantucket include **Cape Air/Nantucket Airlines** (© **800/352-0714**), year-round from Hyannis ($99 round-trip), Boston (about $271 round-trip), Martha's Vineyard ($86 round-trip), and New Bedford ($157 round-trip); **Continental Express** (© **800/525-0280**) from Newark, seasonally (about $520 round-trip); **Island Airlines** (© **508/228-7575**), year-round from Hyannis ($94 round-trip); and **Colgan/US Airways Express** (© **800/428-4322**), year-round from Boston ($383 round-trip) and New York ($499 and up round-trip).

Island Airlines and Nantucket Airlines both offer year-round charter service to the island.

GETTING AROUND

Nantucket is easily navigated on bike, moped, or foot, and also by shuttle bus or taxi. The chamber of commerce strongly suggests that visitors leave their cars behind in order to minimize congestion and environmental impact. If you're staying outside Nantucket Town, however, or if you plan to explore the outer reaches of the island, you might want to bring your car or rent one here. Keep in mind that if you do opt to travel by car, in-town traffic can reach gridlock in the peak season, and parking can be a nightmare.

BY BICYCLE & MOPED   Biking is a great way to get around Nantucket. The island is relatively flat, and paved bike paths abound—they'll get you from Nantucket Town to Siasconset, Surfside, and Madaket. There are also many unpaved back roads to explore, which makes mountain bikes a wise choice. Mopeds are also available, but be aware that local rules and regulations are strictly enforced. Mopeds are not allowed on sidewalks or bike paths. You'll need a driver's license to rent a moped, and state law requires that you wear a helmet.

You can bring your own bike over on the ferries for an additional charge. Otherwise, shops that rent bikes and mopeds (all within walking distance of the ferries) include **Cook's Cycle Shop, Inc.,** 6 S. Beach St. (© **508/228-0800**); **Nantucket Bike Shops,** at Steamboat Wharf and Straight Wharf (© **508/228-1999**); and

Young's Bicycle Shop, at Steamboat Wharf (© 508/228-1151), which also does repairs. Bike rentals average $20 to $30 for 24 hours.

BY SHUTTLE BUS   From June through September, inexpensive shuttle buses, with bike racks and wheelchair lifts, make a loop through Nantucket Town and to outlying spots; for routes and stops, contact the **Nantucket Regional Transit Authority** (© 508/228-7025; www.nantucket.net/trans/nrta) or pick up a schedule at the visitor center on Federal Street or the chamber of commerce office on Main Street. The cost is $1 to $2, and exact change is required. A 3-day pass can be purchased at the visitor center for $10. Dogs are allowed on the bus as long as they are relatively clean and dry.

BY CAR & JEEP   We recommend a car if you'll be here for more than a week or if you're staying outside Nantucket Town. Remember, though, there are no in-town parking lots; parking, although free, is limited.

Rental agencies on the island include **Affordable Rentals of Nantucket,** 6 S. Beach Rd. (© 508/228-3501); **Budget,** at the airport (© 800/527-0700 or 508/228-5666); **Hertz,** at the airport (© 800/654-3131 or 508/228-9421); **Nantucket Windmill Auto Rental,** at the airport (© 800/228-1227 or 508/228-1227); and **Young's 4X4 & Car Rental,** Steamboat Wharf (© 508/228-1151). A standard car costs about $100 per day in season; a four-wheel-drive rental costs about $185 per day (including an Over-Sand Permit).

BY TAXI   You'll find taxis (many are vans that can accommodate large groups or those traveling with bikes) waiting at the airport and at all ferry ports. During the busy summer months, we recommend reserving a taxi in advance to avoid a long wait upon arrival. Rates are flat fees, based on one person riding before 1am, with surcharges for additional passengers, bikes, and dogs. A taxi from the airport to Nantucket Town hotels will cost about $10. Reliable cab companies include **A-1 Taxi** (© 508/228-3330), **All Point Taxi** (© 508/228-5779), **Bev's Taxi** (© 508/228-7874), **Lisa's Taxi** (© 508/228-2223), and **Val's Cab Service** (© 508/228-9410).

VISITOR INFORMATION

For information, contact the **Nantucket Island Chamber of Commerce,** at 48 Main St., Nantucket, MA 02554 (© 508/228-1700; www.nantucketchamber.org). When you arrive, you should also stop by the **Nantucket Visitors Service and Information Bureau,** 25 Federal St. (© 508/228-0925). It's open daily from June to September; and Monday to Saturday from October to May. There are also information booths at Steamboat Wharf and Straight Wharf. Always check the island's newspaper, the *Inquirer & Mirror* (known locally as "The Inky"), for information on events and activities around town.

Nantucket Accommodations, P.O. Box 217, Nantucket, MA 02554 (© 508/228-9559; fax 508/325-7009; www.nantucketaccommodation.com), a 30-year-old private service, arranges advance reservations for inns, cottages, guesthouses, bed-and-breakfasts, and hotels; it has access to 95% of the island's lodging, in addition to houses and cottages available by the night or week (as opposed to most realtors, who will handle rentals for only 2 weeks or more). The charge for the service is $15, assessed only when a reservation is made. Last-minute travelers should keep in mind the **Nantucket Visitors Service and Information Bureau** (© 508/228-0925), a daily referral service for available rooms provided free by the town. It's not a booking service, but it always has the most updated list of accommodations availability and cancellations.

ATMs can be difficult to locate on Nantucket. **Nantucket Bank** (© 508/228-0580) has five locations: 2 Orange St., 104 Pleasant St., Amelia Street, the Hub on Main Street, and the airport lobby, all open 24 hours. **Pacific National Bank** has four locations: A&P Supermarket (next to the wharves), the Stop & Shop (open 24 hr. seasonally), the Steamship Wharf Terminal, and Pacific National Bank lobby (open during bank hours only).

In case of a **medical emergency,** the **Nantucket Cottage Hospital,** 57 Prospect St. (© **508/228-1200**), is open 24 hours.

BEACHES & OUTDOOR PURSUITS

BEACHES   In distinct contrast to Martha's Vineyard, virtually all of Nantucket's 110-mile coastline is open to the public.

- **Children's Beach:** This small beach is a protected cove just west of busy Steamship Wharf. Appealing to families, it has a park, a playground, restrooms, lifeguards, a snack bar, and even a bandstand for free weekend concerts.

- **Cisco Beach** 👧👧: About 4 miles from town, in the southwestern quadrant of the island (from Main St., turn onto Milk St., which becomes Hummock Pond Rd.), Cisco enjoys vigorous waves—great for the surfers who flock here, not so great for the waterfront homeowners. Restrooms and lifeguards are available.

- **Coatue Beach** 👧: This fishhook-shaped barrier beach, on the northeastern side of the island at Wauwinet, is Nantucket's outback, accessible only by four-wheel-drive vehicles, watercraft, or the very strong-legged. Swimming is strongly discouraged because of fierce tides.

- **Dionis Beach** 👧👧👧: About 3 miles out of town (take the Madaket bike path to Eel Point Rd.) is Dionis, which enjoys the gentle Nantucket Sound surf and steep, picturesque bluffs. It's a great spot for swimming, picnicking, and shelling, and you'll find fewer children than at Jetties or Children's beaches. Stick to the established paths to prevent further erosion. Lifeguards patrol here, and restrooms are available.

- **Jetties Beach** 👧👧👧: Located about a half-mile west of Children's Beach on North Beach Street, Jetties is about a 20-minute walk, or an even shorter bike ride, shuttle bus ride, or drive, from town (there's a large parking lot, but it fills up early on summer weekends). It's another family favorite for its mild waves, lifeguards, bathhouse, and restrooms. Facilities include the town tennis courts, volleyball nets, a skate park, and a playground; watersports equipment and chairs are also available to rent. In August, Jetties hosts an intense sand-castle competition, and the Fourth of July fireworks are held here.

- **Madaket Beach** 👧👧👧: Accessible by Madaket Road, by the 6-mile bike path that runs parallel to it, and by shuttle bus, this westerly beach is narrow and subject to pounding surf and sometimes serious crosscurrents. Unless it's a fairly tame day, you might content yourself with wading. It's the best spot on the island for admiring the sunset. Facilities include restrooms, lifeguards, and mobile food service.

- **Siasconset ('Sconset) Beach** 👧👧: The easterly coast of 'Sconset is as pretty as the town itself and rarely, if ever, crowded, perhaps because of the water's strong sideways tow. You can reach it by car, by shuttle bus, or via the Polpis or Milestone bike paths, about an 8-mile trip. Lifeguards are usually on duty, but the closest facilities (restrooms, grocery store, and cafe) are back in the center of the village.

• **Surfside Beach** 𝕮𝕮𝕮: Three miles south of town via a popular bike/skate path, broad Surfside—equipped with lifeguards, restrooms, and a surprisingly accomplished little snack bar—is appropriately named and very popular. It draws thousands of visitors a day in high season, from college students to families, but the free-parking lot can fit only about 60 cars—you do the math, or better yet, ride your bike or take the shuttle bus.

BICYCLING 𝕮𝕮𝕮   Several paved bike paths radiate out from the center of town to outlying beaches. The **bike paths** run about 6 miles west to Madaket, 3.5 miles south to Surfside, and 8 miles east to 'Sconset. To avoid backtracking from 'Sconset, continue north through the charming village, and return on the **Polpis Road bike path** 𝕮𝕮. Strong riders could do a whole circuit of the island in a day, but most will be content to combine a single route with a few hours at a beach.

For a free map of the island's bike paths, stop by **Young's Bicycle Shop,** at Steamboat Wharf (© **508/228-1151**). It's definitely the best place for bike rentals. See "Getting Around," above, for more bike-rental shops.

FISHING   For shellfishing, you'll need a permit from the **harbormaster's office,** at 34 Washington St. (© **508/228-7261**). You'll see surf-casters all over the island (no permit is required); for a guided trip, try Mike Monte of **Surf & Fly Fishing Trips** (© **508/228-0529**). Deep-sea charters heading out of Straight Wharf include Capt. Bob DeCosta's *The Albacore* (© **508/228-5074**), Capt. Josh Eldridge's *Monomoy* (© **508/228-6867**), and Capt. David Martin's *Absolute* (© **508/325-4000**).

NATURE TRAILS   Through preservationist foresight, about one-third of Nantucket's shoreline is protected from development. Contact the **Nantucket Conservation Foundation,** at 118 Cliff Rd. (© **508/228-2884**), for a map of its holdings ($4), which include the 205-acre **Windswept Cranberry Bog** (off Polpis Rd.), where bogs are interspersed amid hardwood forests; and a portion of the 1,100-acre **Coskata–Coatue Wildlife Refuge** 𝕮𝕮, comprising the barrier beaches beyond Wauwinet (see "Organized Tours & Cruises," below). **The Maria Mitchell Association** (see "Museums & Historic Landmarks," below) sponsors guided birding and wildflower walks in season.

WATERSPORTS   **Nantucket Community Sailing** manages the concession at **Jetties Beach** (© **508/228-5358**), which offers lessons and rents out kayaks, sailboards, sailboats, and more. **Sea Nantucket,** on tiny Francis Street Beach off Washington Street (© **508/228-7499**), also rents kayaks; it's a quick sprint across the harbor to beautiful Coatue.

MUSEUMS & HISTORIC LANDMARKS

Hadwen House 𝕮𝕮   During Nantucket's most prosperous years, whaling merchant Joseph Starbuck built the "Three Bricks" (nos. 93, 95, and 97 Main St.) for his three sons. His daughter married successful businessman William Hadwen, owner of the candle factory that is now the Whaling Museum, and Hadwen built this grand Greek Revival home across the street from his brothers-in-law in 1845. Although locals (mostly Quakers) were scandalized by the opulence, the local outrage spurred Hadwen on, and he decided to make the home even grander than he had originally intended. It soon became a showplace for entertaining the Hadwens' many wealthy friends. The home has been furnished with period pieces, and the gardens have been maintained in period style.

96 Main St. (at Pleasant St., a few blocks southwest of the town center). © **508/228-1894**. www.nha.org. Admission included in Nantucket Historical Association's History Ticket ($18 adults, $9 children under 16). AE, MC, V. June–Sept Mon–Sat 10am–5pm, Sun noon–5pm; call for off-season hours. Closed Dec–Mar.

Jethro Coffin House ✿   This 1686 saltbox is the oldest building left on the island. A National Historical Landmark, the brick design on its central chimney has earned it the nickname "The Horseshoe House." It was struck by lightning and severely damaged (in fact, nearly cut in two) in 1987, prompting a long-overdue restoration. It's filled with period furniture such as a trundle bed on wooden wheels.

Sunset Hill Rd. (off W. Chester Rd., about ½ mile northwest of the town center). © **508/228-1894**. www.nha.org. Admission included in Nantucket Historical Association's History Ticket ($18 adults, $9 children). AE, MC, V. Late May to mid-Oct Mon–Sat 10am–5pm; Sun noon–5pm. Closed mid-Oct to late May.

The Maria Mitchell Association ✿✿ *Kids*   This is a group of six buildings organized and maintained in honor of distinguished astronomer and Nantucket native Maria Mitchell (1818–89). The science center consists of astronomical observatories, with a lecture series, children's science seminars, and stellar observation opportunities (when the sky is clear) from the **Loines Observatory,** at 59 Milk St. Extension (© **508/228-8690**), and the **Vestal Street Observatory,** at 3 Vestal St. (© **508/228-9273**).

The **Hinchman House Natural Science Museum** (© **508/228-0898**), at 7 Milk St., houses a visitor center and offers lectures, bird-watching, wildflower and nature walks, and discovery classes for children and adults. The **Mitchell House** (© **508/228-2896**), at 1 Vestal St., the astronomer's birthplace, features a children's history series and adult-artisan seminars, and has wildflower and herb gardens. The **Science Library** (© **508/228-9219**) is at 2 Vestal St., and the tiny, child-oriented **aquarium** (© **508/228-5387**) is at 28 Washington St.

4 Vestal St. (at Milk St., about ½ mile southwest of the town center). © **508/228-9198**. www.mmo.org. Admission to each site: $5 adults, $4 children. Museum pass (for birthplace, aquarium, science museum, and Vestal St. Observatory) $10 adults, $8 children ages 6–14. MC, V. Early June to late Aug Tues–Sat 10am–4pm; call for off-season hours.

Nantucket Life-Saving Museum ✿✿ *Finds*   Housed in a replica of the Nantucket Life-Saving Station, the museum has loads of interesting exhibits, including historic photos and newspaper clippings, as well as one of the last remaining Massachusetts Humane Society surf boats and its horse-drawn carriage.

158 Polpis Rd. (2½ miles east of town) © **508/228-1885**. Admission $5 adults, $2 children. Mid-June to mid-Oct daily 9:30am–4pm.

Whaling Museum ✿✿✿ *Kids*   Reopened in 2005 after a grand multimillion-dollar renovation, this museum is a showpiece in the region. Appropriately, it is housed in a former spermaceti-candle factory (candles used to be made from a waxy fluid extracted from sperm whales). Kids will love the awe-inspiring skeleton of a 43-foot finback whale (stranded in the 1960s), and adults will be fascinated by the exceptional collections of scrimshaw and nautical art. (Check out the action painting, *Ship Spermo of Nantucket in a Heavy Thunder-Squall on the Coast of California 1876,* executed by a captain who survived the storm.) A wall-size map depicts the 'round-the-world meanderings of the *Alpha,* accompanied by related journal entries. The admission price includes daily lectures on the brief and colorful history of the industry, like the beachside "whalebecue" feasts that natives and settlers once enjoyed. Don't miss the gift shop on the way out.

Nantucket Town

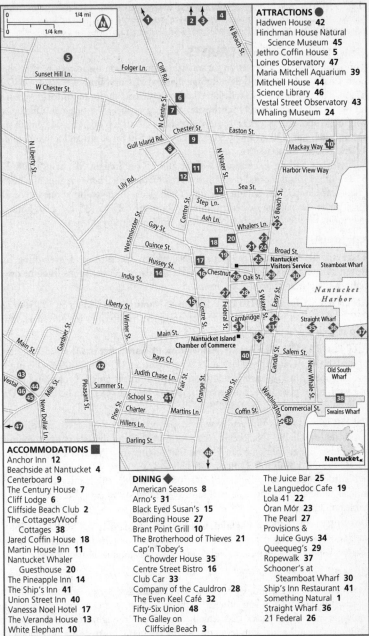

13 Broad St. (in the center of town). ℭ 508/228-1894. www.nha.org. Admission $15 adults, $8 children 5–14. Admission is also included in the Nantucket Historical Associations History Ti cket ($18 adults, $9 children). AE, MC, V. Apr–Nov Mon–Wed 10am–5pm; Thurs 10am–9pm; Fri–Sat 10am–5pm; Sun noon–5pm. Closed Dec–Mar.

ORGANIZED TOURS & CRUISES

The Trustees of the Reservations, a statewide conservation organization, runs the 3-hour **Coskata–Coatue Wildlife Refuge Natural History Tour** ✶✶✶ (ℭ 508/228-6799). The trip via Ford Expedition takes you over sand dunes and through rare habitat out to the **Great Point Lighthouse,** a replica of the 1818 original. On the way, you might spot snowy egrets, ospreys, and terns. Tours are offered mid-May to mid-October, daily at 9:30am and 1:30pm. The cost is $40 for adults and $15 for children 12 and under; call to reserve.

Endeavor **Sailing Excursions** ✶✶, at Slip 15 on Straight Wharf (ℭ 508/228-5585), offers jaunts around the harbor on the *Endeavor,* a 31-foot replica of a historic Friendship sloop. Skipper James Genthner will gladly drop you off at one the beaches for a bit of sunbathing or beachcombing. Rates are $25 to $35 for a 1½-hour sail; reservations are recommended. No sailings November through April.

SHOPPING

There are dozens of upscale shops in Nantucket, specializing in everything from woven sweaters to golden Nantucket basket necklaces. All the shops listed below are right in the center of Nantucket Town.

ANTIQUES/COLLECTIBLES   Tonkin of Nantucket, 33 Main St. (ℭ 508/228-9697), specializes in English and French antiques. Its offerings include silver, china, ship models, and majolica.

ART & CRAFTS   The Artists' Association of Nantucket has the widest selection of work by locals, and the gallery at 19 Washington St. (ℭ 508/228-0294) is impressive. It's open April through January and by appointment only February and March.

Exquisite art glass, as well as ceramics, jewelry, and basketry, can be found at **Dane Gallery,** 28 Centre St. (ℭ 508/228-7779).

FASHION   Martha's Vineyard may have spawned "Black Dog" fever, but this island boasts the inimitable "Nantucket reds"—cotton clothing that starts out tomato-red and washes out to salmon-pink. The fashion originated at **Murray's Toggery Shop,** 62 Main St. (ℭ 800/368-2134 or 508/228-0437).

Nantucket Looms, 26 Federal St. (ℭ 508/228-1908), sells hand-woven cashmere, mohair, and cotton sweaters, as well as scarves, throws, and rugs that are made in the workshop upstairs.

JEWELRY   Diana Kim England, Goldsmiths, 56 Main St. (ℭ 508/228-3766), is a team of five goldsmiths that have over 70 years of combined experience in making jewelry. You'll find gold baskets and pearls, as well as unique custom pieces.

WHERE TO STAY

As with Martha's Vineyard, we've given only summer rates here, because Nantucket is so seasonal. However, if you do visit in the off season, you can find substantial discounts at any of the places that remain open. Note, though, that lodging rates on Nantucket are at high-season levels during the popular Christmas Stroll in December and Daffodil Festival in April.

VERY EXPENSIVE

Cliffside Beach Club ★★★ *Finds* Right on the beach and a 15-minute walk from town, this is the premier lodging on the island. It may not be as fancy as some, but there's a sublime beachy-ness to the whole setup, from the simply decorated rooms and the cheerful, youthful staff to the colorful umbrellas lined up on the beach. All guest rooms have such luxuries as French milled soaps, thick towels, and exceptional linens. Lucky guests on the Fourth of July get a front-row seat for the fireworks staged at Jetties Beach nearby.

46 Jefferson Ave. (about 1 mile from town center), Nantucket, MA 02554. © 800/932-9645 or 508/228-0618. Fax 508/325-4735. www.cliffsidebeach.com. 25 units, 1 cottage. Summer $450–$710 double; $875–$1,745 suite; $900 3-bdrm apt; $1,085 cottage. There is a 5.3% service charge in addition to taxes. Rates include continental breakfast. AE. Closed mid-Oct to late May. **Amenities:** Restaurant (The Galley, an elegant French bistro; p. 306,); exercise facility (Cybex equipment and a trainer on staff); indoor hydrotherapy spa; steam saunas; concierge; climate-controlled massage room; babysitting. *In room:* A/C, TV/DVD, fridge, coffeemaker, hair dryer.

Nantucket Whaler Guesthouse ★★ This 1850s sea captain's house is unique, in that each room is a suite with its own entrance and kitchen facilities. Compared to other B&Bs on the island, the Nantucket Whaler Guesthouse has a particularly private feel, almost like having your own apartment. All rooms are comfortably outfitted with cottage-y furnishings, including overstuffed couches and stacks of games and books.

8 North Water St. (in the center of town), Nantucket, MA 02554. © 800/462-6882 or 508/228-6597. Fax 508/228-6291. www.nantucketwhaler.com. 12 units (8 with tub/shower, 4 with shower only). Summer $325–$495 double; $595–$650 2-bedroom suite. AE, DC, MC, V. Closed mid-Dec to late Apr. No children under age 12. *In room:* A/C, TV/VCR/DVD, CD player, dataport, kitchenette, hair dryer, iron.

Vanessa Noel Hotel *Overrated* This is Nantucket's trendiest inn. Vanessa Noel, a shoe designer whose shoe store is on the first floor, has decorated the eight rooms in this historic building with boutique hotel features like Philippe Starck fixtures, Bulgari toiletries, 15-inch flatscreen televisions, and minibars stocked with the hotel's bottled water. Most of the rooms are tiny (particularly given the prices), though there are two, including a fun attic space, that are fairly spacious. There are more rooms next door at **Vanessa Noel Hotel Green** (© **508/228-5300**), which has an ecological theme, using organic cottons on the bedding and eco-friendly toiletries. **The Café V Bar** (© **508/228-8133**), a caviar and champagne bar on the first floor, serves breakfast fare, like huevos rancheros or a lobster omelet, as well as light dinner fare nightly. The decor includes novelties like leopard-print calfskin banquettes and two swings, and the food is imported from Caviarteria, the New York City caviar emporium.

5 Chestnut St. (in the center of town), Nantucket, MA 02554. © **508/228-5300**. Fax 508/228-8995. www.vanessa noelhotel.com. 8 units. Summer $350–$480 double. AE, DISC, MC, V. *In room:* A/C, TV, minibar, hair dryer.

The Wauwinet ★★ This beachfront retreat is Nantucket's only Relais & Châteaux property. It is also one of the few inns not within walking distance of town, though a shuttle bus offers fairly convenient service. The inn is next to a wildlife sanctuary and is nestled between the Atlantic Ocean and Nantucket Bay. Each lovely room is individually decorated, with pine armoires, plenty of wicker, exquisite Audubon prints, and handsome fabrics, though some are on the small side. Extras include robes, bottled water, and a personalized set of engraved note cards. The staff goes to great lengths to please, ferrying you into town, for instance, or dispatching you on a 21-foot launch across the bay to your own private strip of beach in season.

120 Wauwinet Rd. (P.O. Box 2580), about 8 miles east of Nantucket center, Nantucket, MA 02554. ⓒ **800/426-8718** or 508/228-0145. Fax 508/325-0657. www.wauwinet.com. 25 units, 10 cottages (all with tub/shower). Summer $780–$900 double; $1,000–$1,400 cottage. Rates include full breakfast and afternoon wine and cheese. AE, DC, MC, V. Closed Nov to mid-May. **Amenities:** Restaurant (fine dining); 2 clay tennis courts w/pro shop and teaching pro; croquet lawn; rowboats, sailboats, sea kayaks, and mountain bikes on loan; concierge; room service (8am–9pm). *In room:* A/C, flatscreen TV/DVD, CD player, hair dryer, iron.

White Elephant ⓖⓖⓖ   This luxury property, right on the harbor, is the ultimate in-town lodging. Guest rooms (distributed among 1 building and 12 cottages) are big and airy (the most spacious on Nantucket), with country-chic decor. About half the rooms have working fireplaces, and most have harbor views. The same company owns Breakers, a 25-room hotel next door that offers a less bustling atmosphere. The Brant Point Grill, the pricey restaurant on-site, serves three meals a day. There is a brand-new spa on-site offering a range of services.

50 Easton St. (P.O. Box 1139), Nantucket, MA 02554. ⓒ **800/445-6574** or 508/228-2500. Fax 508/325-1195. www.whiteelephanthotel.com. 53 units (51 with tub/shower, 2 with shower only). Summer $600–$750 double; $730–$1,300 suites. Rates include full breakfast. AE, DC, DISC, MC, V. Closed Dec–Mar. **Amenities:** Restaurant (lobster and steakhouse serving breakfast, lunch, and dinner daily, plus an afternoon raw bar); spa offering facials, body treatments, and massage (in-room or in spa area); exercise room; concierge; business lounge; full room service (7am–11pm); fee-based laundry and dry-cleaning service. *In room:* A/C, TV/DVD, CD, dataport, fridge, hair dryer, iron, safe.

EXPENSIVE

Beachside at Nantucket ⓖ   No ordinary motel, the Beachside has 90 guest rooms that have been lavished with Provençal prints and handsome rattan and wicker furniture; the patios and decks overlooking the central courtyard with its heated pool have been prettified with French doors and latticework. Note that the Beachside has very reasonable off-season rates—$110 a night in the spring.

30 N. Beach St. (about ¾ mile west of the town center), Nantucket, MA 02554. ⓒ **800/322-4433** or 508/228-2241. Fax 508/228-8901. www.thebeachside.com. 90 units (all with tub/shower). Summer $325–$420 double; $750–$850 suite. Rates include continental breakfast. AE, DC, DISC, MC, V. Closed late Oct to late Apr. **Amenities:** Heated outdoor pool. *In room:* A/C, TV, Wi-Fi, fridge, hair dryer, iron. Pet-friendly.

The Cottages/Woof Cottages ⓖⓖ   These small apartments have the best location on the island, stacked up on a wharf that juts out into Nantucket Harbor. If you are looking for a place on Nantucket where you can bring your pooch, these one- and two-bedroom cottages are the perfect choice. All cottages are fresh and sparkling—floors polished, walls painted—and each has an eat-in kitchen and cozy living-room area. Dogs get a welcome basket of treats and a Nantucket bandana. Guests have privileges at the **White Elephant spa,** a sister property.

One Old South Wharf (in the center of town), Nantucket, MA 02554. ⓒ **866/838-9253** or 508/325-1499. Fax 508/325-1173. www.harborviewcottages.com. 33 units (all with tub/shower). Summer $490–$720 studio and 1-bedroom; $590–$1,090 2-bedroom, $990–$1,200 3-bedroom. AE, MC, V. Closed mid-Oct to May. *In room:* TV/VCR/CD, Wi-Fi (fee), kitchenette, hair dryer. Pet-friendly.

Jared Coffin House ⓖⓖ *Kids*   This grand brick manse built in 1845 is the social center of town. Accommodations in two historic buildings range from well-priced singles to spacious doubles. The central location does have a drawback: Front rooms can be quite noisy. Beginning in the summer of 2008, the inn will be the location for the Chinese restaurant, the Harbor Wok. Inn guests get spa privileges and a discount on breakfast and lunch at the Brant Point Grill, the inn's sister property on the harbor.

29 Broad St. (at Centre St.), Nantucket, MA 02554. © 800/248-2405 or 508/228-2400. Fax 508/228-8549. www.jaredcoffinhouse.com. 60 units (52 with tub/shower, 8 with shower only). Summer $280–$450 double. AE, DC, DISC, MC, V. **Amenities:** Restaurant (Chinese); concierge. *In room:* TV, Wi-Fi (fee), fridge, coffeemaker, hair dryer, iron.

The Pineapple Inn 🌟🌟 This beautifully renovated historic inn is one of the premier places to stay on the island. The graceful Quaker entrance of the 1838 home leads to spacious guest rooms decorated with fine reproductions and antiques, Oriental rugs, marble bathrooms, and many four-poster canopy beds. The continental breakfast here is extra deluxe with fresh baked goods, espresso, cappuccino, and freshly squeezed orange juice. Inn guests can use the pool and private Atlantic Ocean beach at one of the inn's sister properties in 'Sconset.

10 Hussey St. (in the center of town), Nantucket, MA 02554. © 508/228-9992. Fax 508/325-6051. www. pineappleinn.com. 12 units (8 with tub/shower, 4 with shower only). Summer $165–$350 double. Rates include continental breakfast. AE, MC, V. Closed early Dec to mid-Apr. No children under age 8. *In room:* A/C, TV, dataport, hair dryer, iron.

Union Street Inn 🌟🌟 *Finds* Innkeepers Deborah and Ken Withrow have a terrific location for their 1770s property, a quiet residential section that's just steps from Main Street. Ken's experience in big hotels shows in the full concierge service offered here. Many guest rooms have canopied or four-poster beds; half have working wood-burning fireplaces. All are outfitted with antique furniture and fixtures. Unlike many Nantucket inns forbidden by zoning laws to serve a full breakfast, this inn's location allows for a superb complete breakfast on the garden patio.

7 Union St. (in the center of town), Nantucket, MA 02554. © 800/225-5116 or 508/228-9222. Fax 508/325-0848. www.unioninn.com. 12 units (1 with tub/shower, 11 with shower only). Summer $345–$445 double; $525 suite. Rates include full breakfast. AE, MC, V. Closed Jan to mid-Apr. *In room:* A/C, TV, CD player, Wi-Fi, hair dryer, no phone.

The Veranda House 🌟🌟 *Finds* This classic guesthouse, formerly known as the Overlook Hotel, has reinvented itself as a "retro chic" hotel with hip decor and deluxe amenities like flatscreen TVs and Simon Pearce lamps. Beds are made up with Frette linens and goose down comforters. The three-story inn, with a view of Nantucket Harbor, is located in a quiet neighborhood, a short walk from the center of town. Wraparound porches surround the inn and serve as the communal area for enjoying the sunshine or meeting fellow guests. The less expensive rooms are on the small side but smartly decorated. Other rooms and suites are quite spacious. Breakfast, which features hot delicacies like artisan cheeses and fresh-baked pastries, is served on the ample front porch.

Three Step Lane (a few blocks from town center), Nantucket, MA 02554. © 877/228-0695 or 508/228-0695. Fax 508/374-0406. www.theverandahouse.com. 18 units, 7 with shared bathroom. Summer $229–$439 double; $219–$589 suites. Rates include continental breakfast. AE, MC, V. Closed Nov to late May. *In room:* A/C, TV/DVD, Wi-Fi, hair dryer.

MODERATE

Anchor Inn 🌟 *Value* This historic gem, an 1806 captain's home, is next to the Old North Church. Another property, 72 Centre St., is three doors down from the inn. Authentic details can be found throughout both houses, in the antique hardware and paneling, wide-board floors, and period furnishings. The five rooms in the 72 Centre St. house are a particularly good value; they are smaller and less expensive.

66 Centre St. (P.O. Box 387, in the center of town), Nantucket, MA 02554. © 508/228-0072. www.anchor-inn.net. 16 units (2 with tub/shower, 14 with shower only). Summer $195–$245 double, $250–$285 suites. Rates include continental breakfast. AE, MC, V. Closed Jan–Feb. *In room:* A/C, TV, hair dryer.

Centerboard 🌸🌸 This updated 1886 home boasts parquet floors, Oriental rugs, lavish fabrics, plush feather mattresses, and lace-trimmed linens. Of the inn's seven bedrooms, the first-floor suite is perhaps the most romantic, with a green-marble Jacuzzi and a private living room with fireplace. Other rooms and bathrooms are on the compact side, as befits a Victorian-era building.

8 Chester St. (in the center of town), Nantucket, MA 02554. © **508/228-9696.** Fax 508/325-4798. www. centerboardguesthouse.com 7 units. Summer $225–$285 double; $365–$450 suite. Rates include continental breakfast. AE, MC, V. Closed Nov–Apr. *In room:* A/C, TV, Wi-Fi, fridge, hair dryer.

The Century House 🌸 This handsome inn offers a homey atmosphere just a short walk to the center of town. One of the highlights is the immense wraparound porch, complete with rocking chairs, where you can relax away an afternoon. Rooms, which are spotlessly clean, range widely in size from the garret rooms on the third floor to more spacious expanses on the second floor. Little extras include luxury bath products and robes. An artist-in-residence program means the walls are hung with numerous interesting paintings.

10 Cliff Rd. (a few blocks from the center of town), Nantucket, MA 02554. © **888/INN-0530** or 508/228-0530 (late Oct to mid-May 561/655-3127). www.centuryhouse.com. 16 units. Summer $145–$495 double; $325–$595 apt. Rates include continental breakfast and afternoon tea. MC, V. Closed late Oct to mid-May. *In room:* A/C, TV/DVD, CD, Wi-Fi, hair dryer.

Cliff Lodge 🌸🌸 *Finds* This charming 1771 whaling captain's house has a country casual style. The cheerful guest rooms feature colorful quilts and splatter-painted floors. Rooms range from a first-floor beauty with king-size bed, paneled walls, and fireplace to the tiny third-floor rooms tucked into the eaves. The spacious apartment in the rear of the house is a sunny delight. Climb up to the widow's walk for a bird's-eye view of the town and harbor.

9 Cliff Rd. (a few blocks from the center of town), Nantucket, MA 02554. © **508/228-9480.** Fax 508/228-6308. www.clifflodgenantucket.com. 12 units. Summer $155 single; $195–$305 double; $475 apt. Rates include continental breakfast. MC, V. Open year-round. No children under 12. *In room:* A/C, TV.

Martin House Inn 🌸🌸 *Value* This is one of the lower-priced B&Bs in town, but also one of the most stylish, with a formal parlor and a spacious side porch, complete with hammock. Some guest rooms in this historic 1803 mariner's home have four-poster beds and working fireplaces. The four garret singles with a shared bathroom are a bargain.

61 Centre St. (btw. Broad and Chester sts.; a couple of blocks from town center), Nantucket, MA 02554. © **508/228-0678.** Fax 508/325-4798. www.martinhouseinn.net. 13 units (4 with tub/shower, 5 with shower only, 4 with shared bathroom). Summer $115 single; $195–$315 double; $365 suite. Rates include continental breakfast. AE, MC, V. *In room:* No phone.

The Ship's Inn 🌸 *Value* This pretty, historic inn is on a quiet side street, just slightly removed—3 blocks—from Nantucket's center. Rooms are comfortable and spacious, considering the house was built in 1831. The decor has a home-y touch. The restaurant downstairs holds its own (see "Where to Dine," below).

13 Fair St. (a few blocks from town center), Nantucket, MA 02554. © **888/872-4052** or 508/228-0040. Fax 508/228-6524. www.shipsinnnantucket.com. 10 units. Summer $195–$250 double. No children under 8. Rates include continental breakfast. AE, MC, V. Closed late Oct to mid-May. **Amenities:** Restaurant (fine dining; p. 308) located in the basement. *In room:* A/C, TV, fridge, hair dryer, iron.

WHERE TO DINE
VERY EXPENSIVE

Brant Point Grill ✸ *Overrated* NEW AMERICAN For the high prices, you can probably do better than this harborside eatery, though it does have some interesting features. Specializing in lobster, steak, and chops, the chef prepares some dishes on a Fire Cone grill, a 21st-century interpretation of a Native American technique that cooks food by radiant heat and imparts it with a smoky mesquite flavor. Two specialties of the chef are tenderloin beef Wellington and an exotic mushroom risotto. If you can't sit on the terrace, try to snag a seat near one of the windows, where you can watch the twilight fade over the harbor. The raw bar is open July through Labor Day from 4 to 7pm for light snacks.

At the White Elephant Hotel (Easton and Willard sts.). ✆ 508/325-1320. Collared shirt and long pants requested for gentlemen. Reservations strongly recommended. Main courses $26–$39 or $45 3-course prix fixe meal. AE, DISC, MC, V. Mid-Apr to early Dec daily noon–2:30pm and 6–10pm. Closed mid-Dec to mid-Apr.

Chanticleer Inn ✸✸✸ MODERN FRENCH The new Chanticleer, in the signature rose-covered cottage in 'Sconset, is the place everyone wants to go for special occasions. Formerly a fancy French restaurant, owners Susan Handy and chef Jeff Worster, who also own Black Eyed Susan's (see below), have reinvented this charming place as a *"brasserie moderne."* Wonderful inventions like cod beignets and traditional appetizers like *moules frites* share the menu with creative versions of steak au poivre and seared Nantucket sea scallops. Tart au citron is among the stellar desserts, but you can also end your meal with a *plats fromage* with three types of succulent cheeses. How French!

9 New St., Siasconset. ✆ 508/257-4499. Reservations strongly recommended. Jacket preferred for men. Main courses $21–$43. AE, DC, MC, V. July and Aug Tues–Sun noon–2pm and 6–10pm; call for off-season hours. Closed Nov–Apr.

Cinco Restaurant and Bar ✸ INTERNATIONAL TAPAS This exquisite restaurant specializes in tapas, those popular little Spanish-style plates of food. This is not the place to come with a big appetite, but it's a great place for a light meal and to enjoy lively atmosphere. There are about 2 dozen choices on the menu; three or four per person would make a small meal, but you'll want to share. The preparations and tastes are unusual and sophisticated. There are cured meats, marinated vegetables, grilled fish, and other delicacies—for example cornmeal-crusted soft-shell crab and Nantucket fluke ceviche.

5 Amelia Dr. (¼ mile from the rotary, just off South Rd.). ✆ 508/325-5151. Reservations recommended. Tapas $11–$31. MC, V. Mid-June to Sept daily 6–10:30pm; call for off-season hours.

Club Car ✸✸ CONTINENTAL For decades one of the top restaurants on Nantucket, this posh venue is popular with locals. The menu has classic French influences. Popular offerings include a first course of octopus in the style of Bangkok with mint and hot peppers, and the classic entree of roast rack of lamb Club Car (with fresh herbs, honey-mustard glaze, and minted Madeira sauce). Some nights, seven-course tasting menus are available for $65 per person. The lounge area/piano bar attracts a lively scene set in an antique car from the old Nantucket railroad.

1 Main St. ✆ 508/228-1101. Reservations recommended. Main courses $24–$45. MC, V. July–Aug daily 11am–3pm and 6–10pm; call for off-season hours. Closed early Dec to late May.

The Galley on Cliffside Beach ☆☆☆ NEW AMERICAN   With the best setting of any restaurant on the island—on a private beach on the property of Cliffside Beach Club (p. 301)—the Galley offers a particularly beachy fine-dining experience. Given the setting, it's no surprise that The Galley specializes in seafood, caught locally by island fishermen. Produce comes from the restaurant's own organic garden. The menu changes often, but noteworthy options include either the signature New England clam chowder with smoked bacon or the lobster spring rolls. As a main course, choose between a Nantucket flounder meunière, native halibut with parsley potatoes and green beans, Black Angus filet, or simply a 2-pound local lobster with truffle butter and all the fixings.

54 Jefferson Ave., Nantucket. © 508/228-9641. Reservations suggested. Main courses $29–$39. AE, MC, V. Daily noon–2pm and 5–10pm. Closed Oct to late May.

The Pearl ☆☆ NEW AMERICAN   Miami Beach meets Nantucket at this swank establishment specializing in "coastal cuisine." The numerous stylish touches include appetizers and desserts served in martini glasses, a contemporary look with bluish lighting and large fish tanks, and an extensive champagne list. Skip the *grande deluxe plateau de mer;* it's not a lot of shellfish for a lot of money. Instead, go for the sashimi of local striped bass, and for a main course, look no further than the wok-fried lobster with lo mein noodles.

12 Federal St. © 508/228-9701. Reservations recommended. Main courses $33–$45. AE, MC, V. Mid-May to mid-Oct daily 6–10pm; call for off-season hours. Closed Jan–Mar.

Straight Wharf ☆☆☆ NEW AMERICAN   Straight Wharf, on the waterfront in the center of town, has long been known for its creative cuisine. The two chefs here like to feature playful takes on old favorites. A starter might be pear celery salad with a main course of wild striped bass with fried green tomatoes. A more affordable "summer grill" menu, served in the bar area, features simpler fare. Make your reservation for 8pm on the deck so you can watch the sun set over the harbor.

Straight Wharf. © 508/228-4499. Reservations recommended. Main courses $34–$38; summer grill menu $16–$22. AE, MC, V. July–Aug Tues–Sun 6–9:30pm; call for off-season hours. Closed late Sept to late May.

The Summer House ☆☆☆ *Finds* FUSION   The classic 'Sconset-style atmosphere distinguishes this fine-dining experience from others on the island: wicker and wrought iron, roses and honeysuckle. A pianist plays nightly—often Gershwin standards, and the pounding Atlantic Ocean is just over the bluff. Though this is one of the few restaurants not in the center of town, it is worth a trip to the far side of the island for the atmosphere and cuisine inspired by Mediterranean cultures. Though the menu changes often, a three-course meal here might begin with sherry lobster bisque. Homemade pastas like chestnut ravioli caprese are not to be missed. One of the specialty entrees is the veal chop stuffed with asparagus and fontina. If it's blueberry season, end your meal with the blueberry pie.

17 Ocean Ave., Siasconset. © 508/257-9976. Reservations recommended. Main courses $33–$39. AE, MC, V. July–Aug daily noon–4pm (at the Beachside Bistro late June to early Sept) and 6–10pm; mid-May to June and Sept to mid-Oct Wed–Sun 6–10pm. Closed mid-Oct to Apr.

Topper's at The Wauwinet ☆☆ REGIONAL/NEW AMERICAN   This 1850 restaurant—part of a secluded resort—is a tastefully subdued knockout, with wicker armchairs, splashes of chintz, and a two-tailed mermaid to oversee a chill-chasing fire. Try to sit at one of the cozy banquettes, if you can. This is Nantucket's most formal restaurant. The menu, a three-course prix fixe with numerous choices, features the finest regional cuisine: Lobster is a major event (it's often sautéed with champagne beurre blanc), and be on the lookout for specials like arctic char. Desserts, like the toasted brioche with poached pears and caramel sauce, are fanciful and fabulous. Topper's is well known for its superlative wine menu. The Wauwinet Inn runs a complimentary launch service in-season to the restaurant for lunch and dinner; it leaves from Straight Wharf at 11am and 5pm, takes 1 hour, and also makes the return trip.

120 Wauwinet Rd. (off Squam Rd.), Wauwinet. ✆ **508/228-8768.** Reservations required for dinner and the launch ride over. Three-course prix fixe $85. AE, DC, MC, V. May–Oct daily noon–2pm and 6–9:30pm. Closed Nov–Apr.

EXPENSIVE

American Seasons ✿✿ REGIONAL AMERICAN   This romantic little restaurant has a great theme: Choose your region (New England, Pacific Coast, Wild West, or Down South) and select creative offerings. Start, for instance, with Louisiana crayfish risotto with fire-roasted onion and fried parsnips in a sweet corn purée from Down South; then move on to the Pacific Coast's aged beef sirloin with caramelized shallot and Yukon potato hash. A lighter tapas menu is available throughout the evening.

80 Centre St. (2 blocks from the center of town). ✆ **508/228-7111.** Reservations recommended. Main courses $24–$30. AE, MC, V. Mid-Apr to Dec daily 6–9pm. Closed Jan to mid-Apr.

Boarding House ✿✿ NEW AMERICAN   This centrally located fine-dining restaurant doubles as one of the most popular bars in town. You can dine in the romantic lower-level dining room or upstairs in the hopping bar area. But on clear summer nights, you'll want to get one of the tables outside on the patio. The menu has definite Asian and Mediterranean influences, but the signature dish is the classic grilled lobster tails with grilled asparagus, mashed potatoes, and champagne beurre blanc. The award-winning wine list offers a range of prices.

12 Federal St. ✆ **508/228-9622.** Reservations recommended. Main courses $26–$36. AE, MC, V. July–Aug daily 6–10pm; call for off-season hours.

Company of the Cauldron ✿✿✿ CONTINENTAL   Considered the most romantic restaurant on the island, this candlelit dining room features a classical harpist in season. The menu is unusual, in that there is a single three- to four-course fixed-price meal each night, so would-be patrons must check the menu out front or call ahead to see which night to go. Dietary preferences can be accommodated with advance notice. The meal might start with a red beet and lobster risotto, then on to pepper-crusted Chateaubriand, and ending with a rustic apple tart. There are just two seatings nightly.

5 India St. (btw. Federal and Centre sts.) ✆ **508/228-4016.** www.companyofthecauldron.com. Reservations required. Fixed-price dinner $50–$55. MC, V. Early July to early Sept Tues–Sun, 2 seatings at 6:45 and 8:45pm; call for off-season hours. Closed mid-Oct to mid-Apr, except Thanksgiving weekend and the first 2 weeks of Dec.

Fifty-Six Union ✿✿ NEW AMERICAN   This understated restaurant offers fine dining without pretensions: just good service, a pleasing contemporary atmosphere, and wonderful food. Diners can sit in the bar area, which tends to be loud and lively, in the quieter Garden Room, or on the outdoor patio. Intriguing appetizers include a Bosc pear salad and crab rangoons with a spicy sauce. Main-course choices range from Javanese fried rice with shrimp and chicken, to a rack of Colorado lamb with mustard crust.

56 Union St. (½ mile from Main St.) ℭ **508/228-6135**. www.fiftysixunion.com. Reservations recommended. Main courses $23–$44. AE, MC, V. Early July to early Sept daily 6–10pm, Sun 10am–1pm; call for off-season hours.

Òran Mór 🏵🏵 NEW AMERICAN

Chef/owner Chris Freeman brings his stellar reputation to this popular upscale restaurant, an intimate second-floor space that has an aura of romance. Chef Freeman specializes in native seafood and local produce, and you will always find Nantucket lobster on the menu, but also unusual appetizers like grilled quail with wild mushrooms. As for entrees, there are local roasted striped bass with littleneck clams, and Peking duck breast with peach ginger salsa.

2 S. Beach St. (in the center of town). ℭ **508/228-8655**. Reservations recommended. Main courses $22–$34. AE, MC, V. July–Aug daily 6–10pm; Sept–June Thurs–Sat and Mon–Tues 6–9pm, Sun noon–9pm. Open year-round.

Ropewalk 🏵 SEAFOOD

This open-air restaurant, which sits at the end of Straight Wharf, doubles as Nantucket's only outdoor raw bar, and it's where the yachting crowd hangs out after a day on the boat. While the food is a bit overpriced, the location is prime. This is a good place to enjoy a light meal or appetizers, such as fried calamari, crab cakes, or fried oysters. The dinner menu includes pineapple-glazed swordfish and bourbon peach barbecue breast of chicken.

1 Straight Wharf. ℭ **508/228-8886**. No reservations. Main courses $23–$33. MC, V. May–Oct daily 11am–10pm. Closed Nov–Apr.

Ship's Inn Restaurant 🏵🏵 NEW AMERICAN

This intimate restaurant in the brick-walled basement of a historic inn is one of the island's most romantic dining options. The waitstaff here is professional and entertaining, a real treat. The menu features a variety of fresh fish, meat, and pasta dishes, including several lighter options made without butter or cream. A flavorful starter here is the Roquefort and walnut terrine with Asian pear. Popular main dishes include the pan-roasted Muscovy duck breast and the grilled yellowtail flounder. For a festive dessert, there's always the Grand Marnier soufflé.

13 Fair St. ℭ **508/228-0040**. Reservations recommended. Main courses $19–$34. AE, MC, V. July–Sept Wed–Mon 5–10pm; call for off-season hours. Closed Nov–Apr.

Trattoria Sfoglia 🏵🏵🏵 NORTHERN ITALIAN

This unpretentious eatery ranks at the top of many people's "my favorite" lists for Nantucket. Dining is in the European style, where you order several courses, beginning with an antipasto, like clams, salami, tomato, and fennel; next, perhaps a corn risotto with lobster and zucchini and a roasted sausage with *contorni* (tasty preparations of farm-fresh vegetables, like beets or eggplant). Light eaters can ask for a half-order of the house-made pasta, which is enough to satisfy the average appetite. The kitchen turns out home-baked bread that some call the island's best, and its own gelato. The only catch is, the restaurant is not in the center of town; visitors without cars will have to take a taxi.

130 Pleasant St. (across from Stop & Shop) ℭ **508/325-4500**. Reservations recommended. Main courses $14–$29. No credit cards. Apr to mid-Oct Mon–Sat 6–10pm; call for off-season hours.

21 Federal 🏵🏵 NEW AMERICAN

This popular restaurant in a historic Greek Revival building in the center of town seems to get better every year. For melt-in-your-mouth pleasure, try the appetizer of Nantucket mussels with walnut pesto cream. The fish entrees, like sautéed halibut with lobster risotto, are the most popular here, although you might opt for the grilled pork chop with a smoked fig and apple chutney. There's also a very happening bar scene here in the summer.

21 Federal St. (in the center of town). © **508/228-2121.** Reservations recommended. Main courses $27–$37. AE, MC, V. Mid-May to mid-Oct (plus Thanksgiving through Christmas Stroll) daily 6–9:30pm. Closed mid-Dec to Mar.

MODERATE

Black Eyed Susan's ✦✦✦ *Finds* ETHNIC ECLECTIC   This is supremely exciting food in a funky diner-style atmosphere. Reservations are accepted for the 6pm seating only, and they go fast. Others must line up outside; the line starts forming around 5:30pm. The menu is in constant flux, as chef Jeff Worster's mood and influences change every 3 weeks. We always enjoy the spicy Thai fish cake and the tandoori chicken with green mango chutney. There's usually a Southwestern touch, like the Dos Equis beer–battered catfish quesadilla with mango slaw, hoppin' john, and jalapeño. There's no liquor license, but you can BYOB. It's also cash only.

10 India St. (in the center of town). © **508/325-0308.** Reservations accepted for 6pm seating only. Main courses $15–$25. No credit cards. Apr–Oct daily 7am–1pm, Mon–Sat 6–10pm; call for off-season hours. Closed Nov–Mar.

The Brotherhood of Thieves ✦ PUB   A recent renovation and expansion has taken away most of the former grittiness of this classic whaling bar, but it is still popular. In July and August, tourists line up for tables in the dark tavern downstairs to chow on burgers and hand-cut curly fries. A new upstairs dining room also has an outside raised terrace. In the fall and winter, locals sit beside the cozy brick hearths downstairs for dinner offerings like fisherman's stew or surf 'n turf. This place serves food later than anyone else in town; you can order off the late-night menu until midnight.

23 Broad St. © **508/228-2551.** Reservations accepted for parties of 6 or more. Main courses $7–$25. MC, V. Mar–Jan Mon–Sat 11:30am–midnight; Sun noon–10pm. Closed Feb.

Centre Street Bistro ✦✦✦ NEW AMERICAN   This tiny fine-dining restaurant in the center of Nantucket town is owned and operated by Ruth and Tim Pitts, who are considered top chefs on the island. It gets top ratings by doing everything right, from atmosphere to service, to the memorable food. This cozy place features wonderful, creative cuisine at reasonable prices, especially compared with other island fine-dining restaurants. The menu changes often, but high points have included the warm goat-cheese tart or the smoked salmon taco to start, and the sesame-encrusted bistro shrimp with mango relish as a main course. Desserts, like the white-chocolate banana tart, are knock-outs.

29 Centre St. © **508/228-8470.** Reservations not accepted. Main courses $19–$25. MC, V. Wed–Sun noon–2:30pm and 6–10pm. Open year-round.

Le Languedoc Cafe ✦✦ NEW AMERICAN   Nantucket's most authentic French cafe offers a cozy atmosphere and reasonable prices. An expensive dining room is upstairs, but locals prefer the casual bistro atmosphere downstairs and out on the terrace. Soups are superb, as are the Angus-steak burgers with garlic french fries, which is on the small but lower-priced bar menu. More elaborate dishes include the roasted tenderloin of pork stuffed with figs and pancetta.

24 Broad St. © **508/228-2552.** www.lelanguedoc.com. Reservations not accepted for cafe; reservations for dining room at 5:30 or 6pm only; others on wait list. Bar menu $14–$22. Dining room $24–$44. AE, MC, V. June–Sept daily 5:30–9:30pm, Tues–Sun 11:30am–2pm; call for off-season hours. Closed Jan to mid-Apr.

LoLa 41 ✦ GLOBAL BISTRO   Sushi is the highlight at Lola's, a fun place dominated by a bar whose servers pour uncommon specialty concoctions at $10 to $12 a pop. The theme is "neoglobal" cuisine: pasta and osso buco from Italy, bacalao (salt cod with polenta and caviar) from Barcelona, and Asian-inspired green and black tea–glazed chicken breast with Buddha's rise. There are even fried clams and calamari—both very good—on the appetizer list. But most people are here for the impressive sushi bar, where you can gorge on nigiri and sashimi to your heart's content. The only thing that might give you pause is the prices: Sushi rolls are $15 to $17 each.

15 S. Beach St. ⓒ **508/325-4001.** Reservations accepted for same-day seating. Main courses $19–$37. AE, MC, V. June–Sept daily 5:30–10pm; call for off-season hours. Closed Jan.

Queequeg's ☆ NEW AMERICAN A cozy bistro atmosphere and good value are the hallmarks of this small restaurant, which is tucked along a side street behind the Athenaeum. Outside seating is available on the patio in good weather. As befits the Moby Dick reference in the name, the specialty here is seafood. The menu offers a range from basics to fancier fare. For example, as an appetizer, you could have the New England clam chowder or Prince Edward Island mussels. The rich and flavorful pan-seared halibut with Parmesan risotto is a favorite with locals. Meat-lovers may enjoy Yankee pot roast or beef tenderloin. A benefit to this menu is, several entrees are available in half-portions, at almost half the price.

6 Oak St. ⓒ **508/325-0992.** Reservations recommended. Main courses $23–$28. MC, V. June–Sept daily 5–10:30pm; call for off-season hours.

Schooner's at Steamboat Wharf AMERICAN This casual family-friendly restaurant near the Steamship Authority dock is noteworthy for the outdoor dining on the screened-in porch. Diners who sit on the second floor have views of the harbor. Prices are reasonable and portions are generous in this casual pub. The most popular dishes are the fajitas, fried clams, fish and chips, and lobster salad. There is a lively late-night bar scene with live acoustic music some nights in season.

31 Easy St. ⓒ **508/228-5824.** Reservations accepted. Main courses $18–$24. AE, MC, V. Apr–Dec daily 11am–10pm. Closed Jan–Mar.

INEXPENSIVE

Arno's (Kids) ECLECTIC A storefront facing the passing parade of Main Street, this institution packs surprising style between its bare-brick walls. The internationally influenced menu yields tasty, bountiful platters for breakfast, lunch, and dinner. Specialties include grilled sirloin steaks and fresh grilled fish. Arno's has a family-friendly atmosphere, and there is a children's menu. Inside the restaurant is a new wine bar called **the 41.**

41 Main St. ⓒ **508/228-7001.** Reservations recommended. Main courses $12–$23. AE, MC, V. Apr–Dec daily 8am–2pm and 5–9pm. Closed Jan–Mar.

Cap'n Tobey's Chowder House ☆ SEAFOOD The specialty at this convenient eatery close to the harbor is seafood, obtained daily from local fishermen. Diners can choose among halibut, yellowfin tuna, and haddock, and have it grilled, baked, or blackened. The raw bar features oysters, littlenecks, and shrimp. Upstairs, **Off Shore at Cap'n Tobey's** has live music in season. Downstairs attracts a sports-bar crowd.

20 Straight Wharf. ⓒ **508/228-0836.** Reservations accepted. Main courses $10–$22. AE, DC, DISC, MC, V. Late June to Sept daily 11:30am–10pm; call for off-season hours. Closed Jan–Apr.

The Even Keel Café AMERICAN This low-key cafe in the heart of town serves breakfast, lunch, and dinner both indoors, at tables or the long counter, and outside, on the patio in the back. Unlike with much of Nantucket's dining scene, you'll find reasonable prices and nonexotic fare here, like burgers, pizza, and sandwiches, as well as Mexican and Italian choices. There are also barbecue baby back ribs, chicken breast in coconut curry sauce, and lobster risotto. There's a kid's menu, as well as high-speed Internet access. On Sunday, they serve a hearty brunch. A small martini bar faces the front window.

40 Main St. ☎ **508/228-1979.** Reservations not accepted. Main courses $10–$22. AE, MC, V. July–Aug daily 7am–10pm; call for off-season hours.

TAKEOUT & PICNIC FARE

You can get fresh-picked produce right on Main Street from the traveling truck from **Bartlett's Ocean View Farm** ⍟, 33 Bartlett Farm Rd. (☎ **508/228-9403**), or head out to this seventh-generation farm where, in June, you get to pick your own strawberries. They also sell sandwiches, quiches, pastries, pies, and more. They're closed January through March.

At **Henry Junior** ⍟, 129 Orange St. (☎ **508/228-3035**), the sub rolls are baked from scratch every morning, as are the chocolate-chip cookies. Bring the family for a cheap and easy lunch. It's closed November through May.

A terrific value on pricey Nantucket, **Something Natural,** 50 Cliff Rd. (☎ **508/228-0504**), turns out gigantic sandwiches, with fresh ingredients piled atop fabulous bread. Save room for their addictive chocolate-chip cookies. Something Natural is closed mid-October to March.

The **Juice Bar** ⍟⍟, 12 Broad St. (☎ **508/228-5799**), is a humble hole in the wall that dishes out some of the best homemade ice cream and frozen yogurt around, complemented by superb homemade hot fudge. It's closed from mid-October to mid-April.

Provisions & Juice Guys, 4 Easy St. (☎ **508/228-4464**), is the spot to get your Nantucket Nectars fix. High-tech blenders mix potent combinations of fresh juice with vitamins, sorbet, yogurt, and holistic enhancers. There are sandwiches, too. It's closed from late December to April.

NANTUCKET AFTER DARK

Acoustic performers from all over the country hold forth in the **Brotherhood of Thieves,** 23 Broad St., in the center of Nantucket Town (no phone), an atmospheric pub where you'll find live folk music just about every night in season; no cover. It's closed in February. The **Chicken Box,** 12 Dave St. (☎ **508/228-9717**), is the rocking spot for the 20-something crowd. It sometimes seems as if the entire population of the island is shoving their way in here. Jimmy Buffett shows up late at night about once a summer, unannounced, and jams with the band. The cover runs from $4 to $15. The **Rose and Crown,** 23 S. Water St. (☎ **508/228-2595**), draws all ages with its loud dance music. The cover for live bands on weekends is $3 to $5. It's closed January through March.

The **Nantucket Arts Alliance** (☎ **800/228-8118** or 508/228-8118) operates Box Office Nantucket, offering tickets for all sorts of cultural events around town. It operates out of the Macy Warehouse on Straight Wharf, in season daily from 10am to 4pm.

Theater buffs will want to spend an evening at the **Actors' Theatre of Nantucket,** Methodist Church, 2 Centre St. (☎ **508/228-6325;** www.nantuckettheatre.com). This shoebox-size theater assays thought-provoking plays as readily as summery farces. The season runs from mid-May to mid-September. Tickets are $12 to $20. You can catch the children's productions ($12) from mid-July to mid-August.

9

Central & Western Massachusetts

by Herbert Bailey Livesey and Leslie Brokaw

While Boston and its maritime appendages of Cape Cod and Cape Ann face the sea and embrace it, inland Massachusetts turns in upon itself. Countless ponds and lakes shimmer in its folds and hollows, often hidden by deep forests and granite outcroppings. Farming and industry grew along the north-south valleys of the Connecticut and Housatonic rivers.

The heartland Pioneer Valley, enclosing the Connecticut River, earned its name in the early 18th century, when European trappers and farmers first began to push west from the colonies clinging to the edges of Massachusetts Bay. They were followed by ambitious capitalists who erected red-brick mills along the river for the manufacture of textiles and paper. Most of those enterprises failed or faded in the post–World War II movement to the milder climate and cheaper labor of the South, leaving a miasma of economic hardship that has yet to be completely resolved. But those industrialists also helped fund several distinguished colleges for which the valley is now known; their educated populations provide much energy and a rich cultural life.

Roughly the same pattern applied in the Berkshires, the twin ranges of rumpled hills that define the western band of the state. The development of this region in the 19th century was prompted mainly by the construction of the railroad from New York and Boston. Artistic and literary folk made a favored summer retreat of it, followed by wealthy urbanites attracted by the region's reputation for creativity and bohemianism. Many of their extravagant mansions, dubbed "Berkshire Cottages," still survive, and to this day the region attracts the town-and-country crowd, who support a vibrant summer schedule of the arts and then steal away as the crimson leaves fall and the Berkshires grow quiet beneath 6 months of snow.

1 Worcester

44 miles W of Boston; 52 miles NE of Springfield

Massachusetts's second-largest city, Worcester (pronounced *Wuss*-ter, or *Woos*-tah locally) has its dilapidated edges, but so, too, do many of the region's urban areas, most of which reached their apogees in the late 19th century. Still, local benefactors have invested in a surprising number of museums, historic buildings, and theatrical venues, and Worcester has enough attractions to justify a stopover or fill an overnight.

The student population draws from over a dozen schools, including Clark University, Worcester Polytechnic Institute, and College of the Holy Cross. Worcester's citizens support frequent bootstrapping efforts, especially downtown around the Romanesque City Hall.

The city was the site of the first National Women's Rights Convention, in 1850. The history of that event is online at the National Park Service website, at www.nps.gov.

ESSENTIALS

GETTING THERE Worcester is 2 miles north of the east-west Massachusetts Turnpike (I-90) via I-290, which bisects the city. Driving can be tricky in Worcester, with the convergence of highways and its one-way streets; getting detailed directions to your destination is advised. **Amtrak** (© **800/USA-RAIL;** www.amtrak.com) stops here daily each way on its route between Boston and Chicago.

VISITOR INFORMATION The **Visitor Center** is on the second floor of the Worcester Historical Museum, 30 Elm St. (© 508/755-7400; www.worcester.org).

WHAT TO SEE & DO

EcoTarium *Kids* This family-oriented institution is set on a woodsy campus traversed by meandering nature trails. Primarily directed at young children, the complex includes an indoor planetarium and a museum with interactive displays about ecology and conservation, and live and taxidermied animals. Outside, there are bald eagles, otters, owls, and a polar bear, and a ⅓ scale model of an 1860s steam engine takes a 12-minute loop through the grounds. For adults and children 7 and older, a Tree Canopy Walkway 40 feet above ground lets you traverse amid oak and hickory trees (summer only). In June and July, there are outdoor jazz concerts at sunset.

222 Harrington Way. © 508/929-2700. www.ecotarium.org. General admission $10 adults, $8 seniors, students, and ages 3–16. Additional fees: Planetarium $5, Explorer Express Train $2.50, Tree Canopy Walkway $9. Tues–Sat 10am–5pm; Sun noon–5pm. From Boston, exit 11 off I-90, north on Rte. 122 (Grafton St.) for 3 miles, right on Plantation St., right on Franklin St., right on Harrington Way.

Higgins Armory Museum *★* Here's where you'll find your knight in shining armor—or at least the armor. This steel-and-glass museum has medieval tapestries, stained-glass windows, and—in the Great Hall, which is fashioned after Gothic castles of yore—dozens of suits of armor, a posed jousting match, and swords and daggers. There's even a suit for a dog. The substantial collection comes from John W. Higgins, president (1912–50) of a Worcester company that processed steel and clearly possessed a keen interest in Renaissance armor and heraldry. The museum added an outpost of the London Brass Rubbings Centre in 2007 for visitors to make rubbings from plates featuring knights, ladies, dragons, and crests. Combat demonstrations are periodically hosted here; Harry Potter fans will be in heaven.

100 Barber Ave. © 508/853-6015. www.higgins.org. Admission $9 adults, $8 seniors, $7 children 6–16, audio tour $2. Tues–Sat 10am–4pm; Sun noon–4pm. From I-190 north, exit 1 onto Rte. 12 north; after a small bridge, take a sharp right (nearly a U-turn) at the first light onto unmarked Barber Ave.

Worcester Art Museum *★★* Occupying most of a large city block, WAM boasts an unexpectedly impressive collection of artworks, from 2nd-century Buddhist pieces to 20th-century American photos, for a total of over 35,000 works. Contemporary special exhibits give some fizz and pop to the hushed classical setting. Particular strengths are the American wing, with canvases by Cassatt, Sargent, and Whistler; some memorable works by anonymous Colonial artists; and silver by Paul Revere. The Europeans on the second floor include Gauguin, Monet, Dürer, and Gainsborough.

There's a Gothic chapter house, once used by Benedictine monks, transported from France and said to be the first medieval room to come to the U.S. A modest cafe offers soups, salads, and sandwiches from 11:30am to 2pm and has an outdoor courtyard in warm months. A new wing is home to educational studios.

55 Salisbury St. (corner of Tuckerman St.) ℂ 508/799-4406. www.worcesterart.org. Admission $10 adults, $8 seniors, free age 17 and under and for all Sat 10am–noon. Wed–Sun 11am–5pm (open at 10am on Sat, and until 8pm on 3rd Thurs of the month).

WHERE TO STAY

Most of the accommodations in and around the city are chain motels. As an alternative, Sturbridge (p. 315), less than 20 miles away, offers some atmospheric choices in a more rural setting.

Beechwood Hotel ✦ The eye-catching feature of this relatively young red-brick boutique hotel is its round core structure, which resembles a medieval keep. Public spaces and guest rooms are agreeably furnished and executive-level rooms and suites have skyline views and newer decor, along with complimentary continental breakfast. Sunday through Thursday, all guests are invited to a manager's reception for a free cocktail (5–7pm). Sunday brunches in the **Harlequin Restaurant** receive local notice. The hotel is located across the street from the University of Massachusetts Medical School and Medical Center complex. Fittingly, the entire hotel is nonsmoking.

363 Plantation St. (at Rte. 9), Worcester, MA 01605. ℂ 800/344-2589 or 508/754-5789. Fax 508/752-2060. www.beechwoodhotel.com. 73 units. $169–$224 double; $159–$430 suite. Rates include continental breakfast. Packages available. AE, DC, DISC, MC, V. Free parking. **Amenities:** Restaurant (New American); bar; 24-hr. room service; 24-hr. fitness room; 24-hr. business center; same-day laundry/dry cleaning service. *In room:* A/C, TV w/free movies, free high-speed Internet, free local and U.S. long-distance calls, 2 phone lines, coffeemaker, hair dryer, iron.

Crowne Plaza Along with its desirable location in the downtown business district, this outlet of the well-known chain delivers on most points of expected conveniences. Buttoned-up bedrooms provide more-than-sufficient elbow room, tripled-sheeted bedding, duvets, and sleep-sound CDs to use with the bedside CD player/clock radio. Concierge-level rooms have unstocked minifridges and a private lounge serving complimentary continental breakfast. Floor eight is the "quiet zone." There are seven suites, each with a living area and kitchenette separated from the bedroom by French glass doors. Fireplaces in the lobby and adjacent dining room are warming notes, and self-parking in the garage directly opposite the main entrance is handy. There's a small on-site theater that hosts comedy shows on the weekends.

10 Lincoln Sq. (corner of Rte. 9 and Major Taylor Blvd.), Worcester, MA 01608. ℂ 800/227-6963 or 508/791-1600. Fax 508/791-1796. www.crowneplaza.com. 243 units. $108–$169 double; suites from $249. Packages available. AE, DC, DISC, MC, V. Valet parking $8; self-parking $5. Pets allowed ($20). **Amenities:** Restaurant (Italian/Continental); bar; heated indoor/outdoor pool w/whirlpool; small exercise room; 24-hr. business center; limited room service; laundry service; dry cleaning; self-serve laundry facilities. *In room:* A/C, TV w/pay movies, Wi-Fi, high-speed Internet, CD player, coffeemaker, hair dryer, iron.

WHERE TO DINE

Just a few blocks east of the downtown train station, a strip of restaurants and cafes line Shrewsbury Street. Among them are the new Italian **VIA,** 89 Shrewsbury St. (ℂ 508/754-4842; www.viaitaliantable.com), and a handsome steakhouse, **111 Chop House,** 111 Shrewsbury St. (ℂ 508/799-4111; www.111chophouse.com). Both are run by the same group behind Sole Proprietor, below.

Sole Proprietor ⭐⭐ SEAFOOD   A chummy, popular, well-run act, from the congenial staff to the long wine card, which includes upward of 30 wines available by the glass. But it's the food that's key, and fish preparations range from bare-bones simple to entrancingly complex. One side of the large rectangular bar is given over to a sushi and raw bar, while the kitchen produces such worthy inventions as tuna steak Barcelona—the fish coated with cracked peppercorns, grilled medium rare, sliced, and laid over a bed of feta cheese, sun-dried tomatoes, scallions, and basil leaves. Lunch specials range from $9 to $11, and portions are generous; they have included bowls piled high with fat scallops, penne pasta, root vegetables, and bacon.

118 Highland St. (Rte. 9) ② 508/798-3474. www.thesole.com. Main courses $17–$40 (sushi rolls $8–$12, lobster dinners $25–$60). AE, DISC, MC, V. Mon–Fri 11:30am–10pm; Sat noon–11pm; Sun 4–9:30pm; bar open with bar food until 1:30am daily.

2 Sturbridge & Old Sturbridge Village

59 miles W of Boston; 22 miles SW of Worcester; 35 miles E of Springfield

Sturbridge is a quiet, pretty New England community, populated by working people. There are two reasons for all the motels and restaurants in this town of 7,837 residents: an antiques show that sets up three times a year in the adjacent town of Brimfield, and **Old Sturbridge Village,** a living museum comprising 19th-century buildings and "residents" who demonstrate the pursuits of the period (see below). One of the top tourist destinations in central Massachusetts, it is deservedly popular.

Note that some "Main Street" addresses are on Route 20 and others are on Route 131.

ESSENTIALS
GETTING THERE   Sturbridge is at the intersection of the Massachusetts Turnpike (I-90) and I-84. Routes 20 and 131 are the main roads in town.

VISITOR INFORMATION   The **Sturbridge Tourist Information Center,** 380 Main Street (Rte. 20 at the exit for Old Sturbridge Village; ② 800/628-8379), is open daily 10am to 5pm. The Sturbridge Area Tourist Association is at **www. sturbridge.org**.

SPECIAL EVENTS   Brimfield is a sleepy village just to the west of Sturbridge, but three times a year some 6,000 dealers gather along a mile of Route 20, the main drag through town, for the **Brimfield Antique and Collectible Shows** ⭐ (② 800/628-8379; www.brimfieldshow.com). Shows run for up to 6 days (Tues–Sun) in mid-May, mid-July, and early September. (Most of the dealers and collectors stay in Sturbridge, so you'll need to reserve a room at least 6 months in advance during show periods.) If you're an antiques collector and visiting when the Brimfield show isn't going on, organizers recommend driving 25 miles south on Route 131 to Putnam, Connecticut. The small town has about a dozen antique shops.

In mid-March, a few dozen establishments participate over 2 weekends in **Sturbridge Area Maple Days** with maple-sugaring demonstrations, pancake breakfasts, and apple-dumpling sampling. Among them is the teeny family operation **K. E. Farm,** 317 Leadmine Road, a few miles past Old Sturbridge Village (② 508/347-9323; www.maplesugarhouse.com), where Ernie and his old wooden sugar shack turn gallons of sap into pints of liquid gold.

WHAT TO SEE & DO

Expect crowds in the area during summer holiday weekends, the Brimfield Antique show, and October foliage season.

Old Sturbridge Village ★★★ *Kids*   Old Sturbridge uses authentic 1800s buildings, many of them moved here from other communities, to re-create a rural settlement of the 1830s. On the large property are a meetinghouse, sawmill, bank, country store, blacksmith shop, school, cooperage, printing office, and parson's home. At the edges of the village are a working farm and herb garden. Lazy boat rides on the adjacent Quinebaug River are popular, as is a hands-on craft center that opened in 2007. Rides on a newly commissioned horse-drawn stagecoach are planned for 2008; the village already features horse-drawn sleigh rides when there's snow.

Costumed docents demonstrate sheep shearing, heirloom gardening, clothes dying, musketry, barrel-making, and more, generally using language true to the period. Special events take place on the Fourth of July and in the Christmas season, and on winter weekends the participatory **Dinner in a Country Village** is great fun: Guests get to stay after-hours to pitch in and make a typical meal on a massive hearth by candlelight, and then gather around a single table to enjoy the fruits of their labor—roast chicken, "beef olives," gourd soup, trifle, fresh-roasted coffee.

After a few dire years financially, the village appears to be on more solid ground. The **Oliver Wright Tavern,** closed for a few years, reopened in 2007, and an aggressive 2006–07 fundraising campaign raised $1.83 million.

1 Old Sturbridge Village Rd. ℂ **800/733-1830** or 508/347-3362. www.osv.org. Admission (2-day pass) $20 adults, $18 seniors, $6 children 3–17. Apr 19–Oct 24 daily 9:30am–5pm; Oct 25–Apr 18 Tues–Sun 9:30am–4pm. Open Thanksgiving and New Year's Day, closed Christmas. Take exit 3B off I-84 or exit 9 off I-90, drive west on Rte. 20, and follow signs to village.

WHERE TO STAY

Familiar chains include the **Comfort Inn & Suites,** 215 Charlton Rd. (Rte. 20) (ℂ **508/347-3306;** www.sturbridgecomfortinn.com), and **Hampton Inn of Sturbridge,** 328 Main St. (Rte. 131) (ℂ **508/347-6466;** www.myhamptoninn.com). The **Heritage Corridor Bed & Breakfast Group** (www.HeritageCorridorBB.com) has links to some of the quainter accommodations in the region.

Publick House ★   This property is the high-profile lodging in the Sturbridge area. The most desirable rooms are the 17 in the main **Historic Inn.** Built in 1771, it's heavy on atmosphere, with Colonial reproduction pieces, quilts on some beds, and floors and ceilings that long ago settled into not-quite-right angles. A downstairs tavern with fireplace, used mainly by guests, is a jovial venue. Suites in the adjacent **Chamberlain House** are larger and somewhat more contemporary. The **Country Motor Lodge,** on the back side of the property, lacks any 18th-century personality whatsoever but has rooms that start at just $69, with cable television and access to a small outdoor pool. The same menu is offered in the tavern as in the more refined **Tap Room,** and a small "bake shoppe" does brisk business throughout the day.

277 Main St. (Rte. 131), P.O. Box 187, Sturbridge, MA 01566. ℂ **800/782-5425** or 508/347-3313. Fax 508/347-5073. www.publickhouse.com. 115 units. $89–$125 double in the Historic Inn; $125–$145 suite in the Chamberlain House; $69–$104 double in Motor Lodge. Packages available. AE, DISC, MC, V. Pets accepted in some rooms of Country Motor Lodge. **Amenities:** 2 restaurants (American); bar; outdoor pool. *In room:* A/C, TV, free Wi-Fi, iron, hair dryer.

WHERE TO DINE

In addition to the establishments listed below, you might sample either of the two restaurants in the **Publick House** (see above).

Cedar Street Restaurant AMERICAN ⭐⭐   Tucked into the first floor of a house on a residential street, Cedar Street is nothing but right notes every step of the way. The decor is traditional with modern touches, the volume on a crowded night is buzzy without being overwhelming, the martini list is long, and the beers include Sam Smith. But we're here for the food, and it doesn't fail to impress: duck with juniper honey drizzle and toasted pistachio dust, and buttermilk fried chicken with red-eye gravy and braised Swiss chard are both as good as you'd find in a big city. Good thing, given the prices, which are at the high end for this region. The experience is worth it. If it's available, go for the chef's favorite to close: strawberry molasses bread pudding with cinnamon gelato and a sugar cookie spoon.

12 Cedar Street, just off of Rte. 20. ℂ **508/347-5800**. www.cedarstreetrestaurant.com. Main courses $16–$32. AE, MC, V. Daily from 5pm.

Rom's ⭐ *Value* ITALIAN/AMERICAN   Fifty years ago, this was a hot-dog-and-fried-clam roadside stand, and it has grown since then like a multigeneration New England farmhouse. Today it seats 750 and remains a good family restaurant, with something for everyone, from homemade pastas and pizzas to full seafood dinners. The lobster roll is twice the size, but about the same price, as those offered on the coast. Buffets at Wednesday and Friday dinner and Sunday brunch are crowd pleasers.

179 Main St. (Rte. 131), 2 miles south of Rte. 20. ℂ **508/347-3340**. Main courses $8.95–$16. AE, DISC, MC, V. Daily 11:30am–9pm (open Sun at 9:30am).

3 Springfield

90 miles W of Boston; 26 miles N of Hartford; 5 miles S of I-90

Times have been tough in this once-prosperous manufacturing city on the east bank of the Connecticut River. But its loyal citizens haven't caved under the pressures of job flight and high unemployment, and evidence of redevelopment can be seen throughout downtown, with recycled loft and factory buildings standing beside modern glass towers. Springfield remains the most important city in western Massachusetts and has enjoyed some success in attracting new enterprises. Vacationers can pass a few hours or a night here, but Springfield is primarily a stopover city.

ESSENTIALS

GETTING THERE   Springfield is located at the juncture of the east-west Massachusetts Turnpike (I-90) and north-south I-91.

Bradley International (ℂ **203/627-3000;** airport code BDL), in Windsor Locks, Connecticut, is the nearest major airport, about 20 miles to the south. Rent a car here from any of the major companies, or catch a bus, cab, or limo into Springfield. Major airlines serving Bradley include **American** (ℂ 800/433-7300), **Continental** (ℂ 800/525-3273), **Delta** (ℂ 800/221-1212), **Northwest** (ℂ 800/225-2525), **United** (ℂ 800/864-8331), and **US Airways** (ℂ 800/428-4322).

Three lines of **Amtrak** (ℂ **800/USA-RAIL;** www.amtrak.com) trains stop in Springfield: the *Lake Shore Limited* running between Boston and Chicago; the *Regional* between Boston and Washington, D.C.; and the *Vermonter* between St. Albans, Vermont (where there are connecting buses from Montreal), and D.C.

VISITOR INFORMATION   The **Greater Springfield Convention and Visitors Bureau** (© 800/723-1548; www.valleyvisitor.com) has downloadable maps of Springfield and other nearby cities at its website. There are visitor centers downtown, at 1441 Main St., Springfield, MA 01103 (© 413/787-1548), and near the Basketball Hall of Fame, at 1200 W. Columbus Ave. (© 413/750-2980). They offer brochures, maps, and discount tickets to local attractions.

SPECIAL EVENTS   During the last 2 weeks in September, **"The Big E"—the Eastern States Exposition** (© 413/737-2443; www.thebige.com) is held on a fairground on the opposite side of the Connecticut River in West Springfield. It's a huge old-fashioned agricultural fair with a 4-H horse show, ox pulling, carnival food such as deep-fried cheesecake, games, a midway, and entertainment from the likes of Joan Jett and Josh Turner. Also on the grounds is **Storrowton Village,** an authentic re-creation of a 19th-century village. It's open from late June through Labor Day, Tuesday through Saturday 11am to 3pm.

WHAT TO SEE & DO

Naismith Memorial Basketball Hall of Fame ★★ *Kids*   A feast for fans, the Basketball Hall of Fame is painless even for those who regard the game as a blur of 7-foot armpits. It has been so popular that this entirely new facility was opened near the original hall in 2002, on a sliver of land between I-91 and the train tracks. Start at the top (third) level at the Honors Ring, with biographies of the players enshrined in the Hall. Interactive displays feature vast quantities of memorabilia and history of the sport, which was invented by Canadian-born Dr. James Naismith in Springfield in 1891 (remember the Chicago Studebakers or the Philadelphia Hebrews?). On the ground floor is a court where clinics and skill challenges are held, and where anyone can pick up a ball and shoot a few. There are several restaurant chain options in the complex, and a Hilton hotel on the other side of the parking lot.

1000 W. Columbus Ave. (at Union St.). © 413/781-6500. www.hoophall.com. Admission $17 adults, $14 seniors, $12 children 5–15. Daily 10am–4pm (until 5pm Sat–Sun).

Six Flags New England *Kids*   The big amusement park of the region, Six Flags offers over 60 rides in total, varying in excitement quotient to satisfy every member of the family. Among the most popular are "Superman—Ride of Steel" and "Batman—The Dark Knight," a floorless roller coaster that puts its deliriously terrified passengers through corkscrew turns, loops, and rolls at speeds of up to 55 mph. In 2007 the park added a "Wiggles World" area for younger children. It's particularly big on water activities, with over 25 water slides, a sand beach, two wave pools, and poolside cabanas. There are frequent celebrations featuring Looney Tunes characters and Thursday night concerts in summer. *Tip:* Tickets can be purchased online at a discount.

1623 Main St. (Rte. 159) Agawam, MA 01001 © 413/786-9300. www.sixflags.com. $50 general admission, $30 anyone under 5'4," free for ages 2 and under. Mid-June through Aug daily 10:30am to at least 8pm most days; check for exact hours. Limited hours mid-Apr to mid-June and Sept–Nov. Closed Nov to mid-Apr. The park is 6 miles south of Springfield.

Springfield Museums at the Quadrangle ★ *Kids*   Four museums and a library surrounding a grassy quadrangle constitute this worthwhile resource. There is a Welcome Center (daily 9am–5pm) on Edwards Street that sells tickets, which are good for all four museums.

Fun Fact **Dr. Seuss's Neighborhood**

The grandparents of the writer and illustrator who called himself Dr. Seuss lived on Springfield's Mulberry Street, and in 1937, he named the first of his dozens of children's books . . . *And to Think That I Saw It on Mulberry Street.* (The book was rejected by 27 publishers before finding a home at Vanguard Press.) Theodor Seuss Geisel followed up with such classics as *The Cat in the Hat* and *How the Grinch Stole Christmas.* Over 200 million copies of his books have been sold, and they've been translated into 15 languages.

Geisel spent most of his adult life in California, but much of his inspiration for his children's books can be traced to Springfield. His drawing of Bartholomew Cubbins's castle bears a strong resemblance to the Howard Street Armory, and some of his landscapes look as if they were recalled from his playtime in Forest Park, near his boyhood home at 74 Fairfield St.

Mulberry Street still has some of the charm of its august years, with Victorian manses outnumbering the undistinguished apartment buildings along its length.

Attached to the center is the **Springfield Science Museum,** which contains a planetarium, dioramas of African animals, and a small Dinosaur Hall.

The **Connecticut Valley Historical Museum** houses a replica 1780s kitchen with its hearth for cooking and low ceilings that kept heat in during New England winters; examples of weapons made by the city's firearms manufacturers in the 1800s; and a yellowing copy of a 1918 newspaper declaring the Red Sox World Series victory.

The **Museum of Fine Arts** ✪ is the most important of the lot, with over a dozen galleries. A Currier & Ives gallery has new exhibits of work by the printmakers every 6 months, while other galleries feature Colonial paintings from Gilbert Stuart and John Copley of the Revolutionary period all the way up to 20th-century abstract expressionists—Frank Stella, Helen Frankenthaler, and George Sugarman.

On the end of the quad near the library is the **George Walter Vincent Smith Art Museum,** housed in an 1896 Italian Renaissance–style mansion. Upstairs are largely sentimental pastoral scenes, with a few small landscapes by George Inness, Thomas Cole, and Albert Bierstadt. The main floor displays Japanese samurai weaponry surrounding a carved 1805 Shinto shrine, as well as a room of full-size casts of classical Greek and Renaissance sculptures.

The Quad itself is a peaceful respite, with marble benches throughout the small park. On the library end is the **Dr. Seuss National Memorial Sculpture Garden,** with sculptures of the author himself (who was born in Springfield), the Cat in the Hat, and the Grinch. The one blemish is that overhanging trees are favorites for birds, with the unfortunate results below.

State and Chestnut sts. ✆ **413/263-6800.** www.springfieldmuseums.org and www.catinthehat.org. Sculpture garden free. Combined admission for all 4 museums: $10 adults, $7 seniors and college students, $5 children 3–17; $3 for the planetarium. Tues–Sun 11am–4pm.

WHERE TO STAY

The two properties listed here are directly across the street from one another.

Sheraton Springfield ★★   A somewhat dreary lobby, with a barking flatscreen TV, is made up for by a friendly staff and renovated rooms on floors 3, 4, and 9 through 12. Updates included new beds, drapery, and carpets. The hotel has a large inner atrium that rooms open onto two concierge-level floors, where guests get breakfast and afternoon hors d'oeuvres. The Sheraton can be a treat after a few nights in idiosyncratic New England B&Bs: Predictable, yes, but with conveniences like two capable restaurants, room service, and an expansive spa and fitness center, charm can suddenly seem overrated.

One Monarch Place, Springfield, MA 01114. ✆ **800/426-9004** or 413/781-1010. Fax 413/747-8065. www.sheraton-springfield.com. 325 units. $109–$189 double. Packages available. Valet parking $13; self-parking $9.95. Pets allowed. AE, MC, V. **Amenities:** 2 restaurants (American); bar; heated indoor pool; health club; sauna; business center; limited room service; dry cleaning. In room: A/C, TV w/pay movies, high-speed Internet access, coffeemaker, hair dryer, iron.

Springfield Marriott ★★   A newly renovated lobby has given this Marriott a sparkling and modern overhaul. The hotel is clean, well appointed, and trim. Freshened guest rooms have new fabrics, dark wood, and marble bathroom floors and sinks. Among the perks are two concierge-level floors. Rooms are on the seventh floor or higher, and some corner rooms have particularly large bathrooms. An in-house sports bar boasts a 10-foot television screen. The entire hotel is nonsmoking and features wireless Internet.

2 Boland Way, Springfield, MA 01105. ✆ **800/228-9290** or 413/781-7111. Fax 413/731-8932. www.marriotthotels.com. 265 units. $89–$204 double. Packages available. Parking $13. AE, DISC, MC, V. **Amenities:** 2 restaurants (Continental/American); 2 bars; heated indoor pool; health club; sauna; business center; limited room service; same-day dry cleaning. In room: A/C, TV w/pay movies, high-speed Internet access and Wi-Fi, coffeemaker, hair dryer, iron.

WHERE TO DINE

Student Prince (The Fort) ★ GERMAN/AMERICAN   In 1935, German immigrants opened the Student Prince and began serving schnitzels and sauerbraten. That might not have seemed the precise historical moment to ensure the success of such an enterprise, but somehow the restaurant thrived. Today it can seat 248. Waitresses rush about in sensible shoes, slapping plates down and tolerating no lip. Monster portions are the rule, with veal shanks as thick as a linebacker's forearm. Weiner schnitzel, roulade, and sauerbraten are to be expected in such a setting, but are no less tasty for that. Be sure to take a peek at the enormous stein collection in the bar, which fills shelves all the way to the high ceiling.

8 Fort St. ✆ **413/788-6628.** www.studentprince.com. Main courses $9.95–$26. AE, DISC, MC, V. Mon–Sat 11am–11pm; Sun noon–9pm.

SPRINGFIELD AFTER DARK

Symphony Hall, 34 Court St., at East Columbus Avenue (✆ **413/788-7033;** www.symphonyhall.com), is a venue for touring musicals such as *Hairspray* and *Chicago,* children's shows, and the **Springfield Symphony Orchestra.** The orchestra's main season runs September through May, and during the summer it performs outdoor concerts locally and in the Berkshires. Its box office is around the corner at 1350 Main St. (✆ **413/733-2291;** www.springfieldsymphony.org).

An ever-changing collection of beer-and-pool joints, music bars, and eateries lies along downtown Worthington and Bridge streets near our two recommended hotels. Among the possibilities are **Theodore's Booze, Blues & BBQ,** 201 Worthington St.

(© 413/736-6000; www.theobbq.com), showcasing blues bands on Friday and Saturday; and the **Fat Cat Bar & Grill,** across the street at 232 Worthington St. (© 413/734-0554), with live music and other entertainment.

4 The Pioneer Valley

Holyoke: 4 miles N of I-90 (via I-91) and 90 miles W of Boston; South Hadley: 5 miles N of I-90; Northampton: 17 miles N of I-90; Amherst: 24 miles N of I-90; Deerfield: 34 miles N of I-90; Turners Falls: 43 miles N of I-90 and 91 miles NW of Boston (via Rte. 2)

Low hills and quilted fields channel the Connecticut River as it runs south toward Long Island Sound, forming the Pioneer Valley. The earliest European settlers came here in the mid-1600s for what proved to be uncommonly fertile soil and were followed in the 19th century by men who harnessed the power of the river and became wealthy textile and paper manufacturers.

These industrialists took the lead in funding the institutions of higher learning that are now the pride of the region. Prestigious Smith, Mount Holyoke, and Amherst are here, as are innovative Hampshire College and the sprawling main campus of the University of Massachusetts, with its 25,600 students. All five contribute mightily to the cultural life of the valley, and the towns of **Northampton, Amherst,** and **South Hadley** are invigorated by the vitality of thousands of college-age young people.

In the north, closer to Vermont, the old section in the village of **Deerfield** preserves the architecture and atmosphere of Colonial New England, while **Turners Falls** is a town-that-time-forgot that artists are now remaking.

Interstate 91 and the smaller Route 5 traverse the valley from south to north, more or less parallel to each other. On the interstate, the region takes less than an hour to drive from edge to edge, while Route 5 tenders more of the flavor of pastoral vistas and colorful mill towns.

The **Massachusetts Office of Travel & Tourism** (© 800/227-6277 or 617/973-8500; www.massvacation.com/lodging) website has an easy-to-use search function for lodgings. Note that room rates pop considerably at graduation time (early May) and when parents come through to drop off students (late Aug and early Sept).

ESSENTIALS

GETTING THERE From Boston and upstate New York, take the Massachusetts Turnpike (I-90) to Springfield, then I-91 or Route 5 north. While there are local buses, you really need a car to explore this area.

The nearest major airport is **Bradley International** (© 203/627-3000; airport code BDL), in Windsor Locks, Connecticut. (See "Springfield," earlier in this chapter, for a list of airlines that serve Bradley.) **Valley Transporter** (© 800/872-8752 or 413/253-1350; www.valleytransporter.com) offers van shuttles between the airport and the towns of the Pioneer Valley. Reservations recommended. **Peter Pan Bus Lines** (© 800/343-9999; www.peterpanbus.com) schedules frequent connections between Springfield and the towns of the Valley.

Amtrak (© 800/USA-RAIL; www.amtrak.com) *Vermonter* line trains stop in Amherst on the route between St. Albans, Vermont, and Washington, D.C., traveling through New York City.

VISITOR INFORMATION Downloadable maps of the Pioneer Valley overall, Holyoke, Northampton, and Amherst are at **www.valleyvisitor.com**.

HOLYOKE

Once an important paper-manufacturing center, Holyoke has suffered a long economic slide since World War II and is nearly all rough edges today, with abandoned factories and a dissolute air. Fans of industrial architecture, however, may well find the city visually intriguing: Canals dug during the city's mid-19th-century heyday still cut through town, and the skyline is bleakly atmospheric.

To take it in, make **Heritage State Park** (© 413/534-1723; www.mass.gov) a destination. The small park runs along a canal, and you'll pass by many of the old mills on the drive there. Follow signs for Main Street (a nondescript commercial road) and turn left onto Appleton Street. The entrance and parking lot is at 221 Appleton St., across from the police station. An interpretive center offers walking tours and exhibits, and there's a **restored antique merry-go-round.** Just beyond the center is the **Volleyball Hall of Fame** (© 413/536-0926; www.volleyhall.org).

SOUTH HADLEY

The essential reason that this stately town pops up on Route 116 amid the farming and working-class communities that are its neighbors is **Mount Holyoke College.** Pioneer educator Mary Lyon founded the school (then a seminary) in 1837, and the college is the oldest of the "Seven Sisters" schools for women.

On the college campus is a worthy **Art Museum** ★ (© 413/538-2245; www.mtholyoke.edu), which focuses on art of Asia, Egypt, and the Mediterranean. Renovation and expansion has brought more of the collection into regular view. Hours are Tuesday through Friday from 11am to 5pm, Saturday and Sunday from 1 to 5pm. Admission is free.

Joseph A. Skinner State Park (© 413/586-0350; www.mass.gov) straddles the border between South Hadley and Hadley. On its 400 acres are picnic grounds, miles of trails, and the historic **Summit House** (May–Oct Sat–Sun 10am to 5pm), with panoramic views of the valley. The 1½-mile road to the summit is open to cars from mid-April to mid-November and to walkers year-round. The park entrance is on Mountain Road, off Route 47, in Hadley.

NORTHAMPTON ★★

Smith College, with its campus sprawling along Main Street just west of the commercial center, is Northampton's dominating physical and spiritual presence. Another of the "Seven Sisters," Smith is now the largest female liberal arts college in the United States.

Northampton, known locally as "Noho," is the cultural center of the valley, with events that range from chamber music to art exhibitions to an **independent film festival** (www.niff.org) each November. The number and diversity of restaurants are far greater than most cities its size can flaunt, and its many stores are as kicky as any devout shopper might ask. Try to allow at least a long day and overnight in the area.

The city has a large gay and lesbian population, and a **Pride March** is held every May (www.northamptonpride.org). A well-received book by Tracy Kidder, *Home Town* (Random House, 1999), profiled Northampton and a number of its citizens.

Tip: The city has a strong tradition of *crosswalk courtesy:* Once a pedestrian puts a toe into a crosswalk, cars in both directions stop. Take note when you're driving.

WHAT TO SEE & DO

President Calvin Coolidge practiced law in Northampton, before and after his occupancy of the Oval Office. He lived in houses at 21 Massasoit St. and on Hampton

The Pioneer Valley

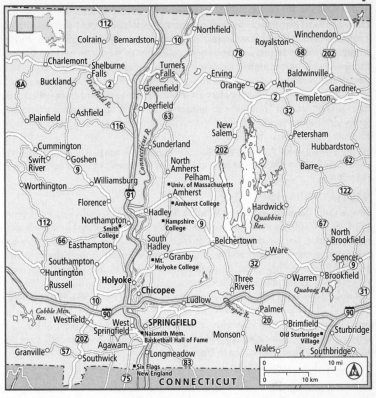

Terrace, but these are not open to the public. However, the **Forbes Library,** 20 West St. (📞 **413/584-6037;** www.forbeslibrary.org), maintains the Calvin Coolidge Presidential Library & Museum, which is open to researchers. A number of Coolidge photos are posted at the Forbes website.

Historic Northampton   This education center used to allow visitors to tour the three 18th- and early-19th-century homes on its property, but no more (there's a chance the 1730 Parsons House might reopen at some point). For now a small museum displays items such as cradles and carved chests from the 1700s, Calvin Coolidge memorabilia, and a dozen ornate silk dresses from 1835 to 1910.

46 Bridge St. (east of the railroad bridge). 📞 413/584-6011. www.historic-northampton.org. Admission $3 adults, $6 family. Mon–Sat 10am–5pm; Sun noon–5pm.

Smith College ✪   Equal parts tranquil and heady, the Smith campus is a bucolic mélange of rolling hills, broad lawns, and Gothic, Greco-Roman, Renaissance, and medieval architecture. Visitors are as likely to hear undergrads who say "See you in glee club!" as they are to see the phrase "Patriarchy Sux!" written in chalk. Frederick Law Olmsted, famed for his design of New York's Central Park, laid out much of the original landscaping, and the campus contains wooded walks and botanic gardens.

Elm St. 📞 413/584-2700. www.smith.edu.

Smith College Museum of Art ⟨★★⟩   With the 2003 conclusion of a $35-million renovation and expansion, this facility stepped up to claim equal footing with New England's finest college art museums, including those at Williams, Harvard, and Yale. It already had an impressive permanent collection of paintings by Degas, Monet, Picasso, and Winslow Homer, among many 19th- and 20th-century Europeans and Americans. Now there is not only more space to show them, but also ample room for an ambitious program of temporary exhibitions. The new third-floor galleries have fine views of town and campus, and allow abundant light for canvases. An atrium cafe serves drinks and snacks. Parking is a challenge (there's no lot specifically for the museum) but is worth the effort.

Elm St. and Bedford Terrace. ⟨€⟩ 413/585-2760. www.smith.edu/artmuseum. Admission $5 adults, $4 seniors, $3 students, $2 ages 6–12. Tues–Sat 10am–4pm; Sun noon–4pm. Second Fri of the month open until 8pm, with free admission 4–8pm.

GETTING OUTSIDE

The **Arcadia Nature Center and Wildlife Sanctuary,** 127 Combs Rd., Easthampton (⟨€⟩ **413/584-3009;** www.massaudubon.org), is a preserve operated by the Massachusetts Audubon Society with 5 miles of trails. Bordering the Connecticut River, the sanctuary contains marshes and woods, and offers **evening canoe rides** in summer. Located 3 miles southwest of Northampton on Route 10, the center is open daily. Admission is $4 for adults, $3 for seniors and children ages 3 to 12.

   Look Memorial Park, 300 N. Main St., Florence (⟨€⟩ **413/584-5457;** www.look park.org), is just northwest of Northampton off Route 9. The park has woods, a lake, pedal boats for rent, miniature golf, tennis courts, and picnic grounds. There are frequent special events for children and families. Admission is $4 weekends from April to October, $2 from November to March.

SHOPPING

Northampton enjoys the most diverse shopping in the valley. Its half-mile-long Main Street, from Bridge Street at the eastern end to the Smith College campus on the western end, is rich with upscale restaurants, art galleries, acupuncture clinics, shops with hand-crafted jewelry, buskers, and clothing boutiques, and has become nearly chic over the past 20 years. It's as easy to find vegan chocolate and organic egg omelets here as Ugg boots and expensive glass artworks.

   A former department store was reconfigured into **Thorne's Marketplace,** 150 Main St. (⟨€⟩ **413/584-5582;** www.thornesmarketplace.com), now containing more than 30 boutiques and casual eating places. Next to the side entrance is **Herrell's,** 7 Old South St. (⟨€⟩ **413/586-9700;** www.herrells.com), a celebrated New England super-premium ice-cream emporium, scooping a huge variety of flavors, including Malted Vanilla, Derby Chocolate Bourbon, and Pumpkin.

   Burnishing the city's reputation as a small town with an unusually vigorous arts community is the prestigious **R. Michelson Gallery,** 132 Main St. (⟨€⟩ **413/586-3964**), which occupies a grand former bank.

   And there are, of course, the used bookstores. "The Pioneer Valley is arguably the most author-saturated, book-cherishing, literature-celebrating place in the nation," wrote the *New York Times.* Nine independent bookstores in downtown vouch for it.

WHERE TO STAY

Anticipate higher rates and limited vacancies during graduation and homecoming, in addition to the usual holiday weekends.

Clarion Hotel ⚘   Renovations have elevated this property from a standard motel into a modest conference center. In the center atrium there's a heated indoor pool with a clear roof that lets in light; poolside and balcony rooms here are priced a little higher. All rooms got comfy new beds and carpeting during the 2006–07 winter season. Units in the A wing, which are bundled more or less around an interior rock garden, are least likely to be housing the frequent sports teams that stay here.

One Atwood Dr. (Rte. 5, 1 mile south of Main St.), Northampton, MA 01060. © 800/582-2929 or 413/586-1211. Fax 413/586-0630. www.hampshirehospitality.com. 122 units. $99–$200 double; $150–$212 suite. Pets accepted ($20). AE, DC, DISC, MC, V. **Amenities:** Restaurant (steakhouse); bar; heated indoor pool; outdoor pool; kiddie pool; tennis court; game room; computer for guests in lobby; limited room service. *In room:* A/C, TV, free Wi-Fi, coffeemaker, hair dryer, iron, safe.

Hotel Northampton ⚘   Built in 1927, this brick building is a grand focal point at the center of town. Classical music and a large spray of flowers greet guests in the lobby. Rooms vary in size and contain Colonial reproductions, feather duvets, and assorted Victoriana. Many front rooms have balconies overlooking King Street, some have fridges, and a few have Jacuzzis. Rooms also have high-tech touches like high-definition 32-inch flatscreen TVs and Wi-Fi, with iPod docking stations expected by year end. Newspapers are delivered each morning. Downstairs, **Wiggins Tavern** is an atmospheric watering hole with dark beams and three stone fireplaces, and the **Coolidge Park Café** has an outdoor terrace in warm weather.

36 King St. (Rte. 5), Northampton, MA 01060. © 800/547-3529 or 413/584-3100. Fax 413/584-9455. www.hotel northampton.com. 106 units. Apr–Nov $165–$230 double; Dec–Mar $145–$215 double. Rates include continental breakfast. AE, DC, DISC, MC, V. Free parking. **Amenities:** 2 restaurants (American); bar; 24-hr. exercise room; 24-hr. business center; limited room service; same-day laundry; dry cleaning. *In room:* A/C, TV, high-speed Internet and Wi-Fi, coffeemaker, hair dryer, iron, safe, robes.

WHERE TO DINE

Eastside Grill ⚘⚘ AMERICAN   This white-clapboard building with a nautical look is particularly appealing to the over-40 set looking for refuge from the prevailing collegiate tone of Northampton. About a third of the entrees involve beef, such as the delicious tenderloins with Gorgonzola and fried leeks, but the seafood choices are impressive, too, especially the sweat pea risotto made with lobster broth and topped with fistfuls of fat scallops, shrimp, and PEI mussels. The grill is noisy and can border on raucous, and service can be slow; it's the place for a good, generous, and fairly priced meal, not a romantic one.

19 Strong Ave. (1 block south of Main St.). © 413/586-3347. www.eastsidegrill.com. Reservations recommended. Main courses $8.50–$21. AE, DC, DISC, MC, V. Mon–Thurs 5–10pm; Fri 5–10:30pm; Sat 4–10:30pm; Sun 4–9pm.

Fitzwilly's AMERICAN   Occupying an 1898 building, this ingratiating pub makes the most of its stamped-tin ceilings and ample space. Copper brewing kettles signal an intriguing selection of beers, and patrons dive into pub faves nachos, burgers, pizzas, crab cakes, and fried calamari. Everything is available for takeout.

23 Main St. (near the bridge). © 413/584-8666. www.fitzwillys.com. Main courses $13–$19. AE, DC, DISC, MC, V. Daily 11:30am–1am.

Green Street Café ⚘ FRENCH   Closed for much of 2007 over a rental issue with Smith College, the much-beloved cafe reopened in late 2007 with a new lease on life and a small attached wine bar. The menu includes escargots and potatoes in parchment, and roast duck leg confit with red cabbage. The restaurant grows its own vegetables in season, and the emphasis throughout the year is on fresh ingredients. There are monthly wine tasting evenings for $25.

64 Green St. (✆ **413/586-5650.** Reservations recommended. Main courses $8–$26. MC, V. Mon–Fri noon–2pm; Sun 10am–2pm; daily 5–10pm. Wine bar open until midnight. Follow Main St. toward the Smith campus, bear left onto West St., turn right on Green St.

Osaka JAPANESE Sushi *and* steak? They're not always paired together, but at Osaka the blend regularly wins the local readers' favorite award—it's the odds-on best of breed in the Valley. Decor includes lots of blond wood, with a sushi bar at the entrance. The menu lists 47 kinds of rolls, over two dozen selections of a la carte sushi and sashimi, and 13 vegetable sushi maki. Then it takes a deep breath before adding soups, chef's specials, teriyaki, hibachi dinners, and so on. The spicy red snapper, ebi tempura, maki, and Naruto roll have all been good.

7 Old South St. (1 block off Main St.). (✆ **413/587-9548.** www.osakanorthampton.com. Rolls $4.50–$13; sushi a la carte $2.50–$12; main courses $11–$26. AE, DC, DISC, MC, V. Mon–Sat 11:30am–11pm (Fri–Sat until midnight); Sun 12:30–11pm.

Spoleto ITALIAN With high ceilings, Tuscan-orange walls, and red banquettes ringing the edges of the room, Mediterranean-rich Spoleto has an upscale-casual Euro flair that fits right into this academic town with its well-traveled populace. The bolognese is justifiably popular: a 12-inch bowl piled high with pasta and a thick sauce of ground sausage, beef, and veil. Paired with a local ale from the Berkshire Brewing Company, it's as hearty a meal as one could ask for. The visual center is a bar that juts into the main room, and it's a comfortable place for solo eaters to dine.

50 Main St. (✆ **413/586-6313.** www.spoletorestaurants.com. Main courses $14–$25. AE, DISC, MC, V. Mon–Thurs 5–10pm (Fri–Sat until 11pm); Sun 4–9pm.

NORTHAMPTON AFTER DARK

Northampton is the nightlife magnet of the valley. For a rundown of what's happening, look for the free *Valley Advocate* (www.valleyadvocate.com).

An old favorite, the **Iron Horse Music Hall,** 20 Center St. (✆ **413/586-8686;** www.iheg.com), hosts a wide variety of artists nearly nightly, from Bruce Cockburn and The Magnetic Fields to regional folk singers and grunge rockers. Cover for live acts is typically between $10 and $20. A sister venue, the **Calvin Theatre and Performing Arts Center,** 19 King St. (✆ **401/584-1444;** www.iheg.com), offers performers as diverse as Lyle Lovett, Steve Earle, and touring ballet companies.

Open since 1891, the **Academy of Music,** 274 Main St. (✆ **413/584-9032;** www.academyofmusictheatre.com), shows art-house and foreign films and provides a venue for symphony concerts, children's shows, and local theater.

Bishop's Lounge, 41 Strong Ave. (✆ **413/586-8900;** www.mulinos.com), a sophisticated update of the funky old Bay State Hotel, has live music of scattered identity 6 nights a week and karaoke on Sunday.

Classical and chamber music is the customary fare at Smith's **Sweeney Concert Hall,** Sage Hall (✆ **413/586-8686**).

The renovated **Pleasant Street Theater**, 27 Pleasant St. (✆ **413/584-5848;** www. pleasantstreettheater.com), is an independent art movie house. It was recently purchased by the independent **Amherst Cinema Art Center,** 28 Amity St., Amherst (✆ **413/253-2547;** www.amherstcinema.org).

AMHERST

Yet another Pioneer Valley town defined by its educational institutions, this one has an even larger student population than most, with distinguished **Amherst College** occupying much of its center, the large **University of Massachusetts** campus to its immediate northwest, and **Hampshire College** off South Pleasant Street.

On the edge of the town green is a seasonal **information booth.** Its hours vary, but if it's closed, visitors can call the **Chamber of Commerce** (© **413/253-0700**).

WHAT TO SEE & DO

The best strolling is within a few blocks any direction of the town green. At the northeast corner of the green is the **Town Hall,** a fortresslike Romanesque Revival creation of Boston's H. H. Richardson.

Amherst College   Named for Baron Jeffery Amherst, a British general during the last of the French and Indian Wars, the illustrious liberal-arts college was founded in 1821. Robert Frost was a member of the faculty for more than a decade. Amherst's campus cuts through the heart of the town and makes for a pretty stroll. The **Mead Art Museum** ✸, routes 116 and 9 (© **413/542-2335**), specializes in American art, including Hudson River School landscapes and modern works by Robert Henri and Frank Stella. Admission is free, and it's open daily except Monday.

S. Pleasant and College sts. © 413/542-2000. www.amherst.edu.

The Emily Dickinson Museum: The Homestead and The Evergreens ✸   Designated a National Historic Monument, the Homestead is where Emily Dickinson was born in 1830 and where she lived until her family moved in 1840, and the Evergreens was the next-door home of Emily's brother Austin and his wife. Emily and her family returned in 1855, and the famous poet stayed here until her death 31 years later. The "Belle of Amherst" was the granddaughter and daughter of local movers and shakers, the source of her support while she produced the poetry that was increasingly celebrated even as she withdrew into near-total seclusion. The two buildings now make up Emily Dickinson Museum, with a free Tour Center, bookshop, and exhibit space in the Homestead, and guided tours of both homes.

280 Main St. (2 blocks east of the Town Hall). © 413/542-8161. www.emilydickinsonmuseum.org. Free to visit the center and bookshop. Entrance to Homestead and Evergreens by guided tour only: $8 adults, $7 seniors and students, $5 ages 6–18, free for children under 6. Center open Mar–Dec 13 Wed–Sun 11am–5pm, guided tours 1–3:30pm. Closed the rest of the year. Reservations recommended.

National Yiddish Book Center   This airy complex on the Hampshire College campus is devoted to rescuing and redistributing Yiddish-language books and to celebrating Yiddish culture through films, lectures, and other public events. In addition to a large book depository, the center has four exhibition galleries, a bookstore, the last Yiddish linotype machine used to publish the *Jewish Daily Forward* newspaper, a library, and a theater—be sure to see the spectacular chandelier here. The center sits in an apple orchard and there are gardens and picnic tables.

1021 West St. (Rte. 116). © 413/256-4900. www.yiddishbookcenter.org. Free admission. Mon–Fri 10am–3:30pm; Sun 11am–4pm.

University of Massachusetts Fine Arts Center   Situated on a sprawling 1,450-acre campus north of the town center, UMass Amherst's FAC books a variety of international dance, flamenco, jazz, and choral groups. The foremost of the campus's six galleries is here, too: The **University Gallery** ⭐ focuses on 20th-century work. Park in the metered public lot behind the visitor center; the FAC is across the street.

UMass campus. 🕐 413/545-2511. www.umass.edu/fac. Free admission. University Gallery Tues–Fri 11am–4:30pm; Sat–Sun 2–5pm.

GETTING OUTSIDE

The **Norwottuck Rail Trail** (🕐 413/586-8706, ext. 12; www.hadleyonline.com/railtrail) follows the former Boston and Maine rail bed for 10 miles through Northampton, Hadley, and Amherst, more or less parallel to Route 9. In the midsection it passes through open farmland. Rentals are available from **Valley Bicycles,** 8 Railroad St., Hadley (🕐 **413/584-4466**).

SHOPPING

The **Jeffrey Amherst Bookshop,** 55 S. Pleasant St. (🕐 **413/253-3381;** www.jeffbooks.com), specializes in Emily Dickinson books. **Scandihoovians,** 25 S. Pleasant St. (🕐 **413/256-0004;** www.scandihoovians.com), features Scandinavian housewares, clothing, jewelry, and Marimekko bags; the original store is in Northampton. **Clay's,** 32 Main St. (🕐 **413/256-4200**), has funky, flowing women's clothes in natural fibers; a small sign on the way to the dressing room says, "You are radiant & beautiful." **Harlow,** 196 Main St. (🕐 **413/584-5233;** www.harlowluggage.com) was founded in 1875 and sells suitcases, wallets, bags, and other travel items.

WHERE TO STAY

Courtyard By Marriott   Open since May 2007, the Marriott is the new jewel of the Hampshire Hospitality chain, which runs six other properties in the area (including the Clarion in Northampton; see above). Rooms have a sleek decor befitting more expensive properties: cherry wood work desks, two telephones in each room, flatscreen TVs. Located on the main drag, Route 9, just at the Hadley/Amherst border, it's convenient to the UMass campus and set back enough to be quiet inside. There's a well-appointed fitness room, and the hotel is entirely smoke-free.

423 Russell St. (Rte. 9), Hadley, MA 01035. 🕐 **800/321-2211** or 413/256-5454. Fax 413/256-5422. www.marriott.com/bdlhd. 96 units. $120–$160 double; $180–$220 suite. AE, DC, DISC, MC, V. **Amenities:** Restaurant (breakfast only); bar; small indoor pool; 24-hr. exercise room; 24-hr. business center; coin-op washers and dryers. *In room:* A/C, TV, free Wi-Fi and high-speed Internet, fridge, coffeemaker, iron, hair dryer.

Lord Jeffery Inn ⭐⭐   Perched directly on the town green, the central location of this small New England town, the Lord Jeff is rich in elegant Colonial decor and offers an environment as warm as the wood fireplace that greets guests in the chilly months. Continually renovated rooms overlook either the common, a private courtyard, or the stone Episcopal church next door. Midpriced preferred rooms, such as no. 44 with a queen bed and sitting area, are nearly suite sized. The **Windowed Hearth** is Amherst's event restaurant, open for dinner Wednesday through Sunday. (Be sure to see the large hearth with its peculiar interior window that gives the room its name.) Pub food is served in the casual **Elijah Boltwood's Tavern** 7am to 10pm daily.

30 Boltwood Ave. (next to the Town Hall), Amherst, MA 01002. 🕐 **413/253-2576.** Fax 413/256-6152. www.lordjefferyinn.com. 48 units. $79–$199 double; suites from $149. AE, MC, V. Pets accepted ($15). **Amenities:** 2 restaurants (creative regional); bar; limited room service. *In room:* A/C, TV, free Wi-Fi, iron, hair dryer.

WHERE TO DINE

Additional options are the restaurants of the Lord Jeffery Inn, above. Also see "Amherst After Dark," below,

Amherst Coffee CAFE If you're looking for the perfect cappuccino, come here: The coffee is strong but not bitter, and it's capped with a thick foam swirled with a decorative leaf pattern. Pair it with a pear-pecan muffin and chill out in the bright room and sea of laptops. There's a large shared wooden table down the center, and wine and nibbles at a small bar area after 5pm.

28 Armory St. ☎ 413/256-8987. www.amherstcoffee.com. Daily 6:30am–11pm (Sun open at 8am).

Chez Albert FRENCH Copper-top tables, French posters, and large picture windows give a Euro touch to this bistro overlooking the town green. For a light lunch, the Chez Salad is fresh with a tang, pairing mesclun greens and dried cherries with duck confit and chopped egg. Paired with the peppery white bean paste that's served with a rustic bread, you'll feel taken care of *and* as if you're following the dining habits of skinny French women. Other lunch options, which are about half the price of dinner main courses, include beef tartine and pork confit with prune.

27 S. Pleasant St. ☎ 413/253-3811. www.chezalbert.net. Main courses $21–$24. AE, DISC, MC, V. Wed–Fri and Sun 11:30am–2pm; Tues–Sat 5–9pm (until 10pm Thurs–Sat).

Judie's ☆☆ CREATIVE AMERICAN Don't leave Amherst without eating at the upbeat Judie's. The vivacious owner does her best to suit every taste. Throughout the day, folks drop by for a cup of seafood bisque or one of the trademark popovers (basil pesto chicken, for example). Typical dinner entrees are the steak and three-mushroom risotto, and the seafood gumbo with shrimp, sausage, scallops, salmon, and lobster. This being a college town, portions run from really big to immense, the better to assuage raging young metabolisms. From 3 to 6pm on weekdays there's "Munchie Madness," when snacks such as potato skins and black bean dip are all half-price.

51 N. Pleasant St. ☎ 413/253-3491. www.judiesrestaurant.com. Main courses $9–$20. AE, DISC, MC, V. Daily 11:30am–10pm (Fri–Sat until 11pm).

AMHERST AFTER DARK

Students and other young adults tend to gravitate toward the livelier music scene in Northampton, but Amherst does offer some nighttime entertainment. Close at hand is **The Black Sheep,** 79 Main St. (☎ 413/253-3442; www.blacksheepdeli.com), active with Celtic and bluegrass music. (The Black Sheep's cafe has sandwiches and a scrumptious dessert case.) At the **Amherst Brewing Company,** 24–36 N. Pleasant St. (☎ 413/253-4400; www.amherstbrewing.com), there's good homemade beer, as well as pool tables, foosball, and big TVs.

Amherst College's **Buckley Recital Hall** (☎ 413/542-2195) hosts chamber music performances that include classical quartets and solo pianists.

DEERFIELD ☆☆☆

Meadows cleared and plowed more than 330 years ago still surround this historic town between the Connecticut and Deerfield rivers. Every morning, tobacco and dairy farmers head out from here to work their land nearby.

Follow the signs to "Old Deerfield" or "Historic Deerfield," a turn-off of Route 5. This small neighborhood has more than 80 homes built in the 17th, 18th, and 19th centuries. Most are private, but 13 can be visited through tours conducted by Historic Deerfield, a local tourism organization (see below). On either side of the main street, students attend the distinguished prep school, **Deerfield Academy,** founded in 1797.

Deerfield is an invaluable fragment of American history (and has been designated a National Historic Landmark village). Massacres of Deerfield's English settlers by the

French and Indian enemies of the British nearly wiped out the town in 1675 and again in 1704. In the latter raid, 47 people were killed and another 112 were taken prisoner and marched to French Quebec.

Special **celebrations** in the town are held on Patriot's Day (the third Mon in Apr), Washington's Birthday, Thanksgiving, and the Christmas holidays. Call the information center in Hall Tavern (© **413/774-5581;** see below) for details.

WHAT TO SEE & DO

The main thoroughfare of Old Deerfield, simply called "**The Street,**" is a mile long. The museum houses are located a few blocks either direction of the visitor center.

Historic Deerfield Walking Tour 🟊🟊🟊 To stroll the main street and visit the properties open for viewing, park in one of the lots behind the Historic Deerfield visitor center (across the street from the teeny post office) or the Flynt Center of Early American Life. Begin with a visit to the **Hall Tavern** (the visitor center), where tickets for guided tours are sold. While there are no charges for walking the neighborhood, the only way to get inside the 13 museum houses is on one of the tours, which depart from here. There's also a booklet that outlines a walking tour of 88 historic locations.

Houses on the guided tour were constructed between 1730 and 1850. They contain furnishings, textiles, ceramics, silver and pewter, and implements used from the mid–17th century to 1850. Included are items made in the Connecticut River Valley during its prominence as an industrial center.

The **Flynt Center of Early American Life** 🟊 has galleries for changing exhibitions of textiles, paintings, and decorative arts relevant to the local history. Call ahead for hours, which can vary from the hours of the house tours.

A free attraction is the **Channing Blake Meadow Walk.** The trail begins beside the Rev. John Farwell Moors House, a Historic Deerfield holding on the west side of The Street. It goes through a working farm, past the playing fields of Deerfield Academy, and through pastures beside the Deerfield River. Along the trail, sheep and cattle are seen up close; for that reason, dogs aren't allowed.

A **Museum Store** (© **413/775-7170**) across the street from the visitor center sells a judicious selection of weather vanes, hand-dipped candles, and reproductions of household items found in the village houses.

80 Old Main St. © 413/775-7214. www.historic-deerfield.org. Admission $7 adults, $5 ages 6–21. Daily 9:30am–4:30pm. Closed Jan–Mar.

Memorial Hall Museum 🟊 Deerfield Academy's original 1798 building was converted into this museum of village history in 1880. A popular, if suggestively grisly, exhibit is the door of a 1698 home that shows the gashes made by weapons of the French and Indian raiders in 1704. Should the point be too subtle, a hatchet is also embedded in the door. Special events include concerts and the September quilt fest.

8 Memorial St. © 413/774-3768. www.old-deerfield.org. Admission $6 adults, $3 children and students, free for children under 6. May–Oct daily 11am–5pm; closed Nov–Apr.

Yankee Candle Village *(Kids)* This emporium is outside the Old Deerfield neighborhood, back on Route 5. The Yankee Candle Company is an empire built on Americans' insatiable love for candles that are scented like cider donuts or vanilla cupcakes. This flagship locale, though, is way more than just a store: It features a year-round Bavarian Christmas Village, a large toy shop, a homemade fudge stand, a candy store, a home furnishings department, an old-fashioned candle-dipping demonstration area, and a stage where the Candle Mountain Boys sing every 30 minutes.

25 Greenfield Rd. (Rte. 5), South Deerfield. © 877/636-7707. www.yankeecandle.com. Free admission.

WHERE TO STAY & DINE

Deerfield Inn ★ Built in 1884, this inn in the middle of The Street in Old Deerfield is one of the best-known stopping places in the valley. The innkeepers have restlessly scoured the establishment over the last few years, replacing all the bathroom fixtures, refinishing the older furniture, installing new carpeting and flatscreen TVs. Antiques and reproductions are judiciously mixed throughout. With blazes in the several fireplaces and an atmospheric tavern in which to linger, this is as pleasant a setting as can be found. That said, the food served in the dining room and in the cafe is no better than ordinary.

81 Old Main St., Deerfield, MA 01342. © 800/926-3865 or 413/774-5587. Fax 413/775-7102. www.deerfield inn.com. 23 units. $145–$240 double. Rates include continental breakfast. Packages available. AE, MC, V. **Amenities:** Restaurant (American); cafeteria; bar; laundry service; dry cleaning. *In room:* A/C, TV/DVD, free Wi-Fi, CD player, coffeemaker, hair dryer, iron.

TURNERS FALLS

The village of Turners Falls was built in the 1860s as a mill town along the Connecticut River, and immigrants from Germany, French Canada, Lithuania, and Ireland all came to chase their dreams. As with other spots in the region, the village began a long economic slide when the mills started closing in the 1940s.

The profile of Turners Falls has begun to rise in recent years, however, thanks to new artistic programming and an active partnership among cultural and commercial groups. Together they're pumping new life in a town that still looks much like it must have 70 years ago, and cafes and boutiques now rub elbows with more modest shops on Avenue A, the main drag.

Start a visit at the new **Great Falls Discovery Center,** 2 Ave. A (© **413/863-3221;** www.greatfallsma.org), which has dioramas of the shoreline and birding culture along the Connecticut River. It's open Tuesday through Sunday June through mid-October, Friday and Saturday the rest of the year. A useful brochure produced by **Turners Falls River Culture** (www.turnersfallsriverculture.org) details a 20-site walking tour that takes in the 19th-century brick buildings that still line the old-fashioned main street. Bicyclists also can park here and take a ride along the new **Franklin County Bikeway's Canalside Trail,** a 4-mile path that opened in early 2008. It starts a block closer to the canal and heads off to the left, to Deerfield.

The **Hallmark Museum of Contemporary Photography,** 52/56 and 85 Ave. A (© **413/863-0009;** www.hmcp.org), opened one gallery in January 2006 and added more snazzy space on the other side of the street in January 2008. Its detailed calendar features a full schedule of openings and public artist talks. The **Shea Theater,** 71 Ave. A (© **413/863-2281;** www.theshea.org), in the Colle Opera House building, was renovated in 2004 and now hosts music, community theater, and dance programs.

For snacks, the **2nd Street Baking Co.,** 69 2nd St. (© **413/863-4455**), makes its own whoopie pies and enormous vegan cookies.

The jewel of the area is about 5 miles away. The **Montague Mill,** 440 Greenfield Rd. (Rte. 47), Montague, is a red gristmill from 1834 that has been repurposed into several small businesses. They include the trim and comfortable **Montague Book Mill** (© **413/367-9206;** www.montaguebookmill.com), whose tagline is "Books you don't need in a place you can't find"; and **The Lady Killigrew Cafe and Pub** (© 413/ 367-9666; www.theladykilligrew.com), a cozy oasis of healthy snacks (brown rice salad, peanut-ginger udon noodles), a choice of wines, and free Wi-Fi (no espresso drinks, however). Its nine tables are perched nearly on top of the small Sawmill River and have spectacularly lovely views—not that all the people working on laptop computers appear to notice. From Turners Falls, head out on 3rd Street and take the right fork; the road turns into Route 47 and the mill comes up on your right after about 4½ miles.

5 The Berkshires

Sheffield: 119 miles N of New York City and 143 miles W of Boston; Great Barrington: 6 miles N of Sheffield; Stockbridge: 8 miles N of Great Barrington; Lee: 4 miles NE of Stockbridge; Lenox: 6 miles north of Stockbridge; Pittsfield: 7 miles north of Lenox; Williamstown and North Adams: 21 miles N of Pittsfield, 202 miles N of New York City, and 131 miles NW of Boston.

More than hills but less than mountains, the Taconic and Hoosac ranges that define this region at the western end of Massachusetts go by the collective name "The Berkshires." The hamlets, villages, and two small cities have long drawn sustenance from the region's kindly Housatonic River and its tranquil tributaries, and are as New England as can be.

Mohawks and Mohegans lived and hunted here, and while white missionaries established settlements at Stockbridge and elsewhere in an attempt to Christianize the native tribes, the Indians eventually moved west. Farmers, drawn to the narrow but fertile flood plains of the Housatonic, were increasingly supplanted in the 19th century by manufacturers, who erected the brick mills that drew their power from the river.

At the same time, artists and writers were attracted by the mild summers and seclusion that these hills and lakes offered. Nathaniel Hawthorne, Herman Melville, and Edith Wharton were among those who put down temporary roots. By the late 19th century and the arrival of the railroad, wealthy New Yorkers and Bostonians had discovered the region and begun to erect extravagant summer "cottages." With their support, culture and the performing arts found a hospitable reception. By the 1930s, theater, dance, and music performances had established themselves as regular summer fixtures. Tanglewood, Jacob's Pillow, and the Berkshire and Williamstown Theatre festivals draw tens of thousands of visitors every summer.

Note that many inns routinely stipulate minimum 2- or 3-night stays in summer and over holiday weekends, and often require advance deposits.

ESSENTIALS

GETTING THERE   The Massachusetts Turnpike (I-90) runs east-west from Boston to the Berkshires, with an exit near Lee and Stockbridge. From New York City, the scenic Taconic State Parkway connects with I-90 not far from Pittsfield, or, to reach the southern end of the county, exit before that on the Taconic at Route 20 heading toward Hillsdale, New York, and Great Barrington, Massachusetts.

Amtrak (© 800/USA-RAIL; www.northeast.amtrak.com) operates the Lake Shore Limited daily between Boston and Chicago, stopping in Pittsfield each way.

VISITOR INFORMATION   The **Berkshire Visitors Bureau,** 3 Hoosac St., Adams, MA (© 800/237-5747 or 413/443-9186; www.berkshires.org), can assist with questions and lodging reservations. Local chambers of commerce and visitor centers maintain information booths at central locations in Great Barrington, Lee, Lenox, Pittsfield, Stockbridge, and Williamstown (see the sections that follow).

The Berkshires

SHEFFIELD ⊕

The first settlement of any size encountered when approaching from Connecticut on Route 7, Sheffield occupies a flood plain beside the Housatonic River, 11 miles south of Great Barrington, with the Berkshires rising to the west.

Agriculture has long been the principal occupation of its residents and still is, to a degree. Everyone else sells antiques, or so it might seem driving along Route 7 (also known as Main St. or Sheffield Plain). The meticulously maintained houses cultivate an impression of prosperous tranquillity.

Memorial Day to Columbus Day, stop by the **Ashley House,** Cooper Hill Road, in Ashley Falls (© **413/298-3239;** www.thetrustees.org). Built by Colonel Ashley himself in 1735, this modified saltbox is believed to be the oldest house in Berkshire County. Ashley was a person of considerable repute in Colonial western Massachusetts: a pioneer settler, an officer during one of the French and Indian Wars, and later a lawyer and a judge. The house is open from 10am to 5pm on Saturday and Sunday. Admission to the grounds is free; tours of the house are $5 for adults and $3 for children 6 to 12. To find it, drive south from Sheffield on Route 7, then veer onto Route 7A toward Ashley Falls. Bear right on Rannapo Road. At the Y intersection, turn right on Cooper Hill Road.

GETTING OUTSIDE

The 278-acre nature reservation called **Bartholomew's Cobble** ⊕, on Route 7A (© **413/229-8600;** www.thetrustees.org), lies beside an oxbow bend in the Housatonic River. A "cobble," by local definition, is a "scenic, rocky eminence rising from the valley floor." These 6 miles of trails cross pastures, penetrate forests, and provide vistas of the river valley from the area's high point, Hurlburt's Hill. Picnicking is permitted. Birders should take binoculars. Trails are open from sunrise to sunset, and the small natural-history museum is open daily from 9am to 4:30pm. Requested donations are $5 for adults and $3 for children 6 to 12.

Canoe tours on the Housatonic have naturalist guides to seek out wildlife along the river. The trips take 3 hours, departing from the visitor center. Fees are $30 for adults, $15 for children 10 to 16 years. Reservations are required; call the number above. To get here, follow the directions for the Colonel Ashley House (see above), except at the end of Rannapo Road, bear left on Weatogue Road.

ANTIQUING

Sheffield lays justifiable claim to the title of "Antiques Capital of the Berkshires"—no small feat, given what seems to be an effort by half the population of the Berkshires to sell collectibles, oddities, and true antiques to the other half. These are canny, knowledgeable dealers who know exactly what they have, so expect high quality and few bargains.

Darr Antiques and Interiors, 34 S. Main St. (© **413/229-7773**), specializes in 18th- and 19th-century English and American furniture. Farther north along Route 7, **Dovetail Antiques,** 440 Sheffield Plain (© **413/229-2628**), features American clocks. Continuing along Route 7, on the left at the edge of town, is **Susan Silver** (© **413/229-8169**), with meticulously restored 18th- and 19th-century English library furniture (desks, reading stands) and French accessories.

There are at least two dozen other dealers along this route. Most of them stock the **free directory** of the Berkshire County Antiques Dealers Association, which lists member dealers from Sheffield to Cheshire and across the border in Connecticut and New York. Look, too, for the pamphlet called *The Antique Hunter's Guide to Route 7.*

SOUTH EGREMONT

If you're coming to the Berkshires from the Taconic Parkway in New York, you can't help but drive through the town of Egremont. Its larger, busier half is South Egremont, once a stop on the stagecoach route between Hartford and Albany. It retains many structures from that era, including mills that utilized the stream that still rushes by. Those circumstances make it a magnet for antiques dealers and restaurateurs.

GETTING OUTSIDE

HIKING   Scenic **Bash-Bish Falls State Park** ★★, on Route 23 (© **413/528-0330;** www.mass.gov), makes a rewarding outing for a day of hiking, birding, and fishing (no picnicking, though). To get here, drive west on Route 23 from town, turning south on Route 41, and immediately right on Mount Washington Road. Watch for signs directing the way to Mount Washington State Forest and Bash-Bish Falls. After 8 miles, a sign indicates a right turn toward the falls; look for it opposite a church with an unusual steeple. The road begins to follow the course of a mountain stream, going downhill. In about 3 miles is a large parking place next to a craggy promontory.

The sign also points off to a trail down to the falls, which should be negotiated only by reasonably fit adults. First, mount the promontory for a splendid view across the plains of the Hudson Valley to the pale-blue ridgeline of the Catskill Mountains. The falls can be heard, but not yet seen, down to the left. If this trail seems too steep, continue driving down the road to another parking area, on the left. From here, a gentler trail, a little over a mile long, leads to the falls. The falls themselves are quite impressive, crashing down from more than 80 feet. The park is open from dawn to dusk. It has 15 campsites, but there are no services inside the park and alcoholic beverages aren't permitted.

SKIING   At the western edge of the township, touching the New York border, is the **Catamount Ski Area,** on Route 23 (© **413/528-1262;** www.catamountski.com). Only about 2 hours from Manhattan, it is understandably popular with New Yorkers. It has over 30 trails, including the daunting Catapult (the steepest run in the Berkshires) and seven chairlifts, as well as a 400-foot half-pipe for snowboarders. Night skiing and rentals are available. On weekends, full-day lift tickets cost $52 for adults, $42 for seniors and children 7 to 13, and $22 for children 6 and under.

WHERE TO STAY

Egremont Inn ★   Guests slip into this friendly former stagecoach stop as easily as into a favorite old flannel robe. The Egremont has been a tavern and inn since 1780. That longevity shows in tilting floors and a grand brick fireplace. Rooms are simple and rustic, with iron bedsteads, rag rugs, wide-board floors, and adequate bathrooms (and no TVs). Dinner is the main event, served Wednesday through Sunday year-round in the dining room, in the tavern, and out on the front porch A singer-guitarist performs Thursday nights, a jazz ensemble Saturday evenings. *Tip:* Rates are negotiable during slow periods and for long stays. Kids are welcome.

Old Sheffield Rd. (1 block off Rte. 23), South Egremont, MA 01258. © **413/528-2111.** Fax 413/528-3284. www.egremontinn.com. 20 units. $100–$200 double; 2–3 nights required on peak-season weekends. Rates include breakfast. Packages available. AE, DISC, MC, V. **Amenities:** Restaurant (American); tavern; outdoor pool; golf course nearby; 2 tennis courts; bike rental. *In room:* A/C.

Weathervane Inn   An affectionate cat welcomes new arrivals to a building that began as a 1735 farmhouse but was renovated in Greek Revival style in 1835. Many guest rooms have four-poster beds with quilts; fireplaces have been added to two units. In summer, a 3-night stay is required on weekends. Children are welcome. Yoga classes are held Monday through Saturday either at the barn at the inn or around the corner at the Berkshire Breathing Project.

Rte. 23, South Egremont, MA 01258. © 800/528-9580 or 413/528-2111. Fax 413/528-1713. www.weathervane inn.com. 10 units. $115–$165 double; $225–$275 suite. Rates include breakfast and afternoon tea. Packages available. AE, DC, MC, V. **Amenities:** Unheated outdoor pool; public golf course next door. *In room:* A/C, dataport.

GREAT BARRINGTON

Even with a population barely over 7,500, this pleasant retail center, 7 miles south of Stockbridge, is the largest town in the southern part of the county. Rapids in the Housatonic provided power for a number of mills in centuries past, most of which are now gone, and in 1886 this was one of the first communities in the world to have electricity on its streets and in its homes.

Great Barrington has no sights of particular significance, leaving time to browse its many antiques galleries and specialty shops. Convenient as a home base for excursions to such nearby attractions as Monument Mountain, Bash-Bish Falls, Butternut Basin, Tanglewood concerts, and the historic houses of Stockbridge, it has a number of unremarkable but entirely adequate motels north of the center along or near Route 7 that tend to fill up more slowly on weekends than the better-known inns in the area. Great Barrington is something of a dining destination, too, with 55 eating places, including, at last count, *four* sushi bars!

A farmer's market is held on Saturday from 9am to 1pm in season at the train station on Castle Street.

The **Southern Berkshire Chamber of Commerce** maintains an information booth at 362 Main St. (© **413/528-1510;** www.southernberkshires.com), near the town hall. It's open Tuesday through Sunday from 10am to 5pm.

GETTING OUTSIDE

The **Egremont Country Club,** on Route 23 (© **413/528-4222;** www.egremont countryclub.com), is open to the public. Its facilities include a scenic 18-hole golf course, tennis courts, and an Olympic-size pool. Greens fees are $45 on weekends and $25 on weekdays for visitors; tee times required.

Butternut Basin, on Route 23, 2 miles east of town (© **413/528-2000,** or 800/438-7669 for snow conditions; www.butternutbasin.com), is known for its strong family ski programs. There's day care for kids ages 2½ to 6, from December 23 until the end of the season, and the Mountaineer program for children 4 to 12 offers packages that include lunch, instruction, and lift tickets for $80 per day. Six double and quad chairlifts provide access to 22 trails. There are also 5 miles of cross-country trails. On weekends, full-day lift tickets cost $50 for adults, $40 for seniors and children 7 to 13, and $15 for children 6 and under.

A little over 4 miles north of town, west of Route 7, is **Monument Mountain,** with two trails to the summit. The easier route is the Indian Monument Trail, about an hour's hike to the top; the more difficult one, the Hickey Trail, isn't much longer but takes the steep way up. The summit, called Squaw Peak, offers splendid views.

SHOPPING

Head straight for Railroad Street, the town's best shopping strip. Start on the corner with Main Street, at **T. P. Saddle Blanket & Trading Co.** (© 413/528-6500). An unlikely emporium that looks as if it was lifted whole from the Rockies, it's packed with boots, hats, Indian jewelry, blankets, and jars of salsa.

Mistral's, 6 Railroad St. (© 413/528-1618), stocks Gallic tableware, linens, fancy foods, and furniture. **Church Street Trading Company,** 4 Railroad St. (© 413/528-6120), defies easy categorization, with walking sticks, dog collars, and candles all on display. Primary wares are sturdily stylish North Country sweaters, shirts, and pants.

The Chef's Shop, 31 Railroad St. (© 413/528-0135), features a bounty of gadgets and cookbooks, as well as cooking classes. Across the street, **La Pace,** 313 Main St. (© 413/528-1888), is an upmarket housewares store with an Italian tilt.

Stay on Route 7, going north of the center, and you'll pass a large mall with an anchoring Kmart. In that unlikely location is one of the best bookstores in the area: **The Bookloft,** Barrington Plaza (© 413/528-1521; www.thebookloft.com).

WHERE TO STAY & DINE

The Old Inn on the Green ★★ This former stagecoach stop from 1760 and the

adjacent 18th-century Thayer House are under the ownership of chef Peter Platt and Meredith Kennard. The five rooms in the main inn are authentically restored and evocative of their original years, with wide floorboards and period latches; several include access to a second-story veranda. Rooms in Thayer House are larger, with a combination of fireplaces, VCRs, and whirlpool tubs. The intimate dining rooms in the pre-Revolutionary tavern have fireplaces, and the only other illumination at dinner is from candles. Menus are quite sophisticated, often featuring such unexpected ingredients as sea urchins, diver scallops, and squab, and closing with a large selection of regional cheeses. Take advantage of the glorious seven-course tasting menu for $85. Reservations are strongly advised, especially on summer weekends and off season. There is outdoor dining in warmer weather.

Rte. 57, New Marlborough, MA 01230. © 413/229-7924. www.oldinn.com. 11 units. $225–$410 double. Rates include breakfast. Packages available. AE, MC, V. Take Rte. 23 east from Great Barrington, picking up Rte. 57 after 3½ miles. After 5¾ miles, The Old Inn is on the left. **Amenities:** Restaurant (creative American); courtyard pool at Thayer House. *In room:* AC, Wi-Fi, hair dryer, iron.

WHERE TO STAY

There are several acceptable motels north of town on Route 7, the most desirable being the **Holiday Inn Express,** 415 Stockbridge Rd. (© 413/528-1810; www.ichotels group.com), which has an indoor pool, whirlpool, small fitness room, and rooms with Jacuzzis and/or fireplaces; rates include breakfast. The **Chamber of Commerce** operates a lodging hot line at © 800/269-4825 or 413/528-4006.

Windflower Inn A roadside lodging built in the middle of the last century in Fed-

eral style, the Windflower commands a 10-acre plot of land opposite the Egremont Country Club, on Route 23 between Great Barrington and South Egremont. The gracious family that has owned and operated the inn through two generations makes everyone welcome. Six rooms have fireplaces; four have canopy beds.

684 S. Egremont Rd. (P.O. Box 25), Great Barrington, MA 01230. © 800/992-1993 or 413/528-2720. Fax 413/528-5147. www.windflowerinn.com. 13 units. $100–$225 double. Rates include full breakfast and afternoon tea. Children under 16 stay in parent's room for $25. AE. **Amenities:** Unheated outdoor pool. *In room:* A/C, TV, free Wi-Fi and high-speed Internet.

WHERE TO DINE

In addition to the places listed below, there's terrific dining at **The Old Inn on the Green** (see above).

Aegean Breeze ☆ GREEK   Readers who associate Greek cuisine with roadside diners or dingy blue-and-white storefronts in strip malls will have their preconceptions swept away by this commendable taverna. Almost hidden on the heavily commercial street leading north from Great Barrington to Stockbridge, it occupies a building with an enclosed porch, an open terrace, and three dining rooms. The menu is laid out in the traditional manner, with sections for *mezedes* (appetizers), *salates,* and *thalasina* (seafood), along with pastas, poultry, and lamb. Execution is what counts here, elevating such standards as *moussaka* (potatoes, eggplant, and ground beef with béchamel) and lamb *plaki* (with mushrooms, Vidalia onions, and feta baked in a clay pot). Especially appealing are the fish and shellfish dishes, 17 of them, utterly fresh and simply prepared. Thursday is lobster night. *Opa!*

327 Stockbridge Rd. © **413/528-4001.** www.aegean-breeze.com. Reservations recommended on weekends. Main courses $15–$31. AE, MC, V. Daily 11am–10pm.

Allium NEW AMERICAN   This new offshoot of a growing northern Berkshire chainlet has the best of intentions: Use of less-toxic paints and recycled materials in construction, and local and seasonal ingredients in the kitchen. Reality insists that the furniture is left over from the previous occupant and the menu includes items imported considerable distance from the immediate region. That doesn't alter the fact that the "field salad" of Garrotxa cheese, Serrano ham, and roasted almonds—all ingredients from Spain—is a tasty start, along with moist, crusty bread dipped in fruity olive oil (European in origin as well). Most entrees are sizeable, if variable in execution. On our last visit, squash-filled ravioli arrived in a too-large puddle of grassy sage pesto, but the cod fritters, crisp outer shells enclosing a creamy brandade with a drizzle of aioli, were as good as the dish can be. With care and a little luck, an entirely satisfactory meal can be had, and the future looks good.

42 Railroad St. © **413/528-2118.** www.mezzeinc.com. Reservations recommended. Main courses $15-$32. AE, DC, MC, V. Sun–Thurs 5–9pm; Fri–Sat 5–10pm.

Aroma (*Value*) INDIAN   Don't be put off by the utterly forgettable non-decor and the pictures of Tuscany on the wall, residual evidence of a long-departed spaghetti joint. Focus on the menu. Apart from especially good deals at lunch, all for under $9, choice is what it's all about. Dinner has over 80 a la carte possibilities, plus 16 breads baked on the premises. That can be daunting, especially for those unaccustomed to this cuisine, but the menu provides useful descriptions. It's hard to go wrong with a couple of vegetable or meat samosas (crispy turnovers), chicken or fish *tikka* (marinated chunks cooked on skewers), sides of basmati rice and mango chutney, and spinach nan (leavened flatbread stuffed with fresh spinach). *A warning:* When the menu or waitress says "spicy," believe it. They'll tone down the heat on request.

485 Main St. © **413/528-3116.** www.aromabarandgrill.com. Main courses $12–$18. AE, DC, MC, V. Daily noon–3pm and 5–10:30pm (until 11pm Fri–Sat).

Bizen ☆ JAPANESE   Pronounced "bee-*zen,*" this was one of the first sushi restaurants to be introduced to The Berkshires. By most accounts, it remains the best. Its well-worn interior makes an off-handed effort to evoke a Japanese *ryokan,* with heavy faux ceiling beams, paper lanterns, and bare blond wood tables and chairs. Two unusually skilled chefs occupy the sushi bar, and they fabricate enormously creative combo rolls. Most are presented in arrays that depend only on the ingredients for their variegated hues, rarely seen in lesser establishments. Throw caution aside and order one of the *omakase* meals, handing over responsibility to the chef's whim. The several categories range in price from $30 to $110—the least expensive will be sufficient for most appetites.

17–21 Railroad St. ℂ 413/528-4343. Main courses $15–$34. AE, MC, V. Daily noon–10pm (until 10:30pm Fri–Sat).

Castle Street Cafe ★★ NEW AMERICAN
This storefront bistro has ruled the Great Barrington roost for some time now, along the way installing what it calls a "Celestial Bar" in the next building, with live jazz piano 6 nights a week in summer and around weekends the rest of the year. Classic foreign films are often shown Monday nights, with three-course dinners at $24. While a Francophilic inclination is apparent in the main room (hello, steak au poivre), it isn't overpowering—rack of lamb and the pistachio-crusted chicken with mango sauce are other possibilities. Have a drink at the bar while you're checking out the night's menu, or stay there for such casual eats as burgers, pizzas, and cheese plates. An award-winning wine list is another reason to stop in.

10 Castle St. (near the Town Hall). ℂ 413/528-5244. www.castlestreetcafe.com. Reservations recommended on weekends. Main courses $16–$28. AE, DISC, MC, V. Sun–Thurs 5–9pm; Fri–Sat 5–10pm (until 10:30pm in the Celestial Bar).

Café Helsinki ECLECTIC
It looks like an eastern European tearoom run by an eccentric fortuneteller, with mismatched tables and even overstuffed living-room armchairs amid the assorted oddments. (In winter, try for a table near the fireplace in the back room.) There are Scandinavian items on the card to justify the name, including Helsinki borscht, "Red Square" smelts, Finnish meatballs, latkes with wild blueberry compote, and blini with gravlax. Refusing the straitjacket, though, the kitchen also puts together a quesadilla du jour, falafel, and a "Bebop Burger." At least they did, on our last visit—expect surprises. There's full bar service. Dinner from the same menu is also served in the adjoining **Club Helsinki** (see below, under "Great Barrington After Dark."

284 Main St. (in back, down the passageway). ℂ 413/528-3394. www.clubhelsinkiweb.com. Reservations recommended on weekends. Main courses $10–$23. DISC, MC, V. Daily 10am–10pm.

Pearl's ★ CONTEMPORARY BISTRO
A share of the credit for Great Barrington's growing rep as a gastronomic destination has to go to this self-assured enterprise. Traditionalists grumble that this follow-up to the owners' stylish Zinc, in Lenox (see later in this chapter), is more Manhattan than Berkshires, and it clearly isn't country cookin'. The presence of a floor-to-ceiling painting of a bull of regal bearing and a large print of a resplendent wild turkey rightly imply that beef and game are the way to go. The New York strip, filet mignon, and curry-rubbed lamb loin come with tasty sides and straightforward preparations that are hard to beat for flavor. Buttermilk fried chicken with fried okra, and breaded pork chops with crawdad and sausage grits are just as satisfying. If they have it, don't resist the caramel banana strudel as a finisher. Since most of the menu items can be cooked quickly, expect to be in and out within an hour, unless you purposely slow down delivery.

47 Railroad St. ℂ 413/528-7767. Reservations recommended. Main courses $23–$31. AE, MC, V. Mon–Sat 5–10pm (until 11pm Fri–Sat); Sun 11am–3pm and 5:30–10pm.

GREAT BARRINGTON AFTER DARK

A grand downtown cinema, the **Mahaiwe Performing Arts Center,** 14 Castle St. (© 413/644-9040; www.mahaiwe.org), has been restored to some of its century-old glory, and it stages a surprising variety of music, dance, and drama. The **Aston Magna Festival** features classical music performed on period instruments. Concerts are held at irregular intervals throughout the year at St. James Church, Main Street and Taconic Avenue (© 800/875-7156 or 413/528-3595; www.astonmagna.org).

Live jazz is often presented at the Castle Street Cafe, and the Union Bar & Grill brings in DJs weekends (see "Where to Dine," above). **Club Helsinki,** 284 Main St. (© 413/528-3394; www.clubhelsinkiweb.com), is a more regular music venue, with as many as 6 nights a week of rock, pop, bluegrass, reggae, and other forms throughout the year; Norah Jones has played there several times. The **Triplex Cinema,** 70 Railroad St. (© 413/528-8886), shows a mixed bag of independent and foreign flicks as well as major studio releases.

STOCKBRIDGE ★★

Stockbridge's ready accessibility from Boston and New York (about 2½ hr. from each and reachable by rail since the mid–19th century) transformed the original frontier settlement into a Gilded Age summer retreat for the rich. The town has long been popular with artists and writers as well. Illustrator Norman Rockwell, who lived here for 25 years, rendered the Main Street of his adopted town in a famous painting. Along and near Main Street are a number of historic homes and other attractions, enough to fill up a long weekend, even without the Tanglewood concert season in nearby Lenox. One of the Berkshires' hottest destinations, Stockbridge is inevitably jammed on warm weekends and during foliage season. A prominent event is the Christmas celebration on the first Sunday in December, when over 50 antique cars are parked along Main Street to help re-create the scene painted by Norman Rockwell decades ago.

Stockbridge lies 7 miles north of Great Barrington and 6 miles south of Lenox. The **Stockbridge Chamber of Commerce** (© 413/298-5200; www.stockbridgechamber.org) maintains an information booth opposite the row of stores depicted by Rockwell. It's open May through October.

WHAT TO SEE & DO

Berkshire Botanical Garden   These 15 acres of flower beds, ponds, and vegetable and herb gardens are an inviting destination for strollers and picnickers. The first weekend in October features a harvest festival.

Routes 102 and 183. © 413/298-3926. www.berkshirebotanical.org. Admission $7 adults, $5 seniors, $3 students, free for children under 12. May–Oct daily 10am–5pm. Tours offered Sat–Sun June–Aug. Drive west from downtown Stockbridge on Main St., picking up Church St. (Rte. 102) northwest.

The Berkshire Theatre Festival ★★   From June to August, and occasionally at other times during the year, The Berkshire Theatre Festival holds its season of classic and new plays, often with marquee names starring or directing. Kevin Kline and Al Pacino are among the many film and theater names who have been participants. Its venue is a "casino" built in 1887 to plans by architect Stanford White. A second venue, the Unicorn Theatre, opened in 1996.

P.O. Box 797, Main St. © 413/298-5576. www.berkshiretheatre.org. Tickets: Main Stage $38–$67, Unicorn Theatre $36–$43.

Chesterwood ★   Sculptor Daniel Chester French, best known for the Lincoln Memorial in Washington, D.C., used this estate as his summer home for more than

30 years. His Minute Man statue at the Old North Bridge in Concord, completed in 1875 when the artist was 25 years old, launched his highly successful career. The 122-acre grounds are used for an annual show of contemporary sculpture. Entrance to the residence and studio is by guided tour only.

4 Williamsville Rd. ✆ **413/298-3579**. www.chesterwood.org. Admission $12 adults, $5 children 6–18. May–Oct daily 10am–5pm. Drive west on Main St., south on Rte. 183 1 mile to the CHESTERWOOD sign.

Mission House   The Rev. John Sergeant had the most benevolent, if paternalistic, of intentions: He sought to build a house among the members of the Housatonic tribe, hoping to convert them to "civilized" (that is, English) ways through proximity to his godly self and his small band of settlers. The weathered Mission House, built in 1739, was the site of this Christianizing process. History buffs, in particular, will enjoy the 45-minute guided tour.

Main and Sergeant sts. (Rte. 102). ✆ **413/298-3239**. www.thetrustees.org. Admission $6 adults, $3 children 6–12. Memorial Day to Columbus Day daily 10am–5pm. Visits are by guided tour only.

Naumkeag ⚘   In 1886, Stanford White designed this 26-room summer house for Joseph Hodge Choate, who served as U.S. ambassador to the Court of St. James. The client dubbed it Naumkeag, a Native American name for Salem, Massachusetts, his childhood home. His house of many gables and chimneys is largely of the New England shingle style, surrounded by impressive gardens with fabulous views to the west. Admission is by guided tour only, worth it for the glimpses of the rich interior, which features extensive use of mahogany and California redwood. One oddity is the chandelier of Murano glass in the shape of a badminton cock. Tucked away in a dark corner upstairs are several original Goya etchings.

Prospect Hill. ✆ **413/298-3239**. www.thetrustees.org. Admission $10 adults, $3 ages 6–12. Memorial Day to Columbus Day daily 10am–5pm. From the Cat & Dog Fountain in the intersection next to The Red Lion Inn, drive north on Pine St. to Prospect Hill Rd., about ½ mile.

Norman Rockwell Museum ⚘⚘   This striking building opened in 1993, at a cost of $4.4 million, to house the works of Stockbridge's favorite son. The illustrator used both his neighbors and the town where he lived to tell stories about an America now rapidly fading from memory. Most of Rockwell's paintings adorned covers of the *Saturday Evening Post:* warm and often humorous depictions of homecomings, first proms, and visits to the doctor. He addressed serious concerns, too, notably with his poignant portrait of a little African-American girl being escorted by U.S. marshals into a previously segregated school. Critics long derided his paintings as saccharine and sentimental, but today a revision of sorts has led to widespread appreciation for his deft brushwork. The lovely 36-acre grounds also contain Rockwell's last studio (closed Nov–Apr). The museum and grounds remain open year-round.

Rte. 183. ✆ **413/298-4100**. www.nrm.org. Admission $13 adults, $7 students, free for children 18 and under. May–Oct daily 10am–5pm; Nov–Apr Mon–Fri 10am–4pm, Sat–Sun 10am–5pm. Take Main St. (Rte. 102) west to the junction with Rte. 183, then turn left (south) at the traffic signal. In about ½ mile, you'll see the entrance to the museum on the left.

WHERE TO STAY & DINE

Inn at Stockbridge ⚘   A little over a mile north of Stockbridge center, the main 1906 building has a grandly columned porch set well back from the road on 12 acres. The innkeepers are eager to please, serving full breakfasts by candlelight and afternoon spreads of wine and cheese. Several bedrooms have fireplaces and whirlpools, and there are four suites in the newly remodeled barn.

30 East St. (Rte. 7), Stockbridge, MA 01262. © **888/466-7865** or 413/298-3337. Fax 413/298-3406. www. stockbridgeinn.com. 16 units. June–Oct $195–$365 double; Nov–May $150–$270 double. Rates include full break-fast and afternoon refreshments. AE, DISC, MC, V. No children under 12. **Amenities:** Heated outdoor pool. *In room:* A/C, TV/VCR, Wi-Fi, CD player, hair dryer, iron.

The Red Lion Inn ★★

So well known that it serves as a symbol of the Berkshires, this busy inn had its origins as a stagecoach tavern in 1773. The rocking chairs on the porch are the place to while away an hour reading or people-watching. An ancient birdcage ele-vator carries guests up to halls and rooms filled with antiques ranging in styles that span 2 centuries. Floors creak and tilt, as might be expected, but modern comforts are pro-vided. Six satellite buildings have gradually been added, all within 3 miles of the inn. Dining choices include the pricey traditional dining room, the casual and marvelously atmospheric **Widow Bingham Tavern,** and, in good weather, the courtyard out back. The basement **Lion's Den pub** also has nightly live entertainment, usually of the folk-rock variety. Book your room far in advance; for a quieter night, ask for an inside room.

Main St., Stockbridge, MA 01262. © **413/298-5545.** Fax 413/298-5130. www.redlioninn.com. 108 units, 14 with shared bathrooms. Jan to late May $89–$265 double, $175–$295 suite; late May to late Oct $105–$275 double, $225–$390 suite; late Oct to mid-Apr $110–$195 double, $185–$395 suite. Packages available. AE, DC, DISC, MC, V. **Amenities:** 3 restaurants (eclectic/American); 2 bars; outdoor pool; golf and tennis privileges nearby; upgraded fit-ness room; limited room service; massage; babysitting; laundry; dry cleaning. *In room:* A/C, TV/VCR, Wi-Fi in some rooms and high-speed Internet in others, unstocked fridges in suites, hair dryer.

Taggart House ★★

Ordinarily, an inn with only four guest rooms wouldn't merit space here. But what rooms! The decor of this outwardly sedate 1850 Victorian/Colo-nial mansion provides guests with a breathtaking immersion in the Gilded Age. Start with the theatrical main floor—the inlaid mahogany dining table was once a center-piece in an Argentine palace. There's a paneled library, a ballroom, a harpsichord, and nine beguiling fireplaces. And upstairs, beds are decorated with fur throws, East Indian silk coverlets, and velvet canopies.

18 Main St. (1 block west of the Red Lion), Stockbridge, MA 01262. © **888/918-2680.** www.taggarthouse.com. 4 units. May–Oct $250–$350 double; Nov–Apr $175–$250 double. Rates include breakfast. Packages available. 2-night minimum stay on weekends. MC, V. Young children not accepted. *In room:* A/C, Wi-Fi, robes.

Once Upon A Table *Value* NEW AMERICAN

Find this down an alley off Main Street, a few yards east of the Red Lion Inn, housed in what looks like a shed leaned against a larger building. Yellow and cream walls with pictures of French waiters con-stitute most of the decor. In high season, a line of hungry patrons often forms outside. In winter, walk right in and start with a cup of hot mulled cider to counter the drafts. The kitchen's aptitude has wavered over its decade of existence but has rarely been less than satisfactory, and often considerably better—and the trend has been up of late. Start with the peppery, woodsy mushroom soup or the "chowdah," where the clam chunks outnumber the potatoes. More venturesome tastes might prefer the escargot potpie or the vegetable dumplings with spicy soy vinaigrette. Continue, perhaps, with goat-cheese ravioli, sautéed gnocchi with tomatoes and pesto, coq au vin, or phyllo-wrapped organic salmon filet.

34 Main St. © 413/298-3870. www.onceuponatablebistro.com. Reservations suggested in high season. Main courses $17–$27. MC, V. Mon–Sat 11am–3pm and 5–9pm, Sun 11am–6pm (shorter hours in winter).

LEE/BECKET

While Stockbridge and Lenox were developing into luxurious recreational centers for the upper crust of Boston and New York, Lee was a thriving paper-mill town. That meant that it was shunned by the wealthy summer people and thus remained essentially a blue-collar town of workers and merchants. It has a somewhat raffish though not unappealing aspect, its center bunched with shops and offices and few of the stately homes that characterize neighboring communities.

The area's contribution to the Berkshire cultural calendar is Jacob's Pillow Dance Festival in Becket, which first thrived as "Denishawn," a fabled alliance between founders Ruth St. Denis and Ted Shawn.

Lee is 5 miles southeast of Lenox. In summer and early fall, the **Lee Chamber of Commerce** (© **413/243-0852;** www.leechamber.org) operates an **information center** on the town common, Route 20 (© **413/243-4929**). It can help you find lodging, often in guesthouses and B&Bs—rarely as grand as those in neighboring Lenox, but nearly always cheaper. That's something to remember when every other place near Tanglewood is either booked or quoting prices of $300 a night.

WHAT TO SEE & DO
Jacob's Pillow Dance Festival ★★★
In 1933, Ted Shawn decided to put on a show in the barn, and so was Jacob's Pillow born. After decades of advance and retreat and evolution, Jacob's Pillow is now to dance what Tanglewood is to classical music. Once a regular summer venue for Shawn and famed dancer and choreographer Martha Graham, one of his early disciples, the theater has long welcomed troupes of international reputation, including the Mark Morris Dance Group, Les Grands Ballets Canadiens, and Twyla Tharp. The season runs from late June to late August, and tickets go on sale April 1; the schedule is usually available by March 1.

Prominent companies are seen in the main Ted Shawn Theatre, while other troupes are assigned to the Doris Duke Studio Theatre. Admission is free to the Inside/Out, an outdoor stage. The growing campus includes a store, pub, dining room, tent restaurant, and exhibition space. Picnic lunches can be preordered 24 hours in advance.

P.O. Box 287, George Carter Rd., Becket. © 413/243-0745. www.jacobspillow.org. Tickets $10–$55. From Lee, take Rte. 20 east about 9 miles, then turn north on Rte. 8 toward Becket.

Santarella ★
With no obligatory historic homes or museums to see in Lee, visitors often make the short excursion to a fairy-tale structure called Santarella, known by most as the "Gingerbread House." Conical turrets top towers, while the shingled roof rolls like waves on the ocean. It served as a studio for sculptor Henry Hudson Kitson from 1930 to 1947, and now is used only for weddings and other special events. The garden is open to visitors.

75 Main Rd. Tyringham. © 413/243-2819. www.santarella.us. Take Rte. 20 south from Lee to Rte. 102, near the no. 2 interchange of the Mass. Pike. Following the signs through the complicated intersection, pick up Tyringham Rd. on the other side and drive south about 4 miles.

GETTING OUTSIDE
October Mountain State Forest (© **413/243-1778**) offers 50 campsites (with showers) and more than 16,000 acres for hiking, canoeing, cross-country skiing, and snowmobiling. To get here, drive northwest on Route 20 into town, turn right on Center Street, and follow the signs.

WHERE TO STAY
Applegate ★ This B&B utilizes a gracious 1920s Georgian Colonial manse to full advantage. The nicest unit has a canopy bed, Queen Anne reproductions, sunlight filtering through gauzy curtains, a steam shower, and a fireplace (with real wood). All

rooms have stoves or fireplaces, and chocolates and brandy await guests at bedside. Breakfast is by candlelight, and the innkeepers set out wine and cheese in the afternoon. Children under 12 are welcome in some of the rooms.

279 W. Park St., Lee, MA 01238. ⓒ **800/691-9012** or 413/243-4451. www.applegateinn.com. 10 units plus a 2-bedroom cottage. June–Oct $270–$385 double; Nov–May $175–$285 double. MC, V. From Stockbridge, drive north on Rte. 7 about ½ mile; take a right on Lee Rd. The inn is 2¼ miles ahead. **Amenities:** Heated outdoor pool; 9-hole golf course across the street; tennis court; access to nearby health club; bikes. *In room:* A/C, Wi-Fi, CD player, hair dryer, robes.

Chambéry Inn ⊛ This was the Berkshires' first parochial school (1885), named for the French hometown of the nuns who ran it. That accounts for the extra-large bedrooms, about 500 square feet each, which were formerly classrooms. Six of them, with 13-foot ceilings and the original woodwork and blackboards, are equipped with whirlpool tubs and gas fireplaces. Some rooms have TV/VCRs, CD players, and fridges. A breakfast basket is delivered to your door each morning.

199 Main St., Lee, MA 01238. ⓒ **800/537-4321** or 413/243-2221. Fax 413/243-0039. www.chamberyinn.com. 9 units. $80–$170 double. Rates include breakfast. Packages available. AE, DISC, MC, V. No children under 16. **Amenities:** Limited room service from neighboring restaurant. *In room:* A/C, TV, free Wi-Fi, coffeemaker, hair dryer, iron.

Devonfield From the road, there's no way to tell what this place is. The sign out front reads only DEVONFIELD, and the large house standing on a rise amid tall hemlocks and 29 acres could as easily be a yoga retreat or a conference center. But an inn it is, of the comfy-casual variety, verging on elegant. Five rooms have fireplaces, and there's a separate cottage with a large sitting room with fireplace, kitchen, Jacuzzi, and king bedroom. Several common rooms invite guests inclined to cocooning. New owners have put a great deal of money into upgrading bathrooms, enclosing two porches, adding new furniture, and installing flatscreen TVs.

85 Stockbridge Rd., Lee, MA 01238. ⓒ **800/664-0880** or 413/243-3298. Fax 413/243-1360. www.devonfield.com. 10 units. June–Oct $190–$300 double; Sept, Nov–May $160–$225 double. Rates include full breakfast. MC, V. No children under 12. **Amenities:** Heated outdoor pool. *In room:* A/C, TV, hair dryer.

LENOX ⊛⊛ & TANGLEWOOD

Stately homes and fabulous mansions mushroomed in this former agricultural settlement from the 1890s until 1913, when the 16th Amendment, authorizing income taxes, put a severe crimp in that impulse. But Lenox remains a repository of extravagant domestic architecture surpassed only in such fabled resorts of the wealthy as Newport and Palm Beach. And because many of the cottages have been converted into inns and hotels, it is possible to get inside some of these beautiful buildings, if only for a cocktail or a meal.

The reason for so many lodgings in a town with a population of barely 5,000 is Tanglewood, a nearby estate where a series of concerts by the Boston Symphony Orchestra is held every summer.

Lenox lies 7 miles south of Pittsfield. The **Lenox Chamber of Commerce** (ⓒ **413/ 637-3646;** www.lenox.org) provides visitor information and lodging referrals.

WHAT TO SEE & DO
Frelinghuysen Morris House & Studio ⊛ Built on 46 acres next to the Tanglewood property in the early 1940s, this Bauhaus-influenced house was the home of abstract artists Suzy Frelinghuysen and George L. K. Morris. Their chosen style was Cubism, which they pursued long after it had been abandoned by better-known practitioners. Works by some of those artists—Braque, Léger, Gris, and Picasso—can be viewed alongside the canvases of the owners. Visits are by tour only.

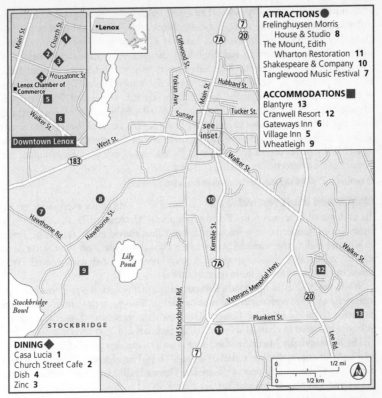

ATTRACTIONS ●
Frelinghuysen Morris
    House & Studio **8**
The Mount, Edith
    Wharton Restoration **11**
Shakespeare & Company **10**
Tanglewood Music Festival **7**

ACCOMMODATIONS ■
Blantyre **13**
Cranwell Resort **12**
Gateways Inn **6**
Village Inn **5**
Wheatleigh **9**

Downtown Lenox

DINING ◆
Casa Lucia **1**
Church Street Cafe **2**
Dish **4**
Zinc **3**

92 Hawthorne St. ☎ 413/637-0166. www.frelinghuysen.org. Admission $10 adults, $3 children 5–16. June 28 to Labor Day Thurs–Sun 10am–4pm; Sept to Columbus Day Thurs–Sat 10am–4pm. Drive south from Tanglewood on Rte. 183, turn left on Hawthorne Rd., then left again on Hawthorne St. (Note that these are 2 different streets.)

The Mount, Edith Wharton Restoration ✦ Wharton, who won a Pulitzer for her novel *The Age of Innocence,* was singularly equipped to write that deftly detailed examination of the upper classes of the Gilded Age and the first decades of the 20th century. She was born into that stratum of society in 1862 and traveled in the circles that made the Berkshires a regular stop on their restless movements between New York, Florida, Newport, and the Continent. Wharton had her villa built on this 130-acre lakeside property in 1902 and lived here 10 years before leaving for France, never to return. She took an active hand in the creation of The Mount, which makes the mansion a notable rarity—it's one of the few designated National Historic Landmarks designed by a woman. In February 2008, however, management announced that The Mount was in danger of being put in foreclosure and launched a "Save the Mount" campaign. Call or check the website for the most up-to-date information.

2 Plunkett St. (at the intersection of rtes. 7 and 7A). ☎ 413/637-1899. www.edithwharton.org. Admission $10 adults, $8 students, free for children under 12. Late Apr to Oct 10am–4pm; guided tours given June–Oct daily 9am–5pm.

Shakespeare & Company ⭐⭐   The repertory company had long used buildings and amphitheaters on the grounds of The Mount (see above) to stage its May-to-December season of plays by the Bard, works by Chekhov and George Bernard Shaw, and efforts by new American and English playwrights. After increasingly bitter conflict with the custodians of the Wharton property, officials of the company purchased a 63-acre property on Kemble Street, closer to downtown Lenox. With construction of a new Founder's Theatre, the Spring Lawn Theatre, the tented Rose Footprint Theatre, an administration building, and planned rehabilitation of other existing buildings, the Company now enjoys its very own campus devoted to the dramatic arts. Walking trails have been developed at the north end of the grounds, and a cafe in the theater lobby serves drinks and light fare. Picnickers are welcome. Free outdoor performances are staged before evening curtain times.

70 Kemble St. ⓒ 413/637-3353. www.shakespeare.org. Tickets $23–$55.

Tanglewood Music Festival ⭐⭐⭐   Lenox is filled with music every summer, and the undisputed headliner is the **Boston Symphony Orchestra** (BSO), conducted by James Levine. Concerts are given at the famous Tanglewood estate, usually beginning in July and ending the weekend before Labor Day. The estate is on West Street (actually in Stockbridge township, although it's always associated with Lenox). From Lenox, take Route 183 1½ miles southwest of town.

While the BSO is Tanglewood's 800-pound cultural gorilla, the program features a menagerie of other performers and musical idioms. These run the gamut from popular artists (James Taylor and Bonnie Raitt) and jazz musicians (Dave Brubeck and Wynton Marsalis) to classical soloists (Itzhak Perlman and Yo-Yo Ma).

The **Koussevitzky Music Shed** is an open auditorium that seats 5,000, surrounded by a lawn where an outdoor audience lounges on folding chairs and blankets. Chamber groups and soloists appear in the smaller **Ozawa Hall.** Major performances are on Friday and Saturday nights and Sunday afternoon.

Tentative programs are available after January 1, and tickets usually go on sale in February and can sell out quickly (you can buy them online). To go at the last minute, take a blanket or lawn chair and get tickets for lawn seating, which is almost always available. You can also attend open rehearsals during the week, as well as the rehearsal for the Sunday concert on Saturday morning.

The estate itself (ⓒ **413/637-5165** June–Aug), with more than 500 acres of lawns and gardens, much of it overlooking the lake called Stockbridge Bowl, was put together starting in 1849 by William Aspinwall Tappan. Admission to the grounds is free when concerts aren't scheduled.

In 1851, a structure on the property called the Little Red Shanty was rented to Nathaniel Hawthorne, who stayed here long enough to write a children's book, *Tanglewood Tales,* and meet Herman Melville, who lived in nearby Dalton. The existing Hawthorne Cottage is a replica (closed to the public). On the grounds is the original Tappan mansion, with fine views.

West St., Stockbridge. ⓒ 617/266-1492. www.tanglewood.org. Tickets $28–$99 Shed and Ozawa Hall, $9–$20 lawn. Lawn tickets for children under 12 are free; children under 5 not allowed in the Shed or Ozawa Hall. Higher prices for opening nights and some special appearances.

GETTING OUTSIDE

Pleasant Valley Wildlife Sanctuary, 472 West Mountain Rd. (ⓒ **413/637-0320;** www.massaudubon.org), has a small museum and 7 miles of hiking and snowshoeing trails crossing its 1,300 acres. Beaver lodges and dams can be glimpsed from a distance, and waterfowl and other birds are found in abundance—bring binoculars. Hours for the nature center are Tuesday through Friday from 9am to 5pm, Saturday and Sunday 10am to 4pm; admission is $3 for adults and $2 for children 3 to 15. Drive north about 6½ miles on routes 7 and 20 and turn left on West Dugway Road.

More extensive trails can be found at **Beartown State Forest,** 69 Blue Hill Rd., in nearby Monterey (② **413/528-0904;** www.mass.gov). The **Appalachian Trail,** which runs from Maine to Georgia, connects here with a loop trail around a small pond with a nice swimming area. Take Route 7 south for 3½ miles, then turn left onto West Road. After 2½ miles, turn left at the T intersection onto Route 102 east. Turn right over the bridge onto Meadow Street, then turn right onto Pine Street and follow the signs.

SHOPPING

The Bookstore, 11 Housatonic St. (② **413/637-3390;** www.bookstoreinlenox.com), with author signings and poetry readings, helps fill a yawning gap in the Berkshires, which are curiously short on comprehensive bookstores. Those in pursuit of art and antiques, on the other hand, cannot easily exhaust the possibilities. For fashion-forward clothing for men and women, much of it Italian-made, check in at **Casablanca,** 21 Housatonic St. (② **413/637-2680**). L.L.Bean, it isn't. Out on Route 7, heading toward Pittsfield, serious cooks should watch for **Different Drummer's Kitchen,** 374 Pittsfield Rd. (② **413/637-0606;** www.differentdrummerskitchen.com).

WHERE TO STAY

The list of lodgings below is only partial, and most can accommodate only small numbers of guests. The Tanglewood concert season is a powerful draw, so prices are highest in summer, as well as during the brief foliage season in mid-October. Rates are of Byzantine complexity, set according to wildly varying combinations of seasons and days of the week as well as facilities offered. Minimum 2- or 3-night stays are usually required during the Tanglewood weeks, foliage, weekends, and holidays. *Note:* For visits during the Tanglewood season, reserve far in advance—February isn't too soon.

Given the substantial number of lodgings available, and limited space here to describe them, admittedly arbitrary judgments have been made to winnow the list. Some inns, for example, are so rule-ridden and facility-free that they come off as crabby—no kids, no pets, no phones, no credit cards, no breakfast before 9am, shared bathrooms—and they cost twice as much as nearby motels that have all those conveniences. We say let them seek clients elsewhere.

If all the area's inns are booked or if you want to be assured the full quota of 21st-century conveniences, routes 7 and 20 north and south of town harbor a number of motels, including the **Mayflower Motor Inn** (② **413/443-4468**), the **Days Inn** (② **413/637-3560**), the **Lenox Motel** (② **413/499-0324**), and the **Comfort Inn** (② **413/443-4714**).

Very Expensive

Blantyre ⊛⊛⊛ This sumptuous 1902 Tudor-Norman mansion used to open only during the warmer months. Now it cossets its guests year-round in its undeniably luxurious public rooms, dining areas, and bedchambers. A long drive curls up through 100 acres to the main manor, where guests enter a baronial lobby packed with imposing antique furniture, a massive fireplace, stuffed animal heads, and a carved and beamed ceiling suitable for the country home of a 19th-century blueblood. The main house holds 8 units and the nearby carriage 12, and there are 4 cottages. Dining—in several interior spaces as well as in the garden and the glassed-in wing that overlooks it—is of the highest order, as dictated by the Relais & Châteaux hotel association, of which the inn is an honored member. Coat and tie are required at dinner. If any place is worth these breathtaking tariffs, it's this one.

P.O. Box 995, Rte. 20, Lenox, MA 01240. ☎ **413/637-3556.** Fax 413/637-4282. www.blantyre.com. 24 units. $550–$850 double. AE, DC, MC, V. From exit 2 on I-90 (Mass. Pike), drive 3 miles on Rte. 20 West. **Amenities:** Restaurant (eclectic); heated outdoor pool; 4 tennis courts; golf nearby; fitness room w/sauna; spa treatments and massage available; 24-hr. room service; same-day dry cleaning. *In room:* fireplace (some), balcony (some), patio (some).

Cranwell Resort ★★★   The main building of this all-season resort looks like a castle in the Scottish Highlands, but no 17th-century laird lived this well. That's where the most expensive rooms are; the rest are in four smaller outlying buildings. Accommodations are outfitted with less concern for adherence to a particular style than for surrounding guests in immediate comfort. The 380-acre property is ringed by views of the surrounding hills, has cross-country ski trails in winter, and boasts a 60-acre golf school. Three dining rooms range from formal to pubby, and live jazz is featured Friday and Saturday nights. An enormous 35,000-square-foot spa was opened in 2002, with pool, lounges with fireplaces, and 17 spa treatment rooms. Services include facial treatments, various massage therapies, exfoliations, and healing wraps. In summer and fall, a satirical cabaret revue is added to the diversions.

55 Lee Rd. (Rte. 20), Lenox, MA 01240. ☎ **800/272-6935** or 413/637-1364. Fax 413/637-4364. www.cranwell.com. 107 units. May–Oct $295–$445 double, Nov to mid-May $195–$345 double. Packages available. AE, DC, DISC, MC, V. **Amenities:** 4 restaurants (eclectic/grill/spa); bar; heated outdoor and indoor pools; 18-hole par-70 golf course; 4 tennis courts; extensive health club; bike rental; salon; limited room service; in-room massage; babysitting; same-day dry cleaning. *In room:* A/C, TV, Wi-Fi, CD player, fridge, coffeemaker, hair dryer, iron, safe, robes.

Wheatleigh ★★   A fountain out front and a lobby fireplace with deeply carved garlands and cherubim set the tone. Beyond, glamorous urbanites often drape themselves in Gatsbyesque poses around the lavishly appointed great hall. Much of the time, they look elaborately bored, no easy feat in this persuasive 1893 replica of a 16th-century Tuscan *palazzo*, which aspires to the highest standards of the moneyed Berkshires. Happily, the interior decor is muted, not florid, utilizing neutral colors and restrained shapes. Wheatleigh has always been very expensive, even though the cheapest rooms average only 11×13 feet. But other places are catching up, and the manager is striving to give requisite value. The dining room rounds out the experience, with painstakingly conceived food presented superbly.

Hawthorne Rd., Lenox, MA 01240. ☎ **413/637-0610.** Fax 413/637-4507. www.wheatleigh.com. 19 units. $650–$1,275 double. AE, DC, MC, V. **Amenities:** 2 restaurants (eclectic); lounge; heated outdoor pool; tennis court; exercise room; bike rental; concierge; in-room massage; babysitting; laundry service; dry cleaning. *In room:* A/C, TV/DVD, CD player, free high-speed Internet, hair dryer.

Moderate–Expensive

Gateways Inn ★★   Harley Procter, who hitched up with a man called Gamble and made a bundle, had this house built in 1912. Its most impressive feature is the staircase that winds down into the lobby. Designed by McKim, Mead, and White, it's a stunner, just the thing for a grand entrance. Equally impressive is the suite named for conductor Arthur Fiedler, with not one but two fireplaces and a big four-poster on the sun porch. Eight rooms have working fireplaces.

Dining in the creative Italian restaurant is one of Lenox's greater pleasures. The bar features 140 grappas and 225 single-malt scotches. A terrace has been added for after-concert light meals and desserts. Lunch is offered on summer weekends, with light fare after dinner to midnight.

51 Walker St., Lenox, MA 01240. © **888/492-9466** or 413/637-2532. Fax 413/637-1432. www.gatewaysinn.com. 12 units. $100–$425 double. Rates include breakfast. Packages available. AE, DC, DISC, MC, V. No children under 12. **Amenities:** Restaurant (eclectic); bar. *In room:* A/C, TV, Wi-Fi.

Moderate

Village Inn An inn off and on since 1775, this place hasn't a whiff of pretense. Its rooms come in considerable variety and are categorized as Deluxe, Superior, Standard, or Economy. That means four-posters in the high-end rooms, some of which have fireplaces, and constricted quarters with smaller beds and no extras at the lower prices. Claw-foot tubs are common. Ask about rooms on the renovated third floor. Afternoon tea and dinner are served in the restaurant, where prices are lower than the town average; light meals are available in the tavern. All rooms have VCRs, and there's a free video library.

16 Church St., Lenox, MA 01240. © **800/253-0917** or 413/637-0020. Fax 413/637-9756. www.villageinn-lenox. com. 32 units. Summer–fall $165–$304 double; winter–spring $143–$202 double. Discount of 30% during midweek in winter/spring. Rates include breakfast. AE, DC, DISC, MC, V. No children under 6. **Amenities:** Restaurant (American); bar. *In room:* A/C, TV/VCR, CD player, hair dryer.

Yankee Inn *Kids* Of the several motels strung along Route 20 east of Lenox center, this is arguably the most desirable, and a place to remember when the area's inns are filled. It is also more congenial for families; children are welcome, as they are not in most B&Bs. Housekeeping is of a reasonably high standard, and furnishings, while routine in design, are as fresh-looking as might be expected in a city hotel. Some rooms have gas fireplaces and unstocked fridges. Long, empty corridors don't enhance the experience, but the indoor/outdoor pool, convenient location, and moderate prices (for the Berkshires) compensate.

461 Pittsfield Rd. (Rte. 20), Lenox, MA 01240. © **800/835-2364** or 413/499-3700. Fax 413/499-3634. www.berkshire inns.com. 96 units. $89–$149 double. Rates include breakfast. AE, DC, DISC, MC, V. **Amenities:** Lounge; heated indoor/outdoor pool w/hot tub; modest exercise room. *In room:* A/C, TV, free Wi-Fi, hair dryer, coffeemaker, iron.

WHERE TO DINE

See also "Where to Stay," above, as many inns have dining rooms. In particular, **Blantyre** (© **413/637-3556**) is worth a splurge. Most of the restaurants recommended below serve lunch, in a region where many don't open until evening. On the other hand, restaurants here are apt to close for an unpredictable few weeks or months in winter, so always call ahead.

Casa Lucia ✦ REGIONAL ITALIAN Here on Lenox's restaurant row, the post-preppie crowd of regulars and weekend refugees from the city is attired in country cashmere and tweed, a taste no doubt honed at campuses of the Ivy League and Seven Sisters. The waitresses display a professionalism rarely experienced in these hills, bringing satisfying starters—carpaccio, grilled calamari, and the like—followed by superior renditions of *osso buco con risotto, bistecca alla Fiorentina,* and six to eight pastas, such as rabbit *tagliatelle.* Dine out on the broad deck in warmer months. Be aware that the restaurant often closes from January to spring; call ahead.

80 Church St. © 413/637-2640. Reservations recommended. Main courses $25–$39. AE, DC, DISC, MC, V. Tues–Sun 5:30–10pm (winter hours fluctuate).

Church Street Cafe ✦✦ ECLECTIC AMERICAN Lenox's most popular eating place delivers fanciful combinations that please the eye and pique the taste buds. Menus change with the seasons, but past options have included baked oysters with leeks and bacon, braised short rib shepherd's pie, and sake-marinated sea bass with shrimp dumplings and shiitakes simmered in soy-ginger broth. Lunch is a busy time here, with gumbo and red chile–roasted chicken quesadillas and crab cake sandwiches among the favorites. The decor is rudimentary, the service friendly but rushed. A large deck fills up whenever the weather allows.

65 Church St. ℂ 413/637-2745. www.churchstreetcafe.biz. Reservations recommended on weekends. Main courses $20–$30. MC, V. May–Oct daily 11:30am–2pm and 5:30–9pm; Nov–Feb Tues–Sat 11:30am–2pm and 5:30–8:30pm. Closed Feb–Apr.

Zinc 🐾🐾 CONTEMPORARY BISTRO   Zinc leapt to the upper echelon of Berkshires dining nearly as soon as it opened. For one thing, it is the best-looking restaurant in town, with its eponymous zinc bar, faux tin ceiling, flowers, lacquered woods, tile floor, and butcher paper over white tablecloths. The cuisine and wine list adhere with some rigor to the French-bistro canon. Start, perhaps, with foie gras adorned with quince and brioche. After that, past menus have listed such toothsome entrees as grilled lamb loin with spinach and chickpea fries, and pan-seared diver scallops with sweet potato and andouille hash. A remarkable 24 wines are available by the glass, most of which go quite well with the five-cheese tasting ($15).

56 Church St. ℂ 413/637-8800. Reservations recommended. Main courses $18–$31. AE, MC, V. Daily 11:30am–3pm and 5:30–9pm (bar until 1am).

PITTSFIELD

Berkshire County's largest city (pop. 45,793) routinely gets little attention in most tourist literature. A commercial and industrial center, it has little of the charm that marks such popular destinations as Stockbridge and Lenox. Something is afoot, though. Always a convenient base for day excursions to other parts of the central Berkshires, this blue-collar city is reinventing itself, with new attractions, more worthwhile restaurants, and an ever livelier nightlife. Emblematic of this shift was the recent reopening of the 1903 Colonial Theatre, once again home to over 200 nights per year of dance, comedy, and music from classical to country.

A recently discovered document banned the playing of baseball within 80 yards of the main church in 1791, giving Pittsfield claim to the invention of the game, 48 years before Cooperstown, New York. In summer, the **Berkshire Black Bears** (ℂ 413/448-2255) play minor-league baseball at Wahconah Park, a 1919 stadium with real wooden box seats.

The **Berkshire Visitors Bureau** (ℂ 800/237-5747 or 413/443-9186; www.berkshires.org) is in the same block of buildings as the Crowne Plaza Hotel, on Berkshire Common.

WHAT TO SEE & DO

Arrowhead   Herman Melville bought this 18th-century house in 1850 and lived here until 1863. It was during this time that he wrote *Moby-Dick*. A nature trail and shop are on-site. In truth, however, the house is of limited interest to visitors other than literature students and avid readers.

780 Holmes Rd. ℂ 413/442-1793. www.mobydick.org. Admission $12 adults, $5 students 15 and older, $3 for ages 6–14. From Fri before Memorial Day to Columbus Day Fri–Wed 10:30am–4pm; rest of year by appointment only. Visits are by guided tour only, given on the hour, 11am–4pm. Drive east from Park Sq. on East St., turn right on Elm St., and turn right on Holmes Rd.

Barrington Stage Company   At intervals throughout the year but with concentrations from late June to late August, this nonprofit theatre company mounts musicals, comedies, and dramas at the **MainStage** on Union Street, the **BSC Stage II** at

1 Wendell Ave., and other sites. Most are new works, such as the Tony-winning *The 25th Annual Putnam County Spelling Bee,* which was given its premiere here before it moved to Broadway.

30 Union St.(℃ 413/526-8888. www.barringtonstage.org. Tickets $15–$25 adults (20% discount for seniors), $10 students.

Berkshire Museum ⊛ It began in 1903 as the "Museum of Natural History and Art," words chiseled in stone above the entrance. The holdings bounce from Babylonian cuneiform tablets to tanks of live fish to archaeological artifacts like a delicate necklace from Thebes dating to at least 1500 B.C. Included in the permanent collections are works by such 19th-century portraitists and landscapists as George Inness, Edwin Church, and Albert Bierstadt. Temporary exhibitions are frequent and professionally mounted. An auditorium seating 300 serves as the "Little Cinema," which shows art and foreign films during the warmer months.

39 South St. (Rte. 7, 1 block south of Park Sq.). ℃ 413/443-7171. www.berkshiremuseum.org. Admission $8 adults, $6.50 seniors and college students, $5 ages 3–18. Mon–Sat 10am–5pm; Sun noon–5pm.

Hancock Shaker Village ⊛⊛⊛ The serenity of the setting, among low hills and meadows, and the carefully considered placement of the buildings and their relationships with each other, are the essence of Shaker philosophy, "Order is Heaven's law." Twenty restored buildings make up the village, which explores the religious practices

Movers & Shakers in Massachusetts

The former Ann Lee, once imprisoned in England for her excess of religious zeal, arrived in New York with eight disciples in 1774, just as the disgruntled American colonies were about to burst into open rebellion. She had anointed herself leader of the United Society of Believers in Christ's Second Coming and was known as Mother Ann. The austere Protestant sect was dedicated to simplicity, equality, and celibacy. They were popularly known as "the Shakers" for their spastic movements when in the throes of religious ecstasy.

By the time Mother Ann died in 1784, the Shakers had many converts, who then fanned out across the country to form communal settlements from Maine to Indiana. One of the most important Shaker communities, **Hancock,** edged the Massachusetts–New York border, near Pittsfield.

Shaker society produced dedicated, highly disciplined farmers and craftspeople whose products were much in demand in the outside world. They sold seeds, invented early agricultural machinery and hand tools, and erected large buildings of several stories and exquisite simplicity. Their spare, clean-lined furniture and accessories anticipated the so-called Danish Modern style by a century and in recent years have drawn astonishingly high prices at auction.

All of these accomplishments required a verve owed at least in part to sublimation of sexual energy, for a fundamental Shaker tenet was total celibacy for its adherents. The society grew through converts and adoption of orphans (who were free to leave, if they wished). But by the 1970s, the movement had a bare handful of believers. The string of Shaker settlements and museums that remain testify to their dictum, "Hands to work, hearts to God."

and lifestyle habits of the austere Protestant sect. Its signature structure is the **1826 round stone barn:** The Shaker preoccupation with functionalism joined with purity of line and respect for materials has never been clearer than it is in the design of this building. Its round shape expedited the chores of feeding and milking livestock by arranging cows in a circle, and the precise joinery of the roof beams and support pillars is a joy to observe.

The second must-see is the brick dwelling that contained the village's communal dining room, kitchens, and sleeping quarters. Sexes were separated at meals, work, and religious services, and there are staircases leading to male and female "retiring rooms."

While artisans and docents demonstrate Shaker crafts and techniques, only some dress in period clothing to portray Shaker inhabitants. All are knowledgeable about their subject, though, and dispense nuggets about the Shaker discipline such as the requirement to dress the right side first and to step with the right foot first. Special programs include sustainable gardening workshops and guided hikes to the Shakers' spiritual retreat on Mount Sinai.

The museum shop is excellent, and a cafe serves lunches in summer and fall, with some dishes based on Shaker recipes.

Routes 20 and 41, Pittsfield. © **800/817-1137** or 413/443-0188. www.hancockshakervillage.org. Admission $15 adults, $5 children 13–17, free for children under 13. Apr 12–May 23 daily 10am–4pm; May 24–Oct 19 daily 10am–5pm; rest of year accessible only by guided tour at 1pm weekdays and 11am and 1pm weekends. Call ahead in off-season to confirm schedule.

GETTING OUTSIDE

Plaine's Bike, Ski & Snowboard, 55 W. Housatonic St., at Center Street (© **413/ 499-0294;** www.plaines.com), rents bikes and carries equipment for all the sports its name suggests. It's on Route 20, west of downtown.

Pittsfield State Forest, entered on Cascade Street (© **413/442-8992;** www. mass.gov), is a little over 3 miles west of the center of town. It includes 65 acres of wild azalea fields that explode in pink blossoms in June. There's also camping, boating, fishing, hiking, biking, and cross-country skiing here. Open daily from 8am to 8pm. Admission is $5 per car from early May to mid-Oct.

BOATING   Onota Boat Livery, 463 Pecks Rd. (© **413/442-1724**), rents canoes and motorboats on Onota Lake, conveniently located at the western edge of the city.

SKIING   **South of the city center, off Route 7 near the Pittsfield city limits, is the **Bousquet Ski Area, Dan Fox Drive (© **413/442-8316** business office, 413/442-2436 snow phone; www.bousquets.com). Bousquet (pronounced *Bos*-kay) has 22 trails, with a vertical drop of 750 feet, two double lifts, and two rope tows. Night skiing is available Monday through Saturday. Rentals and lessons are offered. Lift tickets cost $20 to $37. Snow tubing, weekends and holidays only, costs $18.

Proceeding north on Route 7, watch for the turn west on Brodie Mountain Road and continue 2 miles to **Jiminy Peak** ⊛, Hancock (© **413/738-5500,** or 413/738-7325 for ski reports; www.jiminypeak.com). This expanding resort aspires to four-season activity, so skiing on 28 trails (18 open at night) with seven lifts is supplemented the rest of the year by horseback riding, trapshooting, fishing in a stocked pond, a rock-climbing wall, six tennis courts, mountain biking, pools, and golf at the nearby Waubeeka Springs course. For people staying overnight, lift tickets are included in the room rates. For day-trippers, 4-hour tickets cost adults $48 during the week, $55 on weekends; $38 and $49 for ages 7 to 19; $38 and $39 for seniors; and $17 children under 7.

WHERE TO STAY

Thaddeus Clapp House   The eponymous Mr. Clapp was ahead of his time, incorporating central heating and indoor plumbing in his 1871 manse. He also rejected the excesses of High Victorian design, stripping his home to what amounted—at the time—to near-minimalism. Recent restoration took 18 months and included installation of gas fireplaces and high-speed Internet in the extra-large rooms. The owner/manager is a fervent Pittsfield booster and a font of information about the local dining and cultural scenes.

74 Wendell Ave., Pittsfield, MA 01201. © **888/499-6840** or 413/499-6840. Fax 413/499-6842. www.clapp house.com. 8 units. $125–$295 double. MC, V. *In room:* A/C, TV, CD player, free high-speed Internet, coffeemaker, hair dryer, iron, robes.

The Country Inn at Jiminy Peak *(Kids*   This is one of the better lodging deals in the Berkshires, if your idea of luxury is space. The units, all one- to three-bedroom suites with full kitchens and sofa beds, are perfect for families. Also great for kids are the on-site downhill skiing and abundant recreational facilities (see "Getting Outside," above). Four- and 8-hour lift tickets start any time. In summer, there's downhill mountain-biking for the adventurous, plus bobsled rides on an alpine slide, a bungee-trampoline, a climbing wall, a giant swing, trout fishing, and minigolf. A convenience store on the property has groceries, wine, beer, and a post office. No pets.

Brodie Mountain Rd. (near Rte. 43), Hancock, MA 01237. © **800/882-8859** or 413/738-5500. Fax 413/738-5513. www.jiminypeak.com. 105 units. $129–$999 1- to 3-bedroom suite. Winter rates include lift tickets. Children under 18 stay free in parent's room. AE, DC, DISC, MC, V. **Amenities:** 2 restaurants (eclectic); 2 bars; heated outdoor and indoor pools; 6 tennis courts; exercise room; Jacuzzi; sauna; children's programs; game room; babysitting; coin-op washers and dryers. *In room:* A/C, TV/VCR, free Wi-Fi, kitchenette, coffeemaker, hair dryer, iron.

Crowne Plaza *(Kids*   The tallest building in town at 14 stories, this former Hilton isn't hard to find, although it may take a little 'round-the-block maneuvering to get to the front door. It has the bells and whistles expected of upper-middle chain hotels and is more family-friendly than many smaller lodgings in the region. Kids are welcome and readily occupied with the heated indoor pool and PlayStations in every room. With this many units, there's also a good chance of copping a bed here on Tanglewood weekends. Free self-parking is available in the adjacent garage. Wi-Fi is available in all public areas.

1 West St., Pittsfield, MA 01201. © **877/227-6963** or 413/499-2000. Fax 413/442-0449. www.berkshirecrowne. com. 179 units. Summer $139–$256 double; off season $116–$159 double. AE, DISC, MC, V. **Amenities:** Restaurant (American); bar; heated indoor pool; fitness room w/Jacuzzi; limited room service. *In room:* A/C, TV w/pay movies, free high-speed Internet, coffeemaker, hair dryer, iron.

WHERE TO DINE

Asters STEAK/SEAFOOD   The former Yellow Aster has been converted to this sleek Manhattan(ish) steakhouse, complete with way too much Sinatra on the stereo. The lower floor is a raw bar, and there are several rooms upstairs, two of them with fireplaces. An outdoor fire pit gathers patrons for drinks and dessert. Next to the black onyx bar is a walk-in wine cabinet, signaling the management's enthusiasm for the grape. They offer, for example, a flight of monthly featured wines—2-ounce tastings of three bottles for only $8. Wines by the glass are ample pours, too. Apart from the modest raw-bar choices, you'll find clam chowder, Caesar salad, bruschetta, and crab cakes among the expected starters, most of them competently done, a description that can be given the steaks, chops, and fish as well. In sum, a pleasantly satisfying meal and evening can be had, accompanied by live jazz on Friday and Saturday evenings.

Tips **Pittsfield on Stage**

The **Berkshire Opera Company,** 297 North St. (© **413/442-9955;** www.berkshire opera.org), stages its June productions at the Mahaiwe Theatre in Great Barrington, and its July and August productions of both established and new operas at the Koussevitzky Arts Center of Berkshire Community College in Pittsfield. That venue is also employed by the **Albany Berkshire Ballet,** 116 Fenn St. (© **413/445-5382;** www.berkshireballet.org), with up to 14 performances of two ballets from early July to mid-August.

1015 South St. (Rte. 7) © 413/499-2075. www.berkshiredining.net. Main courses $17–$32. AE, MC, V. Mon–Thurs 4–9pm; Fri–Sat 4–10pm; Sun 10am–2pm and 5–9pm.

Brix Wine Bar ✸ CONTEMPORARY BISTRO   What a refreshing antidote to the largely forlorn Pittsfield dining landscape! The enthusiasm of the owners and staff for their 34-seat enterprise is infectious, the kind that brings patrons back over and over again. Wine is a priority, obviously, and every effort is made to instruct newbies and cosset sophisticates. There are over 50 pressings available by the glass, more than you're likely to see this side of Paris. Flights of four wines cost only $10. The eats are tantalizing and geared to the smallest or largest of appetites, running from such sandwiches as the combination of roasted lamb, pickled red onions, and baby arugula to plates of charcuterie, cheese, and savory tarts—simply keep ordering until sated. Brix, by the way, is named for the inventor of a refractometer used to measure the sugar content of grapes.

40 West St. (opposite Crown Plaza Hotel). © 413/236-9463. www.brixwinebar.com. Main courses $12–$27. AE, MC, V. Tues–Thurs 5–10pm; Fri–Sat 5pm–10:30pm.

WILLIAMSTOWN ✸✸

This community and its prestigious liberal-arts college were both named for Col. Ephraim Williams, who was killed in 1755 in one of the French and Indian Wars. He bequeathed the land for creation of a school and a town. His college grew, spreading east from the central common along both sides of Main Street (Rte. 2). Over the town's long history, buildings have been erected in several styles of the times. That makes Main Street a virtual museum of institutional architecture, with representatives of the Georgian, Federal, Gothic Revival, Romanesque, and Victorian styles (and a few yet to be labeled). Inserted into this diverting display is the '62 Center for Theatre and Dance, a thoroughly contemporary structure that opened in September 2005. It stands at dignified distances from the older buildings, so what might have been a tumultuous visual hodgepodge is instead a stately lesson in historical design. The impressive Clark Art Institute is the best reason to make a special trip, perhaps in conjunction with a performance at the increasingly ambitious Williamstown Theatre Festival.

A free weekly newspaper, the *Advocate* (**www.advocateweekly.com**), produces useful guides to both the northern and southern Berkshires. An **information booth,** at North Street (Rte. 7) and Main Street (Rte. 2), has an abundance of pamphlets and brochures free for the taking.

WHAT TO SEE & DO
Sterling and Francine Clark Art Institute ✸✸✸   Within these walls are canvases by Renoir (34 of them), Degas, Gauguin, Toulouse-Lautrec, Pissarro, and Corot, their

predecessor. Look for Turner's splendid seascape, *Rockets and Blue Lights*. Also on display is the famed Degas sculpture *Little Dancer*, believed to be his only three-dimensional piece and a signature work of the Institute. In addition to these standouts, you'll find works by 15th- and 16th-century Dutch portraitists, European genre and landscape painters, and Americans Sargent and Homer, as well as fine porcelain, silver, and antiques. The Clarks were more disciplined in their acquisitions than most wealthy collectors, and their museum qualifies as one of the great cultural resources of the Berkshires and of the state.

Apart from the collection itself, the Clarks' farsighted endowment funded the modern wing added to the original neoclassical building and has covered all acquisitions, upkeep, and renovations. Their stipulation that there be no admission fee was finally breached, but the charge applies only to adults 4 months a year. A substantial bookstore in the lobby has been joined by a snack counter and an attractive cafe. The first phase of an additional wing was scheduled to open in summer 2008.

225 South St., Williamstown. *(© 413/458-2303. www.clarkart.edu. Admission June–Oct $13 adults, free for students and children; free to all Tues and Nov–June. Day after Labor Day to June Tues–Sun 10am–5pm; July to Labor Day daily 10am–5pm.

Williams College Museum of Art ✷   The second leg of Williamstown's two prominent art repositories exists in large part thanks to the college's collection of almost 400 paintings by the American modernists Maurice and Charles Prendergast. The museum also has works by Gris, Léger, Whistler, Picasso, Warhol, and Hopper. There are frequent special exhibitions and lecture series.

15 Lawrence Hall Dr., Williamstown. *(© **413/597-2429.** www.wcma.org. Free admission. Tues–Sat (and some Mon holidays) 10am–5pm; Sun 1–5pm.

GETTING OUTSIDE
Mount Greylock State Reservation ✷ contains the highest peak (3,491 ft.) in Massachusetts, as well as a section of the Appalachian Trail. A long, narrow, bumpy road allows cars almost to the summit, where the War Memorial Tower affords vistas of the Taconic and Hoosac ranges, far into Vermont and New York (parking $20). The ride down is very popular with mountain bikers. The park's roads and Bascom Lodge are closed for repairs to infrastructure through 2008, so the details below are tentative. Call the number below or check the website for updates.

Ordinarily, the visitor center is open mid-May to mid-October daily from 9am to 5pm, and mid-October to mid-May weekends and holidays from 8am to 4pm. Black bear and deer are often sighted. Trails radiate from the parking lot near **Bascom Lodge,** North Main Street off Route 7 in Lanesboro (*(© **413/743-1591** or 413/443-0011; www.mass.gov), a grandly rustic creation of the Civilian Conservation Corps in the New Deal 1930s. Simple dormitory beds and four private rooms accommodating a total of 32 guests are available for rent from mid-May to mid-October. Family-style dinners are available by reservation.

SHOPPING
In the small downtown shopping district, **Library Antiques,** 70 Spring St. (*(© **413/458-3436;** www.libraryantiques.com), is filled with a wealth of English chess sets, African carvings, Peruvian alpaca sweaters, Polish stoneware, and antique American fishing lures and creels. Open daily. Farther south on Route 7, **Saddleback Antiques,** 1395 Cold Spring Rd. (*(© **413/458-5852**), features country, wicker, and Victorian furniture, and is open every day except Wednesday.

WHERE TO STAY

This is a college town, so in addition to the usual peak periods of July, August, and the October foliage season, accommodations fill up during graduation and on football weekends. The largest lodging in town is the **Williams Inn,** 1090 Main St. (✆ **800/828-0133** or 413/458-9371). Despite the name, it is a standard motel, with a dining room, tavern, and indoor pool. See also the section on nearby North Adams, below.

Field Farm Guesthouse   After an extended vacation of B&B-hopping, there may come a time when one more tilted floor or wobbly Windsor chair will send even a devout inn-lover over the edge. Here's an antidote. This pristine example of postwar modern architecture rose in 1948 on a spectacular 296-acre estate with 4 miles of trails. Most guest rooms look over meadows to Mount Greylock. The living room is equipped with a telescope to view the beavers and waterfowl on the lake. The Scandinavian Modern furniture was made to order for the house, and three units have decks while two have fireplaces. Don't expect a TV or a phone, but there is wireless Internet access in all the rooms. Breakfasts are hearty meals of waffles and five-cheese omelets utilizing fruits, herbs, and vegetables grown on the property.

554 Sloan Rd., Williamstown, MA 01267. ✆/fax **413/458-3135.** http://guesthouseatfieldfarm.thetrustees.org. 5 units. $150–$295 double. Rates include breakfast. DISC, MC, V. Follow Rte. 7 to Rte. 43 and turn west, then make an immediate right on Sloan Rd. Continue 1 mile to the Field Farm entrance, on the right. Closed Mon–Wed from Nov–Apr. **Amenities:** Heated outdoor pool; tennis court. *In room:* Free Wi-Fi, hair dryer.

The Orchards ★★   A sedate choice just right for visiting Williams alumni and parents, the Orchards has an upscale country-club atmosphere; it's the sort of place where afternoon tea is an event. Each of its public and private rooms enjoys a mix of antique and reproduction English-style furniture. Even standard units are sizeable, all with separate dressing cubicles, and those with working fireplaces have chaise lounges and deeply padded chairs. Some have fridges stocked with soft drinks; safes are hidden in places we can't divulge. A recent renovation benefited every corner, including the exercise room, and the kitchen, too, now surpasses the merely competent operation that preceded it. There is live piano in the lounge on weekends. Providing an international touch is an internship program that brings young people from all over the world to staff the front desk and dining room.

222 Adams Rd., Williamstown, MA 01262. ✆ **800/225-1517** or 413/458-9611. Fax 413/458-3273. www.orchards hotel.com. 47 units. Mid-Nov to late May $195–$295 double; late May to mid-Nov $215–$395 double. AE, DC, DISC, MC, V. **Amenities:** Restaurant (international); bar; heated outdoor pool; exercise room w/sauna and whirlpool. *In room:* A/C, TV, free high-speed Internet, alarm clock with MP3 line, coffeemaker, hair dryer, iron, safe.

WHERE TO DINE

A new **Jae's Inn** (✆ **413/458-8032**), has opened a mile south of the town center, at 777 Cold Spring Rd. (Rte. 7). While it was too new for review in this edition, there's every reason to believe it is comparable in style and food to its accomplished sibling in North Adams (p. 359).

Mezze ECLECTIC   Meals here are entirely competent, if less than dazzling. The enthusiasm for small plates is addressed in the name and on the menu, with tapas-type starters like steamed mahogany clams and plates of anchovies, prosciutto, olives, and marinated eggplant. One chef put in time at acclaimed Craft in New York, an experience reflected in such recent dishes as the roasted skate with sautéed arugula, gnocchi, and chanterelles, and the whole-wheat pappardelle with duck confit, oyster mushrooms, and goat cheese. Less esoteric choices are steamed mussels, roast chicken, and the beef duo—short ribs and sirloin. The clientele is composed primarily of professors, administrators, and students with visiting parents in tow.

16 Water St. © 413/458-0123. www.mezzeinc.com. Main courses $13–$27. AE, DISC, MC, V. Sun–Thurs 5–9pm; Fri–Sat 5–10pm.

Spice Root *Value* INDIAN   Catch an irresistible whiff of this Indian eatery from several storefronts away, and thoughts of anything but food vanish. Impecunious students like it for the bargain student-only $11 dinner special, and while the special is pretty good, choices are necessarily limited. The a la carte menu is more rewarding, with 11 starters, five breads, several curries, nine vegetarian dishes, tandoor specialties, and a half-dozen dishes from Bombay. Standouts are the curried salmon, chicken or lamb tikka masala, fiery shrimp vindaloo, and a veggie delight that involves bell peppers stuffed with mashed potatoes, paneer cheese, and spinach accompanied by yellow lentils. Breads are baked on-site, and the version filled with cheese, nuts, and raisins is a particular treat.

23 Spring St. © 413/458-5200. www.spiceroot.com. Main courses $7–$20. AE, DISC, MC, V. Daily 11:30am–2:30pm and 5–10pm.

WILLIAMSTOWN AFTER DARK

The Williams College Department of Music sponsors diverse concerts and recitals. Call its **Concertline** (© 413/597-3146) for information on upcoming events. In addition, the Clark Art Institute (see above) hosts frequent classical-music events.

The '62 Center for Theatre and Dance ★★   Williamstown has long hosted one of the Berkshires' premier summer attractions, the **Williamstown Theatre Festival** (© 413/597-3400; www.wtfestival.org), and now it has a facility that provides a proper showcase. This ambitious center opened in the fall of 2005 (the year in its name is for the class that graduated in 1962), providing three performance venues, as well as studios, classrooms, and rehearsal spaces. Dramatic productions, dance, music, and related cultural events, involving students, alumni, and professionals, can now be mounted all year. Staging classic and new plays during its season from late June to late August, the festival attracts many top actors and directors. The MainStage Theatre presents works by major playwrights, while the CenterStage often features more experimental productions. It's not too difficult to get tickets; even if a performance is said to be sold out, there are often cancellations in the 30 minutes before curtain. Tickets to the Festival itself range from about $20 to $55, while admission to other events is often free, and no more than $10.

1000 Main St. (P.O. Box 517). © 413/597-2425 for box office. www.williams.edu/go/62center.

NORTH ADAMS

In the mid-1990s it seemed impossible that this comatose mill town could recover. Its unemployment rate was the highest in the state, and over two-thirds of its storefronts were empty. A land developer once even suggested that the town be flooded to create lakefront property.

However, North Adams experienced a whiplash turnaround, and today many of those once-abandoned storefronts are taken up with restaurants, galleries, and high-tech start-ups. The unlikely reason, to almost everyone's agreement, is an art museum that opened in 1999. An abandoned industrial complex has been converted, despite early hoots of derision, into a center for the visual and performing arts. It is called the

Massachusetts Museum of Contemporary Art, and it has strikingly altered the socioeconomic dynamic of North Adams.

The first Sunday of October is Fall Foliage Day, with a parade of fire engines, marching bands, and Clydesdales, and balloons, hot dogs, and cotton candy on sale at sidewalk stands.

WHAT TO SEE & DO

Massachusetts Museum of Contemporary Art ★★   A lot of excitement and anticipation surrounded this ambitious project, the conversion of an empty 27-building textile factory into a center for the arts. Even before its official opening, it had a nickname—MASS MoCA—and hosted performances by David Byrne, Patti Smith, and the Merce Cunningham Dance Company. Works on display are often outsized, crossing traditional aesthetic boundaries to marry elements of both performing and visual arts. Its chief virtue—from the standpoint of those contemporary artists who choose to work on a grand scale—is the vastness of the spaces available. But additionally, the museum has hosted a variety of musical events, experimental films, even dance parties, and is attracting small tenant companies working the vineyards of technology, including software, video, and e-commerce. MASS MoCA has attracted hundreds of thousands of visitors and is certainly worth the short detour east from neighboring Williamstown.

The snacky **Lickety Split** (℃ **413/663-3372**) occupies a space on the ground floor of the museum, serving coffee, ice cream, and light fare.

87 Marshall St., North Adams. ℃ **413/662-2111**. www.massmoca.org. Admission $13 adults, $9 students, $5 children 6–16. Wed–Mon 11am–5pm.

WHERE TO STAY

Jae's (see below, under "Where to Dine") also has accommodations.

The Porches ★★   "Retro-rural chic" might describe this row of six detached 19th-century workingmen's houses stitched together by an uninterrupted streetside veranda, the spaces in between roofed over and fitted with indoor catwalks and patios. Rooms are witty tributes to the past, with kitschy lamps and paint-by-numbers pictures on the walls, but are also equipped with DVD players and high-speed Internet access. A computer is provided for guests' use, and laptop rentals are available. Down duvets, bathrobes, and cushy sofas make things even cozier. Ask for one of the second-floor king rooms with balcony. Coffee, croissant, and a newspaper in a rocking chair out on the porch on a warm autumn morning: a singular pleasure for guests. Evening cocktails are available at the front desk.

231 River St., North Adams, MA 01247. ℃ **413/664-0400**. Fax 413/664-0401. www.porches.com. 47 units. Mid-May to early Nov $179–$355 double; mid-Nov to early May $129–$245 double; $175–$329 suite. Rates include breakfast. Packages available. AE, DC, MC, V. Located behind the MASS MoCA complex, ½ block west of Marshall St. **Amenities:** Heated outdoor pool; Jacuzzi; sauna; in-room massage; laundry service (Mon–Fri); free DVD library. *In room:* A/C, TV/DVD, Wi-Fi and high-speed Internet, minibar, hair dryer, iron.

WHERE TO DINE

Café Latino LATIN AMERICAN   Established in Building 11 of the Mass MoCA complex, the cafe is a casual eatery popular with both museum-goers and office workers. The menu displays largely south-of-the-border inclinations, but hardly slavishly—there are too many creative flourishes. The *empanaditas,* for example, are far from traditional, with house-made chorizo combined with red pepper escabeche and spicy mint sauce; or the *latitapas,* bringing together black-bean hummus, chorizo, *queso* *blanco,* guacamole, tostones, and piquillo peppers (a Spanish ingredient). *El Croque Señor* is a barely recognizable take on a Cuban sandwich, a big, messy, delicious assemblage made up of roast pork, ham, avocado, cheddar, and watercress, all on a jalapeño ciabatta. This giddy creativity is underscored by the frequent dinners featuring Japanese-Peruvian cuisine. Thursday through Saturday they bring in jazz combos, folk singers, even a karaoke machine.

1111 Mass MoCA Way ✆ **413/662-2004.** www.mezzeinc.com. Main courses $10–$23. Wed–Sat 11:30am–3pm and 5–9pm.

Gramercy Bistro ✪ CREATIVE AMERICAN   This quiet bistro has come up in the world over the last couple of years and now rules the North Adams culinary roost. It has expanded into the adjacent storefront, applied paint to the walls, hung new artwork, and laid tablecloths over the once-bare tables. On the menu, organic and local meet creative and global. Witness shrimp with spicy red Thai curry; sea scallops with sweet potato, plantain hash, and roasted poblano sauce; sweetbreads with *beurre noir* and pumpkin tortellini; and crab cake with wasabi-soy vinaigrette (about as good as that dish gets). Much of it works, although some tricks amount to good impulses that fall short.

24 Marshall St ✆ **413/663-5300.** www.gramercybistro.com. Main courses $19–$26. Mon, Wed–Thurs 5-9pm; Fri–Sat 5pm–10pm; Sun 10am–1pm and 5–9pm. Closed Tues.

Jae's ✪ ASIAN   The cheerful Korean owner of this inn and restaurant swept from his homeland to Japan to Thailand to assemble his menu, and the result is both entertaining and delicious. He now helms a self-named chain of several restaurants in Boston and The Berkshires. Take the culinary journey with him, beginning with a platter of flawless maki and sushi; continue with the exceptional seafood pancake, made with shrimp, crabmeat, squid, and scallions; and finish with Jae's Special country curry. All the fish is fresh. Or make a meal of appetizers, assembled both in the kitchen and at the sushi bar. From the former, consider *mandoo* (fried meat dumplings) or *hamachi kama* (grilled yellowtail); from the latter, *Naruto* (crab stick, flying fish roe, and avocado roll) or tiger eyes (grilled squid stuffed with smoked salmon). More daring diners might try the spicy kimchi stew or the *bibimbap,* veggies and marinated chicken cooked in a hot stone pot.

The inn features 12 bedrooms, all with air-conditioning, Wi-Fi, TV, and DVD players, which cost $95 to $150 per night.

1111 South State St. (Rte. 8 south). ✆ **413/664-0100.** www.jaesinn.com. Main courses $12–$22. AE, DC, DISC, MC, V. Daily 11:30am–9pm (until 10pm Fri–Sat).

10

Connecticut

by Herbert Bailey Livesey and Leslie Brokaw

Connecticut resists generalization and confounds spinners of superlatives. It doesn't rank at the top or bottom of any important chart of virtues or liabilities, which makes it impossible to pigeonhole. The nation's third-smallest state is certainly compact—only 90 miles wide and 55 miles top to bottom—and while parts of it are clogged with humanity, some corners are as empty and undeveloped as inland Maine.

By many measures, Connecticut's citizens are as wealthy as any in the country, but dozens of its towns are only shells of their prosperous 19th-century selves, beset by poverty as intractable as it gets. The state boasts no dramatic geographical feature, and its highest elevation is only 2,380 feet. Established in 1635 by disgruntled English settlers who didn't like the way things were going at Plymouth Colony, it has long seemed spiritually divorced from the rest of New England—a place to be traversed on the way to Boston.

All this hardly makes Connecticut seem an appealing vacation destination. But a closer look reveals an abundance of reasons to slow down and linger.

To a great extent, the state's personality derives from the presence of water. In addition to having Long Island Sound along its entire southern coast, several significant rivers and their tributaries slice through the hills and coastal plain: the Housatonic, Naugatuck, Quinnipiac, Connecticut, and Thames. They provided power for the mills along their courses and the towns and cities that grew around them. Despite the bucolic image that mention of the state often conjures, industry still drives most of the economy, but the pollution that industry has caused in the rivers and the Sound is being scoured away.

Development appears to have slowed, helping to preserve Connecticut's scores of classic Colonial villages, from the Litchfield Hills in the northwest to the Mystic coast in the opposite corner. These areas are as placid and timeless as they have been since the 1700s—and, at the same time, as polished and sophisticated as transplanted urbanites can make them. A salty maritime heritage is palpable in the old boat-building and fishing villages at the mouths of its rivers, especially those east of New Haven.

Connecticut is New England's front porch. Pull up a chair and stay awhile.

1 The Gold Coast: Fairfield County

Stamford: 40 miles NE of New York City; Norwalk: 50 miles NE of New York City; Westport: 53 miles NE of New York City; Ridgefield: 61 miles NE of New York City

Mansions, marinas, and luxury apartment blocks nudge up against each other along the deeply indented Long Island Sound shoreline in the southwestern corner of the state. This is one of the most heavily developed stretches of the coast and, in terms of

Connecticut

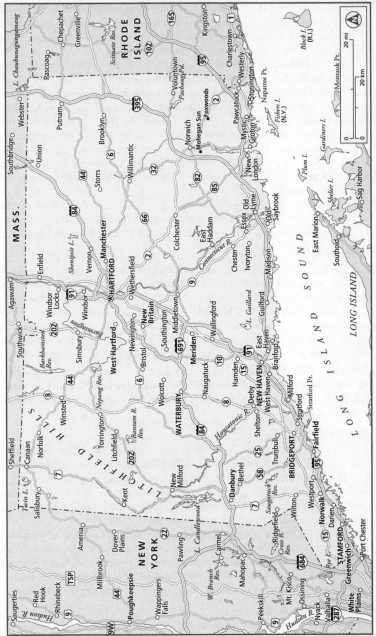

family income, one of the wealthiest. Not for nothing has coastal Fairfield County long been known as the Gold Coast, especially to real estate agents. As the land rises slowly inland from the water's edge, woods thicken, roads narrow, and pockets of New England unfold. Yacht country becomes horse country.

The first suburbs began to form in the middle of the last century, when train rails started radiating north and east from New York's Grand Central Terminal into the countryside. This part of the state was made accessible for summertime refugees from the big city, and eventually weekend houses became permanent dwellings. Corporate executives liked the life of the gentry, so after World War II, they started moving their companies closer to their new homes. Stamford became a city; Greenwich, New Canaan, Darien, and Westport were the bedroom communities of choice—pricey, haughty, redolent of the good life. (Of course, Fairfield County also contains Bridgeport, a depressed city that once considered filing for bankruptcy and has a penchant for political scandal.)

But for visitors, the fashionable "exurbs" (beyond suburban) and their beaches, restaurants, and upscale shops are the draw, along with the villages farther north, especially Ridgefield, that hint of Vermont, all within 1½ hours of midtown Manhattan.

ESSENTIALS

GETTING THERE   From New York and points south, take I-95 or, preferably, the Hutchinson and Merritt parkways. From eastern Massachusetts and northern Connecticut, take I-84 south to Danbury, then Route 7 south into Fairfield County.

The **Metro North** (© **800/METRO-INFO** or 212/532-4900; www.mta.nyc.ny.us/mnr) commuter line has many trains daily from New York's Grand Central Terminal, with stops at Greenwich, Stamford, Darien, Norwalk, Westport, and additional stations all the way to New Haven. Express trains make the trip in 45 to 65 minutes.

VISITOR INFORMATION   Information on the northern part of the county is available at www.litchfieldhills.com, while the **Coastal Fairfield County Convention and Visitor Bureau** (© **800/866-7925;** www.coastalCT.com) can provide materials on the coastal towns.

STAMFORD

In the 1960s, a trickle of Fortune 500 corporations started moving their headquarters from New York 38 miles northeast to Stamford. That flow became a steady stream by the 1980s, and Xerox continues to direct its operations from here, with the Royal Bank of Scotland moving in during 2008. These businesses have erected shiny midrise towers that give the city of 119,000 residents an appearance more like the new urban centers of the Sun Belt than those of the Snow Belt.

One result is a lively downtown that other, less prosperous Connecticut cities surely envy. Roughly contained by Greylock Place, Tresser Boulevard, and Atlantic and Main streets, downtown Stamford has two theaters, tree-lined streets with many shops and a large mall, pocket parks and plazas, and a number of stylish restaurants, sidewalk cafes, and clubs patronized by the city's large cohort of young single professionals.

WHAT TO SEE & DO

Stamford Museum & Nature Center *(Kids*   About 5 miles north of the city center is this fine family-oriented resource. The center has a large lake, an open pen with a pair of river otters, and a real, 10-acre working farm with goats, sheep, cattle, and peacocks. May and June mark the arrival of newborn chicks, kids, calves, and lambs.

On the grounds are a country store, nature trails, a small planetarium, and an oddball Tudor-Gothic house with galleries of art, natural history, and Indian lore.

39 Scofieldtown Rd.(at High Ridge Rd.) (C) 203/322-1646. www.stamfordmuseum.org. Admission $8 adults, $6 seniors and students over 17, and $4 children 4–14. Bendel Mansion & Galleries Mon–Sat and holidays 9am–5pm, Sun 11–5pm; Heckscher Farm daily 9am–5pm (until 4pm Nov–Mar). Feeding time is 9am. The center is 1 mile north of exit 35 off the Merritt Pkwy (Rte. 15).

SHOPPING

United House Wrecking, 535 Hope St. ((C) **203/348-5371;** www.unitedhouse wrecking.com), is a find for dedicated antiques hounds, who will want to make time for this sprawling emporium of oddments. The name may not sound promising, but the company got its start selling architectural remnants salvaged from building demolitions. For years, it featured such items as 1930s gas pumps, stone pigs, and pagodas. Now it showcases far less bizarre imported antiques and reproductions, and has recently added new furnishings to the mix. (It's also rolling out a new name—UHW—as part of the new identity.) It's open Monday through Saturday from 9:30am to 5:30pm, Sunday from noon to 5pm. It's tough to find, though. From exit 9 of I-95, pick up Route 1, then Route 106 north; make a left on Glenbrook Road, which becomes Church Street, and then turn right on Hope Street. Be sure you have a map.

WHERE TO STAY

Stamford Marriott ★★   One of the posher breed of Marriotts, this hotel piles on the extras. Most notable is the **Agora day spa,** off the 2nd floor, with six treatment rooms for facials, body wraps, and waxing, among other services. Steam rooms and 13-head full-body showers are additional attractions. What's more, the hotel has an indoor golf training center with its own staff pro. There is a concierge floor, with lounge. The hotel is smoke-free.

243 Tresser Blvd. (exit 7, I-95), Stamford, CT 06901. (C) **800/732-9689** or 203/357-9555. Fax 203/324-6897. www. marriottstamford.com. 506 units. $169–$284 double. AE, DC, DISC, MC, V. **Amenities:** 2 restaurants (American, steakhouse); lounge; heated indoor/outdoor pool; fitness center and spa; concierge; business center; limited room service; same-day laundry/dry cleaning. *In room:* A/C, TV w/pay movies, high-speed Internet, coffeemaker, hair dryer, iron.

WHERE TO DINE

Dragonfly Lounge ECLECTIC   Though Dragonfly is more a bar than a restaurant, that doesn't mean some good eats can't be had at this newly refurbished gathering place. It looks like a baronial *bierstube,* thanks to faux rough-hewn beams and the leaded panes of neo-Gothic windows. Since booze-fueled mingling is the prevailing activity, food is admittedly ancillary. What is offered by the short card is perhaps necessarily tricky—largely small plates employing such nomenclature as General Tso's Calamari and Kobe Beef Swedish meatballs. While just short of cute, those dishes and their supporting cast are nearly always satisfying, tasty, and not uncommonly pricey. Lobster nachos and grilled pizzas are additional possibilities among the bar offerings, and patrons intent on actual meals can order a "large dish" such as short ribs.

488 Summer St. (C) 203/357-9800. www.dragonflyloungect.com. Small plates $7–$17. AE, MC, V. Sun, Tues–Thurs 5pm–midnight (Fri–Sat until 1am).

Oceans 211 ★ NEW AMERICAN/SEAFOOD   First, know that the hands-on owner put in his apprenticeship at the venerable Oyster Bar in New York's Grand Central Terminal. It shows: The ground-floor bar has a Manhattan sheen, with a curving black marble bar and a long display case of featured wines. The menu (changed daily) is deceptively plain, the entrees listed only by their central ingredients—halibut, Dover sole, wild salmon, snapper—with unflowery descriptions of their preparation. The delights come with what shows up on the plate. One memorable dish was Pacific escolar crusted in Parmesan and served with marinated tomatoes and a purée of broccoli raab. You might have trouble getting past the delectable appetizers and the large selection (most nights) of oysters from the raw bar. Upstairs is a less cozy dining room that seats up to 70.

211 Summer St. ⓒ **203/973-0494.** www.ocean211.com. Reservations suggested on weekends. Main courses $24–$36, with market prices on some dishes. AE, DC, MC, V. Mon–Thurs noon–2:30pm and 5:30–10pm; Fri noon–2:30pm and 5:30–11pm; Sat 5:30–11pm; Sun 5:30–9:30pm.

Smokey Joe's BARBECUE   Smack on the Stamford-Darien line, this wouldn't pass a Fort Worth authenticity test, but it's close enough. Upstairs is a down-and-dirty bar with pool table; downstairs is a classic barbecue joint. Stand in the cafeteria line and select from confusing lists of ribs, brisket, pulled pork, sausage, and birds, supplemented with some Tex-Mex specialties. Then retire to the oil-clothed picnic tables to gorge.

1308 E. Main St. (Rte. 1). ⓒ **203/406-0605.** Main courses $9.95–$25. AE, MC, V. Mon–Thurs 11:30am–9:30pm; Fri–Sat 11:30am–10:30pm; Sun 11:30am–9:30pm (bar daily until 1:30am).

Zinc FRENCH BISTRO   Habitués of the Summer Street restaurant row were happy to note the arrival of this take on the Left Bank bistro model. All the doors in front open onto a raised street-side terrace, the floor inside is covered in tiny black-and-white tiles, and the bar has the requisite zinc top. The theme carries through with a menu that features onion soup, escargots, lobster napoleon, duck confit, and so forth. There are even actual French people in attendance! It's all competently done, and the conviviality ushered in during the 5-to-7pm happy hour (Mon–Fri) continues to flow throughout the evening. They have live music Thursday nights.

222 Summer St. ⓒ **203/252-2352.** www.zincstamford.com. Reservations suggested on weekends. Main courses $19–$35. AE, DC, MC, V. Mon–Sat 11:30am–10pm (until 10:30pm Fri–Sat); Sun 5–9:30pm.

STAMFORD AFTER DARK

The **Stamford Center for the Arts,** Atlantic Street and Tresser Boulevard (ⓒ **203/ 325-4466;** www.stamfordcenterforthearts.org), has two venues. The **Rich Forum,** 307 Atlantic St., presents professional productions, with boldface name actors, of successful Broadway and off-Broadway plays as well as musical and dance presentations. The **Palace Theatre,** 61 Atlantic St., offers rotating appearances by the Stamford Symphony Orchestra, the Connecticut Grand Opera and Orchestra, and the Connecticut Ballet, as well as one-night stands by the likes of B. B. King, the Alvin Ailey Dance Theater, and Bill Cosby.

NORWALK

Given the despair that pervades many New England cities, the continuing betterment of this city's once notorious South Norwalk neighborhood gladdens the heart. The rehabilitation of several blocks of 19th-century row houses is transforming the waterfront into a trendy precinct that has come to be called, inevitably, "SoNo." The **Norwalk Seaport Oyster Festival** (ⓒ **203/838-9444;** www.seaport.org), held in early September, attracts over 90,000 visitors to its tall ships, oyster boats, crafts show, and food booths. There are even skydivers.

Bounded roughly by Washington, Water, and North and South Main streets, SoNo is readily accessible from the South Norwalk railroad station.

WHAT TO SEE & DO

Lockwood-Mathews Mansion Museum   Erected in 1864, this granite mansion in the Second Empire style is covered with peaked and mansard slate roofs, and has 62 rooms arranged around a stunning sky-lit octagonal rotunda. Marble, gilt, marquetry, and frescoes were commissioned and incorporated with abandon. Visits are by guide or audio tour. It has been designated a National Historic Landmark.

295 West Ave. ⓒ 203/838-9799. www.lockwoodmathewsmansion.com. Admission $8 adults, $5 seniors and students, free for children under 12. Mid-Mar to New Year's Day Wed–Sun noon–5pm. From I-95 southbound, take exit 15; from I-95 northbound, take exit 14.

The Maritime Aquarium at Norwalk ✮✮   This is the centerpiece of revitalized SoNo. The present name isn't inclusive, as part of the complex incorporates a section of boat-builders at work as well as exhibits of model ships and full-size vessels, including the *Tango,* which was *pedaled* across the Atlantic. While they don't call it a thrill ride, a submarine simulator takes 18 passengers at a time down to the ocean depths, shaking and shuddering all the way; the climax is a battle between a whale and a giant squid. The main attractions, though, are the marine creatures and mammals on view. Five harbor seals are fed at 11:45am, 1:45pm, and 3:45pm, when they wriggle up on the rocks and even rest their heads in their handler's lap. Additional exhibits include a pair of river otters, an open pool of cow-nosed rays, and tanks alive with creatures found in Sound waters, including sea turtles and sharks. A giant six-story IMAX screen shows nature films that aren't necessarily confined to the seven seas.

10 N. Water St. ⓒ 203/852-0700. www.maritimeaquarium.org. Admission (aquarium only) $11 adults, $10 seniors, $9 children 2–12; IMAX $9 adults, $8 seniors, $6.50 children; combination packages (aquarium plus IMAX movie) $17 adults, $15 seniors, $13 children. July–Aug daily 10am–6pm; Sept–June daily 10am–5pm.

CRUISES

Excursions by 49-passenger ferry to **Sheffield Island** and its historic 1868 lighthouse are offered by the **Norwalk Seaport Association,** 132 Water St. (ⓒ **203/838-9444;** www.seaport.org). The boat departs from Hope Dock, near The Maritime Aquarium. Weather permitting, the boat sets out two to three times daily, on Saturday and Sunday from Memorial Day weekend to late September, as well as Monday through Friday from late June to late September. The round-trip takes about 2½ hours, with a 15-minute layover on the island. Fares are $20 for adults, $18 for seniors (Mon–Wed), $12 for ages 4 to 12, and $5 for ages 3 and under. Thursday evenings from 6 to 9:30pm in season bring clambakes to the island. Other outings include sunset cruises and occasional Sunday picnics. Always call ahead for schedule.

Similarly, the research vessel *Oceanic* has "creature cruises" on weekends from April to June and September to October, as well as daily in July and August, to spot seals and bird life. There are also marine study cruises at other times, a service of The Maritime Aquarium. Fares are $18 per person. Reserve ahead by calling ⓒ **203/852-0700,** ext. 2206.

SHOPPING

Serious shoppers have several choices, primarily among the boutiques and galleries along Washington and Main streets. One shop that may produce a bargain, or at least a surprise, is **Saga,** 119 Washington St. (ⓒ **203/855-1900**). It specializes in folk arts and crafts, as well as jewelry and furnishings from the southwestern United States, Mexico, and points south. Nearby is **A Taste of Holland,** 83 Washington St. (© **203/ 838-6161;** www.kaasnco.com), run by Dutch expatriates, which sells herring, cheese, wooden shoes, candies, and Dutch girl dolls. The original **And Company, Inc.,** 127 Washington St. (© **203/831-8855**), offers bedding, bath products, lamps, tabletop fashions, and soaps. Its success spawned additional stores across the street, at nos. 104 and 108, which sell stylish clothing for men and women.

WHERE TO DINE

For a break from shopping and strolling, drop into **SoNo Caffeine,** 133 Washington St. (© 203/857-4224; www.sonocaffeine.com), which provides breakfast and lunch, offers live jazz and pop some nights—check the website for schedules—and sticks a price tag on virtually every piece of furniture in the place.

Barcelona 🖈 MEDITERRANEAN   Tapas are the featured attraction here, but the kitchen isn't doctrinaire about recipes, which range all over the Mediterranean and even down to South America for inspiration. Two or three tapas per person make a meal, and sharing is inevitable. Start, perhaps, with *charcuteria,* either an assortment of Spanish cheeses, which changes daily, or of cured meats and sausages, usually including nutty-tasting Serrano ham. The day's additional delectables might be *chorizo* with sweet and sour figs, garlic shrimp, or *piquillo* peppers stuffed with potato-cod *brandade.* Other options include *costillas de puerco*—spare ribs with anise-orange glace, and paella for two to six people. The patio is open year-round. Sampler tapas assortments for two or three people cost $48 or $60 (Sun–Thurs).

63–65 N. Main St. (north of Washington St.). © 203/899-0088. www.barcelonawinebar.com. Reservations suggested on weekends. Tapas $3.50–$12; main courses $20–$26. AE, DC, DISC, MC, V. Daily 5pm–1am.

Kazu JAPANESE   The bountiful bento box displayed near the entrance mesmerizes diners awaiting seats. It typically contains a crispy shrimp and calamari salad, salmon skin roll, two vegetable dumplings, a tofu salad, and a chicken *katsu* pizza. At lunch, it's easily enough for two. And given the indifferent decor of plastic room dividers and skimpy representations of irises and lotus blossoms, it's a good thing the focus is on the food to come. Three or four chefs operate at the sushi bar in back, employing truly fresh fish to turn out dumplings and rolls both traditional and cross-cultural in character. In the latter category are jalapeño shrimp with *ponzu* sauce and the mango chicken roll with cilantro, hot peppers, lettuce, and mayo. (Mayo?) Odd or conventional, most items work to happy satisfaction.

64 North Main St. (near West Ave.). © 203/866-7492. Reservations recommended at dinner. Main courses $15–$23. AE, DC, MC, V. Mon–Thurs noon–10pm; Fri noon–11pm; Sat 5:30–11pm; Sun 5–9:30pm.

Match 🖈🖈 NEW AMERICAN   You know a restaurant is hot when the patrons are as young and good-looking as the staff, and they certainly are here (or at least they were when we last visited). Match makes every "Best Of" list in the state, and those tributes are justified. Don't expect elegance: Most of the walls are bare brick, the ceiling has exposed wood joists, and industrial lamps provide most of the lighting. There is the expected martini menu, including pineapple and white chocolate versions for those who don't like the taste of alcohol. Pizzas emerge from the brick oven at the back, delivered to the counter that surrounds it. There is as much eating as drinking going on at the steel-topped main bar, happy diners making the most of such *mmm*-inducing edibles as the "8 hour" *osso buco* with risotto, fried sage, and scallions.

98 Washington St. (btw. Broad and Main sts.). (© 203/852-1088. www.matchsono.com. Reservations strongly recommended on weekends. Main courses $21–$38. AE, DC, MC, V. Daily 5–10pm (sometimes later).

SOUTH NORWALK AFTER DARK

Several of SoNo's restaurants offer musical entertainment on unpredictable schedules. **SoNo Caffeine,** mentioned above, has presented folkies, Brazilian bands, and pop singer-songwriters. The **Black Bear Saloon,** 80 Washington St. (© **203/299-0711;** www.blackbearsono.com), delves into karaoke and brings on cover bands of various enthusiasms. It's open every day from lunch through late evening.

WESTPORT

After World War II, the housing crunch had young couples scouring the metropolitan area for affordable housing along the three main routes of what is now known as the Metro North transit system. Some of them wound up in this pretty village beside the Saugatuck River, several miles inland from Long Island. Most of the new commuter class found Westport to be too far away from Manhattan (1–1½ hr. each way on the train), and it was deemed the archetype of the far-out bedroom communities that were dubbed the exurbs.

Notable for its large contingent of people in the creative crafts, primarily commercial artists, advertising copywriters, art directors, and their fellows, the town was also appealing to CEOs and higher-level executives, many of whom solved their commuting problem by moving their offices to nearby Stamford. The result is a bustling community with surviving elements of its rural New England past wrapped in a sheen of Big Apple panache.

For more information, visit www.coastalCT.com.

GETTING OUTSIDE

Sherwood Island State Park, Green Farms (© **203/566-2305;** www.ct.gov), has two long swimming beaches separated by a grove of trees sheltering dozens of picnic tables with grills. Surf fishing is a possibility from designated areas, and the park has concession stands, restrooms, and an amateurish "nature center." The park is open from Memorial Day to Labor Day, daily from 8am to sunset. Pets are not allowed. By car, take exit 18 off I-95 or U.S. 1, following the road called the Sherwood Island Connector. Admission for out-of-state cars from Memorial Day to September is $10 Monday through Friday, $15 Saturday and Sunday. Cars with Connecticut plates are charged $7 weekdays, $10 weekends.

You can get to Sherwood Island by taking a train to Westport and a taxi from the station to the park. If you don't have a car, you might prefer to use that method to get to **Compo Beach,** the long municipal strand not far from downtown.

West of the town center is **Earthplace** (formerly called the Nature Center for Environmental Activities), 10 Woodside Lane (© **203/227-7253;** www.earthplace.org). Its 62 acres offer walking trails, a wildlife rehab center, and a building with live animals and an aquarium. Open Monday through Saturday from 9am to 5pm, Sunday from 1 to 4pm. Admission $7 adults, $5 for children 12 and under.

Rent a sailboat or kayak or arrange a lesson at the **Longshore Sailing School,** Longshore Club Park, 260 S. Compo Rd. (© **203/226-4646;** www.longshore sailingschool.com), about 2 miles south of Boston Post Road (U.S. 1). Small boat private lessons are $65 per hour.

WHERE TO STAY

Inn at National Hall ☆ A few years ago, this posh riverside hotel was mentioned in the same breath with only a few other Connecticut hostelries. Then hard times set in—two respected restaurateurs gave up on running the dining room and the owner sought permission to go condo. Now the inn is owned by an investment group, and while the future is still uncertain, things have settled down. A good-humored elegance is still in play throughout the 1873 former bank. This is evident upon entering the elevator, which turns out to be a *trompe l'oeil* representation of an estate library. Voluptuous furnishings, antiques, and canopied beds fill both public rooms and duplex suites. It's improbable that you've seen anything like this before. But, oh, those prices!

2 Post Rd., Westport, CT 06880. ☎ **800/628-4255** or 203/221-1351. Fax 203/221-0276. www.innatnationalhall. com. 16 units. $325–$825 double. Rates include breakfast. AE, DC, DISC, MC, V. **Amenities:** Lounge; access to nearby health club; concierge; babysitting; same-day laundry/dry cleaning. *In room:* AC, TV w/pay movies, free Wi-Fi, minibar, hair dryer, safe.

The Westport Inn The building housing this motor hotel has been on the scene since 1935, and while it can't claim the style and elegance of the Inn at National Hall (above), it will likely be around a lot longer. It provides more facilities and services than most motels, including an indoor pool, laundry facility, and fitness room. Guests with a romantic occasion to celebrate can request a room with red satin sheets scattered with rose petals at turndown. Guests have access to the town beach and a nearby golf course. Find it east of the town center. Pets are welcome.

1595 Post Rd. E., Westport, CT 06880. ☎ **203/259-5236.** Fax 203/254-8439. www.westportinn.com. 116 units. $179–$209 double. Rates include breakfast. AE, DC, DISC, MC, V. Pets accepted. **Amenities:** Restaurant (steakhouse); bar; heated indoor pool; small fitness room w/sauna; 24-hr. business center; same-day laundry/dry cleaning. *In room:* A/C, TV, free Wi-Fi, coffeemaker, hair dryer, iron.

WHERE TO DINE

Acqua ☆ MEDITERRANEAN/SEAFOOD A light touch does wonders with such immaculately fresh ingredients as striped bass, halibut, crab, skate, and clams. Presentations are inviting, yet without the appearance of excessive pushing and prodding in the kitchen. The decor consists of murals depicting cherubim, aged-looking tiles, and a bar facing the wood-burning oven, used to bake good designer pizzas and a customer favorite, roasted chicken. Among other possibilities are the open seafood ravioli and pan-roasted sea bass with saffron and couscous. An express lunch in the street-level bar costs only $10, and the midday menu upstairs is far less expensive than dinner.

43 Main St. (near east end of Saugatuck Bridge). ☎ **203/222-8899.** www.acquaofwestport.com. Reservations recommended on weekends. Main courses $16–$38. AE, DC, MC, V. Mon–Thurs noon–2:30pm and 5:30–9:30pm; Fri–Sat noon–2:30pm and 5:30–10:30pm.

Tavern on Main ☆ AMERICAN BISTRO Westporters of all ages, sizes, and colors mount the Tavern's front steps with regularity. Local merchants, widows who lunch, executives, and young moms crowd into the clubby bar to wait for a table. The main room has fragments of the building's earliest 19th-century years—hand-hewn beams and a brick fireplace. While menu items are neither over-the-top nor overly daring, the kitchen does toy with convention. For example, the trademark lobster roll consists of warm (not cool) buttery chunks and shreds of the crustacean filling a hollowed-out, seeded roll. Similar twists are taken with lobster ravioli in a shrimp bolognese sauce and seared ahi tunas over wasabi mashed potato and baby bok choy.

146 Main St. ☎ **203/221-7222.** www.tavernonmain.com. Reservations recommended. Main courses dinner $23–$32. AE, DC, MC, V. Daily 11:30am–4pm and 5:30–10pm (Fri–Sat until 11pm).

Zest ⊛   Phrases like *green and leafy* and *garden fresh* leap to mind with your first look at the menu on other tables. Not that there's a severe shortage of protein on the menu, but it is more often accompanied by salad than by fries, and the tone of the place is decidedly healthy—in a good way. This is by no means Vegan Central, despite the sturdily utilitarian furnishings, the latter necessary to withstand the stresses of an eatery open 16 hours every day. The chef-owner built his rep at the helm of a locally popular Italian restaurant, Da Pietro, and a broadly Mediterranean sensibility informs the food here. There's a pan-seared skate wing, a mushroom risotto with *osso buco,* but also cassoulet and monkfish in a Provence preparation. And you can always start with one of the composed salads as a tribute to the healthy life.

8 Church Lane. ⓒ **203/226-9378.** www.zestcafeandrestaurant.com. Reservations recommended on weekends. Main courses $15–$29. AE, MC, V. Daily 7am–11pm.

WESTPORT AFTER DARK

One of the oldest theaters on the straw-hat circuit, the **Westport Country Playhouse,** 25 Powers Ct. (ⓒ **203/227-4177;** www.westportplayhouse.com), had its first performance in 1931. Revitalized under the leadership of Artistic Director Joanne Woodward and other new administrators, the theater produces a full schedule of comedies, dramas, and musicals from mid-June to mid-September, with performances Monday through Saturday evenings and Wednesday and Saturday matinees. There are single-night or short-term events through the winter season as well. Famous, or at least familiar, actors appear in almost every production (Ms. Woodward even persuaded her husband, Paul Newman, to appear in a production of *Our Town* that went on to Broadway). A music series brings in such acts as Arlo Guthrie, the Preservation Hall Jazz Band, and doo-wop groups. Tickets are priced from about $15 to $48.

RIDGEFIELD

No town in Connecticut has a grander, more imposing main street. Ridgefield's is 132 feet wide, lined with ancient elms, maples, and oaks, and bordered by massive 19th-century houses, most of them in Classical Revival and late Victorian styles. Impressive at any time of the year, it is in its glory during the brief blaze of the October foliage season. Only a little over an hour from New York City (61 miles northeast), the town (pop. 24,000) is nonetheless a true evocation of the New England character. The bustling shopping district has few franchise outlets.

WHAT TO SEE & DO

Aldrich Contemporary Art Museum ⊛⊛⊛   Larry Aldrich was a fashion designer who used his superb collection of paintings and sculptures from the second half of the 20th century to establish this museum. The original 18th-century clapboard structure in which he housed his collection soon doubled in size. But when Aldrich died in 2001, the museum took a sharp turn in another direction. It was decided that it would now be devoted exclusively to "emerging and midcareer artists" and to work no more than 5 years old. To that end, the original collection was almost completely sold off, and the museum was closed for the construction of yet another building. The angular copper-roofed new structure opened in summer 2004. Set back from the road, it contains 12 galleries on two floors, a screening room, and performance spaces, and is a singular contribution to the cultural life of western Connecticut.

258 Main St. (near the intersection of rtes. 35 and 33 at the south end of Main St.). ⓒ **203/438-4519.** www.aldrichart.org. Admission $7 adults, $4 seniors and students, free for youths under 18; Tues free to all. Tues–Sun noon–5pm.

Keeler Tavern This 1713 stagecoach inn was providing sustenance to travelers between Boston and New York long before the Revolutionary War, but that conflict provided it with its object of greatest note. A British cannonball is embedded in one of its walls, presumably fired during the Battle of Ridgefield in 1777. The tavern is now a museum of Colonial life, with period furnishings and costumed guides, and listed in the National Register of Historic Places. And it has another claim to fame: Keeler was long the summer home of architect Cass Gilbert (1849–1934), who designed the Supreme Court Building in Washington, D.C., and was a key figure in the construction of the George Washington Bridge in New York. Visits are by guided tour.

132 Main St. (✆ 203/431-0815. www.keelertavernmuseum.org. Admission $5 adults, $3 seniors, $2 children under 12. Feb–Dec Wed and Sat–Sun 1–4pm.

SHOPPING
Apart from the usual antiques shops and the strip malls north of town on Route 35, **Balducci's**, 21 Governor St. (✆ 203/431-4400), formerly Hay Day Market, is a good stop for devoted food lovers and for anyone contemplating a picnic. Hidden in a shopping center behind Main Street, it is about as fancy a food market as exists outside Manhattan. Sections are devoted to produce, prepared foods, baked goods, charcuterie, cheeses, and fresh flowers. There are also branches in Westport, 1385 Post Rd. (✆ 293/254-5400), and Greenwich, 1050 E. Putnam Ave. (✆ 203/637-7600).

WHERE TO STAY
West Lane Inn ✿✿ An inn that fits most images of a romantic country getaway, this one also works for businesspeople, as it offers Wi-Fi, voice mail, and express checkout. For longer stays, there are two rooms with kitchenettes. A couple of rooms have fireplaces, and all have four-poster beds. The 1849 house stands on a property blessed with giant shade trees. Take breakfast on the porch in good weather; the continental version is included, but hot a la carte dishes are extra. Snacks are available until 9pm. **Bernard's** (below), just across the driveway, serves lunch and dinner.

22 West Lane (off Rte. 35), Ridgefield, CT 06877. (✆ 203/438-7323. Fax 203/438-7325. www.westlaneinn.com. 18 units. $175–$225 double. Rates include breakfast. AE, DC, DISC, MC, V. Driving north from Wilton on Rte. 33, turn west on Rte. 35 at the edge of town. **Amenities:** Concierge; limited room service; laundry service; dry cleaning. *In room:* A/C, TV/VCR, Wi-Fi, fridge, coffeemaker, hair dryer, iron.

WHERE TO DINE
Fans of classy low-brow eats will want to make a special stop at **Chez Lenard** ✿ (no phone), an open-air hot-dog stand on the sidewalk toward the north end of the shopping district, opposite Ballard Park. There are no tables, but these foot-longs come with such trappings as peppers and onions ("Le Hot Dog Excelsior") and cheese fondue ("Logano Suisse"). And the boss gallantly keeps it open right through winter.

Bernard's ✿✿ FRENCH A piano in the main dining parlor is played Friday and Saturday nights and for the festive Sunday brunch, but the primary interests of the owners clearly lie in the kitchen. Imagine sautéed frogs' legs with parsley coulis, roasted garlic custard, and tomato confetti—and that's just to start. Main courses are about fifty-fifty land- and ocean-based proteins. Among the most successful are roasted monkfish wrapped in pancetta and the braised lamb shank with curry-coconut rice galette. Several dinner choices appear as half-priced versions at lunch, but the romance of music and flickering lights is reserved for evenings. Sunday brunch is a fixed-price $35. Adult men might want to wear a jacket.

20 West Lane (near the junction with Rte. 7). ✆ **203/438-8282.** www.bernardsridgefield.com. Reservations recommended on weekends. Main courses $26–$36. AE, DC, MC, V. Wed–Sat noon–2:30pm and 6–9pm (until 10pm Fri–Sat); Sun noon–2:30pm and 5–8pm; shorter hours after Labor Day.

The Elms ⍟⍟ NEW AMERICAN Ridgefield's oldest (1799) operating inn has 20 rooms for overnight visitors, with most of the conveniences travelers expect, but the main attractions are the dining room and tavern. They are in the capable hands of chef Brendan Walsh, who administers fresh twists on regional ingredients without masking their origins. In the main dining room, Connecticut seafood stew and lobster shepherd pie are staples, and the mixed grill of lamb, venison, and sausage is a frequent dinner fixture. Grilled sea scallops with couscous and beans with almonds and mango vinaigrette is of North African inspiration, while the veal medallions sauced with red wine with olives and pepperonata has Tuscan origins. The tavern serves pub grub along the lines of bangers and mash and grilled fish and chicken.

500 Main St. (Rte. 35, at the north end of town). ✆ **203/438-9206.** www.elmsinn.com. Reservations essential on weekends. Main courses $21–$32. AE, DC, MC, V. Wed–Sun 11:30am–9pm.

2 The Litchfield Hills ⍟⍟

New Milford: 82 miles NE of New York City; Lake Waramaug: 92 miles NE of New York City; Litchfield: 112 miles NE of New York City; Norfolk: 133 miles NE of New York City and 136 miles SW of Boston

When the Hamptons got too pricey, too visible, and too chichi back in the 1980s, a lot of stockbrokers, CEOs, and celebs started discovering the Litchfield Hills, arguably the most fetchingly rustic yet still sophisticated part of Connecticut.

The topography and, to an extent, the microculture of the region are defined by the river that runs through it, the Housatonic. Broad but not deep enough for vessels larger than canoes, it waters farms and villages and forests along its course, provides opportunities for recreational angling and float trips, and, over the millennia, has helped to shape these foothills, which merge with the Massachusetts Berkshires.

Men in overalls and CAT caps still stand on the porches of general stores, their breath steaming in the bracing autumn air. Churches hold pancake-breakfast fundraisers; neighbors squabble about development. That's one side of these bucolic hills, less than 2 hours from midtown Manhattan.

Increasingly, the other side is fashioned by refugees from New York. These chic seekers of tranquillity and real estate fled to pre-Revolutionary saltboxes and Georgian Colonials on Litchfield's warren of back roads and brought Manhattan-bred expectations with them. Boutiques fragrant with designer coffees and cachets opened in spaces once occupied by luncheonettes and feed stores. Restaurants discovered sushi and sun-dried tomatoes and just how much money they could get away with charging the newcomers.

Compromises and city-country conflicts aside, the Litchfield Hills remain a satisfying all-season destination for day trips and overnights from metropolitan New York and Connecticut.

ESSENTIALS

GETTING THERE From New York City, follow the Hutchinson River Parkway to I-684 north to I-84 east, taking exit 7 onto Route 7 north. Continue on Route 7 for New Milford, Kent, West Cornwall, and Canaan. For Washington Depot, New Preston, and Litchfield, branch off onto Route 202 at New Milford. An especially attractive entrance into the region is Route 44 from the Taconic Parkway, through Millerton and into Lakeville and Salisbury.

From Boston, take the Massachusetts Turnpike west to the Lee exit, picking up Route 7 south from nearby Stockbridge.

VISITOR INFORMATION   The useful 40-page *Unwind* brochure is produced by the **Northwest Connecticut Convention & Visitors Bureau** (© 800/663-1273; www.litchfieldhills.com).

NEW MILFORD

A gateway to the Litchfield Hills, New Milford was founded in 1703 and functions as a commercial center for the smaller villages that surround it—Roxbury, Bridgewater, Washington, and Brookfield. It is also at the high end of a long stretch of overdeveloped Route 7, which is clogged with strip malls.

New Milford is a welcome stop on the drive north, if only for lunch and a short stroll. Turn right on Route 202 where it splits from Route 7 and crosses the Housatonic River and a railroad track. Up on the left is one end of the long town green. A 1902 fire destroyed many of the buildings around the green, so this isn't one of those picture-book New England settings. Rather, it is a mix of late Victoriana, early Greek Revival, and Eisenhower-era architecture, not to ignore the requisite Congregational church.

Otherwise, there are no obligatory sights, so a walk down Bank Street, west of the green and along Railroad Street, with its crafts shops, a bookstore, and an Art Moderne movie house, won't take long.

GETTING OUTSIDE

Candlewood Lake (© 860/354-6928; www.candlewoodlake.net) is the third-largest man-made lake in the eastern United States. It has a finger that pokes into New Milford, but the area with the most recreational facilities is a few miles to the west. From New Milford, drive north on Route 7 about 2½ miles, turn west on Route 37 toward and through Sherman, then south on Route 39 to **Squantz Pond State Park** (© 203/797-4165; www.ct.gov). With over 170 acres along the lakeshore, it offers swimming, fishing, hiking and cycling trails, picnic grounds, rental canoes, and a boat launch. In the winter, there's ice-skating.

WHERE TO DINE

There are many dining choices along Bank and Railroad streets and out on nearby Route 7.

The Cookhouse ⭐ BARBECUE   Inexplicably, Connecticut is home to some thumping-good barbecue joints. This is the current champ. It's set, appropriately enough, in a converted barn on often-tacky Route 7. Cast aside the diet for the day and start off with hush puppies or Nappy's Nachos, a plate piled with chips, pork, beef, jalapeños, and jack cheese. Continue, if you can, with ribs, chicken, pulled pork, or beef brisket, which are slow-smoked for 10 hours or more. They come with such bountiful sides such as baked beans, collard greens, and mashed potatoes. Separate menu categories list grills, fish, and "comfort foods," the last including burritos, fajitas, macaroni and cheese, and chicken-fried steak.

31 Danbury Rd. (Rte. 7). © 860/355-4111. www.thecookhouse.com. Main courses $15–$22. AE, DC, MC, V. Daily 11:30am–10pm (Fri–Sat until 11pm, Sun until 9pm).

WOODBURY ⭐

The chief distinction of this attractive town strung along Route 6, west of Waterbury, is its over 30 high-end antiques stores. On weekends in good weather, the main road

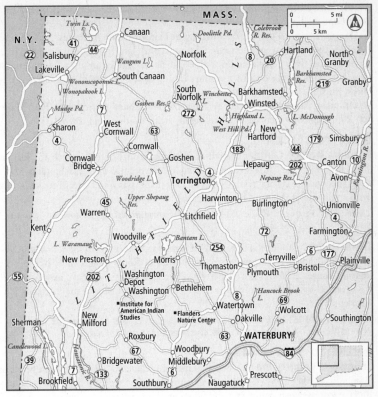

is clogged with cars full of antiquers trolling for treasures, and progress can be slow. The **Woodbury Antiques Dealers Association** (www.antiqueswoodbury.com) offers a directory, which is available in most shops, and an online database listing shops by categories ranging from "folk art" to "wagons, buggies, and sleighs."

The **Litchfield Hills Bed and Breakfast Association** (www.litchfieldhillsbandb. com) includes several members in this town.

ANTIQUING

Shoppers are drawn here for antiques and collectibles of every sort, from funky to obscure to elegant. To winnow down the list, pick up the directory produced by the **Woodbury Antiques Dealers Association** (www.antiqueswoodbury.com) at one of the member stores.

Start off in the building at 289 Main St., at the intersection of routes 6 and 317, which contains **Jennings & Rohn Antiques** (© 203/263-3775). European paintings and furnishings from the 16th century to 1960 are on view, as well as lighting fixtures and some Art Deco. At **Martell & Suffin Antiques** (© 203/263-1913), the owners favor 18th- and early-19th-century European furniture, as well as Asian works of art.

Drive south on Main Street (Rte. 6) to the notable **Wayne Pratt Antiques,** 346 Main St. (© 203/263-5676; www.prattantiques.com), which specializes in 18th-century American furniture, much of it museum-level Chippendale and Queen Anne pieces. Some items are within reach for the rest of us, like the Chinese porcelain boxes for around $12.

Of similar high order are the offerings at **Country Loft Antiques,** 557 Main St. (© **203/266-4500;** www.countryloftantiques.com), largely 19th-century French furnishings and *objets* displayed in a fine old barn. Wares run from biscuit tins to armoires, bolts of fabric to 18th-century dining tables. Be sure to look into the basement, outfitted as a wine cellar.

On most Saturdays in decent weather, the **Woodbury Antiques & Flea Market** (© **203/263-2841**) sets up in a parking lot at the south end of town.

WHAT TO SEE & DO

Flanders Nature Center   North of Woodbury on Route 6, watch for Flanders Road forking to the left. Three miles along, on the right, is the office building for this 1,400-acre nature center. Yearly events include maple syrup and wreath-making, along with a fall festival. Maps of hiking trails are available.

Church Hill and Flanders Rd. © **203/263-3711.** www.flandersnaturecenter.org. Free admission. Office Mon–Fri 9am–5pm; trails daily dawn to dusk.

Glebe House   About the only scrap of surviving history worth mentioning in town is this 1750 house of an Episcopal bishop, west of Route 6 on a street of fine 18th-century houses. A *glebe* was a property given to a preacher as partial compensation for his services. Inside are furnishings true to the period; outside is the Gertrude Jekyll Garden.

Hollow Rd. © **203/263-2855.** www.theglebehouse.org. Admission $5 adults, $2 children 6–12. Garden only $2. May–Oct Wed–Sun 1–4pm; Nov Sat–Sun 1–4pm; other times can be arranged by appointment.

WHERE TO STAY & DINE

Longwood Country Inn ⟨★⟩   South of the town center, this 2-century-old house has been a B&B since 1951. Recent owners pushed out the walls for a 48-seat restaurant, and current overseers completed additional renovations in 2006. Two of the five units are suites, with fireplaces and whirlpool tubs.

The food emerging from the kitchen is contemporary in aspiration and execution, and served at both lunch and dinner from Tuesday through Saturday, with a Sunday buffet brunch from 11am to 3pm (reservations © **203/263-7005**). Dinner entrees are priced from $22 to $35 and include such items as cedar-plank salmon with mango chutney and Long Island duck in a Grand Marnier reduction. There is a live combo on a couple of Friday evenings a month. Children must be over 10 years old.

1204 Main St. (Rte. 6), Woodbury, CT 06798. © **203/266-0800.** Fax 203/263-4479. www.longwoodcountryinn.com. 5 units. $175–$250 double. Rates include breakfast. AE, DC, MC, V. **Amenities:** Restaurant (New American). *In room:* A/C, TV, free Wi-Fi.

Good News Café ⟨★★⟩ NEW AMERICAN   This is a fun spot, one of Connecticut's best, with a cheery staff and rooms doused in ripe primary colors. The food? Make it Europe meets Asia, touching down in various parts of the Americas along the way. The results are spirited but never bizarre, and the menu changes frequently. Examples: Wild boar schnitzel with house-made potato salad, and clams tossed with heirloom tomatoes, pasta, and basil and fennel gremolata. Most of the entrees qualify as heart-healthy, and ingredients, whenever possible, are purchased from local farmers. Desserts, however, tend to be rich, gooey, and caloric—apple spice cake is splendiferous. Saturday nights often feature live jazz, and there's outdoor dining in summer.

694 Main St. (Rte. 6). ✆ **203/266-4663**. www.good-news-cafe.com. Reservations strongly recommended on weekends. Main courses $18–$30. AE, DC, MC, V. Mon, Wed–Sun 11:30am–10pm (from noon on Sun).

WASHINGTON ✿✿ & WASHINGTON DEPOT

Settled in 1734 (its name changed in 1779 to honor the first American president), Washington occupies the crown of a hill beside Route 47. Its village green, with the impressive 1802 Congregational Meeting House surrounded by white buildings and sheltered by shade trees, is an example of a municipal arrangement found all over New England—but rarely to such near-perfection.

Adjacent Washington Depot, down the hill beside the Shepaug River, serves as the commercial center, with a bank and a small cluster of shops. Stop in at the beguiling **Hickory Stick Bookshop,** 2 Greenhill Rd. (✆ **860/868-0525;** www.hickorystick bookshop.com).

Nearby **Steep Rock Reservation** (✆ **860/868-9131;** www.steeprockassoc.org) is a lovely spot for hiking, fly-fishing, or cross-country skiing. (Unfortunately for pet owners, dogs must now be leashed.)

Institute for American Indian Studies   A worthwhile detour takes drivers down Curtis Road to this small repository of Native American crafts and artifacts. They are presented with sensitivity and, for the most part, without polemics. Down a nearby path is a re-creation of an Algonquian village. There's a picnic area on the grounds.

38 Curtis Rd. (off Rte. 199). ✆ **860/868-0518**. www.birdstone.org. Admission $4 adults, $4.50 seniors, $3 children 6–16. Mon–Sat 10am–5pm; Sun noon–5pm (closed Mon–Tues Jan–Mar).

WHERE TO STAY & DINE

Mayflower Inn & Spa ✿✿   Galaxies of stars have already been scattered in abundance over this, one of the state's courtliest manor inns. While the main building is almost entirely new, some elements survive from the original 1894 structure, the most delightful of which is the richly paneled library. Porches look out across manicured lawns to deep woods—58 acres of them. Most bedrooms have fireplaces, and the bathrooms are done with tapestry rugs and mahogany wainscoting—all is as close to perfection as such an enterprise is likely to be, *almost* justifying the breathtaking prices. The clientele can't be described as youthful.

The posh on-site spa features scrubs, wraps, "rituals," and more. The accomplished restaurant features top-drawer ingredients drawn from New England producers and Atlantic fisheries. Execution can be uneven. Perhaps needless to say, the wine cellar is extensive, meticulously chosen, and pricey.

118 Woodbury Rd. (Rte. 47), Washington, CT 06793. ✆ **860/868-9466**. Fax 860/868-1497. www.mayflowerinn.com. 30 units. $440–$640 double; $700–$1,400 suite. AE, MC, V. Take Rte. 202 north 2 miles past New Preston, turn south on Rte. 47 through Washington Depot and up the hill past Washington Common. The entrance is on the left. Children over 12 welcome. **Amenities:** Restaurant (eclectic); pub; heated outdoor pool; nearby golf course; tennis court; elaborate spa; extensive health club; bike rental; same-day laundry; dry cleaning. *In room:* A/C, TV w/pay movies, Wi-Fi, minibar, hair dryer.

WHERE TO DINE

One (pricey) dining option is the restaurant at the **Mayflower Inn** (see above). For a more casual meal, put together a picnic from the delectable array of quiches, pizzas, and salads at **The Pantry,** 5 Titus Rd., Washington Depot (✆ **860/868-0258**). Or eat in there: They recently made room for a dozen tables.

G. W. Tavern ✿ ECLECTIC AMERICAN   The tavern's atmospheric bar has booths and a fireplace, while the simulated attached barn is airier, with a deck that looks down on the Shepaug River. The kitchen concerns itself with interpretations of such robust Americana as crab cakes, meatloaf, chicken potpie, and fish and chips. Daily specials nearly outnumber the items on the regular menu (plus a short card of lighter fare 2:30–5:30pm). It is all quite satisfying, if hardly revelatory. Weekend brunches are popular, as is live jazz Thursday evenings, blues on Monday, and a variety of rock, pop, and folk performers on weekends.

20 Bee Brook Rd. (Rte. 47, a block north of the Washington Depot shopping center). © **860/868-6633**. www.gwtavern. com. Main courses $10–$32. AE, MC, V. Daily 11:30am–10pm (Fri–Sat until 11pm).

NEW PRESTON & LAKE WARAMAUG &&

Never more than a few houses and retailers at the junction of two country roads, the hamlet of New Preston long served primarily as a supplier for locals and, starting in the mid–19th century, the families who summered on nearby Lake Waramaug. More recently, New Preston's small grocery and hardware stores have been converted to antiques emporia of high order, and they find themselves surrounded on weekends by BMWs and Volvos. *Note:* Cellphones do not work in the area.

EXPLORING THE LAKE WARAMAUG AREA

At the northwest tip of the L-shaped lake, 95-acre **Lake Waramaug State Park** &, Lake Waramaug Road (© **860/868-0220;** www.ct.gov), gives the public access to a beautiful body of water that is otherwise monopolized by the private homes and inns that border it. Canoes and paddle boats are for rent, and there's a swimming beach as well as picnic tables, food concessions, and a total of almost 80 camping and RV sites.

Hopkins Vineyard　A former dairy farm on a promontory above Lake Waramaug was converted into a vineyard and winery in 1979. Headquartered in a 19th-century barn across the street from the Hopkins Inn (see "Where to Stay & Dine," below), it produces about a dozen different bottlings. They won't make anyone forget Napa Valley, but prices are fair. Overlooking the lake is a wine bar, where selections of pâtés and cheese can accompany samples of the primary product.

25 Hopkins Rd. © **860/868-7954.** www.hopkinsvineyard.com. Jan–Feb Fri–Sun 10am–5pm (from 11am Sun); Mar–Apr Wed–Sun 10am–5pm (from 11am Sun); May–Dec Mon–Sun 10am–5pm (from 11am Sun).

SHOPPING

In no time, the intersecting streets that form the center of the village have gone from sleepy to spiffy. Notable among the shops is **J. Seitz & Co.,** Main Street/East Shore Road (© **860/868-0119;** www.jseitz.com), featuring bedding, bath products, furniture, and clothing of silk, velvet, cashmere, and suede. Two doors over is **New Preston Kitchen Goods,** 11 East Shore Rd. (© **860/868-1264;** www.newprestonkitchen-goods.com), selling a wide variety of high-end gadgets.

WHERE TO STAY & DINE

The Boulders &&　This once rustic lakeside inn, with a private swimming beach, has scrambled steadily upward in both price and quality. With its sale for $4.3 million in 2002, it took a great leap. The outlying "guesthouses"—four buildings with two spacious units each plus a new carriage house—enjoy private decks, fireplaces, Jacuzzis, and refrigerators. These have contemporary furnishings, while the tone of the bedrooms in the 1895 main house is set by a massive stone fireplace, an elk horn chandelier, and country antiques and reproductions. Drinks at the handsome bar or in the large sitting room precede dinner in the main dining room or on the porch, all with lake views. A serious wine cellar complements the acclaimed cuisine, based on seasonal and local ingredients. The restaurant is closed Monday and Tuesday.

E. Shore Rd. (Rte. 45), New Preston, CT 06777. © 800/455-1565 or 860/868-0541. Fax 860/868-1925. www. bouldersinn.com. 20 units. $350–$425 double. Rates include breakfast or Sun brunch, and afternoon tea. AE, DISC, MC, V. Drive north from New Preston about 2 miles on Rte. 45. No pets. No children under 12. **Amenities:** Restaurant (New American); golf course nearby; tennis court; spa; small fitness room; lake swimming; free canoes and rowboats; game room; limited room service; in-room massage. *In room:* A/C, TV/DVD/CD, hair dryer, iron.

Hopkins Inn *Value*   A family named Hopkins started farming this land in 1787, and its descendants turned the farm into a vineyard and winery in 1979. The farmhouse sits atop a hill with the best views of Lake Waramaug. Food is the main event, since most of the guest rooms are on the spartan side, with phones and TV only in the two-bedroom suite in the annex. Dishes from the Swiss and Austrian Alps are served in hefty portions, with Wiener schnitzel and trout bleu among the options. The restaurant is closed from January through March, but breakfast is still served to overnight guests.

22 Hopkins Rd., New Preston, CT 06777. © **860/868-7295.** Fax 860/868-7464. www.thehopkinsinn.com. 13 units, 11 with private bathroom. $105–$130 double. AE, DISC, MC, V. From New Preston, take Rte. 45 north about 2½ miles and look for the sign on the left. **Amenities:** Restaurant (contemporary Austrian). *In room:* A/C.

LITCHFIELD ⋆⋆

Possessed of a long town common with stately trees reconfigured around the turn of the 20th century by the Frederick Law Olmsted landscaping firm (Olmstead designed New York's Central Park), Litchfield is testimony to the taste and affluence of the Yankee entrepreneurs who built it up, in the late 18th and early 19th centuries, from a Colonial farm community to an industrial center. The factories and mills were dismantled toward the end of the 19th century, and the men who built them settled back to enjoy their riches in their uncommonly large homes.

In recent decades, the town has been discovered by fashionable New Yorkers, who find it less frenetic than the Hamptons. Their influence is seen both in the quality of store merchandise and restaurant fare, as well as in the lofty house prices.

A WALK THROUGH HISTORY

Litchfield's houses and tree-lined streets reward leisurely strollers. From the stores and restaurants along West Street, walk east (to the right when facing the common), and then turn right on South Street. On the opposite corner is the recently expanded **Litchfield History Museum,** at South and East streets (© **860/567-4501;** www. litchfieldhistoricalsociety.org), containing an eclectic array of local historical artifacts, including the world's largest collection of works by the 18th-century portraitist Ralph Earl. It's open from April to mid-November, Tuesday through Saturday from 11am to 5pm and Sunday from 1 to 5pm. Admission is $5 for adults, $3 for seniors, and free for children under 14.

Walking down South Street, on the right, are the **Tapping Reeve House and Law School** (© **860/567-4501;** www.litchfieldhistoricalsociety.org). One of the few historic houses regularly open to the public, the Reeve house was built in 1773, while the adjacent 1784 building was the earliest American law school, established before independence. It counted among its students Aaron Burr and Noah Webster. Hours are the same as those of the Litchfield History Museum (above), which maintains it; one ticket buys admission to both museums.

When the street starts to peter out into more modern houses, walk back toward the common and cross over to the north side. Over there on the right is the magisterial

First Congregational Church, built in 1828. Turn left, then right on North Street, where the domestic architecture matches the quiet splendor of South Street.

NEARBY ATTRACTIONS

Haight Vineyard   Chardonnays and merlots don't spring to mind as likely Connecticut products, but this winery established in 1978 has grown and prospered, presently offering 11 drinkable bottlings. The tasting room is open year-round. It's east of town, off Route 118. There's a second winery in Mystic.

29 Chestnut Hill Rd. (ⓒ 860/567-4045. www.haightvineyards.com. Mon–Sat 10:30am–5pm; Sun noon–5pm.

GETTING OUTSIDE

The **White Memorial Foundation,** 80 Whitehall Rd. (Rte. 202) (ⓒ **860/567-0857;** www.whitememorialcc.org), is a 4,000-acre wildlife sanctuary and nature conservancy about 3 miles southwest of Litchfield. It has campsites and 35 miles of trails for hiking, cross-country skiing, and horseback riding. On the grounds is a small museum of natural history. The Holbrook Bird Observatory looks out on a landscape specifically planted to attract birds. The museum is open year-round, Monday through Saturday from 9am to 5pm and Sunday from noon to 5pm. Admission is $4 for adults, $2 for children 6 to 12.

This is horse country, so consider a canter across the meadows and along the wooded trails of **Topsmead State Forest,** Buell Road (ⓒ **860/567-5694**). The park has a wildlife preserve and a Tudor-style mansion that can be toured the second and fourth weekends of each month from June through October. To get here, follow Route 118 for a mile east of town. The grounds are open from 8am to sunset. Horses can be hired nearby at **Lee's Riding Stable,** 57 East Litchfield Rd., off Route 118 (ⓒ **860/567-0785**). Group trail rides cost $30 per hour per person; half-hour lessons are available.

SHOPPING

Most of the interesting shops are in the row of late-19th-century brick buildings on the south side of the town green. Inserted among the galleries, antique stores, and the inevitable Talbot's is **Kitchenworks,** 23 West St. (ⓒ **860/567-5011;** www.kitchen worksct.com), with a good selection of cookware and tableware, as well as some non-culinary gifts. Around the corner and down a few steep stairs is **Bella Cosa,** corner of West and South streets (ⓒ **860/567-4606**), purveyors of exemplary hand-painted Italian ceramics, pottery, and table linens.

WHERE TO STAY & DINE

Tollgate Hill Inn 𝒢   The centerpiece of this red-barn complex is a 1745 structure known as the Captain William Bull Tavern, listed in the National Register of Historic Places. It houses the bar and restaurant, and it's as atmospheric as all get out, with random-width floors and walls and a marvelously worn bar with a fireplace inglenook. After the new owners brought the kitchen up to code, they turned their attention to the bedrooms in the outlying buildings. Do inspect yours before accepting it, for there are substantial variations in size and configuration. Children and well-behaved pets are welcome.

With relatively few local options, the rejuvenated **restaurant** 𝒢𝒢 was instantly in demand, not least because the menu includes such delights as marinated roasted chicken breast stuffed with pumpkin and served with goat cheese sauce. Open Thursday through Saturday for dinner.

571 Torrington Rd. (Rte. 202), Litchfield, CT 06759. © 866/567-1233 or 860/567-1233. Fax 860/567-1230. www. tollgatehill.com. 20 units. $95–$170 double. Rates include breakfast. AE, DC, MC, V. **Amenities:** Restaurant (international); bar. *In room:* A/C, TV, free Wi-Fi.

WHERE TO DINE

Patty's *Value* AMERICAN/SANDWICHES   Breakfast lovers, Patty's has your back. A roadside eatery outside Litchfield town center, it's *the* local place for apple-sausage omelets, sweet potato pancakes, and sausage and gravy over buttermilk biscuits. Posh it isn't; more like the kind of country cafe seen in scores of other towns—a counter with stools, tables with chairs of a sort first seen sometime around Truman's election. Don't let that stop you—here's food with flavors and earthy panache rarely encountered in such settings, served up with a sense of humor. "Worms in Quicksand," it turns out, is mac and cheese. At lunch, one panino was composed of smoked turkey, red peppers, provolone, thin slices of red onion, leaf spinach, and a pesto sauce. Expect to share the room with farmers, merchants, workmen, and weekenders, but few outsiders. Only breakfast and lunch are served here.

499 Bantam Rd. (Rte. 202). © **860/567-3335.** Most items under $10. No credit cards. Mon–Sat 6am–2pm; Sun 7am–noon.

West Street Grill ✫ NEW AMERICAN   When this contemporary bistro opened well over a decade ago, it was showered with stars by local and big-city reviewers. Known as an incubator for some of Connecticut's best chefs, several of whom went off to open their own places, it hasn't always merited the raves. But despite several important changes, the restaurant's fortunes have more often waxed than waned. Currently, entrees tend toward Italian-style renditions of meats, poultry, and fish, and portions are substantial. It remains the trendiest spot for miles, some of its patrons bearing familiar faces from TV and newspapers. They put out two tables on the sidewalk in warm months.

43 West St. (on the Green). © **860/567-3885.** Reservations recommended for dinner, essential on weekends. Main courses $21–$38. AE, MC, V. Mon–Thurs 11:30am–3pm and 5:30–9pm; Fri–Sat 11:30am–4pm and 5:30–10:30pm.

KENT

A prominent prep school of the same name, a history as an iron-smelting center, and a continuing reputation as a gathering place of artists and writers define this town of fewer than 3,000. Noted 19th-century landscape painter George Inness helped establish that sentiment, and several galleries represent the works of his creative descendants (if not his equals). They are joined by a multiplicity of antiques shops and bookstores, most of them strung along Route 7. South of town on the same road is the hamlet of Bull's Bridge, named for one of the two remaining covered bridges in the state that can be crossed by cars.

Talk of the town is the recent federal recognition of the barely viable Schaghticoke (SKAT-a-cokes) Indian tribe. Ten members occupy a 400-acre reservation next to the prestigious Kent School. It is the fourth tribe in Connecticut to receive formal sovereignty, and controversy is rife locally over what it might do with that status. The prospect of yet another casino looms.

A supersweet local landmark is **Belgique Pâtisserie & Chocolatier** ✫, 1 Bridge St. (© **860/927-3681**), which started life as a restaurant. After the chef-owner tired of the workload, he focused on his calling as chocolatier and pastry chef. Stop in for a superb hot chocolate and examine glass cases full of delicate and creative tarts, cakes, mousses, chocolates, and other confections. There are freshly baked baguettes and croissants, too. Open Thursday through Saturday 9am to 6pm, Sunday 10am to 6pm.

Four miles northeast of Kent is **Kent Falls State Park,** on Route 7 (② **860/927-3238;** www.ct.gov). Its centerpiece, a 250-foot cascade, is clearly visible from the road, and picnic tables are set about the grounds. A path mounts the hill beside the falls. Restrooms are available. A parking fee is charged on weekends and holidays between June and October, but admission is free.

WEST CORNWALL

Not to be confused with Cornwall, 4 miles to the southeast, nor with Cornwall Bridge, 7 miles to the south, this tiny village is best known for its picturesque covered bridge, one of only two in the state that still permits the passage of cars. The bridge connects routes 7 and 128, crossing the Housatonic. With a state forest to the north and a state park to its immediate south, West Cornwall enjoys a piney seclusion that remains welcoming to passersby.

Housatonic Meadows State Park, on Route 7 (② **860/424-3200;** www.ct.gov), comprises 452 acres bordering both sides of the Housatonic River immediately south of West Cornwall. With 95 campsites, it offers access to fishing, canoeing, picnicking, and cross-country skiing. **Housatonic Anglers,** Route 7 (② **860/672-4457;** www.housatonicanglers.com), offers float trips, fly-fishing schools, and guided fishing trips.

Just outside Cornwall proper, off Route 4, is **Mohawk Mountain Ski Area,** 46 Great Hollow Rd. (② **860/672-6100;** www.mohawkmtn.com). "Mountain" is an overstatement, but this is the state's oldest ski resort, with five lifts, 23 trails, snowmakers, and night skiing. All-day lift tickets are $47 for adults, $22 for night skiing (6–10pm). Skis and snowboards are available for rent.

WHERE TO DINE

The Wandering Moose Café (Value) AMERICAN   With more prior incarnations than most people can remember, this location has been serving food of one quality or another for decades. These days, the emphasis on comforting, familiar, and well-prepared meals leaves little room for innovation. Pizza can be topped with scallops, jalapeños, and artichoke hearts. Almond-crusted trout, beef stroganoff, and crab cakes are some of the best bets. Count on clam chowder, burgers, nachos, and baby back ribs, too. Most of it is quite affordable, ensuring that locals of all ages make it their HQ.

Rte. 128 (east end of the covered bridge). ② **860/672-0178.** www.thewanderingmoosecafe.com. Main courses $15–$26. MC, V. Mon–Tues 6:30am–2pm; Wed–Fri 6:30am–3pm and 5:30–9pm; Sat 8am–3pm and 5:30–9pm; Sun 8am–4pm and 5–8pm.

LAKEVILLE & SALISBURY

These two attractive villages share a main street lined with 19th-century houses stretching along Route 44. The "lake" in question is Wononscopomuc, slightly south of the town center.

The discovery in the area of a particularly pure iron ore led to the development of mines and forges as early as the mid-1700s. One of the ironworkers was the eccentric Ethan Allen, later to become the leader of the Green Mountain Boys and a hero for his capture of Fort Ticonderoga from the British in 1775.

Holley-Williams House   One wealthy forge owner, John Milton Holley, bought a 1768 mansion and doubled its size in 1808. The result is a Federal and Greek Revival mix. It contains furnishings assembled by Holley and his descendants over the 173 years the family lived there. There were a lot of them—the outhouse has seven holes.

15 Millerton Rd. (Rte. 44). © 860/435-2878. Free admission (donations welcome). Visits are by guided tour. July 4th to Labor Day Sat–Sun and holidays noon–5pm; rest of year Fri 12–5pm.

WHERE TO STAY & DINE

White Hart ✿ This inn's fortunes have fluctuated in its 180-plus years, but the white-clapboard lodging at the end of Salisbury's main street is continuing its recent rise without a bump. The front porch is a prime summertime perch. Apart from the three suites and the large Ford Room, most of the guest rooms are on the small side. Both the dining rooms and the wine cellar have received excellent notices. Rates have remained stable for some time. VCRs and fridges are available for rent.

Village Green (P.O. Box 545), Salisbury, CT 06068. © 800/832-0041 or 860/435-0030. Fax 860/435-0040. www. whitehartinn.com. 26 units. $135–$300 double. Rates include breakfast. AE, DC, DISC, MC, V. Pets allowed ($25). **Amenities:** Restaurant (New American); cafe; bar. *In room:* A/C, TV, hair dryer.

NORFOLK

Founded in 1758, Norfolk (pronounced NOR-fork) was long popular as a vacation destination for industrialists who owned mills and factories along Connecticut's rivers. At the very least, drive into the center for a look at the village green. It is highlighted by a monument that involved the participation of two of the late 19th century's most celebrated creative people—sculptor Augustus Saint-Gaudens and architect Stanford White.

At the opposite corner is the 90-year-old "Music Shed," the venue for an eagerly awaited series of summer events, the **Norfolk Chamber Music Festival** ✿ (© 860/542-3000; www.yale.edu/norfolk). Held from July to August, it hosts performances by such luminaries as the Tokyo String Quartet and the Vermeer Quartet.

Two prime recreational areas are near each other on Route 272, north of town. A mile from the village green is **Haystack Mountain State Park,** Route 272 (© 860/482-1817; www.ct.gov). Its chief feature is a short trail leading to a three-story stone tower at the 1,715-foot crest. On clear days, the views from the top take in a panorama stretching from the Catskill Mountains to Long Island Sound.

Another 5 miles farther north, on the Massachusetts border, you can enjoy the abundant streams, rapids, and cascades at **Campbell Falls,** Route 272 (© 860/482-1817; www.ct.gov). Fishing, hiking, and picnicking are all possibilities.

WHERE TO STAY

Manor House ✿ This gabled 1898 manse doesn't fit into a stylistic cubbyhole; just call it "Late Victorian Bavarian Tudor." Inside it manages to be both stately and homey, with authentic Tiffany windows and fireplaces in the main salon, dining room, and four bedrooms. The most desirable rooms are on the second floor, notably the English Room, with a king-size bed, and the Lincoln Room, with a half-canopied antique queen-size bed. The least expensive room is on the third floor, tucked under the eaves—when even the owner says the room is very small, believe it. Rates given below are discounted by 20% from December through April.

69 Maple Ave., Norfolk, CT 06058. © 860/542-5690. Fax 860/542-5690. www.manorhouse-norfolk.com. 9 units. $130–$255 double. Rates include breakfast. AE, DISC, MC, V. *In room:* Hair dryer, no phone.

3 New Haven

81 miles NE of New York City

There has been a noticeable, positive uptick in attitude in this Sound-side city in recent years, a palpable sense that things are getting better. This is not to paper over the generalized afflictions of many of Connecticut's cities—nearly a quarter of its citizens live at or below the poverty line, with the attendant urban afflictions that suggests. But all along, the city has had much to offer the leisure traveler: several performing-arts centers and theaters, outstanding museums, autumnal renewals of college football rivalries that date back over 120 years, and a growing number of notable restaurants.

Much of what is worthwhile about New Haven can be credited to the presence of one of the world's most prestigious universities. Yale University both enriches its community and exacerbates the usual town-gown conflicts—a paradox with which the institution and civic authorities have struggled since the Colonial period.

Relatively little serious history has happened here, but there are a number of "firsts" that boosters love to trumpet. Yale awarded the first Doctor of Medicine degree in 1729 to a man who never practiced medicine. Noah Webster compiled his first dictionary here, Eli Whitney perfected his cotton gin, and a local man named Colt invented a revolver in 1836. The first telephone switchboard was made here, necessitated by a Rev. John E. Todd, who was the first person in the world to request telephone service. And the first hamburger was allegedly made and sold here, as was—even less certainly—the first pizza.

ESSENTIALS

GETTING THERE   Interstate 95 between New York and Providence skirts the shoreline of New Haven; I-91 from Springfield, Massachusetts, and Hartford ends here. Connections can also be made from the south along the Merritt and Wilbur Cross parkways. Downtown traffic isn't too congested, except at the usual rush hours, and there are ample parking lots and garages near the Green and Yale University, where most visitors spend their time.

Tweed–New Haven Airport (℃ 203/466-8888; www.flytweed.com; airport code HVN) primarily handles private and charter traffic. Currently, the only commercial passenger flights are offered by **US Air Express** (℃ 800/428-4322; www.usairways.com), and only between New Haven and Philadelphia. The airport is located southeast of the city, near exits 50 and 51 off I-95.

Amtrak (℃ 800/USA-RAIL; www.amtrak.com) has several trains daily that run between Boston and New York and stop in New Haven. New York is 1½ hours away; Boston, about 3 hours. **Metro North** (℃ 800/638-7646 or 212/532-4900; www.mta.nyc.ny.us/mnr) commuter trains make many daily trips between New Haven and New York. Metro North tickets are much cheaper than Amtrak's, but its trains take longer.

VISITOR INFORMATION   The **Greater New Haven Convention & Visitors Bureau** (℃ 203/777-8550; www.visitnewhaven.com) maintains an office at 169 Orange St. Downtown, **INFO New Haven,** at 1000 Chapel St. (℃ 203/773-9494; www.infonewhaven.com), is open daily year-round. In addition to stocks of useful brochures, attendants can make theater and restaurant reservations, and there is a computer terminal at which visitors can check their e-mail.

A bus designed to resemble an electric trolley makes a circuit of downtown, with frequent stops outside important attractions. In operation from 11am to 6pm Monday through Saturday, it passes along its fixed route every 15 or 20 minutes. At this writing, it is free, but check before boarding or call the **New Haven Trolley Line** (℃ 203/288-6282).

New Haven

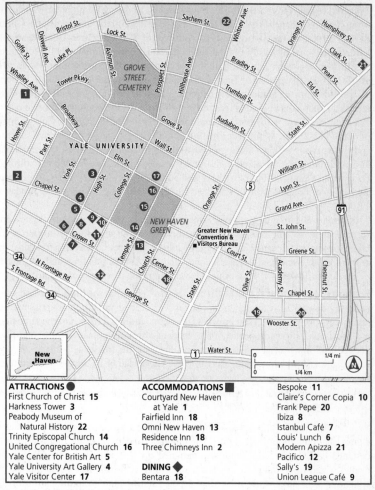

SPECIAL EVENTS   Important events are the new **International Festival of Arts & Ideas** (www.artidea.org), held at many sites around the city in late June, and a free **jazz festival** on the Green from late July to early August. Call INFO New Haven (above) for dates and details.

EXPLORING YALE UNIVERSITY & NEW HAVEN

Most of the major attractions are associated with Yale University and, except for the Peabody Museum, are within walking distance of one another near the **New Haven Green,** which is bounded by Elm, Church, Chapel, and College streets. The Green is divided by north-south Temple Street, with government and bank buildings, including the Gothic Revival City Hall, bordering it on its east. There's a retail district on the south and some older sections of the vast Yale campus to the north and west.

Facing Temple Street are three historic churches, all dating from the early 19th century. Next to Chapel Street is **Trinity Episcopal Church,** a brownstone Gothic Revival structure; the Georgian **First Church of Christ/Center Congregational Church;** and the essentially Federal-style **United Congregational.** The First Church of Christ is of greatest interest, built atop a crypt with tombstones inscribed as early as 1687. Tours are conducted Tuesday through Friday between 10:30am and 2:30pm.

The oldest private home in New Haven has been turned into the **Yale Visitor Center.** It's a Colonial-era building (erected in 1767 by John Pierpont, grandson of one of Yale's founders) facing the north side of the Green at 149 Elm St., near College Street (© **203/432-2300**). While its primary mission is to familiarize prospective students and their parents with a 1-hour **guided walking tour** of the campus, the center also has an introductory video and maps for self-guided tours. It's open Monday through Friday from 9am to 4:30pm, Saturday and Sunday from 11am to 4pm. Guided tours are available Monday through Friday at 10:30am and 2pm, Saturday and Sunday at 1:30pm.

It is impossible to imagine New Haven without Yale, so pervasive is its physical and cultural presence. The most evocative quadrangle of the sprawling institution is the **Old Campus,** which can be entered from College, High, or Chapel streets. Inside, the mottled green is enclosed by Federal and Victorian Gothic buildings and dominated by **Harkness Tower,** a 1920 Gothic Revival campanile that looks much older.

Peabody Museum of Natural History ⸙ Kids

Head to the third floor and work your way down. Up at the top are dioramas with stuffed animals in various environments: bighorn sheep, Alaskan brown bears, bison, and musk oxen. On the same floor is a small but illuminating collection of ancient Egyptian artifacts. The second floor doesn't hold much of general interest, but down on the first is a "bestiary" of large stuffed animals, which leads logically into the Great Hall of Dinosaurs. Guided tours are offered Saturday and Sunday at noon and 1pm.

170 Whitney Ave. (at Sachem St.). © 203/432-5050. www.peabody.yale.edu. Admission $7 adults, $6 seniors, $5 children 3–18; free to all Thurs 2–5pm. Mon–Sat 10am–5pm; Sun noon–5pm.

Yale Center for British Art ⸙⸙

What looks like a parking garage from outside is a great deal more impressive inside. The museum, underwritten by Paul Mellon and designed by Louis I. Kahn (who also designed the Yale University Art Gallery; see below) is said to be the most important repository of British art outside the United Kingdom, with holdings of more than 1,900 paintings and sculptures. Most of the paintings in the permanent collection are from the 16th through the early 19th centuries. It's a dazzling array, with canvases by such luminaries as Hogarth, Gainsborough, Joshua Reynolds, and the glorious J. M. W. Turner.

1080 Chapel St. (at High St.). © 203/432-2800. www.yale.edu/ycba. Free admission. Tues–Sat 10am–5pm; Sun noon–5pm.

Yale University Art Gallery ⸙⸙⸙

The artworks of many epochs and regions are on display, but the museum is most noted for its collections of French Impressionists and American realists of the late 19th and early 20th centuries. It's a satisfying collection for connoisseurs, and won't test the patience of reluctant museum-goers. Take the elevator to the fourth floor and work down. The top floor is utilized primarily for special exhibitions. On the third floor are 14th- to 18th-century Gothic ecclesiastical panels and 16th-century Italian and Dutch portraits, among them paintings by

Rubens and Hals. In sharp contrast are adjoining galleries of 20th-century works—Rothko and Rauschenberg as well as Picasso and Mondrian. The second floor is commanded by compelling African and Asian artworks.

1111 Chapel St. (at York St.). ℂ 203/432-0600. www.artgallery.yale.edu. Free admission (donations appreciated). Tues–Sat 10am–5pm (Thurs until 8pm); Sun 1–6pm.

WHERE TO STAY

New Haven lodgings are both limited and, with one notable exception, largely devoid of either charm or distinctiveness. Still, its motels and hotels fill up far in advance for Yale football weekends, alumni reunions, and graduation. The city visitor center has a **hotel reservations service** (ℂ **800/332-7829**).

Courtyard New Haven at Yale 🐾🐾 At the edge of the older precincts of the sprawling Yale campus, this hotel covers most traveler needs without excess or frippery. The expected components of the Courtyard template are all in place: an adequate fitness room, attached covered parking, a bar, and a dining room serving complementary hot breakfasts. Packaged snacks and bottled water are laid out and a newspaper is at the door in the morning (Mon–Fri). After renovations, this is now one of the more desirable of the local chain hotels. All Courtyard hotels are now smoke-free.

30 Whalley Ave. (near Howe St.), New Haven, CT 06511. ℂ 800/321-2211 or 203/777-6221. Fax 203/772-1089. www.marriott.com. 160 units. $179–$409 double. Parking $12. AE, DC, DISC, MC, V. **Amenities:** Restaurant (breakfast only); bar; 24-hr. business center; exercise room; laundry. *In room:* A/C, TV w/pay movies, CD, free high-speed Internet, fridge, coffeemaker, hair dryer, iron.

Omni New Haven 🐾🐾 Its location couldn't be better, next to the Green and within easy walking distance of theaters, much of the campus, and two of the Yale museums. It's a conventional member of the reliable Omni chain, with a 19th-floor restaurant, John Davenport's, which offers fine views of the Green and surrounding cityscape. Some rooms are equipped with treadmills.

155 Temple St. (south of Chapel St.), New Haven, CT 06510. ℂ 888/444-6664 or 203/772-6664. Fax 203/974-6780. www.omnihotels.com. 306 units. $219–$289 double. AE, DC, DISC, MC, V. **Amenities:** Restaurant; bar; exercise room; concierge; business center; limited room service; same-day laundry; dry cleaning. *In room:* A/C, TV/VCR, Wi-Fi, minibar, coffeemaker, hair dryer, iron.

Three Chimneys Inn 🐾🐾 Once known as the Inn at Chapel West, this 1874 mansion is a favorite of Yalies and their parents. All rooms are outfitted with antiques and mahogany four-poster beds. On chilly days, gas fires burn in seven of the bedrooms and in the dining room and parlor, where a tray of cordials is set out. An honor bar and guest pantry are also at hand. Businesspeople are more in evidence than is usual at inns, many of them here to interview Yale students for jobs.

1201 Chapel St. (btw. Park and Howe sts.), New Haven, CT 06511. ℂ 800/443-1554 out of state, or 203/789-1201. Fax 203/776-7363. www.threechimneysinn.com. 11 units. $220–$295 double. Rates include full breakfast and afternoon tea. AE, DISC, MC, V. No pets. No children under 6. **Amenities:** Exercise room; access to nearby health club; same-day dry cleaning. *In room:* A/C, TV/VCR, high-speed Internet, coffeemaker, hair dryer, iron.

WHERE TO DINE

In addition to the restaurants below, the **Atticus Bookstore & Café** (1082 Chapel St.; ℂ 203/776-4040), what many call the best bookstore in town, devotes half its space to a lunch counter, tables, and a takeout section locally famous for its scones. It's open daily from 8am to midnight.

> ## Tips The New Haven Pizza Wars
>
> On the scene for most of the last century, **Frank Pepe** ✦, 157 Wooster St. (btw. Olive and Brown sts.) (© **203/865-5762**; www.pepespizzeria.com), has long laid claim to the local pizza crown in the face of substantial competition. In exchange for almost unimaginably thin-crusted pies, pilgrims put up with long lines, nothing decor, and an often sullen staff the management prefers to think of as "seasoned." A big fave is the white clam pie.
>
> You can do every bit as well at **Sally's** ✦, 237 Wooster St. (© **203/624-5271**), just down the street. Many knowledgeable pizza lovers believe that **Modern Apizza** ✦, 874 State St. (© **203/776-5306**; www.modernapizza.com), holds the edge over both.

Bentara ✦ SOUTHEAST ASIAN   At this location since 1997, Bentara now finds itself benefiting from a surge in gentrification to its once shabby street. Bare teak tables occupy the spare, roomy front; the back room has tableclothed tables and a second bar. Shadow puppets hang behind opaque panels; carved fertility figures stand along one wall. Billed as Malaysian, the menu encompasses Thai, French, and Vietnamese ingredients and techniques as well. Expect punchy, often fiery flavors, not for those with timid palates. *Ikan goring pedas,* for example, is a memorable golden-fried whole fish in a sweet-spicy sauce; precede it with the pan-simmered mussels in a coconut-curry sauce with slivered onions and red peppers.

76 Orange St. (at Center St.) © 203/562-2511. www.bentara.com. Main courses $12–$27 (but market price for several dishes). AE, DISC, MC, V. Daily noon–2:30pm and 5:30–10pm.

Bespoke ✦✦✦ NEW AMERICAN   This qualifies as the preeminent new restaurant in Connecticut, open since fall of 2006. It would be comfortable in the highest echelons of Manhattan dining, but without the confiscatory tariffs. Food arrives in one dazzling display after another, brought to table by jovial members of a multicultural waitstaff, each of whom is prepared to explain the creations in full detail. The main dining area is below street level, illuminated by dozens of votive candles in wall niches.

The wild-haired chef started up in New Haven with the late-lamented Roomba, a revelatory exercise in the then-fresh Nuevo Latino arena. He and his co-owner wife moved here, barely a block away, and started over. There are hints of that former culinary passion in the Bespoke menu—the seafood chowder in a coconut milk broth, for one—but the range is broader now. Roasted sea bass in a carrot-curry broth with mussels and vegetable couscous was memorable, as was the "Two-Way" duck, an Asian-style leg confit and breast with rhubarb-celery salad and ginger-plum sauce. Just poke a finger at the menu—you're unlikely to be disappointed.

266 College St. (btw. Chapel and Crown Sts.) © 203/562-4644. www.bespokenewhaven.com. Main courses $26–$29. AE, DISC, MC, V. Tues–Thurs 5–9:30pm; Fri–Sat 5-10:30pm; Sun 5–8:30pm.

Claire's Corner Copia (Value) VEGETARIAN   Few college towns are without at least one low-cost vegetarian restaurant, and this one has ruled in New Haven since 1975. Options include curried couscous, eggplant rollatini, six veggie burgers, five flatbread pizzas, and a number of Mexican entrees, including a variety of quesadillas. Fish-eaters will enjoy the tuna salad and open-faced albacore melt sandwiches on offer. Breakfast brings a bounty of plump scones and massive muffins. Place your order at the counter after perusing the very long blackboard menu, pay the cashier, and claim a table. Presently, someone emerges from the kitchen and shouts your name.

1000 Chapel St. (at College St.). 📞 **203/562-3888**. www.clairescornercopia.com. Most items under $10. No credit cards. Sun–Thurs 8am–9pm; Fri–Sat 8am–10pm.

Ibiza 🍷🍷 SPANISH   This used to be Pika Tapas, but it didn't get all that much attention until the owners decided to go upmarket and chefs Bollo and Romero introduced the high-flying modern cuisine and wines of their native land. Their menu includes a few traditional dishes, among them *pasteles de bacalao,* potato-and-cod cakes, and *espinacas a la Catalana,* sautéed spinach with raisins and pine nuts. But they up the ante with vigor, as when they have paired grilled sea scallops with squid-ink pasta or duck breast with diced polenta, bacon, apples, prunes, and tomatoes. To get a better idea of their range, spring for the $58 tasting menu (available Mon–Thurs). Note that lunch is served only on Thursday, and paella only at Tuesday dinner.

39 High St. (south of Chapel St.). 📞 **203/865-1933**. www.ibizanewhaven.com. Reservations essential. Main courses $23–$29. AE, MC, V. Mon–Wed and Fri–Sat 5–10pm (until 11pm Fri–Sat); Thurs noon–2:30 and 5–10pm.

Istanbul Café 🍷 TURKISH   Step through the door into a room that looks very much like a family restaurant in Istanbul's Beyoglu market. An elaborate pewter chandelier looms overhead, Turkish ceramics hang on the walls, tasseled damask drapes are at the windows, and mirror cloth pillows line the bench couch along the wall. The setting is right and so is the food. Plunge further into the mood with the starter platter of *meze*—dollops of hummus, zingy red lentil salad, creamy carrot salad, spinach yogurt, and dolmas (grape leaves wrapped around rice fillings). Crispy rounds of bread give off aromatic steam when they are torn open. Kebabs predominate among the entrees, chunks of chicken, lamb, and/or beef prepared in a number of traditional modes and usually accompanied by rice pilaf and salad. Lamb is wonderful, especially in the Iskender kebab and Yaprak Doner kebab, served only on Friday and Saturday.

245 Crown St. (College St.). 📞 **203/787-3881**. www.istanbulcafect.com. Main courses $14–$19. AE, DC, MC, V. Mon–Thurs noon–10:30pm; Fri–Sun 3–10:30pm (until 11:30pm Fri–Sat).

Louis' Lunch BURGERS/SANDWICHES   The claim, unprovable but gaining strength as the decades roll on, is that America's very first hamburger sandwich was sold in 1900 at this little luncheonette. Although Louis' was moved from its original location to escape demolition, not much else has changed. The wooden counter and tables are carved with the initials of a century of patrons. The beef is freshly ground each day, thrust into gas-fired ovens, and then served (medium rare, usually) on two slices of white toast. The only allowable garnishes are slices of tomato, onion, or cheese. There's no mustard and no ketchup, so don't even ask. And there are no fries, either, just potato chips or potato salad. During late hours from Thursday through Saturday, they add franks and steak sandwiches . . . if the mood strikes them.

261–263 Crown St. (btw. High and College sts.). 📞 **203/562-5507**. www.louislunch.com. All items under $8. No credit cards. Tues–Wed 11am–4pm; Thurs–Sat noon–2am. Closed Aug.

Pacifico 🍷 NUEVO LATINO   The name refers to the cuisines of the long western coastline of Latin America, but it is important to note that the kitchen draws inspiration from that extended region and doesn't engage in slavish replications of traditional dishes. The success of the owners' concept is evident in the small but growing group of similar enterprises both here and in New York. In general, this means lighter, less robustly seasoned food than that found in Mexico, Colombia, Peru, and Ecuador.

Thus, you are offered such inventions as seared tilapia with a yucca crust and artichoke, potato, and Manchego cakes puddled in basil and yellow tomato coulis. Their version of vegetarian paella turns out to be layered quinoa, asparagus, shiitakes, zucchini, plantain, spinach, and more packed into a round pastry basket. Presentations are pretty but unfussy. A particularly good deal is the three-course *prix fixe* lunch at $17. There's a busy under-40 bar scene toward the end of the week.

220 George St. (Temple St.). © 203/772-4002. www.pacificony.com. Main courses $19–$29. AE, DC, MC, V. Mon–Fri 11:30am–3pm and 5–10pm (until 11pm Thurs–Sat).

Union League Café ☆☆ CREATIVE FRENCH   A grand salon that retains an air of the site's aristocratic origins, which date back to 1854—even the name fairly shrieks of the spot's former status as a bastion of WASP privilege, the Union League Club. Things have loosened up considerably, and denim-clad Yalies, their doting parents, philosophizing profs, and deal-making execs are all equally comfortable here. With waiters in aprons and tables covered with butcher paper, the atmosphere is now closer to an updated French brasserie than to that of a gentlemen's sanctuary. Entrees on the order of cod and sweet-potato brandade, saffron monkfish, and braised veal cheeks seem both familiar and fresh. A daily cheese card is proffered instead of, or in addition to, dessert, and the wine list is almost exclusively French. Service is informed and proficient.

1032 Chapel St. (btw. High and College sts.). © 203/562-4299. www.unionleaguecafe.com. Main courses $28–$37. AE, DC, MC, V. Mon–Fri 11:30am–2:30pm and 5–9:30pm; Sat 5–10pm.

NEW HAVEN AFTER DARK

The presence of a highly educated general population ensures a cultural life in New Haven equal to that of many larger cities. A reliable source of information on cultural events and nightlife is the free weekly newspaper the *New Haven Advocate* (www.newhavenadvocate.com).

THE PERFORMING ARTS   Within a couple of blocks of the Green, the **Shubert Performing Arts Center,** 247 College St. (© **800/228-6622** or 203/562-5666; www.shubert.com), presents musicals, opera, plays, cabaret, concerts, and such touring troupes as the Alvin Ailey Dance Theater. The well-regarded **Yale Repertory Theatre** (© **203/432-1234;** www.yalerep.org) mounts an October-to-May season of modern productions as well as classics by Shakespeare, George Bernard Shaw, and Tennessee Williams. It uses three venues: University Theater, 222 York St.; the New Theatre, 1156 Chapel St.; and The Rep, 1120 Chapel St.

Away from downtown, but worth the cab fare, is the prestigious **Long Wharf Theatre,** 222 Sargent Dr. (© **203/787-4282;** www.longwharf.org). It's known for its success in producing new plays that often make the jump to Off-Broadway and even Broadway itself. The season runs from October to June.

Several venues on the Yale campus, including **Sprague Memorial Hall,** 470 College St., and **Woolsey Hall,** at College and Grove streets, host the performances of resident organizations, including the New Haven Symphony Orchestra, New Haven Civic Orchestra, Yale Concert Band, Yale Glee Club, and Yale Philharmonia. For upcoming events, call the **Yale Concert Information Line** (© 203/432-4157).

THE CLUB SCENE   The biggest and best venue for live rock, hip-hop, and pop is **Toad's Place,** 300 York St. (© 203/621-TOAD; www.toadsplace.com), which welcomes the likes of Blonde Redhead, The Mars Volta, and Johnny Winter, with a smattering of tribute bands and regional groups on the schedule, too. Performances are usually from Thursday through Sunday nights.

For something less frenetic, the popular **BAR,** 254 Crown St. (✆ **203/495-1111;** www.barnightclub.com), has a lounge in front—open to the street on warm nights—and a pool table, terrace, and dance floor in back. On Sunday, listen to live jazz or blues. **The Brü Rm,** a brewpub tacked onto the slightly older nightclub, produces rich beers and poses a naked challenge in the eternal New Haven pizza wars; its thinnest-crust pies are leading contenders for the crown long held by Frank Pepe's. The gentrifying Ninth Square neighborhood has a new bar and jazz concert space, **Firehouse 12,** 45 Crown St. (✆ **203/785-0468;** www.firehouse12.com). It's open Wednesday through Saturday nights, featuring half-price drafts and free food some evenings. Combos usually appear on Friday.

4 Hartford

118 miles NE of New York City; 100 miles SW of Boston

Dissidents fleeing the rigid religious dictates of the Massachusetts Bay Colony founded Hartford in 1636. Three years later, they drafted what were called the "Fundamental Orders," the basis of a subsequent claim that Connecticut was the first political entity on earth to have a written constitution, hence the nickname "Constitution State."

Unfortunately, Connecticut's capital and second-largest city endures a drooping uneasiness it hasn't been able to shake. Visitors can't help noticing the miles of distressed housing, weed-strewn lots, and hollow-eyed office structures that radiate out from the center.

Still, Hartford has always pointed gamely to its grand edifices—the divinely overwrought gold-domed capitol, the High Victorian Mark Twain House, and the august Wadsworth Atheneum. Downtown has experienced a construction boomlet in recent years, with a new convention center at riverside among the results, and the gracious Old State House enjoyed a renovation in the mid-1990s. These efforts have encouraged the establishment of some cosmopolitan restaurants. Most of a day trip or overnight visit can be contained within only a few square blocks.

ESSENTIALS

GETTING THERE Interstates 84 and 91 intersect in central Hartford, which is halfway between New York and Boston.

Bradley International (✆ **203/627-3000;** airport code BDL), in Windsor Locks, Connecticut, about 12 miles north of the city, is served by several major airlines, including **American** (✆ 800/433-7300), **Continental** (✆ 800/525-3273), **Delta** (✆ 800/221-1212), **Northwest** (✆ 800/225-2525), **United** (✆ 800/864-8331), and **US Airways** (✆ 800/428-4322).

Amtrak (✆ **800/USA-RAIL;** www.amtrak.com) has several trains that stop daily in Hartford.

VISITOR INFORMATION Connecticut's Commission on Culture & Tourism (✆ **888/288-4778;** www.ctvisit.com) will mail you a free vacation guide if you ask. The website also lists special hotel packages and a "This Weekend" page of suggested activities.

SPECIAL EVENTS In late July, the **Greater Hartford Festival of Jazz** (www.hartfordjazz.com) offers free performances at the pavilion in Bushnell Park.

WHAT TO SEE & DO

Harriet Beecher Stowe House and Library   Stowe's book *Uncle Tom's Cabin*, published in 1852, when she was 41, portrayed the physical, sexual, and emotional abuse endured by enslaved people. It became a best-seller in the United States, England, Europe, and Asia. This home, her last, was built in 1871 and is a smaller version of the adjacent Twain residence (see below). (The authors moved into their respective residences within a year of each other, when Stowe was in her 60s and Twain was nearing 40.) Displays illustrate nineteenth-century women's history, including suffrage, as well as African-American history and racial attitudes in the U.S.

77 Forest St. ⓒ 860/522-9258. www.harrietbeecherstowecenter.org. Admission $8 adults and teens, $7 seniors, $4 children 5–12, free ages 5 and under. Mon–Sat 9:30am–4:30pm; Sun noon–4:30pm. Closed Mon Oct–May. Visits by guided tour only, with separate tours for the garden.

Mark Twain House and Museum ✶✶ *(Kids)*   Samuel Clemens, whose pseudonym, Mark Twain, was a term used by Mississippi River pilots to indicate a water depth of 2 fathoms, lived here from 1874 to 1891, a period when he wrote *The Adventures of Huckleberry Finn* and *A Connecticut Yankee in King Arthur's Court*. The 19-room house is a fascinating example of the late-19th-century style sometimes known as "Picturesque Gothic," with several steeply peaked gables and brick walls whose varying patterns are highlighted by black or orange paint. The High Victorian interior was the work of distinguished designers of the time, including Louis Comfort Tiffany, who provided both advice and stained glass. Twain's enthusiasm for newfangled gadgets— *Life On The Mississippi* is said to be the first novel written on a typewriter—led to the installation of a primitive telephone in the entrance hall.

A guided tour takes about an hour and eventually leads to the top floor and the writer's main workroom, a large space that also has a billiard table (Twain would often wake his butler in the middle of the night to play a few games). A museum, opened in 2003, houses galleries, a small cinema, a cafe, and a shop.

351 Farmington Ave. ⓒ 860/247-0998. www.marktwainhouse.org. Admission $13 adults, $11 seniors, $8 children 6–16, free ages 5 and under. Mon–Sat 9:30–5:30pm; Sun noon–5:30pm. Closed Tues Jan–Mar. Visits by guided tour only. Take exit 46 off I-84, turn right onto Sisson Ave., then right onto Farmington Ave. The house is on the right. From downtown, drive west on Asylum St., bearing left on Farmington Ave. The house is on the left.

The Old State House   After escaping a close call in 1975 (the city wanted to tear it down to build a parking lot), a 4-year, $12-million restoration in the mid 1990s brought the 1796 State House new luster. Upstairs on the right is the Senate chamber, with a full-length painting of the first president by the indefatigable Washington portraitist Gilbert Stuart. Three eras of architecture are represented: Federal (Senate Chamber), Victorian (City Council Chamber), and Colonial Revival (upper hall and stairs). Also on the second floor is the "Museum of Natural and Other Curiosities," which includes a calf with two heads and the horn of a unicorn.

800 Main St. (at Asylum Ave.). ⓒ 860/522-6766. www.ctosh.org. Admission $6 adults, $3 seniors, $3 children 7–17 and students. Tues–Fri 11am–5pm; Sat 10am–5pm.

Wadsworth Atheneum Museum of Art ✶✶✶   Opened in 1842, this was the first public art museum in the United States and remains a repository with few equals in New England. The strength of the collection lies primarily in its American paintings, spanning the period from landscape artists of the 19th century through luminaries of the New York School of the mid–20th century. On the top floor are works by

ATTRACTIONS ●
Harriet Beecher Stowe House **1**
Mark Twain House **1**
The Old State House **7**
Wadsworth Atheneum Museum of Art **9**

ACCOMMODATIONS ■
The Goodwin Hotel **3**
Hartford Marriott Downtown **8**
Hilton Hartford **6**

DINING ◆
Hot Tomato's **2**
Max Downtown **4**
Trumbull Kitchen **5**

Thomas Cole, of the Hudson River School, and his contemporaries Frederick Church and Albert Bierstadt. On the balcony are more Americans—Andrew Wyeth, Milton Avery, Norman Rockwell. The first floor contains rule-bending multimedia works, as well as canvases by abstract expressionists and pop and op artists of the 1950s and 1960s like de Kooning and Rauschenberg.

A new director, Susan Lubowsky Talbott, of the Smithsonian Institution, was appointed in early 2008 and will oversee upcoming renovations of the museum's historic buildings. On the first Thursday of each month, the museum is open until 8pm with live music, cocktails, and special gallery talks and films.

600 Main St. (1 block west of The Old State House). ℂ 860/278-2670. www.wadsworthatheneum.org. Admission $10 adults, $8 seniors, $5 students, free for children 12 and under; $5 admission first Thurs of month 5–8pm. Tues–Fri 11am–5pm; Sat–Sun 10am–5pm (until 8pm first Thurs of most months).

WHERE TO STAY

The Goodwin Hotel ⭐ This quiet hostelry opposite the Civic Center is housed in a Queen Anne–style Victorian built in 1881 as a residence for J. P. Morgan. Its understated public areas are attractive, while its cautiously decorated bedrooms are fully equipped. Valet parking is often slow, but still a blessing along this crowded block. Some of the city's best dining options are short walks away.

1 Haynes St. (at Asylum St.), Hartford, CT 06103. ℂ **800/922-5006** or 860/246-7500. www.goodwinhotel.com. 124 units. $139–$249 double. Packages available. Valet parking $20. AE, DC, DISC, MC, V. **Amenities:** Restaurant (American); lounge; 24-hr. fitness center; concierge; limited room service; same-day dry cleaning. *In room:* A/C, TV, free Wi-Fi, hair dryer, iron.

Hilton Hartford 🐾🐾 *Kids*   This 22-story slab used to be a Sheraton and reopened as a Hilton in 2005 after spending $34 million on both substantive and cosmetic renovations. Hotel chains have been competing with each other to install comfortable mattresses, and guest will love the ones here. Over a hundred adjoining rooms make it attractive to families, and three executive floors have upgraded amenities and a private lounge. The hotel also connects with the Civic Center.

315 Trumbull St., Hartford, CT 06103. ℂ 860/728-5151. Fax 860/240-7247. www.hartford.hilton.com. 404 units. $89–$259 double. Packages available. Self-parking $17. AE, DC, DISC, MC, V. **Amenities:** 2 restaurants (international); bar; indoor pool; fully equipped health club; Jacuzzi; sauna; limited room service; same-day laundry/dry cleaning. *In room:* A/C, TV, high-speed Internet, coffeemaker, hair dryer, iron.

Hartford Marriott Downtown 🐾🐾   This Marriott opened next to the Connecticut Convention Center in 2005 and challenges the existing big guys (above) on every front, with luxury suites, a concierge level, and two splashy restaurants. Guest rooms compete with cushy mattresses as well as iPod docking stations and 27-inch flatscreen TVs that have high-speed Internet access and games. Its main restaurant, **Vivo,** goes in for highly imaginative interpretations of the Tuscan oeuvre, employing wood-fired ovens. The hotel is entirely nonsmoking.

200 Columbus Blvd., Hartford, CT. 06103 ℂ 860/249-8000. Fax 860/249-8181. www.hartfordmarriott.com. 409 units. $169–$319 double. Packages available. AE, DC, DISC, MC, V. **Amenities:** Restaurant (contemporary Italian); bar/lounge; concierge; fitness room and spa; business center; limited room service; same-day laundry/dry cleaning. *In room:* A/C, TV w/pay movies, Wi-Fi, coffeemaker, hair dryer, iron, safe.

WHERE TO DINE

In addition to the restaurants below, consider **Vivo** (ℂ **860/760-2333**), located in the Hartford Marriott (above), which has been picking up local raves.

Hot Tomato's ITALIAN   The renovation of Union Station spawned this popular trattoria in one wing, featuring a glass-sided dining room and terrace. A casually dressed crowd tucks into big bowls of garlicky pasta, the primary offerings here; the lobster *pinchiori,* for one, heaps chunks of the crustacean with portobellos and asparagus in lobster cream sauce over fettuccine. The "Flat Iron" top sirloin is prepared with a Gorgonzola crust.

1 Union Place (corner of Asylum St.). ℂ 860/249-5100. www.hottomatos.net. Reservations advised for patio and on weekends. Main courses $17–$33. AE, DC, DISC, MC, V. Mon–Thurs 11:30am–11pm; Fri 11:30am–midnight; Sat 4pm–midnight; Sun 4–10pm.

Max Downtown 🐾🐾 NEW AMERICAN   Hartford's prime-time power epicenter has a crowd that looks essentially interchangeable with the one that frequents its sister restaurant, Trumbull Kitchen (see below), albeit with a few more suits at midday and a lot of air-kissing at night. The main room has banquettes arrayed behind expanses of glass, with a flashy mural on the back wall. Diners are indulged with hefty chophouse favorites—"Cowboy Cut" beef rib chop with foie gras butter, perhaps—and flightier efforts, such as Moroccan spiced chicken with cinnamon and cranberry couscous. Over two dozen wines are available by the glass.

185 Asylum St. (opposite City Center). © 860/522-2530. www.maxrestaurantgroup.com. Reservations advised on weekends. Main courses $22–$42. AE, DC, MC, V. Mon–Fri 11:30am–2:30pm and 5–10:30pm (Fri until 11:30pm); Sat 5–11:30pm; Sun 4:30–9:30pm.

Rein's ∉ DINER   Rein's is about 15 minutes northeast of Hartford, but it's a good place to keep in mind when you're traveling in the area. It is the region's wildly popular and self-described "New York style" Jewish delicatessen, and top-notch service staff handle the frequent crowds of locals with good cheer. Consistent favorites from the enormous menu include the whitefish salad sandwich, the kasha knish of buckwheat groats, Hebrew National Kosher franks, and nine kinds of Reubens, from straight-up pastrami to a turkey version. Wash it all down with Dr. Brown's peculiar celery-flavored Cel-Ray soda or a classic chocolate egg cream. If there's a line for a table, see if any of the nine counter stools are open. And if you're on the move, take a tip from those who make regular stops here on drives between New York and Boston: Call in an order and have it waiting to go.

435 Hartford Tpk. (Rte. 30), Vernon, CT © 860/875-1344. www.reinsdeli.com. Main courses $5–$13. AE, DISC, MC, V. Daily 7am–midnight. From I-84, take exit 64–65 to Rte. 30 north; Rein's is in a minimall behind the Comfort Inn.

Trumbull Kitchen ∉ ECLECTIC   Looking as though it belongs in a hipper city, this member of the highly successful Max chain (see Max Downtown, above) continues to build upon its initial rush of popularity. Young execs and lawyers frequent it, enjoying a long menu of global grazing noshes including cheese fondues, sushi rolls, and lamb skewers with zucchini tzatziki. A smaller selection of main plates includes a perked-up meatloaf with roasted shallot-garlic sauce and seafood pad Thai. This is fun, diverting food—tasty enough without distracting from the primary mingling.

150 Trumbull St. (near Asylum St.). © 860/493-7417. www.maxrestaurantgroup.com. Main courses $16–$25. AE, DC, MC, V. Mon–Fri 11:30am–11pm (Thurs and Fri until midnight); Sat noon–midnight; Sun 4–10pm.

HARTFORD AFTER DARK

The free weekly *Hartford Advocate* (www.hartfordadvocate.com) provides useful information on cultural, sports, and musical events.

The **Bushnell Center for the Performing Arts,** 166 Capitol Ave. (© 860/987-5900; www.bushnell.org), hosts 350 events a year, including Broadway tours, the Hartford Symphony, children's theater, and comedy shows. The 907-seat Maxwell and Ruth Belding Theater opened in 2001, joining the main hall. The **Hartford Stage,** 50 Church St. (© 860/527-5151; www.hartfordstage.org), mounts a variety of mainstream plays.

The **Arch Street Tavern,** 85 Arch St. (© 860/246-7610; www.archstreettavern.com), is a pub/restaurant with sports on big screens and occasional live music. **Black-Eyed Sally's,** 350 Asylum St. (© 860/278-7427; www.blackeyedsallys.com), known for its ribs and other Southern-style gustatorial treats, presents live blues bands 4 or 5 nights a week.

City Steam Brewery, 942 Main St. (© 860/525-1600; www.citysteambrewery cafe.com), brews about 10 of its own beers, from dark ales to hard ciders, and hosts the Brew HA HA Comedy Club on Thursday through Saturday nights. For beer by the pitcher, along with *Monday Night Football* or the Final Four, **Coach's 06,** 187 Allyn St. (© 860/524-8888; www.coachs06.com), boasts 24 flatscreen TVs, bar snacks, and video games.

5 From Guilford to Old Saybrook *

Guilford: 93 miles NE of New York City; Madison: 98 miles NE of New York City; Old Saybrook: 110 miles NE of New York City

Usually ignored by vacationers anxious to get on to Essex and Mystic and the casinos, the stretch of coast between New Haven and the Connecticut River, known simply as the Shoreline, has its gentle pleasures, enough to justify a short detour for lunch, a walk on a beach, a spell of shopping, or even a proper British high tea (in Madison). When lodgings are difficult to find at the better-known destinations, the Shoreline's inns and resorts are logical alternatives within easy driving distance.

ESSENTIALS

GETTING THERE   The Shoreline can be reached from exit 57 off I-95. Pick up Route 1 (the Boston Post Rd.), which serves as the main street of several Shoreline towns. There are farm stands along the road in the summer and fall.

Several daily **Amtrak** (✆ **800/USA-RAIL;** www.amtrak.com) trains stop at Old Saybrook. The **Shore Line East** (✆ **800/255-7433;** www.shorelineeast.com) commuter line uses the same tracks to service towns between New Haven and New London, but only Monday through Friday.

VISITOR INFORMATION   Information about the towns described in this section is online at **www.newhavencvb.org,** the Greater New Haven website. Other good listings, special hotel packages, and a "This Weekend" page of suggested activities are at www.ctvisit.com, the website of Connecticut's Commission on Culture & Tourism (✆ **888/288-4778**). The Commission has a free vacation guide, too.

Note that the highway signs on I-95 at exit 56 for a "tourist information service" are something of a misnomer: The TA Travel Center in Branford has showers and a laundry primarily for use by truckers, a few fast-food outlets, and just a small rack of brochures.

GUILFORD

One of the state's oldest Colonial settlements (1639), this posh, well-kept village, 13 miles east of New Haven, is embraced by the West and East rivers. It has an uncommonly large public green with a few upscale shops at one corner. There are dozens of historic houses in town, most of them privately owned, but a few open to the public on a limited basis, typically from June to Columbus Day. They include **Hyland House,** 84 Boston St. (✆ **203/453-9477**), an early Colonial saltbox with three walk-in fireplaces and an herb garden, built around 1690, and the **Thomas Griswold House,** 171 Boston St. (✆ **203/453-3176**), with a restored blacksmith shop and Colonial garden, built around 1774. The Hyland House is free; the Griswold House $3 adults, $2 seniors and students.

The Guilford visitor center is located next to the Henry Whitfield State Museum (below). Housed in an 1870 barn, it's open April through December 14 Wednesday through Sunday from 10am to 4:30pm. Additional information is available from the detailed website of the **Guilford Chamber of Commerce** (✆ **203/453-9677;** www.guilfordct.com).

Bishop's Orchards   This huge operation features a farm market, bakery, winery, and pick-your-own fruits, including strawberries and apples, from June through October. In the fall, its Little Red Barn is turned into a sweet family destination, with maple "kettle korn," a hay maze for kids, a make-your-own-scarecrow table, and a riot of mums and pumpkins for sale. Despite its size, Bishop's Orchards retains a down-country feel, perhaps because it's still owned by the same family that started it in 1871. The Orchard's award-winning apple wines are tasty and make nice regional gifts.

1355 Boston Post Rd. (Rte. 1). ℂ 203/453-2338. www.bishopsorchards.com. Free admission. Mon–Sat 8am–7pm; Sun 9am–6pm. Open year-round.

Henry Whitfield State Museum   The Whitfield Museum bills itself as the oldest house in Connecticut and the oldest stone house in New England. Most of what you see now, though, including the leaded windows, dates from a 1930s reconstruction and not from 1639, so it is really more a museum than a historic home. It is still worth a brief visit, however, and the furnishings are authentic to the period. The low stone walls, grass fields, and grand trees of the grounds are also atmospherically evocative of the 17th century.

248 Old Whitfield St. ℂ 203/453-2457. www.whitfieldmuseum.com. Admission $4 adults, $3 seniors and students, $2.50 children 6–17. Wed–Sun 10am–4:30pm Apr–Dec 14; closed rest of the year.

WHERE TO DINE

The Place ⭐ SEAFOOD   Outdoors, under a striped tent if the weather is threatening, The Place cooks its food over open wood fires. You sit on tree stumps and can buy a T-shirt that confirms that you "Put Your Rump On A Stump." In essence, what's served is a clambake, so you are morally obligated to begin with a raft of that bivalve. They are roasted over smoky coals, popped open, dabbed with hot sauce, and run back over the fire as a finish. Corn cooked in the husk and dipped in margarine is another must. You can get bluefish or chicken with that, but why would you? Go for the lobster. Guests are invited to bring along beer, wine, salad, chips, or whatever to fill out a meal. There are several desserts, including slices of pecan pies and hot fudge sundaes, but the carrot cake is the winner. You will leave grinning.

901 Boston Post Rd. (Rte. 1). ℂ 203/453-9276. Main courses $7.95–$21; most under $10. No credit cards. Mon–Fri 5–9pm; Sat 1–9pm; Sun noon–8pm. Late Apr to mid-Oct, plus weekends after mid-Oct weather permitting. From I-95, take exit 58 onto Rte. 77 to Rte. 1, turn left (east). The Place is opposite a shopping mall.

Whitfield's on Guilford Green ⭐ NEW AMERICAN   Several restaurants have occupied this space in recent years, with Whitfield's taking on the mantle in the summer of 2007 with the same owners and same decor, but a new name and a new menu. Typical is the chipotle-orange hanger steak with tomato chutney, and the chef's favorite, a Portuguese-style black cod with chorizo, baby clams, and garlic-tomato broth. A large picture window in the restored Victorian building overlooks the handsome town green, and the bright room attracts well-heeled locals. At lunch, most salads, crab cakes, and sandwiches are under $10. Tuesday through Thursday are half-price wine or drinks evenings, and tasting menus are offered on occasion.

25 Whitfield St. ℂ 203/458-1300. www.whitfieldsonguilfordgreen.com. Reservations recommended. Main courses $6–$31. AE, MC, V. Mon–Fri 11:30am–3pm; Sat–Sun 9am–3pm; daily 5–9pm (until 10pm Fri–Sat).

MADISON

Madison, 19 miles east of New Haven, is home to a historic architectural district that stretches west of the business district along the Boston Post Road, from the main green to the town line, and contains many examples of 18th- and 19th-century domestic styles.

The well-to-do town has completed the transition from colony to seaside resort to year-round community, a process begun when the first house was built in 1651. Today there are two dwellings from the early years that can be visited on limited summer schedules. **Deacon John Grave House,** 581 Boston Post Rd. (© **203/245-4798**), dates from 1685, and the **Allis-Bushnell House,** 853 Boston Post Rd. (© **203/245-4567**), from 1785.

Off the Boston Post Road south of the town center, also reached from exit 62 off I-95, is **Hammonasset Beach State Park** (© **203/245-2785;** www.ct.gov), Connecticut's largest public beach park. On a peninsula jutting into Long Island Sound, its shore is over 2 miles long. The on-site **Meigs Point Nature Center** offers programs and activities from spring through fall, and there are 558 open camp sites. From Memorial Day to Labor Day, cars with out-of-state plates are charged $10 Monday through Friday, $15 on weekends and holidays.

SHOPPING

Madison's commercial district may look ordinary at first glance, but several shops along Boston Post Road and intersecting Wall Street provide entertaining browsing. The stately **R. J. Julia Booksellers,** 768 Boston Post Rd. (© **203/245-3959;** www.rjjulia.com), holds frequent author readings and has a cafe in back; it's open from 8:30am to 9pm.

The Harp & Hearth, 45 Wall St. (© **203/245-1414;** www.harpandhearth.com), stocks gourmet foods and Celtic wares. It has a small bistro for lunch (11am–4pm) and **afternoon tea** (1:30–3:30pm), complete with finger sandwiches and currant scones served with preserves and clotted cream. It's open Tuesday through Saturday.

Five miles from downtown Madison (Rte. 1 east to Rte. 81 north) is **Clinton Crossing,** 20-A Killingsworth Tpk. (© **860/664-0700**), an outlet mall with 70 shops. Clothing stores by such designers as Kenneth Cole, Barneys New York Outlet, and Polo Ralph Lauren are augmented by Coach leather goods and Le Creuset cookware. The mall is directly off I-95 at exit 63.

WHERE TO STAY & DINE

The Inn at Lafayette ❧   The stately Greek Revival portico in the middle of the business district promises a touch of elegance, and the interior delivers. Since 1998, the ground floor has housed **Cafe Allegre** ❧❧, a soothing setting for northern Italian and European food of considerable accomplishment. Fresh regional ingredients are paramount. Main courses, such as lemon chicken and veal Casanova, run from $15 to $29. The bar is a low-key gathering place, popular for lunch, with a piano player on Thursday and Friday nights (closed Mon). The guest rooms upstairs are comfortable enough, with marble bathrooms and king- or queen-size beds.

725 Boston Post Rd., Madison, CT 06443. © **866/623-7498** or 203/245-7773. Fax 203/245-6256. www.innatlafayette.com. 5 units. $125–$150 double. AE, DC, DISC, MC, V. No children under 12. **Amenities:** Restaurant (Italian/European); bar. *In room:* A/C, TV, free high-speed Internet access, hair dryer.

Lenny & Joe's Fish Tale *(Kids* SEAFOOD   At this rough-and-ready fish shack, seafood rules, most of it fried. And while it is sure to elevate triglyceride counts, the nutty coating on superfresh clams, oysters, shrimp, and calamari is hard to resist. Chowders and seafood rolls are the way to go. In this branch, you give your order at the counter and carry it to a table. ***Bonus:*** There's a small old-time carousel and an ice cream stand here, too. A nearby outlet in Westbrook, at 86 Boston Post Rd. (© **860/669-0767**), has table service and a bar, and less of a fast-food feel.

Moments **An Ocean View from a Train Seat**

Riding the Amtrak train along the Connecticut coast is an enormously satisfying way to take in some of the most gorgeous views of the state. The Regional and Acela Express Amtrak routes between New York and Boston both take the coastal track, and for many miles the train hugs the flat shoreline, skimming alongside marshy inlets. If you're traveling north, get a window seat on the right side and settle in for the guided tour.

The sights are rich with coastal New England geography. The section from New Haven to Old Saybrook features green woods and then small harbors dotted with sailboats. At Branford, the train passes a one-lane bridge where fishermen often cast rods. The view opens up to acres of marchland, where wooden perches atop 10-foot poles are homes to birds who set up nests. Passing through Guilford, travelers can catch glimpses of stone walls, then it's more marsh land with canals that curve like a drunkard's walk. In Old Saybrook, the town's large, handsome homes come into sight.

If you time it so that your train arrives in New London around sunset, you'll catch washes of orange and pink light dappling across the ocean. In the stretch between Old Saybrook and New London, the train passes the sandy beaches of Old Lyme and a smattering of teeny islands, some appearing not much bigger than a baseball infield, off the coast. A red-and-white-striped tower signals the initial approach into the industrial zone of New London. The train continues along the water from here to Stonington, passing docks with thousands of sailboats, before moving inland for the trip through Rhode Island up to Massachusetts.

Put down the book, pack away the computer, and daydream out the window. It's good for the soul.

1301 Boston Post Rd., Madison © **203/245-7289.** www.ljfishtale.com. Main courses $5–$22. DC, DISC, MC, V. Daily 11am–9pm (Fri–Sat until 10pm).

OLD SAYBROOK

Its location at the mouth of the Connecticut River (35 miles east of New Haven, 26 miles west of Mystic) is this town's principal lure. Get off Route 1 to see it at its best. Pick up Route 154 (just east of the high school) and take the 6-mile driving loop, which touches the shore and passes through the tony hamlets of Knollwood and Fenwick, and across the causeway to Saybrook Point before ending up back in the main business district.

WHERE TO STAY & DINE

Saybrook Point Inn & Spa 🐟🐟   Resort hotels have existed at this location where the Connecticut River meets the ocean since the late 19th century, and they've gotten the formula down pat at the current facility. It has one of the largest marinas along the coast, an ingratiating restaurant with a clubby bar and a summer dining terrace, a fully equipped fitness room, and a spa offering a full range of body and skin-care services, including mud and seaweed wraps. Bedrooms are spacious, all with wet bars and sitting areas, some with working fireplaces, whirlpool tubs, and balconies.

The **Terra Mar** grill offers definitive versions of clam chowder and lobster roll not to be missed. Sunday buffet brunch is especially popular.

2 Bridge St., Old Saybrook, CT 06475. © **800/243-0212** or 860/395-2000. www.saybrook.com. 80 units. $219–$329 double. Packages available. AE, DC, DISC, MC, V. Take Rte. 154 south from Rte. 1. Pets allowed. **Amenities:** Restaurant (New American); bar; limited room service; indoor and outdoor pool; health club and spa; sauna. *In room:* A/C, TV (DVD available), Wi-Fi, unstocked fridge, hair dryer, iron.

Johnny Ad's SEAFOOD   On what one reviewer accurately described as "a patio of asphalt," this roadside restaurant is distinctive for its year-round schedule and its time-warp atmosphere. This is no faux-oldies place, though: Johnny Ad's has been doing business here since 1957, so it's the real deal. Music of the 1950s is piped through the raw inside rooms and onto an outdoor terrace of picnic tables next to the parking lot. The recommended options, naturally, are fried clams, fish and chips, and the lobster roll. Portions are generous: The small clam strip side order for $8.50 is large enough for at least one and maybe two, depending on your appetite. It's served with a lemon wedge and tarter sauce in a red-and-white cardboard box. Feel free to croon with The Flamingos while you're there.

910 Boston Post Rd. (Rte. 1), Old Saybrook © **860/388-4032**. Main courses $3–$19. No credit cards. Most of the year daily 11am–8pm (Fri–Sat until 8:30pm, Sun until 7pm); in winter daily 11am–3pm.

6 The Connecticut River Valley

Old Lyme: 112 miles NE of New York City; Essex: 114 miles NE of New York City; East Haddam: 124 miles NE of New York City and 132 miles SW of Boston

The Connecticut River, New England's longest, originates in the far north near the Canadian border, 407 miles from where it ends at the Long Island Sound. It separates Vermont from New Hampshire, splits Massachusetts in half, then takes a 45-degree turn just south of Hartford to make its final run to the sea.

Native Americans of the region called the river *Quinnetukut*, which, to the tin ears of the English settlers, sounded like "Connecticut." Because the river was navigable by relatively large ships as far as Hartford, the sheltered lower Connecticut became important for boat-building and industries associated with the international clipper trade. The valley retains that nautical flavor and has miraculously avoided the industrialization, development, and decay that afflict most of the state's other rivers.

River cruises are obvious attractions, supplemented by rides on a steam-powered train, a selection of worthy inns, antiques shops, a venerable musical theater, and even a bizarre castle on a hilltop.

ESSENTIALS

GETTING THERE   Highway 9 runs parallel to the river, along the west side of the valley. It connects I-91 south of Hartford to I-95 near Old Saybrook, making the valley readily accessible from all points in New England.

VISITOR INFORMATION   The state's Central Regional Tourism District (© **800/ 793-4480** or 860/244-8181; www.enjoycentralct.com) is focused on the River Valley. The website of Connecticut's Commission on Culture & Tourism (© **888/288-4778;** www.ctvisit.com) also has a section on the region.

OLD LYME

As quiet a town as the coast can claim, Old Lyme (40 miles east of New Haven, 23 miles west of Mystic) was the favored residence of generations of seafarers and ship captains. Many of their 18th- and 19th-century homes have survived, some as inns and museums. Preservationists and community activists proudly point out that their main street is the only one cut by I-95 that continues to thrive. With its many tree-lined streets largely free of traffic, stressless biking is an attractive option here.

Florence Griswold Museum ⟨ After the shipbuilding and merchant trade had all but flickered out at the end of the 19th century, artists who came to be known as the "American Impressionists" took a fancy to this area. They received encouragement, patronage, and even food and shelter from "Miss Florence," the wealthy daughter of a sea captain. Falling upon hard times later in life, she decided to open her Georgian–Federal 1817 mansion to boarders. It became the temporary home for a number of painters, many of whom left samples of their work in gratitude, sometimes painting directly on the walls of the dining room. Among her grateful guests was Childe Hassam, considered the grand master of the American Impressionists.

Now a National Historic Landmark, the "Flo Gris" was closed for 14 months in 2005 and 2006 for extensive restoration and refurnishing, including the installation of geothermal environmental systems that draw energy for cooling and heating from wells on the property. Visitors can stroll the mansion's property to take in its old-fashioned garden or picnic on the banks of the small Lieutenant River.

96 Lyme St. (Rte. 1). ⟨ 860/434-5542. www.flogris.org. Admission $8 adults, $7 seniors and students, $4 children 6–12. Tues–Sat 10am–5pm; Sun 1–5pm.

GETTING OUTSIDE

One of several state parks at the edge of Long Island Sound, **Rocky Neck State Park,** Route 156 (⟨ **860/739-5471;** www.ct.gov), east of Old Lyme, has a crescent-shaped beach, popular with families, and 160 camping sites. Take I-95 to exit 72 and follow Route 156 south. Open daily from 8am to sunset.

WHERE TO STAY & DINE

Bee and Thistle Inn On 5 acres beside the Lieutenant River, the Bee and Thistle has a core structure that dates from 1756, with later wings and additions. New owners closed it for a few months and reopened in spring 2007, keeping the enjoyable jumble of antiques and collectibles in the public areas. The focus of many guests, though, are the grounds and the dining room, regularly rated "Most Romantic" in the state by reader polls. It's open Wednesday through Sunday for lunch and dinner; jackets are requested for Saturday dinner.

100 Lyme St. (Rte. 1), Old Lyme, CT 06371. ⟨ **800/622-4946** or 860/434-1667. Fax 860/434-3402. www.beeand thistleinn.com. 11 units. $100–$275 double. Packages available. AE, DISC, MC, V. From I-95, take exit 70; turn left off ramp, right at second traffic light, then right on Rte. 1 (Lyme St.). No children under 16. **Amenities:** Restaurant (creative American). *In room:* A/C.

ESSEX ⟨⟨

It is difficult to imagine what improvements might be made to bring this dream of a New England waterside town any closer to perfection. Tree-bordered streets are lined with shops and homes that retain an early-18th-century flavor without the frozen-in-amber quality that can afflict towns as postcard-pretty as this. About 6,500 people live and work and play here, and bustle busily along Main Street, which runs down to Steamboat Dock and its flotilla of working vessels and pleasure craft.

In winter, bald eagles come to the lower reaches of the river, and Essex holds an **Eagle Festival** in mid-February in celebration, with music, Native American dancers, and guided boat and land-based viewing of the raptors. The Connecticut Audubon Society (© 800/714-7201; www.ctaudubon.org) has information.

Other regional information is offered by the Essex Board of Trade (© 860/767-3904; www.essexct.com).

Connecticut River Museum 𝘼   Anglers cast lines from the dock while gulls and ducks hang around hoping for a discarded tidbit. Steamboat service was fully operational here in 1823, and the existing dock dates from 1879. Designated a National Historic Site, the museum proper features model ships, marine paintings, and artifacts that relate the story of shipbuilding in the valley, which began in 1733 and helped make this a center of world trade far into the 19th century. A replica of America's first submarine (1775), the *Turtle,* is also on display. The museum usually has walking-tour maps of Essex, too, making this a good first stop on your visit.

A small cruise boat, the **River Quest** (© 860/662-0577; www.ctriverexpeditions. com), makes 90-minute trips during the day in the warmer months ($20 adults, $15 children; includes museum admission), as well as sunset cruises ($25 adults and children over 12; no children under 12 allowed; includes museum admission). In February and March, it offers eagle-sighting cruises ($40 all passengers; includes museum admission).

Steamboat Dock (at foot of Main St.). © 860/767-8269. www.ctrivermuseum.org. Admission $7 adults, $6 seniors and students, $4 children 6–12. Tues–Sun 10am–5pm.

Essex Steam Train 𝘒𝘪𝘥𝘴   Take a ride on a steam locomotive from the 1920s, chugging along the river to the hamlet of Deep River. The excursion takes about an hour. It can be combined with a cruise on a **Mississippi-style riverboat** (named *Becky Thatcher*) for a 2½-hour tour. Dinner trains include a four-course meal and a 2½-hour ride for $70.

1 Railroad Ave. (Rte. 154). © 800/377-3987 or 860/767-0103. www.essexsteamtrain.com. Train and boat $26 adults, $13 children 2–11; train only $17 adults, $9 children 2–11; family passes available. Daily trips May–Oct; less frequently Nov–Dec; closed Jan–May.

WHERE TO STAY & DINE

Griswold Inn 𝘼𝘼   Nobody doesn't like "The Gris." Rumpled, cluttered, folksy, and forever besieged by drop-in yachties, anglers, locals, and tourists, the main building dates to 1776. The atmospheric taproom started life as a schoolhouse and was moved here in 1800. There's live entertainment every night, be it a Dixieland band or just one man singing sea shanties. The colorful dining rooms are named for their displays of books, antique weapons, or marine paintings. There is a Sunday Hunt Breakfast buffet, and food in the evenings, while still hearty, has taken a turn toward the more innovative. Recent additions include a wine bar with leather furniture and a card of small plates, and wine tastings nearly every week. *Viva Gris!*

36 Main St. (center of town), Essex, CT 06426. © 860/767-1776. Fax 860/767-0481. www.griswoldinn.com. 30 units. $100–$220 double. Rates include breakfast. AE, MC, V. **Amenities:** Restaurant (American); bar. *In room:* A/C.

IVORYTON

Once a center for the ivory trade, where factories fabricated piano keys and hair combs, Ivoryton has since subsided into a residential quietude. A virtual suburb of the only slightly larger Essex, a few miles east, the town perks up a bit in summer, when the **Ivoryton Playhouse,** 103 Main St. (© 860/767-7318; www.ivorytonplayhouse. com), conducts much of its theatrical season, which runs from March to November.

The repertoire includes revivals of well-known shows such as *Evita* and *The Glass Menagerie.*

WHERE TO STAY & DINE

Copper Beech Inn 𝕽𝕽   Despite comparisons with the Griswold Inn in nearby Essex, these are two very different places. Where the Gris is decidedly populist and perennially busy, the stately Copper Beech has much less traffic, and not a single figurative hair out of place. The rooms in the 19th-century main building are replete with character and plenty of antiques, while those in the converted barn Carriage House are spacious, with TVs, Jacuzzis, and decks (the website has room-by-room descriptions and photos). The Copper Beech was already the home to one of the most honored **restaurants** in the region, but the current owners have raised the stakes even higher. Main courses run $28 to $42. The wine list, with over 500 selections and 4,000 bottles, is impressive, and service is seamless.

46 Main St., Ivoryton, CT 06442. ℂ 888/809-2056 or 860/767-0330. www.copperbeechinn.com. 13 units. $195–$350 double. Packages available. AE, DISC, MC, V. Take exit 3 from Rte. 9 and head west on Main St. No children under 16. Dogs allowed. **Amenities:** Restaurant (country French); bar. *In room:* A/C, TV (some units), hair dryers.

CHESTER

Hardly more than a 3-block business center, the riverside hamlet of Chester still deserves savoring. Main Street offers up antiques shops, galleries, and several eateries. **Ceramica,** 36 Main St. (ℂ **800/270-0900;** www.ceramicadirect.com), an outlet of a small chain, carries a line of uniformly gorgeous hand-painted bowls, pitchers, vases, and teapots from Italy.

Nearby is **Devil's Hopyard State Park,** 366 Hopyard Rd., East Haddam (ℂ **860/873-8566;** www.ct.gov), with hiking, camping, a reputation for some of the finest birding in the state, and fishing—brook trout, in particular.

EAST HADDAM / HADLYME

Hadlyme (a jurisdiction of the town of East Haddam), is hardly more than a wide spot in a country road. It wouldn't have attracted much attention at all if a wealthy thespian, William Gillette, hadn't decided to build his hilltop castle here.

To get to the castle and park, take the small **Chester-Hadlyme Ferry** (ℂ **860/594-2551**), at the end of Route 148, slightly less than 2 miles from Chester. A ferry has operated here since 1769, and the current version can take about eight cars and walk-ons ($3 for vehicles, $1 for pedestrians and bicyclists). If it's closed, go north on Route 154 to Haddam and take the bridge to cross to the east side of the Connecticut River, where the castle is located.

Gillette Castle State Park 𝕽   The Hartford-born William Gillette (1853–1937) was a successful actor and playwright known primarily for his portrayals of Sherlock Holmes. He took his money and ran to this hill rearing above the Connecticut River, where he built a 24-room mansion. It's difficult to believe, though, that he really thought the result resembled the medieval fortresses that allegedly were his inspiration: Rock gardens by roadside eccentrics in South Dakota are closer relations. The all-stone exterior has the dripping look of a sandcastle built by wet globs that fell through children's fingers; inside, Gillette designed oddities such as a dining-room table that slid into the wall, an inexplicable space-saving effort.

But no one can argue with his choice of location. The mansion sits atop a hill above the east bank of the Connecticut River, with superlative vistas upriver and down.

Nowhere else is the blessed underdevelopment of the estuary more apparent. The expansive grounds, which are now owned and managed by the state, have picnic areas and nature trails. Because the home's terrace can be entered for free, many visitors come just to take in those **views** ✩✩.

67 River Rd., East Haddam (© 860/526-2336. www.ct.gov. Admission $5 adults, $2 children 6–11. Grounds daily 8am–sunset; castle daily 10am–4:30pm Memorial Day to Columbus Day.

EAST HADDAM AFTER DARK

The dominant building in East Haddam proper is a restored 1876 Victorian of splendid proportions that is now the **Goodspeed Opera House** ✩✩, Goodspeed Landing (© **860/873-8668;** www.goodspeed.org). It mostly stages musicals on the order of *Happy Days: A New Musical* and *Big River: The Adventures of Huckleberry Finn,* but also hosts an annual festival of new artists in January.

7 Mystic ✩✩✩ & the Southeastern Coast

Mystic: 135 miles NE of New York City and 99 miles SW of Boston; Foxwoods and Mohegan Sun casinos: 134 miles NE of New York City and 106 miles SW of Boston

This section of the shoreline is studded with towns that still bear the stamp of their maritime pasts, a string of fishing ports and inlets that segues into the mainland beach resorts of Rhode Island. Inland are a number of still semirural villages, but their futures are uncertain due to the presence of two enormously successful and steadily expanding Indian casino complexes, Foxwoods and Mohegan Sun. They produce gushers of money that are altering forever the character of this region.

The town of Mystic and its twin attractions, Mystic Aquarium and the living museum that is Mystic Seaport, are the prime reasons for a stay—the Seaport alone can easily occupy most of a day, and the two-part town itself sustains a nautical air, with fun shops and restaurants to suit most tastes.

But that's not a complete list of the region's charms. The tranquil neighboring village of Stonington is home to a small but active commercial fishing fleet, the last in the state; there are several enchanting inns in the area; and many companies offer their vessels for whale-watching, dinner cruises, and deep-sea fishing excursions.

If at all possible, avoid July, August, and weekends from May to Columbus Day. That's when the crowds are oppressive, restaurants are packed, and rooms are booked months in advance at very high rates.

ESSENTIALS

GETTING THERE   Take I-95 to exit 84 (New London), exit 86 (Groton), exit 90 (Mystic), or exit 91 (Stonington). If driving from the New York City area, you can avoid the heavy truck and commercial traffic of the western segment of I-95 by taking the Hutchinson River Parkway, which becomes the Merritt Parkway (Rte. 15) and merges with the Wilbur Cross Parkway. Continue to exit 54, connecting with I-95 for the rest of the trip. From Boston, take I-95 straight down.

The **Cross Sound Ferry** (© **860/443-5281;** www.longislandferry.com) provides year-round service for cars between New London and Orient Point on Long Island. The one-way voyage takes about an hour and 20 minutes. One-way fares are $46 for a car and driver, $14 for additional adults, and $6.30 for children. Make reservations in advance when taking a car.

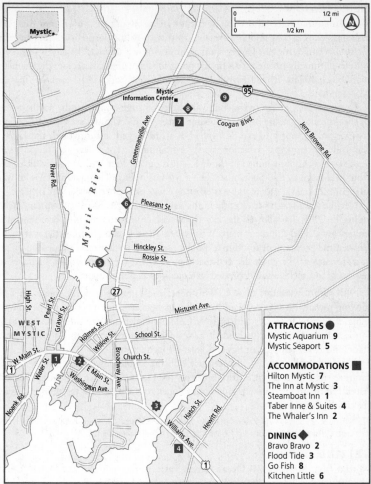

ATTRACTIONS ●
Mystic Aquarium **9**
Mystic Seaport **5**

ACCOMMODATIONS ■
Hilton Mystic **7**
The Inn at Mystic **3**
Steamboat Inn **1**
Taber Inne & Suites **4**
The Whaler's Inn **2**

DINING ◆
Bravo Bravo **2**
Flood Tide **3**
Go Fish **8**
Kitchen Little **6**

Amtrak (☎ **800/USA-RAIL;** www.amtrak.com) runs several trains on its Acela Express and Regional routes between New York, Providence, and Boston, with intermediate stops at New London and Mystic.

The regional bus company **SEAT** (☎ **860/886-2631;** www.seatbus.com) connects many of the towns of the district as well as the casinos.

VISITOR INFORMATION A terrifically helpful source of information is **Mystic Country** (www.mysticcountry.com), which lists, for instance, 83 inn and bed-and-breakfast options and continually updated listings of getaway package specials. They'll also mail out a free **Mystic Country Vacation Kit.**

NEW LONDON

New London's protected deep-draft harbor at the mouth of the Thames River was responsible for its long and influential history as a whaling port. Possessed of an architecturally interesting but largely somnolent downtown district, the city is of note to travelers primarily because it's a transit point for ferry lines connecting the mainland with Block Island, Rhode Island; Long Island, New York; and Martha's Vineyard, Massachusetts.

Connecticut College (www.conncoll.edu) has a large campus at the northern edge of the city, along Route 32 and Williams Street. At the **U.S. Coast Guard Academy** (www.cga.edu), north of exit 82A off I-95, a **full-rigged sailing vessel,** the *Eagle,* is the academy's principal attraction. Used for training current cadets—it's the only such vessel actively commissioned in the U.S.—it is out on tour much of the year, usually from mid-April to mid-September. The *Eagle* was built in Germany in 1936 to train that country's naval cadets and was taken as a war prize after World War II.

New London was more recently in the news as the focus of a U.S. Supreme Court ruling in 2005 that allowed the city to exercise eminent domain to raze residential homes for a redevelopment plan. What made the decision controversial was that it allowed the government to claim a "public use" need for a project headed up by private developers; the court decided that a project that creates new jobs, increases tax revenues, and revitalizes a depressed area qualifies as public use.

Lyman Allyn Museum of Art   This neoclassical granite building stands on a hill looking toward the Coast Guard Academy. Its holdings are the result of the enthusiasms of private collectors and include Colonial American paintings; landscapes by Hudson River School artists Frederic Edwin Church, George Inness, and Albert Bierstadt; and Asian temple castings and Japanese lacquerware.

A notable collection of 19th-century dolls and dollhouses, arranged in detailed room settings right down to tiny ladles on the kitchen counter, is now in **Deshon-Allyn House** on the museum grounds and open to the public on the third Sunday of the month from 1 to 3pm.

625 Williams St. ⓒ 860/443-2545. www.lymanallyn.org. Admission $8 adults, $7 seniors and students, free for children under 12. Tues–Sat 10am–5pm; Sun 1–5pm. From exit 83 off I-95, follow signs.

GETTING OUTSIDE

Not far from downtown is **Ocean Beach Park,** at the south end of Ocean Avenue (ⓒ **800/510-7263** or 860/447-3031; www.ocean-beach-park.com), an expansive recreational facility with a broad sand beach, boardwalk, 50m saltwater pool, carousel and other amusement rids, miniature golf, water slide, bathhouse with lockers and showers, concession stands, and lounge. Parking is $16, which includes park admission for everyone in the car.

From late May to mid-October, **Block Island Express** (ⓒ **860/444-4624;** www.longislandferry.com/bif/home.htm) operates its high-speed catamaran daily between New London and the Old Harbor on Block Island. The passage takes a little over an hour. Round-trip rates are $37 for adults, $18 for children. Passengers and bicycles only. Reservations are essential.

WHERE TO STAY & DINE

Lighthouse Inn Resort 🏵🏵   Designated a National Historic Landmark in 1996, a 1902 Victorian-flavored mansion of a steel magnate is at the center of this multistructure property directly on the Long Island Sound. One of the outbuildings is the

Looking Glass Salon & Day Spa, providing facials, massages, and private fitness training; another is a large carriage house suitable for families. Eleven units are suites with views of the sound; the Waterview Suite was apparently actress Joan Crawford's favorite when she visited. The inn has a private beach with chairs and umbrellas available, and says it's the only hotel in southeastern Connecticut with private access. Chef Timothy Grills (see review of **Timothy's** below) ensures that the several dining rooms are forever full. Meals are also served in the atmospheric tavern, which has live jazz on Friday and Saturday nights.

6 Guthrie Place, New London, CT 06320. ✆ **888/443-8411** or 860/443-8411. Fax 860/437-7027. www.lighthouse inn-ct.com. 51 units. $95–$395 double. Rates include breakfast. Packages available. AE, DISC, MC, V. Guthrie Place is directly off Pequot Ave., which runs along the sound. **Amenities:** Restaurant (New American); bar; heated outdoor pool; Wi-Fi in lobby. *In room:* A/C, TV, high-speed Internet, coffeemaker, hair dryer, iron.

Timothy's ✖✖ NEW AMERICAN   Chef-owner Timothy Grills (talk about names as predestination) was doing just fine in his original contemporary bistro downtown. He's doing even better now, in his more expansive digs in the Lighthouse Inn. While there are always a couple of perky pastas on offer, his menu now has fewer Italian touches. In fact, at first glance, it appears to be entirely conventional, with such stalwarts as Long Island duckling, barbecue salmon, and filet mignon. He doesn't go in for mind-bending innovation, but shoots instead for a high level of execution. His signature dish is the creamy lobster and crabmeat bisque, hardly a rarity in these parts, but with supernal flavorings. Crab cakes, fried calamari, and lollipop lamb chops are regulars, and very good. New London needs more operations like this.

6 Guthrie Place (in the Lighthouse Inn), ✆ **860/443-8411.** www.lighthouseinn-ct.com. Reservations recommended. Main courses $19–$33. AE, DISC, MC, V. Daily 10:30am–3pm and 5–9pm (Fri–Sat until 10pm).

GROTON
The future is more promising for this naval-industrial town on the opposite side of the Thames River from New London. It has long been dependent on the presence of the Electric Boat division of General Dynamics and the Navy's submarine base. There were threats to close the base and, by extension, Electric Boat, but a federal commission issued a reprieve in 2004, and Electric Boat continues to employ 10,500 here and in Quonset Point, Rhode Island.

WHAT TO SEE & DO
A number of companies offer **full- and half-day fishing trips.** Typical of the public boats is the 114-foot *Hel-Cat II,* 181 Thames St. (✆ **860/535-2066** or 860/535-3200; www.visitconnecticut.com/helcat.htm). Trips last from 6 to 10 hours. Check for current prices; the spring 2008 10-hour cod-fishing trip costs $80. Tackle is available for rent. It's located 2 miles south of I-95; take exit 85 if you're driving north on I-95, or exit 87 if you're driving south.

Both charter and party (public) trips are available from the **Sunbeam Fleet,** based at **Captain John's Sport Fishing Center,** 15 First St., Waterford (✆ **860/443-7259;** www.sunbeamfleet.com). Public trips last from 5½ to 9 hours and include night bass fishing from 7pm to 12:30am ($70 plus $5 rod rental; live eels included) and fluke fishing from 7am to 4pm ($68 plus $5 rod rental; bait included). Check for the days and times, which vary between May and November. The same firm runs **historic lighthouse cruises** June through August ($48). Waterford is the town immediately south of New London; the dock is next to the Niantic River Bridge.

History buffs will enjoy a stroll around **Fort Griswold Battlefield State Park,** 57 Fort St. (© **860/449-6877** in season; www.ct.gov). It was here, in 1781, that Benedict Arnold, who originally fought for American independence before trading allegiances, led a British force against American defenders and ruthlessly ordered the massacre of 88 prisoners after they had surrendered. The park is just off Thames Street, which runs along the river.

Submarine Force Library & Museum   The museum's entry hall and adjoining galleries display models of submarines, torpedoes, missiles, deck guns, periscopes, and a full-scale cross section of Bushnell's *Turtle,* the "first submersible ever used in a military conflict," in 1776. Out back, the USS *Nautilus* itself stands at its mooring, ready for inspection. The 362-foot-long sub was commissioned in 1954 and in operation until 1980. The claustrophobic walk through the control rooms, attack center, galley, and sleeping quarters is aided by listening devices handed out to each visitor. Passing through, it is difficult to imagine how the sub could possibly contain a crew of 116 men, especially on its fabled cruise between Pearl Harbor and the North Pole.

1 Crystal Lake Rd. (Naval Submarine Base). © **800/343-0079** or 860/694-3174. www.submarinemuseum.org. Free admission. May 15–Oct 31 daily 9am–5pm, except Tues 1–5pm; Nov 1–May 14 Wed–Mon 9am–4pm. Take exit 86 from I-95, drive north on Rte. 12, and follow signs to the USS *Nautilus.*

WHERE TO STAY

Mystic Marriott Hotel & Spa ✦✦   With the Mystic, built in 2001 at a cost of $47 million, Marriott brings a measure of big-town pizzazz to Groton. Rooms adhere to corporate cookie-cutter standards, but there is little more that a business or leisure traveler might ask for. Room safes are large enough for laptop computers, and on the sixth-floor concierge level, extras include robes, fridges, and a lounge with breakfast and afternoon snacks. The big deal is the **Elizabeth Arden Red Door Spa,** which shares facilities with the excellent fitness center. In addition to manicures, pedicures, hair cut and color, and waxing services, there are 21 facial options, 15 massage options, seaweed wraps, and warm shea-butter body melts. The hotel restaurant, **Octagon** (below), gets high marks.

625 North Rd. (Rte. 117), Groton, CT 06340. © **866/449-7390** or 860/446-2600. Fax 860/446-2601. www.marriott. com. 285 units. $209–$329 double. Packages available. Free on-site parking; $5 valet. AE, DC DISC, MC, V. **Amenities:** 2 restaurants (steakhouse, bistro); bar; heated indoor 50m pool; exhaustively equipped health club and spa; concierge; business center; limited. room service; same-day laundry; dry cleaning. *In room:* A/C, TV w/pay movies, Wi-Fi, coffeemaker, hair dryer, iron, safe.

WHERE TO DINE

Octagon ✦ STEAKHOUSE   While it's not as heavy-handedly masculine as others of its type, the dark, leathery tones of the Mystic Marriott's formal restaurant still manage to look as if midtown Manhattan is just beyond the door. There are options beyond the expected rib-eyes, tenderloins, and strip steaks; an interesting sidebar is the selection of "composed selections" for $19 to $32, with various meats and fish paired with starches or vegetables, such as Tunisian lamb with roasted cauliflower purée and slow braised figs, and chicken cassoulet with root vegetables and baked flageolets (young kidney beans). Starters include Kobe carpaccio and oysters from the raw bar. Nearly 30 wines are offered by the glass.

625 North Rd. (in the Mystic Marriott Hotel). © **860/326-0360.** www.waterfordgrouprestaurants.com/octagon. Reservations recommended. Main courses $19–$40. AE, DC, DISC, MC, V. Daily 5:30–10pm.

Olio CONTEMPORARY BISTRO   Pastas (15 of them) dominate the offerings, with international standards like Thai calamari salad, crab Rangoon spring rolls, quesadillas, and bruschette filling out the menu—tasty and quick for all their familiarity. With bare tables and hard surfaces everywhere, it's loud, and take the reading glasses, because the menu is written in a tiny hand and there are only guttering candles and a few dim pinlights for illumination. The waitstaff is appealing enough that it's easy to forgive their lack of efficiency in keeping glasses full at busy times.

33 Kings Hwy. (south of I-95 at Rte. 1). © **860/445-6546.** www.ckrestaurantgroup.com/olio. Main courses $18–$27. AE, DC, DISC, MC, V. Mon–Sat 11:30am–9pm (until 10pm Fri–Sat); Sun 4:40–9pm.

MYSTIC ✶✶✶

The spirit and texture of the maritime life and history of New England are captured in many ports along its indented coast, but nowhere more precisely than beside the Mystic River estuary and its harbor. This was a dynamic whaling and shipbuilding center during the Colonial period and into the 20th century, but the discontinuation of the first industry and the decline of the second haven't adversely affected the community. No derelict barges or rotting piers degrade the views and waterways (or, at least, not many).

Mystic and West Mystic are stitched together by a drawbridge, the raising of which causes traffic stoppages, at a quarter past every hour, but rarely shortens tempers, except for those of visitors who don't leave their urban impatience behind. There are complaints by some that the town has been commercialized, but T-shirt shops and related tackiness is limited, and the more garish motels and attractions have been restricted to the periphery, especially up near exit 90 off I-95.

The town is home to one of New England's most singular attractions, the Mystic Seaport museum village. It is a re-created seaport of the mid-1800s, with dozens of buildings and watercraft of that romantic era of clipper ships and the China trade.

The **Mystic & Shoreline Visitor Information Center** (© **860/536-1641;** www.mysticinfo.com) is in Building 1D of the **Olde Mistick Village shopping center** (© **860/536-4941;** www.oldmysticvillage.com). To get there, take exit 90 from I-95 and go south on Route 27. Turn left almost immediately onto Coogan Boulevard, and the shopping center will be on your left.

WHAT TO SEE & DO

As in Groton (above), several operators offer **sailing and fishing cruises.** One of the most convenient is **Voyager Cruises,** 15 Holmes St. (© **860/536-0416;** www.voyager mystic.com). It offers trips on the *Argia,* a replica of a 19th-century schooner that docks 100 feet south of the drawbridge in Mystic. Offered are 2 ½-hour "half-day" sailing trips and sunset cruises. Fares are $38 for adults, $35 for seniors, and $28 for children under 18 (must be accompanied by an adult). The same operation also offers 2- to 5-day trips on its tall ship, *Mystic.* Another company, **Windjammer Mystic Whaler,** at City Pier (© **800/697-8420;** www.mysticwhaler.com), offers similar outings on its tall ship, *Mystic Whaler.* Its evening cruise features a classic New England dinner with a 1¼-pound lobster for $80. The season runs from June through mid-October.

Mystic Aquarium & Institute for Exploration ✶✶ (Kids)   If you've never seen a marine show, the sea-lions show here is the place to start. Less gimmicky than similar commercial enterprises in Florida and California, the demonstration illuminates as it entertains and, at 15 minutes in length, doesn't test the attention spans of the very young. The rest of the exhibits are enough to occupy at least another hour. Beluga whales squeal and twirl for their trainers at feeding time, and there are fur seals, endangered Steller sea lions, penguins, and sharks on display with underwater viewing windows. Dozens of rays flutter like butterflies and translucent jellyfish billow and flex in slow-motion dance, a hypnotic display. A 40-minute "Beluga Encounter" program puts visitors right in the water with friendly whales and lets them touch the animals ($99–$149, depending on time of year; reservations strongly suggested), and there is a similar "Penguin Encounter" program. Elsewhere, exhibits on the *Titanic* wreck and other sunken ships, a re-creation of an Amazon rainforest, and a display of glowing, fluorescent coral emphasize conservation and the joys of scientific research.

55 Coogan Blvd. (at exit 90 off I-95). *C* **860/572-5955.** www.mysticaquarium.org. Admission $22 adults, $20 seniors, $17 children 3–12. Mar–Nov daily 9am–6pm; Dec–Feb Mon–Fri 10am–5pm, Sat–Sun and holidays 9am–6pm.

Mystic Seaport ★★★ *Kids*   Dubbed "the museum of America and the sea," the 79-year old Mystic Seaport complex encompasses an entire waterfront settlement, capturing the look and feel of a 19th-century seafaring village. Thirty historic buildings were transported here from all across New England, and there are whaling ships and tall ships to scramble over and a working shipyard where carpenters use historically accurate methods of production. Few visitors fail to be enthralled by *something* in this place that so deeply evokes maritime's golden age, so plan to set aside at least 2 or 3 hours—if not an entire day—for exploring.

The **visitor center** sells tickets and has a daily map guide. Exit the center and head to the village green, which intersects with a street of period-style shops, public buildings, and houses. There's an 1870s hardware and dry-goods store, a one-room schoolhouse, the 1889 Fishtown chapel, and an 1830s home. A **children's museum** for kids up to 7 years old has games characteristic of the era and sailor costumes for dress-up.

From here, the majestic three-masted **Charles W. Morgan,** the proudest possession of the Seaport fleet of over 500 craft, is only a few steps away. It was built in 1841 and was an active whaling ship until 1921. (In fall 2008, the *Morgan* will be taken out of the water for restoration work.)

Fans of scrimshaw and ship "models in bottles" should be sure to continue along the waterfront to the right to the **Stillman Building,** which contains fascinating exhibits of both. Other buildings include a cooperage (where barrels are made), a tavern, an 1833 bank, and other shops and services that did business with the whalers and clipper ships that put in at ports such as this.

The friendly docents in the village are highly competent at the crafts they demonstrate and are always ready to impart as much information as visitors care to absorb. The fact that they aren't dressed in period costumes (except during special events like the Christmas lamplight tours) somehow enhances the village's feeling of authenticity, perhaps by avoiding the contrived air of many such enterprises.

A small **lighthouse**—one of the few buildings at the seaport that is a replica—looks out across the water toward the large riverside houses that line the opposite shore. From here, past the boat sheds, the fishing shacks, and the ketches and sloops that are moored along here in season, is the perky little **SS Sabino,** a steamboat built in 1908. This working ship gives half-hour river rides from mid-May to early October, daily from 11:30am to 3:30pm, and 1½-hour evening excursions Sunday through Thursday at 4:30pm, Friday and Saturday at 4:30 and 6:30pm ($14 adults, $12 children ages 6–17; reservations required). Cruises are offered on other village ships as well. A few steps south is the **Henry B. du Pont Preservation Shipyard,** where the boats are painstakingly restored.

Free water shuttles take visitors from one end of the 19-acre complex to the other. Also on the grounds are the **Galley Restaurant,** which serves pretty good fish and chips, fried clam strips, and lobster rolls; and **Schaefer's Sprouter's Tavern,** which offers snacks and sandwiches (look for the hideaway bed in the corner, where a barman slept to admit late travelers). Across the brick courtyard with the giant anchor is a building containing several **museum stores** as well as an art gallery. These superior shops stock books, kitchenware, fresh-baked goods, nautical prints and paintings, and ship models.

When you exit, ask the gatekeeper to validate your ticket so you can come back the next day for free. Note that not all exhibits are open year-round, so check in advance if there are ones you're especially hoping to see.

75 Greenmanville Ave. (Rte. 27). © **888/973-2767** or 860/572-5315. www.mysticseaport.org. Admission $15 adults, $13 seniors, $9.50 children 6–17 (good for 2 consecutive days). AE, MC, V. Apr–Oct daily 9am–5pm; Nov–Mar daily 10am–4pm. Exit 90 off I-95, south on Rte. 27 for 1 mile. Parking lots are on the left, the entrance on the right.

WHERE TO STAY & DINE
The Inn at Mystic ⊛   A variety of lodgings are on offer at this property occupying 18 acres overlooking Long Island Sound. At the crest of the hill, a 1904 Classical Revival mansion has public rooms as grand as the exterior. Bedrooms there are humbler: antique furniture mixed with merely old stuff, but many have four-poster beds and some have whirlpools. Porches and decks take in both sunrises and sunsets. Down the hill is the intimate Gate House, similarly accoutered. A number of rooms are in a separate motel-style building and are worn but serviceable.

The complex also incorporates the restaurant **Flood Tide** (© **860/536-8140**), with an exhibition kitchen containing a wood-burning grill and brick oven. It's open daily for all three meals and afternoon tea. The dining rooms look out over the sound, so ask for a table by the window.

3 Williams Ave. (at rtes. 1 and 27), Mystic, CT 06355. © **800/237-2415** or 860/536-9604. www.innatmystic.com. 68 units. $75–$295 double. Rates include buffet breakfast and afternoon tea. Packages available. AE, DC, DISC, MC, V. Pets accepted in some units ($15). **Amenities:** Restaurant (contemporary bistro); bar; outdoor pool; 2 putting greens; tennis court; access to nearby health club; free kayaks and boats; limited room service. *In room:* A/C, TV, Internet, fridge, hair dryer.

WHERE TO STAY
There are plenty of ho-hum but adequate area motels that can soak up the traffic at all but peak periods, meaning weekends from late spring to early fall plus weekdays in July and August, when it is necessary to have reservations. The Mystic Country website, at **www.mysticcountry.com**, lists over 50 to choose from.

Hilton Mystic ⊛ *Kids*   Unlike the motels clustered around the I-95 interchange, this is a full-service hotel, providing the amenities expected of its big-city cousins. Renovations in 2008 have warmed up the guest rooms with upscale furniture, marble or granite finishes, and the standard Hilton serenity bed, which features a pillow-top mattress. The hotel has special menus for children, and in summer it sets up a movie room with classic Disney films. It's also just across the street from the Mystic Aquarium. The hotel is owned by the Mashantucket Pequot tribe, so no surprise that there are posters announcing coming attractions at the Foxwoods Casino and a shuttle van to take you there.

20 Coogan Blvd., Mystic, CT 06355. © **800/445-8667** or 860/572-0731. Fax 860/572-0328. www.hiltonmystic.com. 182 units. $149–$349 double. Packages available. AE, DC, DISC, MC, V. Take exit 90 off I-95 and drive south, following signs to the Mystic Aquarium; the hotel is opposite. **Amenities:** Restaurant (Continental); lounge; heated indoor pool; fitness room; bike rental; children's programs; limited room service; same-day laundry; dry cleaning. *In room:* A/C, TV w/pay movies, PlayStation, free Wi-Fi, coffeemaker, hair dryer, iron.

Steamboat Inn 🎖🎖

Mystic's most ingratiating lodging is easily overlooked from land but readily apparent from the river. Perched on the bank of the Mystic River, the yellow-clapboard structure has apartment-size downstairs bedrooms, with Jacuzzis and kitchenettes, while the upstairs units have wood-burning fireplaces. Every room is decorated differently—Laura Ashley was a likely muse—and all but one have views of the water and the sailboats that make up the traffic.

73 Steamboat Wharf, Mystic, CT 06355. © **860/536-8300.** Fax 860/536-9528. www.steamboatinnmystic.com. 11 units. $140–$300 double. Rates include breakfast. Packages available. AE, DISC, MC, V. Parking available in a gated lot. GPS users should use 15 West Main St. (Rte. 1) for directions. Look for the sign pointing down an alley on the west bank of the Mystic River, just before the drawbridge. *In room:* A/C, TV/DVD, Wi-Fi, hair dryer, iron.

Taber Inne & Suites 🎖

Not quite an inn but more than a motel, this small complex has something to suit most tastes and budgets, with seven immaculate buildings containing both simple units and hedonistic suites with fireplaces and decks. The Carriage House, for instance, has a cathedral ceiling, two bedrooms, a sitting room, and a two-person Jacuzzi. Standard rooms are clean, neat, and bland. A building with an indoor pool and fitness center opened in 2004.

66 Williams Ave. (Rte. 1; 2 blocks east of Rte. 27), Mystic, CT 06355. © **866/822-3746** or 860/536-4904. Fax 860/572-9140. www.taberinn.com. 32 units. $110–$185 double. Rates include breakfast. AE, MC, V. **Amenities:** Heated indoor pool; sauna; exercise room, access to nearby health club w/tennis court. *In room:* A/C, TV, Wi-Fi, hair dryer.

The Whaler's Inn 🎖

The previously dispirited aspect of the venerable Whaler's has been banished in recent years. The five structures that constitute the property have all been given fresh fabrics and furnishings, as well as new bathrooms. Best of all (and most expensive) are the eight luxury bedrooms of Hoxie House, all with gas fireplaces and whirlpool baths. Sleigh beds and four-posters are common. Breakfast is taken in the spacious Hospitality Room, which also has an Internet terminal for guest use.

20 E. Main St., Mystic, CT 06355. © **800/243-2588** or 860/536-1506. Fax 860/572-1250. www.whalersinnmystic. com. 41 units. $105–$259 double. AE, DISC, MC, V. Rates include breakfast. Packages available. **Amenities:** Restaurant (contemporary bistro); lounge; jewelry store; access to nearby health club. *In room:* A/C, TV, Wi-Fi, hair dryer, iron.

WHERE TO DINE

Abbott's Lobster in the Rough 🎖 SEAFOOD

This nitty-gritty lobster shack has plenty of picnic tables and not a frill to be found—it's as if a wedge of the Maine coast had been punched into the Connecticut shore. While many options, including hot dogs and chicken, are available, the classic shore dinner rules. That means clam chowder, boiled shrimp, steamed mussels, and a tasty lobster, with coleslaw, chips, and drawn butter thrown in. They don't have a liquor license, but guests are encouraged to bring their own beer or wine.

117 Pearl St., Noank, CT 06340. © **860/536-7719.** www.abbotts-lobster.com. Main courses $5–$34. AE, MC, V. Open daily late May to end of Aug, with weekends early May and in Sept and Oct. Daily noon–9pm in season. From downtown Mystic, go south on Rte. 215 and cross a railroad bridge. At Main St. in Noank, turn left and take an immediate right on Pearl St. Be prepared to ask for directions.

Bravo Bravo ⚜ NEW ITALIAN/AMERICAN   Reserve or plan to wait, because even an expansion into the space next door only made room for more people to squeeze in. It can get as noisy as a disco, aided by bare wood tables and floors, and the waitstaff can be a little scattered. At least half the entrees involve pasta—lobster ravioli, champagne risotto, shrimp with fusilli in a sun-dried tomato vodka sauce—with options for stuffed veal medallion with a garlic spinach cheese or *osso buco*.

20 E. Main St. ✆ 860/536-3228. www.ckrestaurantgroup.com. Reservations recommended. Main courses $18–$27. AE, DC, DISC, MC, V. Tues–Sat 11:30am–2pm; Thurs–Sun 5–9pm (until 10pm Fri–Sat).

Go Fish ⚜ SEAFOOD   Brash and boisterous, Go Fish is dominated by a sprawling granite bar at its center, often surrounded by younger drinkers and grazers. At the far end is an enclosed sushi bar, while near the door is a room usually populated by older folks and families. Local or regional fishery products are employed as much as possible, including Stonington sea scallops and Noank Bluepoint Oysters. Daily specials rely on fresh catches. Portions are abundant, so you might want to skip appetizers, enticing though they are (the creamy bisque, for one). During weekday happy hour, 4:30 to 6pm, the bar menu is half-price.

Olde Mistick Village, at exit 90 off I-95. ✆ 860/536-2662. www.jtkmanagement.com/gofishct. Main courses $17–$30. AE, DISC, MC, V. Mon–Thurs 11:30am–9pm; Fri–Sat 11:30am–9:30pm; Sun noon–9pm.

Kitchen Little ⚜ AMERICAN   Not much more than a shack by the water, this is the sort of place dismissed and passed every day by hundreds of tourists hurrying on to the Seaport. They're missing not only dozens of distinct breakfast choices (try the Portuguese fisherman plate), but also some of the coast's tastiest clam and scallop dishes. At lunch, you should have the clear broth clam chowder, maybe the whole belly clam rolls, and absolutely the fried scallop sandwich. Or consider the lobster roll, with no fillers, only tail and claw flesh. Expect a wait in summer and tight quarters inside. Try to snare a table out back, in view of the tall ships.

135 Greenmanville Ave. (Rte. 27), 1 mile south of I-95. ✆ 860/536-2122. Main dishes $3.45–$13. No credit cards. Mon–Fri 6:30am–2pm; Sat–Sun 6:30am–1pm.

STONINGTON & NORTH STONINGTON

Not much seemed to happen in these slumbering villages, only lightly brushed by the 21st century despite all the thrashing about in heavily touristed Mystic. That suited the residents just fine, explaining why most of them are not thrilled by the continual expansions of the nearby Foxwoods and Mohegan Sun gambling complexes (below).

It is difficult to imagine what those empire might do, eventually, to inland North Stonington, as peaceful a New England hamlet as can be found, with hardly any commercialization beyond a couple of inns. Sound-side Stonington, which marked its 350th anniversary in 1999, has a pronounced maritime flavor, sustained by the presence of the state's only remaining (albeit dwindling) fishing fleet. Its two lengthwise streets are lined with well-preserved Federal-style and Greek Revival homes.

WHAT TO SEE & DO

For an introduction, drive south to **Cannon Square** along Stonington's **Water Street.** Standing in the grassy main square are two cannons that were used to fight off an attack by British warships during the War of 1812. Opposite is a lovely old granite house and, on the corner, a neoclassical bank.

If you continue south to the end of Water Street, you reach **Stonington Point,** where there's a small **town beach.** The misty blue headland directly south across the sound is Montauk Point, the eastern extremity of New York's Long Island.

Here at the point is the **Old Lighthouse Museum,** 7 Water St. (© **860/535-1440;** www.stoningtonhistory.org). The lighthouse was built of stone in 1823, moved to its current site 300 feet away in 1840, and active until 1889. Most of the museum exhibits relate to the maritime past of the area, with scrimshaw tusks and the export porcelain that constituted much of the 19th-century China trade. Admission is $5 for adults, $3 for children 6 to 12. It's open May through October daily from 10am to 5pm.

About 4 miles north is one of the Nutmeg State's handful of earnest wineries, **Stonington Vineyards,** 523 Taugwonk Rd., Stonington (© **800/421-WINE** or 860/535-1222; www.stoningtonvineyards.com), which has a tasting room in a barn beside its vineyard. There are usually five or six pressings to be sampled, with an aged-in-oak chardonnay leading the pack. Bring a picnic, buy a bottle, and take them to tables overlooking the vineyards or the brook than runs past. The winery is open year-round daily from 11am to 5pm, with a cellar tour at 2pm. From downtown Stonington, head north on Main Street until it merges into Taugwonk Road. The vineyard is about 2½ miles after you've passed under I-95. From I-91, take exit 91 and drive north.

WHERE TO STAY

The Inn at Stonington 🏵🏵   Built on the site of a restaurant leveled by fire, The Inn at Stonington harmonizes nicely with its neighbors on the town's main street. Combining the intimacy of a small inn with the comforts of a luxury hotel, it abounds in felicitous flourishes that exceed expectations. Every unit has a gas fireplace, 6 have balconies, and 10 have Jacuzzis. While rooms reflect a single design sensibility, with tailored contemporary interpretations of country decor, no two are alike. Rooms in the annexed building next door are even larger than the originals. The inn has a 400-foot pier with deep water for those arriving on yachts. It's so quiet here, guests might think they are alone, until they enter the bar and find that everyone else has shown up for the evening wine-and-cheese gathering.

60 Water St., Stonington, CT 06378. © **860/535-2000.** Fax 860/535-8193. www.innatstonington.com. 18 units. $180–$445 double. Rates include breakfast and evening wine and cheese. Packages available. AE, DC, MC, V. Take exit 91 off I-95; follow signs into Stonington village. No children under 14. **Amenities:** Well-equipped exercise room; bikes and kayaks available; computer for guests' use. *In room:* A/C, TV, dataport, hair dryer.

Randall's Ordinary 🏵   The oldest structure on this 250-acre estate dates from 1685. All meals are cooked in the Farmhouse in an open-hearth fireplace and served by a staff in period costumes. Considering the primitive circumstances under which the food is prepared, it is always hearty, if simple. Rooms in the 1819 Barn have exposed, rough-hewn beams along with TVs and phones.

41 Norwich Westerly Rd. (Rte. 2), North Stonington, CT 06359. © **877/599-4540.** Fax 860/599-3308. www.randall-sordinary.com. 13 units. $140–$250 double. Packages available. AE, MC, V. I-95 to exit 92, north on Rte. 2. Closed Jan–Apr. *In room:* A/C, TV.

WHERE TO DINE

Noah's AMERICAN   Noah's has been earning raves for years and is a favorite for both locals and travelers, especially among the 30-something set. The restaurant sources locally for its fish, oysters, veggies, and wine (from Stonington Vineyards; see above), among other ingredients. Special point of pride is the homemade deserts;

Noah's website lists 122 options that might be offered any given day, from chocolate raspberry ganache and Kentucky butter cake to red grits (raspberries and tapioca topped with raspberry cream) and the Waldorf-Astoria's signature chiffon cheesecake. The restaurant's on-site bakery also does brisk business.

113 Water St. © 860/535-3925. www.noahsfinefood.com. Main courses $14–$22. Tues–Sun 7:30am–9pm (until 9:30pm Fri–Sat).

Water Street Café NEW AMERICAN   Exposed pipes and industrial-type lighting contrast with rustic walls and banquettes in this cheery restaurant. A blackboard lists creative daily specials, and those are often the best choices. Be sure to start with the local oysters, which are consistently good. Otherwise, hunger pangs can certainly be assuaged by such reliables as barbecue pork sandwiches, burgers, and lobster spring rolls. Expect comforting edibles, shorn of artifice, not artistry. There occasionally is live music of the singer-songwriter variety.

143 Water St. © 860/535-2122. Reservations recommended on weekends. Main courses $10–$19. AE, DISC, MC, V. Daily 11:30am–2:30pm and 5–10pm (until 11pm Fri–Sat); Sat–Sun 8am–2:30pm.

THE CASINOS: FOXWOODS RESORT AND MOHEGAN SUN

What has been wrought in the woodlands north of the Mystic coast in the last 15 years is nothing less than astonishing. There was little but trees here when the Mashantucket Pequot tribe received clearance to open a gambling casino on their ancestral lands in rural southeast Connecticut. Virtually overnight, the tribal bingo parlor was expanded into the full-fledged Foxwoods casino, and a hotel was built. That was in 1992.

Within 3 years, Foxwoods had become enormously profitable. Money cascaded over the Pequot (pronounced *Pee*-kwat) in a seemingly endless torrent. Expansion was immediate—another hotel, then a third, more casinos, golf courses, and a museum devoted to Native American culture. The tribe bought up adjacent lands and nearby inns and hotels, and opened a shipworks to build high-speed ferries. Foxwoods now claims to be the largest casino in the world.

All this wasn't lost on the Mohegan Tribe of Connecticut, which in 1996 opened its own casino complex, Mohegan Sun.

Foxwoods is in the town of Ledyard, and Mohegan Sun is in Uncasville. They're about 5 miles apart as the crow flies, but 11 miles by car, with Foxwoods on the east side of the Thames River and Mohegan Sun on the west.

Residents of surrounding communities have been ambivalent about the development, to put the best face on it. When it was learned that one of the tribe's corporate entities was to be called Two Trees Limited Partnership, a predictable query was, "Is that all you're going to leave us? Two trees?" While there is a continuing danger of damage to the fragile character of this authentically picturesque corner of Connecticut, it is also a fact that thousands of people have found employment here.

WHAT TO SEE & DO

Foxwoods Resort Casino   This casino-hotel complex is forever changing, adding, renovating, and expanding. There are six cavernous gambling rooms. Foxwoods is a member of the **World Poker Tour** and home to the World Poker Finals, held in a room with 100 tables. The 3,600-seat **Bingo Hall** is one of the largest in the world, and the high-tech horse parlor is a dazzler. All the other usual methods of depleting wallets are at hand as well—blackjack, bingo, keno, craps, baccarat, roulette, and money wheels. There are 7,200 slot machines. Some 40,000 people come through the doors every day.

In addition to the gaming, the resort is home to restaurants, high-end boutiques, and three hotels. A fourth, the **MGM Grand at Foxwoods**, was set to open in May 2008 as part of $700-million (!) development project that will include even more gaming venues, restaurants, and convention space. There's an **entertainment center**—great for kids—with a virtual-reality MaxFlight FS2000 Jet simulator and 140 video games. The **Fox Theatre** brings in acts like comedians Bob Saget and Don Rickles, and singers Vanessa Williams and Jackson Browne, and there is a **Hard Rock Cafe** on-site. In the Grand Pequot Tower hotel, a **salon** offers haircuts, facials, and a full menu of nail care. See "Where to Dine," below, for restaurant options. The resort opened the on-site **Lake of Isles Golf Courses** in 2005.

No one is allowed to forget that this whole eye-popping affair is owned and operated by Native Americans. A signature display is *The Rainmaker,* a glass statue of an archer shooting an arrow into the air. Prominently placed around the main buildings are larger-than-life sculptures depicting Amerindians by artists of Chiricahua and Chippewa descent.

39 Norwich-Westerly Rd., Ledyard, CT 06339 Ⓒ 800/369-9663. www.foxwoods.com. From Boston, take I-95 south to exit 92 onto Rte. 2 west. From New Haven and New York, take I-95 north to I-395 north to exit 79A onto Rte. 2A east, picking up Rte. 2 east. Don't bother trying to park in the huge garage: It takes forever and the valet parking at the front door is swift and free.

Mashantucket Pequot Museum & Research Center 🞴🞴

A $193-million trickle from the floods of cash washing over southeastern Connecticut and its resurgent Indian Nation was diverted to create and develop this museum. Opened in 1998 to substantial fanfare, it has justified the hoopla with a carefully conceived mix of film, murals, models, dioramas, and re-creations of scenes of Native American life. The Pequot Village exhibit has wigwams and life-size figures shown fishing, cooking, butchering game, and making baskets. The museum's website offers mountains of historical information. Lunch and snacks are served in the restaurant, and there's a shop with books, jewelry, and crafts. A shuttle bus provided by Foxwoods carries visitors to the museum and back.

110 Pequot Trail. Ⓒ 800/411-9671. www.pequotmuseum.org. Admission $15 adults (ages 16–54), $13 seniors, $10 children 6–15, free for children under 6. Daily 10am–4pm.

Mohegan Sun

In 1996, the barely extant Mohegan tribe opened its gambling casino, and within a few weeks it was drawing 20,000 gamblers a day away from Foxwoods. Expansion followed as quickly here as it did at Foxwoods, and the complex now includes a "Casino of the Sky" wing to complement the original "Casino of the Earth." Both bulge with eager gamblers. "Earth" is circular, with table games from Texas hold 'em to blackjack to craps to baccarat. They're supplemented by keno, a race book, and more than 6,000 slot machines. A new feature called Poker Pro automates the play. Overhead are simulated log constructions meant to suggest ancient lodge houses; it's an aesthetically pleasing space, as casinos go, although few of the avid players seem to notice. "Sky" directly adjoins the **Mohegan Sun Hotel** (below) and is more splashily Vegas in style. In between the two are over 30 pricey shops from Godiva Chocolatier and Brookstone to Coach and Swarovski.

Mohegan has the edge over Foxwoods in its entertainment options. A **10,000-seat arena** nestled between the two wings hosts a professional women's basketball team, the **WNBA's Connecticut Sun,** along with performances by the likes of musicians Billy

Joel, Bon Jovi, and Kenny Chesney; comedian Chris Rock; and magician David Copperfield. The 300-seat **Cabaret Theatre,** in the "Sky" casino, brings in additional comedy shows and events like Ballroom Dancesport Extravaganza. The **Wolf Den,** located smack dab in the center of the "Earth" casino, books dance bands such as Martha Reeves and the Vandellas and the Tower of Power. Its shows are free.

The 22,300-square-foot **Elemis Spa** inside the hotel, open from 7am to 10pm (to 11pm on Fri–Sat), has 15 therapy rooms, including two for "exotic rituals." If you win big—or, conversely, if you want to take the edge off your losses—ritual options include the "Ceremony of the Whirling River," featuring a jasmine-flower bath, massage, Frangipani hair and scalp conditioning, and "conditioning foot delight." It's $250 for 75 minutes. As they say: Easy come, easy go.

See "Where to Dine," below, for restaurant options.

1 Mohegan Sun Blvd., Uncasville. © **888/226-7711.** www.mohegansun.com. Exit 79A from I-395 onto Rte. 2A east. Take exit 2, Mohegan Sun Blvd.

WHERE TO STAY

The first two hotels listed here are in the Foxwoods resort. The third is at Mohegan Sun. The last, The Spa at Norwich Inn, is off-site from both casinos, about 15 minutes from Foxwoods. Note that unlike Las Vegas and other gambling centers, rates aren't kept artificially low at the casino properties as an inducement to gamblers.

Another gigantic hotel, the **MGM Grand at Foxwoods,** was set to open May 2008. It will have 825 rooms and an attached 4,000 theater, with Celine Dion and Michael Bolton among the performers scheduled for later in the year. See www.mgmat foxwoods.com.

Grand Pequot Tower 🏨🏨   The Grand Pequot Tower at Foxwoods handily takes its place among New England's elite resort hotels. The third of the complex's hotels is the grandest of the three in space and concept, and also the most tasteful. The smaller rooms are 450 square feet and include a marble bathtub and vanity area. There's an opulent salon and spa, and polished granite and imported woods and marbles feature extensively in the handsome lobby. The tower's main restaurants, **Paragon** and **Al Dente,** are the high-end operations in the resort.

Foxwoods Resort, 39 Norwich-Westerly Rd., Ledyard, CT 06339. (Mailing address: Rte. 2, Mashantucket, CT 06338.) © **800/369-9663** or 860/885-3000. www.foxwoods.com. 824 units. $145–$295 double; from $400 suite. AE, DC, DISC, MC, V. Free valet parking. **Amenities:** 2 restaurants (French, Italian); bars; indoor pool; golf course on property; health club and spa; concierge; shopping arcade; 24-hr. room service; business center; babysitting; laundry; dry cleaning. In room: A/C, TV, high-speed Internet, coffeemaker, fridge, hair dryer.

Two Trees Inn   This was the first Foxwoods lodging, and it's a 10-minute walk or short shuttle-bus ride from the casino complex. (The free shuttle runs 24 hr. a day.) A conventional motor hotel, it attracts large numbers of bus tours. The junior suite, with beds and a sofa couch, can accommodate six people.

Foxwoods Resort, 39 Norwich Westerly Rd. (Rte. 2), Ledyard, CT 06339. © **800/369-9663** or 860/312-3000. www.foxwoods.com. 280 units. $99–$225 double; suites from $160. AE, DC, DISC, MC, V. **Amenities:** Restaurant; bar; heated indoor pool; fitness room; sauna; Wi-Fi in lobby. In room: A/C, TV w/pay movies, Internet, coffeemaker, hair dryer.

Mohegan Sun Hotel 🏨🏨   This asymmetrical grouping of soaring, silver-skinned wedges provokes the "Wow!" response on first sight, exactly as intended. Every bit the equal of its rival of recent years, the Grand Pequot Tower at Foxwoods, the Mohegan Sun Hotel indulges in jaw-dropping design that begins with the slanting columns arrayed around a reflecting pool in abstract homage to woodland ponds. The front desk is over to the right, the escalators down to the restaurants and shops of the new "Casino of the Sky" on the far side. Rooms, with a minimum of 450 square feet each, are conventionally attractive, albeit utilizing irregular shapes that echo design that was called "modern" in the 1950s.

1 Mohegan Sun Blvd. (off Rte. 2A), Uncasville, CT 06382. (📞 **888/226-7711** or 860/862-8000. www.mohegansun. com. 1,200 units. $150–$375 double. Packages available. AE, DC, DISC, MC, V. Free valet parking. **Amenities:** Many restaurants (steakhouse, fusion, Italian, seafood, American); many bars; large indoor pool; extensive health club and spa; shopping arcade; concierge; 24-hr. room service; babysitting; laundry; dry cleaning. *In room:* A/C, TV w/pay movies, high-speed Internet, hair dryer, fridge, coffeemaker, iron.

The Spa at Norwich Inn 🦆🦆　Set on 42 acres of beautiful grounds, this complex has 49 guest rooms in a main building that are augmented by outlying "villas," which each have a kitchen, a sitting area with fireplace, a separate bedroom, and a private deck. The dining room, **Kensington's,** enjoys a versatile kitchen staff capable of producing meals either conventional or health-minded. The fitness center offers classes in yoga, belly dancing, and Pilates, and the full-service spa is a big-volume operation, with 36 treatment rooms. At that size, some guests have found an impersonal tenor to the experience. While services run from standard-luxurious to silly (Chocolate Chip Aromatherapy Body Wrap, anyone?), the readers of *Connecticut Magazine* have named it the best day spa in the state for 10 years in a row. The property is owned by the Mashantucket Pequots, whose Foxwoods is visible from the front door.

607 W. Thames St. (Rte. 32), Norwich, CT 06360. (📞 **800/275-4772** or 860/886-2401. www.thespaatnorwichinn. com. 100 units. $150–$325 double; from $200 suite (villa). Packages available. AE, DC, MC, V. From I-95, take exit 76 onto I-395 north; take exit 79A onto Rte. 2A east, then immediately exit onto Rte. 32 north and drive 1½ miles to the inn. **Amenities:** Restaurant (eclectic); bar; indoor and outdoor pools; adjacent golf course; fitness center (w/classes) and spa; limited room service. *In room:* A/C, TV/CD, Wi-Fi, fridge, hair dryer, iron.

WHERE TO DINE

At Foxwoods, more than 30 restaurants and fast-food operations situated throughout the hotel-casino complex cover the most popular options. Unlike in Atlantic City or Vegas, there are no bargains to be found: Except at the Festival Buffet (below), expect to pay at least $50 for dinner for two, not including drinks, taxes, and tip.

The high-end options are **Paragon,** with French-influenced cuisine, **Al Dente,** which features designer pizzas and pastas, and **Cedars Steak House,** which grills Angus beef and native seafood. All three expect guests to be dressed for fine dining, and they accept reservations. The most popular dining room is the **Festival Buffet,** with an extensive all-you-can-eat spread. For reservations at any of the Foxwoods restaurants, call the main number (📞 **800/369-9663**) and choose the reservations option.

Mohegan Sun also boasts over three dozen dining options, and those in the new "Casino of the Sky" are the more impressive. Among the top venues are those of celebrity chefs Jasper White and Todd English, with the casual seafood of **Summer Shack** (📞 860/862-9500) and contemporary Italian edibles of **Tuscany** (📞 860/862-3238), respectively, and an outpost of **Michael Jordan's Steakhouse** (📞 888/226-7711). The quality of the food is unexpectedly good, too, within the limits of their missions, at **Big Bubba's BBQ** (📞 860/862-9800), **The Longhouse** (beef and fish; 📞 888/226-7711), **Bamboo Forest** (Southeast Asian; 📞 888/226-7711), and **Pompeii and Caesar** (Italian; 📞 860/226-7711).

11

Rhode Island

by Herbert Bailey Livesey & Leslie Brokaw

Water defines "Little Rhody" as much as mountain peaks characterize Colorado. The Atlantic thrusts all the way to the Massachusetts border, cleaving the state into unequal halves and filling the geological basin that is Narragansett Bay. That leaves 400 miles of coastline and several large islands.

A string of coastal towns runs in a northeasterly arc from the Connecticut border up to Providence, the capital, which lies at the point of the bay, 30 miles from the open ocean. It was here that Roger Williams, banned from the Massachusetts Bay Colony in 1635 for his outspoken views on religious freedom, established his colony. Little survives from that first century, but a large section of the city's East Side is composed almost entirely of 18th- and 19th-century buildings.

Another group of Puritan exiles established their settlement a couple of years after Providence, on an island known to the Narragansett tribe as Aquidneck. Settlers thought their new home resembled the Isle of Rhodes in the Aegean, so the official name became Rhode Island and Providence Plantations, a moniker that was subsequently applied to the entire state and remains the official name.

The most important town on Aquidneck is Newport, and it's the best reason for an extended visit to the state. Its first era of prosperity was during the Colonial period, when its ships not only plied the new mercantile routes to China, but also engaged in the reprehensible "Triangular Trade" of West Indies molasses for New England rum for African slaves. Their additional skill at smuggling and evading taxes brought them into conflict with their British rulers, whose occupying army all but destroyed Newport during the Revolution.

After the Civil War, the town began its transformation from commercial outpost to resort, with the arrival of the millionaires whose lives spawned what Mark Twain sneeringly described as the "Gilded Age." They built astonishingly extravagant mansions, their contribution to Newport's bountiful architectural heritage. Winning the America's Cup and subsequent defenses of yachting's most famous trophy made the town into a recreational sailing center with a packed summer cultural calendar. As a result, travelers who want nothing more than a deep tan by Monday can coexist with history buffs and music lovers.

Finally, there is Block Island, a 1-hour ferry ride from Point Judith. A classic summer resort, it has avoided the imposition of Martha's Vineyard chic and Provincetown clutter. It has also sidestepped history (even though it was first settled in 1661), so there are few mandatory sights. That leaves visitors free simply to explore its lighthouses, hike its cliff-side trails, and hit the beach.

Note: Smoking is now prohibited in all enclosed public spaces, including bars, museums, elevators, restaurants, lobbies, malls, and transportation vehicles and facilities. Up to 50% of hotel rooms can allow smoking, but many inns and hotels ban tobacco entirely.

1 Providence ⭐⭐

45 miles S of Boston; 55 miles NE of New London

Providence delights in its sobriquet, "Renaissance City." No question, the city is moving on up, counter to the trend of so many small and midsize New England cities. Prosperity is evident in the resurgent downcity business center and the emerging adjacent neighborhoods dubbed the Arts & Entertainment and Jewelry districts. More recently on the rise is the West Side, a former industrial enclave adjoining Federal Hill, the city's "Little Italy." All are attracting creative young people and the eating places, shops, bars, and various entertainments they crave.

Rivers have been uncovered to form canals and waterside walkways; distressed buildings of the last century have been reclaimed; and continued construction has added a new hotel behind Union Station as well as Providence Place, a monster mall that brought national department stores here for the first time. The Arts district has its own boutique hotel, too.

Much of the credit for Providence's boom, grudging or exuberant, went to the ebullient six-term mayor Vincent A. "Buddy" Cianci, Jr. But he was sent to prison, caught in an FBI probe into the bribery of local officials. A 97-page federal indictment charged Cianci and others with racketeering, extortion, witness tampering, and mail fraud. Called Operation Plunder Dome, the investigation revived Providence's reputation for tolerance of corruption at high levels. Buddy tried to laugh it off, right up until the verdict. Now out of jail, Buddy's back, without his famed toupee but with his own radio talk show and a spaghetti sauce available for purchase.

Still, continued local pride in the city's revitalization is palpable. A burgeoning dining scene includes ambitious new restaurants that are nearly always less expensive than their counterparts in Boston and New York. College Hill is a National Historic District, the calendar is full of special events, and the presence of the young people attending the city's 12 colleges and universities guarantees a lively nightlife.

Roger Williams knew what he was doing. Admired for his fervent advocacy of religious and political freedom in the early Colonial period, he obviously had good instincts for town building as well. He planted the seeds of his settlement on a steep rise overlooking a swift-flowing river at the point where it widened into a large protected harbor. That part of the city, called the East Side and dominated by the ridge now known as College Hill, remains the most attractive district of a New England city, second only to Boston in the breadth of its cultural life and rich architectural heritage.

College Hill is so named because it is the site of Rhode Island College, which started life in 1764 and was later renamed Brown University. The Hill is further enhanced by the presence of the highly regarded Rhode Island School of Design, whose buildings are wrapped around the perimeter of the Brown campus. In and around these institutions are several square miles of 18th- and 19th-century houses, Colonial to Victorian, lining often gas-lit streets. At the back of the Brown campus is the funky shopping district along Thayer Street, while at the foot of the Hill is the largely commercial Main Street.

While most points of general interest are found on the East Side, the far larger collection of neighborhoods west of the river has its own attractions. The level downtown area is the center for business, government, and entertainment, with City Hall, a new convention center, the best large hotels, some small parks and historic buildings, and several venues for music, dance, and theatrical productions. To its north, across the

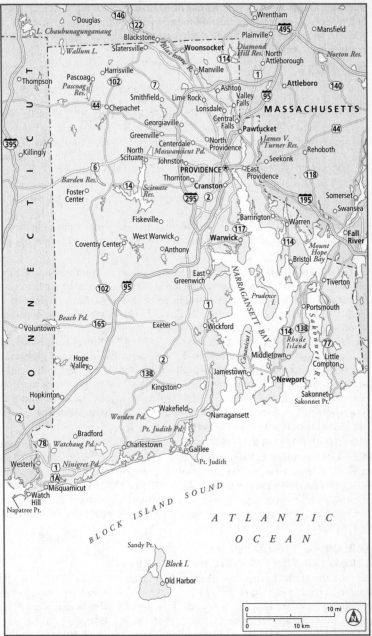

Woonasquatucket River, is the imposing State House, as well as the Amtrak station. And to its west, on the other side of Interstate 95, is Federal Hill, a residential area bearing a strong ethnic identity, primarily Italian, but increasingly leavened by numbers of more recent immigrant groups.

ESSENTIALS

GETTING THERE   I-95, which connects Boston and New York, runs right through the city. From Cape Cod, pick up I-195 west.

T. F. **Green/Providence Airport** (✆ **888/268-7222** or 401/737-8222; www. pvdairport.com) in Warwick, south of Providence (exit 13, I-95), is served by feeder and major airlines, including **American** (✆ 800/433-7300), **Continental** (✆ 800/525-3273), **Delta** (✆ 800/221-1212), **Northwest** (✆ 800/225-2525), **Southwest** (✆ 800/435-9792), **United** (✆ 800/864-8331), and **US Airways** (✆ 800/428-4322). The Rhode Island Public Transit Authority (RIPTA) provides transportation between the airport and the city center. Taxis are also available, costing about $20 for the 20-minute trip.

Amtrak (✆ **800/USA-RAIL;** www.amtrak.com) runs several trains daily between Boston and New York that stop at the attractive new station at 100 Gaspee St., near the State House.

GETTING AROUND   Traffic on local streets isn't bad, even at rush hour. Taxis are not easy to come by, though; few can be found outside even the largest hotels, and they can take up to an hour to arrive when called from restaurants. Alternatives are the **RIPTA buses** of the Green and Gold Lines (✆ **401/781-9400;** www.ripta.com). Made to look like old-time trolleys, these buses have routes that reach most major hotels and tourist destinations. Each ride costs $1.50. RIPTA (the Rhode Island Public Transit Authority) also provides ferry service between Providence and Newport.

A singular attraction is **La Gondola** (✆ **401/421-8877;** www.gondolari.com). A faithful replica of the Venetian original, it carries up to six passengers along the Woonasquatucket and Providence rivers. Especially popular for rides during the WaterFire events, its rates run from $79 to $139 for two persons (about what it would cost in the Italian city itself, minus the airfare).

VISITOR INFORMATION   For advance information, contact the **Providence Warwick Convention & Visitors Bureau,** 1 West Exchange St. (✆ **800/233-1636** or 401/274-1636; www.providencecvb.com). In town, consult the visitor center in the Rhode Island Convention Center, 1 Sabin St. (✆ **800/233-1636** or 401/751-1177), or check with the helpful park rangers at the visitor center of the Roger Williams National Park, at the corner of Smith and North Main streets, open daily from 9am to 4:30pm.

EXPLORING PROVIDENCE
STROLLING THE HISTORIC NEIGHBORHOODS

This is a city of manageable size—the population is about 175,000—that can easily occupy 2 or 3 days of a Rhode Island vacation. One leisurely walk passes most of the prominent attractions and provides a sense of the city's evolution from a colony of dissidents to a contemporary center of commerce and government.

Start downtown, charting a route from the 1878 City Hall on Kennedy Plaza along Dorrance Street 1 block to Westminster. Turn left, then right in 1 block, past The Arcade (see "Quick Bites," later in this section), then left on Weybosset.

Providence

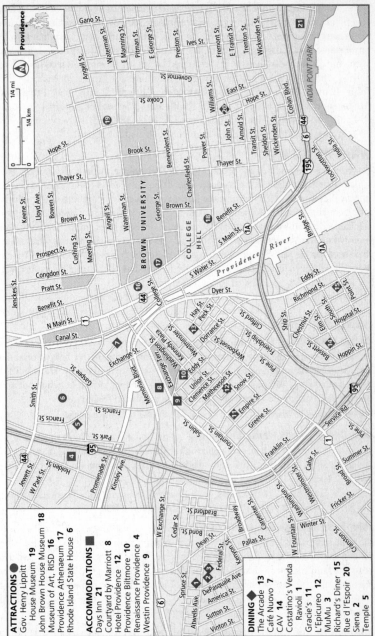

INDIA POINT PARK

Gano St.

Waterman St.
E Manning St.
Pitman St.
E George St.
Preston St.
Ives St.
Fremont St.
E Transit St.
Trenton St.
Wickenden St.
Cohan Blvd.

Governor St.
Angell St.
Cooke St.

Williams St.
East St.
Hope St.
John St.
Arnold St.
Transit St.
Sheldon St.
Wickenden St.

Hope St.
Brook St.
Benevolent St.
Power St.
Thayer St.
Charlesfield St.

Thayer St.
Keene St.
Lloyd Ave.
Bowen St.
Brown St.
Angell St.
Waterman St.
George St.
Brown St.
Benefit St.

BROWN UNIVERSITY
COLLEGE HILL

Providence River

Prospect St.
Cushing St.
Meeting St.

Congdon St.
Pratt St.
Benefit St.
Jenckes St.

S Water St.
S Main St.
Dyer St.

Eddy St.
Richmond St.
South St.
Point St.
Ship St.
Chestnut St.
Elm St.
Hospital St.
Bassett St.
Hoppin St.

N Main St.
Canal St.

Hay St.
Peck St.
Clifford St.
Friendship St.
Weybosset St.
Pine St.

Exchange St.
Gaspee St.

Washington St.
Kennedy Plaza
Westminster St.
Dorrance St.

Smith St.
Francis St.
Park St.
Francis St.

Eddy St.
Union St.
Clemence St.
Mathewson St.
Snow St.

Memorial Blvd.
Exchange Terr.
Sabin St.
Fountain St.
Empire St.
Greene St.

W Park St.
Holden St.
Jewett St.
Promenade St.
Kinsley Ave.

Franklin St.
Service Rd.
Pine St.
Summer St.
Cahir St.

W Exchange St.
Cedar St.
Bond St.
Dean St.
Broadway
Carpenter St.
W Fountain St.
Westminster St.
Washington St.
Fricker St.
Cranston St.
Broad St.

Bradford St.
Pallas St.
Winter St.

Spruce St.
Federal St.
DePasquale Ave.
America St.
Sutton St.
Vinton St.
Atwells Ave.

421

Follow Weybosset until it joins Westminster and continue across the Providence River. Turn right on the other side, walking along South Water Street as far as James Street, just before the I-195 overpass. Turn left, cross South Main, and then turn left on Benefit Street. This is the start of the so-called **Mile of History** ✹✹. Lined with 18th- and 19th-century houses, it is enhanced by gas streetlamps and sections of brick herringbone sidewalks. Along the way are opportunities to visit, in sequence, the 1786 **John Brown House,** the **First Unitarian Church** (1816), the **Providence Athenaeum,** and the **Museum of Art, Rhode Island School of Design.**

The **Rhode Island Historical Society** (✆ 401/438-0463; www.rihs.org) offers 90-minute guided tours of four different neighborhoods of interest.

WHAT TO SEE & DO

Boosters are understandably proud of their **Waterplace Park & Riverwalk** ✹✹, which encircles a tidal basin and borders the Woonasquatucket River down past where it joins the Moshassuck to become the Providence River. It incorporates an amphitheater, boat landings, landscaped walkways, and vaguely Venetian bridges that cross to the East Side. Summer concerts and other events are held here, among them the enormously popular **WaterFire** ✹✹ (✆ 401/272-3111; www.waterfire.org), when a hundred bonfires are set ablaze in braziers set around the basin of Waterplace Park and along the river. WaterFire takes place on evenings in late May through October, with the roar and flicker accentuated by amplified music.

Nearby, in Kennedy Plaza, the **Fleet Skating Center** has an ice rink twice the size of the one in New York's Rockefeller Center, fully utilized almost every winter evening. Skate rentals, lockers, and a snack bar are available.

Brown University   The nation's seventh-oldest college was founded in 1764 and has a reputation as the most experimental institution among its Ivy League brethren. The evidence of its pre-Revolutionary origins is seen in **University Hall,** built in 1771. Tours of the campus are intended primarily for prospective students, but anyone can join; call ahead to reserve—the schedule is altered frequently.

Office of Admissions, 45 Prospect St. (corner of Angell St.). ✆ 401/863-1000. www.brown.edu.

Gov. Henry Lippitt House Museum ✹   This house is as magnificently true to its grandiose Victorian era as any residence on the Continent. Meticulously detailed stenciling, expanses of stained glass, and inlaid floors make this mansion one of the treasures of College Hill. Visits are by guided tour only.

199 Hope St. (at Angell St.). ✆ 401/453-0688. www.preserveri.org. Admission $4 adults, $2 seniors and students. Tours Apr–Dec Tues–Fri 11am–3pm on the hour; Sat–Sun and Jan–Mar by appointment only.

John Brown House Museum   Quite unlike the fiery 19th-century abolitionist of the same name, *this* John Brown was an 18th-century slave trader who amassed a fortune in the China trade. He contributed much of that fortune to the university that bears the family name. The style of his 1786 mansion is Georgian, although after the Revolution, he no doubt preferred to think of it as Federal. Visits are by guided tour.

52 Power St. (at Benefit St.). ✆ 401/273-7507. www.rihs.org. Admission $7 adults, $5.50 seniors and students, $4 children 7–17. Apr–Dec Tue–Fri 1:30–4pm, Sat 10:30am–4pm; Jan–Mar Fri–Sat only.

Museum of Art, Rhode Island School of Design ✹✹   Prestigious RISD (pronounced *Riz*-dee) supports this ingratiating center of fine and decorative arts. Of the many excellent college and university museums in New England, this ranks near the top for the breadth of its collection. Those holdings include Chinese terra cotta, Greek statuary, and French Impressionist paintings. Probably of greatest interest are the works by such masters as Monet, Cézanne, Rodin, Picasso, and Matisse. But allow ·time for the American wing, which contains paintings by John Singleton Copley and John Singer Sargent. The Gorham silver collection alone is nearly worth the admission.

224 Benefit St. (btw. Waterman and College sts.). Ⓒ 401/454-6500. www.risdmuseum.org. Admission $8 adults, $5 seniors, $3 college students with ID, $2 children 5–18; free to all the 3rd Thurs of the month 5–9pm, Sun 10am–1pm, last Sat of month. Tues–Sun 10am–5pm (Thurs until 9pm).

Providence Athenaeum   The Providence Athenaeum commissioned this 1838 Greek Revival building to house its lending library, the fourth-oldest in the United States and an innovative concept at the time. Edgar Allan Poe courted Sarah Whitman, his "Annabel Lee," among these shelves. Glances through the old card catalog reveal handwritten cards dating well back into the 1800s; bibliophiles will lose themselves in this evocative place. Rotating exhibits of rare books and works by local artists are additional attractions. The library has money problems that have contributed to a contretemps over ways to raise funds, specifically a decision to sell off an Audubon folio valued at $7 million.

251 Benefit St. (at College St.). Ⓒ 401/421-6970. www.providenceathenaeum.org. Free admission. Mon–Thurs 9am–7pm; Fri–Sat 9am–5pm; Sun 1–5pm. Closed first 2 weeks in Aug.

Rhode Island State House   Constructed of white Georgian marble that blazes in the sun, the 1900 capitol dominates the city center. This near-flawless example of neo-classical governmental architecture (by McKim, Mead & White; 1891–92) boasts one of the largest self-supported domes in the world. The gilded figure on top represents "Independent Man," the state symbol. Inside, a portrait of George Washington is given pride of place, one of many depictions painted by Gilbert Stuart, a Rhode Island native.

82 Smith St. (btw. Francis and Hayes sts.). Ⓒ 401/277-2357. Free admission. Guided tours by appointment Mon–Fri 8:30am–noon.

Roger Williams Park Zoo ⚡ *Kids*   The zoo is divided into three principal habitats: Tropical America, the Farmyard, and the Plains of Africa. A newer exhibit is devoted to Australia, with the zoo's first saltwater aquarium. A walk-through aviary and under-water viewing areas with polar bears, sea lions, and harbor seals are additional attractions, and there are a museum of natural history and a planetarium. The facility has looked a bit bedraggled of late, but not enough to deter visits.

1000 Elmwood Ave. (at exit 17 off I-95). Ⓒ 401/785-3510. www.rogerwilliamsparkzoo.org. Admission $12 adults, $8 seniors, $6 children ages 3–12. Early Apr–Oct Mon–Fri 9am–5pm; mid-Oct to mid-Apr daily 9am–4pm. Driving south on I-95, take exit 17; driving north, take exit 16.

SHOPPING

Thayer Street, the main commercial district for the university, is home to the official **Brown Bookstore,** at no. 244 (at the corner of Olive St.). Also in the vicinity are **Silverberry's,** at no. 220, with dressy and casual clothes for college-age women, and **Hillhouse,** no. 135, long in the business of providing male Brownies with Ivy dress-up clothes for interview weeks and parents' days.

WHERE TO STAY

The clusters of motels around most of the exits from I-95 and I-195 offer decent value. Among these possibilities are the **Days Hotel,** 220 India St. (© **401/272-5577;** www.daysinn.com), and the **Ramada Inn,** 940 Fall River Ave., Seekonk, MA (© **508/336-7300;** www.ramada.com). Rates at area inns and motels invariably go up on alumni and parents' weekends and during graduation weeks.

Courtyard by Marriott ✿   This Downcity hotel's style and exterior materials harmonize with the adjacent former Union Station complex, and it completed a 3-month renovation in early 2008. As a midpriced entry designed primarily for businesspeople, its rooms are equipped with two-line phones, free Wi-Fi, and well-lit desks. It is just as comfortable for leisure travelers, with several of our recommended restaurants, the new Providence Place mall, and WaterFires only minutes away. While the on-site cafe doesn't serve dinner, meals can be delivered from nearby restaurants.

32 Exchange Terrace, Providence, RI 02903. © **800/321-2211** or 401/272-1191. Fax 401/272-1416. www.courtyard. com. 216 units. $159–$279 double. AE, DC, DISC, MC, V. **Amenities:** Cafe/bar (breakfast and cocktails); indoor pool w/whirlpool; exercise room; business center; coin-op laundry; same-day dry cleaning. In room: A/C, TV w/pay movies, free Wi-Fi, coffeemaker, hair dryer, iron.

Hotel Providence ✿✿   A dazzling contribution to the emerging downtown Arts and Entertainment District, this boutique hotel, combining two buildings, gained instant membership in the selective Small Luxury Hotels of the World marketing group. The owners filled the lobby and main halls with fine 18th- and 19th-century European antiques and artworks, and commissioned custom reproductions for the bedrooms to carry through with the image thus created. There are wireless hotspots in public areas. Guests are serenaded at 15-minute intervals by the pealing of the 16 bells of Grace Church, across the street, so light sleepers will want a room away from that side of the hotel.

311 Westminster St., Providence, RI 02903. © **800/861-8990** or 401/861-8000. Fax 401/861-8002. www.thehotel providence.com. 80 units. $189–$359 double. Packages available. AE, DC, DISC, MC, V. Valet parking $18. Small pets allowed. **Amenities:** Restaurant (Italian); piano bar; small fitness room; concierge; business center; room service; same-day laundry; dry cleaning. In room: A/C, TV w/movies, free Wi-Fi, CD player, coffeemaker, hair dryer, iron, robes, safe.

Providence Biltmore ✿✿   A grand staircase beneath the stunning Deco bronze ceiling dates the centrally located building to the 1920s, and a plaque in the lobby shows the nearly 7-foot-high water level of the villainous 1938 hurricane. From the lobby, the dramatic glass elevator shoots skyward, exiting outdoors to scoot up the side of the building. Most guest rooms are large, half of them with more than 600 square feet of floor space; some of the 20 suites have kitchenettes. King or California king beds are standard. There's an Elizabeth Arden Red Door Spa on-site, too. No pets.

11 Dorrance St., Providence, RI 02903. © **800/294-7709** or 401/421-0700. Fax 401/455-3127. www.providencebiltmore. com. 289 units. $199–$229 double. AE, DC, MC, V. Valet parking $24. **Amenities:** Restaurant; bar; fitness center; concierge; business center; limited room service; babysitting; laundry; dry cleaning. In room: A/C, TV, VCR available, Wi-Fi, coffeemaker, hair dryer, iron.

Renaissance Providence ✿✿✿   Here's a story: In the late 1920s, the Masons were building a neoclassical temple a couple of blocks west of the State House. The Masons ran out of money and construction suddenly ended, leaving the building an empty shell. There it stood for 78 years, unoccupied, a magnet for graffiti vandals and thieves. But over $100 million has transformed it into this ambitious luxury hotel, a rival to the best the city has to offer. A grand lobby with a fireplace welcomes guests, some of whom choose one of the two executive floors, with their private club lounge. An up-to-the-minute fitness center is up there, too. Only 2 weeks after opening in the summer of 2007, the staff proved to be carefully trained, cheerful, and efficient. **Temple**, the flashy restaurant-bar downstairs, was an instant hit with locals as well as hotel guests.

5 Ave. of the Arts (labeled on most maps as Brownell St.), Providence, RI 02903. *©* **800/468-3571** or 401/276-0010. Fax 401/276-0023. www.renaissancehotels.com. 272 units. $179–$299 double. AE, DC, DISC, MC, V. Valet parking $21. **Amenities:** 1 restaurant (fusion); 1 bar; fitness center w/spa; concierge; business center; room service; babysitting; same-day laundry; dry cleaning. *In room:* A/C, TV w/pay movies, high-speed Internet, minibar, coffeemaker, hair dryer, iron, safe.

Westin Providence 🟊🟊🟊   This is easily the city's most important hotel, with a luxurious interior and a downtown location. Skyways connect the hotel with the Providence Place mall and the convention center. Bedrooms are equipped with the patented Heavenly Bed sheets, pillows, and mattresses. The architectural grandeur of the lobby rotunda and other public spaces is only improved by the sunny dispositions of the staff. Off the lobby is a lounge with the buffed glow of an exclusive men's club. **Agora,** the main dining room, gets excellent reviews from critics and serves all meals. A 31-story, 200-unit tower was recently added to the main building. Westin hotels are non-smoking.

1 West Exchange St., Providence, RI 02903. *©* **800/937-8461** or 401/598-8000. Fax 401/598-8200. www.starwood hotels.com/westin. 364 units. $229–$314 double. AE, DC, DISC, MC, V. Valet parking $18. **Amenities:** 2 restaurants (eclectic, American); 2 bars; indoor pool; fully equipped health club w/Jacuzzi and sauna; concierge; business center; limited room service; babysitting; same-day laundry; dry cleaning. *In room:* A/C, TV w/pay movies, high-speed Internet, fridge, coffeemaker, hair dryer, iron, safe.

WHERE TO DINE

Providence has a sturdy Italian heritage, resulting in a profusion of tomato-sauce and pizza joints, especially on Federal Hill, the city's "Little Italy" west of downtown and I-95. That identity is starting to change, with an influx of more international shops and restaurants, but a stroll along the main drag of the district, Atwells Avenue between Bradford and Sutton, can set off furious hunger alarms, satisfied by a stop at **Costantino's Venda Ravioli,** 265–275 Atwells Ave. (*©* **401/421-9105;** www.venda ravioli.com). It started out as a simple retail pasta store but has expanded into a little empire of prepared foods, an espresso bar, large cheese and meat sections, packaged Italian specialties, and cafe tables inside and out on the terrace.

One fruitful strip to explore for lower-cost dining options is that part of **Thayer Street** bordering the Brown University campus. It counts Thai, Tex-Mex, barbecue, and Indian restaurants among its possibilities.

Cafe Nuovo 🟊🟊🟊 FUSION   This spacious room of glass, marble, and burnished wood occupies part of the ground floor of a downtown office tower that overlooks the confluence of the Moshassuck and Woonasquatucket rivers. (It makes an ideal overlook for the WaterFire events.) Unlike its local competitor, Al Forno, which gets the greater share of praise and ink (largely undeserved), Cafe Nuovo takes reservations, is open for lunch *and* dinner, and impresses with every course, from dazzling appetizers to stunning pastries. The fare may be grounded in the Italian repertoire, but it skips lightly among other inspirations, too—Greek and Portuguese among them. That culinary restlessness leads to such dishes as the macadamia-and-goat-cheese-crusted rack of lamb with Swiss chard and white zinfandel sauce. There's music on weekends and outdoor dining in warm weather. Restaurants come and go, but Cafe Nuovo endures, steady and embracing.

1 Citizens Plaza (access is from the Steeple St. bridge). ⓒ **401/421-2525.** www.cafenuovo.com. Reservations advised. Main courses $24–$36. AE, DC, DISC, MC, V. Mon–Fri 11:30am–3pm; Mon–Thurs 5–10:30pm; Fri–Sat 5–11pm. Closed 1st week in Jan.

CAV 👁👁 ECLECTIC   No corporate design drudge had a hand in *this* warehouse interior, a Jewelry District pioneer. CAV is an acronym for "Cocktails/Antiques/Vict-uals," and patrons are surrounded by tribal rugs, African carvings, and assorted antiques (most for sale). Turkish kilims under glass cover the tables. The resulting bohemian air is not unlike Greenwich Village in the 1960s, complete with live jazz or blues on weekends ($5 cover usually). Attractive servers bring dishes prepared by folks quite accomplished at their craft. Select from such strenuous menu swings as pista-chio-crusted crab cake with sriracha aioli and fried lotus root to the delectable overkill of roasted venison rack with grilled venison sausage, potato and fruit samosa, long beans, and anise-star demiglace. Every day brings a choice of special soup, appetizer, pasta, and a crispy thin-crusted pizza or two.

14 Imperial Place (near Basset St.). ⓒ **401/751-9164.** www.cavrestaurant.com. Reservations recommended. Main courses $16–$29. DISC, MC, V. Mon–Thurs 11:30am–10pm; Fri–Sat 11:30am–1am; Sun 10:30am–10pm.

Chez Pascal 👁👁 FRENCH   It's a longish drive north from the Brown campus, but this warm little bistro is worth it. Candlelight trembles over sponged ochre walls and dark wainscoting. The kitchen works in the French tradition but isn't dogmatic about it. The variety of house-made pâtés and charcuterie is unusually large; the enthusiasm for them prompted the chef to set up a gourmet hot dog cart in the park across the street in summer. Order a "pork sampler," and they bring chops, sausage, and barbe-cue on a bed of leeks and spinach with a potato pancake on top. The desires of vege-tarians aren't ignored, with a vegetable cassoulet and a three-course dinner of potato terrine, eggplant, peppers, and onions as a starter. To bring in patrons on slow Tues-days, Wednesdays, and Thursdays there's a fixed-price menu for $28. A bell-ringer dessert is the apple galette—bread pudding with a ball of cinnamon ice cream.

960 Hope St. (corner of 9th St.). ⓒ **401/421-4422.** www.chez-pascal.com. Reservations advised. Main courses $22–$27. AE, DC, MC, V. Tues–Thurs 5:30–9:30pm; Fri–Sat 5:30–10pm.

Gracie's 👁 NEW AMERICAN   Moved to the downtown Arts District from its for-mer Federal Hill address, this longtime favorite hasn't lost a smidgen of its old verve. Pinlights in the ceiling hint at the night sky, a theme carried out with rather too much enthusiasm in the proliferation of five-pointed stars scattered over the rest of the room. That aside, there are unlikely to be legit complaints about either the food or the people who bring it. It all starts with an *amuse bouche*—on one occasion, a tiny cup of broccoli soup with lemon oil. The first course can be the artisanal cheese tasting accompanied by pistachios, pepper jelly, and blueberry compote. Carnivores will be more than sated by the loin of lamb with an olive and almond crust with haricot verts and morel bordelaise. While the entrees mostly involve grilled or roasted meats, an elaborate tasting of fruits and vegetables is also available. A three-course theater menu for $40 is available from 5 to 7pm (the Trinity Repertory Company is across the street), and on Thursday they hold a free wine and cheese tasting from 5 to 7pm.

194 Washington St. ⓒ **401/272-7811.** www.graciesprov.com. Reservations advised. Main courses $24–$30. AE, DC, MC, V. Tues–Sat 5–10pm; Sun 4pm–10pm.

Tips Big Tastes Hide in Little Rhody

You'd think, in an age of instant communication, that no ingratiatingly fla-vorful edible tidbit or preparation would stay unknown for long. Worthy regional specialties fast become national staples—think Buffalo wings, Carolina blooming onions, Texan burritos. But Rhode Islanders are tight-fisted about their food secrets, and even residents of neighboring states are in the dark. So while you're visiting, try to check out some of the following:

- **Rhode Island clam chowder** is a clear broth, neither tomato- nor cream-based, as are, respectively, the far better-known Manhattan and New England versions.

- **Stuffies** come in as many versions as there are cooks. At Flo's Clam Shack in Newport, big quahog clams are chopped up with hot and sweet pep-pers and bread crumbs, packed inside the two shell halves, and shut, the whole held together by a rubber band and baked. The mixture assumes the consistency of setting plaster but is no less tasty for that.

- **Johnnycakes** (also known as jonnycakes) are breakfast fodder, some as thin as crepes, others as thick as standard griddlecakes. The difference from the conventional pancakes is the primary ingredient, cornmeal. Honey is a common topping.

- **Clam cakes** are as inaccurately named as Brooklyn egg creams (which have neither eggs nor cream). These aren't cakes, but deep-fried fritters, and the clams therein are notable primarily for their virtual absence.

- **Coffee milk** and **cabinets** are the obligatory beverages to go with Rhody chow. The first is made with sweet coffee syrup, while the second is what the rest of America thinks of as a milkshake.

- **New York System Wieners** have only a passing acquaintance with Big Apple franks. In Rhode Island, the wieners are short—3 or 4 inches long—served on soft steamed buns and topped (usually) with a chili-type meat sauce, minced onion, and mustard. Nobody eats just one—the typical ration is four or more.

So step up to the counter and demand "Four all the way, extra sauce, and a coffee milk." You thus commence your initiation into the mysteries of the Rhode Island food culture. And did we mention Gray's Ice Cream (p. 430).)?

MuMu ★★ ASIAN   Smack in the middle of the busiest, most Italian part of Federal Hill is this Chinese restaurant that looks the part, with a black and scarlet color scheme, little vases of fresh flowers on each table, and a menu that goes on forever. But there is a knowing presence in command here. The middle-aged woman in sweater set and slacks who might welcome you is the owner of this and several other restaurants in China, Taiwan, and the U.S. She's behind the sorcery of the *xiao long bao*, pork dumplings with a tablespoon of broth *inside*, which bursts over your chin if you're not careful. Additional specialties include Sichuan chili ravioli, which is what it sounds like and delectable, tender beef with mustard greens in black bean sauce, and boneless spareribs with sautéed garlic. If you've never had Peking duck because of the advance ordering requirement, try it here, where it will arrive by the time you've downed your appetizer. Or make a meal of *dim sum*—there are eight of them.

220 Atwells Ave. (near Dean St.). ⓒ **401/369-7040**. Main courses $7.25–$16. AE, MC, V. Sun–Mon, Wed–Thurs 11am–10pm; Fri–Sat 11am–11pm.

Rue de l'Espoir AMERICAN BISTRO   When everyplace else on College Hill is closed, full, or downright tacky, there's always The Rue. It serves breakfast or brunch, lunch, and dinner every day, a rebuke to those restaurateurs who can barely bring themselves to open 5 nights a week for a couple of hours. It is filled with people of all ages, from Brown frosh to retirees. Easily the most popular brunch in town proffers "Rue Melt," an irresistible assemblage of English muffin, Thai crab cake, poached eggs, home fries, and lemon-grass aioli. The brunch prices don't hurt, either: only $9 to $12 for main courses. During the week, dinners run to bouillabaisse, miso-glazed halibut, and lamb served two ways. The three-course dinner prix-fixe costs $25.

99 Hope St. ⓒ **401/751-8890**. www.therue.com. Reservations recommended, essential on weekends. Main courses $25–$32. AE, DC, MC, V. Daily 7:30–11am, 11:30am–2:30pm, and 5–9pm.

Siena 🕊 ITALIAN   Federal Hill's days as a tomato gravy and pizza destination are fading, replaced by upbeat, contemporary chefs and owners who value quality and are alert to trends. Siena isn't your grandpa's spaghetti joint: With "Tuscan Soul Food," it draws all ages (including an occasional shrieking child) and is among the hottest new places in town. That ardor might cool, but for the moment, it is full and loud. Waitstaff is more knowledgeable and attentive than average. There are pizzas, the thin, wood-grilled, upscale kind, and the antipasti may distract your attention from the rest of the card. Give full consideration, though, to the *pollo al Diavolo,* the chicken breasts with an herb and hot red pepper rub; and the *aragosta cioppino,* the San Francisco fish stew of lobster, shrimp, clams, mussels, swordfish, and calamari in a spicy broth. You won't be disappointed.

238 Atwells Ave. ⓒ **401/521-3311**. www.sienaprovidence.com. Reservations strongly advised. Main courses $16–$29. AE, DC, MC, V. Mon–Fri 5–10pm; Sat 4:30–11pm; Sun 3–10pm.

Temple 🕊 AMERICAN BISTRO   At this writing, this restaurant in the new Renaissance Providence hotel (see above) enjoys the avid interest of young professionals and older sophisticates, and that's only a month after the soft opening. Walking in, you may think you've wandered through a wrong door into a disco. The music and crowd of seekers-after-companionship are in full voice. The mirrors, tiles, and other hard surfaces in the dining room ensure that the noise level restaurateurs love doesn't dip much below 70 decibels.

That aside, the waitstaff is earnest and good-looking, and the food, while short of truly memorable, proves to be fun variations of old favorites. It's a little tricky to ferret out the best choices, given their listing under such menu headings as "Flatbreads," "Snacks," "Field" (vegetables), and "Templates" (mains). Typical are the stuffies, a twist on the Rhody staple, here served as breaded clams with chorizo baked in open shells. The plate of fried calamari is easily enough for two, and mussels in cream sauce come with a paper cone of Belgian-style *frites.*

120 Francis St. (Ave. of the Arts). ⓒ **401/919/5050**. www.temple-downtown.com. Reservations advised. Main courses $15–$26. Mon noon–1am; Tues–Sat 6:30am–1am; Sun 6:30am–midnight.

QUICK BITES

Providence claims the invention of the diner, starting with a horse-drawn wagon transporting food down Westminster Street in 1872. The tradition is carried forward by the likes of the **Seaplane Diner,** 307 Allens Ave. ((*© 401/941-9547**), a silver-sided classic with tableside jukeboxes, and **Richard's Diner,** 377 Richmond St. ((*© 401/331-8541**), so small you can walk across it in six strides.

A bona fide National Historic Landmark is an unlikely venue for snarfing up cookies, souvlaki, and egg rolls, but **The Arcade,** 65 Weybosset St. ((*© 401/598-1199**), is a 19th-century progenitor of 20th-century shopping malls, an 1828 Greek Revival structure that runs between Weybosset and Westminster streets. Its main floor is given over largely to fast-food stands and snack counters of the usual kinds—yes, the Golden Arches, too—while the upper floor is primarily boutiques and souvenir shops.

Another local culinary institution arrives in Kennedy Plaza on wheels every afternoon around 4:30pm. The grungy aluminum-sided **Haven Bros.** ((*© 401/861-7777**) is a food tractor-trailer with a counter and six stools inside and good deals on decent burgers and even better fries sold from its parking space next to City Hall. No new frontiers here, except that it hangs around until way past midnight to dampen the hunger pangs of club-goers, lawyers, night people, and workaholic pols.

PROVIDENCE AFTER DARK

This being a college town, there is no end of music bars, small concert halls, and pool pubs. A good source of information is the free weekly *Providence Phoenix* (www.providencephoenix.com).

THE PERFORMING ARTS   The **Opera Providence** ((*© 401/331-6060;** www.operaprovidence.org) stages three or four productions a season at various locations, including the Veterans Memorial Auditorium. The **Rhode Island Philharmonic** ((*© 401/831-3123;** www.ri-philharmonic.org) usually appears at the Providence Performing Arts Center or the Veterans Memorial Auditorium. Big-ticket touring musicals on the order of *Rent, The Producers,* and *Monty Python's Spamalot,* as well as traveling dance companies and other attractions, are showcased at the **Providence Performing Arts Center,** 220 Weybosset St. ((*© 401/421-ARTS;** www.ppacri.org), while new plays share space with Chekov, Albee, and Shakespeare at the **Trinity Repertory Company,** 201 Washington St. ((*© 401/351-4242;** www.trinityrep.com). The **Dunkin' Doughnuts Center,** 1 La Salle Sq. ((*© 401/331-2211;** www.dunkindonutscenter.com), between the Convention Center and the Holiday Inn Downtown, hosts stellar performers and acts (Bruce Springsteen, among them), along with up-and-comers.

THE CLUB & MUSIC SCENE   A tragic nightclub fire in 2003 at the Station in Warwick killed 100 patrons. Strict and expensive regulations were imposed on nightclubs and other music venues, compelling some places to suspend operations or close permanently.

One prominent survivor is **Lupo's Heartbreak Hotel,** 79 Washington St. ((*© 401/272-5876;** www.lupos.com). Formerly at 239 Westminster St., it still hosts a variety of live concerts 2 or 3 nights a week. Tickets can be purchased at www.etix.com; they usually cost between $18 and $35.

For jazz and blues 5 to 7 nights a week, head to the **Hi-Hat,** 3 Davol Sq. ((*© 401/453-6500;** www.thehihat.com). Find it near the west end of the Point Street bridge.

If a heavy bar scene isn't appealing, there's always **AS220,** 115 Empire St. (✆ **401/ 831-9327;** www.as220.org), which describes itself as "a nonprofit community arts center with work studios" for mostly local visual, musical, and performance artists. It hosts 10 to 12 events every week. Similar in mission is **Tazza Caffee & Lounge,** 250 Westminster St. (✆ **401/421-3300;** www.tazzacaffe.com), an espresso bar open daily from early morning to late night that puts on fashion shows, sculpture exhibits, and poetry readings to go with films and jazz and blues combos.

Many restaurants in the city engage musical groups 2 or more nights a week. These include **CAV,** described under "Where to Dine," above. At the **Trinity Brewhouse,** 186 Fountain St. (✆ **401/453-2337;** www.trinitybrewhouse.com), live jazz and blues share attention with boutique beers, a pool table, and a deck.

MOVIES   For art-house films and midnight cult movies, check the **Avon Cinema,** 260 Thayer St., near Meeting Street (✆ **401/421-3315;** www.avoncinema.com), or the **Cable Car,** 204 South Main St. (✆ **401/272-3970;** www.cablecarcinema.com), which has comfy sofas and free popcorn refills.

2 Sakonnet Point

As a break from the urbanity of Providence or the concentration of sights and activities that is Newport, a side trip down the length of the oddly isolated southeastern corner of Rhode Island is a soothing excursion.

No one has thought to throw a bridge or run a ferry across the water between Newport and Sakonnet Point, prospects the reclusive residents would no doubt resist to the last lawsuit. They have been known to steal road signs to discourage summer visitors, and almost no enterprises are specifically geared to attract tourists. Things are quiet in these parts, and they intend to keep it that way.

To get here from Providence or Boston, pick up I-195 east, then Route 24 south, toward Newport. Take exit 4 for Route 77 south, just before the Sakonnet River Bridge. From Newport, take Route 138 toward Fall River, and exit on Route 77 south immediately after crossing the bridge.

After a welter of small businesses, most of them involved in some way with the ocean, Route 77 smoothes out into a pastoral Brigadoon, not quite rural, but more rustic than suburban. Colonial farmhouses, real or replicated, bear sidings of weathered shakes the color of wood smoke. They are centered in tidy lawns, bordered by miles of low stone walls. No plastic deer, no tomato plants in front yards—it's as if a requirement of residence were attendance at a school of good taste.

WHAT TO SEE & DO

There are a few antiques shops and roadside farm stands along the way, and a cluster of shops and eating places at Tiverton Four Corners, about halfway down the point. The building on the near-right corner of that intersection is **Provender,** 3883 Main Rd. (✆ **401/624-8084**), a lunch counter famed for its veggie sandwich, the "Great Garbanzo." It's closed from Christmas until spring. On the far-left corner, at the edge of the parking lot, is a destination dear to the hearts of Rhode Islanders. **Gray's Ice Cream,** 16 East Rd. (✆ **401/624-4500**), scoops out 32 flavors of the super-premium dessert, along with 11 more sherbets and frozen yogurts. Coffee is the best-selling flavor. It's open daily from 6:30am to 7pm in winter, until 9pm in summer.

Another good reason to pull off the road is **Sakonnet Vineyards** ⋆, 162 W. Main Rd. (✆ **401/635-8486;** www.sakonnetwine.com), with an entrance road on the left, about 3 miles south of Tiverton Four Corners. In operation since 1975, it is one of New England's oldest wineries and produces 30,000 cases of creditable wines annually. Types range from a popular pinot noir to an honored vidal blanc. Bring along a picnic lunch, then buy a bottle and retire to one of the tables beside the pond. There's also a tasting room open daily from 10am to 6pm in summer, 11am to 5pm in winter. They charge $7 for tastings of six wines (from a list of 12), and you get to keep the glass.

Continuing south on Route 77, the road skirts Little Compton and heads on to **Sakonnet Point,** where the inland terrain gives way to stony beaches and coastal marshes. There's a wetlands wildlife refuge, a small harbor with working boats, and not much else.

Now head back north on Route 77, watching for the sign pointing toward Adamsville. Take the right turn at the triangular traffic island just beyond, onto a road that seems to have neither name nor number. Shortly, it arrives at a T intersection with a Congregational church and the C. R. Wilbur general store. This is downtown **Little Compton.** Long situated next to the store was a communal gathering spot, the **Common's** restaurant. It burned to the ground in 2005 but has been rebuilt and is the likeliest place for a snack or lunch in the area. Turn left (north), and you're back in the country. In less than 2 miles, the road ends at Peckham Road. Turn left to return to Route 77, and turn right (north) to return to your original destination.

WHERE TO DINE

Boat House ✦ SEAFOOD   Opened in 2005, largely as a service to the occupants of the condo development rising on the hill behind it, the restaurant emphasizes fish. Originally, it was on a May-to-Columbus-Day schedule, but it proved so popular, management decided to keep it open all year. That's understandable: There's that wide vista of Sakonnet Bay, and the food is fresh, clean, and varied. Raw clams and oysters are from the region, the seafood stew has local ingredients, and the salads are large enough to serve as light lunches, especially when you choose to add chicken, salmon, or shrimp. Among the listed "munchies" are Thai mussels steamed in coconut curry with Asian vegetables and soba noodle. Most of the entrees are uncomplicated but tasty, from fish-and-chips to tuna and the double-thick pork chop. This is good place to try out the wines of Sakonnet Vineyards.

227 Schooner Dr., Tiverton. ⓒ **401/624-6300.** www.boathousetiverton.com. Main courses $14–$32. AE, DISC, MC, V. Mon–Sat 11:30am–9pm (until 10pm Fri–Sat); Sun 11am–9pm. Take exit 5 coming from Newport; the restaurant is north of the Sakonnet River Bridge.

Evelyn's Drive-In ⟨Value⟩ SEAFOOD   No Rhody food adventure is complete without a visit to an authentic clam shack. There are at least a dozen dotted along the coast beside beaches and inlets, and Evelyn's is one of the first a local is likely to recommend. There's a takeout window in front, a dining room with air-conditioning, and many more tables on the terrace out back, some roofed over, others with umbrellas. The menu lists all the seaside essentials—clear clam chowder, clam cakes, stuffies, calamari, fried scallops, lobster rolls—see p. 427 for descriptions of some of these peculiarly native treats. Fried clams are either whole-bellied (for purists) or strips (who find the bellies squishy), but all are committed to the snapping-hot oil not one second longer than necessary to reach nutty crispiness. There are plenty of nonmarine dishes, including a popular chicken pie and meat loaf. There's a full-service bar.

2335 Main Rd. (Rte. 77), Tiverton. ⓒ **401/624-3100.** www.evelynsdrivein.com. Main courses $5–$15. MC, V. Daily 11:30am–8pm (until 8:30pm Fri–Sun).

3 Newport (★(★(★

75 miles S of Boston; 115 miles NE of New Haven

"City by the Sea" is the unimaginative nickname an early resident unloaded on Newport. At least it was accurate, because for a time during the Colonial period it rivaled Boston and even New York as a center of New World trade and prosperity. Newport occupies the southern tip of Aquidneck Island in Narragansett Bay and is connected to the mainland by three bridges and a ferry.

Wealthy industrialists, railroad tycoons, coal magnates, financiers, and robber barons were drawn to the area in the 19th century, especially between the Civil War and World War I. They bought up property at the ocean's rim to build what they called summer "cottages"—which were, in fact, mansions of immoderate design and proportions patterned after European palaces.

The principal toys of the Newport elite were equally extravagant yachts meant for pleasure, not commerce, and competition among them established Newport's reputation as a sailing center. In 1851, the schooner *America* defeated a British boat in a race around the Isle of Wight. The prize trophy became known as the America's Cup, which remained in the possession of the New York Yacht Club (with an outpost in Newport) until 1983. In that shocking summer, *Australia II* snatched the Cup away from *Liberty* in the last race of a four-out-of-seven series. An American team regained the cup in 1987, but in 1995 a New Zealand crew took it away. The strong U.S. yachting tradition has endured despite the loss of the Cup, and Newport continues as a bastion of world sailing and a destination for long-distance races.

The perimeter of the city resembles a heeled boot, its toe pointing west, not unlike Italy. About where the laces of the boot would be is the downtown business and residential district. Several wharves push into the bay, providing support and mooring for flotillas of pleasure craft. Much of the strolling, shopping, eating, quaffing, and gawking is done along this waterfront and its parallel streets: America's Cup Avenue and Thames Street. (The latter used to be pronounced "Tems," in the British manner but was Americanized to "Thaymz" after the Revolution.)

The navy pulled out its battleships, causing a decline in the local economy, but it hasn't proven to be the disaster predicted by some, and Newport has been spared the coarser intrusions that afflict so many coastal resorts. T-shirt emporia have kept within reasonable limits—a remarkable feat, considering that Newport has nearly 4 million visitors a year.

Immediately east and north of the business district are blocks of Colonial, Federal, and Victorian houses of the 18th and 19th centuries, many of them designated National Historic Sites. Happily, they are not frozen in amber but are very much in use as residences, restaurants, offices, and shops. Taken together, they are as visually appealing in their own way as the 40-room cottages of the super-rich.

So despite Newport's prevailing image as a collection of stupefyingly ornate mansions and regattas of sailing ships inaccessible to all but the rich and famous, the city is, for the most part, middle class and not too immoderately priced. Scores of inns and B&Bs ensure lodging even during festival weeks, at rates and fixtures from budget to ultraluxury level. In almost every respect, this is the "First Resort" of the New England coast.

ESSENTIALS

GETTING THERE   From New York City, take I-95 to the third Newport exit, picking up Route 138 east (which joins briefly with Rte. 4) and crossing the Newport toll bridge slightly north of the downtown district. From Boston, take Route 24 through Fall River, picking up Route 114 into town.

T. F. Green/Providence Airport (© 401/737-8222) in Warwick, south of Providence (exit 13, I-95), handles national flights into the state. Major airlines serving this airport include **American** (© 800/433-7300), **Continental** (© 800/525-3273), **Delta** (© 800/221-1212), **Northwest** (© 800/225-2525), **Southwest** (© 800/435-9792), **United** (© 800/864-8331), and **US Airways** (© 800/428-4322). A few of the larger Newport hotels provide shuttle service, as does **Cozy Cab** (© 401/846-2500).

The **Rhode Island Public Transit Authority,** or **RIPTA** (© **800/244-0444** or 401/781-9400; www.ripta.com), runs up to 28 buses a day on the 70-minute ride between Providence's Kennedy Plaza and the Newport Gateway Visitor Center. One-way fare is $1.50.

RIPTA also has **ferry service** between Point Street Landing in Providence and Perrotti Park, near Newport's Gateway Center. From mid-May to mid-October, there are six departures daily. One-way fare is $8 for adults and $6 for seniors and children 5 to 11; younger children ride free.

VISITOR INFORMATION   For advance information available 24 hours, call **visitor information** (© **800/976-5122** outside Rhode Island, 800/556-2484 in Rhode Island; www.goNewport.com). In town, stop by the excellent **Newport Gateway Visitor Center,** 23 America's Cup Ave. (© **800/326-6030** or 401/849-8048). Open daily from 9am to 5pm (until 6pm Fri–Sat), it has attendants on duty, a lodging-availability service, a cafe, and panoramic photos showing the locations of mansions, parks, and other landmarks. A TV monitor lists regularly updated lists of inns and hotels with available rooms. The building is shared with the bus station.

PARKING & GETTING AROUND   Most of Newport's attractions, except for the mansions, can be reached easily on foot, so leaving your car at your hotel or inn is wise. Parking lots aren't cheap, especially at the waterfront, and many streets are narrow. The metered parking along Thames Street is closely monitored by police, and fines are steep (although Nov–Apr the meters are hooded and parking is free for up to 3 hr.). Renting or bringing a bicycle is an attractive option.

RIPTA, the **Rhode Island Public Transit Authority** (© 401/781-9400), has several trolley/bus routes through town, making stops at major sights. Service originates at the Gateway Information Center. Fare is $1.50.

SPECIAL EVENTS   Arrive any day in summer, and you can expect to find at least a half-dozen festivals, competitions, or other events in progress. Following is only a partial list. (Call ahead to confirm dates: © **800/263-4636** outside Rhode Island, or 401/848-2000 in Rhode Island).

While there are a few substantive events in the off season, notably **Christmas in Newport** (© **401/849-6454;** www.christmasinnewport.org) and the February **Winter Festival** (© **401/847-7666;** www.newportwinterfestival.com), which focuses on food and winter sports, the pace ratchets up in June, starting with the **Great Chowder Cook-Off** (© **401/846-1600;** www.newportfestivals.com).

In the third week of July is the **Black Ships Festival** (© **401/846-2720;** www.newportevents.com), a celebration of all aspects of Japanese culture.

August brings the **Newport Folk Festival** (www.newportfolk.com) and the 4-day **JVC Jazz Festival—Newport** (© **866/468-7619;** www.festivalproductions.net), both

Newport

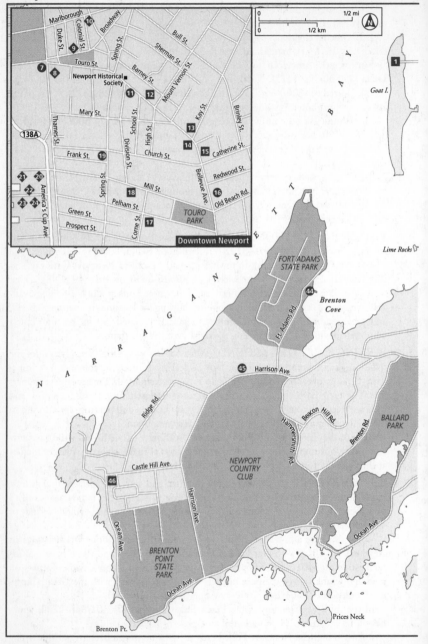

Downtown Newport

- Marlborough
- Broadway
- Duke St.
- Colonial St.
- Bull St.
- Spring St.
- Sherman St.
- Barney St.
- Touro St.
- Mount Vernon St.
- Newport Historical Society
- Mary St.
- Thames St.
- School St.
- High St.
- Kay St.
- Brinley St.
- Frank St.
- Division St.
- Church St.
- Catherine St.
- Redwood St.
- Bellevue Ave.
- Old Beach Rd.
- Mill St.
- Spring St.
- Pelham St.
- Green St.
- Corne St.
- America's Cup Ave.
- Prospect St.
- TOURO PARK

138A

1/2 mi
1/2 km

NARRAGANSETT BAY

Goat I.

Lime Rocks

FORT ADAMS STATE PARK

Ft. Adams Rd.

Brenton Cove

Harrison Ave.

Ridge Rd.

Beacon Hill Rd.

Hammersmith Rd.

Brenton Rd.

BALLARD PARK

NEWPORT COUNTRY CLUB

Castle Hill Ave.

Harrison Ave.

Ocean Ave.

BRENTON POINT STATE PARK

Ocean Ave.

Brenton Pt.

Prices Neck

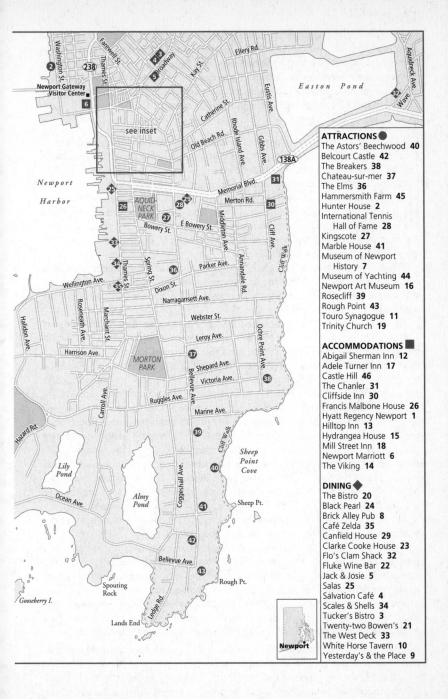

ATTRACTIONS ●
The Astors' Beechwood **40**
Belcourt Castle **42**
The Breakers **38**
Chateau-sur-mer **37**
The Elms **36**
Hammersmith Farm **45**
Hunter House **2**
International Tennis
 Hall of Fame **28**
Kingscote **27**
Marble House **41**
Museum of Newport
 History **7**
Museum of Yachting **44**
Newport Art Museum **16**
Rosecliff **39**
Rough Point **43**
Touro Synagogue **11**
Trinity Church **19**

ACCOMMODATIONS ■
Abigail Sherman Inn **12**
Adele Turner Inn **17**
Castle Hill **46**
The Chanler **31**
Cliffside Inn **30**
Francis Malbone House **26**
Hyatt Regency Newport **1**
Hilltop Inn **13**
Hydrangea House **15**
Mill Street Inn **18**
Newport Marriott **6**
The Viking **14**

DINING ◆
The Bistro **20**
Black Pearl **24**
Brick Alley Pub **8**
Café Zelda **35**
Canfield House **29**
Clarke Cooke House **23**
Flo's Clam Shack **32**
Fluke Wine Bar **22**
Jack & Josie **5**
Salas **25**
Salvation Café **4**
Scales & Shells **34**
Tucker's Bistro **3**
Twenty-two Bowen's **21**
The West Deck **33**
White Horse Tavern **10**
Yesterday's & the Place **9**

held at Fort Adams State Park. In early September, the gardens of the Point section of town are open to visitors during the **Secret Garden Tour** (© 401/847-0514; www.secretgardentour.com). The **Waterfront Irish Festival** (© 401/846-1600; www. newportwaterfrontevents.com) arrives in early September, **Oktoberfest** (www.newport festivals.com) on Columbus Day weekend, and the **Bowen's Wharf Seafood Festival** (© 401/849-2120; www.bowenswharf.com) in the third week of October.

THE COTTAGES

"The Cottages" is what wealthy summer people called the almost unimaginably sumptuous mansions they built in Newport in the last decades before the 16th Amendment to the Constitution permitted an income tax.

Say this for the wealthy of the Gilded Age, many of whom obtained their fortunes by less than honorable means: They knew a good place to put down roots when they saw it. These are the same ones, after all, who developed Palm Beach in winter, the Hudson Valley in spring, the Berkshires in autumn, and Newport in summer, sweeping from house to luxurious house with the insouciance of a bejeweled matron dragging her sable down a grand staircase.

When driving or biking through the cottage district (walking its length is a serious trek for most people), consider the fact that most of these astonishing residences are still privately owned. That's almost as remarkable as the grounds and interiors of the nine that are open to the public.

Six of the mansions are maintained by the **Preservation Society of Newport County,** 424 Bellevue Ave. (© 401/847-1000; www.newportmansions.org), which also operates the 1748 Hunter House, the 1860 Italianate Chepstow villa, the 1883 Isaac Bell House, and the Green Animals Topiary Gardens in Portsmouth. The Society sells a **combination ticket,** good for a year, to five of its properties; the cost is $31 for adults, $10 for children 6 to 17. Individual tickets for The Breakers are $16 for adults, $4 for children 6 to 17; and for Hunter House $25 for adults, $4 for children 6 to 17. Individual tickets for Kingscote, The Elms, Chateau-sur-mer, Marble House, and Rosecliff are $11 for adults, $4 for children 6 to 17. They can be purchased at any of the properties. Credit cards are accepted at most, but not all, of the cottages. Children under 6 are free, but note that strollers are not allowed in the properties. Special events, such as the festive Thanksgiving and Christmas celebrations, cost extra. The Society also conducts specialty tours, including holiday evenings at the mansions and "behind the scenes" at The Elms. Parking is free at all the Society properties.

The mansions that aren't operated by the Preservation Society but are open to the public are Belcourt Castle, Beechwood, and Rough Point.

During the winter, the mansions of the Society take turns each year staying open through the period, with an additional one or two openings on weekends. Following are descriptions of the cottages in the order in which they're encountered when driving south from Memorial Boulevard along Bellevue Avenue, then west on Ocean Drive.

You might want to visit only one or two estates per day because their sheer opulence can become numbing. Each residence requires 45 minutes to an hour for its guided tour. If at all possible, go during the week to avoid crowds and traffic.

Kingscote ⚐   This mansion (on the right side of the avenue) is a reminder that well-to-do Southern families often had second homes north of the Mason-Dixon line to avoid the sultry summers of the deep South. Kingscote was built in 1841, nearly 40 years before the Gilded Age (usually regarded as the era between the end of the

Civil War and the beginning of World War I). But it is considered one of the New-port Cottages because it was acquired in 1864 by the sea merchant William Henry King, who furnished it with porcelains and textiles accumulated in the China trade. Architect Richard Upjohn designed the mansion in the same Gothic Revival style he used for Trinity Church in New York. The firm of McKim, Mead & White was com-missioned to design the 1881 dining room, notable for its Tiffany glass panels.

Bowery St. (west of Bellevue Ave.). Late Mar to Apr Sat–Sun 10am–5pm; May to Columbus Day daily 10am–5pm. See above for admission details. As you drive down Bellevue, the Isaac Bell House is btw. Kingscote and The Elms.

The Elms ✸✸

Architect Horace Trumbauer is said to have been inspired by the Château d'Asnières outside Paris, and a first look at the ornate dining room of The Elms, suitable for at least a marquis, buttresses that claim. So do the sunken gardens, laid out and maintained in the formal French manner. The owner was a first-generation million-aire, a coal tycoon named Edward J. Berwind. His cottage was completed in 1901, and he filled it with Louis XIV and XV furniture, as well as paintings and accessories true to the late 18th century. It was one of the first fully electrified mansions in Newport. Visi-tors can opt for a self-guided audio tour as well as lunch in The Elms Carriage House.

Bellevue Ave. Daily 10am–5pm. Closed Thanksgiving and Dec 24–25. See above for admission details.

Chateau-sur-mer ✸

William S. Wetmore was yet another merchant who made his fortune in the China trade. The entrance to this "Castle by the Sea" is on the left side of Bellevue, driving south. High Victorian in style, which means it drew from many inspirations (including Italian Renaissance and French Second Empire), the Chateau features a central atrium that reaches up three levels to a stained-glass skylight, with balconies at every level. One of Wetmore's parties attracted 3,000 guests. A park designed in a style true to the period of the cottage has copper beech and weeping wil-low trees standing around its garden pavilion.

Bellevue Ave. Jan to mid-Apr Sat–Sun and holidays 10am–4pm; mid-Apr to Oct daily 10am–5pm. See above for admission details.

The Breakers ✸✸✸

If you have time to see only one of the cottages, make it this one. Architect Richard Morris Hunt was commissioned to create this replica of a generic Florentine Renaissance palazzo, replacing a wood structure that burned down in 1892. He was unrestrained by costs: The high iron entrance gates alone weigh over 7 tons, and the 50×50-foot great hall has 50-foot-high ceilings, forming a giant cube, and is sheathed in marble. The Breakers took nearly 3 years to build (1892–95), with platoons of artisans imported from Europe to apply gold leaf, carve wood and marble, and provide mural-size baroque paintings. The bathrooms, far from common at the time, were provided with both fresh and salt running water, hot and cold.

Such mind-numbing extravagance shouldn't really be surprising—Hunt's patron was, after all, Cornelius Vanderbilt II, grandson of railroad tycoon Commodore Van-derbilt. Had Vanderbilt been European royalty, The Breakers would have provided motive for a peasant revolt. Vanderbilt's small family and their staff of 40 servants had 70 rooms in which to roam.

The furnishings on view are original. Evenings of classical and Broadway music are often presented.

Ochre Point Ave. (east of Bellevue Ave.). ✆ 401/847-1000. Mid-Apr to Jan 1 daily 10am–5pm (until 6pm Fri–Sat in July–Aug); Nov 24 and Dec 1, 8, 15, and 29 also 6–8pm. See above for admission details. Turn left on Ruggles Ave. after Chateau-sur-mer, then left again on Ochre Point Ave. The Breakers is on the right; a parking lot is on the left.

Rosecliff ⚘   Stanford White thought the Grand Trianon of Louis XVI at Versailles a suitable model for this 1902 commission for the flamboyant Tessie Fair Oelrichs, heiress to the Comstock Lode. With 40 rooms, it doesn't overwhelm on the scale of, say, The Breakers (above). But it has the largest ballroom of all the cottages and a storied heart-shaped grand staircase. All this was made possible by one James Fair, an immigrant who made his fortune after he unearthed the thickest gold and silver vein of Nevada's Comstock Lode and bought this property for his daughters.

In 1941, the mansion and its contents were sold for $21,000. It was used as a setting for some scenes in the Robert Redford movie of Fitzgerald's *The Great Gatsby* (1974). On a humid summer day, keep in mind that the mansion is air-conditioned.

Bellevue Ave. Mid-Apr to late Oct daily 10am–5pm. See above for admission details. From The Breakers, return to Bellevue Ave. and turn left (south); Rosecliff is on the left.

The Astors' Beechwood ⚘⚘   Mrs. William Backhouse Astor—*the* Mrs. Astor, as every brochure and guide feels compelled to observe—was, during her active life, the arbiter of exactly who constituted New York and Newport society. "The 400" list of socially acceptable folk was influenced or perhaps even drawn up by her, and that roster bore meaning, in some quarters, well into the second half of the 20th century. Being invited to Beechwood was absolutely critical to a social pretender's sense of self-worth, and elaborate machinations were set in motion to achieve that goal.

Rebuilt in 1857 after a fire destroyed the original version, the mansion isn't as large or impressive as some of its neighbors. But unlike those managed by the Preservation Society, it provides a little theatrical pizzazz with a corps of actors who pretend to be friends, children, and servants of Mrs. Astor. In set pieces, they share details about life in the late Victorian era. Frequent special events are held, often replicating those that took place when she held court, including costume balls and specially decorated banquets with Victorian music and dancing.

There are several regularly scheduled tours and events—Living History, Murder Mystery, Speakeasy (no minors), and the Christmas tours. Many involve vignettes performed by the resident acting troupe, and admission prices vary.

580 Bellevue Ave. ✆ 401/846-3772. www.astors-beechwood.com. Admission $20–$30 adults, $16–$26 seniors, $8–$15 children 6–12. Mid-May to early Nov daily 10am–5pm (tours every 20 min.); Christmas events Nov–Dec Wed–Sun; Feb to mid-May Fri–Sun 10am–4pm (tours every 30 min.). Closed Jan.

Marble House ⚘⚘⚘   Architect Richard Morris Hunt outdid himself for his clients William and Alva Vanderbilt. Several types of marble were used both outside and in, with a lavish hand that rivals the palaces of the Sun King, especially Le Petit Trianon at Versailles. It reaches its apogee in the ballroom, which is encrusted with three kinds of gold. It cost William $11 million to build and decorate Marble House, but Alva divorced him 4 years after the project was finished. She got the house, which she soon closed after marrying William's friend and neighbor. When her second husband died, Alva discovered the cause of female suffrage and reopened Marble House in 1913 to hold a benefit for the campaign for women's right to vote. (Dishes in the scullery bear the legend "Votes for Women.")

Bellevue Ave. Mid-Apr to Jan 1 daily 10am–5pm (Fri–Sat until 6pm); Nov Sat–Sun 10am–4pm; Jan–Mar Sat–Sun and holidays 10am–4pm. See above for admission details.

Belcourt Castle ⚘⚘   This was the only slightly less grand mansion down the road from Marble House to which Alva Vanderbilt repaired after her second marriage.

While the Vanderbilts were avid yachtsmen, her new husband, Oliver Hazard Perry Belmont, was a fanatical horseman. His 60-room house contained extensive stables on the ground floor where his beloved steeds slept under monogrammed blankets. (The Belmonts were instrumental in building New York's famed Belmont Racetrack.)

The castle, intended to resemble a European hunting lodge, has a ponderously masculine character, understandable in that it was designed for the bachelor Belmont before he won over vivacious Alva. It contains artifacts from the medieval era through the 19th century, including stained glass, Japanese cabinetry, a full-size replica of a gaudy Portuguese coronation carriage, and French Renaissance furniture. Thomas Edison designed the lighting. There are 14 secret doors and a tunnel to the kitchens, which were located 2 blocks away for fear of fire. The castle sold for a mere $25,000 in the early 1940s to the family of Harold B. Tinney, members of which still live here.

There are evening ghost and candlelight tours (with champagne) on some nights; tickets are $15 and reservations are wise. Leave the young ones at home.

657 Bellevue Ave. (at Lakeview Ave.). © 401/846-0669. www.belcourtcastle.com. Admission $12 adults, $8 seniors and college students, $7 children 13–18, $5 children 6–12. Feb–May Sat–Sun and holidays 10am–3pm; Memorial Day to mid-Oct daily 9:30am–4:30pm; mid-Oct to Nov daily 10am–4pm; Dec (special tours) 10am–3pm daily. Closed Jan.

Rough Point ★★ The fabled 1887 Gothic-Tudor home of the late tobacco heiress Doris Duke made its long-awaited opening in 2000. Only a portion of the 105 rooms are open for viewing. The heiress's collections include a wealth of Ming-dynasty vases, Flemish and French tapestries, and paintings by Van Dyck and Gainsborough. Watch for the ivory inset side tables bearing the marks of Catherine the Great in what is called the Yellow Room.

While those who knew her reject suggestions that Duke was reclusive or troubled, hers was, at the least, an often darkly eventful life. It was here at Rough Point in 1967 that the story of the tobacco heiress and her interior decorator/companion unfolded. Eduardo Tirella was killed after being crushed against the iron entrance gates by Duke's station wagon. Duke later claimed that she accidentally hit the accelerator when Tirella got out of the car to open the gates. The police chief declared it "an unfortunate accident," but local tongues wagged.

Duke died in 1993, bequeathing Rough Point to the Newport Restoration Foundation, along with all clothing, jewelry, and furniture in the house. Visits are by guided tour only. Tickets are sometimes available on the spot or at the Newport Gateway Visitors Center, but a better option is to make reservations and purchase tickets online.

Bellevue Ave. © 401/849-7300. www.newportrestoration.org. Admission $25, free under 12 years. Visits by guided tour only; mid-Apr to mid-May Thurs–Sat 9:45–1:45pm, mid-May to early Nov Tues–Sat 9:45–1:45pm. To get here from Belcourt Castle, continue south on Bellevue. Rough Point is on the left, just before a sharp turn west along what becomes Ocean Dr. There's no parking at the mansion; minibuses shuttle visitors from the Newport Gateway Visitors Center.

ADDITIONAL ATTRACTIONS

Historic Hill is the large district of Colonial Newport that rises from America's Cup Avenue, along the waterfront, to Bellevue Avenue, the beginning of Victorian Newport. **Spring Street** ★ serves as the Hill's main drag, and it's a treasure trove of Colonial, Georgian, and Federal structures. Chief among its visual delights is the 1725 **Trinity Church** ★, at the corner of Church Street. Said to have been influenced by the work of the legendary British architect Christopher Wren, it certainly reflects that inspiration in its belfry and distinctive spire, seen from all over downtown Newport and dominating Queen Anne Square, a greensward that runs down to the waterfront.

Hammersmith Farm Built for John W. Auchincloss in 1887, this shingled Victorian mansion was used for the wedding reception of John F. Kennedy and Jacqueline Bouvier (whose mother was married to an Auchincloss), in 1953. It subsequently became the unofficial summer White House of the short Kennedy presidency. It was sold in 1997 and sold again 2 years later, and it is no longer open to the public. It can still be seen from the road, however.

Ocean Dr. (past Castle Hill Ave.).

Hunter House 🞴 Another property of the Preservation Society, this 1754 Georgian Colonial is one of the most impressive dwellings in the neighborhood known as the Point, north of downtown. Above the doorway is a carved wooden pineapple. This symbol of welcome derived from the practice of placing a real pineapple at the door to announce that the sea-captain owner had returned from his long voyage and was ready to receive guests. The interior displays furniture crafted by Newport's famed 18th-century cabinetmakers, Townsend and Goddard.

54 Washington St. (at Elm St.). ℂ **401/847-1000**. See "The Cottages," above, for admission details. Late May to early Oct daily 10am–5pm.

International Tennis Hall of Fame On Bellevue Avenue, there was (and is) an exclusive men's club called the Newport Reading Room. One member was James Gordon Bennett, Jr., the wealthy publisher of the *New York Herald*. He persuaded a friend to ride a horse into the club. The outraged members reprimanded Bennett, who had an instant snit that they hadn't enjoyed his little jest. He went right out and bought a property on the other side of Memorial Boulevard, and ordered a structure built for his own social and sports club.

McKim, Mead & White produced a shingle-style edifice of lavish proportions, with turrets and verandas and an interior piazza for lawn games, equestrian shows, and a new game called tennis. It is now given to a permanent grass court. As Bennett hoped, his Newport Casino swiftly became the premier gathering place of his privileged compatriots. Now the pavilion hosts professional tournaments, and its courts are open to the public for play (call ahead to make reservations May–Oct). The building itself houses the Hall of Fame, of interest primarily to fans of the game. A restaurant ((ℂ **401/847-0418**) serves lunch, sunset dinners, and weekend brunch.

194 Bellevue Ave. (at Memorial Blvd.). ℂ **800/457-1144** or 401/849-3990. www.tennisfame.org. Admission $9 adults, $7 seniors and students, $5 children 16 and under. Daily 9:30am–5pm (except during tournaments and major holidays).

Museum of Newport History Maintained by the Newport Historical Society, this museum is in the refurbished 1772 Brick Market (not to be confused with the nearby shopping mall Brick Marketplace). The architect was Peter Harrison, also responsible for the Touro Synagogue (see below). The museum houses boat models, marine charts, antique silverware, and a ship figurehead, and also features videos on Newport history.

127 Thames St. (at Touro St.). ℂ 401/841-8770. www.newporthistorical.org. Donation only. Thurs–Sat 10am–4pm; Sun 1–4pm.

Newport Art Museum Across the avenue from Touro Park, this was the first Newport commission of Richard Morris Hunt, who went on to design many of the cottages along Bellevue Avenue. Unlike most of his later Newport houses, the 1862 main structure is in the Victorian stick style, a wood construction that had origins in earlier

Carpenter Gothic. It now mounts art exhibitions and serves as a venue for concerts. Featured in the collection are the works of artists from southeastern New England from the Colonial era to today.

76 Bellevue Ave. (at Old Beach Rd.). © 401/848-8200. www.newportartmuseum.com. Voluntary donation, recommended $6 adults, $5 seniors, and $4 students. Memorial Day to Labor Day Mon–Sat 10am–5pm, Sun noon–5pm; Labor Day to Memorial Day Mon–Sat 10am–4pm, Sun noon–4pm.

Touro Park   Opposite the Newport Art Museum, this small park provides a shaded respite. At its center is the Old Stone Mill. Dreamers like to believe that its eight columns were erected by Vikings. Realists say it was built by Benedict Arnold, a governor of the colony long before his great-great-grandson committed his infamous act of treason during the War of American Independence.

Bellevue Ave. (btw. Pelham and Mill sts.).

Touro Synagogue   This is the oldest existing synagogue in the United States, dating from 1763. A Sephardic Jewish community, largely refugees from Portugal, lived in Newport from the mid–17th century, over 100 years before this building was erected. It was designed by Peter Harrison, who was also responsible for the Brick Market (see Museum of Newport History, above). The synagogue was designated a National Historic Site in 1946.

85 Touro St. (Spring St.). © 401/847-4794. www.tourosynagogue.org. Free admission. July 1 to Labor Day Sun–Fri 10am–5pm; Labor Day to June 30 Sun 11am–3pm, Mon–Fri 1–3pm; Nov 1–Apr 30 Sun 11am–3pm, Mon–Fri at 1pm (groups of 10 or more by appointment only). Guided tours only, beginning every half-hour; call for the current schedule.

OUTDOOR PURSUITS: THE BEACH & BEYOND

Fort Adams State Park, Harrison Avenue (© 401/841-0707; www.fortadams.org), is on the thumb of land that partially encloses Newport Harbor. It can be seen from the downtown docks and reached by driving or biking south on Thames Street and west on Wellington Avenue (a section of Ocean Dr., which becomes Harrison Ave.). The sprawling 1820s fort for which the park is named has been under restoration since 2003, work that can be viewed by guided tour. Admission is $10 for adults, $5 for ages 6 to 18, and free for 5 and under. The park is the site of music festivals and war reenactments. Boating, ocean swimming, fishing, and sailing are all possible in the park's 105 acres. Open from mid-May through October. Also on the grounds is the **Museum of Yachting** (© 401/847-1018; www.moy.org), housed in a stone barracks from the early 19th century. Open from mid-May through October daily from 10am to 5pm, by appointment the rest of the year. Admission is $5 for adults, $4 for seniors and children under 12.

Farther along Ocean Drive, past Hammersmith Farm, is **Brenton Point State Park** ★★, a scenic preserve that borders the Atlantic, with nothing to impede the waves rolling in and collapsing on the rock-strewn beach. Scuba divers are often seen surfacing offshore, anglers enjoy casting from the long breakwater, and on a windy day, the sky is dotted with colorful kites.

There are other beaches more appropriate for swimming. The longest and most popular is **Easton's Beach** ★, which lies along Route 138A, the extension of Memorial Boulevard, east of town. There are plenty of facilities, including a bathhouse, eating places, picnic areas, lifeguards, a carousel, and the **Newport Aquarium** (© 401/849-8430). Parking costs $8 weekdays, $10 on weekends.

On Ocean Drive, less than 2 miles from the south end of Bellevue Avenue, is **Gooseberry Beach** ★, which is privately owned but open to the public. Parking costs

$15 Monday through Friday, $20 Saturday and Sunday. Chair rentals, showers, and changing rooms are available.

Cliff Walk ★★ skirts the edge of the southern section of town where most of the cottages were built and provides better views of many of them than can be seen from the street. Traversing its length, high above the crashing surf, is more than a stroll but less than an arduous hike. For the full 3.5-mile length, start at the access point near the intersection of Memorial Boulevard and Eustis Avenue. For a shorter walk, start at the Forty Steps, at the end of Narragansett Avenue, off Bellevue. Leave the walk at Ledge Road and return via Bellevue Avenue. Figure 2 to 3 hours for the round-trip, and be warned that there are some mildly rugged sections to negotiate, no facilities, and no land phones. The walk is open from 9am to 9pm.

A popular winter enterprise, the outdoor **Sovereign Bank Family Skating Center** (© **401/846-3018;** www.skatenewport.com) is set up at the Newport Yachting Center, on America's Cup Avenue. An oval rink 90 by 120 feet long, it's open daily from mid-November into March, depending upon weather. Skate rentals are available.

Biking is one of the best ways to get around town, especially out to the mansions and along **Ocean Drive** ★★. Among several rental shops are **Ten Speed Spokes,** 18 Elm St. (© **401/847-5609;** www.tenspeedspokes.com), and **Scooters,** 411 Thames St. (© **401/619-0573;** www.scootersofnewport.com).

Adventure Sports Rentals, at the Inn on Long Wharf, 142 Long Wharf (© **401/ 849-4820**), rents not only bikes and mopeds, but also outboard boats, kayaks, and sailboats; parasailing outings can be arranged.

Guided fly-fishing trips and fly-casting instruction are offered by the **Saltwater Edge,** 561 Lower Thames St. (© **401/842-0062;** www.saltwateredge.com). Anglers are taken out on half- and full-day quests for yellowfin tuna, bluefish, striped bass, and white marlin.

ORGANIZED TOURS & CRUISES

Several organizations conduct tours of the mansions and the downtown historic district. Between May 15 and October 15, the **Newport Historical Society,** 82 Touro St. (© **401/846-0813;** www.newporthistorical.org), offers a few different itineraries of considerable variety and length. Tickets cost as little as $4 and as much as $12. They can be purchased at the Society or at the Gateway Visitor Center (see "Visitor Information," earlier in this section).

Viking Tours, based at the Gateway Visitor Center, 23 America's Cup Ave. (© **401/ 847-6921;** www.vikingtoursnewport.com), has narrated bus tours of the mansions and harbor cruises on the excursion boat *Viking Queen.* Bus tours—daily in summer, Saturday from November to April—are 1½ to 4 hours and cost $23 to $49 for adults, $14 to $21 for children 5 to 11. Boat tours, from mid-May to mid-October, are 1 hour in length and cost $13 for adults, $11 for seniors, and $6 for kids. In July and August, the cruise can be extended to include a stop and tour of Fort Adams; $18 for adults, $16 for seniors, and $9 for children.

Classic Cruises of Newport ★, Bannister's Wharf, schedules narrated cruises on its 72-foot schooner *Madeleine* (© **401/847-0298;** www.cruisenewport.com). There are daily departures from spring to late fall; fares are $27 or $35 (children under 12 $5 off). The company's classic powerboat *RumRunner II* (© **401/847-0299;** same website) offers cruises daily over the same period. Rates are $18 per person for most outings, $25 for the cocktail cruise.

The *Spirit of Newport* ⚓, 2 Bowen's Wharf (© **401/849-3575**), offers daily 1½-hour cruises of the bay and harbor from May 1 to Columbus Day; fares are $14 for adults, $12 for seniors, $7 for children ages 4 to 12. Another possibility is the *Adirondack* ⚓, a 78-foot schooner that makes 2-hour cruises from the Newport Yachting Center (© **401/846-3018**; www.sail-newport.com). Its ticket booth is on America's Cup Avenue at Commercial Wharf; reservations must be made in advance. Daily departures cost $27 to $35, depending on the time of day.

The **Newport Touring Company,** 19 America's Cup Ave. (© **800/398-7427** or 401/841-8700; www.newportdinnertrain.com), features 90-minute round-trip excursions in vintage railroad trains along the edge of the bay. Fares are $13 for adults, $11 for seniors; kids 10 and under are free, but only one per paying adult; additional kids are charged $8.95. The company also has a **dinner train** that operates Thursday through Saturday mid-April to mid-December. Variations include a rail-and-cruise luncheon, and cabaret and murder mystery dinners, with prices per person from $44 to $55. In addition, the company offers a combined train/cruise package at $22 for adults, $19 for seniors, and $15 for additional children.

SHOPPING

At the heart of the downtown waterfront, **Bannister's Wharf, Bowen's Wharf,** and **Brick Marketplace** have about 60 stores among them, although few are especially compelling.

More interesting, if only for their quirky individuality, are the shops along **Lower Thames Street.** Eco-conscious shoppers must check out **Chartreuse** (no. 411), where the stock is comprised of handcrafted recyclable materials from developing countries. Would you believe purses fashioned from foil candy wrappers and the pop tabs off soda cans? **Aardvark Antiques** (no. 475) specializes in salvaged architectural components. Books, nautical charts, and sailing videos are offered at **Armchair Sailor** (no. 543), and for vintage clothing, visit **Cabbage Rose** (no. 493).

Spring Street is noted for its antiques shops and purveyors of crafts, jewelry, and folk art. One of these is **MacDowell Pottery** (no. 140), a studio selling ceramics and gifts by Rhode Island artisans; the nearby **J. H. Breakell & Co.** (no. 132) is a good source for handcrafted jewelry. Antique boat models are displayed along with marine paintings and navigational instruments at **North Star Gallery** (no. 105). **The Drawing Room/The Zsolnay Store** (nos. 152–154) stocks estate furnishings and specializes in Hungarian Zsolnay ceramics.

Spring intersects with **Franklin Street,** which harbors even more antiques shops in its short length. **Newport China Trade Co.** (no. 8) deals in export porcelain and objects associated with 19th-century China. Take a fat wallet to the **John Gidley House** (no. 22) for European antiques of high order. **Patina** (no. 26) is another dealer in Americana and folk art.

Bellevue Avenue has possibilities, too. One of the most alluring shops is **Karen Vaughan** (no. 148), with its delightful collection of high-style and witty gifts, antiques, china, rugs, and the unclassifiable.

WHERE TO STAY

The **Gateway Visitor Center** (© **800/976-5122** or 401/849-8040; www.go newport.com) lists vacancies in motels, hotels, and inns on a large TV monitor. Most can be called from free direct-line phones located nearby. Less impulsive travelers should reserve in advance, especially on weekends (2 months ahead for weekends from

Memorial Day to Labor Day). On short notice, though, you can try **Newport Reservations** (© 800/842-0102; www.newportreservations.com).

Many of the better motels are located in Middletown, about 2 miles north of downtown Newport. Possibilities include the **Courtyard by Marriott,** 9 Commerce Dr. (© 401/849-8000; www.marriott.com); **Newport Ramada Inn,** 936 W. Main Rd. (© 401/846-7600; www.ramada.com); and **Newport Gateway Hotel,** 31 W. Main Rd. (© 401/847-2735; www.historicinnsofnewport.com). Newport itself has a **Marriott,** 25 America's Cup Ave. (© 401/849-1000).

The rates given below generally have very wide ranges depending upon seasonal demand, so a $300 room on weekends in July might be half that in spring. The summer season is usually defined as Memorial Day to Columbus Day, with lower prices in effect the rest of the year.

VERY EXPENSIVE

Abigail Stoneham Inn ✦✦   The third property of the company that also operates the Cliffside Inn and Adele Turner Inn (below), this inn, the smallest of the group, displays the trademark fixtures and services of its siblings. These include exquisite decor; marble bathrooms with double Jacuzzis in every room; prebreakfast room delivery of juice, coffee, and newspaper of your choice; and extraordinary afternoon teas with scones, cakes, and finger sandwiches. But it also has distinctive touches: a bar set up like a little pub . . . for designer waters, and an intimate room where couples can have tea for just two. And the level of sensuality has been amped up: Separate menus list long rosters of soaps and bath products, there are over 20 different kinds of pillows to add to or substitute for those already on the bed, and at bedtime, there are strawberries and cream with the turndown.

102 Touro St., Newport, RI 02840. © 800/845-1811. www.abigailstonemaninn.com. 5 units. $275–$695 double. Rates include breakfast and afternoon tea. A surcharge of $50 applies on weekends and holiday Sun May 1–Oct. AE, DC, DISC, MC, V. No pets. No children under 12. **Amenities:** Concierge; limited room service; same-day laundry/dry cleaning. *In room:* A/C, TV, free Wi-Fi (most rooms), iPod docking station, hair dryer.

Castle Hill ✦✦✦   The setting—40 oceanfront acres on a near-island—is the overwhelming attraction of this, the highest-profile resort in Newport. But after roof-to-foundation renovations of the 1874 Victorian mansion and its outbuildings, even a visit in foul weather is a treat. There is no more enticing ritual in Newport than taking to one of the Adirondack chairs that dot the slope from the inn down toward the water, cocktail in hand, watching boats returning from the fishing grounds while the sun turns the water to gold. Best values are the Harbor Houses, which have been gutted and overhauled and have porches overlooking the bay. Breakfast buffets are expansive, and dinners (inside or on the terrace) are among the most accomplished in Newport. The kitchen applies Asian and European notions and techniques to the Hudson Valley duck, Farmstead artisan cheese, and Georges Bank scallops.

590 Ocean Dr., Newport, RI 02840. © 888/466-1355 or 401/849-3800. Fax 401/849-3838. www.castlehillinn.com. 27 units. Summer $419–$1,509 double; fall–spring $259–$1,079; winter $239–$659 double (higher prices are for suites). Rates include breakfast and afternoon tea. AE, DISC, MC, V. Open weekends only Nov–Apr. Closed Jan. Children under 12 not accepted in main house. **Amenities:** Restaurant (eclectic); bar; laundry; dry cleaning. *In room:* A/C, TV, hair dryer.

The Chanler ✦✦✦   Newport hoteliers keep topping themselves, but it will be a long while before they can best what has been wrought here. A boutique hotel with only 20 units, the French Empire main structure dates from 1873. It stands above the northern end of the Cliff Walk, overlooking the surf that rolls through the bay. All rooms have gas fireplaces, separate sitting areas, and, except for one suite, double Jacuzzis, supplemented by multinozzled shower stalls. Each is jaw-droppingly decorated to a different theme—Mediterranean, Renaissance, Tudor—but chairs, sofas, and mattresses are uniformly plush, deep, and all but impossible to leave. In peak season, there are about three staff members for every guest. Be sure to get a tutorial on the controls of the shades, TV, door lock, and showers. The restaurant, **Spiced Pear** (✆ **401/847-2244**), has surged to elite status, using Kobe beef, Kurobuta pork, Iranian caviar, and the like.

117 Memorial Blvd., Newport, RI 02840. ✆ **401/847-1300.** www.thechanler.com. 20 units. June–Oct $795–$1,195; Nov–May $275–$475 double. Rates include breakfast. AE, DC, MC, V. **Amenities:** Restaurant (fusion); bar; concierge; 24-hr. room service; access to nearby health club; in-room massage; laundry; dry cleaning. *In room:* A/C, TV/DVD, free Wi-Fi, CD player, wet bar, hair dryer, safe.

EXPENSIVE

Adele Turner Inn ★★ While it is unlikely that the Adele Turner will ever match its estimable sibling Cliffside (see below) virtue for virtue—its rooms are smaller, for one thing—it comes close enough to merit this high recommendation. And in one area, it is preferable: Once you are here, most of the downtown attractions are within walking distance. Each room has a fireplace; some have been restored, others are newly installed. Some of the units have hot tubs. Full breakfasts and afternoon teas are nothing less than sumptuous.

93 Pelham St., Newport, RI 02840. ✆ **800/845-1811** or 401/857-1811. Fax 401/848-5850. www.adeleturnerinn.com. 13 units. $130–$575 double. Room rates are $50 higher on weekends May–Oct. Rates include breakfast and afternoon tea. AE, DC, MC, V. **Amenities:** Concierge; limited room service; same-day laundry/dry cleaning; free video library. *In room:* A/C, TV/DVD/VCR, CD player, free Wi-Fi (most rooms), hair dryer, iron.

Cliffside Inn ★★★ This tops the list of grand Newport inns. All units have at least one working fireplace, and most have whirlpool baths. A suite in the outlying Seaview Cottage has a bathroom that has to be seen: The tub features both standard and handheld shower heads, eight spray nozzles, and a built-in TV and CD player! Antiques are generously deployed, including Eastlake and Tiffany originals and Victorian fancies that include (in room no. 11) an amusing "bird cage" shower from 1890. A favorite unit is the Garden Suite, a duplex with private garden and big double bathroom with radiant heat beneath the Peruvian tile floors. Coffee, juice, and the newspaper of your choice are delivered to your room even before the full breakfast.

2 Seaview Ave. (near Cliff Ave.), Newport, RI 02840. ✆ **800/845-1811** or 401/847-1811. Fax 401/848-5850. www.cliffsideinn.com. 16 units. $155–$695 double. Room surcharge of $50 on weekends May–Oct, as well as winter holiday weekends. Rates include breakfast and afternoon tea. AE, DISC, MC, V. No children under 13. **Amenities:** Limited room service; laundry; same-day dry cleaning. *In room:* A/C, TV/DVD/VCR, Wi-Fi, CD player, hair dryer, iron.

Francis Malbone House ★★ In 1996, nine modern rooms were added in a wing attached to this original 1760 Colonial house. They are very nice, with king-size beds and excellent reproductions of period furniture. Four of them share two sunken gardens, and three have Jacuzzi tubs built for two. Given a choice, though, take a room in the old section, where antiques outnumber repros, Oriental rugs adorn buffed wide-board floors, and silks and linens are deployed unsparingly. All but two units enjoy gas fireplaces. In 2000, the owners bought the adjacent Benjamin Mason House, a colonial home from 1750, and added a suite and another guest room to their offerings. An opulent tea service is set out each afternoon. The most interesting parts of the waterfront are right outside the property.

392 Thames St. (east of Memorial Blvd.), Newport, RI 02840. *©* **800/846-0392** or 401/846-0392. Fax 401/848-5956. www.malbone.com. 20 units. Apr 16–Nov 14 $255–$355 double; Nov 15–Apr 15 $99–$175; suites from $200. Weekend surcharge $50. Rates include breakfast and afternoon tea. AE, MC, V. No children under 12. *In room:* A/C, TV/VCR, CD player, dataport, hair dryer, iron.

Hilltop Inn ⟨★⟩   Recently purchased and renovated by the owners of Francis Malbone House (see above), this Craftsman-style inn endeavors to measure up to the standards of its sibling. It's close enough, with an excellent location at the end of Bellevue Avenue, a short uphill walk from the wharf area, and with a useful little fitness room in the carriage house. Nine rooms have fireplaces, and turn-of-the-last-century ceramic tiles and elaborate woodwork abound. To avoid the climb up the long staircase, reserve the first-floor Stewart Room, which has its own porch and whirlpool tub. Most rooms have king-size beds.

2 Kay St., Newport, RI 02840. *©* **800/846-0393** or 401/619-0054. Fax 401/619-2536. www.hilltopnewport.com. 5 units. Summer $275–$475 double; off season $245–$345 double. AE, MC, V. **Amenities:** Fitness room. *In room:* A/C, TV, free Wi-Fi, CD player, unstocked fridge, iron, robes.

Hyatt Regency Newport ⟨★⟩   More than 25 years old, the Hyatt is notable for its complete roster of hotel services, its location on an island at the northern end of Newport Harbor, and its full-service spa. You might expect such a place to be impersonal, but the staff endeavors to be pleasant. Delightful views of the harbor and town can be had from the restaurant and most of the guest rooms. Beds feature pillow-top mattresses, and newspapers are delivered to guest doors in the mornings.

1 Goat Island, Newport, RI 02840. *©* **800/233-1234** or 401/851-1234. Fax 401/846-7210. www.newport.hyatt.com. 264 units. Summer $279–$446 double; winter $199–$329 double. AE, DC, DISC, MC, V. Parking $16. No pets. **Amenities:** 2 restaurants (American, regional); bar; indoor freshwater and outdoor saltwater pools; 2 tennis courts; well-equipped health club and spa; concierge; airport courtesy van; business center; limited room service; massage; babysitting; same-day laundry; dry cleaning. *In room:* A/C, TV w/pay movies, Wi-Fi, coffeemaker, hair dryer, iron.

Hydrangea House ⟨★⟩   This long-established inn can't quite match up with its more expensive competitors, but don't assume you'll feel deprived here. The deep violet exterior catches the eye, and the front door opens onto a dim common area furnished with antiques and a fireplace. That leads, in turn, into the breakfast room, with one long table beneath a glass chandelier. Fourteen upholstered chairs surround it, which leads easily into conversation. Morning coffee can be taken on the veranda in back. Upstairs bedrooms and suites are named rather than numbered, each distinctively decorated; all have steam showers and gas fireplaces, and some have Jacuzzis. The ample parking lot in back has enough space for all guests.

16 Bellevue Ave., Newport 02840. *©* **800/945-4667** or 401/846-4435. www.hydrangeahouse.com. 9 units. $265–$475 double. Rates include breakfast. AE, MC, V. *In room:* A/C, TV, free Wi-Fi, hair dryer.

MODERATE

Mill Street Inn   Something different from most Newport inns, this 19th-century sawmill was scooped out and rebuilt from the walls in. Minimalist decor, furnishings, and service pertain, but this is an all-suite facility, where even its smallest unit has a queen-size bed and a sofa bed. The duplexes have private balconies, but everyone can use the rooftop decks, where breakfast is served on warm days. Where full breakfasts and afternoon teas of inns at other properties in the area are often lavish, they are skimpy here. The spacious rooms, excellent beds and bedding, and relatively modest prices compensate. There are three floors but no elevator.

75 Mill St. (2 blocks east of Thames), Newport, RI 02840. *©* **800/392-1316** or 401/849-9500. Fax 401/848-5131. www.millstreetinn.com. 23 units. June–Sept $179–$219 suite; Oct–May $129–$169 suite. Rates include breakfast and afternoon tea. Packages available. Children under 16 stay free in parent's room. Packages available. AE, DC, MC, V. Free adjacent parking. **Amenities:** Access to nearby health club; dry cleaning. *In room:* A/C, TV w/pay movies, Wi-Fi, minibar, hair dryer, safe, robes.

The Viking   On the Newport scene since 1926, this neo-Georgian sprawl of a hotel was built to accommodate the summer guests of Newport's wealthiest families. Today its assets outnumber deficiencies, although it poses no challenge to Castle Hill or The Chanler, described above. On the plus side, it is cheaper than its rivals and has a new fitness room and spa, an indoor pool, a good location, and a pleasant staff. Renovations completed in 2007 transformed the rooms in the original front third of the hotels to a degree of comfort that constitutes a vast improvement over the bland Reagan-era furnishings and fixtures of the remaining units. Ask for a front room on the second through fifth floors. The rooftop bar with views of the harbor is an outstanding feature.

1 Bellevue Ave., Newport, RI 02840. *©* **800/556-7126** or 401/847-3300. www.hotelviking.com. 237 units. $119–$689 double. Packages available. AE, DC, DISC, MC, V. Pets accepted ($75 cleaning fee). **Amenities:** Restaurant (regional); bar; health club and spa; limited room service; laundry; dry cleaning. *In room:* A/C, TV, Wi-Fi, hair dryer, iron, robes.

WHERE TO DINE

There are far too many restaurants in Newport to give full treatment to even just the best among them. Equal in many ways to those recommended below are **Canfield House,** 5 Memorial Blvd. (*©* **401/847-0416**); **Yesterday's & the Place,** 28 Washington Sq. (*©* **401/847-0116**); and **The West Deck,** 1 Waites Wharf (*©* **401/847-3610**). And for bargain dining in pricey Newport, the bountiful pastas of **Salas,** 343 Thames St. (*©* **401/845-8772**), are a perfect choice for hungry families.

The dining rooms at Castle Hill and The Chanler ("Where to Stay" above) are unsurpassed in this resort town of many good restaurants. They are open to any members of the public who are unintimidated by the expenditures required. Do make reservations. Figure about $200 to $300 for dinner for two.

Cut costs but not enjoyment by assembling a picnic at **Max's Market,** 469 Lower Thames St. (*©* **401/849-8088**). Special sandwiches include a crab cake with rémoulade, a lemon hummus wrap, quesadillas, and a dilled shrimp construction. There are 10 salads and other items along the lines of barbecue pulled pork.

Winter hours and days of operations vary considerably. Call ahead to avoid disappointment.

EXPENSIVE

Black Pearl ⍟ SEAFOOD/AMERICAN   This long building near the end of the wharf has you covered. The Tavern contains an atmospheric bar and a room with marine charts on the walls. The pricier Commodore's Room is more formal, with linens, candles, real silver, and 19th-century sailing prints. In either setting, most of the preparations of fish, duck, lamb, and beef are familiar but of good quality. In the popular Tavern, don't miss the definitive Newport chowder, which has been winning prizes since forever, followed by a Pearlburger or one of the other overstuffed sandwiches. Chicken pot pie arrives with a high golden-brown dome that explodes in steam when punctured. In summer, the menu is similar at the patio and open-air bar on the wharf, and there is a separate "Hot Dog Clam Chowder Annex." No cellphones.

30 Bannister's Wharf. ⓒ 401/846-5264. www.blackpearlnewport.com. Reservations and jackets for men required for dinner in Commodore's Room. Main courses $17–$30 in Tavern, $21–$39 in Commodore's Room. AE, MC, V. Tavern daily 11:30am–1am; Commodore daily 11:30am–3pm and 6–10pm. Closed Jan and 1st 2 weeks in Feb.

Café Zelda ⓖ STEAK/SEAFOOD   The bar at the corner is a local favorite populated by neighborhood regulars; the entrance to the two-level dining room is on the left, more often occupied by 40-plus tourists. Engravings of sailboats line the walls, oil lamps gutter in squat tumblers on each table. Remember your reading glasses, or just say, "bouillabaisse," one of the winners, with fish and shellfish in a somewhat bland leek and tomato saffron broth. The big deal, though is chicken-fried lobster, in which the flesh is taken out of the shell, dipped in a pancake-like batter and flash-fried, producing a dish resembling tempura. Otherwise, wood-grilled hanger steak with *frites* is commendable. Bread, served with a dish of olive oil, is boring, but the chardonnay from Newport Vineyard is worthwhile. At lunch, by all means go for the Zelda burger.

529 Thomas St. ⓒ 401/849-4002. www.cafezelda.com. Reservations advised for dinner. Main courses $18–$35. AE, MC, V. Mon–Thurs 5–10pm; Fri–Sat 11:30am–3pm and 5–10:30pm; Sun 11am–3pm and 5–9pm.

Clarke Cooke House ⓖⓖⓖ ECLECTIC   For many, this is the quintessential Newport restaurant. The picturesque 19th-century structure was moved to the wharf from America's Cup Avenue in the 1970s. Most of its several levels are open to the air in summer and glassed-in in winter. Several bars lubricate conversation. Up on the formal third floor, the staff sautés your lobster out of the shell while you put away such appetizers as stuffed zucchini blossoms, perhaps moving on to a rack of lamb *persillade* with minted tarragon glaze. If that seems too rich, spare the walk upstairs and stop in at the Bistro/Grille, which wraps around a fireplace and center bar. The main floor, called the Candy Store, serves full meals, snacks, sandwiches, and drinks, and below that is the Boom Boom Room, with dancing on weekends from 9pm to whenever. All levels have access to the wide choices of a big wine cellar. No cellphones in the dining areas.

Bannister's Wharf. ⓒ 401/849-2900. www.clarkecooke.com. Reservations recommended on summer weekends. Main courses $18–$39 in Candy Store and Grille, $27–$44 upstairs. AE, DC, DISC, MC, V. Candy Store and Grille summer daily 11:30am–10:30pm, winter Fri–Sun 11:30am–10:30pm; dining rooms summer daily 6–10pm, winter Wed–Sun 6–10pm.

Tucker's Bistro ⓖ CONTEMPORARY BISTRO   You can't miss it at night: Cascades of tiny lights swirl around the long facade. The eponymous owner is an avid yard-sale attendee who has filled his red walls with prints and mirrors in ornate gold frames and crowded his shelves with books, ceramics, and glassware—all oddly harmonious in their entirety. Anyway, Mr. Harris keeps the lights so low his staff provides flashlights to read the menu. The food is up to the visual extravagance, crying out for a meal of the provocative appetizers. Snapping taste buds to attention are the Thai shrimp nachos, actually crisp wontons topped with the grilled prawns, garnished with scallions and red pepper strips! Exclamation points are warranted as well for the pan-fried lobster and banana cakes with almond aioli (!) and the entree of George's Bank scallops with tiny ricotta and potato ravioli with sweet pepper tapenade! After these combinations, the rococo environment starts to look downright restrained.

150 Broadway. ⓒ 401/846-3449. www.tuckersbistro.com. Reservations advised. Main courses $21–$36. AE, DC, MC, V. Daily 6–10pm (until 10:30pm Fri–Sat).

Twenty-Two Bowen's ⓖⓖ STEAKHOUSE   On a wharf? Surrounded by water and fishing boats and unlimited tureens of clam chowder? Counterintuitive though it might seem, that's where the owners of the Castle Hill Inn decided to open their unabashed beef emporium. They guessed right: It's been full since the first day and, unlike many of its competitors, busy enough to stay open straight through the winter. The three rooms and bar have the burnished dark wood and polished brass of an old-time yacht club. Patrons are of an age and apparent income level to be comfortable with the steep prices, and possessed of sufficient knowledge to make assured choices from the extensive wine list. Light, briny oysters from the raw bar are the preferable preface to a pound or two of perfectly charred prime sirloin or porterhouse. Thick veal and lamb chops are possible alternatives, as are lobsters. All meats are served alone on the plate—sides are extra, from $5 to $9. In spring and summer, there's an outdoor patio. Service is as professional as any in Newport.

22 Bowen's Wharf. ⓒ **401/841-8884.** www.22bowens.com. Reservations recommended for dinner and weekend brunch. Main courses $26–$47. AE, DC, MC, V. Daily 11:30am–3:30pm and 5–10pm (Fri–Sat until 11pm).

MODERATE

Brick Alley Pub ⭐ *Kids* ECLECTIC   The Brick is loud and good-natured, Newport's favorite hangout. Families, tourists, working stiffs, and yachtsmen squeeze through the doors into the thronged dining rooms, the bar, and the terrace. Just so you know what you're getting into, the cab of a 1938 Chevy pickup truck is next to the soup-and-salad bar (there's another truck on the roof). Decor also incorporates kid-size vehicles, license plates, vintage photos, and a model train. The voluminous menu is pub grub squared: stuffed clams, Cajun catfish, nachos, burgers, pizzas, steaks, stuffies, meatloaf, and squid-ink spaghetti with cream, scallops, and crabmeat. Entrees include salad or the soup/salad/bread buffet *plus* potatoes and vegetables. Newport Storm Amber Ale is on draft.

140 Thames St. ⓒ **401/849-6334.** www.brickalley.com. Reservations recommended for dinner. Main courses $16–$29. AE, DISC, MC, V. Mon–Fri 11:30am–10pm (Fri until 11pm); Sat 11am–11pm; Sun 11am–10pm. Closed the week after Super Bowl.

Fluke Wine Bar ⭐⭐⭐ *Finds* ECLECTIC   Opened in summer 2007 in the three-story building that housed Le Bistro for 30 years, write this down as a must-dine on any weekend visit. The second-floor dining room is marginally more formal—there are tablecloths—but climb the steps to the third level. The tables are bare, but it's a happier space, with the bar, views of the harbor, and a convivial crowd to enjoy them. Set the mood with one of their specialty cocktails, the Stone Fruit Whiskey Smash, perhaps, or one of nearly a score of wines by the glass. Pours are generous. The chef has a New Orleans background, so spicy flavors are to be expected. Order his version of quahog chowder, unusually thick and earthy, both better and unlike any other chowder you're likely to encounter. When the potato croquettes arrive, they might seem ordinary, but one bite and they reveal themselves as Ping-Pong-ball-shaped crispy shells enclosing air, a tangy dipping sauce at the ready. Large plates include lobster, lamb chops, and Hudson Valley foie gras with a reduced balsamic drizzle.

41 Bowen's Wharf. ⓒ **401/849-7778.** www.flukewinebar.com. Reservations suggested. Main courses $17–$36. AE, MC, V. Daily 11:30am–3pm and 5:30–10pm.

Salvation Café ⭐ ECLECTIC   As funky-hip as Newport gets, this is a gathering place so popular with locals that the tourists who discover it are barely visible. A monster Gulf sign and amateurish oil paintings occupy the walls. The steel-topped bar is given primarily to diners, at least in the early evening hours. The stereo plays 1940s big bands or Tom Jones or Gene Autry, and the menu, too, hops and skips around the map. It plucks pad Thai here, *malai kofta* there, and the no-doubt tasty spinach and tofu concoction from a place not known. But unfocused though it might be, a lot of satisfying food can be had here. Linguine with chipotle shrimp gets a nod, as do pork vindaloo over lemon coconut rice and the meltingly tender flesh from long-braised short ribs topped with mole sauce. Truth to tell, though, most people probably wind up with the 10-ounce Salvation burger with bacon and cheddar.

140 Broadway. ✆ **401/847-2620**. www.salvationcafe.com. Main courses $9.50–$22. AE, DC, MC, V. Mon–Sat 5–10pm.

Scales & Shells ★★ SEAFOOD   The graceless name reflects the uncompromising character of this clangorous fish house. Diners who insist on a modicum of elegance should head for the upstairs room, called Upscales. Immediately inside the door is the open kitchen, which provides some guidance as to which of the myriad fish and shellfish to order. They're listed on the big blackboard on the back wall, offered in guileless preparations that allow the natural flavors to prevail. Substantial portions, too: The "large" appetizer of fried calamari is enough for four. Swordfish grilled over hardwood and topped with roasted sweet peppers is typical. Or have linguini with your choice of clams, calamari, or shrimp. Expect no meat or fowl, but there are some vegetarian pastas. Note that credit cards aren't accepted.

527 Lower Thames St. ✆ **401/846-3474** for main floor, 401/847-2000 for Upscales. www.scalesandshells.com. Reservations recommended May–Sept. Main courses $14–$29. No credit cards. Sun–Thurs 5–10pm; Fri–Sat 5–11pm; Sun 4–10pm (slightly shorter hours in winter). Closed Mon Jan–May and from last week in Dec to 1st 2 weeks in Jan.

INEXPENSIVE

Flo's Clam Shack SEAFOOD   Just past Easton's Beach over the Newport/Middletown line, this old-timer is more than a lopsided strand-side shanty—but not *much* more. Step up to the order window, choose from the handwritten menu, and receive a stone with a number painted on it. What you'll get, if you're wise, are clams, on a plate or on a roll. Cooked swiftly to order, they're as tender as any to which you might have set your teeth. This is also the place to sample "chowda"—red, white, or clear—and that Rhode Island specialty, stuffies. Clam cakes are inexplicably tasty, given the lack of clams therein. "Find a clam, get a prize," jokes the owner. The menu also suggests two hot dogs with a bottle of Moët for $50. Few patrons take that opportunity. Upstairs are a raw bar and deck even more happily ramshackle than below. Sunday features live music from 2 to 6pm.

4 Wave Ave., Middletown, RI ✆ **401/847-8141**. Main courses $9–$19. No credit cards. Apr–Dec 11am–9pm. Closed Jan–Mar.

Jack & Josie NEW AMERICAN   Fun is on the menu at this quirky corner spot, a sort of pool room/luncheonette/sports bar/Internet cafe. Within the airy, well-lit space are five computer terminals ($10 per hour), a pool table, plasma TVs, and an eating area with brushed aluminum tables. Food? Mostly soups, salads, and sandwiches, along with contemporary twists, as in the warm pear and goat cheese salad and "The Jack," thin slices of sirloin with caramelized onions, fig compote, and arugula sage blue cheese. But the owner—who is neither Jack nor Josie, which are actually the names of her dogs—has added several entrees, including a quiche of the day, roasted pork tenderloin, and meatloaf. Bring your own wine or beer; otherwise, herbal teas, smoothies, and specialty coffee drinks are options.

111 Broadway. ✆ **401/851-6900**. www.jackandjosies.com. All items under $10. AE, MC, V. Sun–Mon 10am–5pm; Wed–Sat 10am–10pm. Closed 1 week in Mar.

NEWPORT AFTER DARK

The most likely places to spend an evening lie along **Thames Street.** One of the most obvious possibilities, **The Red Parrot,** 348 Thames St., near Memorial Boulevard (© **401/847-3140;** www.redparrotrestaurant.com), has the look of an Irish saloon and features jazz combos Thursday through Sunday.

A full schedule of live music is on the plate at the **Newport Blues Café** ⊛, 286 Thames St., at Green Street (© **401/841-5510;** www.newportblues.com), plus a Sunday gospel brunch. With its fireplace, dark wood, and massive steel back door that used to guard the safe of this former bank, the cafe has a lot more class than most of the town's bars. Meals are available nightly in summer, Thursday through Sunday nights off season. It might close for 2 or 3 months in winter.

H2O, 359 Thames St. (© **401/849-4466;** www.h2onewport.com), is one of Newport's newest clubs and has an expansive waterfront deck with a harbor view. Singers with acoustic guitars prevail some afternoons, and things punch up after dinner with live rock and reggae on the deck Friday, Saturday, and additional nights in summer. **Mudville,** 8 W. Marlborough St. (© **401/849-1408**), is a bar for sports dudes and the women who put up with them. A dozen TVs, including a couple of big-screen plasmas, are fed by both satellite and cable, ensuring that no sporting event anywhere will be unavailable. A fireplace and fake Tiffany lamps constitute the decor.

Several restaurants offer music, as with deejays for dancing and live music in the bar at **The Landing,** 30 Bowen's Wharf (© **401/847-4514;** www.thelandingrestaurant newport.com). Also check out **Christie's,** 351 Thames St. (© **401/847-5400**), and **The West Dock,** 1 Waites Wharf (© **401/847-33610**).

4 South County: From Narragansett to Watch Hill

Narragansett: 32 miles SW of Providence; 14 miles W of Newport

Travelers rushing along the Boston–New York corridor inevitably choose I-95 to get from Providence to the Connecticut border. They either do not have the time for a detour or don't know that the nearby shore has some of the best beaches and most congenial fishing and resort villages of New England. This is called South County, a designation that has no official status but refers to the coast that is the southerly edge of Bristol County. Bypassed by the inland I-95, it has escaped much of the commercial development that besets many parts of the New England coast.

Rhode Islanders certainly know about the beguilements of South County, though, so try to avoid weekends in July and August, when the crush of day-trippers can turn these two-lane roads into parking lots.

Definitions are fuzzy, but for our purposes, South County runs from Narragansett, a little over 30 miles south of Providence, west to Westerly, nudging Connecticut. See the map on p. 419 to locate towns discussed in this section.

ESSENTIALS

GETTING THERE   To get to South County from Providence or Boston, take I-95 south, leaving it at exit 9 to pick up Route 4, also a limited-access highway. This merges with Route 1, arriving in Narragansett in about 20 miles. Turn east on Route 1A for a few miles to reach Narragansett Pier. From Newport, cross the Newport and Jamestown bridges on Route 138 to Route 1A south, and follow it to Narragansett, the center of South County's beach country. It is 14 miles west of Newport.

VISITOR INFORMATION The attendants at the **tourist information office** (✆ **401/783-7121;** www.narragansettri.com), in the landmark Towers on Route 1A in Narragansett, can help visitors find lodging. Contact the **South County Tourism Council,** 4808 Tower Hill Rd., Wakefield, RI 02879 (✆ **800/548-4662** or 401/789-4422; www.southcountyri.com), to request the useful brochure *South County Style.*

NARRAGANSETT & THE BEACHES ☄☄

Following Route 1A south, the pace quickens, at least from late spring to foliage season. After crossing the Narrow River Inlet, the road bends around toward **Narragansett Pier.** Along here and several miles on south to Port Judith and Jerusalem are some of the most desirable beaches in New England, with swaths of fine sand, relatively clean waters, and summer water temperatures that average about 70°F (21°C). When there are storms down south, the water kicks up enough to justify getting out the surfboard, and this is thought to be the best place in the state to catch the waves.

After a few blocks, Route 1A makes a sharp right turn (west), but stick to the shore, proceeding south on Ocean Road. Straight ahead is the **Towers,** a massive stone structure that spans the road between cylindrical towers with conical roofs. It is all that remains of the Gilded Age Narragansett Casino, designed by McKim, Mead & White, but lost in a 1900 fire. In the seaward tower is the Narragansett **tourist information office** (see "Essentials," above).

WHERE TO DINE

Amalfi MEDITERRANEAN BISTRO   At least three restaurants preceded this one, in this same space, but Amalfi seems to be a survivor. Its bank of windows looks out over Route 1A to the beach and ocean. On yet another menu that encourages a meal of appetizers, the carpaccio of beef is sliced as thin as butterfly wings and the calamari frito are tossed with a savory mix of sun-dried tomatoes, Kalamata olives, and spicy peppers. Main dishes swing from paella to lobster ravioli to red pepper gnocchi with Tuscan veal stew. A less expensive bistro menu in the bar area has pastas and sandwiches. The staff is pleasant, if not terribly professional. The restaurant is in the sprawling complex that is the **Village Inn,** 1 Beach St., Narragansett, RI 02882 (✆ **800/842-7437** or 401/783-6767; www.v-inn.com). It's probably the best lodging of an unattractive few in the area. Rooms run around $140 to $240.

1 Beach St. ✆ **401/792-3999.** www.amalfiri.com. Main courses $16–$30. AE, DC, MC, V. Daily 5–9pm (until 10pm Fri–Sat).

Coast Guard House SEAFOOD/AMERICAN   Adjacent to the Towers is this 1888 former Coast Guard headquarters, now an increasingly popular restaurant that enjoys unobstructed views of the beach and breakers crashing a few feet below its windows—a diversion from the corporate-looking interior. Despite the venue, the menu features as many meat dishes as seafood, executed with equal parts sophistication and unevenness. Seafood stew packs in lobster, fish, mussels, Italian sausage, kale, fennel, and potatoes in a tomato-saffron broth. Lobster comes steamed, broiled, or baked. Another bar is on the deck upstairs.

40 Ocean Rd. ✆ **401/789-0700.** Main courses $18–$36. AE, DC, DISC, MC, V. Mon–Thurs 11:30am–3pm and 5–9pm; Fri–Sat 11:30am–3pm and 5–10pm; Sun 10am–2pm and 4–10pm (shorter hours in winter; call ahead). Closed Jan.

Spain ☄ SPANISH   South of Scarborough Beach, this is deservedly the most popular restaurant on this stretch of shore. Partly it's the congenial staff, partly the terraces overlooking the sea. But the greatest share of credit goes to the stellar interpretations of the Spanish tapas tradition and such favorites as *paella Valenciana*. Authenticity doesn't head the list of the kitchen's concerns: The irresistible fried calamari are tossed with very un-Spanish hot peppers. Do sample the *espinacas a la Catalana*—spinach sautéed with garlic, raisins, and pine nuts. The several dishes listed on the menu as "Shellfish Combinations" deserve particular consideration.

1144 Ocean Rd. (C) **401/783-9770.** Reservations accepted only for parties of 6 or more. Main courses $13–$30. AE, DC, DISC, MC, V. Tues–Sat 4–10pm (Fri–Sat until 11pm); Sun 1–9pm.

FROM NARRAGANSETT TO POINT JUDITH

Follow scenic Ocean Road south from the Towers, soon arriving at **Scarborough State Beach** 𝕽𝕽 ((C) **401/789-2324;** www.riparks.com). Noticeably well kept, with a row of pavilions for picnicking and changing, it has ample parking and surroundings unsullied by brash commercial enterprises. The beach is largely hard-packed sand. While the mild surf makes this a good option for families with young children, sections are often also jammed with teenagers and college students.

Continuing on Ocean Road to the end, you'll reach the **Point Judith Lighthouse,** 1460 Ocean Rd. ((C) **401/789-0444**). Built in 1816, the brick beacon is a photo op that can be approached but not entered.

GALILEE

Backtrack along Ocean Road, turning left on Route 108, then left again on Sand Hill Cove Road, past the dock of the only year-round ferries to Block Island, and into the Port of Galilee. At the end, past a cluster of restaurants beside the channel connecting Point Judith Pond with the ocean, is the redundantly named **Salty Brine State Beach.** Protected by a breakwater, it is a good choice for families with younger children, but popular with teenagers as well. On the opposite side of the channel is popular **East Matunuck State Beach,** where waves break upon the sand at an angle, producing enough action to permit decent surfing on some summer days.

To get a better sense of the area from the water, consider the 1¾-hour tour on the *Southland* ((C) **401/783-2954;** www.southlandcruises.com), which departs from State Pier in Galilee. Daily departures from mid-June to Labor Day; weekends only from Labor Day to mid-October. Prices are $15 to $18 for adults, $13 to $16 for seniors, $10 for children 4 to 12, free for ages 3 and under.

Numerous **party and charter boats** leave for fishing expeditions from Point Judith. Another possible excursion is a **whale-watching cruise** with the **Frances Fleet,** 2 State St., Point Judith ((C) **800/662-2824** or 401/783-4988; www.francesfleet.com). Cruises launch from late June August Monday through Saturday from 1 to about 5:30pm. It isn't cheap, at $40 for adults and $25 for children under 12, but the sight of a monster humpback leaping from the water is unforgettable.

WHERE TO DINE

George's of Galilee SEAFOOD/AMERICAN   The impulse to drive as far as you can without winding up in the drink may account for part of the popularity of George's, in business for over 50 years. It can't be the food, which is good enough but unexceptional, despite the accolades of enthusiastic readers of regional magazines. Anyway, the decks serve as a good vantage point to watch the boat traffic in the channel. As for food, give the fried smelts, stuffies, fish and chips, and clam and cod cakes a thought, perhaps carrying them from the takeout window over to the picnic tables by the beach. After Labor Day, the twin lobsters go for $25.

250 Sand Hill Cove Rd. ℂ **401/783-2306.** www.georgesofgalilee.com. Main courses $14–$25 (market prices for lobster). AE, DISC, MC, V. May–Oct daily noon–10pm; Nov–Apr Thurs–Sun noon–2:30pm and 6–9:30pm.

WATCH HILL ⚓

Although much of Westerly township remains peacefully semirural, it contains more than a dozen villages, notably the peninsular resort of Watch Hill, and several contiguous public beaches on slender barrier islands enclosing large saltwater ponds.

A pretty land's-end village that achieved its resort status during the post–Civil War period, Watch Hill has retained it ever since. It helped that it is the closest of South County's beach towns to New York. Many grand summer mansions and Queen Anne gingerbread houses remain from that time. The north side of the point occupied by the village is the harbor, packed with pleasure boats. Stretching from the eastern edge of Westerly township to the southwesternmost tip of the state at Watch Hill are **Dunes Park Beach** ⚓ and **Atlantic Beach,** followed by **Misquamicut State Beach** ⚓, a gathering place for large numbers of adolescents, and **Napatree Point Barrier Beach** ⚓, a wildlife preserve notable for its white crescent beach. While you can enter the Napatree preserve for free, there are no facilities, a reason for its generally sparser crowds. All the beaches are noted for their fine-grained sand and gentle surf with gradual drop-offs.

South of town on Watch Hill Road is the picturesque 1856 **Watch Hill Lighthouse,** open from 1 to 3pm Tuesday and Thursday. Back in town at the small **Watch Hill Beach,** younger children get a kick out of the nearby **Flying Horse Carousel,** which dates to 1867. Only kids are allowed to ride; tickets are 50¢. The carousel is open daily from mid-June to early September. Parents will have to settle for the more than 50 shops that fill the commercial blocks.

To get to Watch Hill from Providence and points north, take exit 1 off I-95, south on Route 3, which passes through Westerly and continues to Watch Hill. From Connecticut, take exit 92 from I-95, going south briefly on Route 2, picking up Route 78 (the Westerly Bypass) down along Airport Road into Watch Hill. Free parking is extremely limited, so if you arrive after 8am, expect to pay up to $15 in the commercial lot behind the main street.

Amtrak trains traveling between Boston and New York stop in Westerly several times daily. There is a pull-over **information office** on I-95 near the Connecticut border, and a **Chamber of Commerce** office at 74 Post Rd. in Westerly (ℂ **800/732-7636;** www.westerlychamber.org).

WHERE TO STAY

Pleasant View Inn ⭐   Two miles east of Watch Hill, this is a small resort with a private strand that adjoins 4 miles of Misquamicut Beach. The front desk can arrange guaranteed tee times at a nearby course. Five categories of rooms are assigned, most of the better ones facing the ocean, with balconies; some have fridges and microwaves. The cheapest rooms overlook a parking lot.

65 Atlantic Inn, Westerly, RI 02891. ℂ **800/782-3224** or 401/348-8200. www.pvinn.com. 112 units. May–June and Sept–Oct $85–$175 double; July–Aug $172–$270 double. Packages available. AE, MC, V. Closed Nov–Apr. No pets. **Amenities:** 2 restaurants (American); bar; heated outdoor pool and Jacuzzi; fitness room w/Jacuzzi and sauna; game room. *In room:* A/C, TV.

Shelter Harbor Inn ⭐   If it's time to stop for the night, for dinner, or for a spectacular Sunday brunch (reservations essential), watch for the entrance to this venerable inn off U.S. 1, about 6 miles east of Westerly. Parts of the main building date to

1810, accounting for the creaking floorboards and doors that don't quite close. A genteel tone prevails. Several bedrooms have fireplaces, decks, or both. They might have been furnished by Ye Olde Inne central warehouse but are comfortable enough. A shuttle takes guests to the private beach a mile away. A cautiously creative restaurant and honored wine cellar round out the picture. Only one dinner entrees exceeds $25; portions are large. The inn and restaurant are open 365 days a year.

10 Wagner Rd., Westerly, RI 02891. ℭ 800/468-8883 or 401/322-8883. Fax 401/322-7907. www.shelterharborinn. com. 24 units. Summer $186–$238 double; off-season $96–$198 double. Rates include breakfast. AE, DC, DISC, MC, V. **Amenities:** Restaurant (regional); bar; rooftop hot tub; paddle tennis; croquet. *In room:* A/C, TV, Wi-Fi.

The Villa ⭐ A Dutch Colonial manor with many Italianate overlays on Route 1A outside of town, The Villa is most often recommended for its extensive gardens and warm hospitality. All units are suites with fridges and microwaves. Three have Jacuzzi tubs built for two, and a couple have gas fireplaces. The breakfasts are continental during the week, but enhanced with hot dishes on weekends. Unlike most lodgings in the area, it is open all year.

190 Shore Rd., Westerly, RI 02891. ℭ 800/722-9240 or 401/596-1054. Fax 401/596-6268. www.thevillaatwesterly. com. 6 units. Summer $235–$305 double; rest of year $115–$235 double. Rates include breakfast. Packages available. AE, DISC, MC, V. **Amenities:** Outdoor pool w/Jacuzzi. *In room:* A/C, TV/DVD, CD player, fridge, coffeemaker, hair dryer.

Watch Hill Inn Savor sunsets from the veranda of this century-old clapboard lodge. Bedrooms are mostly of good size, with nothing special by way of decor, apart from the four-posters and occasional antiques. There's access to a beach. Meals are largely in the seafood-and-pasta tradition, but with superb views, taken in from the Grille Room and four decks.

38 Bay St., Watch Hill, RI 02891. ℭ 800/356-9314 or 401/348-6300. Fax 401/348-6301. www.watchhillinn.com. 16 units. Summer $300–$450 double; winter $175–$275 double. Rates include breakfast. Packages available. MC, V. **Amenities:** Restaurant; bar. *In room:* A/C, TV.

WHERE TO DINE

Olympia Tea Room ⭐ NEW AMERICAN The genteel tone of Watch Hill is undergirded by the Olympia, long a favorite meet-and-eat retreat. This version of an even older restaurant opened in 1939 and long retained its soda fountains and wooden booths. The fountain is now a full bar, but the kitchen continues to crank out pretty imaginative food. If available, jump for the appetizer of plump, lightly fried oysters on wilted spinach and corn salsa. The stuffies and lobster rolls are as good as you're likely to enjoy in coastal New England, and the "easy lobster casserole" contains more meat than a whole lobster. Be sure to read the "Watch Hill History" in the front of the menu—it's quite entertaining.

74 Bay St. ℭ 401/348-8211. Reservations not accepted. Main courses $20–$32. AE, MC, V. June to Columbus Day daily 11am–10pm and Apr–May Thurs–Sun 11am–9pm. (Hours and days vary frequently; call ahead.) Closed Nov to Easter.

The Up River Café ⭐ NEW AMERICAN An up-and-down history as a restaurant under other names and chefs has preceded in this converted old woolen mill cantilevered over the river that runs through town. The current occupant chooses to avoid experimentation, with a resulting menu that strides along a workmanlike path. The main dining room is a two-tiered affair allowing water views; the smaller adjacent room has a fireplace. It all has a North Woods look, with bare wide-board floors, carried through in the homey tavern beside the entry hall. Although listed as a starter, the fried calamari tossed with banana peppers, peanuts, and crisp rice noodles in a Thai chile sauce is a meal by itself. Entrees are half sea-based, half land-based on a card that changes seasonally. Dishes utilizing sea scallops harvested by the local Stonington fleet are reliable, as is the New Zealand lamb that is usually on offer.

37 Main St. ℂ 401/348-9700. www.theuprivercafe.com. Reservations suggested on weekends. Main courses $15–$34. AE, MC, V. Mon–Sat 11:30am–10pm (until 11pm Fri–Sat); Sun 5–9pm (closing an hour earlier after Labor Day).

5 Block Island ★★

Viewed from above or on a map, Block Island looks like a pork chop with a big bite taken out of the middle. Only 7 miles long and 3 miles wide, it is edged with long stretches of beach lifting at points into dramatic bluffs. The interior is dimpled with undulating hills, only rarely reaching above 150 feet in elevation. Its hollows and clefts cradle over 300 sweet-water ponds, some no larger than a backyard swimming pool. That "bite" out of the western edge of the "chop" is **Great Salt Pond,** which almost succeeds in cutting the island in two but, as it is, serves as a fine protected harbor for fleets of pleasure boats.

The only significant concentration of houses, businesses, hotels, and people is at **Old Harbor,** on the lower eastern shore, where most of the ferries from the mainland arrive and most of the remaining fishing boats moor.

Named for Adrian Block, a Dutch explorer who briefly stepped ashore in 1641, the island's earliest European settlement was in 1661, and it has since attracted the kinds of people who nurture fierce convictions of independence, fueled in part by the streaks of paranoia that led them to live on a speck of land with no physical connection to the mainland. In the past, that has meant farmers, pirates, fishermen, smugglers, scavengers, and entrepreneurs, all of them willing to deal with the realities of isolation, lonely winters, and occasional killer hurricanes. Today there are about 1,000 permanent residents of similar pluck and enterprise who tough it out 9 months a year waiting for the sun to stay awhile.

Vacationers are wont to describe this as paradise—and they are correct, at least if sun and sea and zephyrs are paramount considerations. Those elements transformed the island from an offshore afterthought into an accessible summer retreat for the urban middle class after the Civil War, in America's first taste of mass tourism.

Unlike other such regions throughout the country that have lost their sprawling Victorian hotels to fire or demolition, Block Island has preserved many of its buildings from that time. They crowd around Old Harbor, providing most of the lodging base. Smaller inns and B&Bs add more tourist rooms, most in converted houses built at the same time as the great hotels. There are only a few establishments that even resemble motels, and building stock is marked, with few exceptions, by tasteful Yankee understatement. Despite the ominous presence of a few houses that resemble those plunked down in potato fields in ultrachic precincts of New York's Long Island, development so far remains under control, and there exist no franchised eateries or shops of any kind—this is not the place to have a Big Mac attack.

Away from the sand and surf, it is an island of peaceful pleasures and gentle observations. Police officers wear Bermuda shorts and ride bikes. Children tend lemonade stands in front of picket fences and low hedges. Clumps of hydrangeas tangle with beach roses and honeysuckle, hiding the foundations of saltboxes and Victorian farmhouses with shingles scoured gray by sea winds. No squirrels, chipmunks, possums, or

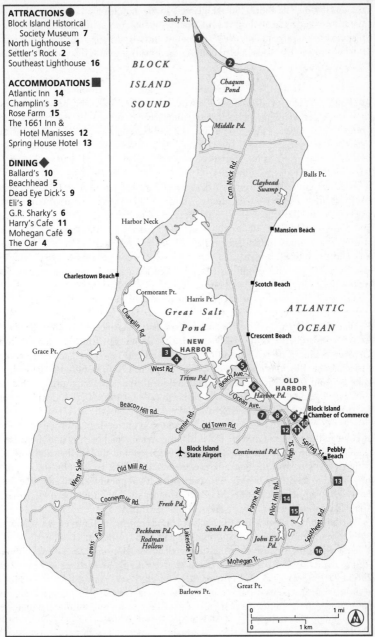

Block Island

ATTRACTIONS ●
Block Island Historical
    Society Museum **7**
North Lighthouse **1**
Settler's Rock **2**
Southeast Lighthouse **16**

ACCOMMODATIONS ■
Atlantic Inn **14**
Champlin's **3**
Rose Farm **15**
The 1661 Inn &
    Hotel Manisses **12**
Spring House Hotel **13**

DINING ◆
Ballard's **10**
Beachhead **5**
Dead Eye Dick's **9**
Eli's **8**
G.R. Sharky's **6**
Harry's Cafe **11**
Mohegan Café **9**
The Oar **4**

Sandy Pt.

BLOCK

ISLAND

SOUND

Chaqum Pond

Middle Pd.

Balls Pt.

Corn Neck Rd.

Clayhead Swamp

Harbor Neck

■ Mansion Beach

Charlestown Beach ■

Cormorant Pt.

Harris Pt.

Great Salt

Pond

■ Scotch Beach

ATLANTIC

OCEAN

■ Crescent Beach

Grace Pt.

Champlin Rd.

NEW
HARBOR

West Rd.

Trims Pd.

Beach Ave.

OLD
HARBOR

Harbor Pd.

Ocean Ave.

Block Island
Chamber of Commerce

Beacon Hill Rd.

Center Rd.

Old Town Rd.

High St.

Spring St.

Pebbly
Beach

West Side

Block Island
State Airport

Continental Pd.

Old Mill Rd.

Cooneymus Rd.

Fresh Pd.

Lakeside Dr.

Payne Rd.

Pilot Hill Rd.

Southeast Rd.

Lewis Farm Rd.

Peckham Pd.
Rodman
Hollow

Sands Pd.

John E's
Pd.

Mohegan Tr.

Barlows Pt.

Great Pt.

0   1 mi

0   1 km

raccoons live on The Block, but the island is in the middle of a prominent flyway for migratory birds, and egrets, ducks, goldfinches, and kingfishers are seen in abundance. Deer were introduced about 30 years ago, to the islanders' current regret, bringing Lyme disease and the four-hoofed enthusiasm for turning flowerbeds into salad bars.

ESSENTIALS

GETTING THERE   The **Interstate Navigation Company,** New London, CT (© **860/442-7891** or 401/783-4613; www.blockislandferry.com), provides most of the surface service. This includes year-round passenger-and-vehicle ferries between Point Judith and Old Harbor on The Block and passenger-only ferries on daily runs between Newport and Block Island from July 1 to September 5. The Point Judith boats depart as many as nine times daily in high season, as few as two times daily in winter; sailing time is 50 minutes.

The Newport ferries leave Fort Adams at 9:15am and return from Old Harbor on Block Island at 4:45pm. Sailing time is 2 hours. While reservations aren't required for passengers, get to the dock early, as the boats tend to fill up quickly.

Getting a car to Block Island is something of a hassle and considerably more expensive. At this writing, round-trip fares are $17 to $21 for adults, $16 to $20 for seniors, and $8.20 to $12 for children. Passenger vehicles cost an additional $90 to $109, and there is a long list of different fees for bicycles, mopeds, and motorcycles. **Car reservations** must be made by phone at © **866/783-7996.** Drivers, be prepared: You are expected to *back* your car into the close quarters of the ferry's main deck.

High-speed passenger-only service is in operation from both Point Judith and New London, Connecticut. **Island Hi-Speed Ferry,** Port of Galilee, RI (© **86/783-7996;** www.blockislandferry.com), makes several daily round-trips from late May to early October. Sailing time is about 30 minutes; round-trip passenger fare is $30 adults, $14 children. **Block Island Express,** New London, CT (© **860/444-4624;** www. goblockisland.com), has cut the previous average time to the Block nearly in half, to a little over an hour. Service is from late May to early October 10; round-trip fares are $35 to $40 for adults, $18 to $20 for children.

Given the cost of taking a car, consider parking in one of the nearby long-term lots at Point Judith or New London. Block Island is small, rental bicycles and mopeds are readily available, there are cabs for longer distances, and most hotels and inns are within a few blocks of the docks. There are even car-rental agencies on the island. If you intend to take a car anyway, understand that it's important to make ferry reservations well in advance, at © **866/783-7996** Monday through Friday between 5am and 4pm. Two months isn't too early for weekend departures.

One last thing: Try to avoid the last ferry Sunday nights in summer, when boisterous weekend drunks roll on board from the bars along Water Street.

Westerly State Airport, near the Connecticut border, is the base for over a dozen regular flights to and from Block Island via **New England Airlines** (© **800/243-2460,** 401/596-2460 in Westerly, or 401/466-5881 on Block Island; www.block-island.com/nea). Flights depart hourly in summer, taking 12 to 15 minutes. Fares are $84 round-trip for adults, $69 for children. Make advance reservations and allow for the possibility that coastal fogs or high winds will delay or even cancel flights.

VISITOR INFORMATION   The **Block Island Chamber of Commerce** has a year-round information office at the ferry landing at Old Harbor (© **800/383-BIRI** or 401/466-2474; www.blockislandchamber.com). Its attendants can answer questions

---

> **Tips A Note on Accommodations**
>
> If you arrive on Block Island without reservations, here's one approach to getting an inexpensive bed for the night: show up at an inn an hour or so after the last ferry has departed. Management will often lower quoted rates if rooms are still available.

---

and help visitors find lodging. In the same building are lockers for day-trippers and one of the island's few ATMs. A building at Corn Neck Road and Ocean Avenue contains the only bank, which also has an ATM.

Most streets on Block Island have no house numbers, and some roads have no names. Best leave your dog at home: Hotels, inns, and B&Bs won't accept them, they are banned from the beaches, and they are supposed to be leashed at all times.

Daily newspapers from Boston, New York, and Providence are sold at the **Island Bound Bookstore,** Water Street (© **401/466-8878;** www.islandboundbookstore. com), next to the Post Office, and at **B.I.G.** (© **401/466-2949**), the grocery store on Ocean Avenue (near Corn Neck Rd.). When they become available, however, depends on the ferry from Port Judith to which they are delivered each morning.

GETTING AROUND   Cars are allowed on the island, but roads are narrow, winding, and without shoulders, and drivers must contend with runners and flocks of bicycles and mopeds. Unless your party includes people with mobility problems or small children, we recommend leaving your car on the mainland and joining the two-wheelers. If you'd like to rent a car after you arrive by boat or plane, **Block Island Bike & Car Rental,** on Ocean Avenue (© **401/466-2297**), has offices near Payne's Dock and at the airport; reserve ahead. If you decide to bring your car to the island, top off the gas tank before rolling onto the ferry. There is only one rudimentary gas station, behind Sharky's restaurant.

Rental bikes and mopeds are available at several shops and stands. Convenient sources near Old Harbor include **The Moped Man,** Water Street (© **401/466-5444**), on the main business street, renting bikes as well as mopeds; **Old Harbor Bike Shop,** at the ferry dock (© **954/270-4721;** www.oldharborbikeshop.com); and **Island Moped & Bikes,** Chapel Street, behind the Harborside Inn (© **401/466-2700**). Rates for bikes are typically $18 to $30 a day, less with widely available discount coupons. Moped rates vary but are usually from $75 to $90 for half to full days. Bargaining often brings prices down, especially early in the week after the weekenders have left, or for 3 or more days. Keep in mind that mopeds aren't allowed on dirt roads, which provide access to many beaches.

Some inns also rent bicycles, so a possible plan is to take a taxi from the ferry or airport to your inn, drop off luggage, and get around by bike after that. Two such inns are the **Seacrest,** 207 High St. (© **401/466-2882**), and **Rose Farm,** on Roslyn Road (© **401/466-2034**), but inquire about rentals when making room reservations at other places as well.

EXPLORING THE ISLAND

With no golf course and a lone museum that takes only about 15 minutes to see, little on the island distracts from the central missions of sunning, cycling, hiking, lolling, and ingesting copious quantities of lobster, clams, chowder, and alcohol. Add a couple of lighthouses, a wildlife refuge, and three topographical features of note, and that's about it, enough to provide destinations for a few leisurely bike trips. A driving tour of every site on that list takes no more than 2 hours.

A couple of miles south of Old Harbor on what starts out as Spring Street is the **Southeast Lighthouse** (© 401/466-5009; www.nps.gov). A tablet by the road claims that, in 1590, the Manisseans, the Indians of Block Island, drove a war-party of 40 Mohegans over the bluffs. An undeniably appealing Victorian structure, built in 1874, the lighthouse's claim for attention lies primarily in the fact that it had to be moved 245 feet back from the eroding precipice a few years ago to save it. That was expensive, and now another $1 million or two is desperately needed to renovate this National Historic Landmark. While a small exhibit on the ground floor can be seen for free, the admission fee to the top is $5.

Continuing along the same road, which goes through other names and soon makes a sharp right turn inland, watch for the left turn onto West Side Road. In a few hundred yards, pull over near the sign for **Rodman's Hollow,** a geological dent dug by a passing glacier. It's deeper than it looks, the bottom a few feet below sea level and laced with walking trails beneath a thick mantle of low trees. Much of what you see here is designated forever wild, for the Nature Conservancy has purchased about a third of the island's surface to protect it from development. A map of the 12-mile trail network can be purchased at the Chamber of Commerce building at the ferry landing.

From Old Harbor, proceed north on Corn Neck Road, skirting Crescent Beach, on the right. The paved road eventually ends at **Settler's Rock** ★★★, with a plaque naming the English pioneers who landed here in 1661. This is one of the loveliest spots on the island, with mirrored **Chaqum Pond** behind the Rock and a scimitar beach curving out to **North Lighthouse,** erected in 1867. In between is a **national wildlife refuge** that is of particular interest to birders. The lighthouse, best reached by foot along the rocky beach, is now an interpretive center of local ecology and history, open from July 5 to Labor Day daily from 10am to 4pm.

Back in Old Harbor, the **Block Island Historical Society Museum,** Old Town Road and Ocean Avenue (© 401/466-2481), was an 1871 inn that now contains a miscellany of photos, ship models, and tools. Upstairs is a room set up to reflect the Victorian period.

The beaches on Block Island will suit every taste. Immediately south of the Old Harbor, past the breakwater, is the northern end of **Pebbly Beach,** a section informally known as **Ballard's Beach** for the popular restaurant located there (see "Where to Dine," below). Crowded with sunbathers and swimmers, it is one of only two on the island with lifeguards. The surf is often rough. Drinks are served at your towel. North of Old Harbor, beyond the Surf Hotel, starts the 3-mile-long **Crescent Beach** (also known as Frederick J. Benson Town Beach or simply Town Beach). The southern section, with a sandy bottom that stays shallow well out into the gentle surf, is known as **Kid Beach** because of its relative safety for children. Farther along is the main part, a broad strand served by a pavilion with a snack bar, bathrooms, and showers. Chairs, umbrellas, and boogie boards can be rented. The surf is higher along here and rolls straight in; lifeguards are on duty. Continuing north, and with a small parking lot reached by a dirt road off Corn Neck Road, is **Scotch Beach.** Consider this grown-up and R-rated, dominated by young summer workers and residents. Still farther north is **Mansion Beach,** with a dirt road of the same name leading in from Corn

Neck Road. Somewhat more secluded, it is usually less crowded than the others. On the west side of the island, running south from the jetty that marks the entrance to New Harbor, is **Charlestown Beach.** Uncrowded and relatively tranquil during the day, it draws anglers from dusk into the night surf-casting for striped bass.

Apart from sunbathing, the island's most popular pursuit is **bicycling.** The ferries allow visitors to bring their own bikes (for a small fee), but several local agencies rent bikes as well (see "Getting Around," above).

Parasailing has become popular here, and chutes can be seen lifting riders up to heights of 1,200 feet above the ocean. Call **Block Island Parasail** (© **401/864-2474;** www.blockislandparasail.com) with questions, but you must make reservations in person at the office near the Old Harbor ferry landing. Fares start at $70 and go up, gauged by altitude; observers are charged $20 each. The company also offers banana boat and jet boat rides, as well as dive trips.

A more old-fashioned form of transportation is provided by **Rustic Rides Farm,** on West Side Road (© **401/466-5060**). A walking attendant handles the reins and protects the littlest ones on the trail. A 1-hour slow ride costs $40; a 1-hour sunset ride costs $65, and a 2-hour beach ride is $100.

Fishing, kayaking, and canoeing are hugely popular, and one name to know is **Pond & Beyond** (© **401/742-5460**). The owners possess encyclopedic knowledge of the island, and their rental kayaks put in at the head of the gentle inland ponds off the Great Salt Pond (New Harbor). Guided tours are limited to five kayakers of any skill level. Tours last 2½ hours and cost $50 per person. **Block Island Fishworks,** Ocean Avenue (© **401/466-5392;** www.bifishworks.com), sells fishing tackle and arranges charter boat outings for both inshore and deep-water angling. Another source of boat rentals is **Champlin's Resort,** on Great Salt Pond (© **401/466-5811;** www.champlins resort.com), which has bumper boats and Zodiacs as well as kayaks.

WHERE TO STAY

Most inns are in buildings over 100 years old, so expect wavy floors, narrow hallways, steep staircases, and rooms of odd configuration. Air-conditioning is rare on the island, and such amenities as TV and Wi-Fi cannot be assumed. With what amounts to a 4-month year for businesses serving tourists, the differences in cost between moderate and very expensive room rates are narrow. Two- or 3-night minimum stays are routinely required.

Atlantic Inn 🐸🐸   Perched upon 6 rolling acres south of downtown, this 1879 Victorian hotel beguiles with its long veranda and broad views. Bedrooms are furnished mostly with antiques. Drawn by the restaurant's changing menu of special appetizers—braised pheasant with cranberry beans was one—people start assembling at 4pm each summer day. They take up the Adirondack chairs on the sloping lawn to settle in for the spectacular sunsets, lubricated by cocktails and the most diverse beer and wine selection on the island. Bill Clinton stopped by for dinner when he was President, drawn by the reputation of the kitchen, one of the two most accomplished on Block Island. It can be assumed he had no trouble getting a table, but the rest of us need reservations from June to September.

High St., Box 188, Block Island, RI 02807. © **800/224-7422** or 401/466-5883. Fax 401/466-5678. www.atlantic inn.com. 21 units. Mid-Apr to mid-Oct $165–$289 double. Rates include breakfast. DISC, MC, V. Closed Nov–Apr. **Amenities:** Restaurant (eclectic); bar; 2 tennis courts; bike rental.

Champlin's ★★ *Kids*   Families are welcome at this all-inclusive resort, with 225 slips in the marina for visiting yachters. Those who are put off by the idiosyncratic adornments of Victorian inns will be pleased by the simpler lines and muted fabrics of the bedrooms here. All rooms have fridges and microwaves (another plus for families). There's live music in the bars on weekends, picnic grounds with grills, a pizza bar and ice-cream parlor, a laundry facility, and even a theater showing first-run movies. Once you've unpacked, there isn't much to compel you to leave, but a shuttle van is provided for trips to other parts of the island. Cars, mopeds, kayaks, and pontoon boats are available for rent.

Great Salt Pond, P.O. Box J, Block Island, RI 02807. ✆ **800/762-4541** or 401/466-7777. Fax 401/466-2638. www. champlinsresort.com. 30 units. $275–$335 double. AE, MC, V. Closed mid-Oct to early May. From Old Harbor, drive west on Ocean Ave. and turn left on West Side Rd. The entrance road to Champlin's is on the right. Ferries from Long Island dock here. **Amenities:** Restaurant; 2 bars; large outdoor pool; 2 tennis courts; kayak, bumper boat, and paddle-boat rentals; moped and bike rentals; game room; car rental; coin-op washers and dryers. *In room:* A/C, TV, unstocked fridge.

Rose Farm ★   Spot deer and pheasant on the 20 acres of the 1897 farmhouse that was the original inn. It is complemented by an additional house across the driveway. Four of the rooms in the new building feature Jacuzzis and decks. Some have canopied beds, most have ocean views, and their furnishings are often antique. A few share bathrooms. Afternoon refreshments, usually iced tea and pastries, are served. There are 24 bicycles available for rent.

Roslyn Rd., Box E, Block Island, RI 02807. ✆ **401/466-2034**. Fax 401/466-2053. www.rosefarminn.com. 19 units, 2 with shared bathroom. $119–$259 double. Rates include breakfast. AE, DISC, MC, V. Closed Nov–Mar. From Old Harbor, drive west on High St. and turn left on paved driveway past the Atlantic Inn. Children over 12 welcome. **Amenities:** Bike rental; coin-op washers and dryers.

The 1661 Inn/Hotel Manisses ★★   Emus, llamas, black swans, two camels, and a Scottish Highland ox graze in the meadow behind the Hotel Manisses, the most visible property of a island-wide hospitality empire. The Victorian hotel tends toward older couples. Guest rooms utilize oak antiques and lots of wicker; some have fireplaces. The Manisses parlor serves desserts and flaming coffees in the evening, and stylish dining is featured in the main dining room, with comparable fare in the more casual Gatsby Room. Picnic lunches are also prepared for guests.

The 1661 Inn, up the hill, is where substantial champagne breakfast buffets and afternoon wine and cheese are served to guests of all nine of the properties. (Children are welcome in seven of the buildings; smoking is allowed in one.) The 1661 Inn is now open year-round, although the restaurants are closed in winter.

1 Spring St., P.O. Box 1, Block Island, RI 02807. ✆ **800/626-4773** or 401/466-2421/2063. Fax 401/466-3162. www. blockislandresorts.com. 17 units in hotel, 9 units in the inn, additional units in satellite properties. $70–$440 double. Rates include breakfast. MC, V. **Amenities:** 2 restaurants; bar; concierge; babysitting. *In room:* TV/VCR, fridge, hair dryer.

Spring House Hotel ★   Marked by its red mansard roof and wraparound porch, the island's oldest hotel (1852) has hosted Ulysses S. Grant, Mark Twain, and the Kennedy clan. The young staff is congenial, if occasionally a bit scattered. Bedrooms in the two buildings come in three styles, with queen-size beds and pullout sofas; most are large. A significant attraction is the all-you-can-eat barbecue lunch on the veranda. More formal meals are served in the all-white dining room. Swimming is allowed in the freshwater pond on the property. The hotel sponsors concerts of classical and pop music on its grounds in July and August.

902 Spring St., P.O. Box 902, Block Island, RI 02807. © **800/234-9263** or 401/466-5844. www.springhousehotel. com. 50 units. $125–$400 double. Rates include breakfast. AE, MC, V. Closed mid-Oct through Mar. **Amenities:** Restaurant; bar.

WHERE TO DINE

Expect mostly lobsters, fried and grilled fish and chicken, and routine burgers and beef cuts. Chowders are usually surefire, especially the creamy New England version. Clam cakes appear less frequently on menus than before but are still a staple. Actually deep-fried fritters containing more dough than clams, they are still fun eating, especially when dipped in tartar sauce. Lobster dishes are usually sold at market prices, higher than those listed below.

Several inns and hotels have dining rooms worth noting (see "Where to Stay," above), but even there, neither jackets nor ties are required. Due to the seasonal nature of the resort island, its restaurants can change policies, menus, and, most important, chefs, in a twinkling. Keep that in mind if any of the observations below prove to undervalue or overstate a restaurant's virtues.

Ballard's ⭐ *Kids* AMERICAN   Sooner rather than later, everyone winds up at Ballard's. Behind the long front porch is a warehouselike hall where a monster whale skeleton hangs, and beyond that a terrace beside a crowded beach. Several bars and frequent live bands fuel drinkers and diners from lunch until midnight. The menu is all over the map, with something for everyone. Complementing the lobster rolls and fish and chips are yellowfin tuna au poivre and roasted monkfish medallions with shrimp and sweet pepper. Kids have their own menu, and they can make as much noise and mess as they want. It gets pricey for families, though, so you might want to go for lunch, not dinner, and have sandwiches, not entrees.

Old Harbor. © **401/466-2231.** www.ballardsinn.com. Main courses $9–$24. AE, MC, V. Daily 11am–midnight. Closed Oct to mid-May.

Beachhead ⭐ *Kids* ECLECTIC   After changes in management, the menu has been expanded from the former tavern limitations to one of the more ambitious slates on the island. The casual atmosphere remains, making this a likely destination for families in afternoon and early evening (dinner prices are steep, though). In peak season, at least, the noise level is high enough to mask childish squeals. Plenty of seating is available inside and on the porch. There's a pizza of the day, seafood and meats are prepared in more imaginative ways than before, and the selection of beers and wines is attractive.

Corn Neck Rd. © **401/466-2249.** www.thebeachead.com. Main courses $16–$25. MC, V. Daily 11:30am–9pm (later in summer).

Eli's ITALIAN/AMERICAN   This place used to be just a spaghetti-and-grinders drop-in, but it's evolved into one of the island's most popular eateries. Problem is, it can serve only 50 voracious diners at a time, and the no-reservations policy means waits of up to 2 hours. Once inside at table, tuna nachos are a popular appetizer, and marinated chicken with Thai curry fried rice is tops. Rack of lamb comes crusted in oregano and almonds with a bulgur salad, tomatoes, and feta cheese with a lemon-caper brown butter sauce. Such combinations are undeniably full-flavored, although the diverse ingredients are often mashed together as if in a thick stew, losing some of their individuality. Huge portions defy anyone to finish.

Chapel St. © **401/466-5230.** Main courses $19–$28. DISC, MC, V. May–Oct daily 6–9pm (Sat–Sun until 10pm); Nov–Dec Sat–Sun 5:30–10pm. Closed Jan–Apr.

Tips **Do-It-Yourself Shore Dinners**

Should you have housekeeping facilities in your lodging, you might wish to put together a New England shore dinner. Lobster is the central component, of course, and you can buy yours straight off the fishing boats. Each afternoon from about 4 to 5:30pm, boats put in at both Old Harbor and the Great Salt Pond. Depending upon their catches of the day, they charge from $6 to $8 per pound. A more reliable source is **Finn's Fish Market,** at the Old Harbor ferry landing (© **401/466-2102**). Its lobster prices are similar, and it also carries oysters, clams, shrimp, and fish.

For the other fixings—corn, tomatoes, bread, sausage, chicken—stop at either the **Block Island Grocery** (known as the B.I.G.), near Ocean Avenue and Corn Neck Road (© **401/466-2949**), a conventional supermarket; or **Block Island Depot,** Ocean Avenue (© **401/466-2403**), which carries a line of cheeses and organic foods. The best-stocked wine and liquor store is the **Red Bird Package Store,** on Dodge Street (© **401/466-2441**), around the corner from the north end of Water Street. **Seaside Market,** toward the other end of Water Street (© **401/466-5876**), has a good wine selection and some grocery products.

G. R. Sharky's AMERICAN   With its kicked-back atmosphere and pub-style menu, this entry opposite Crescent Beach has a clear kinship with at least a dozen casual eateries on the island. Mounted fish, deer heads, and sports memorabilia decorate the bar. Expect the usual burgers and cheesesteak pretenders, but know that the people handling the fried-fish dishes have a superbly light hand—go for the definitive fish and chips. Daily specials lean to the likes of blackened this or that—mako shark, for one—while regular dinner entrees run to fettuccine Alfredo and rib-eye steak. Children are welcome.

Corn Neck Rd. © 401/466-9900. Main courses $14–$27. MC, V. Daily 5–10pm. Closed late Oct to mid-May.

Harry's Café ECLECTIC   A former deli has been expanded into this perky new eatery near the post office with side windows looking out over New Harbor. It's furnished with oak tables and bentwood chairs, and there are a few tables out on the terrace. Order at the counter in front of the open kitchen in back, and they bring the food to you. Trust their menu when they describe their burritos as "BIG!" And expect the other choices to bounce around the continents, what with jerk scallops, ginger chicken wontons, and ravioli diablo. Most items sampled proved to be a cut or two above the island standard. Alcohol isn't served.

Water St. © 401/466-5400. www.harryscafe.com. Main courses $16-$25. Daily noon–10pm.

The Oar ☆ AMERICAN   This former good-time bar is now open for a buffet breakfast and full-service lunch and dinner, and the menu has been plumped up with a few more choices. Grilled swordfish, sirloin, and fried chicken flesh out the old roster of nachos, lobster rolls, and calamari. A deck and a bar with a picture window take in dramatic views of storms over the mainland and of the fleet of pleasure boats in the Great Salt Pond. Enclosing the deck with clear plastic and adding heat lamps has extended the season. Inside, the ceiling and walls are hung with scores of oars—all of them painted with cartoons, graffiti, and assorted messages of obscure or ribald intent.

West Side Rd. (Block Island Marina). ℭ 401/466-8820. Main courses $14–$25. AE, MC, V. Daily 8am–midnight (bar until 1am). Closed late Oct to May.

BLOCK ISLAND AFTER DARK

Nightlife isn't of the raunchy, rollicking South Florida variety, but the bars don't close at sunset, either. Among the prime candidates for a potential rockin' good time is **Captain Nick's,** on Ocean Avenue (ℭ 401/466-5670), opposite the Block Island Grocery. It has pool, three bars, and a large dance floor inside, as well as dollar beers, cheap burgers, and live music most nights in season out on the terrace. A block away, **McGovern's Yellow Kittens,** on Corn Neck Road (ℭ 401/466-5855), also presents live bands in summer, inside or out on the deck. Darts, pool tables, foosball, and video games help fill the winter nights. Pub food, pool tables, video games, and foosball are also attractions at **Club Soda,** on Connecticut Avenue (ℭ 401/466-5397).

Ballard's (see "Where to Dine," above) has live rock or pop most afternoons out on the terrace and nightly inside. An occasional live-music venue is the lounge of the **National Hotel,** on Water Street (ℭ 401/466-2901). Yachtsmen and other sailors docked or moored at Champlin's Marina settle in on the end of the main dock at **Trader Vic's,** at New Harbor (ℭ 401/466-2641). The bar is downstairs, with a DJ or band out on the deck most afternoons. In addition to the sunset drinks and tapas on the front lawn of the **Atlantic Inn** (see "Where to Stay," above), many visitors settle in on the porch of the equally well-situated (and less expensive) **Narragansett Inn,** on Water Street (ℭ 401/466-2626).

Island residents try to keep **Mahogany Shoals,** on Payne's Dock at the end of Water Street (ℭ 401/466-5572), to themselves. What they come for is the barbed humor of Wally McDonough. He sings Irish folk ballads and banters with the audience, invariably giving better than he gets. Wally occupies his corner Wednesday through Sunday nights, assuming he feels like it. Get there around 10pm.

12

Vermont

by Paul Karr

Vermont's rolling, cow-spotted hills, shaggy peaks, sugar maples, world-champion fall foliage, and quaint towns give it a distinct sense of place. This state is filled with the dairy farms, dirt roads, and small-scale enterprises that bring joy to the hearts of back-road travelers. And the towns are home to an intriguing mix of old-time Vermonters, back-to-the-landers who showed up in VW buses in the 1960s and never left (many got involved with municipal affairs or put down business roots—think Ben & Jerry); and newer, moneyed arrivals from New York or Boston who came to ski or stay at B&Bs and ended up buying second homes. Some of those second homes ended up becoming first homes.

The place captures a sense of America as it once was—because, here it still *is*. Vermonters share a sense of community, and they still respect the ideals of thrift and parsimony above those of commercialism. (It took years for Wal-Mart to get approval to build its first big-box store in Vermont.) Locals prize their villages, and understand what makes them special. That counts for a lot in an age when so many other small towns have been swallowed up by suburban creep or otherwise faded away with the changing of the times.

For travelers, Vermont remains a superb destination of country drives, mountain rambles, and overnights at country inns. A good map opens the door to back-road adventures, and it's not hard to get a taste of Vermont's way of life. The state's total population is just a shade over 600,000, making it one of only a handful of states with more senators (two) than representatives (one) in Congress. It does sometimes feel like the cows still outnumber the humans here.

Southern Vermont has mostly resisted the encroachments of progress (except at ski resorts on winter weekends), and remains a great introduction to the state. You'll find plenty of antiques shops, handsome inns, fast-flowing streams (with fish!), and inviting restaurants. The area is anchored at each corner by the towns of Bennington and Brattleboro; between them runs the spine of the Green Mountains and a national forest district, both of which reward explorers in search of Robert Frostian views and experiences. These hills also host many of the state's popular ski resorts.

Northern Vermont is different. On the region's western edge, along the shores of Lake Champlain, Burlington—the state's largest, most lively city—is ringed by fast-growing suburban communities and fun startup companies. But drive an hour east and you're deep in the Northeast Kingdom, the state's least developed, most lost-in-time region.

There are remnants of industry here—marble quarries near Rutland, converging train tracks at White River Junction, brick factories in Springfield and Bellows Falls—but mostly it's still rural living: cow pastures high in the hills, clapboard farmhouses under spreading trees, maple-sugaring operations, the distant sound of timber being cut in woodlots. New and old co-exist here peaceably, and there are few places in America I'd rather be on a summer or fall afternoon.

1 Bennington, Manchester & Southwestern Vermont

Bennington: 143 miles NW of Boston; 126 miles S of Burlington. Manchester: 24 miles N of Bennington

BENNINGTON 🐝

Bennington, Vermont's third-largest city, owes its fame (such as it is) to a handful of eponymous moments, places, and things: the Battle of Bennington, fought in 1777 during the American War of Independence; Bennington College, a small, prestigious liberal arts school; and Bennington pottery, which traces its ancestry back to the original factory in 1793 and is still prized by collectors for its superb quality.

Today visitors will find a Bennington of two faces. Historic Bennington (more commonly known as Old Bennington), with its white clapboard homes, sits atop a hill west of town off Route 9. (Look for the obelisk and you're there.) Modern downtown Bennington, on the other hand, is a pleasant but no-frills commercial center stocked with real estate offices, plumbers, diners, and stores that still sell what people actually need—not so much a tourist destination as a handy supply depot.

ESSENTIALS

GETTING THERE Bennington is at the intersection of state routes 9 and 7. If you're coming from the south, the nearest interstate access is via the New York Thruway at Albany, about 35 miles away. (But you have to drive through the city of Troy first, which takes time; figure 45 minutes or more from the Thruway to downtown Bennington.) From the east, I-91 is about 40 miles away at Brattleboro.

VISITOR INFORMATION The **Bennington Area Chamber of Commerce,** 100 Veterans Memorial Dr. (🕐 **800/229-0252** or 802/447-3311; www.bennington.com), maintains a **visitor center** on Route 7 about 1 mile north of the downtown, near the veterans' complex and a small park. This office is open Monday to Friday from 9am to 5pm year-round, and also Saturday and Sunday from 10am to 4pm from mid-May until mid-October. There's also a **downtown welcome center** (🕐 **802/442-5758**) in a former blacksmith shop at South and Elm streets; look for the big blue flag. Operated by the *other* BBC—the Better Bennington Corporation, of course—it's open Monday through Saturday from 9am to 5pm year-round and has a big map of the area to orient you.

EXPLORING THE TOWN

You can't miss the **Bennington Battle Monument** 🐝🐝 (🕐 **802/447-0550**) if you're passing through the countryside. This 306-foot obelisk of blue limestone atop a low rise was dedicated in 1891. It resembles a shorter, paunchier Washington Monument. Note also that it's about 6 miles southeast from the actual site of the battle; this monument marks the spot where munitions were stored. The monument's viewing platform, which is reached by elevator, is open daily from 9am to 5pm from mid-April through October. A small fee ($2 adults, $1 children age 6–14) is charged.

Near the monument, you'll find distinguished old homes lushly overarched with ancient trees. Be sure to spend a few moments exploring the old burying ground, where several Vermont governors and the poet Robert Frost are buried. The chamber

Moments **"I Had a Lover's Quarrel with the World."**

That's the epitaph on the tombstone of Robert Frost, who is buried in the cemetery behind the 1806 First Congregational Church where Route 9 makes two quick bends west of downtown and down the hill from the Bennington Monument. Signs point the way to the Frost family grave. Travelers often stop here to pay their respects to the man many still consider to be *the* true voice of New England. (Frost was born in California, but was raised in Massachusetts from the age of 11 and lived mostly in New Hampshire and Vermont the rest of his life.) Closer to the church, look for the old tombstones—some decorated with urns and skulls—of other Vermonters who lived much less famous lives.

of commerce (see above) provides a walking-tour brochure that helps you make sense of this neighborhood's formerly vibrant past.

Bennington College ✪ was founded in the 1930s as an experimental women's college. It has since gone co-ed and garnered a national reputation as a leading liberal arts school. Bennington has a great reputation for the teaching of writing; W. H. Auden, Bernard Malamud, and John Gardner all taught here. In the 1980s, Bennington produced a fresh wave of prominent young authors, including Donna Tartt, Bret Easton Ellis, and Jill Eisenstadt. The pleasant campus north of town is worth wandering.

The Bennington Museum ✪✪   This eclectic and intriguing collection is one of the best small museums in northern New England. The museum traces its roots back to 1875, although it has occupied its current stone-and-column home overlooking the valley since "only" 1928. The expansive galleries feature a wide range of exhibits on local arts and industry, including early Vermont furniture, glass, paintings, and Bennington pottery. Of special interest are the many colorful primitive landscapes by Grandma Moses (1860–1961), who lived much of her life nearby. (The museum has the largest collection of Moses paintings in the world.) Look also for the glorious 1925 luxury car called the Wasp, just 16 of which were handcrafted in Bennington between 1920 and 1925, and rotating special exhibitions, like the 2007 Impressionist show of rarely shown works from Renoir, Monet, Degas, and the like.

75 W. Main St. (Rte. 9 btw. Old Bennington and the town center). ⓒ 802/447-1571. www.benningtonmuseum.org. Admission $8 adults, $7 seniors and students, free for children under 18; $19 family. Daily 10am–5pm.

WHERE TO STAY
The Four Chimneys Inn ✪✪   This 1912 Colonial Revival catches your eye as you roll into Bennington from the west; it's at the edge of Old Bennington, so the towering Bennington Monument looms just over its shoulder. Set back from Route 7 on an 11-acre, nicely landscaped lot, this imposing white three-story structure features—no surprise—four prominent chimneys. It was once a fancy-pants restaurant where such luminaries as Liz Taylor and Walt Disney supped. Today, the guest rooms (in the main inn, an ice house, and a carriage house) are inviting and homey; some sport real fireplaces burning actual wood, and some have nice Jacuzzis, four-poster beds, and/or mountain views. The overall atmosphere seems to be improving with the latest owners, the Greens, who married at the inn.

Vermont

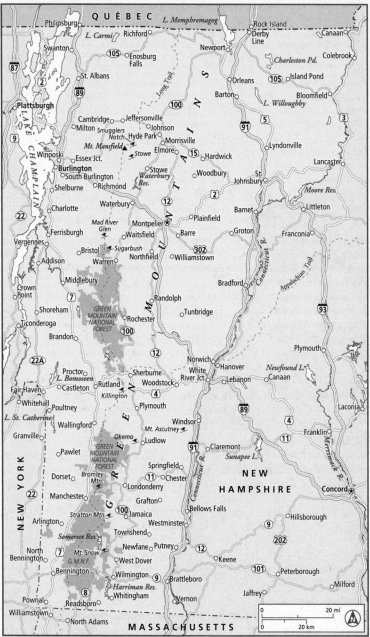

21 West Rd., Bennington, VT 05201. ✆ **802/447-3500.** Fax 802/447-3692. www.fourchimneys.com. 11 units. $125–$275 double. Rates include full breakfast. 2-night minimum stay foliage and holiday weekends. AE, DISC, MC, V. Children 12 and over accepted. **Amenities:** Restaurant. *In room:* A/C, TV, dataport, hair dryer, iron/ironing board, Jacuzzi (some units), fireplace (some units).

Paradise Motor Inn ★ (Kids)

Paradise by the dashboard light? Well, this is Bennington's best motel, even if prices have shot up in recent years; it's uncommonly clean and well-managed, sits across from the Hemmings gas station, and is walking distance to town. The tidy, generously sized accommodations are further bolstered by such surprising amenities as full kitchens in some of the suites, tennis courts, a heated pool, and a decent coffee shop. The central location and views aren't bad, either. Try to reserve a spot in the North Building, in spite of its dated 1980s styling—each unit has an outdoor terrace or balcony. The more up-to-date Office Building is done in Colonial Revival style.

141 W. Main St., Bennington, VT 05201. ✆ **800/575-5784** or 802/442-8351. Fax 802/447-3889. www.theparadise motorinn.com. 78 units. $85–$130 double, $110–$240 suite. DC, DISC, MC, V. **Amenities:** Restaurant; heated outdoor pool; 2 tennis courts; fitness room; coin-op laundry. *In room:* A/C, TV, Jacuzzis (some), kitchenette (some units).

South Shire Inn ★★

A locally prominent banking family hired architect William Bull in 1880 to design and build this impressive Victorian home. The spacious downstairs has leaded glass on its bookshelves and intricate plasterwork in the dining room. The five guest rooms in the main inn are richly hued, and most have canopied beds and working fireplaces using Duraflame-type logs. The best room is one of the old master bedrooms, with its king-size canopied bed, tile-hearth fireplace, and beautiful bathroom with hand-painted tile. Four newer, more modern guest rooms—with such names as "Jim Dandy"—are in the carriage house; here, the downstairs rooms are slightly more formal, while the upstairs rooms more intimate, with low eaves and skylights over their tubs. These rooms have televisions with VCRs, ceiling fans, and (in one case) even a wet bar. There's a daily afternoon tea served in the main house.

124 Elm St., Bennington, VT 05201. ✆ **888/201-2250** or 802/447-3839. Fax 802/442-3547. www.southshire.com. 9 units. $110–$225 double. Rates include breakfast. MC, V. Not appropriate for children. *In room:* A/C, TV (some units), hair dryer, fireplace, Jacuzzi (some units).

WHERE TO DINE

Alldays & Onions ★ ECLECTIC

This casual spot was named after an early-20th-century British automobile manufacturer. Locals flock here to enjoy wholesome, tasty sandwiches, deli salads, and tasty soups; the atmosphere is that of a small-town restaurant gussied up for a big night out. Expect anything from pot roast and turkey with fixings to Cajun seafood pasta, grilled steaks or shrimp, pastrami sandwiches, burgers, or tortellini. More ambitious items might include a Southwest cowboy steak or stir-fried soba noodles and vegetables. Breakfast, served Saturday and Sunday only, is good.

519 Main St. ✆ **802/447-0043.** Reservations accepted for dinner only. Breakfast items $2–$8; sandwiches $3–$7; dinner main courses $15–$19. AE, DISC, MC, V. Mon–Wed 11am–3pm; Thurs–Fri 11am–3pm and 5–9pm; Sat 7:30am–10:30am, 11am–3pm, and 5–9pm; Sun 9am–1pm.

Blue Benn Diner ★ (Value) DINER

Diner aficionados make pilgrimages to enjoy the ambience of this 1945 Silk City classic—so classic that the blue-plate dinner specials might also include vegetables, rice, soup or salad, rolls, and rice pudding for one price. A bit incongruously, fancier and vegetarian fare is also available, such as a grilled portobello on sourdough. But that's not why you're here. You come here for reliable New England diner staples such as turkey with gravy, fried haddock, slabs of cornbread

French toast, great omelets, fruity pancakes, homemade doughnuts, and a signature butterscotch Indian pudding served warm with a scoop of vanilla ice cream.

314 North St. (Rte. 7). ℂ 802/442-5140. Breakfast $1.50–$5.95; sandwiches and entrees $1.95–$5.75; dinner specials $7.95–$8.95. No credit cards. Mon–Tues 6am–5pm; Wed–Fri 6am–8pm; Sat 6am–4pm; Sun 7am–4pm.

Pangaea ✰✰ ECLECTIC   This upscale little culinary campus is a bit hard to find (it's tucked away in workaday North Bennington), but it's well worthwhile for gourmands to make the effort. This is one of the better restaurants in southern Vermont. Chef/owner Bill Scully delivers excellent meals (using local and organic ingredients whenever possible) in no less than five distinct dining spaces. Start with something intriguing such as Vermont boar-and-Brie Wellington, spring rolls, or a chèvre-cardamom strudel. Entrees could include a pan-roasted breast of Long Island duck, saltimbocca, Thai green curry, maple-glazed pork loin, or a piece of pan-roasted wild-caught striped bass; sauces are accented with hints of Asia and Europe. There's also a cozy lounge next door, serving a lighter menu of burgers, pasta, cassoulet, Cobb salads, stir-fries, and worldwide beers that wouldn't be out of place in a chic Manhattan hotel lounge.

1 Prospect St., N. Bennington (from Bennington, go west on Rte. 9 a half-mile, turn right onto Rte. 67A near Hemmings, and continue 4½ miles to N. Bennington. Restaurant is in center of village). ℂ 802/442-7171. Dinner main courses $19–$34; lounge items $6–$21. V, MC. Tues–Sun 5–9pm.

ARLINGTON, MANCHESTER & DORSET ✰✰✰

This trio of closely spaced villages is Vermont at its, well, Vermont-est, making them an ideal collective destination for a romantic getaway, aggressive antiquing, or even some serious outlet shopping. Each of the three towns is worth visiting, and each has its own unique charm and vibe.

Arlington ✰ has a town center that borders on microscopic. With its auto-body shops, hub-of-town gas station, and redemption center (all remnants of a time when the main highway artery passed right through town), it gleams a bit less than its compatriots just to the north.

Manchester ✰✰ (also known as Manchester Village) and **Manchester Center** share a blurred town line, yet maintain distinct characters. The more southerly Manchester Village has an old-world, old-money elegance and a prim, campuslike town centered on the resplendently columned Equinox Resort. Just to the north, Manchester Center is the major mercantile hub in these parts, with dozens of outlet stores offering discounts on big-name clothing, accessories, and housewares.

Another worthy detour off the beaten track is **Dorset** ✰✰, an exquisitely preserved little village of white clapboard architecture and marble sidewalks. It's a bit farther to the north; to get there, follow Route 30 north out of Manchester Center.

ESSENTIALS

GETTING THERE   Arlington, Manchester, and Manchester Center all lie north of Bennington on Historic Route 7A, which runs parallel to and west of Route 7; you can take either route. Dorset is north of Manchester Center on Route 30, which diverges from Route 7A in Manchester Center. **Vermont Transit** (ℂ 800/552-8737; www.vermonttransit.com) provides bus service to Manchester Center; the bus stop (and ticket sales) are located at 119 Canal St.

VISITOR INFORMATION   The **Manchester and the Mountains Regional Chamber of Commerce** (ℂ 800/362-4144 or 802/362-2100; www.manchester vermont.net) maintains a year-round information center at 5080 Main St. (Rte. 7A

North) beside the small village green in Manchester Center. Its open Monday through Saturday from 10am to 5pm, and from Memorial Day weekend through October, it's also open on Sundays from noon to 5pm and until 7pm on Friday and Saturday nights. If you're staying in **Arlington,** that hamlet maintains its own small self-serve visitor information center at the Stewart's gas station on Route 7A. Just take what you need.

For information on outdoor recreation, the **Green Mountain National Forest** maintains a district ranger office (© **802/362-2307**) in Manchester on routes 11 and 30 east of Route 7. It's open Monday through Friday from 8am to 4:30pm.

MUSEUMS & HISTORIC HOMES

American Museum of Fly Fishing ⋆⋆ *Finds* If you loved *A River Runs Through It* and you're crazy about fly-fishing, you've come to the right place: This is home to the world's largest collection of angling art and items. The complex, which includes a gallery space, library, reading room, store, and historical resources, was specially built for the purpose; browse through the impressive collection of antique rods (including those of Daniel Webster, Ernest Hemingway, and Winslow Homer), reels, and 200-year-old flies, as well as photos, instructional videos, sketchbooks, and historical items. A Greek historian wrote of a fly-fishing-like practice in A.D. 200—who knew? This is a surprisingly fun place to while away an hour; about the only thing missing is, well, fish. The museum is right on Route 7A between the Equinox and Manchester Center's shops, just south of the Orvis flagship store.

4104 Main St. (Rte. 7A), Manchester, VT 05254. © **802/362-3300**. www.amff.com. $5 adults, $3 children ages 5–14. Daily 10am–4pm (closed major holidays).

Hildene ⋆⋆ When you first drive up the gravel road to this estate, you may not realize that you're face to face with both U.S. history and natural history. Robert Todd Lincoln, son of the tragically assassinated U.S. president, summered in this stately 24-room Georgian Revival mansion between 1905 and 1926, and delighted in showing off its remarkable features; they include a sweeping staircase and a 1908 Aeolian organ with 1,000 pipes (you can hear it played on the house tour). This place is more regal than ostentatious, and it was built with an eye toward quality. Lincoln also had formal gardens designed after the patterns in a stained-glass window and planted on a gentle promontory outside with outstanding views of the flanking mountains—today, that view is one of the southern Vermont's most popular wedding spots each summer and fall. The home and lovely, expansive grounds can be viewed on group tours that start at an informative visitor center; allow time following the tour to explore those grounds. In summer, there are fun wagon rides to the Hildene farm for $1 extra, and cross-country skiing and snowshoeing are allowed with admission to the grounds in winter.

Historic Rte. 7A, off Rte. 30, Manchester. © **802/362-1788**. www.hildene.org. Tours $12 adults, $4 children, free for children under 6. Grounds $5 adults, $2 children 6–14. Daily 9:30am–4:30pm.

Southern Vermont Art Center ⋆⋆ This fine-art center is well worth the short detour from town. Located partly in a striking Georgian Revival home surrounded by more than 400 pastoral hillside acres (it overlooks land that once belonged to Charles Orvis of fly-fishing fame), the center features a series of galleries displaying works from its well-regarded collection, as well as frequently changing exhibits of contemporary Vermont artists. An inventive and appealing modern building across the drive, designed to display more of the 800-piece permanent collection, opened in 2000. (It was designed by the noted contemporary architect Hugh Newell Jacobsen.) Check the center's schedule before you arrive; you may be able to sign up for an art class or workshop while you're in town. Also, leave time to enjoy a light lunch at the **Garden Cafe** and wander the lovely grounds, exploring both the sculpture garden and the woods beyond.

West Rd. off Rte. 30 (P.O. Box 617), Manchester. ℂ **802/362-1405**. www.svac.org. Admission $8 adults, $3 students, free for children under 13. Tues–Sat 10am–5pm; Sun noon–5pm.

AREA SKIING

Bromley Mountain Ski Resort ☝ *Kids*   Bromley is a great place to learn to ski. Gentle and forgiving, the mountain also has long, looping, intermediate runs that are tremendously popular with families; *SKI Magazine* once named it the second-best ski destination in the nation for families. The slopes are mostly south-facing, which means they receive the warmth of the sun and some protection from the harshest winter winds. (It also means that the snow may melt more quickly than at other ski resorts.) The base lodge scene is mellower than at many resorts, and your experience is almost guaranteed to be relaxing. This is *not* a fancy-pants resort, and the runs do not feature any extreme by-the-seat-of-your-pants skiing; if you want that, bypass this one. But for what it is, Bromley is very nice.

3984 Rte. 11, Peru (P.O. Box 1130, Manchester Center, VT 05255). ℂ **802/824-5522**, or 800/865-4786 for lodging. www.bromley.com. Adult lift tickets $25–$63 day, $25–$52 half-day; discounts for youths and seniors.

Stratton Mountain Ski Resort ☝☝   Founded in the 1960s, Stratton labored in its early days under the belief that Vermont ski areas needed to be Tyrolean to be successful—hence, the overly Swiss-chalet feel of the architecture, and for a while this mountain felt like Vail's slightly poorer cousin. In recent years, though, Stratton has worked to shed its image as a haven of alpine quaintness. In a bid to attract a younger, edgier set, new owners have spent more than $25 million in improvements (mostly in snowmaking). Now it's consistently ranked among the nation's top ten best-groomed mountains by skiers, and also gathers kudos for its lifts, dining options, and customer service. The slopes here are especially popular with snowboarders; expert skiers should check out Upper Middlebrook, a twisting run off the summit.

RR 1, Box 145 Stratton Mountain, VT 05155. ℂ **802/297-4000**, or 800/STRATTON for lodging. www.stratton.com. Adult day lift tickets $69–$72; discounts for seniors and children.

OTHER OUTDOOR ACTIVITIES

HIKING & BIKING   Scenic hiking trails ranging in difficulty from challenging to easy-as-an-after-dinner-stroll can be found up in the hills a short drive from town. At the Green Mountain District Ranger Station (see "Visitor Information," above), ask for the free brochure *Day Hikes on the Manchester Ranger District,* which lists 19 hiking trails easily reached from Manchester.

A scenic drive 30 to 40 minutes northwest of Manchester Center takes you to the **Delaware and Hudson Rail-Trail,** approximately 20 miles of which have been built in two sections in Vermont. The southern section of the trail runs about 10 miles from West Pawlet to the state line at West Rupert, over trestles and past vestiges of former industry, such as the old Vermont Milk and Cream Co. Like most rail-trails, this one is perfect for exploring by mountain bike. You'll bike sometimes on the original ballast, other times through grassy growth. To reach the trail head, drive north on Route 30 from Manchester Center to Route 315, then continue north on Route 153. In

West Pawlet, park across from the old-timey general store (a good place to pick up refreshments), then set off on the trail southward from the old D&H freight depot across the street.

The hills around Manchester are full of other great touring rides, too; your headquarters should be **Battenkill Sports Bicycle Shop** (© 800/340-2734 or 802/362-2734), at 1240 Depot St. in downtown Manchester Center. It's a wonderful little place, with free local bike maps and a range of rentals from hybrids to touring cycles to mountain bikes.

CANOEING   For a duck's-eye view of the rolling hills, stop by **BattenKill Canoe Ltd.,** on Rte. 7A in Arlington (© 800/421-5268 or 802/362-2800; www.battenkill. com). This friendly outfit offers daily canoe rentals for exploring the Battenkill River and surrounding areas. Trips range from 2 hours to a day, and the firm specializes in multiple-night, inn-to-inn canoe packages. The shop is open daily in season (which runs from about May–Oct) from 9am to 5:30pm, and usually from Wednesday through Friday during the rest of the year (but check ahead if you're coming during those months).

FLY-FISHING   Why not learn from the best? Aspiring anglers can sign up for fly-fishing classes taught by skilled instructors affiliated with **Orvis** (© 800/235-9763), the famous fly-fishing supplier and manufacturer based in Manchester. The 2-day classes (about $430 per person) include instruction in knot tying and casting, plus some catch-and-release fishing on a company pond and the Battenkill River. Classes are held from late April until mid-October, and special rates are available at the Equinox Resort (see "Where to Stay," below) for visiting Orvis students.

WHERE TO STAY
EXPENSIVE

Barrows House 🏵🏵   Within easy strolling distance of Dorset stands this compound of eight Early American buildings, set on 12 nicely landscaped acres studded with birches, firs, and maples. Built in 1784, the main house has been an inn since 1900. Its primary distinctions are its historical lineage and its convenience to Dorset; the rooms are more comfortable than elegant, with sturdy dressers, bedside tables, and the like. Some add gas or wood fireplaces, and three cottages (one of which doubles as the pool house) offer additional space and privacy for families. A few units here have phones, but most still don't—ask in advance if that's important to you. This place will certainly please history buffs. Those looking for more amenities, though, may prefer to book a place in Manchester.

Rte. 30, Dorset, VT 05251. © 800/639-1620 or 802/867-4455. Fax 802/867-0132. www.barrowshouse.com. 28 units. $145–$190 double; $175–$245 suite and cottage. 2-night minimum stay Sat–Sun and some holidays. AE, DISC, MC, V. Pets allowed in 2 cottages. **Amenities:** Restaurant; outdoor pool; 2 tennis courts; sauna; bike rental; game room. *In room:* A/C, TV (some units), dataport (some units), fireplace (some units), Jacuzzi (some units), no phone (some units).

The Equinox Resort 🏵🏵🏵   Under new ownership, the venerable Equinox is changing, yet remains a longtime blue blood (and wedding-party) favorite; its white clapboard and stately columns define Manchester Village. The place's roots date to 1769, but don't be misled: This is a full-blown and modern resort, complete with a full-service spa, lovely indoor pool, scenic golf course, and extensive sports facilities. Rooms are tastefully appointed, if not terribly large, and are being updated as we go to press. The resort recently acquired the nearby **1811 House,** one of the best B&Bs

in the state; it offers cozy rooms with authentically uneven pine floors and antique furniture, and is also being modernized. Suites in the adjacent Charles Orvis Inn are big
and modern, with use of a private billiards room included. A bonus: The resort offers
plenty of activities on its 1,300-plus acres of grounds, such as skeet shooting, falconry,
and guided hikes up Mount Equinox.

Rte. 7A (P.O. Box 46), Manchester Village, VT 05245. (C) **800/362-4747** or 802/362-4700. Fax 802/362-1595.
www.equinoxresort.com. 183 units. Main inn peak season $279–$449 double, $449–$639 suite; off-season $179–
$399 double, $399–$629 suite; Charles Orvis Inn $609–$899 suite. Packages available. AE, DISC, MC, V. **Amenities:**
4 restaurants; indoor pool; outdoor pool; golf course; 3 tennis courts; spa; sauna; concierge; salon; limited room service; babysitting; laundry service; dry cleaning; croquet; falconry school. *In room:* A/C, TV, dataport, hair dryer, iron.

Inn at Ormsby Hill ★★ The oldest part of the striking Inn at Ormsby Hill dates
to 1764 (the revolutionary Ethan Allen is rumored to have hidden out here). Today,
it's a harmonious medley of eras and styles, with inspiring views of the Green Mountains. Free cookies baked by the owner/chef welcome all guests, who then enjoy those
cookies (and those views). Delicious, truly gourmet breakfasts are served in a dining
room that was built by prominent 19th-century attorney Edward Isham to resemble
the interior of a steamship. Each of the inn's rooms has a two-person Jacuzzi and a fireplace. Among the best units: the Taft Room, with its vaulted wood ceiling, and a first-
floor Library, where many of Isham's books still line the shelves.

1842 Main St. (Rte. 7A, near Hildene south of Manchester Village), Manchester Center, VT 05255. (C) **800/670-2841**
or 802/362-1163. Fax 802/362-5176. www.ormsbyhill.com. 10 units. Mon–Fri $195–$315 double; Sat–Sun
$235–$355 double; foliage season and holidays $345–$435. Rates include breakfast. 2-night minimum stay on
Sat–Sun. Mid-week discounts sometimes available. DISC, MC, V. Closed briefly in Apr. Children 14 and older welcome.
In room: A/C, hair dryer, fireplace, Jacuzzi.

The Reluctant Panther ★★★ New owners took over this luxury inn, a quick walk
from the Equinox, in the fall of 2005 . . . and 30 days later, the main house burned
to the ground. Remarkably, it reopened within a year with upgraded furnishings.
Gone is the all-purple paint scheme; all units now sport a fireplace (or two), a Jacuzzi,
thick duvets, and flatscreen televisions. In the main inn, the woodsy Akwanok room
is furnished with Orvis nightstand lamps and a birch headboard handcrafted in the
Adirondacks. Other rooms are decorated according to themes as well: horses in the
John Morgan Suite, flowery murals in the Florist Suite. In the outbuildings, the Garden Suite has a living room and see-through fireplace, while the Panther Suite is popular for its four-poster bed, grandiose bathroom, and regal, columned Jacuzzi. The
Pond View Suite is blue-themed and bigger than most Vermont cottages. A basement-
level pub pulls local beers and hosts live jazz.

17–39 West Rd., Manchester Village, VT 05254. (C) **800/822-2331** or 802/362-2568. Fax 802/362-2586. www.reluctant
panther.com. 20 units. $219–$579 double and suite. Off-season rates lower; holiday and foliage-season rates higher.
Rates include full breakfast. AE, DC, DISC, MC, V. Pets allowed on limited basis ($50 per night charge). **Amenities:**
Restaurant; pub. *In room:* A/C, TV/DVD, coffeemaker, hair dryer, iron/ironing board, fireplace, Jacuzzi.

MODERATE

Arlington Inn ★★ This stout, columned Greek Revival house (1848) would be
perfectly at home in the Virginia countryside; it anchors its village well, set back from
Route 7A on a lawn bordered by sturdy maples. Inside, the inn boasts a similarly
courtly feel, with unique wooden ceilings adorning first-floor rooms and a tavern that
borrows atmosphere from an English hunt club. The 18 units are divided, 6 apiece,
among three buildings: the main building, an 1830 parsonage next door (best if you
prefer modern comforts and extra touches), and the detached carriage house, which is

home to the quietest units because they're farthest removed from the traffic sounds—such as they are—of Route 7A. Most rooms sport four-poster beds, fireplaces, and/or a Jacuzzi; the Remember Baker's room, in the parsonage, even has its own private porch with two rocking chairs.

Rte. 7A at Rte. 313, Arlington, VT 05250. © **800/443-9442** or 802/375-6532. Fax 802/375-6534. www. arlingtoninn.com. 18 units. Aug–Oct $127–$257 double, rest of the year $97–$197 double. Rates include full breakfast. MAP plan available. 2-night minimum stay most weekends. AE, DISC, MC, V. **Amenities:** Restaurant; pub; tennis court; babysitting. *In room:* A/C, TV, dataport, fireplace (some units), Jacuzzi (some units).

Barnstead Inn 🌀 If you're looking for a bit of history with your lodging but feel shell-shocked by area room rates, consider this congenial place within walking distance of Manchester's commercial center. All but two of the guest rooms are in an 1830s hay barn; many are decorated in a rustic country style, some with exposed beams. Expect vinyl bathroom floors, industrial carpeting, and a mix of motel-modern and antique furnishings. Among the more desirable units are the two rooms (nos. 11 and 12) above the office, each with two double beds and original round beams, and the two suites—including the recently renovated Green River Lodge, which comes with a fireplace of hand-laid stone, nice Persian-style rugs, a kitchenette, and a two-person Jacuzzi. A few rooms at this inn are even priced under $100, which is remarkable considering the town it's in. All in all, this place offers good value.

Bonnet St. (P.O. Box 988), Manchester Center, VT 05255. © **800/331-1619** or 802/362-1619. www.barnsteadinn. com. 14 units. $89–$310 double and suite; foliage-season rates higher. AE, MC, V. Children over 12 welcome. **Amenities:** Outdoor pool. *In room:* A/C, TV, dataport, kitchenette (1 unit), fridge (1 unit), coffeemaker, Jacuzzi (1 unit).

The Inn at Manchester 🌀🌀 *Finds* Originally built as a private country home in the late 19th century, this property was converted to lodging in 1978; it's just a half-mile from the budget shopping that draws so many visitors to Manchester. Rooms are in the main inn, built as a private home in 1889, as well as in the adjacent carriage house from the mid-1800's—both are listed on the National Register of Historic Places. Each of the 18 rooms, suites, and carriage-house units—all named for flowers or herbs—are clean and fresh, with distinctive looks. The place is decorated with art and sculpture from around the world; and most, but not all, rooms have televisions, and some have good direct views of Mount Equinox. Buoyant owners Frank and Julie Hanes not only work hard to upgrade and maintain their inn, but they're also as kind and helpful as can be. Four acres of grounds, a brook, and a porch with chairs only add to the peaceful ambience.

Historic Route 7A (P.O. Box 41), Manchester Village, VT 05254. © **800/273-1793** or 802/362-1793. Fax 802/375-6534. www.innatmanchester.com. 18 units. $155–$295 double. Rates include full breakfast. AE, DISC, MC, V. **Amenities:** Dining room; pub; outdoor pool. *In room:* A/C, TV (some units), hair dryer, fireplace (some).

West Mountain Inn 🌀 Sitting atop a grassy bluff at the end of a dirt road a half-mile from Arlington center, this rambling, white-clapboard building dates back a century and a half. It's a perfect place for travelers striving to get away from the hum of the city. Guest rooms, named after famous Vermonters, are nicely furnished with country antiques and Victorian reproductions; they vary widely in size and shape, but even the smallest has plenty of charm and character. The expansive Rockwell Kent Suite offers a four-poster canopy bed in a heavily wood-paneled bedroom, plus a wood-burning fireplace in a sitting room with French-style couches. Three townhouses feature kitchens, and there's a 100-year-old post-and-beam barn good for weddings, reunions, and other gatherings. The 150 acres of grounds are ideal for exploring.

River Rd. and Rte. 313, Arlington, VT 05250. © 802/375-6516. Fax 802/375-6553. www.westmountaininn.com. 20 units. Summer, spring, and Sat–Sun in winter $165–$293 double; foliage season $239–$324 double; winter Mon–Fri $165–$205 double; town houses $185–$299 (without breakfast). Most rates include full breakfast. MAP plans also available. 2-night minimum stay Sat–Sun. AE, DISC, MC, V. **Amenities:** Restaurant; massage; babysitting. *In room:* A/C, TV (some units), kitchenette (some units), no phone.

Wilburton Inn ⍟   This impressive Tudor estate (built in 1902) is sumptuously appointed and its common spaces are filled with European antiques, Persian carpets, and even a baby grand piano. Throughout the brick mansion you'll find works from a modern-art collection amassed by the inn's owners, Albert and Georgette Levis. Guest rooms are divided among the main house and several outbuildings of various vintages, sizes, and styles. In the outbuildings, the best unit might be spacious room no. 24, which has a private deck with views of Mount Equinox and the property's quirky outdoor sculptures. The good **dining room** ⍟ flies under the local radar but is worth a look for dinner. This inn hosts a lot of weddings in summer and fall, so Monday to Friday is often a quieter time to visit during the high season.

River Rd., Manchester Village, VT 05254. © 800/648-4944 or 802/362-2500. Fax 802/362-1107. www.wilburton. com. 35 units. $125–$250 double. Rates include full breakfast. 2- to 3-night minimum stay Sat–Sun and holidays. AE, MC, V. **Amenities:** Restaurant; outdoor pool; 3 tennis courts. *In room:* A/C, TV (some units), hair dryer, iron, fireplace (some units).

INEXPENSIVE

Dorset Inn ⍟⍟   Set in the center of genteel Dorset, this former stagecoach stop was built in 1796 and claims to be the oldest continuously operating inn in Vermont. With 30 rooms, it's fairly large and impersonal (by Vermont inn standards, I mean), and might not provide the completely rustic experience you're expecting, but it's certainly professionally run. And prices are surprisingly reasonable given those of the competition down in Manchester. The carpeted guest rooms, some located in a well-crafted addition right next door that dates from the 1940s, are furnished in an upscale country style and a mix of reproductions and antiques, including canopied and sleigh beds. All rooms are air-conditioned, though most still lack televisions and phones. The restaurant and tavern mean you don't have to drive miles to find a restaurant (this is a rural area), and a day spa has recently been added to increase the pampering.

8 Church St. at Rte. 30, Dorset, VT 05251. © 877/367-7389 or 802/867-5500. Fax 802/867-5542. www.dorsetinn. com. 30 units. Late May to mid-Nov $150–$225 double; rest of the year $120–$150 double. Rates include full breakfast. MAP plans available. AE, MC, V. Children over 5 welcome. Pets allowed by prior permission. **Amenities:** Restaurant; pub; spa. *In room:* A/C, TV (some units), no phone (most units).

Palmer House Resort Motel ⍟   This "resort motel" is several notches above the run-of-the-mill motels in the area. Owned and operated by the same family for about a half-century, its rooms are furnished with antiques and other unexpected niceties; ask for one of the somewhat larger rooms in the newer rear building if you value space. In 2000, ten spacious suites were added, each with a king bed, gas fireplace, wet bar, two-person Jacuzzi, and private deck overlooking a trout-stocked pond and the mountains beyond. The buildings are set on 22 nicely tended acres, and the motel even has its own small golf course. (There's no charge either to play golf on the course or to borrow a couple of fishing rods for a few hours.) Rooms here tend to book up early in the season.

Rte. 7A, Manchester Center, VT 05255. © 800/917-6245 or 802/362-3600. Fax 802/362-3600. www.palmerhouse. com. 50 units. Summer $85–$175 double; $190–$300 suite. 2-night minimum stay some weekends. Children 12 and older welcome. AE, DISC, MC, V. **Amenities:** Outdoor pool; heated indoor pool; golf course; 2 tennis courts; exercise room; Jacuzzi; sauna. *In room:* A/C, TV, dataport, fridge, coffeemaker, hair dryer, fireplace (some units), Jacuzzi (some units).

WHERE TO DINE

In addition to the selections below, most of the inns listed above offer good to excellent dinners on site in their dining rooms, often in romantic settings. For informal dining or a beer, locals head for **Mulligan's** (© 802/362-3663), a pubby family eatery on Rte. 7A near the Equinox resort and the fly-fishing museum. I also like picking up a dozen sinkers for the drive or flight home at **Mrs. Murphy's Donuts** (© 802/362-1874), a locals-only spot on the outlet strip.

Chantecleer ✰✰✰ CONTINENTAL   If you like superbly prepared Continental fare, but are put off by the stuffiness of highbrow Euro-wannabe restaurants, this is the place for you. Rustic elegance is the best description for this century-old dairy barn. The oddly tidy exterior, which looks as if it could house a chain restaurant, doesn't offer a clue to how pleasantly romantic the interior is. The chef changes his menu every 3 weeks; specializing in game, he might feature veal with a roasted garlic, sage, and balsamic demiglace one night; Swiss air-dried beef, veal chops, Wiener schnitzel, or slow-roasted duck with sesame seeds and hoisin sauce on others. Especially good is the Dover sole, which is filleted right at your table. Finish with a delicious "Matterhorn" sundae of vanilla ice cream shingled with toasted hazelnut nougatine, and topped (for good measure) with a mix of Swiss and French hot fudges.

Rte. 7A (3½ miles north of Manchester Center). © 802/362-1616. Reservations recommended. Main courses $26–$35. AE, MC, V. Wed–Sun 6–9pm. Closed Nov and mid-Apr to mid-May.

Little Rooster Cafe ✰ CONTEMPORARY/REGIONAL   You've got to love a place where the seats are painted like birds' nests. They really take the farm motif to the extreme at this appealing spot near the outlets, which is open only for breakfast and lunch, but it's the best choice in town for either of these meals. Breakfast choices include creative Cajun omelets, corned-beef hash with béchamel sauce, and flapjacks served with real maple syrup. Lunches feature a creative sandwich selection—you might find good roast beef sandwiches with pickled red cabbage and horseradish dill sauce, for instance.

Rte. 7A S., Manchester Center. © 802/362-3496. Breakfast items $4.50–$6.75; lunch $6.50–$8.25. No credit cards. Daily 7am–2:30pm. Closed Wed in off season.

Mistral's at Toll Gate ✰✰ FRENCH   The best tables at Mistral's are along the windows, which overlook a lovely creek that's spotlighted at night. Inside the tollhouse of a long-since-bypassed byway, this restaurant is a romantic mix of modern and old. Its menu changes seasonally, with dishes that could include salmon cannelloni stuffed with lobster or grilled filet mignon with Roquefort ravioli. The kitchen is run with great aplomb by the chef/owner, who does an admirable job ensuring consistent quality and has been recognized with *Wine Spectator* awards since 1994.

Toll Gate Rd. (east of Manchester off Rte. 11/30). © 802/362-1779. Reservations recommended. Main courses $22–$32. AE, MC, V. July–Oct Thurs–Tues 6–10pm; Nov–June Thurs–Mon 6–10pm.

The Reluctant Panther ✰✰✰   This award-winning dining room—built as part of the renovation of the inn by the same name (see "Where to Stay," above)—has become one of the best fine-dining restaurant options in Manchester. The handsome, newly created space looks out onto Mount Equinox and a small pond; waitstaff are incredibly professional and knowledgeable about the expansive wine list and the cuisine of chef Daniel Jackson, formerly of the Woodstock Inn. The kitchen reaches for and attains a high level of quality with cuisine that's Continental with flair: Starters might include a panko-crusted ahi tuna roll, a salad of local greens and cheese, or signature lobster-crab cakes with rémoulade; for main courses, you might find maple-glazed organic chicken breast, seared halibut, "lacquered" duckling, chargrilled beef tenderloin paired with a nicely crunchy quiche of Maytag blue cheese, or a spicy, fabulous bouillabaisse packed with salmon, shrimp, and other Atlantic seafood.

17-39 West Rd., Manchester Village, VT 05254. © **800/822-2331** or 802/362-2568. www.reluctantpanther.com. Reservations required. Main courses $22–$32. AE, DC, DISC, MC, V. Tues–Sat 5:30–9:30pm.

SHOPPING

Manchester Center has perhaps the best concentration of high-end outlets in New England. Among the notable retailers with cut-rate shops are Brooks Brothers, Coach, Baccarat, BCBGMAXAZRIA, Giorgio Armani, Mikasa, Polo/Ralph Lauren, Theory, and many more; there's something for shoppers young and old. Most of the shops are in tasteful mini-mall clusters in and around a T-intersection in the heart of Manchester Center. Hungry from all the shopping and window-shopping? In season there's an outdoor stand with Vermont's very own Ben & Jerry's ice cream.

If your interests include fishing or rustic, outdoorsy fashion, seek out **Orvis,** a Manchester-based local company that has crafted a worldwide reputation for manufacturing its top-flight fly-fishing equipment. The **Orvis Company Store** ✦ (© **802/362-3750**) is between Manchester and Manchester Center and sells housewares, men's and women's clothing—both for daily wear and sturdy outdoor use—and, of course, fly-fishing equipment. Two small ponds just outside the shop allow prospective customers to try the gear before buying. A sale room, with even more deeply discounted items, is directly behind the main store.

2 Brattleboro & the Southern Green Mountains

Brattleboro: 105 miles NW of Boston; 148 miles SE of Burlington

The hills and valleys around the bustling town of Brattleboro, in Vermont's southeast corner, have some of the state's best-hidden treasures. Driving along the main valley floors—on roads along the West or Connecticut rivers, or on Route 100—tends to be only moderately interesting. To really soak up the region's flavor, then, turn off the main roads and wander up and over rolling ridges into the narrow folds of mountains hiding peaceful villages. If it looks as though the landscape hasn't changed all that much in the past 2 centuries, you're right. It really hasn't.

THE WILMINGTON / MOUNT SNOW REGION ✦

Wilmington has a nice selection of antiques shops, boutiques, and pizza joints. Except on busy holiday weekends, when it's inundated by visitors driving oversized SUVs, it feels like a gracious mountain village untroubled by the times. From Wilmington, the ski resort of Mount Snow is easily accessible to the north via Route 100, which is brisk, busy—and close to impassable on sunny weekends in early October. Heading north, you'll first pass through West Dover, an attractive classic New England town with a prominent steeple and acres of white clapboard.

ESSENTIALS

GETTING THERE   Wilmington is at the junction of Route 9 and Route 100. Route 9 offers the most direct access. The Mount Snow area is north of Wilmington on Route 100.

> ## ⌐Tips Looking for More Information?
>
> The best source of information for the region is the great state visitor center
> (© 802/254-4593), off I-91 in Guilford (just south of Brattleboro, a few miles
> after crossing the Massachusetts border); you can only reach it traveling from
> the south on I-91, not from the north. The attractive building, inspired by Ver-
> mont's barns, is filled with maps, brochures, and videos on activities in the
> region. Helpful staff dole out up-to-the-minute information, make reservations,
> and otherwise guide you; there are even bake sales outside in good weather.
> The vending machines and spotless bathrooms are priceless for families.

VISITOR INFORMATION   The **Mount Snow Valley Chamber of Commerce**
(© 877/887-6884; www.visitvermont.com) maintains a visitor center at 21 W. Main
St. in Wilmington. Open year-round daily from 10am to 5pm, the chamber offers a
room-booking service, which is helpful for smaller inns and B&Bs; they also put
together a comprehensive guide to the region. For on-mountain accommodations,
check with Mount Snow's Lodging Bureau and Vacation Service (© 800/245-7669).

THE MARLBORO MUSIC FESTIVAL

The renowned **Marlboro Music Festival** ✰✰✰ has classical concerts, performed by
accomplished masters as well as by highly talented younger musicians, on Saturdays
and Sundays from mid-July to mid-August in the agreeable town of Marlboro, east of
Wilmington on Route 9. The retreat was founded in 1951 and has hosted countless
noted musicians, including Pablo Casals, who participated between 1960 and 1973.
Concerts take place in the 700-seat auditorium at Marlboro College, and advance
ticket purchases are strongly recommended. Call or write for a schedule and a ticket
order form. Ticket prices usually range from about $15 to $35. Between late August
and mid-June, contact the festival's winter office at Marlboro Music, 1616 Walnut St.,
Suite 1600, Philadelphia, PA 19103 (© 215/569-4690). In summer, write Marlboro
Music, Box K, Marlboro, VT 05344, or call the box office (© 802/254-2394). The
website is at **www.marlboromusic.org**.

DOWNHILL SKIING

Mount Snow ✰   Mount Snow is noted for its widely cut runs on the front face of the
mountain (disparaged by some skiers as "vertical golf courses"), yet it also remains an
excellent destination for intermediates and advanced intermediates. More advanced
skiers migrate to the North Face, which is its own little world of bumps and glades. This
is also an excellent spot for snowboarding. Because it's the closest Vermont ski area to
Boston and New York (about a 4-hr. drive from Manhattan), the mountain can get even
more crowded than other Vermont hills on the weekends—maybe that's why the resort's
lift-ticket prices have surged in recent years. Mount Snow's village is attractively arrayed
along the base of the mountain; the most imposing structure is a balconied hotel overlooking a small pond, but the overall character here at the bottom is still shaped mostly
by unobtrusive smaller lodges and homes. Once famed for its groovy singles scene, the
hill's post-skiing activities have mellowed somewhat and embraced the family market,
although 20-somethings can still find a good selection of après-ski activities.

Mount Snow, VT 05356. © 800/245-7669 or 802/464-2151. www.mountsnow.com. Adult day lift tickets $63–$72,
half-day lift tickets $47–$54; discounts for youth and seniors.

WHERE TO STAY

The Mount Snow area has a surfeit of lodging options, ranging from basic motels to luxury inns to slope-side condos; rates in most of them drop quite a bit in summer, when the region slips into a pleasant lethargy. In winter, the high prices reflect the relatively easy drive to New York and Boston. The best phone call to make first is to Mount Snow's lodging line (ⓒ **800/245-7669**) to ask about vacation packages and condo accommodations.

Deerhill Inn and Restaurant ⟨★⟩

The Deerhill Inn, on a hillside above Route 100 with views of the rolling mountains, was built as a ski lodge in 1954, but the helpful innkeepers have given it a more gracious country gloss. In summer, it features attractive gardens and a stonework pool; in winter, the slopes are a short drive away. Guests have access to two comfortable sitting areas upstairs, stocked with a television and books. Guest rooms vary from very cozy to spacious, and most are decorated with a countryish flair; several are located in a motel-like addition, and these rooms have balconies. The best rooms are the two with cathedral ceilings.

14 Valley View Rd. (P.O. Box 136), West Dover, VT 05356. ⓒ **800/993-3379** or 802/464-3100. Fax 802/464-5474. www.deerhill.com. 14 units. $130–$320 double; $240–$345 suite. Rates include breakfast. 2-night minimum stay Sat–Sun. AE, MC, V. Children 8 and older welcome. **Amenities:** Restaurant; outdoor pool; bike rental. *In room:* Jacuzzi (some), fireplace (some), no phone.

Inn at Quail Run ⟨★⟩ *Kids*

Quail Run is a hybrid of the sort New England could use more of: an intimate B&B that welcomes families (and even pets, in certain rooms). Set on 15 acres in the hills east of Route 100, the converted ski lodge features guest rooms in a contemporary country style. Family accommodations include king-size and bunk beds; the standard rooms are motel-size, and a few have gas fireplaces. The inn also sports an attractive heated outdoor pool and an eight-person Jacuzzi.

106 Smith Rd., Wilmington, VT 05363. ⓒ **877/784-6835** or 802/464-3362. www.thequailruninn.com. 13 units. $165–$210 double. Rates include full breakfast. 3-night minimum stay holiday weekends; 2-night minimum stay foliage season. AE, DISC, MC, V. Pets allowed in some rooms ($15 per night). **Amenities:** Outdoor pool; Jacuzzi; sauna; game room. *In room:* A/C (1 unit), TV.

Inn at Sawmill Farm ⟨★★⟩

The Inn at Sawmill Farm is spread over 28 acres, and it was one of the very first inns in New England to cater to affluent travelers—a lead that many, many others have since followed. (The impressive wine cellar is a tip-off.) Guest rooms in this old farmhouse, parts of which date back to 1797, are distinctive, but all share a similar look, with contemporary country styling and Colonial reproduction furniture. Among the best are Cider House No. 2, with its rustic beams and oversize canopy bed, and the Woodshed, a quiet cottage with a beautiful brick fireplace and a cozy loft. Some guests report that in recent years the inn has lost a bit of its burnish, and, especially given the high room rates, service is no longer as good.

Crosstown Rd. and Rte. 100 (P.O. Box 367), West Dover, VT 05356. ⓒ **802/464-8131**. Fax 802/464-1130. www.the innatsawmillfarm.com. 20 units. $300–$725 double; foliage season $375–$850. Rates include breakfast and dinner. AE, DC, MC, V. Closed Apr–May. **Amenities:** Restaurant; outdoor pool; tennis court. *In room:* A/C, hair dryer, iron/ironing board, fireplace (some units), Jacuzzi (some units).

Trail's End ⟨★⟩

Just a short drive off Route 100 on 10 nicely tended acres, this establishment is an updated 1960s ski lodge with attractive rooms and abundant common space. The guest rooms are spotlessly clean, styled in country fashion and well-kept by innkeeper Lois Smith and family. Many rooms feature fireplaces and/or Jacuzzis, and the suites are perfect for midwinter cocooning with their microwaves, refrigerators, and VCRs/DVD players; some have queen sleigh beds. The best room? Maybe no. 6, with a lovely fireplace and oak accents. Other spots to linger include the main common room with its big stone fireplace, a stone-floored library, and a game room.

5 Trail's End Lane (look for the turn btw. Haystack and Mount Snow), Wilmington, VT 05363. (C) **800/859-2585** or 802/464-2055. www.trailsendvt.com. 14 units. $110–$200 double. Rates include breakfast. 2- to 3-night minimum stay Sat–Sun and holidays. AE, DISC, MC, V. Children 7 and older welcome. **Amenities:** Outdoor pool; tennis court; Jacuzzi; game room; babysitting. *In room:* TV, fireplace, Jacuzzi, no phone.

Vintage Motel *(Value)*   A good budget choice for those planning to spend little time in their rooms, this motel has basic rooms with industrial carpeting, durable furniture, and a few nice touches such as quilts and a family room with a microwave and VCR (one unit with a DVD player). Bathrooms have curious 4-foot-square tubs (with showers), which are odd but appealing—and this has got be one of the few budget motels you'll ever book that has its own driving range on-site. In winter, the place is very popular with snowmobilers (a trail passes through the backyard) and skiers.

195 Rte. 9 (P.O. Box 222), Wilmington, VT 05363. (C) **800/899-9660** or 802/464-8824. www.vintagemotel.net. 18 units. $45–$85 double; $100–$200 suite. Holiday rates higher. AE, DISC, MC, V. 2-night minimum stay some weekends; 3 nights on holidays. Pets allowed in some units. **Amenities:** Outdoor pool; driving range. *In room:* TV.

White House of Wilmington *✦*   This grand Colonial Revival mansion sits atop the crest of an open hill just east of Wilmington. Built in 1915 by a lumber baron, the interior has hardwood floors, arched doorways, and nice detailing throughout. It's often a lively and bustling place, especially in winter, with cross-country skiers, snowshoers, and snow tubers all milling about (there's a great hill out front). The guest rooms are simply furnished in Colonial Revival style; nine have wood fireplaces, four have whirlpools. The best include room no. 1, a corner unit with lovely wood floors, a fireplace, and a vintage white-tile bathroom; and no. 3, which has its own balcony and sitting room with fireplace.

178 Rte. 9, East Wilmington, VT 05363. (C) **800/541-2135** or 802/464-2135. Fax 802/464-5222. www.whitehouse inn.com. 25 units. $118–$268 double, foliage season higher. Rates include breakfast. 2-night minimum stay Sat–Sun. AE, MC, V. Children 8 and older welcome in main inn; all ages welcome in guesthouse. **Amenities:** Outdoor pool; indoor pool; sauna; steam room; snowshoe rental; cross-country ski trails. *In room:* Fireplace (some units), Jacuzzi (some units), no phone.

WHERE TO DINE

Dot's *✦* *(Value)* DINER   Wilmington is justly proud of Dot's, an institution that has stubbornly remained loyal to its longtime clientele, offering good, inexpensive food in the face of creeping boutique-ification elsewhere in town. (A second, more modern Dot's is located in Dover.) Right in the village, Dot's is a classic, with pine paneling, swivel stools at the counter, and checkerboard linoleum tile. It's famous for its chili and berry pancakes and hot open-faced turkey sandwiches, but don't overlook other fare such as the Cajun skillet—a medley of sausage, peppers, onions, and home fries sautéed and served with eggs and melted Monterey Jack cheese.

3 West Main St., Wilmington. (C) 802/464-7284. Breakfast $3–$7; lunch $3–$8; dinner $3–$13. DISC, MC, V. Daily 5:30am–8pm (to 9pm Fri–Sat).

Inn at Sawmill Farm *✦✦* CONTINENTAL   More than 30,000 bottles of wine lurk in the custom-made wine cellar of this inn, which has earned a coveted "Grand Award" from *Wine Spectator* magazine. The wine is one of the reasons the inn consistently attracts well-heeled diners; chef/proprietor Brill Williams is the other. The food is deftly prepared, with entrees that could range from roasted poussin stuffed with shallots to salmon filet with a sorrel cream sauce to potato-crusted sea bass with wild mushrooms, oven-roasted cod, or Indonesian curried chicken breast. A bistro menu adds lighter items too. The signature desert is ice cream with dark chocolate, butter, and nut sauce. The barn-and-farmhouse atmosphere is romantic, the service superb.

Crosstown Rd. and Rte. 100, West Dover. (C) 802/464-8131. www.theinnatsawmillfarm.com. Reservations recommended. Main courses $28–$39. AE, DC, MC, V. Daily 6–9:30pm. Closed mid-Apr to Memorial Day weekend.

Maple Leaf Malt & Brewing Co. PUB FARE   This is the place for those nights you don't feel like anything fancy but Dot's is a bit *too* authentic for your mood. This neighborly bar (just around the corner from Dot's, in fact) serves oversized sandwiches, burgers, wraps, and the occasional pasta special. It's all perfectly fine, if unexciting. The food makes a nice accompaniment to a dozen or so brews crafted on the far side of the glass walls in the downstairs dining room.

3 N. Main St., Wilmington. (C) 802/464-9900. Main courses $7–$16. AE, DISC, MC, V. Restaurant daily noon–10pm; bar daily noon–midnight.

BRATTLEBORO ✦

Set in a scenic river valley, the commercial town of Brattleboro is more than just a wide place in the road to fill the gas tank and stock up on provisions (though some parts of town do lend themselves only to that). In fact, it has a funky, slightly dated charm; the rough brick texture of this compact, hilly city has aged nicely, its flavor different from that of other Vermont towns due to a suspiciously high concentration of ex-flower children who moved here, grew up, cut their hair, and settled in. They now operate many local enterprises and institutions—some with a New Age-y tinge.

ESSENTIALS

GETTING THERE   From the north or south, Brattleboro is easily accessible by car via exits 1 and 2 on I-91. From the east or west, Brattleboro is best reached via Route 9, which comes in from Bennington; Keene, New Hampshire; and Albany, New York. Brattleboro is also a stop on the **Amtrak** (C) **800/872-7245**) line from Boston to northern Vermont.

VISITOR INFORMATION   The **Brattleboro Chamber of Commerce,** 180 Main St. (C) 877/254-4565 or 802/254-4565; www.brattleborochamber.org), provides travel information year-round, Monday through Friday between 8:30am and 5pm.

EXPLORING THE TOWN

Here's a simple, straightforward strategy for exploring Brattleboro: Park and walk. The commercially vibrant downtown is blessedly compact, and strolling around is the best way to appreciate its human scale and handsome commercial architecture. A town of cafes, bookstores, antiques stores, and outdoor recreation shops, it invites browsing. One shop of special note is **Sam's Outdoor Outfitters,** 74 Main St. (C) **802/254-2933**), filled to the eaves with camping and fishing gear; it's open daily.

Enjoyable for kids and curious adults is the **Brattleboro Museum & Art Center** (C) **802/257-0124;** www.brattleboromuseum.org) at the Union Railroad Station, 10 Vernon St. (it's the stone building downtown near the bridge to New Hampshire). Wonderful exhibits highlight the history of the town and the Connecticut River Valley. The museum is open from Wednesday through Monday from 11am to 5pm. Admission is $4 for adults, $3 for seniors, $2 for students, and free for children under 6.

OUTDOOR PURSUITS

A soaring aerial view of Brattleboro can be found atop **Wantastiquet Mountain,** which is just across the Connecticut River in New Hampshire (figure on a round-trip of about 3 hr.). To reach the base of the "mountain" (a term that's a bit grandiose), cross the river on the two green steel bridges, then turn left on the first dirt road; go one-fifth mile to a parking area on your right. The trail begins here via a carriage road (stick to the main trail and avoid the side trails) winding about 2 miles through a forest and past open ledges to the summit, which is marked by a monument dating from 1908. From here, you'll be rewarded with sweeping views of the river, town, and landscapes beyond.

Bike rentals and advice on day-trip destinations are available at the **Brattleboro Bicycle Shop,** 165 Main St. (© **800/272-8245** or 802/254-8644; www.bratbike.com). Hybrid bikes ideal for exploring area back roads can be rented by the day or week.

WHERE TO STAY

Several chain motels flank Route 5 north of Brattleboro. Perhaps the best choice is the **Quality Inn & Suites,** 1380 Putney Rd. (© **866/254-8701** or 802/254-8701; www.qualityinnbrattleboro.com), featuring a restaurant, a fitness center with a sauna, and both an indoor and an outdoor pool. Double-room rates generally range from about $49 to $129, depending on size and season.

Chesterfield Inn 🏆🏆   Just a 10-minute drive east of Brattleboro in New Hampshire, this attractive inn sits in a field just off a busy state highway, but inside it's more quiet and refined than you might imagine. The original farmhouse dates back to the 1780s, but it has been expanded and modernized, and today has a casual contemporary sensibility with antique accents. Nine guest rooms are located in the main inn, and six more are in cottages nearby; all are spacious and comfortably appointed in a mix of modern and antique furniture. The two priciest units have fireplaces, double Jacuzzis, and private decks with mountain and meadow views, but more than half of the rest of the rooms also have wood-burning or gas fireplaces.

20 Cross Rd. (Rte. 9), W. Chesterfield, NH 03466. © 800/365-5515 or 603/256-3211. Fax 603/256-6131. www. chesterfieldinn.com. 15 units. $150–$295 double; foliage season and holidays $175–$320 double. 2-night minimum stay foliage season and holidays. AE, DC, DISC, MC, V. Pets allowed with prior permission. **Amenities:** Restaurant; babysitting. *In room:* A/C, TV, dataport, minibar, coffeemaker, hair dryer, iron, fireplace (some units), Jacuzzi (some units).

Colonial Motel & Spa *Value*   Operated by the same family since 1975, this sprawling compound set back from the main highway is well-maintained and offers the best value in town. Opt for the back building's larger and quieter rooms, which are furnished with armchairs and sofas. This motel's best feature is the 75-foot indoor lap pool in the spa building, and there's a sauna and an outdoor pool, too. *Tip:* Skiers who present their lift tickets receive a $20 discount.

Putney Rd., Brattleboro, VT 05301. © 800/239-0032 or 802/257-7733. www.colonialmotelspa.com. 68 units. $60–$140 double and suite. Rates include continental breakfast (Mon–Fri only). AE, DISC, MC, V. Take exit 3 off I-91; turn right and continue a half-mile. **Amenities:** Restaurant; indoor pool; outdoor pool; Jacuzzi; sauna. *In room:* A/C, TV.

Forty Putney Road 🏆   Built in the early 1930s, this compact French château–style home has five guest rooms, including a two-room suite in an adjacent cottage. All are attractively appointed with a mix of modern country furnishings and reproductions. A few units have gas fireplaces. The cottage suite, with its foldaway sofa in the living

Brattleboro

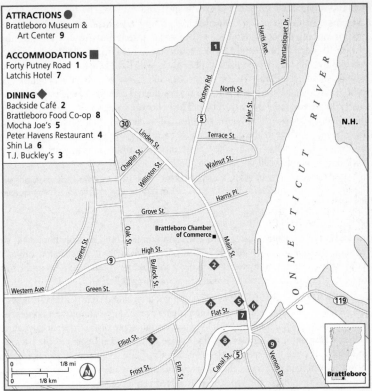

ATTRACTIONS ●
Brattleboro Museum &
Art Center **9**

ACCOMMODATIONS ■
Forty Putney Road **1**
Latchis Hotel **7**

DINING ◆
Backside Café **2**
Brattleboro Food Co-op **8**
Mocha Joe's **5**
Peter Havens Restaurant **4**
Shin La **6**
T.J. Buckley's **3**

room, is popular with small families and couples (or pairs of couples traveling together). The inn is a short stroll from town, on a busy road.

40 Putney Rd., Brattleboro, VT 05301. ℂ **800/941-2413** or 802/254-6268. Fax 802/258-2673. www.putney.net/ 40putneyrd. 5 units. Peak season $199–$259 double; off-season $159–$199 double. Rates include breakfast. AE, DISC, MC, V. Pets allowed with prior permission. **Amenities:** Pub. *In room:* A/C, TV/VCR, dataport, fridge, hair dryer, iron.

Latchis Hotel 🅰 *(Value)* This downtown hotel fairly leaps out in Victorian-brick Brattleboro. Built in 1938 in an understated Art Deco style, the Latchis was once the cornerstone for a small chain of hotels and theaters. It no longer has its own orchestra or commanding dining room (though the theater remains), but still has an authentic—if at times somewhat outdated-feeling—flair. For the most part, the accommodations are compact and comfortable, if not exactly luxurious. About two-thirds of the units have limited views of the river, although those also come with the sounds of cars on Main Street. (If you want quiet, sacrifice the views and ask for a room in the back.) Rooms here all have minifridges. From the hotel it's easy to explore town on foot: You're right at the foot of the commercial district.

50 Main St., Brattleboro, VT 05301. ℂ **800/798-6301** or 802/254-6300. www.brattleboro.com/latchis. 30 units. $75–$165 double; foliage season rates higher. Rates include continental breakfast. AE, MC, V. **Amenities:** Restaurant; movie theater. *In room:* A/C, TV, minifridge, coffeemaker, iron/ironing board.

Naulakha ☆ This unique property, owned and managed by the British-inspired Landmark Trust, would be a superb place to unwind (there are 55 acres of lovely grounds) even without its rich history. But what makes this two-story, shingled home in the hills outside Brattleboro more extraordinary is its literary heritage: The home was built for the British writer Rudyard Kipling, who lived here for several years in the mid-1890s while working on *The Jungle Book* and *Captains Courageous*. Kipling never quite fit into rural Vermont, where he was considered eccentric; he left abruptly, selling the home and much of its furniture. The home can be rented by the night or week, and while the prices may cause the fainthearted to blanch at first look, remember that it sleeps eight—three of the bedrooms have twin beds, while the other one has a double bed. Bring friends—even at the most expensive times of year, your nightly rate works out to about $100 per bedroom.

707 Kipling Rd., Dummerston, VT 05301. ✆ **802/257-6868**. Fax 802/257-7783. www.landmarktrustusa.org. 1 4-bedroom house (up to 8 people). $1,350–$2,300 per week or $275–$425 per night. MC, V. Pets allowed. **Amenities:** Tennis court.

WHERE TO DINE

In addition to the choices listed below, the subterranean (and possibly homesick) coffee shop **Mocha Joe's** (✆ **802/257-7794**) at 82 Main St. is a collection point for locals with a friendly, funky feel, good cup of joe, and fresh-squeezed ades in the summer. Try a maple latte if you're looking for something different.

Backside Café ☆ AMERICAN This is a good local choice for either breakfast or lunch. There's nothing fancy on the menu here; everything is simple and homemade, and it's less—how to put it—crunchy-granola than some of the other local eateries. The cafe is in an open, airy second-floor space with wooden booths in the back of a building that once housed a Chrysler dealership. Lunches include familiar favorites such as grilled ham and Swiss cheese, spicy chili, homemade soups, and some modest exotica such as spinach, tomato, and roasted red pepper on focaccia.

Midtown Mall, 22 High St. (btw. High and Elliot sts., off the public parking lot). ✆ **802/257-5056**. Main courses $2–$5 at breakfast; $3–$5 at lunch. AE, DISC, MC, V. Tues–Fri 7:30am–3pm; Sat 8am–3pm; Sun 9am–3pm.

Brattleboro Food Co-op ☆ DELI This co-op has been selling wholesome foods since 1975, and its location, in a small strip mall downtown near the New Hampshire bridge, has plenty of parking (though the old-timey plaza it's in is a bit tricky to spot from the main road). The huge store has a deli counter great for takeout; snag a quick, filling lunch that won't necessarily be tofu and sprouts—you can get a smoked turkey and Swiss cheese sandwich, or opt for a crispy salad. Check out the eclectic wine selection and the cheeses in the store, too, especially the award-winning Vermont Shepherd cheeses, which are made nearby in Putney. Other interesting finds here could include natural bath products, house-made sausages, and hand-cut steaks from the good meat section. One more plus: The store section is open until 9pm every single night, a boon in early-closing Vermont.

Brookside Plaza, 2 Main St. ✆ **802/257-0236**. Sandwiches $3.50–$6; prepared foods usually $4–$5 per lb. MC, V. Mon–Sat 8am–9pm; Sun 9am–9pm.

Peter Havens Restaurant ☆☆ REGIONAL/AMERICAN You're likely to feel instantly at home in this popular dining spot, which has just 10 tables; chef-owned Peter Havens has been serving up reliable fare to locals in town since 1989. Situated in a pleasantly contemporary building, this eatery may not bowl you over with its menu at first look, but you'll be impressed by whatever you're served. Meals are prepared with choice ingredients and served with panache. Seafood is a specialty, and offerings might include such choices as salmon with a chipotle pepper rémoulade. The jazz sometimes playing in the background makes a nice accompaniment.

32 Elliot St. ℭ **802/257-3333**. Reservations strongly recommended. Main courses $19–$24. MC, V. Tues–Sat 6–9pm.

Shin La *Value* KOREAN/JAPANESE   This is your best bet in Brattleboro for inexpensive Asian food. With wooden booths and mismatched furniture, it has the character of a pizza shop yet consistently good fare. Half the menu features a range of sushi rolls and plates, as well as other traditional Japanese bar fare such as yakitori, katsu (fried cutlets), and tempura; the other half, meanwhile, offers something pretty hard to find in New England—Korean country fare such as *bool ko ki* (sliced sirloin), Korean barbecue, and *shu'mai* (steamed dumplings). This is an inexpensive change of pace when you're tired of the usual choices.

57 Main St. ℭ **802/257-5226**. Main courses $6–$10. MC. V. Mon–Sat 11am–9pm.

T. J. Buckley's ✦✦✦ NEW AMERICAN   Brattleboro's best restaurant, and one of the better choices in Vermont, the Lilliputian T. J. Buckley's is housed in a classic old diner on a dim side street—but this is far from diner food. Renovations such as slate floors and golden lighting have created an intimate restaurant that seats about 20, and no secrets exist between the chef, sous-chef, and the server, all of whom remain within a couple of dozen feet of one another (and you) throughout the meal—the entire place is smaller than the kitchen of most restaurants. The menu here is limited, with just a few each night, but the food has absolutely nothing in common with simple diner fare. Ingredients are fresh and select, the preparation more concerned with melding flavors than dazzling with architectural flourishes.

132 Elliot St. ℭ **802/257-4922**. Reservations strongly recommended. Main courses $25–$32. No credit cards. Winter Thurs–Sun 6–9pm; rest of year Wed–Sun 6–9pm (sometimes later).

NEWFANE ✦ & TOWNSHEND ✦

These two villages, about 5 miles apart on Route 30, are the picture-perfect epitome of Vermont. Set within the serpentine West River Valley, both are built around town greens. Both towns consist of impressive white-clapboard homes and public buildings that share the grace and scale of the surrounding homes. Both boast striking examples of Early American architecture, notably Greek Revival. Don't bother looking for strip malls, McDonald's, or video outlets here; Newfane and Townshend seem to have idled on a sidetrack for decades while the rest of America steamed ahead.

ESSENTIALS

GETTING THERE   Newfane and Townshend are located on Route 30 northwest of Brattleboro. The nearest interstate access is off exit 3 from I-91.

VISITOR INFORMATION   No formal information center serves these towns. Brochures describing local inns and attractions are available at the **state visitor center** (ℭ **802/254-4593**) on I-91 in Guilford, south of Brattleboro. The website **www.newfane.com** provides good local information for the town of Newfane.

EXPLORING THE AREA

The **National Historic District** ✦✦ comprises some 60 buildings around the green and on nearby side streets. You'll find styles ranging from Federal through Colonial

Revival, although Greek Revival appears to carry the day. A strikingly handsome courthouse—where cases are still heard, as they have been for nearly 2 centuries—dominates the shady green. This structure was built in 1825; its imposing portico was added in 1853. For more details on area buildings, get a copy of the free walking-tour brochure at the Moore Free Library, on West Street, or at the Historical Society (see below).

Explore Newfane's history at the engaging **Historical Society of Windham County** $\mathcal{R}$, on Route 30 across from the village common. Housed in a handsome 1930s Colonial Revival brick building, it has an eclectic assemblage of local artifacts (dolls, melodeons, rail ephemera), along with changing exhibits that give intriguing snippets of local history. It's open from late May through mid-October, Wednesday through Sunday, from noon until 5pm; admission is by donation.

More than two dozen **antiques shops** on or near Route 30 in the West River Valley allow for good grazing on lazy afternoons; they are also fine resources for serious collectors.

WHERE TO STAY & DINE

Four Columns Inn $\mathcal{R}\mathcal{R}$ You can't help noticing the Four Columns when in Newfane: It's the regal, white-clapboard building with (obviously) four Ionic columns just off the green. This perfect village setting conceals an appealing inn within. Rooms in the main house and the "garden" wing are larger and more expensive than those above the restaurant, and some have been made over as luxury suites with double Jacuzzis. The best choice may be room no. 12, a suite with a Shaker-style king bed, Jacuzzi, skylight, gas fireplace, and sitting area. Room no. 4 has a nice view of the village green (which means street traffic as well), cathedral ceilings, Jacuzzi, and a double-sided fireplace. The **dining room** $\mathcal{R}$ has served the likes of Nicole Kidman, Henry Kissinger, and Paul Newman. The inn owns 150 acres of property interlaced by hiking trails.

21 West St. (P.O. Box 278), Newfane, VT 05345. $\mathcal{C}$ **800/787-6633** or 802/365-7713. Fax 802/365-0022. www.four columnsinn.com. 15 units. $165–$235 double; $265–$385 suite. Rates include full breakfast and afternoon tea. AE, DISC, MC, V. Pets allowed with prior permission ($10 per pet per night). **Amenities:** Restaurant; outdoor pool; babysitting. *In room:* A/C, hair dryer, fireplace (some units), Jacuzzi (some units), no phone.

Three Mountain Inn $\mathcal{R}\mathcal{R}$ The lovely Three Mountain Inn is in the middle of the appealing village of Jamaica, in a historic white clapboard home of lovely wide-board pine walls. It has benefited from major upgrades under ambitious innkeepers, who have refurbished the rooms in a restrained country style. The accommodations range from cozy and basic rooms to outright sumptuous suites outfitted with whirlpools, gas fireplaces, and televisions with DVD players. Seven of the units are located in the adjacent Robinson House, and there's also a private detached cottage with such luxury trimmings as a double Jacuzzi, surround-sound entertainment system, skylights, and a private front porch. The inn is a good base for exploring southern Vermont; in winter, skiing at Stratton is a short drive away, and in summer you can walk to Jamaica State Park, where there's an easy serpentine hike along the river on an old rail bed. The **award-winning dining room** $\mathcal{R}$ serves wonderful prix-fixe meals Wednesday through Sunday.

Rte. 30, Jamaica, VT 05343. $\mathcal{C}$ **800/532-9399** or 802/874-4140. www.threemountaininn.com. 15 units. $165–$270 double; $295–$330 suite; $325–$360 cottage. Rates include breakfast. Packages available. AE, MC, V. Pets allowed with restrictions (call first). Children 12 and older welcome. **Amenities:** Restaurant; outdoor pool. *In room:* A/C, TV (some units), dataport, hair dryer, fireplace (some units), Jacuzzi (some units).

Windham Hill Inn 🔆🔆   This inn is about as good as it gets, especially if you're in search of a romantic getaway. Situated on 160 acres at the end of a dirt road in a high upland valley, the inn was built in 1823 as a farmhouse and remained in the same family until the 1950s, when it was converted into an inn. Today it mixes the best of old and new; guest rooms are wonderfully appointed in elegant country style. A number have Jacuzzis or soaking tubs, balconies or decks, and gas fireplaces—and all rooms have good views. Especially nice: the Jesse Lawrence Room, with its lovely modern soaking tub, writing desk, plush chairs, cherry four-poster king bed, and gas wood-stove; and the Forget-Me-Not, which has a similar setup. The game room is the place to gather at night, and the excellent **dining room** 🔆 features creative and delightfully arranged cooking; outside, the inn maintains 6 miles of groomed cross-country ski trails.

311 Lawrence Dr., West Townshend, VT 05359. ℂ **800/944-4080** or 802/874-4080. Fax 802/874-4702. www.windham hill.com. 21 units. $195–$430 double. Rates include full breakfast. 2- to 3-night minimum stay Sat–Sun and some holidays. Packages available. AE, DISC, MC, V. Closed the week prior to Dec 27. Turn uphill across from the country store in West Townshend and continue uphill 1¼ miles to the dirt road (Lawrence Drive); turn right and continue to end. Children 12 and older welcome. **Amenities:** Restaurant; outdoor heated pool; tennis court. *In room:* A/C, hair dryer, iron, fireplace (some units), Jacuzzi (some units).

3 Woodstock & Environs 🔆

Woodstock: 16 miles W of White River Junction; 140 miles NW of Boston; 98 miles SE of Burlington

For more than a century, the resort community of Woodstock has been considered one of New England's most exquisite villages, and its attractiveness has benefited from the largesse of some of the country's most affluent citizens. Even the surrounding countryside is, by and large, unsullied—it's pretty difficult to drive to Woodstock via any route that *isn't* pastoral and scenic, and by the time you're here you're already feeling as if you're back in some other, slower-paced era. Few New England villages can top Woodstock for sheer grace and elegance; its tidy downtown is compact and neat, populated by galleries and boutiques. The lovely village green is surrounded by handsome homes, creating what amounts to a comprehensive review of architectural styles of the 19th and early 20th centuries.

In addition to Woodstock, this region also takes in nearby White River Junction, Quechee, and Norwich, three towns of distinctly different lineages along the Connecticut River on the New Hampshire border. In fact, while here you'll want to cross over the river to Hanover, New Hampshire (p. 558), a lovely town that's home to Dartmouth College.

WOODSTOCK 🔆🔆

Much of Woodstock is on the National Register of Historic Places already, and—as if that weren't enough—the Rockefeller family deeded 500 acres surrounding Mount Tom (see below) to the National Park Service to protect even more of it from developers. In fact, locals occasionally joke that downtown Woodstock itself could be renamed Rockefeller National Park, given the attention and cash the Rockefeller family has lavished on this town in the interest of preservation. (For starters, Rockefeller money built the faux-historic Woodstock Inn and paid to bury unsightly utility lines around town.)

The town is also notable as a historic center of winter outdoor recreation. The nation's very first ski tow (a rope tow powered by, yes, an old Buick motor) was built in 1933 at the Woodstock Ski Hill near today's Suicide Six ski area. There are no huge mountains hereabouts, and maybe that's why this is definitely no longer the center of Vermont's skiing universe (maybe Stowe is?)—but that's actually a very good thing. Low-key Woodstock is growing more upscale, yet it remains one of my very favorite small towns in New England—a great place summer, winter, or fall to hike, bike, skate, cross-country ski, snowshoe, or simply window-shop and leaf-peep.

ESSENTIALS

GETTING THERE   Woodstock is 13 miles west of White River Junction on Route 4 (take exit 1 off I-89). Woodstock is 20 miles east of Killington on Route 4.

VISITOR INFORMATION   The **Woodstock Area Chamber of Commerce,** 18 Central St. (© **888/496-6378** or 802/457-3555; www.woodstockvt.com), staffs a helpful information booth on the green, open June through October daily, usually from 9:30am to 5:30pm.

EXPLORING THE TOWN

The heart of the town is the shady, elliptical **Woodstock Green.** The famous Admiral George Dewey spent his later years in Woodstock, and local wags may try to convince you that the green was laid out in the shape of Dewey's flagship. This is such a fine and believable explanation for the odd, cigar-shaped green that you'll be forgiven a moment of distress when you discover that the green was actually already in place—in the same shape—by 1830, or 7 years before Dewey was born. Oh, well.

To put other local history in similar perspective, stop by the **Woodstock Historical Society** ✪, 26 Elm St. (© **802/457-1822**). Housed in the 1807 Charles Dana House, this beautiful home has rooms furnished in Federal, Empire, and Victorian styles, and has displays of dolls, costumes, and early silver and glass. The Dana House and adjoining buildings with more exhibits are open from mid-June to the end of October, Tuesday through Sunday from 10am to 5pm. Admission is $5 to the Dana House (which includes tours on the hour), or $3 to view only the gallery and barns sections, which are open the same dates but only until 3pm.

Billings Farm and Museum ✪✪✪   This remarkable working farm offers a striking glimpse into a grander era when Vermont was still Rockwellian, as well as an introduction to the oddly interesting history of scientific farming. This extraordinary spot was the creation of Frederick Billings, a native Vermonter who was credited with completing the Northern Pacific Railroad. (Billings, Montana, is named after him.) Billings returned home to create a managed forest along the principles of the pioneering ecologist George Perkins Marsh, who was born here in Woodstock and had lived on this estate. As a 19th-century dairy farm, it was renowned for its scientific breeding of Jersey cows and fine architecture, particularly its gabled 1890 Victorian farmhouse. A tour includes hands-on demonstrations of farm activities, exhibits of farm life, a look at an heirloom kitchen garden, and a visit to active milking barns. You can buy a 2-day combination ticket granting admission to the farm and the historic park (see below).

River Rd., about a half-mile north of town on Rte. 12. (P.O. Box 489, Woodstock) © **802/457-2355.** www.billings farm.org. Admission $10 adults, $9 seniors, $8 children 13–17, $6 children 5–12, $3 children 3–4, free for children under 3. May–Oct daily 10am–5pm; also Sat–Sun at Thanksgiving and Christmas week.

Marsh-Billings-Rockefeller National Historic Park ✪✪✪   The Billings Farm and the National Park Service have teamed up to manage this new park, the first and only national park focused on the history of conservation; it's more or less across the street from the Billings Farm (see above), and is closely related. Here you'll learn about

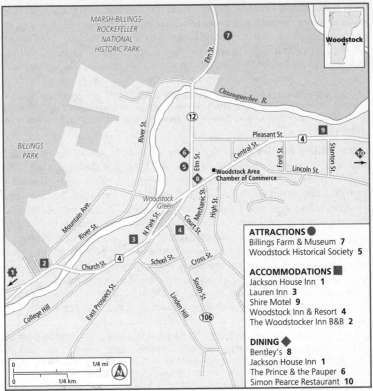

ATTRACTIONS ●
Billings Farm & Museum **7**
Woodstock Historical Society **5**

ACCOMMODATIONS ■
Jackson House Inn **1**
Lauren Inn **3**
Shire Motel **9**
Woodstock Inn & Resort **4**
The Woodstocker Inn B&B **2**

DINING ◆
Bentley's **8**
Jackson House Inn **1**
The Prince & the Pauper **6**
Simon Pearce Restaurant **10**

the life of George Perkins Marsh, the author of *Man and Nature* (1864), considered one of the first and most influential books in the history of the environmental movement. You'll also learn how Woodstock native and rail tycoon Frederick Billings, who read *Man and Nature*, eventually returned and purchased Marsh's boyhood farm, putting into practice many of the principles of good stewardship that Marsh espoused. The property was subsequently purchased by Mary and Laurance Rockefeller, who in 1982 established the nonprofit farm; a decade later, they donated more than 500 acres of forest land and their mansion, filled with exceptional 19th-century landscape art, to the National Park Service. Visitors can tour the elaborate Victorian mansion, walk the graceful carriage roads surrounding Mount Tom, and view one of the oldest professionally managed woodlands in the nation. Mansion tours accommodate only a limited number of people; advance reservations are recommended.

54 Elm St. (P.O. Box 178), Woodstock. 𝄢 802/457-3368. www.nps.gov/mabi. Free admission to grounds; mansion tour $8 adults, $4 seniors, free for children under 16. Late May–Oct daily 10am–5pm.

WHERE TO STAY
Jackson House Inn ⊕ In 2006 new ownership took over this property, a 5-minute drive west of the Woodstock village center. The home was built in 1890 in a Queen Anne style by a lumber baron who hoarded the best wood for himself; the cherry and

maple floors here are beautiful. An addition in 1997 created a wing of four suites with additional amenities such as fireplaces and Jacuzzis. Most rooms are well appointed with antiques, though some older rooms are a bit small. At evening hors d'oeuvres-and-wine get-togethers, guests seem to enjoy the social time. There's also a 3-acre backyard with formal gardens, and a pond where you can swim. The inn's restaurant (see "Where to Dine," below) is very good most nights, if a bit pricey.

114–3 Senior Lane, Woodstock, VT 05091. ℭ **800/448-1890** or 802/457-2065. Fax 802/457-9290. www.jackson house.com. 15 units. $220–$330 double; $310–$440 suite. Rates higher in foliage season. 2-night minimum stay most Sat–Sun. AE, MC, V. Children 14 and older welcome. **Amenities:** Restaurant. *In room:* A/C, hair dryer, no phone (some units).

Kedron Valley Inn ✿✿ You might recognize this inn, one of Vermont's oldest, even if you've never been here: For years, it's been featured in the background of Bud-weiser's Christmas TV commercial, with Clydesdales stomping gamely through the snow. In a complex of Greek Revival buildings at a tiny crossroads 5 miles south of Woodstock, the inn is run by a cordial couple who offer guests a mix of history and style. Attractive guest rooms in three buildings are furnished in both antiques and reproductions, and all have heirloom quilts; most have wood-burning fireplaces, and a few have Jacuzzis. Rooms in the newer, motel-like log building by the river are equally well furnished (and less expensive), with canopied beds, custom oak wood-work, and fireplaces; one even has a private streamside terrace. Room nos. 12 and 17 (both suites) in the main house are among the most popular, as both have fireplaces and double Jacuzzis, and the inn's **dining room** ✿ is excellent. Some readers have noted the inn's rooms can be on the chilly side in deep winter.

Rte. 106 (P.O. Box 145), South Woodstock, VT 05071. ℭ **800/836-1193** or 802/457-1473. Fax 802/457-4469. www. kedronvalleyinn.com. 24 units. $133–$299 double; foliage season and Christmas week $171–$337 double. Rates include breakfast. Discounts available Mon–Fri in off-season. AE, DISC, MC, V. Closed Apr and briefly prior to Thanks-giving. Pets occasionally accepted with prior permission ($15 per night). **Amenities:** Restaurant; swimming pond. *In room:* A/C, TV, fridge (some units), fireplace (most units), Jacuzzi (some units), no phone.

Lauren Inn This sturdy brick Greek Revival B&B with a white clapboard ell just off the west end of the Woodstock green has found new ownership, new pricing, a new restaurant, and a makeover that transformed a formerly simple place into one where all the rooms now sport king-size beds (except 1 room, which has a queen), tele-phones with voicemail, iPod docking stations, and flatscreen televisions. The property is well situated for exploration of the village, and in back is a lovely porch overlook-ing the inn's 3 acres—a great spot for enjoying breakfast or just sitting quietly. Guest rooms are furnished in a sometimes-odd mix of styles, and while the restaurant and customer service are still finding their footing, this is still a notch higher on the accommodations scale than it used to be.

3 Church St., Woodstock, VT 05091. ℭ **802/457-1925.** Fax 802/457-1990. www.thelaureninn.com. 11 units, 5 units share 2 bathrooms. $169–$223 double; $275–$325 suite. Higher rates during foliage season and Christmas week. Rates include breakfast. MC, V. Closed Apr. Pets allowed ($5 per pet per night). **Amenities:** Restaurant; outdoor pool; tennis court. *In room:* TV.

Shire Motel The convenient Shire Motel is within walking distance of the green and the rest of the village, and with its attractive Colonial decor, it's better appointed than your average motel. Rooms are bright and have more windows than you might expect, most facing the river that runs behind the property. (The downside: some thin bed sheets and scuffed walls.) At the end of the second-floor porch is an outdoor kitchen where you can sit on rockers overlooking the river and enjoy a cup of coffee.

The yellow clapboard house next door has three spacious and modern suites, all with gas fireplaces and Jacuzzis.

46 Pleasant St., Woodstock, VT 05091. © 802/457-2211. www.shiremotel.com. 36 units. $78–$218 double. Foliage season rates higher. AE, MC, V. *In room:* A/C, TV, dataport, fridge, Jacuzzi (some units).

Twin Farms *Finds* ✦✦✦   Twin Farms offers uncommon luxury, privacy, and romance at uncommon prices. Housed on the 300-acre farm that was once home to Nobel prize–winning novelist Sinclair Lewis and his wife, it's a tasteful small resort. The compound consists of a main inn (four units), lodge (two units), farmhouse (four units), and 10 outlying cottages. All accommodations are rustic yet cleanly modern, with Scandinavian furnishings, modern art, and other master touches; the Aviary cottage, for instance, has a delightful bathtub of hand-set stone in the living room that looks like a birdbath and seems to flow from the stone fireplace. The owners are noted art collectors, and work on display includes originals by David Hockney, Roy Lichtenstein, and William Wegman. This is as close to all-inclusive as New England gets: Rates include three chef-prepared gourmet meals daily, an open bar, use of all the resort's recreational equipment, and transport from local airports.

Royalton Tpk., a dirt road near center (from Woodstock take Route 12 north to Barnard; P.O. Box 115, Barnard, VT 05031. © 800/894-6327 or 802/234-9999. www.twinfarms.com. 14 units. $1,100–$1,650 double; $1,750–$2,750 cottage. Rates include 3 meals daily and all liquor. AE, MC, V. Closed Apr. No children under 18 accepted. **Amenities:** Restaurant; lake swimming; 2 tennis courts; fitness center; Jacuzzi; watersports equipment rental; bike rental; game room; concierge; car rental; courtesy car; limited room service; in-room massage. *In room:* A/C, TV/VCR/DVD player, minibar, coffeemaker, hair dryer, iron, no phone.

Woodstock Inn & Resort ✦✦✦   This is possibly central Vermont's best full-scale resort. In an imposing brick structure right off the town green, the inn at first glance appears to be a venerable and long-established institution. But it's not—it was only opened in 1969. The inn adopted a Colonial Revival look well suited for Woodstock. Inside, guests are greeted by a broad stone fireplace and sitting areas tucked throughout the lobby; guest rooms are tastefully decorated in country pine or a Shaker-inspired style. The best units, in the newer wing built in 1991, have plush carpeting, refrigerators, and fireplaces. In recent years the inn has gone for a new, more contemporary look and a younger clientele, with the result that most rooms have been refitted with king bedding and added amenities. A big bonus here for guests is the free use of the inn's downhill and cross-country skiing facilities nearby; the fitness center has squash courts, racquetball, and steam rooms.

14 The Green, Woodstock, VT 05091. © 800/448-7900 or 802/457-1100. Fax 802/457-6699. www.woodstockinn. com. 141 units, 3 suites. $149–$434 double; $360–$664 suite. Off-season rates lower. Packages available. 2-night minimum stay Sat–Sun. AE, MC, V. **Amenities:** 2 restaurants; indoor pool; outdoor pool; golf course; putting green; 12 tennis courts; fitness center; bike rental; concierge; limited room service; babysitting; laundry service; dry cleaning. *In room:* A/C, TV, dataport, fridge (some units), hair dryer, iron, safe.

The Woodstocker Inn B&B ✦✦ *Finds*   At the foot of Mount Tom, this inn—so yellow it's impossible to miss—is owned by two cheerful ex-British publishing executives who employ green practices and display some mighty fine hospitality. They're slowly renovating with bright paints, stylish fixtures, and a sense of humor. The 1830s Cape now offers beds fitted with organic duvets, recycled-paper tissues, energy-efficient lighting and appliances, and natural bath products. Pastel walls and lovely exposed wood floors predominate. There's also Wi-Fi access, a well-stocked library, and baskets of complimentary candy bars. The romantic bathroom in the Westminster unit features cast iron clawed-foot tubs placed side by side beneath a skylight, while the Richmond suite's big recliners face a Bose home-theater system. And the whimsical Chelsea has a bright red Italian tub-and-sink combo. Breakfasts are a high point, featuring terrific homemade and locally sourced yogurt, fruit compote, porridge, sausage, bacon, and English-style cooked tomatoes and beans.

61 River St., Woodstock, VT 05091. ℂ 802/457-3896. Fax 802/457-3897. www.woodstockervt.com. 9 units. $110–$300 double. Rates include full breakfast. AE, MC, V. Children not allowed. *In room:* A/C, TV, no phone.

WHERE TO DINE

Bentley's ✦✦ AMERICAN   Bentley's adopts an affluent English gentlemen's club feel and is Woodstock's best choice for lunch. The dining room, set beyond an Anglophilic bar, affects a Victorian elegance, though it's not ostentatious. Lunch is the time to pick up one of the juicy burgers, barbecue plates, stews, flatbreads, or highly creative sandwiches (grilled chicken with Gouda, mango chutney, and almonds, for instance). The dinner menu leans more toward resort standards such as chicken and shrimp pescatore and steak flambéed tableside with Yukon Jack bourbon, but also cracks its doors to admit slightly more ambitious fare such as duck with apricot and plum sauce. It's often quite crowded here at night, when it becomes the closest thing in town to a "scene" after 10pm (a top women's magazine recently tabbed it as a "hot spot," though that's a reach); reserve a table. At the fine brunches on Sunday, try New England corned-beef hash with poached eggs and hollandaise sauce.

3 Elm St. ℂ 877/457-3232 or 802/457-3232. www.bentleysrestaurant.com. Reservations recommended for parties of 4 or more. Main courses $9–$15 at lunch; $11–$23 at dinner. AE, DC, DISC, MC, V. Mon–Sat 11:30am–9:30pm; Sun 11am–9:30pm. Open later for cocktails and dancing on weekends.

Jackson House Inn ✦✦ CONTINENTAL   The Jackson House dining room is a modern addition to the original inn (see above), and is now its starring attraction. Its centerpiece is a 16-foot-high stone fireplace, and it boasts soaring windows with views of the gardens. Once settled, you'll sample cuisine that's usually ingeniously conceived, deftly prepared, and artfully arranged by Chef Jason Merrill. The three-course meals begin with offerings such as Maine crabmeat and field greens with shaved fennel, or a foie gras "BLT." The main courses do an equally good job combining the earthy with the celestial; expect dishes such as crispy-skin salmon with a shiitake compote, mustard-encrusted lamb loin chops, an Angus filet served with white-corn polenta and an onion marmalade, or pan-roasted day boat scallops with a fruity salsa. For dessert, you might find a banana-walnut soufflé, crème brûlée with a cranberry compote, a grilled peach served with a rooibos-tea reduction and cannoli, or a steamed lemon pudding. The wine list is extensive.

114–3 Senior Lane. ℂ 800/448-1890 or 802/457-2065. Reservations highly recommended. 3-course prix-fixe dinner about $55; chef's tasting menu about $95. AE, MC, V. Wed–Sun 6–9pm.

The Prince and the Pauper ✦✦ NEW AMERICAN   It takes a bit of sleuthing to find this spot, down Dana Alley (next to the Woodstock Historical Society's Dana House), but it's worth the effort. This is one of Woodstock's best dining rooms, in an intimate but surprisingly informal setting. It's a bit more casual than most of the other restaurants in town. Ease into your evening with a libation in the taproom, then move to the rustic yet elegant little dining room. The good-value fixed-price menu (which doesn't include dessert) changes often. You might start with Maine smoked salmon over toast, lobster ravioli, or French onion soup spiked with Vermont apple cider, then move on to five-spiced duckling, filet mignon with peppercorn sauce, grilled ahi tuna from Hawaii with Asian spices, or the house specialty: a boneless rack of lamb baked in puff pastry with spinach and mushroom duxelles. Those on a tight budget can enjoy the lounge and the bistro menu, which is available daily except Saturdays and on holidays—it's full of good stuff like pulled-pork sandwiches, pizzas, steaks, fish, and crab cakes.

24 Elm St. ☎ 802/457-1818. www.princeandpauper.com. Reservations recommended. Prix-fixe dinners $46; bistro entrees $13–$21 (not available Sat). AE, DISC, MC, V. Sun–Thurs 6–9pm; Fri–Sat 6–9:30pm. Lounge opens at 5pm.

Simon Pearce Restaurant ★★ NEW AMERICAN   The setting here can't be beat. Housed in a restored 19th-century woolen mill with wonderful views of a water-fall, Simon Pearce is a collage of exposed brick, pine floorboards, and handsome wooden tables and chairs. Meals are served on Simon Pearce pottery and glassware—if you like your place setting, you can buy it afterward at the sprawling retail shop in the mill. The atmosphere is a good mix of formal and informal. Lunch dishes include madras curry chicken salads, beef and Guinness stew, lamb burgers, shepherd's pie, and crispy calamari with field greens. At dinner, look for entrees such as horseradish-crusted cod, grilled steak with smoked sea salt, crispy roast duckling with mango chut-ney, roasted chicken with a sage bread pudding, or pan-roasted wild salmon.

1760 Main St. (inside The Mill), Quechee. ☎ 802/295-1470. www.simonpearce.com. Reservations recommended for dinner. Main courses $8–$16 at lunch; $22–$29 at dinner. AE, DC, DISC, MC, V. Daily 11:30am–9pm.

4 Killington & Rutland

Killington: 12 miles E of Rutland; 160 miles NW of Boston; 93 miles SE of Burlington

In 1937, a travel writer described the village near Killington Peak as "a church and a few undistinguished houses." The rugged, remote area was isolated from Rutland to the west by imposing mountains and accessible only through the daunting Sherburne Pass.

That was before Vermont's second-highest mountain was developed as the North-east's largest ski area; before a wide, 5-mile-long access road was slashed through the forest right to the mountain's base. And it was before Route 4 was widened and upgraded, improving access to Rutland considerably. Today this is one of the most heavily traveled routes through the Green Mountains, and that early travel writer would be hard-pressed to recognize the region today.

Killington is plainly *not* the Vermont pictured on calendars and postcards. The region around the mountain boasts Vermont's most active winter scene, with loads of distractions both on and off the mountain. The area has a frenetic, where-it's-happen-ing feel in winter. Those most content here are skiers who like their skiing BIG, sin-gles in search of aggressive mingling, and travelers who want a wide selection of amenities and are willing to sacrifice some of that quintessential New England charm for a broader range of diversions.

About a dozen miles to the west, the rougher-edged city of Rutland lacks the imme-diate charm of other Vermont towns, but has a rich history and an array of conven-ient services for travelers. (It's also home to a huge annual state fair each fall.)

KILLINGTON

Killington lacks a town center, a single place that makes you feel you've arrived, and perhaps a soul as well; Killington is wherever you park. This town is so tied to the ski hill that it actually renamed itself after the mountain and resort in 1999; before that, it had been called Sherburne. Since the mountain was first developed for skiing in 1958, dozens of restaurants, hotels, and stores have sprouted up along Killington Road to accommodate the legions of skiers who descend upon the area during the ski season, which typically runs from October well into May, and sometimes even into June. Suburban-style theme restaurants dot the area, along with dozens of hotels and condos ranging from fancy to dowdy.

ESSENTIALS

GETTING THERE   Killington Road, the access road to the mountain, extends southward from routes 4 and 100 (it's still marked on some older maps as Sherburne). It's about 12 miles east of Rutland on Route 4. Many local inns offer shuttles to the Rutland airport, and **Amtrak** (© 800/USA-RAIL; www.amtrak.com) offers a slow daily service from New York City to Rutland, with connecting shuttles to the mountain and various resorts.

The Marble Valley Regional Transit District (© 802/773-3244; www.thebus.com) operates the **Skibus,** a handy daily, dawn-to-dusk shuttle service between Rutland and Killington daily in winter. Rides cost $2 per person one-way.

VISITOR INFORMATION   The **Killington Chamber of Commerce** (© 800/ 337-1928 or 802/773-4181; www.killington-chamber.org) has information on lodging and travel packages, and staffs an information booth on Route 4 at the base of the access road; it's open weekdays from 9am to 5pm and shorter hours on weekends. For information on accommodations in the area and travel to Killington, contact the resort's lodging service (© 800/621-6867) directly.

DOWNHILL SKIING

Killington 🏂🏂   A love-it or hate-it kind of place, New England's largest and most bustling ski area offers a greater vertical drop than any other New England mountain. It's certainly exciting, you've got to give it that. You'll find the broadest selection of slopes here, with trails ranging from long, narrow, old-fashioned runs to killer bumps high on its flanks. Thanks to this diversity, it has long been the Vermont destination of choice for serious skiers. That said, it's also the skiing equivalent of the Mall of America: a huge operation run with efficiency and not much personality. It's easy for kids to get separated from friends and family, and the resort seems to attract boisterous packs of young adults out for a good time. Families probably want to look elsewhere; places such as Sugarbush (see later in this chapter), Stowe, or Suicide Six are better options. But for a big-mountain experience, with lots of evening activities and plenty of challenging terrain, this is still a great choice.

4763 Killington Rd., Killington, VT 05751. © 800/621-6867 or 802/422-6200. www.killington.com. Day lift tickets $76 adults; discounts for children and seniors.

CROSS-COUNTRY SKIING

Nearest to the ski area (just east of Killington Rd. on Rte. 100/Rte. 4) is **Mountain Meadows Cross Country Ski Resort** 🏂 (© 802/775-7077 or 802/775-0166; www. xcskiing.net), with 36 miles of trails groomed for both skating and classic skiing. The trails are largely divided into three sections, with beginner trails closest to the lodge, an intermediate area a bit farther along, and an advanced 6-mile loop farthest away. Rentals and lessons are available at the lodge. For adults, a 1-day pass is $18, and a half-day (after 1pm) pass is $15. Kids ages 6 to 12 pay $8 per day, $6 per half-day.

The intricate network of trails at the **Mountain Top Nordic Ski & Snowshoe Center** 🏂🏂 (© 802/483-6089), part of the Mountain Top Inn, has long had a loyal following. The 50-mile trail network offers pastoral views through mixed terrain, most of it groomed. The trails are often deep with snow owing to the inn's ridge-top position

---

(Tips **Skiing on a Budget? Think Rutland!**

Skiers on a budget should consider home-basing it in Rutland at one of the city's many chain hotels and motels, then commuting to the mountain via car or the $2 shuttle bus. See the "Rutland" section below for a few suggestions.

---

high in the hills east of Rutland, and snowmaking along key portions of the trail ensures you won't have to walk across any bare spots during snow droughts. Adults pay $19 for 1-day trail passes, $16 for half-day passes (after 1pm). This is challenging and picturesque terrain.

GOLF

Vermont is loaded with fine golf courses, public and private, lovely in summer and outstandingly scenic in fall. The acknowledged top dog is the graceful **Green Mountain National Golf Course** ★★ (© **888/483-4653** or 802/422-4653; www.greenmountainnational.com) on Route 100 in Killington. Greens fees run from $49 to $69 per adult, not including the cost of a motorized cart (mandatory on weekends). There are discounts if you begin after 3pm. Rentals, instruction, and a driving range are also available.

A HISTORIC SITE

President Calvin Coolidge State Historic Site ★★   When told that Calvin Coolidge had died, literary wit Dorothy Parker is said to have responded, "How can they tell?" Even in death, the nation's most taciturn president fought for respect. But a trip to the Plymouth Notch Historic District should restore Silent Cal's reputation once and for all among visitors, who'll get a strong sense of the president reared in this mountain village. The only president born on Independence Day, Coolidge was a man shaped by the harsh weather, isolation of his high upland valley, and a strong sense of community and family who always remained a hero (and still is) to many Vermonters. The historic district consists of a group of about a dozen unspoiled buildings open to the public, plus a number of other private residences that may be observed from the outside only. Coolidge grew up here, and in August 1923 it was here in his boyhood home—the Coolidge Homestead, now open for tours—that the then-Vice President was awakened and informed that President Warren Harding had died. His own father, a notary public, administered the presidential oath of office. Coolidge is buried in the cemetery right across the road, where every July 4th a wreath is laid at his simple grave in a quiet ceremony. The bright foliage in the surrounding hills is another reason to visit here. Be sure to stop by **Frog City Cheese** (© 802/672-3650), just uphill from the Coolidge Homestead. The factory is open daily from 9:30am to 5pm throughout the historic site's season, same hours as the site itself.

Rte. 100A, Plymouth. © 802/672-3773. Admission $7.50 adults, $2 children 6–14; $20 family. Late May to mid-Oct daily 9:30am–5pm.

WHERE TO STAY

Blueberry Hill Inn ★   The homey Blueberry Hill Inn lies in the heart of the Moosalamoo recreation area, on 180 acres along a quiet road about 45 minutes northwest of Killington, perhaps midway to Middlebury. With superb hiking, biking, canoeing, swimming, and cross-country skiing, it's a good destination for those inclined toward spending time outdoors, away from the bother of everyday life. From an inn brochure: "We offer you no radios, no televisions, no bedside phones to disturb your vacation." There are also no Jacuzzis or double-sided fireplaces, either, a bit surprising given the high room rates. But there are plenty of country-design quilts and simple pieces of furniture; this is a place for true rustication. The inn dates to 1813, though one graceful addition is the greenhouse walkway leading to the cozy guest rooms. Family-style meals are served in a rustic dining room, with a great stone fireplace and homegrown herbs drying from the wooden beams. Remember that rates here are charged *per person*, not per room; kids are charged half-price.

Goshen-Ripton Rd., Goshen, VT 05733. © **800/448-0707** or 802/247-6735. Fax 802/247-3983. www.blueberry hillinn.com. 12 units. $130–$160 per adult, $65–$80 per child age 5–12. Rates include breakfast and dinner. MC, V. **Amenities:** Sauna; bike rental; babysitting. *In room:* No phone.

Cortina Inn & Resort ★★

The innkeepers here do a fine job making this inn, with nearly 100 rooms, feel smaller and more intimate than that. Great attention is paid to service and detail; the staff has even been spotted brushing off guests' car windows after a snow. The lodge, set back slightly from busy Route 4, has retro ski-chalet charm dating from the original construction—note the sunken conversation pit with its two-sided fireplace and a spiral staircase twisting up to a second level. Guest rooms vary, but all are nicely furnished—a few suites even come equipped with wet bars, refrigerators, and Jacuzzis. The indoor lap pool is lovely, and there's a pond on which you can take fly-fishing lessons and practice casting; two reading rooms to hang out in; and a small mountain biking center for rentals or guided tours through the hills. Watch for off-season room specials.

103 U.S. Rte. 4 (1½ miles west of Pico), Killington, VT 05751. © **800/451-6108** or 802/773-3333. Fax 802/775-6948. www.cortinainn.com. 96 units. $109–$335 double; discounts for multiple days. Rates include full breakfast. Packages available. 5-night minimum stay Christmas week; 3-night minimum stay Columbus and Presidents' Day weekends. AE, DC, DISC, MC, V. Pets allowed ($10 per pet per night). **Amenities:** 2 restaurants; indoor pool; 8 tennis courts; fitness room; Jacuzzi; sauna; 2 game rooms; children's center; concierge; shuttle (ski season only); limited room service; babysitting; laundry service; dry cleaning. *In room:* A/C, TV, dataport, hair dryer, fridge (some units), iron, fireplace (some units), Jacuzzi (some units).

Inn at Long Trail ★

The Inn at Long Trail is situated in an architecturally undistinguished building at an ecologically important crossroads: It's at the intersection of Route 4 and the Long and Appalachian trails (about a 10-min. drive from Killington's ski slopes). The interior of this rustic inn is far more charming than the exterior. Tree trunks support the beams in the lobby, which also sports log furniture and stairway banisters of yellow birch. The older rooms in the three-floor hotel (built in 1938 as an annex to a long-gone lodge) are furnished simply, in ski-lodge style. Comfortable, more modern suites with fireplaces, telephones, and TVs are in a motel-like addition. The dining room is fun and appealing, maintaining the Keebler-elfy theme with a stone ledge that juts through the wall from the mountain behind.

709 U.S. Rte. 4, Killington, VT 05751. © **800/325-2540** or 802/775-7181. Fax 802/747-7034. www.innatlongtrail. com. 19 units. Summer and fall $75–$105 double; foliage-season rates higher. Rates include breakfast. 2-night minimum stay weekends and during foliage season. AE, MC, V. Closed late Apr–late June. Pets allowed with prior permission. **Amenities:** Dining room; pub; Jacuzzi; laundry service. *In room:* TV (some units), phone (some units).

Inn of the Six Mountains ★

With its profusion of gables and dormers, Inn of the Six Mountains ranks among the most architecturally memorable of the many hotels lined up along Killington Road. The lobby is welcoming in a modern, Scandinavian sort of way, with lots of blond wood and stone, and the location is convenient to

Killington's base lodge, just a mile up the road. The guest rooms are tastefully decorated in a Shaker-inspired sort of way, but for a luxury hotel that offers only "deluxe" rooms and suites, the attention to detail can come up short, with some routine maintenance that apparently has been put off.

2617 Killington Rd., Killington, VT 05751. ℂ **800/228-4676** or 802/422-4302. www.sixmountains.com. 103 units. Mid-May to Nov $89–$159 double, $139–$209 suite; Dec to mid-Apr $129–$259 double, $179–$309 suite. Foliage season rates higher. Closed mid-Apr to mid-May. Rates include breakfast. AE, DC, DISC, MC, V. **Amenities:** Restaurant; indoor pool; outdoor pool; tennis court; fitness center; Jacuzzi; sauna; game room; business center; massage; limited room service. *In room:* TV, dataport, fridge, coffeemaker, hair dryer, safe.

Killington Grand Resort Hotel ★★

This is a good (though pricey) choice for travelers seeking contemporary accommodations right on the mountain. More than half of the units have kitchen facilities, and most are quite spacious, though decorated in a generic country-condo style. Some units can sleep up to six people, and the resort has placed an emphasis on catering to families. You pay a premium for convenience compared with other spots near the mountain, but that convenience is hard to top during ski season; the helpful service is a notch above that typically experienced at large ski hotels, and you can literally ski to the mountain over a special bridge. A new addition to the hotel is the Killington Grand Spa, offering Swedish massage, Vichy showers, stone massages, and more.

228 E. Mountain Rd. (near Snowshed base), Killington, VT 05751. ℂ **877/4KTIMES.** Fax 802/422-6881. www.the killingtongrand.com. 200 units. Fall and winter $336–$395 double, suites from $508; off-peak $129–$310 double, suites from $175. Packages available. 5-night minimum stay during Christmas and school holidays; 2-night minimum stay Sat–Sun. AE, DISC, MC, V. **Amenities:** 2 restaurants; 2 bars; outdoor pool; 2 tennis courts; spa; fitness center; Jacuzzi; sauna; children's programs; concierge; limited room service; massage; dry cleaning. *In room:* A/C, TV, dataport, coffeemaker, hair dryer, iron, safe.

The Mountain Top Inn & Resort ★★

It really *is* on top of a mountain. Situated on 1,300 lovely ridge-top acres, this pond-side property sports one of New England's best views and a relaxing, summery feel, from the expansive front porch of Adirondack chairs to croquet games and horse rides. Carved out of a former turnip farm, the inn has left its root-vegetable heritage far behind: Even the lowest-priced rooms have been updated in woods, leathers, and tartans, and six expanded suites—including High Meadow (with a wall of windows looking out on the scenery) and comfy Mamey's Retreat, across the hall from where Ike stayed back in 1955—come wonderfully outfitted with such modern amenities as flatscreen TVs, sofas, double-sided fireplaces, jetted tubs, and kitchenettes. Activities abound: riding, clay-bird shooting, fly-fishing lessons, free canoeing and kayaking, dog-sledding (really), and performances of jazz and classical music. This is about a 25-minute drive from Killington.

195 Mountain Top Rd., Chittenden, VT 05737. ℂ **800/445-2100** or 802/483-2311. Fax 802/483-6373. www.mountain topinn.com. 55 units. Spring and late fall $150–$315 double; summer and winter $225–$495 double; foliage season and holidays $255–$545 double. AE, MC, V. **Amenities:** 2 restaurants; bar; outdoor pool; kayaks and canoes; activities center. *In room:* A/C, TV, dataport, kitchenette (some units), fireplace (some units), Jacuzzi (some units).

The Summit Lodge ★

Plaid carpeting and Saint Bernard dogs: Those two motifs set the tone at this lodge on a rise just off Killington's access road. Though built only in the 1960s, the inn has a somewhat historical character; much of the common space was constructed of salvaged barn timbers, and there are fieldstone fireplaces to warm yourself by in winter. The guest rooms here are undistinguished, with clunky pine furniture and little ambience, though all of them do have balconies or terraces. You might not spend much time in your room, anyway, since the common spaces are so nice. I will say this. The lodge has more character than most self-styled resorts along the access road, and it offers decent value, so give it a look—especially if you love Saint Bernards. At last count, two resided here.

Killington Mountain Rd. (P.O. Box 119), Killington, VT 05751. ✆ 800/635-6343 or 802/422-3535. Fax 802/422-3536. www.summitlodgevermont.com. 45 units. $78–$140 double; holiday and foliage season rates higher. 3- to 4-night minimum fall-foliage weekends and some holidays. Winter rates include breakfast. Minimum-stay policy on holidays. AE, DC, MC, V. **Amenities:** Restaurant; pub; 2 outdoor pools; tennis courts; Jacuzzi; game room; limited room service; massage. *In room:* TV.

WHERE TO DINE

Charity's 1887 Saloon PUB FARE   Bustling and laid-back, this is the place if you like your food big and simple (wings, beer, shrimp, rinse, repeat) and your crowd young. A barn-like place adorned with stained-glass lamps and Victorian prints, the tavern is centered on a handsome old bar that was crafted in Italy, shipped to West Virginia, used for a century, then packed up again and sent here in the early '70s. This rather extended history of the bar top turns out to be much more interesting than the food: The menu's mostly burgers and wings, plus a few vegetarian choices.

Killington Rd. ✆ 802/422-3800. Reservations not accepted. Main courses $6–$9 at lunch, $13–$19 at dinner. AE, MC, V. Daily 11:30am–10pm.

Choices Restaurant and Rotisserie ✦ BISTRO   Locals seem to like this unpretentious place, located on the access road across from the Outback. Full dinners come complete with salad or soup and bread, and restore calories lost out on the slopes or the trail. Fresh pastas are a specialty (try Cajun green-peppercorn fettuccine if it's available); other entrees include meats from a rotisserie. The atmosphere is nothing to write home about, and the prices are higher than at the burger joints nearby, but the quality of the food and care taken in preparation are better than most at Killington, too.

Killington Rd. (at Glazebook Center). ✆ 802/422-4030. Main courses $13–$22. AE, MC, V. Mon–Thurs 5–10pm; Fri–Sat 5–11pm; Sun 11am–2pm.

Hemingway's ✦✦✦ NEW AMERICAN   Killington seems an unlikely place for a culinary adventure, yet Hemingway's provides one. On an arrow-flat stretch of highway, Hemingway's is one of the best restaurants in northern New England. Housed in a former stagecoach stop, the restaurant staff seats guests in one of three formal areas; two upstairs rooms are especially well appointed in damask linen, crystal goblets, and fresh flowers. Your meal might start with Maine scallops; good cream of garlic soup; or a quail sandwich. The main courses might take in a filet of red snapper, served with grilled shrimp and risotto; a cut of salmon; herbed poussin with truffled potatoes; duck with peaches; or slow-roasted veal with couscous and vegetables. Finish with a Vermont cheese plate or desserts such as a warm lavender cake, semolina pudding with figs, or fruit soup. Dress casually yet neatly (no shorts or T-shirts).

4988 Rte. 4 (btw. Rte. 100 N. and Rte. 100 S.). ✆ 802/422-3886. www.hemingwaysrestaurant.com. Reservations highly recommended. Main courses $28–$34; prix-fixe menus more expensive. AE, MC, V. Wed–Thurs and Sun 6–9pm; Fri–Sat 6–10pm. (Also selected Mon–Tues during ski and foliage seasons; call ahead.) Closed mid-Apr to mid-May and early Nov.

The Highlands Dining Room ✦✦ AMERICAN/CONTINENTAL   The Mountain Top Inn & Resort's dining room delivers surprisingly sophisticated cuisine from its woodsy, folksy perch. (Though jackets are requested of gentlemen, there are also racks of moose antlers for lighting and accouterment, if that gives you some idea). With Chef Will Hollinger and Sous Chef Shawn Casey, meals begin with appetizers such as truffled scallops, beef capriccio, or a martini glass of buttermilk-fried calamari with aioli and basil, move on to seasonal fruit-nut or smoked salmon salads, then continue with main dishes that sway both toward France (filet mignon with fried oysters, pan-seared duck) and Asia (seared sesame tuna with a miso risotto). The attached **Highlands Tavern** serves a simpler and lower-priced but equally fine menu of hearty meat loaf, pastas, ale-battered fish and chips and the like—with the added bonus of outdoor terrace seating.

195 Mountain Top Rd., Chittenden, VT 05737. $©$ **800/445-2100** or 802/483-2311. Reservations recommended. Main courses $25–$40. AE, DC, MC, V. Daily 6–9pm.

Wally's American Grill 𝄞 *Kids* AMERICAN/ECLECTIC This 1950s-retro restaurant is a festive, upbeat place—often crowded with visitors and locals who've just enjoyed a long day on the slopes or trails. Situated in a strip-mallish complex near the top of Killington Road, the restaurant's interior sets a subdued, yet good, mood. The menu here is simple diner fare, expanded for a slightly sophisticated clientele; expect omelets, eggs, hotcakes, and combo specials like the "All In" and the "Jackpot" at breakfast (check out the active orange juicer); salads and sandwiches for lunch; and dinner entrees including New Zealand shrimp, pasta, lobster ravioli, seared salmon, steaks, and even Quebec-style poutine. There are plenty of beers on tap as well.

Killington Rd. $©$ **802/422-3177.** Reservations not accepted. Lunch and dinner main courses $8–$18. AE, DC, MC, V. Sun–Thurs 7am–9pm; Fri–Sat 7am–midnight.

RUTLAND

Rutland is a no-nonsense, blue-collar city that never had a reputation for charm. Today, it's undergoing a low-grade renaissance, attracting a small clutch of new residents who enjoy the small-city atmosphere, free summer outdoor concerts, cheaper real estate, and quick access to the mountains—Killington is just minutes away. But this place remains working-class at heart, and it probably always will.

Rutland also remains the regional hub for central Vermont, with a long line of big-box stores, fast-food chain restaurant, and businesses stretched out along busy Route 7 both north and south of downtown. (The local airport is nearby, too.) At times, the downtown comes perilously close to looking like one big (and outdated) strip mall. That said, Rutland still has the feel of a real place with real Vermont people, a good antidote for anyone who has spent too much time trapped in cuckoo-clock shops and lift lines.

ESSENTIALS

GETTING THERE It's easy to get to Rutland. By car, the city is at the intersection of two old U.S. highways, U.S. Route 7 and U.S. Route 4. Burlington is 67 miles to the north and Bennington is 56 miles to the south via Route 7; Woodstock is 25 miles east on Route 4, across the mountains. **Amtrak** ($©$ **800/USA-RAIL;** www.amtrak. com) offers daily train service from New York City via the Hudson River Valley; the ride takes about 5½ hours. Surprisingly, Rutland is also served by daily direct flights from Boston on **Continental Connection** ($©$ **800/523-3273;** www.continental. com); the flight takes 1 hr.

VISITOR INFORMATION The **Rutland Region Chamber of Commerce,** 256 N. Main St., Rutland, VT 05701 ($©$ **800/756-8880** or 802/773-2747; www.rutland vermont.com), staffs an information booth at the corner of Route 7 and Route 4 West; it's open daily from Memorial Day to Columbus Day. The chamber's main office is open year-round Monday through Friday 8am to 5pm.

FESTIVALS   The **Vermont State Fair** ⍟ (🕿 **802/775-5200;** www.vermontstatefair. net) has attracted fairgoers from throughout Vermont and beyond for more than a century and a half. Expect clowns, carnival rides, live music, cows (and lots of other agricultural exhibits), and plenty more; admission is about $6 per adult per day, with discounts for kids. There's also a small charge for parking. It's held from late August through the first week of September at the expansive fairgrounds on U.S. Route 7, just south of the city center on the right-hand side as you leave town. Gates open at 8am daily.

EXPLORING THE TOWN

A stroll through Rutland's historic downtown delights architecture buffs. Look for the detailed marblework on many of the buildings, such as the Opera House, the Gryphon's Building, and along Merchant's Row. Note especially the fine marble exterior of the Chittenden Savings Bank at the corner of Merchants Row and Center Street. Nearby South Main Street (Route 7) also has a good selection of handsome homes built in elaborate Queen Anne style.

Another stop worth making, especially as a rainy-day diversion, is the **Chaffee Art Center** ⍟, at 16 S. Main St. (🕿 **802/775-0356**). Housed in a Richardsonian structure dating from 1896, with a characteristically prominent turret and a mosaic floor in the archway vestibule—this building is on the National Register of Historic Places, with glorious parquet floors restored to their original luster—the center showcases the abundant local artistic talent concealed in Rutland and the hills beyond. While it owns no permanent collections, the center does feature changing exhibits of local work, much of it for sale. It's open daily except Tuesdays from 10am to 5pm (Sun noon–4pm); admission is by donation.

OUTSIDE OF TOWN

A worthy detour from Rutland is to the amiable town of **Proctor,** about 6 miles northwest of Rutland center. (Take Rte. 4 west, then follow Rte. 3 north.) This quiet town is nestled in the folds of low hills; some of its homes and bridges are made of local marble, appropriate since this was once a noted center for quarrying the fine-grained local marble (which found its way to the U.S. Supreme Court, Lincoln Memorial, and other important structures).

In 1991, the quarries closed and the factory shut down, but the heritage lives on at the expansive, popular **Vermont Marble Museum** ⍟ (🕿 **800/427-1396** or 802/459-2300; www.vermont-marble.com), which touts itself as the world's largest marble exhibit. View an 11-minute video about marble, walk through "Earth Alive" displays about local geology, see a sculptor working in marble, and explore the Hall of Presidents, with life-size bas-relief sculptures of all the past presidents. The sheer size of this former factory is impressive. The gift shop has a great selection of reasonably priced marble products.

The museum is open daily from Memorial Day through October from 9am to 5:30pm, and closed the rest of the year. Admission is $7 for adults, $5 for seniors, $4 for students 13 to 18, and free for children under 13. (Prices are $1 cheaper if you book them in advance by phone.) Look for signs to the exhibit from Route 3 in Proctor.

WHERE TO STAY

Rutland has a selection of basic roadside motels and chain hotels, mostly clustered on or along Route 7 south of town.

Inn at Rutland ✿ Built as a family home in the 1890s by the grain-empire Burdett family, this is an imposing Victorian B&B overlooking U.S. Route 7 on the north side of town. It's elaborate on the outside, but even more so on the inside; gracefully curving walls, stamped plaster wainscoting, oak trim, and leather wallpaper are some of the noteworthy details. The downstairs parlors are formal in an Edwardian sort of way, and guest rooms are surprisingly spacious. Rooms facing Route 7 are a bit noisier, but the house was solidly wrought and seems to buffer most of it. The third-floor rooms are generally less detailed, but the Washington and the Rutland—both large and quiet—are still two of the best in the house. The Washington room was also one of two units recently outfitted with a Jacuzzi tub; the Orleans room is the other. The Franklin room sports a really nice brick fireplace.

70 N. Main St. (Rte. 7), Rutland, VT 05701. ✆ 800/808-0575 or 802/773-0575. www.innatrutland.com. 8 units. $120–$175 double; holidays and fall-foliage season $150–$220 double. Rates include full breakfast. AE, DISC, MC, V. *In room:* TV, fireplace (some units), Jacuzzi (2 units).

WHERE TO DINE

In addition to the choices listed below, **Clem's Café** (✆ **802/775-3337**) is a casually hip cafe housed in a former bank, right downtown at 100 Merchants Row. Grab a seat at a sidewalk table or move inside and choose a room. (The bank vault is tiny and nicely painted, and you can have a lively conversation there—with an echo.) A good selection of coffees is available, plus baked goods such as banana-nut tarts, croissants, and cheese Danishes. It's open Monday to Friday until 2pm, to 1pm on Saturday and Sunday.

And, for families, there's an outlet of the popular northern New England fish-house chain **Weathervane** (✆ **802/773-0382**), which I happen to like (and find that kids seem to enjoy, too). It's located at 124 Woodstock Ave., which is Route 4 a few blocks uphill (going toward Killington) from the central crossroads of Routes 4 and 7. How they get fresh fish all the way from the Maine coast over here to Rutland every morning is beyond me, but it's worth checking out.

Little Harry's ✿ GLOBAL Little Harry's is an offshoot of the great Harry's restaurant outside Ludlow. This one is located in downtown Rutland, on the first floor and in the basement of a strikingly unattractive building; yet this place has a wonderfully eclectic menu, just like its papa, with main selections ranging from grilled steak sandwiches to duck in a "searing" red Thai curry. Appetizers are equally eclectic, with choices along the lines of marinated olives, gazpacho, pad Thai, and hummus. Dishes span the globe and will appeal to anyone with an adventurous palate.

121 West St. ✆ 802/747-4848. Reservations recommended. Main courses $11–$17. AE, MC, V. Daily 5–10pm.

5 Middlebury ✦/✦

Middlebury is 35 miles S of Burlington, 85 miles N of Bennington, and 65 miles NW of White River Junction

Middlebury is a gracious college town amid rolling hills and empty, pastoral countryside, its town center idyllic in a New-England-as-envisioned-by-Hollywood kind of way. For many travelers, it provides the perfect combination of small-town charm, access to the outdoors (the Adirondacks and Green Mountains are both close at hand), and a dash of sophistication. The influence of college students and out-of-staters has resulted in a natural foods store, ethnic restaurants, and more arts, crafts, and books than you would expect to find in a place several times its size.

ESSENTIALS

GETTING THERE   Middlebury is on Route 7 about midway between Rutland and Burlington. From upstate New York by car, you can drive to Fort Ticonderoga and taking the "cable ferry" (© **802/897-7999**) across the Lake Champlain. The ferry operates from mid-May to late October, about three times per hour; the cost for autos is a steep $8 one-way, $14 round-trip per car, but it takes just 7 minutes.

VISITOR INFORMATION   The **Addison County Chamber of Commerce,** 2 Court St. (© **800/733-8376** or 802/388-9300; www.midvermont.com), is in a handsome, historic white building just off the green, facing The Middlebury Inn. Brochures and assistance are available from Monday through Friday during business hours (9am–5pm), and often on Saturday and Sunday from early June to mid-October. Ask for the map and guide to downtown Middlebury. It lists town shops and restaurants and is published by the Downtown Middlebury Business Bureau.

EXPLORING THE TOWN

The best place to begin a tour of Middlebury is at the Addison County Chamber of Commerce's information center (see above); be sure to request the chamber's self-guided walking-tour brochure.

The **Vermont Folklife Center** ★ (© **802/388-4964;** www.vermontfolklifecenter. org) recently relocated to 88 Main St. Here you'll find a gallery of changing displays of various folk arts from Vermont and beyond, including music and visual arts. The gift shop has intriguing items, such as heritage foods and traditional crafts. It's open Tuesday through Saturday from 10am to 5pm; admission is by donation.

The historic **Otter Creek** ★★ district, set on a steep hillside by the rocky creek, is well worth exploring. Here you can peruse top-flight Vermont crafts at the **Vermont State Crafts Center at Frog Hollow** ★★, 1 Mill St. (© **888/388-3177;** www.frog hollow.org). In a picturesque setting overlooking the tumbling stream, the center is open daily (closed Sun in winter) and shows the work of some 300 Vermont craftspeople in various galleries. Their wares range from extraordinary carved wood desks to metalwork to glass and pottery. There are also a pottery studio, with a resident potter who's often busy at work, and plenty of arts classes; visit the center's website for an updated listing of the current exhibits and courses. The Crafts Center also maintains shops in Manchester Village and at the Church Street Marketplace in Burlington.

From Frog Hollow, take the footbridge over the river and find your way to **The Marble Works** ★, an assortment of wood and rough-marble industrial buildings on the far bank, converted to a handful of interesting shops and restaurants.

Atop a low ridge with beautiful views of the Green Mountains to the east and farmlands rolling toward Lake Champlain in the west, prestigious **Middlebury College** ★★ has a handsome, well-spaced campus of gray limestone and white marble buildings that are best explored by foot. The architecture of the college, founded in 1800, is primarily Colonial Revival, giving it a rather stern Calvinist ambience. Especially appealing is the prospect from the marble Mead Memorial Chapel, built in 1917 and overlooking the campus green.

At the edge of campus is the **Middlebury College Center for the Arts,** which opened in 1992. This architecturally engaging center houses the small **Middlebury College Museum of Art** ★ (© **802/443-5007**), with a selective sampling of European and American art, both ancient and new. Classicists will savor the displays of Greek painted urns and vases; modern-art aficionados can check out the museum's

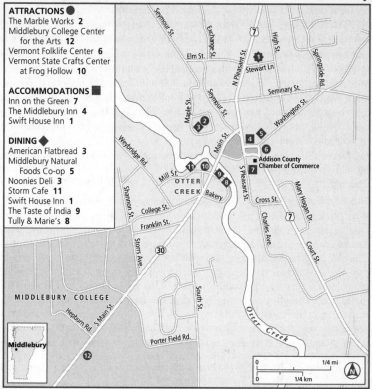

ATTRACTIONS ●
The Marble Works **2**
Middlebury College Center
  for the Arts **12**
Vermont Folklife Center **6**
Vermont State Crafts Center
  at Frog Hollow **10**

ACCOMMODATIONS ■
Inn on the Green **7**
The Middlebury Inn **4**
Swift House Inn **1**

DINING ◆
American Flatbread **3**
Middlebury Natural
  Foods Co-op **5**
Noonies Deli **3**
Storm Cafe **11**
Swift House Inn **1**
The Taste of India **9**
Tully & Marie's **8**

Seymour St.
Exchange St.
Elm St.
High St.
Springside Rd.
N Pleasant St.
Stewart Ln.
Seminary St.
Maple St.
Seymour St.
Washington St.
Weybridge Rd.
Main St.
Addison County
Chamber of Commerce
S Pleasant St.
Mill St.
OTTER CREEK
Bakery
Shannon St.
College St.
Cross St.
Mary Hogan Dr.
Franklin St.
Charles Ave.
Court St.
Storrs Ave.
30
MIDDLEBURY COLLEGE
Hepburn Rd. S Main St.
South St.
Otter Creek
Middlebury
Porter Field Rd.

0   1/4 mi
0   1/4 km

permanent and changing exhibits. The museum is on Route 30 (S. Main St.) and is open Tuesday through Friday from 10am to 5pm, Saturday and Sunday from noon to 5pm; note that it's closed for half of August and most of December, times when the college is out of session. Admission is free.

Finally, one recommended walk for people of all abilities—and especially those of poetic sensibilities—is the **Robert Frost Interpretive Trail** ⍟, dedicated to the memory of New England's poet laureate. Frost lived in a cabin on a farm across the road for 23 summers. (The cabin is now a National Historic Landmark.) On Route 125 approximately 6 miles east of Middlebury, this relaxing loop trail is just a mile long, with excerpts of Frost's poems placed on signs along the trail. Also posted is information about the trail's natural history. Managed by the Green Mountain National Forest, the trail offers pleasant access to the lovely intermountain lowlands.

WHERE TO STAY

The outskirts of Middlebury, particularly Route 7 just south of the village green, are home to a handful of budget motels and inns. The 1960s-era **Blue Spruce Motel,** 2428 Rte. 7 S. (© **802/388-4091**), has about two dozen basic rooms, plus some cottages; families lingering in the area for a few days should inquire about a suite with its own full kitchen, sleeping loft, and carport. Rates run from about $68 to $98 for the double rooms, $135 to $150 for the suite. The **Greystone Motel,** at 1395 Rte. 7 S. (℃ **802/388-4935**), has 10 clean rooms with small bathrooms; rates for a double room can range from around $55 to $125, with winter being the least-expensive time.

The Inn on the Green 🐦🐦 This handsome village inn occupies a house that dates to 1803 (it was Victorianized with a mansard tower later in the century). It's both historic and comfortable. The rooms are furnished with a mix of antiques and reproductions; wood floors and boldly colored walls of harvest yellow, peach, and burgundy lighten the architectural heaviness of the house. The suites are naturally the most spacious, but all units offer plenty of elbow room. Those in the front of the house are wonderfully flooded with afternoon light.

71 S. Pleasant St., Middlebury, VT 05753. ℃ **888/244-7512** or 802/388-7512. www.innonthegreen.com. 11 units. July–Oct $179–$229 double, $279–$329 suite; Nov–June $129–$199 double, $189–$329 suite. Rates include continental breakfast. 2-night minimum stay Sat–Sun. AE, DC, DISC, MC, V. *In room:* A/C, TV, dataport, hair dryer, iron.

The Middlebury Inn 🐦 The historic Middlebury Inn traces its roots to 1827, when Nathan Wood built the Vermont Hotel, a brick public house. It now consists of four buildings containing 75 modern guest rooms equipped with most conveniences. Rooms are on the large side, and most are outfitted with a sofa or upholstered chairs, Colonial-reproduction furniture, and some vintage bathroom fixtures. Room nos. 116 and 246 are spacious corner units entered via a dark foyer/sitting room; no. 129, though smaller, has a four-poster bed, a view of the village green, and a Jacuzzi. Guest rooms in the Porterhouse Mansion next door also have a pleasant, historical feel. (An adjacent motel is decorated in an Early American motif, but underneath the veneer it's just a standard-issue motel; stick with the main inn if you want a taste of history.)

14 Court Sq., Middlebury, VT 05753. ℃ **800/842-4666** or 802/388-4961. Fax 802/388-4563. www.middleburyinn. com. 70 units. Mon–Fri $88–$245 double, $235–$240 suite; Sat–Sun $98–$270 double, $270–$375 suite. Rates include continental breakfast. AE, DC, MC, V. Pets allowed in some rooms. **Amenities:** Restaurant; tavern; business center; laundry service. *In room:* A/C, TV, dataport, hair dryer, iron.

Swift House Inn 🐦🐦 This historic complex of three whitewashed houses sits on a hillside 2 blocks from downtown Middlebury, and it was always a favorite. New owners have improved it with such touches as chai tea in the rooms, a friendly barkeep, and improved pricing of the inn's fine restaurant. The lower-priced rooms in the roadside gatehouse have a B&B feel and have been updated with upscale carpets, gorgeous wooden floors, and bathrooms. The nine rooms in the main Federal-style inn (built in 1814) are thoroughly imbued with the intriguing history of the place: A Vermont governor lived here at one time. Inside, it's decorated in a simple, historical style of antiques and reproduction furnishings, including the Clark Room—two former rooms combined into one, it has a love seat and looks out over lovely lawns and grounds. The carriage house's six suites—ideal for honeymooners and business travelers—are the inn's most luxurious, and most have Jacuzzis and fireplaces.

25 Stewart Lane, Middlebury, VT 05753. ℃ **866/388-9925** or 802/388-9925. Fax 802/388-9927. www.swifthouse inn.com. 20 units. Main inn $110–$185 double; gate house $110–$135 double; carriage house $235–$255 suite. Rates include full breakfast. 2-night minimum stay some weekends. AE, MC, V. **Amenities:** Restaurant; limited room service (breakfast only). *In room:* A/C, TV, dataport, hair dryer, iron, fireplace (some units), Jacuzzi (some units).

Waybury Inn 🐦 Photos of Bob Newhart and "Larry, his brother Darryl and his other brother, Darryl," grace the wall behind the desk at this 1810 inn. This inn was featured in the classic TV show *Newhart*—the exterior, anyway. (The interior was created on a Hollywood sound stage.) The architecturally handsome Waybury has loads of integrity in a simple, farmhouse sort of way. Rooms vary in size, as they do in most old inns; the more you pay, the more space you'll get (three of the rooms are considered suites, with enhanced amenities such as four-posted king beds, Jacuzzis, or claw-footed bathtubs). This inn is close to the road, thus its front-facing rooms can be a bit noisy at night from highway noise; the two attic rooms are cozy, if a bit darker and more garretlike.

457 E. Main St. (Rte. 125), East Middlebury, VT 05753. ℂ 800/348-1810 or 802/388-4015. Fax 802/388-1248. www. wayburyinn.com. 15 units, 1 with detached private bathroom. $115–$180 double; $175–$250 suite. Rates include breakfast. Call for information about packages. AE, DISC, MC, V. Pets allowed with restrictions (call first). **Amenities:** Restaurant. *In room:* A/C, no phone.

WHERE TO DINE

In addition to the eateries listed below, Middlebury possesses an abundance of delis, sandwich shops, and the like—perfect for a quick lunch or a picnic.

The Storm Cafe ★★ NEW AMERICAN   This tiny, casual spot with great river views on the ground floor of a stone mill in Frog Hollow is a chef-owned restaurant popular with locals and travelers alike. The menu is beguilingly simple, but tremendous care is taken in the selection of ingredients and the preparation; salads are especially good. Eclectic lunch selections include "The Dude" (bacon, cheese, and vegetables on ciabatta), the 'Frisco Chick (chicken, pistachios, golden raisins, and salad in a tomato wrap), and a pile of mussels steamed in wine, lime, and spices; dinner selections might include seafood lasagna, penne carbonara, Cuban grilled pork loin, sirloin tournedos, and a daily seafood special. Desserts run to a Bavarian torte, blackberry bread pudding, and that old New England standby: a whoopie pie. The wine list isn't bad, either. As a fine-dining spot, this is one of the town's best.

3 Mill St. ℂ 802/388-1063. Reservations recommended. Main courses $6–$9 lunch; $16–$23 dinner. MC, V. Tues–Sat 11:30am–2:30pm and 5–9pm.

Swift House Inn ★★ NEW AMERICAN   This inn restaurant consists of two dining rooms on the ground floor of the main house. It's a wonderfully homey place to get a fancy meal in town. Meals may start with a fresh salad, some pan-crisped white bean cakes, or mussels, followed by grilled lamb top round with delicately grilled zucchini, or maybe an oven-roasted duck breast over garlic polenta, grilled strip steak, Scottish salmon with soba noodles, or some basil pasta with eggplant "meatballs." Finish with a boca negra chocolate cake with coconut whipped cream, a wonderful cappuccino-flavored crème brûlée with caramelized pecans, or whatever else is on the menu. Some tables look out onto the grounds—and, by default, sunset over the mountains to the west.

25 Stewart Lane, Middlebury, VT 05753. ℂ 802/388-9925. Reservations recommended. Main courses $15–$21. AE, MC, V. Thurs–Mon 6–9pm.

Tully and Marie's ★ NEW AMERICAN/GLOBAL   Tully and Marie's is a bright and colorful Art Deco–inspired restaurant overlooking the creek, made all the more appealing by its surprising location down a small, dark alley. This is a fun, low-key eatery that puts you in a good mood the moment you walk in. Angle for a table perched over the creek, then inspect a menu specializing in New American cuisine—with plenty of clear influences from Asia and Mexico. At lunch expect burgers, burritos, and an exceptionally creative array of sandwiches and wraps of crab cakes, salmon, brie, and other fresh ingredients. At dinner you might find grilled jumbo sea scallops glazed with chipotle peppers and maple syrup, house-smoked pork barbecue, fajitas, Moroccan-spiced salmon, jerk chicken, and a daily steak special.

7 Bakery Lane. (℃) **802/388-4182.** www.tullyandmaries.com. Reservations recommended Sat–Sun. Main courses $7–$8 at lunch; $10–$24 at dinner. AE, MC, V. Daily 11:30am–3pm and 5–9pm (to 10pm Fri–Sat).

6 The Mad River Valley (★/★

Warren: 3 miles S of Waitsfield; 205 miles NW of Boston; 43 miles SE of Burlington

Save for a couple of telltale signs, you could drive Route 100 through the sleepy villages of **Warren** and **Waitsfield** and never realize you're close to some of the choicest skiing in the state. The region hasn't fallen prey (yet) to unbridled condo or strip-mall development, and the valley seems to have learned from the overdevelopment that afflicts such ski resort areas as Mount Snow and Killington. Even the Mad River Green, a tidy strip mall on Route 100 just north of Route 17, is disguised as an old barn; it's scarcely noticeable from the main road. Some veteran Vermont travelers say approvingly that the valley today looks much like the Stowe of 30 years ago did.

The region's character becomes less pastoral along the access road to the **Sugarbush** ski resort, but even there development isn't too heavily concentrated. The best lodges and restaurants tend to be tucked into the forest or set along streams; make sure you have good directions before setting out in search of accommodations or food, and try not to do so at night unless necessary—most of these roads do not come with street-lights. (That's why you're in Vermont, remember?) Hidden up a winding valley road, **Mad River Glen,** the area's older ski area, has a pleasantly dated quality that still eschews glitz in favor of rustic charms. It's many Vermonters' favorite ski hill for that reason.

ESSENTIALS

GETTING THERE   Warren and Waitsfield are on Route 100 between Killington and Waterbury. The nearest interstate access is from exit 10 (Waterbury) on I-89; drive south on Route 100 for 14 miles to Waitsfield.

VISITOR INFORMATION   The **Mad River Valley Chamber of Commerce** (℃ **800/828-4748** or 802/469-3409; www.madrivervalley.com) is at 4601 Main St. (Rte. 100) in the General Wait House, next to the elementary school. It's open daily from 9am to 5pm during summer, foliage season, and ski season; during slower times, expect more limited opening hours and days.

SKIING & OTHER WINTER SPORTS

Downhill skiing is abundant in the valley (see below). For slower-paced activity, the outdoorsy folks at Clearwater Sports (℃ **802/496-2708;** www.clearwatersports.com), on Main Street in Waitsfield, rent snowshoes and telemark skis—and also dispense advice—in the winter.

Mad River Glen ★/★/★ (Finds   Mad River Glen is the curmudgeon of the Vermont ski world—just what you'd expect from a place whose motto used to be "Ski it if you can." High-speed detachable quads? Forget it. Until early 2007, the main ski lift was a 1948 *single*-chair lift that creaked its way a mile up to the summit. Snowmaking? Don't count on it. This hill is nearly entirely dependent on the whims of Mother Nature. Snowboarding? Nope; it's forbidden. Toll-free telephone numbers? A fancy website? Hardly. This hill long ago attained cult status among one-with-the-mountain connoisseurs, and its fans seem determined to keep it that way: Owned and operated by a cooperative of Mad River skiers since 1995, it claims to be the only cooperative-owned ski area in the country. But don't mistake this gentler approach for easy skiing—the slopes here are twisting and narrow, and hide some of the steepest drops in New England (nearly half the slopes are classified as "expert"). A ski school and kids' program are offered, and care is taken to preserve (and explain) the mountain's ecology. A renegade spirit remains here—even in the face of the sport's, and Vermont's, inexorable process of upscaling.

PO Box 1089, Waitsfield, VT 05763. *©* **802/496-3551.** www.madriverglen.com. Day lift tickets $35–$56 adults, half-day tickets $29–$45 adults. Discounts for youths and seniors.

Sugarbush 🎿🎿   Sugarbush is a fine intermediate-to-advanced ski resort comprising two ski mountains linked by a 2-mile, 10-minute high-speed chairlift that crosses three ridges. (A shuttle bus offers a warmer way to traverse the mountains.) The number of high-speed lifts (four) and excellent snowmaking capabilities make this a desirable destination for serious skiers. While an improved Sugarbush has generated some buzz since large-scale improvements began in the mid-1990s, it remains a low-key area with great intermediate cruising runs on the north slopes and some challenging, old-fashioned expert slopes on Castlerock. Sugarbush is a good choice if you find the sprawl of Killington overwhelming but don't want to sacrifice great skiing for a quieter and more intimate resort.

Sugarbush Access Rd., Warren, VT 05674. *©* **800/537-8427** or 802/583-6300. www.sugarbush.com. Day lift tickets $46–$70 adult, half-day tickets $38–$56 adult. Discounts for youths and seniors.

EXPLORING THE VALLEY

BIKING   A rewarding 14-mile **bike trip** 🎿🎿 along paved roads begins at the village of Waitsfield. Park near the covered bridge, then follow East Warren Road past the Inn at Round Barn Farm and up into the hilly, farm-filled countryside. (Don't be discouraged by the unrelenting hill at the outset.) Near the village of Warren, turn right at Brook Road to connect to Route 100. Return north on the bustling but often scenic Route 10 to Waitsfield, minding the traffic carefully.

   Clearwater Sports, at 4147 Main St. (Rte. 100) in Waitsfield north of the covered bridge (*©* **802/496-2708**; www.clearwatersports.com), offers mountain-bike rentals from a blue-and-white Victorian-era house (in addition to its main business of renting kayaks). The staff is helpful, offering suggestions for routes and tours.

HIKING   Hikers in search of good exercise and a spectacular view should strike out for **Mount Abraham** ✸✸, west of Warren. Drive west up Lincoln Gap Road (it leaves Rte. 100 just south of Warren Village) and continue to the crest, where you cross the intersection with the Long Trail. Park here and hike north on the trail; after about 2 miles, you reach the Battell Shelter. Push on another .8 mile up a steep ascent to reach panoramic views atop 4,006-foot Mount Abraham. Enjoy, and then retrace your steps. Allow 4 or 5 hours for this round-trip hike.

For a less demanding adventure that still yields great views, head *south* from Lincoln Gap Road on the Long Trail. In about .6 mile, look for a short spur trail to **Sunset Rock** ✸, with sweeping westward vistas of the farms of the Champlain Valley, along with Lake Champlain and the knobby Adirondacks beyond. A round-trip hike here requires a little more than an hour.

WHERE TO STAY

Inn at the Mad River Barn ✸ *Value*   This classic 1960s-style ski lodge attracts a clientele that's nearly fanatical in its devotion to the place. One reason might be charismatic (and opinionated) owner Betsy Pratt, who was formerly co-owner with her late husband of Mad River Glen before she sold it to the cooperative that runs the mountain today. Don't come expecting a fancy place—carpets and furniture tend toward the threadbare. Instead, come expecting to have fun. It's all knotty pine; spartan guest rooms and rustic common rooms help visitors feel at home putting their feet up. Accommodations are in the two-story barn behind the white clapboard main house and in an annex building, which is a bit fancier but with less character. In winter, dinners are served in boisterous family style. In summer, the mood is slightly more sedate but enhanced by a beautiful pool a short walk away in a grove of birches.

2849 Mill Brook Rd. (Rte. 17), Waitsfield, VT 05673. (℡) **800/631-0466** or 802/496-3310. Fax 802/496-6696. www.madriverbarn.com. 15 units. $77–$115 double. Holiday and foliage-season rates higher. Mon–Fri discounts available. Rates include breakfast. 2-night minimum stay holiday and Sat–Sun in winter. AE, DISC, MC, V. **Amenities:** Restaurant (winter only); lounge; outdoor pool; fitness room; sauna; game room. *In room:* TV (most units), fridge (some units), no phone.

Inn at Round Barn Farm ✸✸   You pass through a covered bridge just off Route 100 to arrive at one of the most romantic B&Bs in northern New England, a regal barn and farmhouse on 235 sloping acres with views of fields all around. The centerpiece of the inn is the Round Barn, a beautiful 1910 structure that's used for weddings, art exhibits, and even Sunday church services. Each guest room is furnished in understated country elegance. The less expensive rooms, in the older part of the house, are comfortable if small; larger luxury units in the attached barn sport soaring ceilings beneath old log beams, and include such extras as steam showers, gas fireplaces, Jacuzzis, and in-room phones.

1661 E. Warren Rd., Waitsfield, VT 05673. (℡) **802/496-2276.** Fax 802/496-8832. www.innattheroundbarn.com. 12 units. $165–$315 double. Rates include breakfast. 3-night minimum stay during holidays and foliage season. AE, DISC, MC, V. Closed Apr 15–30. Children 15 and older welcome. **Amenities:** Indoor pool; game room; cross-country ski center. *In room:* A/C, hair dryer, Jacuzzi (some units), no phone (most rooms).

The Pitcher Inn ✸✸✸   This Relais & Châteaux property is one of Vermont's finest. Set in the timeless village of Warren, the inn was built in the 1990s from the ground up following a fire that leveled a previous home; only the barn is original. Architect David Sellars created an inn that seamlessly blends modern conveniences, whimsy, and classic New England styling. The common areas fuse several styles: Colonial

Revival, mission, and (if this can be called a style) Adirondack-sporting-camp. There isn't a bad room in the house; all are designed with such wit that they're more like elegant puzzles. (One great feature: The carved "in-flight" goose on the ceiling of the Mallard Room is attached to a weathervane on the roof, and it rotates to indicate wind direction.) Most units have wood-burning or gas fireplaces, and some have steam showers. Rates here are pricey, but include not only breakfast but also afternoon tea service and—from Sunday through Thursday—a full three-course dinner.

275 Main St. (P.O. Box 347), Warren, VT 05674. © 802/496-6350. Fax 802/496-6354. www.pitcherinn.com. 11 units. $350–$600 double; $700 suite. Rates include breakfast and afternoon tea (also dinner Sun–Thurs). Golf and ski packages available. 2-night minimum stay Sat–Sun; 3-night minimum on holiday weekends; 5-night minimum Christmas. AE, MC, V. Children under 16 accepted in suites only. **Amenities:** Restaurant; spa; Jacuzzi; game room; limited room service; in-room massage; babysitting. *In room:* A/C, TV/VCR, dataport, hair dryer, Jacuzzi (some).

West Hill House 🐝🐝 Under the ownership of the MacLarens since 2006, this is among the more casual and relaxed inns in the valley, in part because of its quiet hillside location, and in part because of the easy camaraderie among guests. Set on a lightly traveled country road, the inn offers the quintessential New England experience, just a few minutes from the slopes at Sugarbush. Built in the 1850s, the farmhouse boasts three common rooms, including a bright, modern addition with a handsome fireplace for warmth in winter, an outdoor patio for summer lounging, and a game room with a pool table. Guest rooms are each decorated in an updated country style, and all of them now sport air-conditioning; gas fireplaces or woodstoves; and either a steam shower or a Jacuzzi. The owners will provide you snowshoes (a nice touch), and they maintain lovely perennial gardens and ponds.

1496 W. Hill Rd., Warren, VT 05674. © 800/898-1427 or 802/496-7162. www.westhillbb.com. 8 units. $140–$225 double. Rates include breakfast. Packages available. 3-night minimum stay preferred for foliage and holiday weekends; 2-night minimum stay other weekends. AE, DISC MC, V. Children 12 and older welcome. **Amenities:** Honor-system bar; in-room massage; snowshoes. *In room:* A/C, TV/VCR, dataport, hair dryer, iron, Jacuzzi (some units).

WHERE TO DINE

On Friday and Saturday nights in Waitsfield, the **American Flatbread** 🐝🐝 bakery (© 802/496-8856), on Route 100 in Waitsfield, serves terrific-tasting, organic-flour pizzas to the public from 5:30 to 9pm. Come up to an hour early and place your name on the waiting list, since no reservations are taken; if you get in, you'll experience founder George Schenk's vision of whole foods.

The Common Man 🐝🐝 EUROPEAN It sounds like a pedestrian pub, but the Common Man is anything but. Housed in a century-old barn, the interior is soaring and dramatic. Chandeliers, floral carpeting on the walls (weird, but it works), and candles on the tables meld successfully and coax all but the most coldhearted of guests into a relaxed frame of mind. You'll be halfway through the meal before you notice there are no windows. The menu strives to be as ambitious and appealing as the decor, and sometimes succeeds. Starters such as sautéed rabbit livers in mustard sauce, beet goat-cheese salad, and handmade tagliatelle are followed by entrees that might range from grilled duck with molasses-mashed sweet potatoes and cherry glaze to lamb tenderloin, pan-seared scallops, or panko-crusted soft shell crabs.

3209 German Flats Rd., Warren. © 802/583-2800. www.commonmanrestaurant.com. Reservations recommended in peak season. Main courses $25–$30. AE, DISC, MC, V. Daily 6–9pm in ski season; closed Sun–Mon rest of the year.

The Den 🐝 AMERICAN This place offers good food, decent service, and no frills. A local favorite since 1970 for its well-worn, neighborly feel, this is the kind of spot

where you can plop down in a pine booth, help yourself to the salad bar while awaiting your main course, and cheer on the Red Sox on the tube over the bar. The menu
offers usual pub fare, such as burgers, fries, Reubens, roast-beef sandwiches, meal-size
salads, and pork chops with applesauce.

Junction of routes 100 and 17, Waitsfield. (𝖈 **802/496-8880.** Main courses $5–$7 at lunch; $9–$14 at dinner. AE,
MC, V. Sun–Thurs 11:30am–10pm; Fri–Sat 11:30am–11pm.

John Egan's Big World Pub & Grill 𝖋 GRILL   Gonzo skier John Egan starred in
ten Warren Miller skiing films, but he *really* took a risk when he opened this restaurant on Route 100. In a 1970s-style motel dining room decorated with skiing memorabilia (including a bar made of ski sections signed by skiing luminaries), the
restaurant serves a small but above-average pub menu that the chef often pulls off with
unexpected flair: Menu options could include rack of lamb, goulash, paella, or steaks
in a garlicky wine sauce. Wood-grilled pizzas are popular, too.

Rte. 100, Warren. (𝖈 **802/496-3033.** Main courses $9–$18. AE, MC, V. Daily 5–9:30pm; Sun also 10am–2pm.

The Spotted Cow 𝖋𝖋 NEW AMERICAN/FRENCH   Set on the ground floor of
a small, rustic retail complex in Waitsfield, the Cow is a low-ceilinged, modern, nat-
ural-wood spot with cherry banquettes and windows facing out onto a walkway. The
place has the cozy feel of a bistro that only locals know about, with a more cultivated
than funky air. The kitchen succeeds with creative approaches to old favorites; venison is almost always on the menu, as is fresh fish. The duck and lamb cassoulet, if it's
on the menu, is a good choice, as is fish chowder made with a splash of rum. A vegetarian special is usually available, too.

Bridgestreet Marketplace (at corner of Rte. 100 and E. Warren Rd.), Waitsfield. (𝖈 **802/496-5151.** Reservations recommended. Main courses $18–$24. MC, V. Wed–Thurs 7:30am–2:30pm; Fri–Sat 7:30am–2pm and 5:30–8pm.

The Warren House Restaurant 𝖋 NEW AMERICAN/FRENCH   With a cozy
location in a 1958 sugarhouse, this is a popular spot not far from the slopes. The
menu is creative and increasingly cooked with a French accent—it's getting to be less
and less "eclectic comfort food" and more in the fine-dining vein. Starters could
include steamed mussels, a simple salad of tomato and Vermont goat cheese, or escargots baked with roasted garlic. For main courses, look for such items as a roasted rack
of lamb, crispy duck confit leg, grilled filet mignon with cabernet sauce, diver scallops
in a lemon-caper sauce, and grilled swordfish.

2585 Sugarbush Access Rd., Warren. (𝖈 **800/817-2055** or 802/583-2421. Reservations recommended. Main courses
$14–$20. AE, MC, V. Wed–Sun 5:30–9:30pm (until 10pm Fri–Sat). Call first in summer and fall. Closed 1st 2 weeks of
May and Nov.

7 Montpelier, Barre & Waterbury

Montpelier: 13 miles SE of Waterbury; 9 miles NW of Barre; 178 miles NW of Boston; and 39 miles SE of Burlington

Montpelier 𝖋𝖋 may very be the most down-home, low-key state capital in the U.S.
(and it's certainly the one with the smallest population); the glistening, iconic gold
dome of the capitol building is about the only showy or pretentious thing in the entire
city. Rising up behind it isn't a bank of mirror-sided skyscrapers but a thickly forested
hill. Montpelier, it turns out, isn't a self-important center of politics, just a small town
that happened to become home to state government. Restaurants, coffee shops, and
diverse cultures flowed in as a result, and today it's quite an agreeable place to pass an
afternoon or stay a night if you yearn to know how small-town Vermont really ticks.

Yes, the capitol is worth a quick visit, as is the local historical society; more than that, though, Montpelier is worth visiting to experience a small, clean New England town that's more than a little friendly and cultured.

Montpelier is centered on two main boulevards: State Street, lined with government buildings, and Main Street, where many of the town's stores and restaurants are found. It's all quite compact and cordial—and walkable. The downtown sports a pair of hardware stores next door to each another, good shops, and the **Savoy Theater** (© **802/229-0509** or 802/229-0598), one of the best art movie houses in northern New England. A large cup of cider and popcorn slathered with real, unclarified butter here costs less than a small popcorn at a mega-mall cinema anywhere else.

Nearby **Barre** (pronounced "Barry") is more commercial and less charming, with more of a blue-collar, red-state ethos than Montpelier, and it shares an equally important past: This was once the hub of Vermont's huge granite quarrying industry.

About 10 miles west of Montpelier, **Waterbury** ✪ is at the juncture of Route 100 and I-89, making it a commercial center by default if not by design. Set along the Winooski River, it tends to sprawl more than other Vermont towns, perhaps in part because of the flood of 1927, which came close to leveling the town. It's also because the town has attracted an inexplicable number of food companies (including Ben & Jerry's Ice Cream Store and Green Mountain Coffee) that have built factories and outlets in what were once pastures. With its location between Montpelier and Burlington, and its easy access to Stowe and Sugarbush, Waterbury has begun to attract those looking for the good life.

Downtown, with its brick commercial architecture and sampling of handsome early homes, is worth a brief tour, but most travelers are either passing through or looking for "that ice-cream place." Despite its drive-through quality, Waterbury makes a decent home base for further explorations in the Green Mountains; in Burlington, 25 miles to the west; and in Montpelier just to the east.

ESSENTIALS

GETTING THERE   Montpelier is accessible by car via exit 7 off I-89. For Barre, take exit 8; Waterbury is at exit 10. For bus service to Montpelier or Waterbury, contact **Vermont Transit** (© **800/451-3292** or 802/229-9220; www.vermonttransit. com). For train service to Waterbury, contact **Amtrak** (© **800/872-7245;** www. amtrak.com), whose *Vermonter* makes daily departures from New York City. The trip time one-way is about 9 hours.

VISITOR INFORMATION   The **Central Vermont Chamber of Commerce** (© **802/229-4619;** www.central-vt.com) is on Stewart Road off exit 7 of I-89. Turn left at the first light; it's a half-mile farther on the left. The chamber is open Monday through Friday from 9am to 5pm.

EXPLORING MONTPELIER & BARRE

Start your exploration of Montpelier with a visit to the gold-domed **State House** ✪ at 115 State St. (© **802/828-2228**), guarded out front by a statue of Ethan Allen. Three capitol buildings have risen on this site since 1809; the present building retained the portico designed during the height of Greek Revival–style in 1836. Modeled after the temple of Theseus in Athens, it's made of Vermont granite. Self-guided tours are offered whenever the capitol is open, Monday through Friday (except holidays) from 8am to 4pm. Free guided tours are offered every half-hour between July and mid-October, Monday through Friday from 10am to 3:30pm and Saturday from

Fun Fact The Story of Ben & Jerry

Doleful cows standing amid a bright green meadow on Ben & Jerry's ice cream pints have almost become a symbol for Vermont, but Ben & Jerry's cows—actually, they're Vermont artist Woody Jackson's cows—also symbolize friendly capitalism ("hippie capitalism," as some prefer).

The founding of the company is a legend in business circles. Two friends from Long Island, New York, Ben Cohen and Jerry Greenfield, started the company in Burlington in 1978 with $12,000 and a few mail-order lessons in ice-cream making. The pair experimented with flavor samples obtained free from salesmen, and sold their product out of an old downtown gas station. Embracing the outlook that work should be fun, they gave away free ice cream at community events, staged outdoor films in summer, and plowed profits back into the local community. Their free-spirited approach, along with the exceptional quality of their product, built a hugely successful corporation.

While competition from other gourmet ice-cream makers, and a widespread desire to cut back on fat consumption, have both made it tougher to have fun and turn a profit, Ben and Jerry are still at it, expanding their manufacturing plants outside New England and concocting new products. Though Ben and Jerry sold their interest to a huge multinational food concern—a move that raised not a few eyebrows among its grass-roots investors—the company's heart and soul (and manufacturing) remain squarely in Vermont.

The main factory in Waterbury may be one of Vermont's most popular tourist attractions. The plant is located about a mile north of I-89 on Route 100, and the grounds have a festival marketplace feel to them, despite the fact that there's no festival and no marketplace. During summer season, crowds mill about waiting for the 30-minute factory tours. Tours are first-come, first-served, and run at least every 30 minutes from 9am to 9pm in July and August (shorter hours in the off-season, but always open at least 9am–5pm); afternoon tours fill up quickly, so get there early to avoid a long wait.

Once you've got your ticket, browse the small ice-cream museum (learn the long, strange history of Cherry Garcia), buy a cone of your favorite flavor at the scoop shop, or lounge along the promenade, which is scattered with Adirondack chairs and picnic tables. Tours are $3 for adults, $2 for seniors, and free for children under 12. There's also a package deal where you get a tour, a T-shirt, and a pint of the good stuff for $20.

Kids can enjoy the "Stairway to Heaven," which leads to a playground, and a "Cow-Viewing Area," which is self-explanatory. The tours are informative and fun, and conclude with a sample of the day's featured product. For more information, call © **866/BJTOURS** or 802/882-1240.

11am to 2:30pm. The informative and fun tour is worthwhile if you're in the area, but not worth a major detour.

A short stroll from the State House is the **Vermont Historical Society Museum** Ⱃ, 109 State St. (⒞ **802/828-2291;** www.vermonthistory.org). The museum is housed in a replica of the elegant old Pavilion Building, a prominent Victorian hotel, and contains a number of artifacts, including a gun once owned by Ethan Allen. It's normally open Tuesday to Saturday from 10am to 4pm (also May–Oct Sun noon–4pm). Admission is $5 for adults, $3 for students or seniors, and $12 for families. There's also a store on the premises.

Rock of Ages Quarry ⰓⰓ   When in or around Barre, listen for the deep, throaty hum of industry. That's the Rock of Ages Quarry, set on a hillside high above town near the aptly named hamlet of Graniteville. A visitor center presents informative exhibits, a video about quarrying, a glimpse of an old granite quarry (no longer active), and a selection of granite gifts. Self-guided tours of the old quarry are free. For a look at the active quarry (the world's largest), sign up for a guided half-hour tour on a shuttle for a small charge; an old bus groans up to a viewer's platform high above the 500-foot, man-made canyon, where workers cleave huge slabs of fine-grained granite and hoist them out using 150-foot derricks anchored with a spider's web of 15 miles of steel cable. It's an operation to behold. There's also a new exhibit, which lets you try your hand at blasting and cutting stone by hand. Let me just quote from the NASCAR-like public relations material: "Grab the gun, squeeze the trigger, and feel the pulsating throb of up to 110 PSI of abrasive and air leap from the nozzle as you learn to cut in stone . . ." What red-blooded guy could resist an offer like that?

773 Graniteville Rd. (P.O. Box 482, Barre, VT 05641), Graniteville. ⒞ **802/476-3119.** www.rockofages.com. Visitor center open May–Oct Mon–Sat 8:30am–5pm, Sun 10am–5pm (in foliage season daily 8:30am–5:30pm); self-guided tours free, small charge for narrated tours. From Barre, drive south on Rte. 14, turn left at lights by McDonald's; watch for signs to quarry.

WHERE TO STAY
IN MONTPELIER

Capitol Plaza Hotel Ⱃ   The favored hotel of folks on business with the state government, it's also well located (across from the capitol) to serve visitors exploring the town. The small lobby has a Colonial cast to it; guest rooms on the three upper floors adopt a light, faux-Colonial tone, and have more amenities than you might expect. Still, it has the feel of a place best suited for conventions—it's nothing immaculate, but it does offer clean, comfortable, and convenient digs. Some rooms add wingback chairs and Ralph Lauren bedding, and three still-fancier suites add Jacuzzis, fridges, sofas, and bigger televisions.

100 State St., Montpelier, VT 05602. ⒞ **800/274-5252** or 802/223-5252. Fax 802/229-5427. www.capitolplaza.com. 56 units. $98 double; foliage season from $119 double; $118–$168 suite. AE, DISC, MC, V. **Amenities:** Restaurant; conference center. *In room:* A/C, TV, dataport, fridge (suites only), hair dryer, iron, Jacuzzi (suites only).

Inn at Montpelier ⰓⰓ *(Finds)*   Two historic in-town homes make up the Inn at Montpelier, and both are welcoming accommodations appealing to those who enjoy historic architecture and eye-catching interior design. The main cream-colored Federal-style building was built in 1827 (though this only became an inn in 1988), and has a mix of historical and up-to-date furnishings, a sunny sitting room, and a deck off the rear of the second floor. Room no. 27 is especially pleasant, with a huge cherry-wood

---

Finds **Hope Cemetery: Written in Stone**

For a poignant display of a nearly lost art, head to Barre's **Hope Cemetery**, located on a hillside in a wooded valley north of Barre on Route 14 (from the middle of town, follow Maple Avenue north). The cemetery, established in 1895, is filled with columns, urns, and human figures carved from the fine-grained local granite; more than just a memorial park, it's also a kind of outdoor museum celebrating the remarkable talent of local stonecutters.

---

king bed, Martha Washington chair, Chippendale desk—and a big private outdoor deck with lounge chairs. But there are plenty of other nice choices, too, including several rooms with wood-burning fireplaces. The property is decorated somewhat sparely rather than in the overly florid manner of many New England inns, and this is actually quite appealing. (Head to Waitsfield or Warren if you're in search of the quintessential Vermont inn). This inn is also an easy stroll from downtown, and the included continental breakfast features lemon curd, healthy cereals, and pastries from La Brioche Bakery & Cafe (see "Where to Dine," below.)

147 Main St., Montpelier, VT 05602. (C) 802/223-2727. Fax 802/223-0722. www.innatmontpelier.com. 19 units. $120–$202 double. Rates include continental breakfast. AE, DC, DISC, MC, V. **Amenities:** Bike rental; in-room massage; dry cleaning. *In room:* A/C, TV, dataport.

IN WATERBURY

The Old Stagecoach Inn *𝒜* This handsome, gabled home, within walking distance of downtown, is full of wonderful details such as painted wood floors, a pair of upstairs porches, an old library with a stamped tin ceiling, and a chessboard. Originally built in 1826, the house was gutted and revamped in 1890 in ostentatious period style by an Ohio millionaire. After some years of quiet disuse, it was converted to an inn in the late 1980s by owners who preserved the historical detailing. Guest rooms are furnished in an understated Victorian style, mostly with oak and pine furniture and antiques. It's not a polished inn, but it's quite comfortable. The two third-floor rooms have retained the original exposed beams and skylights, and feel pleasant and open because of this. The three back rooms share a bathroom and offer guests more the feel of a friendly (and shared) farmhouse.

18 N. Main St., Waterbury, VT 05676. (C) 800/262-2206 or 802/244-5056. Fax 802/244-6956. www.oldstage coach.com. 11 units, 3 with shared bathroom. $70–$130 double; foliage season, Christmas week, and Presidents' Day weekend $80–$180 double. Rates include breakfast. 2-night minimum stay during peak periods. AE, DISC, MC, V. **Amenities:** Restaurant. *In room:* TV (some units).

Thatcher Brook Inn *𝒜* On busy Route 100 not far from the Ben & Jerry's factory (see above), guests here have the illusion they are considerably farther away from this major artery than they actually are. The late-19th-century white-clapboard building has a pleasing historical character, and though it has undergone significant renovations and expansions during the intervening years, these additions have somehow kept the inn's Queen Anne-style intact. The common areas downstairs are worn to a nice patina. Guest rooms are carpeted and decorated with furniture varying from Ethan Allen new to flea-market oak, though the overall character takes its cue from a somewhat fussy country look. Room nos. 14 through 17 are larger and more spacious than most here; nos. 8 through 11 have back balconies that face a wooded hillside. Some rooms have air-conditioning.

1017 Waterbury Stowe Rd. (Rte. 100), Waterbury, VT 05676. © 800/292-5911 or 802/244-5911. www.thatcher brook.com. 16 units. $89–$175 double; foliage season, holidays, Christmas week, and Presidents' Day weekend $135–$225 double; $325–$399 suite. Rates include breakfast. 2-night minimum stay during foliage season; 3-night minimum stay during Christmas. Packages available. AE, DC, DISC, MC, V. **Amenities:** Restaurant; access to nearby fitness center. *In room:* Fireplace (some units), Jacuzzi (some units).

WHERE TO DINE

A creation of the New England Culinary Institute, **La Brioche Bakery & Cafe** (© 802/229-0443) occupies the corner of Montpelier's State and Main streets. It's a little bit of Europe in one of New England's more Continental cities. A deli counter offers baked goods such as croissants and baguettes. Get them to go, or settle into a table in the afternoon sun outdoors. It's open daily from as early as 6:30am until late afternoon.

I've spent many a wintry (or fall, or summery) afternoon inside the cleverly named **Capitol Grounds** , at 27 State St. (© 802/223-7800), a stone's throw from the gold dome of the state capitol building. One of my favorite coffeehouses in New England, it's a great, youthful spot to order an espresso, hot chocolate, soup, delicious sandwich, or baked goods while you peer out at the goings-on of town, watch the snow fall, or leaf through the newspaper. You'll find everyone from mothers and their kids to State House interns to Greenpeace members hanging out here. There's now live folk music twice a week.

IN MONTPELIER
Main Street Grill & Bar AMERICAN/ECLECTIC   This modern, comfortable restaurant serves as classroom and ongoing exam for students of the New England Culinary Institute, just down the block. It's not unusual to see knots of students, toques at a rakish angle, walking between the restaurant and class. You can eat in the first-level dining room, watching street life through the broad windows, or hang out in the homey bar downstairs. Dishes change every 3 months, but lunch may include a poached pear and Stilton salad to start, followed by a hanger steak salad, grilled salmon, crab cakes, pulled pork tacos, or fish and chips. Dinner may feature a grilled leg of lamb, steaks, pasta with mussels, a tofu stir fry (vegetarian dishes are always on the menu), or a fancy version of meat loaf.

118 Main St., Montpelier. © 802/223-3188 (Grill & Bar) or 802/229-9202 (Chef's Table). Limited reservations accepted. Main courses $4–$12 lunch; $12–$19 dinner. AE, DISC, MC, V. Tues–Sat 11:30am–2pm and 5:30–9pm; Sun 10am–2pm and 5:30–9pm.

IN WATERBURY
Marsala Salsa *Finds* INDIAN/MEXICAN   The owner of Marsala Salsa was born in Trinidad, raised on the cuisine of India, and worked at a Mexican restaurant in Nevada. The result? Marsala Salsa, a hybrid of two international cuisines, both well-prepared at reasonable prices. The restaurant, in a funky storefront in Waterbury's historic downtown, is decorated with a light and culturally ambiguous touch. Mexican entrees include carne asada and *bistec picado,* strips of sirloin charbroiled with homemade avocado-lime butter. If you're more tempted by the Asian subcontinent, try the curries or tandoori chicken, or wonderful shrimp *shaag*—a light curry with sautéed shrimp, spinach, and carrots. It's an unexpected oasis deep behind local culinary battle lines manned primarily by cheddar cheeses and maple syrups.

13-15 Stowe St. © 802/244-1150. Reservations recommended Sat–Sun. Main courses $7–$13. MC, V. Mon–Sat 5–9pm.

8 Stowe

Stowe is 10 miles N of Waterbury, 35 miles E of Burlington, and 75 miles NE of White River Junction

Stowe is a wonderful destination in summer, fall, or winter. One of Vermont's first winter destination areas, it has managed the decades-long juggernaut of growth with patience. Condo developments and strip mall–style restaurants have arrived, to be sure, but the village has mostly preserved its essential character and balance—including an old-fashioned main street and great views of surrounding mountains and across the farmlands of the valley floor. Thanks to its history and charm, this area tends to attract a more affluent clientele than, say, Killington or Okemo.

Downtown Stowe is quaint and compact, home to what may be Vermont's most gracefully tapered church spire (atop the Stowe Community Church). Because the ski hill is a few miles away from the village, there's actual life here year-round (in other words, the town doesn't suffer that woebegone emptiness many ski villages do in summer). You can actually explore it on foot or by bike, which isn't the case at places that have developed around large parking lots and condo clusters.

Tucked into the roads leading to the mountain are an amazing variety of lodging and restaurants. Stowe offers more choice than you'd expect. Most of this growth has taken place along Mountain Road (Rte. 108), which runs northwest from the village to the base of Mount Mansfield and the Stowe ski resort. Here you'll find an array of motels, restaurants, shops, bars, and even a three-screen cinema, many of which are carefully designed or at least tastefully tucked out of view of the main road; this road has all the convenience of a strip mall, but little of the scenic blight.

ESSENTIALS

GETTING THERE   Stowe is on Route 100, about 10 miles north of Waterbury. In summer, Stowe can also be reached from Burlington or Montpelier (after some back-roading) via Smugglers' Notch on Route 108. This scenic pass, which squeezes narrowly between rocks and is not recommended for RVs or trailers, is one of the state's most scenic drives—but is closed in winter (and absolutely packed in Oct).

Stowe has no direct train or bus service, but **Amtrak's** (© **800/USA-RAIL;** www.amtrak.com) *Vermonter* service from New York City stops in Waterbury, 10 miles south, after a 9-hour ride. You can rent a car there from **Thrifty** (© **802/244-8800;** www.thrifty.com) or call a local taxi or car service.

VISITOR INFORMATION   The **Stowe Area Association** (© 877/467-8693 or 802/253-7321; www.gostowe.com) maintains a handy office at 51 Main St. in the village center. It's open Monday through Friday from 9am to 8pm, Saturday and Sunday from 10am to 5pm in summer, fall-foliage season, and winter (more limited hours during slower seasons).

The **Green Mountain Club** (© 802/244-7037), a statewide association devoted to building and maintaining backcountry trails in the mountains, also has a visitor center on Route 100 between Waterbury and Stowe.

SPECIAL EVENTS   The weeklong **Stowe Winter Carnival** (© 802/253-7321) has taken place annually, from the middle to the end of January, since 1921. The fest features a number of wacky events involving skis, snowshoes, and skates, as well as nighttime entertainment. Don't miss the snow-sculpture contest or snow golf, played on the (snow-covered) Snow Country Club.

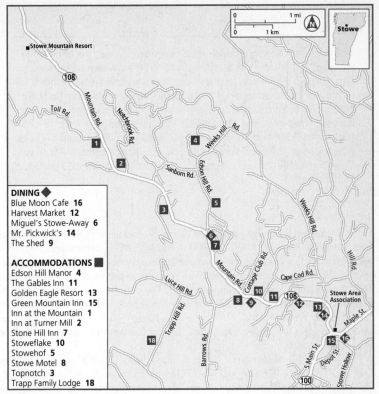

DINING ◆
Blue Moon Cafe **16**
Harvest Market **12**
Miguel's Stowe-Away **6**
Mr. Pickwick's **14**
The Shed **9**

ACCOMMODATIONS ■
Edson Hill Manor **4**
The Gables Inn **11**
Golden Eagle Resort **13**
Green Mountain Inn **15**
Inn at the Mountain **1**
Inn at Turner Mill **2**
Stone Hill Inn **7**
Stoweflake **10**
Stowehof **5**
Stowe Motel **8**
Topnotch **3**
Trapp Family Lodge **18**

DOWNHILL SKIING

Stowe Mountain Resort 🎿🎿🎿   Stowe was one of the first, and one of the classiest, ski resorts in the world when it opened in the 1930s. Its regional dominance has eroded somewhat in the years since—Killington, Sunday River, and Sugarloaf, among others, have snagged big shares of the New England ski market. But the historic resort still has loads of charm and plenty of excellent runs. It's one of the best places to get the full New England ski experience: a combination of beautiful ski trails and views. This is a tremendous challenge for advanced skiers, with winding, old-style trails—especially notable are the legendary "Front Four" trails (National, Starr, Lift Line, and Goat), which have humbled more than a handful of folks. The mountain also has four good, long lifts that go all the way from bottom to top—not the usual patchwork of shorter lifts you find at many other ski areas.

5781 Mountain Rd., Stowe, VT 05672. ✆ **800/253-4754** or 802/253-3000. www.stowe.com. Adult day lift tickets $54–$79; half-day adult tickets $61–$64. Discounts for youths and seniors.

CROSS-COUNTRY SKIING

Stowe is an outstanding destination for cross-country skiers, offering several groomed ski areas with a combined total of more than 100 miles of trails traversing everything from gentle valley floors to challenging mountain peaks.

> ### Tips   The Vermont Ski Museum
>
> When you're schussing through little downtown Stowe, the **Vermont Ski Museum**, at 1 South Main St. (© 802/253-9911; www.vermontskimuseum.org), makes a serviceable stop; it's filled with memorabilia and exhibits on such topics as the history of ski lifts, and the interesting Vermont Ski Hall of Fame is on the mezzanine level. Inductees include Mead Lawrence (who won two medals in the 1950 Winter Olympics) and Billy Koch (a silver medalist in 1976), both of whom trained in Vermont. The museum is open Wednesday to Monday from noon to 5pm (closed Nov and mid-Apr to late May). Technically it's free to enter; the suggested donation is $3 per adult or $5 per family.

The **Trapp Family Lodge Nordic Ski Center** ⚄, on Luce Hill Road about 2 miles from Mountain Road (© 800/826-7000 or 802/253-8511; www.trappfamily.com), was the nation's first cross-country ski center. It remains one of the most gloriously situated in the Northeast, set atop a ridge with views across the broad valley and into the folds of mountains flanking Mount Mansfield. The center maintains about 30 miles of groomed trails (plus some 60 miles of ungroomed backcountry trails) on its 2,700 acres of rolling forestland; basically, for the cross-country ski nut, this is heaven. Rates are $20 per adult for a full-day trail pass (less for kids and half-days), and $20 for equipment rental.

The **Edson Hill Manor** (see "Where to Stay," below) maintains a **Ski Touring Center** (© 800/621-0284 or 802/253-7371) with 15 miles of wooded trails just off Mountain Road; it cost about $10 for a day pass in past years. Good ski touring is also enjoyed at the **Stowe Mountain Resort Cross-Country Touring Center** (© 800/253-4754 or 802/253-3000), with 20 miles of groomed trails and 25 miles of backcountry trails at the base of Mount Mansfield; full-day passes cost $17 to $19 for adults, about half that much for ages 6 to 12. Private and group lessons are also available here.

SUMMER OUTDOOR PURSUITS

Stowe's history is linked to winter recreation, but it's also a great fair-weather destination, surrounded by lush, rolling green hills and open farmlands and towered over by craggy **Mount Mansfield,** Vermont's top peak at 4,393 feet.

There are several ways to get to the top of Mansfield. Part of Stowe Mountain Resort, the **auto toll road** ⚄ (© 802/253-3500) traces its lineage back to the 19th century, when it served horse-drawn vehicles bringing passengers to a former hotel near the mountain's crown. (That hotel was demolished in the 1960s.) Drivers now twist their way up the road and park, still below the summit; a 2-hour hike along well-marked trails is required to get to the very top, which offers unforgettable views. The toll road is open 9am to 4pm from late May to mid-October. The fare is $21 per car with up to six passengers, $6 per additional person. Ascending on foot is free, but bicycles and motorcycles are prohibited for some reason.

Another option is the **Stowe gondola** ⚄ (© 802/253-3500), which whisks visitors to the summit at the Cliff House Restaurant. Hikers can explore the rugged, open ridgeline, and then descend on the gondola before twilight. The gondola runs from mid-June to mid-October. The full round-trip costs $20 for adults, $16 for seniors, and $12 for children ages 6 to 12. There are family discounts. The lift is open for summer sightseeing 10am to 5pm daily from late June through mid-October. The **restaurant** 𝔊, by the way, is no snack bar—this is a fine-dining experience, with lunches daily from summer to early fall, plus Saturday-night candlelit five-course dinners (at the top of the state) featuring wine and cheese, Vermont meats, and the like.

The budget route up Mount Mansfield—the most rewarding, but of course the most physically demanding—is entirely **on foot** 𝔊, with at least nine options for an ascent. This requires a good map. Ask for information from the tourism office or knowledgeable locals (your inn may be able to help), or stop by Green Mountain Club headquarters, on Route 100, 4 miles south of Stowe; it's open Monday through Friday. GMC also offers advice on other area trails.

One of the most understated local attractions is the **Stowe Recreation Path** 𝔊𝔊, winding 5.3 miles from behind Stowe Community Church up the valley toward the mountain, ending behind the Topnotch Tennis Center. This exceptionally appealing pathway, completed in 1989, is heavily used by locals in summer; in winter it serves as a cross-country ski trail. Connect to the pathway at either end, or at points where it crosses side roads leading to Mountain Road. No motorized vehicles or skateboards are allowed.

All manner of recreational paraphernalia is available for rent at the **bike & ski shop** (© **802/253-7919**) on the Rec Path, including full-suspension demo bikes, baby joggers, and bike trailers. The shop is on Mountain Road (across from the Golden Eagle Resort), open from 9am to 6pm daily in summer.

AJ's Ski & Sports, at 350 Mountain Rd. (© **800/226-6257**; www.ajssports.com), rents bikes for $8 per hour or $27 per day, less for kids.

Fans of paddle sports should seek out **Umiak Outdoor Outfitters**, at 849 S. Main St. in downtown Stowe (© **802/253-2317**; www.umiak.com). The folks here provide a slew of guided river trips (flat water or light rapids) and instruction (learn how to roll that kayak). Also available are canoe, kayak, and raft rentals. The same outfit runs outstanding snowshoeing tours by moonlight in winter, some culminating in gourmet dinners.

Finally, anglers should allow ample time to peruse **The Fly Rod Shop** (© **802/253-7346**), located on Route 100 about 2 miles south of the village. This well-stocked shop has fly and spin tackle, along with camping gear, antique fly rods, and rentals of canoes and fishing videos.

WHERE TO STAY
EXPENSIVE
Stone Hill Inn 𝔊𝔊   With just nine rooms, the contemporary yet romantic Stone Hill Inn (built in 1998) offers personal service and a handy location, along with fancy amenities in all rooms such as four-poster king-size beds, Egyptian cotton towels, double-sided gas fireplaces that front double Jacuzzis in sizable bathrooms, and flatscreen televisions with DVD players and VCRs. Rooms don't have phones, but there's a private phone booth off the lobby. Room layouts are roughly the same, each coming with a small sitting area. High-ceilinged common rooms sport fireplaces and billiard tables, and a well-stocked guest pantry offers complimentary beverages around the clock. An outdoor hot tub provides a relaxing soak. Breakfast is served in a bright morning

room, and free hors d'oeuvres are set out each evening. Stone Hill lacks history, but you'll happily forego timeworn character in exchange for the quiet, luxury, and romance.

89 Houston Farm Rd. (off Mountain Rd. midway btw. village and ski resort), Stowe, VT 05672. (C) **802/253-6282.** www.stonehillinn.com. 9 units. $295–$395 double. Rates include breakfast. 2-night minimum stay Sat–Sun and foliage season; 3-night minimum stay holiday weekends; 4-night minimum stay Christmas week. Closed mid-Apr to early May and mid-Nov to early Dec. AE, DC, DISC, MC, V. Not suitable for children. **Amenities:** Jacuzzi; game room; self-service laundry; movie library; snowshoes and toboggan. *In room:* A/C, TV/VCR, hair dryer, safe, Jacuzzi.

Stoweflake 🏕🏕 This resort with the cutesy name is on Mountain Road en route to the mountain, less than 2 miles from the village; lately it has been playing catch-up with the more upscale Topnotch resort and spa (see below), adding better amenities to its most expensive rooms. As a result, the newest guest rooms are now nicer than those at Topnotch—they're regally decorated and have amenities such as two phones and wet bars. The resort has several categories of guest rooms in two wings; the "superior" rooms in the old wing are a bit cozy, okay for an overnight, but you're better off requesting "deluxe" level or better if you will be staying a few days. Many of these units have tubs with jets. The spa and fitness facilities are adequate, even if they lack the over-the-top elegance of Topnotch's (what, no waterfalls?); there's a decent-sized fitness room with Cybex equipment, a squash/racquetball court, co-ed Jacuzzi, and a small indoor pool. Stoweflake also manages a small collection of fine townhouses nearby.

1746 Mountain Rd. (P.O. Box 369), Stowe, VT 05672. (C) **800/253-2232** or 802/253-7355. Fax 802/253-6858. www.stoweflake.com. 95 units. Peak winter season $170–$270 double, $390 suite; holiday season $180–$290 double, $340 suite; off-season $150–$250 double, $360 suite. Packages available. 2-night minimum stay on most weekends; 4-night minimum stay during holidays. AE, DC, DISC, MC, V. **Amenities:** 2 restaurants; indoor pool; outdoor pool; 2 tennis courts; racquetball/squash court; health club; spa; bike rental; children's center; game room; business center; salon; limited room service; in-room massage; babysitting; laundry service; dry cleaning. *In room:* A/C, TV, dataport, fridge (some units), coffeemaker (some units), hair dryer, iron, Jacuzzi (some units).

Topnotch 🏕🏕🏕 The boxy, uninteresting exterior of Topnotch hides a surprisingly creative interior and upscale facility (voted 1 of the top resort spas in the U.S. by *Condé Nast Traveler* readers). The main lobby is in ski-lodge style, with lots of stone, wood, and a huge moose head on the wall; guest rooms are attractively appointed, mostly in country pine. Some units have wood-burning fireplaces; some have Jacuzzis; and third-floor rooms sport cathedral ceilings. The main attractions are the huge 35,000-square-foot **spa** 🏕, free for guests (nonguests pay a $50 fee). This spa has such nice touches as fireplaces in the locker rooms and a range of aerobics classes, weight training programs, and revitalizing treatments for face, skin, and body. Outdoors, you can ramble on 120 acres of grounds, doing anything from horseback riding to cross-country skiing to indoor tennis. There are three pools (2 outdoor, 1 indoor) and a Jacuzzi for loosening after-ski muscles.

4000 Mountain Rd., Stowe, VT 05672. (C) **800/451-8686** or 802/253-8585. Fax 802/253-9263. www.topnotch-resort.com. 92 units. $180–$320 double, $315–$755 suite; holidays $380–$495 double, $500–$860 suite. 6-night minimum stay Christmas week. AE, DC, DISC, MC, V. Pets allowed. **Amenities:** 2 restaurants; indoor pool; 2 outdoor pools; tennis courts (4 indoor, 10 outdoor); fitness room; spa; Jacuzzi; sauna; concierge; limited room service; horseback riding. *In room:* A/C, TV, dataport, fridge, coffeemaker, hair dryer, iron, safe, Jacuzzi (some units).

Trapp Family Lodge 🏕 The Trapp family of *Sound of Music* fame bought this sprawling farm high up in Stowe in 1942, just 4 years after fleeing the Nazi takeover of Austria. Descendants of Maria and Baron von Trapp continue to run this Tyrolean-flavored lodge today, on 2,700 mountainside acres. It's a comfortable resort hotel, if designed more for efficiency than for elegance. The wood-paneled guest rooms are a notch or two better than run-of-the-mill hotel rooms, and most come with fine valley views and private balconies. Though they are slowly being made more upscale with thick duvets, Jacuzzis and fridges in some suites, and so forth, rooms here are not cheap; they offer access to nice facilities, but better value can be found elsewhere in the valley. The lodge also has villas and house rentals, although again these are steeply priced. Sunday concerts are held in the meadow in summer, a nice touch.

700 Trapp Hill Rd. (P.O. Box 1428), Stowe, VT 05672. ℂ 800/826-7000 or 802/253-8511. Fax 802/253-5740. www. trappfamily.com. 120 units. $195–$585 double, $295–$880 suite. Rates include meals during holidays and foliage season. 3-night minimum stay Presidents' Day weekend and foliage season; 5-night minimum stay Christmas week. AE, DC, MC, V. Depart Stowe westward on Rte. 108; in 2 miles bear left at fork near white church; continue up hill following signs for lodge. **Amenities:** 2 restaurants; heated indoor pool; 2 outdoor pools (1 for adults only); 4 tennis courts; fitness center; sauna; children's programs; game room; limited room service; in-room massage; babysitting; coin-op washers/dryers; dry cleaning. *In room:* A/C, TV, fridge (a few units), Jacuzzi (a few units).

MODERATE

Edson Hill Manor 🏔️🏔️
The Edson Hill Manor sits atop a long, quiet drive 2 miles from Mountain Road and has an ineffably quirky charm. The main lodge dates to the 1940s; the four carriage houses just up the hill are of newer vintage. The compound is set amid a rolling landscape of lawns, hemlocks, and maples, with a comfortable common room in the main house like a movie set for a country retreat—tapestries, pastels, and oils adorn the walls. Most of the nine guest rooms in the main lodge have pine walls and floors, wood-burning fireplaces, Colonial maple furnishings, wingback chairs, and four-poster beds. The 16 carriage-house rooms, 4 to each house, are somewhat larger but lack the cozy charm of the main inn and feel a bit like motel units (really *nice* motel units).

1500 Edson Hill Rd., Stowe, VT 05672. ℂ 800/621-0284 or 802/253-7371. www.edsonhillmanor.com. 25 units. $159–$219 double; off-season rates lower, holiday rates higher. Rates include breakfast; MAP plans also available. Ask about packages. AE, DISC, MC, V. Pets and young children welcome in carriage-house units only. **Amenities:** Restaurant; access to nearby pool; riding stables (lessons available). *In room:* A/C (some units), TV (some units).

The Gables Inn 🏔️
This cozy and comfortable inn, housed in a gray farmhouse facing Mountain Road, is a relaxed place—the hot tub next to the front door makes that point clear. The main farmhouse has 12 rooms of varying size and shape, simply furnished with country antiques; the smaller rooms are quite small. A more contemporary "carriage house" in the back offers four nicely sized rooms, most with cathedral ceilings, canopy beds, fireplaces, Jacuzzis, and air-conditioning. Two "Riverview Suites" in another adjacent building are better appointed, with Jacuzzis, telephones, televisions with VCRS, small refrigerators, fireplaces, and the like.

1457 Mountain Rd., Stowe, VT 05672. ℂ 800/422-5371 or 802/253-7730. Fax 802/253-8989. www.gablesinn.com. 18 units. $78–$190 double; $150–$235 suite. Foliage-season and holiday rates higher. All rates include breakfast. 2-night minimum stay Sat–Sun, holidays, and foliage season. AE, DC, DISC, MC, V. **Amenities:** Restaurant; outdoor pool; Jacuzzi. *In room:* A/C, TV (some units), fridge (some units), Jacuzzi (some units), no phone (most units).

Golden Eagle Resort 🏔️ 🧒
Of the numerous lodgings lined up along Mountain Road, few are more family-friendly than this one. The Golden Eagle gets it right with a children's play area, three pools, two ponds for fishing, a regulation tennis court, 80 acres of private woods laced with hiking trails, and even a small spa offering kids' massages. Adults enjoy the place, too, particularly the romantic cottages and suites with fireplaces and whirlpools behind the main building. The spa also has a popular indoor Jacuzzi, and the mornings-only cafe serves breakfasts of local eggs, dairy, and bacon.

Don't come if you're expecting white-glove service, valet parking, and a fancy restaurant; the Golden Eagle is perfect for family rustication. There are also a few apartment units with full kitchens or kitchenettes, and even a house for rent.

511 Mountain Rd. (P.O. Box 1090), Stowe, VT 05672. ⓒ **800/626-1010** or 802-253-4811. Fax 802-253-2561. www.goldeneagleresort.com. 94 rooms. Spring, summer, and fall $99–$174 double, $144–$319 suite; winter, holidays, and foliage season $114–$304 double, $164–$514 suite. AE, DISC, MC, V. **Amenities:** Cafe; 2 outdoor pools; indoor pool; tennis court; spa; Jacuzzi. *In room:* Fridge, coffeemaker, fireplace (some units), Jacuzzi (some units).

Green Mountain Inn ✸✸✸

This handsome, historic structure sits right in the village, and it's probably the best choice in town for those seeking a sense of New England history along with a bit of pampering. A sprawling hostelry with about 100 guest rooms spread among several buildings old and new, it feels far more intimate, with accommodations tastefully decorated in an early-19th-century motif that befits the 1833 vintage of the main inn. More than a dozen units have Jacuzzis and/or gas fireplaces, and the Mill House has rooms with CD players, sofas, and Jacuzzis that open into the bedroom from behind folding wooden doors. The deluxe Mansfield House (which opened in 2000) adds double Jacuzzis, marble bathrooms, and 36-inch TVs with DVD players; all these expensive rooms are superb. Other rooms are smaller and simpler, but certainly offer a fine taste of Vermont.

Main St. (P.O. Box 60), Stowe, VT 05672. ⓒ **800/253-7302** or 802/253-7301. Fax 802/253-5096. www.greenmountain inn.com. 100 units. $129–$329 double, $229–$409 suite; foliage season $169–$269 double, $309–$439 suite; Christmas week $269–$399 double, $429–$829 suite. 2-night minimum stay summer and winter weekends and in foliage season. AE, DISC, MC, V. Pets allowed in some rooms (call ahead; $20 per night). **Amenities:** Restaurant; heated outdoor pool (year-round); fitness room; Jacuzzi; sauna; steam room; game room; limited room service; in-room massage; laundry service. *In room:* A/C, TV, hair dryer.

Inn at The Mountain ✸

Owned and operated by Stowe Mountain Resort, this is the resort's "official" hotel—though not nearly as fancy as one would imagine it to be. A low-key spot, it's more like an upscale motel than like a fancy lodge, with clean, attractive rooms that are more spacious than average motel rooms. Inside you'll find veneer furniture, small refrigerators, and tiny balconies facing the pool or the woods. It's located near the base of the mountain, although not close enough to ski-in and ski-out to your room. Also ask about the 40 or so condos nearby, suitable for families.

5781 Mountain Rd., Stowe, VT 05672. ⓒ **800/253-4754** or 802/253-3000. www.stowe.com. 33 units. $119–$359 double; apartments and town houses higher. Holiday season rates higher. 5-night minimum stay Christmas week. Packages available. AE, DC, DISC, MC, V. **Amenities:** Restaurant; outdoor pool; 9 tennis courts; fitness center; Jacuzzi; sauna; limited room service. *In room:* A/C, TV, fridge, fireplace (some units).

Stowehof ✸

High on a hillside, this inn feels far removed from the hubbub of the valley. The exterior architecture has an aggressive, neo-Tyrolean ski-chalet styling, but inside the place comes close to magical—it's pleasantly woodsy, folksy, and rustic, with heavy beams and pine floors, ticking clocks, and maple tree trunks carved into architectural elements. Common spaces feature nooks and fireplaces. Furnished without a lot of fanfare, guest rooms are decorated individually: Some are bold and festive with sunflower patterns, others more subdued and quiet. The smaller units are quite simple, like a country bed-and-breakfast, while fancier rooms have wood-burning fireplaces, wingback chairs, and air-conditioning. But one and all feature good views. The outdoor pool has a view of Mansfield, while the indoor pool building is simple and lovely, with a sauna and hot tub; the lodge is also next to Wiessner Woods, 80 acres laced with hiking and cross-country ski trails. Stowehof offers horseback riding and tennis lessons on the property for an additional charge.

434 Edson Hill Rd. (P.O. Box 1139), Stowe, VT 05672. © **800/932-7136.** www.stowehofinn.com. 46 units, 2 guest-houses. $99–$285 double; holidays and foliage season $210–$500 double. Off-season discounts available. Rates include full breakfast. Ask about packages. 2-night minimum stay on some weekends; 4-night minimum stay during holidays. AE, DC, MC, V. **Amenities:** Restaurant; pub; heated outdoor pool; indoor pool; 4 tennis courts; Jacuzzi; sauna; game room; business center; in-room massage; laundry service; dry cleaning. *In room:* A/C (some units), TV, fireplace (some units).

INEXPENSIVE

Inn at Turner Mill   Set in a narrow wooded valley along a tumbling stream, this homey 1936 building (barn-red, in the shape of a ski chalet) was built as a residence and inn. The inn is eclectic in style, with everything from orange wall-to-wall carpeting to attractively rustic log furniture. There's a memorable, monolithic stone walk-way outside and a steep staircase to the upper floors. The inn is a short trip from the mountain and across the road from the Rec Path, making it a good destination for bike-trippers; snowshoes can also be obtained upon request.

56 Turner Mill Lane, Stowe, VT 05672. © **800/992-0016** or 802/253-2062. www.turnermill.com. 8 units. $75–$110 double; $100–$285 apartment. Summer and fall rates include breakfast. AE, MC, V. *In room:* TV, fridge, coffeemaker.

Stowe Motel *Value*   This is one of Stowe's best choices for those traveling on a slim budget. The motel has 60 or so units, spread out among three buildings; rooms here are basic, but a bit larger than average, and have some comfortable touches such as couches and coffee tables. All of the units have small fridges, and the slightly more expensive efficiency units add two-burner stoves for in-room cooking. Surprisingly, you get access to tennis courts, a pool, hammocks, and an outdoor hot tub—a pretty good setup for such a budget-priced place. They will even rent you snowshoes or mountain bikes (there are 16 acres of grounds here). Not big enough? The motel also rents out some local houses and apartments nearby, some quite nice with hot tubs, washer/dryers, and the like.

2043 Mountain Rd., Stowe, VT 05672. © **800/829-7629** or 802/253-7629. Fax 802/253-9971 www.stowemotel. com. 60 units. $78–$158 double. AE, DISC, MC, V. Pets allowed (1 per room, $10 per night). **Amenities:** Outdoor heated pool; Jacuzzi; tennis court; game room; snowshoes. *In room:* A/C, TV, dataport, fridge, coffeemaker.

WHERE TO DINE

The **Harvest Market** ✱, at 1031 Mountain Rd. (© **802/253-3800**), is a great place for picking up takeout gourmet. You can browse Vermont products and imports and snag some fresh-baked goods to bring back to the ski lodge or take for a picnic along the bike path. Slightly high prices may cause your eyebrows to arch, but if you're not on a tight budget, it's a good place to splurge.

Blue Moon Cafe ✱✱✱ NEW AMERICAN   Delectable crusty bread on the table, Frank Sinatra crooning in the background, and vibrant local art on the walls are clues that this isn't your typical ski-area pub-fare restaurant. A short stroll off Stowe's main street, in an older home with a contemporary interior, the Blue Moon offers the village's finest dining. The wonderful menu changes every Friday, but count on lamb, beef, and veggie dishes, plus seafood dishes and even venison. The kitchen staff has superb instincts for spicing, and creates rather inventive dishes for Vermont such as sweet-and-sour braised rabbit, grilled lamb steak, orange-beet soup, polenta-crusted shrimp, grilled tuna with tomatillo, and a banana-leaf steamed halibut with Thai curry. Desserts, which are pure delights, might include a Belgian chocolate pot, a white chocolate mousse with caramelized banana, a lemon curd tart, or a Vermont cheese plate.

35 School St. ⓒ **802/253-7006.** Reservations recommended. Main courses $17–$32. AE, DISC, MC, V. Daily 6–9:30pm. In shoulder seasons, sometimes Sat–Sun only; call ahead.

Miguel's Stowe-Away ⭑ MEXICAN/SOUTHWEST   In an old farmhouse midway between the village and the mountain, Miguel's packs in folks looking for the tangiest Mexican and Tex-Mex food in the valley. Start off with a margarita or Vermont beer, and then order up appetizers such as empanadas, nachos, or jalapeños. Follow up with sizzling fajitas, the good chicken Santa Fe or fish chimichangas, or a filling combo plate. Desserts range from the complicated (apple-mango compote with cinnamon tortilla and ice cream) to the simple (chocolate-chip cookies). Miguel's is popular enough to offer its own brand of chips, salsa, and other products. Expect a boisterous atmosphere on busy nights.

3148 Mountain Rd. ⓒ **800/254-1240** or 802/253-7574. www.miguels.com. Reservations recommended Sat–Sun and in ski season. Main courses $11–$18 (most dishes under $14). AE, DISC, MC, V. Daily 5–10pm (from 5:30pm in summer). Lunch in winter only noon–3pm.

Mr. Pickwick's ⭑⭑ PUB FARE/CONTINENTAL   Mr. Pickwick's is a pub and restaurant that's part of Ye Old English Inne. It could justly be accused of being a theme-park restaurant, with the theme being "ye olde Englande"—but it's slowly changing. Run since 1983 with creative gusto by British ex-pats Chris and Lyn Francis, it's hard not to enjoy yourself here; begin by admiring the Anglo decor while relaxing at handsome wood tables in the booths (dubbed "pews"). Sample from among some 150 beers (many of them British) before ordering longtime lunch specialties such as a ploughman's lunch or fish and chips. Dinner still offers the fish and chips, but has become something more upscale than it used to be: Korean-spiced hanger steak, roasted duck breast with figs, veal loin chops, and the like now make appearances.

433 Mountain Rd. ⓒ **802/253-7064.** Reservations accepted for parties of 6 or more. Main courses $10–$19 at lunch, $19–$35 at dinner; dinner tasting menu $60 per person. AE, DC, MC, V. Daily 11am–1am.

The Shed ⭑ PUB FARE/BREWERY   Stowe has plenty of options for pub fare, but The Shed is the most consistently reliable. Since it opened more than 3 decades ago, this friendly, informal place has won fans by the sleigh-load with filling fare and feisty camaraderie (join the "Hall of Foam" by ordering a microbrew sampler). It has a bar area with popcorn and a good selection of beverages, ranging from craft beers brewed on the premises to frozen rum drinks to homemade root beer. The dining room has a chain-restaurant feel, but the bright solarium in the rear is a perfect spot to perch during sunny Sunday brunch. Meals are pub-fare eclectic: nachos, burgers, ribs, fish and chips, chicken, prime rib, shepherd's pie, simple seafood, sandwiches, and the like.

1859 Mountain Rd. ⓒ **802/253-4364.** Reservations recommended weekends and holidays. Main courses $8–$11 at lunch, $8–$21 at dinner. AE, DC, DISC, MC, V. Sun–Thurs 11:30am–10pm; Fri–Sat 11:30am–11pm.

9 Burlington

Burlington: 215 miles NW of Boston; 98 miles S of Montreal; 154 miles NE of Albany, NY

Burlington is a vibrant college town—it's home to the University of Vermont, known as UVM—that's continually and valiantly resisting the onset of "middle age." After all, this was the birthplace of Ben & Jerry's, founded by two hippies-gone-big-time and perpetual kids at heart. (Look for the sidewalk plaque at the corner of St. Paul and College streets commemorating their original ice-cream shop.) This city elected a socialist mayor in 1981, Bernie Sanders, who's now the only independent member of

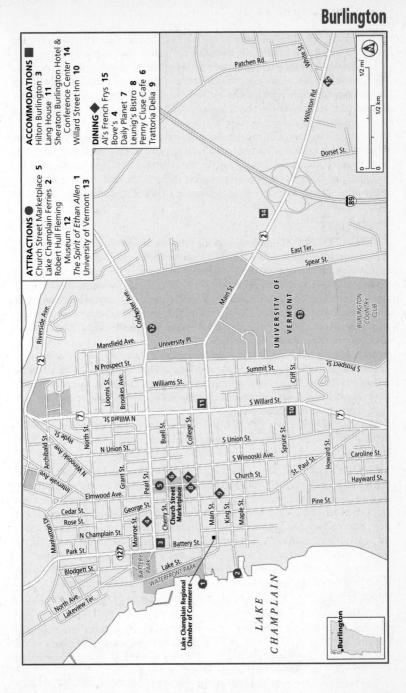

Burlington

ACCOMMODATIONS ■
Hilton Burlington **3**
Lang House **11**
Sheraton Burlington Hotel &
Conference Center **14**
Willard Street Inn **10**

DINING ◆
Al's French Frys **15**
Bove's **4**
Daily Planet **7**
Leunig's Bistro **8**
Penny Cluse Cafe **6**
Trattoria Delia **9**

ATTRACTIONS ●
Church Street Marketplace **5**
Lake Champlain Ferries **2**
Robert Hull Fleming
Museum **12**
The Spirit of Ethan Allen **1**
University of Vermont **13**

Lake Champlain Regional
Chamber of Commerce

LAKE CHAMPLAIN

WATERFRONT PARK

BATTERY PARK

CHURCH STREET MARKETPLACE

UNIVERSITY OF VERMONT

BURLINGTON COUNTRY CLUB

Patchen Rd.
White St.
Williston Rd.
Dorset St.
East Ter.
Spear St.
Main St.
University Pl.
Mansfield Ave.
N Prospect St.
Summit St.
Cliff St.
S Willard St.
Williams St.
Loomis St.
Brookes Ave.
N Willard St.
Buell St.
College St.
S Union St.
S Winooski Ave.
Church St.
Spruce St.
St. Paul St.
Caroline St.
Hayward St.
Howard St.
North St.
N Union St.
Grant St.
Pearl St.
Elmwood Ave.
Cherry St.
Main St.
King St.
Maple St.
Pine St.
George St.
Cedar St.
Rose St.
N Champlain St.
Monroe St.
Battery St.
Lake St.
Park St.
Blodgett St.
North Ave.
Lakeview Ter.
Riverside Ave.
Colchester Ave.
Archibald St.
N Winooski Ave.
Hyde St.
Intervale Ave.
Manhattan Dr.
S Prospect St.

89
2
7
127
2

Burlington

1/2 mi
1/2 km

(and the only self-described socialist in) the U.S. Senate. Burlington was also the birthplace of the rock band Phish, legendary for their meandering jam sessions.

It's no wonder Burlington has become a magnet for those seeking an alternative to big-city life: The downtown occupies a superb position overlooking Lake Champlain and the Adirondack Mountains of New York. To the east, the Green Mountains rise dramatically, with two of their highest points (Mount Mansfield and Camel's Hump) stretching above an undulating ridge.

The pedestrian mall (Church St.), that quizzical creation that has failed in so many other cities for unknown reasons, actually *works* here: People stroll, eat, shop, and seem to enjoy the relative lack of auto traffic (and parking). New construction has brought large stores downtown, reversing the flight to the mall that has plagued so many other towns. The city's scale is pleasantly skewed toward pedestrians—walk whenever possible.

ESSENTIALS

GETTING THERE   Burlington is at the junction of I-89, Route 7, and Route 2. **Burlington International Airport (BTV),** about 3 miles east of downtown, is served by **Continental Express** (© 800/525-0280; www.continental.com) nonstop from Boston and Newark; **Delta Connection** (© 800/221-1212; www.delta.com) nonstop from Atlanta and Cincinnati; **JetBlue** (© 800/538-2583; www.jetblue.com) daily from New York City, **United** (© 800/241-6522; www.united.com), from Chicago and Washington's Dulles airport, and **US Airways Express** (© 800/428-4322; www. usair.com) from New York City, Philadelphia, and Washington's National airport.

Amtrak's (© **800/USA-RAIL;** www.amtrak.com) *Vermonter* service offers daily departures for Burlington from New York, New Haven, Springfield, Massachusetts, and points beyond such as Baltimore and Washington, D.C. It's a pretty cheap ride ($44 one-way from New York at least check)—but it also takes 9½ hours from New York, longer from most other points.

Vermont Transit Lines (© 802/864-6811; www.vermonttransit.com), with a depot at 345 Pine St., has bus connections from Albany, Boston, Hartford, New York's JFK Airport, and other points in Vermont, Massachusetts, and New Hampshire.

VISITOR INFORMATION   The **Lake Champlain Regional Chamber of Commerce,** 60 Main St. (© 877/686-5253 or 802/863-3489; www.vermont.org), maintains an information center in a stout 1929 brick building just up from the waterfront and a short walk from Church Street Marketplace. Hours are Monday through Friday from 8am to 5pm. On Saturday and Sunday, helpful maps and brochures are left in the entryway for visitors. A summer-only information booth is also staffed at the Church Street Marketplace at the corner of Church and Bank streets (no phone).

The free local weekly, *Seven Days* (www.7dvt.com), carries topical and lifestyle articles, along with a very good weekly listing of local events and happenings.

SPECIAL EVENTS   First Night Burlington (© 802/863-6005; www.firstnight burlington.com) turns downtown into a stage on New Year's Eve. Hundreds of performers—from rockers to vaudevillians—play at nearly three dozen venues (mostly indoors) for 10 hours beginning at 2pm. The evening finishes with a bang at the midnight fireworks. Admission is $20 for adults (or $12 if you purchase before Christmas), $6 for children, and covers all performances.

The **Vermont Mozart Festival** (© 802/862-7352; www.vtmozart.com) takes place in and around Burlington (and farther afield) from mid-July to August. (The festival also has a winter series.) Ticket prices vary considerably. Call for a schedule and information, or check the website.

EXPLORING BURLINGTON

Downtown centers on the **Church Street Marketplace,** a pedestrian mall alive with activity throughout the year. This is the place to wander without purpose and watch the crowds; you can always find a cafe or ice-cream shop to rest your feet. While the shopping and grazing is good here, don't overlook the superb historic commercial architecture that graces much of downtown either. A number of side streets radiate from Church Street, with a mix of restaurants, shops, and offices.

Ethan Allen Homestead Museum A quiet retreat on one of the most idyllic, least-developed stretches of the Winooski River, the Ethan Allen Homestead is a shrine to Vermont's favorite son; years later, he and his Green Mountain Boys are still larger-than-life figures here. Though Allen wasn't actually born in Burlington, he settled here later in life on property confiscated from a British sympathizer during the Revolution. This reconstructed farmhouse is an enduring tribute to the war hero; an orientation center gives an intriguing multimedia accounting of Allen's life and other points of regional history. The house is open for tours for a small charge from mid-October to mid-May by appointment only (a day's advance notice is required), while the grounds are open year-round daily from dawn to dusk and free of charge.

Rte. 127, Colchester (from I-89, take exit 17 to North Ave. or exit 15 to Rte. 15). © 802/865-4556. Admission $3 adults, $4 seniors, $2.50 children 5–17, $15 per family. May–Oct daily 9am–5pm. Closed Nov–Apr. Take Rte. 127 northward from downtown; look for signs.

Lake Champlain Ferries Car ferries chug across the often placid, sometimes turbulent waters of Lake Champlain from Burlington to Port Kent, New York, between late May and early October, and it's a good way to cut out miles of driving if you're heading west toward the Adirondacks. It's also a great way to see the lake, leaves, and mountains on a pleasant, inexpensive 1-hour cruise. Reservations are taken for the Burlington route only, which operates 10 to 20 times per day when it's running. Travelers are advised to make reservations at least a day in advance. Two other ferries also cross the lake—much more quickly, in just 12 to 20 minutes—linking Grande Isle, Vermont, with Plattsburgh, New York, and Charlotte, Vermont, with Essex, New York; note that credit cards are not accepted for fares on these two shorter rides. Between June and mid-October, narrated, musically accompanied, or dinner-inclusive lake cruises are also offered by the ferry company; call © **802/864-9669** for details. Note that these three ferries are not affiliated with the "cable ferry" at Ticonderoga (see above), a fourth lake-crossing point between Vermont and New York State.

King St. Dock. © **802/864-9804.** www.ferries.com. Burlington to Port Kent: $17 one-way fare for car and driver from Burlington, $4.70 per additional adult, $2.05 per additional child 6–12; round-trip fares slightly discounted. Charlotte to Essex and Grande Isle to Cumberland Head: $9 one-way for car and driver, $3.50 additional adult passenger, $1.50 children 6–12.

Robert Hull Fleming Museum This University of Vermont facility houses a fine collection of art and anthropological displays, with a permanent collection of African, ancient Egyptian, Asian, and Middle Eastern art. A selection of paintings by 20th-century Vermont artists is also on permanent display, and changing exhibitions reflect varied cultures. On weekdays, you must feed the museum's meters to park and also get a pass from the reception desk; on Saturday and Sunday, there's an additional lot available. Call or check the museum website for a schedule of lectures and other special events.

61 Colchester Ave. (UVM campus). ℂ **802/656-0750.** www.flemingmuseum.org. Admission $5 adults, $3 seniors and students, $10 family. Labor Day–Apr Tues–Fri 9am–4pm, Sat–Sun 1–5pm; May–Labor Day Tues–Fri noon–4pm, Sat–Sun 1–5pm.

Shelburne Museum ★★★ Established in 1947 by Electra Havemeyer Webb, the museum contains one of the nation's most singular collections of American decorative, folk, and fine art. The Shelburne occupies some 37 buildings spread over 45 rolling acres, just 7 miles south of Burlington. No less than the *New York Times* has opined, "There is nothing like Shelburne in the museum universe," and Shelburne's holdings of some 150,000 items certainly testify to that. As expected, some of the more mundane exhibits chronicle quilts, early tools, decoys, weather vanes, and the like; but the museum also collects and displays entire *buildings* from around New England and New York, including an 1890-vintage railroad station, a lighthouse, a stagecoach inn, an Adirondack lodge, and a round barn from Vermont. Even a 220-foot steamship is eerily landlocked on the museum's grounds. Additions over the years include a wonderful 1950s ranch house (furnished in period style) and an architecturally engaging Collector's House, made creatively of prefab metal structures and other materials and featuring folk art displays. Rotating special exhibits periodically highlight particular aspects of Americana such as Shaker design, African-American quilting, and the art of John James Audubon.

Rte. 7 (P.O. Box 10), Shelburne. ℂ **802/985-3346.** www.shelburnemuseum.org. Summer admission $18 adults, $9 children 6–18. Discounted rates after 3pm. Late May–Oct daily 10am–5pm; selected buildings also open Apr–late May and mid-Oct to Dec 31; call for information.

The Spirit of Ethan Allen ★ Accommodating 500 passengers on three decks, the *Ethan Allen III* (brought to Lake Champlain in 2002 and 40% larger than its predecessor) offers a more genteel touring alternative to the ferry. The vistas of Lake Champlain and the Adirondacks haven't changed much since Samuel de Champlain first explored the area in 1609. The enclosed decks are air-conditioned, and food and drink is served from a deli and cash bar; in addition to four-times-daily narrated tours (1½ hr.), there are many specialty cruises involving dinner, music, or a murder (dramatically for mystery buffs, not a real one). Parking is available at additional cost.

Burlington Boathouse. ℂ **802/862-8300.** www.soea.com. Narrated tours $13 adults, $6 children 3–11; specialty cruises $18–$44 adults, $13–$31 children 3–11. Narrated cruises daily mid-May to mid-Oct; specialty cruises early June to mid-Oct.

University of Vermont Founded in 1791, and funded by a state donation of 29,000 acres of forest land across 120 townships, the university now has grown to accommodate some 8,000 undergraduates and more than a thousand graduate students, plus a few hundred medical students. The campus is set on 400 acres atop a small hill overlooking downtown and Lake Champlain to the west; it also has a glorious view of the Green Mountains to the east. The campus is large, with more than 400 buildings, many of which were designed by noted architects of their day including H. H. Richardson, and McKim, Mead & White. (By the way, it's UVM, not UVT; the initials stand for *Universitas Virdis Montis,* or University of the Green Mountains.) A controversial new student center opened in 2007, dwarfing some of the surrounding buildings with both its size and boxlike design, but it's here to stay.

Ethan Allen, Patriot & Libertine

In 1749, the governor of New Hampshire began giving away land to settlers willing to brave the howling wilderness that is now Vermont. Two decades later, New York State courts decreed those grants void, opening the door for New York speculators to flood the region and push the original settlers out of the valleys and up into the less hospitable Green Mountains.

Unsurprisingly, this decision didn't sit well with those already settled in, and they established a network of military units—the Green Mountain Boys—to drive out the New Yorkers. A fellow named Ethan Allen headed up this new militia, launching a series of harrying raids against the impudent Gothamites. His Boys destroyed homes, drove off livestock, and chased those Big Apple sheriffs back across the border from whence they had come.

The American Revolution soon intervened; Allen and his Green Mountain Boys now took up the revolutionary cause with equal vigor. They helped sack Fort Ticonderoga in 1775, rallied to the cause at the famed Battle of Bennington, and continued to confound the British effort throughout the remainder of the war. Allen's fame grew as word spread about him; a hard-drinking, fierce-fighting, large-living sort of guy, he supposedly could bite the head off a nail, and was so tough (they say), a rattlesnake that bit him promptly died.

While Allen's apocryphal exploits endured long after his death in 1789, he also left a more significant legacy: Vermont's statehood in 1791 was due in large part to the independence and patriotism the region developed under his leadership, and today you still can't drive far in Vermont without a reminder of Allen's historical presence. Parks are named for him, inns boast that he once slept there, and you'll still hear the occasional story about his bawdy exploits. Amen.

What UVM *doesn't* have is the usual college neighborhood of beery bars, bagel shops, and bookstores immediately adjacent to campus. Downtown serves that function, 5 blocks away, connected via College Street. In fact, a free daily shuttle that looks like an old-fashioned trolley runs along College Street between the Community Boathouse on the waterfront and the campus, year-round from 11am to 9pm. Use it.

The Waterfront   The waterfront has benefited from a $6 million renovation centered on Union Station at the foot of Main Street. The renovation includes some newly constructed buildings such as the **Wing Building,** an appealingly quirky structure of brushed steel and other nontraditional materials, blending in with the more rustic parts of the waterfront. Next door is the **Cornerstone Building,** with a restaurant and offices, offering better views of the lake from its higher vantage point. Nearby, the city's **Community Boathouse** is an inviting destination on a summer's day (see below). Bear in mind that Burlingtonians accept a fairly liberal definition of the adjective "lakeside." In some cases, it can mean a shop or restaurant 300 feet away.

WHERE TO STAY

There are several excellent resort properties with a half-hour's drive or so of the city. If those are too rich for your blood, a number of chain motels cluster along Route 7 (Shelburne Rd.) in South Burlington, about a 5- to 10-minute drive from downtown. While they lack even a trace of New England charm, they're generally modern, clean, and reliable.

Basin Harbor Club ⭐⭐ *Kids*   This is one of Vermont's best rustic resorts in which to kick back and simply enjoy lake breezes and lovely scenery. The best units are cottages facing out onto Champlain from clifftop perches; they feel wonderfully isolated, yet many sport carpets, fireplaces, comfy beds, work desks, sofas, and Jacuzzis. You *won't* find televisions, so borrow or rent bikes, kayaks, canoes, or a speedboat; hit the golf course; and grab a tennis racquet (lessons available). Art classes, lectures, great gardens, Adirondack-style chairs, three good restaurant choices on the dining plan, and an excellent kids' program complete the sense of having stepped into an upscale summer camp. Summertime bonus: Thursday nights bring lobster dinners and live jazz to the beach.

4800 Basin Harbor Rd., Ferrisburgh, VT 05456. From Burlington, take U.S. 7 about 23 miles south into Vergennes, turn right at signs just after bridge, and continue 7 miles to resort property. © **800/622-4000** or 802/475-2311. Fax 802/475-6545. www.basinharbor.com. 123 units. $150–$550 double and cottage. Rates include breakfast, lunch, and dinner mid-June to early Sept only. Rates do not include 18% service fee. B&B and MAP plans and rates also available. 2-night minimum stay some weekends. 7-night minimum stay in cottages July–Aug. MC, V. Closed mid-Oct to mid-May. "Well-behaved" pets allowed in cottages ($10 per pet per night). **Amenities:** 3 restaurants; outdoor pool; golf course; 5 tennis courts; fitness center; bike rentals; children's programs; concierge; babysitting; laundry service; dry cleaning; boat rentals. *In room:* A/C, dataport, coffeemaker, fridge (some units), hair dryer, iron/ironing board, Jacuzzi (some units).

Hilton Burlington ⭐⭐   This nine-story Hilton hotel—formerly flagged as a Radisson and then as a Wyndham property—has great views if you spend extra for a lakeside room. It's a sleek glass box built in 1976 (and it looks like it), and renovations have kept the aging process mostly at bay. It's also the most centrally located of any hotel in city, tucked right between the waterfront and Church Street Marketplace, each about a 5-minute walk away. Five cabana rooms open right up to the pool area and are especially good for families.

60 Battery St., Burlington, VT 05401. © **802/658-6500** or 800/445-8667. Fax 802/658-4659. www.hilton.com. 257 units. Summer $159–$269 double; winter $139–$179 double. Ask about packages. AE, DISC, MC, V. Self-parking in garage $5.50 per day. **Amenities:** Restaurant; indoor pool; fitness room; Jacuzzi; concierge; business center; conference rooms; room service; babysitting; laundry service; dry cleaning. *In room:* A/C, TV, dataport, coffeemaker, hair dryer, iron/ironing board, safe.

The Inn at Essex ⭐⭐   This inn makes a persuasive case that it truly is "Vermont's Culinary Resort": Its chefs come straight from the acclaimed New England Culinary Institute in Montpelier. The 120 rooms here are every bit as impressive as the food, and 20 acres of grounds on a majestic hillside setting enhance the experience of staying; it's not only about the eats. Rooms and suites are fitted with reproduction furniture and decked in flowery wallpaper and bed covers; many are further gussied up with fireplaces, two-line phones, CD players, Jacuzzi tubs, handsome four-poster beds, and rocking chairs. There are even some suites outfitted for longer stays, built with separate full kitchens including Hearthstone gas stoves—for those who prefer to become the "Top Chef" themselves. For more on the inn's dining options, see "Where to Dine," below.

70 Essex Way, Essex, VT 05452. (C) **800/727-4295** or 802/878-1100. Fax 802/878-0063. http://vtculinaryresort.com. 120 units. May–Oct $209–$309 double, $249–$529 suite; Nov–Apr $169–$239 double, $209–$479 suite. AE, DC, MC, V. **Amenities:** 2 restaurants; outdoor pool; golf course; fitness center; spa; room service; bike rentals; massage. *In room:* A/C, TV, dataport, fridge (some units), fireplace (some units), Jacuzzi (some units).

The Inn at Shelburne Farms ✸✸
The numbers behind this elaborate mansion on the shores of Lake Champlain tell the story: 60 rooms, 10 chimneys, 1,400 acres. It's a tourist attraction in and of itself (and there's an admission charge to the extensive farms on the property). Yet you can sleep here and pretend it's all yours. Built in 1899, the sprawling Edwardian "farmhouse" is a place to fantasize about the lifestyles of the rich and famous. Noted architect Frederick Law Olmsted helped shape the grounds, and the guest rooms vary in decor and upkeep—many have day beds. If you're feeling flush, rent Overlook, the original master bedroom of owner Lila Webb; it has frilly draperies, a big king bed, and great views of the lake, meadows, and grounds. The Louis XVI room was furnished with whitewashed furniture in 1899, and it's still here. Some budget units have shared bathrooms, of which the Oak Room is best.

Harbor Rd., Shelburne, VT 05482. (C) **802/985-8498.** www.shelburnefarms.org. 26 units, 7 with shared bathrooms. $235–$410 double with private bathroom; $140–$200 double with shared bathroom; $235–$340 cottage. 2-night minimum stay Sat–Sun. AE, DC, DISC, MC, V. Closed mid-Oct to mid-May. **Amenities:** Restaurant; lake swimming; tennis court; children's farmyard; babysitting; farm tours. *In room:* Kitchenette (2 units).

Lang House ✸
This stately, white Queen Anne mansion (1881) sits on the hillside between downtown and the University of Vermont. Not as extravagant as the similar Willard Street Inn, it's nevertheless comfortably appointed and almost lavish with rich cherry and maple woodwork. Rooms vary, though most have small bathrooms and small TVs; two of the best rooms are corner units: No. 101, on the first floor, has a wonderfully old-fashioned bathroom with wainscoting, while no. 202 has a cozy sitting area tucked into the turret that gets lots of afternoon light. Breakfast is largely organic (even the maple syrup) and quite good. The B&B has a liquor license, and can sell you a bottle of wine or beer. It also has a special connection to the university nearby, too—the owner and her son are both graduates.

360 Main St., Burlington, VT 05401. (C) **877/919-9799** or 802/652-2500. Fax 802/651-8717. www.langhouse.com. 11 units. $145–$245 double. Rates include breakfast. AE, DISC, MC, V. *In room:* A/C, TV, hair dryer, iron/ironing board.

Sheraton Burlington Hotel & Conference Center ✸
The largest conference facility in Vermont, the Sheraton also does a decent job catering to individual travelers and families. This sprawling and modern complex (it has 15 conference rooms!) just off the interstate is a 5-minute drive east of downtown, on the way to the airport; it features a sizable indoor garden area. All guest rooms have two phones and in-room Nintendo systems; rooms in the newer wing are a bit nicer, furnished in a simpler, lighter country style. Ask for a room facing east if you want to enjoy views of Mount Mansfield and the Green Mountains.

870 Williston Rd., Burlington, VT 05403. (C) **800/866-6117** or 802/865-6600. Fax 802/865-6670. 309 units. $89–$229 double. AE, DC, DISC, MC, V. **Amenities:** Restaurant; lounge; indoor pool; fitness room; 2 Jacuzzis; concierge; limited room service; laundry service. *In room:* A/C, TV, dataport, coffeemaker, hair dryer, iron/ironing board.

Willard Street Inn ✸✸
This impressive and historic inn is housed in a splendid Queen Anne–style brick mansion a few minutes' walk from the university. The inn has soaring first-floor ceilings, cherry woodwork, and a beautiful window-lined breakfast room. The home was built in 1881 by a local bank president, and once served as a retirement home before it became an inn. Four-poster beds and rather frilly decor

are the norms. Among the best units are no. 12, which boasts a small sitting area and views of the lake, and spacious no. 4, with a sizable bathroom and more lake views; all are decorated with genuine and reproduction antiques, and some have down comforters and fireplaces. Walk down the marble staircase to admire the solarium, lawns, and English gardens.

349 S. Willard St. (2 blocks south of Main St.), Burlington, VT 05401. © **800/577-8712** or 802/651-8710. Fax 802/651-8714. www.willardstreetinn.com. 14 units, 1 with detached bathroom. $130–$230 double. Rates include full breakfast. 2-night minimum stay Sat–Sun. AE, DC, DISC, MC, V. *In room:* A/C, TV, dataport, fireplace (some units).

WHERE TO DINE

Al's French Frys *Finds* BURGERS & FRIES   Ignore the technically incorrect spelling. Al's is where Ben and Jerry (*the* Ben and Jerry) go to satisfy french-fry cravings, and it's a must-hit roadside joint when you're in town. Al's is both fun and efficient, and the vats of fries (you can order a cup, a pint, or a quart) draw locals back time and again. Other offerings—hamburgers, hot dogs, sloppy-joe-like barbecue, wraps, chicken wings, and grilled cheese sammies (for less than a buck!)—are okay, if nothing special, but they do nicely complement the fries. Add a side order of cheese or chili sauce for the fries if you dare. No beer here; instead you can order a coke, a shake (five flavors), or—this being Vermont—a cup of plain or chocolate milk.

1251 Williston Rd. (Rte. 2, just east of I-89), South Burlington. © **802/862-9203.** Sandwiches and burgers $1–$5, fries $1–$4. No credit cards. Mon–Thurs 10:30am–11pm; Fri–Sat 10:30am–midnight; Sun 11am–11pm.

Bove's *Value* ITALIAN   A Burlington landmark since 1941, Bove's is a classic red-sauce-on-spaghetti joint a couple of blocks from the Church Street Marketplace. It's got true character, and, amazingly, nothing here costs more than 9 bucks—*still*. The facade is black and white, its octagonal windows closed to prying eyes by Venetian blinds. Step through the doors and into a lost era, grab a seat at a vinyl-upholstered booth, and browse the menu: spaghetti with butter sauce, spaghetti with meat sauce, spaghetti with meatballs . . . you get the idea. The red sauce here is tangy, the vodka-cream sauce rich and award-winning, and the garlic sauce packs enough punch to knock you out of your booth and keep you from getting kissed all night. (They jar and sell their sauces, in case you want to take some home.) Not feeling hungry for pasta? Bove's also fixes grinders—which should be the *only* correct term for a sub/hero/hoagie, in my view—and serves inexpensive cheesecake slices topped with maple (never seen that before), cherry, or chocolate. I can't resist telling you this, either: The restaurant operates a van around town known as the Meatball-Mobile, serving little portions of (yes) meatballs, ravioli, and soft-serve ice cream.

68 Pearl St. © **802/864-6651.** www.boves.com. Sandwiches $2–$5.40; dinner items $5.75–$9. No credit cards. Tues–Thurs 2–8:30pm; Fri–Sat 11am–8:30pm.

The Daily Planet ECLECTIC   Named for Superman alter-ego Clark Kent's day-job newspaper (I think), this popular spot is often brimming with college students and downtown workers on evenings and weekends. It's so cutting-edge that it's hard to believe it's been here for more than 20 years. The mild mayhem adds to the charm, enhancing an eclectic, fun menu—and the food is better prepared than you might expect from a place that takes its cues from a pub (and probably has college students moonlighting as sous chefs). Look for such items as a blackened grouper sandwich, peach-glazed grilled salmon, pan-seared duck breast in plum-ginger sauce, cold noodles in spicy Szechwan sauce, and a mustard-swathed pork steak. Desserts are equally creative and good-tasting. Don't forget to check the specialty martini menu.

15 Center St. ℂ **802/862-9647.** Reservations recommended for parties of 5 or more. Main courses $5.75–$7.95 at lunch; $7–$22 at dinner. AE, DISC, MC, V. Daily 4pm–2am.

Inn at Essex ★★ REGIONAL/CONTINENTAL   The Inn at Essex, about a 15-minute drive from Burlington, is the auxiliary campus of the Montpelier-based New England Culinary Institute. It offers both formal and informal dining rooms with meals prepared and served by New England's rising culinary stars. The two inn restaurants are housed in a large faux-farmhouse complex along the fringe of Burlington's suburban sprawl; inside, the setting is quiet and comfortable. In the light and airy **Tavern** (that's its name), you may be tempted by nachos, Yankee pot roast, seared scallops, prime rib, lasagna, buffalo wings, gnocchi, or salmon-crab cakes. Amid the more intimate, country-inn elegance of **Butler's,** the dinner fare is a bit more ambitious, with entrees that might run to a cheese flight (including a twice-baked Grafton cheddar soufflé), a pave of sole or salmon, grilled lamb chops, pan-roasted duck, and a number of seafood specials. There's also a Sunday brunch buffet; ask about kitchen tours, too.

70 Essex Way, Essex Junction. ℂ **800/727-4295** or 802/878-1100. http://vtculinaryresort.com. Reservations recommended at Butler's, not needed at the Tavern. Tavern main courses $5.50–$15; Butler's entrees $7–$25. AE, DC, DISC, MC, V. Tavern daily 2–11pm; Butler's daily 11:30am–10pm.

Leunig's Bistro ★★ REGIONAL/CONTINENTAL   This boisterous, fun place right on the pedestrian mall has a retro old-world flair, with washed walls, a marble bar, crystal chandeliers, and oversized posters. The inventive, large menu here features regional foods prepared with a continental touch. An upscale brunch is served on Saturday and Sunday, with duck tacos, gravlax flatbread, and the like; lunch runs to good sandwiches. But dinner is where things *really* get cranked up: Items change seasonally, and you might find roasted duck à l'Orange, free-range veal scaloppini in a grapefruit sauce, salade Niçoise, a rhubarb-y rack of pork, and a marinated lamb loin.

115 Church St. ℂ **802/863-3759.** Reservations recommended Sat–Sun and holidays. Main courses $8–$14 at lunch; $18–$26 at dinner. AE, DISC, MC, V. Mon–Thurs 11am–10pm; Fri 11am–11pm; Sat 9am–11pm; Sun 9am–10pm.

Penny Cluse Cafe ★★ *Finds* CAFE/LATINO   This gets my vote as the city's best choice for lunch or breakfast. A block off the Church Street Marketplace, Penny Cluse is a casual, bright, and popular spot decorated in a vaguely Southwestern motif. Among the better breakfasts: the buttermilk or gingerbread pancakes, breakfast sandwiches, a popular "tofu scram," and the Zydeco breakfast of two eggs (cooked any style), black beans, andouille sausage, and corn muffins; polenta with eggs is another filling choice. Lunch items range from salads to fish tacos to chicken-'n-biscuits to sandwiches (the veggie Reuben with mushrooms, spinach, and red onions is excellent), and there are also more elaborate choices such as adobo pork chops with plantain cake. Some breakfast prices are at the high end of the Vermont breakfast price scale—but they leave you satisfied, so you might not mind. Good coffees and teas abound, too.

169 Cherry St. ℂ **802/651-8834.** Breakfast and lunch entrees $5–$8.50. MC, V. Breakfast and lunch Mon–Fri 6:45am–3pm; Sat–Sun 8am–3pm.

Trattoria Delia ★★ *Finds* ITALIAN   Locally foraged mushrooms served over polenta with fontina—if that causes you to sit up and take notice, this is your place. Serving the best Italian food in Burlington, Lori and Tom Delia's eatery is in a low-traffic location, almost hidden through a speakeasy-like door beneath a large building. But locals never fail to find it; be sure to reserve ahead if you're coming. Inside is culinary magic, with genuinely Italian specialties such as veal shanks, herb-and-red wine-braised wild boar, filet mignon in white-truffle butter, sirloin sautéed in chianti, seafood stew, and classic pasta dishes such as tagliatelle alla Bolognese, spaghetti and Gulf shrimp baked in a parchment paper, and rigatoni baked in the oven in a clay pot with basil-tomato sauce and meat. Then choose from Italian dessert wines and traditional desserts such as gelati, torte, tiramisu, and panna cotta. It's a great find.

152 Saint Paul St. ⓒ 802/864-5253. Reservations recommended. Main courses $14–$27. DC, MC, V. Daily 5–10pm.

10 The Northeast Kingdom

St. Johnsbury is 60 miles N of White River Junction, 75 miles E of Burlington, and 125 miles N of Brattleboro

Vermont's Northeast Kingdom has a more wild and remote character than much of the rest of the state. Consisting of Orleans, Essex, and Caledonia counties, the region was given its memorable nickname in 1949 by Vermont Sen. George Aiken, who understood the area's allure at a time when few others paid it much heed. What gives this region its character is its stubborn, old-fashioned insularity.

In contrast to the dusky narrow valleys of southern Vermont, the Kingdom's landscape is open and spacious, with rolling meadows ending abruptly at the hard edge of dense boreal forests. The leafy woodlands of the south give way to spiky woods of spruce and fir. Accommodations and services for visitors aren't plentiful or easy to find here, but a growing number of good inns are sprouting up in these hills and forests.

The entire tour described below, from Hardwick to St. Johnsbury by way of Newport, Derby Line, and Lake Willoughby, is approximately 90 miles by car. Allow a full day or more if you plan to take advantage of hiking and biking in the region.

Visitor information for the region is available from the **Northeast Kingdom Chamber of Commerce** (ⓒ **800/639-6379** or 802/748-3678; www.nek chamber.com) at 51 Depot Square, Suite #3, in downtown St. Johnsbury.

DRIVING TOUR   THE NORTHEAST KINGDOM

Start:	Hardwick
Finish:	St. Johnsbury
Time:	One full day

Start your tour at Hardwick, which is at the intersection of routes 14 and 15, about 23 miles northwest of St. Johnsbury and 26 miles northeast of Montpelier:

❶ Hardwick

A small town with rough edges set on the Lamoille River, Hardwick has a compact commercial main street with some intriguing shops, a couple of casual, family-style restaurants, and one of Vermont's best little natural foods stores (the Buffalo Mountain Food Co-op).

From here, head north on Route 14 about 7 miles to the turnoff to Craftsbury and:

❷ Craftsbury Common

An uncommonly graceful village, Craftsbury Common is home to a small academy and a large number of historic homes and buildings spread along a central green and the village's main street. The town occupies a wide upland ridge and offers sweeping views to the east and west; be sure to stop by the old cemetery on the south end of town, too, where you can wander among historic tombstones of pioneers—they date back to the 1700s. Craftsbury is an excellent destination for mountain biking and cross-country skiing.

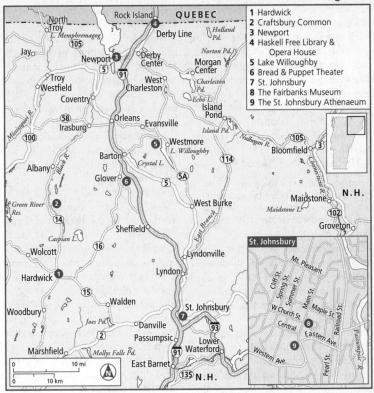

1 Hardwick
2 Craftsbury Common
3 Newport
4 Haskell Free Library & Opera House
5 Lake Willoughby
6 Bread & Puppet Theater
7 St. Johnsbury
8 The Fairbanks Museum
9 The St. Johnsbury Athenaeum

From Craftsbury, continue north to reconnect to Route 14. Pass through the towns of Albany and Irasburg as you head north. At the village of Coventry, veer north on Route 5 to the lakeside town of:

❸ Newport

This commercial (and commercial-looking) outpost is set on the southern shores of Lake Memphremagog, a stunning 27-mile-long lake that's just 2 miles wide at its broadest point (the bulk of it lies across the border in Canada). From Newport, continue north on Route 5, crossing under I-91, about 7 miles more to the border town of Derby Line. This outpost has a handful of restaurants and antiques shops; if you have a passport, you can also park and walk across the bridge to poke around the Canadian town of Rock Island.

Back in Derby Line, look for the:

❹ Haskell Free Library & Opera House

At the corner of Caswell Avenue and Church Street (✆ **802/873-3022**), this handsome neoclassical building contains a public library on the first floor and an elegant opera house on the second, which is modeled after the old Boston Opera House. The theater opened in 1904 with advertisements promoting a minstrel show featuring "new songs, new jokes, and beautiful electric effects." It's a beautiful theater, with a scene of Venice painted on the drop curtain and carved cherubim adorning the balcony.

What's most curious about the structure, however, is that it lies half in Canada and half in the U.S. (The Haskell family donated the building jointly to the towns of Derby Line and Rock Island.) A thick black line runs beneath the seats of the opera house, indicating who's in the U.S. and who's in Canada. Because the stage is set entirely in Canada, apocryphal stories abound from its early days of frustrated U.S. officers watching fugitives perform on stage. More recently, the theater was used for the occasional extradition hearing.

The library is open Tuesday to Saturday.

From Derby Line, retrace your path south on Route 5 to Derby Center and the juncture of Route 5A. Continue south on Route 5A to the town of Westmore on the shores of:

⑤ Lake Willoughby

This glacier-carved lake is best viewed from the north, where its shimmering sheet of water appears to be pinched between the base of two low mountains at its southern end. There's a distinctive alpine feel to the scene; this underappreciated lake is one of the most scenic in Vermont. Route 5A along the eastern shore is lightly traveled, and ideal for biking or walking. For information about ascending the nearby mountains on foot, see "Outdoor Pursuits," below.

Head southwest on Route 16, which branches off Route 5A just north of the lake. Follow Route 16 through the peaceful villages of Barton and Glover. About 1 mile south of Glover, turn left on Route 122. On your left, look for the farmstead that serves as home to the:

⑥ Bread & Puppet Theater

For nearly 3 decades, until 1998, Polish artist and performer Peter Schumann's Bread and Puppet Theater staged an elaborate annual summer pageant at this farm, attracting thousands of attendees who gaped at the theater's brightly painted puppets (crafted of fabric and papier-mâché, they could be an amalgam of Ralph Nader and Hieronymus Bosch). The huge puppets marched around the farm grounds, acting out dramas that typically featured rebellion against

tyranny of one sort or another. It was like Woodstock, minus the music.

Alas, the event became too popular—and attracted drifters of questionable character. In 1998, a murder at an adjacent campground prodded Schumann to shut down the circus for a while. His troupe still designs and builds puppets here, however, and periodically takes its unique shows on the road—or offers live performances in Glover. (For the latest schedules, check the troupe's website, www.breadandpuppet.org.)

Between June and October, you can still visit the venerable, slightly tottering barn, home of the **Bread and Puppet Museum** ⚐ (ℂ **802-525-3031** or 802-525-1271), which preserves many of the puppets from past events. This remarkable display shouldn't be missed if you're near the area. Downstairs, in former cow-milking stalls, smaller displays include mournful washerwomen doing laundry and King Lear addressing his daughters. Upstairs, the vast hayloft is filled with soaring, haunting puppets, some up to 20 feet tall. Admission is free, though donations are encouraged.

From Glover, continue south through serene farmlands to Lyndonville, where you pick up Route 5 south to:

⑦ St. Johnsbury

This is the largest community in the Northeast Kingdom, and its major center of commerce. First settled in 1786, the town enjoyed a buoyant prosperity in the 19th century, largely stemming from the success of platform scales (invented here in 1830 by Thaddeus Fairbanks), which are still manufactured here. The town, which still hasn't been overtaken by sprawl, outlet shops, tourist boutiques, or brewpubs, features an abundance of fine commercial architecture in two distinct areas, joined by steep Eastern Avenue.

The commercial part of town lies along Railroad Street (Rte. 5) at the base of the hill. The more ethereal part of town runs along Main Street at the top of the hill; here, you'll find the local library (with its fine art museum), the St. Johnsbury Academy, and a second grand museum (see below for details on the two museums). This northern end of Main Street is also notable for its grand residential architecture.

In St. Johnsbury, at the corner of Main and Prospect streets, find the:

⑧ Fairbanks Museum

This imposing Romanesque red-sandstone structure was constructed in 1889 to hold the accumulations of obsessive amateur collector Franklin Fairbanks, grandson of the inventor of the platform scale. Fairbanks was once described as "the kind of little boy who came home with his pockets full of worms." In adulthood, his propensity to collect continued unabated. His collections include four stuffed bears, a huge moose with full antlers, art from Asia, and 4,500 stuffed native and exotic birds—and that's just the tip of the proverbial iceberg. (In fact, it's surprising there isn't *an* iceberg here as well.)

The soaring, barrel-vaulted main hall, reminiscent of an old-fashioned railway depot, embodies Victorian grandeur. Amid the assorted clutter, look for the, er, unique mosaics of John Hampson: He depicted famous moments in American history—such as Washington bidding his troops farewell—made entirely out of mounted insects. (In the Washington scene, iridescent green beetles form the epaulets and the regal great coat comprises hundreds of purple moth wings.) These works alone are worth the price of admission, and capture the peculiar oddity of the place.

The museum (*C* **802/748-2372;** www.fairbanksmuseum.org) is open Tuesday through Saturday from 9am to 5pm, and Sunday from 1 to 5pm; from April to October, it's also open Monday from 9am to 5pm. Admission is $6 for adults, $5 for seniors and children ages 5 to 17, and $18 per family (maximum of 2 adults). There's a planetarium *☆* here as well—the only one in Vermont.

Also on Main Street, just south of the museum at 1171 Main St, find the:

⑨ St. Johnsbury Athenaeum

In an Edward Hopper-esque brick building with a truncated mansard tower and prominent keystones over the windows, St. Johnsbury's public library also houses an extraordinary art gallery dating to 1873. It claims to be the oldest unadulterated art gallery in the nation.

Your first view of the gallery is spectacular: After winding through a cozy library and past its ticking regulator clock, you round a corner and find yourself gazing across Yosemite National Park. The luminous 10×15-foot oil painting was created by noted Hudson River School painter Albert Bierstadt, and the gallery was built specifically to accommodate this work. (Not everyone was happy about it moving here. "Now *The Domes* is doomed to the seclusion of a Vermont town, where it will astonish the natives," groused the *Boston Globe* at the time.) The natural light flooding in from the skylight above enhances the painting.

Another 100 or so other works fill the remaining walls of the museum. Most are copies of other paintings (that was a common teaching tool in the 19th century), but look for originals by other Hudson River School painters including Asher B. Durand, Thomas Moran, and Jasper Cropsey.

The Athenaeum (*C* **802/748-8291;** www.stjathenaeum.org) is open Monday and Wednesday from 10am to 8pm; Tuesday, Thursday, and Friday from 10am to 5:30pm; and Saturday from 9:30am to 4pm. Admission is free, but donations are encouraged.

DOWNHILL SKIING

Jay Peak 🌟🌟🌟 Just south of the Canadian border, Jay Peak is a great choice for those who prefer to avoid the glitz and clutter that seem to plague many ski resorts these days. While some new condo development has been taking place at the base of the mountain, Jay still has the feel of a remote, isolated destination, accessible by a winding road through unbroken woodlands. Thanks to its staggering snowfall (an average of about 30 feet annually, more than anywhere else in New England), there is extensive glade skiing between the trees here. The resort's ski school specializes in running the glades, too, making this a fitting place for advanced intermediates to learn how to navigate the exciting, challenging trails. Even in summer, there's a golf course, aerial tram (like a gondola), and swimming pool for the family to enjoy here.

4850 Rte. 242, Jay, VT 05859. © 800/451-4449 or 802/988-2611. www.jaypeakresort.com. Day lift tickets $59 adults; half-day tickets $44 adults. Discounts for youths, students, seniors, and Vermont residents.

CROSS-COUNTRY SKIING

The same folks who offer mountain biking at the Craftsbury Outdoor Center also maintain about 60 miles of groomed cross-country trails through the gentle hills surrounding Craftsbury. The forgiving, old-fashioned trails, maintained by **Craftsbury Nordic Center** 🌟🌟 (© 802/586-7767), emphasize pleasing landscapes rather than fast action; they even "guarantee" skiable snow from January until the second Sunday in March. Another option is the **Highland Lodge Ski Touring Center** 🌟 (© 802/533-2647; www.highlandlodge.com), on Caspian Lake in Greensboro, with more than 30 miles of packed trails (about 10 miles of which are further groomed) through rolling woodlands and fields. Should you care to stay here, there are double rooms and cottages on the property (see "Where to Stay," below).

WHERE TO STAY & DINE

Comfort Inn & Suites 🌟 Built in 2000, this interstate-side property consists of more than 100 units and has a number of nice touches, such as granite vanity counters and high-backed desk chairs. Rooms are pleasantly appointed, more like an inn than a motel chain, and the basement houses an appealing (if small) pool, fitness center, and game room outfitted with air hockey and a billiards table. This hotel is outside town, right off I-91, about a mile south of downtown St. Johnsbury.

703 Rte. 5 S. (exit 20 on I-91), St. Johnsbury, VT 05819. © 866/464-2408 or 802/748-1500. Fax 802/748-1243. 107 units. June to mid-Oct $139–$399 double and suite; mid-Oct to May $89–$139 double and suite. Rates include continental breakfast. AE, DISC, MC, V. **Amenities:** Indoor pool; fitness room; game room; coin-op washers/dryers. *In room:* A/C, TV, dataport, coffeemaker, hair dryer, iron.

Highland Lodge 🌟 Built in the mid–19th century, this all-inclusive lodge has been accommodating guests since 1926. Just across the road from lovely Caspian Lake, it has 11 rooms furnished in a comfortable country style, plus 11 nearby cottages, 9 of which are equipped with kitchenettes. A stay here is supremely relaxing: The main summer activities include swimming or boating on the lake, and tennis on a clay court. In winter, the lodge maintains its own cross-country ski area (see above) with miles of packed and groomed trails. Behind the lodge is an attractive nature preserve that invites quiet exploration. Rates here include breakfast, dinner, and free use of the canoes, kayaks, and most of the other equipment and facilities scattered about the property (except for the mountain bikes). Note that, unlike at most lodging establishments in America, you can get a single room here for a fair price—about 60% of the double-occupancy rates below. Also note that children and teens are charged depending on age; this charge can range from $100 for an 18-year-old to $40 for a 2-year-old. (Infants are not charged.)

Caspian Lake, Greensboro, VT 05841. ℂ **802/533-2647.** Fax 802/533-7494. www.thehighlandlodge.com. 22 units. $237–$330 double. Rates include breakfast and dinner. DISC, MC, V. Closed mid-Mar to May and mid-Oct to Christmas. From Hardwick, take Rte. 15 east 2 miles to Rte. 16, and then drive 2 miles north to East Hardwick. Continue west and follow signs to the inn. **Amenities:** Dining room; tennis court; watersports equipment; bike rentals; children's program; game room; babysitting; laundry service; cross-county ski trails. *In room:* Kitchenette (some units), no phone.

Inn on the Common ✹✹

This handsome complex of three Federal-era townhouse buildings anchors the charming ridge-top village of Craftsbury Common, a quintessential New England village. This is a wonderful place, mixing just the right measures of history and pampering; it's well-managed by owners Jim and Judi Lamberti, who spent more than a decade at the fine Inn at Essex before purchasing this inn in 2003. It's a social place, attracting both families and couples seeking a romantic getaway; you won't find any phones or televisions in the rooms. Some of the best units here have fireplaces or wood-burning stoves, and guests enjoy using the outdoor pool, deck, and tennis courts. Dinner is served in the Trellis restaurant 4 to 5 nights per week, often by candlelight.

1162 N. Craftsbury Rd. (P.O. Box 75), Craftsbury Common, VT 05827. ℂ **800/521-2233** or 802/586-9619. Fax 802/586-2249. www.innonthecommon.com. 16 units. May–late Sept $165–$225 double, $275 suite; fall-foliage season $195–$275 double, $325 suite; late Oct–March, $135–$225 double, $255 suite. 2-night minimum stay most weekends. Rates include full breakfast. Closed Apr. AE, DISC, MC, V. Pets allowed with prior permission ($25 per stay). **Amenities:** Restaurant; outdoor pool; tennis court; massage; babysitting; croquet. *In room:* Hair dryer, no phone.

WilloughVale Inn ✹✹

An elegant inn on a low rise at the northern end of Lake Willoughby, the WilloughVale possesses stunning views of twin mountains bracketing the other end of the lake. It's an ideal location for a quiet retreat; Robert Frost stayed here in 1909 and wrote a poem about it ("A Servant to Servants"). The 9 rooms in the main lodge are tastefully appointed, with much of their furniture crafted in Vermont; some have private sections of porch and are thoroughly updated with Jacuzzis, big-screen televisions, and fireplaces. The cottages—four right on the lake with kitchenettes, four others nearby with views—give more of a rustic, Adirondack-lodge feeling. Some have fireplaces or Jacuzzis, and they still feel like country retreats. The inn's restaurant serves well-prepared meals with a superb view of the lake, and there's also a small tavern on site.

793 Rte. 5A South, Westmore, VT 05860. ℂ **800/594-9102** or 802/525-4123. Fax 802/525-4514. www.willoughvale. com. 17 units. Mid-June to mid-Oct $153–$263 double, $253–$325 cottage; mid-Oct to late Dec $103–$213 double, $174–$259 cottage. Weekly discounts available in summer only. Christmas week rates higher. Closed Jan to mid-June. Rates include continental breakfast (some units). 2-night minimum stay for all cottages; also 2-night minimum stay in lodge in July, Aug, and fall-foliage season. Ski packages available. AE, MC, V. 1 small or medium dog sometimes allowed per room (call ahead; $20 per night). **Amenities:** Restaurant; tavern; bike rentals; watersports equipment rental. *In room:* A/C, TV, coffeemaker (some units), fridge (some units), Jacuzzi (some units).

13

New Hampshire

by Paul Karr

Okay, I admit it. I love New Hampshire. Yes, I know it's not quite as postcard-worthy as Vermont, and not nearly so lobster-loaded as Maine. The state charges everyone, even residents, an annoying $2 to traverse a measly 15 miles of coastal interstate highway (with no views). Beaches are nearly nonexistent. The fields here are full of rocks, and the winters are much too long.

That "Live Free or Die" license plate? It's for real. Granite Staters regard zoning as a grand conspiracy to undermine property rights. Last time I checked, the state did not have any bottle-return laws, bills banning billboards, legislation requiring motorcyclists to wear helmets, nor sales or income taxes on its books. Longtime resident Robert Frost once famously opined that "Good fences make good neighbors," and folks here still mostly agree.

Yet that's what makes this place so wonderful to visit: its authenticity. You'll hear real accents, and witness real ingenuity and parsimony. New Hampshire savors its reputation as an outpost of plucky, heroic, independent citizens fighting the good fight against intrusive laws and irksome bureaucrats—the same sort of folks who took up arms and thumbed their noses at King George way back when.

This rebellious attitude has had consequences, of course. State legislators have had to become extremely creative when financing public services. Many are funded either by lottery sales or through the state's stiff "tourist tax" (8% on meals and hotel lodging), or by hefty local property taxes that hit residents hard. Candidates for virtually every local, state, or national office must take "The Pledge," vowing to fight any effort to impose a sales or income tax here. To shirk "The Pledge" is tantamount to political suicide.

Get beyond New Hampshire's affable crankiness, though, and you find at its core is a tough independence and a laconic acceptance that—no matter what—you can't change the weather, and you can't expect the Red Sox to win. (Well, scratch the latter—the Sox did win. "Twice." Hallelujah!) Travelers passing through can find these attitudes in spades—plus pickup trucks, pancake houses, hunting caps, and country-rock music.

It's not *all* about flannel shirts and rifle racks here, though. For one thing, you'll find that Granite Staters know how to have fun: comic actor Adam Sandler comes from here, and the guys from Aerosmith still hang out in their adopted home. You'll also find wonderfully diverse terrain—from beaches to broad lakes to impressive hills and mountains. Within an hour's drive here, you can toss a Frisbee on a long beach, ride bikes along country lanes, hike rugged granite hills blasted by some of the most severe weather in the world, and canoe or boat on a placid lake in the company of moose and loons.

You'll also find good country inns and home cooking. Most of all, you'll find a strong dose of the wily independence that has defined New England since the first settlers arrived 3½ centuries ago.

1 Portsmouth ★★

Portsmouth: 11 miles N of Hampton; 10 miles NE of Exeter; 55 miles N of Boston; 54 miles S of Portland

Novice travelers are often surprised when they learn that New Hampshire isn't land-locked—it actually has coastline. Granted, it isn't much of one (just 18 miles), but travelers quickly learn that it manages to pack a lot of variety (and real-estate value) into that little bit of space. The coast has honky-tonk beach towns, eye-popping mansions, vest-pocket state parks with swaths of warm sand, and a historic seaport city with a vibrant maritime history and culture. Ecologically speaking, there are dunes, lush hardwood forests, and a complex system of salt marshes that has prevented development from overtaking the region entirely.

A short drive inland, colonial-era historic towns and a slower way of life have so far resisted the inexorable creep of Boston's suburbs. While strip malls are belatedly appearing throughout the region (particularly along Rte. 1), the quiet downtowns are holding their own, several establishing themselves as fertile breeding grounds for small-scale entrepreneurs who've shunned the hectic life of bigger cities.

Portsmouth is the sort of place that tugs you back to visit again and again, a civilized little seaside city of bridges, brick, and seagulls—and quite a lot of culture. Filled with elegant architecture that's more intimate than intimidating, this Boston-in-miniature projects a strong, proud sense of its local heritage without being overly precious about it. Part of the city's appeal is its variety: Upscale coffee shops and art galleries share main-street space with junk shops, barbers, tattoo parlors, and pierced local girls and boys. The upscale crowd has begun steadily elbowing old-time businesses out of the main square, but despite the influx of new money lately, this town retains an earthiness that serves as a great balance to more touristed and, well, saccharine coastal towns. Portsmouth's humble and historic waterfront is so understated that you actually have to seek it out; it's still a working waterfront, as you'll learn if you manage to locate it.

This city's history runs deep, a fact that is evident on even a quick walk through town. For the past 3 centuries, Portsmouth has been the hub of the coastal Maine/New Hampshire region's maritime trade. In the 1600s, Strawbery Banke (it wasn't called Portsmouth until 1653) was a major center for the export of wood and dried fish to Europe. Later, in the 19th century, it prospered as a center of regional trade. Just across the Piscataqua River in Maine (so important a connection that there are four bridges from Portsmouth to that state), the Portsmouth Naval Shipyard—founded way back in 1800—evolved into a prominent base for the building, outfitting, and repairing of U.S. Navy submarines. Today, Portsmouth's maritime tradition continues with a lively trade in bulk goods; look for the scrap metal and minerals stockpiled along the shores of the river on Market Street. The city's de facto symbol is the tugboat, one or two of which are almost always tied up in or near the waterfront's picturesque "tugboat alley."

Visitors to Portsmouth will discover a surprising amount of available experiences in such a small space, including good shopping in the boutiques that now occupy much of the historic district; good eating at many small restaurants and bakeries; and plenty of history to explore among the historic homes and museums set on almost every block of Portsmouth.

ESSENTIALS

GETTING THERE   Portsmouth is served by exits 3 through 7 on I-95. The most direct access to downtown is via Market Street (exit 7), which is the last New Hampshire exit, just before crossing the big bridge and the river to Maine. Take that exit, then bear right (coming from the south) or left (from the north). You'll come straight into town.

Amtrak (© 800/872-7245; www.amtrak.com) operates four to five trains daily from Boston's North Station to downtown Dover, New Hampshire; a one-way ticket is about $17 per person, and the trip takes about 1½ hours. You can then take the no. 2 **COAST** bus (© 603/743-5777; www.coastbus.org) from Dover station to the center of downtown Portsmouth, a 45-minute trip that costs just $1 (50¢ for seniors).

Bus is not a bad choice. **Greyhound** (© 800/231-2222; www.greyhound.com), **C&J Trailways** (© 800/258-7111 or 603/430-1100; www.cjtrailways.com), and **Vermont Transit** (© 800/552-8737; www.vermonttransit.com) all run about five buses daily from Boston's South Station to Portsmouth, plus one to three daily trips from Boston's Logan Airport. Each service has a different pickup point: Greyhound's is the main bus stop in Market Square, Vermont Transit's is a food shop on Hanover Street (downhill from the main square, near the city parking garage), and C&J's is at a modern but distant bus station about 5 miles south at the former Pease air base (call a taxi or rent a car). The one-way cost for any of the three trips is about $16 per person; C&J purportedly prohibits passengers from talking on cellphones.

A one-way Greyhound trip from New York City's Port Authority bus station to downtown Portsmouth is about $45 and takes about 6½ hours.

VISITOR INFORMATION   The **Greater Portsmouth Chamber of Commerce,** 500 Market St. (© 603/436-3988; www.portcity.org), has an information center between exit 7 and downtown across the road from the piles of salt and scrap metal. From Memorial Day to Columbus Day, it's open Monday through Wednesday from 8:30am to 5pm; Thursday and Friday from 8:30am to 7pm; and Saturday and Sunday from 10am to 5pm. The rest of the year, it's open Monday to Friday only, 8:30am to 5pm. During the summer, a second staffed booth opens right out in Market Square (in front of the Breaking New Grounds coffee shop with the outdoor tables).

HISTORIC BUILDINGS

John Paul Jones House 🎯   Scottish Revolutionary War hero John Paul ("I have not yet begun to fight") Jones is believed to have lived in this 1758 home during the war, while he was here to oversee construction of his sloop, the *Ranger,* likely the first ship to sail under the U.S. flag (a model is on display). He took a ragtag crew of locals to England and gave them no end of bother. The house is immaculately restored and maintained by the Portsmouth Historical Society; costumed guides lead tours.

43 Middle St. © 603/436-8420. Admission $8 adults, free for children. Daily 11am–5pm, last tour begins at 4:30pm. Closed mid-Oct to mid-May.

Moffatt-Ladd House 🎯🎯   Built for a family of prosperous merchants and traders, this 1763 home is as notable for its elegant gardens as it is for the home's great hall and elaborate carvings. Now a National Historic Landmark, it belonged to a single family from 1763 until 1913, when it became a museum. As a result, many furnishings never left the premises; aficionados of Early American furniture and painting, take note.

154 Market St. © 603/436-8221. www.moffattladd.org Admission to house and gardens $6 adults, $2.50 children under 12; gardens only, $2 per person. Tours mid-June to mid-Oct Mon–Sat 11am–5pm, Sun 1–5pm.

Strawbery Banke 🎯🎯🎯   In 1958, the city of Portsmouth was finalizing plans to raze this neighborhood (which was settled in 1653!) to make way for "urban renewal." A group of local citizens resisted the move, and they prevailed, establishing an outdoor

New Hampshire

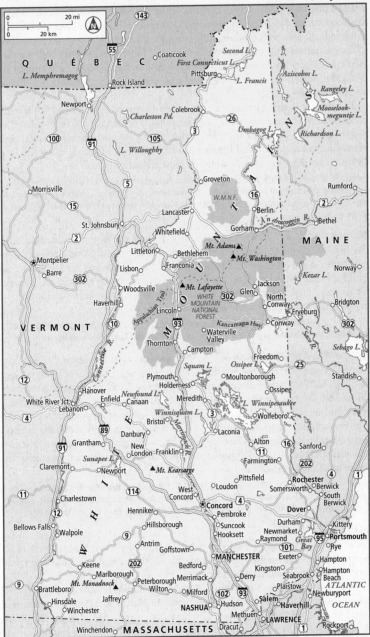

history museum that's become one of the largest and best in New England. Today the attraction consists of 10 prime downtown acres and more than 40 historic buildings. Ten buildings have been restored with period furnishings; eight more feature exhibits. (The rest can be only viewed from the exterior, but are mostly very well restored.) While Strawbery Banke employs staffers to assume the character of historical residents, the emphasis is more on the buildings, architecture, and history than the costumed reenactors.

The neighborhood surrounds an open lawn (formerly an inlet) and has a settled, picturesque quality. At three working crafts shops, watch coopers, boatbuilders, and potters at work. The most intriguing home is the split-personality Shapley-Drisco House, half of which depicts life in the 1790s and half of which shows life in the 1950s, nicely demonstrating how houses grow and adapt to each era.

Hancock St. © **603/433-1100.** www.strawberybanke.org. Summer admission $15 adults, $10 children 5–17, free for children 4 and under, $40 per family; winter rates discounted. May–Oct open daily for self tours 10am–5pm; Nov–Apr 90-min. guided tours on the hour Sat–Sun only, 10am–2pm. Extra tours in Dec. Look for directional signs posted around town.

Warner House ⚝   This house, built in 1716, was the governor's mansion during the mid–18th century, when Portsmouth was the state capital. After a period as a private home, it was opened to the public in the 1930s. This stately brick structure with graceful Georgian architectural elements is a favorite among architectural historians for its wall murals (said to be the oldest murals still in place in the U.S.), early wall marbleizing, and original white pine paneling.

150 Daniel St. © **603/436-8420.** www.warnerhouse.org. Admission $5 adults, $4 seniors, $2.50 children 7–12, free for children 6 and under. Mid-June to mid-Oct Mon–Sat 11am–4pm; Sun noon–4pm. Closed Nov–early June.

Wentworth-Gardner House ⚝⚝⚝   Arguably the most handsome mansion in the Seacoast region, this is considered one of the nation's best examples of Georgian architecture. The 1760 home features many period elements, including pronounced quoins (blocks on the building's corners), pedimented window caps, plank sheathing (to make the home appear as if made of masonry), an elaborate doorway with Corinthian pilasters, a broken scroll, and a paneled door topped with a pineapple, the symbol of hospitality. Perhaps most memorable is its scale—though a grand home of the Colonial era, it's modest in scope; some architectural circles today may not consider it much more than a pool house.

50 Mechanic St. © **603/436-4406.** Admission $5 adults, $2 children 6–14, free for children 5 and under. Tues–Sun noon–4pm. Closed mid-Oct to mid-June. From rose gardens on Marcy St. across from Strawbery Banke, walk south 1 block, turn left toward bridge, make a right before crossing bridge; house is down the block on your right.

BOAT TOURS

Portsmouth is especially attractive when seen from the water. A small fleet of tour boats ties up at Portsmouth, taking scenic tours of the Piscataqua River and the historic Isle of Shoals throughout the summer and fall.

The **Isles of Shoals Steamship Co.** ⚝⚝ (© **800/441-4620** or 603/431-5500; www.islesofshoals.com) sails from Barker Wharf on Market Street and is the most established of the city's tour companies. The firm takes a variety of tours on the 90-foot, three-deck M/V *Thomas Laighton* (a modern replica of a late-19th-c. steamship). Most popular are the excursions to the Isle of Shoals, at which passengers can disembark and wander about Star Island, a dramatic, rocky landmass that's part of an island cluster far out in the offshore swells. Reservations are strongly encouraged. Other popular

Portsmouth

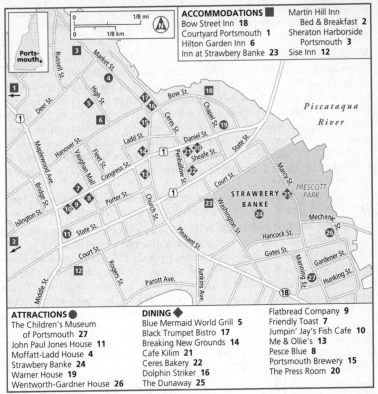

trips include a sunset lighthouse cruise. Fares for the tips to the Isles of Shoals in 2007 ranged from $10 to $25 per adult, depending on the length of the cruise; dinner cruises cost extra. Parking is an additional charge, as well.

Portsmouth Harbor Cruises ✪ (© 800/776-0915 or 603/436-8084; www. portsmouthharbor.com) specializes in tours of the historic Piscataqua River aboard the *Heritage,* a 60-foot, 49-passenger cruise ship with plenty of open deck space. It leaves from the Ceres Street docks, beside the tugboats. Cruise past five old forts or enjoy the picturesque tidal estuary of inland Great Bay, a scenic trip upriver from Portsmouth. Trips run daily; reservations are suggested. Fares are $12 to $20 for adults, $10 to $18 for seniors, and $8 to $13 for children ages 2 to 12.

ESPECIALLY FOR KIDS

The Children's Museum of Portsmouth ✪ *Kids* The Children's Museum is a bright, lively little arts-and-science museum that offers a morning's worth of hands-on exhibits of interest to younger artisans and scientists. (It's designed to appeal to children between the ages of 1 and 11.) Popular displays include exhibits on earthquakes, dinosaur digs, and lobstering, along with a miniature yellow submarine and space shuttle cockpit, both of which invite the youngsters to clamber around inside of them.

280 Marcy St., 2 blocks south of Strawbery Banke. ⓒ 603/436-3853. www.childrens-museum.org. Admission $6 adults and children, $5 seniors, free for children 1 and under. Tues–Sat 10am–5pm; Sun 1–5pm (also Mon during summer and school vacations).

WHERE TO STAY

Downtown accommodations are preferable, as everything is within walking distance, but prices tend to be high. The fairly new **Courtyard Portsmouth** (ⓒ 603/436-2121), at 1000 Market St., is big and modern, with business amenities and comfortable beds; it's right off I-95 about 2 or 3 minutes' drive from downtown. But the service here is highly variable; hopefully that will improve. It books up fast on summer weekends or when conventions come to town, so specify and confirm your room type in advance. Since 2006, there's also been a brand new **Hilton Garden Inn** (ⓒ 603/431-1499) in a very central downtown location, with a nice indoor pool. It's a little pricier than the Sheraton (see below).

In addition to the options below, also see the **Portsmouth Harbor Inn and Spa,** in chapter 14; it's located right across the river in Kittery, a quick walk from downtown.

Bow Street Inn Bed and Breakfast　This is an adequate destination for travelers who are willing to accept so-so accommodations in order to save money or get a central location. The former brewery was made over in the 1980s in a bit of inspired recycling; condos occupy the top floor, the Seacoast Repertory Theatre occupies the ground floor, and the middle floor makes up this inn, a 10-room property in the center of the historic district. The rooms, off a sterile hallway, are frankly quite small and unexceptional except for nos. 6 and 7, which provide some views of the harbor; a premium is charged for those rooms. Parking is free in a church lot across the street.

121 Bow St., Portsmouth, NH 03801. ⓒ 603/431-7760. Fax 603/433-1680. www.bowstreetinn.com. 10 units. Peak May–Oct $145–$180 double; rest of the year $99–$160 double. Rates include continental breakfast. 2-night minimum stay on some holidays. AE, DISC, MC, V. *In room:* A/C, TV, dataport, hair dryer.

Inn at Strawbery Banke ⭐ *Finds*　This historic little inn is tucked away in an 1814 home on Court Street, an ideal base for exploring Portsmouth: Strawbery Banke is just a block away, and Market Square (the center of the city's cafe action) is just 2 blocks away. The friendly innkeepers have done a nice job of taking a cozy antique home and making it comfortable for guests. Rooms are tiny and simply furnished, yet brightened up by stenciling, pencil-poster beds, wooden shutters, and their beautifully preserved pine floors; one has a bathroom down the hall. Two sitting rooms are stocked with TVs, phones (there are none in the rooms), and lots and lots of books; you take full breakfast in a dining room each morning.

314 Court St., Portsmouth, NH 03801. ⓒ 800/428-3933 or 603/436-7242. www.innatstrawberybanke.com. 7 units, 1 with detached bathroom. Mar–Sept $145–$150 double; Nov–Feb $100–$115 double. Rates include full breakfast. 2-night minimum stay Sat–Sun in Aug and Oct. AE, DISC, MC, V. Children 10 and older welcome. *In room:* A/C, no phone.

Martin Hill Inn Bed & Breakfast ⭐⭐　This B&B in a residential neighborhood is just a short walk from downtown. The inn consists of two period buildings: a main house (built around 1815) and a second guesthouse built 35 years later. All rooms have queen-size beds, writing tables, and sofas or sitting areas, and are variously appointed with distinguished wallpapers, porcelains, antiques, love seats, four-poster or brass beds, and the like. The relaxing, expansive Greenhouse Room is basically a suite with its own sitting room and wicked-furnished sun porch. More good stuff: a stone path from the inn leads to a small, beautiful water garden, and the included full breakfast is a highlight. It might consist of johnnycakes (a delicious New England specialty of cornmeal pancakes), "goldenrod" eggs, quiche, nutty waffles, or cooked fruit. When checking out, remember there's an automatic $3 charge for housekeepers' tips.

404 Islington St., Portsmouth, NH 03801. © **603/436-2287.** 7 units. May–Oct $130–$210 double; rest of the year $115–$160 double. Holiday rates higher. Off-season discounts available. 2-night minimum stay summer and holiday weekends. Rates include full breakfast. MC, V. No children under 16. *In room:* A/C.

Sheraton Harborside Portsmouth 🏵🏵

This five-story, in-town brick hotel is nicely located on the way into town—the attractions of downtown Portsmouth are virtually at your doorstep (Strawbery Banke is about a 10-min. walk, and waterfront bars are a block or two away). With plenty of parking both underground and across the street, a stay here makes for a relatively stress-free visit. The modern building was inspired by the low brick buildings of the city, and it wraps around a circular courtyard. It's a well-maintained and -managed property popular with business travelers as well as with leisure travelers looking for the amenities of a larger hotel. (Decor, however, is a bit bland). Some rooms and suites have views of the working harbor.

250 Market St., Portsmouth, NH 03801. © **888/627-7138** or 603/431-2300. Fax 603/431-7805. www.sheraton portsmouth.com. 200 units. $130–$310 double and suite; off-season discounts available. AE, DISC, MC, V. **Amenities:** Restaurant; fitness center; spa; business center; limited room service; executive rooms. *In room:* A/C, TV, dataport, minibar, coffeemaker, hair dryer, iron.

Sise Inn 🏵

A modern, elegant hotel in the guise of a country inn, this solid Queen Anne–style home was built for a prominent merchant in 1881; the hotel addition was constructed in the 1980s, amid other renovations. The effect is happily harmonious, with antique stained glass and copious oak trim meshing well with the more contemporary elements. An elevator serves the three floors; modern carpeting is throughout, but many rooms have antique armoires, updated Victorian styling, and whirlpool or soaking tubs. I like no. 302, a bi-level, two-bedroom suite with a claw-footed tub; no. 406, a suite with soaking tub and private sitting room; no. 120, with its private patio; and no. 216 (in the carriage house), with a working sauna, a two-person whirlpool, and lovely natural light. This is a popular hotel for business travelers (partly thanks to inn-wide Wi-Fi access).

40 Court St. (at Middle St.), Portsmouth, NH 03801. © **877/747-3466** or 603/433-0200. Fax 603/433-1200. www. siseinn.com. 34 units. $120–$280 double and suite. Rates include continental breakfast. AE, DISC, MC, V. **Amenities:** Laundry service. *In room:* A/C, TV, iron/ironing board, hair dryer, Jacuzzi (some units).

Three Chimneys Inn 🏵🏵

About 20 minutes northwest of Portsmouth at the edge of the university town of Durham, this is a wonderful retreat. The main section of the inn dates to 1649, but later additions and a full-scale renovation in 1997 have given it more of a regal Georgian feel now. All of the units are above average in size, and have been lushly decorated with four-poster or canopied beds, mahogany armoires, and Belgian carpets. Most rooms sport either gas or Duraflame log fireplaces. One of my favorites is the William Randolph Hearst Room, with photos of starlets on the walls and a massive bed that's a replica of one at San Simeon. Five rooms on the ground-floor level beneath the restored barn have private entrances, Jacuzzis, and gas fireplaces; these tend to be a bit more cavelike than the other units, but they're luxurious and romantic. This is a popular place for weddings on summer weekends, and it's always booked up long in advance of University of New Hampshire events such as graduation, football games, and homecoming weekend. Be sure to reserve well ahead at those times.

17 Newmarket Rd., Durham, NH 03824. ℂ **888/399-9777** or 603/868-7800. Fax 603/868-2964. www.threechimneys inn.com. 23 units. $139–$239 double. MAP rates available. Rates include full breakfast. 2-night minimum stay on Sat–Sun in Sept–Oct. AE, DISC, MC, V. Children 6 and older welcome. **Amenities:** 2 restaurants; bar. *In room:* A/C, TV, coffeemaker.

Wentworth by the Sea ★★★

The reopening of this historic resort in 2003 was a major event; it's now one of the top resorts in New England. The photogenic grand hotel, which opened on New Castle Island in 1874 but later shut down, was refurbished by the owners of the Samoset Resort in Rockland, Maine (p. 633) and is operated jointly with Marriott in professional, luxurious fashion. As befits an old hotel, rooms vary in size, but most are spacious with good views of ocean or harbor. Particularly interesting are the suites occupying the three turrets. Some rooms have gas-powered fireplaces or private balconies; all have luxury bath amenities, new bathroom fixtures, and beautiful detailing and furnishings. Families will appreciate that many contain two queen beds. A set of luxury suites beside the marina are truly outstanding; they have water views, modern kitchens, and marble bathrooms with Jacuzzis. A full-service spa offers a range of treatments and body wraps.

Wentworth Rd. (P.O. Box 860), New Castle NH 03854. ℂ **866/240-6313** or 603/422-7322. Fax 603/422-7329. www. wentworth.com. 161 units. $229–$459 double and suite; off-season discounts and packages available. AE, DISC, MC, V. **Amenities:** 2 restaurants; bar; indoor pool; outdoor pool; spa; golf course privileges. *In room:* A/C, TV, kitchenette (some units), coffeemaker, hair dryer, fireplace (some units), Jacuzzi (some units).

WHERE TO DINE

For two more dining options beyond those listed below, visit the **Wentworth by the Sea** resort (see "Where to Stay," above) on Rte. 1B a few miles south of the city. There are two choices: a main dining room and a casual bar and grill. The **dining room** fare is top-rate, served beneath a remarkable (and original) frescoed dome; entrees might include grilled swordfish, lobster with filet mignon, seared yellowfin tuna, a clambake, a lobster pie, or something more continental. There is a moderate dress code: Men are asked to wear a collared shirt. The **Latitudes** grill has a simpler menu, but offers something the main inn can't—an outdoor patio of tables with lovely views overlooking the water. It's softly lit at night.

Downtown Portsmouth now also has a branch of the terrific **Flatbread Company** (ℂ **603/436-7888**) pizzeria, at 138 Congress St. It's *the* place to eat a terrific organic-wheat crust pizza.

Black Trumpet Bistro ★★ BISTRO/WINE BAR

When the owners of the popular Lindbergh's Crossing—formerly in this space—decided to pack up and sell in early 2007, their own executive chef, Evan Mallett, jumped at the chance to buy it. He cooks exotically spiced comfort food in an intimate, two-story building within a former warehouse. The menu is subtly influenced by Spain and Latin America: You partake of starters that might include quahog chowder, tomato-y octopus with chorizo, bacalao salad, local mussels steamed in porter, or a Moroccan-spiced beetroot soup. Among the entrees, the Black Trumpet burger is fun, incorporating foraged mushrooms and Gouda cheese, as is an ostrich filet served with pine nuts in a Concord grape demiglace. The wine list is strong. If you don't have reservations and they're full, sit in the bar.

29 Ceres St. ℂ 603/431-0887. www.blacktrumpetbistro.com. Reservations recommended. Main courses $16–$26. AE, DC, MC, V. Sun–Thurs 5:30–9:30pm; Fri–Sat 5:30–10pm.

Tips Portsmouth: Coffee Capital

Portsmouth has perhaps the best cafe scene in all of northern New England. I'd even rate it comparable to Cambridge's or Boston's, slightly better than Portland's, and way better than Burlington's. There are at least 10 places in the compact downtown alone where you can get a very good cup of coffee and better-than-average baked goods, and new coffeehouses open all the time. There's a Starbucks (of course), but my favorite spots to enjoy a coffee drink or pot of tea with a book are, in this order: **Breaking New Grounds** (*©* **603/436-9555**), 14 Market Sq., with outstanding espresso shakes, good tables for chatting out on the square, and late hours; **Caffe Kilim** (*©* **603/436-7330**), at 79 Daniel St., across from the post office, a more bohemian choice; and **Me and Ollie's** (*©* **603/436-7777**), at 10 Pleasant St., well-known locally for its good bread, sandwiches, and homemade granola.

If you want a bit more of a bite to go with your coffee, Portsmouth's got that covered, too. Two outstanding places leap to mind. The tie-dyed **Friendly Toast** (*©* **603/430-2154**), at 121 Congress St., serves a variety of eggs and other breakfast dishes all day long, plus heartier items such as burgers. And the funky **Ceres Bakery** (*©* **603/436-6518**), at 51 Penhallow St. (a side street off the main square), has a handful of tiny interior tables; grab a sandwich, cookie, or slice of cake to go, and walk to the waterfront rose gardens nearby.

Blue Mermaid Island Grill ★★ *Finds* GLOBAL/ECLECTIC   The Blue Mermaid is a Portsmouth favorite for its good food, good value, and refusal to take itself too seriously. A short stroll from Market Square, in a historic area called the Hill, it's not pretentious—locals congregate here, Tom Waits tunes play in the background, and the service is casual but professional. The menu is adventurous in a low-key, global way, leaning ever so slightly toward Mexico and the Caribbean—you might try a tortilla pizza or a salmon club sandwich for lunch, or a dinner of short ribs in guava-soy sauce, served with cornbread; Bimini-style grilled chicken with bananas and walnuts in bourbon sauce, sided with a sweet potato hash; or beef medallions spiced up with horseradish cream and chipotle peppers. For fun, make a dinner out of small-plate offerings like wontons, Jamaican beef patties, and the seafood-coconut wrap. They also cook seafood on a wood-fired grill, burgers, pasta, and pizzas. Libations include local draft brews plus a full menu of coolers, mojitos, Goombay smashes, and margaritas.

409 The Hill (at Hanover and High sts., facing the municipal parking garage). *©* 603/427-2583. www.bluemermaid. com. Reservations recommended for parties of 6 or more. Main courses $6–$12 at lunch; $16–$22 at dinner. AE, DISC, MC, V. Mon–Thurs 11:30am–9pm; Fri–Sat 11:30am–10pm; Sun 10am–9pm.

Dolphin Striker ★ NEW ENGLAND   Housed in a historic brick warehouse in Portsmouth's most charming area, the Dolphin Striker serves traditional New England seafood dishes—some of them dressed up in new ways such as a mushroom-crusted filet of cod or a piece of salmon "lacquered" in tomato-y balsamic vinaigrette and then grilled. But the redoubtable Maine lobster pot pie hasn't changed since, well, probably 1700. Seafood loathers can find refuge in a duet of organic beef (hanger steak and wine-braised ribs), a rack of lamb when it's on the menu, or the grilled duck breast with risotto and fruity sauce. The main dining room here has a rustic, public-house atmosphere with wide pine-board floors and wooden furniture; downstairs is a comfortable pub known as the Spring Hill Tavern, with quite good acoustic acts. After 9pm, the Striker shelves the heavy fare and switches over to a lighter "tavern" menu.

15 Bow St. ℂ 603/431-5222. www.dolphinstriker.com. Reservations recommended. Main courses $21–$27 at dinner. AE, DC, DISC, MC, V. Daily 5–11pm.

The Dunaway 🐟🐟🐟 NEW AMERICAN/FRENCH   Right across the road from lovely little Prescott Park, restaurateur Jay McSharry's latest project is a very welcome addition to the Strawbery Banke complex. Dunaway chef Ben Hasty grew up on a farm in southern Maine and cooked at the prestigious The French Laundry in San Francisco and Arrows in Ogunquit before joining the Dunaway's opening team in 2005. His menu draws both on local ingredients (lobster, the catch of the day, Maine-raised organic beef) and techniques from faraway lands—chiefly, but not only, France. Witness entrees of sea bass, lemony stuffed sole, pan-roasted duck breasts with duck bacon and polenta, and rib eyes with Calvados sauce. Many of the herbs, fruits, and vegetables are cultivated and plucked right from Strawbery Banke's gardens. But the real capping touch here is the elegant interior decor, which preserves the period feel of the building (lots of exposed wood and candles) yet also feels like a romantic night out.

66 Marcy St. (across from Prescott Park). ℂ 603/373-6112. www.dunawayrestaurant.com. Reservations recommended. Main courses $9–$18 at lunch; $26–$36 at dinner. AE, DC, DISC, MC, V. Mon–Thurs 5:30–9:30pm; Fri–Sat 5–10pm; Sun 5–9pm. Also, lunch daily 11:30am–2pm mid-Apr to Sept.

Jumpin' Jay's Fish Café 🐟🐟 SEAFOOD   One of Portsmouth's best eateries, Jay's is a welcome destination for those who like seafood more sophisticated than whatever's pulled out of the deep-fryer. A sleek and spare dining room dotted with splashes of color, it has an open kitchen and a polished-steel bar; people seem to have fun eating here, one reason Jay's attracts a younger, more culinary-attuned clientele than most spots in town. The fresh catch of the day is posted on blackboards; you pick your fish, then pair it with card of sauces such as a spicy orange-sesame glaze, a lobster velouté, a citrusy mustard sauce, or simple olive oil and herbs. Pasta dishes are also an option—add scallops, mussels, or chicken as you like. The food is great, and the attention to detail by the kitchen and waitstaff is admirable.

150 Congress St. ℂ 603/766-3474. www.jumpinjays.com. Reservations recommended. Dinner main courses $19–$25. AE, DISC, MC, V. Mon–Thurs 5:30–9:30pm (till 9pm in winter); Fri–Sat 5–10pm; Sun 5–9pm.

Pesce Blue 🐟🐟🐟 SEAFOOD/ITALIAN   Another upscale seafood eatery in downtown Portsmouth? Yes, and again it's a smashing success, thanks to a youthful drive that starts with ownership and trickles on down. Chef James Walter serves seafood and other dishes with a strong Italian accent. Lunch might be a piece of grilled flatbread topped with smoked salmon; a "salad" of mussels, San Marzano tomatoes, marinated olives, and capers; or a cut of pan-roasted haddock with baccala-whipped potatoes and ramps. Plenty of antipasti are available as well. Dinner entrees could include a crispy piece of sockeye salmon, lasagna with house lamb sausage, oil-poached halibut, a mixed seafood grill, a wild boar steak, a small plate of tuna tartare with pickled apples and capers (the small plates are great), or a whole salt-baked branzino. The house desserts include mascarpone-ricotta cheesecake, fennel-flavored panna cotta, molten chocolate cake, gelati, and a lovely olive oil-orange cake topped with vanilla cream.

106 Congress St. ℂ 603/430-7766. www.pesceblue.com. Main courses $9–$21 at lunch; $14–$30 at dinner. AE, DISC, MC, V. Mon–Tues 5–9pm; Wed–Sun 11:45am–2pm and 5–9pm.

Portsmouth Brewery ☞ ECLECTIC/PUB FARE   In the heart of the historic district (look for the tipping tankard suspended over the sidewalk), New Hampshire's first brewpub opened in 1991 and still draws a loyal clientele with its superb beers. The tin-ceiling, brick-wall dining room is open, airy, echoey, and redolent of hops. Brews are made in 200-gallon batches and include specialties such as Old Brown Dog ale and a delightfully creamy Black Cat Stout. An eclectic menu complements these robust beverages. It includes the expected pizzas, burgers, and sandwiches (including a "steak bomb"), but also offers a changing rotating of some pretty adventurous selections such as tamarind grilled shrimp, crispy green tomatoes with Parmesan cheese, artichoke-stuffed ravioli, and cioppino. The food here is getting better every year; the beer is already excellent.

56 Market St. ⓒ 603/431-1115. www.portsmouthbrewery.com. Reservations accepted for parties of 10 or more. Main courses $7–$22. AE, DC, DISC, MC, V. Daily 11:30am–12:30am.

The Press Room TAVERN FARE   Locals flock here more for convivial atmosphere and easy-on-the-budget prices than for creative cuisine. An in-town favorite since 1976, The Press Room boasts that it was the first place in the area to serve Guinness beer, so it's appropriate that the place has a rustic, vaguely Gaelic charm. On cool days, a fire burns in the woodstove, and drinkers throw darts in at atmosphere of brick walls, pine floors, and heavy wooden beams. Choose from a bar menu of inexpensive selections such as burgers, fish and chips, and stir-fries. The jazz here is justifiably popular among locals (See "Portsmouth After Dark," below).

77 Daniel St. ⓒ 603/431-5186. Reservations not accepted. Sandwiches $4–$7; main courses $8–$13. AE, DISC, MC, V. Sun–Thurs 5–11pm; Fri–Sat 11:30am–11pm.

Victory 96 State Street ☞☞ CONTINENTAL   Chef/owner Duncan Boyd, who opened this dining room and gentlemen's bar in a brick corner space just off lovely Prescott Park, trained under legendary Boston grillman Jasper White and star chef Todd English. He learned very, very well: The food here emphasizes the New England harvest of clams, corn, cod, pumpkin, lobster, and so forth, and successfully carries a summery whiff of salty Cape Cod air throughout. The menus change seasonally. Starters run to such things as foie gras with brandied peaches and Pemaquid oysters on the half-shell; main courses have included leg of lamb, roasted venison, or roasted duck with a beach plum sauce. You might finish with Maine wild blueberry tarts, chocolate soufflé cake, or plates of artisan cheese. The **bar area** ☞ is a special treat, with plenty of luxurious couches and chairs and a separate menu of small plates and big burgers.

96 State St. ⓒ 603/766-0960. www.96statestreet.com. Reservations recommended. Entrees $19–$27. AE, MC, V. Tues–Sun 5:30–9pm (lounge area from 5pm).

PORTSMOUTH AFTER DARK
PERFORMING ARTS
The Music Hall ☞☞   This historic theater dates back to 1878 and was restored to its former glory by a local arts group. A variety of shows are staged here, from film festivals and comedy revues to *The Nutcracker* and concerts by visiting symphonies and pop artists (David Crosby and Graham Nash played here in 2007). Call or check the website for a current calendar. 28 Chestnut St. ⓒ 603/436-2400. www.themusichall.org.

BARS & CLUBS
Muddy River Smokehouse   Blues are the thing in Muddy River's upstairs eating room and downstairs lounge. Saturday and Sunday offer reggae and blues, sometimes

played by well-known performers. Cover charges vary; admission is free for some shows if you arrive early. I recommend the music here more than the barbecue, which is only middling. 21 Congress St. © 603/430-9582. www.muddyriver.com.

The Press Room ⍟   A popular local bar and restaurant (see "Where to Dine," above), the Press Room also offers casual entertainment almost every night, either upstairs or down. It's best known locally for its live jazz; the club brings in quality performers from Boston and beyond. You might also hear beat poetry or blues. 77 Daniel St. © 603/431-5186.

Spring Hill Tavern   Quality acoustic noodling, live jazz, classical guitar, and low-key rock is offered most evenings of the week here. It's the pub located right beneath the popular Dolphin Striker seafood restaurant (see "Where to Dine," above). 15 Bow St. © 603/431-5222.

2 The Monadnock Region & the Connecticut River Valley ⍟

Peterborough: 71 miles NW of Boston; 38 miles SW of Manchester, NH

New Hampshire's southwestern corner is a pastoral region of rolling hills, small villages, rustic farmsteads, and winding back roads. What the area lacks in major attractions, it makes up for in peacefulness and bucolic charm—plus one good-sized mountain. The inns here tend to be more basic and less luxurious than those across the river in southern Vermont, but their prices will appeal to budget travelers looking for a taste of history with their bed and breakfast. It's becoming a popular area for Bostonians seeking a respite from city life, and in fall thousands of them stream steadily north to this region for the excellent fall foliage, some of the best in New England.

For many visitors, the main activities here are woodland strolls, afternoons reading on the porch, and idle drives to nowhere. In fact, the best strategy for exploring this area may be to put away the map and turn randomly down side roads to see where they lead. Wherever you go, odds are good that you'll find a Currier & Ives tableau.

PETERBOROUGH ⍟⍟

Peterborough, settled in 1749, is no quaint colonial town gathered primly around a village green. Instead, it has the feel of a once-prosperous commercial center, where the hum of industry provided stability. That hum is a lot quieter now, but Peterborough hasn't been left behind the times—or, if it has, it is making book on that fact. This is still a beautiful town, with diverse architecture, set in a valley at the confluence of the Contoocook and Nubanusit rivers. Improbably, the town and its surroundings have even carved out a fresh niche for themselves as centers of publishing and technology.

ESSENTIALS

GETTING THERE   Peterborough is situated between Keene and Nashua on cross-state Route 101. A decent map is essential for exploring the many fine little villages and towns nearby on winding state and county roads.

VISITOR INFORMATION   The **Greater Peterborough Chamber of Commerce,** P.O. Box 401, Peterborough, NH 03458 (© **603/924-7234;** www.peterborough chamber.com), provides advice either over the phone or at a year-round information center at 10 Wilton Rd. (at the intersection of Route 101 and Route 202). The center is open Monday to Friday year-round, and Saturday from mid-June through the end of October.

OUTDOOR PURSUITS

Mount Monadnock rises impressively above the gentler hills of southern New Hampshire. Though only 3,165 feet high (about half the height of Mount Washington to the north), it has a solitary grandeur that has attracted hikers for more than 2 centuries. The knobby peak was climbed by New England literary luminaries such as Ralph Waldo Emerson and Henry David Thoreau. Today, more than 100,000 hikers follow their lead and head for the summit each year. It's not a place for solitary walks.

Some 40 miles of trails lace the patchwork of public and private lands on the slopes of the mountain. The most popular (and best-marked) trails leave from near the entrance to **Monadnock State Park** 𝖠𝖠 (ⓒ **603/532-8862**), about 4 miles northwest of Jaffrey Center off Rte. 124. (Head west on Rte. 124; after 2 miles, follow the park signs to the north.) A round-trip hike on the most direct routes will take someone in decent shape about 3 to 4 hours. The park is open year-round (a ranger is on duty until 9pm in summer). Admission to the park costs $3 for adults and children 12 and older, $1 for children ages 6 to 11, free for children age 5 and under and senior residents of New Hampshire. No pets are allowed in this park. There's also camping at 28 sites in a small camp area, 10 available by reservation only, for $23 per night.

WHERE TO STAY

Benjamin Prescott Inn 𝖠   Col. Benjamin Prescott fought at the Battle of Bunker Hill before retiring to Jaffrey in 1775. This three-story home built by his sons dates to 1853, a handsome yellow Greek Revival farmhouse along an (often busy) road about 2 miles east of Jaffrey's town center. Throughout this pleasant inn, you'll find a strong sense of history and a connection to the past. All guest rooms have ceiling fans and phone jacks (phones provided on request), and two of the suites have air-conditioning. Best rooms in the house? Maybe cranberry-hued Col. Prescott's Room, bright and airy and furnished with two comfortable armchairs and a writing desk. Susannah's Suite has a brass bed and a sitting room. Guests can wander the farmlands beyond the inn or set off to hike Mount Monadnock, just a short drive down the road.

433 Turnpike Rd. (Rte. 124), Jaffrey, NH 03452. ⓒ **888/950-6637** or 603/532-6637. Fax 603/532-1142. www. benjaminprescottinn.com. 10 units. $85–$175 double. Rates include full breakfast. 2-night minimum some holidays and peak-season weekends. AE, MC, V. In room: A/C (2 units), no phone.

Birchwood Inn 𝑉𝑎𝑙𝑢𝑒   This quiet retreat offers good rooms at good prices, plus a thoroughly British experience as a bonus. Thoreau visited the inn on one of his many rambles through New England; neither the town nor the inn seems to have changed much since then. A handsome, historic brick farmhouse with a white-clapboard ell, it's in the middle of the country crossroads town of Temple, near the town Grange and a park with three war memorials (including one to the heroes of 1776). It's also an easy stroll to a historic cemetery with headstones dating back to the 18th century. The inn is decorated in a pleasantly informal country style; all seven rooms are named for an important city in England, and each has a different theme (musical instruments, train memorabilia, country store, and so on) bordering on kitschy without overdoing it. Rooms have small, non-cable TVs; one has two twin beds, and two of them share a bathroom. The on-site tavern opens 5 nights a week and serves pub food and beer.

340 Rte. 45, P.O. Box 23, Temple, NH 03084. ⓒ **603/878-3285**. 7 units, 2 with shared bathroom. $75–$109 double. Rates include full breakfast. 2-night minimum stay during foliage season. No credit cards. Children older than 10 welcome. Drive 1½ miles south on Rte. 101. **Amenities:** Restaurant; pub; game room. In room: TV, no phone.

Hancock Inn ☆☆   The austere and simple Hancock Inn, built in 1789, claims to be New Hampshire's oldest. (But the Birchwood, above, makes a similar claim.) Like the Birchwood, it's on the main street of a small town that doesn't appear to have changed much since the 18th century. You'll find classic Americana inside, from creaky floors and braided oval rugs to guest rooms appointed in understated Colonial decor. The Rufus Porter Room has an evocative full-length wall mural from the inn's early days, plus two fireplaces. The Ballroom is also intriguing: It has a high, vaulted ceiling (it really used to be the ballroom) and a Jacuzzi. The Bell Tower Room comes furnished with a cannonball king-size bed, gas fireplace, and another Jacuzzi; it overlooks the garden. And the Moses Eaton Room helpfully reproduces original designs of Eaton, a famed stencil artist who lived in the town for a time. This inn has all the historical charm of similar inns in the area, yet a slightly more upscale sensibility.

33 Main St., Hancock, NH 03443. © **800/525-1789** or 603/525-3318. www.hancockinn.com. 14 units. $125–$295 double. Rates include breakfast. AE, DC, DISC, MC, V. Pets allowed in 1 unit. Children 12 and older welcome. **Amenities:** Restaurant. *In room:* A/C, TV, hair dryer, fireplace (some units), Jacuzzi (some units).

The Inn at Jaffrey Center ☆   In the middle of one of New Hampshire's most gracious villages, this lovely, architecturally eclectic inn was built back around 1830. After years of turnover and decline, the inn got a much-needed makeover in 2000, when its rooms were updated in traditional New England style, some with four-poster or canopy beds. Rooms that formerly shared a bathroom all got their own, and fixtures such as old claw-footed tubs (in some rooms) were refurbished and reinstalled. Some rooms have TVs; all have goose-down comforters. The lawns are attractive, the local foliage is great, and downtown's churches and lanes are nearby.

379 Main St. (P.O. Box 484), Jaffrey Center, NH 03452. © **877/510-7019** or 603/532-7800. Fax 603/532-7000. www.theinnatjaffreycenter.com. 11 units. June–Oct $110–$160 double; Nov–May $75–$110 double. Rates include continental breakfast. Minimum stays required during foliage and holiday weekends. MC, V. **Amenities:** Restaurant; pub. *In room:* No phone.

WHERE TO DINE

Acqua Bistro ☆☆ MEDITERRANEAN/BISTRO   This is Peterborough's best choice for a well-crafted meal. Hidden off Peterborough's main thoroughfares, near Twelve Pine and the Sharon Arts Center, Acqua Bistro is a modern, agreeable spot overlooking a little steam. It offers some Mediterranean twists on the usual continental fare. Entrees may include the likes of venison chops, braised lamb shanks, ginger-crusted salmon, bison steaks, and an onion cassoulet. There's always something for them on the menu for vegetarians and vegans, too. Creative, alternative-topping pizzas (chicken sausage, shrimp with wasabi cream) are baked in a stone oven nightly as well, and Sunday mornings feature a stylish bistro brunch.

9 School St., Peterborough. © **603/924-9905**. Reservations accepted for parties of 5 or more. Main courses $12–$28. MC, V. Tues–Sat 4–10pm; Sun 11am–10pm.

Peterborough Diner ☆ *Finds* *Kids* DINER   This classic throwback to the 1940s is hidden on a side street, but it's worth locating. Behind that faded yellow-green exterior is a cozy diner of wood, aluminum, tile, and ceiling fans, along with a mellow jukebox. The meals are just as you'd expect: filling, cheap, and basic. Look for good hot-oven grinders (served with fries), plates of hot turkey with cranberry sauce, deep-fried fish, and veal parmigiana. (Though blasphemous to diner aficionados, chicken cordon bleu and wraps are also on the menu.) Of course they have milkshakes and banana splits, too. Really hungry? Come early and order the "belly buster" (about $12). You get three of everything: three eggs, slices of bacon, slices of toast, sausage patties, pancakes, and slices of French toast. Plus some home fries. Knock yourself out.

10 Depot St., Peterborough. © 603/924-6202. Breakfast items $2–$6; lunch and dinner $4–$8. AE, DISC, MC, V. Daily 6am–9pm.

Twelve Pine ⚘ UPSCALE DELI   This inviting deli and market, in an airy former railroad building behind Peterborough's main street, is a great spot to nosh and linger; you select a pre-made meal (say, chicken burritos or one of the homemade soups of the day) from a deli counter, and it's popped in a microwave if need be. You bring it to a table. You enjoy it. Easy, just as lunch should be. Sandwiches are made with homemade bread and heaping fillings; excellent cheeses are available by the pound, and fresh juices round out the meal. It's a relaxed place offering good value.

11 School St. (in Depot Sq.), Peterborough. © 603/924-6140 or 877/412-7463. www.twelvepine.com. Sandwiches around $6; other items priced by the pound. MC, V. Mon–Fri 8am–7pm; Sat 9am–5pm; Sun 9am–4pm.

CORNISH ⚘

Artists flocked to the bucolic Connecticut River valley region north of Claremont in the late 19th century; the gentle beauty of the Cornish area, still evident today, makes it clear why. The first artists to arrive were painters and sculptors, who showed up in the late 1880s and early 1890s, building modest homes in these hills. They were followed by politicians and then affluent city folk, who eventually established a summer colony. Among those who populated the hills that look across the river toward Mount Ascutney were sculptor Daniel Chester French, painter Maxfield Parrish, and *New Republic* editor Herbert Crowley. Visitors included Ethel Barrymore and presidents Woodrow Wilson and Theodore Roosevelt.

ESSENTIALS

GETTING THERE   Don't bother looking for a main street. Cornish is a few scattered villages and crossroads with names like Cornish Flat, Cornish Mills, South Cornish, and (come on, people) Cornish City. The best route is north up Route 12A from Claremont. Route 120 passes through inland parts of Cornish en route to Hanover.

VISITOR INFORMATION   The **Greater Claremont Chamber of Commerce** (© **603/543-1296;** www.claremontnhchamber.org), dispenses travel information from the Moody Building on Tremont Square. Cornish's town website, **www.cornishnh.net**, provides additional historical information.

EXPLORING THE CORNISH AREA

The region's premier monument to the former arts colony is the **Saint-Gaudens National Historic Site** ⚘⚘ (© **603/675-2175;** www.nps.gov/saga), off Route 12A. The sculptor Augustus Saint-Gaudens first arrived in this valley in 1885, shortly after receiving an important commission to create a statue of Abraham Lincoln. His friend Charles Beaman, a Manhattan lawyer who owned several homes and much land in the Cornish area, assured him that he could find a plenty of "Lincoln-shaped men" in the area. Saint-Gaudens came, found them, and stayed here more or less for the rest of his life.

His hillside home and studio, which he called Aspet, after the village in Ireland where he was raised, are superb places to learn more about this extraordinary artist. A brief tour of the house, which is kept mostly as it was when Saint-Gaudens lived here, provides a brief introduction to the man. Visitors then learn about Saint-Gaudens the artist at several outbuildings and on the grounds, where many replicas of his most famous statues are on display.

The 150-acre grounds are laced by short nature trails where you can explore the hilly woodlands, passing along streams and a millpond. The grounds are open year-round; the historic site's buildings are open for touring daily from late May through the end of October, 9am to 4:30pm. Admission is $5 for adults, free for children under 17. There's no charge to visit the grounds in the off-season.

Covered-bridge aficionados should seek out the **Cornish-Windsor Covered Bridge** (★), which is the nation's longest covered bridge. Spanning the Connecticut River between Vermont and New Hampshire, this bridge has an long, interesting lineage. A toll bridge was first built in 1796 to replace a ferry; the current bridge was built in 1866, then restored in 1989. When the late afternoon light hits it just right, it makes for a great photograph.

HANOVER ★★

If your idea of the perfect New England experience involves a big green space surrounded by stately brick buildings, be sure to visit Hanover, a thriving university town in the Connecticut River Valley about a half-hour's drive north of Cornish and right across the river from Norwich, Vermont. Settled in 1765, the town was first home to early colonists who were granted a charter by King George III to establish a college here. The school was named for the second Earl of Dartmouth, its first trustee, and ever since it has had a profound impact in shaping this community.

The handsome, oversized village green marks a permeable border between college and town. In summer, the green is an ideal destination for strolling and lounging. The best way to explore Hanover is on foot, so your first job is to park your car, which can be trying during peak seasons (fall foliage and whenever school is in session or when there are events here). Try the municipal lots west of Main Street if you can't find a meter. Once here, the chief attraction is the campus of **Dartmouth College** itself. But downtown also offers fine restaurants, galleries, bookstores, and taverns.

ESSENTIALS

GETTING THERE   Hanover is just north of Lebanon, New Hampshire, via Route 10 or Route 120. From Boston, Concord, or Manchester to the south, take I-93 to I-89 north. From Brattleboro or St. Johnsbury, Vermont, take I-91. From Montpelier or Burlington, Vermont, take I-89 south to I-91 north in White River Junction, head north a few miles, then exit for Norwich and cross the river.

Even for the car-less, Hanover is well-connected. **Dartmouth Coach** (✆ 800/637-0123; www.concordcoachlines.com) buses pull into town from Boston at least a half-dozen times a day, an easy 2½ hour ride costing $40 to $55 round-trip. Furthermore, **Amtrak** (✆ 800/872-7245; www.amtrak.com) trains from New York City pull into White River Junction, Vermont, which isn't far away, once per day.

VISITOR INFORMATION   Dartmouth College alumni and local chamber of commerce volunteers maintain an **information center** on the town green in summer. It's open daily from 10am to 5pm in June and September, daily from 9:30am to 5pm in July and August. In the off-season, head for the **Hanover Area Chamber of Commerce** (✆ 603/643-3115) office, at 47 S. Main Street, across from the post office. It's open Monday through Friday, from 9am to 4:30pm.

SPECIAL EVENTS   In early to mid-February, look for the fantastic and intricate ice sculptures marking the return of the annual **Dartmouth Winter Carnival;** call

---

Tips **Orozco's Hidden Artwork at Dartmouth**

Dartmouth's **Baker Memorial Library**—that tall, church-like building at the back of the green—houses a wonderful hidden treasure downstairs: a set of fresco murals by the Mexican painter José Clemente Orozco, who painted *The Epic of American Civilization* while teaching here between 1932 and 1934. The huge paintings, 24 panels covering 3,200 square feet, wrap around an entire study room almost unnoticed by napping and chatting students. Ask for a fact sheet interpreting the colorful, metaphorical murals at the library's front desk.

Dartmouth College's student affairs office at © **603/646-3399** for more information on this traditionally beer-soaked event.

EXPLORING HANOVER & THE VICINITY

Hanover is a superb town to explore on foot, by bike, or even by canoe. Start by picking up a map of the **Dartmouth campus** ✦✦, available from the college's information center on the green (summer and fall only) or at The Hanover Inn across the street. Free guided tours of the campus also offered in summer, and the expansive, leafy campus is a delight to walk through.

South of the green, next to The Hanover Inn, is the modern **Hopkins Center for the Arts** ✦✦ (© **603/646-2422**); Dartmouth students just call it "The Hop." The center attracts national acts to its 900-seat concert hall, and stages top-notch dance and theatrical performances in its Moore Theater. Wallace Harrison, the architect who later went on to fame for designing Lincoln Center in New York, designed this building. You can find a comprehensive schedule of upcoming events at the Hop at its website, **http://hop.dartmouth.edu**.

Enfield Shaker Museum ✦✦ This is a Shaker museum, not a living community like the one in Canterbury, but it's still worth visiting. A cluster of historic buildings on Lake Mascoma about a 20-minute drive southeast of Hanover, "The Chosen Vale" (as its first inhabitants called this valley) was founded in 1793. By the mid-1800s, the community had swelled to 350 members and 3,000 acres. From that high point, though, its ranks then dwindled, and by 1927 Shakers had abandoned the Chosen Vale and sold the village off, lock, stock, and barrel. Today, much of the property is owned either by the state of New Hampshire or the museum.

Dominating the village is the **Great Stone Dwelling,** an austere but gracious granite five-plus-story structure erected between 1837 and 1841. When constructed, it was the tallest building north of Boston, and it remains the largest dwelling house built in any Shaker community. The Enfield Shakers lived and dined here, as many as 150 of them eating together at once at trestle tables. In 1997, the museum acquired the stone building and in 2005 moved the museum into it. A self-guided walking tour of the surrounding village (check out the Stone Mill Building, too) is free with admission to the museum. Some of the historical feel here is compromised by recent condominium development along the lake's shores, though the scale and design of these structures are (so far) remaining fairly sympathetic to the original village's proportions.

447 Rte. 4A, Enfield. © 603/632-4346. www.shakermuseum.org. Admission $7.50 adults, $6.50 seniors, $5 college students, $3 children 10–17, free for children under 10. Memorial Day to mid-Oct Mon–Sat 10am–5pm, Sun noon–5pm; rest of the year, tours noon–2pm on Wed and Fri–Mon.

Tips Exploring Newport & Lake Sunapee

While visiting the Hanover, Concord, or Cornish areas, don't forget to side-trip over to the Newport–Lake Sunapee region. The commercial center of the area is **Newport** ★★, an old mill town with grit, character, and substantial history in a pretty valley setting. This town produced Sarah Josepha Hale, author of the children's poem "Mary Had a Little Lamb" and creator of the Thanksgiving holiday (President Lincoln was sufficiently impressed by her persistence to make it official). Hale was also among the first American women to serve as editor of a national publication, *Godey's Lady's Book*. She's just one of the famous folks who grew up here.

Today the town's historical attractions include a quilt project documenting Newport's industrial past and the immigrants (including healthy numbers of Finns, Polish, Greeks, and Italians) who pitched in to turn the engines of commerce here; an antique 1815 Hunneman "handtub," a wheeled apparatus built by an apprentice of Paul Revere and once used by firemen to pump water while fighting blazes (it's on display inside the Lake Sunapee Bank, at 9 Main St.); and a wooden **covered bridge** ★, painstakingly built by a local craftsman to replicate the priceless original, which was torched by an arsonist in 1993.

Drop by the town's **Richards Free Library** ★ (© 603/863-3430), at 58 N. Main Street, to get oriented; for my money, it's one of the best small-town libraries in America. (Tantalizing historical tidbit: President Kennedy was invited to accept a writing award at this library on the night of November 22, 1963. He politely declined, due to commitments in Dallas.) Ponder that over a delicious pizza at **Newport Village Pizza** (© 603/863-3400), 7 S. Main St., which makes one of my favorite pies in New England. For more details about town and the area, contact the helpful Newport Chamber of Commerce (© **603/863-1510**). There's a good, volunteer-run **info kiosk** on the town common (that big space green space right in the middle) during the summer months.

Hood Museum of Art ★★   Often overlooked by visitors to Hanover (it's not visible from the street), this modern, open building right beside the Hopkins Center houses one of the oldest college museums in the nation and holds some 65,000 items. Its current incarnation—an austere, modern three-story structure—was built in 1986. The permanent collection includes a superb selection of 19th-century American landscapes; significant holdings of African-American and Native American art and artifacts; and six stone reliefs dating from 900 B.C. Assyria. Special exhibits are frequent and high-quality; in 2005, the Hood hosted a show by the artist Fred Wilson, who arranged hidden items from the museum's collection in thought-provoking, sometimes disturbing ways.

Wheelock St. (From the Hanover green, facing the Hopkins Center, cross Wheelock St. and take the footpath to the left of the Hopkins Center.) © 603/646-2808. http://hoodmuseum.dartmouth.edu. Free admission. Tues and Thurs–Sat 10am–5pm; Wed 10am–9pm; Sun noon–5pm.

Ledyard Canoe Club ★★   An idyllic way to spend a lazy afternoon in Hanover is to drift along the Connecticut River in a canoe, assuming you know how to paddle one

Six miles away, big **Lake Sunapee** ⭐⭐ is said to be one of the purest in the nation; it's much deeper than it looks, which helps. Sunapee is a longtime favorite summer resort of Bostonians, and offers excellent swimming, boating, and fishing. The short, steep mountain across the way—which, together with the beach, forms **Mount Sunapee State Park** (© 603/763-5561)—is a fine place to hike, ski, snowboard, or catch a gondola ride for expansive foliage and lake views. There's a $3 charge ($1 for kids) to enter either the beach or mountain portion of the park; you can rent skis from a hut at the mountain, or at **Bob Skinner's Ski & Sports** (© 603/763-2920) outside the park entrance near the traffic circle. Early August brings an outstanding arts event to the park, the weeklong **Craftsman's Fair** ⭐ (© 603/224-3375)—expect plenty of high-quality, handcrafted art pieces. Two-day admission tickets to the fair cost $10 per adult, $8 per senior or student; children under 12 are admitted free.

The main commercial harbor for the lake, **Sunapee Harbor**, is a few miles away at the junction of Route 103B and Route 11. This is the place to put in your boat, grab an ice-cream cone at sunset, or just sit watching the lakeside cottages light up. You might see a famous face; members of the band Aerosmith and their families own lakefront or island homes in the area, for instance. On the back side of the lake, pretty **New London** ⭐⭐ is an attractive college town with more than its share of fine homes and upscale restaurants. Without ever straying off Main Street, you can settle down for a full meal at the tony **Millstone** (© 603/526-4201); relax over eggs and java or bistro dinners at **Jack's** (© 603/526-8003); or go British pub-style with a shared table of bread, cheeses, sandwiches, pot roast, and beer at **Peter Christian's Tavern** (© 603/526-4042).

safely. Dartmouth's historic boating club is just down the hill from the campus. While much of the club's focus is on competitive racing, it's also a place where travelers can rent a boat for a few hours and explore the tree-lined river. Instruction is also available. Life jackets must be carried at all times, and worn by children and non-swimmers.

Off W. Wheelock St. (turn upstream at the bottom of the hill west of bridge; follow signs to the clubhouse). © 603/643-6709. www.dartmouth.edu/~lcc. Canoe and kayak rentals $10 per hour, $20 per day ($30 on Sat–Sun). Summer Mon–Fri 10am–8pm, Sat–Sun 9am–8pm; spring and fall Mon–Fri noon–6pm, Sat–Sun 10am–6pm. Open whenever river temperature is higher than 50°F (10°C).

WHERE TO STAY

Mid-priced chain hotel and motel properties are clumped together just off the interstate in West Lebanon, about 5 miles south of Hanover. Take exit 20 off I-89 to find most of them.

There are also lodgings in Norwich, Vermont (right across the river from Hanover), and White River Junction, Vermont (a few miles downriver via I-91). See chapter 12 for details on those areas.

The Hanover Inn 🎭🎭 The white-and-brick Hanover Inn is the Upper Valley's best-managed and most up-to-date luxury hotel, perfectly situated for exploring both the Dartmouth campus and the compact downtown. The inn is located directly across Hanover's big central green from the college. Established in 1780, most of the present-day five-story structure was actually added in successive stages—first in 1924, then again in 1939, and finally in 1968. The result somehow manages to keep its architectural balance (more or less), and the inn offers professional service, attractive rooms, fine dining, and subterranean walkways connecting you to both the college's Hood art museum and its Hopkins Center performing arts spaces. Most of the rooms here have canopy or four-poster beds and down comforters; some even overlook the pretty green and the busy street. Dining options here include a fancy dining room (see "Where to Dine," below), a terrace of outdoor tables fronting the green, and a wine bistro.

Wheelock St. (P.O. Box 151), Hanover, NH 03755. ⓒ 800/443-7024 or 603/643-4300. Fax 603/643-4433. www.hanoverinn.com. 92 units. From $259 double; from $309 suite. Off-season discounts available. AE, DISC, MC, V. Valet parking $12 per day. Pets allowed ($15 per night). **Amenities:** 3 restaurants; 2 bars; access to fitness equipment; limited room service; massage; babysitting; dry cleaning. *In room:* A/C, TV, dataport, coffeemaker, hair dryer, iron.

WHERE TO DINE

If you're in a hurry, the **Dirt Cowboy Café,** at 7 S. Main St., is a good choice for coffee and a snack. The beans are roasted right downstairs, then served upstairs in a number of inventive combinations (I like the breve shot) alongside smoothies and good baked items. Sit at a table, twiddle at your laptop, or just eavesdrop on professors and students enjoying their down time.

Another good spot for a quick bite or drink is **Zins** 🎭, an informal wine bistro offering about 30 wines by the glass, concealed off the lobby inside the Hanover Inn (see "Where to Stay," above) on Wheelock St. It's open daily, serving light meals of sandwiches, salads, burgers, and grilled fish with the wine. Helpfully, they also offer a short menu of kids' meals.

Daniel Webster Room 🎭🎭 CONTEMPORARY AMERICAN The main dining room in the Hanover Inn will appeal to anyone looking for fine dining in a formal New England atmosphere. The Colonial Revival room is reminiscent of a 19th-century resort hotel, with big fluted columns, floral carpeting, and regally upholstered chairs. Produce and beef from the college's organic farm and local farmers is used seasonally here; the menu isn't terribly inventive but it gets the job done. Changing entrees at lunch and dinner might include salads, a club sandwich, braised rabbit leg with truffled pappardelle, grilled Shetland salmon with polenta, center-cut sirloin steaks with pan-roasted potatoes, a bowl of soba noodles with tofu or chicken, local bratwurst, or simply boiled scrod. A brand-new dinner menu was unveiled in early 2008.

Hanover Inn, Wheelock St. ⓒ 603/643-4300. Reservations recommended. Main courses $7–$20 at lunch; $20–$30 at dinner. AE, DISC, MC, V. Mon 7–10:30am and 11:30am–1:30pm; Tues–Fri 7–10:30am, 11:30am–1:30pm, and 6–9pm; Sat 7–10:30am and 6–9pm; Sun 11am–1:30pm.

Lou's 🎭 *Value* BAKERY/DINER Lou's has been a Hanover institution since 1947, attracting hungry, hung-over hordes of students for breakfast on the weekends and a steady local clientele of working folk dropping by for eggs or lunch during the week. The look is no-frills New Hampshire, with a black-and-white linoleum checkerboard floor, maple-and-vinyl booths, and a harried but efficient crew of waiters setting the tone. Breakfast is served all day (real maple syrup on your pancakes costs extra—go ahead and splurge), and the sandwiches, served on fresh-baked bread, are huge and good. Locals pop in after the dining room closes in the late afternoon; while the staff preps for the next morning's rush, you can buy baked goods (if any are left) until 5pm.

30 S. Main St. © 603/643-3321. Breakfast items $3–$7; lunch $5–$8. AE, MC, V. Mon–Fri 6am–3pm; Sat–Sun 7am–3pm (opens 8am Sun in winter). Bakery open to 5pm daily.

3 The Lake Winnipesaukee Region ⍟

Meredith is 40 miles N of Concord, 60 miles NW of Portsmouth, and 110 miles N of Boston

Huge Lake Winnipesaukee, carved by glaciers from nearly the dead center of New Hampshire, is *easily* the state's biggest, with a 180-mile shoreline. Yet it's so irregularly shaped, edged with dozens of inlets, coves, and bays, and dotted by more than 250 islands. As a result, when you're actually out on the lake, it doesn't seem very big at all. The lake gives the illusion of being a chain of much smaller lakes and ponds, rather than one massive body of water, which makes it more welcoming than a single monolithic body of water.

The best bases for the lake include towns like Center Harbor, Moultonborough, and Wolfeboro (see below); and Meredith. For more advice on where to set up camp, see the box "Choosing a Home Base on Winnipesaukee," below.

MEREDITH ⍟

The village of Meredith sits at the northwestern facet of the (roughly diamond-shaped) jewel that is Winnipesaukee. There are good views across a nice bay from almost anyplace in town, but Meredith lacks the quaintness and broad selection of activities that many travelers want—a busy road cuts the tidy little downtown right off from the lake's shore, and strip malls have also intruded as well. Still, this town is stocked with life's necessary services (restaurants, gas station, souvenir shops, pizza places, full-sized grocery stores), and it's also home to several desirable inns. Foremost among its qualities is its superb location.

ESSENTIALS

GETTING THERE   Reach **Meredith** by taking I-93 to exit 23. Drive 9 miles east on Route 104 to Route 3, turn left, and continue downhill to the town and the lakefront. **Concord Coach** (© 800/639-3317; www.concordcoachlines.com) provides twice-daily bus service from points south, including to and from Boston; pick it up at the Irving gas station on Main St.

The same buses also stop in **Center Harbor,** which has a new ticket office at the Village Car Wash and Laundromat (in the Dunkin' Donut plaza—hey, this is small-town New Hampshire, remember?).

VISITOR INFORMATION   The **Meredith Area Chamber of Commerce** (© 877/ 279-6121 or 603/279-6121; www.meredithcc.org) maintains an office in the white

---

(*Fun Fact* **What-the-Winnipesaukee?**

How do you say it? All together, now: Win-ah-pa-SOCK-ee. What does it mean? It's a little hazy. Either "Smile of the great spirit," in the tongue of local Abenaki peoples who were living here when colonists arrived, or possibly "Pretty lake in a high spot." (Pretty *big* lake would have been even better.)

house on Route 3 (on the left when driving down the hill from Rte. 104). It's open daily in summer from 9am to 5pm; closed Saturday and Sunday in winter.

EXPLORING THE AREA

Meredith's attractive, though now largely bypassed, Main Street ascends a hill from Route 3 at an elbow in the middle of town. A handful of shops, galleries, and boutiques offer low-key browsing. The creative re-adaptation of an early mill at the **Mill Falls Marketplace** has about 20 shops, including a well-stocked bookstore, pizzeria, ice-cream shop, and art gallery. It's connected to The Inns at Mill Falls (see "Where to Stay," below), at the intersection of Route 3 and Route 25.

An excellent fair-weather trip is an excursion to 112-acre **Stonedam Island** 𝕗𝕗, one of the largest protected islands in the lake. (You need a boat, canoe, or kayak to get there, obviously.) Owned by the Lakes Region Conservation Trust (ⓒ **603/279-3246**), the island has a trail that winds through wetlands and forest. About 2½ miles southeast of downtown Meredith, it's an ideal destination for a picnic.

Rent a canoe or kayak for a half-day, day, or week at **Wild Meadow Canoes & Kayaks** 6 Whittier Hwy, Center Harbor, NH 03226 (ⓒ **800/427-7536** or 603/253-7536; www.wildmeadowcanoes.com), in Center Harbor. The shop, open daily, is less than 5 miles from Meredith, the next town north on Route 25 (the route tracing the bay).

WHERE TO STAY

The Inns at Mill Falls 𝕗𝕗𝕗 This expanding complex is gradually dominating Meredith, but has managed its growth pretty well so far. Accommodations are spread among four buildings, each subtly different, all well-tended and comfortable. The main inn is in a former mill complex and has attractive, simple rooms. Units in the more upscale Chase House all have gas fireplaces; most also have balconies with rockers. The Inn at Bay Point is on 2,000 feet of lakefront, and most rooms have balconies with sensational views. In 2004, the inn unveiled Church Landing, a converted church right on the lakefront (it's connected to the other by a footpath). This annex offers rooms and suites with gas fireplaces, double Jacuzzis, and balconies. A pool and health club were also added to this new section, as well as marina space and a restaurant—one of eight in the inns, ranging from sub sandwiches to more upscale fare.

Rte. 3, Meredith, NH 03253. ⓒ **800/622-6455** or 603/279-7006. www.millfalls.com. 159 units. $109–$429 double and suite. Minimum stay some weekends. AE, DC, DISC, MC, V. **Amenities:** 8 restaurants; bar; indoor pool; fitness center; spa; Jacuzzi; shopping arcade; limited room service; massage; babysitting; laundry service; dry cleaning. In room: A/C, TV, dataport, hair dryer, iron/ironing board, fireplace (some units), Jacuzzi (some units).

Manor on Golden Pond 𝕗𝕗𝕗 This regal stucco-and-shingle mansion, about 9 miles north of Meredith, was built between 1903 and 1907 on a low hill overlooking pretty Squam Lake (the "Golden Pond" of tear-jerking film fame). Inside, it has the feel of an English manor house, with oak paneling and leaded windows; the options to play croquet, horseshoes, or tennis on a clay court add to the summery feel. Most rooms have wood-burning fireplaces, and some have Jacuzzis; some also have knockout views of the hills and water that make you feel a bit like the king of a realm. The best units: Sandwich, Yorkshire, Savoy Court, Buckingham, Stratford, and Dover Cottage, all lavishly appointed. Fourteen landscaped acres of grounds, good for strolling, are studded with pines. The dining room is "dressy casual" (no shorts or jeans) and excellent, and there are a pub and a bistro for guests who left sport coats or heels behind.

Rte. 3, Holderness, NH 03245. ⓒ **800/545-2141** or 603/968-3348. Fax 603/968-2116. www.manorongoldenpond. com. 25 units (fewer in winter). $210–$445 double. Rates include full breakfast and afternoon tea. 2-night minimum

BACKCOUNTRY FEES

The White Mountain National Forest requires anyone using the backcountry—for hiking, mountain biking, picnicking, skiing, or any other activity—to pay a recreation fee. Anyone parking at a trail head must display a backcountry permit on the car dashboard. Those lacking a permit face a fine. Permits are available at ranger stations and many stores in the region. An annual permit costs $20, and a 7-day pass is $5. You can also buy a day pass for $3, but it covers only one site. (If you drive anywhere else in the mountain later in the afternoon and park again, you'll have to pay the $3 again.) You're much better off with the 7-day or annual pass. For information, contact the **Forest Service's White Mountains office** (⊘ 603/528-8721; www.fs.fed.us/r9/white).

RANGER STATIONS & INFORMATION

The Forest Service's **central White Mountains office** is located at 719 N. Main St. in Laconia (⊘ **603/528-8721**), near Lake Winnipesaukee. Your best general source of information while in the mountains, though, is probably at the **Saco Ranger Station,** 33 Kancamagus Hwy., 300 feet west of Route 16, Conway (⊘ **603/447-5448**). Other district offices that might be more convenient to your route include the **Androscoggin Ranger Station,** 300 Glen Rd., in Gorham (⊘ **603/466-2713**); the Pemigewasset Ranger Station's **Plymouth office,** 1175 Route 175 in Holderness near the Plymouth town line (⊘ **603/536-1315**); and the Pemigewasset station's **Bethlehem office,** 660 Trudeau Rd. in Bethlehem (⊘ **603/869-2626**).

The good **Evans Notch Ranger Station** (⊘ **207/824-2134**), which covers the Maine portion of the White Mountains (about 50,000 acres), is also not far off if you're in the easternmost parts of the mountains; it's located in Bethel, Maine, at 18 Mayville Rd., just off Route 2 north of the Bethel downtown.

The National Parks Service also maintains two helpful visitor centers. The **Gateway Visitor Center** ⊙ (⊘ **603/745-3816**) is just off exit 32 of Interstate 93, well-stocked and in a good position en route to many attractions. It's open daily, year-round. Then there's the **Lincoln Woods Visitor Center** (⊘ **603/630-5190**), about 5 miles east of Lincoln right on the Kancamagus Highway. There's **suspension bridge** very near this visitor center, too, accessible via a footpath.

Finally, even more info and advice on recreation in the White Mountains is available at the **AMC's Pinkham Notch Visitor Center** (⊘ **603/466-2721**), on Route 16 between Jackson and Gorham. The center is open daily, year-round, from 6am to 10pm. It has a cafe and a travel store, too.

CAMPING

The White Mountain National Forest maintains two dozen drive-in campsites scattered throughout the region, from small to large. Campsites mostly cost in the $16 to $20 per night range. Reservations are accepted at many of these through the **National Recreation Reservation Service** (⊘ **877/444-6777;** www.recreation.gov). Most campsites are basic (some with pit toilets only), but all are well-maintained. Remember that some require reservations at least 1 week in advance (in other words, no walk-ins) and 2- to 3-night minimum stays on some Saturdays and Sundays.

Of these **national forest campgrounds,** the largest and least personal is **Dolly Copp Campground** (⊘ **603/466-2713**), near the base of Mount Washington. But it has a superior location and great views from the open sites. Along the Kancamagus Highway, I'm partial to the **Covered Bridge Campground** (⊘ **603/447-2166**), 6 miles west of Conway, which is adjacent to an 1858 covered bridge and a short drive

---

stay on holidays and in foliage season. AE, DISC, MC, V. Children 12 and older welcome. **Amenities:** 2 restaurants; pub; outdoor pool; tennis court; spa; watersports equipment rental; limited room service; massage. *In room:* A/C, TV, dataport, fridge (some units), coffeemaker (some units), hair dryer, iron/ironing board.

WHERE TO DINE

Abondante ITALIAN/TRATTORIA   This casual storefront market and deli has good atmosphere—maple floors, copper-topped tables, herbs drying from the joists overhead, and classical music. Both table service and to-go orders are available, with a tasty selection of fresh pastas (the lobster ravioli is very popular) and rustic breads, not to mention imported chocolates. This is a good spot for a casual dinner.

30 Main St., Meredith. ⊘ **603/279-7177.** Main courses $13–$23. AE, DISC, MC, V. Summer daily 5–9pm (until 10pm Fri–Sat); off-season Wed–Sat 5–9pm, Sun 4–8pm.

Hart's Turkey Farm Restaurant *Kids* TURKEY/AMERICAN   Hart's Turkey Farm Restaurant is bad news . . . if you're a turkey. It's Thanksgiving every day here: On a typical busy day, this place dishes up more than a *ton* of America's favorite bird to a loyal clientele of regulars and tourists. Opened in 1954, it hasn't changed much since then. This is a comfortable, New England family restaurant without any fuss, in a big dining space (the most seats in the entire lakes region, claim the proprietors). Service here is afflicted with the same rushed efficiency found in any place that sees lots of bus tours, but it's New Hampshire–friendly enough. There's a cute gift shop, too, where you can find even more turkeys—and they sell carryout pies in the lobby.

Junction of routes 3 and 104, Meredith. ⊘ **603/279-6212.** www.hartsturkeyfarm.com. Main courses $10–$25; sandwiches less. AE, DISC, MC, V. Summer daily 11:15am–9pm; fall–spring daily 11:15am–8pm.

WOLFEBORO ⋆⋆

The handsome town of Wolfeboro, on Lake Winnipesaukee's eastern shore, claims to be the first-ever summer resort in the U.S. The documentation makes a pretty good case for it. In 1763 John Wentworth, nephew of a former governor, was granted land for a summer estate on what's now called Lake Wentworth, a small lake connected to Winnipesaukee by a tiny river. Blue-blood types (and grand hotels) eventually followed him to the area, and the village that prospered has been a great success both as a summer retreat and a year-round community.

In contrast to the low-brow tourist attractions of Weirs Beach, this town has a more prim sensibility and takes its own preservation quite seriously. You'll find impeccably maintained 19th-century homes, attractive downtown shops, and a refined sense of place. There's the requisite private boarding school (Brewster Academy), which dates from 1820. You might even see a famous face at the hardware store or ice-cream shop—well-known celebrities and politicians often vacation here, and some own summer homes in the area.

ESSENTIALS

GETTING THERE   Lake Winnipesaukee's eastern shore is best explored using Route 28 (from Alton Bay to Wolfeboro) and Route 109 (from Wolfeboro to Moultonborough).

VISITOR INFORMATION   The **Wolfeboro Chamber of Commerce** (⊘ 800/516-5324 or 603/569-2200; www.wolfeboroonline.com/chamber) provides regional information and advice from its offices in a converted railroad station at 32 Central Ave., a block off Main Street in Wolfeboro. It's open daily in summer, Monday to Friday the rest of the year.

SPECIAL EVENTS   The **Great Waters Music Festival** (© **603/569-7710;** www. greatwaters.org) is an amazingly eclectic series held on the campus of Brewster Academy throughout summer. Performers really run the gamut, from swing bands (the Glen Miller Orchestra) to big-time jazz (Dianne Reeves, Wynton Marsalis) to good old-fashioned folk (Judy Collins, Arlo Guthrie).

EXPLORING WOLFEBORO

Wolfeboro has a vibrant, homey downtown, easily explored on foot. Park near Depot Square and the Victorian-style train station, and stock up on brochures and maps at the Chamber of Commerce office. Behind the station, a trail runs along the old tracks past Back Bay to a set of small cascades.

To help you see the lake from a Wolfeboro base, several **boat tours** depart from the docks just behind the shops on Main Street. One of the most fun is the wind-in-your-face, zippy half-hour tour aboard the ***Millie B.*** ⊛ (© **603/569-1080**), a 28-foot mahogany speedboat constructed by HackerCraft. (Ticket prices have zoomed in recent years, too: The ride costs $20 per adults, $10 for children ages 4 to 12.)

For more conventional travelers, the impressive **MS *Mount Washington*** ⊛⊛ (© **888/ 843-6686** or 630/366-5531; www.cruisenh.com) is a handsome, 230-foot-long vessel that sails out of Weirs Beach daily in summer and calls at Wolfeboro's docks several times per week—check at the docks for a current schedule. Day cruises (2–3 hours each) cost $25 to $40 for adults, less for children.

Alternately, you could arrange a chartered excursions on the ***Winnipesaukee Belle*** ⊛ (© **603/569-3796**), a faux 65-foot steamship with a canopied upper deck operated by the Wolfeboro Inn (see "Where to Stay," below)—though the charters start at about $800 for a 2-hour cruise. Needless to say, if you're paying that much, bring lots of friends (it holds up to 150 passengers), plus good camera and video equipment.

For a much cheaper, self-propelled afternoon, kayak rentals and guided tours are available from **Winnipesaukee Kayak** ⊛, 17 Bay St., at the Back Bay Marina (© **603/ 569-9926**). On a relatively windless day, few activities beat exploring by paddle from Wolfeboro Bay to the cluster of islands just to the south. (Watch for recreational boaters, who occasionally get out of hand and too close to small craft.)

Quiet lake swimming is available at **Wentworth State Park** ⊛ (© **603/271-3556**), which has a nice beach and a shady picnic area. The park is 5 miles east of Wolfeboro on Rte. 109. It's open daily mid-June to Labor Day. The entrance fee is $3 per adult, $1 per child ages 6 to 11. No pets are allowed into this park.

Castle in the Clouds ⊛⊛   About 15 miles north of Wolfeboro is a rather unusual sight. Shoemaker-turned-millionaire Thomas Gustave Plant built this eccentric stone edifice on top of a little mountain overlooking Winnipesaukee in 1913, at a cost of $7 million (in 1913 dollars!) as a retreat from his factory in Boston. Known as "Lucknow" at the time, the home is a sort of rustic, smaller San Simeon East, with cliff-hugging rooms, stained-glass windows, and unrivaled views of surrounding hills and lakes. Park at the carriage house; from there, you're led through the house by knowledgeable tour guides. Look for mannequin knights in suits of armor, old shotguns, exotic wood carvings, tusks—guy stuff, basically. Even if the castle holds no interest for you, the 5,200-acre grounds and their views (which get even better in foliage season) is worth the price of admission. So is the long access road, which can be harrowingly narrow and winding in spots but rewards the steely nerved traveler with wonderful vistas and turnouts for stopping along the way. Take time to explore while you're driving up; the road back down is straight and uninteresting.

Rte. 171 (4 miles south of Rte. 25), Moultonborough. © **603/476-5900.** www.castleintheclouds.org. Admission $10 adults, $8 seniors, $5 students 7–17, free for children under 6. Grounds only $6 adults, free for children. Mid-May to late May Sat–Sun 10am–4:30pm; June to mid-Oct daily 10am–4:30pm. Closed mid-Oct to mid-May.

WHERE TO STAY & DINE

Wolfeboro Inn ⊛⊛   This small, elegant resort hotel strives to mix modern and traditional, and succeeds admirably. An easy stroll from downtown Wolfeboro, the property dates back to 1812 but was expanded and updated during the mid-1980s. The modern lobby has a small atrium with wood beams, a slate floor, and a brick fireplace, retaining old-world elegance. Most of the comfortable guest rooms are furnished with Early American reproductions and quilts. Deluxe rooms have better views, and about a dozen have balconies overlooking the lake as well. The dining room here is considered excellent, but the inn's sliver of lake shore has only a very tiny beach.

90 N. Main St. (P.O. Box 1270), Wolfeboro, NH 03894. © **800/451-2389** or 603/569-3016. Fax 603/569-5375. www.wolfeboroinn.com. 44 units. Mid-May June $150–$220 double, $220–$310 suite; July–Oct $190–$270 double, $265–$320 suite; Nov–Dec $110–$185 double, $160–$200 suite. Packages available. Closed Jan to mid-May. Rates include continental breakfast. 2-night minimum stay in peak season. AE, DISC, MC, V. **Amenities:** Restaurant; pub; watersports equipment rental; concierge; limited room service; babysitting; laundry service; dry cleaning. *In room:* A/C, TV, fridge (some units), coffeemaker, hair dryer, iron.

4 The White Mountains ⊛⊛⊛

The White Mountain range is northern New England's outdoor recreation capital. This high range of peaks is a sprawling, rugged playground that calls out to legions of intrepid kayakers, mountaineers, rock climbers, thrill-seeking skiers, mountain bikers, bird-watchers, and backpacking hikers.

The **White Mountain National Forest** organizes and administrates much of this vast landscape, encompassing nearly 800,000 acres of rocky, forested terrain, more than 100 waterfalls, dozens of backcountry lakes, and miles of clear brooks and cascading streams. An elaborate network of hiking trails (more than 1,000 miles' worth) dates back to the 19th century, when city folk took to these mountains to build character and experience nature first-hand. Trails ranging from easy to vertical lace the forests, trade the rivers, and traverse knife-like ridgelines where the weather can change so quickly and dramatically it can do you in, if you're not ready for it.

The heart of the White Mountains is their highest point: 6,288-foot **Mount Washington,** an ominous, brooding peak that's often cloud-capped and mantled with snow both early and late in the season. It's so big, you can see it from Portland, Maine, 100 miles away. An often-blustery peak, it's accessible by cog railway, car, and foot, making it one of the more popular destinations in the region. You won't find untouched wilderness here, but you will find abundant natural drama.

Flanking Washington is the brawny **Presidential Range,** a series of similarly wind-blasted granite peaks, similarly named for U.S. presidents and offering similarly eye-popping views. Beyond this range, plenty of lesser-known ridges also beckon hikers seeking an elemental test.

If your idea of fun *doesn't* involve steep cliffs or icy dips in mountain streams, you can still enjoy the scenery via spectacular drives. The most scenic is the **Kancamagus Highway** between Conway and Lincoln, offering plenty of pull-outs to picnic and snap great photos.

You'll need a home base. North Conway is the lodging capital, with hundreds of motel units; Loon Mountain and Waterville Valley are condo villages; and Bethlehem, Jackson, and the Franconia and Crawford notches offer old-style inns and hotels.

The White Mountains

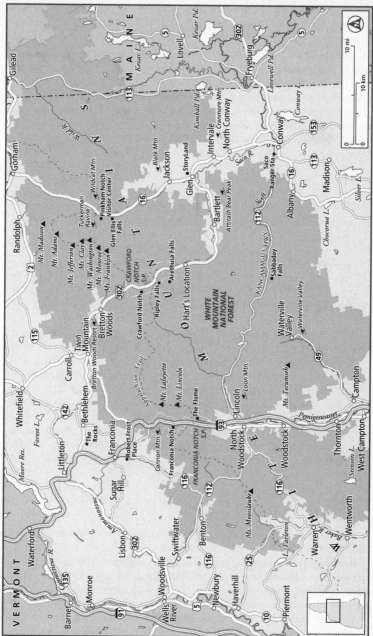

Activities in the White Mountains

BACKPACKING   The White Mountains allow for some of the most challenging and scenic backpacking in all of the Northeastern U.S. The best trails are within the huge **White Mountain National Forest**, which encompasses several 5,000-plus-foot peaks and more than 100,000 acres of designated wilderness. Its trails range from easy walks along bubbling streams to demanding ridgeline paths buffeted by fierce winds.

The **Appalachian Mountain Club** (© 603/466-2727; www.amc-nh.org) is an excellent source of general information about the region's outdoors offerings. It's a major supplier of lodging, too. Eight sturdy mountain huts ⓐ (small cabins) offer bare-bones, bunkroom-style shelter and great campfire conviviality in dramatic settings; hearty breakfasts and dinners are included with your rates. The AMC maintains a clutch of other cabins and lodges in the mountains, too, such as the Shapleigh Bunkhouse in Crawford Notch and the Joe Dodge Lodge in Pinkham Notch, which has some four-person family rooms. Other AMC-operated overnight options include the Hermit Lake Shelters (about $10 per night) and a dozen other more primitive shelters and campsites, about half of which are free. The rest charge a nominal fee of $8 per person. Check AMC's national website (www.outdoors.org) for all the lodging details and to make reservations, which are essential for all of these lodgings in summer.

In addition, a number of three-sided Adirondack-style shelters exist throughout the backcountry and can be used on a first-come, first-served basis. Some are free, others have a small fee. (Simply pitching a tent in the backcountry is free, subject to certain restrictions, with no permits required.) Check with the **White Mountain National Forest** headquarters (© 603/528-8721; www.fs.fed.us/r9/white) or a district ranger station for rules and regulations concerning these shelters.

Everything you could possibly need for a day or overnight hike, including sleeping bags and pads, tents, and backpacks, is available for rent at **Eastern Mountain Sports** (© 603/356-5433) on Main St. in North Conway at reasonable rates. It's open daily.

to delightful river swimming at the Rocky Gorge Scenic Area. Both are open seasonally, from around mid-May until mid-October.

Backcountry tent camping is free throughout the White Mountains, and no permit is needed. (You will need to purchase a parking permit to leave your car at the trail head; see above.) Check with a ranger station for current restrictions on camping in the backcountry. Three-sided log lean-tos are also scattered throughout the White Mountain backcountry, providing overnight shelter for campers. Some shelters are free; at others, a backcountry manager will collect a small fee. Contact any ranger station (see above) for details and locations.

There are also eight **state park campgrounds** located in northern New Hampshire (© 603/271-3628; www.nhstateparks.org).

HIKING   The White Mountains offer more than 1,000 miles of trails. The essential guide to hiking in this region is the Appalachian Mountain Club's *White Mountain Guide*, which contains up-to-date and detailed descriptions of every trail in the area. The guide is available at most bookstores and outdoor shops (and even at some filling stations) in the region.

ROCK CLIMBING   The White Mountains are renowned for their impressive, towering granite cliffs, especially Cathedral and White Horse ledges, attracting legions of rock climbers from throughout the U.S. and Europe. Ascents range in difficulty from "pretty easy" to "extraordinarily hard; my life flashed before my eyes." The North Conway area hosts three climbing schools, and experienced and aspiring climbers alike have plenty of options for improving their skills. Classes range from 1 day to a week.

Contact the Eastern Mountain Sports Climbing School (© 800/310-4504; www.emsclimb.com), the International Mountain Climbing School (© 603/356-7064; www.ime-usa.com/imcs), or the Mountain Guides Alliance (© 603/356-5310) for more information.

SKIING   The best downhill ski areas in the White Mountains are Cannon Mountain, Loon Mountain, Waterville Valley, Wildcat, and Attitash Bear Peak, with vertical drops of 2,000 feet and all the services one would expect of a professional ski resort. See below in this chapter for details on these ski hills.

The state also boasts two dozen cross-country ski centers, which groom a combined total of more than 500 miles of trails. The state's premier cross-country destination is **Jackson** (© **800/927-6697** or 603/383-9355; www.jacksonxc.com), with more than 50 miles of trails in and around a scenic village near the base of Mount Washington. Two more good Nordic ski centers are located at **Bretton Woods Resort** (© **800/314-1752** or 603/278-3322) at the western entrance to Crawford Notch, and the spectacularly remote **Balsams/Wilderness** cross-country ski center (© **800/255-0600** or 603/255-3400) in the northerly reaches of the state. Adults must pay $15 to $17 per day to ski the trails at any of these facilities (there are discounts for kids and seniors), and all of them can rent you a set of good skis.

NORTH CONWAY

North Conway is 150 miles N of Boston and 62 miles NW of Portland

For better or worse, North Conway is the commercial heart of the White Mountains. Outdoor purists abhor the place, considering it a garish interloper to be avoided at all costs—except, maybe, when seeking a post-hike pizza and a beer. Shoppers, on the other hand, are drawn magnetically to the outlets and accouterments of commerce perched along routes 302 and 16, the two highways that overlap in town.

No, North Conway itself won't strike anyone as a natural wonderland. The strip south of the village is basically one long turning lane flanked with outlet malls, motels, and chain restaurants of every architectural stripe. On rainy weekends and during foliage season, the road can resemble a linear parking lot. There's so much clutter here you often forget to look *up*—which is where the peaks of the Whites are standing. Behind that big grocery store.

Sprawl notwithstanding, North Conway is beautifully situated along the eastern edge of the broad and fertile Saco River valley (also called the Mount Washington Valley). The village is trim and attractive (if often congested), with an open green, some colorful shops, Victorian frontier-town commercial architecture, and a distinctive little train station. It's a good place to park, stretch your legs, and find a cup of coffee or a snack. (There's a Ben & Jerry's "scoop shop" off the green, near the train station.)

ESSENTIALS

GETTING THERE   North Conway and the Mount Washington Valley sit on Route 16 and U.S. Route 302. Route 16 connects to the Spaulding Turnpike, then to I-95 to Boston and New York; Route 302 zigzags from Maine to Vermont. Traffic can be vexing in the Mount Washington Valley on holiday weekends in summer, and (especially) foliage weekends in fall, when backups of several miles are common. Try to plan around these busy times in order to preserve your own sanity.

Concord Coach (© 800/639-3317; www.concordcoachlines.com) runs two daily buses from Boston, picking up and dropping off in North Conway at the Eastern Slope Inn (Rte. 16/302) and in Conway at the First Stop Market gas station, right on Main Street.

VISITOR INFORMATION   Contact the **Mount Washington Valley Chamber of Commerce** (© 800/367-3364 or 603/356-5701; www.mtwashingtonvalley.org), which operates a seasonal information booth opposite the village green. Staff can help arrange for local accommodations. It's open daily in summer, and in winter on Saturday and Sunday only.

RIDING THE RAILS

The **Conway Scenic Railroad** ★★ (© 800/232-5251 or 603/356-5251; www.conwayscenic.com) provides mountain excursions in comfortable rail cars (including a dome car and a dining car) pulled by either steam or early diesel engines. Trips depart from a distinctive 1874 train station, off the village green, recalling an era when trains regularly pulled in from Boston and New York to enjoy the country air for a month or two each summer. The 1-hour excursion heads south, but only to Conway; you're better off signing up for the more picturesque 1¾-hour trip northward to the village of Bartlett. Or, for the best show, select the 5-hour excursion through dramatic Crawford Notch, with stupendous views of the mountains from high along this beautiful glacial valley.

Some trains run from mid-April right up until Christmas, while others only run in summer—each train has a different schedule, so check ahead. Coach, first-class, and dome-car fares are available; the first-class passengers sit in "Gertrude Emma," an 1898 parlor car with wicker and rattan chairs, mahogany woodwork, and an observation platform. Depending on the class of service you choose, tickets for shorter excursions are $12 to $31 per adult, with an extra charge for the dining car because a meal is included; it costs $42 to $62 per person for the Crawford Notch trip. There are discounts for kids and toddlers. Some trains do not take advance reservations.

DOWNHILL SKIING

Cranmore Mountain Resort ★ *Value*   Mount Cranmore claims to be the oldest operating ski area in New England, and ski pioneer Hannes Schneider did in fact practically single-handedly bring a new form of downhill skiing to America here, beginning in 1939. (The resort was also famous, for half a century, for its tracked ski lift,

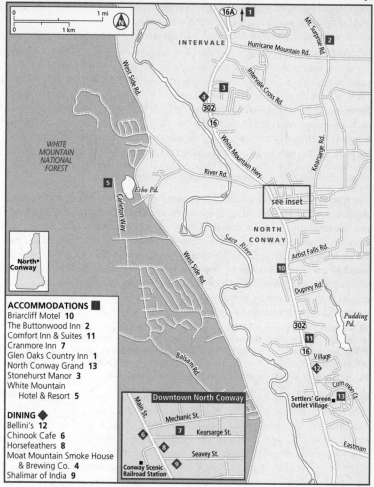

INTERVALE

WHITE
MOUNTAIN
NATIONAL
FOREST

NORTH
CONWAY

Hurricane Mountain Rd.

Mt. Surprise Rd.

Intervale Cross Rd.

Kearsarge Rd.

White Mountain Hwy.

River Rd.

see inset

Saco River

Artist Falls Rd.

Duprey Rd.

Pudding
Pd.

Echo Pd.

West Side Rd.

Carleton Way

Balsam Rd.

West Side Rd.

Village

Settlers' Green
Outlet Village

Common Ct.

Eastman

North
Conway

ACCOMMODATIONS ■
Briarcliff Motel **10**
The Buttonwood Inn **2**
Comfort Inn & Suites **11**
Cranmore Inn **7**
Glen Oaks Country Inn **1**
North Conway Grand **13**
Stonehurst Manor **3**
White Mountain
    Hotel & Resort **5**

DINING ◆
Bellini's **12**
Chinook Cafe **6**
Horsefeathers **8**
Moat Mountain Smoke House
    & Brewing Co. **4**
Shalimar of India **9**

Downtown North Conway

Main St.

Mechanic St.

Kearsarge St.

Seavey St.

Conway Scenic
Railroad Station

---

known as the Skimobile—now sadly gone by the wayside.) Cranmore's slopes are unrepentantly old-fashioned, but the mountain has restyled itself as a snow-sports mecca—look for snow tubing, snow scooters, and ski bikes. These slopes aren't likely to challenge advanced skiers, but they delight many beginners and intermediates, as well as those who enjoy diversion with the ski toys. It's ideal for families, thanks to the relaxed attitude, range of activities, and not-outrageous ticket prices.

1 Skimobile Rd. (PO Box 1640), North Conway, NH 03850. © **800/786-6754**. www.cranmore.com. Adult day lift tickets $47; discounts for kids, teens, and seniors.

WHERE TO STAY

In addition the choices I've selected below, **Route 16** in North Conway is packed to the gills with basic motels, which are reasonably priced in the off-season (you can sometimes find a room for around $40–$50 per night in spring or late fall), but getting surprisingly expensive during peak travel times such as summer, ski-season weekends, and fall foliage season. Fronting the commercial strip, these motels don't offer much in the way of a pastoral environment, but most are comfortable and conveniently located.

Briarcliff Motel Among North Conway's dozens of roadside motels, the Briarcliff is a decent option. A basic U-shaped motel with standard-size rooms about a half-mile south of the village center, all its units have been redecorated in rich colors, much like B&B rooms. You will pay extra for a room with a "porch" and mountain view, but these are a little peculiar—the porches are actually part of a long enclosed sitting area, each unit separated from its neighbor by cubicle-height partitions. (Save your money.) If you can ignore the traffic noise and the nagging signs, the Briarcliff is a value.

Rte. 16 (P.O. Box 504), North Conway, NH 03860. ℂ 800/338-4291 or 603/356-5584. www.briarcliffmotel.com. 30 units. Summer and fall $99–$179 double; rest of the year $59–$112 double. 2-night minimum stay holidays and foliage season. AE, DISC, MC, V. **Amenities:** Outdoor pool. *In room:* A/C, TV, fridge.

The Buttonwood Inn ☆ Just a few minutes' drive from the outlets and restaurants, the Buttonwood has more of a classic country-inn feel than any other North Conway inn. It's set on 17 quiet acres on the side of Mount Surprise in an 1820s-era home, with a tastefully appointed interior inspired by the Shaker style. Most guest rooms tend toward the small and cozy, but two common rooms (one with a television) allow guests plenty of space to unwind. Two units have gas fireplaces, one has a Murphy bed, and one has a large Jacuzzi (it's also wheelchair-accessible). The hosts are uncommonly helpful with the planning of day trips, no matter your interests. Breakfasts, a highlight, tend toward the country elegant; the rhubarb coffeecake is a hit.

Mt. Surprise Rd., North Conway, NH 03860. ℂ 800/258-2625 or 603/356-2625. Fax 603/356-3140. www.buttonwoodinn.com. 10 units, 2 with detached private bathroom. Late June–Oct $165–$270 double; rest of the year $95–$210 double. Rates include breakfast. 2- to 3-night minimum stay Sat–Sun and holidays. Packages available. AE, DISC, MC, V. Closed Apr. Children 6 and older are welcome. **Amenities:** Outdoor pool; cross-country ski trails. *In room:* A/C, TV (some units), dataport, hair dryer, fireplace (2 units), Jacuzzi (some units).

Comfort Inn & Suites ☆ *Kids* This tidy chain hotel consists entirely of "suites" (which are mostly just big rooms, rather than units with a separate living room) spread out among three stories, giving travelers a bit more elbow room than at most of the motels in town. It's a good choice for families, because it's close to outlet shopping and near a separately owned elaborate, pirate-themed miniature golf course (which gives a slight discount to the hotel's guests). A few rooms have gas fireplaces.

2001 White Mountain Hwy. (Rte. 16), North Conway, NH 03860. ℂ 866/647-8483 or 603/356-8811. Fax 603/356-7770. 58 units. $99–$199 double; executive suites to $249. Rates include continental breakfast. AE, DISC, MC, V. **Amenities:** Heated indoor pool; fitness room. *In room:* A/C, TV, dataport, fridge, coffeemaker, hair dryer, iron, fireplace (some units).

Cranmore Inn ☆ *Kids* The Cranmore Inn has the feel of a 19th-century boardinghouse—which is appropriate, because that's what it is. Open since 1863, this three-story Victorian home is a short walk from North Conway's village center. Its heritage—it's the oldest continuously operating hotel in North Conway—adds charm and quirkiness, but comes with occasional drawbacks such as uneven water pressure. Still, it offers good value thanks to the handy location, the hospitality of the innkeepers, and the layout of the guest rooms. Interestingly, some of the 16 units in the main inn consist of two bedrooms, connected in the middle by one private hallway bathroom; these are very family-friendly. Three additional big "kitchen units" are housed in an annex; these elaborate suites come with their own kitchens, gas woodstoves, separate dining rooms, living rooms, and even personal computers. Again, great for families.

80 Kearsarge St. (P.O. Box 1349), North Conway, NH 03860. ℭ 800/526-5502. www.cranmoreinn.com. 19 units, some with private bathroom in hallway. Peak season $79–$164 double, off-season $59–$134 double. Rates include full breakfast (except in kitchen units). 2-night minimum stay Sat–Sun, holidays, foliage season. Packages and Mon–Fri discounts available. AE, DISC, MC, V. **Amenities:** Outdoor pool. *In room:* TV (some units), kitchenette (some units).

Glen Oaks Country Inn ⚜

Just 10 minutes north of North Conway is a spur road that leads through the village of Intervale, which has several lodges and a feeling of being removed from the clutter of outlet shops. Glen Oaks was built in 1850, with a mansard-roofed third floor added when it opened as an inn in 1890. Typical for the era, the rooms are more cozy than spacious, and today are decorated mostly with reproductions and some country Victorian antiques. Some rooms have private bathrooms across the hallway. The best units might be the two in the nearby stone cottage (the Cottle Room has a wood-burning fireplace, wing chairs, and a small porch with Adirondack chairs) or the newer Forest Cottage, with a two-person Jacuzzi and small refrigerator.

Rte. 16A (P.O. Box 37), Intervale, NH 03845. ℭ 877/854-6535 or 603/356-9772. Fax 603/356-5652. www.glenoaksinn. com. 11 units. Mid-June to mid-Oct $105–$180 double; mid-Oct to Dec $105–$160 double. Rates include full breakfast. 2-night minimum stay most weekends and holidays. AE, DISC, MC, V. Children 6 and older welcome. **Amenities:** Outdoor pool. *In room:* A/C, TV, fridge (some units), fireplace (some units), Jacuzzi (some units).

North Conway Grand ⚜⚜ *Kids*

If you're looking for convenience, amenities, and easy access to outlet shopping, this former Sheraton is your best bet. Built on the site of North Conway's former airfield, the Grand is a four-story, gabled hotel with a pond adjacent (and architecturally similar) to Settlers' Green, one of the town's key shopping complexes. Kids enjoy chatting with Monty, the talking moose in the lobby. The hotel offers clean, comfortable, and basic rooms with the usual chain-hotel furnishings. Recently the hotel's amenities have been ramped up, including now year-round access to the outdoor pool and Jacuzzi (the patio is heated); there's another brick-terraced pool inside with his-and-her saunas, plus a newly constructed outdoor kiddie pool and play area featuring spray jets and other fun features. High-speed Internet access here is free.

Rte. 16 at Settler's Green (P.O. Box 3189), North Conway, NH 03860. ℭ 800/655-1452 or 603/356-9300. www.north conwaygrand.com. 200 units. Summer $109–$219 double; off-season $79–$149 double. AE, DC, DISC, MC, V. **Amenities:** Restaurant; indoor pool; outdoor pool; 4 tennis courts; fitness room; Jacuzzi; sauna; children's programs; travel desk; coin-op laundry; executive rooms. *In room:* A/C, TV, dataport (some units), fridge, coffeemaker, hair dryer, iron/ ironing board, Jacuzzi (some units).

Stonehurst Manor ⚜

This imposing, architecturally eclectic Victorian stone-and-shingle mansion, originally built for the family that owned the Bigelow carpet firm, is set amid acres of white pines on a rocky knoll above Route 16. It's about 1 mile north of North Conway. It wouldn't seem at all out of place in either the south of France or the moors of Scotland. One would assume that it caters to the stuffy and affluent, yet the main focus here is on outdoor adventurers, so it attracts a surprisingly youngish crowd. Request a room in the regal original 1876 mansion if you can; another 10 units are housed in a comfortable but less elegant wing added in the 1950s.

Rte. 16 (P.O. Box 1937), North Conway, NH 03860. ℭ 800/525-9100 or 603/356-3113. www.stonehurstmanor.com. 25 units. Mon–Fri $110–$170 double, Sat–Sun $140–$200 double. Holiday and foliage season rates higher. MAP plans available. 2-night minimum stay Sat–Sun, 3-night minimum on holiday weekends. MC, V. Pets allowed in some rooms ($25 per pet per night). **Amenities:** Dining room; outdoor pool; tennis court; Jacuzzi. *In room:* A/C, TV, fireplace (some units), Jacuzzi (some units).

White Mountain Hotel and Resort ⚜⚜

This contemporary resort has the best location of any hotel close to the Conways. Sited at the base of dramatic White Horse

Ledge near Echo Lake State Park, in a modern golf-course community, the hotel was built in 1990 but its style borrows from classic area resorts. The designers have somehow managed to take some of the more successful elements of a friendly country inn—a nice deck with a view, comfortable seating in the lobby and a clubby tavern area—and incorporate them into a thoroughly modern resort. The comfortably appointed guest rooms here are a solid notch or two above standard hotel furnishings.

2600 West Side Rd. (5½ miles west of town center), North Conway, NH 03860. © 800/533-6301. Fax 603/356-7100. www.whitemountainhotel.com. 80 units. $99–$209 double; $109–$249 suite. B&B rates available. 2-night minimum stay on Sat–Sun. Packages available. AE, DISC, MC, V. **Amenities:** Dining room; tavern; outdoor pool; golf course; 2 tennis courts; fitness center; Jacuzzi; sauna; limited room service; babysitting; laundry service; dry cleaning. *In room:* A/C, TV, dataport, fridge, coffeemaker, hair dryer, iron/ironing board.

WHERE TO DINE

North Conway is a bastion of family-style restaurants, fast-food chains, and bars that happen to also serve food. If you want more refined dining, you're best off heading for The Inn at Thorn Hill in Jackson, about 10 minutes north (see below).

Bellini's ⊛ SOUTHERN ITALIAN   Bellini's is run by the third generation of the Marcello family, who opened their first place in Rhode Island in 1927. The food here runs the gamut from fettuccine chicken pesto and braciola to steaks, beef carpaccio, and (in homage to Rhode Island) stuffed quahogs. Almost everything is homemade—soups, breads, pastas, and desserts. Especially good are the toasted ravioli appetizers. Drinks include a martini menu, including espresso martinis.

Rte. 16, North Conway. © 603/356-7000. www.bellinis.com. Reservations not accepted. Main courses $12–$22. AE, DISC, MC, V. Mon–Thurs 4–10pm; Fri–Sun 4–11pm.

Chinook Café ⊛ ECLECTIC   The Chinook Café opened in 1998 in Conway, a pretty village about a 10-min. drive south of North Conway. It began as a small, mostly takeout place, but its popularity led it to move down the street and expand. Now you'll find healthy, vaguely gourmet fare for breakfast (polenta with goat cheese, oatmeal pancakes) and lunch (smoked salmon and white-bean, portobello sandwiches), with a good selection of vegetarian items too. There are changing daily specials, and the homemade baked goods are a fitting conclusion to a hike.

80 Main St. (across from fire station), Conway. © 603/447-6300. Breakfast and lunch items $5–$7. MC, V. Mon–Sat 7am–4pm; Sun 7am–3:30pm.

Horsefeathers ⊛ PUB FARE   In a town where pub food is the rule, Horsefeathers has been leading the pack since 1976. Set in the village, across from the train station, this local hangout is often loud and boisterous, filled with everyone from families to off-duty bartenders. The music has become more of a draw in recent years. The food is sometimes hard to pin down, ranging from tortilla soup to eggplant ravioli with a red-pepper cream sauce, but it tends to gather strength in the middle: chicken wings, grilled steaks, burgers, grilled fish, an apple-smoked bacon cheddar burger. The lobster-crab cakes are good, as is the Harvey—a house pastrami sandwich with onions, tomato, and poppy-seed dressing—and the buttery lobster-scallop pie.

Main St., North Conway. © 603/356-2687. www.horsefeathers.com. Reservations not accepted. Main courses $6.95–$18. AE, MC, V. Daily 11:30am–11:45pm.

Moat Mountain Smoke House and Brewing Co. ⊛ BARBECUE/PUB FARE
This is the local spot for fresh, on-site brewed beer, smoked meats, and wood-fired pizza. It's casual and relaxed, with a more intriguing variety of eats than other North

Conway beer joints. You can choose from a selection of smoky barbecued items, obviously (the brisket and ribs are popular), and other dishes include smoked trout, salmon, wood-grilled pizzas, burgers, quesadillas, wraps, and nachos—including one variant with smoked salmon and mango-pineapple salsa. About a dozen beers are on tap most nights, including half that are house-brewed.

3378 White Mountain Hwy. (Rte. 16), North Conway (about 1 mile north of the village). © 603/356-6381. www.moatmountain.com. Reservations not accepted. Main courses $7–$20. AE, MC, V. Daily 11:30am–9pm (until 10pm Fri–Sat).

Shalimar of India ⭐ NORTHERN INDIAN   Shalimar is a pleasant surprise in a town where "adventurous ethnic cuisine" usually means vegetables on your nachos. Shalimar offers a wide variety of tasty, tangy dishes from India such as tandoori dishes, biryani, vegetarian entrees, and a tangy lamb vindaloo. Meals are well-prepared, and the chef will adjust the spice level to your taste. Shalimar is just a short walk from the village green. Like many places in town, they offer a kids' menu, too.

27 Seavey St., North Conway. © 603/356-0123. www.shalimarofindia.com. Reservations recommended on peak summer and winter weekends. Main courses $6–$7 at lunch; $11–$14 at dinner. DISC, MC, V. Sat–Sun noon–3pm and 5–9:30pm; Mon 5–9:30pm; Tues–Fri 11am–2:30pm and 5–9:30pm.

JACKSON & ENVIRONS ⭐⭐

The gateway village to Mount Washington and its massive surrounding peaks, **Jackson** ⭐⭐ is a quiet place in a picturesque valley off Route 16, just 15 minutes to the north of North Conway. The village center, approached via a single-lane covered bridge, remains tiny and touches of old-world elegance remain—vestiges of a time when Jackson was a favored destination of the East Coast upper middle class, who fled the summer heat of the cities to relax here in rambling wooden hotels and second homes.

Thanks to its revamped golf course and one of the most elaborate, well-maintained cross-country ski networks in the nation, Jackson has found renewed life as a resort both in summer and winter. Though no longer undiscovered, it still feels a shade out of the mainstream and is a peaceful spot, especially when compared to the busy scene just to the south.

ESSENTIALS
GETTING THERE   Jackson is just off Route 16, about 11 miles north of North Conway. Heading north, look for the covered bridge on the right. Surprisingly, **Concord Coach** (© 800/639-3317; www.concordcoachlines.com) offers one daily bus here to and from Boston. Wait at the covered bridge and wave down the driver.

VISITOR INFORMATION   The **Jackson Area Chamber of Commerce** (© 800/866-3334 or 603/383-9356; www.jacksonnh.com), based in offices at the Jackson Falls Marketplace on Route 16B, can answer questions about area attractions and make lodging reservations.

EXPLORING MOUNT WASHINGTON ⭐⭐⭐
Mount Washington (also known as "The Rockpile"), just north of Jackson in the heart of the White Mountain National Forest, is often described with impressive facts and figures that don't always succeed at evoking the windblown, hellishly scenic peak. But here are a few anyway. At 6,288 feet, Washington is the highest mountain in the Northeast. It's said to have the worst weather in the world outside the polar regions. It still holds the world's record for the highest surface wind speed ever recorded—231

Tips **You'll Never Walk Alone**

Despite the raw power of its weather, Mount Washington's summit is *not* the place for those seeking true wilderness. The top is home to a train platform, a parking lot, a snack bar, a gift shop, a museum, and a handful of outbuildings housing a weather observatory. There are also plenty of crowds on clear days, all seeking that prized red-and-blue THIS CAR CLIMBED MT. WASHINGTON bumper sticker New Englanders' cars wear like badges of courage. Then again, the views here can't be beat, extending into four states and out to the ocean. It's worth seeing. But keeping all those other folks out of the frame of your digital shots and Handycam footage? Now, *that's* an extreme sport.

---

mph in 1934, something Granite Staters take a perverse pride in. (There's a weatherman posted at the top of the mountain year-round, and there used to be a small TV crew here, too, documenting the craziness.) Winds topping 150 mph are routinely recorded 9 months out of the year, a result of the mountain's position at the confluence of three major storm tracks.

Washington might also be the New England mountain with the most options for getting to its summit. Visitors can ascend via a special cog railway (see the "Crawford Notch" section, later in this chapter); in their cars, along a snaky toll road to the summit; in an all-terrain vehicle (ATV), using the same road; by guide-driven van; or on foot.

The best place to learn about Mount Washington and its approaches is rustic **Pinkham Notch Visitor Center** (© **603/466-2721**), operated by the Appalachian Mountain Club. At the crest of Route 16 between Jackson and Gorham, the center offers overnight accommodations and meals (see below), maps, a limited selection of outdoor supplies, and plenty of advice from its helpful staff. A number of hiking trails also depart from here, with several loops and side trips.

About a dozen **trails** in all lead to the mountain's summit, ranging in length from about 4 to 15 miles. (Detailed information is available at the visitor center.) The most direct and dramatic way is via the **Tuckerman Ravine Trail** ✦✦✦, which departs right from Pinkham Notch. It's a true full day's endeavor. Healthy hikers should allow 4 to 5 hours for the ascent, 2 to 4 hours for the return trip. Be sure to allow enough time to enjoy the dramatic glacial cirque of Tuckerman Ravine, which attracts extreme skiers to its sheer drops as late as June, and often holds patches of snow well into the summer.

The **Mount Washington Auto Road** ✦✦ (© **603/466-3988;** www.mount washingtonautoroad.com) opened in 1861 as a carriage road, and has since remained a wildly popular attraction. The steep, winding 8-mile road (with an *average* grade of 12%) is partly paved and incredibly dramatic; your breath will be taken away at one curve after another. The ascent will test your iron will; the descent will test your car's brakes. This trip is not worth doing, though, if the summit is in the clouds; wait for a clear day.

Located on Route 16 just north of Pinkham Notch, the road is open daily from early May until late October from 8am to 5pm (hours may be slightly different early or late in the season). The cost is $20 per vehicle and driver, plus $7 for each additional adult ($5 for extra children ages 5–12); it's $12 for a motorcycle and its operator. This price includes an audiocassette or CD narration pointing out sights along the way (available in English, French, or German) and the famous bumper sticker.

No trailers, RVs, or mopeds, are allowed, which makes sense. But management has also imposed some other slightly curious vehicle restrictions to protect against breakdowns and logjams; for example, Acuras, Hondas, Saturns, Sterlings, and Jaguars with automatic transmissions must show a "1," "L," or "S" on the shifter to be allowed on the road; only H-3 version Hummers can ascend; and no Lincoln Continentals from before 1969 are permitted. (Darn it!) But taxis and police cars are okay (whew!), so long as the first gear is operational.

If you'd prefer to leave the driving to someone else, **van tours** ascend throughout the day, allowing you to relax, enjoy the views, and learn about the mountain from informed guides. The cost is $26 for adults, $23 for seniors, and $11 for children ages 5 to 12, and includes a half-hour stay on the summit. (Longer tours are currently being developed.)

One additional note: The average temperature atop the mountain is 30°F (–1°C). (The record low was–43°F/–6°C, and the warmest temperature ever recorded atop the mountain, in August, was 72°F/22°C.) Even in summer, visitors should come ready for blustery, cold conditions.

EXPLORING PINKHAM NOTCH 🐾🐾🐾

The AMC's Pinkham Notch Visitor Center is at the height of land on Route 16. Just south, look for signs for **Glen Ellis Falls** 🐾🐾, worth a quick stop. From the parking area, you'll pass through a pedestrian tunnel and walk along the Glen Ellis River for a few minutes until it seemingly drops off the face of the earth. The stream plummets 64 feet down a cliff; observation platforms are situated at the top and near the bottom of the falls, which are one of this region's most impressive after a heavy rain. From the parking lot to the base of the falls is less than a half-mile walk.

From the same visitor center, it's about 2.5 miles up to **Hermit Lake** and **Tuckerman Ravine** 🐾🐾🐾 via the Tuckerman Ravine Trail (see above). Even if you're not planning to continue on to the summit, the ravine—with its sheer sides and lacey cataracts—might be the most dramatic destination in the White Mountains. If you're in good shape, it's well worth the 2-hour climb in anything except the most miserable weather. The trail is wide and only moderately demanding. Bring a picnic and lunch on the massive boulders that litter the ravine's floor.

In summer, an enclosed gondola known as the **Wildcat Express** 🐾 at the Wildcat ski area (see below) hauls passengers up the mountain for views of Tuckerman Ravine and Mount Washington's summit. The lift operates Saturday and Sunday from Memorial Day to mid-June, then daily through the mid-October. The ski resort's base lodge is just north of Pinkham Notch on Route 16. It cost $13 per adult, with discounts for seniors and kids, but it doesn't run in bad weather.

CROSS-COUNTRY SKIING

Jackson regularly ranks among the top cross-country ski resorts in the nation. The reason is the nonprofit **Jackson Ski Touring Foundation** (© **800/927-6697** or 603/383-9355; www.jacksonxc.com), which created and maintains the extensive trail network. The terrain is wonderfully varied; many of the trails are rated "most difficult," which will keep advanced skiers from getting bored. But novice and intermediate skiers also have plenty of good options spread out along the valley floor.

Start at the base lodge, near the Wentworth Resort in the center of Jackson. There's parking here, and you can ski right through the village and into the hills. Gentle trails traverse the valley floor, with more advanced trails winding up the mountains. One-way ski trips with shuttles back to Jackson are available; ask if you're interested. Given how extensive and well-maintained the trails are, passes are a good value at $17 for adults, $12 for seniors, and $8 for children ages 10 to 15. Rentals are available at the ski center (ticket/rental packages are available); snowshoes can be rented, too—there are specifically groomed for snowshoers.

DOWNHILL SKIING

Black Mountain ✦ *Kids*   Dating back to the 1930s, Black Mountain is one of the White Mountains' pioneer ski areas. It remains a quintessential family mountain—modest in size, non-threatening, ideal for beginners—though there's also glade skiing for more advanced skiers. A day here feels a bit like you've trespassed in some farmer's unused hayfield, which really adds to the charm. It's also surprisingly inexpensive compared with the other resorts around the Whites. The ski area also offers two compact terrain parks for snowboarders, as well as lessons, rentals, a day-care center for small kids, a ski school, and a base lodge with a cafeteria and pub.

P.O. Box B, Jackson, NH 03846. ✆ 800/475-4669 or 603/383-4490. www.blackmt.com. Adult day lift tickets $22–$32; half-day lift tickets $23; discounts for seniors and kids.

Wildcat ✦✦   Set high within Pinkham Notch, Wildcat Mountain combines a rich heritage as a venerable ski resort with the best views of any ski area in the White Mountains. This mountain offers a bountiful supply of intermediate trails, as well as some challenging expert terrain. It's skiing the way it used to be—no base-area clutter, just a single lodge with an unpretentious cafeteria and a pub. While that also means there are no on-slope hotels, condos, or other accommodations, there are lots of lodging options within an easy 15-minute drive. Ask about ticket packages combining your lift ticket with downhill ski rentals and, if you need, lessons.

Rte. 16, Pinkham Notch, NH 03846. ✆ 888/754-9453 or 603/466-3326. www.skiwildcat.com. Adult day lift tickets $59; half-day lift tickets $39; discounts for seniors, teens, and kids 6 to 12.

ESPECIALLY FOR KIDS

Parents with young children (age 10 and under) can buy peace of mind at **Story Land** ✦✦, at the northern junction of routes 16 and 302 (✆ **603/383-4186;** www.storylandnh.com). This old-fashioned (mid-1950s) fantasy village is filled with 30 acres of improbably leaning buildings, magical rides, fairy-tale creatures, and other enchanted beings. A "sprayground" features a 40-foot-tall water-spurting octopus—kids can get a good summer soaking. Story Land is open Saturday and Sunday from Memorial Day to mid-June, 9am to 5pm; daily 9am to 6pm from mid-June to Labor Day; and Saturday and Sunday 9am to 5pm until Columbus Day. Admission is a flat $23 per person for all visitors age 4 and older; toddlers under age 4 enter free.

WHERE TO STAY

Covered Bridge Motor Lodge ✦ *Value*   This pleasant, family-run motel on 5 acres between Route 16 and the burbling river is right next to Jackson's covered bridge. Rooms are priced affordably for the area. The best units have balconies that overlook the river; the noisier rooms facing the road are a bit cheaper. Ask about the two-bedroom apartment units with kitchens and fireplaces. While basic, the lodge has gardens

Tips **Gorham: Budget Beds, Low-Cost Lunches**

White Mountains travelers on a slim budget would do well to look at **Gorham** as their base for mountain explorations. This tidy commercial town 10 minutes north of Pinkham Notch lacks charm, but it does have a great selection of clean mom-and-pop motels and family-style restaurants. If you're planning to spend most of your time out hiking or canoeing, this won't matter so much anyway.

and other appealing touches like a hot tub, a pool, and a set of riverside barbecue grills (bring marshmallows) that make it a good pick for families stretching a buck.

Rte. 16 (Box V), Jackson, NH 03846. ℂ **800/634-2911** or 602/383-9151. Fax 603/383-4146. www.jacksoncovered bridge.com. 32 units. $79–$139 double; $109–$229 suite. Rates include continental breakfast. AE, DISC, MC, V. **Amenities:** Outdoor pool; tennis court; Jacuzzi. *In room:* A/C, TV, kitchenette (some units), fridge, coffeemaker (some units).

Eagle Mountain House ✿✿   The white wooden Eagle Mountain House is a handsome relic that has happily survived the ravages of time, fire, and the fickle tastes of tourists. Built in 1916, the gleaming, classic five-story hotel is set in an idyllic valley above Jackson. Guest rooms are furnished in a country-pine look with stenciled blanket chests, armoires, and feather comforters. You'll pay a premium for rooms with mountain views, though it's not really necessary to spend the extra cash. Instead, just plan to spend most of your free time lounging on the long, wide wraparound porch with views across the golf course and out to the mountains beyond.

Carter Notch Rd. (P.O. Box E), Jackson, NH 03846. ℂ **800/966-5779** or 603/383-9111. Fax 603/383-0854. www.eaglemt. com. 93 units. $79–$179 double; $109–$229 suite. 2-night minimum some weekends and peak periods. Ask about packages. AE, DISC, MC, V. **Amenities:** 2 restaurants; tavern; outdoor pool; golf course; 2 tennis courts; health club; Jacuzzi; sauna; massage; dry cleaning. *In room:* TV, fridge (some units), iron/ironing board.

The Inn at Thorn Hill ✿✿✿   This elegant inn is a superb choice for a romantic getaway. The classic shingle-style home (now swathed in light yellow siding) was designed by famed architect Stanford White in 1895, just outside Jackson's village center and surrounded by wooded hills. Inside, the place has a comfortable Victorian feel. Rooms are luxuriously appointed; you'll find it hard to leave them. Some of the nicest include the Katherine Suite, with a fireplace and two-person Jacuzzi, and the little yellow Notch View Cottage with its classic screened front porch and a double Jacuzzi with a forest view. The hospitality here is top-notch, and the main dining room's three-course dinners (see "Where to Dine," below) are among the best in the Mount Washington Valley; you're almost certain to sample it, since nearly all rates include a full breakfast, afternoon tea service, and dinner in the dining room or more casual lounge. Recently added is a quite lovely spa area with nice facilities (a wooden sauna, whirlpool-like tubs) and a full menu of services from hydrotherapy and facials to prenatal massage and yoga.

Thorn Hill Rd. (P.O. Box A), Jackson, NH 03846. ℂ **800/289-8990** or 603/383-4242. www.innatthornhill.com. 25 units. $189–$430 double. Rates include full breakfast, afternoon tea, and dinner. Packages available. 2- to 3-night minimum stay Sat–Sun and some holidays. AE, DISC, MC, V. Children 8 and older welcome. **Amenities:** 3 restaurants; bar; outdoor pool; spa; Jacuzzi; limited room service; babysitting; laundry service. *In room:* A/C, TV, fireplace (some units), Jacuzzi (some units).

Joe Dodge Lodge at Pinkham Notch *(Finds)*

Guests come to the Pinkham Notch Visitor Center more for the camaraderie than for the accommodations. Situated spectacularly at the base of Mount Washington, far from commercial clutter and with easy access to many hiking and skiing trails, this center is operated by the Appalachian Mountain Club like a tightly run youth hostel, with guests sharing simple bunkrooms, dormitory-style bathrooms, and optional meals at family-style tables in the main lodge. (A set of private rooms provide double beds or family accommodations, with breakfast and dinner included in the price.) The two huge pluses here are a festive atmosphere and a can't-be-beat location. You can also buy a trail lunch to go in the cafeteria.

Rte. 16, Pinkham Notch, NH. (Mailing address: AMC, P.O. Box 298, Gorham, NH 03581.) © **603/466-2721.** www.outdoors.org. 108 beds in 32 rooms of 2, 3, and 4 beds, all with shared bathroom. Double rooms $130–$150 including breakfast and dinner. Bunkrooms peak season $51 per adult, $28 per child 15 and under (discount for AMC members); off-season $43 per adult, $25 per child; MAP plans also available. Holiday rates higher. MC, V. Children 3 and older welcome. **Amenities:** Cafeteria. *In room:* No phone.

Wentworth Resort Hotel *(★★★)*

The venerable Wentworth sits in the middle of Jackson Village, all turrets, eaves, and awnings. Built in 1869, this Victorian shingled inn once consisted of a campus-like set of 39 buildings (including a dairy and an electric plant), but it had edged to the brink of deterioration by the mid-1980s. Then the seven remaining buildings were refurbished, with a number of condominium clusters added around the expanded and upgraded golf course. The inn has since upgraded again; you'll feel like a prince (or princess). The hugely spacious, standard and superior double rooms are lavishly decorated with quality, Victorian-inspired furnishings. Suites (all with king-size beds) are stocked with such amenities as propane fireplaces, whirlpools, outdoor hot tubs, and claw-footed tubs. Visitors of stout constitution can stroll right up the road and plunge into the icy waters of Jackson Falls.

1 Carter Notch Rd. (P.O. Box M), Jackson, NH 03846. © **800/637-0013** or 603/383-9700. Fax 603/383-4265. www.thewentworth.com. 76 units. Peak season $185–$245 double, $305–$355 suite; off-season $155–$185 double, $225–$265 suite. Rates include full breakfast and 5-course dinner. B&B and no-meals plans also available. AE, DC, DISC, MC, V. **Amenities:** Restaurant; outdoor pool; golf course; tennis court; cross-country ski center. *In room:* A/C, TV (some units), fireplace (some units), Jacuzzi (some units).

Wildcat Inn & Tavern *(★)*

The Wildcat Inn occupies a three-story building in the center of Jackson village. It's a comfortable, informal spot better known for its cozy restaurant and tavern than for its accommodations. Guest rooms are mostly small, two-room suites, carpeted and furnished with a mishmash of furniture. Most of the sitting rooms have contemporary sofas, chairs, and pine furniture, offering cozy sanctuary after a day of hiking or skiing. Two rooms directly above the tavern offer good privacy for families or friends traveling together, though noise from performing musicians may filter upward. There's also one cottage with a kitchen. The main dining room resembles a country farmhouse, with old wood floors and pine furniture; in the winter, stake out a toasty spot in front of the **tavern** *(★★)* fireplace, one of the most popular gathering spots in the valley. Sip a drink and order from a the bar menu.

Rte. 16A, Jackson, NH 03846. © **800/228-4245** or 603/383-4245. www.wildcattavern.com. 15 units. $79–$129 double; $99–$259 suite and cottage. Foliage season rates higher. Rates include full breakfast. AE, DC, MC, V. **Amenities:** Dining room; tavern. *In room:* A/C, TV, kitchenette (1 unit).

WHERE TO DINE

The Inn at Thorn Hill *(★★★)* NEW AMERICAN

The romantic Inn at Thorn Hill is a great choice for a memorable meal. The dining room faces the forested hill behind the inn. Start with a glass of wine from the good wine list (the restaurant has won the *Wine Spectator* award of excellence), then browse the menu, which has leaned away from Asian accent to more solidly Continental or French fare of late. Appetizers might include mussels steamed in Vermouth, a salad of lobster claw meat with bacon and leeks, a Serrano ham and pine-nut salad. Entrees could be a grilled New York sirloin steak, a rack of lamb with goat cheese–flavored grits, salmon with endive, seared tuna with couscous, or a roasted chicken breast with mushrooms. Desserts are great; try the chèvre cheesecake, sour-cream panna cotta with strawberries, chocolate pavé, apple-rhubarb crisp, or rosewater granita (if they're on the menu).

Thorn Hill Rd., Jackson. ℭ 603/383-4242. www.innatthornhill.com. Reservations recommended. Main courses $23–$31. AE, DISC, MC, V. Daily 6–9pm.

Thompson House Eatery ✰✰ ECLECTIC   This friendly, old-fashioned spot in a 19th-century Cape-style "plank" farmhouse sits at the edge of Jackson's golf course. It attracts crowds for the fare, which is pricier than it used to be. Dining is both indoors and out. For lunch, there are a variety of fun salads, meat loaf, and deli-style sandwiches. For dinner, expect barbecue-spiced pork tenderloin, a seafood mélange cooked in sherry, lamb chops with the classic mint jelly, bronzed duck breast over duck sausage, and several vegetarian items like a meaty, Parmesan-crusted eggplant layered with smoked cheddar and mushrooms. Desserts and martinis here are excellent; there's also a bar on the premises with its own substantial menu.

193 Main St. (off Rte. 16A, near intersection with Rte. 16), Jackson. ℭ 603/383-9341. Reservations recommended for dinner. Main courses $7–$10 at lunch; $17–$30 at dinner. AE, DISC, MC, V. Summer and fall Mon–Thurs 11:30am–3pm and 5:30–9pm; Fri–Sun 5:30–9pm; rest of the year, call for hours.

CRAWFORD NOTCH ✰✰

Crawford Notch is a wild, rugged mountain valley that angles right through the heart of the White Mountains. There's a surplus of legend and history here. For years after its discovery by European settlers in 1771, this was an impenetrable wilderness—and a literal barrier to commerce, because it blocked trade between the upper Connecticut River Valley and the busy harbors in Portland and Portsmouth. Eventually some plucky bunch got through the pass, and it developed into an important route.

By the way, don't get confused by directions referring to the towns of Twin Mountain and Bretton Woods. These are the *same* village; it has two different names.

ESSENTIALS

GETTING THERE   Route 302 runs through Crawford Notch for approximately 25 miles between the towns of Bartlett and Twin Mountain. Pick up 302 from Portland, Maine (coming from Maine or Boston), I-93 (exit for Bethlehem) from the White Mountains, or I-91 (exit for Wells River, Vermont) from New York City.

VISITOR INFORMATION   The **Twin Mountain-Bretton Woods Chamber of Commerce** (ℭ 800/245-8946; www.twinmountain.org) provides general information and lodging referrals from a booth near the intersection of U.S. Route 302 and U.S. Route 3. It's open from mid-May through the middle of October.

HIKING

The Appalachian Mountain Club's **Highland Center at Crawford Notch** ✰✰ (ℭ 603/278-4453), on Route 302 in Bretton Woods, is a newish, multipurpose facility on 26 acres of AMC-owned land. It's a great headquarters for hikes into the surrounding mountains. Under one roof, you can book a tour, hike the path that passes nearby, bunk down for the night in the Highland Lodge, eat communal dinners, or use L.L.Bean gear for free (yes, really). It's open year-round.

From June through mid-October (but only Sat–Sun after mid-September), the Center is also the hub for two AMC-operated **hiker shuttles** (① **603/466-2727**). These vans cruise the mountains, depositing and picking up hikers; they're useful, though pricey—but if you haven't brought a car, this is really your only option. Rides cost $14 one-way, regardless of length; AMC members get a $2 discount.

SKIING

Attitash ✦✦   This is one of New England's most scenic ski areas, and Attitash is also a good mountain for families and skiers at the intermediate-edging-to-advanced level. The resort consists of 70 or so trails across two peaks, 1,750-foot Attitash and adjacent Bear Peak. Dotted with rugged rock outcroppings and full of sweeping views of Mount Washington and the Presidential Range (there's also an observation tower on the main summit), this is an eye-popping place—but the skiing is fine, too. Look for great cruising runs and a handful of challenging drops. There's also a terrain park for snowboarders. The base area here tends to get sleepy at night, though; those looking for true nightlife should pile into the car and drive 15 minutes to North Conway.

Rte. 302 (P.O. Box 308), Bartlett, NH 03812. ① 877/677-7669 or 603/374-2368. www.attitash.com. Adult day lift tickets $59–$65; discounts for seniors and students.

Bretton Woods Resort ✦✦ *Kids*   Bretton Woods tapped controversial Olympic ski medalist Bode Miller as director of skiing, and the newer trails and lifts bringing a welcome vitality to the mountain, which has long been popular with beginners and families. Trails here include plenty of glades and wide cruising runs, as well as some more challenging options for advanced skiers. The challenge level still doesn't rival that of the most demanding slopes in Vermont or Maine, but one section features "Bode's Run," an expert trail partly designed by Miller. The resort also continues to do an award-winning job taking care of kids (tons of programs for the little ones) and retains a low-key attitude that families seem to adore. Accommodations are available both on the mountain and nearby, notably at the grand, red-roofed Mount Washington Hotel (see "Where to Stay," below), though nightlife here tends to consist of a quiet hot tub or catching the late news on TV. There's also night skiing here; three snowboard terrain parks; and (for those so inclined) an excellent cross-country ski center nearby. Still not sold? How about this: You can eat barbecue up on top of West Mountain. Grab some before skiing the glades or riding the Cog Railway.

Rte. 302, Bretton Woods, NH 03575. ① 800/314-1752 or 603/278-3320. www.brettonwoods.com. Adult day lift tickets $59–$69; half-day lift tickets $59–$69; discounts for teens, young children, and seniors.

A HISTORIC RAILWAY

Mount Washington Cog Railway ✦✦   Mount Washington's Cog Railway was a marvel of engineering when it opened in 1869, and it remains so today. Part moving museum, part slow-motion roller-coaster ride, the Cog Railway steams to the mountain's summit at a determined, "I think I can" pace of about 4 mph. But you'll still get some adrenaline thrills, especially when the train crosses Jacob's Ladder, a rickety-seeming trestle 25-feet high that angles upward at a grade of more than 37%. Passengers enjoy the expanding view on this 3-hour round-trip (which includes important stops to add water to the steam engine, check the track switches, and allow other trains to ascend or descend). A 20-minute stop at the summit allows you to browse around. Be aware that this ride is noisy, breezy, and sulfurous. *Don't* wear white. If you dress warmly in a jacket and sweater, and expect to get covered with a light patina of cin-der and soot, you'll be okay. There's now also a shorter, 1-hour ride, operating twice daily all winter, through the lovely, snow-covered vistas.

Base Rd., Bretton Woods (from Rte. 302, turn onto Base Rd. at Fabyan's Station Restaurant and continue 6 miles to railway base station). ✆ **800/922-8825** or 603/278-5404. www.thecog.com. Fare $59 adults, $54 seniors, $39 chil-dren 4–12, free for children 3 and under. Winter fares lower. MC, V. Runs daily (usually on the hour, 9am to 3 or 4pm; check website or call for schedule), Memorial Day–late Oct and Sat–Sun in May. Shorter excursions twice daily Nov–Mar. Reservations recommended.

WHERE TO STAY & DINE

Bernerhof Inn 🎯 _Value_   Overlooking busy Route 302 on the way to Crawford Notch, the Bernerhof occupies a century-old home that's all gables and squared-off turrets. Inside, guest rooms are eclectic and fun, crafted with odd angles and corners; all are tastefully furnished in a simple country style light on the froufrou. The third-floor Mountain Shadow suite is tucked under the eaves with a two-person Jacuzzi and in-room sauna, for instance. Other rooms have Jacuzzis under a skylight, stained-glass windows, wood floors, brass beds, and handsome cherry furniture; one even has a clover-shaped tub in an alcove. In addition to a decent dining room serving suitably wheels-on-the-road Germanic fare (schnitzel, fondue, knockwurst) and a woody pub, the new lounge is a good place to catch up on e-mail or read the paper over coffee.

Rte. 302, Glen, NH 03838. ✆ **800/548-8007** or 603/383-9132. Fax 603/383-0809. www.bernerhofinn.com. 9 units. $99–$199 double. Rates include full breakfast. Packages available. 2-night minimum stay peak season and Sat–Sun. AE, DISC, MC, V. **Amenities:** Restaurant; pub. _In room:_ A/C, TV, hair dryer, fireplace (some units), Jacuzzi (some units).

The Mount Washington Hotel 🎯🎯 _Kids_   At the foot of New Hampshire's highest peak, this five-story resort, with gleaming white clapboards and a cherry-red roof, almost seems like a Bavarian castle appearing out of the mist. Built in 1902, it once drew such luminaries as Babe Ruth, Thomas Edison, and Woodrow Wilson. It's one of my favorite properties in the state; I especially enjoy the 900-foot-long back porch, looking directly up at the massive mountain and down onto a golf course, pool, and tennis court. Guest rooms vary in size and decor; many have grand views. Meals are taken in an impressive, lost-in-time octagonal dining room while an orchestra plays. There are lots of family and kids' programs and activities (such as fly-casting lessons), and innkeepers are making overdue improvements. Though the hotel can still feel a bit unfinished at times, it remains a classic New England resort in an unbeatable setting.

U.S. Rte. 302, Bretton Woods, NH 03575. ✆ **800/314-1752** or 603/278-1000. www.mtwashington.com. 200 units. $145–$525 double; $910–$1,750 suite. Rates include breakfast and dinner. Minimum stay during holidays. AE, DISC, MC, V. **Amenities:** 2 restaurants; indoor pool; outdoor pool; 2 golf courses; 12 tennis courts; Jacuzzi; sauna; bike rental; children's programs (summer); concierge; shopping arcade; room service; babysitting. _In room:_ TV.

Notchland Inn 🎯🎯   Off Route 302 in a wild section of Crawford Notch, this inn looks every bit like something out of a Sir Walter Scott novel. Built of hand-cut gran-ite in the mid-1800s, Notchland is classy yet informal, perfectly situated for exploring the wilds of the White Mountains. The front parlor was designed by Gustav Stickley, a founder of the Arts & Crafts movement, in suitably wood-heavy style; check out the unique fireplace. Guest rooms are outfitted with antiques, wood-burning fireplaces, high ceilings, and individual thermostats. Some of the five suites have Jacuzzis and/or private decks; two are located in an adjacent former schoolhouse (the one upstairs has a wonderful soaking tub) and there are three new cottages, all with kitchens or wet bars. You may want to add the five-course dinner to your plan—because the closest restaurant is a long, dark drive away. Nonguests can dine here, too.

Rte. 302, Hart's Location, NH 03812. (© **800/866-6131** or 603/374-6131. www.notchland.com. 16 units. $195–$225 double, $275–$315 cottage and suite; foliage season and holidays $255–$275 double, $325–$365 cottage and suite. Rates include breakfast. 2- to 3-night minimum stay Sat–Sun, foliage season, and some holidays. AE, DISC, MC, V. Children 12 and older welcome. **Amenities:** Dining room; Jacuzzi; babysitting. *In room:* A/C (some units), hair dryer, kitchenette (some units), iron/ironing board, fireplace (most units), no phone.

FRANCONIA NOTCH 𝒢𝒢

Franconia Notch *is* classic New Hampshire. As travelers head north on I-93, the Kinsman Range to the west and the Franconia Range to the east begin converging, and the road swells upward as though to meet them. Soon, the mountain ranges press inward on either side like a closing book, forming dramatic **Franconia Notch,** which offers little in the way of civilization or services but a whole lot of natural drama. Most of the notch is in a well-managed state park that to most travelers will be indistinguishable from the national forest. Travelers should plan on a leisurely ride through the notch, allowing time to get out of the car and explore forests, craggy peaks, and local eateries. Franconia Notch is more developed for recreation (and thus more crowded with day-trippers) than equally rugged Crawford Notch to the northeast (see earlier in this chapter), and outdoorsy types might enjoy it more as a result.

ESSENTIALS

GETTING THERE   I-93 runs right through Franconia Notch, narrowing from four lanes to two (and becoming the Franconia Notch Pkwy.) in the most scenic parts. Several scenic roadside pull-offs dot the route. **Concord Coach** (© **800/639-3317;** www.concordcoachlines.com) runs one daily bus to and from Boston. There is no ticket office in Franconia; wait at Mac's Market, right off I-93 at exit 38.

VISITOR INFORMATION   Information on the park and surrounding area is available at the **Flume Gorge & Visitor Center** (© **603/745-8391**), at exit 34A off I-93. North of the notch, the **Franconia Notch Chamber of Commerce** (© **603/823-5661;** www.franconianotch.org) maintains a helpful little hut of visitor information on Main Street next to the town hall, open spring through fall.

EXPLORING FRANCONIA NOTCH STATE PARK 𝒢

Franconia Notch State Park's (© **603/745-8391**) 8,000 acres, nestled within the much bigger White Mountain National Forest, host an array of scenic attractions easily accessible from I-93 and the Franconia Notch Parkway.

The Flume 𝒢𝒢 is a rugged 800-foot gorge through which the Flume Brook tumbles. A popular attraction in the mid–19th century, it's 800 feet long, 90 feet deep, and as narrow as 20 feet at the bottom; visitors explore by means of a network of boardwalks and bridges on a 2-mile walk. Early photos of the chasm show a boulder wedged in overhead; this was swept away in an 1883 avalanche. If you're just looking for an easy, quick hit of nature, it's worth the money. But otherwise set off into the mountains and seek your own sights without the crowds and cost. It's open from mid-May through mid-October, weather permitting, 9am to 5pm (a half-hour later in July and Aug). Admission is $10 for adults, $7 for children ages 6 to 12. Walk or snowshoe the grounds for free in the off-season.

Echo Lake 𝒢 is a picturesquely situated recreation area, with a 28-acre lake, a handsome swimming beach, and picnic tables scattered about, all within view of Cannon Mountain on one side and Mount Lafayette on the other. A bike path runs alongside the lake and meanders up and down the notch for a total of 8 miles. Take exit

34C to get to Echo Lake Beach; admission to the state park is $3 for visitors over age 12, $1 for visitors age 12 and under.

For a high-altitude view of the region, set off for the alpine ridges on the **Cannon Mountain Aerial Tramway** ⬧⬧ (℗ **603/823-8800**). The old-fashioned cable car serves skiers in winter; in summer, it whisks up to 80 travelers at a time to the summit of the 4,180-foot mountain. Once up top, you can strike out on foot along the Rim Trail for superb views. Be prepared for cool, gusty winds. The tramway opens from lay May to late October and costs $11 round-trip for adults, $7 for children ages 6 to 12.

DOWNHILL SKIING
Cannon Mountain ⬧ (Value)   During downhill skiing's formative years, this state-run ski area was *the* place to ski in the East. One of New England's very first ski mountains, Cannon remains famed for its challenging runs and exposed faces, and the mountain still attracts skiers who are serious about getting down the hill in style. Many of the old-fashioned New England–style trails are narrow and fun (but often icy, because they're constantly scoured by the notch's winds), and the enclosed tramway is an elegant way to get to the summit (see above). With no base lodge scene to speak of, skiers must retire to inns in Franconia or Sugar Hill, or else retreat southward to the condo country that is Lincoln. Interestingly, lift-ticket prices haven't risen appreciably here in at least 2 or 3 years, which is unheard of at New England ski resorts.

Franconia Notch Pkwy., Franconia. ℗ **603/823-8800**. www.cannonmt.com. Adult day lift tickets $42–$54; half-day lift tickets $26–$40; discounts for seniors, teens, and youth.

LITERARY HISTORY
The Frost Place ⬧   Robert Frost lived in New Hampshire from the time he was 10 until he was 45. The Frost Place is a humble farmhouse where the poet once lived with his family, one of several northern New England abodes he inhabited during his career (Derry, New Hampshire, and Arlington, Vermont, are two others covered in this book). Today, appropriately, his former farmhouse is a quietly respectful tribute in the form of an arts center and gathering place for local writers. Walking the grounds, it's not hard to see how his granite-edged poetry evolved here at the fringes of the White Mountains. First editions of Frost's works are on display; a nature trail in the woods nearby is posted with excerpts from some of his poems. In early July each year, there's a Frost Day celebration with readings from resident poets and lectures.

Ridge Rd. (Box 74), Franconia. ℗ **603/823-5510**. www.frostplace.org. Admission free; suggested donation $4 adults, $3 seniors, $2 children 6–12, free for children under 6. Late May–June Sat–Sun 1–5pm; July–early Oct Wed–Mon 1–5pm. From Franconia, travel south 1 mile on Rte. 116 to Ridge Rd. (a gravel road); turn off and follow signs a short way to the house, parking in lot below the house.

WHERE TO STAY & DINE
Franconia Inn ⬧   This welcoming inn is set on a quiet road in a bucolic valley 2 miles from the village of Franconia. Built in 1934 after a fire destroyed the original 1886 structure, the inn has an informal feel, with wingback chairs around the fireplace in one common room, and jigsaw puzzles half completed in the paneled library. Guest rooms are appointed in a relaxed country fashion; a few have gas fireplaces, and a few have Jacuzzis. The inn is a haven for cross-country skiers—about 40 miles of groomed trails start right outside the front door—and breakfast (optional for an extra most of the year) is delicious, with a set of gourmet choices available.

1300 Easton Rd., Franconia, NH 03580. ℗ **800/473-5299** or 603/823-5542. www.franconiainn.com. 34 units. $111–$191 double and suite; foliage season $155–$235 double and suite. Rates include breakfast in foliage season. B&B and

MAP rates also available year-round. 3-night minimum stay on holiday weekends. Mon–Fri discounts available off-season. AE, MC, V. Closed Apr to mid-May. **Amenities:** Restaurant; bar; outdoor pool; 4 tennis courts; Jacuzzi; sauna; free bikes; bridle trails; horse rentals; cross-country ski trails. *In room:* No phone.

Polly's Pancake Parlor ★★ *(Finds) (Kids)* This family-style eatery, in a shaggy wooden-sided building dating from around 1830 a few miles uphill from the little village of Sugar Hill, is one of my favorite breakfast stops in New England (or anywhere). Besides possessing possibly the best views of any pancake house in the Western world, the restaurant serves a wonderful assortment of pancakes (order a combo of three kinds; I like the chocolate chip and cornmeal flapjacks). Of course, all are served with real New Hampshire maple syrup and maple sugar from the "sugar farm" on which Polly's sits. Kids love this place, and there's also a good gift shop for adults that doubles as a display for antique farm implements. They serve sandwiches and salads here, too (but that's not why you're here), and maple-inflected desserts (which is). Breakfast and American-road food aficionados should not miss a chance to experience Polly's. It's open from spring through foliage season, and you can also mail-order syrup year-round using the toll-free number.

672 Route 117, Sugar Hill. ℭ **603/823-5575** or 800/432-8972. Most items $4–$10. May–late Oct Mon–Fri 7am–2pm; Sat–Sun 7am–3pm.

Sugar Hill Inn ★★ A classic New England inn, with wraparound porch and sweeping mountain panoramas occupying 16 acres on lovely Sugar Hill, this welcoming, comfortable spot is a great base for exploring the western White Mountains. Bette Davis stayed here once upon a time, no doubt for the great expansive views out back. A new owner purchased the place in 2006, and so far he has improved the property with central air-conditioning and an in-ground pool, the inn's first. (He's said to be adding a cottage to the property soon as well.) Rooms are graciously appointed in antique country style, some influenced by Shaker sensibility; many have gas Vermont Castings stoves for heat and atmosphere. The **dining room** ★, one of the area's best, serves upscale eclectic four-course dinners in a cozy, fire-lit-tavern setting to both inn guests and the general public—a point of pride for the new owner, who received culinary training in New York. The restaurant is closed Wednesdays.

116 Rte. 117, Sugar Hill, NH 03586. ℭ **800/548-4748** or 603/823-5621. www.sugarhillinn.com. 12 units. $140–$290 double; $155–$380 suite and cottage. Rates include breakfast. Packages available. AE, MC, V. Closed Apr. Children 12 and older welcome. **Amenities:** Restaurant; outdoor pool; massage. *In room:* A/C (some units), no phone.

14

Maine

by Paul Karr

Humor columnist Dave Barry once suggested that Maine's state motto should be changed to "Cold, but damp," thereby emphasizing its two primary qualities.

Well, that's somewhat true. Spring tends to last for just a few blustery days; November features bitter winds alternating with gray sheets of rain; and the interminably long winter brings a mix of blizzards and ice storms.

Ah, but summer. Summer in Maine brings osprey diving for fish off spruce-cloaked points, gleaming cumulus clouds building over the rounded peaks of the western mountains, and the haunting whoops of loons echoing off dense forest walls bordering sapphire-clear lakes. Summer brings languorous days when the sun rises off the Atlantic early, well before the tourists do (but the lobstermen still beat it to work); by 8am, it already feels like noon. Maine summers offer an experience of peacefulness that simply can't be duplicated easily elsewhere in the lower 48; a few days in the right spot can rejuvenate even the most jangled nerves.

The trick is in *finding* that right spot. U.S. Route 1 along the Maine coast is mostly an amalgam of convenience stores, tourist boutiques, and restaurants catering to bus tours; you have to get off this beaten track a little bit before you can really start to unwind. The loop road, beach, and most popular mountain peaks of popular Acadia National Park can get pretty congested in summer—you simply won't believe how many New York, New Jersey, and Massachusetts license plates have made their way this far north and east. Look for a nice fishing village instead. And it goes without saying, but I'll say it: arriving in Maine without a room reservation in high season (Memorial Day to Columbus Day, plus a short foliage season in October) is just a bad idea.

So long as you avoid those most-congested areas, Maine's remote position and size really works to your advantage. The state has an amazing 5,500 miles of coastline, plus 3,000 or so coastal islands, and miles of mountain trails with few other hikers (except maybe moose and deer) for company. With a little homework, you can find that perfect little cove, island, or village, book a room in advance, and get ready to enjoy Maine's lovely scenery.

Getting to know the locals is fun, too. Mainers were mostly fishermen (as opposed to the farmers who colonized the rest of New England) and other seafaring folk, so today Mainers—even the transplanted ones—still exhibit a wry sense of humor and gregariousness. There's a Bait's Motel in Searsport (complete with worm-hanging-off-its-hook motif), and a tiny street called Fitz Hugh Lane in Somesville. Take the time to get to know folks here; you'll be rewarded by it.

And for specific coverage of the Maine coastline so detailed that you'll practically be able to spot every last seagull sitting on top of a rock, pick up my *Frommer's Maine Coast* guidebook. It's a great resource that will help you enjoy that slice of this region even more fully.

1 The Southern Maine Coast ★ ★

York is 45 miles SW of Portland, 10 miles NE of Portsmouth, and 65 miles NE of Boston

Maine's southern coast runs roughly from the state line at Kittery to Portland, and is the primary destination of most travelers to the state. (These statistics include many day-trippers from the Boston area). While it takes some doing to find privacy or remoteness here, there are at least two excellent reasons to come: the long, sandy beaches and a sense of history in the coastal villages (some of them, anyway).

Thanks to quirks of geography, nearly all of Maine's sandy shores are along this stretch of coastline. It's not hard to find a relaxing spot whether you prefer dunes, the lulling sound of breaking waves, or a carnival-like atmosphere in a beach town. Waves depend on the weather; during a good Northeast blow, they pound the shores, rise above the roads, and threaten beach houses built decades ago. During balmy midsummer days, though, the ocean can be as gentle as a farm pond, its barely audible waves lapping timidly at the shore as the tide creeps in, inch by inch, covering tidal pools full of crabs, snails, and starfish.

One thing all the beaches here share in common: They're washed by the chilled waters of the Gulf of Maine, which makes for invigorating swimming. Though the beach season is generally brief and intense, running only from July 4th to Labor Day, some towns are making an effort to stretch the tourist season out into fall. However, this idea hasn't really taken hold yet (the frigid water might have something to do with), and once Labor Day weekend is finished, oceanside communities reliably adopt a slower, almost somnolent pace.

KITTERY & THE YORKS ★ ★

For travelers driving into Maine from the south, **Kittery** ★ is the first town to appear after crossing the big bridge spanning the Piscataqua River from New Hampshire. Once famous for its (still operating) naval yard, Kittery is now better known for its dozens of factory outlets.

"The Yorks," just to the north, are three towns that share a name, but little else. In fact, it's rare to find three such well-defined and diverse New England archetypes within such a compact area. **York Village** ★ is full of 17th-century American history and architecture in a compact area, and has a good library. **York Harbor** ★ ★ reached its zenith during America's late Victorian era, when wealthy urbanites constructed cottages at the ocean's edge; it's the most relaxing and scenic of the three. Finally, **York Beach** ★ ★ is a fun beach town with amusements, taffy shops, a small zoo, gabled summer homes set in crowded enclaves, a great lighthouse, and two excellent beaches with sun, sand, rocks, surf, surfers, fried-fish stands, and lighthouse views.

ESSENTIALS

GETTING THERE   Kittery is accessible from either **Interstate 95** or **Route 1,** with well-marked exits. Coming from the south, the Yorks are reached most easily by heading for (but not taking) the Maine Turnpike; follow I-95 to a point just south of the turnpike exit, then exit to the right ("last exit before tolls"). Coming from the north, pay your toll exiting the turnpike and then take the first exit, an immediate right.

Maine

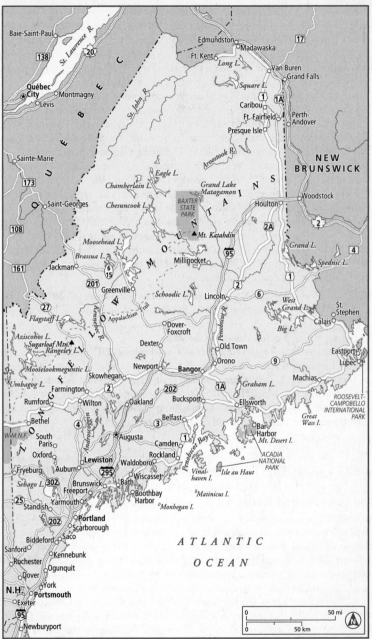

Amtrak (© 800/872-7245; www.amtrak.com) operates four to five Downeaster trains daily from Boston's North Station (which does not connect to Amtrak's national network; you must take a subway or taxi from Boston's South Station first) into southern Maine, stopping outside Wells, about 10 miles away from the Yorks; a one-way ticket costs $19, and the trip takes 1¾ hours. From Wells, though, you'll need to phone for a taxi or arrange for a pickup to get to your final destination.

No bus lines serve the stretch of Maine between Portland and Kittery. However, no less than *three* competing lines run regular buses daily from Boston's South Station to downtown Portsmouth, New Hampshire, which is very close to Kittery (you can actually walk over a bridge into Maine from Portsmouth). For more details, see "Essentials" in the Portsmouth section of chapter 13. Taking a bus from New York City's Port Authority to Portsmouth costs about $45 one-way and takes about 6½ hours; from Boston, figure a fare of $17 or $18 one-way and a 1-hour ride.

From mid-June through Labor Day, a trackless **trolley** (a bus gussied up to look like an old-fashioned trolley) links the two beaches (Short Sands and Long Sands) in York and provides a convenient way to explore both. The "trolley" costs $1.50 each way. An all-day pass on a longer, circular sightseeing route through the Yorks costs $8 per adult, $4 for kids age 3 to 10; hop on at well-marked stops. The chief advantage of this route is that is passes out to Nubble Light (see below), a very scenic point that is too far for most folks to from the beaches.

VISITOR INFORMATION   The **Kittery Information Center** (© 207/439-1319) is at a well-marked rest area on I-95. It's full of info and helpful staff; has a pet exercise area and copious vending machines; and is open daily from 8am to 6pm in summer, from 9am to 5:30pm the rest of the year.

The **Greater York Region Chamber of Commerce** (© 207/363-4422) also operates another helpful **visitor center,** one that mirrors the shape of a stone cottage. It's set back from Rte. 1, right across from the Maine Turnpike exit 1 (beside the Stonewall Kitchen headquarters). In peak season, it's open Monday to Saturday from 9am to 5pm and Sunday from 10am to 4pm; from Labor Day through June, it's open Monday to Friday 9am to 4pm and Saturday from 10am to 2pm.

EXPLORING YORK

York is split into several village centers, described above; the best for walking around in is **York Village** ✦✦, a fine destination for those curious about early American history. First settled in 1624, the village opens several homes to the public.

Old York Historical Society ✦✦✦   York's local historical society oversees the bulk of the town's collection of historic buildings, some of which date to the early 18th century, and most of which are astonishingly well preserved or restored. Tickets are available to eight Old York–operated properties in all; one good place to start is at the **Jefferds' Tavern** ✦, across from the handsome **old burying ground** ✦. Changing exhibits document various facets of early life. Next door is the School House, furnished as it might have been in the last century. A 10-minute walk along lightly traveled Lindsay Road brings you to **Hancock Wharf,** next door to the **George Marshall Store.** Also nearby is the Elizabeth Perkins House, with its well-preserved Colonial Revival interiors. Finally, there are two "don't-miss" buildings in the society's collection: the **Old Gaol** ✦✦, which still has its (now-musty) dungeons, was built in 1719 as a jail to hold criminals, debtors, and other miscreants. It's the oldest surviving public building in the United States. Then, just down the knoll from the jail, is the

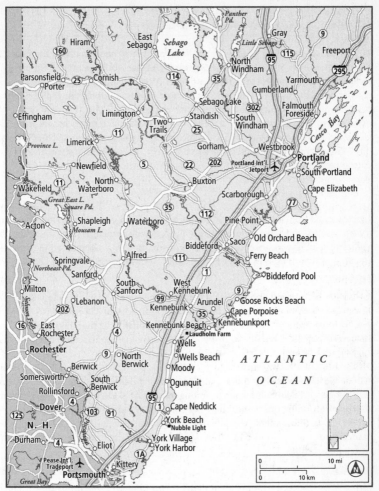

Emerson-Wilcox House , built in the mid-1700s and periodically added onto through the years. It's a virtual catalog of architectural styles and early decorative arts.

207 York St., York. ✆ **207/363-4974.** www.oldyork.org. Admission per building $5 adult, $4 seniors, $3 children 3–15; pass to all buildings $10 adult, $9 seniors, $5 children 4–15. Museum Mon–Sat 10am–5pm; some properties shorter hours. Closed mid-Oct to mid-June.

BEACHES

York Beach actually consists of *two* beaches, **Long Sands Beach** 🎫🎫 and **Short Sands Beach** 🎫, separated by a rocky headland. Both have plenty of room for sunning and Frisbees when the tide is out. When the tide is in, though, both become narrow and cramped. Short Sands fronts the honky-tonk town of York Beach, with its candlepin bowling, taffy-pulling machine, and video arcades. It's a better pick for families traveling with kids who have short attention spans. Long Sands runs along Route 1A,

---

Finds Sayward-Wheeler House

For those who'd like a taste of local history but lack the stamina for the full-court Old York visit, stop by the **Sayward-Wheeler House** ✿ in York Harbor, run by the group **Historic New England**. In this well-preserved merchant's home dating back to 1760, you'll see china captured during the 1745 Siege of Louisbourg, which routed the French out of Nova Scotia. It's open Saturday and Sunday only, June through October. Tours are given hourly from 11am to 4pm. Admission is $5. For information, call the house (© **207/384-2454**) or the organization's office in Boston (© **617/227-3956**; www.historic newengland.org).

---

directly across from a line of motels, summer homes, and convenience stores. Parking at *both* beaches is metered in summer; pay heed, as enforcement is strict and you must pay until 9pm, 7 days a week. (At the end of summer, they decapitate the meters—literally—and parking is then free and plentiful until the next Memorial Day.)

SHOPPING

Kittery has become a shopping mecca thanks to the establishment of colonies of little factory outlet shopping malls clustered along both sides of U.S. Route 1, about 4 miles south of York. More than 100 of these outlets flank the highway, in more than a dozen strip malls. It's aesthetically ugly, but if you're looking to score a deal, you just might find it beautiful.

Name-brand retailers with factory shops here purveying cut-rate designer stuff include Coach, Orvis, Samsonite, Gap, Eddie Bauer, Banana Republic, Calvin Klein, Brookstone, and Polo Ralph Lauren, among many others. On rainy summer days, lots of people (including this author) have been spotted whiling away hours here. Parking can be tight. Information on current outlets is available from the **Kittery Outlet Association.** Call © **888/KITTERY (548-8379)** or visit the website at www.the kitteryoutlets.com.

WHERE TO STAY

York Beach is stocked with plenty of motel rooms right on Long Sands Beach. Quality is highly variable, since all these properties are individually owned, but all of them can correctly boast that you can walk across the street and be at the beach. Reserve ahead during high season, or inquire at the York visitor center about vacancies if you're arriving without a room at the last minute (which, in summer, is a bad idea).

In Kittery

Portsmouth Harbor Inn and Spa ✿✿ This handsome 1899 home is just across the river from downtown Portsmouth, New Hampshire (p. 543), a pleasant, half-mile walk across a drawbridge. Innkeepers Nat and Lynn Bowditch extend homey touches such as fresh cookies and complimentary drinks. Rooms are tastefully restored and furnished with eclectic antiques, and though some are on the small side, all are boldly furnished and fun—the Valora room has ruby-red walls, harbor views, attractive antiques, and an above-average-size bathroom with historic accents. The King George room comes with a king-size bed (of course) and kingly skyline and bridge views. The

Dido's two single beds can be adapted into an extra-long king. The whimsically decorated sitting room has two couches, on which you can sprawl and browse through intriguing books. Spa services in an annex are quite popular with guests and locals alike; try to book your treatment ahead if you're coming.

6 Water St., Kittery, ME 03904. (C) **207/439-4040.** Fax 207/438-9286. www.innatportsmouth.com. 5 units. Mon–Fri $120–$190 double; Sat–Sun $120–$200 double. Rates include full breakfast. 2-night minimum sometimes required. MC, V. Not recommended for children under 12. **Amenities:** Spa; Jacuzzi. *In room:* A/C, TV, dataport, hair dryer.

In The Yorks

Dockside Guest Quarters ✦ David and Harriet Lusty established this quiet retreat in 1954, and recent additions (mostly new cottages) haven't changed the friendly, maritime flavor of the place. Situated on an island connected to the mainland by a small bridge, the inn occupies nicely landscaped grounds shady with maples and white pines. Five of the rooms are in the cozy main house, built in 1885, but the bulk of the accommodations are in small, shared, town-house-style rustic cottages constructed between 1968 and 1998 and scattered by the water. These are simply furnished but bright and airy; most have private decks overlooking the entrance to York Harbor. Several also have woodstoves, fireplace, and/or kitchenettes (you pay quite a bit extra for the kitchenette units). Overall, it's a friendly place with good views. The lawn is a good place to sit; the inn also maintains a simple restaurant and offers boat tours of the harbor, which leave from its own dock.

Harris Island (P.O. Box 205), York, ME 03909. (C) **888/860-7428** or 207/363-2868. Fax 207/363-1977. www.dockside gq.com. 25 units. Mid-June to mid-Oct $121–$216 double, $173–$276 cottage rooms; May to mid-June and mid-Oct to Dec $98–$125 double, $104–$197 cottage rooms. Rates include breakfast. Closed Jan–Apr and closed Mon–Fri in May, Nov, and Dec. 2-night minimum stay in summer. DISC, MC, V. Drive south on Rte. 103 from Rte. 1A in York Harbor; cross bridge over York River, turn left and follow signs to end. **Amenities:** Restaurant; rowboats; boat tours; bike rentals; laundry service; badminton; croquet. *In room:* A/C, TV, kitchenette (some units), fireplace (some units).

Stage Neck Inn ✦ Recovered from a February 2007 fire, this remains one of the better mid-range choices in the York area because of its position right on a York Harbor beach. Since about 1870, a hotel in one form or another has been housing guests on this windswept bluff between the harbor and the open ocean. This most recent incarnation was built in 1972, furnished with an understated, country club–like elegance. It does create some sense of old-fashioned intimacy, though the accommodations and amenities do not reach resort-level status. Almost every room here has a view of the water (nonoceanview rooms are much less expensive), and guests can enjoy recreational facilities such as tennis courts and the sandy beach just steps away without ever leaving the property. There are two year-round dining rooms, both serving three meals daily, plus a poolside snack bar and terrace lounge open in peak season only. Book ahead in summer, when the inn becomes a very popular New England wedding destination.

Stage Neck Rd. (P.O. Box 70), York Harbor, ME 03911. (C) **800/340-1130** or 207/363-3850. Fax 207/363-2221. www. stageneck.com. 58 units. Mid-May to Oct $205–$385 double; late Feb to mid-May and Nov–Dec $145–$225 double. Closed Jan–late Feb. 2-night minimum stay Sat–Sun, 3-night minimum holiday weekends. Off-season packages available. AE, DC, DISC, MC, V. Head north on 1A from Rte. 1; make 2nd right after York Harbor post office. **Amenities:** 2 restaurants; indoor pool; outdoor pool; ocean swimming; tennis courts; fitness room; Jacuzzi; sauna; massage. *In room:* A/C, TV/VCR, CD player.

Union Bluff Hotel ✦ With its stumpy turrets, dormers, and prominent porches, the Union Bluff has the look of an old-fashioned, 19th-century beach hotel; it's a surprise to learn it was only built in 1989. Inside, the hotel is a generic-modern building;

rooms have oak furniture, wall-to-wall carpeting, and small refrigerators. Step outside and you're 10 seconds from the Short Sands beach, downtown T-shirt and shell shops, and bowling alley and game arcade (great for kids). There are also about 20 rooms in a motel annex next door, but stick with the main inn for the prime rooms and views; the best units are the suites on the top floor, which have beach vistas (and some have Jacuzzis or fireplaces). There's also a simple wood-paneled lounge and a restaurant on site. It's amazing how low the rates plummet here mid-week and off-season, when the hotel becomes among the most inexpensive places to stay in all of southern Maine. Also remember that parking is pretty tight on this hotel's little street; RVs will need to park their rigs in the public pay lot adjacent.

8 Beach St. (P.O. Box 1860), York Beach, ME 03910. ⓒ 800/833-0721 or 207/363-1333. www.unionbluff.com. 61 units. Mid-May to late Oct $69–$249 double, $139–$329 suite; rest of the year $49–$129 double, $99–$189 suite. Packages available. AE, DISC, MC, V. **Amenities:** 2 restaurants; pub. *In room:* A/C, fridge (some units), fireplace (some units), Jacuzzi (some units).

WHERE TO DINE

Bob's Clam Hut FRIED SEAFOOD   Operating since 1956, Bob's manages to retain an old-fashioned flavor—despite now being surrounded on all sides by factory outlet malls, and with prices that have steadily escalated out of the "budget eats" category. It still fries up heaps of clams and other seafood, sides them with french fries and coleslaw in baskets, and puts them out with tremendous efficiency. Order at the window, get a soda, and stake out a table inside or on the deck (with its lovely view of, er, Rte. 1) while waiting for your number to be called. The food is surprisingly light, cooked in cholesterol-free vegetable oil; the onion rings are especially good. To ensure that your diet plans are irrevocably busted, Bob's also serves ice cream at an adjacent scoop shop. Now that's overkill.

Rte. 1 (west side), Kittery. ⓒ 207/439-4233. Reservations not accepted. Sandwiches $4–$13; dinners $8–$29. AE, MC, V. Memorial Day–Labor Day Mon–Thurs 11am–8pm, Fri–Sat 11am–9pm, Sun 11am–7:30pm; hours vary in off-season.

Goldenrod Restaurant *Kids* TRADITIONAL AMERICAN   Follow the neon inside this beach-town classic, which is *the* place in York Beach for unfancy local color—it has been a summer institution here since it opened in 1896. It's easy to find: Look for visitors gawking through plate-glass windows at ancient taffy machines hypnotically churning out taffy in volumes (millions of candies a year), enough to make truckloads of dentists wealthy. The restaurant, right behind the candy-making operation, is low on frills but long on atmosphere. Diners sit on stout oak furniture around a stone fireplace or elbow-to-elbow at an antique soda fountain (my preference). Breakfast offerings are New England diner standards, and for lunch you can eat soups, burgers, and overpriced sandwiches. But what saves the place is the outstanding candy counter, where you can line up to buy boxes of wax-wrapped taffy "kisses" (check the striping on each candy for its flavor; I like the molasses and peppermint best), almond-pocked birch bark, and other penny-candy treats. The shakes, malts, and sundaes are on the sweet side, but not bad.

Railroad Rd. and Ocean Ave., York Beach. ⓒ 207/363-2621. www.thegoldenrod.com. Main courses $4–$15 for lunch and dinner. MC, V. Memorial Day–Labor Day daily 8am–10pm (until 9pm in June); Labor Day to Columbus Day Wed–Sun 8am–3pm. Closed Columbus Day–Memorial Day.

Lobster Cove ✦ SEAFOOD/FAMILY FARE   Right across the street from the pounding surf of Long Sands Beach, dependable Lobster Cove is a good choice when the family is too tired to drive far in search of a feed. And a "feed" is what you'll get here. Breakfast consists of standard, inexpensive choices like omelets, pancakes, and eggs Benedict. Lunch runs to burgers and sandwiches, but dinner is prime time, when a standard shore dinner of lobster, corn on the cob, clam chowder, and steamed clams is hefty and good. Lobster pie is an old-fashioned New England favorite. They also do lobster rolls, clam rolls, steaks, broiled seafood, and traditional Maine desserts such as wild blueberry pie and warm bread pudding with whiskey sauce.

756 York St., York (south end of Long Sands Beach). ✆ 207/351-1100. Main courses $7–$21. AE, MC, V. Daily 7:30am–9pm.

Stonewall Kitchen Café 🕹🕹 CAFE   Stonewall Kitchen's York-based gourmet foods operation has taken a step forward with this quality, inexpensive cafe, smartly located in its York headquarters/store right beside the local tourist information office. The cafe serves simple, hearty items such as fish chowder, soups, lobster rolls (and lobster BLTs), muffulettas (a New Orleans–style, olive-salami sandwich), turkey wraps with cranberry spread, and much more. Check the board to find out what's served that day. Finish with a dessert such as lemon squares, brownies, or fresh-baked cookies. The cafe kitchen also prepares gourmet meals to go.

Stonewall Lane (set back from U.S. Rte. 1), York. ✆ 207/351-2719. www.stonewallkitchen.com. Sandwiches and salads $7–$11. AE, DC, DISC, MC, V. Mon–Sat 8am–3pm (takeout until 5pm); Sun 9am–3pm (takeout until 5pm).

OGUNQUIT 🕹🕹

Ogunquit is a bustling beachside town that has attracted vacationers and artists for more than a century. Though certainly notable for its abundant and elegant summer-resort architecture, Ogunquit is most famous for its 3½-mile white-sand beach, backed by grassy dunes. This beach serves as the town's front porch, and most everyone drifts over there at least once a day when the sun is shining. Since the latter part of the 19th century, the town has also found another sort of fame as a destination for gay travelers; many local enterprises here are run by gay entrepreneurs.

Despite its architectural gentility and overall civility, the town can become overrun with tourists (and cars) during peak summer season, especially on Saturday and Sunday. If you don't like crowds, try to visit in the off-season.

ESSENTIALS
GETTING THERE   Ogunquit is right on U.S. Route 1, midway between York and Wells. It's accessible from both exit 7 and exit 19 (from the north) of the Maine Turnpike.

VISITOR INFORMATION   The **Ogunquit Welcome Center,** P.O. Box 2289, Ogunquit, ME 03907 (✆ **207/646-2939;** www.ogunquit.org), is on U.S. Route 1, south of the village center. It's open daily 9am to 5pm Memorial Day to Columbus Day (until 8pm Sat–Sun during the peak summer season), and Monday to Saturday during the off-season—and it has restrooms.

GETTING AROUND   Ogunquit centers on a three-way intersection that seems fiendishly designed to cause massive traffic foul-ups in summer. Parking in and around the village is tight and relatively expensive for small-town Maine ($6 per day or more in various lots). As a result, Ogunquit is best navigated on foot or by bike.

EXPLORING OGUNQUIT
The village center is good for an hour or two of browsing among the boutiques, or sipping a cappuccino at one of the several coffee emporia.

Tips **Try the Trolley**

A number of trackless "trolleys" (© 207/646-1411)—actually buses—with names like *Dolly* and *Ollie* (you get the idea) run all day from mid-May to Columbus Day between Perkins Cove and the Wells town line to the north, with detours to the sea down Beach and Ocean streets. These trolleys are very handy, and they stop everywhere. (There's a map of stops posted online at **www.ogunquit.com/trolley.cfm**.) Rides cost $1.50 one-way (children free), or you can buy a day pass for $5 per adult and $3 per child under 10; it might be worth the expense to avoid driving and parking hassles and limits.

From the village, you can walk to scenic Perkins Cove along **Marginal Way** ✦✦, a mile-long oceanside pathway that departs across from the Seacastles Resort on Shore Road. It passes tide pools, pocket beaches, and rocky, fissured bluffs, all worth exploring. The seascape can be spectacular, but Marginal Way can also be extremely crowded during fair-weather weekends, so head out in the early morning.

Perkins Cove ✦, accessible either from Marginal Way or by driving south on Shore Road and veering left at the Y intersection, is a small, well-protected harbor that attracts many visitors and is often heavily congested. A handful of galleries, restaurants, and T-shirt shops cater to the tourist trade from a cluster of quaint buildings between harbor and sea. (If teeming crowds and tourist enterprises are *not* the reason you came to Maine, steer clear of Perkins Cove.) An intriguing pedestrian drawbridge is operated by whoever happens to be handy.

Not far from the cove is the **Ogunquit Museum of American Art** ✦✦✦, 543 Shore Rd. (© 207/646-4909; www.ogunquitmuseum.org), one of the best and most beautiful small art museums in the nation (that's not just me talking; the director of New York's Metropolitan Museum of Art said so, too). It's only open in summer and early fall, however. Set back from the road in a grassy glen overlooking the rocky shore, the museum has a spectacular view that initially overwhelms the artwork as visitors walk through the door. But stick around for a few minutes—the changing exhibits in this architecturally engaging modern building of cement block, slate, and glass will get your attention soon enough; its curators have a track record of staging superb shows and attracting national attention, and the permanent collection holds work by seascape master Marsden Hartley and many members of the Ogunquit Colony, including Woodbury, Hamilton Easter Field, and Robert Laurent. The museum is open from July to October, Monday to Saturday from 10:30am to 5pm and Sundays from 2 to 5pm. Admission costs $7 for adults, $5 for seniors, and $4 for students; it's free for all children under the age of 12.

For evening entertainment, head for the **Ogunquit Playhouse** ✦ (©207/646-2402), a 750-seat summer stock theater right on U.S. Route 1 (just south of the main town intersection) with an old-style look that has garnered a solid reputation for its careful, serious attention to stagecraft. The theater has entertained Ogunquit since 1933, attracting noted actors such as Bette Davis, Tallulah Bankhead, and Sally Struthers. Performance tickets generally cost in the range of $30 to $45 per person.

WHERE TO STAY

In addition to the selections below, there are many family-owned budget- to moderately priced motel operations around town. Simply cruising **U.S. Route 1** can yield

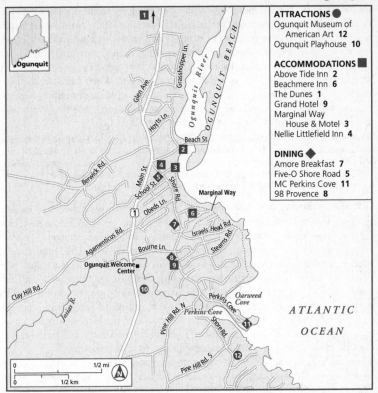

ATTRACTIONS ●
Ogunquit Museum of
   American Art **12**
Ogunquit Playhouse **10**

ACCOMMODATIONS ■
Above Tide Inn **2**
Beachmere Inn **6**
The Dunes **1**
Grand Hotel **9**
Marginal Way
   House & Motel **3**
Nellie Littlefield Inn **4**

DINING ◆
Amore Breakfast **7**
Five-O Shore Road **5**
MC Perkins Cove **11**
98 Provence **8**

dividends (don't forget your AAA card if you're a member). In July and August you'll be hard-pressed to find a bargain, but try the following three economical choices first for a combination of affordability and amenities.

Above Tide Inn   This nicely located inn rises from where a lobster shack once stood, until a 1978 blizzard took it to sea. That fact (and the inn's name) should suggest its great setting: on a lazy tidal river between town and the main beach, which is an easy stroll away. It's right by the start of Marginal Way, the town's popular walking path. Location is the prime draw here, since rooms are a bit smaller and darker than one might expect at a beach property. If the weather's good, you're in luck—each room has its own outdoor sitting area, most connected to the room (though two tables are reserved on a front deck for guests in back that don't face the water). Room no. 1 has a nice view of the river. Remember that this inn doesn't accept small children or pets.

66 Beach St. (P.O. Box 1288), Ogunquit, ME 03907. ⓒ 207/646-7454. www.abovetideinn.com. 9 units. Mid-June to Labor Day $170–$250 double; mid-May to mid-June and Labor Day to Columbus Day $110–$180 double. Rates include continental breakfast. MC, V. 3-night minimum stay in summer. Not appropriate for young children. Closed Columbus Day to mid-May. *In room:* A/C, TV, fridge, no phone.

Beachmere Inn ⍟   Run by the same family since 1937, the Beachmere Inn sprawls across a grassy hillside (the inn occupies about 4 acres); nearly every room has a view northward up the beach. Guests choose from two buildings on the main grounds. The Victorian section, all turrets and porches, dates from the 1890s. Next door is Beachmere South, a motel-like structure of concrete slathered with a stucco finish; rooms here are spacious (some are minisuites, which cost more) and interestingly angled, and all have private balconies or patios with great views. The inn is right on the Marginal Way footpath, terrific for walks and access to the beach. When rooms in the main buildings are filled, guests are offered accommodations in cottages nearby—these are spacious and appropriate for families. Larger groups might inquire about Hearthstone, an elegant cottage with a fireplace a short walk from the inn.

62 Beachmere Pl., Ogunquit, ME 03907. ℭ 800/336-3983 or 207/646-2021. Fax 207/646-2231. www.beachmereinn. com. 53 units. June–Aug $170–$250 double, cottage $145–$390; May and Sept to mid-Oct $95–$234 double, $75–$280 cottage; Apr and mid-Oct to early Dec $75–$170 double, $60–$210 cottage. Rates include continental breakfast. 3-night minimum in summer. AE, DC, DISC, MC, V. Closed early Dec–Mar. **Amenities:** Beach access. *In room:* A/C, kitchenettes (in some), fireplaces (in some), patios and balconies (in some).

Cliff House Resort and Spa ඇඇ

Say what you want about the set of modern buildings that replaced a former grand hotel here, but the new Cliff House must have the best ocean views of any hotel in Maine: nearly a 360-degree panorama. This was for years an old-money seaside resort of classic architecture. Now the new complex offers a number of different styles of rooms, most with comforts such as digital televisions and recliners; other improvements include new beds and furniture in the Cliffscape wing, a new conference space with an amphitheatre, and a covered corridor linking all terraces and guest rooms with the dining areas. A lovely vanishing-edge pool fronting the sea does indeed seem to disappear into the blue, and there's a good upscale restaurant with knockout vistas. The state-of-the-art spa and fitness facility dispenses a wide range of soothing treatments and exercise programs.

Shore Rd. (P.O. Box 2274), Ogunquit, ME 03907. ℭ 207/361-1000. Fax 207/361-2122. www.cliffhousemaine.com. 200 units. July–Aug $275–$350 double, mid-Apr–June and Sept–early Dec $155–$295 double. Meal plans available. 3-night minimum stay July–Aug and holiday weekends; 2-night minimum other weekends. Packages available. AE, DISC, MC, V. Closed early Jan–late Mar. **Amenities:** Restaurant; bar; indoor pool; 2 outdoor pools; fitness center; spa; Jacuzzi; room service. *In room:* A/C, TV, hair dryer.

The Dunes ඇඇ

This classic motor court (built around 1936) has made the transition into the modern luxury age more gracefully than any other vintage motel I've seen. It has one six-unit motel-like building, but most of the rooms are in gabled cottages of white clapboard and green shutters; these have full kitchens and bathrooms. Plenty of old-fashioned charm remains in many of the units, with vintage maple furnishings, oval braided rugs, maple floors, knotty pine paneling, and louvered doors. Most of the cottages also have wood-burning fireplaces. The complex is set on 12 acres, wedged between busy Rte. 1 and the ocean, but somehow stays quiet and peaceful; Adirondack chairs overlook a lagoon, and guests can borrow a rowboat to get across to the beach.

518 U.S. Rte. 1 (P.O. Box 917), Ogunquit, ME 03907. ℭ 888/295-3863. www.dunesmotel.com. 36 units. Summer $100–$285 double, $180–$335 cottage; spring $75–$190 double, $130–$255 cottage. MC, V. July–Aug 1-week minimum stay in cottages; 3-night minimum stay in motel. All other weekends, 2-night minimum stay in motel. Closed Nov–late Apr. **Amenities:** Outdoor pool; watersports equipment rental. *In room:* A/C, TV, dataport, fridge, coffeemaker.

Grand Hotel ⓥalue ඇ

The modern Grand Hotel, built in 1990, seems a bit out of place in Victorian Ogunquit; but the hotel centers on a three-story atrium and consists entirely of two-room suites. The modern rooms have a generic, chain-hotel character, but each has a private deck from which to enjoy the Maine air (no ocean views).

All rooms also have refrigerators, microwaves, and TVs, as well as VCRs and DVD players (with tapes available for rent), making it a good deal for families. The top-floor penthouses are airy and bright, with cathedral ceilings and Duraflame-log fireplaces. The hotel is about a 10-minute walk to the beach, and guests can use a nearby health club. Other nice touches: Parking (one car per party) is underground and connected to the rooms by elevator, and there's a small indoor pool.

276 Shore Rd. (P.O. Box 1526), Ogunquit, ME 03907. ℂ 800/806-1231 or 207/646-1231. www.thegrandhotel.com. 28 suites. Late June to Labor Day $139–$269 double; late Mar to late June and Labor Day to mid-Nov $59–$219 double. Rates include continental breakfast. 2- or 3-night minimum Sat–Sun, holidays, and other peak season dates. DISC, MC, V. Underground parking. Children accepted in some suites. Closed mid-Nov to late Mar. **Amenities:** Indoor pool; Jacuzzi. *In room:* A/C, TV/VCR/DVD player, kitchenette, fridge, microwave, fireplace (some units).

Marginal Way House and Motel ⓕ

This old-fashioned, nothing-fancy compound centers on a four-story, mid-19th-century guesthouse with summery, basic rooms and white-painted furniture; the whole affair is plunked down on a large, grassy lot on a quiet cul-de-sac, and it's hard to believe you're smack in the middle of beehive-busy Ogunquit. But it's true: Both the beach and the village are just a few minutes' walk away. Room no. 7 is among the best, with a private porch and canopy and ocean views. The main house is surrounded by four contemporary buildings that lack charm, yet the motel-style rooms here are generally comfortable and bright. All rooms have refrigerators and none have phones; one- and two-bedroom efficiencies are available for longer stays, and rooms on higher-floors are most desirable.

Wharf Lane (P.O. Box 697), Ogunquit, ME 03907. ℂ 207/646-8801. www.marginalwayhouse.com. 30 units (1 with private bathroom down hall). Early June–Labor Day $82–$199 double; mid-Apr to early June and early Sept to mid-Oct $49–$159 double. Minimum stay requirements on some weekends. MC, V. Closed mid-Oct to mid-Apr. Pets allowed in off-season only; advance notice required. *In room:* A/C, TV (most units), fridge, no phone.

Nellie Littlefield House ⓕ

This 1889 home stands impressively at the edge of Ogunquit's compact commercial district. This prime location and the handsome Queen Anne architecture are the main draws here. All rooms are carpeted and feature a mix of modern and antique reproduction furnishings; several have refrigerators. Four rooms to the rear have private decks, although views are limited—mostly looking out onto the motel next door. The most spacious room is the third-floor J. H. Littlefield suite, with two TVs and a Jacuzzi. The most unique unit? The circular Grace Littlefield room, located in the upper turret and overlooking the street. The basement features a compact fitness room with modern equipment.

27 Shore Rd. (P.O. Box 1341), Ogunquit, ME 03907. ℂ 207/646-1692. www.visit-maine.com/nellielittlefieldhouse. 8 units. June–Sept $108–$230 double; Mar–May and Oct–Dec to $85–$170 double. Holiday rates higher. Rates include full breakfast. 3-night minimum on high-season weekends and holidays. DISC, MC, V. Closed Jan–Feb. Children over 12 are welcome. **Amenities:** Fitness center. *In room:* A/C, TV, fridge (some units), Jacuzzi (few units).

WHERE TO DINE

Amore Breakfast ⓕ *Value* BREAKFAST It's breakfast-only at this homey little Shore Road spot halfway between Main Street and Perkins Cove, but what a breakfast it is. This is *not* the place for dainty pickers and waist-watchers. (But, hey, you're on vacation, right?) Look for numerous variations on the eggs Benedict theme (including a popular one with a big hunk of lobster on top), plus Belgian waffles, wonderful bananas Foster–style French toast with pecans outside and cream cheese inside, and more than a dozen types of yummy omelets. Coffee is from a small-batch San Diego coffee roaster. And they've got heart, too: Annual benefit meals are held, with the proceeds going to care packages for a Dominican orphanage. Italian owner Leanne Cusimano deserves (and gets local) kudos.

178 Shore Rd. © 866/641-6661 or 207/646-6661. www.amorebreakfast.com. Breakfast items $4.95–$13. MC, V. Summer daily 7am–1pm. Closed Wed–Thurs in off-season.

Arrows ☆☆☆ NEW AMERICAN When owner/chefs Mark Gaier and Clark Frasier opened Arrows in a gray farmhouse outside town in 1988, they quickly put Ogunquit on the national culinary map (and it's still ranked among the nation's top 15 by *Gourmet* magazine). They've done so not only by creating an elegant and intimate atmosphere, but by serving up some of the freshest, most innovative cooking in New England. The emphasis is on local products—often very local. The salad greens are grown in gardens on the grounds, and much of the rest is produced or raised locally. The food transcends traditional New England fare and is deftly prepared with exotic twists and turns. The menu changes nightly, but among the more popular recurring appetizers is the house-cured prosciutto—hams are hung in the restaurant to cure in the off-season. Entrees might include some interpretation of lobster; wild salmon in four preparations (including a portion steamed with pine needles); roasted squab in a "crystal lantern" with tangerine and fermented black beans; or halibut cooked three ways. The wine list is top-rate. Note that there is a moderate dress code: jacket preferred for men, no shorts allowed.

41 Berwick Rd. © 207/361-1100. www.arrowsrestaurant.com. Reservations strongly recommended. Main courses $42–$44; tasting menus $95–$135. MC, V. July–Labor Day Tues–Sun 6–9:30pm; rest of the year, call ahead for open hours or check website. Closed Jan–Mar. Turn uphill at the Key Bank in the village; the restaurant is 2 miles on your right.

Five-O Shore Road ☆☆ SEAFOOD/NEW AMERICAN A fine choice if you're looking for a more casual alternative to the more formal restaurants listed, Five-O is one of those spots where just reading the menu is a decent evening's entertainment. Chef Zachary Crosby has transformed a formerly Caribbean-inspired menu into one that roams around the map: You might eat a char-grilled filet or rope-caught local mussels, but also duck nachos, escargot with shallots, local mussels roasted with almonds, wild salmon poached in lobster-saffron bullion, mole-spiced pork, or fresh haddock stuffed with seafood. Of course, you can get a Maine lobster in season, too, perhaps served over a bed of mussels steamed with bleu cheese, sweet cream, and cracked pepper. There's also a cool cocktail lounge and club, and a strong wine list. Is this Maine or Manhattan? Either way, it's a winner.

50 Shore Rd. © 207/646-5001. www.five-oshoreroad.com. Reservations strongly recommended in summer. Main courses $24–$33. AE, DISC, MC, V. Valet parking. Memorial Day–Labor Day daily 5–9pm; call for hours outside peak season.

MC Perkins Cove ☆☆ SEAFOOD/NEW AMERICAN The loss of Hurricane could have been a serious blow to Ogunquit, but chef-partners Mark Gaier and Clark Frasier (the M and C in MC) of Arrows (see above) have opened this bistro in its place, which manages to be fun rather than stuffy. Expect big food, even on the "small" plates: lobster rolls, chopped salads, oysters on half shell, and crab cakes give way to progressively more sophisticated starters like cockle clams in coconut milk and corn-fried calamari. For your entree, choose a steamed lobster, sesame-grilled trout, Kobe burger, tuna, or hanger steak, then add aioli or another sauce and one of the "evil carbos" (french fries, onion rings, and so on). Finish up with a buttery brownie served with burnt orange caramel and orange peel, little whoopee pies, apple-blueberry turnovers, a bittersweet chocolate cake, or peppermint stick ice cream with cookies.

Perkins Cove. © 207/646-6263. www.mcperkinscove.com. Reservations recommended. Main courses $8–$19 at lunch; $24–$33 at dinner. DC, DISC, MC, V. June–Sept daily 11:30am–2pm and 5:30–11pm; closed Tues in off-season. Closed Jan.

98 Provence ★★ BISTRO Chef Pierre Gignac incorporates fresh, local ingredients (such as lobster) in a menu that changes thrice yearly to reflect the seasons but never gets too fusion-minded; instead, it's solidly French throughout. Start with such appetizers as an escargot stew with morels and asparagus, a shepherd's pie of duck, fisherman's soup, or a sweetish shallot and foie gras tart. Entrees wander the barnyard and sea, from veal mignon with a mushroom-port sauce to pork shank to beef short ribs, spring lamb loin with a rosemary crust and garlic cream, roast duck, or halibut with salmon caviar. A fixed-price table d'hôte (appetizer, main course, and dessert) menu features set meals such as vichyssoise, stewed chicken, and lemon tart; mussels with bleu cheese, monkfish, and pineapple tart; and soft-shell crab with halibut confit and Provence-style nougat, served frozen. The summery, classy interior decor is about as close as you'll get in New England to a Provençal feel.

262 Shore Rd. © 207/646-9898. www.98provence.com. Reservations recommended. Main courses $21–$30; table d'hôte menus $29–$39. AE, MC, V. Summer Wed–Mon 5:30–9:30pm; off-season Thurs–Mon 5:30–9pm.

THE KENNEBUNKS ★★

"The Kennebunks" consist of the side-by-side villages of **Kennebunk** and **Kennebunkport,** both situated along the shores of small rivers and both claiming a portion of rocky coast. The region was first colonized in the mid-1600s and flourished after the American Revolution, when ship captains, boat builders, and prosperous merchants constructed imposing, solid homes. The Kennebunks are famed for their striking historical architecture and expansive beaches; make time to explore both.

ESSENTIALS

GETTING THERE Kennebunk is just off exit 25 of the Maine Turnpike; follow signs east into town. You can also get here by taking U.S. 1 from York and Ogunquit. To reach Kennebunkport, exit for Kennebunk and continue through town on Port Road (Rte. 35) 3½ miles. At the traffic light, turn left and cross the small bridge.

VISITOR INFORMATION The **Kennebunk-Kennebunkport Chamber of Commerce,** 17 Western Ave. (P.O. Box 740), Kennebunk, ME 04043 (© 800/982-4421 or 207/967-0857), can answer questions year-round by phone or at its offices on Route 9, next to the H.B. Provisions grocery store. The **Kennebunkport Information Center** (© 207/967-8600), operated by an association of local businesses, is off Dock Square (next to Ben & Jerry's) and is open daily in summer and fall.

GETTING AROUND The local trolley (actually a bus) makes several stops in and around Kennebunkport and also serves the beaches; it stops once per hour from 10am until 5pm. The fare comes in the form of a day pass, which costs $11 per adult or $6 per child ages 3 to 14; it includes unlimited trips. Call © 207/967-3686, or check **www.intowntrolley.com** for details.

EXPLORING KENNEBUNK

Kennebunk's downtown is inland, just off the turnpike, and is a dignified, small commercial center of white clapboard and brick. The **Brick Store Museum** ★, 117 Main St. (© 207/985-4802), hosts shows of historical art and artifacts throughout the summer, switching to contemporary art in the off-season. The museum is housed in a historic former brick store—yes, a store that once sold bricks!—and three adjacent buildings. The buildings have been renovated and all have the polished gloss of a well-cared-for gallery. Admission is free (though a $3 donation is suggested), and tours cost $5 per person. The museum is open Tuesday to Friday 10am to 4:30pm and Saturday from 10am to 1pm.

EXPLORING KENNEBUNKPORT

Dock Square has a pleasantly wharflike feel to it, with low buildings of mixed vintages and styles, but the flavor is mostly clapboard and shingles. The side streets are lined with one of the nation's richest assortments of Early American homes; many have been converted to B&Bs (see "Where to Stay," below).

Ocean Drive from Dock Square to **Walkers Point** ⚓ and beyond is lined with opulent summer homes overlooking surf and rocky shore. You'll likely recognize the Bush family compound right out on Walkers Point when you arrive. If it's not familiar from the time it has spent in the national spotlight, look for crowds with telephoto lenses. If they're not out, look for a shingle-style secret service booth at the head of a driveway. That's the place. There's nothing to do here, though, but park for a minute, snap a picture, and then push on.

BEACHES

The coastal area around Kennebunkport is home to several of the state's best beaches. Southward across the river (technically, this is Kennebunk, though it's much closer to Kennebunkport) are **Gooch's Beach** and **Kennebunk Beach** ⚓. Head eastward on Beach Street (from the intersection of routes 9 and 35) and you'll soon wind into a handsome colony of eclectic shingled summer homes. The narrow road twists past sandy beaches and rocky headlands. It may be congested in summer; avoid gridlock by exploring on foot or by bike.

WHERE TO STAY

Beach House Inn ⚓⚓   This is a good choice if you'd like to be close to the people-watching, dog-walking action on and above Kennebunk Beach. The inn was built in 1891 but has been extensively modernized and expanded; in 1999 it was purchased by the folks who own the White Barn Inn (see below), and was gussied up with down comforters, pillows, and other upgrades. The rooms here aren't necessarily historic, but they are carpeted and most have Victorian furnishings and accents, plus nice framed photographs of beach landscapes. Suites have panoramic views of the ocean. But the main draw here might be the lovely porch, where you can stare out at the pebble beach across the road and idly watch the bikers and in-line skaters. The inn has bikes and canoes for guests to use and provides beach chairs and towels.

211 Beach Ave., Kennebunk, ME 04043. ✆ 207/967-3850. Fax 207/967-4719. www.beachhseinn.com. 35 units. Late June to mid-Sept $255–$390 double; early June–late June and mid-Sept to Oct $185–$399 double; Nov–Dec $155–$300 double. Closed Jan–May. Rates include continental breakfast and afternoon tea. Packages available. 2-night minimum Sat–Sun. AE, MC, V. **Amenities:** Canoes; bikes. *In room:* TV.

The Colony Hotel ⚓⚓   One of a handful of oceanside resorts that has preserved the classic New England vacation experience, this mammoth white Georgian Revival (from 1914) lords over the ocean and the mouth of the Kennebunk River. All rooms in the three-story main inn have been renovated recently; they're bright and cheery, simply furnished in summer-cottage antiques. Rooms in two of the three outbuildings carry over the rustic elegance of the main hotel; the exception is the East House, a 1950s-era motel at the back edge of the property with uninteresting motel-style rooms. Staff encourages guests to socialize downstairs in the lobby, on the porch, on the putting green, or at a shuffleboard court that's lighted for nighttime play.

140 Ocean Ave. (P.O. Box 511), Kennebunkport, ME 04046. ⓒ **800/552-2363** or 207/967-3331. Fax 207/967-8738. www.thecolonyhotel.com/maine. 123 units. $99–$625 double. Rates include breakfast. 3-night minimum on summer weekends and holidays in main hotel. Closed late Oct to mid-May. AE, MC, V. Pets allowed ($25 per pet per night). **Amenities:** Restaurant; lounge; heated saltwater pool; putting green; bike rentals; room service; library. *In room:* A/C (some units), TV (some units), safe.

Old Fort Inn ⭐⭐

The sophisticated Old Fort Inn sits on 15 acres in a quiet, picturesque neighborhood of late-19th-century summer homes 2 blocks from the ocean. Guests check in at a tidy antiques shop and park around back at the large carriage house, an interesting amalgam of stone, brick, shingle, and stucco. Rooms here all have creature comforts, yet retain the charm of yesteryear: They are solidly wrought and delightfully decorated with antiques and reproductions. About half the rooms have in-floor heated tiles in the bathrooms; all have such welcome amenities as robes, refrigerators, Aveda bath products, discreet self-serve snack bars, microwaves, and sinks. There are two large suites in the main house; light-filled no. 216 faces east and looks out over the pool. A full buffet breakfast is also served in the main building.

Old Fort Rd. (P.O. Box M), Kennebunkport, ME 04046. ⓒ **800/828-3678** or 207/967-5353. Fax 207/967-4547. www. oldfortinn.com. 16 units. High season $175–$395 double; low season $125–$295 double. Rates include full breakfast and 1 hr. free tennis. 2-night minimum Sat–Sun and July–Labor Day, 3-night minimum holiday weekends. AE, DC, DISC, MC, V. **Amenities:** Heated outdoor pool; tennis court; laundry service and self-serve laundry; dry cleaning. *In room:* A/C, TV, minibar, fridge, microwave, coffeemaker, hair dryer, iron/ironing board.

White Barn Inn ⭐⭐⭐

The White Barn pampers its guests to no end, and is perhaps the state's best hotel (with its best dining room; see "Where to Dine," below.) Upon checking in, guests are shown to a parlor and served a drink while valets gather luggage and park cars. The atmosphere is distinctly European, with an emphasis on service. Rooms are individually decorated in an upscale country style. Nearly half the rooms have wood-burning fireplaces, while the suites (in an outbuilding across from the main inn) are spectacular; each has a separate color theme and most have flatscreen televisions, whirlpools, or similar perks. There are plenty of unexpected niceties such as fresh flowers and turndown service. In 2003, the inn acquired a handful of cottages on the Kennebunk River across the road—these are cozy and nicely equipped with modern kitchens and bathrooms, a wonderful addition to a property that had lacked nothing except water views.

Ocean Ave. (¼ mile east of junction of routes 9 and 35; P.O. Box 560-C), Kennebunk, ME 04043. ⓒ **207/967-2321.** Fax 207/967-1100. www.whitebarninn.com. 25 units, 4 cottages. $280–$540 double; $565–$785 suite; $630–$1,260 cottage. Rates include continental breakfast and afternoon tea. 2-night minimum Sat–Sun; 3-night minimum holiday weekends. AE, MC, V. Free valet parking. **Amenities:** Outdoor heated pool; free bikes; concierge; conference rooms; limited room service (breakfast only); in-room massage. *In room:* A/C, TV, safe, fireplace (some units), Jacuzzi (some units).

The Yachtsman Lodge & Marina ⭐⭐

The White Barn Inn took over this riverfront motel in 1997 and made it an appealing base for exploring the southern Maine coast. Within walking distance of Dock Square, nice touches abound, such as down comforters, granite-topped vanities, high ceilings, CD players, and French doors that open onto patios just above the river. Every room is located on the first floor and is similarly appointed, but while standard motel size, their simple, classical styling is far superior to anything you'll find at a chain motel.

Ocean Ave. (P.O. Box 2609), Kennebunkport, ME 04046. ℂ 207/967-2511. Fax 207/967-5056. www.yachtsman lodge.com. 30 units. $189–$369 double. Rates include continental breakfast. AE, MC, V. 2-night minimum stay Sat–Sun and holidays. *In room:* A/C, TV/VCR, dataport, fridge, coffeemaker, hair dryer, iron, CD player.

WHERE TO DINE

Federal Jack's Restaurant and Brew Pub PUB FARE   This light, airy, and modern restaurant, named after a schooner built at Cape Porpoise a century ago, is in a retail complex of recent vintage that sits a bit uneasily amid the boatyards lining the south bank of the Kennebunk River. From the second-floor perch (look for a seat on the spacious three-season deck in warmer weather), you can gaze across the river toward the shops of Dock Square. The upscale pub menu features regional fare with a creative twist and also offers standards such as hamburgers, steamed mussels, and pizza. This is a good bet for a basic meal without any pretensions; locals keep a sharp eye on the specials board, which features such treats as grilled crab and havarti sandwiches. The restaurant is best known for its Shipyard ales, lagers, and porters, which they've been brewing since 1992 and are among the best in New England.

8 Western Ave., Lower Village (south bank of Kennebunk River), Kennebunk. ℂ 207/967-4322. www.federaljacks. com. Main courses $2.95–$16 at lunch and dinner; lobster dinners priced to market. AE, DISC, MC, V. Daily 11:30am–9pm (bar to 1am); Sun brunch served 10:30am–2pm.

Hurricane ☆☆ AMERICAN/ECLECTIC   Originally an offshoot of Brooks and Luanne MacDonald's award-winning restaurant in Ogunquit, this is now the only Hurricane still blowing. The late open hours are a boon in early-closing Maine. Lunch might start with a cup of lobster chowder, the "Ice Cube" (a block of iceberg lettuce with bleu cheese dressing, toasted pecans, roasted pears, and croutons), a lobster Cobb salad, a bento box of shrimp, or pepper-seared tenderloin carpaccio; the main course could be a gourmet sandwich, some pan-roasted halibut over coconut purple rice, tuna burgers, a muffuletta sandwich, or seared diver-caught scallops. Dinner entrees run to such items as lobster cioppino, grilled veal chops, "stuffed" risotto, roasted chicken on a cheddar biscuit, rack of lamb with a white-bean ragout, or baked or boiled lobster. Finish with a vanilla bean crème brûlée, Key lime tart with coconut rum sauce, a raspberry/lemon panna cotta, or a course of cheeses.

29 Dock Sq., Kennebunkport. ℂ 207/967-1111. www.hurricanerestaurant.com. Reservations recommended. Main courses $15–$45; small plates $8–$22. AE, DC, DISC, MC, V. Daily 11:30am–10:30pm (winter to 9:30pm).

Pier 77 Restaurant ☆☆ CONTEMPORARY NEW ENGLAND   Long a tony restaurant with a wonderful ocean view, Pier 77 was recently renovated and renamed by husband-and-wife team Peter and Kate Morency. The food, drawing on Peter's training at the Culinary Institute of America and 20 years in top kitchens in Boston and San Francisco, is more contemporary and skillful than almost anything else in Maine. The menu has traditional favorites (filet mignon, lobster in the rough) along with slightly more adventurous dishes, such a trio of duck courses and a tomato-ey seafood stew. The restaurant has earned *Wine Spectator*'s awards of excellence since 1993.

77 Pier Rd., Cape Porpoise (Kennebunkport). ℂ 207/967-8500. www.pier77restaurant.com. Reservations recommended. Main courses $14–$25. AE, MC, V. Memorial Day–Labor Day daily 11:30am–2:30pm and 5–10pm; off-season, call for hours.

White Barn Inn ☆☆☆ REGIONAL/NEW AMERICAN   The White Barn Inn's (see above) classy dining room attracts gourmands from New York and Boston. The restaurant is housed in a rustic barn attached to the inn, with a soaring interior and an eclectic collection of country antiques displayed in a hayloft. Chef Jonathan

Cartwright's menu also changes frequently, nearly always incorporating local ingredients: You might start with a signature lobster spring roll of daikon, carrots, snow peas, and Thai sauce, or locally caught pan-seared diver scallops; glide through an *intermezzo* course of fruit soup or sorbet; and then graduate to a pan-seared filet of salmon, a grilled chicken breast over creamed spinach, or a simply steamed lobster over fettuccine with cognac coral butter sauce. The tasting menu runs to seasonal items such as three variations of oyster; sautéed smoked haddock rarebit; Québec foie gras roulade; and peekytoe crab with a roast pineapple salad. Service is astonishingly attentive and knowledgeable, capping the experience. It's no surprise this has been selected one of America's top inn restaurants by readers of *Travel + Leisure* magazine.

Beach Ave., Kennebunkport. © 207/967-2321. Reservations recommended. Fixed-price dinner $91; tasting menu $125 per person. AE, MC, V. Mon–Thurs 6:30–9:30pm; Fri 5:30–9:30pm. Closed 2 weeks in Jan.

2 Portland ★★

Portland: 106 miles N of Boston

Maine's largest city, Portland sits on a hammerhead-shaped peninsula extending into scenic Casco Bay. It's easy to drive right past on I-295, admiring the skyline at 60 miles an hour, and be on your way to the villages and headlands farther up the coast. After all, one doesn't usually think of urban life when envisioning a vacation in Maine.

But Portland is well worth an afternoon's detour or even a weekend stay. This historic city has plenty of charm—especially the renovated (and touristed) Old Port, with its brick sidewalks and cobblestone streets, but not only there. Travelers who stop in Portland are also rewarded with ferries to offshore islands, boutique shops, historic homes, architectural treasures, graceful neighborhoods—and top-shelf dining. Portland is the culinary mecca of northern New England, blessed with an uncommonly high number of excellent restaurants for a city its size.

ESSENTIALS

GETTING THERE Coming from the south by car, downtown Portland is most easily reached by taking exit 44 off the Maine Turnpike (I-95), then following I-295 (which is free) into town. exit I-295 onto Franklin Arterial (exit 7), then continue straight uphill and downhill until you arrive at the city's ferry terminal. Turn right onto Commercial Street, and continue a few blocks to parking meters and the visitor center on the right (see below).

Amtrak (© 800/872-7245; www.amtrak.com) runs the daily Downeaster service from Boston's North Station to Portland (passengers from other cities must change stations from South Station to North Station in Boston by taxi or subway). The train makes four to five round-trips daily, for about $23 one-way. Downtown is a short city bus ride or a 30- to 45-minute walk from the station.

Two bus lines, **Concord Coach** (© 800/639-3317 or 207/828-1151; www.concord coachlines.com) and **Vermont Transit** (© 800/552-8737 or 207/772-6587; www. vermonttransit.com), provide bus service to Portland from Boston and Bangor. The Vermont Transit bus terminal is at 950 Congress St., about a mile downhill from, and south of, the downtown core. Concord Trailways, which is a few dollars more expensive, has movies and headsets on its trips; its terminal is inconveniently set on Thompson Point Road (a 35-min. walk from downtown), but it is served by city buses and taxis.

Portland International Jetport (© 207/874-8877; www.portlandjetport.org), airport code PWM, is the largest airport in Maine. It's served by flights from **Continental**

(© **800/523-3273;** www.continental.com), **Delta** (© **800/221-1212;** www.delta. com); **JetBlue** (© **800/538-2583;** www.jetblue.com), **Northwest** (© **800/225-2525;** www.nwa.com), **United Express** (© **800/864-8331;** www.ual.com), and **US Airways** (© **800/428-4322;** www.usair.com). The airport has grown by fits and starts in recent years (ongoing construction and tight parking can be frustrating at times), but is still quite easily navigated; car rentals are available, and a taxi to the city center runs about $15.

VISITOR INFORMATION The **Convention and Visitor's Bureau of Greater Portland,** 245 Commercial St., Portland, ME 04101 (© **207/772-5800** or 207/772-4994; www.visitportland.com), stocks a large supply of brochures and is happy to dispense information about local attractions, lodging, and dining. The center is open year-round, Monday to Friday from 8am to 5pm and shorter hours on Saturday, depending on the season. There are three more tourist information kiosks scattered around town: one at the **Portland International Jetport** (© **207/775-5809**), open daily until 10:30pm; one in **Deering Oaks Park** near the Forest Avenue exit off I-295, open at least 6 days a week year-round; and one ad hoc kiosk that opens up outside the **cruise ship terminal** on Commercial Street for 4 hours after any cruise ship arrives.

Portland also has a free weekly newspaper, the *Portland Phoenix,* offering good listings of local events, films, nightclub performances, and the like. Copies are widely available at restaurants, bars, and convenience stores.

EXPLORING THE CITY

Any visit to Portland should start with a stroll around the historic **Old Port** ⊀. Bounded by Commercial, Congress, Union, and Pearl streets, this area near the waterfront has the city's best commercial architecture, a mess of boutiques, restaurants, and bars. (The Old Port tends to transform at night, with crowds growing younger and rowdier.) The narrow streets and intricate brick facades reflect a mid-Victorian era; most of the area was rebuilt following a devastating fire in 1866. Exchange Street is the heart of the Old Port, with other attractive streets running off and around it.

The city's finest harborside stroll is along the **Eastern Prom Pathway** ⊀, which wraps for about a mile along the waterfront beginning at the Casco Bay Lines ferry terminal at the corner of Commercial and Franklin streets. This paved pathway is suitable for walking or biking, and offers expansive views of the islands and boat traffic on the harbor. The pathway skirts the lower edge of the **Eastern Promenade** ⊀, a 68-acre hillside park with broad, grassy slopes extending down to the water. The tiny East End Beach is also here, but the water is often off-limits for swimming (look for signs). The pathway continues on to Back Cove Pathway, a 3½-mile loop around tidal Back Cove.

Atop Munjoy Hill, above the Eastern Promenade, is the distinctive **Portland Observatory** (© **207/774-5561**). It's a quirky shingled tower, dating from 1807, used to signal the arrival of ships into port. Exhibits inside provide a quick glimpse of Portland's past, but the real draw is the expansive view from the top of the city and the harbor. It's open daily (when flags are flying from the cupola) from Memorial Day through Columbus Day, 10am until 5pm; the last tour leaves at 4:30pm. Admission is $6 for adults, $4 for children ages 6 to 16.

Children's Museum of Maine ⊀ (Kids)

The centerpiece exhibit in Portland's good kids' museum is its camera obscura, a room-size "camera" located on the top floor of this stout, columned downtown building next to the art museum. Children gather

Portland

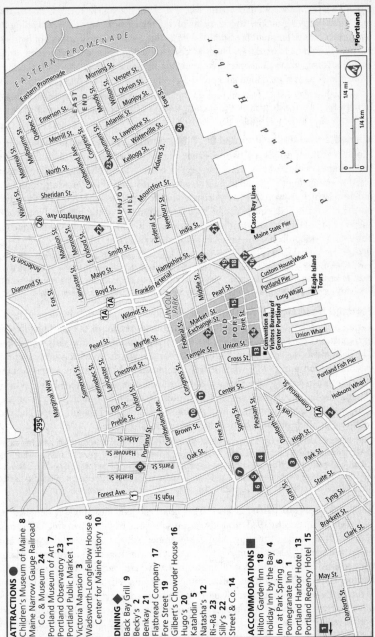

Portland

Harbor

Portland Head

EASTERN PROMENADE

Eastern Promenade

EAST END

Morning St.
Vesper St.
Obrion St.
Wilson St.
Moody St.
Munjoy St.
Fore St.
Atlantic St.
St. Lawrence St.
Waterville St.
Adams St.
Kellogg St.

Emerson St.
Quebec St.
Melbourne St.
Merrill St.
Montreal St.
Cumberland Ave.
Congress St.
Monument St.
North St.

Walnut St.
Sheridan St.
Washington Ave.
MUNJOY HILL
Mountfort St.
Federal St.
Newbury St.
India St.

Anderson St.
Madison St.
Monroe St.
E. Oxford St.
Smith St.
Hampshire St.
Middle St.
Pearl St.

Diamond St.
Fox St.
Lancaster St.
Mayo St.
Boyd St.
Franklin Arterial
Wilmot St.
LINCOLN PARK

Casco Bay Lines
Maine State Pier
Custom House Wharf
Portland Pier
Eagle Island Tours
Long Wharf
Union Wharf

Pearl St.
Myrtle St.
Federal St.
Market St.
Exchange St.
OLD PORT
Fore St.
Temple St.
Union St.
Cross St.

Somerset St.
Kennebec St.
Lancaster St.
Chestnut St.
Congress St.
Center St.
Spring St.
Pleasant St.
Commercial St.
Convention & Visitors Bureau of Greater Portland
Portland Fish Pier
Hobsons Wharf

Marginal Way
Elm St.
Oxford St.
Preble St.
Cumberland Ave.
Brown St.
Free St.
York St.
High St.

295
Alder St.
Hanover St.
Oak St.
Danforth St.
Park St.
State St.

Forest Ave.
Parris St.
Brattle St.
High St.
Gray St.
Tyng St.
Brackett St.
Clark St.
May St.
Danforth St.

1/4 mi
1/4 km

ATTRACTIONS ●
Children's Museum of Maine **8**
Maine Narrow Gauge Railroad
Co. & Museum **24**
Portland Museum of Art **7**
Portland Observatory **23**
Portland Public Market **11**
Victoria Mansion **3**
Wadsworth-Longfellow House &
Center for Maine History **10**

DINING ◆
Back Bay Grill **9**
Becky's **2**
Benkay **21**
Flatbread Company **17**
Fore Street **19**
Gilbert's Chowder House **16**
Hugo's **20**
Katahdin **5**
Natasha's **12**
Ri-Rá **23**
Silly's **22**
Street & Co. **14**

ACCOMMODATIONS ■
Hilton Garden Inn **18**
Holiday Inn by the Bay **4**
Inn at Park Spring **6**
Pomegranate Inn **1**
Portland Harbor Hotel **13**
Portland Regency Hotel **15**

609

around a white table in a dark room, where they see magically projected images that include cars driving on city streets, boats plying the harbor, and seagulls flapping by. This never fails to enthrall, providing a memorable lesson in the workings of lenses—ours, and the camera obscura's. That's just one attraction; there are plenty more, from a simulated supermarket checkout counter to a firehouse pole to a mock space shuttle that kids pilot from a high cockpit.

142 Free St. (next to the Portland Museum of Art). (© 207/828-1234. www.childrensmuseumofme.org. Admission $6. Free 5–8pm 1st Fri of each month. AE, MC, V. Mon–Sat 10am–5pm; Sun noon–5pm. Closed Mon fall–spring. Discounted parking at Spring St. parking garage.

Maine Narrow Gauge Railroad Co. & Museum ★ Kids
In the late 19th century, Maine was home to several narrow-gauge railways, operating on rails 2 feet apart. Most of these versatile trains have disappeared, but this nonprofit organization is dedicated to preserving the examples that remain. There's a small fee for admission to the museum, which is waived if you purchase a more expensive ticket for the short ride on the little train that chugs along Casco Bay at the foot of the Eastern Promenade. Views of the islands are outstanding; the ride itself is slow-paced and yawn-inducing, but young ones probably will enjoy it. Bring the video camera.

58 Fore St. (© 207/828-0814. www.mngrr.org. Museum admission $2 adults, $1 seniors and children ages 3–12; train fare (includes free museum admission) $10 adults, $9 seniors, $6 children ages 3–12, free for children 2 and under. Memorial Day–Columbus Day, daily 11am–4pm (trains run on the hour); rest of the year Sat–Sun only 10am–4pm. From I-295, take Franklin Arterial exit to Fore St.; turn left and continue to museum on right.

Portland Head Light & Museum ★★
A short drive (15–20 min. depending on traffic) from downtown Portland, this 1794 lighthouse is one of the most picturesque in the nation. You'll probably recognize it from advertisements, calendars, or posters. The light marks the entrance to Portland Harbor and was occupied continuously from its construction until 1989, when it was automated and the graceful keeper's house (1891) was converted to a small town-owned museum focusing on the history of navigation. The lighthouse itself is still active; thus closed to the public; but visitors can stop by the museum or browse for lighthouse-themed gifts in a gift shop. The surrounding grounds of Fort Williams Park are great for picnics.

In Fort Williams Park, 1000 Shore Rd., Cape Elizabeth. (© 207/799-2661. www.portlandheadlight.com. Free admission for grounds; museum admission $2 adults, $1 children 6–18. Park grounds daily year-round sunrise–sunset (until 8:30pm in summer); museum daily Memorial Day–Columbus Day 10am–4pm Sat–Sun only mid-Apr to mid-May and mid-Oct to late Dec. From Portland, follow State St. across bridge to South Portland; bear left on Broadway. At 3rd light, turn right on Cottage Rd. (Rte. 77), which becomes Shore Rd.; follow several more miles to park on left.

Portland Museum of Art ★★★
This bold, modern museum was designed by I.M. Pei & Partners in 1983, and it features selections from its own fine collections along with a parade of touring exhibits. (Summer exhibits are usually targeted at a broad audience.) The museum is particularly strong in American artists with Maine connections, including Winslow Homer, Andrew Wyeth, and Edward Hopper, and it has fine displays of Early American furniture and crafts. The museum shares the Joan Whitney Payson Collection with Colby College (the college gets it one semester every other year), which includes wonderful European works by Renoir, Degas, and Picasso. Special exhibitions have brought the landscape paintings of Frederic Church, art by Native American high-school students from northern Maine, and a mysterious *Mona Lisa* that may have been a preparatory study for the famous work. Guided tours are given daily at 2pm.

7 Congress Sq. (corner of Congress and High sts.). ✆ 207/775-6148. www.portlandmuseum.org. Admission $10 adults, $8 students and seniors, $4 students 6–17. Free admission Fri 5–9pm. Year-round Tues–Sun 10am–5pm, Fri to 9pm; Memorial Day to mid-Oct also Mon 10am–5pm.

Victoria Mansion ★★ *Finds*   Widely regarded as one of the most elaborate Victorian brownstone homes ever built in the U.S., this mansion (also known as the Morse-Libby House) is often mentioned in books on American architecture. It's a remarkable display of high Victorian style. Built between 1858 and 1863 for a Maine businessman who had made his fortune in New Orleans, the towering, slightly foreboding home is a prime example of Italianate style. Inside, craftsmen and artisans have gone to town with murals and other detailing. The decor is somber, but the home offers an engaging look into a bygone era. It's a must for architecture buffs. The weeks leading up to Christmas bring an annual round of special tours and events.

109 Danforth St. ✆ 207/772-4841. www.victoriamansion.org. Admission $10 adults, $9 seniors, $3 children 6–17, free for children under 6. Christmas slightly higher. May–Oct Mon–Sat 10am–4pm, Sun 1–5pm; late Nov–Dec Tues–Sun 11am–5pm. Tours twice per hour. Closed Nov and Jan–Apr. From the Old Port, head west on Fore St., and veer right on Danforth St. at light near Giobbi's restaurant; proceed 3 blocks to the mansion, at the corner of Park St.

Wadsworth-Longfellow House & Center for Maine History   The Maine Historical Society's "history campus" includes three widely varied buildings along busy Congress Street in downtown Portland. The austere brick Wadsworth-Longfellow House dates from 1785 and was built by Gen. Peleg Wadsworth, father of noted poet Henry Wadsworth Longfellow. It's furnished in an early-19th-century style, with many samples of Longfellow family furniture on display. Adjacent to the home is the Maine History Gallery, in a garish postmodern building, formerly a bank. Changing exhibits here explore the rich texture of Maine history. Just behind the Longfellow house is the library of the Maine Historical Society, a popular destination among genealogists.

489 Congress St. ✆ 207/774-1822. www.mainehistory.org. $7 adults, $6 seniors and students, $3 children (6–18). Longfellow House May–Dec Mon–Sat 10:30am–4pm, Sun noon–4pm.

ON THE WATER

Casco Bay Lines   Six of Casco Bay's islands have year-round populations and are served by scheduled ferries from downtown Portland. Except for Long Island, the islands are part of the city of Portland. The ferries provide an inexpensive way to view the bustling harbor and get a taste of island life. Trips range from a 20-minute (one-way) excursion to Peaks Island (the closest thing to an island suburb, with 1,200 year-round residents), to the 5½-hour cruise to Bailey Island (connected by bridge to the mainland south of Brunswick) and back. All the islands are well suited for walking; Peaks Island has a rocky back shore that's easily accessible via the island's paved perimeter road (bring a picnic lunch). There's also a bike-rental outfit a few blocks from the island's ferry dock. Long Island has a good hidden beach. Cliff Island is the most remote of the six-pack, with a sedate turn-of-the-20th-century character.

Commercial and Franklin sts. ✆ 207/774-7871. www.cascobaylines.com. Fares vary depending on the run and the season; summer rates $6–$9 round-trip. Frequent departures 6am–10pm.

Eagle Island Tours ★   Eagle Island was the summer home of famed arctic explorer and Portland native Robert E. Peary, who claimed in 1909 to be the first person to reach the North Pole. (His accomplishments have been the subject of exhaustive debates among arctic scholars, some of whom insist he inflated his claims.) In 1904, Peary built a simple home on a remote, 17-acre island at the edge of Casco Bay; in

Kids Take Me Out to the Sea Dogs

The Portland Sea Dogs are a minor league Double-A team affiliated with the Boston Red Sox (a perfect marriage in baseball-crazy northern New England). They play through summer at Hadlock Field (217 Park Ave.; © **800/936-3647** or 207/879-9500; www.seadogs.com) a small stadium near downtown that still retains an old-time feel despite aluminum benches and other updating. Activities are geared toward families, with lots of entertainment between innings and a selection of food that's a couple of notches above basic hot dogs and hamburgers. (Try the tasty french fries and grilled sausages.) You might even catch future pro stars—Josh Beckett, Brad Penny, Alex Gonzalez, Charles Johnson, and Kevin Millar all did time here as farmhands before they made "the show." The season runs around April until about Labor Day.

1912, he added flourishes in the form of two low stone towers. After his death in 1920, his family kept up the home; they later donated it to the state, which has since managed it as a state park. The home is open to the public, maintained much as it was when Peary lived here. Eagle Tours takes one trip daily from Portland. The 4-hour excursion includes a 1½-hour stopover on the island.

Long Wharf (Commercial St.) © 207/774-6498. www.eagleislandtours.com. $26 adults, $24 seniors, $15 children age 3–12 (includes state park fee). Tour departs daily at 10am from late June–Labor Day, Sat–Sun only early June and Sept.

WHERE TO STAY

In a pinch, check around the **Maine Mall** in **South Portland**; chain hotels abound. If you're looking for something more central, the **Hilton Garden Inn** at 65 Commercial St. (© 207/780-0780) is convenient to the Old Port—not to mention the islands of Casco Bay. You'll pay for the privilege of being in the heart of the waterfront, though: double rooms mostly run from about $189 up to $369 per night.

The **Holiday Inn by the Bay,** 88 Spring St. (© 800/345-5050 or 207/775-2311), offers great views of the harbor from about half the rooms, along with the usual chain-hotel creature comforts. Peak-season rates are approximately $180 for a double. Budget travelers seeking chain hotels typically head toward the area around the Maine Mall in South Portland, about 8 miles south of the attractions of downtown.

Inn at Park Spring This small, tasteful B&B is located on a busy downtown street in a historic brick home that dates back to 1835. It's well located for exploring the city on foot. The Portland Museum of Art is just 2 blocks away, the Old Port is about 10 minutes away, and great restaurants are all within easy walking distance. Guests can linger or watch TV in a front parlor, or chat at the communal dining table in the adjacent room. The accommodations are all corner rooms, and most are bright and sunny. Especially nice is "Spring," with its great morning light and wonderful views of the historic row houses on Park Street, and "Gables," on the third floor, which gets abundant afternoon light and has a nice bathroom.

135 Spring St., Portland, ME 04101. © 800/437-8511 or 207/774-1059. www.innatparkspring.com. 6 units. Mid-June to Oct and holidays $149–$175 double; rest of the year $99–$165 double. 2-night minimum Sat–Sun. Rates include full breakfast and off-street parking. AE, MC, V. No children under 10. *In room:* A/C, hair dryer, iron/ironing board.

Pomegranate Inn 🏛🏛   Housed in an imposing, dove-gray 1884 Italianate home in the architecturally distinctive Western Prom neighborhood, this home is decorated with whimsy and elegance. Look for bold, exuberant wall paintings by a local artist and eclectic antique furniture collected and tastefully arranged by the owner. If you have the chance, peek into an unoccupied room—they're all different, with painted floors and faux-marble woodwork. Most have gas fireplaces; the best room is in the carriage house, which comes with its own private terrace, kitchenette, and fireplace. Tea and wine are served upon arrival, and sit-down breakfasts take place in a cheery dining room. This inn is well situated for strolling the West End, and downtown is about a 20-minute walk away.

49 Neal St., Portland, ME 04102. (℃) **800/356-0408** or 207/772-1006. Fax 207/773-4426. www.pomegranateinn.com. 8 units. Memorial Day–Oct $175–$265 double; rest of the year, $95–$165 double. Rates include full breakfast. 2-night minimum summer weekends and holidays. AE, DISC, MC, V. On-street parking. From the Old Port, take Middle St. (which turns into Spring St.) to Neal St. in the West End (about 1 mile); turn right and proceed to inn. Children 16 and older welcome. **Amenities:** Tea and wine service. *In room:* A/C, TV, kitchenette (1 unit), fireplace (some units).

Portland Harbor Hotel 🏛🏛   Adjacent to Portland's busy nightlife on the corner of Fore and Union streets, only steps from a long row of bars and restaurants, this semi-circular town-house-like structure is designed to fit in with the brick facades that prevail throughout the Old Port. The hotel, with its many amenities, appeals to the boutique crowd. The interior courtyard throws off European ambience; large, exquisite rooms are furnished with comfy queen- and king-size beds and spacious work desks. Even the standard rooms are outfitted with big, deep bathtubs in granite-faced bathrooms; armoires; comfy duvets and down coverlets; two-line phones; and big TVs with 70 channels each. Deluxe rooms and suites add Jacuzzis and sitting areas, and many units look out onto the attractive garden area. The front desk now rents bicycles inexpensively for local sightseeing. Remember that the proximity to so many bars means some late-night weekend noise.

468 Fore St., Portland, ME 04101. (℃) **888/798-9090** or 207/775-9090. Fax 207/775-9990. www.portlandharbor hotel.com. 100 units. Mid-May to mid-Oct $229–$249 double, $329 suite; off-season $159–$179 double, $259 suite. Packages available. AE, DC, DISC, MC, V. Valet parking in garage $10 per day. **Amenities:** Dining room; bar; fitness center; bike rental; concierge; limited room service; dry cleaning. *In room:* A/C, digital TV, Internet access, hair dryer, safe, Jacuzzis (some units).

Portland Regency Hotel 🏛🏛🏛   Centrally located on a cobblestone courtyard in the middle of the trendy Old Port, the Regency boasts one of the city's premier hotel locations. But it's got more than location—this is also one of the most architecturally striking and better-managed hotels in southern Maine. Housed in an 1895 brick armory, the hotel is thoroughly modern and offers attractive rooms, appointed and furnished with all the expected amenities. There are several types of rooms and suites, each fitted to the place's unique architecture; for a splurge, ask for a luxurious corner room with a handsome (nonworking) fireplace, sitting area, city views out big windows, and a Jacuzzi. Staff is professional, the small health club is among the best in town (it includes a sauna and hot tub), and the downstairs level conceals a **restaurant** and a **bar** 🏛 that's the best quiet place in town to sip a drink.

20 Milk St., Portland, ME 04101. (℃) **800/727-3436** or 207/774-4200. Fax 207/775-2150. www.theregency.com. 95 units. Early July–late Oct $249–$269 double; $289–$389 suite; off-season $159–$219 double, $209–$329 suite. AE, DISC, MC, V. Valet parking $8 per day. **Amenities:** Restaurant; bar; fitness club w/aerobics classes; Jacuzzi; spa; sauna; courtesy car to airport; business center; conference rooms; limited room service; babysitting (with prior notice); dry cleaning (Mon–Fri). *In room:* A/C, TV, minibar, safe.

WHERE TO DINE
EXPENSIVE

Back Bay Grill ✦✦ NEW AMERICAN   Back Bay Grill has long been one of Portland's consistently best restaurants, with an upscale, contemporary ambience; the only trouble is finding it, in a rather pedestrian neighborhood near the city's central post office. There's light jazz on the stereo and bold artwork on the walls that goes several notches above the usual bistro atmosphere. Chef Larry Matthews has been cooking here since 1997, and he bought it from founder Joel Freund in 2002; his menu, revamped seasonally, emphasizes local produce and meats as much as possible. Diners might start with some Maine crab cakes in a Thai chili aioli sauce, beef carpaccio, crispy duck confit, or roasted acorn squash soup. Among the main courses, look for such dishes as a sausage of locally raised lamb, grilled filet mignon in red-wine sauce, monkfish with pesto-whipped potatoes, or salmon crusted in horseradish and served with roasted beets and basmati rice. Memorable, too, are the fresh pastas, such as hand-rolled fettuccini with truffles or lobster tortellini with lobster foam.

65 Portland St. ✆ **207/772-8833**. www.backbaygrill.com. Reservations recommended. Main courses $17–$33. AE, DC, DISC, MC, V. Mon–Thurs 5:30–9:30pm; Fri–Sat 5:30–10pm.

Fore Street ✦✦ CONTEMPORARY GRILL   Fore Street has emerged as one of northern New England's most celebrated restaurants. Chef Sam Hayward's secret is simplicity: Local and organic ingredients whenever possible. The dining space centers on a busy open kitchen where a team of chefs constantly stoke the wood-fired brick oven and grill. The menu changes nightly; the best entrees utilize the grill and oven to the fullest, such as spit-roasted pork loin and chicken or grilled marinated hanger steak. Wood-roasted mussels are also a big hit. Finish with a dessert of chocolate soufflé, hand-dipped chocolates, or gelato; these are often accented in summer by seasonal Maine berries and fruits. During the long summer evenings, light floods in through the loftlike space's huge windows; later at night, soft lighting against the brick walls, maple floors, and coppery tables lend a more intimate glow to the place, which is always bustling. Though it can be mighty hard to snag a reservation here, particularly on summer weekends, management sets aside a few tables each night for walk-ins.

288 Fore St. ✆ **207/775-2717**. www.forestreet.biz. Reservations recommended. Main courses $13–$29. AE, MC, V. Mon–Thurs 5:30–10pm; Fri–Sat 5:30–10:30pm; Sun 5:30–9:30pm.

Hugo's ✦✦✦ ECLECTIC/NEW AMERICAN   The resurrection of Hugo's under New England–native Chef Rob Evans is nothing short of amazing. Just a decade ago, the place was fading, but Evans and partner Nancy Pugh changed all that. Evans has brought a philosophy of using locally produced ingredients wherever possible; the result is a set of experimental, exciting menus that begin in familiar territory, and then take off into the stratosphere. Even the basic four-course menu might include such twists as "four-textured mini-lobster," "a love affair with cod," or four treatments of duck. Tasting menus expand the palate further; representative stops on the journey might include Maine mussels and periwinkles, soy-glazed pork belly, rabbit-stuffed quail, or soft-shell lobsters. Dessert could be a roasted-apple French toast, pine-nut-and-gooseberry cheesecake, pistachio-buttermilk ice cream, or a tasting of chocolate dishes. A great little tapas menu is available at the bar, and the proprietors also recently opened a sandwich-and-Belgian-fries shop right down the same street.

88 Middle St. ✆ **207/774-8538**. www.hugos.net. Reservations highly recommended (required for Chef's Menu). Prix-fixe menus $68–$90 per person; bar tapas menu $6–$16 per item. AE, MC, V. Tues–Thurs 5:30–9pm; Fri–Sat 5:30–9:30pm.

Street & Co. ★★★ MEDITERRANEAN/SEAFOOD   A pioneering establishment on now-bustling Wharf Street, Dana Street's intimate, brick-walled bistro specializes in seafood. You pass the open kitchen as you're seated, and then watch talented chefs somehow perform their magic in a tiny space. The fish is as fresh as can be (the docks are close by), and cooked just right. Diners sit at copper-topped tables, designed so waiters can deliver steaming skillets directly from the stovetop. Looking for lobster? Try it grilled and served over linguine in a butter-garlic sauce. Other good choices include tuna, fresh mussels, or a grilled piece of whatever's come in (swordfish, perhaps)—the catch of the day is often a highlight. This place often fills up early, so reservations are strongly recommended, though some tables are reserved for walk-ins; it can't hurt to check if you're in the neighborhood. During summer, outdoor seating is available at a few precious tables on the alley.

33 Wharf St. © 207/775-0887. Reservations recommended. Main courses $14–$24. AE, MC, V. Mon–Thurs 5:30–9:30pm; Fri–Sat 5:30–10pm. Lounge opens 30 min. earlier.

MODERATE

Beale Street BBQ ★ *Finds* BARBECUE   Beale Street BBQ owner Mark Quigg once operated a takeout grill on Route 1 outside Freeport, but author Stephen King got wind of his cooking; soon he was catering movie shoots, joining forces with his two brothers, and the Quiggs have never looked back. Of the barbecue joints in Maine, this is probably my favorite, with an appealing roadhouse atmosphere, friendly staff, and great smoked meats. Check the board for intriguing daily specials, which usually include a fish preparation as well as Creole or Cajun offerings; I also like the barbecue sampler ("All You Really Need to Know About BBQ"), which entitles you to a choice of pulled pork, chicken, or beef brisket; sweet, crunchy cornbread; a half slab of ribs; a quarter chicken; delicious spicy smoked links that remind me of east Texas; and a mound of barbecued beans and coleslaw. Two people could comfortably split it. There's another, fancier location (© **207/442-9514**) at 215 Water St., in the town of Bath, a half-hour north up U.S. Route 1, also open daily and until late.

727 Broadway, South Portland. © 207/767-0130. Reservations not accepted. Main courses $9–$18. MC, V. Daily 11:30am–10pm.

Benkay ★ *Value* JAPANESE/SUSHI   Of Portland's sushi restaurants, Benkay is the hippest, usually teeming with a lively crowd lured by good value. It's also the most authentic: Chef Seiji Ando trained in his native Osaka and in Kyoto. The sushi, sashimi, and maki roll menus are inexpensive and deliver a lot for the money, with a pretty wide assortment of choices. Standard Japanese treats like tempura, gyoza, teriyaki, tempura, katsu, and udon round out the menu. Expect harried service on busy nights. It stays open until 12:30am Friday and Saturday—a boon in early-closing Portland. Finish with green-tea ice cream.

2 India St. (at Commercial). © 207/773-5555. www.sushiman.com. Reservations not accepted. Main courses $8–$17. AE, MC, V. Mon–Thurs 11:30am–2pm and 5–9:30pm; Fri 11:30am–2pm and 5pm–12:30am; Sat 5pm–12:30am; Sun 5–9:30pm.

Flatbread Company ★ PIZZA   This upscale, hippie-chic pizzeria—an offshoot of the original Flatbread Company in Waitsfield, Vermont—might have the best waterfront location in town. It sits on a slip overlooking the Casco Bay Lines terminal, so you can watch fishermen and ferries while you eat. (Picnic tables are set out on the deck in fair weather.) The inside brings to mind a Phish concert, with Tibetan prayer flags and longhaired staffers stoking wood-fired ovens and slicing nitrate-free pepperoni and organic vegetables. The laid-back, smoky atmosphere really makes the place; the pizza is quite good, too.

72 Commercial St. (℃) 207/772-8777. Reservations accepted for parties of 10 or more. Pizzas $12–$15. AE, MC, V. Mon–Tues 5–9pm; Wed–Sun 11:30am–9pm.

Katahdin 🕁🕁 CREATIVE NEW ENGLAND   Katahdin is a lively, often noisy spot that prides itself on its eclectic cuisine. Artists on slim budgets dine on Chef Becky Lee Simmons' nightly specials, which could be something basic or something delicate, such as sea scallops with smoked bacon and green-pea tendrils; Maine shrimp in a buttery fondue with house-made gnocchi; or roast duck with a citrusy confit. There's a small but decent selection of wines. Reservations are not accepted, but you can enjoy a glass of northern California vintage or one of the restaurant's famous house martinis while waiting at the bar for your table.

106 High St. (℃) 207/774-1740. www.katahdinrestaurant.com. Reservations not accepted. Main courses $12–$18. DISC, MC, V. Tues–Thurs 5–9:30pm; Fri–Sat 5–10:30pm.

Natasha's 🕁 NEW AMERICAN/ASIAN   Natasha's menu is delightfully creative in its simplicity and its blending of Maine foods with Asian and Latin accents: A lobster stew with leek and potatoes, a Maine lump crab cake, or some chipotle-flecked mussels might serve as typical starters. Dinner items could include a pad Thai-like Cambodian bowl of wok-fried vegetables and meat spiced with pineapple, mint, cilantro, peanuts, and fried banana; a lovely mixed grill (including a choice of duck); chai-spiced tuna with bamboo rice; or filet mignon with prosciutto-wrapped scallops. Lunch is inviting, too, with creative sandwiches, salads, wraps, fish tacos, and noodle dishes. There's also a brunch service on Saturday and Sunday.

82 Exchange St. (℃) 207/541-3663. Reservations recommended. Main courses $4.50–$9.95 at lunch (mostly $5–$6); $19–$32 at dinner. AE, DISC, MC, V. Mon–Fri 11am–9pm; Sat–Sun 9am–9pm.

Rí~Rá 🕁 IRISH PUB   This fun place is styled after a friendly Irish pub. The doors were imported from a shop pub in Kilkenny, and the back bar and counter are from County Louth. Old and new blend pretty seamlessly; it's fairly authentic, except for the lack of smoke and the Patriots and Red Sox on TV instead of Celtic soccer. Upstairs beyond the pub is a nice dining room with a view of the ferry dock; look for basic fare such as smoked turkey wraps, fish and chips, meat loaf, shepherd's pie, and Guinness bread pudding, along with a smattering of upscale dishes and Irish specialties such as crab-filled salmon, Derrybeg pork (glazed with apricot, mustard, and cider), and broxty: a scallion-potato pancake topped with parsley sauce and meat.

72 Commercial St. (℃) 207/761-4446. www.rira.com. Main courses $9–$20. AE, MC, V. Mon–Sat 11:30am–10pm; Sun 11am–10pm.

INEXPENSIVE

Becky's BREAKFAST/LUNCH   Becky's has been written up in *Gourmet* magazine, but that obviously hasn't gone to the proprietor's head. This waterfront institution is in a squat maroon building of concrete of concrete on the not-so-quaint end of the waterfront. It has drop ceilings, fluorescent lights, and scruffy counters, booths, and tables. It opens early (4am) to cater to local fishermen grabbing a cup of joe and some eggs before heading out onto (or back in from) the water; later in the day, it attracts high-school kids, businesspeople, and just about everyone else. The menu is extensive, offering about what you'd expect: sandwiches (fried haddock and cheese, corn dogs, tuna melt) and a milky bowl of chowder. It's also noted for its breakfasts, including

---

(*Fun Fact* **To Market, To Market . . . Once Again**

The Portland Public Market has moved—and the local library almost did, too. It's been an interesting couple of years for the city's public market, which was originally conceived and funded by the late benefactress Betty Noyce in the 1990s. A few blocks downhill from Portland's main drag, the 37,000-square-foot space was, for a short while, one of the best and hippest places in northern New England to pick up a coffee in the morning, a sandwich at lunch, a lobster and some vegetables to cook for dinner, and other gourmet goods. Sadly, the market closed its doors in 2007 and the property was sold after Noyce's nonprofit foundation determined it could no longer subsidize the lower-than-market rents being charged to food vendors. The market appeared to have dissolved for good, and city residents were understandably disheartened.

But a small consortium of vendors banded together and bought a building in the center of the city, rechristening it the **Public Market House** (28 Monument Square). Today the market thrives once more. The vacant former market building? City voters defeated a 2007 referendum that would have purchased the space and converted it into a new city library. But stay tuned.

---

more than a dozen different omelets; eggs any way you want them; and fresh fruit bowls, pancakes, and French toast. Where else can you choose from among five different types of home fries? This is a Portland institution.

390 Commercial St. © 207/773-7070. www.beckysdiner.com. Breakfast items $2.25–$7.50; lunch and dinner items $2–$8. AE, DISC, MC, V. Daily 4am–9pm.

Gilbert's Chowder House CHOWDER/SEAFOOD   Gilbert's is a popular waterfront spot that's nautical without being too cute. The chowders are okay; if you're looking to stay full, consider getting yours in a bread bowl. Other choices here include fried clams, haddock sandwiches, and seafood available broiled or fried. There's also a basic lobster dinner with corn on the cob and a cup of clam chowder. Limited microbrews are on tap, and the cheesecake makes a fitting dessert.

92 Commercial St. © 207/871-5636. Reservations not accepted. Chowders $2.50–$9.75; sandwiches $2.25–$9.95; main courses $6.95–$23. AE, DISC, MC, V. Mon–Thurs 11am–10pm; Fri–Sat 11am–11pm; Sun 11am–9pm (closed earlier in winter).

Silly's *Finds Kids* ECLECTIC/TAKEOUT   Silly's is the favorite cheap-eats joint for hip Portlanders. Situated on a commercial street near the Eastern Promenade, the interior is informal, bright, and funky, with mismatched 1950s dinettes and a hodgepodge back patio beneath trees. There's also a weird fascination with Einstein here; like Einstein, the menu is creative, and everything is made fresh and from scratch. The place is noted for its roll-ups ("fast Abdullahs"), a series of tasty fillings piled into soft tortillas. I like the shish kebab with feta or the sloppy "Diesel," made with pulled pork barbecue and coleslaw. The fries here are hand-cut, the burgers big and delicious, and there's beer on tap. Newer menu additions include the "slop bucket," which has a messy, layered-burrito feel. Don't overlook the playful, changing dessert menu of cookies, pies, ice creams, and cakes, either—nor the huge milkshakes. Silly's whips 'em up with peanut butter, tahini, bananas, malt—just about anything you could imagine and some things (cranberry sauce, marshmallow crispies) you couldn't have.

40 Washington Ave. (✆ **207/772-0360**. www.sillys.com. Most items $5–$13; pizzas to $18. MC, V. Tues–Sun 11:30am–9pm.

PORTLAND AFTER DARK
FILM

Downtown Portland is still blessed with two downtown movie houses, enabling travelers in the mood for a flick to avoid the disheartening slog out to the boxy, could-be-anywhere mall megaplexes. **Nickelodeon Cinemas,** 1 Temple St. ((✆ **207/772-9751**), has six screens showing first- and second-run films at reasonable prices. **The Movies** ✵, 10 Exchange St. ((✆ **207/772-9600** or 207/772-8041), is a compact art-film showcase in the heart of the Old Port featuring a lineup of foreign and independent films of recent and historic vintage.

PERFORMING ARTS

Portland has a growing creative corps of performing artists. Theater companies typically take the summer off, but it doesn't hurt to call or check the local papers for special performances.

Portland Stage Company ✵   The most polished and consistent of the Portland theater companies, Portland Stage offers crisply produced shows starring local and imported equity actors in a handsome, second-story theater just off Congress Street. About a half-dozen shows are staged throughout the season, which runs from October to May. Recent productions have included *Proof, Arcadia, Fences, Noises Off,* Shakespeare's *Much Ado About Nothing,* and *Augusta* (a drama about small-town Maine). Performing Arts Center, 25A Forest Ave. (✆ **207/774-0465**. www.portlandstage.com. Tickets $25–$35 adults, discounts for students and seniors.

Portland Symphony Orchestra ✵✵   The well-regarded Portland Symphony, now headed by Robert Moody, offers a variety of performances throughout the season (typically Sept–May), ranging from pops concerts to Mozart; half the orchestra are Mainers, the rest New Englanders, and all are talented. Summer travelers should consider a Portland detour the week of July 4th, when the "Independence Pops" is held (weather permitting) at various sites around southern Maine, including the grounds of the Portland Head Lighthouse in Cape Elizabeth. There are also special Christmas shows. 477 Congress St. (✆ **207/842-0800** for tickets or 207/773-6128 for information. www.portland symphony.com. Tickets $16–$57, discounts for students and seniors.

3 Midcoast Maine

Bath: 33 miles NE of Portland. Boothbay Harbor: 23 miles E of Bath; 41 miles SW of Rockland

Veteran Maine travelers contend that this part of the coast, long known as the "Midcoast," is fast losing its native charm—it's too commercial, they say, too developed, too highfalutin . . . in short, too much like the *rest* of the United States. These grousers have a point, especially along U.S. Route 1. But get off the main roads and you'll swiftly find pockets of another Maine, some of the most pastoral and picturesque meadows, mountains, peninsulas, and harbors in the entire state.

Beyond local tourist huts and chambers of commerce, the best source of information for the Midcoast region in general is found at the **Maine State Information Center** ((✆ **207/846-0833**) just off exit 17 of I-295 in Yarmouth, which isn't really *in* the Midcoast—but you'll almost certainly pass through to get there. This state-run center is stocked with hundreds of brochures, and is staffed with a helpful crew that can provide

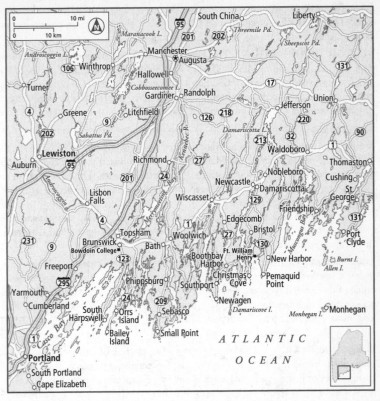

information about the entire state but that is particularly well informed about the middle reaches of coast. It's open daily from 8am to 6pm (8:30am–5pm in winter), and the attached restroom facilities are always open.

FREEPORT ⊛

If **Freeport** were a mall (which is not all that far-fetched an analogy), L.L.Bean would be the anchor store. It's the business that launched this town to prominence, elevating its status from just another Maine fishing village near the interstate to one of the state's major tourist draws for the outlet centers that sprang up here in Bean's wake. Freeport still has the look of a classic Maine village, but it's a village that's been largely taken over by the national fashion industry; most of the old historic homes and stores have been converted into upscale factory shops purveying name-brand clothing and housewares at cut-rate prices. Banana Republic occupies an exceedingly handsome brick Federal-style home; a Carnegie library became an Abercrombie & Fitch pumping club music (oh, the inhumanity); and even the McDonald's is inside a tasteful, understated Victorian farmhouse—you really have to look for the golden arches.

Seeking the real Maine? Head at some point for **South Freeport,** which consists of a boat dock, general store, and lobster shack at the end of a finger of land reached via a numberless side road off U.S. Route 1.

ESSENTIALS

GETTING THERE   Freeport is on U.S. Route 1, though the downtown is most easily reached via I-295 from either exit 20 or exit 22.

VISITOR INFORMATION   The **Freeport Merchants Marketing Association,** P.O. Box 452, Freeport, ME 04032 (ℭ **800/865-1994** [automated] or 207/865-1212; www.freeportusa.com), publishes a map and directory of businesses, restaurants, and overnight accommodations. The free map is widely available around town, or you can contact the association to have one sent to you.

SHOPPING

Freeport has more than 140 retail shops spaced out between exit 20 of I-295 (at the far lower end of Main Street) and Mallet Road, which connects to exit 22. Some shops have even begun to spread south of exit 20 toward Yarmouth. The bulk of them are "factory" or "outlet" stores. If you don't want to miss a single one, get off at exit 17 and head north on U.S. Route 1.

These stores are typically open daily 9am to 9pm during the busy summer and close much earlier (at 5 or 6pm) in other seasons; between Thanksgiving and Christmas, they remain open late once more.

Cuddledown   Cuddledown started producing down comforters in 1973, and now makes a whole line of products much appreciated in northern climes and beyond. Some of the down pillows are made right in the outlet shop, which also carries a variety of European goose-down comforters in all sizes and weights. Look for linens, blankets, moccasins, and home furnishings, too. 475 U.S. Rte. 1 (btw. exits 17 and 20). ℭ **207/865-1713** or 207/865-4993. www.cuddledown.com.

Freeport Knife Co. ✶   This place sports a wide selection of knives for kitchen and camp alike, including blades from Germany, Switzerland, and Japan. Look for their custom line, or just bring in your dull blade for a sharpening. They also sell replacement parts and do repairs on all brands of knives. 181 Lower Main St. ℭ **207/865-0779.** www.freeportknife.com.

L.L.Bean ✶✶✶   Monster outdoor retailer L.L.Bean traces its roots from the day Leon Leonwood Bean decided that what the world really needed was a good weatherproof hunting shoe. He joined a watertight gum shoe to a laced leather upper. Hunters liked it; the store grew. An empire was born. Today L.L.Bean sells millions of dollars' worth of clothing and outdoor goods nationwide through its well-respected catalogs, and it continues to draw hundreds of thousands of customers through its doors to a headquarters building and several offshoots around town. The modern, multilevel main store is about the size of a regional mall, but it's very tastefully done with its own

---

⎛Fun Fact⎠ **All Bean's, All the Time**

One of the big reasons that L.L.Bean's flagship shop is such a tourist draw is that it's open 365 days a year, 7 days a week, 24 hours a day—note the lack of any locks or latches on the front doors. As such, it's a popular spot even in the dead of night, especially during summer or around holidays. Folks have been known to set out from New Hampshire at 1 or 2 in the morning to enjoy the best deals (and empty aisles) on their middle-of-the-night arrival.

Tips Need an Outlet?

In addition to the main store, L.L.Bean now maintains two new **satellite shops** (🕾 877/552-3268) stocking small, rapidly changing inventories of specialized goods, some of them used; this pair of shops replaced the old factory store just downhill from the flagship campus. **The Bike, Boat & Ski Store** is near L.L.Kids (behind the flagship store) and holds lots of canoes, kayaks, paddles, cycles, and helmets. The **Hunting & Fishing Store** opened in November 2007, just south of town on U.S. 1 (past the gas station) and houses fly-fishing gear, hunting boots, and the like.

---

indoor trout pond and lots of natural wood. Selections include Bean's own trademark clothing, along with home furnishings, books, shoes, and plenty of outdoor gear for camping, fishing, and hunting (there's a particularly good section). The staff is incredibly knowledgeable—Bean's encourages staff to take the gear home and try it out to better serve customers. A minute's walk away, behind the main store down a pathway, is the L.L.Kids store with similar goods for a (much) younger set. 95 Main St. (at Bow St.). 🕾 800/559-0747. www.llbean.com.

Mangy Moose A souvenir shop with a twist: Virtually everything in this place is moose-related. Really. There are moose wineglasses, moose trivets, moose cookie cutters, and (of course) moose T-shirts. Somehow, this merchandise is a notch above what you'll find in most other souvenir shops around the state. 112 Main St. 🕾 800/606-6517 or 207/865-6414. www.themangymoose.com.

Thos. Moser Cabinetmakers ★ Classic furniture reinterpreted in lustrous wood and leather is the focus at this shop, which—thanks to a steady parade of ads in the *New Yorker* and a Madison Avenue branch—has become nearly as representative of Maine as L.L.Bean has. Shaker, mission, and modern styles are wonderfully reinvented by Tom Moser and his designers and woodworkers, who produce heirloom-quality signed pieces. Nationwide delivery is easy to arrange. There's a good selection of knotted rugs, too, made by an independent artisan, and a good gallery of Maine art on site. 149 Main St. 🕾 207/865-4519 or 800/708-9041. www.thomasmoser.com.

WHERE TO STAY

Harraseeket Inn ★★ The Harraseeket is a large, thoroughly modern hotel 2 blocks north of L.L.Bean. Despite its size, a traveler could drive down Main Street and not immediately notice it—and that's a good thing. A late-19th-century home is the soul of the hotel, though most of the rooms are in later additions, built in 1989 and 1997. Guests can relax in the dining room, read the paper in a common room with the baby-grand player piano, or sip a cocktail in the homey Broad Arrow Tavern (with its wood-fired oven and grill, it serves dinner as well as lunch). Guest rooms are large and tastefully furnished, with quarter-canopy beds and a mix of contemporary and antique furnishings; some have gas or wood-burning fireplaces, more than half now have whirlpools, and some are even done up with wet bars and refrigerators. This inn is especially pet-friendly, with doggy beds and treats for four-footed guests.

162 Main St., Freeport, ME 04032. 🕾 800/342-6423 or 207/865-9377. www.harraseeketinn.com. 84 units. $125–$304 double and suite. All rates include full breakfast and afternoon tea. MAP rates available. Pets welcome ($25 per pet per night). AE, DC, DISC, MC, V. Take exit 22 off I-295 to Main St. **Amenities:** 2 restaurants; bar; indoor pool;

concierge; business center; conference rooms; room service; laundry service; dry cleaning. *In room:* A/C, TV, dataport, fridge (some units), coffeemaker, hair dryer (some units), safe, fireplace (some units), Jacuzzi (some units).

Kendall Tavern Bed & Breakfast

If you want to avoid some of downtown's crowds without ever straying more than walking distance from the primo shopping, Kendall Tavern is your solution. This handsome B&B is in a cheerful yellow farmhouse on 3½ acres of land at a bend in the road a half-mile north of the center of Freeport. Rooms are simple, plushly carpeted, and comfortable. Everything is decorated in bright and airy style, with framed prints of New England scenes and Victorian ladies on the walls and mixes of antique and new furniture; some rooms have Vermont-style electric stoves. Rooms facing Main Street are a bit noisier due to traffic.

213 Main St., Freeport, ME 04032. ⓒ 800/341-9572 or 207/865-1338. Fax 207/865-3544. www.kendalltavern.com. 7 units. $140–$185 double; off-season and Mon–Fri discounts available. Rates include full breakfast. Children over age 8 welcome. AE, DISC, MC, V. **Amenities:** Jacuzzi. *In room:* A/C, no phone.

Maine Idyll Motor Court *(Value)*

Talk about a throwback to a happier time: This motel doesn't take any credit cards, but they will take your personal check. This 1932 "motor court" is a Maine classic—a cluster of 20 cottages scattered around a grove of oak and beech trees. Most cottages come with a tiny porch, wood-burning fireplace (birch logs are provided), television (yes, color), modest kitchen facilities (no ovens), and time-worn furniture. These cabins are not very big, but they're comfortable enough and kept clean; some have showers, some bathtubs. Kids might enjoy the swing set in the play area, dog-walkers the nature trails attached to the property, and picnickers the grill sets. The only interruption to the idyll here is the omnipresent drone of traffic: I-295 is just through the trees to one side, and U.S. 1 to the other side. Get past that, and you'll find good value for your money here. They even have free Wi-Fi throughout.

1411 U.S. Rte. 1, Freeport, ME 04032. ⓒ 207/865-4201. www.maineidyll.com. 20 units. $59–$107 double; spring rates lower. Rates include continental breakfast. No credit cards. Closed Nov–Apr. Pets on leashes allowed. *In room:* Kitchenette, fireplace (most units), fridge, no phone.

WHERE TO DINE

Gritty McDuff's BREWPUB

Spacious, informal, and air-conditioned in summer, Gritty's is an offshoot of Portland's first brewpub. It's a short drive south of the village center, and is best known for its varied selection of house-brewed beers like the unfiltered Black Fly Stout. The pub offers a wide-ranging bar menu of reliable salads, burgers, steaks, stone-oven pizzas, cheesesteak sandwiches, quesadillas, and pub classics such as shepherd's pie and fish and chips. There's a kids' menu as well.

187 Rte. 1 (Main St.), Freeport. ⓒ 207/865-4321. Reservations not accepted. Main courses $10–$17. AE, DISC, MC, V. Daily 11:30am–11pm.

Harraseeket Lunch & Lobster *(Finds)* LOBSTER

At a boatyard on the Harraseeket River about a 10-minute drive from Freeport's shopping district, this lobster pound gets crowded on sunny days—although, with its heated dining room, it's a worthy destination any time it's open. Point to and order a lobster sized according to your hunger level, then take in river views from the dock as you wait for your number to be called. Come in late afternoon to avoid the lunch and dinner hordes. You can also get fried fish, burgers, chowder, or an ice cream.

Main St., South Freeport. ⓒ 207/865-4888. Lobsters market price (typically $8–$15). No credit cards. Mid-June to Labor Day daily 11am–8:45pm; May to mid-June and early Sept to mid-Oct daily 11am–7:45pm. Closed mid-Oct to Apr. From Portland, take I-295 to exit 17 and head north on U.S. Rte. 1; turn right on S. Freeport Rd. at big Indian statue to South Freeport. Turn right and drive to waterfront. From downtown Freeport, take South St. (off Bow St.) to South Freeport and turn left at stop sign.

Jameson Tavern ⟡ AMERICAN/PUB FARE   In another historic farmhouse literally in the shadow of L.L.Bean (on the north side), Jameson Tavern touts itself as the birthplace of Maine. And it is: In 1820, papers were signed here legally separating Maine from Massachusetts. Mainers still appreciate that pen stroke. Today, the tavern sports two restaurants under the same ownership; as you enter the door, the historic Tap Room is to your left, a compact and often crowded spot filled with the smell of fresh popcorn, draft beer, and pubby food. The other part of the house is the Dining Room, more formal in a country-Colonial sort of way. Meals here are hearty fare, but healthier than they were in days of yore: filet mignon wrapped in bacon, yes, but also poached salmon, baked haddock, fresh pastas, and seafood salads.

115 Main St. (✆ **207/865-4196**. Reservations recommended. Main courses $7–$18 in tap room and dining room at lunch; $15–$26 dining room dinner. AE, DC, DISC, MC, V. Tap room daily 11am–11pm; dining room daily in summer 11am–10pm, winter 11:30am–9pm.

WISCASSET ⟡⟡ & THE BOOTHBAYS ⟡

Wiscasset is a cute riverside town just inland from the Atlantic (no views), and it's not shy about letting you know: THE PRETTIEST VILLAGE IN MAINE boasts a sign at the edge of town and on many brochures. Whether or not you agree with this assessment (and not all locals do), the town is indeed attractive, even if the charm is diminished somewhat by summertime traffic snaking through the town center. Still, it makes a good stop for stretching one's legs and grabbing a bite to eat en route to other coastal destinations.

The **Boothbays,** on Route 27 about 11 miles south of Route 1, are a string of small, scenic villages—East Boothbay, **Boothbay Harbor,** and Boothbay—on a peninsula.

ESSENTIALS

GETTING THERE   Wiscasset is right on U.S. Route 1, between Bath and Damariscotta. Boothbay Harbor is off Route 1, southeast down a peninsula on Route 27; coming from the south, turn right shortly after crossing the bridge in Wiscasset.

VISITOR INFORMATION   As befits a place where tourism is a major industry, the Boothbay region has *three* visitor information centers in and around town. On U.S. Route 1, at the Route 27 turnoff, there's an info center open seasonally, a good place to stock up on initial brochures. A mile before you reach the villages is the also-seasonal **Boothbay Information Center** (open June–Oct). If you zoom past that one or it's closed, don't fret: The year-round **Boothbay Harbor Region Chamber of Commerce,** P.O. Box 356, Boothbay Harbor, ME 04538 (✆ **800/266-8422** or 207/633-2353; www.boothbayharbor.com), is at the intersection of routes 27 and 96.

EXPLORING WISCASSET

Aside from enjoying the town's handsome architecture and general quaintness, there are a few quirky, low-key attractions good for a break while traveling along the coast. You'll also find a handful of worthwhile antiques shops and eateries.

Castle Tucker ⟡   This fascinating museum at the edge of town overlooking the river was first built in 1807 in the style of a Scottish mansion, then was radically added onto and altered in a more ostentatious style in 1858 (that's when the dramatic piazza was added). The home remains more or less in the same state it was in when reconfigured by cotton trader Capt. Richard Tucker. Tours of the lower floor are offered by the Society of New England Antiquities, which was given the house by its former owner, Richard's daughter Jane (ask about her story) in 1997. The detailing is exceptional and offers insight into the life of an affluent sea captain in the late 19th century. Be sure to note the extraordinary elliptical staircase and the painted plaster trim (which is not oak, though it looks like it).

Lee St. (at High St.). ℭ **207/882-7169.** Admission $5. June to mid-Oct, tours depart hourly Wed–Sun, 11am–4pm; closed the rest of the year.

Musical Wonder House ✦ *(Finds)* Danilo Konvalinka has been collecting music boxes for decades, and nothing seems to delight him more than playing them for awestruck visitors; this offbeat museum, filling a 32-room sea captain's manse with some 5,000 of them (yes, *thousand*), is the happy result. The collection includes massive, ancient music boxes as resounding as orchestras (such as an 1870 Girard music box from Austria), as well as many smaller contraptions emitting tinnier, more tinkly sounds. The music boxes are displayed and played in four rooms of the 1852 home; admission is charged per room, and a tour can get quite pricey. *Tip:* If you're undecided about whether it's worth it, try this: Visit the free gift shop and sample some of the coin-operated 19th-century music boxes in the adjoining hallway first. Intrigued? Sign up for the next tour—there are three tiers of pricing.

18 High St. ℭ **207/882-7163.** www.musicalwonderhouse.com. 2-room tour $10, 3-room tour and quick upstairs walk-through $20, full tour $45; discounts for seniors. Late May–Oct daily 10am–5pm. Closed Nov to mid-May.

EXPLORING THE BOOTHBAY REGION

Though the attractions listed below are fine, the best way to see the Boothbays is from the deck of a boat. Nearly two dozen tour boats berth at the harbor or nearby. **Balmy Days Cruises** (ℭ **800/298-2284** or 207/633-2284; www.balmydayscruises.com), for instance, runs a half-dozen short trips daily ($12 for adults, $6 for children) around the harbor in summertime. If you'd rather be sailing, ask about the 90-minute cruises aboard the sloop *Friendship* ($20 per person; 5 daily in summer). Schedules are reduced in spring and fall; call ahead for reservations.

Coastal Maine Botanical Gardens ✦ This expansive complex of waterside gardens is a work in progress, but it's well worth exploring. It's a natural habitat being gently coaxed into a more manicured state, with pathways through the mossy forest featuring gardens with different themes and flowers, plus an alley of more than 1,000 birch trees. Throughout, the walks are quiet and lush; one of the best trails runs along much of the tidal shoreline that's part of the property.

Barters Island Rd., Boothbay (near Hodgdon Island). ℭ **207/633-4333.** www.mainegardens.org. Admission $10 adults, $8 seniors, $5 children ages 5–17, $25 family. Mon–Fri 9am–5pm; Sat–Sun 9am–6pm. From Rte. 27 in Boothbay Center, bear right at monument, then make the first right onto Barters Island Rd.; drive 1 mile to stone gate on the left.

Maine State Aquarium *(Kids)* Operated by the state's Department of Marine Resources, this compact aquarium offers a context for the marine life in the Atlantic. Kids can view rare albino and blue lobsters, or get their hands wet in a 20-foot touch tank—a sort of petting zoo of the slippery and slimy. The aquarium is located on a point across the water from Boothbay Harbor, and parking is tight; visitors are urged to take the free shuttle bus from downtown that runs daily until 5pm.

McKown Point Rd., West Boothbay Harbor. ℭ **207/633-9542.** Admission $5 adults, $3 children 5–18 and seniors. Late May–Aug daily 10am–5pm; Sept Wed–Sun 10am–5pm; closed Oct–Memorial Day.

WHERE TO STAY

One of the coast's best campgrounds, the **Chewonki Campground** ⚐ (✆ **800/465-7747** or 207/882-7426; www.chewonkicampground.com), is located between Bath and Wiscasset. Campsites cost from $28 to $49 per night, which is at the high end of the camping price scale for Maine—but worth it. Drive 7 miles east of Bath on U.S. Route 1; turn right on Route 144, then take the next right past the airport and follow signs to the campground.

Five Gables Inn ⚐   East Boothbay was once home to a dozen summer hotels; now there's just one left. The handsome Five Gables was painstakingly restored in the late 1980s, and sits proudly amid a small colony of summer homes on a quiet road above a peaceful cove. It's nicely isolated from the confusion and hubbub of Boothbay Harbor. Nearly all of the pleasantly appointed rooms look out onto the water, and five have fireplaces burning manufactured logs; some also sport four-poster beds. Don't come expecting televisions or phones—it's a quiet place lacking both. Room no. 8 is a corner unit with brilliant morning light and good coastal views; no. 14 is the biggest and most frequently requested room, with more views and a fireplace with a marble mantle. Some first-floor rooms open onto a common deck, which means a little privacy. The inn's included breakfast buffet is very good.

Murray Hill Rd. (P.O. Box 335), East Boothbay, ME 04544. ✆ **800/451-5048** or 207/633-4551. www.fivegablesinn.com. 16 units. $130–$225 double. Rates include breakfast. MC, V. Closed mid-Oct to mid-May. Drive through East Boothbay on Rte. 96; turn right at blinking light onto Murray Hill Rd. Children 12 and older are welcome. *In room:* Fireplace (some units), no phone.

The Lawnmere Inn   The Lawnmere, a short hop from Boothbay on the northern shore of Southport Island, offers easy access to town and a restful environment. It does indeed sit on a nice green lawn. The main inn was built as a guesthouse in the late 19th century, and has since been updated (with a slight loss of charm). Nearly two-thirds of the guest rooms, however, are housed in two motel-like annexes known as the "wings"; these rooms have private balconies with views of the quiet waterway separating Southport Island from the mainland. Good regional and global cuisine is served in a comfortable, homey **dining room** ⚐ overlooking the water; it's some of the most reliable food in a town that has seen more than its share of restaurant turnover. Nonguests can also dine here; reservations are recommended.

Rte. 27 (P.O. Box 29), Southport, ME 04576. ✆ **800/633-7645** or 207/633-2544. www.lawnmereinn.com. 28 units. June to mid-Oct $89–$169 double; $169–$189 suite. 2-night minimum on holiday weekends. Packages available. MC, V. Closed mid-Oct to May. Pets accepted on limited basis; $10 per pet. Drive south through Boothbay Harbor on Rte. 27; cross bridge onto Southport Island. Inn is just past bridge, on the right. **Amenities:** Dining room; pub; free bikes. *In room:* A/C (some units).

Topside   This old gray house, on the hilltop looming above dated motel buildings, looks a bit spooky at first glance. Fear not; Topside has spectacular ocean views at a reasonable price. The inn—a former boardinghouse for shipyard workers—has simple, clean, comfortable rooms mostly done in whites and pastels, furnished with a mixture of antiques and contemporary furniture. At the edge of the lawn there are two outbuildings stocked with basic motel-style units; these are on the smallish side, with dated paneling and furniture, though two end units (nos. 9 and 14) might have the best views on the entire property. Most units have some glimpse of the water, in fact, and many have decks or patios. At press time, Topside was updating about one-third of its rooms and will unveil new designs for them in the spring of 2008.

60 McKown St., Boothbay Harbor, ME 04538. ℂ **888/633-5404** or 207/633-5404. Fax 207/633-2206. www.topside inn.com. 21 units. $120–$185 double. Rates include full breakfast. 2-night minimum Sat–Sun, 3-night minimum holiday weekends. Children 6 and older welcome. DISC, MC, V. Closed Nov–Apr. *In room:* TV, fridge (some units).

WHERE TO DINE
In Wiscasset

Red's Eats ⭐ *(Finds* LOBSTER/TAKEOUT   Red's is a tiny red shack next to Route 1 smack in downtown Wiscasset—right where the traffic maddeningly backs up at the bridge. It's received more than its fair share of national ink and TV attention for its famous lobster rolls. And they *are* good, consisting of big, moist, meaty chunks of chilled lobster in a toasted hot-dog roll with a little mayo on the side. (No skimpy pieces or celery here!) Be aware that they're pricey—you can find less expensive, less filling versions anywhere else. But these are the best-tasting in Maine. As a result, expect to stand in line for a while. The few tables behind the stand fill up quickly in summer; you can also walk downhill to the public riverfront dock a minute away. Besides the lobster rolls, very cheap fare (hot dogs, sandwiches) dominates the rest of the menu. You can also get very good ice cream cones here.

U.S. 1 at Water St. (just before bridge). ℂ **207/882-6128.** Sandwiches $2–$5; lobster rolls typically $13–$14. No credit cards. Mon–Thurs 11am–11pm; Fri–Sat 11am–2am; Sun noon–6pm. Closed Oct–Apr.

Sarah's Cafe ⭐ *(Value* SANDWICHES/TRADITIONAL   Sarah's is a friendly Wiscasset family favorite that opened in 1987, then moved down the block to a place with a view of Sheepscot River a decade later. Expect personable service and filling, well-prepared food: lobster, pizzas, a changing menu of soups, stews, and more. It's usually crowded for lunch and early dinner, with items such as pita pockets, croissant sandwiches, and a cheesy local favorite called a whaleboat; the lobster rolls are uniformly excellent, and so are the dessert pies. Just want some takeout? They'll do a "bucket" of ravioli to go. This is a great choice for an informal lunch break when you're motoring up Route 1 and don't feel like standing in the long lines at Red's. The adjacent Twin Schooner Pub, also owned by Sarah's, is good for a beer.

Water St. and U.S. Rte. 1 (across street from Red's). ℂ **207/882-7504.** Sandwiches and meals mostly $5–$10; pizzas $5–$18. AE, DISC, MC, V. Daily 11am–8pm (until 9pm Fri–Sat).

In the Boothbays

More creative dining can be found in the dining rooms of both the Spruce Point Inn and The Lawnmere Inn (see "Where to Stay," above).

Boothbay Lobster Wharf SEAFOOD   Across the harbor from downtown Boothbay, this place offers no-frills lobster and seafood; it's the best pick from a cluster of lobster-in-the-rough places lining the waterfront nearby. Lobsters are priced to market, and there are the usual fried-food baskets and sandwiches for those who don't dig crustaceans. This is a fine place for a classic Maine outdoor meal on a sunny day, but it's probably uninteresting in rain or fog. There's now a new fish market here, open year-round, where you can pick up cooked or live lobsters and the day's fresh catch even after the restaurant closes down for the season.

97 Atlantic Ave., Boothbay Harbor. ℂ **207/633-4900.** Reservations not accepted. Fried and grilled foods $2–$10; dinners $7–$15. DISC, MC, V. Mid-May to mid-Oct daily 11:30am–9pm. By foot, cross footbridge and turn right; follow road for ⅓ mile to co-op.

Lobsterman's Wharf SEAFOOD   On the water in East Boothbay, the Lobsterman's Wharf has the comfortable, pubby feel of a popular neighborhood bar, complete with pool table. That makes it popular with locals, but the kitchen also serves better-than-standard meals and knows how to make out-of-towners feel at home. Specials have included a mixed-seafood grill, a barbecue shrimp-and-ribs platter, grilled swordfish with béarnaise sauce, seafood fettuccine, tuna sashimi, and lobsters served at least four different ways. Blueberry pie and chocolate cake make good finishers. At lunch, there are burgers, baked haddock, lobster rolls, and steamed lobsters. Sensing a theme?

224 Ocean Pt. Rd. (Rte. 96), East Boothbay. (C) **866/733-2057.** Reservations only accepted for parties of 6 or more. Main courses $5–$14 at lunch; $14–$25 (mostly $14–$16) at dinner. AE, MC, V. Apr–Oct daily 11:30am–10pm. Closed Nov–Mar.

PEMAQUID PENINSULA 🏵🏵

Pemaquid Peninsula is an irregular, rocky wedge driven deep into the Gulf of Maine. Far less commercial than Boothbay Peninsula across the Damariscotta River, it's much more suited to relaxed exploration and nature-appreciation than its cousin. Rugged and rocky Pemaquid Point, at the extreme southern tip of the peninsula, is one of the most dramatic destinations in Maine when the ocean surf pounds the shore.

ESSENTIALS

GETTING THERE The Pemaquid Peninsula is accessible from the south and west by taking U.S. Route 1 to Damariscotta, then turning south down Route 129/130. Coming from the north or northeast, take U.S. 1 through Waldoboro, then turn south down Route 32 just south of town.

VISITOR INFORMATION The **Damariscotta Region Chamber of Commerce,** P.O. Box 13, Damariscotta, ME 04543 ((C) **207/563-8340**), is a good source of local information and maintains a seasonal information booth just off U.S. Route 1 during the summer months. To get there, follow Route 27 south, leaving Route 1 just east (across the bridge) after Wiscasset.

EXPLORING THE PEMAQUID PENINSULA

The Pemaquid Peninsula invites slow driving and frequent stops. South on Route 129 toward Walpole is Damariscotta, a sleepy head-of-the-harbor village. On the left is the austerely handsome Walpole Meeting House, dating from 1772. Usually not open to the public, services are held here during the summer and the public is welcome.

Then head down Route 129 to picturesque **Christmas Cove,** so named because Capt. John Smith (of Pocahontas fame) anchored here on Christmas Day in 1614. While wandering about, look for the rustic **Coveside Bar and Restaurant** ((C) **207/ 644-8282**), a popular marina with a pennant-bedecked lounge and basic dining room.

About 5 miles north of South Bristol, turn right on Pemaquid Road, which will take you to Route 130. Continue south on Route 130 to the village of New Harbor, then look for signs to **Colonial Pemaquid** ((C) **207/677-2423**). Open daily from Memorial Day to Labor Day, this state historic site has exhibits on the original 1625 settlement here; archaeological digs take place in the summertime. The $2 admission charge (free for children under age 12) includes a visit to stout **Fort William Henry,** a 1907 replica of a supposedly impregnable fortress. Nearby **Pemaquid Beach** is good for a (chilly) ocean dip or a picnic with the family.

Pemaquid Point 🏵🏵, owned by the town of **Bristol,** should be your final destination; it's the place to while away an afternoon ((C) **207/677-2494**). Bring a picnic and a book, and find a spot on the dark, fractured rocks to settle in. The ocean views are superb, and the only distractions are the tenacious seagulls that might take a profound interest in your lunch.

WHERE TO STAY

Bradley Inn ⚓ The Bradley Inn is within easy hiking or biking distance to the point, but there are plenty of reasons to lag behind at the inn, too. Wander the nicely landscaped grounds or settle in for a game of cards at the pub. The rooms are tastefully appointed with four-poster cherry beds (though no televisions). The third-floor rooms are the best (despite the hike up the stairs), thanks to distant glimpses of John's Bay, and a high-ceilinged second-floor suite occupying the entire floor is equipped with a full kitchen and dining room. The inn is popular for summer weekend weddings, so ask in advance if you're seeking solitude and quiet. New in 2007 was a seaside spa with a menu of wellness services.

Rte. 130, 3063 Bristol Rd., New Harbor, ME 04554. ☎ 800/942-5560 or 207/677-2105. Fax 207/677-3367. www. bradleyinn.com. 17 units. $160–$235 double, $225–$325 suite and cottage. Rates include full breakfast and afternoon tea. Packages available. AE, MC, V. Closed Nov–Mar. **Amenities:** Dining room; pub; spa; free bikes; room service. *In room:* Kitchen (1 unit), fireplace (some units).

Hotel Pemaquid *Value* This 1889 coastal classic isn't directly on the water—it's about a 1- or 2-minute walk from Pemaquid Point—but the main inn has the flavor of an old-time boardinghouse. Outbuildings are a bit more modern. Though most rooms now do have private bathroom, the inn is still old-fashioned at heart, with a no-credit cards policy, narrow hallways, and antiques, including a great collection of old radios and phonographs. The two- and three-bedroom suites—one with a sun porch and one with a kitchen—are good for families, and there are cottages and a carriage house available by the week.

Rte. 130, Pemaquid Point (Mailing address: 3098 Bristol Rd., New Harbor, ME 04554). ☎ 207/677-2312. www.hotel pemaquid.com. 23 units, 4 with shared bathrooms. $80–$100 double with private bathroom; $65–$75 double with shared bathroom; $125–$240 suite; cottages $775–$825 weekly. 2-night minimum stay Sat–Sun. No credit cards. Closed mid-Oct to mid-Apr. *In room:* TV (some units), no phone.

WHERE TO DINE

Shaw's Fish and Lobster Wharf ⚓ LOBSTER Shaw's attracts hordes of tourists, and it's no trick to figure out why: It's one of the best-situated lobster pounds, with postcard-perfect views of the working harbor. You can stake out a seat on either the open deck or the indoor dining room (go for the deck), or order up some appetizers from the raw bar. This is one of the few lobster joints in Maine with a full liquor license.

On the water, New Harbor. ☎ 207/677-2200. Lobster priced to market (typically $7 per lb.). MC, V. Mid-May to mid-Oct daily 11am–8pm (until 9pm July–Aug). Closed mid-Oct to mid-May.

MONHEGAN ISLAND ⚓⚓⚓

Monhegan Island is Maine's premier island destination. Visited by Europeans as early as 1497, the wild, remote island was settled by fishermen attracted to the sea's bounty in offshore waters. In the 1870s, artists discovered the island and stayed for a spell, including Rockwell Kent (the artist most closely associated with the island), George Bellows, Edward Hopper, and Robert Henri.

It's not hard to figure out why artists have been attracted to this place, with its almost-mystical sense of tranquillity. It's also a superb destination for hikers, since most of the island is undeveloped and laced with footpaths.

Just be aware that this is not Martha's Vineyard. There's one ATM on Monhegan, and few pay phones—heck, even electricity is scarce. That's what most visitors seem to like about it, and an overnight at one of the island's very simple inns is strongly recommended if you've got time; the island's true character doesn't emerge until the last day boat sails back to the mainland. If you just can't stomach the complete quiet and the lack of phones, TV's, and late-night takeout, day trips are also easy to arrange.

ESSENTIALS

GETTING THERE   Access to Monhegan Island is via boat from New Harbor, Boothbay Harbor, or Port Clyde. The picturesque trip from Port Clyde is the favorite route of longtime visitors; the boat passes the Marshall Point Lighthouse and a series of spruce-clad islands before reaching the open sea and plying its way toward Monhegan.

Two boats make the run to Monhegan from little Port Clyde. The *Laura B* is a doughty workboat (building supplies and boxes of food are loaded on first; passengers fill in the available niches on the deck and in the small cabin), and makes the run in about 70 minutes. A newer boat—the slightly faster, passenger-oriented *Elizabeth Ann*—makes the run in about 50 minutes and offers a large heated cabin and more seating. You'll need to leave your car behind, so pack light and wear sturdy shoes. The fare is $30 round-trip for adults, $16 for children ages 2 to 12, and $5 for pets. They do take credit cards, but reservations are advised. Contact **Monhegan Boat Line,** P.O. Box 238, Port Clyde, ME 04855 (*©* **207/372-8848;** www.monheganboat.com). Parking is available just off the Port Clyde dock for $4 per day.

VISITOR INFORMATION   Monhegan Island has no formal visitor center, but it's small and friendly enough that you can make inquiries of just about anyone you meet on the island pathways. Clerks at the ferry dock in Port Clyde may also be helpful. Be sure to pick up the inexpensive map of the island's hiking trails at the ticket office or various shops around the island. Also, a good website maintained by an island resident dispenses info to first-time visitors: **www.monheganwelcome.com**.

EXPLORING MONHEGAN

Walking is the chief activity on the island; it's genuinely surprising how much distance you can cover on these 700 acres (about 1½ miles long and ½ mile wide). The village clusters tightly around the harbor; the rest of the island is mostly wild land, laced with 17 miles of trails. Much of the island is ringed with high, open bluffs atop fissured cliffs; pack a picnic lunch and hike the **perimeter trail** 🍀🍀🍀, spending much of the day sitting, reading, and enjoying the surf rolling in against the cliffs.

The inland trails are appealing in a far different way. Deep, dark **Cathedral Woods** 🍀🍀 is mossy and fragrant; sunlight only dimly filters through the evergreens to the forest floor. **Birding** is also a popular spring and fall activity. The island is right on the Atlantic flyway, and a wide variety of birds stop here during annual migrations.

The sole attraction on the island is the good **Monhegan Museum** 🍀 (www. monheganmuseum.org), next to the 1824 lighthouse on a high point above the village. The museum, open for a few hours in the middle of each day from late June through September, has a quirky collection of historic artifacts and provides context for this rugged island's history. Nearby is a small and select art museum that opened in 1998 and features changing exhibits showcasing the works of illustrious island artists, including Rockwell Kent.

The spectacular **view** 🍀🍀 from the grassy slope in front of the lighthouse is the real prize, though. The vista sweeps across a marsh, past one of the island's most historic hotels, past Manana Island, and across the sea beyond. Get here early if you want a good seat for the sunset; folks often congregate here after dinner for the view.

Artists are still attracted to this island in great numbers, and many open their **studios** to visitors during posted hours in summer.

WHERE TO STAY & DINE

Things have changed, a little, since the day when you had zero options for sleeping or dining overnight on Monhegan, and had to retreat to the mainland. There are a handful of cottages, simple inns, and plain restaurants on the island. In a pinch, hit the **North End Market** (© 207/594-5546) for picnic supplies.

Monhegan House ⋆   The handsome Monhegan House has been accommodating guests since 1870, and it has the comfortable, worn patina of a venerable lodging house. The accommodations at this four-story walk-up are austere but comfortable, more so after recent renovations; there are no closets, and everyone uses clean dormitory-style bathrooms except guests who rent the new two-bedroom suite (with a queen bed and a double sofa). The downstairs lobby with fireplace is a welcome spot to sit and take the fog-induced chill out of your bones, since it can get cool on the island, even in August. A dining room serves dinner nightly during the short summer season, and Monhegan's first public Wi-Fi hotspot (never thought I'd be writing *that* sentence) and ATM are in the casual eatery, **The Novelty,** behind the inn.

Monhegan Island, ME 04852. © 207/594-7983. www.monheganhouse.com. 31 units (most with shared bathroom). $109–$140 double, $165–$185 suite. Rates include breakfast. MC, V. Closed Oct–late May. **Amenities:** 2 restaurants; Wi-Fi; ATM. *In room:* No phone. Located across road from island's church.

Trailing Yew   At the end of long summer afternoons, guests congregate near the flagpole in front of the main building of this simple, rustic hillside compound. They're waiting for the ringing of the bell that signals the start of the included-with-the-price dinner, just like at summer camp. Inside, guests sit around long tables, introduce themselves to their neighbors, and wait for the family-style repast. This is a friendly, informal place popular with hikers and birders. Guest rooms are simply furnished in a pleasantly dated, summer-home style. Only one of the four guest buildings has electricity, however—guests in rooms without electricity are provided kerosene lamps and instructions for their use. Also, all rooms are unheated. Rates here are charged per person: $90 for adult in 2007, less for children (pro-rated according to age).

Lobster Cove Rd., Monhegan Island, ME 04852. © 207/596-0440. 37 units (36 with shared bathrooms). $180 double (2 adults); children rates differ according to age. Rates include breakfast, dinner, taxes, and tips. No credit cards. Closed early Oct to mid-May. **Amenities:** Dining room. *In room:* No phone.

4 Penobscot Bay

Camden: 230 miles NE of Boston; 8 miles N of Rockland; 18 miles S of Belfast

You'll find some of Maine's most distinctive coastal scenery in the Penobscot Bay region, which is dotted with broad offshore islands and hills rising high above the ocean shore. Though the mouth of the bay is occupied by two large islands, its waters still churn when the winds and tides are right.

ROCKLAND & ENVIRONS

On the southwest edge of Penobscot Bay, Rockland has long been proud of its brick-and-blue-collar waterfront reputation. Built around the fishing industry, Rockland historically dabbled in tourism on the side, but with the decline of fisheries and the rise of Maine's tourist economy, the balance has shifted. Rockland is swiftly being colonized

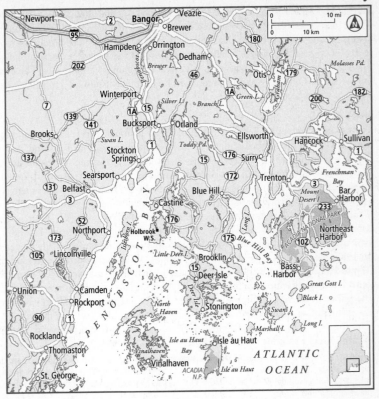

by creative restaurateurs, innkeepers, artisans, and other folks who are transforming from fish-processing center to arts-and-crafts center.

ESSENTIALS

GETTING THERE By car, U.S. Route 1 passes directly through the center of Rockland. **Concord Coach** (*C* **800/639-3317;** www.concordcoachlines.com) offers two to three daily buses from Portland and Boston.

Surprisingly, Rockland's tiny **airport** (Knox County Regional Airport, airport code RKD) is served by daily direct flights from Boston on **U.S. Airways Express** (*C* **800/428-4322;** www.usairways.com). There's a local taxi on call, and a single rental-car kiosk at the terminal. The airport itself is actually in Owls Head, off Route 73.

From spring through fall (and again in December), the **Maine Eastern Railroad** (*C* **866/637-2457;** www.maineeasternrailroad.com) runs excursion trains between Brunswick and Rockland. Round-trip fares in 2007 were $40 per adult, $35 for seniors, and $20 for children ages 5 to 15.

VISITOR INFORMATION The **Penobscot Bay Regional Chamber of Commerce,** P.O. Box 508, Rockland, ME 04841 (*C* **800/562-2529** or 207/596-0376; www.therealmaine.com), staffs an information desk at Harbor Park. It's open daily Memorial Day to Labor Day 9am to 5pm, and on Monday to Friday the rest of the year.

SPECIAL EVENTS   The **Maine Lobster Festival** (℡ 800/562-2529 or 207/596-0376) takes place at Harbor Park the first weekend in August (plus the preceding Thursday and Friday). Entertainers and vendors of all sorts of Maine products—especially, of course, the famous Maine crustaceans—fill the waterfront parking lot for thousands of festival-goers who enjoy the pleasantly buttery atmosphere. The event includes the Maine Sea Goddess Coronation Pageant. Admission is $7 to $10 per day; food, of course, costs extra.

MUSEUMS

Farnsworth Museum 𝒜𝒜𝒜   Rockland, for all its rough edges, has long and historic ties to the arts. Noted sculptor Louise Nevelson grew up in Rockland, and in 1935 philanthropist Lucy Farnsworth bequeathed a fortune to establish the Farnsworth Museum, which has since become one of the most respected little art museums in New England. Located right downtown, the Farnsworth has a superb collection of paintings and sculptures by renowned American artists with connections to Maine—not only Nevelson but three generations of Wyeths (N. C., Andrew, and Jamie), plus Rockwell Kent, Childe Hassam, and Maurice Prendergast. The exhibit halls are modern, spacious, and well designed, and shows are professionally prepared. In 1998, the museum expanded with the opening of the **Farnsworth Center for the Wyeth Family,** housed in a former Methodist church. The Farnsworth also owns two other buildings that are open to the public. One is the Farnsworth Homestead, behind the museum, offering a glimpse into the life of prosperous coastal Victorians. Even more interesting is the **Olson House** 𝒜, a 25-minute drive away, in the village of Cushing; it's perhaps Maine's most well-known home, immortalized in Andrew Wyeth's famous painting *Christina's World.*

356 Main St., Rockland. ℡ 207/596-6457. www.farnsworthmuseum.org. Museum $10 adults, $8 seniors and students 18 and older, free for children 17 and under (includes admission to Olson House and Farnsworth Victorian Homestead); Olson House only $4 per person. MC, V. Memorial Day–Columbus Day daily 10am–5pm; rest of the year Tues–Sun 10am–5pm.

Owls Head Transportation Museum 𝒜 *(Finds)*   You don't need to be a car or plane buff to enjoy this museum, though it helps. Founded in 1974 and located 3 miles south of Rockland on Route 73, the museum has an extraordinary collection of cars, motorcycles, bicycles, and planes, nicely displayed in a tidy, hangarlike building at the edge of the Knox County Airport. Look for the beautiful early Harley Davidson and a sleek Rolls-Royce Phantom dating from 1929.

Rte. 73, Owls Head. ℡ 207/594-4418. www.ohtm.org. $8 adults, $7 seniors, $5 children 5–17, $20 families. Apr–Oct daily 10am–5pm; Nov–Mar daily 10am–4pm.

WHERE TO STAY

Captain Lindsey House Inn 𝒜   The three-story, brick Captain Lindsey House is a couple of minutes' walk from the Farnsworth Museum. It was originally built as a hotel in 1835, then went through several subsequent incarnations, including one as headquarters of the Rockland Water Co. Guests enter through a doorway a few steps off Rockland's Main Street into an opulent first-floor common area done up in rich tones, dark-wood paneling, and a mix of antique and contemporary furniture. The upstairs rooms are decorated in simple country style with back-in-time beds, coffee tables, rocking chairs, and desks; even smaller rooms are well done, and rooms on the third floor have attractive exposed pine floors and Oriental carpets. All the beds are covered with feather duvets, though only two rooms have tubs. This isn't the most luxurious option in town, but it does have plenty of throwback-Maine character.

5 Lindsey St., Rockland, ME 04841. ✆ **800/523-2145** or 207/596-7950. Fax 207/596-2758. www.lindseyhouse.com. 9 units. $120–$211 double. Rates include breakfast. AE, DISC, MC, V. **Amenities:** Fax service. *In room:* A/C, TV, hair dryer.

East Wind Inn ☆ Here's how *you* become the "tenants" in Tenants Harbor: Head for the East Wind, acclaimed in such publications as *Architectural Digest*. It's a former sail loft converted to lodgings, perfectly situated beside the harbor with water views from all rooms and a long wraparound porch. This is your classic seaside hostelry of simple beds with white bedspreads, busy wallpaper, simple Colonial reproduction furniture, and tidy rooms. Some units have twin beds, though no. 1 is a good corner suite with a queen bed and a sofa. (There are more rooms across the way at a former sea captain's house.) The atmosphere is relaxed almost to the point of ennui, and the service is good. Traditional New England fare is served in an Edwardian-era dining room from spring through fall.

P.O. Box 149, Tenants Harbor, ME 04860. ✆ **800/241-8439** or 207/372-6366. Fax 207/372-6320. www.eastwind inn.com. 22 units (6 with shared bathroom). $66–$109 double with shared bathroom, $126–$149 double with private bathroom; $156–$201 suite; $176–$201 apartment. Rates include full breakfast. 2-night minimum stay Sat–Sun. AE, DISC, MC, V. Drive south on Rte. 131 from Thomaston to Tenants Harbor; turn left at post office. Pets allowed with advance notice ($15 per pet per night), but not in public rooms of inn. **Amenities:** Dining room.

LimeRock Inn ☆☆ This beautiful Queen Anne–style inn is on a quiet side street 2 blocks off Rockland's Main Street. Its latest owners have done a commendable job keeping this one of the area's very best B&B choices. Attention has been paid to detail throughout, from the kingly choices of country Victorian furniture to the Egyptian cotton bed sheets. All guest rooms are welcoming. Among the best are the Island Cottage Room, a bright and airy south-of-France-like chamber wonderfully converted from an old shed (it has a private deck and a Jacuzzi); the Turret Room, with a lovely canopy bed, cherry daybed, and French doors leading into a bathroom with a clawfooted tub and shower; and the elegant Grand Manan Room, with a big four-poster mahogany king bed, fireplace, and double Jacuzzi that puts one in mind of a Southern plantation home.

96 Limerock St. Rockland, ME 04841. ✆ **800/546-3762.** www.limerockinn.com. 8 units. $110–$229 double. Rates include full breakfast. DISC, MC, V. *In room:* Hair dryer, fireplace (some units), Jacuzzi (some units).

Samoset Resort ☆☆ The Samoset is a something of a Maine coast rarity—a modern, self-contained resort with contemporary styling, ocean views, and lots of golf. Both the hotel and town houses here are surrounded by the handsome golf course, with expansive views of it (and the ocean beyond) from almost every window on the property. The lobby is constructed of massive timbers recovered from an old grain silo in Portland, and guest rooms all have balconies or terraces plus newly installed flatscreen TVs and improved vanities, makeup mirrors, and fixtures. Bathrooms are extra-big, many with soaker tubs. Golfers like the place for its scenic 18-hole course with several waterside holes, and there's a golf school. Families can always find plenty of activities for kids here (including a summer camp during high season, and babysitting year-round). The health club, with three separate areas, is excellent.

220 Warrenton St., Rockport, ME 04856. ✆ **800/341-1650** or 207/594-2511. www.samoset.com. 178 units. Early July–late Aug $259–$289 double ($369 suite); mid-Apr to early July and late Aug–early Oct $179–$289 double ($259–$289 suite); winter starting at $129 double ($209 suite). Cottage $539–$769. MAP rates available. AE, DC, DISC, MC, V. **Amenities:** 3 restaurants; indoor pool; heated outdoor pool; golf course; golf school; 4 tennis courts;

health club; Jacuzzi; sauna; children's programs; concierge; courtesy car; business center; room service; shopping arcade; massage; babysitting; laundry service; dry cleaning. *In room:* A/C, TV, coffeemaker, hair dryer, iron/ironing board, safe.

WHERE TO DINE

Cafe Miranda 🎯🎯 *Finds* WORLD CUISINE

Hidden away on a side street, this tiny contemporary restaurant has a huge menu with big flavors and a welcoming, hip attitude. "We do not serve the food of cowards," owner-chef Kerry Altiero has said. The fare draws liberally from cuisines around the globe. (Mr. Altiero again: "It's comfort food for whatever planet you're from.") Given its wide-ranging culinary inclinations, it's surprising how good everything is. The menu changes so often that the following list is undoubtedly partly or completely out of date, but previous delicious bites have included: char-grilled pork and shrimp cakes with a ginger-lime-coconut sauce; pork ribs in smoked jalapeño sauce; Indian almond chicken; Ducks of Spanish Pleasure (a sort of duck curry, perhaps created in homage to Bob Dylan?); and small plates like gazpacho, roasted corn with pickled banana peppers, grilled rare beef with wasabi, and fried oysters with buttermilk sherry vinegar. Sunday brunch is a recent addition, featuring eggs, "really good" hot dogs, salads, and smoked haddock cakes. This place provides some of the best value (and wine and beer lists) in Maine.

15 Oak St., Rockland. ✆ 207/594-2034. www.cafemiranda.com. Reservations strongly recommended. Small plates and main courses $9–$22. DISC, MC, V. Mon–Sat 5:30–9:30pm; Sun 10:30am–2:30pm and 5:30–9:30pm.

Cod End Cookhouse 🎯 *Kids* LOBSTER POUND

Part of the allure of Cod End is its hidden and scenic location—it seems as though you've stumbled upon a secret spot. Situated between the Town Landing and the East Wind Inn in little Tenants Harbor, it's a classic lobster joint with fine views of said harbor. You walk through a fish market (where you can buy fish or lobster to go, along with various lobster-related souvenirs) and place your order at an outdoor shack. Lobsters are the main draw here, naturally, but there's plenty more to eat including chowders, stews, linguini with seafood, clam and haddock rolls, and a simple kids' menu of burgers, dogs, and sandwiches (including peanut butter and jelly) for the youngsters.

Commercial St. (next to the town dock), Tenants Harbor. ✆ 207/372-6782. www.codend.com. Main courses $5–$10 at lunch; $8–$15 at dinner. DISC, MC, V. Memorial Day–Sept daily 11am–8:30pm; closed Oct to mid-May.

Primo 🎯🎯🎯 MEDITERRANEAN/NEW AMERICAN

Primo opened in April 2000 and quickly developed a buzz as one of New England's best. The restaurant, owned by chef Melissa Kelly and pastry chef Price Kushner, occupies two nicely decorated floors of a century-old home a short drive south from downtown Rockland. Start with an appetizer such as mushroom pie with white truffle oil, steak salad with Vidalia onions, ale-battered soft-shell crab, planked quail, or a cream of (Maine) asparagus soup. Entrees might run to saffron tagliolini with steamed mussels, Maine lobster with peas, grilled leg of lamb with ricotta gnocchi and fava beans, rhubarb-glazed duck, or seared halibut over a corn-risotto cake paired with local fiddleheads. Finish with one of Kushner's inventive desserts: warmed Belgian chocolate cake, an espresso float, a rhubarb-strawberry tartlet with vanilla gelato and strawberry sauce, homemade cannoli, hot doughnuts tossed in cinnamon and sugar, or a *crostata* made from local apples. The wine list is outstanding. It's hard to get a last-minute table here during peak summer season, but, failing that, order at the bar.

2 S. Main St. (Rte. 173), Rockland. ✆ 207/596-0770. www.primorestaurant.com. Reservations highly recommended. Main courses $23–$38. AE, DC, DISC, MC, V. Summer daily 5:30–9pm; call for dates/hours in off-season.

CAMDEN 🎖🎖

A quintessential coastal Maine town at the foot of wooded Camden Hills, the affluent village of Camden sits on a picturesque harbor that no Hollywood movie set could improve on. It has been attracting the gentry of the Eastern Seaboard for more than a century. The mansions of the moneyed set still dominate the town's shady side streets (many have been converted into bed-and-breakfasts), and Camden is possessed of a grace and sophistication that eludes many other coastal towns.

The best way to enjoy Camden is to park your car—this may require driving a block or two off U.S. Route 1, which unfortunately runs right up through the center of town. The village is of a perfect scale to explore on foot, with plenty of boutiques and galleries. Don't miss the hidden town park (look behind the library), either: It was designed by none other than the firm of Frederick Law Olmsted, the famed landscape architect who designed New York City's Central Park.

ESSENTIALS

GETTING THERE   By car, Camden is right on U.S. Route 1. Coming from the south, you can shave a few minutes off the trip here by turning left onto state Route 90 about 6 miles past Waldoboro, bypassing the downtown streets of the city of Rockland. **Concord Coach** (© **800/639-3317;** www.concordcoachlines.com) runs bus service (2 to 3 trips daily) to Camden from Boston and Portland.

VISITOR INFORMATION   The **Camden-Rockport-Lincolnville Chamber of Commerce,** P.O. Box 919, Camden, ME 04843 (© **800/223-5459** or 207/236-4404; www.camdenme.org), dispenses helpful information from its center at the Public Landing in Camden, where there's also free parking (although spaces are scarce in summer). The chamber is open year-round Monday to Saturday. In summer, it's also open Sundays from about 10am to 4pm.

EXPLORING CAMDEN

Camden Hills State Park 🎖🎖 (© **207/236-3109**) is about a mile north of the village center on Route 1. This 6,500-acre park has an oceanside picnic area, camping at 107 sites, a winding toll road up 800-foot Mount Battie with spectacular views from the summit, and a variety of well-marked hiking trails. The day-use fee is $3 for adults and $1 for children ages 5 to 11. It's open from mid-May to mid-October.

If hikes and mild heights don't bother you, I definitely recommend an ascent to the ledges of **Mount Megunticook** 🎖🎖, preferably early in the morning before the crowds have amassed (and while mists still linger in the valleys). Leave from near the state park's campground—the trail head is clearly marked—and follow the well-maintained path to open ledges. The hike takes only 30 to 45 minutes; spectacular views of the harbor await, plus glimpses of smaller hills and valleys. Depending on your stamina level, you can keep walking on the park's trail network to Mount Battie, or into lesser-traveled woodlands on the east side of the Camden Hills.

The Camden area is also great for exploring by bike. A nice loop several miles long takes you from Camden into the cute little village of **Rockport** 🎖, which has an equally scenic harbor and fewer tourists. There's a boat landing, small park, cafe, one of the state's best art galleries, and a very highly regarded school of photography (see "Rocking It in Rockport" box).

The Camden-Rockport Historical Society has prepared a 9-mile bike (or car) tour with brief descriptions of some of the historic properties along the way. The brochure describing the tour is free; check for it at the chamber of commerce at the town's Public

Moments Rocking It in Rockport

Rockport ⍟ is absolutely worth a few hours' time during any trip to Camden. Try this route, either by bike or by car: Take Bayview Street from the center of Camden out along the bay, passing by opulent seaside estates. The road soon narrows and becomes quiet and pastoral, overarched by leafy trees. At the stop sign just past the cemetery, turn left and continue into Rockport. (Along the way, you might pass happily grazing cows.) In Rockport, snoop around the historic harbor and stop by the **Center for Maine Contemporary Art** ⍟⍟, 162 Russell Ave. (© 207/236-2875; www.artsmaine. org), a stately gallery with rotating exhibits of local painters, sculptors, and craftspeople. Admission is $5 per adult (free for children); the gallery is open Tuesday to Saturday from 10am until 5pm and Sunday from 1 to 5pm.

Also visit the **Prism Glass Studio & Gallery** (© 207/230-0061; www.prism-glassgallery.com). This combination glass-blowing gallery and cafe is at 297 Commercial St. in the heart of the village; it's open Wednesday through Sunday. Patti Kissinger and Lisa Sojka own the 6,500-square-foot facility, which showcases glass blown by top blowers; maintains a studio for stained glass (Tiffany lamp reproductions and the like); and serves up impressive high cuisine in the Gallery Café.

Landing (see above), or ask for one at the Whitehall Inn (see below). The brochure also includes a 2-mile walking tour of downtown Camden. Bike rentals, repairs, maps, and local riding advice are available in town at **Ragged Mountain Sports** (© 207/236-6664), at 46 Elm St.

WHERE TO STAY

It's best to reserve well in advance. You might also try **Camden Accommodations and Reservations** (© 800/344-4830 or 207/236-6090; www.camdenac.com), which provides assistance with everything from booking rooms at local B&Bs to finding cottages for seasonal rentals.

Also, there's camping at seasonally open **Camden Hills State Park** (see "Exploring Camden," above). Sites cost $20 to $30 per night for non-Maine residents in summer, depending on whether you snag one of the new water-and-electrical hookup sites or not. There's a $7 to $10 discount from mid-September until the park closes.

Blue Harbor House ⍟   On busy Route 1 just south of town, this pale-blue 1810 farmhouse has been an inn since 1978, decorated throughout with a feminine country look. Rooms and suites vary in size; some are smallish, but all include such touches as four-poster beds, claw-footed tubs, wicker furniture, Jacuzzis, triptych mirrors, writing desks, or slipper chairs. The best rooms are the carriage-house suites, with their private entrances and extra amenities. The dining room serves nice candlelit prix-fixe dinners and lobster feeds to guests.

67 Elm St., Camden, ME 04843. © **800/248-3196** or 207/236-3196. Fax 207/236-6523. www.blueharborhouse.com. 11 units. $95–$155 double; $145–$185 suite. Rates include breakfast. AE, DISC, MC, V. Pets allowed in some units with prior permission. Closed mid-Oct to mid-May. **Amenities:** Dining room. *In room:* A/C, TV, hair dryer, fireplace (some units), Jacuzzi (some units).

Camden

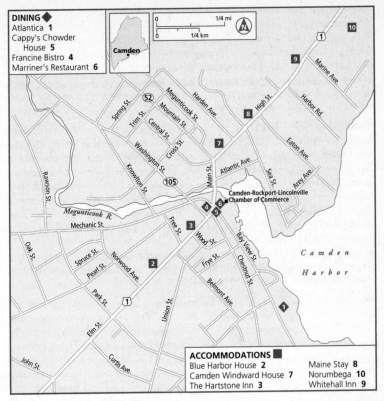

Camden

Camden Windward House ✦✦   One of the big complaints from travelers staying on Camden's High Street was the noise from passing traffic. The Windward's owners solved that problem by installing double windows on their historic 1854 home; as a result, when you close the door behind you, the village feels miles away. Welcoming common rooms are decorated with a light Victorian hand and cranberry glass; in the library, you'll find a refrigerator, icemaker, and afternoon libations for fixing. Rooms vary in size, but all have flatscreen televisions, phones, and air-conditioning; some suites have gas fireplaces, Jacuzzis, claw-footed tubs, or private decks. Even the simpler, elegant Brass Room has a private deck. Guests choose from lots of hot breakfast entrees, served in a pleasant dining room of maple tables. This place is better and friendlier than you might expect.

6 High St., Camden, ME 04843. ⓒ **877/492-9656** or 207/236-9656. www.windwardhouse.com. 8 units. Peak season $190–$280 double; off-season $110–$240 double. Rates include full breakfast and afternoon tea. AE, MC, V. No children under 12. **Amenities:** Library; bar. *In room:* A/C, TV, dataport, hair dryer, Jacuzzi (some units).

The Hartstone Inn ✦✦ *(Finds)*   Chef/innkeeper Michael Salmon draws raves for his cooking at this downtown Camden inn, but the accommodations in the early-19th-century Victorian home are fine, too. He and his wife previously operated a resort in Aruba; you'll be glad they traded down in weather. Now expanded to 21 units, the Hartstone's rooms are studded with antiques and some of the most beautiful decor on the entire Midcoast; all suites include Jacuzzis. The full breakfasts are a major reason to come, and five-course **dinners** 𝒜𝒜 marry local Maine seafood with Caribbean chilies, spices, and cooking techniques—lobster with vanilla beurre blanc, anyone? This is definitely a unique dining experience on a coastline full of B&Bs, and one worth traveling to find. There's a cooking school on the premises, as well.

41 Elm St., Camden, ME 04843. ℂ 800/788-4823 or 207/236-4259. www.hartstoneinn.com. 21 units, 1 with bathroom across hall. $105–$190 double; $150–$265 suite. Closed late Nov–late Apr. MC, V. **Amenities:** Restaurant. *In room:* A/C, TV, dataport, fireplace (some units), Jacuzzi (some units).

Maine Stay 𝒜𝒜   The Maine Stay is one of Camden's premier bed-and-breakfasts. In a home dating from 1802 (expanded in Greek Revival style in 1840), it's a classic slate-roofed New England home set in a shady yard within walking distance of both downtown and Camden Hills State Park. The guest rooms, spaced out over three floors, have ceiling fans (and a few have televisions); each is distinctively furnished in antiques, and the lovely wooden floors are often exposed. Top-floor rooms have foreshortened ceilings with interesting angles. One favorite unit is the downstairs Carriage House Room, away from the buzz of Route 1, with French doors leading to its own stone patio and a Vermont Castings stove to keep warm.

22 High St., Camden, ME 04843. ℂ 207/236-9636. Fax 207/236-0621. www.mainestay.com. 8 units. $110–$250 double and suite. Rates include full breakfast. Packages available. AE, MC, V. Children over 10 welcome. *In room:* TV (some units), kitchenette (1 unit), fireplace (some units).

Norumbega 𝒜𝒜𝒜 *(Finds)*   You'll have no problem finding Norumbega; head north out of town and look for the castle on the right. This 1886 stone mansion, built by telegraph system inventor Joseph Stearns, is wonderfully eccentric, full of wondrous curves, angles, and materials; it's on the National Historic Registry. There's extravagant carved-oak woodwork in the lobby, a stunning oak-and-mahogany inlaid floor, and a kingly downstairs billiards room. Guest rooms have been meticulously restored and furnished with antiques; some have fireplaces, three ground-level units sport private decks, and most now have televisions. Two suites rank among the finest in northern New England: the amazingly bright and airy Library Suite, in the original two-story library (it has an interior balcony) and the sprawling Penthouse with its superlative bay views, king-sized bed, and huge oval tub. Don't miss Norumbega's "Murder Mystery" weekends; solve the mystery first, and you win a free stay!

63 High St., Camden, ME 04843. ℂ 877/363-4646 or 207/236-4646. www.norumbegainn.com. 12 units. July to mid-Oct $285–$475 double and suite; mid-May to June and late Oct $125–$275 double and suite; Nov to mid-May $225–$375 double and suite. All rates include full breakfast and evening snacks and refreshments. 2-night minimum in summer, Sat–Sun, and holidays. AE, DISC, MC, V. Children age 7 and older welcome. **Amenities:** Billiards room. *In room:* TV (most units), fireplace (some units).

Whitehall Inn 𝒜   The Whitehall is a venerable Camden establishment, thanks (but only partly) to local poetess Edna St. Vincent Millay, who was "discovered" here by a guest who encouraged Edna to study writing (the guest went on to fund Edna's college education); the room where the discovery happened still has the 1904 Steinway Edna played. Set at the edge of town on busy Route 1, the three-story inn has a striking architectural integrity of columns, gables, a long roofline, and atmospherically winding staircases. The antique furnishings—including a handsome Seth Thomas clock, Oriental carpets, and cane-seated rockers on the front porch—are cared for impeccably. Guest rooms are simple yet appealing; many lack phones and TVs, and a few double up on shared bathrooms, but even these "economy" rooms have sturdy Maine charm. The only drawback? That traffic—try to get a room in back.

52 High St., Camden, ME 04843. ✆ **800/789-6565** or 207/236-3391. www.whitehall-inn.com. 50 units, 8 with shared bathroom. July to mid-Oct $149–$199 double; mid-May to June $99–$159 double. Rates include full breakfast and afternoon tea. AE, MC, V. Closed mid-Oct to mid-May. **Amenities:** 2 restaurants; tennis court; tour desk; conference rooms; babysitting. *In room:* TV (some units), no phone (some units).

WHERE TO DINE

Atlantica 🕸🕸 SEAFOOD/ECLECTIC   Atlantica gets high marks for its seafood menu, always well-prepared under the management of executive chef Ken Paquin, a graduate of the Culinary Institute of America (and former top dog at a number of other establishments, including the Equinox in Vermont). On the waterfront with a small indoor seating area and an equally small deck, Paquin cooks subtly creative fare such as seared day boat scallops over lemon risotto with a steamed lobster; roasted breast of duck with a sweet-corn béarnaise sauce; butter-poached lobster in a mushroom fondue; porcini-dusted bass; chipotle-rubbed pork; creamy chowders; Pemaquid oysters; and the catch of the day, perhaps plated with a pistachio "crumble," a red-beet puree, or a polenta cake.

1 Bayview Landing. ✆ **888/507-8514** or 207/236-6011. www.atlanticarestaurant.com. Reservations recommended. Main courses $26–$36. AE, MC, V. Wed–Mon 5:30–9pm. Closed Nov–Mar.

Cappy's Chowder House *(Kids* SEAFOOD/AMERICAN   "People always remember their meals here," say local fans of Cappy's, an institution smack in the middle of Camden for close to 3 decades. Well, maybe. Travelers—especially families—do drift in here to drink up the atmosphere and fill up on the famous thick clam chowder (it's even been noted in *Gourmet* magazine). There's also seafood stew, rotating special chowders, burgers, club sandwiches, fried fish, lobster and lobster rolls in summer, and . . . a wine list? Why, yes. It's all well worth a quick stop if you're looking for a reasonably priced and filling meal for the family late at night. By the way, Cappy is an old salt who worked the local docks for years; he's not with us any longer—but his name lives on. There's also a little bakery around the side.

1 Main St. ✆ **207/236-2254.** www.cappyschowder.com. Main courses $8–$20. MC, V. Daily 11:30am–9pm.

Francine Bistro 🕸 FRENCH BISTRO   This place feels more like a French brasserie in Manhattan's Meatpacking District than a coastal seafood joint—and that's a good thing. A meal from chef Brian Hill might begin with fish, onion, or lentil soup; a ceviche of halibut, serrano chilies, and red onions; mussels in Bordeaux and shallots; or skewers of grilled lamb served with white pesto, orange, and endive. What a refreshing wakeup call in a section of coast dominated by fried/baked cod/haddock and lobsters. The night's entrees might run to roast chicken with a chèvre gratin or a cauliflower-cheese hash; duck a l'orange; a crispy skate wing with Jerusalem artichokes; a roasted sea bass in caramelized garlic sauce; seared halibut with shrimp; a haddock stuffed with scallops; or reliable steak frites. Eat at simple tables from church-pew-like seating.

55 Chestnut St., Camden. ✆ **207/230-0083.** www.francinebistro.com. Reservations recommended. Main courses $17–$25. MC, V. Tues–Sat 5:30–10pm.

Marriner's Restaurant DINER   "The last local luncheonette" is how Marriner's sums itself up, and has used a sign with the legend DOWN HOME, DOWN EAST, NO FERNS, NO QUICHE to also get its message across: Namely, that this is a small and no-frills affair, totally Maine, so don't expect snootiness or pretense. Done up in a not-too-subtle nautical theme of pine booths and vinyl seats (some of which are sometimes taped together with duct tape), These folks have been dishing up filling breakfasts and lunches for the locals since 1942; it's a great place for early risers to get a quick start on the day and check out the local characters. Lunches are basic and good, too, especially the chowders and lobster and crab rolls—and don't miss the homemade pies.

35 Main St., Camden. ℰ 207/236-4949. Most breakfast items $4–$6; lunch items $4–$12 (most under $7). MC, V. Daily 6am–2pm.

5 The Blue Hill Peninsula 🟊🟊

Blue Hill is 136 miles NE of Portland: 23 miles N of Stonington: and 14 miles SW of Ellsworth

Forming the eastern boundary of Penobscot Bay—though you must drive north and then *south* to get there, diverging from Route 1 by a good 15 miles or more—the Blue Hill Peninsula is a little back-roads paradise. If you like to get lost on country lanes that end at the ocean, or loop back on themselves with nothing but green trees and salt air for company, this is the place for you. The roads are hilly, winding, and narrow, passing through forests and along old saltwater farms, touching on the edges of inlets here and there.

They take extra time to reach, but villages like **Castine** and **Blue Hill** are well worth building into any Maine-coast itinerary. They'll hold you captive with their simple water views, boatyards, tiny artists' communities, local fresh eats, and grassroots radio.

CASTINE & ENVIRONS 🟊🟊

Quiet little Castine, off the beaten track, might be one of the most gracious villages in Maine. It's not so much the handsome, meticulously maintained mid-19th-century homes that fill the side streets. Nor is it the location on a quiet peninsula, 16 miles south of tourist-clotted Route 1. No, what lends Castine most of its charm are the splendid, towering elm trees that still overarch many of the village's streets. Before Dutch elm disease ravaged the nation's elms, much of America once looked like this. Through perseverance and a measure of good luck, Castine has managed to keep several hundred of its elms alive, and it's worth the drive here to see them.

You'll have to work (which means drive significant distances) to find nightlife and dining, but if you like your towns quiet, you'll love it here.

ESSENTIALS

GETTING THERE Castine is 16 miles south of U.S. Route 1. Turn south on Route 175 in Orland (east of Bucksport) and follow it to Route 166, which winds its way to Castine. Route 166A offers another, alternate route along Penobscot Bay.

VISITOR INFORMATION Castine lacks a formal information center, though the clerks at the **town office** (ℰ 207/326-4502) are often helpful with local information. (Don't abuse this privilege, though, since they have actual work to do running the town.) The town office is open Monday to Friday from 11am to 3pm. The **Blue Hill Peninsula Chamber of Commerce** (see later in this chapter) handles tourist inquiries in a more formal manner.

EXPLORING CASTINE

One of the town's more intriguing attractions is the **Wilson Museum** 🟊 (ℰ 207/ 326-9247; www.wilsonmuseum.org), on Perkins Street, an appealing and quirky anthropological museum constructed in 1921. This small museum contains the collections of John Howard Wilson, an archaeologist and collector of prehistoric artifacts from around the globe. His gleanings are neatly arranged in a staid, classical arrangement of the sort that proliferated in the late 19th and early 20th centuries. The museum is open from the end of May to the end of September, Tuesday to Sunday from 2 to 5pm; admission is free.

Next door is the affiliated **John Perkins House** (same phone number as the museum), Castine's oldest home. It was occupied by the British during the Revolution and the War of 1812, and a tour features demonstrations of old-fashioned cooking techniques. This house is only open in July and August, and only Wednesdays and Sundays (2–5pm). There is a fee for guided tours of the home. Two additional attractions in the Wilson-Perkins complex (it's almost like a little historical campus, really) include a **blacksmith shop** and the **Hearse House,** which are free to tour; both of these outbuildings have the same limited hours as the Perkins House.

Castine is also home to the **Maine Maritime Academy** (✆ **207/326-4311**), which trains sailors for the rigors of life at sea with the merchant marine. The campus is on the western edge of the village, and the 500-foot T.S. (for Training Ship) *State of Maine* ⚓, a hulking black-and-white vessel, is often docked here—all but overwhelming the village. (It's off cruising to places like Odessa, Germany, and Gibraltar when it's not here.) Free half-hour tours of the ship are offered in summer when the ship is in port.

WHERE TO STAY

Castine Harbor Lodge ⚓ *Kids*   Housed in a red-roofed 1893 mansion, this is a good place for families to hole up for a night or two. The only inn actually on the water in Castine, it's run with a good cheer that allows kids to feel at home amid the regal architecture. The main parlor is good for a game of pool, while the spacious rooms are eclectically furnished with a mix of antiques and modern furniture. Two of the guest rooms share an adjoining bathroom, but that's almost okay—the bathrooms at this hotel have some of best "loo" views in the state.

147 Perkins St. (P.O. Box 215), Castine, ME 04421. ✆ 207/326-4335. www.castinemaine.com. 16 units (2 with shared bathrooms), 1 cottage. $85–$245 double; cottage $1,250 weekly. Rates include continental breakfast. MC, V. Pets allowed ($10 per pet per night). **Amenities:** Dining room; bar; pool table.

Castine Inn ⚓   The Castine Inn is a Maine Coast rarity: a hotel that was originally built as a hotel, not a residence, in 1898. This handsome, cream–colored inn, designed in an eclectic Georgian Federal Revival–style, has a great wraparound porch and attractive gardens. The lobby takes its cue from the 1940s, with wingback chairs and loveseats and a fireplace in the parlor. Guest rooms on the two upper floors are attractively (sometimes unevenly) furnished in Early American style with graceful prints, pastel walls, pencil-poster beds, and sofas; three suites have recently been added, consolidating formerly smaller rooms and upping the amenities a bit. The elegant dining room (see "Where to Dine," below) serves some of the coast's best dinners.

Main St. (P.O. Box 41), Castine, ME 04421. ✆ 207/326-4365. Fax 207/326-4570. www.castineinn.com. 17 units. Peak season $90–$245 double; off-season rates lower. Rates include full breakfast. Closed early Oct–late Apr. 2-night minimum July–Aug. MC, V. Children 8 and older welcome. **Amenities:** Dining room; sauna.

Pentagöet Inn ⚓⚓   At the Pentagöet, "activities" consist of sitting on the wraparound front porch on cane-seated rockers watching the hum (though I hesitate to call it that) of Main Street. This quirky, yellow-and-green (ca. 1894) inn with the prominent turret is tasteful and sturdily built. The lobby features hardwood floors, oval braided rugs, and a woodstove; it's all comfortable without being prissy, professional without being chilly. Most units sport king-size beds with ornate headboards and lacy white coverlets—some have claw-footed bathtubs and/or fireplaces, and one even includes a balcony with flowers. Rooms on the upper two floors of the main house are furnished eclectically in a mix of antiques and collectibles, while five units in the adjacent Perkins Street building (an austere, Federal-era house) are furnished more simply and show off painted wooden floors. The amazingly character-filled **pub** ⍟ and delicious fare in the **dining room** ⍟ are both excellent.

26 Main St. (P.O. Box 4), Castine, ME 04421. ⍟ 800/845-1701 or 207/326-8616. www.pentagoet.com. 16 units (2 with private hallway bathrooms). Peak season $115–$245 double; off-season rates lower. Rates include full breakfast. MC, V. Closed Nov–Apr. Pets by reservation only. Suitable for older children only. **Amenities:** Dining room; pub; bikes. *In room:* Fireplace (some units).

WHERE TO DINE
Castine Inn ⍟⍟ NEW AMERICAN   Castine Inn chef/owner Tom Gutow served stints at such acclaimed places as Bouley and (now-shuttered) Verbena in the brutal restaurant climate of New York City, so he isn't timid about experimenting with local meats and produce here in mid-coastal Maine. The menu changes too regularly to be pinned down, but expect permutations riffing on some of the same notes as dinner entrees like lobster with vanilla butter, mango mayonnaise, and a tropical-fruit salsa or lamb loin with eggplant, green lentils, tomatoes, and a rosemary *jus*. There's also an attached wine bar.

Main St. ⍟ 207/326-4365. Reservations recommended. Main courses $26–$33. MC, V. Daily 6–9pm. Closed early Oct–late Apr.

Dennett's Wharf Restaurant & Oyster Bar PUB FARE   In a soaring waterfront sail loft with dollar bills tacked all over the high ceiling, Dennett's Wharf serves upscale bar food in a lively setting leavened by a good selection of microbrews. When the weather is decent, there's outside dining beneath a bright yellow awning with superb harbor views. Look for sandwiches, salads, and fried clams at lunch; dinner includes local lobsters, baby-back ribs, pad Thai (yes, really), and hanger steak. The newish oyster bar serves (obviously) oysters on the half-shell. But how did all those bills get on the ceiling? Ask your server; it will cost you exactly $1 to find out.

15 Sea St. (next to the town dock). ⍟ 207/326-9045. Reservations recommended in summer and for parties of 6 or more. Lunch items $5–$13; dinner items $9–$27. AE, DISC, MC, V. Daily 11am–midnight. Closed mid-Oct to Apr.

BLUE HILL ⍟
Blue Hill, population 2,400, is easy to find—just look for the dome of Blue Hill itself, which lords over the northern end of Blue Hill Bay. Set between the mountain and the bay is the quiet and historic town, clustered along the bay's shore and a little stream. There's never much going on here, which seems to be exactly what attracts repeat summer visitors; it might also explain why two excellent bookstores are located in this dot of a town. Many old-money families maintain lovely retreats along the water or in the hills around here, but the village center offers a couple of choices for lodging even if you don't have local connections. It's a good place for a quiet break.

ESSENTIALS
GETTING THERE   Blue Hill is southeast of Ellsworth, at the juncture of routes 15 and 172. From Bar Harbor, follow Route 3 through Ellsworth, cross the bridge, then follow Route 172 about 14 miles to Blue Hill. Coming from the south (Rockland or

Belfast) on Route 1/Route 3, turn south onto Route 15 about 5 miles east of Bucksport, and drive about 12 miles.

VISITOR INFORMATION   Blue Hill does not maintain a true staffed visitor information booth. Look for the "Blue Hill, Maine" brochure and map at state information centers, or write to the **Blue Hill Peninsula Chamber of Commerce** (© 207/374-3242; www.bluehillpeninsula.org), 28 Water St., Blue Hill, ME 04614. Locals are usually able to answer any questions you may have.

EXPLORING BLUE HILL

A good way to start your exploration is to ascend the open summit of **Blue Hill** ✦✦, from which you'll gain superb views of the bay and the bald mountaintops on nearby Mount Desert Island. To reach the trail head from the center of the village, drive north on Route 172 about 1½ miles, then turn west (left) on Mountain Road at the Blue Hill Fairgrounds. Drive another ¾ mile and look for the well-marked trail; park on the shoulder of the road. The fairly easy ascent is about a mile, and takes about 45 minutes. Bring a picnic lunch.

Even if you're not given to swooning over historic homes, you owe yourself a visit to the intriguing **Parson Fisher House** ✦ (© 207/374-2459; www.jonathanfisher house.org), on routes 176 and 15, a half-mile west of the village. Fisher, Blue Hill's first permanent minister, was a small-town-Maine version of a Renaissance man when he settled here in 1796. Educated at Harvard, Fisher not only delivered sermons in six different languages (including Aramaic), but was also a writer, painter, and inventor of boundless energy. On a tour of his home, which he built himself in 1814, you can see a clock with wooden works he fashioned, as well as books he wrote, published, and bound by hand (all by himself). The house is open from July to mid-September, Thursday through Saturday from 1 to 4pm. Admission is by donation; $5 per person is suggested.

WHERE TO STAY

Blue Hill Farm Country Inn   Comfortably situated on 48 acres about 2 miles north of the Blue Hill's village center, the Farm Country Inn (not to be confused with its neighbor; see below) has some of the most relaxing and comfortable common areas you'll find; the first floor of a big barn was converted into a spacious living room, with sitting areas arrayed so that you can opt either for the privacy or the company of others. Guest rooms are smallish and lightly furnished, though—none have anything larger than a double bed. The more modern rooms are upstairs in the barn loft and are nicely decorated in a country farmhouse style, though they're a bit motel-like. The seven older rooms in the farmhouse have more character, and share a single bathroom with a small tub and hand-held shower.

Rte. 15 (P.O. Box 437), Blue Hill, ME 04614. © 207/374-5126. www.bluehillfarminn.com. 14 units (7 with shared bathroom). $90–$110 double with private bathroom; $80–$90 double with shared bathroom. Rates include continental breakfast. AE, MC, V. *In room:* No phone.

Blue Hill Inn ✦✦   The Blue Hill Inn has been hosting travelers since 1840. On one of the village's main streets, and within walking distance of almost everything, this Federal-style lodging house displays a convincing Colonial American motif, its authenticity enhanced by creaky floors. Friendly innkeepers have pleasantly furnished all the rooms with antiques and down comforters; four units in the main house have wood-burning fireplaces, although these rooms are open only from mid-May through the end of October. A large contemporary suite in an adjacent, free-standing building has a cathedral ceiling, fireplace, full kitchen, living room, and deck; this Cape House Suite is available to guests year-round. Ask about packages that include kayaking, hiking, or sailing.

40 Union St. (P.O. Box 403), Blue Hill, ME 04614. ☎ **800/826-7415** or 207/374-2844. Fax 207/374-2829. www.blue hillinn.com. 12 units. $138–$195 double; $165–$285 suite. Rates include full breakfast and afternoon tea. 2-night minimum in summer. DISC, MC, V. Main inn closed Dec to mid-May, 1 cottage open year-round. Children 13 and older are welcome. **Amenities:** Dining room. *In room:* A/C, kitchenette (1 unit), fireplace (some units).

WHERE TO DINE

The **Fish Net** (☎ 207/374-5240), at the north end of Main St. (near the junction of Routes 172 and 177), is a longtime local favorite for its lobster rolls, fried clam baskets, ice-cream cones, and the like; it has all the atmosphere of a carhop place. It's open seasonally.

There's also a new dining spot in town called **The Wescott Forge** (☎ 207/374-9909), at 66 Main St. (the barn-red building at the bridge). The lunch menu comprises mostly sandwiches, salads, and pizzas, while duck, steaks, and seafood are served for dinner. This building has held a number of restaurants over the years, but none of them has succeeded for long; let's see what happens this time.

Arborvine 🔭🔭 SEAFOOD/FUSION   The Arborvine gives this sleepy town a topflight eatery. In a beautifully renovated Cape Cod–style house, the restaurant's interior is warm and inviting—think rough-hewn timbers, polished wooden floors, and a cozy bar area. The owners are careful to use locally procured ingredients, such as Bagaduce River oysters on the half-shell as an appetizer. The intriguing nightly main courses change but might run to haddock Niçoise, broiled Stonington halibut with grilled polenta, coriander-crusted ahi with seaweed and Japanese flavorings, galettes of Maine crab and shrimp, or seared local scallops in a garlicky saffron broth. The non-seafood choices are equally exciting: a rack of lamb in pine nuts and basil, beef medallions over a dollop of Vermont chèvre, crispy roast duckling glazed with kumquat with apple-ginger chutney, or just a simple boneless rib eye with duxelle sauce. Yummy desserts could include a Grand Marnier–spiked chocolate mousse; a gingery vanilla crème brûlée; or a Bartlett pear in puff pastry sided with macadamia nut-flavored cream, pomegranate sauce, and a bit of cinnamon ice cream.

Main St., Blue Hill, ME 04614. ☎ 207/374-2119. www.arborvine.com. Dinner $27–$30. MC, V. Summer daily 5:30–8:30pm; off-season Fri–Sun 5:30–8:30pm.

6 Mount Desert Island & Acadia National Park 🔭🔭🔭

Bar Harbor: 270 miles NE of Boston, 160 miles NE of Portland

Mount Desert Island is home to spectacular Acadia National Park, and for many visitors, the two places are one and the same. Yet the park's holdings are only part of the appeal of this popular island, which is connected to the mainland by a short causeway. Besides the parklands, there are scenic harbor-side villages and remote backcountry roads aplenty, lovely B&Bs and fine restaurants, oversize 19th-century summer "cottages," and the historic tourist town of Bar Harbor.

Mount Desert Island is split in two by an inlet. Most of the park's land is on the eastern side of the island, though there are some vast holdings in the west, too. The eastern side is much more heavily developed. **Bar Harbor** is the island's center of commerce and entertainment, a once-charming resort now in danger of being swallowed

Mount Desert Island & Acadia National Park

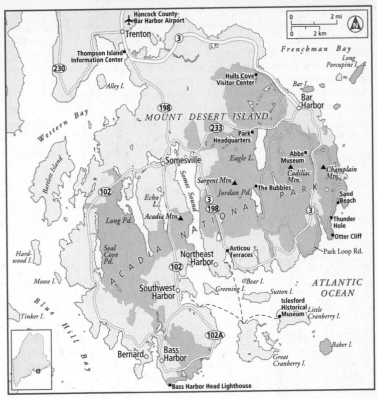

up by T-shirt and trinket shops. The western side has a quieter, more settled air and teems with more wildlife than tourists; here, the villages are mostly filled with fisherman and second-homers rather than actual commerce.

ACADIA NATIONAL PARK &&&

It's not hard to understand why Acadia is one of the crown jewels of the U.S. national park system. (It draws the second-most visitors annually of any national park.) The landscape here is a rich tapestry of rugged cliffs, pounding ocean surf, fishing and leisure boats lolling in harbors, and quiet forest paths.

Acadia's terrain, like so much of the rest of northern New England, was shaped by the cutting action of the last great glaciers moving into and then out of the region about 18,000 years ago. A mile-high ice sheet rumbled slowly over the land, scouring valleys into deep U shapes, rounding many once-jagged peaks, and depositing boulders at odd places in the landscape—including the famous 10-foot-tall Bubble Rock, which appears perched precariously on the side of South Bubble Mountain. You can see bald eagles soaring overhead, and whales breaching below. In between, you'll find remote coves perfect for beach picnics, lovely offshore islands accessible only by sea kayak, clear ponds and lakes with nary a boat, and uncrowded mountaintops (reached by car or foot) with views of it all.

ESSENTIALS

GETTING THERE   Acadia National Park is near Ellsworth, reach via Route 3. Normally travelers take U.S. Route 1 to Ellsworth from southern Maine, but you can avoid coastal congestion by taking the Maine Turnpike to Bangor, then picking up I-395 to Route 1A and continuing south into Ellsworth. Though this is longer in terms of miles, it's the quicker route in summer.

Year-round, there are several flights daily from Boston on small planes to the **Hancock County-Bar Harbor airport** (airport code BHB; www.bhbairport.com) in Trenton, just across the causeway from Mount Desert Island. Contact **U.S. Airways Express** (© 800/428-4322; www.usairways.com). From here, call a taxi, rent a car, or ride the free shuttle bus (late June through mid-October only) to downtown Bar Harbor.

It's difficult to get here by bus. In summer only, **Vermont Transit** (© 800/552-8737; www.vermonttransit.com), affiliated with Greyhound, runs buses from Boston's South Station to Bangor, continuing onward once daily to Bar Harbor. **Concord Coach** (© 800/639-3317; www.concordcoachlines.com) also runs a few buses daily to Bangor from Boston, but does not continue onto the island; you'll need to change to a taxi (a long expensive ride) or to Vermont Transit.

GETTING AROUND   A free **summer shuttle bus service** ⭐⭐ known as the *Island Explorer* (www.exploreacadia.com) was inaugurated in 1999 as part of an effort to reduce the number of cars on the island's roads. It's working; the propane-powered buses—equipped with racks for bikes—serve multiple routes covering nearly the entire island, and will stop anywhere you request outside the village centers, including trail heads, ferries, small villages, and campgrounds. Bring a book; there are lots of stops. All routes begin or end at the Village Green in Bar Harbor, but you can and should pick up the bus almost anywhere else to avoid parking hassles in town. Route no. 3 runs from Bar Harbor along much of the Park Loop, offering easy free access to some of the park's best hiking trails. The buses operate from late June through mid-October (with fewer, but still enough, buses running from September to mid-October); ask for a schedule at island information centers, in shops, or at your hotel or campground.

GUIDED TOURS   **Acadia National Park Tours** (© 207/288-0300; www.acadia tours.com) offers 2½-hour park tours departing twice daily (10am and 2pm) from downtown Bar Harbor. The bus tour includes three stops (Sieur De Monts Springs, Thunder Hole, and Cadillac Mountain) and plenty of park trivia, courtesy of the driver. This is an easy way for first-time visitors to get a quick introduction to the park before setting out on their own side trips. Tickets are available at Testa's Restaurant, 53 Main St., in Bar Harbor; the cost is $25 for adults, $10 for children under 12.

(*Tips* Cost-Effective Acadia

No daily pass to Acadia is available, so if you'll be here more than 2 weeks, purchase a $40 annual Acadia pass for your car instead of several $20 weekly passes. Or consider buying an $80 National Parks Pass, which allows you and your vehicle entry to *all* national parks during a calendar year.

ENTRY POINTS & FEES   Entrance fees to the park are collected at several gates and points from May through October; the rest of the year, entrance is free—one of this nation's great outdoor bargains either way. A 1-week pass, which includes unlimited trips on the Park Loop Road (closed in winter), costs $20 per car from late June through early October and $10 per car in spring and fall; there's no additional charge per passenger once you've bought the pass. Hikers, cyclists, and anyone else traveling without a vehicle (that is, motorcyclists or boaters) must pay a $5-per-person fee.

You can enter the park at several points in the interwoven network of park and town roads—a glance at a park map, available free at the visitor center, will make these access points self-evident. The main point of entry to Park Loop Road, the park's most scenic byway, is near the official park visitor center at **Hulls Cove** (on Route 3 just north of Bar Harbor); the entry fee is collected at a tollbooth on the loop road, a half-mile north of Sand Beach.

VISITOR CENTERS & INFORMATION   Acadia staffs two visitor centers. The **Thompson Island Information Center** (☎ 207/288-3411) on Route 3 is the first you'll pass as you enter Mount Desert Island. This center is maintained by the local chambers of commerce, but park personnel are often on hand to answer inquiries. Open daily 6am to 10pm from May to mid-October, it's a good first stop for general lodging and restaurant information.

If you're interested primarily in information about the park itself, continue on Route 3 to the National Park Service's **Hulls Cove Visitor Center,** about 7½ miles beyond Thompson Island. This attractive, stone-walled center has professionally prepared park-service displays, such as a large relief map of the island, natural history exhibits, and a short introductory film. You can also request free brochures about hiking trails and the carriage roads, or purchase postcards and more detailed guidebooks. The center is open daily mid-April through October from 8am to 4:30pm (to 6pm July–Aug, to 5pm Sept–Oct). Information is available year-round, by phone or in person, from the park's **headquarters** (☎ 207/288-3338), on Route 233 between Bar Harbor and Somesville, open 8am to 4:30pm daily. You can also ask questions online at their website, **www.nps.gov/acad.**

DRIVING TOUR   **DRIVING THE PARK LOOP ROAD**

The 20-mile **Park Loop Road** ⭑⭑ is to Acadia what Half Dome is to Yosemite—the park's premier attraction, and a magnet for the largest crowds. This remarkable roadway starts near the Hulls Cove Visitor Center and follows the high ridges above Bar Harbor before dropping down along the rocky coast. Here, spires of spruce and fir cap dark granite ledges, making a sharp contrast with the white surf and steel-blue sea. After following the picturesque coast and touching on several coves, the road loops back inland along Jordan Pond and Eagle Lake, with a detour to the summit of the island's highest peak, Cadillac Mountain.

Ideally, visitors should try to make two circuits of the loop road. The first time, go for the sheer exhilaration of it and to get the lay of the land. On the second time around, plan to stop frequently and poke around on foot, setting off on trails or scrambling along the coastline. Scenic pull-offs are staggered at frequent intervals. The two-lane road is one-way along its coastal sections; the right-hand lane is set aside for parking, so you can stop wherever you'd like, admire the vistas, and click away.

From about 10am until 4pm in July and August, anticipate big crowds along the loop road, at least on days when the sun is shining. Parking lots often fill up and close at some of the most popular destinations, including Sand Beach, Thunder Hole, and the Cadillac Mountain summit, so try to visit these spots early or late in a day. Alternatively, make the best of cloudy or drizzly days by letting the weather work to your advantage; you'll sometimes discover that you have the place nearly to yourself.

From the Hulls Cove Visitor Center, the Park Loop initially runs atop:

❶ Paradise Hill

The tour starts with sweeping views eastward over Frenchman Bay. You'll see the town of Bar Harbor far below, and just beyond it the Porcupines, a cluster of islands that look like, well, just what you'd expect from the name.

Following the Park Loop Road clockwise, you'll dip into a wooded valley and come to:

❷ Sieur de Monts Spring

Here you'll find a rather uninteresting natural spring, unnaturally encased, along with a botanical garden with some 300 species showcased in 12 habitats. The original **Abbe Museum** (✆ **207/288-3519**) is here, featuring a small but select collection of Native American artifacts. It's open daily from late May to early October, 9am to 4pm; admission is $2 for adults, $1 for children ages 6 to 15. (A larger and more modern branch of the museum in Bar Harbor features more and better curated displays; a ticket here gets you a $2 discount there. See "Exploring Bar Harbor," below, for details.)

The Tarn is the chief reason to stop here; a few hundred yards south of the springs via a footpath, it's a slightly medieval-looking and forsaken pond sandwiched between steep hills. Departing from the south end of the Tarn is the fine **Dorr Mountain Ladder Trail** (see "Hiking," below).

Continue the clockwise trip on the loop road; views eastward over the bay soon resume, almost uninterrupted, until you get to:

❸ The Precipice Trail

The park's most dramatic trail, this ascends sheer rock faces on the east side of Champlain Mountain. Only about ¾ of a mile to the summit, it's rigorous, and involves scrambling up iron rungs and ladders in exposed places (those with a fear of heights and those under 5 ft. tall should avoid this trail). The trail is often closed midsummer to protect nesting peregrine falcons. Rangers are often on hand in the trail-head parking lot to point out the birds and suggest alternative hikes.

Between the Precipice Trail and Sand Beach is a tollbooth where visitors have to pay the park entrance fee.

Picturesquely set between the arms of a rocky cove is:

❹ Sand Beach

Sand Beach 🄰 is virtually the only sand beach on the island, although swimming these cold waters (about 50°F/10°C) is best enjoyed on extremely hot days or by those with a freakishly robust metabolism. When it's sunny out, the sandy strand is crowded midday with picnickers. (The water at the far end of the beach—where a gentle stream enters the cove—is often a few degrees warmer than the part beside the access stairway.)

Two worthwhile hikes start near this beach. **The Beehive Trail** overlooks Sand Beach (see "Hiking," below); it starts from a trail head across the loop road. From the east end of Sand Beach, look for the start of the **Great Head Trail,** a loop of about 2 miles that follows on the bluff overlooking the beach, then circles back along the shimmering bay before cutting through the woods back to Sand Beach.

About a mile south of Sand Beach is:

⑤ Thunder Hole

Thunder Hole ⑥ is a shallow oceanside cavern into which surf surges, compresses, and bursts out on days when the seas are rough. (A walking trail on the road allows you to leave your car parked at the beach). On those days, you can feel the ocean's power and force resonating under your sternum. *Tip:* The best viewing time is 3 hours before high tide; check tide tables, available at local hotels, restaurants, and info kiosks.

Just before the road curves around Otter Point, you'll be driving atop:

⑥ Otter Cliffs

This set of 100-foot-high precipices is capped with dense stands of spruce trees. From the top, look for spouting whales in summer. In early fall, thousands of eider ducks can sometimes be seen floating in big, raft-like flocks just offshore. A footpath traces the edge of the crags.

At Seal Harbor, the loop road veers north and inland back toward Bar Harbor. On the route is:

⑦ Jordan Pond

Jordan Pond ⑥⑥ is a small but beautiful body of water encased by gentle, forested hills. A 3-mile hiking loop follows the pond's shoreline (see "Hiking," below), and a network of splendid carriage roads converges at the pond. After a hike or mountain-bike excursion, spend some time at a table on the lawn of the Jordan Pond House restaurant (see "Where to Dine," below).

Shortly before the loop road ends, you'll pass the entrance to:

⑧ Cadillac Mountain

Reach this **mountain** ⑥ by car, ascending an early carriage road. At 1,528 feet, it's the highest peak on the Atlantic between Canada and Brazil. During much of the year, it's also the first place on U.S. soil touched by the rays of sunrise. But because Cadillac Mountain is the only mountaintop in the park accessible by car, and because it's also the island's highest point, the parking lot at the summit can get jammed. Some lower peaks accessible only by foot—such as Acadia and Champlain mountains—have equally excellent views and far fewer crowds.

GETTING OUTSIDE

CARRIAGE RIDES ⑥⑥   Several types of carriage rides are offered by the park-managed **Wildwood Stables** (✆ 207/276-3622; www.acadia.net/wildwood), about a half-mile south of the Jordan Pond House. The tours depart daily in season and take in sweeping ocean views from a local mountaintop, ramble over the Rockefeller bridges, or drop by the Jordan Pond House for (optional) tea and popovers (extra charge). The tours cost from $16 to $22 per adult, or $4.50 to $9 per child ages 2 to 12. There's a special carriage designed for passengers with disabilities, and you can even charter your own carriage for a private group. Reservations are recommended.

GOLF   There are 2 good golf courses on Mount Desert Island. The **Kebo Valley Golf Club** (✆ **207/288-3000**) is one of the oldest in America, open since 1888. The **Northeast Harbor Golf Club** (✆ **207/276-5335**) is another good choice. Greens fees at both range from about $40 to $80 per person for 18 holes in season.

HIKING   Hiking is the quintessential Acadia activity, and it should be experienced by everyone at least one. The Hulls Cove Visitor Center has a chart summarizing area hikes. Cobble together different loop hikes to make your trips more varied, and be sure to plan your hiking according to the weather; if it's damp or foggy, you'll stay drier and warmer strolling the carriage roads. If it's clear and dry, head for the highest peaks (Cadillac, the Bubbles) with the best views.

MOUNTAIN BIKING The 57 miles of **carriage roads** 🏵🏵🏵 in the park make for very smooth biking. Note that bikes are also allowed onto the island's free shuttle buses (see "Getting Around," above). A useful map of the carriage roads is available free at any visitor center; more detailed guides can be purchased at area bookshops, but they really aren't necessary. Remember that anywhere carriage roads cross private land (mostly btw. Seal Harbor and Northeast Harbor), they're closed to mountain bikes, which are also banned from hiking trails.

Mountain bikes can be rented along Cottage Street in Bar Harbor, with rates usually $20 or less for a full day, $12 to $15 for a half-day (which is 4 hr. in the bike-rental universe). Most bike shops include locks and helmets as basic equipment, but ask what's included before you rent. Also ask about closing times, since you'll be able to get in a couple of extra hours with a late-closing shop. The **Bar Harbor Bicycle Shop** (℗ **207/288-3886**), at 141 Cottage St., gets many people's vote for most convenient and friendliest. You could also try **Acadia Bike** (℗ **800/526-8615;** www.acadiabike.com), at 48 Cottage St., which is very good.

CAMPING

The National Park Service maintains two campgrounds within Acadia National Park. Both are extremely popular; during July and August, expect both of them to fill up by early to mid-morning.

The more popular of the two is **Blackwoods** 🏵🏵 (℗ **207/288-3274**), on the island's eastern side, with about 300 sites. To get there, follow Route 3 about 5 miles south out of Bar Harbor; bikers and pedestrians have easy access to the loop road from the campground via a short trail, and the Island Explorer bus stops here as well. This campground has no public showers or electrical hookups, but an enterprising business just outside the campground entrance provides clean showers for a modest fee. Camping fees at Blackwoods are $20 per night from May through October, $10 per site in April and November. Advance **reservations** can be made to Blackwoods by calling ℗ **877/444-6777** between 10am and midnight (only until 10pm in winter), or by using a new reservations system online at **www.recreation.gov**. An Acadia pass (see above) is also required for campground entry.

The **Seawall** 🏵 (℗ **207/244-3600**) campground is located over on the quieter, western half of the island, near the tiny fishing village of Bass Harbor (one of the Island Explorer bus routes also has a stop here). Seawall has about 215 sites, and it's a good base for cyclists or those wishing to explore several short coastal hikes within easy striking distance. However, it's quite a ways from Bar Harbor and Sand Beach on the other side of the island; for families, it might not be the best choice. The campground is open mid-May through the end of September, but they *do not take reservations*. It's first-come, first-served all the way—and the lines form early. In general, if you get here by 9 or 10am you're pretty much assured of a campsite, especially if you want a walk-in site.

Camping fees at Seawall are $14 to $20 per night, depending on whether you want to drive directly to your site, or can pack a tent in for a distance of up to 150 yards. There are also no electrical or water hookups here, and (as it is with Blackwoods) prior acquisition of an Acadia entrance pass is required to stay at the campground.

WHERE TO DINE

Jordan Pond House 🏵🏵 *Finds* AMERICAN The secret to the Jordan Pond House? Location, location, location. The restaurant traces its roots from 1847, when a farm was established on this picturesque property at the southern tip of Jordan Pond looking north toward The Bubbles, a picturesque pair of glacially sculpted mounds. In 1979, the original structure and its birch-bark dining room were destroyed by fire. A more modern, two-level dining room was built in its place—it has less charm, but it still has the island's best dining location, on a nice lawn. Afternoon tea with popovers and jam is a hallowed tradition here. The lobster stew is expensive but very good. Dinners include classic entrees like prime rib, steamed lobster, and baked scallops.

Park Loop Rd. (near Seal Harbor), Acadia National Park. © 207/276-3316. www.jordanpond.com. Advance reservations not accepted; call before arriving to hold a table. Main courses $8.50–$18 at lunch; $17–$20 at dinner. AE, DISC, MC, V. Mid-May to late Oct daily 11:30am–8pm (until 9pm July–Aug).

BAR HARBOR 🏵

Bar Harbor provides most of the meals and beds to travelers coming to the island, as it has since the grand resort era of the late 19th century, when wealthy vacationers first discovered the Acadia region. Some see the town as a tacky tourist mecca, replete with T-shirt vendors, ice-cream shops, and souvenir palaces, as well as crowds spilling off the sidewalks into the street and appalling traffic for such a small town. That is all somewhat true. Yet the town's history, distinguished architecture, and beautiful location on Frenchman Bay *still* make it a desirable base for exploring the island anyway, and it has by far the best selection of lodging, meals, supplies, and services. If you want to shop, fine-dine, or go out at night, you've pretty much got to stay here. Otherwise, consider elsewhere on the island (see below).

ESSENTIALS

GETTING THERE   Bar Harbor is on Route 3, about 10 miles southeast of the causeway leading onto Mount Desert Island. For plane and bus access, see "Getting There," in the Acadia National Park section above.

VISITOR INFORMATION   The **Bar Harbor Chamber of Commerce,** P.O. Box 158, Bar Harbor, ME 04609 (© 207/288-5103; www.barharborinfo.com), stockpiles a huge arsenal of information about local attractions, both at its offices on 1 West St. (at the pier) and in a welcome center on Route 3 in Trenton, just before the bridge onto the island. Write, call, or e-mail in advance for a directory of area lodging and attractions. The chamber's website is chock-full of information and helpful links.

EXPLORING BAR HARBOR

The best water views in town are from the foot of Main Street at grassy **Agamont Park,** which overlooks the town pier and Frenchman Bay. From here, set off past The Bar Harbor Inn on the **Shore Path** 🏵🏵, a wide, winding trail that follows the shoreline for half a mile along a public right of way. The pathway passes in front of many elegant summer homes (some converted to inns), offering a superb vantage point from which to view the area's architecture.

The **Abbe Museum** 🏵, 26 Mount Desert St. (© **207/288-3519;** www.abbemuseum.org), opened in 2001 as an in-town extension of the smaller, simpler museum at the Sieur de Monts spring in the national park (see above). showcasing a top-rate collection of Native American artifacts. A 17,000-square-foot gallery, this downtown branch has an orientation center and a glass-walled lab where visitors can see archaeologists at work preserving recently recovered artifacts, along with changing exhibits and videos that focus largely tribes from Maine and other parts of New England. From late May through October, it opens daily from 10am to 6pm; then, from November through late April, it's open Thursday to Saturday (same hours). In late April and most of May, it's open Friday to Sunday only. Admission is $6 for adults, $2 for children ages 6 to 15.

WHALE-WATCHING

Bar Harbor is a base for several ocean endeavors, including whale-watching tours. Operators offer excursions in search of humpbacks, finbacks, minke, and the infrequently seen, endangered right whale. The sleekest is the Bar Harbor Whale Watch Company's *Friendship V* ((C) **888/942-5374** or 207/288-2386; www.whalesrus.com), which operates from the municipal pier at 1 West St. in downtown Bar Harbor. Tours are on a fast, twin-hulled, three-level excursion boat that can hold 200 passengers in two heated cabins. The tours run 3 hours plus; the cost is $49 per adult, $26 per child age 6 to 14, and $8 per child under age 6. A puffin- and whale-watching tour is also offered for the same prices, and there are shorter seal-watching tours for about half the price. There's free on-site parking and a money-back guarantee that you'll see whales. The daily tours begin each season in late May and run through fall; call ahead for dates.

WHERE TO STAY
Expensive

Bar Harbor Grand Hotel ⭐   Bar Harbor's newest big hotel (it opened in 2003) fills a lodging gap between quaint, expensive inns and B&Bs and the island's family-owned motels, hotels, and cottages. The hotel's blocky, two-tower design faithfully copies the style of the Rodick House, a now-defunct 19th-century lodging in Bar Harbor that could once boast of being Maine's largest hotel; the Grand, however, does the former one better with spacious rooms and bathrooms and, of course, all-modern fixtures. Rooms and suites are decked out in the same floral bedspreads and curtains you'd expect in any upscale business hotel, and the access to downtown Bar Harbor and the nearby ocean are big pluses. Concessions to business and tourist travelers include a guest laundry facility, gift shop, and high-speed Internet access (for a fee). Not surprisingly, they're getting a lot of tour groups here. Expect comfort, rather than island character.

269 Main St., Bar Harbor, ME 04609. (C) **888/766-2529** or 207/288-5226. www.barharborgrand.com. 70 units. Mid-June to mid-Nov $145–$205 double; mid-Apr to mid-June $79–$129 double. Suites more expensive. Rates include continental breakfast. Packages available. DISC, MC, V. Closed mid-Nov to mid-Apr. **Amenities:** Heated outdoor pool; fitness room; Jacuzzi; gift shop; coin-op laundry. *In room:* A/C, TV, fridge, coffeemaker.

Bar Harbor Hotel-Bluenose Inn ⭐⭐   This resort-style complex—situated in two buildings—offers stunning views of the surrounding terrain. Facilities here are more modern, too: Expect spacious carpeted rooms with huge bathrooms, small refrigerators, and balconies, as well as a good fitness center, indoor and outdoor pools (the indoor pool is fairly palatial), and one of the island's best dining rooms, the **Rose Garden** (see "Where to Dine," below). The two buildings are slightly different in character, but in either case upper-floor rooms with sea views are worth the extra cost, especially if the weather is good. Staff here is professional and friendly.

90 Eden St., Bar Harbor, ME 04609. (C) **800/445-4077** or 207/288-3348. www.bluenoseinn.com. 97 units. Mid-June to mid-Oct $145–$405 double; spring and late fall $75–$299 double. AE, DC, DISC, MC, V. Closed Nov–Apr. **Amenities:** Restaurant; indoor pool; outdoor pool; fitness center; spa; Jacuzzi. *In room:* A/C, TV, fridge, coffeemaker, hair dryer, iron/ironing board, fireplace (some units).

The Bar Harbor Inn ⭐⭐   The Bar Harbor Inn, just off Agamont Park, nicely mixes traditional and contemporary. On shady grounds just a minute's stroll from downtown, the inn offers convenience and gracious charm. The shingled main inn, which

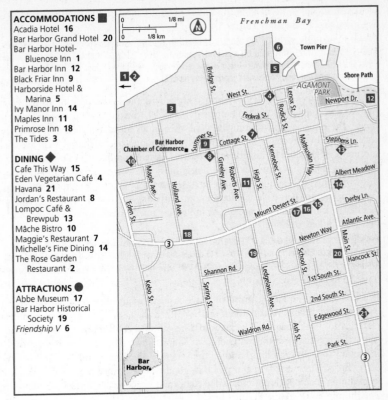

ACCOMMODATIONS ■
Acadia Hotel **16**
Bar Harbor Grand Hotel **20**
Bar Harbor Hotel-
    Bluenose Inn **1**
Bar Harbor Inn **12**
Black Friar Inn **9**
Harborside Hotel &
    Marina **5**
Ivy Manor Inn **14**
Maples Inn **11**
Primrose Inn **18**
The Tides **3**

DINING ◆
Cafe This Way **15**
Eden Vegetarian Café **4**
Havana **21**
Jordan's Restaurant **8**
Lompoc Café &
    Brewpub **13**
Mâche Bistro **10**
Maggie's Restaurant **7**
Michelle's Fine Dining **14**
The Rose Garden
    Restaurant **2**

ATTRACTIONS ●
Abbe Museum **17**
Bar Harbor Historical
    Society **19**
Friendship V **6**

dates from the turn of the 19th century, has a settled, old-money feel, with its semi-circular dining room and a buttoned-down lobby; guest rooms, located in the Main Inn and two additional structures, are decidedly more contemporary. Units in the Oceanfront Lodge and Main Inn both offer spectacular bay views, and many have private balconies; the less expensive Newport Building lacks views but is comfortable and up-to-date. In 2006 the inn added a spa with Vichy showers, aromatherapy, heated-stone treatments, and facial treatments. The semiformal **Reading Room** serves resort meals with the best dining-room views in town.

Newport Dr. (P.O. Box 7), Bar Harbor, ME 04609. ℂ **800/248-3351** or 207/288-3351. www.barharborinn.com. 153 units. Late May–late Oct $119–$379 double; late Mar–late May and late Oct–late Nov $79–$215 double. Rates include continental breakfast. AE, DISC, MC, V. Closed Dec to mid-Mar. **Amenities:** Dining room; heated outdoor pool; fitness room; spa; Jacuzzi; conference room; limited room service. *In room:* A/C, TV, hair dryer.

Harborside Hotel & Marina ℱ   Formerly an inexpensive, family-style motel, the Harborside now offers upscale digs. It promises a range of studios and two- and three-bedroom suites sporting fancier bathrooms, business-hotel amenities, and big televisions. The priciest suites will be similar to condominium units, with various combinations of Jacuzzis, fireplaces, balconies, water views, and even some full kitchens and dining rooms. Guests are taken care of: There's a bar in the pool, a plush chandeliered-and-tapestried bar in the Bar Harbor Club building, and a formal dining room and an Italian trattoria.

55 West St., Bar Harbor, ME 04609. ✆ **800/328-5033** or 207/288-5033. www.theharborsidehotel.com. 187 units. $139–$259 double; $225–$850 suite. Off-season rates sometimes lower. DISC, MC, V. Closed Nov–Apr. **Amenities:** 2 restaurants; 2 bars; outdoor pool; fitness center; spa; Jacuzzi; conference room. *In room:* A/C, TV, dataport, kitchenette (some units), fireplace (some units), Jacuzzi (some units).

Ivy Manor Inn ✪   The Ivy Manor quickly proved a welcome addition to Bar Harbor's upscale lodging pool when it opened in 1997. Located in a 1940s-era Tudor-style house, the inn has been thoroughly done over in an understated French Victorian style, mostly in rich colors such as burgundy. The rooms here are larger than average; most are carpeted and furnished with attractive, tasteful antiques from the innkeeper's collection. Some have antique claw-footed tubs; others have small outdoor sitting decks. Among the best units: no. 6, a small suite with a private sitting room and small fireplace; and no. 1, the Honeymoon Room, with king-size bed and imposing walnut headboard and matching armoire. The inn restaurant, **Michelle's,** is one of the town's best (see "Where to Dine," below).

194 Main St., Bar Harbor, ME 04609. ✆ **888/670-1997** or 207/288-2138. www.ivymanor.com. 8 units. Mid-June to Oct $200–$325 double; Apr to mid-June $185–$275 double. Rates include full breakfast. Closed Nov–Mar. 2-night minimum on holiday weekends. AE, DISC, MC, V. Children over 12 welcome. **Amenities:** Restaurant; lounge. *In room:* A/C, TV, fireplace (some units).

The Tides ✪   The Tides consists of just four guest rooms (three of which are suites) in a sprawling yellow mansion built in 1887. It's at the head of a long, lush lawn that descends to water's edge, on 1½ acres in a neighborhood of imposing homes within easy walking distance of the center of town. Guests unwind in one of two spacious living rooms (one on each floor) and on the veranda, which has a unique outdoor fireplace. Breakfast is served on this porch in good weather; otherwise, it's enjoyed in a regal dining room, with polished wood floors and views out to Bar Island. There's a 2-night minimum stay at all times here.

119 West St., Bar Harbor, ME 04609. ✆ **207/288-4968.** www.barharbortides.com. 4 units. Peak season $275 double, $375–$395 suite; off-season rates lower. Rates include full breakfast. 2-night minimum stay year-round. AE, DISC, MC, V. **Amenities:** Restaurant. *In room:* TV, dataport, fireplace (most units).

Moderate

Acadia Hotel ✪ *(Value)*   The Acadia Hotel is nicely situated overlooking Bar Harbor's village green, easily accessible to in-town activities and the free shuttles dispersing to elsewhere on the island. All things considered, it's an amazing value (prices have actually gone down in the last couple of years). A handsome, simple home dating from the late 19th century, it has a wraparound porch and guest rooms decorated in nice floral motifs. Rooms vary widely in size and amenities. Some units have whirlpool tubs, phones, and/or king beds; one has a kitchenette, and about half have small refrigerators. It's a simple place, but quite clean and well run.

20 Mt. Desert St., Bar Harbor, ME 04609. ✆ **888/876-2463** or 207/288-5721. www.acadiahotel.com. 11 units. July to mid-Oct $119–$149 double; Apr–June and mid-Oct to mid-Nov $59–$99 double. Packages available. AE, MC, V. *In room:* A/C, TV, fridge (some units), no phone (some units).

Black Friar Inn ✪   The Black Friar Inn, tucked on a side street overlooking a parking lot, is a yellow-shingled structure with quirky pediments and a somewhat eccentric air. It offers decent value. A former owner "collected" interiors and installed them throughout the home, among them a replica of a namesake pub in London with elaborate carved-wood paneling (now a common room), stamped-tin walls (now in the breakfast room), and a doctor's office (now a guest room). Rooms are carpeted and furnished in a mix of antiques; most are smallish, though the big suite features nice paneling, a sofa, wingback chair, and gas fireplace. Other rooms sport such touches as rose-tinted stained-glass windows, brass beds, and a mini-spiral staircase. The least expensive units are two garret rooms on the third floor, each of which has a detached private bathroom down the hall.

10 Summer St., Bar Harbor, ME 04609. ℭ 207/288-5091. Fax 207/288-4197. www.blackfriar.com. 7 units, 2 with private hallway bathrooms. Peak season $110–$160 double; off-season rates lower. Rates include full breakfast. 2-night minimum mid-June to mid-Oct. DISC, MC, V. Closed Dec–Apr. Children 12 and older welcome. **Amenities:** Sea-kayaking and fly-fishing tours (for a fee). In room: A/C, fireplace (1 unit).

Maples Inn ⍟   A modest home tucked away on a side street among other Bar Harbor B&Bs, the Maples is located an easy walk from downtown—perfect for those who want to see a movie or eat out. It's a popular destination for those attracted to outdoor activities, too, and you'll often find guests swapping stories about the day's adventures on the handsome front porch, or lingering over breakfast to compare notes about hiking trails. The innkeeper, an interior designer, has a way of making guests comfortable; rooms are small to medium-size, but you're not likely to feel cramped—they have private bathrooms, wicker furniture, pencil poster beds, and handsome antique wooden writing desks. The two-room White Birch has a fireplace, a lacy canopy bed with a down comforter, and a bright blue-and-white decor; Red Oak has a private deck with plastic lounge chairs. Gourmet breakfasts are served in a sunny dining room.

16 Roberts Ave., Bar Harbor, ME 04609. ℭ 207/288-3443. www.maplesinn.com. 6 units. Mid-June to mid-Oct $85–$120 double; May to mid-June and mid-Oct to mid-Nov $125–$170 double. Memorial Day weekend $20 higher. Rates include full breakfast. 2-night minimum stay, 3-night minimum on holiday weekends. DISC, MC, V. Closed mid-Nov to Apr. Not appropriate for children. In room: Fireplace (1 unit), no phone.

Primrose Inn ⍟   This handsome Victorian stick–style inn, originally built in 1878, is one of the most notable properties on the "mansion row" along Mount Desert Street. Its distinctive architecture has been preserved, and was perhaps even enhanced during a 1987 addition of rooms, private bathrooms, and balconies. This inn is comfortable, furnished with "functional antiques" and modern reproductions; many rooms have a floral theme, thick carpets, and adjacent sitting or reading rooms. Two newer, "premium" rooms have private entrances and are stocked with king beds, gas fireplaces, and such other amenities as a porch or whirlpool tub. Note that a 2-night minimum stay is required and pets are no longer allowed.

73 Mount Desert St., Bar Harbor, ME 04609. ℭ 877/846-3424 or 207/288-4031. www.primroseinn.com. 13 units. Late June–Aug $145–$245 double; late May–late June and Sept–Oct $95–$195 double. Daily rates include full breakfast and afternoon tea. 2-night minimum stay. AE, DISC, MC, V. Closed late Nov–late May. In room: A/C, TV, hair dryer, iron/ironing board, fireplace (some units), Jacuzzi (1 unit).

Inexpensive

The Colony (Value)   Owned by the same family since 1950, the Colony is a vintage motor court consisting of a handful of motel rooms plus a battery of cottages arrayed around a long green. It's best appreciated by those with a taste for things retro; others might decide to look for something fancier. But the price is right. Rooms are furnished in a simple '70s style that won't win any awards for decor, but they're adequate; there are two classes of motel room, regular and luxury—the difference being better views and bigger beds (queens and kings instead of paired doubles). Some of the cottages have phones and kitchenettes, some don't, but all have TVs. This complex is just across Route 3 from a cobblestone beach, and about a 10-minute drive into Bar Harbor.

Rte. 3 (P.O. Box 56), Hulls Cove, ME 04644. ✆ 207/288-3383. www.acadia.net/thecolony. 55 units. Peak season $65–$125 double; off-season rates lower. AE, DC, DISC, MC, V. *In room:* A/C (some units), TV, kitchenette (some units), fridge (some units), no phone (some units).

WHERE TO DINE
Expensive

Michelle's Fine Dining ✶✶ FRENCH/SEAFOOD   Michelle's is located in the graceful Ivy Manor Inn (see "Where to Stay," above), and it offers one of the island's best dinner experiences. The three dining rooms are elegant, and there's outside seating when the weather's good. The extensive menu elaborates on traditional French cuisine with New England twists; as you'd expect, the seafood selection is extensive. Nightly appetizers might include smoked salmon layered with a chervil mousse, or foie gras with black truffles. Main courses are even more elaborate, with dishes such as chateaubriand for two (carved tableside); roasted lobster in a basil-cream sauce; rack of lamb; and a bouillabaisse of lobster, mussels, clams, and scallops. Finish with the house's unique "bag of chocolate," which comes with berries and is served in an edible chocolate bag, or one of several excellent soufflés.

194 Main St. ✆ 207/288-0038 or 888/670-1997. www.michellesfinedining.com. Reservations required during peak season. Main courses $26–$40. AE, DISC, MC, V. Daily 6–9pm. Closed late Oct–early May.

The Rose Garden Restaurant ✶✶✶ NEW AMERICAN   One of only a handful of fine-dining establishments in Bar Harbor that delivers a big-league dining experience, this unassuming room in the Bluenose Inn (see "Where to Stay," above) turns out wonderful meals. The a la carte and prix-fixe menus aren't cheap, but they're very good. Appetizers might include smoked salmon, foie gras, crab cakes, strudel filled with asparagus and Gruyère, or lobster bisque with sweet brandy cream. Main courses could include seared tenderloin steaks, grilled salmon with mustard sauce and a potato cake, fresh lobster meat over pasta, a roasted rack of lamb, or peppery venison with squash puree and cranberry sauce. When they're on the menu, the chocolate-mousse cake, crème brûlée, apple tarts, or mascarpone cheesecake are good dessert choices.

90 Eden St. ✆ 800/445-4077 or 207/288-3348. Reservations recommended. Breakfast $10–$17; dinner prix-fixe menu $63; a la carte entrees $40. MC, V. May–late Oct breakfast 6–10:30am; dinner 5:30–9:30pm. Closed late Oct–Apr.

MODERATE

Cafe This Way ✶✶ ECLECTIC   Cafe This Way is the kind of place where they know how to do wonderful Asian and Mediterranean things with simple ingredients. It has the feel of a hip coffeehouse, yet it's much more airy and creative than that. Bookshelves line one wall, and there's a small bar tucked into a nook; oddly, they serve breakfast and dinner but no lunch. Breakfasts are excellent though mildly sinful-it's more like brunch. Go for the burritos, corned beef hash with eggs, a range of omelets (build your own if you like), and the calorific Café Monte Cristo: a French toast sandwich stuffed with fried eggs, ham, and cheddar cheese served with fries and syrup. Yikes. Dinners are equally appetizing, with tasty starters that might run to Maine crab cakes in tequila-lime sauce, grilled chunks of Cyprus cheese, or lobster spring rolls. The main-course offerings of the night could include anything from lobster stewed in spinach and Gruyère cheese to sea scallops in vinaigrette, steaks, grilled lamb, peachy pork chops, or the filling Korean stir-fry dish known as bibimbap.

14½ Mount Desert St. © 207/288-4483. www.cafethisway.com. Reservations recommended for dinner. Breakfast items $5–$8, dinner main courses $7–$24. MC, V. Mid-Apr to Oct Mon–Sat 7–11am; Sun 8am–1pm; dinner daily 5:30–9pm.

Havana 🏛🏛 LATINO/FUSION   Havana set a new culinary bar for Bar Harbor's restaurants when it opened in 1999 in what was then a town of fried fish and baked stuffed haddock. The spare, sparkling decor in an old storefront is as classy as anything you'll find in Boston, and the menu could hold its own in any big city, too. Chef/owner Michael Boland says his menu is inspired by Latino fare, which he melds nicely with New American ideas. While the offerings change weekly, expect items like appetizers of monkfish ceviche, Cuban-style beef tenderloin-and-pineapple brochettes, or Thai tofu with a plantain crust. Entrees could include choices as adventurous as spicy Chilean black-bean stew, tuna seasoned with *guajillo* chilies, grilled pork chops rubbed with maple sugar and chilies, and filet mignon rubbed with Cuban coffee and black pepper with a topping of garlic butter and spicy honey. Finish with an equally dazzling dessert such as pistachio-mousse popovers with chocolate Cointreau sauce, a pecan tart sided with cinnamon gelato, or a *tres-leches* (three-milk) cake.

318 Main St. © 207/288-2822. www.havanamaine.com. Reservations recommended. Main courses $16–$33. AE, DC, DISC, MC, V. Daily 5–10pm.

Mâche Bistro 🏛🏛 BISTRO   Little Mâche Bistro has developed a devoted local following among those who know good food; its soothing yet plain decor conceals a sophisticated kitchen—you wouldn't expect an imported-cheese course offered in a place with plywood floors, but there is one. The menu here changes monthly; appetizers could include a salad of Maytag blue cheese, apples, and truffle vinaigrette; garlic-seared shrimp; or a cheese plate. Main courses might include coq au vin, sirloin steaks roasted in a mushroom jus, good duck breast braised in an orange-ginger sauce, braised lamb shank, pan-fried tempeh and vegetables with a ponzu sauce, sole meunière, or a smoky seafood stew.

135 Cottage St. © 207/288-0447. www.machebistro.com. Reservations recommended. Main courses $12–$21. AE, MC, V. Tues–Sun 5–9pm.

Maggie's Restaurant 🏛🏛 SEAFOOD   The slogan for Maggie's is "Notably fresh seafood," and the place invariably delivers on that understated promise. (Only locally caught fish is used.) It's a casually elegant spot, good for a romantic evening while you enjoy the soothing music, attentive service, and excellent seafood. Appetizers could include grilled cherrystone clams in white-wine sauce or lobster stew; main courses might be bronzed cod with a lime-tartar sauce, lobster crepes, Gulf shrimp with feta and olives over rice, pan-seared scallops, or salmon seared in Indian spices and served with cucumber-mint salsa. They also do nice steaks and chicken, but that's not why you dine here. Desserts are homemade and it's worth leaving room for them: blueberry pie, lemon curd, and dark chocolate pudding cakes, and a delicious menu of sundaes—the island's best.

6 Summer St. © 207/288-9007. www.maggiesbarharbor.com. Reservations recommended July–Aug. Main courses $16–$24. MC, V. Mon–Sat 5–9:30pm.

INEXPENSIVE
Eden Vegetarian Café 🏛🏛 *(finds)* VEGETARIAN   Have you ever seen a vegetarian restaurant where people dress up for dinner? Now you have. Right across from the harbor, Bar Harbor's only vegetarian eatery is operated by Mark Rampacek, who brings high culinary flair and atmosphere to his cause. Most dishes here use organic

and/or locally grown ingredients, and all are wonderfully inventive and tasty. The menu changes during the three seasons of the year the cafe is open; depending on the time of year, it might offer starters such as pumpkin soup, shiitake crepes, or a beet carpaccio. Main courses include a "bento box" of grilled tofu, edamame, and Japanese rolls and salads; Korean-style hot pots of local mushrooms, onions, and broth over udon noodles; Thai "drunken" noodles and vegetables and tofu in a sweet-and-sour tamarind broth; or a lovely carbonara pasta subbing in a local smoked-dulse cream for the bacon. For dessert, you might find chocolate fondue, dairy-free ice creams, or sponge cake with lemon curd or blueberries. There's also a full range of coffees and teas and a full bar.

78 West St. ℭ 207/288-4422. www.barharborvegetarian.com. Reservations strongly recommended. Main courses $9–$17. MC, V. Summer daily 5–9pm. Closed Sun in spring and fall; call for exact hours.

Jordan's Restaurant *(Value* DINER   This unpretentious breakfast-and-lunch joint has been dishing up filling fare since 1976, and offers a glimpse of the old Bar Harbor. It's a popular haunt of local working folks and retirees, but staff is also genuinely friendly to tourists. Diners can settle into one of the pine booths or at a laminated table and order off the placemat menu, choosing from basic fare such as grilled cheese with tomato and a slight but serviceable hamburger. The soups and chowders are all homemade. Breakfast is the specialty here, with a broad selection of three-egg omelets, along with muffins and locally famous pancakes made with wild Maine blueberries. With its atmosphere of "seniors at coffee klatch" and its rock-bottom prices, this is not a gourmet experience, but fans of Americana and dinerlike places might enjoy it.

80 Cottage St. ℭ 207/288-3586. Breakfast $2.95–$6.75; lunch $2.25–$8.25. MC, V. Daily 4:30am–2pm. Closed Feb–Mar.

Lompoc Cafe and Brewpub ★ AMERICAN/ECLECTIC   The Lompoc Cafe has a well-worn, neighborhood-bar feel to it—little wonder, since waiters and other workers from around Bar Harbor congregate here after-hours. The cafe consists of three sections: the original bar, a tidy beer garden just outside (try your hand at bocce), and a small and open barn-like structure at the garden's edge to handle the overflow. The brewery next door produces several unique beers, including a blueberry ale (ask for a sample before ordering a full glass) and a smooth porter. Bar menus are usually yawn-inducing, but this one actually has some pleasant surprises, like Caesar salads; lobster quesadillas; local mussels in white wine, Dijon mustard, and cream; grilled miso tofu; chicken-and-green chili burritos; bourbony barbecue pork sandwiches; and grilled portobello slices over soba noodles in a spicy peanut sauce. The outdoor tables are appealing, and live music acts frequently play here.

36 Rodick St. ℭ 207/288-9392. www.lompoccafe.com. Reservations not accepted. Main courses $4–$13. MC, V. May–Nov daily 11:30am–1am. Closed Dec–Apr.

ELSEWHERE ON THE ISLAND ★★

You'll find plenty to explore outside Acadia National Park and Bar Harbor. Quiet fishing villages, deep woodlands, and unexpected ocean views are among the jewels you can turn up once you get beyond Bar Harbor town limits.

ESSENTIALS
GETTING AROUND   The eastern half of the island is best navigated using Route 3, which forms a rough loop from Bar Harbor through Seal Harbor and past Northeast Harbor, then runs up along the eastern shore of Somes Sound. Route 102 and

Route 102A provide access to the island's western half. Without a car, use the free Island Explorer shuttle (see "Getting Around," in the Acadia National Park section, above).

VISITOR INFORMATION   The Thompson Island Information Center as you enter the island is a great info source. Locally, the **Southwest Harbor-Tremont Chamber of Commerce,** P.O. Box 1143, Southwest Harbor, ME 04679 (© **800/ 423-9264** or 207/244-9264) and the **Mount Desert Chamber of Commerce,** P.O. Box 675, Northeast Harbor, ME 04662 (© **207/276-5040**) can also help.

EXPLORING THE REST OF THE ISLAND

On the tip of the eastern lobe of Mount Desert Island is the staid, prosperous little village of **Northeast Harbor** ⋒, long a favorite retreat of well-heeled folks up and down the Eastern seaboard. You can see their shingled palaces poking out of the forest and along the shore, but the village itself (which consists of one short main street and a marina) is also worth investigating.

One of the best, least-publicized places for enjoying views of the harbor is from the understatedly spectacular **Asticou Terraces** ⋒⋒. Finding the parking lot can be tricky: Head a half-mile east (toward Seal Harbor) on Route 3 from the junction with Route 198, and look for the small gravel lot on the water side of the road with a sign reading ASTICOU TERRACES. Park here, cross the road on foot, and set off up a magnificent path made of local rock that ascends the sheer hillside, with expanding views of the harbor and the town.

When leaving Northeast Harbor, plan to drive out via Sargent Drive. This one-way route runs through Acadia National Park along the shore of Somes Sound, affording superb views of this glacially carved inlet. On the far side of Somes Sound, there's good hiking (see above) and the towns of **Southwest Harbor** ⋒ and **Bass Harbor.** These are both home to fishermen and boat-builders, and though the character of these towns is changing, they're still far more humble than Northeast and Seal harbors.

WHERE TO STAY

Asticou Inn ⋒   The once-grand Asticou Inn, which dates from 1883, still occupies a prime location at the head of Northeast Harbor and is desirable for many even as it shows signs of tiring. The weathered gray shingles and profusion of overhanging eaves give it a stern demeanor, but it also has elements of eccentricity; despite some incipient shabbiness, a cozy old-world gentility seems to arise from the creaking floorboards and through the thin guest-room walls. Rooms are furnished in a simple summer-home style; some rooms have claw-footed tubs, and a few have fireplaces or kitchenettes, but none have phones or TVs. Dinner in the airy, wooden-floored main dining room focuses, as expected, on seafood entrees served with class.

Rte. 3 (P.O. Box 337), Northeast Harbor, ME 04662. © 800/258-3373 or 207/276-3344. www.asticou.com. 44 units. July–Aug $230–$340 double; May and Sept–Oct $135–$245 double. Rates include breakfast. MAP plans available July–Aug only. DISC, MC, V. Valet parking. Closed Nov–Apr. No children under 6. **Amenities:** Dining room; outdoor pool; tennis court; concierge; business center; limited room service; babysitting; laundry. *In room:* Kitchenette (few units), fireplace (few units), no phone.

The Claremont ⋒   Early prints of the Claremont show an austere, four-story wooden building overlooking Somes Sound from a grassy rise; it hasn't changed much since. The place offers nothing fancy or elaborate, just classic New England grace. It's somehow appropriate that the state's largest croquet tournament (yes, really) is held here for a week each August. Common areas and dining rooms are pleasantly appointed in country style; there are a library, fireplace, and puzzles aplenty. Most of the guest rooms are bright and airy, outfitted with antiques, old furniture, and modern bathrooms. Guests opting for meal plans get dibs on rooms overlooking the water, which are nice (though the fare is middling). There's also a set of cottages of varied vintages and styles in the woods and on the water, all with fireplaces and kitchenettes.

P.O. Box 137, Southwest Harbor, ME 04679. (C) 800/244-5036. www.theclaremonthotel.com. 44 units. Inn rooms: July–Aug $184–$245 double; mid-June to late June and Sept to mid-Oct $115–$175 double. Cottages July–Aug $203–$291 double; late May–June and Sept to mid-Oct $150–$218 double. Rates include breakfast. MAP rates available for inn rooms only. MC, V. 3-night minimum in cottages. Closed mid-Oct to late May; inn rooms closed until mid-June. **Amenities:** 2 restaurants; lounge; tennis court; rowboats; free bikes; babysitting; croquet. *In room:* Kitchenette (some units).

Inn at Southwest (★) There's a decidedly late-19th-century air to this mansard-roofed Victorian home, but it holds back on overdoing the frills. All guest rooms, named for Maine lighthouses, are outfitted with both contemporary and antique furniture. All rooms have ceiling fans and down comforters. Among the most pleasant rooms is Blue Hill Bay, on the third floor, with its yellow-and-blue color scheme, large bathroom, sturdy oak bed and bureau, and glimpses of the scenic harbor; Pumpkin Island, featuring a sleigh bed and a rosewood sofa; and the Winter Harbor Suite, which has a pencil-poster canopy bed, French doors, and a gas-log fireplace. Breakfasts here give lodgers good incentive to rise and shine, with changing specialties such as Belgian waffles with raspberry sauce, poached pears, and blueberry-stuffed French toast.

371 Main St. (P.O. Box 593), Southwest Harbor, ME 04679. (C) 207/244-3835. www.innatsouthwest.com. 7 units. $105–$185 double. Rates include full breakfast. DISC, MC, V. Closed Nov–late Apr. *In room:* No phone.

Kingsleigh Inn (★) In a 1904 Queen Anne–style home right on Southwest Harbor's Main Street, the Kingsleigh has long been a reliable stop. Its living room features a wood-burning fireplace and fine art, while sitting and breakfast rooms offer further refuge. All rooms are outfitted with sound machines (to drown out ambient noise), wine glasses, and robes; some also have air-conditioners. The huge third-floor suite has outstanding views (with a telescope to see them better), VCR and DVD players, a fireplace, and a king-size bed, though other rooms are only small to moderately sized. The three-course breakfasts are filling and artistic, with choices such as asparagus frittata, fruit crepes, Belgian waffles, and stuffed French toast. Other nice touches include walking sticks for guest use and all-day, self-service espresso.

373 Main St. (P.O. Box 1426), Southwest Harbor, ME 04679. (C) 207/244-5302. Fax 207/244-7691. www.kingsleigh inn.com. 8 units. $130–$195 double, $245–$305 suite. Closed Nov–Mar. Rates include full breakfast. Children 13 and older welcome. AE, MC, V. *In room:* A/C (some units), hair dryer, no phone.

Lindenwood Inn (★★) Innkeeper Jim King gave up cabinetmaking to open a string of successful B&Bs in Southwest Harbor, and this latest one is his best; it feels as if you're renting a home for the weekend with friends. In a handsome Queen Anne–style sea captain's home (built in 1904) over the harbor's edge, the Lindenwood has modern rooms done in simple, bold colors and accented with items from King's collections of African and aboriginal art. Most units have balconies and lots of windows, some also have fireplaces or French doors, and all contain wonderfully comfy beds. The breakfast room, lobby, and lounge are very appealing (and have recently been redesigned), as is the heated in-ground pool. Breakfasts of French toast, thick blueberry pancakes, or whatever else is cooking are always good, and there's a small honor bar for fixing a late-night cocktail. The biggest draw, however, is the outstanding hospitality.

118 Clark Point Rd. (P.O. Box 1328), Southwest Harbor, ME 04679. ℂ 800/307-5335 or 207/244-5335. www.lindenwood inn.com. 8 units. July–Oct $125–$195 double; $225–$325 suite. Nov–June $85–$175 double; $165–$295 suite. Rates include full breakfast. AE, MC, V. **Amenities:** Bar; heated outdoor pool; Jacuzzi. *In room:* TV, kitchenette (1 unit), fridge (2 units), no phone.

WHERE TO DINE

Beal's Lobster Pound ⭑ LOBSTER POUND   Purists claim this is among the best lobster shacks in Maine. It's certainly got the atmosphere: Creaky picnic tables on a plain concrete pier that overlooks a working-class harbor and is next to the Coast Guard base. Translation: Don't wear a jacket and tie. You go inside to pick out lobster from a tank (pay by the pound), then choose side dishes (corn on the cob, slaw, steamed clams) and wait for your number to be called. Your meal will arrive on Styrofoam or paper plates, but you won't care. There's also a takeout window across the deck serving fries, fried clams, and fried fish (sensing a theme?), plus ice-cream cones.

182 Clark Point Rd., Southwest Harbor. ℂ **207/244-7178** or 207/244-3202. www.bealslobster.com. Lobsters market price. AE, DISC, MC, V. Summer daily 9am–8pm; after Labor Day 9am–5pm. Closed Columbus Day–Memorial Day.

The Burning Tree ⭑⭑ *Finds* REGIONAL/SEAFOOD   Located on a busy straightaway of Route 3 between Bar Harbor and Otter Creek, The Burning Tree is an easy restaurant to speed right past; that would be a mistake. This low-key place, with its bright, open, and sometimes noisy dining room, serves up some of the best and freshest dinners on the island. Much of the produce and herbs comes from its own gardens, with the rest of the ingredients supplied locally whenever possible. Seafood is the specialty here, and it's consistently prepared with imagination and skill—expect unusual spicing (like New Orleans-style lobster) and combinations.

Rte. 3, Otter Creek. ℂ 207/288-9331. Reservations recommended. Main courses $18–$23. DISC, MC, V. Mid-June to Columbus Day Wed–Mon 5–10pm. Closed Columbus Day–late May.

Fiddlers' Green ⭑⭑ *Kids* ECLECTIC/NEW AMERICAN   Island native chef Derek Wilbur's bistro is a big hit in these seafaring parts. Begin with something from the cold seafood bar: smoked salmon wrapped in gravlax and horseradish chèvre, oysters on the half shell, or Wilbur's sashimi martini—a cup of smoked mussels, scallop *ceviche*, and raw tuna in a pear-tahini marinade. Or start with such small plates as Thai-curried shrimp with coconut milk, fried catfish filet with a Cajun rémoulade, or smoked baby-back ribs. There are always lots of steaks and a few excellent pasta dishes on the menu, such as lobster strozzapreti with a *vinho verde* cream sauce, and meatier main dishes could include Asian hot pots, Creole-spiced roasted half chickens, pork Cubano, tempura-fried scallops, lobster pot pie, or a good old steamed lobster. There's quite an extensive wine list, and martini drinkers should take note: Wilbur's bar serves a long list of classic and obscure versions. There's even a kids' menu.

411 Main St., Southwest Harbor. ℂ 207/244-9416. www.fiddlersgreenrestaurant.com. Reservations recommended. Main courses $16–$32. AE, DISC, MC, V. Tues–Sun 11:30am–3pm and 5:30–9pm. Closed Columbus Day–Memorial Day.

Red Sky ⭑⭑ CONTINENTAL/NEW AMERICAN   Despite a change in ownership and chefs, Red Sky continues to bring big-city dining sensibilities to its little village. Meals takes New England ingredients to creative heights, using French and other Continental techniques and accents. Begin with intriguing starters like organic chicken-liver pâté, baked oysters stuffed with crab and bacon, duck-pork sausage, or a crispy, layered polenta. Salads here are excellent, and main courses run to choices like a New York strip steak grilled and topped with Maytag blue cheese, Dijon-baked salmon, spicy molasses-flavored grilled scallops, pan-roasted breast of duck with blueberry Chambord sauce, and maple-glazed baby-back ribs. Finish with a very lemony lemon cake, bittersweet Belgian chocolate pudding, toasted gingerbread with caramel sauce and brandied whipped cream, or one of the sorbets or ice creams.

14 Clark Point Rd., Southwest Harbor. © 207/244-0476. www.redskyrestaurant.com. Entrees $19–$30. AE, DISC, MC, V. July–Sept Wed–Sun 5:30–9pm; rest of the year, closed Sun. Closed Jan.

7 Western Maine ⟨★⟩

Bethel is 70 miles NW of Portland, 135 miles NE of Concord, and 180 miles N of Boston

Maine's western mountains are in a rugged, brawny region that stretches northeast between the White Mountains and the Carrabassett Valley. The Whites are bigger, and the Maine coast is a lot more commercialized and convenient, than this region. The villages here aren't nearly as quaint as those in Vermont. But you will find natural wonders here that those other places can't touch: huge azure lakes and sparkling little ponds; forests thick with spruce and fir; mossy, mossy woods (to borrow from Thoreau); and more mountains and foothills than you could tramp through in a lifetime.

BETHEL ⟨★★⟩

Until pretty recently, **Bethel** was a sleepy resort town with one of those family-oriented ski areas that seemed destined for mothballs. But then the **Sunday River** ski area changed hands to those of a brash entrepreneur, who dusted it up, turned it upside down, and eventually remade it over into one of New England's most vibrant and challenging ski destinations.

With the rise of Sunday River, the sturdy New England town of Bethel (about 7 miles from the ski area) has been dragged into the modern era, and it hasn't (yet) taken on the artificial, packaged flavor of most other New England ski towns. This village is still defined by the stoic buildings of the respected Gould Academy prep school; a broad village common; and The Bethel Inn, a sprawling, old-fashioned resort that's managed to stay ahead of the tide by adding condos without ever losing its pleasant, timeworn character.

ESSENTIALS

GETTING THERE   Downtown Bethel is a simple turnoff from the intersection of two busy roads, Route 26 and U.S. 2. Get there from Portland or Boston via the Maine Turnpike (I-95), taking exit 63 ("Gray") and heading west on Route 26 for about 1 hour. From New Hampshire, drive east of Gorham on U.S. Route 2 for 20 to 30 minutes.

There's a very helpful free shuttle, the **Mountain Explorer** (© **207/784-9335**), between downtown Bethel and the ski resort. It runs on Saturday and Sunday from Thanksgiving until just before Christmas, and then daily until early April, from around 6:30am to midnight.

VISITOR INFORMATION   The **Bethel Area Chamber of Commerce,** 30 Cross St., Bethel, ME 04217 (© **800/442-5826** or 207/824-2282; www.bethelmaine.com), has offices at 8 Station Place, behind the movie theater. It's open Monday to Friday until 8pm, Saturdays to 6pm, and Sundays to 5pm.

GRAFTON NOTCH STATE PARK

Grafton Notch State Park ★★ straddles Route 26 as it angles northwest from Bethel into New Hampshire. This 33-mile drive, one of my favorites in the state, is both picturesque and dramatic, and unlike the Kancamangus Highway, it's never stop-and-go (there are no services along the way; gas up if needed). You begin by passing through fertile farmlands in a broad river valley before ascending through bristly forests to a glacial notch hemmed in by rough, gray cliffs on the hillsides above. Foreboding **Old Speck Mountain** towers to the south; views of **Lake Umbagog** open to the north as you continue into New Hampshire. The foliage is excellent in early October most years as well. This route attracts few crowds, though it's popular with Canadian tourists (and Canadian logging rigs loaded up with big trees) heading for the Maine coast.

Public access to the park consists of a handful of roadside parking lots near scenic areas. The best of the bunch is **Screw Auger Falls** ★, where the Bear River drops through several small cascades before tumbling dramatically into a narrow, corkscrewing gorge carved long ago by glacial runoff through granite bedrock. Picnic tables dot the forested banks upriver of the falls, and kids seem inexorably drawn to splash and swim in the smaller pools on warm days. From mid-May through mid-October, $2 per person admission is charged to the 3,000-acre park (discounted for kids, free for seniors); get a pass at a self-pay station in a parking lot.

DOWNHILL SKIING

Sunday River Ski Resort ★★★   Sunday River has grown at stunning speed and swiftly become one of the best ski mountains in New England for its terrain and conditions. (The resort scene still lags a bit, though there's a good brewery on site.) Unlike ski areas that developed around a single tall peak, Sunday River expanded along an undulating ridge 3 miles wide that encompasses a total of *seven* peaks. Simply traversing the resort, stitching a run together via the various chairlift rides, can take an hour or more. As a result, you're rarely bored. The descents offer something for everyone, from deviously steep bump runs to wide, wonderful intermediate trails. Sunday River is also blessed with plenty of water for snowmaking, and makes tons of the stuff using a proprietary system. The superb skiing conditions are, alas, offset by an uninspiring base area. The lodges and condos here tend toward the architecturally dull. Trails here are so good that they're often crowded on Saturdays and Sundays, even though there isn't a significant population center of size for miles; come Monday to Friday, though, and you'll pretty much have the place to yourself.

P.O. Box 450, Bethel, ME 04217. ℂ 207/824-3000. www.sundayriver.com. Adult day lift tickets $69–$72; adult half-day lift tickets $52; discounts for seniors, youth, and children.

OTHER OUTDOOR PURSUITS

GOLF   The Bethel Inn's **Country Club** (ℂ **207/824-6276)** is an unusually scenic 18-hole golf course right next to the inn. Greens fees for 18 holes cost $30 to $50 per person. Clubs and golf carts can be rented, and the club also has a driving range; tee times are not mandatory, but they're strongly recommended in high season.

HIKING   The **Appalachian Trail** ★★★ crosses the Mahoosuc Range northwest of Bethel. Many who have hiked the entire 2,000-mile trail say this stretch is the most demanding on knees and psyches, but also one of the mostly weirdly beautiful. The trail doesn't forgive; it foregoes switchbacks in favor of sheer rocky ascents and descents. It's also hard to find water along the trail here during dry weather. Still, it's worth the effort for the views and unrivaled sense of remoteness.

One stretch of the trail crosses **Old Speck Mountain** ✿, which at 4,170 feet is (surprisingly) Maine's third-highest peak. Views from the wooded summit are nonexistent since an old fire tower closed, but an easy-to-moderate spur trail on the lower end of the trail ascends an 800-foot cliff called "The Eyebrow" (not for those afraid of heights) with a good vantage point on the rugged terrain of the Notch. Or you can continue past the summit down into a bowl containing Old Speck Lake and a primitive campsite. Look for the well-signed parking lot where Route 26 intersects the trail the state park; park, pay, strap on boots (spots are muddy), and head south on the A.T. to climb Old Speck; in one-tenth of a mile, you'll intersect the Eyebrow Trail, which you can follow to the overlook. Continuing upward, you'll encounter mild cascades and increasing views of the valley foliage.

Across Route 26, the A.T. runs east and up **Baldpate Mountain** (the face and top have patches of open ledge) on its meandering way toward the trail's finish line at Mount Katahdin (p. 667). Baldpate is higher than you might think: Its summit is only about 400 feet lower than the rival it directly faces.

The Appalachian Mountain Club's *Maine Mountain Guide* contains detailed information about these and other area hikes; pick up a copy if you're a serious walker.

WHERE TO STAY

The Bethel Inn Resort ✿   A classic, old-fashioned resort set on 200 acres right in Bethel village, this inn has a quiet and settled air—appropriate, since it was built to house patients of one Dr. John Gehring, who put Bethel on the map by treating nervous disorders here through a regimen of healthy country living. (The town was once known as "the resting place of Harvard" for the legions of faculty treated here.) The quaint, homey rooms aren't especially spacious, but they are pleasingly furnished with country antiques. Rooms and suites added to the inn in the late 1990s are more modern, with amenities such as DVD players or Jacuzzis in some, and air-conditioning (which the main inn lacks). You give up some of the charm of the main building here, but gain elbow room and creature comforts. Some spa services have recently been added, and the **cross-country ski center** ✿ and golf course are each scenic and excellent.

On the Common, Bethel, ME 04217. ℂ **800/654-0125** or 207/824-2175. www.bethelinn.com. 150 units. Summer $198–$418 double; winter $158–$454 double. Rates include breakfast and dinner. Packages available. 2-night minimum stay summer weekends and ski season; 3-night minimum stay during winter school vacations. AE, DISC, MC, V. Pets allowed ($10 per night). **Amenities:** 2 restaurants; bar; outdoor pool; golf course; tennis court; fitness center; Jacuzzi; sauna; shuttle to ski areas; watersports equipment rental; massage; babysitting; laundry service. *In room:* A/C (some units), TV, hair dryer, iron/ironing board, fireplace (some units), Jacuzzi (some units).

Jordan Grand Resort Hotel ✿ *Kids*

The anchor for expanded development in the far-flung Jordan Bowl area, this hotel feels miles away from the rest of the resort, largely because it is—even the staff makes *The Shining* jokes about its remoteness. A modern if sprawling hotel, it offers little personal touch or flair, but boasts a great location for skiers who want to be first on untracked slopes each morning. Owing to the quirky terrain, parking is inconvenient; you often have to walk some distance to your room (opt for valet parking). Rooms are simply furnished in a durable condo style. Many are quite spacious and most have balconies. It's a popular destination with families, so not the best choice for couples seeking a quiet getaway. Sunday River has improved its food service; its two restaurants are a notch above ski-area hotel fare.

Sunday River Rd. (P.O. Box 450), Bethel, ME 04217. © 800/543-2754 or 207/824-5000. Fax 207/824-2111. www. sundayriver.com. 195 units. $117–$332 double. AE, DC, DISC, MC, V. Valet parking. **Amenities:** 2 restaurants; outdoor pool; fitness room; Jacuzzi; sauna; steam room; children's center; concierge; business center; coin-op laundry; limited room service; massage; babysitting; dry cleaning. In room: A/C, TV, dataport, kitchenette (some units), coffeemaker.

The Victoria 𝒢𝒢   Built in 1895 and damaged by lightning some years back, the homey Victoria was restored in 1998 with antique lighting fixtures, period furniture, and the original, formidable oak doors. It's a good sleeper pick when you want to get away from resortville. Guest rooms have a luxurious, William Morris feel, with richly patterned wallpaper and handmade duvet covers. Room no. 1 is a luxurious master suite, with a turret window and sizable bathroom; no. 3 is the only unit with wood floors (all the others are carpeted), but it has a tiny bathroom. Most intriguing are the four "loft" rooms in an attached carriage house, each with a gas fireplace, Jacuzzi, and soaring ceilings revealing some of the rugged original beams. These suites have small second-story sleeping lofts, and sleep up to eight guests each. The dining room is worth a look as a fancy night out (see "Where to Dine," below).

32 Main St. (P.O. Box 249), Bethel, ME 04217. © 888/774-1235 or 207/824-8060. www.thevictoria-inn.com. 15 units. $89–$179 double; $169–$309 suite. Rates include full breakfast. 2-night minimum stay Sat–Sun and holidays. AE, MC, V. Pets sometimes allowed ($30 per night). **Amenities:** Restaurant (see below). In room: A/C, TV, dataport, hair dryer, fireplace (some units), Jacuzzi (some units).

WHERE TO DINE

The **Sunday River** ski resort is probably your best bet: It offers a total of eight dining experiences at last count, most of the pub food variety; of these eight, however, the three inside the resort's two hotels—the **Grand Summit Resort** and the **Jordan Grand Resort**—are pretty decent.

Sunday River Brewing Company PUB FARE   This modern brewpub, on prime real estate at the corner of Route 2 and the Sunday River access road, is a good choice if your objective is to quaff locally brewed ales and porters. Its motto? "Eat Food. Drink Beer. Have Fun." That about says it. The beers are good; the food (burgers, nachos, wings, pork sandwiches) doesn't strive for culinary heights. Come early if you're looking for a quiet bite, as it can sometimes get loud later when bands take the stage.

Rte. 2 (at Sunday River Rd.), Bethel. © 207/824-4253. Reservations not accepted. Main courses $8–$16. AE, MC, V. Mon–Thurs 11:30am–9:30pm; Fri–Sun 11:30am–11:30pm.

8 Baxter State Park & Environs 𝒢𝒢𝒢

Baxter State Park is one of Maine's crown jewels, even more spectacular in some ways than Acadia National Park. This 200,000-plus-acre park in the remote north-central part of the state is unlike most state parks you may be accustomed to in New England—don't look for fancy bathhouses or groomed picnic areas. When you enter Baxter State Park, you enter near-wilderness.

Former Maine governor and philanthropist Percival Baxter single-handedly created the park, using his inheritance and investment profits to buy the property and donate it to the state in 1930. Baxter stipulated that it remain "forever wild." Caretakers have done a good job fulfilling his wishes: You won't find paved roads, RVs, or hook-ups at the campgrounds. (Size restrictions keep all RVs out.) Even cellphones are banned. You will find rugged backcountry and remote lakes. You'll also find Mount Katahdin, a granite monolith that rises above the sparkling lakes and boreal forests around it.

> ⟨*Tips* **Grinning and Bearing It In Baxter**
>
> There are a few dozen black bears in Baxter State Park, and while they are not out to eat you, they do get ornery when disturbed, and they do get hungry at night. The park has published these tips to help you keep a safe distance:
>
> • Put all food and anything else with an odor (toothpaste, repellent, soap, deodorant, perfume) in a sealed bag or container and keep it in your car.
> • If you're camping in the backcountry without a car, put all your food, dinner leftovers, and other "smelly" things in a bag and hang it between two trees (far from your tent) so that a bear can't reach it easily. Never keep any food in your tent.
> • Take all your trash with you from the campsite when you leave.
> • Do I need to say this? Don't feed the bears, and don't toss food on the trail.

ESSENTIALS

GETTING THERE   Baxter State Park is 85 miles north of Bangor. Take I-95 to Medway (exit 244), then head west 11 miles on Route 11/157 to the mill town of Millinocket, the last major stop for supplies. Go through town and follow signs to Baxter State Park. Another, less-used entrance is in the park's northeast corner. Follow I-95 to exit 259, then take Route 11 north through Patten and west on Route 159 to the park. The speed limit in the park is 20 mph; motorcycles and ATVs are not allowed.

VISITOR INFORMATION   Baxter State Park provides maps and information from its **park headquarters,** at 64 Balsam Dr. in Millinocket (✆ **207/723-5140;** www.baxterstateparkauthority.com). Note that no pets are allowed into the park, and all trash you generate must be brought back out. For information on canoeing and camping *outside* of Baxter State Park, contact **Maine Woods, Inc.,** 92 Main St. (P.O. Box 421), Ashland, ME 04732 (✆ **207/435-6213;** www.northmainewoods.org). This is the consortium of paper companies, other landowners, and concerned individuals which controls and manages recreational access to private parcels of the Maine woods.

For help finding cottages, rentals, and tour outfitters in the area, contact the **Katahdin Area Chamber of Commerce,** 1029 Central St., Millinocket, ME 04462 (✆ **207/723-4443;** www.katahdinmaine.com), open Monday to Friday from 9am to 1pm.

FEES   Baxter State Park visitors driving cars with out-of-state license plates are charged a per-day fee of $12 per car. (It's free to Maine residents, as well as to any occupants of a rental car bearing Maine plates.) This fee is charged only once per stay if you're coming to camp; otherwise, you need to re-pay each day you enter the park.

OUTDOORS PURSUITS

BACKPACKING   The park maintains about 180 miles of backcountry hiking trails and more than 25 backcountry campsites, some of them accessible only by canoe. Most hikers coming to the park are intent on ascending **Mount Katahdin** (see below), Maine's highest peak; but dozens of other peaks are well worth scaling as well, and simply walking through the deep woods here is a sublime experience in stretches; you will hear no chainsaws. Reservations are required for backcountry camping; many of the best spots fill up quickly in early January when reservations open for a calendar year (see "Camping," below).

En route to Katahdin, the Appalachian Trail winds through the "100-mile Wilderness," a remote stretch where the trail crosses few roads; it's a wild, spare land of loons and moose. Get trail maps from the **Appalachian Trail Conference,** P.O. Box 807, Harpers Ferry, WV 25425 (© **304/535-6331;** www.appalachiantrail.org).

CAMPING   Baxter State Park has eight **campgrounds** accessible by car and two more backcountry camping areas that must be walked into; most are open from mid-May until mid-October. Don't count on finding a spot if you show up without reservations in mid-summer; the park starts processing requests on a first-come, first-served basis the first week in January. Call well in advance (as in, during the previous year) for the forms to mail in. Camping inside the park costs $9 to $18 per site, with some cabins and bunkhouses available at rates ranging from $10 to $30 per person. Reservations can be made by mail, in person at the headquarters in Millinocket (see "Visitor Information," above), or (sometimes) by phone—but *only* less than 14 days from arrival. Don't call them about any other dates.

HIKING   With 180 miles of maintained backcountry trails and 46 peaks (including 18 that are higher than 3,000 ft.), Baxter State Park is a serious destination for serious hikers. The most imposing peak is 5,267-foot **Mount Katahdin** ★★★, the northern terminus of the **Appalachian Trail.** An ascent up this rugged, glacially scoured mountain is a trip you'll not soon forget. The raw drama and grandeur of the rocky, windswept summit is equal to anything you'll find in the White Mountains.

Allow at least 8 hours for the round-trip, and turn back if the weather takes turns bad en route. The most popular route departs from **Roaring Brook Campground**— so popular it's closed to day hikers when the parking lot fills. Get there early. You ascend first to dramatic **Chimney Pond,** which is set like a jewel in a glacial cirque, then continue upward toward Katahdin's summit via one of two trails. (The **Saddle Trail** is the most forgiving, the **Cathedral Trail** ★ the most dramatic.) From here, descent begins along the tricky **Knife Edge,** a narrow, rocky spine between Baxter Peak and Pamola Peak. Do *not* take this trail if you are afraid of heights, or in windy weather: In spots, it narrows to just 2 or 3 feet wide, with a drop hundreds of feet down on either side. From the Knife Edge, the trail follows a long, gentle ridge back to Roaring Brook.

Appendix: Fast Facts, Toll-Free Numbers & Websites

1 Fast Facts: New England

AMERICAN EXPRESS American Express offers travel services, including check cashing and trip planning, through a number of affiliated agencies in the region. Call © **800/221-7282** for the nearest location.

AREA CODES **Massachusetts** is now divided into a number of area codes: 617 and 857 for Boston; 781 and 339 for a suburban ring surrounding Boston; 508, 978, 774, and 351 for central Massachusetts and Cape Cod; and 413 for western Massachusetts.

Connecticut uses 860 and 959 for Hartford and northern and eastern parts of the state, 203 and 475 for roughly the southwestern quarter of the state (the part closest to New York City).

Rhode Island's area code is 401. **Vermont's** is 802. **New Hampshire's** is 603. **Maine's** is 207.

ATM NETWORKS See "Money & Costs," p. 51.

AUTOMOBILE ORGANIZATIONS Motor clubs will supply maps, suggested routes, guidebooks, accident and bail-bond insurance, and emergency road service. The **American Automobile Association (AAA)** is the major auto club in the United States. If you belong to a motor club in your home country, inquire about AAA reciprocity before you leave. You may be able to join AAA even if you're not a member of a reciprocal club; to inquire, call AAA (© **800/222-4357**; www.aaa.com). AAA is actually an organization of regional motor clubs, so look under "AAA Automobile Club" in the White Pages of the telephone directory. AAA has a nationwide emergency road service telephone number (© 800/AAA-HELP).

BUSINESS HOURS Banks are generally open Monday to Friday 9am to 3pm. Drive-in teller hours are longer. Shops are usually open Monday to Friday from 9am to 6pm, Saturday from 10am to 6 or 7pm, and Sunday from noon until 5 or 6pm. In bigger cities or in shopping-mall or outlet-shop areas, these hours will be somewhat extended, as late as 9pm during peak summer shopping season.

CAR RENTALS See "Toll-Free Numbers & Websites," p. 675.

DRINKING LAWS The legal age for purchase and consumption of alcoholic beverages is 21; proof of age is required and often requested at bars, nightclubs, and restaurants, so it's always a good idea to bring ID when you go out.

Do not carry open containers of alcohol in your car or any public area that isn't zoned for alcohol consumption. The police can fine you on the spot. And nothing will ruin your trip faster than getting a citation for DUI ("driving under the influence"), so don't even think about driving while intoxicated.

DRIVING RULES See "Getting There & Getting Around," p. 45.

ELECTRICITY Like Canada, the United States uses 110 to 120 volts AC (60 cycles), compared to 220 to 240 volts AC (50 cycles) in most of Europe, Australia, and New Zealand. Downward converters that change 220–240 volts to 110–120 volts are difficult to find in the United States, so bring one with you.

If you're coming from Europe, bring a **connection kit** of the right power and phone adapters, a spare phone cord, and a spare Ethernet network cable—or find out whether your hotel supplies them to guests.

EMBASSIES & CONSULATES All embassies are located in the nation's capital, Washington, D.C. Some consulates are located in major U.S. cities, and most nations have a mission to the United Nations in New York City. If your country isn't listed below, call for directory information in Washington, D.C. (© 202/555-1212), or check **www.embassy.org/embassies**.

The embassy of **Australia** is at 1601 Massachusetts Ave. NW, Washington, DC 20036 (© **202/797-3000;** www.austemb.org).

The embassy of **Canada** is at 501 Pennsylvania Ave. NW, Washington, DC 20001 (© **202/682-1740;** www.canadianembassy.org). Other Canadian consulates are in Buffalo (New York), Detroit, Los Angeles, New York, and Seattle.

The embassy of **Ireland** is at 2234 Massachusetts Ave. NW, Washington, DC 20008 (© **202/462-3939;** www.irelandemb.org). Irish consulates are in Boston, Chicago, New York, San Francisco, and other cities. See website for complete listing.

The embassy of **New Zealand** is at 37 Observatory Circle NW, Washington, DC 20008 (© **202/328-4800;** www.nzembassy.com). New Zealand consulates are in Los Angeles, Salt Lake City, San Francisco, and Seattle.

The embassy of the **United Kingdom** is at 3100 Massachusetts Ave. NW, Washington, DC 20008 (© **202/588-7800;** www.britainusa.com). Other British consulates are in Atlanta, Boston, Chicago,

Cleveland, Houston, Los Angeles, New York, San Francisco, and Seattle.

EMERGENCIES For fire, police, and ambulance, find any phone and dial © **911.** If this fails, dial 0 (zero) and report an emergency.

GASOLINE (PETROL) At press time, in the U.S., the cost of gasoline (also known as gas, but never petrol), is abnormally high. Gas prices in New England are about average for the U.S., in spots a big higher. Taxes are included in the price listed on gas station signs. One U.S. gallon equals 3.8 liters or .85 imperial gallons. Fill-up locations are known as gas or service stations.

HOLIDAYS Banks, government offices, post offices, and many stores, restaurants, and museums are closed on the following legal national holidays: January 1 (New Year's Day), the third Monday in January (Martin Luther King, Jr., Day), the third Monday in February (Presidents' Day), the last Monday in May (Memorial Day), July 4 (Independence Day), the first Monday in September (Labor Day), the second Monday in October (Columbus Day), November 11 (Veterans' Day/Armistice Day), the fourth Thursday in November (Thanksgiving Day), and December 25 (Christmas). The Tuesday after the first Monday in November is Election Day, a federal government holiday in presidential-election years (held every 4 years, and next in 2008).

Some states have their own special state holidays, too. Maine and Massachusetts celebrate **Patriots Day** on a Monday in mid-April, while Vermont observes **Town Meeting Day** on the first Tuesday in March and also **Bennington Battle Day** in mid-August. All state offices are closed on these days. Most state offices in the states also close on the day after Thanksgiving, which changes annually.

For more information on holidays, see "New England Calendar of Events," in chapter 3.

INSURANCE Health Insurance Although it's not required of travelers, health insurance is highly recommended. Most health insurance policies cover you if you get sick away from home—but check your coverage before you leave.

International visitors to the U.S. should note that, unlike many European countries, the United States does not usually offer free or low-cost medical care to its citizens or visitors. Doctors and hospitals are expensive and, in most cases, will require advance payment or proof of coverage before they render their services. Good policies will cover the costs of an accident, repatriation, or death. Packages such as **Europ Assistance's Worldwide Healthcare Plan** are sold by European automobile clubs and travel agencies at attractive rates. **Worldwide Assistance Services, Inc.** (© 800/777-8710; www.worldwideassistance.com), is the agent for Europ Assistance in the United States. Though lack of health insurance may prevent you from being admitted to a hospital in nonemergencies, don't worry about being left on a street corner to die: The American way is to fix you now and bill the daylights out of you later.

If you're ever hospitalized more than 150 miles from home, **MedjetAssist** (© 800/527-7478; www.medjetassistance.com) will pick you up and fly you to the hospital of your choice in a medically equipped and staffed aircraft 24 hours a day, 7 days a week. Annual memberships are $225 individual, $350 family; you can also purchase short-term memberships.

Canadians should check with their provincial health plan offices or call **Health Canada** (© 866/225-0709; www.hc-sc.gc.ca) to find out the extent of their coverage and what documentation and receipts they must take home in case they are treated in the United States.

Travelers from the U.K. should carry their European Health Insurance Card (EHIC), which replaced the E111 form as proof of entitlement to free/reduced-cost medical treatment abroad (© **0845 606 2030;** www.ehic.org.uk). Note, however, that the EHIC covers only "necessary medical treatment," and for repatriation costs, lost money, baggage, or cancellation, travel insurance from a reputable company should always be sought (see www.travelinsuranceweb.com).

As a safety net, you may want to buy travel medical insurance, particularly if you're traveling to a remote or high-risk area where emergency evacuation might be necessary. If you require additional medical insurance, try **MEDEX Assistance** (© 410/453-6300; www.medexassist.com) or **Travel Assistance International** (© 800/821-2828; www.travelassistance.com; for general information on services, call the company's **Worldwide Assistance Services, Inc.**, at © 800/777-8710).

Travel Insurance The cost of travel insurance varies widely, depending on the destination, the cost and length of your trip, your age and health, and the type of trip you're taking, but expect to pay between 5% and 8% of the vacation itself. You can get estimates from various providers through **InsureMyTrip.com.** Enter your trip cost and dates, your age, and other information, for prices from more than a dozen companies.

U.K. citizens and their families who make more than one trip abroad per year may find an annual travel insurance policy works out cheaper. Check **www.moneysupermarket.com**, which compares prices across a wide range of providers for single- and multitrip policies.

Most big travel agents offer their own insurance and will probably try to sell you their package when you book a holiday. Think before you sign. **Britain's Consumers' Association** recommends that you insist on seeing the policy and reading the fine print before buying travel insurance. **The Association of British**

Insurers (✆ 020/7600-3333; www.abi.
org.uk) gives advice by phone and publishes Holiday Insurance, a free guide to policy provisions and prices. You might also shop around for better deals: Try **Columbus Direct** (✆ 0870/033-9988; www.columbusdirect.net).

Trip Cancellation Insurance Trip-cancellation insurance will help retrieve your money if you have to back out of a trip or depart early, or if your travel supplier goes bankrupt. Trip cancellation traditionally covers such events as sickness, natural disasters, and State Department advisories. The latest news in trip-cancellation insurance is the availability of **expanded hurricane coverage** and the **"any-reason"** cancellation coverage—which costs more but covers cancellations made for any reason. You won't get back 100% of your prepaid trip cost, but you'll be refunded a substantial portion. **Travel-Safe** (✆ 888/885-7233; www.travel-safe.com) offers both types of coverage. Expedia also offers any-reason cancellation coverage for its air-hotel packages. For details, contact one of the following recommended insurers: **Access America** (✆ 866/807-3982; www.accessamerica.com), **Travel Guard International** (✆ 800/826-4919; www.travelguard.com), **Travel Insured International** (✆ 800/243-3174; www.travelinsured.com), or **Travelex Insurance Services** (✆ 888/457-4602; www.travelex-insurance.com).

INTERNET ACCESS Many public libraries in New England have terminals with free Internet access. For the most part, Internet cafes have come and gone in the last few years; it's best to ask around locally, or try visiting **www.netcafe guide.com** or **www.cybercafe.com**.

LEGAL AID If you are "pulled over" for a minor infraction (such as speeding), never attempt to pay the fine directly to a police officer; this could be construed as attempted bribery, a much more serious crime. Pay fines by mail or directly into the hands of the clerk of the court. If accused of a more serious offense, say and do nothing before consulting a lawyer. Here the burden is on the state to prove a person's guilt beyond a reasonable doubt, and everyone has the right to remain silent, whether he or she is suspected of a crime or actually arrested. Once arrested, a person can make one telephone call to a party of his or her choice. International visitors should call their embassy or consulate.

LOST & FOUND Be sure to tell all of your credit card companies the minute you discover your wallet has been lost or stolen and file a report at the nearest police precinct. Your credit card company or insurer may require a police report number or record of the loss. Most credit card companies have an emergency toll-free number to call if your card is lost or stolen; they may be able to wire you a cash advance immediately or deliver an emergency credit card in a day or two.

Visa's U.S. emergency number is ✆ 800/847-2911 or 410/581-9994. American Express cardholders and traveler's check holders should call ✆ 800/221-7282. MasterCard holders should call ✆ 800/307-7309 or 636/722-7111. For other credit cards, call the toll-free number directory at ✆ 800/555-1212.

If you need emergency cash over the weekend when all banks and American Express offices are closed, you can have money wired to you via **Western Union** (✆ 800/325-6000; www.westernunion.com).

MAIL At press time, domestic postage rates were 27¢ for a postcard and 42¢ for a letter. For international mail, a first-class letter of up to 1 ounce costs 94¢ (72¢ to Canada and Mexico); a first-class postcard costs the same as a letter. For more information go to **www.usps.com** and click on "Calculate Postage."

If you aren't sure what your address will be in the United States, mail can be sent to you, in your name, c/o General Delivery at the main post office of the city or region where you expect to be. (Call © **800/275-8777** for information on the nearest post office.) The addressee must pick up mail in person and must produce proof of identity (driver's license, passport, and so on). Most post offices will hold your mail for up to 1 month, and are open Monday to Friday from 8am to 6pm, and Saturday from 9am to 3pm.

Always include zip codes when mailing items in the U.S. If you don't know your zip code, visit www.usps.com/zip4.

MAPS All the New England states offer free maps at well-stocked visitor information centers; ask at the counter if you don't see them. For incredibly detailed maps, consider purchasing one or more of the **DeLorme** atlases, which depict every road and stream, along with many hiking trails and access points for canoes. DeLorme's headquarters and map store (© **800/561-5105** or 800/642-0970) are in Yarmouth, Maine, but their products are available at bookstores and convenience stores throughout the region.

MEASUREMENTS See the chart on the inside front cover of this book for details on converting metric measurements to nonmetric equivalents.

MEDICAL CONDITIONS If you have a medical condition that requires **syringe-administered medications,** carry a valid signed prescription from your physician; syringes in carry-on baggage will be inspected. Insulin in any form should have the proper pharmaceutical documentation. If you have a disease that requires treatment with **narcotics,** you should also carry documented proof with you—smuggling narcotics aboard a plane carries severe penalties in the U.S.

For **HIV-positive visitors,** requirements for entering the United States are somewhat vague and change frequently. For up-to-the-minute information, contact **AIDSinfo** (© **800/448-0440** or 301/519-6616 outside the U.S.; www.aids info.nih.gov) or the **Gay Men's Health Crisis** (© **212/367-1000;** www.gmhc. org).

NEWSPAPERS & MAGAZINES Almost every small city and town has a daily or weekly newspaper covering local happenings. The largest **daily papers** include the *Boston Globe* (Massachusetts), *Hartford Courant* (Connecticut), *Portland Press Herald* (Maine), *Manchester Union Leader* (New Hampshire), and *Burlington Free Press* (Vermont). Boston, Burlington, Portland, and a few other cities also have **free alternative weeklies** that are very handy sources of information on concerts and shows at local clubs. The *Wall Street Journal* and the *New York Times* are also distributed widely throughout New England, although they can sometimes be hard to find in small or remote towns.

PASSPORTS The websites listed provide downloadable passport applications, as well as the current fees for processing applications. For an up-to-date, country-by-country listing of passport requirements around the world, go to the "International Travel" tab of the U.S. State Department at **http://travel.state. gov**. International visitors to the U.S. can obtain a visa application at the same website. *Note:* Children are required to present a passport when entering the United States at airports. More information on obtaining a passport for a minor can be found at http://travel.state.gov. Allow plenty of time before your trip to apply for a passport; processing normally takes 4–6 weeks (3 weeks for expedited service) but can take longer during busy periods (especially spring). And keep in mind that if you need a passport in a hurry, you'll pay a higher processing fee.

For Residents of Australia You can pick up an application from your local post office or any branch of Passports Australia, but you must schedule an interview at the passport office to present your application materials. Call the **Australian Passport Information Service** at ℂ **131-232,** or visit the government website at www.passports.gov.au.

For Residents of Canada Passport applications are available at travel agencies throughout Canada or from the central **Passport Office,** Department of Foreign Affairs and International Trade, Ottawa, ON K1A 0G3 (ℂ **800/567-6868;** www.ppt.gc.ca). *Note:* Canadian children who travel must have their own passport. However, if you hold a valid Canadian passport issued before December 11, 2001, that bears the name of your child, the passport remains valid for you and your child until it expires.

For Residents of Ireland You can apply for a 10-year passport at the **Passport Office,** Setanta Centre, Molesworth Street, Dublin 2 (ℂ **01/671-1633;** www.irlgov.ie/iveagh). Those under age 18 and over 65 must apply for a 3-year passport. You can also apply at 1A South Mall, Cork (ℂ **21/494-4700**), or at most main post offices.

For Residents of New Zealand You can pick up a passport application at any New Zealand Passports Office or download it from their website. Contact the **Passports Office** at ℂ **0800/225-050** in New Zealand or 04/474-8100, or log on to www.passports.govt.nz.

For Residents of the United Kingdom To pick up an application for a standard 10-year passport (5-yr. passport for children under 16), visit your nearest passport office, major post office, or travel agency, or contact the **United Kingdom Passport Service** at ℂ **0870/521-0410** or search its website at www.ukpa.gov.uk.

For Residents of the United States Whether you're applying in person or by mail, you can download passport applications from the U.S. State Department website at **http://travel.state.gov.** To find your regional passport office, either check the U.S. State Department website or call the **National Passport Information Center** toll-free number (ℂ **877/487-2778**) for automated information.

POLICE For police, dial ℂ **911.** If this fails, dial 0 (zero) and report an emergency.

SMOKING Smoking is now banned in all workplaces and public places (restaurants, bars, offices, hotel lobbies) in all five New England states, though there are some exceptions—casinos in Connecticut, for example, and some private clubs.

TAXES The United States has no value-added tax (VAT) or other indirect tax at the national level. Every state, county, and city may levy its own local tax on all purchases, including hotel and restaurant checks and airline tickets. These taxes will not appear on price tags.

The current state sales taxes in New England, as of early 2008, are: Connecticut, 6% (and 12% on lodging); Maine, 5% (but 7% on lodging and 10% on auto rentals); Massachusetts, 5% (plus local sales taxes such as Boston city or airport taxes on lodging); New Hampshire, no general sales tax but an 8% tax on lodging and dining; Rhode Island, 7% (plus a 5% surtax on lodging); and Vermont, 6% (but 9% on lodging and dining and 10% on alcohol served in restaurants).

TELEPHONES Many convenience groceries and packaging services sell **prepaid calling cards** in denominations up to $50; for international visitors, these can be the least expensive way to call home. Many public pay phones at airports now accept American Express, MasterCard, and Visa credit cards. **Local calls** made from pay phones in most locales cost either 25¢ or 35¢ (no pennies, please). Most long-distance and international calls can be dialed directly from any phone. **For calls within the United States and to Canada,** dial 1 followed by the area code and the seven-digit number. **For other international calls,** dial 011 followed by the country code, city code, and number you are calling.

Calls to area codes **800, 888, 877,** and **866** are toll-free. However, calls to area codes **700** and **900** (chat lines, bulletin boards, "dating" services, and so on) can be very expensive—usually a charge of 95¢ to $3 or more per minute, and they sometimes have minimum charges that can run as high as $15 or more.

For **reversed-charge or collect calls,** and for person-to-person calls, dial the number 0 then the area code and number; an operator will come on the line, and you should specify whether you are calling collect, person-to-person, or both. If your operator-assisted call is international, ask for the overseas operator.

For **local directory assistance** ("information"), dial 411; for long-distance information, dial 1, then the appropriate area code and 555-1212.

TELEGRAPH, TELEX & FAX Tele-graph and telex services are provided primarily by **Western Union** (© **800/ 325-6000;** www.westernunion.com). You can telegraph (wire) money, or have it telegraphed to you, very quickly over the Western Union system, but this service can cost as much as 15% to 20% of the amount sent.

Most hotels have **fax machines** available for guest use (be sure to ask about the charge to use it). Many hotel rooms are wired for guests' fax machines. A less expensive way to send and receive faxes may be at stores such as **The UPS Store.**

TIME The continental United States is divided into four time zones: Eastern Standard Time (EST), Central Standard Time (CST), Mountain Standard Time (MST), and Pacific Standard Time (PST); in addition, Alaska and Hawaii each have their own time zones.

All of New England is in the **Eastern Standard Time zone.** When it's noon in Boston and Portland, it's 11am in Chicago (CST), 10am in Denver (MST), 9am in Los Angeles (PST), and 5pm in London (GMT).

Daylight saving time is in effect from 1am on the second Sunday in March to 1am on the first Sunday in November, except in Arizona, Hawaii, the U.S. Virgin Islands, and Puerto Rico. Daylight saving time moves the clock 1 hour ahead of standard time.

TIPPING Tips are a very important part of certain workers' income, and gratuities are the standard way of showing appreciation for services provided. (However, tipping is certainly not compulsory if service is poor.) In hotels, tip **bellhops** at least $1 per bag ($2–$3 if you have a lot of luggage) and tip the **chamber staff** $1 to $2 per day (more if you've left a disaster area for him or her to clean up). Tip the **doorman** or **concierge** only if he or she has provided you with some specific service (for example, calling a cab for you or obtaining difficult-to-get theater tickets). Tip the **valet-parking attendant** $1 every time you get your car.

In restaurants, bars, and nightclubs, tip **service staff** 15% to 20% of the check, tip **bartenders** 10% to 15%, tip **checkroom attendants** $1 per garment, and tip **valet-parking attendants** $1 per vehicle.

As for other service personnel, tip **cab drivers** 15% of the fare, tip **skycaps** at airports at least $1 per bag ($2–$3 if you have a lot of luggage), and tip **hairdressers** and **barbers** 15% to 20%.

TOILETS You won't find public toilets or "restrooms" on the streets in most U.S. cities but they can be found in hotel lobbies, bars, restaurants, museums, department stores, railway and bus stations, and service stations. Large hotels and fast-food restaurants are often the best bet for clean facilities. Restaurants and bars in resorts or heavily visited areas may reserve their restrooms for patrons.

USEFUL PHONE NUMBERS

U.S. Dept. of State Travel Advisory: ℂ 202/647-5225 (manned 24 hrs.)

U.S. Passport Agency: ℂ 202/647-0518

U.S. Centers for Disease Control International Traveler's Hotline: ℂ 404/332-4559

VISAS For information about U.S. visas, go to **http://travel.state.gov** and click on "Visas." Or go to one of the following websites:

Australian citizens can obtain up-to-date visa information from the **U.S. Embassy Canberra,** Moonah Place, Yarralumla, ACT 2600 (ℂ **02/6214-5600**), or by checking the U.S. Diplomatic Mission's website at **http://us embassy-australia.state.gov/consular**.

British subjects can obtain up-to-date visa information by calling the **U.S. Embassy Visa Information Line** (ℂ **0891/200-290**) or by visiting the "Visas to the U.S." section of the American Embassy London's website at **www.us embassy.org.uk**.

Irish citizens can obtain up-to-date visa information through the **Embassy of the USA Dublin,** 42 Elgin Rd., Dublin 4, Ireland (ℂ **353/1-668-8777**), or by checking the "Consular Services" section of the website at **http://dublin.usembassy.gov**.

Citizens of **New Zealand** can obtain up-to-date visa information by contacting the **U.S. Embassy New Zealand,** 29 Fitzherbert Terrace, Thorndon, Wellington (ℂ **644/472-2068**), or get the information directly from the website at **http://wellington.usembassy.gov**.

MAJOR U.S. AIRLINES

(*flies internationally as well)

American Airlines*
ℂ 800/433-7300 (in U.S. or Canada)
ℂ 020/7365-0777 (in U.K.)
www.aa.com

Cape Air
ℂ 800/352-0714
www.flycapeair.com

Continental Airlines*
ℂ 800/523-3273 (in U.S. or Canada)
ℂ 084/5607-6760 (in U.K.)
www.continental.com

Delta Air Lines*
ℂ 800/221-1212 (in U.S. or Canada)
ℂ 084/5600-0950 (in U.K.)
www.delta.com

Frontier Airlines
ℂ 800/432-1359
www.frontierairlines.com

Midwest Airlines
ℂ 800/452-2022
www.midwestairlines.com

Nantucket Airlines
ℂ 800/635-8787
www.nantucketairlines.com

Northwest Airlines
ℂ 800/225-2525 (in U.S.)
ℂ 870/0507-4074 (in U.K.)
www.nwa.com

United Airlines*
ℂ 800/864-8331 (in U.S. and Canada)
ℂ 084/5844-4777 in U.K.
www.united.com

US Airways*
ℂ 800/428-4322 (in U.S. and Canada)
ℂ 084/5600-3300 (in U.K.)
www.usairways.com

Virgin America*
ℂ 877/359-8474
www.virginamerica.com

MAJOR INTERNATIONAL AIRLINES

Air France
℃ 800/237-2747 (in U.S.)
℃ 800/375-8723 (U.S. and Canada)
℃ 087/0142-4343 (in U.K.)
www.airfrance.com

Air New Zealand
℃ 800/262-1234 (in U.S.)
℃ 800/663-5494 (in Canada)
℃ 0800/028-4149 (in U.K.)
www.airnewzealand.com

Alitalia
℃ 800/223-5730 (in U.S.)
℃ 800/361-8336 (in Canada)
℃ 087/0608-6003 (in U.K.)
www.alitalia.com

American Airlines
℃ 800/433-7300 (in U.S. and Canada)
℃ 020/7365-0777 (in U.K.)
www.aa.com

Bahamasair
℃ 800/222-4262 (in U.S.)
℃ 242/300-8359 (in Family Islands)
℃ 242/377-5505 (in Nassau)
www.bahamasair.com

British Airways
℃ 800/247-9297 (in U.S. and Canada)
℃ 087/0850-9850 (in U.K.)
www.british-airways.com

Continental Airlines
℃ 800/523-3273 (in U.S. or Canada)
℃ 084/5607-6760 (in U.K.)
www.continental.com

Delta Air Lines
℃ 800/221-1212 (in U.S. or Canada)
℃ 084/5600-0950 (in U.K.)
www.delta.com

Finnair
℃ 800/950-5000 (in U.S. and Canada)
℃ 087/0241-4411 (in U.K.)
www.finnair.com

Icelandair
℃ 800/223-5500 ext. 2, prompt 1
    (in U.S. and Canada)

℃ 084/5758-1111 (in U.K.)
www.icelandair.com
www.icelandair.co.uk (in U.K.)

Japan Airlines
℃ 012/025-5931 (international)
www.jal.co.jp

Lufthansa
℃ 800/399-5838 (in U.S.)
℃ 800/563-5954 (in Canada)
℃ 087/0837-7747 (in U.K.)
www.lufthansa.com

Qantas Airways
℃ 800/227-4500 (in U.S.)
℃ 084/5774-7767 (in U.K. or Canada)
℃ 13 13 13 (in Australia)
www.qantas.com

South African Airways
℃ 271/1978-5313 (international)
℃ 0861 FLYSAA (086/135-9722)
    (in South Africa)
www.flysaa.com

Swiss Air
℃ 877/359-7947 (in U.S. and Canada)
℃ 084/5601-0956 (in U.K.)
www.swiss.com

Turkish Airlines
℃ 90 212 444 0 849
www.thy.com

United Airlines*
℃ 800/864-8331 (in U.S. and Canada)
℃ 084/5844-4777 (in U.K.)
www.united.com

US Airways*
℃ 800/428-4322 (in U.S. and Canada)
℃ 084/5600-3300 (in U.K.)
www.usairways.com

Virgin Atlantic Airways
℃ 800/821-5438 (in U.S. and Canada)
℃ 087/0574-7747 (in U.K.)
www.virgin-atlantic.com

BUDGET AIRLINES

Aer Lingus
✆ 800/474-7424 (in U.S. and Canada)
✆ 087/0876-5000 (in U.K.)
www.aerlingus.com

AirTran Airways
✆ 800/247-8726
www.airtran.com

Air Berlin
✆ 087/1500-0737 (in U.K.)
✆ 018/0573-7800 (in Germany)
✆ 180/573-7800 (all others)
www.airberlin.com

Frontier Airlines
✆ 800/432-1359
www.frontierairlines.com

JetBlue Airways
✆ 800/538-2583 (in U.S.)
✆ 801/365-2525 (in U.K. or Canada)
www.jetblue.com

Southwest Airlines
✆ 800/435-9792 (in U.S., U.K., and Canada)
www.southwest.com

Spirit Airlines
✆ 800/772-7117
www.spiritair.com

Index

See also Accommodations index, below.

ACCOMMODATIONS